TENTH EDITION

Business

Its Legal, Ethical, and Global Environment

Bo Chambers/Flickr/Getty Images

Marianne Moody Jennings

Arizona State University

CENGAGE
Learning®

Australia • Brazil • Canada • Mexico • Singapore • Spain • United Kingdom • United States

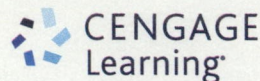
CENGAGE
Learning·

Business: Its Legal, Ethical, and Global Environment, Tenth Edition
Marianne M. Jennings

Vice President, General Manager, Social Science & Qualitative Business: Erin Joyner

Product Director: Michael Worls

Product Manager: Vicky True-Baker

Content Developer: Sarah Blasco

Product Assistant: Tristann Jones

Market Director: Kristen Hurd

Senior Content Project Manager: Tamborah Moore

Senior Media Developer: Kristen Meere

Manufacturing Planner: Kevin Kluck

Marketing Coordinator: Christopher Walz

Production Service: Charles Emmanuel, diacriTech

Rights Acquisitions Specialist: Anne Sheroff

Image Research & Permissions: Sundar Ananthapadmanabhan/PMG

Text Permissions Research: Sarah Andrews/PMG

Sr. Art Director: Michelle Kunkler

Internal and Cover Designer: Ke Design

Cover Image: © Bo Chambers/Flickr/Getty Images

For product information and technology assistance, contact us at
Cengage Learning Customer & Sales Support, 1-800-354-9706
For permission to use material from this text or product, submit all requests online at **www.cengage.com/permissions**
Further permissions questions can be emailed to
permissionrequest@cengage.com

Library of Congress Control Number: 2013950684

ISBN 13: 978-1-285-42826-0

ISBN 10: 1-285-42826-9

Cengage Learning
200 First Stamford Place, 4th Floor
Stamford, CT 06902
USA

Cengage Learning is a leading provider of customized learning solutions with office locations around the globe, including Singapore, the United Kingdom, Australia, Mexico, Brazil, and Japan. Locate your local office at: **www.cengage.com/global**

Cengage Learning products are represented in Canada by Nelson Education, Ltd.

To learn more about Cengage Learning Solutions, visit **www.cengage.com**

Purchase any of our products at your local college store or at our preferred online store **www.cengagebrain.com**

Printed in Canada
1 2 3 4 5 6 7 17 16 15 14 13

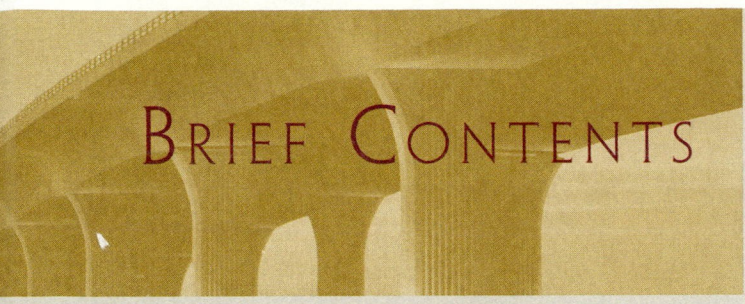

BRIEF CONTENTS

Bo Chambers/Flickr/Getty Images

CONTENTS

Chapter 3

The Judicial System 72

Chapter *7*

International Law 208

Chapter *8*

Business Crime 236

Chapter *9*
Business Torts 276

Chapter *10*
Cyberlaw, Social Media, and Privacy 308

Chapter *11*
Environmental Regulation and Sustainability 336

Part 3
BUSINESS SALES, CONTRACTS, AND COMPETITION 367

Chapter 12
Contracts and Sales: Introduction and Formation 368

Chapter 13
Contracts and Sales: Performance and Remedies 410

Chapter 14

Product Advertising and
Liability 446

Chapter 15

Products: Business Intellectual
Property 484

Chapter 16

Business Competition: Antitrust 516

Part 4

BUSINESS MANAGEMENT AND GOVERNANCE 549

Chapter 17

Management of Employee Conduct: *Agency* 550

Chapter 18

Governance and Structure: Forms of Doing Business 586

Chapter 19

Governance and Regulation 626

Chapter 20
Management of Employee Welfare 668

Chapter 21
Management: Employment Discrimination 706

Appendices A-1

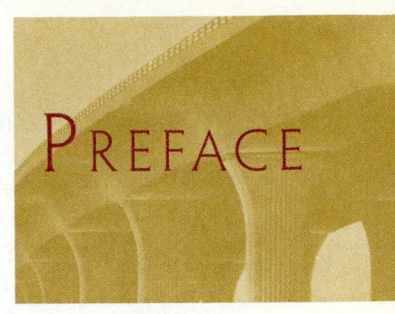

A Different World, but the Same Issues

The seventh edition was published amidst the fallout from the legal, ethical, and, too often, financial collapses of Enron, WorldCom, Adelphia, HealthSouth, Parmalat, Arthur Andersen, Kmart, and others. With Sarbanes–Oxley on the books and new regulatory demands on corporations, we thought perhaps we had turned the corner. But the eighth edition was published as Wall Street and the economy were reeling from the fallout of a subprime mortgage market operating under regulatory radar without a great deal of disclosure on portfolio risk. When the ninth edition was published, the SEC had just settled a civil suit it brought against Goldman Sachs for allegedly selling securities to clients it was betting against as a short-seller in a scheme that saw its profits reach double-digit billions. Goldman paid a fine of $550 million. In late 2009, Goldman's CEO, Lloyd Blankfein, uttered the same words that Jeffrey Skilling did in 2000: "We are doing God's work." Now, as the tenth edition goes to press, there are questions about the fairness of the scrutiny of taxpayers by an administrative agency, the Internal Revenue Service, and the Justice Department's tapping of phones of news corporations. Book publishers signed antitrust consent decrees for agreeing to fix prices in order to compete with Amazon. JPMorgan Chase lost $6 billion because a London trader exceeded the bank's risk limits and the bank's reporting requirements were modified. A factory in Bangladesh, that produced clothing for U.S. retailers, collapsed, killing over 600 employees, a collapse that was caused by noncompliance with safety and code standards.

The patterns of business behavior that push the envelope of law and ethics continue. A good portion of the members of the New York legislature were indicted on corruption charges, companies from Ralph Lauren to Avon paid fines for violations of the Foreign Corrupt Practices Act, and BP paid the largest fines in U.S. history for the safety and environmental violations that resulted from the explosion of its Deepwater Horizon oil rig in the Gulf. Colleges and universities struggled with terminations of coaches for everything from losing to the failure to supervise the criminal activity of assistant coaches. The issues of law and ethics are still at the forefront of business, sports, and government. It has become a tall order just to keep up with all the events!

These companies and organizations and their employees and executives certainly could have benefited from understanding and keeping at the forefront of their decision processes the basics of law and ethics! The legal and ethical environments of business are center stage. Several editions ago, Congress made massive regulatory reform a reality with the passage of the Sarbanes–Oxley legislation on corporate governance, accounting regulation, and criminal penalties. But the SEC missed Bernie Madoff's $50 billion Ponzi scheme for 18 years and Congress passed additional reforms for financial market regulation in 2010. Credit card solicitations, billing, and terms have changed completely and are now under a new Consumer Protection

Bureau housed within the Federal Reserve so that all aspects of credit cards are now consolidated and regulated in one place. Business is even more international, and we are witnessing the need for thoughtful legal and ethical analysis as companies enter new markets. Even Apple struggled with backlash from conditions in its supplier's factories. Suicides and child labor at Foxconn damaged the Apple brand. There were so many FCPA cases that the Justice Department issued new guidelines to help companies better construct their compliance programs for controlling bribes in international operations.

The world and business continue to change and grow, but law and ethics have retained their role and importance. In fact, now more than ever, we need to understand the legal and ethical issues that affect our businesses and our lives. The knowledge base and even the questions in law and ethics remain the same, but the underlying facts have changed. For example, we still debate the social responsibility role of business. Now we raise that issue in the context of whether Apple and Google should take advantage of offshore tax loopholes. We continue to delve into the pros and cons of sending production to other countries. We still have the question of when a contract is formed, but now we face that question with "point and click" technology rather than faxes and letters. We continue to be concerned about our privacy as consumers, but now we wonder who really has access to our Facebook page. We still wonder about the extent of copyright law. The file-sharing programs have never quite gone away and the film industry now litigates the downloading of copyrighted films. The world is different, but law and ethics form the constant framework into which we fit the issues of the day. In the materials that follow, you have the chance to understand the marvelous stability of this framework and the ease with which you can apply it to this very different world. Be sure to look for descriptions of the new structure as well as the continuing features in the book, such as the "Consider..." tutorials, the ethics issues, and the "Business Strategy" application exercises.

Building the Bridge: Applying Legal and Ethical Reasoning to Business Analysis

I gave my students a midterm exam—a review of Apple and its various business issues, including the conditions in its supplier factories in China. These students are in the second year of their master's degree studies. They have been trained in economics, marketing, management, and finance. But as they completed their analysis of what went wrong with the world's most admired and emulated company, they had an epiphany. A company can get the finance issues right (Apple saves about 30 percent in production costs by outsourcing to China), have the right brand appeal and great products, and even yield terrific sales figures. However, it can all fall apart over the legal issues. China's standards for plant safety, wages, and working hours are different from those of the United States—and regulatory oversight is spotty. When suicides among plant workers were being covered internationally and child labor issues emerged, there was a chilling effect on Apple and Apple sales. The differing legal standards in international business were at the heart of this major setback for a company, one that would cause a drop in its stock. And when it comes to problems with factory standards and safety, the protests and boycotts follow. They are very capable *business* students. However, they did not realize until this midterm exam how much of business turns on anticipating the legal issues and getting them resolved correctly. And they also realized that all of our discussions of ethics and social responsibility had a role in doing business.

TANSTAAFL—"there ain't no such thing as a free lunch" when it comes to international outsourcing. There are costs associated with using the much cheaper labor and factories in other countries. And those costs come from legal issues, which, if handled poorly, can affect a company's value and tarnish its brand name.

Why couldn't these students see the interconnection and critical roles of law and ethics in business until this case for their midterm? It was not for lack of exposure to the law. I taught my course "by the book," so to speak. Students could recite the components of a valid contract, rattle off the requirements for bankruptcy, and recall from memory the antitrust statutes. Yet, I was coming to realize, this rote knowledge was not enough. One of my best former students, who had gone on to medical school, came to me perplexed about her office lease. She said that the complex in which she wanted to open her practice had a "no advertising" policy. In fact, she said that when she toured the premises with a leasing agent, the leasing agent turned to her and said, "You're not one of those doctors who advertises, are you? Because if you are, we can't lease to you. We have a policy against it." One of my best students, who knew the antitrust statutes well, could not apply them to her everyday business. Worse, perhaps, she could not *recognize* when to apply these statutes: She did not see the antitrust implications of the agent's statements nor the problems with the physicians in the complex taking such an approach to screening tenants.

I have reached the conclusion that there have always been shortcomings in the standard approach to teaching business students law and ethics. Students were not ignorant of the law; rather, they simply lacked the necessary skills to recognize legal and ethical issues and to apply their knowledge of law and ethics to business decision making. As instructors, we were not integrating legal and ethical reasoning with business analysis. My conclusion led me to develop my own materials for classroom use and eventually led to the publication of the first edition of this book. Now in its tenth edition, *Business: Its Legal, Ethical, and Global Environment* brings to the classroom the most integrated approach to learning law and ethics available in the market today. Throughout every chapter and in every feature, students and instructors are continually reminded of how various legal and ethical principles apply in business contexts. For all areas of law and ethics, this book answers the question: How does this concept affect a business? This book builds a bridge for the student between knowledge of law and ethics and application of both in business. My 37 years of teaching law and ethics finally brought this realization: Business ethics is not easily grasped nor practiced in business because we depersonalize ethical issues. If we just allow the company or organization to make the decision, our ethics are not in question; the company's are. The ethical issues in the book require students to bring ethical issues into their lives, their circumstances, their world. This feature also forces them to answer this question in a wide variety of contexts: "If it were you, and you were faced with the dilemma and required to make a decision, what would you do?"

Strengthening the Bridge: New Content, Business Applications, and Learning Aids

For the tenth edition, *Business: Its Legal, Ethical, and Global Environment* has undergone further refinement. New content has been added, new business applications have been integrated into every chapter, and the learning aids have been modified and refocused to help students understand and apply legal and ethical concepts.

NEW CONTENT

The tenth edition of *Business: Its Legal, Ethical, and Global Environment* continues to meet its goal of helping students with their understanding of how law and ethics apply to the business world. The organizational structure, based on feedback from those who use the text, has been changed. The four parts remain, but there is a new mix of topics in those four parts. Part 1 offers the student an overview of the legal, ethical, and judicial environments of business. Part 2 covers the regulatory environments of business, including environmental regulation and sustainability as well as a new chapter on cyberlaw. Part 3 has been reorganized to provide a more logical flow of material and covers all aspects of sales and competition. Part 4 has also been reorganized and covers business management and corporate governance. This newly restructured section covers all issues related to employees, boards, agents, and how to keep all of these groups coordinated while taking legal and ethical actions.

ETHICS

Chapter 2: Business Ethics and Social Responsibility offers new examples and insights on the application of ethics to business decision making. Chapter 2 is chock full of the examples the last two years have netted—including Dr. Drew's conflict of interest and a note from the jurors about the ethics of Wall Street executives in their acquittal verdict of one of them. Ethics coverage is also integrated throughout all chapters.

Business Applications

BIOGRAPHY

A "Biography" feature appears at the end of each chapter. These biographies provide students with business history through the study of individuals and companies involved with the area of law and ethics covered in the chapter. For example, Chapter 10 has a biography of Kim Dotcom, the man responsible for a high percentage of movie copyright infringement who awaits trial on an international level. Chapter 13 provides the story of Charlie Sheen's contract dispute following his termination from his popular television series. Chapter 15 gives a biography of Mattel and its Bratz dolls and its long intellectual property battle over who had the idea for the dolls.

FOR THE MANAGER'S DESK

Each chapter also contains at least one "For the Manager's Desk" feature. These readings provide students the opportunity to see how business interrelates with ethics and law. Some of the readings are excerpts from business publications, such as the *Wall Street Journal*, while other excerpts from the *Harvard Business Review*, *Corporate Finance Review*, and the *American Business Law Journal* offer the latest in academic studies and insights.

Learning Aids

... AND THE LAW

Each chapter contains a popular feature to further integrate law and ethics with the other "silos" of business. The "... and the Law" feature puts law and ethics in the context of economics, human resources, public policy, strategy, finance, and other areas to illustrate the ways knowledge of the where and how for the fit of law and ethics can help make better managers and better decisions. For example, Chapter 18 presents the pros and cons of giving shareholders a say on CEO compensation packages. Chapter 17 includes a discussion of the organizational behavior lessons learned from the legal problem Penn State experienced as a result of a former assistant football coach molesting children in the facilities of the school's football program. Chapter 5's "Economics and the Law" takes a look at the issue in increasing eminent domain proceedings. These features apply the principles from business disciplines to understand more fully the depth and breadth of management issues.

CASE HEADLINES

Every court case has a case headline that summarizes what issues are involved in the case. In Chapter 12, students read *Paramount Contracting Co. v DPS Industries, Inc.*, a case that addresses the issue of what constitutes the sales of goods and what constitutes the sale of services. The case title is memorable: "Dirt Is Cheap, But It Is Still a Good." In Chapter 6, the case *Hornbeck Offshore Services, L.L.C. et al. v Salazar* deals with an issue of whether agency action was arbitrary and capricious in issuing a moratorium on offshore drilling, and the case title is "Drilling Down to the Facts Supporting a Rule." The vivid one-line description and colorful facts of the case, a common thread throughout the case choices in the text, help students internalize the rules and lessons about not destroying evidence for a potential lawsuit.

CHAPTER OPENERS

Chapters begin with an opening problem, titled "Consider...," which presents a legal dilemma relevant to the chapter's discussion and similar to those business managers need to handle. These are revisited and answered in the body of the chapter. For example, Chapter 6 has a new chapter opening on a proposed regulation on food calorie content disclosure that would affect movie theater popcorn. Chapter 20 has a new opening on Boeing's battle to open a new plant for the production of its new 787 in South Carolina that would be nonunion. Moreover, answers to these opening "Consider..." features are referenced in the text and clearly marked. In Chapter 6, the chapter opening scenario is woven throughout the chapter to explain the rulemaking process and business interaction with that process. Next, opening statements discuss the major topics of the chapter and present the general goals for the chapter in the form of questions to be answered. Finally, quotations, often humorous, pique students' interest and focus the chapter on the major issues.

CHAPTER SUMMARY

Each chapter concludes with a summary that reinforces the major concepts of the chapter. Each summary is constructed around the key questions introduced at the start of the chapter and key terms presented throughout the chapter.

BUSINESS STRATEGY APPLICATIONS

Each chapter has a business strategy connection designed to help students understand where law and ethics fit in developing effective business strategies. For example in Chapter 5, the "Business Strategy" feature deals with how companies are coping with Internet sales tax issues. This feature shows how important legal issues are in determining costs and margins in business. The Chapter 13 "Business Strategy" deals with how restaurants are coping with no-shows in their reservations and their contract rights when someone makes a reservation but never shows up.

Organization and Features: A Structure to Guide Students to Reasoning and Analysis

The classic features have been updated and strengthened. The organization has been retained to continue to meet student needs in the classroom.

ORGANIZATION

As noted, there are now four parts in the book, which serve to organize the materials around four basic areas: (1) understanding the legal environment, (2) understanding the regulatory environment, (3) dealing with sales, contracts and competition, and (4) management and governance. Every chapter integrates international and ethical topics.

PART 1

In four chapters, Part 1 offers an introduction to law, an introduction to business ethics and the judicial system, and a discussion of litigation and alternative dispute resolution. Part 1 provides students with a foundation in law and ethics as well as legal and ethical reasoning, necessary for the areas of law in the chapters that follow. By being brief (four chapters), Part 1 offers instructors an early and logical break for exams.

PART 2

In seven chapters, Part 2 covers the regulatory environment of business, including the following topics: constitutional law, administrative and international law, business crimes and business torts, cyberlaw, and environmental regulation. The new cyberlaw chapter, Chapter 10: Cyberlaw, Social Media, and Privacy, deals with what may be one of the law's fastest growing areas. What are my rights when it comes to posting information online? And, what are the rights of my employer or college admission officer to see that information? At the completion of Parts 1 and 2, students have a grasp of the legal system, ethical boundaries, and the laws that affect business operational decisions, even those in cyberspace.

PART 3

The five chapters in Part 3 present students with the legal and ethical issues surrounding contracts, sales, and competition. Part 3 includes the following topics: contract formation and performance (including coverage of consumer issues); product liability; intellectual property; trade restraints; and business competition and antitrust. From the negotiation of price to the collection of accounts, this segment of the book covers all aspects of selling business products and services. This section is structured so that the contracts discussion precedes the complexities of property and competition.

PART 4

The five chapters in Part 4 discuss business management and governance. Topics include the management of employees, from agency law to employment regulation to employee rights to issues in discrimination. However, Part 4 now includes the governance issues of business structure and management, including financing and securities law issues. This section covers the issues of running, managing, and financing a business.

FEATURES

COURT CASES

Edited court language cases provide in-depth points of law, and many cases include dissenting and concurring opinions. Case questions follow to help students understand the points of law in the case and think critically about the decision. The courts have been active since the last edition, and many 2011–2013 case decisions are presented throughout the book. Students will be able to study Donald Trump's claim for defamation when a writer misstated his net worth. Can a company avoid Foreign Corrupt Practices Act violations when it has its agent appointed a government official in another country? What happens when a young man saves his Pepsi points to claim a Harrier Jet that he sees in a Pepsi spoof ad for "Pepsi stuff"? Does he get his jet?

CONSIDER...

"Consider…" problems, along with "Ethical Issues" and "Business Planning Tips," have been a part of every chapter since the first edition. The "Consider…" features, often based on real court cases, ask students to evaluate and analyze the legal and ethical issues discussed in the preceding text. Because these issues are integrated into the text, students must address and think critically about these issues as they encounter them. Through interactive problems, students learn to judge case facts and determine the consequences. "Consider…" brings the most current topics into the book and the classroom. Students can think about fracking and environmental law and issues of sustainability. The issues of privacy and professionalism arise in a "Consider…" on a wet t-shirt contest that results in an embarrassing moment for a television news anchor.

THINKING, APPLYING, AND ANSWERING: "CONSIDER..." TUTORIALS—A GUIDE FOR REASONING

One "Consider…" per chapter is solved for the students in a methodical walk-through that helps them understand how to apply the legal principles or case precedent that they have just studied. The facts of the case or hypothetical are presented and the students are asked to recall what they have just learned. Next, students are walked through applying those principles to the current facts. Finally, they are given the answer and the reason that answer is consistent with their thinking and applying.

ETHICAL ISSUES

The "Ethical Issues" feature appears in every chapter and presents students real-world ethical problems to grapple with. "Ethical Issues" help integrate coverage of ethics into every chapter. These ethical issues include personal and real-life examples that help students relate to the pervasive nature of ethical dilemmas that they do and will continue to face. For example, the release of 9-1-1 calls as public records raises issues about an individual's privacy as students examine the content of the Demi Moore 9-1-1 call and the issues about her condition released during the call in Chapter 6.

BUSINESS PLANNING TIPS

Students are given sound business and legal advice through "Business Planning Tips." With these tips, students not only know the law but also know how to anticipate issues and ensure compliance.

CYBERLAW

In addition to the new cyberlaw chapter (Chapter 10: Cyberlaw, Social Media, and Privacy), most chapters also include a segment on cyberlaw. These chapter-by-chapter materials, marked by an icon, give students the chance to see how new technology fits into the existing legal framework.

EXHIBITS

Exhibits include charts, figures, and business and legal documents that help highlight or summarize legal and ethical issues from the chapter. With the credit and financial market reforms and the changes in criminal penalties, many of the charts are either new or updated.

END-OF-CHAPTER PROBLEMS

Many end-of-chapter problems have been updated and now focus more on actual cases. There are new chapter problems throughout the book of varied lengths for different instructor needs.

The Informed Manager: Who Should Use This Book?

With its comprehensive treatment of the law, integrated business applications, and full-color design, *Business: Its Legal, Ethical, and Global Environment* is well suited for both undergraduate and MBA students. The book is used extensively in undergraduate education programs around the country. In addition, this edition has been class-tested with MBA students, and it is appropriate for MBA and executive education programs.

A NOTE ON AACSB STANDARDS

The strong presence of ethics, social responsibility, international law and issues, and the integration of other business disciplines make the book an ideal fit for meeting AACSB standards and curriculum requirements. The AACSB standards emphasize the need for students to have an understanding of ethical and global issues. The tenth edition continues with its separate chapter on ethics as well as ethical issues and dilemmas for student discussion and resolution in every chapter. The separate chapter on international law continues its expanded coverage from the last edition, and each chapter has a segment devoted to international law issues. The tenth edition includes readings on office romance, the challenges of ethics and law in international business, the role of lawyers in other countries, and attitudes outside the United States on insider trading and antitrust laws.

This edition presents students with the legal foundation necessary for business operations and sales but also affords the students the opportunities to analyze critically the social and political environments in which the laws are made and in which businesses must operate. An examination of the lists of companies and individuals covered in the biographies, and of the publications from which the "For the Manager's Desk" readings are taken, demonstrates the depth of background the tenth edition offers in those areas noted as critical by the AACSB. The materials provide a balanced look at regulation, free enterprise, and the new global economy.

Supplements

Business: Its Legal, Ethical, and Global Environment offers a comprehensive and well-crafted supplements package for both students and instructors.

Weekly Ethics and Law Updates. Available at **mariannejennings.com**, the weekly updates contributed by the author offer at least 12 current events per month for discussion and analysis. The update features new decisions, new statutes, new regulations, new ethical dilemmas, and a host of examples and cites to current periodicals. The tenth edition includes references to these updates in the text.

Instructor's Manual. The *Instructor's Manual*, written by the author, provides the following for each chapter: a detailed outline; answers to "Considers...," "Ethical Issues," case problems, and the end-of-chapter Questions and Problems; briefs of all cases; summaries of key features; supplemental readings; and interactive/cooperative learning exercises.

PowerPoint® Lecture Review Slides. Developed by the author, these Power-Point slides consist of lecture outlines and select tables and figures used in the book. The slides are available for use by students as an aid to note taking, and by instructors for enhancing their lectures.

Test Bank. The Test Bank for instructors includes more than 2,000 questions in true/false, multiple-choice, and essay format. The questions vary in levels of difficulty, and meet a full range of tagging requirements, including AACSB standards.

Cognero. Cengage Learning Testing Powered by Cognero is a flexible, online system that allows you to:

- author, edit, and manage Test Bank content from multiple Cengage Learning solutions
- create multiple test versions in an instant
- deliver tests from your LMS, your classroom, or wherever you want

Start right away! Cengage Learning Testing Powered by Cognero works on any operating system or browser.

- No special installs or downloads needed
- Create tests from school, home, the coffee shop—anywhere with Internet access

What will you find?

- Simplicity at every step. A desktop-inspired interface features drop-down menus and familiar, intuitive tools that take you through content creation and management with ease.
- Full-featured test generator. Create ideal assessments with your choice of 15 question types (including true/false, multiple choice, opinion scale/likert, and essay). Multi-language support, an equation editor, and unlimited metadata help ensure your tests are complete and compliant.
- Cross-compatible capability. Import and export content into other systems.

CourseMate. CourseMate brings course concepts to life with interactive learning, study, and exam-preparation tools—including an e-book—that support the printed textbook. Revised for this edition, student study materials and a set of auto-gradable, interactive quizzes allow students to instantly gauge their comprehension of the material. Built-in engagement tracking tools allow instructors to follow students' study activities and assess their progress.

CengageNOW™. CengageNOW™ is an online teaching and learning resource that gives you more control in less time and delivers better outcomes—NOW. Brand new to this edition, CengageNOW for *Business: Its Legal, Ethical, and Global Environment* allows instructors to customize additional test and study materials for their students. Written by Ray Teske of University of Texas at San Antonio, each of the 21 chapters provides several categories of multiple-choice questions that stress different aspects of the chapter materials: Chapter Review, Business Hypotheticals, Legal Reasoning, and IRAC. Along with pre- and post test questions, all quiz content is tagged to specific standards. These online resources ensure that students possess the study materials needed to understand and apply the legal principles covered in the book.

Business Law Digital Video Library. The Digital Library offers more than 90 videos and helps your students link their everyday experiences to legal ideas, spark classroom discussion, and reinforce core concepts. The Business Law Digital Video Library is organized into six series: Legal Conflicts in Business (includes specific modern business and e-commerce scenarios); Ask the Instructor (presents straightforward explanations of concepts for student review); Drama of the Law (features classic business scenarios that spark classroom participation); LawFlix (contains clips from many popular films); Real World Legal (presents legal scenarios encountered in real businesses); and Business Ethics in Action (presents ethical dilemmas in business scenarios). For more information about the Digital Video Library, visit www.cengage.com/blaw/dvl. Access for students is free when bundled with a new textbook or can be purchased separately. Students must register for and purchase access to the Digital Video Library at www.cengagebrain.com.

KnowNOW Blog. A professor's dream—a daily blog, written by the author and other professors, on eye-catching legal issues that allows students the opportunity to engage in discussion and really master concepts because of the nature of the subject matter. Insider trading is something that may not grab their attention until you share with them the story of the famous Notre Dame football player, Rudy, who settled pump-and-dump charges by the SEC. And a breached sale-of-fabric contract sounds like a dull session unless you are able to use the Lululemon problem—the company made thousands of yoga pants with the fabric only to discover through customer complaints that the fabric was see-through and those customers wanted their money back. Even antitrust law comes to life when you use the merger of Corona with Bud Light to cover market share and monopoly power.

Cengage Learning's Global Economic Watch (GEW) Resource Center. This is your source for turning today's challenges into tomorrow's solutions. This online portal houses the most up-to-date content concerning the economic crisis. Organized by discipline, the GEW Resource Center offers the solutions instructors and students need in an easy-to-use format. Included are an overview and timeline of the historical events leading up to the crisis, links to the latest news and resources, discussion and testing content, an instructor feedback forum, and a Global Issues Database. Visit www.cengage.com/thewatch for more information.

Professor Marianne Jennings is an emeritus professor of legal and ethical studies in business from the W. P. Carey School of Business at Arizona State University, having retired in 2011 after 35 years of teaching there. She returned to part-time teaching there in 2013, and continues to teach graduate courses in business ethics at colleges around the country.

During her tenure at ASU, she served in many different capacities: director of the Joan and David Lincoln Center for Applied Ethics (1995–1999); faculty director for the MBA Executive Program (2006–2007); associate dean (1986–1987); chair of the University Hearing Board (1995–2011); and faculty athletic representative to the NCAA and PAC-10 (1986–1987).

Professor Jennings earned her undergraduate degree in finance and her J. D. from Brigham Young University. Her internships were with the Federal Public Defender and U.S. Attorney in Nevada, and she has done consulting work for law firms and businesses and professional groups, including AES, Boeing, Dial Corporation, Mattel, Motorola, CFA Institute, Southern California Edison, the Arizona Auditor General, the Cities of Phoenix, Mesa, and Tucson, the Institute of Internal Auditors, Coca-Cola, DuPont, Blue Cross Blue Shield, Motorola, Mattel, Pepsi, Hy-Vee Foods, IBM, Bell Helicopter, Amgen, Raytheon, and VIAD.

Professor Jennings has authored hundreds of articles in academic, professional, and trade journals. Currently, she has six textbooks and monographs in circulation. The eighth edition of her textbook, *Case Studies in Business Ethics*, and the tenth edition of her textbook, *Business: Its Legal, Ethical and Global Environment*, will be published in January 2014. Her first textbook, *Real Estate Law*, had its tenth edition published in January 2013. She was added as a co-author to *Anderson's Business and the Legal Environment* in 1997, a text whose 22nd edition was published in January 2013. Her book, *Business Strategy for the Political Arena*, was selected in 1985 by *Library Journal* as one of its recommended books in business/government relations. *A Business Tale: A Story of Ethics, Choices, Success, and a Very Large Rabbit*, a fable about business ethics, was chosen by *Library Journal* in 2004 as its business book of the year. *A Business Tale* was also a finalist for two other literary awards in 2004. In 2000, her book on corporate governance was published by the *New York Times* MBA Pocket Series. Professor Jennings' book on long-term success, *Building a Business Through Good Times and Bad: Lessons from Fifteen Companies, Each With a Century of Dividends*, was published in October 2002 and has been used by Booz, Allen, Hamilton for its work on business longevity. Her book on organizational ethical culture, *The Seven Signs of Ethical Collapse*, was published by St. Martin's Press and continues to be used by many organizations as a framework for assessing culture. Her books have been translated into five languages. Her latest book, *Somewhere Between Ezekiel and Miss Havisham*, a book of essays on grief, was published in 2012.

Her columns have been syndicated around the country, and her work has appeared in the *Wall Street Journal, Chicago Tribune, New York Times, Washington Post*, and *Reader's Digest*. A collection of her essays, *Nobody Fixes Real Carrot Sticks Anymore*, first published in 1994, is still being published. She was given an Arizona Press Club award in 1994 for her work as a feature columnist. She has been a commentator on business issues on *All Things Considered* for National Public Radio.

She has conducted more than 500 workshops and seminars in the areas of business, personal, government, legal, academic, and professional ethics. She was named professor of the year in the College of Business in 1981, 1987, 2000, and 2010 and was the recipient of a Burlington Northern teaching excellence award in 1985. In 1999, she was given best article awards by the Academy of Legal Studies in Business and the Association for Government Accountants. She was given best article awards by the Institute of Internal Auditors and Association of Government Accountants in 2001 and 2004. She was a Dean's Council of 100 Distinguished Scholar from 1995–2011. In 2000, the Association of Government Accountants inducted her into its Speakers Hall of Fame. In 2005, she was named an All-Star Speaker by the Institute of Internal Auditors. In 2006, her article, "Ethics and Investment Management: True Reform," was selected by the United Kingdom's *Emerald Management Review* from 15,000 articles in 400 journals as one of the top 50 articles in 2005. She was named one of the Top 100 Thought Leaders by Trust Across America in 2010. In 2012, she was named one of the 100 Most Influential People in Business Ethics by *Ethisphere* magazine.

She is a contributing editor for the *Real Estate Law Journal, New Perspectives, The Smart Manager*, and *Corporate Finance Review*. She served on the Board of Editors for the *Financial Analysts Journal* from 2007–2012. She served as editor-in-chief of the *Journal of Legal Studies Education* during 2003–2004. During 1984–1985, she served as then–Governor Bruce Babbitt's appointee to the Arizona Corporation Commission. In 1999, she was appointed by Governor Jane Dee Hull to the Arizona Commission on Character. From 1986–1987, she served as ASU's faculty athletic representative to the NCAA and PAC-10. From 1999–2009, she served as president of the Arizona Association of Scholars.

She is a member of twelve professional organizations, including the State Bar of Arizona, and has served on four boards of directors, including Arizona Public Service (now Pinnacle West Capital) from 1987–2000, Zealous Capital Corporation, and the Center for Children with Chronic Illness and Disability at the University of Minnesota. She served as chair of the Bonneville International Advisory Board for KHTC/KIDR from 1994–1997 and was a weekly commentator on KGLE during 1998. She was appointed to the board of advisers for the Institute of Nuclear Power Operators in 2004. She has appeared on *CNBC, CBS This Morning*, the *Today Show*, and *CBS Evening News*.

Personal: Married since 1976 to Terry H. Jennings, Maricopa County Attorney's Office Deputy County Attorney; five children: Sarah, Sam, and John, and the late Claire and Hannah Jennings.

ACKNOWLEDGMENTS

By its tenth edition, a book has evolved to a point of trademark characteristics. This book is known for its hands-on examples and readings for business managers. That trademark evolves because of the efforts of many. They are the reviewers and adopters of the text who provide ideas, cases, and suggestions for improvement and inclusion. For this edition, the following colleagues offered their seasoned advice:

Shawn Abbott *(College of the Siskiyous)*
Suzanne Bechtel *(State College of Florida)*
Robert H. Breakfield *(Winthrop University)*
Leslee Brock *(Southwest Mississippi Community College)*
Emmy Buboltz *(Minnesota State University Mankato)*
Linda Christiansen *(Indiana University Southeast)*
Robert H. Doud *(Adelphi University)*
Dr. Christopher C. Esgar *(Penn State University)*
Peter Fagan *(Embry-Riddle Aeronautical University)*
M. M. Forsyth *(University of Southern Mississippi)*
Andy Garcia *(Bowling Green State University)*
Brian Gardner *(Transylvania University)*
Yolande Gardner *(Lawson State Community College)*
Richard R. Gerken *(Plymouth State University)*
Ilene Goldberg *(Rider University)*
Arlene M. Hibschweiler *(University at Buffalo)*
Robert Kenny, Esq. *(Rider University)*
Lora Koretz *(Arizona State University)*
Gail Petravick *(Bradley University)*
Leslie Sekerka *(Menlo College)*
Jeannine Shafer *(Western Michigan University)*
Wayne Tanna *(Chaminade University of Honolulu)*
Regina Webb *(Southern University at Shreveport)*
Russell Welch *(University of North Texas)*

Any edition of a book bears the mark of the editors who work to design, refine, market, and produce it. Seven editions ago, Rob Dewey saw potential for the book and applied his enthusiasm and market insights to mold a somewhat ugly duckling into a four-color swan. The book also carries the imprimatur of Steve Silverstein, who confronted me with a profound question, "Why can't those in business see these ethical dilemmas when they are in the midst of them?" His question forced me back to the drawing board and resulted in the more personal ethical dilemmas. Vicky True, now in Rob's role, understands the needs of instructors because of her intense road schedule, holds a keen sense of market direction, and offers the insights of both to help to shape this new edition. Sarah Blasco, new as the editor for this edition, gives new meaning to "supportive editor" and "organized." She applies a steady hand as she watches for consistencies, dates, and clarity. Tristann Jones serves as a patient administrator and coordinator for all of us. Tamborah Moore, the production editor, once again brought her eye for detail, her experience, and her insightful questions to the long haul of copyedit and page proofs. Kris Tabor has been with me since the first edition, helping with word processing, IMs, study guides, test banks, and venting. We mark 26 years of a terrific partnership with this edition.

This book also carries the unmistakable liveliness of an author who shares her life with helpful and delightful children and one tolerant husband. Since the first edition of this book, I have added four children to our first, witnessed two graduate from college, one from law school, grieved over the loss of two, and seen the others grow up all too quickly in a household in which "Mom, the UPS guy is here with page proofs" was their first spoken sentence. They now simply witness me hovering over my computer from dawn's light until I fall asleep on the keyboard. My children and my husband, collectively my family, are the most charming people I know. They have brought me stories, pop culture, and good sense with their, "Uh-oh, here we go!" Even from their now–globally dispersed positions, they call and ask, "How's the writing going?" Their vibrancy is found in the color and charm of these pages. I am grateful for their unanimous and unwavering support for my work. Finally, I am grateful to my parents who taught me through their words and examples of the importance and rewards of ethics and hard work.

Marianne Moody Jennings

Part 1

BUSINESS: ITS LEGAL, ETHICAL, AND JUDICIAL ENVIRONMENT

Simply stated, you cannot run a successful business without knowing the law. What is legal? Where can I find the laws I need to know? How do I make decisions about legal conduct that is ethically troublesome to me? What if I have a disagreement with a customer, employee, or shareholder? How and where can I resolve our differences?

This portion of the book explains what law is, where it can be found, how it is applied, and how legal disputes are resolved. But beyond the legal environment of a business, there are the ethical issues. Just because what you are doing is legal does not mean it is ethical. And why should a manager make ethical choices and behave honorably in business? Law and ethics are inextricably intertwined. A commitment to both is part of a sustainable business model.

1

INTRODUCTION TO LAW

Most people understand the law through personal experiences. Some are exposed to law through traffic tickets. Others encounter the law when a problem arises with a landlord or lease. Many wonder about their rights when search engines and other Internet companies gather information about them without their realizing such efforts were ongoing. Since 2008, many have come to understand the law as they faced fore-closures on their homes and needed to know their rights. Their understanding of the law may be limited by the anger they feel about having their email scanned or getting a traffic ticket. However, without traffic laws, the roads would be a study in survival of the fittest. The law is your source of assurance that if you face a foreclosure, you will have not only rights but also time to respond to your lender's actions. Each day businesses find and face legal and ethical issues in everything from privacy rights on Facebook to proper documentation of employees' citizenship.

The types of laws and the penalties for violating them vary from state to state and from city to city but, however much they vary, laws exist everywhere and at every level of government. Indeed, law is a universal, necessary foundation of an orderly society. Law helps maintain order, imposing on us certain minimum standards of conduct. When we fall short of those standards, we risk penalties. Law is made up of rules that control people's conduct and their interrelationships. Traffic laws control not only our conduct when we are driving but also our relationships with other drivers using the roads. In some instances, traffic laws give other drivers a right-of-way and we are liable to them for any injuries we cause by not following those laws.

This chapter offers an introduction to law. How is law defined? What types of laws are there? What are the purposes and characteristics of law? Where are laws found, and who enacts them?

UPDATE
For up-to-date legal news, go to **mariannejennings.com**

Consider...

YouTube was founded in February 2005 by three former employees of Paypal. When YouTube was launched in December 2005, a press release described it as a "consumer media company" that "allows people to watch, upload, and share personal video clips." YouTube achieved rapid prominence and profitability, eclipsing competitors such as Google Video and Yahoo Video by wide margins. In November 2006, Google acquired YouTube for $1.65 billion. By March 2010, site traffic on YouTube had soared to more than 1 billion daily video views, with more than 24 hours of new video uploaded to the site every minute.

Viacom, other film companies, and copyright holders discovered that their films and other video materials were posted on YouTube and filed suit against YouTube and Google for copyright infringement. Google and YouTube maintained that those who posted the videos were responsible for infringement and that they only provided an Internet site and service. Are YouTube and Google responsible for the copyright infringement of others?

1-1 Definition of Law

Philosophers and scholars throughout history have offered definitions of law. Aristotle, the early Greek philosopher, wrote that "the law is reason unaffected by desire" and "law is a form of order, and good law must necessarily mean good order." Oliver Wendell Holmes Jr., a U.S. Supreme Court justice of the early twentieth century, said, "[L]aw embodies the story of a nation's development through many centuries." Sir William Blackstone, the English philosopher and legal scholar, observed that law was "that rule of action which is prescribed by some superior and which the inferior is bound to obey." *Black's Law Dictionary* defines law as "a body of rules of action or conduct prescribed by the controlling authority, and having legal binding force."[1] Law has been defined at least once by every philosopher, statesman, and police officer.

Law is simply the body of rules governing individuals and their relationships. Most of these rules become law through a recognized governmental authority. Laws give us basic freedoms, rights, and protections. Law also offers a model of conduct for members of society in their business and personal lives and gives them certainty of expectation. Plans, businesses, contracts, and property ownership are based on the expectation that the law will provide consistent protection of rights. Without such constancy in legal boundaries, society would be a mass of chaos and confusion.

1-2 Classifications of Law

1-2a PUBLIC VERSUS PRIVATE LAW

Public law includes those laws enacted by some authorized governmental body. State and federal constitutions and statutes are all examples of public laws, as are the state incorporation and partnership procedures, county taxation statutes, and local zoning laws.

Private law, on the other hand, is developed between two individuals. For example, landlords usually have regulations for their tenants, and these regulations are private laws. Homeowners' associations have developed an important body of private law that regulates everything from the type of landscaping for homes in a subdivision to whether homeowners can erect basketball hoops in their driveways. The terms of a contract are a form of private law for the contracting parties. Although the requirements for forming and the means for enforcing that contract may be a matter of public law, the terms for performance are the private law the parties agree to as the rules for governing their relationships. Employer rules in a corporation are also examples of private law; as long as those rules do not infringe any public rights or violate any statutory or constitutional protections, those rules define a private law relationship between employer and employee. For example, most companies now have Twitter and Facebook policies that limit the type of information and comments employees can post about their employers in social media outlets. Interestingly, both state legislatures and the U.S. Congress have proposed legislation that would control employer restrictions on employees' posts. Public law is being changed to reflect technological areas that are not yet addressed in employment law.

1-2b CRIMINAL VERSUS CIVIL LAW

A violation of a **criminal law** is a wrong against society. A violation of a **civil law** is a wrong against another person or persons. Criminal violations have penalties such as fines and imprisonment. When you run a red light, you have committed a criminal violation and owe society a penalty, such as a fine or imprisonment. Violations of civil laws, on the other hand, require restitution: Someone who violates a civil law must compensate the harmed party. If you do run a red light and strike and injure a pedestrian, your criminal case is society's remedy. The civil wrong in the same action requires you to pay damages to that pedestrian.

If you drive while intoxicated, you are breaking a criminal law and are subject to a fine, jail term, or license suspension. If you have an accident while driving intoxicated, you commit a civil wrong against anyone you injure. People who are injured as a result of your driving while intoxicated can file a civil suit against you to recover for injuries to their persons and property (cars).

Other differences also distinguish civil laws from criminal laws and their enforcement. For example, different rights and procedures are used in the trials of criminal cases (see Chapter 8 for more details).

1-2c SUBSTANTIVE VERSUS PROCEDURAL LAW

Substantive laws are those that give rights and responsibilities. **Procedural laws** provide the means for enforcing substantive rights. For example, if Zeta Corporation has breached its contract to buy 3,000 microchips from Yerba Corporation, Yerba has the substantive right to expect performance and may be able to collect damages for breach of contract by bringing suit. The laws governing how Yerba's suit is brought and the trial process are procedural laws. Procedural laws are also used in criminal cases, such as grand jury proceedings or arraignments and pleas (see Chapter 8 for more information).

1-2d COMMON VERSUS STATUTORY LAW

The term **common law** has been in existence since 1066, when the Normans conquered England and William the Conqueror sought one common set of laws for governing a then-divided England. The various customs of each locality were conglomerated so that all fiefdoms could operate under a "common" system of law. The common law came about as judges in different areas settled disputes in similar ways by consulting their fellow judges on their previous decisions before making decisions. This principle of following other decisions is referred to as *stare decisis*, meaning "let the decision stand." This process of legal reasoning is still followed today. The courts use the judicial decisions of the past in making their judgments in order to provide the consistency and constancy of the law.

As much of an improvement as it was, the common law was still just uncodified law. Because of increased trade, population, and complexities, the common law needed to be supplemented. As a result, **statutory law**, which is passed by some governmental body and written in some form, was created.

Today, in the United States, we have common law and statutory law. Some of our common law still consists of principles from the original English common law. For example, how we own and pass title to real property are areas largely developed from English common law. The body of common law continues to grow, however: the judicial system's decisions constitute a form of common law that is used in the process of *stare decisis*. Courts throughout the country look to other courts' decisions when confronted with similar cases.

Statutory law exists at all levels of government—federal, state, county, city, borough, and town. Our statutory law varies throughout our nation because of the cultural heritages of various regions. For example, the southwestern states have marital property rights statutes—often referred to as community property laws—that were influenced by the Spanish legal system implemented in Mexico. The northeastern states have different marital property laws that were influenced by English laws on property ownership. Louisiana's contract laws are based on French principles because of the early French settlements there.

1-2e LAW VERSUS EQUITY

Equity is a body of law that attempts to do justice when the law does not provide a remedy, when the remedy is inadequate, or when the application of the law is terribly unfair. Equity, which originated in England, came into being because the technicalities of the common law often resulted in unresolved disputes or unfair resolutions. The monarchy allowed its chancellor to hear those cases that could not be resolved in the common law courts; eventually, a separate set of equity courts developed that were not bound by rigid common law rules. These courts could get more easily to the heart of a dispute. Over time, they developed remedies not available under common law. Common law, for example, usually permitted only the recovery of monetary damages. Courts of equity, on the other hand, could issue orders, known as **injunctions**, prohibiting certain conduct or ordering certain acts. The equitable remedies available in the **courts of chancery** were gradually combined with the legal remedies of the common law courts so that now parties can have their legal and equitable remedies determined by the same court.

Today's courts award equitable remedies when the legal remedy of money damages would be inadequate. For example, the copyright infringement cases brought by the recording and motion picture industries sought against the individuals and companies that provided the technological means for making individual copies of movies and songs (the file-sharing programs). The record companies, the movie producers, and the artists could never be adequately compensated with money for these forms of infringement because the continued activity caused the loss of their exclusive copyrights. The remedy that they sought and were given were injunctions that, within certain parameters, ordered a halt to the sites and programs that facilitated the unauthorized downloading of copyrighted materials.

1-3 Purposes of Law

1-3a KEEPING ORDER

Laws carry some form of penalty for their violation. Antitrust violations carry a fine or imprisonment or both. Violations of civil laws also carry sanctions. If an employer discriminates against you by refusing to give you a raise or promotion because of your age, gender, or race, you can seek money damages. A driver who injures another while driving intoxicated can be prosecuted but must also pay for the damages and the costs of the injuries the other person experiences. These civil and criminal penalties for violations of laws prevent feuds and the use of primitive methods for settling disputes, such as force.

The USA Patriot Act addresses a variety of legal issues, from search warrants to reporting requirements for banks and others engaged in high-dollar transactions (see Chapters 8, 12, and 9). The Patriot Act was passed for the purpose of preventing terrorist activities through early detection of plots and the control of funds used for financing terrorist activities.

1-3b INFLUENCING CONDUCT

Laws also influence conduct in a society. For example, securities laws require companies to make certain disclosures about those securities before they can be sold to the public. The antitrust laws passed in the early twentieth century prohibited some methods of competition, such as price fixing, and limited others, such as mergers (see Chapter 16). These types of laws continue to change the way businesses operate. For example, Google recently agreed to stop restricting its advertisers from working with other search engines.

1-3c HONORING EXPECTATIONS

Businesses commit resources, people, and time to ventures, expansion, and product development with the expectation that the contracts for those commitments will be honored and enforced according to existing law. Investors buy stock with the knowledge that they will enjoy some protection of that investment through the laws that regulate both the securities themselves and the companies in which they have invested. Laws allow prior planning based on the protections inherent in the law.

1-3d PROMOTING EQUALITY

Laws have been used to achieve equality in those aspects of life in which equality is not a reality. For example, the equal-right-to-employment acts (see Chapter 21) were passed to bring greater equality to the job market. The social welfare programs of state and federal governments were created to further the cause of economic justice. The antitrust laws attempt to level the playing field for the free enterprise system to operate efficiently.

1-3e LAW AS THE GREAT COMPROMISER

A final and important purpose of law is to act as the great compromiser. Few people, groups, or businesses agree philosophically on how society, business, or government should be run. Law serves to mesh different views into one united view so that all parties are at least partially satisfied. When disputes occur, the courts apply the law to the parties' situation in an attempt to strike a compromise between two opposing views. The U.S. Supreme Court has provided compromises for the rights of businesses to be involved in the political process and make donations to candidates (see Chapter 5). In the relationship between freedom of speech and advertising regulation, the law serves as the mediator.

1-4 Characteristics of Law

1-4a FLEXIBILITY

CYBERLAW

© iStockPhoto.com/ dra_schwartz

As society changes, the law must change with it. When the United States was an agricultural nation, the issues of antitrust, employment discrimination, and securities fraud rarely arose. However, as the United States became an industrialized nation, those areas of law expanded, and they continue to expand today. As the United States further evolves into a technological and information-based society, still more areas of law will be created and developed. Computer fraud and identity theft, for example, were unknown issues 35 years ago; today, both state and federal laws address these issues through criminal statutes (see Chapter 10). The introduction of the fax machine required courts to reexamine how offers and acceptances of contracts are made, and the Internet has resulted in legislation allowing electronic signatures to have the same force and effect as signatures on paper (see Chapter 12).

Circumstances change through technology, sociology, and even biology. The law must address those changes. The "Consider..." at the beginning of the chapter demonstrates how the development of new technology presented new legal issues. What are the rights of copyright holders when an Internet company creates a system that allows users to post videos that are copyrighted? With billions of users and millions of videos, how do we protect copyrighted materials?

1-4b CONSISTENCY

Although the law must be flexible, it still must be predictable. Law cannot change so suddenly that parties cannot rely on its existence or protection. Being able to predict the outcome of a course of conduct allows a party to rely on a contract or dissuades a party from the commission of a crime. For a contract, a judicial remedy can be ordered for breach or nonperformance; for a crime, a prescribed punishment is the result.

1-4c PERVASIVENESS

The law must be pervasive and cover all necessary areas, but at the same time, it cannot infringe on individual freedoms or become so complex that it is difficult to enforce. For example, laws cover the formation, operation, and dissolution of corporations. Laws govern corporate management decisions on expanding, developing, and changing the nature of the corporation. Laws also ensure that shareholders' rights are protected. The corporation has great flexibility in management, as long as it stays within these legal boundaries.

CYBERLAW

In the two following cases, the courts struggle as they try to honor the law's purposes of keeping order and honoring expectations while also grappling with the unique issues raised by modern technology and its applications and use in the context of balancing those purposes. The principle of *stare decisis* is at work in these two cases (see Chapter 3). You will be able to see how the law has evolved to address new issues that have resulted from technological developments. Case 1.1, the *Grokster* case, is briefed in Exhibit 1.1. A **brief** is a tool used by lawyers, law students, and judges to help them summarize a case and focus on its facts and the key points of the decision by the court. Case 1.2, the *Viacom* case, answers the questions posed in the "Consider…" problem at the beginning of the chapter.

| **CASE 1.1** | *Metro-Goldwyn-Mayer Studios Inc. v Grokster, Ltd.*
545 U.S. 913 (2005)[2] |

Copyright Infringement? Really, It's Just a Little Peer-to-Peer File Sharing

FACTS

Grokster, Ltd., and StreamCast Networks, Inc. (respondents/defendants) distribute free software products that allow computer users to share electronic files through peer-to-peer networks. With no central computer server required in these networks, the issue of storage space for high-bandwidth-capacity servers disappears. Because copies of a file (particularly a popular one) are available on many users' computers, file requests and retrievals move faster than on other types of networks, and can take place between any computers that remain connected to the network without risk of a server glitch. Peer-to-peer networks are used by universities, government agencies, corporations, and libraries to store and distribute electronic files.

Grokster and StreamCast software users have generally used the software networks for sharing copyrighted music and video files without authorization. A group of copyright holders (MGM for short, but including motion picture studios, recording companies, songwriters, and music publishers—petitioners) sued Grokster and StreamCast for their users' copyright infringements through the distribution of their software that allows users to reproduce and distribute copyrighted works in violation of the Copyright Act.

Grokster and StreamCast do not know when files are copied, but MGM commissioned a statistician to conduct a systematic search, and his study showed that nearly 90 percent of the files available for download were copyrighted works. Grokster and StreamCast dispute this figure and argue that free copying even of copyrighted works may be authorized by the rightholders. They also argue that potential noninfringing uses

of their software are significant, although infrequent in use. Some musical performers have gained new audiences by distributing their copyrighted works for free across peer-to-peer networks, and some distributors of unprotected content have used peer-to-peer networks to disseminate files, Shakespeare being an example. StreamCast has given Morpheus users the opportunity to download the briefs in this very case, though their popularity has not been quantified.

StreamCast gave away a software program of a kind known as OpenNap, designed as compatible with the Napster program. The OpenNap program was engineered "to leverage Napster's 50 million user base."

One StreamCast proposed ad read: "Napster Inc. has announced that it will soon begin charging you a fee. That's if the courts don't order it shut down first. What will you do to get around it?" Another proposed ad touted StreamCast's software as the "#1 alternative to Napster" and asked "[w]hen the lights went off at Napster … where did the users go?" StreamCast even planned to flaunt the illegal uses of its software; when it launched the OpenNap network, the chief technology officer of the company averred that "[t]he goal is to get in trouble with the law and get sued. It's the best way to get in the new[s]." Grokster launched its own OpenNap system called Swaptor and inserted digital codes into its website so that computer users using Web search engines to look for "Napster" or "[f]ree filesharing" would be directed to the Grokster website, where they could download the Grokster software.

Grokster and StreamCast receive no revenue from users, who obtain the software itself for nothing. Instead, both companies generate income by selling advertising space, and they stream the advertising to

CONTINUED

Grokster and Morpheus users while they are employing the programs. As the number of users of each program increases, advertising opportunities become worth more. While there is doubtless some demand for free Shakespeare, the evidence shows that free access to copyrighted work is most important to users.

The District Court held that those who used the Grokster and Morpheus software to download copyrighted media files directly infringed MGM's copyrights, but granted summary judgment in favor of Grokster and StreamCast as to any liability arising from distribution of the then current versions of their software. The Court of Appeals affirmed. MGM appealed.

JUDICIAL OPINION

SOUTER, Justice

The question is under what circumstances the distributor of a product capable of both lawful and unlawful use is liable for acts of copyright infringement by third parties using the product….

Digital distribution of copyrighted material threatens copyright holders as never before, because every copy is identical to the original, copying is easy, and many people (especially the young) use file-sharing software to download copyrighted works. As the case has been presented to us, these fears are said to be offset by the different concern that imposing liability, not only on infringers but on distributors of software based on its potential for unlawful use, could limit further development of beneficial technologies.

The argument for imposing indirect liability in this case is, however, a powerful one, given the number of infringing downloads that occur every day using StreamCast's and Grokster's software. When a widely shared service or product is used to commit infringement, it may be impossible to enforce rights in the protected work effectively against all direct infringers, the only practical alternative being to go against the distributor of the copying device for secondary liability on a theory of contributory or vicarious infringement.

In *Sony Corp. v Universal City Studios*, 464 U.S. at 434, this Court addressed a claim that secondary liability for infringement can arise from the very distribution of a commercial product…. Because the VCR was "capable of commercially significant noninfringing uses," we held the manufacturer could not be faulted solely on the basis of its distribution.

In sum, where an article is "good for nothing else" but infringement, there is no legitimate public interest in its unlicensed availability, and there is no injustice in presuming or imputing an intent to infringe…. Conversely, the doctrine absolves the equivocal conduct of selling an item with substantial lawful as well as unlawful uses, and limits liability to instances of more acute fault than the mere understanding that some

of one's products will be misused. It leaves breathing room for innovation and a vigorous commerce.

Grokster and StreamCast reply by citing evidence that their software can be used to reproduce public domain works, and they point to copyright holders who actually encourage copying. Even if infringement is the principal practice with their software today, they argue, the noninfringing uses are significant and will grow.

Because the Circuit found the StreamCast and Grokster software capable of substantial lawful use, it concluded on the basis of its reading of *Sony* that neither company could be held liable, since there was no showing that their software, being without any central server, afforded them knowledge of specific unlawful uses.

This view of *Sony*, however, was in error, converting the case from one about liability resting on imputed intent to one about liability on any theory.

…Nothing in *Sony* requires courts to ignore evidence of intent if there is such evidence, and the case was never meant to foreclose rules of fault-based liability derived from the common law.

The classic case of direct evidence of unlawful purpose occurs when one induces commission of infringement by another, or "entic[es] or persuad[es] another" to infringe, Black's Law Dictionary 790 (8th ed. 2004), as by advertising. Thus at common law a copyright or patent defendant who "not only expected but invoked [infringing use] by advertisement" was liable for infringement "on principles recognized in every part of the law."

For the same reasons that *Sony* took the staple-article doctrine of patent law as a model for its copyright safe-harbor rule, the inducement rule, too, is a sensible one for copyright. We adopt it here, holding that one who distributes a device with the object of promoting its use to infringe copyright, as shown by clear expression or other affirmative steps taken to foster infringement, is liable for the resulting acts of infringement by third parties. We are, of course, mindful of the need to keep from trenching on regular commerce or discouraging the development of technologies with lawful and unlawful potential. The inducement rule, instead, premises liability on purposeful, culpable expression and conduct, and thus does nothing to compromise legitimate commerce or discourage innovation having a lawful promise.

Here, the summary judgment record is replete with other evidence that Grokster and StreamCast, unlike the manufacturer and distributor in *Sony*, acted with a purpose to cause copyright violations by use of software suitable for illegal use.

…[e]ach company showed itself to be aiming to satisfy a known source of demand for copyright infringement, the market comprising former Napster users. StreamCast's internal documents made constant reference to Napster, it initially distributed its Morpheus software through an OpenNap program compatible

CONTINUED

with Napster, it advertised its OpenNap program to Napster users, and its Morpheus software functions as Napster did except that it could be used to distribute more kinds of files, including copyrighted movies and software programs. Grokster's name is apparently derived from Napster, it too initially offered an OpenNap program, its software's function is likewise comparable to Napster's, and it attempted to divert queries for Napster onto its own Web site. Grokster and StreamCast's efforts to supply services to former Napster users, deprived of a mechanism to copy and distribute what were overwhelmingly infringing files, indicate a principal, if not exclusive, intent on the part of each to bring about infringement.

[Neither company] attempted to develop filtering tools or other mechanisms to diminish the infringing activity using their software. As the record shows, the more the software is used, the more ads are sent out and the greater the advertising revenue becomes. Since the extent of the software's use determines the gain to the distributors, the commercial sense of their enterprise turns on high-volume use, which the record shows is infringing. This evidence alone would not justify an inference of unlawful intent, but viewed in the context of the entire record its import is clear.... The unlawful objective is unmistakable.

We hold that one who distributes a device with the object of promoting its use to infringe copyright, as shown by clear expression or other affirmative steps taken to foster infringement, is liable for the resulting acts of infringement by third parties. The judgment of the Court of Appeals is vacated, and the case is remanded for further proceedings consistent with this opinion.

CASE QUESTIONS

1. What is the difference between Sony's Betamax and Grokster's software program?

2. What did Grokster argue as a means for avoiding vicarious liability for copyright infringement? What is the significance of "other lawful means of use"?

3. List the critical facts that tipped the Court's decision against Grokster.

EXHIBIT 1.1 Sample Case Brief

Name of case:	*Metro-Goldwyn-Mayer Studios Inc. v Grokster, Ltd.*
Court:	U.S. Supreme Court
Citation:	545 U.S. 913 (2005)
Parties and their roles:	Grokster, Ltd. and StreamCast Networks, Inc. (respondents/defendants); Metro-Goldwyn Mayer and other film companies and recording studios (petitioners/plaintiffs)
Facts:	MGM and others sued Grokster and StreamCast for their users' copyright infringements, alleging that they knowingly and intentionally distributed their software to enable users to reproduce and distribute the copyrighted works in violation of the Copyright Act.
Issues:	Can Grokster and StreamCast be held liable for copyright infringement based on third parties' unlawful use of its software? What are the legal rights of those whose copyrights are infringed by others using a tool provided by companies such as Grokster?
Lower court decision:	The District Court held that those who used the Grokster and Morpheus software to download copyrighted media files directly infringed MGM's copyrights, but granted summary judgment in favor of Grokster and StreamCast as to any liability arising from distribution of the then current versions of their software. The Court of Appeals affirmed. MGM appealed.
Decision:	Groksters and StreamCast could be held liable.
Reasoning:	The court held that Grokster and StreamCast can be held liable for the infringement by others, not on the grounds of no other lawful use (for there are other lawful uses of their technology), but rather for their intent established by their methods of advertising, their advice to users, and their lack of control over the use of their software and their knowledge regarding its use for infringement purposes.

The following case builds on the precedent of the *Grokster* case and also provides the answer for the chapter opening "Consider…."

CASE 1.2

Viacom International, Inc. v YouTube, LLC
676 F.3d 19 (2nd Cir. 2012)

A Few Episodes of the "Family Guy" Here and There, But Am I My Users' Keeper?

FACTS

YouTube was founded in February 2005 by Chad Hurley, Steve Chen, and Jawed Karim, three former employees of Paypal. When YouTube was launched in December 2005, a press release described it as a "consumer media company" that "allows people to watch, upload, and share personal video clips." YouTube achieved rapid prominence and profitability, eclipsing competitors such as Google Video and Yahoo Video by wide margins. In November 2006, Google acquired YouTube for $1.65 billion. By March 2010, site traffic on YouTube had soared to more than 1 billion daily video views, with more than 24 hours of new video uploaded to the site every minute. Viacom and other film studios and organizations (plaintiffs), relying on *Metro–Goldwyn–Mayer Studios Inc. v Grokster, Ltd.*, 545 U.S. 913 (2005), filed suit alleging direct and secondary copyright infringement of 79,000 audiovisual "clips" of their copyrighted materials on the YouTube website. The district court granted summary judgment to YouTube and Google. The plaintiffs appealed.

JUDICIAL OPINION

CABRANES, Judge

The Digital Millennium Copyright Act (DMCA) limits the liability of online service providers for copyright infringement. A party that qualifies as a service provider (to obtain limited liability] must also satisfy certain "conditions of eligibility," including the adoption and reasonable implementation of a "repeat infringer" policy that "provides for the termination in appropriate circumstances of subscribers and account holders of the service provider's system or network." In addition, a qualifying service provider must accommodate "standard technical measures" that are "used by copyright owners to identify or protect copyrighted works." [§ 512(i)(1)(B), (i)(2)]

Title II of the DMCA, separately titled the "Online Copyright Infringement Liability Limitation Act"

(OCILLA), was designed to "clarif[y] the liability faced by service providers who transmit potentially infringing material over their networks." A party [seeking a safe harbor under OCILLA] must satisfy certain "conditions of eligibility," including the adoption and reasonable implementation of a "repeat infringer" policy that "provides for the termination of subscribers and account holders of the service provider's system or network." In addition, a provider must accommodate "standard technical measures" that are "used by copyright owners to identify or protect copyrighted works."

Section 512(c) also requires service providers to "designate[ ] an agent to receive notifications of claimed infringement," and specifies the components of a "takedown notice" to that agent. Actual knowledge of infringing material, awareness of facts or circumstances that make infringing activity apparent, or receipt of a takedown notice each trigger an obligation to expeditiously remove the infringing material.

With the statutory context in mind, we now turn to the facts of this case.

THE YOUTUBE AWARENESS ISSUE

YouTube founder Jawed Karim prepared a report in March 2006 which stated that, "[a]s of today[,] episodes and clips of the following well-known shows can still be found [on YouTube]: Family Guy, South Park, MTV Cribs, Daily Show, Reno 911, [and] Dave Chapelle [sic]." Karim further opined that, "although YouTube is not legally required to monitor content … and complies with DMCA takedown requests, we would benefit from preemptively removing content that is blatantly illegal and likely to attract criticism." He also noted that "a more thorough analysis" of the issue would be required. At least some of the TV shows to which Karim referred are owned by Viacom. A reasonable juror could conclude from the March 2006 report that Karim knew of the presence of Viacom-owned material on YouTube. A reasonable juror could also conclude

CONTINUED

that Karim believed the clips he located to be infringing (since he refers to them as "blatantly illegal"), and that YouTube did not remove the content from the website until conducting "a more thorough analysis," thus exposing the company to liability in the interim. [i]n a July 4, 2005 e-mail exchange, YouTube founder Chad Hurley sent an e-mail to his co-founders with the subject line "budlight commercials," and stated, "we need to reject these too." Steve Chen responded, "can we please leave these in a bit longer? another week or two can't hurt." Karim also replied, indicating that he "added back in all 28 bud videos." Similarly, in an August 9, 2005 e-mail exchange, Hurley urged his colleagues "to start being diligent about rejecting copyrighted/inappropriate content," noting that "there is a cnn clip of the shuttle clip on the site today, if the boys from Turner would come to the site, they might be pissed?" Again, Chen resisted: "but we should just keep that stuff on the site. i really don't see what will happen. what? someone from cnn sees it? he happens to be someone with power? he happens to want to take it down right away. he gets in touch with cnn legal. 2 weeks later, we get a cease & desist letter. we take the video down."

We are persuaded that the plaintiffs have raised a material issue of fact regarding YouTube's knowledge or awareness of specific instances of infringement. Accordingly, we hold that summary judgment to YouTube on all clips-in-suit, especially in the absence of any detailed examination of the extensive record on summary judgment, was premature.

THE MONITORING ISSUE

DMCA safe harbor protection cannot be conditioned on affirmative monitoring by a service provider. For that reason, § 512(m) is incompatible with a broad common law duty to monitor or otherwise seek out infringing activity based on general awareness that infringement may be occurring

Our recent decision in *Tiffany (NJ) Inc. v eBay Inc.*, 600 F.3d 93 (2nd Cir. 2010), lends support to this result. In *Tiffany*, we rejected a willful blindness challenge, holding that although eBay "knew as a general matter that counterfeit Tiffany products were listed and sold through its website," such knowledge "is insufficient to trigger liability." In so holding, however, we rested on the extensive findings of the district court with respect to willful blindness. The *Tiffany* holding counsels in favor of explicit fact-finding on the issue.

VICARIOUS LIABILITY

The plaintiffs [argue] that [the] common law imposes liability for vicarious copyright infringement "[w]hen

the right and ability to supervise coalesce with an obvious and direct financial interest in the exploitation of copyrighted materials—even in the absence of actual knowledge that the copyright mono [poly] is being impaired." In light of our holding that § 512(c)(1)(B) does not include a specific knowledge requirement, we think it prudent to remand to the District Court to consider in the first instance whether the plaintiffs have adduced sufficient evidence to allow a reasonable jury to conclude that YouTube had the right and ability to control the infringing activity and received a financial benefit directly attributable to that activity.

THE INDEXING AND "RELATED VIDEOS" ISSUE

The § 512(c) safe harbor is only available when the infringement occurs "by reason of the storage at the direction of a user of material that resides on a system or network controlled or operated by or for the service provider." In this case, the District Court held that YouTube's software functions fell within the safe harbor for infringements that occur "by reason of" user storage. The relevant case law makes clear that the § 512(c) safe harbor extends to software functions performed "for the purpose of facilitating access to user-stored material."

A similar analysis applies to the "related videos" function, by which a YouTube computer algorithm identifies and displays "thumbnails" of clips that are "related" to the video selected by the user. The plaintiffs claim that this practice constitutes content promotion, not "access" to stored content, and therefore falls beyond the scope of the safe harbor.

The record makes clear that the related videos algorithm "is fully automated and operates solely in response to user input without the active involvement of YouTube employees." Furthermore, the related videos function serves to help YouTube users locate and gain access to material stored at the direction of other users. Because the algorithm "is closely related to, and follows from, the storage itself," and is "narrowly directed toward providing access to material stored at the direction of users," we conclude that the related videos function is also protected by the § 512(c) safe harbor.

THIRD-PARTY CONTRACTS

The final software function at issue here—third-party syndication—is the closest case. In or around March 2007, YouTube transcoded a select number of videos into a format compatible with mobile devices and "syndicated" or licensed the videos to Verizon Wireless and other companies. The plaintiffs

CONTINUED

argue—with some force—that business transactions do not occur at the "direction of a user" within the meaning of § 512(c)(1) when they involve the manual selection of copyrighted material for licensing to a third party. The parties do not dispute, however, that none of the clips-in-suit were among the approximately 2,000 videos provided to Verizon Wireless. In order to avoid rendering an advisory opinion on the outer boundaries of the storage provision, we remand for fact-finding on the question of whether any of the clips-in-suit were in fact syndicated to any other third party.

The order granting summary judgment to YouTube is VACATED and the cause is REMANDED.

CASE QUESTIONS

1. Explain why the statutes are important in deciding this case.

2. Explain what conduct of YouTube the court focuses on to remand the case on copyright infringement issues.

3. What can you learn about e-mail communications between and among business owners?

Consider...

Demand Media owns Cracked.com, a comedy website. Along with the site's own humorous content, registered users may post items to their personal profiles. Cracked has a policy of terminating Cracked user accounts if it receives one or more complaints that a user has infringed an author's copyright.

Austin Obodai filed suit against Demand Media for infringement alleging that a registered user with the screen name "socialway" published 32 items of Obodai's on his Cracked profile. Obodai owns the copyrights for these items. The items have titles such as "How to Pick a Credit Card Now," "How to Bank With Good Institutions," and "How to Become Awful at Math."

Before filing suit, Obodai did not notify Cracked.com about the problems with "socialway's" posts. When Demand Media received the notice from its designated copyright agent about the infringement, it removed Obodai's materials immediately. There was evidence in the case that Cracked "responds expeditiously to notifications of claimed infringement on Cracked.com."

Obodai says Demand Media is still liable because the materials were in the profile of a user and should be monitored. What should the court do? Remember to apply the *Grokster* and *Viacom* cases. [*Obodai v Demand Media, Inc.*, 2012 WL 2189740 (S.D.N.Y.)]

THINK: Before answering this problem, review the decisions in the *Grokster* and *Viacom* cases. Recall the following.

1. Technology that permits copying of copyrighted materials is not an automatic violation of copyright law if:
   a. The service provider would not be able to monitor posting of items that were infringing copyrights.
   b. The service provider has a means for copyright holders to notify it of problems.
   c. The service provider takes action when it is notified or is aware of infringement.

2. It is possible for a service provider to be "vicariously liable" for infringement if they are aware that their technology or product is used for infringement, they benefit from the infringement uses, and they take no steps to halt the infringement despite the capability to do so.

APPLY: The requirements for an exemption appear to be present for Demand Media because of its notification procedures and response.

ANSWER: You can answer this "Consider..." by reviewing the issues these facts have in common with the facts from the *Grokster* and *Viacom* cases. Think through the following questions: Does the service provider have an agent for notice? Does the service provider have notice of infringement? Does the service provider remove infringing materials? Once you have answered these questions, you have your answer.

ETHICAL ISSUES

Evaluate the ethics of the founders of YouTube as they e-mailed among each other about the presence of full copyrighted shows on YouTube and their reluctance to take them down or take down CNN videos that they knew would be a problem.

FOR THE MANAGER'S DESK

Re: Grokster Friends and Foes

One of the interesting pieces of background information on the *Grokster* case is the parties, in addition to MGM and Grokster, who filed *amicus curiae* (friend of the court) briefs in the case.

Managers in many companies and industries realized their strategic interests in the outcome of this case. Looking at the following list, discuss whose position you believe these parties took when they wrote their briefs in support.

a. Intellectual Property and Technology Law Professors for the U.S. Public Policy Committee of the Association for Computing Machinery

b. The American Library Association

c. The Consumer Electronics Association

d. Intel Corporation

e. The Cellular Telecommunications & Internet Association

f. The American Civil Liberties Union

g. Office of the Commissioner of Baseball; the National Basketball Association; the National Football League

h. Don Henley, Glenn Frey, Joe Walsh, and Timothy B. Schmit (the Eagles); Jimmy Buffett; Kenny "Babyface" Edmonds; Mickey Hart and Bill Kreutzmann (of the Grateful Dead); Sheryl Crow; and Kix Brooks

i. Napster, LLC; Tennessee Pacific Group, LLC, d/b/a Pass Along Networks; Wurld Media, Inc.; and Virtual Music Stores Ltd.

1-5 The Theory of Law: Jurisprudence

Law is the compromise of conflicting ideas. Not only do people differ in their thinking on the types of specific laws, they also differ on the theory behind the law or the values a legal system should try to advance or encourage. Many can agree on the definition of law and its purposes but still differ on how those purposes are best accomplished. The incorporation of theories or values into the legal process is, perhaps, what makes each society's laws different and causes law to change as society changes its values. These different theories or value bases for law are found in an area of legal study called **jurisprudence**, a Latin term meaning "wisdom of the law." In many cases, how the law should work is unclear. Conflicting philosophical views often come together in litigation. Judges and lawmakers must struggle to do the best good for the most members of society.

1-5a THE THEORY OF LAW: POSITIVE LAW

There are some who see law as simply written orders that we must keep. Known as the positive law school of thought, those who subscribe to it believe that the critical part of the law is obedience so that we can have an orderly society.

BUSINESS STRATEGY

The Dangers of Lawsuits as a Strategy

Another important lesson of both the *Grokster* and *Viacom* cases is the importance of business strategy. Napster was the first music downloading site and although litigation put it out of business, the seeds of technology began to take hold. The possibilities now seem endless as the technology has evolved to allow us to purchase music in very different, more convenient, and less costly ways. Artists can now release music to fans directly and need not deal with record companies. Some artists have commented that they enjoy the direct link to fans and the ability to get music to those fans very quickly.

The free downloading of songs was curbed by copyright laws, and the law is one business tool that can be used to enforce rights and protect stability. However, sometimes the law is a stopgap measure or even interferes with the strategic planning for technological changes. Litigation is often not the best resolution for a problem. Here, record and film industries needed to look at the technology's possibilities and use it, not try to stop it. By 2006, online song purchases were the most popular method for purchasing music. Fueled by Apple and its iTunes site, the focus of the music industry has shifted completely. Today, we have the ability through Netflix and Hulu to purchase television episodes and films at our convenience. Perhaps the copyright owners should have worked on delivery systems for their products rather than trying to stop the inexorable march of others using technology to create this consumer convenience. The litigation and infringement were symptoms of a lack of vision and strategy within the industry for technology's new ways for buying music.

© yxowert/Shutterstock.com

1-5b THE THEORY OF LAW: NATURAL LAW

Another theory of jurisprudence is that of natural law, a theory that holds that we have certain rights that cannot be taken away by law. The United States of America's form of government was grounded in the natural law theorists' views that we have certain unalienable rights that cannot be taken away by any law. Any law that purports to take away those rights is invalid and must be challenged, either through the courts or through civil disobedience. An example would be slavery. While slavery was legal in the United States and other countries for many years, it was constantly met with dissent, disobedience, and eventually civil war. Natural law trumped the positive law and slavery was eliminated because it was declared a violation of the law.

1-5c THE THEORY OF LAW: THE PROTECTION OF INDIVIDUALS AND RELATIONSHIPS

Justice Oliver Wendell Holmes, in "Natural Law," his famous essay written in 1918 at the height of World War I, he rejected the notion of natural law. His essay began with the famous phrase, "The life of the law has not been logic; it has been experience." Holmes's opinion is that our interactions with each other constitute the foundation of law.

> If I do live with others they tell me what I must do if I wish to remain alive. If I do live with others they tell me what I must do and abstain from doing various things or they will put the screws to me.[3]

In other words, the law is what keeps the peace among us, and should we choose to ignore it, those around us will take control and bring us into compliance.

Business Planning Tip

Failure to anticipate technological changes results in significant revenue losses under contracts for copyrighted works or patented products. For example, many actors, writers, and others involved with television shows of the 1950s and 1960s do not enjoy the royalties from their shows, which run in what seems to be perpetual syndication on networks such as TV Land and Nick at Nite that feature only television shows of other generations. Those involved in the production of these shows did not foresee what technology would permit. Walt Disney and Universal did not anticipate the video tape recorder, downloading, file-sharing, or streaming, and their capability.

Technology clauses in royalty agreements for patents and copyrights that cover any future means of distribution, whether by wire, sound, computer, or satellite, provide an open-ended agreement for royalty coverage from evolving technology.

© Grounder/Shutterstock.com

Consider...

Apply the theories of jurisprudence to the following situations.

1. Maj. Gen. Antonio M. Taguba led an investigation of the conduct of U.S. soldiers in the Abu Ghraib prison in Iraq. The 54-page report documented brutal treatment of Iraqi prisoners, torture, and humiliation, all in violation of either the Geneva Convention for the treatment of prisoners of war or the standards of the Red Cross. Gen. Taguba referred to the treatment of the prisoners as consisting of "egregious acts and grave violations of international law."[4] One of the findings of the report is that the soldiers serving as prison guards had little training. General Taguba recommended training for soldiers in when to disobey orders. A fellow officer said of General Taguba, "If you want the truth; he's going to tell you the truth. He's a stand-up guy."[5]

   General Taguba's father was Staff Sgt. Tomas Taguba, a man who fought in the Battle of Bataan and was taken prisoner by the Japanese. He escaped from prison there and joined the fighters in Japan who opposed the government.

   Based on these brief descriptions of these two men, what philosophy of law do you think they would follow?

2. A supervisor has ordered an employee to inflate the company's earnings for the quarter so that their unit can meet their goals and attain their bonuses. Must the employee obey?

3. Is a businessperson who believes the tax system to be unconstitutional justified in refusing to pay taxes? How will society react to such a position?

4. Is there any example of a law that is accepted by everyone in society? What about the laws against speeding? What about the laws that restrict who can marry? What happens, according to the philosophers, when there is no common agreement on what the law should be?

5. Refer back to the *Viacom* case. What school of thought on jurisprudence do you think Mr. Chen and the other founders of YouTube followed, based on the content of their e-mails?

1-5d THE THEORY OF LAW: THE SOCIAL CONTRACT

Roscoe Pound, another legal philosopher and dean of Harvard Law School for 20 years, had a different view of jurisprudence from Justice Holmes. His view was that law exists as the result of those who happen to be in power, that there is a type of social contract that we mutually honor. In 1941, Pound wrote his famous credo, called "My Philosophy of Law."

> *I think of law as in one sense a highly specialized form of social control in a developed politically organized society—a social control through the systematic and orderly application of the force of such a society. Moreover, it operates through a judicial process and an administrative process, which also go by the name of law… .[6]*

1-6 Sources of Law

Laws exist in different forms at every level of government. As discussed earlier, law exists not only in statutory form but also in its common law form through judicial decisions. Statutory law exists at all levels of government. Statutes are written laws enacted by some governmental body with the proper authority—legislatures, city governments, and counties—and published and made available for public use and knowledge. These written statutes are sometimes referred to as codified law, and their sources, as well as constitutions, are covered in the following sections.

1-6a CONSTITUTIONAL LAW

The U.S. Constitution and the constitutions of the various states are unique forms of law. **Constitutions** are not statutes because they cannot be added to, amended, or repealed with the same ease as can statutes. Constitutions are the law of the people, and are changed only by lengthier and more demanding procedures than those used to repeal statutes.

Constitutions tend to protect general rights, such as speech, religion, and property (see Chapter 5 for a more complete discussion). They also provide a framework for all other forms of laws. The basic rights and protections afforded in them cannot be abridged or denied by the other sources of law. In other words, a statute's boundaries are formed by constitutionally protected rights. Exhibit 1.2 is an illustration of the sources of law; constitutional law is at the base of the pyramid diagram because of its inviolate status.

1-6b STATUTORY LAW AT THE FEDERAL LEVEL

Congressional Law

Congress is responsible for statutory law at the federal level. The laws passed by Congress become part of the **United States Code** (U.S.C.). Examples of such laws are the 1933 and 1934 Securities Acts (see Chapter 19), the Sherman Act and other antitrust laws (see Chapter 16), the Equal Employment Opportunity Act (see Chapter 21), the National Labor Relations Act (see Chapter 20), the Truth-in-Lending Act (see Chapter 12), the USA Patriot Act (see Chapters 8 and 19), and the Internal Revenue Code (see Chapter 18).

Statutes from the U.S.C. are referenced or *cited* by a standard form of legal shorthand, often referred to as a **cite** or **citation**. The number of the title is put in front of

EXHIBIT 1.2 Sources of Law

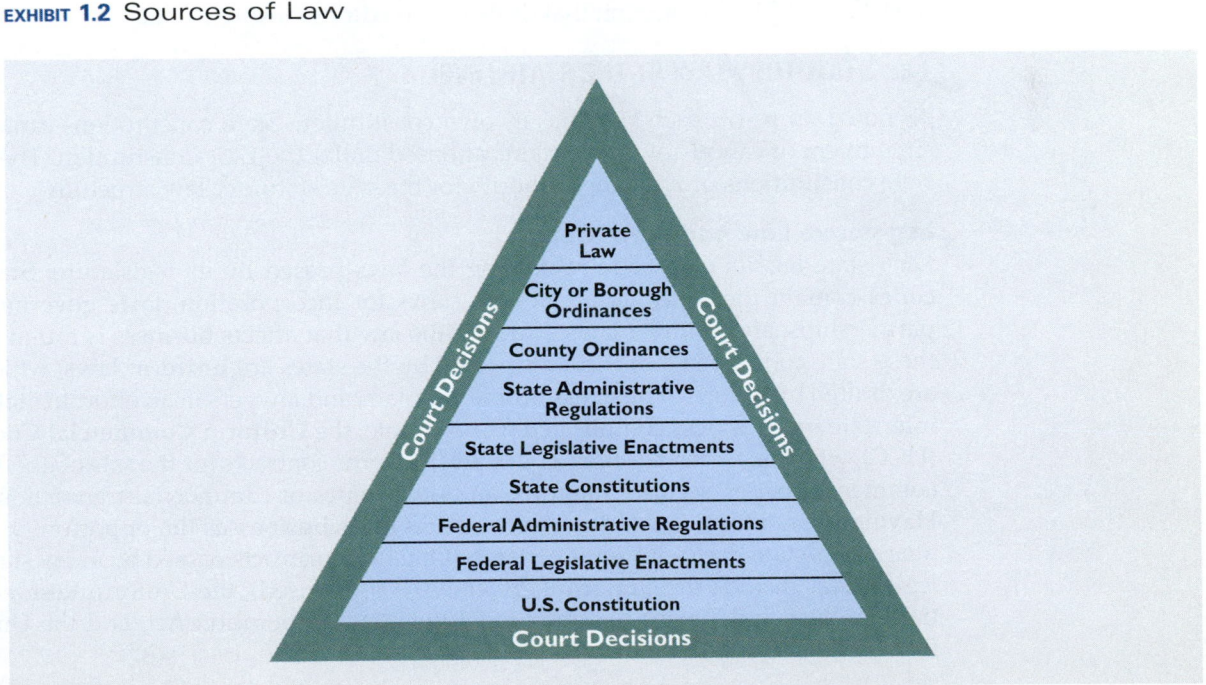

© Cengage Learning

"U.S.C." to tell which volume of the Code to go to. For example, "15 U.S.C." refers to Title 15 of the U.S. Code (Title 15 happens to cover securities). There may be more than one volume that is numbered "15," however. To enable you to find the volume you need, the reference or cite has a section (§) number following it. This section number is the particular statute referenced, and you must look for the volume of Title 15 that contains that section. For example, the first volume of Title 15 contains §§ 1–11. A full reference or cite to a United States Code statute looks like this: 15 U.S.C. § 77. When a U.S.C. cite is given, the law cited will be a federal law passed by Congress.

Executive Orders

Executive orders are laws of the executive branch of the federal government and deal with those matters under the direct control of that branch. For example, on his second day in office, President Barack Obama issued an executive order prohibiting the use of waterboarding in questioning military combatants who are in U.S. custody. In 2012, President Obama issued an executive order that gave a path to citizenship for certain young people who were brought to the United States by their parents and had served in the military and/or graduated from high school (or its equivalent) and did not have a felony criminal record.

Federal Administrative Regulations

The federal government has administrative agencies that serve the functions of promulgation of rules (called regulations) for developing specifics such as forms and time requirements for carrying out the legislative enactments of Congress, in addition to enforcing both the laws and regulations (see Chapter 6 for more details). Examples of federal agencies include the Environmental Protection Agency (EPA), the Equal Employment Opportunity Commission (EEOC), and the Securities and Exchange Commission (SEC).

Federal regulations are found in the Code of Federal Regulations (CFR), a set of paperback volumes that is published once each year. A citation from the CFR has a structure similar to that of a U.S.C. cite. For example, 12 C.F.R. §226 is volume 12 of the CFR and §226 is a section that deals with credit disclosure rights.

1-6c STATUTORY LAW AT THE STATE LEVEL

As noted on p. 17., each state has its own constitution. State constitutions cannot circumvent or cancel any of the rights afforded under the U.S. Constitution. These state constitutions provide the authority for the state statutory law structure.

Legislative Law and State Codes

Each state has its own code containing the laws passed by its legislature. **State codes** contain the states' criminal laws, laws for incorporation, laws governing partnerships, and contract laws. Much of the law that affects business is found in these state codes. Some of the laws passed by the states are **uniform laws**, which are drafted by groups of business people, scholars, and lawyers in an effort to make interstate business less complicated. For example, the **Uniform Commercial Code** (UCC), which has been adopted in 49 states, governs contracts for the sale of goods, commercial paper, security interests, and other types of commercial transactions. Having this uniform law in the various states gives businesses the opportunity to deal across state lines with some certainty. Other uniform acts passed by many state legislatures include the Uniform Partnership Act (Revised), the Uniform Residential Landlord and Tenant Act, the Model Business Corporation Act, and the Uniform Probate Code.

State Administrative Law

Just as at the federal level, state governments have administrative agencies with the power to pass regulations dealing with the statutes and powers given by the state legislatures. For example, most states have an agency to handle incorporations and the status of corporations in the state. Most states also have a tax agency to handle income or sales taxes in the state.

1-6d LOCAL LAWS OF CITIES, COUNTIES, AND TOWNSHIPS

In addition to federal and state statutes, local governments can pass **ordinances** or statutes within their areas of power or control. For example, cities and counties have the authority to handle zoning issues, and the municipal code outlines the zoning system and whatever means of enforcement and specified penalties apply. These local laws govern lesser issues, such as dog licensing, curfews, and loitering. However, local governments are often responsible for national legal trends. For example, city and county bans on Styrofoam containers have resulted in the transformation of the fast-food industry by the use of new types of containers. City ordinances often affect national companies and the companies make changes nationwide to comply with local ordinances.

1-6e PRIVATE LAWS

Private laws are a final source of written law and are found, for example, in contracts and landlord regulations. These private laws are enforceable provided they are not inconsistent with rights and protections afforded under the other sources of law (see Chapters 3 and 4).

1-6f COURT DECISIONS

Looking at Exhibit 1.2, you can see that all of the sources of law just covered are surrounded in the pyramid by the term "Court Decisions." Often the language in a statute is unclear, or perhaps whether the statute or ordinance applies in a particular situation is unclear. When these ambiguities or omissions occur in the statutory language, courts provide interpretation or clarification of the law when disputing parties bring suit. These court decisions are then read along with the statutory language in order to give a complete analysis of the scope and intent of the statute. The *Grokster* and *Viacom* cases illustrate how laws are interpreted and applied on issues related to the federal copyright statutes and infringement through new technologies.

1-7 Introduction to International Law

Business is global. Companies headquartered in Japan have factories in the United States, and U.S. firms have manufacturing plants in South America and subcontractors and suppliers in China. Trade and political barriers to economic development no longer exist. Businesses must be adept at trading across country boundaries and such trade requires an understanding of international law.

International law is not a neat body of law like contract law or the UCC. Rather, it is a combination of the laws of various countries, international trade customs, and international agreements. Article 38(1) of the Statute of the

International Court of Justice (a court of the United Nations that countries consent to have resolve disputes) is a widely recognized statement of the sources of international law:

(a) *international conventions, whether general or particular, establishing rules expressly recognized by the contesting states;*

(b) *international custom as evidence of a general practice accepted as law;*

(c) *the general principles of law recognized by civilized nations;*

(d) *judicial decisions and the teachings of the most highly qualified publicists of the various nations, as subsidiary means for the determination of rules of law.*

1-7a   CUSTOM

Every country has its boundaries for allowable behavior, and these boundaries are unwritten but recognized laws. The standards of behavior are reflected in statements made by business people and government officials. Custom develops over time and through repeated conduct. For example, working conditions in factories around the world have improved over the past 20 years not through changes in laws but through the business custom of inspections, monitors, and transparent disclosure of supply chain resources. Business custom is now one of assuming responsibility for the conditions in factories that supply parts and labor for goods produced around the world.

In addition to operations, businesses must develop a knowledge of and sensitivity to individual country customs related to negotiations and relationships. For example, unlike the United States, most countries do not offer a warranty protection on goods and instead follow a philosophy of *caveat emptor*, "Let the buyer beware." Other countries also do not recognize the extensive rules of insurance and risk followed here with respect to the shipment of goods. Multinational firms must make provisions for protection of shipments in those countries with different standards. Differing laws can affect product content and quality. For example, lead-based paint is not permitted for use on children's toys in the United States, but in China, at one point, lead-based paint was standard in toy production. A toy manufacturer must learn to specify legal standards for suppliers because custom and laws in that country may find the suppliers assuming the same standards they use apply to production for businesses outside their country.

At one time, the customs of China with respect to intellectual property, most particularly computer software, lagged behind those of Europe and the United States. Chinese custom was to separate infringement into two categories: ordinary acts and serious acts. Ordinary infringement is not regarded as a legal issue and requires only that the party apologize, destroy the software, and not engage in infringement again. Courts were rarely involved in ordinary infringement cases. However, the U.S. government demanded more protection for its copyright holders by imposing trade sanctions, and China eventually agreed to revise its customs and laws to afford protection. In this case, China's customs had to be changed to provide protection similar to that afforded in other countries.

1-7b   TREATIES

A **treaty** is an agreement between or among nations on a subject of international law signed by the leaders of the nations and ratified by the nations' governing bodies. In the United States, treaties are ratified by the Senate and are included in the pyramid (Exhibit 1.2) as federal legislative enactments.

Treaties can be between two nations—**bilateral treaties**—or **multilateral treaties**, those that are made among several nations. Other treaties, recognized by almost all nations, are called general or **universal treaties**. Universal treaties are a reflection of widely followed standards of behavior. For example, the Geneva Convention is a universal treaty covering the treatment of prisoners of war. The Vienna Convention is a universal treaty covering diplomatic relations. The Warsaw Convention is a treaty that addresses issues of liability for injuries to passengers and property during international air travel. For more discussion on trade treaties, see Chapter 7.

1-7c PRIVATE LAW IN INTERNATIONAL TRANSACTIONS

Those businesses involved in multinational trade and production rely heavily on private law to assure performance of contractual obligations. Even though each country has a different set of laws, all of them recognize the autonomy of parties in an international trade transaction and allow the parties to negotiate contract terms that suit their needs, as long as none of the terms is illegal. **Party autonomy** allows firms to operate uniformly throughout the world if their contracts are recognized as valid in most countries. For example, most international trade contracts have a choice-of-law clause whereby the parties decide which country's law will apply to their disputes under the contract.

1-7d INTERNATIONAL ORGANIZATIONS

Some international organizations provide the means for facilitating multinational commercial transactions. For example, the World Trade Organization (WTO) (see Chapter 7 for more details) provides a Dispute Settlement Body (DSB), a forum for resolving trade disputes related to multilateral treaties.

1-7e THE DOCTRINES OF INTERNATIONAL LAW

There are a number of principles of international law that are widely accepted and honored by most countries. These include the **act of state doctrine**, a theory that

FOR THE MANAGER'S DESK

Re: How International Ice Skating Scandals Are Resolved

In an example of private law at work, the International Olympic Committee (IOC) dealt with issues of vote exchanges among judges for the pairs figure skating competition. Canadian skaters David Pelletier and Jamie Sale were awarded a silver medal after what was called "the performance of a lifetime" in the competition. Their performance was flawless, although not as difficult as that of Elena Berezhnaya and Anton Sikharulidze, who were awarded the gold medal despite several errors in their performance.

The French judge on the panel, Marie Reine Le Gougne, said she was pressured by the Russians to rank the Russian team first. There may have been a *quid pro quo* arrangement with the French to assure the Russian vote

for the French competitors in ice dancing if the Russians could have the French vote in pairs.

Following public outcry and an investigation, the IOC awarded a second gold medal to the Canadian skaters. The decision was based on IOC rules, internal policies, and an internal fact-finding group. No criminal laws were broken, and it was up to the private body to take appropriate action for rules violations.

What ethical issues do you see in these events? Was the remedy appropriate? Would you have accepted the gold medal if you were the Canadian team?

Source: Selena Roberts, "Canadian Skaters Awarded Share of Olympic Gold; French Judge Suspended, Her Scoring Thrown Out," *New York Times*, February 16, 2002, A1, B21.

protects governments from reviews of their actions by courts in other countries. In any action in which the government of a country has taken steps to condemn or confiscate property, the courts of other countries will not interfere (see Chapter 7 for a full discussion of this and other doctrines of international law).

1-7f   TRADE LAW AND POLICIES

The importance of trade laws, tariffs, and policies has increased directly with the rising numbers of international business transactions. Chapter 7 provides additional details on trade laws, tariffs, restrictions, and trade agreements.

1-7g   UNIFORM INTERNATIONAL LAWS

Because trade barriers have been largely eliminated, contracts have been and are being formed between and among businesses from virtually all nations. However, not all nations have the same approach to contracts. Indeed, some nations have no contract laws or commercial codes. In an attempt to introduce uniformity in international contract law, the UN developed its Contracts for the International Sale of Goods (CISG), which has been adopted widely and allows businesses to opt in or out of its application in adopting countries. Similar to the UCC (see Chapter 12), the CISG has provisions on contract formation, performance, and damages. More information on the CISG can be found in Chapters 7, 12, and 13.

1-7h   THE EUROPEAN UNION

Once referred to as the Common Market, and later known as the European Community (EC), the European Union (EU) is a tariff-free group of European countries that have joined together to enjoy the benefits of barrier-free trade. Formed in 1992, the single economic community requires member nations to subscribe to the same monetary standard, the elimination of immigration and customs controls, universal product and job safety standards, uniform licensing of professionals, and unified taxation schedules. The EU continues to evolve and is experiencing tension because of the weaker economies of some of its members and the need for other members to provide economic support for failing government finances. More details on the governance of the EU and its laws and tensions can be found in Chapter 7.

BIOGRAPHY   The Humble Frequent-Flier Mile—So Complicated!

Those airline bonus miles that you get when you travel are a gift, right? And those frequent-flier miles that credit card companies let you earn are also a gift from the credit card company, a sort of incentive for using their card, right? Well, the Internal Revenue Code, part of the United States Code, concludes that it depends on the meaning and/or source of those frequent-flier miles.

For example, if your credit card company gives you 30,000 frequent-flier miles for signing up for a credit card, that award is enough to get you a round-trip ticket to many destinations. That round-trip ticket is worth something and the something came from a bank or credit card

company, and that would be payment of personal gain to you. In 2012, Citibank customers who received the mileage sign-on bonus got a 1099 income form from Citibank because the IRS says the account holder received benefits that are taxable if worth more than $100. Any round-trip ticket anywhere is worth more than $100, so you owe taxes on your signing bonus.

However, the IRS has been kind enough to issue a number of interpretations of the IRC as to when we owe taxes on our mileage awards. If you earn miles from an airline as a frequent flier on that airline, they are treated as a rebate, so no tax is due on those bonuses.

The same is true if you earn those miles because you were flying for business—still not taxable income.

Any miles given by any company to lure you to their business (credit card companies, mutual funds, and even plumbing companies) are considered income, just as free gifts (iPhones, etc.) awarded for opening such accounts are considered income.

Some creative charities and employers are using award miles as raffles for raising money. However, whoever wins the raffle and gets the frequent-flier miles must pay income tax on that prize, just as those who win

$50,000 on *Jeopardy* must pay taxes on that money. A prize in cash or a prize in miles is still income.

Statutory interpretation comes alive with the simple question about the taxability of frequent-flier miles. The answer that threads through all of the examples is that if those miles look like prizes or customer rewards, they are as taxable as being given a bonus, which is exactly what frequent-flier miles are when awarded by anyone other than an airline.

Source: Laura Saunders, "Frequent-Flier Tax Traps," *Wall Street Journal,* February 4–5, 2012, p. B9.

Summary

How is law defined?

- Law is a form of order. Law is the body of rules of society governing individuals and their relationships.

What types of laws are there?

- Public law—codified law; statutes; law by government body
- Private law—rules created by individuals for their contracts, tenancy, and employment
- Civil law—laws regulating harms and carrying damage remedies
- Criminal law—laws regulating wrongful conduct and carrying sentences and fines
- Statutory law—codified law
- Common law—law developed historically and by judicial precedent
- Substantive laws—laws giving rights and responsibilities
- Procedural laws—laws that provide enforcement rights

What are the purposes of law?

- Keep order; influence conduct; honor expectations; promote equality; offer compromises

What are the characteristics of law?

- Flexibility; consistency; pervasiveness
- Jurisprudence—theory of law

Where are laws found and who enacts them?

- Constitution—document that establishes structure and authority of a government
- Federal statutes—laws passed by Congress: the U.S. Code
- State statutes—laws passed by state legislatures, including uniform laws on contracts and business organizations
- Ordinances—local laws passed by cities, counties, and townships

What are the sources of international law?

- Customs—the standards of conduct and norms in a country
- Treaties—agreements between and among nations regarding their political and commercial relationships
- Private law—party autonomy recognized in all nations
- International doctrines—widely accepted principles of law followed in most countries
- European Union—group of nations working collectively for uniform laws and barrier-free trade
- Uniform laws—Contracts for the International Sale of Goods (CISG)

Questions and Problems

1. Bryant Gunderson is a sole proprietor with a successful bungee-jumping business. He is considering incorporating his business. What levels and sources of law would affect and govern the process of incorporation?

2. Jeffrey Stalwart has just been arrested for ticket scalping outside the Great Western Forum in Los Angeles. Jeffrey sold a ticket to an Alanis Morrissette concert to an intense fan for $1,200; the face value of the ticket was $48. Ticket scalping in Los Angeles is a misdemeanor. Will Jeffrey's court proceedings be civil or criminal?

3. In 1933, Walt Disney Company entered into a contract with Irving Berlin, Inc., assigning musical copyrights in exchange for a share of Berlin revenues. The agreement exempted from copyright protection Disney's use of the assigned music in motion pictures. The music was used in several Disney feature-length cartoons (*Snow White* and *Pinocchio*) that were later made available for sale on videocassette. Mr. Berlin's heirs brought suit, alleging infringement. Was this new technology an infringement? Could videocassettes have been anticipated? [*Bourne v Walt Disney Co.*, 68 F.3d 621 (2nd Cir. 1995)]

4. Define and contrast the following:
   a. Civil law and criminal law
   b. Substantive law and procedural law
   c. Common law and statutory law
   d. Private law and public law

5. During the 2001 baseball season, Barry Bonds, a player with the San Francisco Giants, hit 73 home runs in one season, a new record that went beyond the 72 set by Mark McGwire in 2000. Mr. Bonds made his record-breaking home run in San Francisco. When he hit the home run, the ball went into the cheap seats. All agree that Alex Popov had his glove on the home-run ball. However, Patrick Hayashi ended up with the ball.

   Mr. Popov filed suit alleging that Mr. Hayashi assaulted Mr. Popov in order to get the ball. A substantial amount of videotape shows Mr. Popov's "gloving" of the ball. Mr. Popov says the ball belongs to him because he held that ball in a "Sno-cone position" and others wrested it from his control.

   Mark McGwire's ball from his record-breaking home run sold for $3 million. The battle for the Bonds home-run ball carries high financial stakes. What areas of law will be involved in the judge's determination of who gets the baseball? (Peter Page, "Ownership of historic baseball is in extra innings," *National Law Journal*, November 12, 2001.)

6. Gottfrid Svartholm Warg, Peter Sunde, Fredrik Neij, and Carl Lundstrom are four Swedish lads who operated the Pirate Bay website. Pirate Bay allowed its users to have free access to copyrighted movies, music, and more. The site had 22 million users and was based in Sweden, a signatory country to the mutual agreement among countries for enforcement of each other's copyright laws. U.S. music companies and filmmakers asked the Swedish government to take action against Pirate Bay for its role in facilitating copyright infringement. When the Swedish government brought criminal copyright charges against Pirate Bay, the four lads said that they were just promoting free information. They did not actually "host" any of the copyrighted materials, and also did not profit from the exchange of music and films. "We earn $1,000,000 per year from advertising placed on the site, not from users." Is there copyright infringement? What laws apply?

7. Around 5:00 a.m. on January 1, 2004, Matthew Schmucker, who was eighteen at the time, was traveling alone in a horse and buggy near the intersection of Indiana State Road 37 and Notestine Road in Harlan, Indiana. He was intoxicated at the time and failed to stop at an intersection, thereby colliding with the side of a 2003 Dodge Stratus carrying David Candon and Monica Young, who is now paralyzed from the neck down as a result of the accident. Schmucker was charged with being a minor in possession of alcohol and failing to stop at a throughway. Candon, Young, and their children, who were in the car at the time of the auto/buggy collision, brought suit against Schmucker. Schmucker declared bankruptcy and asked to be discharged from his obligations to Candon and Young. Candon and Young argued that the injury was a "willful and malicious injury by a vessel" under the bankruptcy code and was thus a nondischargeable debt. Schmucker said a horse and buggy is not a vessel. Discuss the role of the court in this case. What would the court look to in making its decision? What is the impact of the court's decision on the ability of the family to recover for injuries? [*Young v Schmucker*, 409 B.R. 477 (N.D. Ind. 2008)]

8. Ms. Paris Hilton, a well-known celebrity with a ubiquitous presence on television and in *People* magazine, had her driver's license suspended by the state of California because of driving under the influence (DUI) or while intoxicated (DWI). She was then pulled over by officers for DUI while driving with a suspended license. Following a hearing on the second traffic stop, a judge sentenced Ms. Hilton to 45 days in jail for failure to honor the terms of her DUI probation, including driving while intoxicated.

List all the types of laws that apply to Ms. Hilton in her situation and also where the specific California laws would appear on the pyramid of the sources of law. If Ms. Hilton asked for a pardon or commutation of her sentence by the governor of California, would the law allow it?

9. Classify the following subject matters as substantive or procedural laws:
   a. Traffic law on speeding
   b. Small claims court rules
   c. Evidence
   d. Labor law
   e. Securities

10. The New York Attorney General began an investigation of Monster Energy Drinks (Monster Beverage), Pepsi's AMP (PepsiCo), and 5-Hour Energy Drinks (Living Essentials) to determine whether the companies are adequately disclosing the amount of caffeine in their drinks. The investigation focuses on the fact that there are other ingredients in the drinks such as black tea extract and guarana that are disclosed on the labels of the drinks, but the labels don't disclose that there may be additional caffeine in the additional ingredients.

The Food and Drug Administration (FDA) has already issued a warning about combining these energy drinks with alcohol consumption because of several resulting deaths. In addition, the Department of Health and Human Services (HHS) has issued a report warning about the negative health impact of excessive caffeine consumption. The report documented reports from emergency room physicians about young people requiring emergency room treatment because of consumption of alcohol and energy drinks. Neither agency has, however, taken any action against the makers of these drinks.

List all of the applicable layers of law involved in this energy drink situation. What statutory interpretations do you think there will have to be as a result of the investigation? (Nelson D. Schwarz, "New York State Is Investigating Energy Drink Makers," *New York Times*, August 29, 2012, p. B1.)

ECONOMICS, ETHICS, THE LAW

The Cost of Corporate Wrongdoing

© Ron and Joe/Shutterstock.com

Read and analyze "Paying the Piper: An Empirical Examination of Longer-Term Financial Consequences of Illegal Corporate Behavior," 40 *Academy of Management Journal* 129 (1997), by Melissa S. Baucus and David A. Baucus. Then answer the following questions.

a. What financial impact does illegal corporate behavior have on a company?

b. How long does a company feel the impact of illegal behavior?

c. How does the market react to illegal corporate behavior?

d. What are the financial costs of violating the law?

Notes

1. Reprinted with permission of Thomson Reuters.

2. On remand, the federal district court granted summary judgment to the plaintiffs. [*Metro-Goldwyn-Mayer Studios Inc. v Grokster, Ltd.*, 454 F. Supp. 2d 966 (C.D. Cal. 2006)] The court later granted a permanent injunction against Grokster. [518 F. Supp. 2d 1197 (C.D. Cal. 2007)]

3. Oliver Wendell Holmes, "Natural Law," 32 *Harvard Law Review* 40 (1918). Copyright © 1918 by The Harvard Law Review Association.

4. Douglas Jehl, "Head of Inquiry on Iraq Abuses Now in Spotlight," *New York Times*, May 11, 2004, A1, A12.

5. *Id.*

6. From *My Philosophy of Law* by Roscoe Pound. © 1941 West Publishing Corporation. Reprinted with permission of West Group.

2 BUSINESS ETHICS AND SOCIAL RESPONSIBILITY

The dawn of the new century brought us the scandals of Enron, WorldCom, Adelphia, Tyco, HealthSouth, and others, and the resulting Sarbanes-Oxley reforms (see Chapters 8, 18, and 19), but the new regulations and stiffer criminal penalties for white-collar crime did not stop over 250 companies from backdating stock options for their executives, a practice that required restatements of income and resulted in financial losses to shareholders and loss of trust in these executives. In the government sector, we lost governors, senators, mayors, and presidential candidates to various kickback and personal scandals. In 2008, two 150-year-old Wall Street firms collapsed and, as a result, the banking and insurance industries teetered and the economy faltered. We learned that the portfolios of the collapsed firms were chock full of high-risk mortgage securities that had been represented as AAA quality. While we were still reeling from 2008 and the resulting Dodd-Frank financial market reforms, we learned mortgage lenders had falsified foreclosure documents and that banks were fixing the international lending rate and profiting from their market positions based on their advance knowledge—something other investors did not know. Then we finally learned that Lance Armstrong had taken performance-enhancing drugs and was stripped of all of his Tour de France titles as well as his Nike sponsorships. A 2012 Josephson Institute study found that 76 percent of high-school students copied others' homework and 49 percent of them cheated on tests.[1] And a 2011 study found that 43 percent of young people post false information to their Facebook, Twitter, and LinkedIn sites. No one even bothered to survey what is false on dating sites. We learned through criminal activity that not all participants were who and what they said they were.

What happened to ethics? Is doing business just a matter of lying and getting away with it? Does anybody really care about ethics in business now? Has society drifted, and is business conduct just a reflection of changing ethical norms? And what does it mean

UPDATE
For up-to-date news on ethical issues, go to **mariannejennings.com**

to be ethical in our lives and in business? This chapter discusses these questions and answers several others: What is ethics? How does ethics affect me? What is business ethics? Why is business ethics important? What ethical standards should a business adopt? How do employees recognize ethical dilemmas? How are ethical dilemmas resolved? How does a business create an ethical atmosphere?

> *Goodness is the only investment that never fails.*
>
> **Henry D. Thoreau**
> Walden, "Higher Laws"

> *Of all the passions, the passion for the Inner Ring is most skillful in making a man who is not yet a very bad man do very bad things.*
>
> **C.S. Lewis**
> "The Inner Ring"

Consider...

1. Who said, "I have done absolutely nothing wrong"?
2. What CEO said, "In today's regulatory environment, it's virtually impossible to violate the rules. It's impossible for a violation to go undetected, certainly not for a considerable period of time"?
3. What CEO said, "We are the good guys. We are on the side of angels"?
4. Who said, "Go after the men who seek out prostitutes"?
5. Who said, "It'll give me a chance to show my innocence"?
6. What company had a 64-page, award-winning code of ethics?*

*ANSWERS: 1. Former Illinois governor Rod Blagojevich, charged with attempting to fill President Obama's Senate seat in exchange for favors and perks and convicted of lying to the FBI. 2. Bernie Madoff, former CEO of Bernard L. Madoff Investment Securities LLC, a firm that perpetrated a $50 billion Ponzi scheme. 3. Jeffrey Skilling, former CEO of Enron, and Lloyd Blankfein, CEO of Goldman Sachs. 4. Former New York governor Eliot Spitzer, in 2004, when he was establishing a task force as New York attorney general to halt prostitution in New York. Mr. Spitzer resigned when his long-standing relationship with a call girl was uncovered in a sting operation. 5. John Kinnucan, former owner of Broadband Research LLC, a Wall Street analyst firm, who later entered a guilty plea to all charges of insider trading. 6. Enron.

> *A bad reputation is like a hangover. It takes a while to get rid of, and it makes everything else hurt.*
>
> **James Preston**
> Former CEO, Avon

> *There is a big difference between what we have the right to do and what is right.*
>
> **Hon. Justice Potter Stewart**
> Associate Justice, U.S. Supreme Court, 1958–1981

> $P = f(x)$
> *The probability of an ethical outcome is a direct function of the amount of money involved; the more money, the less likely the ethical outcome.*
>
> **CFA Institute**

The chapter's opening "Consider…" teaches us that often we look at what companies and business executives say and do and the fact that the companies are doing well, and assume that they must all have high ethical standards. The quotes are ironic because these individuals and/or their companies then crossed the ethical lines they touted as standards.

We look at these individuals' behaviors and wonder why they thought they could get away with their poor ethical choices, or why they believed they were immune from the laws and our ethical standards. We like to think of ourselves as so different from those who cross ethical and/or legal lines. But all of them were college graduates, nearly all with business degrees. All of them were respected by their friends and were active in community projects and institutions. These individuals were "good" people, but they lost sight of personal ethics, business ethics, and the importance of ethics in success. Before they committed their business crimes, the worst that could have been said about many white-collar criminals who are serving 6-month to 25-year prison sentences is that they had parking and speeding tickets. Keeping ethics with us, in life and in business, can help us avoid the kinds of mistakes that so many bright and capable businesspeople have made. But, we wonder, what are ethics? How do we know when we have them? How do we keep them when we face pressures, whether on an important exam or in meeting the quarterly numbers or our sales quota at work? This chapter answers these questions.

2-1 What Is Ethics?

When we learn that the Government Services Administration (GSA) held a meeting at a Las Vegas hotel at a cost of nearly $1 million to taxpayers, we label that conduct "unethical." When we read that Jonah Lehrer, a young and rising star writer at the *New Yorker* fabricated quotes from Bob Dylan, we use the term *unethical*. When we learn that Beyoncé may have lip-synced "The Star-Spangled Banner" at the 2013 presidential inauguration, we feel that we have been duped.

2-1a "IT'S JUST NOT RIGHT!"

We read about these types of situations in the newspaper each day. From politics to journalism to business to our favorite sports and Hollywood icons, references to ethics run through the stories. But we also face ethical dilemmas ourselves. Two students purchase tickets at a theater to see *Lincoln*, and when they emerge from the theater they realize they are in an open area with access to other theaters. If they wanted to, they could slip into *Zero Dark Thirty* or another movie without paying for another ticket. "Who's to know?" they might think. "Hollywood makes too much money anyway." "It doesn't really hurt anyone." These thoughts are similar to those that may have run through the minds of the GSA administrators, the young writer, and the singer who did not analyze the risk factors in their conduct. Although we may believe we are different from business executives and others involved in scandals, we all face ethical dilemmas each day. Do I tell the clerk that he gave me too much change? Do I tell the lender on my loan application that my salary was just cut 25 percent? Do I go back to pay for the laundry detergent that slipped through on the bottom of my cart? Do I do what my boss says when he tells me to write a fake review online for our company's services? Do I tell a potential buyer of my car about the hairline crack in the engine block? Do I tell my clients that I am selling off the investments I am trying to get them to buy?

The fact pattern changes slightly. The parties' names and the subject matter vary, but the ethical issues are the same. Some conduct is more harmful, such as those situations in which a criminal statute is violated. Still, regardless of the law, we look at the conduct of government employees, the writer, the students in the theater, the company employee writing reviews, and the seller of the car, and we conclude, "It's just not right!" We probably agree that they all behaved unethically. We may not be able to zero in on what bothers us about their conduct, but we know an ethics violation, or an ethical breach, when we see one.

2-1b NORMATIVE STANDARDS: HOW WE BEHAVE TO KEEP ORDER

But what do we mean when we say that someone has acted unethically? Ethical standards are not the standards of the law. In fact, they are a higher standard. Sometimes referred to as *normative standards* in philosophy, ethical standards are the generally accepted rules of conduct that govern society. Ethical rules are both standards and expectations for behavior, and we have developed them for nearly all aspects of life. For example, no statute in any state makes it a crime for someone to cut in line in order to save the waiting time involved by going to the end of the line.[2] But we all view those who "take cuts in line" with disdain. We sneer at those cars that sneak along the side of the road to get around a line of traffic as we sit and wait our turn. We resent those who tromp up to the cash register in front of us, ignoring the fact that we were there first and that our time is valuable too.

2-1c LINE-CUTTING AND ETHICS

If you have ever resented a line-cutter, you understand ethics and have applied ethical standards in life. Waiting your turn in line is a societal expectation. "Waiting your turn" is not an ordinance, a statute, or even a federal regulation. "Waiting your turn" is an age-old principle developed because it was fair to proceed with first in time, first to be served. "Waiting your turn" exists because large groups wait for the same road, theater tickets, or fast food at noon in a busy downtown area. We recognize that lines ensure order and that waiting your turn is the just way to allocate the limited space and time allotted for the traffic, the tickets, or the food. "Waiting your turn" is an expected but unwritten behavior that plays a critical role in an orderly society.

So it is with ethics. Ethics consists of those unwritten rules we have developed for our interactions with each other. These unwritten rules govern us when we share resources or honor contracts. "Waiting your turn" is a higher standard than the laws passed to maintain order. Those laws apply when individuals use physical force or threats to push to the front of the line. Assault, battery, and threats are forms of criminal conduct for which the offenders can be prosecuted. But the law does not apply to the stealthy line-cutter who simply sneaks to the front, perhaps using a friend and a conversation as a decoy. No laws are broken, but the notions of fairness and justice are offended by one individual putting him- or herself above others and taking advantage of others' time and position.

Because line-cutters violate the basic procedures and unwritten rules for line formation and order, they commit an ethical breach. We don't put line-cutters in jail, but we do refer to them as unethical. Other examples of unethical behavior also carry no legal penalty. A married person who commits adultery does not commit the type of crime that lands you in jail, but does create a breach of trust with his or her spouse. We do label their conduct with adjectives such as *unfaithful*, and even use a lay term to describe adultery: *cheating*.

Speaking of cheating, looking at someone else's paper during an exam is not a criminal violation. If you cheat on a test, your professor may sanction you and your college may impose penalties, but the county attorney will not prosecute you for cheating. Your conduct is unethical because you did not earn your standing and grade under the same set of rules applied to the other students. Just like the line-cutter, your conduct is not fair to those who spent their time studying. Your cheating is unjust because you are getting ahead using someone else's work.

These examples of cutting in line, committing adultery, and cheating on exams bring certain common adjectives to our minds: "That's not *fair*!" "That was *dishonest*!" "That was *unjust*!" You have just defined ethics for yourself. Ethics is more than common, or normative, standards of behavior. Ethics is honesty, fairness, and justice. The principles of ethics, when honored, ensure that the playing field is level, and that we earn our achievements by using our own work and ideas. Being ethical means being honest and fair in our interactions with each other, whether personally or in business.

FOR THE MANAGER'S DESK

Re: A State of the Union on Academic Ethics

Ethics is not so difficult to understand, but it is difficult to practice. Data are available on the ethics of everyone from school-age children to graduate school students. In 1992, the Josephson Institute found that 61 percent of high school students reported that they had cheated at least once during a school year. By 2008, that number had risen slightly to 64 percent, but then fell to 49 percent in 2012.[3] According to the Center for Academic Integrity, about 75 percent of college students confess that they have cheated in some way in college.[4] The rate for graduate students is 50 percent. They describe taking notes and answers into exams, copying others' work, downloading and buying term papers from the Internet, and not contributing to team projects but still receiving credit for them. Graduate students at Columbia University extended the time clock for an online exam. Harvard Business School candidates tapped into the school's admission database. Thirty-four students at Duke's Fuqua Business School faced discipline for collaborating on a take-home exam. Several New York high school students faced criminal charges related to a cheating conspiracy on SAT exams. One student took the exam for 20 students, who paid him an average of $2,500 for his efforts at scholastic identity deception.

Consider...

Why do we worry about ethics in school? What is the point of teaching young people to be honest? Why do we impose penalties for cheating? How does cheating affect those who do not cheat? What are some of the long-term consequences if those who cheat are permitted to pass courses, graduate with honors, and pursue careers in their fields? What happens when the 75 percent of those who admit cheating in college reaches 100 percent?

2-2 What Is Business Ethics?

Many have referred to "business ethics" as an oxymoron. The little jibe suggests that it is impossible to be in business and be ethical. Some see the pursuit of profit as being at odds with ethics. However, the term *business ethics* is actually a complex one with many layers of meaning. The first layer consists of basic values (covered in the following section) such as being honest, keeping promises, and not taking things that do not belong to you. Another layer consists of notions of fairness (also covered in the next section) such as how we treat others, including customers and employees who report to us. Still a third layer consists of issues related to how a business interacts with the community, the environment, and its neighbors.

The three layers of business ethics bring back into the purely quantitative models of business the elements of a fair playing field. Business ethics involve the study of fairness and ethical standards amidst the pressure of earning a profit and providing returns to shareholders and others who have invested in the business.

A business faces the special problem of having to develop ethical standards for a group of people who work together toward the common goal of profit for the firm. Individuals in the group have personal ethical standards, but too often employees find that the ethical standards imposed by managers at the top of a company result in possible harm to those at the bottom or to others outside the

ETHICAL ISSUES

Gerry Roscoe was the "Outstanding Graduating Senior" for the class of 2013 at State University. By tradition, the graduate chosen for this honor speaks at the commencement ceremonies for the university. Gerry was scheduled to give the student commencement address and had a job awaiting him on Wall Street at one of the nation's largest investment banking firms.

Jill Swain and Eric Bourdeaux were also graduating seniors who knew Gerry. Jill and Eric knew that, at least twice, Gerry had taken exams for others. One was a final exam during their sophomore year. The class was an economics course with 500 students. The exam was held in a large lecture hall and proctored by graduate students. ID was not required, and Gerry took the exam twice, once for his section and at another time for a friend who was having trouble with the course. Without a B on the mid-term, Gerry's friend would have failed the course and lost his scholarship. The second instance involved a final exam in finance. Finance 300 had been taught in sections of 50 students, but a common final

was given with, again, 500 students in the room. The exam was proctored by one finance professor and graduate students. Gerry had taken Finance 300 one year before his girlfriend, Anissa Foulger, had, and she struggled through the course. She needed a B on the final exam in order to pass the course. If she did not pass, she jeopardized her transfer to a college in New York upon Gerry's graduation and employment there. Jill and Eric saw Gerry enter the common final for Finance 300, and he explained that he was taking the final for Anissa: "You understand. Everything is off if she doesn't make it through. She doesn't need this stuff. She is going into advertising. I can take it for her and she'll get her B."

If you were Jill or Eric, what would you have done at the time of the exams? What would you do now that Gerry has been given this "Outstanding Graduating Senior" honor? Does his dishonesty really hurt anyone? Wasn't Gerry just being noble by taking the exam for his friend? For his girlfriend? Is it any of your business? How is anyone harmed by what Gerry did?

firm. An employee may feel compelled to resolve the conflict between loyalty to an employer and the performance of an illegal or unethical act ordered by that employer by simply following the employer's direction. In other words, in developing standards of business ethics, an employee has personal economic interests in continuing employment that may compromise personal ethical standards. Businesses face the additional challenges of developing business standards that are consistent with individual standards and helping employees understand that their personal standards of honesty and fairness need not be different at work. To accomplish this meshing, business managers should understand the various sources of ethical standards.

2-2a ETHICAL STANDARDS: POSITIVE LAW AND ETHICS

Ethical standards can be derived from different sources, and ethicists often debate the origins of these standards. One theory is that our ethical standards are the same as actual or positive law, and that our ethical decisions are made simply upon the basis of whether an activity is legal. **Positive law**, or codified law, establishes the standard for ethical behavior. But compliance with positive law is not always ethical. For example, one of the most frequently asked questions about the 2008 financial crisis is, "How come no one has been convicted of any crimes?" The federal government has brought three cases against fund managers and analysts in an attempt to attain convictions. However, in all three cases, the juries returned acquittals in the cases. In the third case, the jury sent the judge a note along with

Reprinted with permission of Jim Brown (c) 1991.

its acquittal that read, "This verdict should not deter the S.E.C. from continuing to investigate the financial industry, review current regulations and modify existing regulations as necessary." The jury found that there was not criminal conduct because violation of the law, but they called the conduct "appalling." The three acquittals illustrate that ethical and legal standards are not the same. Conduct may be legal, but not ethical.

2-2b ETHICAL STANDARDS: NATURAL LAW AND ETHICS

Others believe that our ethical standards are derived from a higher source and that they are universal. Often labeled **natural law,** this school of ethical thought supports the notion that some standards do not exist because of law (and, indeed, may exist despite laws). For example, as discussed in Chapter 1, at one time the United States permitted slavery. Even though the positive law allowed the activity and the standard of positive law considered slave ownership ethical, natural law dictated that the deprivation of others' rights was unethical.

2-2c ETHICAL STANDARDS: MORAL RELATIVISM AND ETHICS

Moral relativism (also called *situational ethics*) establishes ethical standards according to the situation in which the dilemma is faced. Violation of the law, for example, is permitted if you are stealing to provide food for your starving family. Under moral relativism, adultery is justified when you are caught in an unhappy marriage, as is the business situation in which you engage in lying to avoid offending a coworker or a customer. Bribery is illegal in the United States, and most companies even have firm policies against accepting gifts, because doing so may create conflicts of interest; but some companies still use a relativist approach and argue that being competitive in international markets is different. They adhere to a philosophy of "When in Rome, do as the Romans do," following the standards and customs in a given country even though those same behaviors in the United States would be unacceptable and even illegal.

2-2d ETHICAL STANDARDS: RELIGION AND ETHICS

A final source of moral standards is religious beliefs or divine revelation. The source of standards can be the Bible, the Koran, or any inspired book or writing that is the cornerstone of a religion or faith and believed to have resulted from divine revelation.

2-3 What Are the Categories of Ethical Dilemmas?

Regardless of the root or source of a company's or individual's ethical standards, certain categories of conduct involve ethical issues. The following 12 categories were developed and listed in *Exchange*, the magazine of the Brigham Young University School of Business.

2-3a TAKING THINGS THAT DON'T BELONG TO YOU

Everything from the unauthorized use of the Pitney-Bowes postage meter at your office for mailing personal letters to exaggerations on travel expenses to the downloading of music from the Internet without authorization to not working your required hours at your job but accepting full pay as if you had belongs in this category of ethical violations. A CFO (chief financial officer) of a large electric utility reported that, after taking a cab from LaGuardia International Airport to his midtown Manhattan hotel, he asked for a receipt. The cab driver handed him a full book of blank receipts and drove away. Apparently, the problem of accurately reporting travel expenses involves more than just employees.

2-3b SAYING THINGS YOU KNOW ARE NOT TRUE

A salesperson who tells a potential customer that a product carries a "money-back guarantee" when the salesperson knows that only an exchange is possible has said something that is not true, committed an ethical breach and possibly a violation of the law, and misled the customer. If a car dealer assures a customer that a car has not been in an accident and it has, an ethical breach has occurred. If a homeowner tells a buyer that a home has not had any water damage when, in fact, the basement had been flooded, this false statement is an ethical breach too.

2-3c GIVING OR ALLOWING FALSE IMPRESSIONS

An urban legend that has circulated among marketing departments around the country is the story of an infomercial that offered two CDs with the hits of the 1980s on them. The infomercial emphasized over and over again, "All songs by original artists." Even the CDs carried the line, "All songs by original artists." When purchasers read the label with a closer eye and listened to the CDs, they discovered that all the songs were performed by one group, a group called "The Original Artists." While technically true, the advertising left a false impression with customers who assumed they would be buying songs as performed by the recording artists who made the songs popular.

2-3d BUYING INFLUENCE OR ENGAGING IN CONFLICT OF INTEREST

A company awards a construction contract to a firm owned by the father of the state attorney general while the state attorney general's office is investigating that company. A county official who has the responsibility for selecting the contractor who will build the county's new baseball stadium travels around the country at the contractor's expense to view existing stadium sites. The county official should see as many sites and samples of work as there are bidders on the new stadium, but when the contractors pay, there is an ethical issue. A physician researcher whose work concludes that a company's product is meritorious needs to disclose the consulting fees he receives from that company.

All of these examples illustrate conflicts of interest. Those involved in situations such as these often protest, "But I would never allow that to influence me." That they have to insist they are not or would not be influenced is evidence of the conflict. Whether the conflict can or will influence those it touches is not the issue, for neither party can prove conclusively that a *quid pro quo* was not intended. The possibility exists, and it creates suspicion.

ETHICAL ISSUES

The temptation is remarkable. The run is long. The body screams, "No more!" So, it happened again in the New York City Marathon for 2008. Cheating on this form of a physical final examination became international news when, in 1979, Boston Marathon runner and winner Rosie Ruiz combined her running with a hitch on the train to earn first place. She repeated the ploy in the 1980 Boston Marathon, when her creative approach was discovered.

The New York Road Runners Club, the sponsors and managers of the New York City Marathon, disclosed multiple subway riders in their 2008 race on the eve of the 2009 Marathon with the hope of encouraging the 42,000 runners to go the distance, the real distance. For 2008, there were 71 runners disqualified from the race, 46 of them for taking the subway in order to go the distance. The club discovers these free-riders when it investigates what it believes to be extraordinary times for runners who have not been able or should not have

been able to achieve their recorded times. In at least two situations, the runners who took the subway also took first place in their age categories and deprived the real winners of their Tiffany trophies as well as the thrill of quaffing the elixir of victory on the day of the marathon. The real winners in these age categories from 2008 were not notified of their victories until July 2009 because of the time the investigations take.

A spokesperson from the Road Runners Club said that the greatest temptation in the race comes when the runners enter Manhattan via the Queensboro Bridge. That entry to the city is close to Central Park and the finish line, but the race first takes a turn there for another 10 miles into Harlem and the Bronx. Most cheaters simply skip those boroughs and head right into Central Park and the finish line.

Are there any laws that govern this situation with the runners? Discuss the ethical issues of the runners. Is anyone really hurt if runners cheat?

Consider...

Dr. Drew Pinsky, the host of a cable health show, recommended GlaxoSmithKline's antidepressant Wellbutrin to physicians and patients but did not disclose that he received $275,000 from Glaxo-SmithKline for "services related to Wellbutrin." Dr. Drew, as he is known on television, participated in town hall meetings, published writings, and hosted multimedia activities that touted the benefits of Wellbutrin. When asked about his failure to disclose the payments, Dr. Drew said that all of his commentary and writing were consistent with his clinical experience and that, "how does a doctor choose one specific antidepressant medication for a certain patient from the many excellent medications available? The vast majority of doctors attending my lectures stated that they felt I answered this question and did so in an unbiased and scientifically sound manner." Is there a conflict of interest? Did Dr. Drew manage the conflict correctly? Is there any significance to Dr. Drew's statement that doctors felt that he answered their questions in a scientific and unbiased manner?
(Jeanne Whalen, "'Dr. Drew' Was Paid by Glaxo," *Wall Street Journal*, July 5 2012, B3.)

Steps for Analyzing Ethical Dilemmas and Case Studies in Business

1. Make sure you have a grasp of all the available facts.

2. List any information you would like to have but don't and what assumptions you would have to make, if any, in resolving the dilemma.

3. Take each person involved in the dilemma and list the concerns they face or might have. Be sure to consider the impact on those not specifically mentioned in the case. For example, product safety issues don't involve just engineers' careers and company profits; shareholders, customers, customers' families, and even communities supported by the business are affected by a business decision on what to do about a product and its safety issue.

4. Develop a list of resolutions for the problem. Apply the various models for reaching this resolution. As you apply the various models to the dilemma, you may find additional insights for questions 1, 2, and 3. If the breach has already occurred, consider the possible remedies and develop systemic changes so that such breaches do not occur in the future.

5. Evaluate the resolutions for costs, legalities, and impact. Try to determine how each of the parties will react to and be affected by each of the resolutions you have proposed.

6. Make a recommendation for the actions that should be taken.

Some Help for You on the Dr. Drew Case

THINK: To help in your analysis, consider the following list of the parties affected by this dilemma.

- GlaxoSmithKline—the company's credibility is affected by Dr. Drew's conduct, recommendations, and disclosures.

- The doctors who listened to Dr. Drew's recommendations without knowing about his compensation.

- The patients who asked for or used the drug Wellbutrin without knowing about Dr. Drew's conflict.

- Other drug manufacturers whose drugs may have been more appropriate or worthy of recommendation but were not mentioned because of Dr. Drew's loyalty to Wellbutrin and GlaxoSmithKline.

APPLY: To further assist you in your analysis, consider the following categories:

- Conflict of interest: Dr. Drew had an obligation to disclose his financial interest in promoting the drug. Those who listened to his analysis, read his recommendations, or used the drug deserved to know before they made their decision that he did have a financial interest.

- Giving or allowing false impressions: Dr. Drew gave the impression of being a detached clinician who had prescribed the drug and had patients who benefited, but he did not disclose that he was paid by GlaxoSmithKline for his work in recommending the drug.

ANSWER: Because the conduct has already occurred, your role becomes one of recommendation. You need to provide a recommendation that affords protection to all the parties listed as affected by the conduct. For example, to protect the credibility of the pharmaceuticals, the companies and their experts need to develop a policy on accepting compensation, as well as one for disclosures of these programs of compensation. These policies may require not only disclosure but also prohibitions on certain types of conduct (such as doctors receiving stock ownership in the pharmaceutical companies) if the conflict seems too difficult to overcome. Two approaches can be taken in regard to a conflict of interest: (1) don't do it, or (2) disclose the conflict to those affected. Sometimes disclosure is insufficient and one party must not engage in the conduct. Regulators may force these new standards on physicians and pharmaceutical firms.

2-3e HIDING OR DIVULGING INFORMATION

Taking your firm's product development or trade secrets to a new place of employment constitutes an ethical violation: divulging proprietary information. Failing to disclose the results of medical studies that indicate that your firm's new drug has significant side effects is an ethical violation: hiding information that the product could be harmful to purchasers.

2-3f TAKING UNFAIR ADVANTAGE

New credit card regulations went into effect in 2010 and 2012 because so many businesses took unfair advantage of customers on payment due dates, late fees, and increases in interest rates. Not all of the charges were spelled out clearly in the credit card terms prior to the regulatory changes. These new credit disclosure requirements and other truth-in-lending provisions all resulted because businesses took unfair advantage of consumers who could not easily follow the jargon of long and complex agreements.

Consider...

Eagle Gate College hired an admission consultant from Stevens-Henager College named Janna Miller. Ms. Miller hired others from Stevens-Henager to join her at Eagle Gate. Those who came along to join Ms. Miller also brought along lists of potential students for recruiting purposes. Those lists of potential students are very valuable to for-profit colleges because of the need for new students. In addition, the information left behind at Steven-Henager was altered so that the data base of potential recruits could not be reached due to incorrect phone numbers and/or e-mails. Stevens-Henager could not contact the potential students from their own data base.

Are there ethical issues in this situation? Or is this just competition?

[*Stevens-Henager College v Eagle Gate College*, 248 P.3d 1025 (Utah 2011)]

2-3g COMMITTING ACTS OF PERSONAL DECADENCE

While many argue about the ethical notion of an employee's right to privacy, it has become increasingly clear that personal conduct outside the job can influence performance and company reputation. During 2012, a number of CEOs and the former head of the CIA, General David Petraeus, had to resign their positions because of affairs with employees or extramarital affairs. The CEOs' personal conduct created tension within their companies and resulted in loss of respect from the employees. For General Petraeus, his role as the chief executive for the organization protecting national security was in jeopardy because the affair with a younger woman left him vulnerable to threat and also meant he was not complying with the agency standards that applied to all employees. Personal conduct by those who are in leadership positions affects organizational reputation, morale, and credibility.

2-3h PERPETRATING INTERPERSONAL ABUSE

A manager sexually harasses an employee. Another manager is verbally abusive to an employee. Still another manager subjects employees to humiliating correction in the presence of customers. In some cases, laws protect employees. But at the heart of this category is unfair treatment.

2-3i PERMITTING ORGANIZATIONAL ABUSE

Many multinational firms, such as Walmart, Ikea, Apple, and Nike, have faced issues of organizational abuse. The unfair treatment of workers in international operations appears in the form of child labor, demeaning wages, excessive working hours, and factory safety standards. Even though a business cannot change the culture of another country, it can perpetuate—or alleviate—abuse through its operations there.

2-3j VIOLATING RULES

Many rules, particularly those in large organizations that tend toward bureaucracy from a need to maintain internal controls or follow lines of authority, seem burdensome to employees trying to serve customers and other employees. However, those rules do serve a purpose and should be followed so that harms are avoided. For example, Yale University senior Michele Dufault was killed in a lab accident when her hair was caught in a lathe in the machinery lab. The physics and astronomy major did not follow the simple safety rule of tying your hair back before beginning work with the heavy equipment. She was also working in the lab at 2:30 a.m., a time when there were no people near the lab and she violated a basic safety standard of not working alone around the large machines. Sometimes these rules seem superfluous and we feel that we have more expertise and experience and need not follow them. However, there is an ethical issue here in that as a student she had agreed to follow the safety rules of the lab and the university. Not following those rules was a breach of that promise. As a result of Ms. Default's accident, Yale and other colleges and universities have revamped their rules, enforcement, and training to encourage compliance.

2-3k CONDONING UNETHICAL ACTIONS

In this breach of ethics, the wrong results from the failure to report the wrong. What if you witnessed a fellow employee embezzling company funds by forging his signature on a check that was supposed to be voided? Would you report that violation? A winking tolerance of others' unethical behavior is in itself unethical. Suppose that as a product designer, you were aware of a fundamental flaw in your company's new product—a product predicted to catapult your firm to record earnings. Would you pursue the problem to the point of halting the distribution of the product? Would you disclose what you know to the public if you could not get your company to act? Toyota experienced the cost of employees not passing along information about customer accidents and complaints when it recalled 8.5 million vehicles, answered class-action suits, and repaired relationships with government regulators over its alleged failure to disclose important data and issues about its cars' safety. One former employee of Lehman Brothers, whose sales efforts and structuring of securities investments "helped lead to the demise of the bank he loved and to an economic unraveling worldwide confessed, 'I have blood on my hands.'"[5] His remorse comes from his failure to speak up and raise his concerns about the ethical issues he saw even as he was rewarded for his work.

2-3i BALANCING ETHICAL DILEMMAS

In some situations, the answers are neither right nor wrong; rather, the situations present dilemmas to be resolved. For example, Google has struggled for years with its decision to do business in the People's Republic of China because of known human rights violations and censorship by the government there. Its eventual decision was to remain in China despite the government's censorship of its search engine there. Other companies debated whether to do business in South Africa when that country's government followed a policy of apartheid. In some respects, the presence of these companies would help by advancing human rights and, certainly, by improving the standard of living or communications for at least some international operations workers. On the other hand, their presence could help such governments sustain themselves by enabling them to point to economic successes despite human rights violations.

2-4 Resolution of Business Ethical Dilemmas

So far, you know what business ethics is and you have a list of the areas that cover most ethical dilemmas. But if you were faced with an ethical dilemma, how would you resolve it? The resolution of ethical dilemmas in business is often difficult, even in firms with codes of ethics and cultures committed to compliance with ethical models for decision making. Managers need guidelines for making ethical choices. Several prominent scholars in the field of business ethics have developed models for use as guides in difficult situations. This section covers those models.

2-4a BLANCHARD AND PEALE

The late Dr. Norman Vincent Peale and management expert Kenneth Blanchard offer three questions that managers should ponder in resolving ethical dilemmas: "Is it legal?" "Is it balanced?" "How does it make me feel?" If the answer to the first question, "Is it legal?" is no, for business ethics purposes, your ethical analysis is done. While there is room for conscientious objection to many laws on an ethical basis, a manager is not given the authority to break the law, and agencies such as the Internal Revenue Service (IRS) and the Securities Exchange Commission

(SEC) are not known for helping companies ease their consciences through refusals to pay taxes or file required securities disclosures and reports. The Hewlett-Packard board hired private investigators to determine the source of leaks about its board meetings, activities, and decisions. The investigators hired (actually a subcontractor of a contractor) used a technique known as "pretexting" in the trade. They posed as others in order to obtain access to phone records of directors and reporters to determine who was calling who, an activity prohibited by a California statute.[6] Eventually, the investigators as well as some within the company, including HP's ethics officer, were charged with violations. These managers failed to stop when the answer to the question of legality was "no."

Answering the second question, "Is it balanced?" requires a manager to step back and view a problem from other perspectives—those of other parties, owners, shareholders, or the community. For example, an M&M/Mars cacao buyer was able to secure a low price on cacao for his company because of pending government takeovers and political disruption. M&M/Mars officers decided to pay more for the cacao than the negotiated figure. Their reason was that someday their company would not have the upper hand, and then they would want to be treated fairly when the price became the seller's choice.

Answering "How does it make me feel?" requires a manager to do a self-examination of the comfort level of a decision. Some decisions, though they may be legal and may appear balanced, can still make a manager or employee uncomfortable. For example, Gil Meche, a pitcher for the Kansas City Royals, was entitled to $12 million in compensation for his final contract year with the royals. However, his shoulder and arm had significant pain from years of pitching and he opted not to have surgery for repairs. Under the terms of his contract, all he had to do was report for spring training and the season and go through the motions of rehabilitation. Mr. Meche retired because he said, "When I signed my contract, my main goal was to earn it. Once I started to realize I wasn't earning my money, I felt bad. I was making a crazy amount of money for not even pitching. Honestly, I didn't feel I deserved it. I did not want to have those feelings again."[7] Known as the element of conscience, this test for ethics requires businesspeople to find the source of their discomfort in a particular dilemma or proposed decision.

2-4b THE FRONT-PAGE-OF-THE-NEWSPAPER TEST

One simple ethical model requires only that a decision maker envision how a reporter would describe a decision on the front page of a local or national newspaper. When Salomon Brothers illegally cornered the U.S. government's bond market, the *BusinessWeek* headline read, "How Bad Will It Get?" Nearly two years later, a follow-up story on Salomon's crisis strategy was headlined "The Bomb Shelter That Salomon Built." During the aftermath of the bond market scandal, the interim chairman of Salomon, Warren Buffett, told employees, "Contemplating any business act, an employee should ask himself whether he would be willing to see it immediately described by an informed and critical reporter on the front page of his local paper, there to be read by his spouse, children, and friends. At Salomon we simply want no part of any activities that pass legal tests but that we, as citizens, would find offensive."[8]

There are other examples, such as that involving the Government Services Administration (GSA) when it held a retreat for employees in Las Vegas, "GSA Head Resigns Over Las Vegas Boondoggle."[9] This headline is one for employees to consider if they are contemplating a day off for obtaining and playing a new video game: "Calling in Sick to Heed 'Call of Duty.'"[10] And "Chief's DUI Arrest Roils the FAA (Federal Aviation Administration)," tells all leaders that they need to exercise caution and discretion in their personal lives.[11]

When Wall Street firms were reporting multibillion-dollar losses due to their highly leveraged portfolios of risky instruments, the headline on the cover of *Fortune* magazine read, "What Were They Smoking?" (November 26, 2007). The headline test helps us to put our decisions into a longer-term perspective.

2-4c LAURA NASH AND PERSPECTIVE

Business ethicist Laura Nash has developed a series of questions that business managers should ask themselves as they evaluate their ethical dilemmas. One of the questions is, "How would I view the issue if I stood on the other side of the fence?" For example, in 1993, federal guidelines required meat to be cooked to 140 degrees Fahrenheit. At that time, however, the state of Washington proposed imposing a higher temperature requirement of 155 degrees. Burger King cooked its hamburgers to 160 degrees and Wendy's, Hardee's, and Taco Bell cooked their meat to 165 degrees.

Health and food industry experts supported a minimum cooking temperature of 155 degrees to be certain *E. coli* bacteria are eliminated. Jack-in-the-Box followed the legal minimum of 140 degrees. Would you want that information as a consumer? Given the trend toward higher temperatures and the pending regulation, would you want your meat cooked to a higher temperature? Although the cooking temperature was legal, an ethical issue arises in continuing to follow only the law when health experts are concerned about the adequacy of the law. Jack-in-the-Box did, in fact, experience an *E. coli* outbreak: one child died and 300 other customers became ill.[12]

Other questions in the Nash model include, "Am I able to discuss my decision with my family, friends, and those closest to me?" "What am I trying to accomplish with my decision?" "Will I feel as comfortable about my decision over time as I do today?" The Nash model forces managers to seek additional perspectives as decisions are evaluated and implemented. For example, when the late William Aramony served as the CEO of United Way, he enjoyed such perks as an annual salary of close to $400,000, flights on the Concorde, and limousine service. Even though these benefits were about the same as those of other CEOs managing comparable assets, it would still be difficult to justify such benefits to a donor who earns $22,000 a year and has pledged 5 percent of it to United Way.

2-4d THE *WALL STREET JOURNAL* MODEL

The *Wall Street Journal* model for resolution of ethical dilemmas consists of compliance, contribution, and consequences. Like the Blanchard–Peale model, any proposed conduct must first be in compliance with the law. The next step requires an evaluation of a decision's contributions to the shareholders, the employees, the community, and the customers. For example, furniture manufacturer Herman Miller, in a decision that was prescient in relation to the sustainability initiatives of 2010, decided both to invest in equipment that would exceed the requirements for compliance with the 1990 Clean Air Act and to refrain from using rain forest woods in producing its signature Eames chair. The decision was costly to the shareholders at first, but ultimately they, the community, and customers enjoyed the benefits.

Finally, managers are asked to envision the consequences of a decision, such as whether headlines that are unfavorable to the firm may result. The initial consequence of Miller's decisions was a reduction in profits because of the costs of the changes. However, the long-term consequences were the respect of environmental regulators, a responsive public committed to rain forest preservation, and Miller's long-standing recognition as one of America's top 20 corporate citizens.

2-4e OTHER MODELS

Of course, much simpler models for making ethical business decisions are available. One stems from Immanuel Kant's categorical imperative, loosely similar to the Golden Rule: "Do unto others as you would have them do unto you." Treating others or others' money as we would want to be treated is a powerful evaluation technique in ethical dilemmas. (See Exhibit 2.5 and p. 63 for more discussion.)

2-5 Why We Fail to Reach Good Decisions in Ethical Dilemmas

Very often, we look at the harmful conduct of corporate executives and wonder, "Where were their minds, and what were they thinking when they decided to engage in such bad behavior?" Often those involved did not walk through the steps in resolving ethical dilemmas discussed earlier. But they probably also slipped into rationalizations rather than analysis. The following sections provide a list and summary of each of the frequent statements of rationalization that we use to avoid facing ethical dilemmas (see Exhibit 2.1).

2-5a "EVERYBODY ELSE DOES IT"

When former Tour de France winner (now stripped of those titles) Lance Armstrong admitted that he had used performance-enhancing drugs throughout his career he said, "Doping was organized and everywhere in the peloton. In my mind, the choice was 'do it or go home.' For me that was not a choice."[13] "Everybody else does it" is a rationalization, but it is not an analysis of the ethical issues involved in conduct.

2-5b "IF WE DON'T DO IT, SOMEONE ELSE WILL"

The rationalization of competition is one that finds us reasoning that if someone is going to do it and make money, it might as well be us. For example, a friend asks if

---

EXHIBIT 2.1 The Language of Rationalization

"Everybody else does it."
"If we don't do it, someone else will."
"That's the way it has always been done."
"We'll wait until the lawyers tell us it's wrong."
"It doesn't really hurt anyone."
"The system is unfair."
"I was just following orders."
"You think this is bad, you should have seen . . ."
"It's a gray area."

he can pay you for the use of your subway pass, a pass that says it is nontransferable. You could easily say, "If I don't do it, he will just get someone else to do it, so I might as well benefit." The fact that others may engage in unethical conduct does not require you to join them. Think through the consequences if we relied on this notion that they are going to do it anyway, so we might as well participate. There is an impact on the sale of tokens, the ability to trust pass-holders, and the overall revenues of the transportation system if everyone participates in such a sharing program.

2-5c "THAT'S THE WAY IT HAS ALWAYS BEEN DONE"

Corporate or business history and business practices are not always sound. The fact that for years nothing has changed in a firm may indicate the need for change and an atmosphere that invites possible ethical violations. For example, when the New Orleans Saints bounty program was uncovered by the NFL, a program under which some players were able to double their salaries by taking out certain players or inflicting physical injuries on players in exchange for cash bonuses, the players all said that they came into the culture that had always done this kind of thing. They also said that they knew it was a mistake, but because it was accepted behavior in their organizations, they did it anyway.

2-5d "WE'LL WAIT UNTIL THE LAWYERS TELL US IT'S WRONG"

Lawyers are trained to provide only the parameters of the law. In many situations, they offer an opinion that is correct in that it does not violate the law. Whether the conduct they have judged as legal is also ethical is a different question. Allowing law and lawyers to control a firm's destiny ignores the opportunity to make wise and ethical choices. For example, the SEC has given very little guidance to companies and lawyers about when they need to disclose health issues of their CEOs. So, when Steve Jobs had his liver transplant and when he was experiencing significant health issues in the years following the transplant, Apple made no disclosures other than that Mr. Jobs was taking a leave of absence and when he would return. Nonetheless, Apple's stock dropped as a result of the nondisclosures because speculation ran rampant. Apple met its legal disclosure requirements, but withholding material information resulted in losses to the shareholders. Apple's response to those who raised questions about Apple's candor was that it had followed the advice of legal counsel. (See Chapter 19 for more information on required disclosures.)

2-5e "IT DOESN'T REALLY HURT ANYONE"

When we are the sole rubbernecker on the freeway, traffic remains unaffected. But if everyone rubbernecks, we have a traffic jam. If all of us made poor ethical choices, we would cause significant harm. A man interviewed after he was arrested for defrauding insurance companies through staged auto accidents remarked, "It didn't really hurt anyone. Insurance companies can afford it." The second part of his statement is accurate. The insurance companies can afford it—but not without cost to someone else. Such fraud harms all of us because we must pay higher premiums to allow insurers to absorb the costs of investigating and paying for fraudulent claims.

2-5f "THE SYSTEM IS UNFAIR"

Often touted by students as a justification for cheating on exams, this rationalization eases our consciences by telling us we are cheating only to make up for deficiencies in the system; yet just one person cheating can send ripples through an entire system. The credibility of grades and the institution come into question as students obtain grades through means beyond the system's standards. In countries in which corruption is a way of life and government employees award contracts and rights to do business on the basis of payments rather than on the merits of a given company or its proposal, the bribery only results in greater unfairness within and greater costs to those countries. Many economists have noted that a country's businesses and economy will not progress without some fundamental assurance of trust that comes through a belief that there is a level playing field where the quality of products and services matter.

2-5g "I WAS JUST FOLLOWING ORDERS"

In many criminal trials and disputes over responsibility and liability, managers disclaim their responsibility by stating, "I was just following orders." Sometimes, individuals should not follow the directions of supervisors because they have been asked to do something illegal or immoral. Judges who preside over the criminal trials of war criminals often remind defendants that an order is not necessarily legal, ethical, or moral. Values require us to question or depart from orders when others will be harmed or wronged. In the days prior to the financial collapse of MF Global, employees were asked to transfer funds from clients' accounts in order to cover hedging losses, something that is prohibited by law. During the investigation, the employees said that they did what they were ordered to do. However, the result was significant losses for their customers. When the allegations of prisoner abuse in Iraq emerged, along with photos, one of the first defenses raised by lawyers for the soldiers being court-martialed for their role in the abuses was, "I was just following orders." Sometimes following orders is not the ethical thing to do.

2-5h "YOU THINK THIS IS BAD, YOU SHOULD HAVE SEEN…"

This rationalization finds employees looking back at earlier times and reminding others that the company's safety policies or accounting practices used to be much worse. At one company, when some employees objected to backdating contracts to slip the earnings into the quarter, some employees reassured them by saying, "At least we're not using the 35-day month we used to use to meet targets."

2-5i "IT'S A GRAY AREA"

The gray area is a comfort level for us when we are in the midst of an ethical dilemma. Once we enter the gray area, we have a fine line that crosses into illegality and also an opportunity to explore an issue beyond bare legal requirements. An attorney for former HP general counsel Ann Baskins says that Ms. Baskins now realizes that she should have focused on questioning whether the pretexting was ethical, not just on whether it was legal. "She regrets that she did not do so."[14] Kevin Hunsaker, a deputy general counsel and chief ethics officer, asked internal HP security employees about the legality of the pretexting operations, and one responded, "I think it's on the edge, but above board." Hunsaker responded with what have become the infamous words in the investigation, "I shouldn't have asked." On the edge and in a gray area often lands us in legal difficulty and controversy. Even though many of the charges were dismissed or reduced, five individuals, including Mr. Hunsaker, were charged with criminal misconduct in the HP pretexting case and the company paid a $14 million fine to settle the charges.

ETHICAL ISSUES

Indy driver Danica Patrick gave an interview to *Sports Illustrated* writer and radio host Dan Patrick, a transcript of which follows.

> *Dan: If you could take a performance-enhancing drug and not get caught, would you do it if it allowed you to win Indy?*
>
> *Danica: Well then it's not cheating, is it? If nobody finds out?*
>
> *Dan: So you would do it?*
>
> *Danica: Yeah, it would be like finding a grey area. In motorsports we work in the grey areas a lot. You're trying to find where the holes are in the rule book.*

After the interview, in an interview with *USA Today*, Ms. Patrick indicated that she was just joking. The head of the USADA (U.S. Anti-Doping Agency) called the interview "totally irresponsible," and added, "Although joking about the use of dangerous and unhealthy drugs that cheaters use to rob clean athletes of their dreams is no laughing matter."

Identify the rationalizations in Ms. Patrick's statements. Why do you think she answered the questions as she did? Was the joke still an ethical issue?

Sources: Danpatrick.com, http://www.sportsillustrated.cnn.com, accessed June 2, 2009; Eddie Pells, AP wire story, June 2, 2009.

© martan/Shutterstock.com

2-6 Social Responsibility: Another Layer of Business Ethics

So far in this chapter we have covered two layers of business ethics: the basic categories, and notions of fairness. A third layer of ethics focuses on relationships and conflicts among relationships.

In some ethical dilemmas in business, the interests of the shareholders might be different from the interests of the employees. Lower wages bring higher profits and returns, at least temporarily, to shareholders, but is shipping work overseas to countries where the wages are low or work conditions unhealthy taking unfair advantage? In this third layer of business ethics, we look at the interests of those who are affected by business decisions, often called the stakeholders of the business. For example, suppose the business discovers that its air pollution control equipment is not state-of-the-art technology and that, although no laws are being violated, more pollution is being released than is necessary. To correct the problem, its factory must be shut down for a minimum of three months. The pollution will harm the air and the community, but the shutdown will harm the workers and the shareholders. The business must consider the needs and interests of all its stakeholders in resolving the ethical dilemma it faces. Much discussion and disagreement continue to surround this particular issue. In the following interview excerpt, economist Milton Friedman offers a different perspective on this ethical dilemma.

Q: Quite apart from emission standards and effluent taxes, shouldn't corporate officials take action to stop pollution out of a sense of social responsibility?

Milton Friedman: *I wouldn't buy stock in a company that hired that kind of leadership. A corporate executive's responsibility is to make as much money for the shareholders as possible, as long as he operates within the rules of the game. When an executive decides to take action for reasons of social responsibility, he is taking money from someone else—from the stockholders, in the form of lower dividends; from the employees, in the form of lower wages; or from the consumer, in the form of higher prices. The responsibility of a corporate executive is to fulfill the terms of his contract. If he can't do that in good conscience, then he should quit his job and find another way to do good. He has the right to promote what he regards as desirable moral objectives only with his own money. If, on the other hand, the executives of U.S. Steel undertake to reduce pollution in Gary for the purpose of making the town attractive to employees and thus lowering labor costs, then they are doing the stockholders' bidding. And everyone benefits: The stockholders get higher dividends; the customer gets cheaper steel; the workers get more in return for their labor. That's the beauty of free enterprise.... To the extent that pollution caused by the U.S. Steel plant there is confined to that city and the people there are truly concerned about the problem, it's to the company's advantage to do something about it. Why? Because if it doesn't, workers will prefer to live where there is less pollution, and U.S. Steel will have to pay them more to live in Gary, Indiana.*[15]

2-6a ETHICAL POSTURES FOR SOCIAL RESPONSIBILITY

Often, decisions in dilemmas that involve stakeholders depend on the overall attitude of a company and its perspective on the role of business in society. The ethical perspective of a business often sets the tone for its operations and employees' choices. Historically, the philosophical debate over the role of business in society has evolved into four schools of thought on ethical behavior based on the responses to two questions: (1) Whose interest should a corporation serve? (2) To whom should a corporation be responsive in order to best serve that interest? These questions have only two answers—"shareholders only" and "the larger society"—and the combination of those answers defines the school of thought. The following discussion is summarized in Exhibit 2.2.

Inherence

According to the inherence school of thought, managers answer only to shareholders and act only with shareholders' interests in mind. This type of manager would not become involved in any political or social issues unless it was in the shareholders' best interests to do so, provided the involvement did not backfire and cost the firm sales. Milton Friedman's philosophy, as previously expressed,

---

EXHIBIT 2.2 Social Responsibility of Corporations

	MORAL QUESTION: WHOSE INTEREST SHOULD THE CORPORATION SERVE?	POLICY QUESTION: BEST WAY TO SERVE INTEREST IF THE CORPORATION IS RESPONSIVE TO:
Inherence	Shareholders only	Shareholders only
Enlightened self-interest	Shareholders only	Larger society
Invisible hand	Larger society	Shareholders only
Social responsibility	Larger society	Larger society

Source: Adapted with permission of *American Business Law Journal*, from Daryl Hatano, "Should Corporations Exercise Their Freedom of Speech Rights?" 22 *American Bus.L.J.* 165 (1984).

is an example of inherence. To understand how a business following the inherence school of thought would behave, consider the issue of a proposed increase in residential property taxes for school funding. A business that subscribes to the inherence school would support a school tax increase only if the educational issue affected the company's performance and only if such a position did not offend those who opposed the tax increase.

Enlightened Self-Interest

According to this school of thought, the manager is responsible to the shareholders but serves them best by being responsive to the larger society. Enlightened self-interest is based on the view that, in the long run, business value is enhanced if business is responsive to the needs of society. In this school, managers are free to speak out on societal issues without the constraint of offending someone, as in inherence. Businesses would anticipate social changes and needs and be early advocates for change. For example, many corporations today have instituted job sharing, child-care facilities, and sick-child care in response to the changing structure of the American family and workforce. This responsiveness to the needs of the larger society should also be beneficial to shareholders because it enables the business to retain a quality workforce.

The Invisible Hand

The invisible hand school of thought is the opposite of enlightened self-interest. According to this philosophy, business ought to serve the larger society and it does this best when it serves the shareholders only. Such businesses allow government to set the standards and boundaries for appropriate behavior and simply adhere to these governmental constraints as a way of maximizing benefits to their shareholders. They become involved in issues of social responsibility or in political issues only when society lacks sufficient information on an issue to make a decision. Even then, their involvement is limited to presenting data and does not extend to advocating a particular viewpoint or position. This school of thought holds that it is best for society to guide itself and that businesses work best when they serve shareholders within those constraints.

Social Responsibility

In the social responsibility school of thought, the role of business is to serve the larger society by responding to society's needs as a first priority. A business following this school of thought would advocate full disclosure of product information to consumers in its advertising and would encourage political activism on the part of its managers and employees on all issues, not just those that affect the corporation. These businesses adhere to the belief that their sense of social responsibility contributes to their long-term success.

2-7 Why Business Ethics?

Now that you have background on the types of ethical issues businesses face, background on social responsibility, and a framework for analysis of ethical issues, you may still be skeptical: "But why should a business worry about these things beyond just complying with the law? Why not just maximize under the system?" Some compelling reasons promote choosing ethical behavior, as discussed in the following sections.

2-7a PERSONAL ACCOUNTABILITY AND COMFORT: BUSINESS ETHICS FOR PERSONAL REASONS

Before looking at business data on the value of ethics, it is important to realize that the choices we make in our business lives must still feel personally comfortable. And it would be misleading to say that every ethical business is a profitable business. First, not all ethical people are good managers or possess the necessary skills for making a business a success; but many competent businesspeople have suffered for being ethical, and many others seem to survive despite their lack of ethics. Columnist Dave Barry noted that every time an oil spill occurs, the oil companies ready themselves for the higher prices and profits that come because all that oil is lost at sea. Despite his conviction and jail term related to junk bond sales in the 1980s, Michael Milken decades later earned a $50 million fee for helping Ted Turner negotiate a merger with Time Warner.[16] Many whistle-blowers, although highly respected, have been unable to find employment in their industries. If ethical behavior does not guarantee success, then why have ethics? The answer has to do with personal ethics applied in a business context. One investment banker who worked on Drexel Burnham's trading desk during the Michael Milken days of that firm and who is now chairman of GoldTree Asset Management said, "Just to be able to sit on the desk and see the calls start at 4:15 in the morning, Boesky and Perelman and Diller and Murdoch …"[17] But Mr. Wagner said that he took not just the memories of the power of Drexel with him but a powerful lesson as well: "There's a difference between being very competitive and can-do, and winning at all costs. All costs is costly."

Business ethics is really nothing more than a standard of personal behavior applied to a group of people working together to make a profit. Some people are ethical because it enables them to sleep better at night. Some people are ethical because of the fear of getting caught. But being personally ethical is a justification for business ethics—it is simply the correct thing to do. Bowen McCoy's "The Parable of the Sadhu" focuses on business ethics for personal reasons.

FOR THE MANAGER'S DESK

Re: The Parable of the Sadhu

[In 1982], as the first participant in the new six-month sabbatical program that Morgan Stanley has adopted, I enjoyed a rare opportunity to collect my thoughts as well as do some traveling. I spent the first three months in Nepal, walking 600 miles through 200 villages in the Himalayas and climbing some 120,000 vertical feet. On the trip my sole Western companion was an anthropologist who shed light on the cultural patterns of the villages we passed through.

During the Nepal hike, something occurred that has had a powerful impact on my thinking about corporate ethics. Although some might argue that the experience has no relevance to business, it was a situation in which a basic ethical dilemma suddenly intruded into the lives of a group of individuals. How the group responded I think holds a lesson for all organizations no matter how defined.

The Sadhu

The Nepal experience was more rugged and adventuresome than I had anticipated. Most commercial treks last two or three weeks and cover a quarter of the distance we traveled.

My friend Stephen, the anthropologist, and I were halfway through the 60-day Himalayan part of the trip when we reached the high point, an 18,000-foot pass over a crest that we'd have to traverse to reach the village of Mukinath [sic], an ancient holy place for pilgrims.

Six years earlier I had suffered pulmonary edema, an acute form of altitude sickness, at 16,500 feet in the vicinity of Everest base camp, so we were understandably concerned about what would happen at 18,000 feet. Moreover, the Himalayas were having their wettest spring in 20 years; hip-deep powder and ice had already driven us off one ridge. If we failed to cross the pass, I feared that the last half of our "once in a lifetime" trip would be ruined.

The night before we would try the pass, we camped at a hut at 14,500 feet. In the photos taken at the camp, my face appears wan. The last village we'd passed through was a sturdy two-day walk below us, and I was tired.

During the late afternoon, four backpackers from New Zealand joined us, and we spent most of the night awake, anticipating the climb. Below we could see the fires of two other parties, which turned out to be two Swiss couples and a Japanese hiking club.

To get over the steep part of the climb before the sun melted the steps cut in the ice, we departed at 3:30 A.M. The New Zealanders left first, followed by Stephen and myself, our porters and Sherpas, and then the Swiss. The Japanese lingered in their camp. The sky was clear, and we were confident that no spring storm would erupt that day to close the pass.

At 15,500 feet, it looked to me as if Stephen were shuffling and staggering a bit, which are symptoms of altitude sickness. (The initial stage of altitude sickness brings a headache and nausea. As the condition worsens, a climber may encounter difficult breathing, disorientation, aphasia, and paralysis.) I felt strong, my adrenaline was flowing, but I was very concerned about my ultimate ability to get across. A couple of our porters were also suffering from the height, and Pasang, our Sherpa sirdar (leader), was worried.

Just after daybreak, while we rested at 15,500 feet, one of the New Zealanders, who had gone ahead, came staggering down toward us with a body slung across his shoulders. He dumped the almost naked, barefoot body of an Indian holy man—a sadhu—at my feet. He had found the pilgrim lying on the ice, shivering and suffering from hypothermia. I cradled the sadhu's head and laid him out on the rocks. The New Zealander was angry. He wanted to get across the pass before the bright sun melted the snow. He said, "Look, I've done what I can. You have porters and Sherpa guides. You care for him. We're going on!" He turned and went back up the mountain to join his friends.

I took a carotid pulse and found that the sadhu was still alive. We figured he had probably visited the holy shrines at Mukinath [sic] and was on his way home. It was fruitless to question why he had chosen this desperately high route instead of the safe, heavily traveled caravan route through the Kali Gandaki gorge. Or why he was almost naked and with no shoes, or how long he had been lying in the pass. The answers were not going to solve our problem.

Stephen and the four Swiss began stripping off outer clothing and opening their packs. The sadhu was soon clothed from head to foot. He was not able to walk, but he was very much alive. I looked down the mountain and spotted below the Japanese climbers marching up with a horse.

Without a great deal of thought, I told Stephen and Pasang that I was concerned about withstanding the heights to come and wanted to get over the pass. I took off after several of our porters who had gone ahead.

On the steep part of the ascent where, if the ice steps had given way, I would have slid down about 3,000 feet, I felt vertigo. I stopped for a breather, allowing the Swiss to catch up with me. I inquired about the sadhu and Stephen. They said that the sadhu was fine and that Stephen was just behind. I set off again for the summit.

Stephen arrived at the summit an hour after I did. Still exhilarated by victory, I ran down the snow slope to congratulate him. He was suffering from altitude sickness, walking fifteen steps, then stopping, walking fifteen steps, then stopping. When I reached them, Stephen glared at me and said: "How do you feel about contributing to the death of a fellow man?"

I did not fully comprehend what he meant.

"Is the sadhu dead?" I inquired.

"No," replied Stephen, "but he surely will be!"

After I had gone, and the Swiss had departed not long after, Stephen had remained with the sadhu. When the Japanese had arrived, Stephen had asked to use their horse to transport the sadhu down to the hut. They had refused. He had then asked Pasang to have a group of our porters carry the sadhu. Pasang had resisted the idea, saying that the porters would have to exert all their energy to get themselves over the pass. He had thought they could not carry a man down 1,000 feet to the hut, reclimb the slope, and get across safely before the snow melted. Pasang had pressed Stephen not to delay any longer.

The Sherpas had carried the sadhu down to a rock in the sun at about 15,000 feet and had pointed out the hut another 500 feet below. The Japanese had given him food and drink. When they had last seen him he was listlessly throwing rocks at the Japanese party's dog, which had frightened him.

We do not know if the sadhu lived or died.

For many of the following days and evenings Stephen and I discussed and debated our behavior toward the sadhu. Stephen is a committed Quaker with deep moral vision. He said, "I feel that what happened with the sadhu is a good example of the breakdown between the individual ethic and the corporate ethic. No one person was willing to assume ultimate responsibility for the sadhu. Each was willing to do his bit just so long as it was not too inconvenient. When it got to be a bother, everyone just passed the buck to someone else and took off. Jesus was relevant to a more individualist stage of society, and how do we interpret his teaching today in a world filled with large, impersonal organizations and groups?"

I defended the larger group, saying, "Look, we all cared. We all stopped and gave aid and comfort. Everyone did his bit. The New Zealander carried him down below the snow line. I took his pulse and suggested we treat him for hypothermia. You and the Swiss gave him clothing and got him warmed up. The Japanese gave him food and water. The Sherpas carried him down to the sun and pointed out the easy trail toward the hut. He was well enough to throw rocks at a dog. What more could we do?"

"You have just described the typical affluent Westerner's response to a problem. Throwing money—in this case food and sweaters—at it, but not solving the fundamentals!" Stephen retorted.

"What would satisfy you?" I said. "Here we are, a group of New Zealanders, Swiss, Americans, and Japanese who have never met before and who are at the apex of one of the most powerful experiences of our lives. Some years the pass is so bad no one gets over it. What right does an almost naked pilgrim who chooses the wrong trail have to disrupt our lives? Even the Sherpas had no interest in risking the trip to help him beyond a certain point."

Stephen calmly rebutted, "I wonder what the Sherpas would have done if the sadhu had been a well-dressed Nepali, or what the Japanese would have done if the sadhu had been a well-dressed Asian, or what you would of done, Buzz, if the sadhu had been a well-dressed Western woman?"

"Where, in your opinion," I asked instead, "is the limit of our responsibility in a situation like this? We had our own well-being to worry about. Our Sherpa guides were unwilling to jeopardize us or the porters for the sadhu. No one else on the mountain was willing to commit himself beyond certain self-imposed limits."

Stephen said, "As individual Christians or people with a Western ethical tradition, we can fulfill our obligations in such a situation only if (1) the sadhu dies in our care, (2) the sadhu demonstrates to us that he could undertake the two-day walk down to the village, or (3) we carry the sadhu for two days down to the village and convince someone there to care for him."

"Leaving the sadhu in the sun with food and clothing, while he demonstrated hand-eye coordination by throwing a rock at a dog, comes close to fulfilling items one and two," I answered. "And it wouldn't have made sense to take him to the village, where the people appeared to be far less caring than the Sherpas, so the third condition is impractical. Are you really saying that, no matter what the implications, we should, at the drop of a hat, have changed our entire plan?"

The Individual versus the Group Ethic

Despite my arguments, I felt and continue to feel guilt about the sadhu. I had literally walked through a classic moral dilemma without fully thinking through the consequences. My excuses for my actions include a high adrenaline flow, a superordinate goal, and a once-in-a-lifetime opportunity—factors in the usual corporate situation, especially when one is under stress.

Real moral dilemmas are ambiguous, and many of us hike right through them, unaware that they exist. When, usually after the fact, someone makes an issue of them, we tend to resent his or her bringing it up. Often, when the full import of what we have done (or not done) falls on us, we dig into a defensive position from which it is very difficult to emerge. In rare circumstances we may contemplate what we have done from inside a prison.

Had we mountaineers been free of physical and mental stress caused by the effort and the high altitude, we might have treated the sadhu differently. Yet isn't stress the true test of personal and corporate values? The instant decisions executives make under pressure reveal the most about personal and corporate character. Among the many questions that occur to me when pondering my experience are: What are the practical limits of moral imagination and vision? Is there a collective or institutional ethic beyond the ethics of the individual? At what level of effort or commitment can one discharge one's ethical responsibilities?

Not every ethical dilemma has a right solution. Reasonable people often disagree; otherwise there would be no dilemma. In a business context, however, it is essential that managers agree on a process for dealing with dilemmas.

The sadhu experience offers an interesting parallel to business situations. An immediate response was mandatory. Failure to act was a decision in itself. Up on the mountain we could not resign and submit our résumé to a headhunter. In contrast to philosophy, business involves action and implementation—getting things done. Managers must come up with answers to problems based on what they see and what they allow to influence their decision-making processes. On the mountain, none of us but Stephen realized the true dimensions of the situation we were facing.

One of our problems was that as a group we had no process for developing a consensus. We had no sense of purpose or plan. The difficulties of dealing with the sadhu were so complex that no one person could handle it. Because it did not have a set of preconditions that could guide its action to an acceptable resolution, the group reacted instinctively as individuals. The cross-cultural nature of the group added a further layer of complexity. We had no leader with whom we could identify and in whose purpose we believed. Only Stephen was willing to take charge, but he could not gain adequate support to care for the sadhu.

Some organizations do have a value system that transcends the personal values of the managers. Such values, which go beyond profitability, are usually revealed when the organization is under stress. People throughout the organization generally accept its values, which, because they are not presented as a rigid list of commandments, may be somewhat ambiguous. The stories people tell, rather than printed materials, transmit these conceptions of what is proper behavior.

For twenty years I have been exposed at senior levels to a variety of corporations and organizations. It is amazing how quickly an outsider can sense the tone and style of an organization and the degree of tolerated openness and freedom to challenge management.

Organizations that do not have a heritage of mutually accepted, shared values tend to become unhinged during stress, with each individual bailing out for himself. In the great takeover battles we have witnessed during past years, companies that had strong cultures drew the wagons around them and fought it out, while other companies saw executives, supported by their golden parachutes, bail out of the struggles.

Because corporations and their members are interdependent, for the corporation to be strong the members need to share a preconceived notion of what is correct behavior, a "business ethic," and think of it as a positive force, not a constraint.

As an investment banker I am continually warned by well-meaning lawyers, clients, and associates to be wary of conflicts of interest. Yet if I were to run away from every difficult situation, I wouldn't be an effective investment banker. I have to feel my way through conflicts. An effective manager can't run from risk either; he or she has to confront and deal with risk. To feel "safe" in doing this, managers need the guidelines of an agreed-on process and set of values within the organization.

After my three months in Nepal, I spent three months as an executive-in-residence at both Stanford Business School and the Center for Ethics and Social Policy at the Graduate Theological Union at Berkeley. These six months away from my job gave me time to assimilate twenty years of business experience. My thoughts turned often to the meaning of the leadership role in any large organization. Students at the seminary thought of themselves as antibusiness. But when I questioned them they agreed they distrusted all large organizations, including the church. They perceived all large organizations as impersonal and opposed to individual values and needs. Yet we all know of organizations where people's values and beliefs are respected and their expressions encouraged. What makes the difference? Can we identify the difference and, as a result, manage more effectively?

The word "ethics" turns off many and confuses more. Yet the notions of shared values and an agreed-on process for dealing with adversity and change—what many people mean when they talk about corporate culture—seem to be at the heart of the ethical issue. People who are in touch with their own core beliefs and the beliefs of others and are sustained by them can be more comfortable living on the cutting edge.

At times, taking a tough line or a decisive stand in a muddle of ambiguity is the only ethical thing to do. If a manager is indecisive and spends time trying to figure out the "good" thing to do, the enterprise may be lost.

Business ethics, then, has to do with authenticity and integrity of the enterprise. To be ethical is to follow the business as well as the cultural goals of the corporation, its owners, its employees, and its customers. Those who cannot serve the corporate vision are not authentic business people and, therefore, are not ethical in the business sense.

At this stage of my own business experience I have a strong interest in organizational behavior. Sociologists are keenly studying what they call corporate stories, legends, and heroes as a way organizations have of transmitting the value system. Corporations such as Arco have even hired consultants to perform an audit of their corporate culture. In a company, the leader is the person who understands, interprets, and manages the corporate value system. Effective managers are then action-oriented people who resolve conflict, are tolerant of ambiguity, stress, and change, and have a strong sense of purpose for themselves and their organizations.

If all this is true, I wonder about the role of the professional manager who moves from company to company. How can he or she quickly absorb the values and culture of different organizations? Or is there, indeed, an art of management that is totally transportable? Assuming such fungible managers do exist, is it proper for them to manipulate the values of others?

What would have happened had Stephen and I carried the sadhu for two days back to the village and become involved with the villagers in his care? In four trips to Nepal my most interesting experiences occurred in 1975 when I lived in a Sherpa home in the Khumbu for five days recovering from altitude sickness. The high point of Stephen's trip was an invitation to participate in a family funeral ceremony in Manang. Neither experience had to do with climbing the high passes of the Himalayas. Why were we so reluctant to try the lower path, the ambiguous trail? Perhaps because we did not have a leader who could reveal the greater purpose of the trip to us.

Why didn't Stephen with his moral vision opt to take the sadhu under his personal care? The answer is because, in part, Stephen was hard-stressed physically himself, and because, in part, without some support system that involved our involuntary and episodic community on the mountain, it was beyond his individual capacity to do so.

I see the current interest in corporate culture and corporate value systems as a positive response to Stephen's pessimism about the decline of the role of the individual in large organizations. Individuals who operate from a thoughtful set of personal values provide the foundation of a corporate culture. A corporate tradition that encourages freedom of inquiry, supports personal values, and reinforces a focused sense of direction can fulfill the need for individuality along with the prosperity and success of the group. Without such corporate support, the individual is lost.

That is the lesson of the sadhu. In a complex corporate situation, the individual requires and deserves the support of the group. If people cannot find such support from their organization, they don't know how to act. If such support is forthcoming, a person has a stake in the success of the group, and can add much to the process of establishing and maintaining a corporate culture. It is the management's challenge to be sensitive to individual needs, to shape them, and to direct and focus them for the benefit of the group as a whole.

For each of us the sadhu lives. Should we stop what we are doing and comfort him; or should we keep trudging up toward the high pass? Should I pause to help the derelict I pass on the street each night as I walk by the Yale Club en route to Grand Central Station? Am I his brother? What is the nature of our responsibility if we consider ourselves to be ethical persons? Perhaps it is to change the values of the group so that it can, with all its resources, take the other road.

Discussion Question

Consider the closing questions Mr. McCoy poses. How do they apply to you personally and to businesses?

Source: Reprinted by permission of *Harvard Business Review.* From "The Parable of the Sadhu," by Bowen H. McCoy, May–June 1997. Copyright © 1997 by Harvard Business School Publishing Corporation; all rights reserved.

ETHICAL ISSUES

In 2006, David Sharp, 34, from Britain, was not handling a climb to Mt. Everest well. He was a victim of oxygen deprivation and eventually collapsed on the ground. Forty other climbers passed him by and, unable to move, Mr. Sharp froze to death. Those who passed him by indicated that the conditions are rugged and that climbers know going in that they may have to pay the ultimate price.

Lincoln Hall, 50, from Australia, was discovered by an American guide after he had spent a night on the freezing mountainside. The MyHeroProject describes Mr. Hall's condition as follows, "He was sitting on the trail with his jacket around his waist, wearing no hat or gloves. The group stopped to investigate and found he was suffering from symptoms of edema, frostbite and dehydration. He was alone and hallucinating; and generally incoherent in

his responses to their offers of help. He was without any of the proper equipment for survival in such conditions. Apparently, Mr. Hall had collapsed the previous day on his way down from the summit."

Mr. Dan Mazur and his team abandoned their climb and stayed with Mr. Hall until rescuer sherpas could come to help. Mr. Hall's team assumed that he was dead and had called his wife the evening before to tell her.

In the years since 1953, 3,000 climbers have made it to the Everest summit, but 200 climbers have died. A climb with a guide costs about $60,000. What do you think makes the difference in the decision process between those who stop to help and those who continue their climbs?

Source: Adapted from Alan Cowell, "Adventurers Change. Danger Does Not," *New York Times,* June 4, 2006, p. WK 5.

2-8 Importance of Ethics in Business Success and the Costs of Unethical Conduct

As you learn in other disciplines, from economics to management, business is driven by the bottom line. Profits control whether the firm can obtain loans or gain investors and serve as the sole indicator of the firm's success—and, in most cases, its employees' success, as well. Indeed, business firms can be defined as groups of people working together to obtain maximum profits. The pursuit of the bottom line, however, can occasionally distort the perspective of even the most conscientious among us. The fear of losing business and, consequently, losing profits and capital support can persuade people to engage in conduct that, although not illegal, is unethical. But those who pursue only the bottom line fail to recognize that a successful business is more like a marathon than a sprint, requiring that ethical dilemmas be resolved with a long-term perspective in mind. Indeed, those firms that adhere to ethical standards perform better financially over the long run. A 2010 study indicates that if companies are not ever-vigilant in adhering to ethical standards, they slip into illegal activity and destroy their profitability, often to the point of bankruptcy.[18]

The Tylenol tampering incident of 1982 offers one of the most telling examples of the rewards of being ethical. When Tylenol capsules were discovered to have been tainted with deadly poison, Tylenol's manufacturer, McNeil Consumer Products Company, a subsidiary of Johnson & Johnson, followed its code of ethics, which required it to put the interests of the consumer first. In what many financial analysts and economists considered to be a disastrous decision and a dreadful mistake, McNeil recalled all Tylenol capsules from the market—31 million bottles with a retail value of about $100 million. A new and safer form of a noncapsule Tylenol caplet was developed, and within a few months Tylenol regained its majority share of the market. The recall had turned out to be neither a poor decision nor a financial disaster. Rather, the company's actions enhanced its reputation and served to create a bond between Tylenol and its customers that was based largely on trust and respect for the integrity of the company and the product. Johnson & Johnson and McNeil enjoyed decades of goodwill and deferential treatment arising from their recall. The two companies had a near immunity from questions about their products and practices until 2010, when the companies' conduct differed substantially from the 1982 recall. In 2010, the FDA found metal particles in the company's liquid Infant's Tylenol. That can happen in production, but the key is to stop production, issue a recall, and confess. Instead, however, one officer resigned and the FDA levied penalties against McNeil over its lack of cooperation, mishandling of materials, lax documentation, and failure to follow up on customer complaints.[19] An April 2010 FDA site visit to one plant found 20 violations of the agency's good manufacturing processes. One violation was releasing seven batches of cherry-flavored Infants' Tylenol after the employees had found the metal from processing pistons in the product. Not only did McNeil not issue a recall, it did not even notify the government about the issue. The result of these decisions has been declining profits, federal monitoring, and a loss of trust by consumers.

Nestlé provides another example of the consequences for poor ethical choices, consequences that can span generations. Nestlé has endured many consumer boycotts since the early 1970s as a result of its intense—and what came to be perceived by the public as exploitative and unethical—marketing of infant formula in then–Third World nations, where the lack of sanitation, refrigeration, and education led to serious health problems in infants given the formula. In 1989, nearly 20 years after the infant formula crisis, Nestlé's new "Good Start" formula was slow in market infiltration and, because of continuing consumer resistance, did not perform as well as its quality and innovativeness would have predicted. Nestlé has never gained the market share or reputation its quality product deserves. As the Nestlé experience illustrates, a firm's reputation for ethical behavior is the same as an individual's reputation: It takes a long time to gain, but it can be lost instantly as the result of one bad choice.

BP, the oil and natural gas company, was performing well, with operations in 100 countries, 96,000 employees, and nearly 24,000 retail service stations around the world. As the second-largest oil company in the world and one of the world's 10 largest corporations, BP had also been a perennial favorite of NGOs and environmental groups. For example, *Business Ethics* named BP the world's most admired company and one of its top corporate citizens. Green Investors named BP its top company because of BP's continuing commitment to investment in alternative energy sources. But BP had issues percolating as it gained these recognitions. In 2005, an explosion at one of BP's refineries, located in Texas City, Texas, resulted in the death of 15 employees and injuries to 170 others. Both an internal investigation and a government report indicated that the accident would have been avoidable if the company had not cut maintenance costs at the expense of safety. The accident followed on the heels of charges that the company's traders were manipulating the price of propane in the markets by holding back on supplies.

Also, the company's oil fields at Prudhoe Bay, Alaska, burst in 2006, resulting in a 267,000-gallon oil spill on pristine Alaskan tundra.[20] Industry standards require "smart-pigging" (ultrasonic checking) of pipelines every five years to detect weaknesses or corrosion. At the time of the March 2006 spill, BP disclosed that it had not done smart-pigging on the Prudhoe Bay line since 1998 and that the pipes had not been cleaned since 1992. The BP field manager at Prudhoe Bay said, following the spill, "If we had it to do over again, we would have been pigging those lines."[21] The line had to be closed down and, again, an internal report revealed that the cost-cutting drive at BP affected the decisions in the oil fields. Following the oil spill, BP's stock price fell more than 15 percent in three months.

Oil production dropped 75 percent and BP spent $1 billion to fix the Texas refinery. One expert noted at that time that it would take years for BP to recover financially and even longer to restore its credibility with the market and regulators. That prescient remark has proved to be even truer after BP's Deepwater Horizon well in the Gulf of Mexico sprung a "leak" and began gushing oil in April 2010. The evidence of compromises on well construction and rig safety was so overwhelming that BP paid a $4 billion fine following a guilty plea to environmental and safety violations.

As General Motors prepared to release its Chevrolet Malibu for production in 1976, an engineer drafted a memo about some issues with the placement of the car's gas tank and the likelihood of its explosion in the event of a rear-end collision. The memo discussed both the potential liability for such accidents and the costs of modifying the design. The Malibu went forward without production and design changes. By 1981, the company faced some litigation related to rear-end collisions involving the Malibu and gas tank explosions. A lawyer working on the cases found the 1976 memo and explained the need to keep the engineer's thoughts and analysis from being disclosed. In December 1999, a jury awarded the victims of a Malibu rear-end collision and explosion more than $107 million compensatory damages and $4.8 billion punitive damages (later reduced to $1.2 billion on appeal) and explained that its high damage verdict was directly attributable to the memo, the knowledge, and the failure to disclose that information or take corrective action.

The poor ethical choices of the aforementioned firms resulted in tremendous financial setbacks and, in some cases, destruction. The core values of a firm give it long-standing profitability. "The Tony Bennett Factor" offers some insight into longevity, profitability, and values.

FOR THE MANAGER'S DESK

Re: The Tony Bennett Factor

I had blocked out the background noise offered courtesy of MTV and my teenager, but I glanced up and saw Tony Bennett. My parents raised me on Tony Bennett LPs back in the '50s. "I Left My Heart in San Francisco" enjoyed hours of play in Tyrone, Pa. And here he was back, "Tony Bennett Unplugged." Mr. Bennett has not changed. Yet his success has spanned generations. Suddenly my work with a colleague, Prof. Louis Grossman, had new meaning. We had been studying business longevity, trying to determine what makes some businesses survive so successfully for so long.

Prof. Grossman and I began our study when we spotted a 1982 full-page ad in this newspaper placed by Diamond Match Co. The ad touted the company's 100 years of consistent dividend payments. Today's standards tell us that 100 quarters of dividend payments would be stellar. What kind of company was this? Were there others?

We discovered seven other industrial firms that could boast of making at least an annual dividend payment for a string of 100 years or more: Scovill, Inc.; Ludlow Corp.; Stanley Works; Singer Co.; Pennwalt, Inc.; Pullman, Inc.; and Corning Glass Works. Pullman, Ludlow and Stanley had unbroken chains of a century of quarterly dividend payments as well.

Mr. Bennett and our eight companies have survival in common. These survivors' tools make management theories of today seem trite. They had no shifting paradigms. No buzzwords.

Mr. Bennett recognized his strength as a balladeer and stuck with it, through everything from the Beatles to Hootie and the Blowfish. Although each of our companies recognized the importance of diversification, they all held fast to a WBAWI—or "what business are we in?"—philosophy. They knew their strengths, developed strong market presences based on those strengths, and never forgot their roots. Mr. Bennett never performed without singing "I Wanna Be Around." Singer never left its sewing machines. Pullman never deserted its train cars. Diamond held on to its matches.

The firms diversified only when their strengths allowed. Scovill began as a brass button manufacturer and backed into brass manufacturing because it knew brass. Scovill bought Hamilton Beach because Hamilton Beach was a major brass purchaser. Scovill understood this customer's business.

Other companies have forgotten the WBAWI lesson and paid the price. Sears abandoned its catalog, insurance and real estate businesses and now struggles to find a retail presence. IBM has suffered for not understanding its business was the workplace, not mainframe computers. Its Lotus takeover shows it may recognize the PC as the workplace.

All Mr. Bennett needs are a microphone and a pianist to make music. All eight of our companies were low-cost producers. All eight were cost conscious. Scovill executive vice presidents with worldwide responsibilities shared a secretary. Spartan company headquarters were the rule for these firms. There were barely six-figure salaries for executives. By contrast, IBM's Louis Gerstner hired an executive chef at $120,000 just last month.

Mr. Bennett has used the same musical arranger for nearly 30 years. Our eight companies' management team histories are in direct contrast to the executive recruiting practices in vogue today. Scovill, founded during the Jefferson administration in 1803, had only 12 CEOs during its 100-year dividend run. Three of the companies (Singer, Stanley and Diamond) had CEOs who served for more than 40 years. Seven of the companies never had a CEO serve for fewer than 10 years. They were not afraid of home-grown management. Their officers and CEOs came up through the ranks. Management succession is found in all eight companies.

Perhaps this information demonstrates the importance of continuity and stability. The executives appreciated the tension between short-term results and long-term performance, but the short term did not control decision making. Donald Davis, chairman and CEO of Stanley Works, put it this way: "The tension is always there. One of the top management's toughest jobs really is to mediate between the two viewpoints—short-term profit results now versus investment for future development."

Mr. Bennett did and does spend time on the road in concert, in direct contact with audiences—no mega-tours, just constant gigs. And a full century before we heard of customer service, these firms sent their sales forces and vice presidents alike out on the road to talk directly with customers. They had interesting marketing studies: one-on-one feedback. Sales calls, follow-ups, replacements, and refunds allowed them to remain in the customers' minds and good graces.

One officer said it best: "Anyone can read the monthly financial reports: What we need to do is to interpret them so we can spot trends. We call on customers, on suppliers, we look at the bottom line of course, but we know how that line reached the bottom."

Mr. Bennett has never made a bad recording or disappointed during a live performance. Our eight firms had strong commitments to integrity. Their mantra was: "If there's integrity, there will be quality and profits." Their integrity manifested itself in more than just quality. Frederick T. Stanley, founder of Stanley Works, spoke of the intricate balance between automation and employees: "Machines are no better than the skill, care, ingenuity and spirit of the men who operate them. We can achieve perfect harmony when shortening of an operation provides mutual advantages to the workman and the producers." Ethics before its time. Re-engineering done correctly in the 1800s. Nothing at the expense of the customer or the employee.

Our firms were no less remarkable than Mr. Bennett and his success with Generation X—his third generational conquest. The sad part of their stories is what happened following the takeover battles of the '80s. But that is a story for another time. For now, it is reassuring to realize that cost-consciousness, focus, customer service, home-grown management and integrity are keys to longevity. Today's management fads seem as shallow as Ice T (aka Ice-T) and Madonna. There is a simple Tony Bennett factor in success that makes today's fads much easier to debunk and infinitely easier to question.

Source: "The Tony Bennett Factor," by Marianne M. Jennings, from *The Wall Street Journal,* June 26, 1995, p. A12.

2-8a ETHICS AS A STRATEGY

Ethical behavior not only increases long-term earnings; it also enables businesses to anticipate and plan for social needs and cultural changes that require the firm or its product to evolve. One of the benefits of a firm's ethical behavior and participation in community concerns is the goodwill that such involvement fosters. Conversely, the absence of that goodwill and consequent loss of trust can mean the destruction of the firm.

When methyl isocyanate gas leaked from the Union Carbide plant in Bhopal, India, in 1984, the deadly gas left more than 2,500 dead and 200,000 injured. Investigations revealed that the plant had experienced problems with some of the equipment designed to prevent such leaks. Although actual liability issues were hotly debated in court, many ethical questions were raised regarding the plant and Union Carbide. Was it a wise decision to build the plant in a country with little expertise in the relevant technology? Did the people in the town know of the potential dangers of the plant? Why was a city of shacks allowed to be erected so close to the plant?

According to the Indian government, the plant had been operated well within legal and regulatory requirements, and Union Carbide's management had been cooperative in installing any additional equipment needed. Should Union Carbide have done more than was legally required? Did the plant operators need more training for such emergencies? Finally, the Bhopal incident raises many questions about the relationship between U.S. businesses and their operations in developing countries that may not be prepared to deal with the latest technologies and may not be fully informed about the associated risks. And the effect on Union Carbide's market capitalization continued for years following the accident. Union Carbide really never recovered from the damage to its reputation despite the fact that several reports conclude the accident was the result of a deliberate act of sabotage. Eventually Dow acquired Union Carbide and the curse of the Union Carbide accident ended as the company was absorbed. Reputations and conduct move markets.

2-8b THE VALUE OF A GOOD REPUTATION

A reputation, good or bad, stays with a business or an individual for a long time. Richard Teerlink, the former CEO of Harley-Davidson, has said, "A reputation, good or bad, is tough to shake." Once a company makes poor ethical choices, it carries the baggage of those choices despite successful and sincere efforts to reform. Salt Lake City struggled to regain its credibility as the trials from the bribery allegations surrounding its winning the bid for the 2002 Winter Olympics progressed and companies withdrew sponsorships. Businesses were, at that time, unsure about the reputations and trustworthiness of those running the Salt Lake City Olympic operations. It took new leadership and a commitment to high ethical standards from Mitt Romney, who went on to become a two-term governor of Massachusetts and presidential candidate in 2008 and 2012, to restore confidence in the Salt Lake City 2002 Winter Olympics.

2-8c LEADERSHIP'S ROLE IN ETHICAL CHOICES

George Fisher, the former CEO of Motorola and Kodak, has defined leadership as the ability to see around corners. In other words, a leader sees a problem before it becomes a legal issue or liability and fixes it, thus saving company time and money. All social, regulatory, and litigation issues progress along a timeline. As the issue is brought to the public's attention, either by stories or by the sheer magnitude of the problem, the momentum for remedies and reforms continues until behavior is changed and regulated. Ethical choices afford firms opportunities to take positions ahead of the curve. Firms can choose to go beyond the law and perhaps avoid regulation that might be costly or litigation that can be devastating. For example, the issues relating to the problems with asbestos dust in the lungs of asbestos workers and installers were clear in the 1930s. More studies needed to be done, but there was sufficient evidence to justify lung protection for workers and the development of alternative forms of insulation. However, the first litigation relating to asbestos and asbestos workers did not arise until 1968. For that 30-year period, those in the business of producing and selling asbestos insulation products had the opportunity to take preventive actions. They chose to wait out the cycle. The results were a ban on asbestos and litigation at levels that forced the largest producer, Johns-Manville (now Manville), into bankruptcy. Leadership choices were available in the 1930s for offering warnings, providing masks, and developing alternative insulators. Johns-Manville chose to continue its posture of controlling information releases and studies. The liability issue progressed to a point of no choice other than bankruptcy and reorganization.

Every business regulation that exists today controls business conduct in an area that was once not subject to control but, rather, provided an opportunity for businesses to self-regulate by making good value choices. Problems resulting from a lack of candor in payday loans and in the so-called subprime loan market have surfaced at all levels of our economy. "We made so much money, you couldn't believe it. And you didn't have to do anything. You just had to show up,"[22] was the comment of Kal Elsayed, a former executive at New Century Financial, a mortgage brokerage firm based in Irvine, California. With his red Ferrari, Mr. Elsayed enjoyed the benefits of the growth in the subprime mortgage market. However, those risky debtors, whose credit histories spelled trouble, defaulted on their loans. New Century Financial declared bankruptcy under the weight of its portfolio of $39.4 billion in subprime loans. "Subprime mortgage lending was easy until the market changed" is the hindsight comment of mortgage brokers and analysts. And the Wall Street instruments tied to those mortgages carried the defaults throughout the economy. The mortgage lending market is now greatly controlled and limited by state and federal regulations. Wall Street firms not under federal controls are nevertheless subject to increased regulation.[23]

Ethical choices give businesses the freedom to make choices before regulators mandate them. Breaches of ethics bring about regulation and liability with few opportunities to choose and less flexibility. The notions of choices and leadership are diagrammed in Exhibit 2.3, which is explained in the following discussion. Every issue progresses along a cycle that begins with a *latency* phase, in which the industry is aware of a problem. The use of private information about consumers' buying patterns was well known in the marketing industry, but few consumers were aware of that use. The *awareness* stage begins when the popular press reports on an issue and raises questions. Once the public has knowledge of a problem, it responds by demanding assurance that the problem either is resolved or is not really an issue—or by calling for reform. The *activism* stage is one in which members of the public ask for either voluntary or regulatory reform. If voluntary reform is not forthcoming, those affected may sue or lobby for reform, or both. For example, a group of parents, police officers, and shareholders protested Time

EXHIBIT 2.3 Leadership and Ethics: Making Choices before Liability and Regulation

Source: Adapted from James Frierson, "Public Policy Forecasting: A New Approach," *SAM Advanced Management Journal*, Spring 1985, pp. 18–23.

Warner's production of "Cop Killer," a song by the rap music artist Ice T (a.k.a. Ice-T). The public outcry was strong both in the press and at Time Warner's shareholder meeting. Congress was considering holding hearings on record labels and record content. Time Warner eventually made a choice to voluntarily withdraw the song, later in the regulatory cycle when public outcry was strong but still in time to avert regulation.

During 2004, the public again became active in demanding changes in the content of entertainment when Janet Jackson and Justin Timberlake's performance at the halftime show at the Super Bowl resulted in partial nudity on prime-time television. In 2007, CBS Radio and MSNBC pulled the Don Imus show because of questionable comments he made. Entertainment and television executives undertook voluntary controls to prevent government controls. The televised Academy Awards are now on a five-second delay so that any mishaps can be edited out before broadcast. Some artists are not permitted to appear on awards shows because of their past behaviors on similar shows. Voluntary self-control averts government regulation.

Few people realize one aspect of the Tylenol poisonings case (noted earlier in the chapter), which is that the issue of tamper-proof packaging had been a concern in the industry long before the poisonings involving Tylenol occurred. Those in the industry were concerned that packaging that did not signal unauthorized entry so that a buyer could spot tampering could open the door to the tragedy that eventually occurred. However, no one in the industry, despite knowledge of this issue, took steps to create tamper-proof packaging. The law did not require such a step; additional costs were associated with the packaging and retooling production; and some were worried that they would be at a competitive disadvantage if their products were harder to use than those that did not have the tamper-proof packages. By not solving the problem voluntarily, companies faced unpleasant results: first, the tragedy of the deaths, and second, additional regulations and costs imposed as the government required tamper-proof packaging.

2-9 Creation of an Ethical Culture in Business

2-9a THE TONE AT THE TOP AND AN ETHICAL CULTURE

Employees work under the pressures of meeting quarterly and annual goals and can make poor choices if the company's priority with respect to values and ethics is not made clear. Employees must see that those who evaluate and pay them really do care about ethics. Employees are convinced that ethics is important when they see officers comply with all of the provisions in the company code of ethics. They see the right tone at the top when ethical employees are rewarded and unethical conduct is punished. The tone at the top comes from actions by officers and executives that show they "walk the talk" about ethics.

2-9b DODD-FRANK, SARBANES-OXLEY, SENTENCING, AND AN ETHICAL CULTURE

Following the collapses of Enron, WorldCom, and other companies noted in the chapter's opening "Consider...," Congress passed the most extensive reforms of corporate governance and financial reporting since the enactment of the 1933 and 1934 securities laws following the 1929 stock market crash. Following the 2008 financial markets collapse and the bankruptcies of many financial firms, Congress added additional reforms through what is called the Dodd-Frank Act (Wall Street Reform and Consumer Financial Protection Act; see Chapters 18 and 19 for more information on these two statutes). Although both statutory reforms impose many requirements on accountants, lawyers, directors, and officers, they also increased criminal penalties and empowered the Federal Sentencing Commission to examine the types of things companies could do that would improve the ethical culture, thereby reducing the risk of misconduct and earning sentence reductions for companies that attempt to create an ethical culture but still have an ethical or legal lapse.

The Federal Sentencing Commission has determined that factors such as the following would be helpful in setting the tone of the company:

- A code of ethics
- Training for employees in the code and in ethics
- A means for employees to report misconduct anonymously
- Follow-up on reports employees make on misconduct
- Action by the board, including follow-up and monitoring, on complaints and reports made by employees
- Self-reporting and investigation of legal and ethical issues
- Sanctions and terminations for those within the company who violate the law and company rules, including officers
- A high-ranking officer, with the ability to communicate with the CEO and board, who is responsible for the code of ethics and ethics training in the company

The guidelines for company practices incorporate the factors most experts agree are critical to setting an ethical culture in a company.

2-9c REPORTING LINES: AN ANONYMOUS ETHICS LINE FOR AN ETHICAL CULTURE

An anonymous reporting line is a minimum requirement for companies working to achieve and maintain an ethical culture. The reporting line can be received internally or, in best-practices companies, the report goes out to a third-party contractor who then keeps track of the issue and its progress toward resolution within the company. In addition to encouraging employees to discuss issues with their supervisors, anonymous reporting allows employees to raise issues without the fear and concern that might deter them from reporting to a supervisor. Under the sentencing guidelines, companies that can show they fostered an atmosphere of education and discussion in which employees were encouraged to come forward will fare much better in terms of fines and other punishments if any missteps occur. Many companies have developed ethical news bulletins to offer employees examples of and guidelines on ethical dilemmas. DuPont delivers an ethics bulletin to employees through its e-mail system. Blue Cross Blue Shield has given employees Slinky toys for their desks with the hotline reporting number on them so that as employees think and perhaps use the Slinky to relieve pressure and stress, they will be reminded to

Business Planning Tip

In the past, company ethics officers tended to come from HR and PR. Now, ethics officers at companies have unprecedented power: They are given full access to speak to all employees, have direct lines to boards and CEOs, and appear to have an edge in knowing how to question employees in terms of halting activities. A number of former prosecutors have become ethics officers at companies that have experienced legal or ethical difficulties:

- Richard C. Breeden, former SEC chairman, was an outside monitor at KPMG and is now the CEO of Breeden Capital Management LLC.

- Eric R. Dinallo, formerly with Eliot Spitzer at the New York attorney general's office, was chief compliance officer at Morgan Stanley from 2003 to 2006. Since 2006 he has been general counsel for Willis Group Holdings, an insurance broker.

- Beth L. Golden, also formerly with Spitzer's office, was chief compliance officer at Bear Stearns until its collapse in 2008 and subsequent acquisition by JP Morgan.

- Mari B. Maloney, formerly with the National Association of Securities Dealers (NASD) (now Financial Industry Regulatory Authority, FINRA) and the Manhattan DA's office, was chief compliance officer at AIG and is now the chief compliance officer at Standard & Poor's.

© Grounder/Shutterstock.com

BUSINESS STRATEGY

The Ethical Culture

Leadership by Example

Company Policies and Compensation Systems Reward Ethical and Moral Behavior

**Ethics Codes
Ethics Training: Annual/Scenarios
Investigations/Enforcement/Feedback**

© Cengage Learning

A strategic pyramid can help in understanding how to implement an ethical culture. At the base of the pyramid are the facial trappings of ethics: codes. Even Enron had a 64-page, award-winning code of ethics. Some companies have progressed beyond annual training seminars to regular ethics scenarios circulated throughout the company for employees to consider and discuss before the ethics office offers its insights and guidance on the hypothetical or reality-based scenario that has been presented. Some companies regularly report to employees on number of ethics questions/reports, the investigations, and the outcomes (within the bounds of privacy constraints). For example: "The ethics office investigated 323 matters and employee disciplinary action was taken in 175 of those matters. The form of discipline included terminations, warnings, loss of bonus [and whatever other sanctions were imposed]." The purpose of this data-based feedback is to let employees know, particularly those who reported anonymously and

wish to remain anonymous, of the ethics office activity, the results of investigations, and, perhaps most importantly, the enforcement.

The next layer involves compensation for and recognition of the role of individuals' moral development and the differing roles employees play in terms of organizational behavior parameters in moving the company toward ethical behavior and an ethical culture.

The final or top layer, and the area conquered by so few companies, requires leadership at the executive level and dramatic shifts in both internal and external policies and behaviors of the company. Exploring these top two layers can provide ethics officers and ethics programs within companies with the next step in the evolution of not just "best practices in ethics programs," but in the creation of an ethical culture.

Source: Adapted from Marianne M. Jennings, "Taking Ethics Programs to the Next Level: Why CFOs Are Critical," *Corporate Finance Review* 10, no. 3 (2005), pp. 38–42. Reprinted by permission of Thomson Reuters.

report any problems. The federal government has an ethics encyclopedia online for its employees to use. The encyclopedia is filled with examples of government employees' misconduct and the sanctions they received.

2-9d DEVELOPING AN ETHICS STANCE

Both individuals and firms should decide up front what types of conduct they would never engage in and be certain that the rules are in writing, that everyone understands the rules, and that the rules will be enforced uniformly. Individuals

© yxowert/Shutterstock.com

can vary in their responses to various ethical dilemmas. For example, a woman who had taken $12,000 from her employer was terminated immediately upon the company's discovery of the embezzlement. At the company's next board meeting, the board members discussed the issue and had varying views. One director felt that taking something that does not belong to you is wrong and that termination was the appropriate action. Another director said that his remedy would be determined by whether the money was taken all at once or over a period of time. Another director said that his remedy would be determined according to why the employee took the money. Still another director noted that perhaps the employee did not understand that this type of action is wrong. The directors varied in their views on ethics. One is pragmatic—it is simply wrong. Another applies a relative approach—why did she take the money? Exhibit 2.4 diagrams the ethical stances of the directors.

Knowing where you stand as a company sends clear signals to employees. Knowing where you stand as an individual sends clear signals for the behavior of those around you. Taking a position on a set of values helps a company avoid the either/or conundrum in which tough situations are boiled down to something such as, "Either we release this product now with its flaws and meet the deadline and start getting earnings, or we don't and the company collapses." A value-based decision is one that says, "We as a company do not cheat our customers with poorly designed or manufactured products, and we don't hurt them with defective ones. Because of that value, we retool quickly to correct the problem and get the product out there as soon as possible." With this value-based decision, the company also makes a good business decision, for it has chosen to avoid the often-destructive costs of releasing a defective product despite knowledge of that defect. The GM Malibu case discussed earlier represents the destructive costs of deciding not to take action based on values but, rather, taking action based only on immediate returns.

EXHIBIT 2.4 Your Ethics Stance: The Embezzling Employee

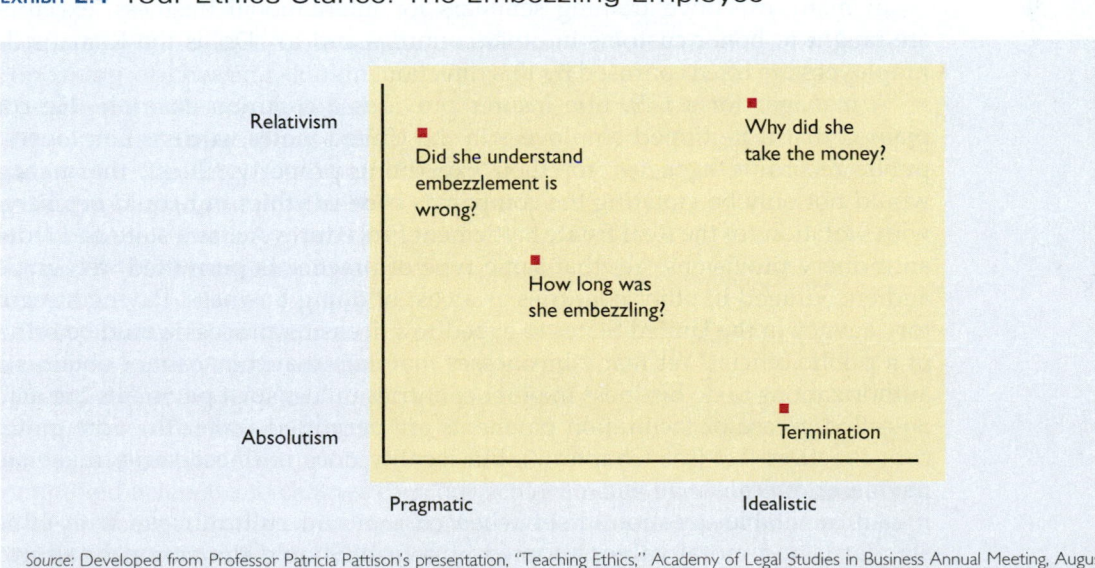

Source: Developed from Professor Patricia Pattison's presentation, "Teaching Ethics," Academy of Legal Studies in Business Annual Meeting, August 11–15, 1994, Dallas, Texas as adapted from "Teaching Ethics" by D. R. Forsych, *Journal of Personality and Social Psychology.*

2-9e BEING CAREFUL ABOUT PRESSURE AND SIGNALS

Doing the right and ethical thing often gets lost in the pressures employees felt with respect to goals and number quotas. These types of signals create a pressured environment in which employees fall into ethical lapses that often lead to illegal behavior. Just the disparity between the amount of time devoted to discussion of results versus ethics is a signal. For example, most employees will say that they discuss performance goals every day and then add, "Without fail, we sign off on the ethics policy once each year!" The signal, however unwitting, is that performance matters most.

In the subprime mortgage meltdown that affected so many Wall Street investment houses, there were clear differences between the firms that collapsed and those that survived. Stan O'Neal at Merrill Lynch, a company that led the pack with over $25 billion in losses and an eventual takeover, was an indefatigable "numbers guy" who took Merrill Lynch from its position of being a safe, trading house to a leveraged player, and O'Neal expected employees to produce results. One Merrill Lynch executive noted the pressure, "It got to the point where you didn't want to be in the office on Goldman earnings days." The pressure for goals was so intense that no one really questioned the numbers and how they were getting the results. Employees called operations meetings "staged." The result was Merrill Lynch's demise, even as employees became concerned but were pressured to just keep going despite the clear consequences.

2-10 Ethical Issues in International Business

The global market presents firms with more complex ethical issues than they would experience if operations were limited to one country and one culture. Moral standards vary across cultures. In some cases, cultures change and evolve to allow conduct that was not previously acceptable. For example, tipping hospital employees is common practice in some countries. In the United States, such behavior could be illegal in the case of government-run hospitals.

In many executive training seminars for international business, executives are taught to honor customs in other countries and to "Do as the Romans do." Employees are often confused by this direction.

A manager for a U.S. title insurer provides a common example. He complained that if he tipped employees in the United States, such as employees at public recording agencies, for their expediting property filings, the manager would not only be violating the company's code of ethics but could be charged with violations of the Real Estate Settlement Procedures Act and state and federal antibribery provisions. Yet that same type of practice is permitted, recognized, and encouraged in other countries as a cost of doing business. Paying a regulatory agency in the United States to expedite a licensing process would be bribery of a public official. Yet many businesses maintain that they cannot obtain such authorizations to do business in other countries unless such payments are made. So-called grease or facilitation payments are permitted under the Foreign Corrupt Practices Act (see Chapter 7), but legality does not necessarily make such payments ethical.

An inevitable question arises when custom and culture clash with ethical standards and moral values adopted by a firm. Should the national culture or the company code of ethics prevail? Typical business responses to the question of whether cultural norms or company codes of ethics should control decisions in international business operations are: Who am I to question the culture of another country? Who am I to impose U.S. standards on all the other nations of the world? Isn't legality the equivalent of ethical behavior? The attitude of businesses is one that permits ethical deviations in the name of cultural sensitivity. Many businesses fear that the risk of offending those in other countries is far too high to impose U.S. ethical standards on the conduct of business in other countries.

Part of the misunderstanding about ethics in international business on the part of U.S.-based businesses is that ethical standards in the United States vary significantly from the ethical standards in other countries. Operating under this misconception can create a great deal of ethical confusion among employees. Strategically, businesses and their employees are more comfortable when they operate under uniform standards. What is known as the "Golden Rule" in the United States actually has existed for some time in other religions and cultures and among philosophers. Exhibit 2.5 offers a list of how this simple rule is phrased in different writings. The principle is the same even if the words vary slightly.

The successful operation of commerce depends on the ethical roots of business. A look at the three major parties in business explains this point. These parties are the risk-takers, the employees, and the customers. Risk-takers—those furnishing the capital necessary for production—are willing to take risks on the assumption that customers will judge their products as valuable. Employees are willing to offer production input, skills, and ideas in exchange for wages, rewards, and other incentives. Consumers and customers are willing to purchase products and services as long as they receive value in exchange for their furnishing, through payment, costs, and profits to the risk-takers and employees. To the extent that the interdependency of the parties in the system is affected by factors outside of their perceived roles and control, the intended business system does not function on its underlying assumptions.

Although the roots of business have been described as primarily economic, this economic system cannot survive without recognition of some fundamental values. Some of the inherent—indeed, universal—values built into our capitalistic economic system, as described here, are as follows: (1) the consumer is given value in exchange for the funds expended; (2) employees are rewarded according

---

EXHIBIT 2.5 A Possible Uniform Standard for Ethical Choices

Categorical imperative: How would you want to be treated?
    Would you be comfortable with a world with your standards?
Christian principle: The Golden Rule
    And as ye would that men should do to you, do ye also to them likewise. (Luke 6:31)
    Thou shalt love . . . thy neighbor as thyself. (Luke 10:27)
Confucius: What you do not want done to yourself, do not do to others.
Aristotle: We should behave to our friends as we wish our friends to behave to us.
Judaism: What you hate, do not do to anyone.
Buddhism: Hurt not others with that which pains thyself.
Islam: No one of you is a believer until he loves for his brother what he loves for himself.
Hinduism: Do nothing to thy neighbor which thou wouldst not have him do to thee.
Sikhism: Treat others as you would be treated yourself.
Plato: May I do to others as I would that they should do unto me.

to their contribution to production; and (3) the risk-takers are rewarded for their investment in the form of a return on that investment. Exhibit 2.6 depicts this relationship. Everyone in the system must be ethical. An economic system is like a four-legged stool. If corruption seeps into one leg, the economic system is off balance. In international business, often the government slips into corruption, with bribes controlling which businesses are permitted to enter the country and who is awarded contracts in that country. In the United States, the wave of reforms at the federal level since 2008 was the result of perceived corruption in the financial markets that resulted in a lack of transparency.

To a large extent, all business is based on trust. The tenets for doing business are dissolved as an economy moves toward a system in which one individual can control the market in order to maximize personal income.

Suppose, for example, that the sale of a firm's product is determined not by perceived consumer value but, rather, by access to consumers, which is controlled by government officials. That is, your company's product cannot be sold to consumers in a particular country unless and until you are licensed within that country. Suppose further that the licensing procedures are controlled by government officials and that those officials demand personal payment in exchange for your company's right to even apply for a business license. Payment size may be arbitrarily determined by officials who withhold portions for themselves. The basic values of the system have been changed. Consumers no longer directly determine the demand.

Beyond just the impact on the basic economic system, ethical breaches involving grease payments introduce an element beyond a now-recognized component in economic performance: consumer confidence in long-term economic performance. Economist Douglas Brown has described the differences between the United States and other countries in explaining why capitalism works here and not in all nations. His theory is that capitalism depends on an interdependent

EXHIBIT 2.6 The Interdependence of Trust, Business, and Government

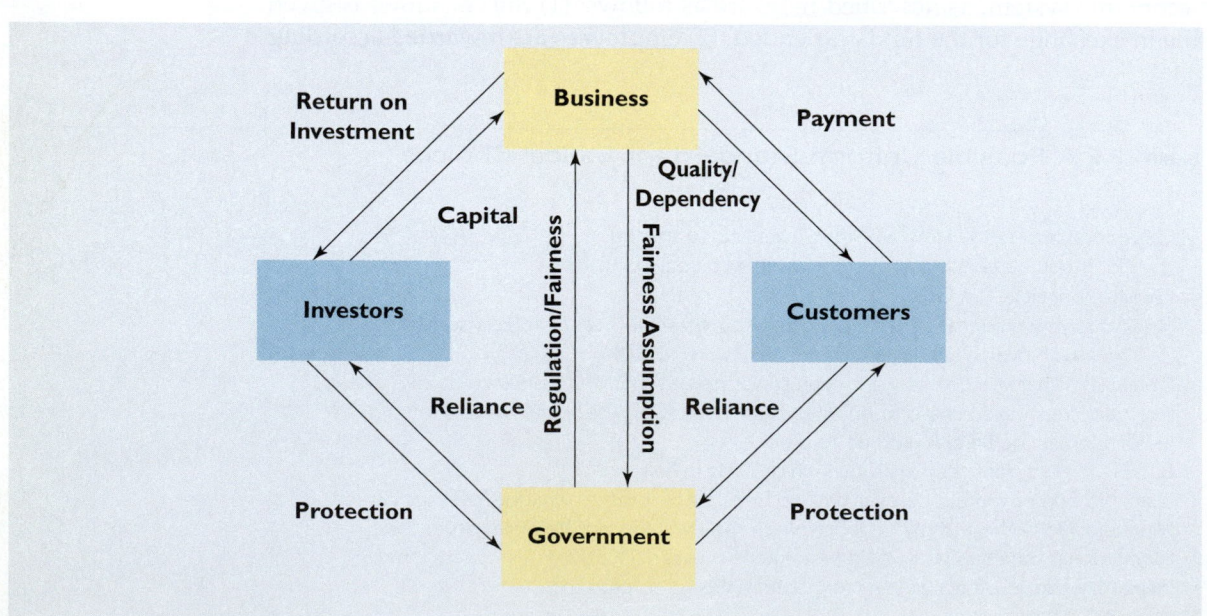

© Cengage Learning

system of production. For economic growth to proceed, consumers, risk-takers, and employees must all feel confident about the future, about the concept of a level playing field, and about the absence of corruption. To the extent that consumers, risk-takers, and employees feel comfortable about a market driven by these basic assumptions, the investment and commitments necessary for economic growth via capitalism will be made. Significant monetary costs are incurred by business systems based on factors other than customer value, as discussed earlier. In developing countries where "speed" or grease payments are required and corrupt government officials are in control, the actual money involved may not be significant in terms of the nation's culture. Such activities and payments introduce an element of demoralization and cynicism that thwarts entrepreneurial activity when these nations most need risk-takers to step forward.

Consider...

Transparency International publishes an annual index of perceptions of corruption. Business executives are asked to rank countries on a scale from 1 to 10, with 10 being the least corrupt. The results for 2012 are as follows.

LEAST CORRUPT	MOST CORRUPT
• New Zealand	• Somalia
• Denmark	• Korea (North)
• Finland	• Myanmar
• Sweden	• Afghanistan
• Singapore	• Uzbekistan
• Norway	• Turkmenistan
• Netherlands	• Sudan
• Australia	• Iraq
• Switzerland	• Haiti
• Canada	• Venezuela
• Luxembourg	• Equatorial Guinea
• Hong Kong	• Burundi
• Iceland	• Libya
• Germany	• Democratic Republic of Congo
• Japan	• Chad
• Austria	• Yemen
• Barbados	• Kyrgyzstan
• United Kingdom	• Guinea
• Belgium	• Cambodia
• Ireland	• Zimbabwe
• Bahamas	• Paraguay
• Chilé	• Papua Guinea
• Qatar	• Nepal
• United States	• Laos
• France	• Kenya
• Santa Lucia	

Why do you think the index appears as it does? Do you see a correlation between economic development or its absence and corruption?

Bribes and *guanxi* (gifts) in China given to establish connections with the Chinese government are estimated at 3 to 5 percent of operating costs for companies, totaling an estimated $5 billion of China's foreign investment. But China incurs costs from the choices government officials make in return for payments. For example, *guanxi* are often used to persuade government officials to transfer government assets to foreign investors for substantially less than their value. Chinese government assets have fallen more than $50 billion in value during the same period of economic growth, primarily because of the large undervaluation by government officials in these transactions with foreign companies. China's economy was adrift because of this underlying corruption. Economic progress began with the elimination of graft.

Perhaps Italy and Brazil provide the best examples of the long-term impact of corruption in foreign business practices. Although the United States, Japan, and Great Britain have had scandals such as the savings and loan failures, political corruption, and insurance regulation, these forms of misconduct do not indicate corruption that pervades entire economic systems. The same cannot be said about Italy. Elaborate connections between government officials, the Mafia, and business executives were unearthed in the 1990s. As a result, half of Italy's cabinet resigned at one time, and hundreds of business executives were indicted. It has been estimated that the interconnections of these three groups cost the Italian government $200 billion, as well as compromising the completion of government projects. Italy is known for its 40-year freeway project. In over 40 years of work, it has not been able to complete a single highway designed to connect the northern and southern parts of the country.

In Brazil, the level of corruption has led to a climate of murder and espionage. Many foreign firms have elected not to do business in Brazil because of so much uncertainty and risk—beyond the normal financial risks of international investment. Why send an executive to a country where officials may use force when soliciting huge bribes?

The *Wall Street Journal* offered an example of how Brazil's corruption has damaged the country's economy despite growth and opportunity in surrounding nations. The governor of the northeastern state of Paraiba in Brazil, Ronaldo Cunha Lima, was angry because his predecessor, Tarcisio Burity, had accused Mr. Lima's son of corruption. Mr. Lima shot Mr. Burity twice in the chest while Mr. Burity was having lunch at a restaurant. The speaker of Brazil's Senate praised Mr. Lima for his courage in doing the shooting himself as opposed to sending someone else. Mr. Lima was given a medal by the local city council and granted immunity from prosecution by Paraiba's state legislature. No one spoke for the victim, and the lack of support reflected a culture controlled by self-interest that benefits those in control. Unfortunately, these self-interests preclude economic development.

Economists in Brazil document hyperinflation and systemic corruption. A São Paulo businessman observed, "The fundamental reason we can't get our act together is we're an amoral society." This businessperson probably understands capitalism. Privatization that has helped the economies of Chile, Argentina, and Mexico cannot take hold in Brazil because government officials enjoy the benefits of generous wages and returns from the businesses they control. The result is that workers are unable to earn enough even to clothe their families, 20 percent of the Brazilian population lives below the poverty line, and crime has reached the level of nightly firefights. Brazil's predicament occurred over time, as graft, collusion, and fraud became entrenched in the government-controlled economy.[24]

BIOGRAPHY

The Stories and Risks of the Celebrity Endorsement

Lance Armstrong, who was stripped of his Tour de France wins and subsequently admitted to using performance-enhancing drugs, was once ranked as the 60th most effective product spokesperson in the world. He was right up there with Brad Pitt. Now, he is ranked 1,410, with rapper Nicki Minaj.

The companies that have not renewed Mr. Armstrong's endorsement agreements or have terminated them include Nike, Radio Shack, Trek Bicycle, Easton-Bell (the makers of the Giro helmets Mr. Armstrong wore in his races), FRS Energy Foods, Anheuser-Busch, 24 Hour Fitness, and Nissan. Mr. Armstrong earned between $15 and $17 million per year from the endorsement contracts.

Celebrity endorsement contracts always have some form of a morals clause, a clause that allows the sponsor to terminate the contract for a variety of reasons, such as an arrest. However, the clauses generally have additional grounds for termination, such as conduct by the celebrity that bring negative publicity or boycotts to the company. The termination rights are basically a judgment call on the part of the company. There is not much wiggle room for the celebrities. In fact, there is a long history of terminations.

Olympian Michael Phelps lost his endorsement contract with Kellogg's when photos of him smoking a bong pipe at a campus party showed up on the Internet in 2009. Model Kate Moss lost her endorsement contracts with Burberry and Chanel when, in 2005, a grainy videotape emerged that showed her using cocaine. In 2007, Verizon withdrew its sponsorship of the Gwen Stefani tour when a raunchy video of her opening act, Akon, appeared online. The video showed Akon engaged in questionable on-stage behavior with a fan under the age of 18. The video resulted in considerable coverage and outrage from parents and commentators. Uniquely, the Stefani endorsement contract was terminated for her association with another artist who had displayed questionable behavior.

Perhaps the best example of discretion in using the morals clauses came when Tiger Woods was in a car crash near his Florida home and the extent of his marital infidelity came to light. Mr. Woods lost endorsement contracts with Accenture, AT&T, and Gatorade. Gatorade did, however, continue its relationship with the Tiger Woods Foundation. Nike did not drop its sponsorship and Nike chairman and cofounder Phil Knight explained that these problems with athletes are just "part of the game" when you sign them. Tag Heuer did not drop Woods because, as a spokesperson explained, "He's the best in his domain. We respect his performance in the sport. Woods' personal life is not our business." Tag Heuer did, however, stop running its ads featuring Mr. Woods. Gillette also stopped running Woods ads but did not terminate the relationship until later. When the charges leveled by the U.S. Anti-Doping Agency were detailed against Lance Armstrong, Nike originally stood by their man. However, when the agency released its documentation, Nike called the evidence "insurmountable" that Mr. Armstrong had participated in doping for more than a decade.

There can also be redemption and new contracts. Michael Vick lost his Nike contract when he entered a guilty plea and went to prison for charges related to a dog-fighting business. However, Mr. Vick now has most of his endorsements back. Michael Phelps' calmer life and additional 2012 Olympic medals rewarded him with restored contracts.

Mr. Armstrong has resigned as chairman of his Live Strong foundation, and many companies, including Nike, have agreed to continue their support for this charity that does have Armstrong-branded products that it sells to raise money.

Questions for Discussion

1. When can a company use a morals clause? Why do companies use moral clauses? What difference does it make what celebrities and sports figures do in their personal lives?

2. Is the use of a morals clause a matter of strict contract interpretation?

Summary

What is ethics?
- Behavior beyond the law
- Day-to-day nature of ethics

What is business ethics?
- Ethical standards—normative standards of behavior set by culture
- Ethical standards—standards of behavior set by natural law
- Ethical standards—moral relativism; moral standards by situation
- Ethical standards—religion and ethics

What are the categories of ethical dilemmas in business?
- Taking things that don't belong to you
- Saying things you know are not true
- Giving or allowing false impressions
- Buying influence or engaging in conflict of interest
- Hiding or divulging information
- Taking unfair advantage
- Committing acts of personal decadence
- Perpetrating interpersonal abuse
- Permitting organizational abuse
- Violating rules
- Condoning unethical actions
- Balancing ethical dilemmas

How do employees resolve ethical dilemmas?
- Blanchard and Peale
- Front-page-of-the-newspaper test
- *Wall Street Journal* and stakeholders
- Laura Nash and perspective
- Categorical imperative

Why do we fail to reach good ethical decisions?
- "Everybody else does it."
- "If we don't do it, someone else will."
- "That's the way it has always been done."
- "We'll wait until the lawyers tell us it's wrong."
- "It doesn't really hurt anyone."
- "The system is unfair."
- "I was just following orders."
- "You think this is bad, you should have seen . . . "
- "It's a gray area."

What is social responsibility and how does a business exercise it?
- Positive law—codified law
- Inherence—serves shareholders' interests
- Enlightened self-interest—serves shareholders' interests by serving larger society
- Invisible hand—serves larger society by serving shareholders' interests
- Social responsibility—serves largest society best by serving larger society

Why is business ethics important?
- Profit
- Leadership
- Reputation
- Strategy

How does a business create an ethical atmosphere?
- Tone at the top
- Frank-Dodd and corporate sentencing guidelines
- Code of ethics
- Reporting hotlines
- Ethical posture and developing an ethical stance

What are the ethical issues in international business?
- Corruption issues
- Economic systems and ethics

Questions and Problems

1. E. & J. Gallo, the world's largest winery, announced that it would stop selling its Thunderbird and Night Train Express wines in the Tenderloin, the skid row of San Francisco, for six months. Gallo took the action after meeting with an activist group called Safe and Sober Streets, which has asked grocers to remove the high-alcohol wine from the district, where citizens say drunks create a menace. One retailer in the district said, "If I don't sell this, I will have to close my doors and go home."

Discuss the actions of E. & J. Gallo and the dilemma of the retailers in the district. Be sure to discuss the type of philosophy each of them holds with respect to social responsibility and ethical dilemmas.

2. Paul Backman is the head of the purchasing department for L. A. East, one of the "Baby Bells" that came into existence after the divestiture of AT&T. Mr. Backman and his department purchase everything for the company, from napkins to wires for equipment lines.

S. C. Rydman is an electronics firm and has been a major supplier for L. A. East since 1984. Rydman is also the cosponsor of an exhibit at Wonder World, a theme park in Florida.

Rydman's vice president and CFO, Gunther Fromme, visited Mr. Backman in his office on April 3, 2004. Rydman had no bids pending at that time, and Mr. Fromme told Mr. Backman that he was there "for goodwill." Mr. Fromme explained that Rydman had a block of rooms at Wonder World because of its exhibit there and that Mr. Backman and his group could use the rooms at any time, free of charge.

Should Mr. Backman and his employees use the block of rooms? Why or why not?

3. Scott Thompson, who was made CEO of Yahoo in March 2012, stated on his résumé that he has an accounting and computer science degree from Stonehill College, earned in 1979. However, Stonehill College did not offer a degree in computer science until the early 1980s. Mr. Thompson had carried the degree information on his résumé for some time, including during his time as an executive at Paypal. One of Yahoo's investors, the hedge fund, Third Point, uncovered the information and pointed out that the company's website as well its SEC 10K report included the information about the computer science degree. Mr. Thompson says that Third Point's CEO, Daniel Loeb, has a "personal vendetta" against him. Discuss the ethical issues.

4. Kenneth Branch was an employee with Lockheed Martin in 1996. At that time Lockheed Martin was competing head-to-head with the Boeing Company for a government contract worth $5 billion. Mr. Branch interviewed for a job in Boeing's rocket division in 1996 and began employment at Boeing in January 1997.[25]

The government awarded the contract to Boeing. An internal investigation by Boeing revealed that Mr. Branch and his supervisor, William Erskine, had thousands of pages of proprietary documents from Lockheed Martin, including detailed information about Lockheed Martin's costs and specifications for the rocket contract. Boeing turned over 11 boxes of documents to Lockheed in 2003, some of which were marked "Proprietary."

Applying the model on steps for analyzing ethical dilemmas and case studies in business you learned in the "Consider . . .," feature, determine whether there were any ethical breaches in Boeing's conduct.

The author has performed consulting work for Boeing on changing its ethical culture. Why is this disclosure important in this text? Why is this disclosure important to you?

5. During the 2012 presidential inauguration, a controversy arose: Did Beyoncé lip-sync the national anthem? No definitive answer was offered by those involved. What was clear was that the National Marine Band did not play during her performance, that a tape was played, and that those in charge of the event felt a live performance was too risky because the singer had not had the opportunity to rehearse with the band prior to her performance. Are there any ethical issues here? Does this action fit into any of the ethical categories? Could you offer any advice to those involved about the ethical issues?

6. Richard M. Scrushy, the former CEO of HealthSouth and now a convicted felon (bribery), was the subject of a probation hearing. Prosecutors said that Mr. Scrushy was trying to leave the country in February 2007 via his 92-foot yacht, the *Chez Soiree*. The yacht journey was nixed when bad weather hit the Alabama coast. Mr. Scrushy protested the allegations, testifying that he had permission to travel to South Florida as part of a vacation that had been approved for him and his family (including going to Disney World). He said he did not tell the probation officer about the trip to Miami because her questions were not specific enough, "I can't answer the question unless she asks me."[26] The federal magistrate said that Mr. Scrushy was being "coy" with his probation officers. Discuss whether Mr. Scrushy breached any ethical standards with his conduct and interpretation of the terms of his probation.

7. Marilee Jones, the dean of admissions of MIT, resigned in 2007 after 28 years as an administrator in the admissions office. The dean for undergraduate education received information questioning Ms. Jones's academic credentials. Her résumé, used when she was hired by MIT, indicated that she had degrees from Albany Medical College, Union College, and Rensselaer Polytechnic Institute. In fact, she had no degrees from any of these schools or from anywhere else. She had attended Rensselaer Polytechnic as a part-time nonmatriculated student during the 1974–1975 school year but the other institutions had no record of any attendance at their schools. When Ms. Jones arrived at MIT for her entry-level position in 1979, a degree was probably not required. She then progressed through the ranks of the admissions office and, in 1997, she was appointed dean of admissions. She explained that she wanted to disclose her lack of degrees at that point but that she had gone on for so long that she did not know how to come clean with the truth.

Ms. Jones had been on a national book tour from 2006 to 2007 promoting her book, *Less Stress, More Success: A New Approach to Guiding Your Teen Through College Admissions and Beyond.* The book advises, "Holding integrity is sometimes very hard to do because temptation may be to cheat or cut corners. But just remember that 'what goes around comes around,' meaning that life has a funny way of giving back what you put out."

Ms. Jones was known around the campus for her sense of humor as well as her common sense and outspokenness. She resigned because the chancellor, Philip M. Clay, said, "There are some mistakes people can make for which 'I'm sorry' can be accepted, but this is one of those matters where the lack of integrity is sufficient all by itself."

In her letter of resignation, Ms. Jones said she "did not have the courage to correct my resume." Apply what you have learned in this chapter to help analyze what went wrong with Ms. Jones's decision process. What mistakes did she make through the whole process in her actions and responses?

8. Gold Peak Tea, a Coca-Cola brand, sponsored it's "Take the Year Off" contest. The prize was one year off work and $100,000. Entrants were required to submit a video. Theodore A. Scott, a Decatur, Georgia, attorney, won the grand prize based on votes for his video. His video began with him describing how he had missed out with his family because of his career demands and vowed to spend time with his wife, children, and grandchildren if he won the prize. He also said that he would drink, of course, iced tea.

After Gold Peak told Mr. Scott that he had won, the company received a tip (and the company will not identify who gave them the tip) that Mr. Scott had gone to About.com, a site that has information on contests and sweepstakes, and made a pitch to voters there. Mr. Scott asked them to vote for him.

When Gold Peak learned of the post, it disqualified Mr. Peak and gave the prize to the next entrant in line. Rule 6B of the "Take the Year Off" contest provides that contestants were prohibited from obtaining votes by "offering prizes or other inducements to members of the public, vote farming, or any other activity that artificially inflates such finalists' votes as determined by sponsor in its sole discretion."

Mr. Scott has defended his action by saying that the people who voted for him were real people and that he did not use robotics or Facebook accounts. An expert on sweepstakes agrees, "In my opinion, that's not cheating if those are real people who aren't being induced." Is Mr. Scott correct? Did he cheat?

9. Heinz Ketchup holds 54 percent of the U.S. ketchup market, and 9 of every 10 restaurants feature Heinz ketchup. However, Heinz has learned that many restaurant owners simply refill Heinz bottles with cheaper ketchup, thereby capitalizing on the Heinz name without the cost. One restaurant owner explains, "It's just ketchup. The customers don't notice." There are no specific health regulations that apply, and owners are not breaking the law by refilling the bottles. Do you think this practice is ethical?

10. Gerald Grinstein, the former CEO of Delta Air Lines, refused to take any bonuses, stock options, or extra compensation for 2006 and instead would only take his base salary of $338,000. Grinstein arranged to have $1 billion distributed to about 39,000 nonunionized employees and 1,000 managers within 12 to 15 months after the airline emerged from bankruptcy. "I'm the dawning of the old age," was the comment the 74-year-old CEO made when asked why he was taking such an unprecedented step.[27] Grinstein is giving up an estimated $10 million. He also added, "Corporate pay packages have gotten out of control. It has become a salary derby out there." Grinstein still arranged to have bonuses for top executives if they hit certain profit targets and explained, "You have got to have a program that attracts executives but at the same time you've got to take care of the relationships with frontline employees."[28] Apply the various schools of social responsibility to Mr. Grinstein and decide which he followed. Think about the regulatory cycle's application to the issue of CEO pay. What do you think regulators will do?

ECONOMICS, ETHICS, & THE LAW

Self-Interest vs. Selfishness

Adam Smith, in what has been called the seminal work on free-market economics, wrote, "It is not from the benevolence of the butcher, the brewer, or the baker, that we can expect our dinner, but from their regard to their own interest."[29] Self-interest, then, is what Smith believed to be the motivator for economic engagement and growth. Is there a difference between self-interest and selfishness? Where would social responsibility fit in the Smith view of the relationship between ethics and economics? However, 17 years before writing *Wealth of Nations*, Smith wrote *The Theory of Moral Sentiments*, and included the following observation about ethics and business: "How selfish soever man may be supposed, there are evidently some principles in his nature which interest him in the fortune of others and render their happiness necessary to him though he derives nothing from it except the pleasure of seeing it."[30] What does this quote reveal about Smith's attitudes toward social responsibility?

Notes

1. Josephson Institute, http://www.josephsoninstitute.org, accessed December 20, 2012. For information on cheating in college, see Donald L. McCabe, Kenneth D. Butterfield, and Linda KlebeTreviño, "Academic Dishonesty in Graduate Business Programs: Prevalence, Causes, and Proposed Action," 5 *Academy of Management Learning and Education* 294 (2006).

2. There is a misdemeanor statute in Seattle that makes it illegal to cut in line in front of other drivers who are waiting to board a ferry.

3. See http://www.josephsoninstitute.org.

4. Professor Donald McCabe of Rutgers University has conducted surveys on academic integrity for many years. His latest survey involved 4,500 student respondents nationwide. See Center for Academic Integrity at Clemson University, http://www.academicintegrity.org, for more information.

5. Louise Story and Landon Thomas, Jr., "Tales from Lehman's Crypt," *New York Times*, September 12, 2009, p. SB1.

6. Steve Stecklow et al., "Sonsini Defended HP's Methods in Leak Inquiry," *Wall Street Journal*, September 8, 2006, p. A1.

7. Tyler Kepner, "Pitcher Spurns $12 Million, To Keep Self-Respect," *New York Times*, January 27, 2011, p. A1.

8. Leah Nathan Spiro, "The Bomb Shelter Salomon Built," *BusinessWeek*, September 9, 1991, pp. 78–80.

9. *Washington Post*, April 2, 2012, p. A1.

10. *USA Today*, November 12, 2012, p. 1B.

11. *Wall Street Journal*, December 6, 2011, p. A3.

12. Catherine Yang and Amy Barrett, "In a Stew Over Tainted Meat," *BusinessWeek*, April 12, 1993, p. 36.

13. Dorothy Rabinowitz, "Is Lance Armstrong Really Sorry?" *Wall Street Journal*, January 18, 2013.

14. Sue Reisinger, "Runaway Train Hits H-P's GC," *National Law Journal*, December 18–25, 2006, pp. 8–9.

15. From "Interview: Milton Friedman," *Playboy*, February 1973. © 1973 *Playboy*.

16. Mr. Milken was required by the Securities and Exchange Commission to pay a fine for his involvement in the negotiations (see Chapter 21).

17. Mr. Wagner is referring to Ivan Boesky, another financier who served a prison sentence; Ron Perelman, the chairman of Revlon, Inc.; Barry Diller, former chairman of Paramount and Fox and owner of the Home Shopping Network; Rupert Murdoch, the media mogul who now owns Fox; and Jenny Anderson, "The Drexel Diaspora," *New York Times*, February 6, 2005, 3-1, Money & Business.

18. Yuri Mishina, et al., "Why 'Good' Firms Do Bad Things: The Effects of High Aspirations, High Expectations, and Prominence on the Incidence of Corporate Illegality," 53 *Academy of Management Journal* 701 (2010).

19. Jonathan D. Rockoff, "J&J Lapses Are Cited in Drugs for Kids," *Wall Street Journal*, May 27, 2010, p. B1.

20. For complete information about BP's presence in Alaska and its contribution to the economic base there, go to http://alaska.bp.com.

21. Chris Woodward, Paul Davidson, and Brad Heath, "BP Spill Highlights Aging Oil Field's Increasing Problems," *USA Today*, August 14, 2006, pp. 1B, 2B.

22. Julie Creswell and VikasBajas, "A Mortgage Crisis Begins to Spiral, and the Casualties Mount," *New York Times*, March 5, 2007, pp. C1, C4.

23. For a summary of the state legislation on predatory lending practices, see Therese G. Franzén and Leslie M. Howell, "Predatory Lending Legislation in 2004," 60 *Business Lawyer* 677 (2005).

24. Barnaby J. Feder, "An Abrupt Departure Is Seen as a Harbinger," *New York Times*, May 1, 2002, pp. C1, C2.

25. Anne Marie Squeo and Andy Pasztor, "U.S. Probes Whether Boeing Misused a Rival's Documents," *Wall Street Journal*, May 5, 2003, pp. A1, A7.

26. Andrew Backover, "Report Slams Culture at WorldCom," *USA Today*, November 5, 2002, p. 1B.

27. Annual report for 1998, posted at http://www.worldcom.com. (*Note:* Because WorldCom no longer exists, company information can be found only in the Edgar database at http://www.sec.gov.)

28. Bernard Ebbers's letter to shareholders in the annual report for 1999, posted at http://www.worldcom.com. (*Note:* Because WorldCom no longer exists, information about the company can be found only in the Edgar database at http://www.sec.gov.)

29. Adam Smith, *An Inquiry into the Nature and Causes of the Wealth of Nations* (1776). Book 1, Chapter 2, Paragraph 2, Edited by Edwin Cannan. Chicago: University of Chicago Press, 1976. Accessed online March 5, 2010 at http://www.econlib.org/library/Smith/smWN.html.

30. *The Theory of Moral Sentiments* (1759). Part 1, Section 1, Chapter 1, Paragraph 1, Edited by D. D. Raphael and A. L. Macfie. Oxford: Clarendon Press; New York: Oxford University Press, 1976. Accessed online March 5, 2010 at http://www.econlib.org/library/Smith/smMS.html.

Chapter 3 THE JUDICIAL SYSTEM

Our introduction to law included discussions of statutory law and common law. With so many statutes at so many levels, you perhaps might think that statutory law is a complete source of law. However, sometimes statutes need interpretation. Someone must determine when, how, and to whom statutes apply. Statutory law is not even half of all the law. The bulk of the law is found in judicial decisions. These decisions contain statutory interpretations and common law. This chapter covers the parties involved in these decisions, as well as the courts that make them—what they decide, when they can decide, and how those decisions are made.

For as thou urgest justice,
be assured thou shalt
have justice, more than
thou desirest.

Portia
The Merchant of Venice, Act IV,
Scene I

Consider...

Patricia Baker was a passenger aboard a Royal Caribbean Cruise Lines ship. She had purchased a ticket to participate in a mock pirate ship excursion tour in the Cayman Islands from E & H Cruises, a Cayman Islands corporation. While boarding the E & H mock pirate ship, Ms. Baker fell and was injured. She brought suit in Florida federal district court against both Royal Caribbean and E & H to recover for her injuries. E & H moved to dismiss the suit because it did not do business in the United States and was not subject to U.S. courts. Ms. Baker argues that she bought the pirate excursion ticket in Florida, so E & H was doing business in the United States. Is she correct? Can E & H be required to come to the United States to defend the suit?

3-1 Types of Courts

All U.S. court systems include two different types or levels of courts: trial courts and appellate courts.

3-1a TRIAL COURTS

A **trial court** is the place in the judicial system where the facts of a case are presented. This court is where the jury sits if the case is a jury trial. Here the evidence and witnesses are presented and the first decision in the case is made, by either judge or jury. The procedures for trials and trial courts are covered in Chapter 4.

3-1b APPELLATE COURTS

At least one other court, an **appellate court**, reviews the conduct during the trial of the judge, the lawyers, the witnesses, and the jury. This process of review helps assure that the lower court applied the law correctly and followed the rules of procedure. Further, this review system provides uniformity. In some appeals, the appellate court issues published opinions, which can then be referred to and used as resources in deciding future cases. However, in many cases the appellate court issues unpublished opinions. Unpublished opinions have become a controversial issue; and although no law prohibits citing such opinions, a cite should always make clear that the opinion is an unpublished one.

3-2 How Courts Make Decisions

3-2a THE PROCESS OF JUDICIAL REVIEW

Appellate courts do not hold trials. Rather, they review what has been done by trial courts to determine whether the trial court, also referred to as the lower court, made an error in applying the substantive or procedural law in the case, through the process of **judicial review**.

The atmosphere in the appellate court is different from that of the trial court. No witnesses, no jury, and no testimony play a role. No new evidence is considered; only the evidence presented at trial is reviewed. The court reviews a transcript of the trial along with all the evidence presented at trial to determine whether an error was made.

In addition to the transcript and evidence, each of the parties to a case can present the appellate court with a **brief**, which is a summary of the case and the legal issues being challenged on appeal. The appellate brief is each side's summary of why the trial court decision or procedures were correct or incorrect. The parties make their arguments for their positions in the brief and support them with statutes and decisions from other cases. The brief serves as a summary of the major points of error the parties allege occurred during the trial. This type of brief, called an **appellate brief**, is very detailed. In fact, many refer to "briefs" as a misnomer because they are generally quite lengthy. Note that these briefs differ from the case brief presented in Exhibit 1.1.

Many appellate courts permit the attorneys for the opposing parties to make timed oral arguments in their cases. An **oral argument** is a summary of the points that have been made in each party's brief. The judge can also ask questions of the attorneys at that time. At the trial level, one judge makes all decisions. At the appellate level, more than one judge reviews the actions of the lower court in a case. The typical number is three, but, in the case of state supreme courts and the U.S. Supreme Court, the full bench of judges on the court hears each case. For example, in U.S. Supreme Court decisions, all nine justices review the cases before the Court unless they have recused (disqualified) themselves because of some conflict.

The panel of appellate judges reviews the case and the briefs, hears the oral argument, and then renders a decision. The decision in the case could be unanimous or could be a split vote, such as 2 to 1. In the case of a split vote, a justice who is not in the majority will frequently draft a **dissenting opinion**, which is the judge's explanation for a vote different from that of the majority.

Checking for Error

A **reversible error** is one that might have affected the outcome of the case or influenced the decision made. Examples of reversible errors include the refusal to allow some evidence to be admitted that should have been admitted, the refusal to allow a particular witness to testify, and misapplication of the law.

When a reversible error has been made, the appellate court **reverses** the lower court's decision. However, in some cases, the appellate court will also **remand** the case, which means the court sends the case back to the trial court for further proceedings. For example, when the court orders a reversal because some evidence should have been admitted that was not, the case is remanded for a new trial with that evidence admitted (i.e., allowed).

If the appellate court does not find a reversible error, it simply **affirms** the decision of the lower court. The fact that a decision has been affirmed does not mean no mistakes were made at the trial; rather, it means that none of the mistakes was a reversible error. The appellate decision is written by a member of the court who has voted with the majority. The decision explains the facts and the reasons for the court's reversal, remand, or affirmation.

In some appellate cases, the court will **modify** the decision of a lower court. The full case is neither reversed nor affirmed; instead, a portion or portions of the case are reversed or modified. For example, a trial court verdict that found a defendant negligent might be affirmed, but the appellate court could also hold that the damages awarded were excessive. In this type of decision, the case is remanded for a redetermination of damages at the trial court level.

Statutory Interpretation

In addition to checking for error, appellate courts render interpretations of statutes. Often, statutes seem perfectly clear until a new factual situation not covered by the statute arises.

3-2b THE DOCTRINE OF *STARE DECISIS*

Judicial review by appellate courts of lower court decisions by appellate courts provides the database for the doctrine of *stare decisis*, a Latin term meaning "let the decision stand." The decisions of the appellate courts are written and often published so that they may be analyzed, reviewed, and perhaps applied in the future.

Setting Precedent

When reviewing the decisions of lower courts, courts examine their own previous decisions, along with decisions of other courts on the same topic. This process of examining other decisions for help in a new case uses case **precedent**, which is the doctrine of *stare decisis*. Judges examine all prior cases in the same area of law or related to a statute to determine whether the issue has already been decided and, if so, whether the current case should be decided in the same way. Following case precedent does not mean similar cases will be decided identically; several factors influence the weight given to precedent.

The Quality of Precedent

Where the case originated is one of the factors that influence the use of precedent in a case. In federal courts, precedent from other federal courts is strongest when the case involves federal issues.

In state courts, prior decisions within a particular state's own court system are given greater weight than decisions from other states' courts. One state's courts are not obliged to follow the precedent of another state's courts; they are free to examine it and use it, but, as with all precedent, it is not a mandatory requirement to follow another state's decisions.

The Purposes of Precedent

The purposes of precedent are the same as the purposes of law. Law offers some assurance of consistency and reliability. The judiciary recognizes these obligations in applying precedent. Stability and predictability are necessary in the way law functions. No exact formula applies when deciding a case, but consistency is a key element in the use of precedent.

In addition to consistency, however, judges must remember the law's need for flexibility. As new twists in facts arise and technology develops, the judiciary must adapt the law to those changes. For example, in Chapter 1, the *Grokster* and *Viacom* cases illustrate the need for a reexamination of the scope of a law because of evolved technology and its role in copyright law and protections.

The Interpretation of Precedent

Using precedent involves more than just finding similar cases. Every case decision has two parts. One is the actual rule of law, which technically is the precedential part. However, judges never offer just a rule of law in a case. The rule of law is given at the end of the case decision after a full discussion of reasoning and precedent. This discussion is called the *dicta* of the case, which includes case precedent of benefit to each party. In some instances, the rule of law may benefit one party while the *dicta* benefit the other party.

A dissenting opinion is *dicta* and is often quoted in subsequent cases to urge a court to change existing precedent. Application of precedent is not a scientific process, and it often leaves much room for interpretation and variation.

Consider...

Then a third-year law student, Andrew Rausa was spending July 4 with some friends on the porch or stoop area of one of the brownstone homes in Brooklyn, New York. The area in front of the brownstone is enclosed in a fence with a gate entry. Mr. Rausa and his friends were also enjoying several rounds of beer. Two police officers came by, noted the group inside the wrought-iron fence, and cited them all for drinking in public. Mr. Rausa looked up the code section on his phone and found that a public place for purposes of the "no drinking in public" code provision was defined as:

[one] to which the public or a substantial group of persons has access, including, but not limited to a park, sidewalk, or beach.

There are exceptions for neighborhood block parties and events covered by permits. The group of friends decided to fight the violations because they did not want them to be part of their permanent records. How should the court interpret the code provision? Consider the following questions in interpretation. What if you were drinking in your house, but your front door was open? A window?

When Precedent Is Not Followed

Precedent may not be followed for several reasons. Some of those reasons have already been given: the precedent is from another state, or the precedent is interpreted differently because of the *dicta* in that precedent. Precedent is also not followed when the facts of cases can be "distinguished," which means that the context of the facts in one case is different enough from those in other cases that the precedent cannot be applied. For example, suppose that a court decided that using roadblocks to stop motorists to check for drunk drivers is constitutional. Another court then decides that using roadblocks just to check for drivers' licenses is not constitutional. The first case can be distinguished because of the purpose of the roadblocks: to prevent a hazardous highway condition. The court may not see the same urgency or safety issue in roadblocks used for checking for drivers' licenses. The precedent can be distinguished.

The theories of law discussed in Chapter 1 may also control whether precedent is applied. Courts struggle with issues of fact and law and with changes in society as they apply precedent and consider modifications.

For example, a court may not follow a precedent because of an ethical reason or because of the need to change the law on the basis of what is moral or what is right. A precedent may also be abandoned on an economic theory; in this case, the court changes the law to do the most good for the most people. For example, a factory may be a nuisance because of the noise and pollution it creates, and ample case law probably supports shutting down the factory as a nuisance. However, the factory may also be the town's only economic support, and its shutdown will mean unemployment for virtually the whole town. In balancing the economic factors, the nuisance precedent may not be followed or it may be followed in only a modified way.

3-3 Parties in the Judicial System (Civil Cases)

3-3a PLAINTIFFS

Plaintiffs are the parties who initiate a lawsuit and are seeking some type of recovery. In some types of cases those who initiate the court action are called petitioners (such as in an action for divorce). Plaintiffs file their suits in the appropriate court, and this filing step begins the litigation process.

3-3b DEFENDANTS

Plaintiffs seek recovery from **defendants**, who are named in the suit as having committed some violation of the law or the rights of the plaintiff. Another name for a defendant is **respondent**.

3-3c LAWYERS

In most cases, each of the parties is represented by a **lawyer**. Lawyers have other functions besides representing clients in a lawsuit. Many lawyers offer "preventive" services. Lawyers draft contracts, wills, and other documents to prevent legal problems from arising. One role that lawyers play is advising clients in advance in order to minimize clients' legal problems and costs.

The attorney–client relationship is a fiduciary one that carries a protected privilege. The attorney is expected to act in the best interests of the client and can do so without the fear of having to disclose the client's thoughts and decisions. The **attorney–client privilege** keeps the relationship confidential and assures that others (even an adversary in a lawsuit) have limited access to lawyer–client conversations. One of the key areas of discussion and debate, under Sarbanes-Oxley (SOX), related to corporate lawyers' duty to report fraud and other financial misdeeds of their client companies. Lawyers were concerned about the need for client confidentiality, and regulators and investors were concerned that lawyers have remained silent as financial frauds have been ongoing in companies. Under the law, lawyers are not required to blow the whistle on their clients, but they are required to take steps to notify the audit committee and board about misconduct, and ultimately resign if the conduct is not changed and rectified. (For more details of the role of general counsel, the privilege, and auditors' responsibilities regarding financial fraud, refer to Chapters 8, 18, and 19.)

Under the American Bar Association's Model Rules for Professional Responsibility, attorneys are obligated to represent clients with persuasive force. An attorney who agrees to represent a client must represent that client to the best of the lawyer's ability. Because of the privilege, many lawyers know that their clients actually did commit a crime or breach a contract. However, the client's confession to an attorney is confidential. Even with knowledge of a client's guilt, an attorney must represent the client in a manner that gives the client all rights and protections under the law. There is a difference between a client's confession to a crime and the proof required for conviction of

Business Planning Tip

Be careful to protect your lawyer–client privilege. Business letters and memos to lawyers should be marked as privileged and include limitations on access to those letters and memos. If you reveal information to someone other than your lawyer, you may lose your privilege on that information. Holding a conversation or meeting with your lawyer with others present may cost you your privilege, too. Privileged communications should be with your lawyer(s) only.

that crime. A lawyer's obligation is to see that the other side meets its burdens and responsibilities in proving a case against the client. Lawyers *do* represent guilty people. Their role is to, as many lawyers phrase it, "keep the system clean." Protecting the rights of the guilty is required in order to ensure that the rights of the innocent are also preserved. However, lawyers are not required to remain silent under the privilege if a client is about to commit a crime. A lawyer representing a client accused of murder cannot disclose that the client confessed. However, a lawyer whose client vows to kill someone must make a disclosure in order to prevent a crime.

Lawyers and their titles and roles vary from country to country. Great Britain and most of Canada have *solicitors* and *barristers*. Solicitors prepare legal documents, give legal advice, and represent clients in some of the lesser courts. Barristers are the only "lawyers" who can practice before higher courts and administrative agencies. Quebec and France have three types of lawyers: the *avocat*, who can practice before the higher courts and give legal advice; the *notaire*, who can handle real property transactions and estates and can prepare some legal documents; and the *juriste* (legal counselor), who can give advice and prepare legal documents. In Germany, a lawyer who litigates is called *Rechtsanwalt* and a lawyer who advises clients but does not appear in court is called *Rechtsbeistand*. Japan has only one class of lawyers, called *Bengosh*, but does have the *Shiho-Soshi*, a type of advanced notary with the authority to incorporate companies, prepare documents, and create wills. In Italy, the two types of lawyers—whose roles are similar to those in the dual British system—are *avocati* and *procuratori*.

FOR THE MANAGER'S DESK

Re: The Privilege of Lawyers

To whom does the attorney–client privilege belong? An attorney who is employed as general counsel for a corporation, or a lawyer representing that corporation in a particular matter, owes a duty to the corporation. The corporation, in those circumstances, is the client. Employees are not. The privilege, therefore, applies to corporate client communications. Even though officers and employees provide the attorney with the information about what the corporation did, the lawyer does not represent those officers and employees. In most situations, the interests of the officers and employees are the same as those of the corporation, and a lawyer can work closely with the officers and employees to represent the corporation. However, in some circumstances the corporation's interests are different from those of the employees. For example, suppose that a general counsel for a corporation learned that its officers had engaged in price-fixing. (See Chapter 8 for more discussion of criminal prosecutions of officers of a corporation and Chapter 16 for discussion of price-fixing and antitrust violations.) The general counsel would discuss the issue with the board (see

Chapters 18 and 19) and perhaps conclude that it is best to disclose what has happened to the Justice Department. The officers involved might object, but they are not protected by any privilege with the corporation's attorney. The attorney is protecting a client, the company, by disclosing the misconduct and perhaps providing assurance that the board was unaware of the price-fixing, which would then reduce any penalties the company might be required to pay. The issue of client confidentiality for corporate officers' discussions with corporate counsel continues to be a contentious issue that is on a path to the U.S. Supreme Court. In *U.S. v Graf*, 610 F.3d 1148 (9th Cir. 2010), the court developed a complex test of five factors for determining whether employees of an insurance company waived their privilege in talking with corporate counsel. The result has been a series of complex decisions on when and if the privilege applies and a need for clarification.

[*Hernandez v Creative Concepts*, 2013 WL 638696 (D. Nev. 2013)]

3-3d JUDGES

Judges control the proceedings in a case and, in some instances, the outcome. Trial judges control the trial of a case, from presiding over the selection of a jury to ruling on evidence questions. (See Chapter 4 for more details on trial procedures.) Appellate judges review the work of trial court judges. They do not actually hear evidence. Rather, they review the record of the case to determine whether there has been reversible error.

Judges are selected in various ways throughout the country. Some judges are elected to their offices. Some states have merit appointment systems wherein judges are appointed on the basis of their qualifications. In some states, judges are appointed by elected officials subject to the approval of the legislature. In some states with appointed judges, the judges are put on the ballot every other year (or at some other interval) for retention; voters in these states do not decide whom they want as judges but do decide whether they want to keep them once they are in office. Federal judges are appointed for life by the president with Senate approval.

3-3e NAME CHANGES ON APPEAL

The lawyers and the parties stay in the "game" even after a case is appealed. However, the names of the parties do change on appeal. The party appealing the case is called the **appellant**. Some courts also call the party appealing a case the **petitioner**. The other party (the one not appealing) is called the **appellee** or **respondent**.

Some states change the name of the case if the party appealing the case is the defendant. For example, suppose that Smith sues Jones for damages in a car accident. The name of the case at trial is *Smith v Jones*. Smith is the plaintiff, and Jones is the defendant. If Smith wins the case at trial and Jones decides to appeal, Jones is the appellant and Smith is the appellee. In some courts, the name of the case on appeal becomes *Jones v Smith*. Other courts leave the case name the same but still label Jones the appellant and Smith the appellee.

3-4 The Concept of Jurisdiction

Courts are found at every level of government, and every court handles a different type of case. In order for a court to decide or try a particular case, both parties to the case and the subject matter of the case must be within the established powers of the court. The established powers of a court make up the court's **jurisdiction**. *Juris* means law, and *diction* means to speak.

Jurisdiction is the authority or power of a court to speak the law. Some courts can handle bankruptcies, whereas others may be limited to traffic violations. Some courts handle violations of criminal laws, whereas others deal only with civil matters. The subject matter of a case controls which court has jurisdiction. For example, a case involving a federal statute belongs in a federal district court by its subject matter; however, federal district courts are found in every state. *In personam* **jurisdiction**, or jurisdiction over the person, controls which of the federal district courts will decide the case. Determining which court can be used is a two-step process; subject matter and *in personam* jurisdiction must fit in the same court.

3-5 Subject Matter Jurisdiction of Courts: The Authority Over Content

The two general court systems in the United States are the federal court system (see Exhibit 3.1) and the state court system.

3-5a THE FEDERAL COURT SYSTEM

The Trial Court of the Federal System

The **federal district court** is the general trial court of the federal system. However, federal district courts are limited in the types of cases they can hear; that is, their subject matter jurisdiction is limited. Federal district courts can hear three types of cases: those in which the United States is a party, those that involve a federal question, and those that involve diversity of citizenship.

Jurisdiction When the United States Is a Party

Any time the U.S. government is a party in a lawsuit, it will want to be tried in its own court system—the federal system. The United States is a party when it brings suit or when it is the defendant named in a suit. For example, many businesses have brought suit against the Department of Health and Human Services, a federal agency, regarding the constitutionality of that agency's rules related to the implementation of Obama Care, the nickname given to national health care reform. Because an agency of the federal government is the defendant in the case, the federal district court has exclusive jurisdiction over the suits.

Federal Jurisdiction for a Federal Question

The federal district court also has jurisdiction over cases involving federal questions. For example, if a business is suing for treble damages (a remedy of three times the amount of damages experienced) under the federal antitrust laws

EXHIBIT 3.1 The Federal Court System

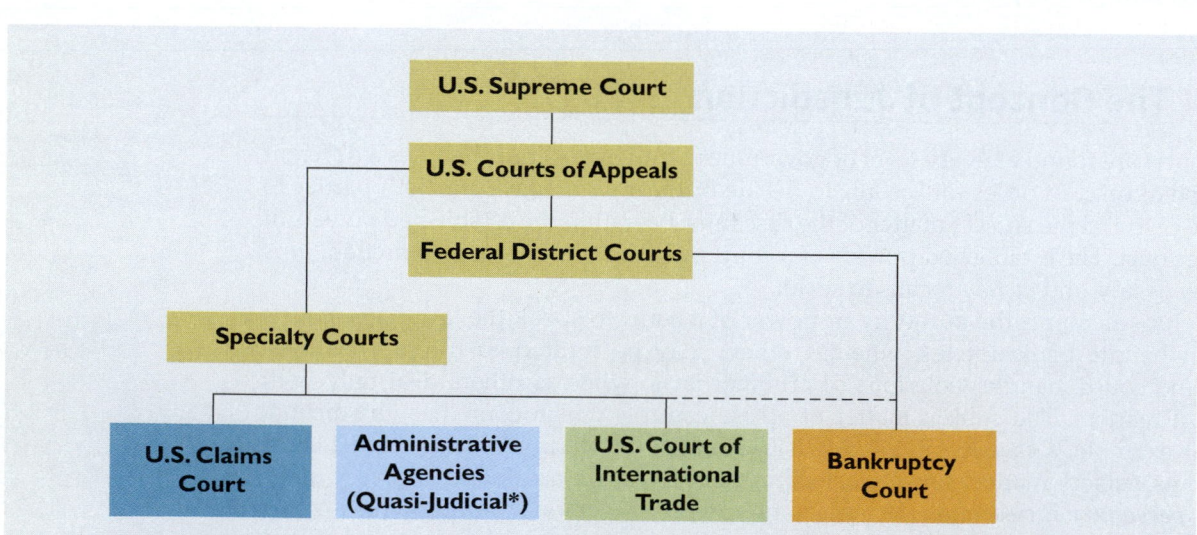

*For example, the Federal Trade Commission (FTC) or the National Labor Relations Bureau (NLRB).

© Cengage Learning

(see Chapter 16), the case involves a federal question and may be brought in federal district court. A suit charging a violation of the Equal Protection Clause of the U.S. Constitution (see Chapter 5 for more details) also involves a federal question and can be brought in federal district court. Prosecutions for federal crimes also involve federal questions, and the United States will be a party as the prosecutor; these criminal cases are tried in federal district court.

Many federal questions can also be heard by a state court. For example, most state constitutions include the same Fifth Amendment protections included in the U.S. Constitution. A plaintiff often has a choice between federal and state court, and the decision to proceed in one forum as opposed to the other may be a strategic one based on the nature of the case, rules of procedure, and other factors related to differences between the two court systems.

Jurisdiction by Diversity

Most of the civil cases in federal district court are not there because they are federal questions or because the United States is a party. Most civil cases are in federal district court because the plaintiff and defendant are from different states and their case involves damage claims in excess of $75,000. Cases in which the parties are from different states qualify for **diversity of citizenship** status, and federal district courts have the authority to hear these diversity cases. That authority is not exclusive; a state court can also hear diversity cases as long as neither party chooses to exercise the right to a federal district court trial. In diversity cases, state and federal courts have **concurrent jurisdiction**. Concurrent jurisdiction means that two courts have the authority to hear a case. By contrast, **exclusive jurisdiction** means that only one court has the authority to hear the case. For example, federal district courts have exclusive jurisdiction over cases in which the United States has charged an individual or corporation with a federal crime.

Federal courts decide controversies among citizens of different states for reasons that go back to fears about state court judges giving preferential or favorable treatment to citizens of their state, as opposed to nonresident parties. If the case is held in one side's state court, that side might have an unfair advantage or built-in prejudice because of the location of the court.

When corporations are parties to suits, the diversity issue is more complex. The citizenship of a corporation can be its state of incorporation or the state in which its principal office is located. This citizenship test is used for subject matter jurisdiction. The citizenship test for *in personam* jurisdiction has been greatly expanded.

It is important to understand that when a federal court tries a case on the basis of diversity, it is simply trying the case under the same state laws but without the local prejudice that might exist in a state court. In other words, federal courts do not rule under a different set of laws; they simply apply the state law in a different setting.

Limited Jurisdiction: The Special Trial Courts of the Federal System

Not all cases in which the United States is a party or in which a federal question is involved are decided in federal district courts. The federal system also has specialized trial courts to handle limited matters. For example, the jurisdiction of the Tax Court in the federal system is limited to tax issues. If you challenge the Internal Revenue Service because it would not allow one of your deductions, your case would be heard in Tax Court. The bankruptcy courts make up a well-used limited court system within the federal system and have exclusive jurisdiction over all bankruptcies. No other court can handle a bankruptcy or bankruptcy issues, and bankruptcy courts do not handle any other type of trial or suit.

The U.S. Claims Court is another specialized federal court: It handles disputes that involve government contracts and other claims against the federal government, such as eminent domain issues. (See Chapter 5 for more discussion of eminent domain and "takings.")

The U.S. Court of International Trade is a specialized court that focuses on international trade transactions regulated by federal agencies in various ways and also on customs issues.

Another court that is often discussed along with the federal system is the Indian Tribal Court. This court, the court of the Native American nations, has exclusive jurisdiction over criminal and civil matters on the reservations. Indian tribal courts are unique because of their limited jurisdiction and their exclusivity, which arises from their sovereign nature.

The Structure of the Federal District Court System

Each state has at least one federal judicial district. The number of federal districts in each state is determined by the state's population and caseload. States such as Wyoming and Nevada have only one federal district each, whereas states such as Illinois and New York have many. The number of courts and judges in each federal district is also determined by the district's population and caseload. Even in those states with just one district, the district has several judges and multiple courtrooms for federal trials. Ninety-four federal districts serve the 50 states, the District of Columbia, Puerto Rico, Guam, the Virgin Islands, and the Northern Mariana Islands.

The Importance of Federal District Court Decisions

The subject matter of cases that qualify for federal district court jurisdiction is important. These cases involve the interpretation of federal statutes, and often the resolution of constitutional issues. Because of the importance of these decisions, the opinions of federal district judges are published in a reporter series called the *Federal Supplement*, which reprints most opinions issued by federal district judges in every federal district. (Decisions of the Court of International Trade are also found in the *Federal Supplement*.) Cases in the *Federal Supplement* provide excellent precedent for interpretation and application of federal statutes. In addition to the system for citing statutes (see Chapter 1), a specific system is used for citing case opinions. Such a system is necessary so that precedent can be found easily for use in future cases.

All case cites consist of three elements: an abbreviation for the reporter, the volume number, and the page number. The abbreviation for the *Federal Supplement* is "F. Supp." or, for the second series, after volume 999, "F. Supp. 2d," or, the third series, "F. Supp. 3d." The volume number always appears in front of the abbreviation, and the page number appears after it. A formal cite includes in parentheses the federal district in which the case was decided and the year the case was decided. A sample federal district court cite of a case decided in the D.C. district that dealt with business challenge to Obama Care looks like this:

National Federation of Independent Business v Sebelius, 780 F. Supp. 2d 1307 (N.D. Fla. 2011)

This method of uniform citation not only helps ease the burden of research but also provides an automatic way to know where a case came from and how it can be used.

The Appellate Level in the Federal System

Cases decided in federal district court and the specialized trial courts of the federal system can be appealed. These cases are appealed to the U.S. courts of appeals (formerly called the U.S. circuit courts of appeals).

Structure.   All of the federal district courts are grouped into **federal circuits** according to their geographic location. Exhibit 3.2 is a map that shows the 13 federal circuits. Note that 11 of the circuits are geographic groupings of states; the twelfth circuit is the District of Columbia, and the thirteenth is a nongeographic circuit created to handle special cases such as those involving patent disputes and issues, and appeals from the Court of Claims and Court of International Trade. Some scholars and members of Congress have proposed creating a fourteenth circuit by dividing the very large Ninth Circuit.

Each circuit has its own court of appeals. The office of the court's clerk is located in the city named in each of the federal circuits in Exhibit 3.2. The number of judges for each of the federal circuits varies according to caseload. However, most cases are heard by a panel of three of the circuit judges. It is rare for a case to be heard *en banc* (by the "whole bench," meaning all the judges in that circuit). One of the more famous cases to be heard *en banc* following a three-judge panel decision involved a father's challenge to his child being required to recite the Pledge of Allegiance because the phrase "under God" was in the pledge: *Elk Grove Unified School Dist. v Newdow*, 292 F.3d 597 (9th Cir. 2002) and 313 F.3d 500 (9th Cir. 2002) with *en banc* rehearing denied, 328 F.3d 466 (9th Cir. 2003).[1]

Procedures.   The U.S. courts of appeals are appellate courts and operate by the same general procedures discussed earlier in the chapter. An appeal consists of a

---

EXHIBIT 3.2 The 13 Federal Judicial Circuits

Source: Administrative Office of the U.S. Courts.

record of the trial in the court below (here, the federal district court), briefs, and possible oral argument. The standard for reversal is reversible error. Because the right of appeal is automatic, the appellate courts have tremendous caseloads. A full opinion is not given in every case. In the cases that are affirmed, the opinion may consist of that one word. Other decisions are issued as memorandum opinions for the benefit of the parties but not for publication.

Opinions.   The opinions of the U.S. courts of appeals are published in the *Federal Reporter*. The system of citation for these cases is the same as for federal district court opinions. The abbreviation for the *Federal Reporter* is "F." (or sometimes "F.2d" or "F.3d"; the "2d" means the second series, which was started after the first "F" series reached volume 300, and this series is now followed by a third series—"F.3d"). A formal cite includes in parentheses the federal circuit and date of the decision. A sample U.S. court of appeals cite, the appeal of a case challenging the constitutionality of a California law regulating video-game violence, would look like this:

Brown v Entertainment Merchants Assoc.
556 F.3d 950 (9th Cir. 2010)

The U.S. Supreme Court

A decision by a U.S. court of appeals is not necessarily the end of a case. One more appellate court is part of the federal system—the **U.S. Supreme Court**. However, the Supreme Court's procedures and jurisdiction are slightly different from those of other appellate courts.

Appellate Jurisdiction and Process.   The Supreme Court handles appeals from the U.S. courts of appeals. This appeal process, however, is not an automatic right. The Supreme Court must first decide whether a particular case merits review. That decision is announced when the Court issues a *writ of certiorari* for those cases it will review in full. The Supreme Court, in its *writ*, actually makes a preliminary determination about the case and whether it should be decided. Only a small number of cases appealed to the Supreme Court are actually heard. In 1945, 1,460 cases were appealed to the Court. By 1960, that number had grown to 2,313. Now the number averages about 7,000 each year for fiscal year 2012 (the latest year available from the Court), having 7,713 cases. The court grants *certiorari* in about 100 cases and hears oral arguments and issues written opinions in about 70 to 80 cases. For example, in the 2012 term, the Supreme Court heard oral arguments in 79 cases and issued 64 written opinions. All of the Supreme Court opinions issued in one year total about 5,000 pages, including the majority, concurring, and dissenting opinions.

The court grants *writs of certiorari* in cases as a matter of discretion. *Certiorari* may be granted because of a conflict among the circuits about the law, such as the differing decisions among the circuits on the constitutionality of Obama Care, or because the case presents a major constitutional issue, such as with corporate political donations. This *writ of certiorari* procedure also applies to other sources of appellate cases, such as those coming up through state supreme courts, which can be appealed to the U.S. Supreme Court. For example, in 2012, the U.S. Supreme Court granted *certiorari* in several cases that involved product liability issues against generic drug manufacturers for failure to provide adequate warnings. Some states allowed the suits to go forward and others states did not because of preemption issues. The issue was whether the federal regulation of of drug instructions and warnings preempted state product liability laws. The plaintiffs in the case were

FOR THE MANAGER'S DESK

Re: A Look at What Appellate Courts Do

The following chart, organized by federal circuits, shows the percentage of lower court decisions the U.S. Supreme Court reversed in 2012.

CIRCUIT	CASES TAKEN	CASES REVERSED	REVERSAL RATE
1st	4	2	55.6%
2nd	9	7	71.9%
3rd	2	1	68.2%
4th	5	5	61.2%
5th	5	3	72.5%
6th	5	5	72.9%
7th	1	1	55.3%
8th	4	4	68.3%
9th	16	13	80%
10th	2	2	75%
11th	3	0	60%
Federal Circuit			**83.3%**

granted *certiorari* because they argued that state product liability standards should apply because of the failure to warn. The U.S. Supreme Court granted *certiorari* for purposes of clarifying the federal law and preemption issues. That case, *Mutual Pharmaceutical Co., Inc. v Bartlett*, 133 S.Ct. 2466 (2013), because of its significance regarding federal law preempting state law (see Chapter 5 for more discussion), resulted in a significant decision and opinion on preemption.

The U.S. Supreme Court also acts as a trial court (called a court of **original jurisdiction**) in certain cases. When one state is suing another state, the U.S. Supreme Court becomes the states' trial court. For example, the water dispute among California, Arizona, Colorado, and Nevada has been tried over a period of years by the U.S. Supreme Court. The Court also handles the trials (on espionage charges, for example) of ambassadors and foreign consuls.

Structure.   The U.S. Supreme Court consists of nine judges, who are nominated as justices to the Court by the president and confirmed by the Senate. The appointment is for life. A president who has the opportunity to appoint a Supreme Court justice is shaping the structure of the Court and the resulting decisions. U.S. Supreme Court justices are often labeled "conservative" or "liberal." The makeup of the bench controls the philosophy and decisions of the Court.

Opinions.   Because the Court is the highest in the land, its opinions are precedent for every other court in the country. The importance of these opinions has resulted in three different volumes of reporters for U.S. Supreme Court opinions. The first is the *United States Reports* (abbreviated "U.S."). These reports are put out by the U.S. Government Printing Office and are the official reports of the Court. Because these reports are often slow to be published, two private companies also publish opinions in the *Supreme Court Reporter* (abbreviated "S. Ct.") and the *Lawyer's Edition* (abbreviated "L. Ed." or "L. Ed. 2d"). The three-part cite for *Citizens United v Federal Election Com'n* (the Court's decision on corporate speech during elections) follows:

558 U.S. 310 (2010)
130 S.Ct. 876 (2010)
175 L.Ed.2d 753 (2010)

3-5b THE STATE COURT SYSTEMS

Although each state court has a different structure for its court system and the courts may have different names, the basic structure in each state is similar to the federal system. Exhibit 3.3 provides a diagram of a sample state court system.

State Trial Courts

Each state has its own general trial court. This court is usually called a circuit, district, county, or superior court. It is the court in which nondiversity civil cases are heard and state criminal cases are tried.

In addition to its general trial court, each state also has its own group of "lesser courts." They are courts with **limited jurisdiction** and are comparable to the specialty courts of the federal system. For example, most states have a **small claims court** in which civil cases with minimal damage claims are tried. In a true small claims court attorneys are not used. Parties represent themselves before a judge. Such a setting offers parties the chance to have a judge arrive at a solution without the expense of attorneys. The amount recoverable in small claims court is indeed small: $200–$15,000 is the typical range.

Most states also have a lesser court that allows the participation of lawyers but limits the amount that can be recovered. The idea is to take the burden of lesser cases away from the usually overburdened general trial courts. These courts are called **justice of the peace courts** or **county courts**.

Most cities also have their own trial courts, which are limited in their jurisdiction to the trial of lesser crimes, such as violations of city ordinances. Many states call these courts **traffic courts** because city ordinances involve so many traffic regulations.

EXHIBIT 3.3 Typical State Court System

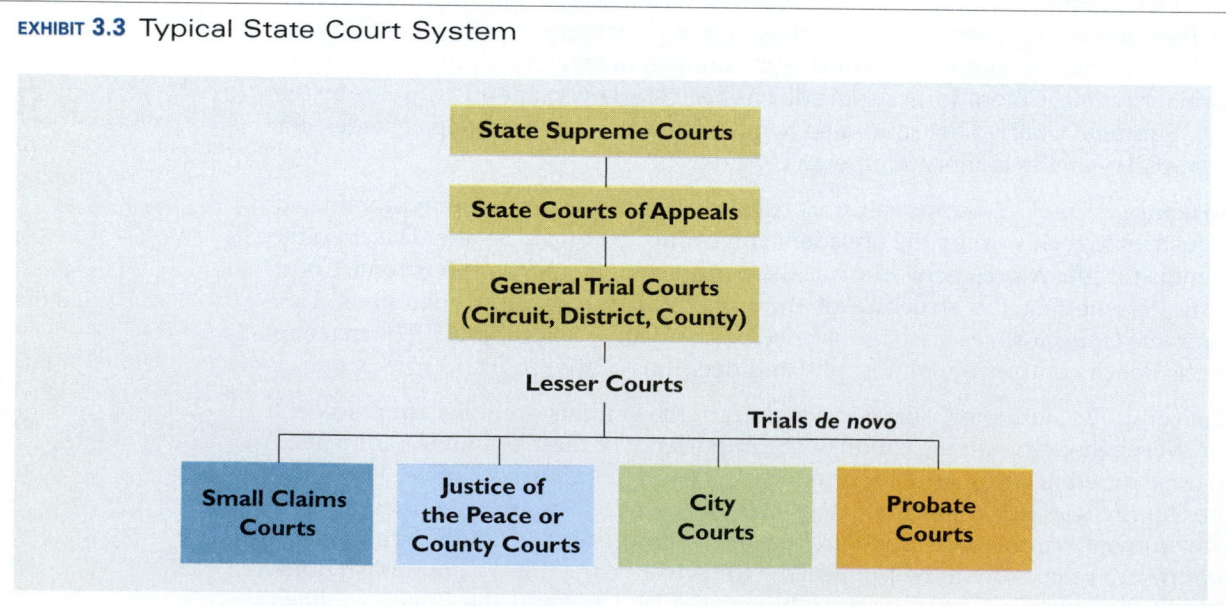

© Cengage Learning

In addition to these courts, some states have specialized courts to handle matters that are narrow in their application of law but frequent in occurrence. For example, although probating (processing) a will and an estate involves narrow issues of law, the supply of this type of case is constant. Many states have special courts to handle this and related matters, such as guardianships for incompetent persons.

Many of the lesser courts allow appeals to a general state trial court for a new trial (**trial** *de novo*) because not all judges in these lesser courts are lawyers, and constitutional protections require a right of *de novo* appeal in those situations.

State Appellate Courts

State appellate courts serve the same function as the U.S. courts of appeals. The court system provides an automatic right of review in these courts. Some states have two appellate-level courts to handle the number of cases being appealed. The opinions of these courts are reported in the state's individual reporter, which contains the state's name and some indication that an appellate court decided the case. For example, state appellate decisions in Colorado are reported in *Colorado Appeals Reports* (abbreviated "Colo. App."). These opinions are also reported in a **regional reporter**. All states are grouped into regions, and opinions of state appellate courts are grouped into the reporter for that region. Exhibit 3.4 presents the various regions and state groupings. For example, Nevada is part of the Pacific region, and its appellate reports are found in the *Pacific Reporter* (abbreviated "P.," "P.2d," or "P.3d"). The following is a cite from a Wisconsin state appellate court

---

EXHIBIT 3.4 National Reporter System Regions

Pacific (P. or P.2d)	Northwestern (N.W. or N.W.2d)	Northeastern (N.E. or N.E.2d)	Southeastern (S.E. or S.E.2d)
Alaska	Iowa	Illinois	Georgia
Arizona	Michigan	Indiana	North Carolina
(California)	Minnesota	Massachusetts	South Carolina
Colorado	Nebraska	(New York)	Virginia
Hawaii	North Dakota	Ohio	West Virginia
Idaho	South Dakota	**Atlantic (A. or A.2d)**	**Southern (So. or So.2d)**
Kansas	Wisconsin	Connecticut	Alabama
Montana	**Southwestern (S.W. or S.W.2d)**	Delaware	Florida
Nevada		District of Columbia	Louisiana
New Mexico	Arkansas	Maine	Mississippi
Oklahoma	Kentucky	Maryland	
Oregon	Missouri	New Hampshire	
Utah	Tennessee	New Jersey	
Washington	Texas	Pennsylvania	
Wyoming		Rhode Island	
		Vermont	

Note: California and New York each have their own reporter system.
Source: The national reporter system was developed by West Publishing Company. Reprinted with permission of West Publishing Company.

decision—a case dealing with the ability of a caretaker in a group home to consent to the search of the bedroom of one of the residents:

> *State v Gracia*, 808 N.W.2d 743 (Wis.App. 2011)

State Supreme Courts

State supreme courts are similar in their function and design to the U.S. Supreme Court. These courts do not hear every case because the right of appeal is not automatic. These supreme courts have some discretion in deciding which cases they will hear. State supreme courts also act as trial courts in certain types of cases and so are also courts of original as well as appellate jurisdiction. For example, if two counties within a state have a dispute, the state supreme court would take the trial to ensure fairness. A state supreme court's decision is not necessarily the end because there is the possibility of an appeal to the U.S. Supreme Court if the case also involves a federal question or an issue of constitutional rights.

The opinions of state supreme courts are significant and are reported in the regional reporters discussed earlier. Many states also have their own reporters for state supreme court opinions. For example, California has the *California Reporter*. The state supreme court reporters are easily recognized because their abbreviations are the abbreviation of each state's name. The following cite is for the state supreme court decision in the *Garcia* case:

> *State v Garcia*, 826 N.W.2d 87 (Wis. 2013)

3-5c JUDICIAL OPINIONS

Although the published opinions of the courts just discussed vary in their places of publication, the format is the same. Exhibit 3.5 shows a sample page from a reporter, with each part of the excerpt identified. Opinions are reported consistently in this manner so that precedent can be found and used easily through the research keys highlighted at the beginning.

3-5d VENUE

The concept of jurisdiction addresses the issue of which court system has the authority to try a case. The concept of **venue** addresses the issue of the location of the court in the system. For example, a criminal case in which a defendant is charged with a felony can be tried in any of a state's general trial courts. Heavy media coverage, however, may result in a judge's changing the venue of a case from the place where the crime was committed to another trial court in an area where there is less publicity about the case and it is easier to obtain an impartial jury. However, the bar is a tall one for establishing the need for a change of venue. In *Skilling v U.S.*, 130 S.Ct. 2896 (2010), the U.S. Supreme Court held that the daily and ongoing coverage of Enron's collapse and the role of former CEO Jeffrey Skilling in that collapse were not enough to require that Mr. Skilling's trial for criminal fraud be moved from Houston, where the company was headquartered, to another federal court in Texas or outside the state.

3-6 *In Personam* Jurisdiction of Courts: The Authority Over Persons

Once the proper court for the subject matter in a case is determined, only half the job is done. For example, a case may involve a million-dollar claim between citizens of different states, in which case a federal district court has subject matter

EXHIBIT 3.5 Sample Page of a Case in a National Reporter

CASTEEL v STATE ——————————— case name
Cite as 131 P.3d 1 (Nev. 2006) ——————————— case cite

case name ——— ┌ **Dion Fabion CASTEEL, Appellant,**
v
└ **The STATE of Nevada, Respondent.**

docket ——— **No. 42436.**
number

court ——— Supreme Court of Nevada.

March 30, 2006.

Rehearing Denied May 17, 2006.

Reconsideration en banc Denied
June 12, 2006.

Background: Defendant was convicted in the Eighth Judicial District Court, Clark County, Joseph T. Bonaventure, J., of 10 counts of sexual assault of a minor and 12 counts of use of a minor under age of 14 in production of pornography. He appealed.

Holdings: The Supreme Court, Maupin, J., held that:

1. consent to search of apartment given by defendant's live-in girlfriend authorized police officers to search apartment;

2. girlfriend had authority to consent to officers' search of defendant's gym bag;

3. trial court's findings supported its conclusion that defendant was not in custody for *Miranda* purposes when he was interrogated by officer; but

4. defendant could be convicted only of four counts of use of a minor under age of 14 in production of pornography.

decision of the court ——— Affirmed in part, reversed in part, and remanded.

decision issue research tool ——— ┌ **1. Searches and Seizures 177**
Consent to search of apartment given by defendant's live-in girlfriend authorized police officers to search apartment; girlfriend had equal control over apartment, which she shared with defendant.
└ U.S.C.A. Const.Amend. 4.

2. Criminal Law 1139
Appellate court reviews the lawfulness of a search de novo because such a review requires consideration of both factual circumstances and legal issues. U.S.C.A. Const.Amend. 4.

3. Searches and Seizures 177
A warrantless search is valid if police officers acquire consent from a cohabitant who possesses common authority over the property to be searched. U.S.C.A. Const.Amend. 4.

4. Searches and Seizures 186
Defendant's live-in girlfriend had authority to consent to police officers' search of his gym bag, which was located in closet inside apartment that he shared with girlfriend; girlfriend gave officers valid consent to search apartment, and defendant apparently took no special steps to secure privacy interest in gym bag and did not deny girlfriend all access to apartment, given that both girlfriend and minor victim knew contents of gym bag and knew that it could be found in closet. U.S.C.A. Const.Amend. 4.

5. Searches and Seizures 177
A warrantless search is valid based on the consent of one occupant, despite the physical presence of the nonconsenting occupant. U.S.C.A. Const.Amend. 4.

Philip J. Kohn, Public Defender, and Sharon G. Dickinson and Jordan S. Savage, Deputy Public Defenders, Clark County, for Appellant.

George Chanos, Attorney General, Carson City; David J. Roger, District Attorney, James Tufteland, Chief Deputy District Attorney, and Ross J. Miller, Deputy District Attorney, Clark County, for Respondent.

attorneys for parties

Before MAUPIN, GIBBONS and HARDESTY, JJ.

judge deciding case

MAUPIN, J. ———————————

In this appeal, we hold that a warrantless search of a residence is valid based on the consent of one occupant where the other occupant fails to object. We also resolve questions concerning custody for purposes of *Miranda v Arizona*.[1] Finally, we conclude that only 4 counts of production of child pornography may stand because the State failed to prove production depicting separate sexual performances.

opinion

BUSINESS STRATEGY

Strategic Geography on Courts and Higher Damages

Not all states have the same laws, not all jurors see issues the same way, and not all courts are as fussy about experts and evidence as others. Businesses must know where to go, court-wise, in order to maximize the results of their litigation.

Companies that purchase patents and file suit against large corporations for infringement have favored the Eastern District of Texas (Tyler and Marshall, Texas) for their suits for the past decade because those who live in this area (including lawyers and jurors) believe in patents in the same way they believe in oil and gas rights. If you find it, you own it, and all the rights and royalties that come with that ownership. Most cases filed there are settled because everyone involved understands the area dynamics. If a case does go to trial, the verdicts are Texas-size. Versata Software recovered $345 million

from SAP following a patent infringement trial held in Marshall, Texas. That verdict is the 10th largest in patent infringement history. When Microsoft lost its Eastern District of Texas court case to I4i, it paid $200 million in damages.

There are also geographical differences in how product liability cases are viewed. Philadelphia, Pennsylvania is a favorite for product liability plaintiffs because the court there is known for its "rocket docket" (fast-moving cases) and because Pennsylvania places no limits on damage claims in product liability suits.

Businesses and individuals have learned to choose their courts' locations very carefully. As seen in these examples, geography matters in results.

Source: Susan Decker, "A Crackdown on Patently Absurd Lawsuits," *BusinessWeek*, May 14–20, 2012, 33.

jurisdiction over the parties. So which of the 94 federal district courts will hear the case? The case will be heard by the federal district court with *in personam* jurisdiction over the parties. Subject matter jurisdiction is one issue; the other jurisdictional issue is power over the parties involved in the case.

The various criteria for determining *in personam* jurisdiction are examined here and are outlined in Exhibit 3.6.

3-6a OWNERSHIP OF PROPERTY WITHIN THE STATE

A party who owns real property in a state is subject to the jurisdiction of that state's courts for litigation related to that property. Actually, this type of jurisdiction gives the court authority over the person because the person owns a thing in the state. Technically, this type of jurisdiction through property ownership is called *in rem* **jurisdiction**.

3-6b VOLUNTEER JURISDICTION

A court has jurisdiction over a person who agrees to be subject to that court. In some contracts, for example, the parties agree that any lawsuits will be brought in the seller's state. The seller's state courts then have jurisdiction over that volunteer buyer. Most Internet contracts have a venue clause.

3-6c PRESENCE IN THE STATE

The third and final way a state court can take jurisdiction is by the "presence" of a party in the state, which is determined by different factors.

Residence

Individuals are present in a state if they have a residence in that state. Different definitions of residency are used for tax and election laws, but the requirement here is simply that the person live in the state some time during any given year.

EXHIBIT 3.6 Personal Jurisdiction

© Cengage Learning

Corporations are residents of the states in which they are incorporated. A corporation is also a resident, for purposes of judicial jurisdiction, of any state in which it has a business office with employees.

"Minimum Contacts"

Both corporations and residents can be subject to a state court's jurisdiction if they have "minimum contacts" in that state. The standard for **minimum contacts** is a fairness standard, which was established by the U.S. Supreme Court in *International Shoe v Washington*, 326 U.S. 310 (1945). This decision requires states to notify out-of-state defendants of a suit and determine that those defendants have some contact with the state. Such contact can come through the voluntary acts of shipping products or advertising products or services in the state. The courts look at the extent of involvement in the state as a standard for fairness. However, fairness does not require an office or an employee in the state. These standards for *in personam* jurisdiction are more liberal than the citizenship requirements for diversity actions.

Long-Arm Statutes: The Tools of Minimum Contacts

In order to follow the Supreme Court's ruling on fairness, all of the states have adopted **long-arm statutes**. These statutes are appropriately named: They give courts the power to extend their "arms of jurisdiction" into other states. For example, suppose that Zeta Corporation is incorporated in Ohio and has its manufacturing plant there. Zeta ships its glass baking dishes to every state in the country, although it has no offices anywhere except in Ohio. Joan Berferd, who lives in Alabama, is injured when one of Zeta's baking dishes explodes. Can the Alabama courts allow

Berferd to file suit there and require Zeta to come to Alabama to defend the suit? Yes, because a long-arm statute is fair if it covers businesses shipping products to the state. Zeta entered the Alabama market voluntarily and must be subject to the Alabama courts. Long-arm statutes generally cover businesses with offices in the state, businesses shipping products into the state, and businesses that cause a **tort** to be committed in that state.

E & H Cruises, Ltd. v Baker (Case 3.1) deals with a long-arm issue and provides an answer for the chapter's opening "Consider…"

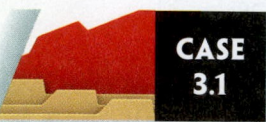

| CASE 3.1 | *E & H Cruises, Ltd. v Baker*
88 So.3d 291 (Fla. App. 2012) |

Slips-and-Falls on Pirate Ships: A Jurisdictional Problem

FACTS

Patricia Baker (plaintiff) was a passenger aboard the MV *Mariner of the Seas*, which was operated by Royal Caribbean Cruise Lines, Inc. ("RCCL"). Ms. Baker purchased a ticket to participate in a mock pirate ship excursion tour in the Cayman Islands. The Excursion Tour was operated by E & H Cruises, Ltd., a Cayman Islands corporation. While transferring to the mock pirate ship, Ms. Baker was injured. She filed suit against RCCL and E & H (Defendants) under various theories of liability. The defendants filed a motion to dismiss for lack of personal jurisdiction and forum *non conveniens*. The trial court denied the motion to dismiss, and the defendants appealed.

JUDICIAL OPINION

CORTIÑAS, Judge

When determining whether personal jurisdiction exists over a non-resident defendant, the trial court conducts a two-step inquiry. The trial court must first determine whether the plaintiff has alleged sufficient jurisdictional facts in the complaint such that the action is within the ambit of Florida's long-arm statute. When making this determination, the trial court "must strictly construe the statute in favor of the non-resident defendants." For the second step, the trial court must make a determination as to "whether 'sufficient minimum contacts exist between Florida and the defendant to satisfy due process requirements.'"

In support of her argument in favor of general jurisdiction, the plaintiff asserts that E & H has maintained a membership in the Florida-Caribbean Cruise Association ("FCCA") for several years, has traveled to Florida for annual FCCA networking events, and had also maintained connections to Royal Marine Insurance Group and Total Bank. Although E & H's principal admitted to traveling to Miami on more than one occasion for the purpose of attending an annual FCCA charity dinner, he specified that he had "attended that . . . more on [his] personal behalf." He acknowledged that he joined the FCCA in order to "build a relationship with the cruise lines," and further testified that in addition to the charity dinner in Miami, he has also "been to a few of the FCCA conventions that they hold on the different islands every year." Mere attendance at fundraisers that happen to be held in Miami, particularly where it is acknowledged that related events are held "on the different islands every year" does not meet the statutorily required threshold of "continuous and systematic contacts" with Florida.

Furthermore, the fact that E & H utilized a Florida broker to obtain an insurance policy, which covered only potential claims arising out of its activities outside of the United States, is insufficient to establish personal jurisdiction.

At no time did E & H maintain any offices or employees in Florida, own any assets or real estate in Florida, or directly sell any of its services in Florida. E & H did not advertise in Florida. Accordingly, we do not find the requisite "systematic and continuous" contact with Florida necessary for general jurisdiction.

Plaintiff argues that RCCL and E & H entered into a Tour Operator Agreement in relation to the pirate excursions and that E & H thereby was conducting business in Florida through an agency or joint venture relationship with RCCL. The Tour Operator Agreement specifies that E & H "acknowledges that the control and responsibility of the Shore Excursion remains exclusively with E & H." RCCL has no control over, nor say in, how the Excursion Tours are operated. The plaintiff can point to no evidence to the contrary. Because we

CONTINUED

find that this necessary element is lacking, there can be no joint venture between E & H and RCCL for purposes of determining personal jurisdiction.

The plaintiff's argument that E & H had an agency relationship with RCCL is also meritless. Here, the Tour Operator Agreement clearly specifies that E & H is an independent contractor and, again, the plaintiff simply cannot show that RCCL had any control over E & H's actions with respect to how the Excursion Tours were operated, or vice-versa.

We further note that the mere fact that tickets to E & H's Excursion Tours are available for purchase in Florida through RCCL is also insufficient to constitute "[o]perating, conducting, engaging in, or carrying on a business or business venture."

The plaintiff was not a resident of Florida, the injury occurred in the territorial waters of the Cayman Islands, and there was no property involved in the plaintiff's injury that was located within Florida at the time of contracting.

The plaintiff further asserts that personal jurisdiction may be found pursuant to the indemnification provision found in the Tour Operator Agreement. The plaintiff, however, overlooks that she was not a party to that agreement, and that she cannot [therefore] use same as a basis for jurisdiction.

Reversed and remanded.

CASE QUESTIONS

1. List the factual issues Ms. Baker raised in trying to establish jurisdiction.

2. What factors for the court determine what is important in denying jurisdiction?

3. What did you learn about your rights as a traveler on an off-shore excursion?

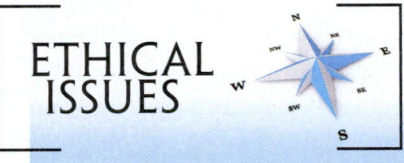

ETHICAL ISSUES

Evaluate the ethics of off-shore companies selling their services and products to U.S. citizens and being able to avoid being sued when those buyers are harmed.

© martan/Shutterstock.com

3-6d INTERNET COMPANIES AND LONG-ARM JURISDICTION

One of the active areas of *in personam* jurisdiction involves the question of when companies that do business solely over the Internet can be required to travel to a state to defend a lawsuit that is the result of their sales of goods in that state. In making the determination of jurisdiction, courts look at five factors: (1) the nature and quality of the contacts with the state; (2) the quantity of contacts with the state; (3) the relation of the suit to the contacts; (4) the interest of the state in allowing its residents to recover; and (5) the convenience of the parties. These factors are applied differently, but Internet immunity seems to be winning the day. For example, in *Johnson v Arden*, 614 F.3d 785 (8th Cir. 2010), the court held that a Colorado-based Internet site owner could not be required to come to Missouri to defend a defamation suit based on what was posted on its website about a Missouri company's business. The result of this and other differing decisions is that the Internet companies enjoy an immunity from long-arm statutes and, often, because of limited resources, an immunity from claims by Internet customers. The U.S. Supreme Court will ultimately need to grant *certiorari* to clarify *in personam* jurisdiction in Internet cases.

Consider...

Panagea, Inc., an Arkansas corporation, operates a restaurant called "The Flying Burrito Company" in Fayetteville, Arkansas. The restaurant trademark was registered on January 11, 2005. Flying Burrito LLC is a limited liability company organized by Matthew Goodman under Iowa law that operates a restaurant in Ames, Iowa called "The Flying Burrito." The Iowa restaurant opened in August 2004 and Robert Moore managed the restaurant from that date until August 2007. Moore is a citizen of Iowa.

Shortly after his Iowa restaurant opened, Mr. Goodman learned of the Panagea trademark application. Mr. Goodman and Mr. Moore traveled to Arkansas to ask permission to use Panagea's trademark. The permission was not given, but both the Flying Burrito, Arkansas and Flying Burrito, Iowa continued to use the name. Panagea filed an infringement suit against the Flying Burrito in Arkansas for trademark infringement. The lower court dismissed the case for lack of jurisdiction over the Iowa parties and Panagea appealed. What should the appellate court decide?

Steps for Analyzing This Case Study

THINK:

1. Determine how much of a presence Goodman, Moore, and the Iowa Flying Burrito had in Arkansas.

2. List the contacts each had with folks in Arkansas.

3. Determine whether there will be any suit or remedy if the case must be moved to Iowa.

APPLY: Goodman and Moore did travel to Arkansas for a meeting. However, the Flying Burrito did not have a presence in Arkansas through products, sales, or sale representatives. If the case is not heard in Arkansas, the Panagea owners will have to pursue the remedy in Iowa and they may not have the means to pursue the case there, but, on the other hand, the likelihood of anyone being confused about the nature of the two businesses is small.

ANSWER: The facts of this case do not provide a sufficient basis for granting jurisdiction over the Arkansas Flying Burrito. Panagea can be required to come to Iowa to bring the suit. [*Panagaea, Inc. v Flying Burrito LLC*, 647 F.3d 741 (8th Cir. 2011)]

3-7 The International Courts

The decisions of international courts provide precedent for parties involved in international trade. However, one of the restrictions on international court decisions is that the decision binds only the immediate parties to the suit on the basis of their factual situation. International courts do not carry the enforcement power or authority of courts in the U.S. federal and state systems. They are consensual courts and are used only when the parties agree to use them.

The **International Court of Justice** (ICJ) is the most widely known international court. It was first established as the Permanent Court of International Justice (PCIJ) in 1920 by the League of Nations. In 1945, the United Nations (UN) changed the name and structure of the court. The ICJ is made up of 15 judges, no more than 2 of whom can be from the same nation, who are elected by the General Assembly of the UN. The court has been described as having **contentious jurisdiction**, which is to say that the court's jurisdiction is consensual: When a dispute occurs, the parties can agree to submit the dispute to the ICJ.

In addition to the ICJ, other international courts include the European Union's **Court of Justice of European Communities** and the **European Court of Human Rights**, as well as the **Inter-American Court of Human Rights**. Jurisdiction in these courts is also consensual.

The decisions of these courts and decisions from individual countries' courts dealing with international law issues can be found in *International Law Reports*.

In recent years, London's Commercial Court, established more than 100 years ago, has become a popular forum for the resolution of international commercial disputes. Over half the cases in this court involve foreign enterprises. Some companies choose London's Commercial Court as the forum for their disputes for several reasons, even though neither they nor their transactions have any connection with England. First, the court has the advantage of being a neutral forum. Second, for U.S. firms, the use of the English language in the court is important. Third, the court has a wide range of experience in international disputes, from shipping contracts to joint trading ventures. Fourth, the judges on the court were all once commercial litigators themselves and bring their depth of experience to the cases. Fifth, the court is known for its rapid calendar, moving cases along quickly. Major cases are heard within one year from the service of summons. Finally, the court has used a variety of creative remedies. The Commercial Court has issued pretrial injunctions to freeze assets, and its ties to the English government afford the injunctions international recognition. Perhaps the most famous of the Commercial Court's cases is its handling of the 20 class actions against Lloyd's of London.

3-7a JURISDICTIONAL ISSUES IN INTERNATIONAL LAW

The jurisdiction of courts within a particular country over businesses from other countries is a critical issue in international law. A common subject in international disputes is whether courts in the United States, for example, can require foreign companies to defend lawsuits within the United States.

3-7b CONFLICTS OF LAW IN INTERNATIONAL DISPUTES

The courts and judicial systems of countries around the globe vary, as do the procedural aspects of litigation. For example, Japan has no discovery process that permits the parties to examine each other's documents and witnesses prior to trial (see Chapter 4 for more details on discovery and the Japanese court system), and the United States permits lawyers to collect contingency fees and also permits broader tort recovery than would be available in most other countries.

Because of liberal discovery and recovery rules in the United States, many plaintiffs injured in other countries by products manufactured by U.S.-based firms want to bring suit in the United States to take advantage of our judicial system's processes and rules. However, the California Supreme Court has ruled in *Stangvik v Shiley, Inc.*, 819 P.2d 14 (Cal. 1991) that if a plaintiff's home country provides an adequate forum for a dispute, the case cannot be brought in the United States. The suit involved family members of various patients who had died when their heart valves, manufactured by Shiley of Irvine, California, failed. The decision of the California Supreme Court required the plaintiffs to return to their home countries, where the recovery would be substantially less. However, states do differ on their conclusions about *forum non conveniens*; see *Ison v E.I. DuPont de Nemours and Co., Inc.*, 729 A.2d 832 (Del. 1999) and *Martinez v E.I. DuPont Nemours and Co., Inc.*, 2012 WL 6840578 (Del. Super. 2012).

Business Planning Tip

With national and international business transactions becoming so frequent, many contracts now include "forum selection" clauses. These portions of a contract stipulate that if litigation is required, a particular court in a particular state or country will have jurisdiction over both parties. For example, a franchisor might have the forum selection clause provide that all litigation by franchisees would be in the state and city where the franchisor's principal office is located. Checking a contract carefully for these clauses will enable you to decide, before signing, whether you want to agree to travel to another state or country if litigation becomes necessary.

© Grounder/Shutterstock.com

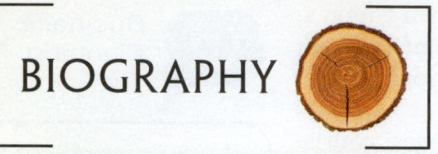

BIOGRAPHY The Judges and Their Words

The judges who handle trials and appeals often find themselves dealing with serious statutory interpretations and legal issues even as they are faced with whimsical factual patterns. Below are some sample excerpts from judicial opinions that illustrate the tall order judges have in managing their court rooms and in issuing their wisdom, precedent, and decisions.

Where, on a murder trial, the argument of counsel for the state is applauded, and cries of "Hang him!" proceed from the listeners, it is the duty of the judge to ascertain the guilty persons, and punish them to the extent of the law.
Woolfolk v State, 8 S.E. 724 (Ga. 1889)

That golfers do not always hit their golf balls straight is a matter of common knowledge; it is a fact that needs no supporting evidence, a principle that needs no citation of authority.
Geddes v Mill Creek Country Club, Inc., 751 N.E.2d 1150 (Ill. 2001)

Discharge of sworn juror based on purported misconduct, because other jurors had complained that juror emitted a foul body odor and was flatulent, was improper, where trial court failed to conduct inquiry, especially where defense counsel objected.
People v Westbrook, 576 N.Y.S.2d 372 (N.Y. App. Div. 1991)

Juror note sent during deliberations, asking for the opportunity to thank all concerned for privilege of serving, mentioning breakup of her marriage and her view that the male lawyer who sat in second chair at the prosecution table was a "Cutie," and asking to be given that lawyer's telephone number when trial was over, did not require the juror's disqualification; trial judge interviewed the juror in counsel's presence, explained to her that the note was inappropriate, and obtained her assurance that nothing, including her favorable impression of a prosecutor, would prevent her from being fair to both sides.
People v Lewie, 953 N.E.2d 760 (N.Y. 2011)

© Fekete Tibor/Shutterstock.com

Summary

What is the judicial process?

- Judicial review—review of a trial court's decisions and verdict to determine whether any reversible error was made
- Appellate court—court responsible for review of trial court's decisions and verdict
- Brief—written summary of basis for appeal of trial court's decisions and verdict
- Reversible error—mistake by trial court that requires a retrial or modification of a trial court's decision
- Options for appellate court:
  - Reverse—change trial court's decision
  - Remand—return case to trial court for retrial or reexamination of issues
  - Affirm—uphold trial court's decisions and verdict

- Modify—overturn a portion of the trial court's verdict
- *Stare decisis*—Latin for "let the decision stand"; doctrine of reviewing, applying, and/or distinguishing prior case decisions
- Case opinion—written court decision used as precedent; contains *dicta* or explanation of reasoning and, often, a minority view or dissenting opinion

Who are the parties in the judicial system?

- Plaintiffs/petitioners—initiators of litigation
- Defendants/respondents—parties named as those from whom plaintiff seeks relief
- Lawyers—officers of the court who speak for plaintiffs and defendants

- Attorney–client privilege—confidential protections for client conversations
- Appellant—party who appeals lower court's decision
- Appellee—party responding in an appeal

What factors decide jurisdiction?

- The power of the court to hear cases
  - Subject matter jurisdiction—authority of court over subject matter
  - Jurisdiction over the parties: *in personam* jurisdiction
  - Voluntary
  - Through property
  - Presence in the state: minimum contacts
  - Residence
  - Business office

What are the courts and court systems?

- Federal court system
  - Federal district court—trial court in federal system; hears cases that involve a federal question, the United States as a party, or a plaintiff and defendant from different states (diversity of citizenship) and $75,000 or more at issue; opinions reported in *Federal Supplement*
  - Limited jurisdiction courts—bankruptcy courts, court of claims
  - U.S. Courts of Appeals—federal appellate courts in each of the circuits; opinions reported in *Federal Reporter*
  - U.S. Supreme Court—highest court in United States; requires *writ of certiorari* for review; acts as trial court (original jurisdiction) for suits involving states and diplomats
- State court system
  - Lesser courts—small claims, traffic courts, justice of the peace courts
  - State trial courts—general jurisdiction courts in each state
  - State appellate courts—courts that review trial court decisions
  - State supreme courts—courts that review appellate court decisions
- International courts
  - Voluntary jurisdiction
  - International Court of Justice—UN court; contentious (consensual) jurisdiction; reported in *International Law Reports*
  - London Commercial Court—voluntary court of arbitration

Questions and Problems

1. The brokerage firm of E. F. Hutton was charged with federal criminal violations of interstate funds transfers. In reviewing the case, the lawyers for the government discovered internal memoranda from and between branch managers in several states that outline a process for check kiting (a literal stringing together of checks and deposits) that enabled E. F. Hutton to earn interest on phantom deposits. Where will the case be tried? Which court system? Which court? Why?

What are the lawyers' obligations with respect to the documents? What is the company's obligation? If you were a manager at E. F. Hutton, would you voluntarily disclose the documents to the government?

2. Pharmaceutical manufacturer Merck is experiencing ongoing litigation over its drug Vioxx because of customers who say they had cardiovascular side effects from taking the anti-arthritis pain drug. As of mid-2007, Merck was facing 9,500 lawsuits that a federal judge ruled could not be tried as class actions because of the different health issues among the plaintiffs who were bringing the suits against Merck. A jury in a federal court in New Orleans cleared Merck of any responsibility for the death of Richard Irvin, a Florida resident who had a fatal heart attack one month after he began to take Vioxx. In 2005, Merck won one state court verdict in New Jersey and lost another state court trial in Texas. Why would some of the cases be tried in state court and some in federal court? Explain the differing decisions.

3. N-the-Water Publishing, Inc. dba Still N the Water Publishing produces hip-hop and rap music through sampling, the process of copying portions of prior master sound recordings directly onto new sound recordings and then rapping on top of the new sound recording. Bridgeport Music is the owner of the copyright for the music that Still N the Water has used for its rap and hip-hop song productions. Bridgeport is headquartered in Nashville, Tennessee, and Still N the Water is part of a series of record companies based in Florida and Texas. Bridgeport brought suit against Still N the Water in federal district court in Tennessee. Under Tennessee's long-arm statute, jurisdiction may be asserted on "any basis not inconsistent with the constitution of this state or of the United States." [Tenn. Code Ann. § 20–2–214(a)(6)] Still N the Water sells CDs in all 50 states, with sales spread equally among the states and marketing plans for each of the states.

Can Still N the Water be required to come to Tennessee to defend the lawsuit? [*Bridgeport Music, Inc. v Still N The Water Pub*, 327 F.3d 472 (6th Cir. 2003); *cert. denied* 540 U.S. 948 (2003)]

4. The domain name aol.org was registered by Korea DNS, a South Korean entity, on September 3, 2001, and subsequently transferred first to an individual, Sujin Jeon, and thereafter to an individual listed simply as "Will E." Here in the United States, the domain name AOL.COM is registered to its parent company and owner, Time Warner/AOL. That name has been held since 1996. On July 30, 2002, America Online, the original holder of registered U.S. trademarks for AOL and AOL.COM, filed suit against the Korean company and individuals for infringement and violation of the Anticybersquatting Act. The Korean defendants filed a motion to dismiss on the grounds that the federal district court in Virginia, where AOL had filed suit and where its company headquarters are situated, did not have *in personam* jurisdiction over aol.org because it had no presence in the U.S. Should the motion to dismiss be granted? [*America Online, Inc. v Aol.Org*, 259 F. Supp. 2d 449 (E.D. Va. 2003)]

5. Determine which court(s) would have jurisdiction over the following matters:
   a. The sale of securities without first registering them with the Securities and Exchange Commission, as required under 15 U.S.C. § 77 *et seq.*
   b. A suit between a Hawaiian purchaser of sunscreen lotion and its California manufacturer for severe sunburn that resulted in $65,000 in medical bills

6. Where will the following cases be tried?
   a. A will contest that challenges the validity of a will
   b. A suit by a homeowner against his building contractor for $1.5 million for the failure to provide termite protection on the home the contractor built
   c. A suit by a defense contractor against the U.S. Army for nonpayment on drones delivered to Iraq

7. The following rule appears in State University's current catalog:

A course in which a grade of C or better has been earned may not be repeated. The second entry will not be counted in earned hours or grade point index for graduation.

Rod took his business math course and earned a C. Not satisfied with his grade but unaware of the catalog regulation, Rod took the math course again and this time earned a D. The registrar has entered the D grade in Rod's cumulative average. Rod objects based on the catalog rule, but the registrar says the rule applies only if a higher grade is earned. What should Rod do? Should the grade count?

8. Eulala Shute lived in Arlington, Washington, and through a local travel agent purchased a seven-day Carnival cruise. The cruise began in Los Angeles went to Puerto Vallarta, Mexico, and then returned to Los Angeles. Carnival Cruise Lines, Inc., the owner of the ship and the firm responsible for the cruise, is a corporation based in Miami, Florida. While the cruise ship was in international waters off of Mexico, Shute tripped and fell on a deck mat during a guided tour of the ship's galley.

Shute filed suit in federal district court in the state of Washington against Carnival to recover for her injuries. Could the Washington court take *in personam* jurisdiction over Carnival? [*Carnival Cruise Lines, Inc. v Shute*, 499 U.S. 585 (1991)]

9. Gail Lindgren is an entrepreneur who runs a small business called Moonbeams, based in West Des Moines, Iowa. Ms. Lindgren designed and began selling JEANJANGLES, jewelry that hangs from the belt loops on jeans. Ms. Lindgren obtained a patent for the trinkets and, in addition to storming the Iowa jeans-wearing market, sold the JEANJANGLES on her website, www.jeanjangles. com (the company's original website). A California company, GDT, began selling "Jeans for the Hip," called JEAN JEWEL. Ms. Lindgren became aware of GDT, its website, and its product when *People* magazine did a feature story on the jean trinkets and friends called to congratulate her on her national success. Ms. Lindgren filed suit in federal district court in Iowa against GDT for infringement. GDT maintains that it has never been to Iowa, has no stores in Iowa, has no salespeople or other employees in Iowa, and cannot be required to come to Iowa to defend a lawsuit. Ms. Lindgren says that GDT has a website and is selling its jewels to residents in Iowa and must come to Iowa to defend a suit there because it is doing business there. Who is correct? [*Lindgren v GDT, LLC*, 312 F. Supp. 2d 1125 (S.D. Iowa 2004)]

10. The words "I've fallen and I can't get up!" were part of a TV commercial for a device whose marketing was directed at the elderly and whose appeal was that the device was hooked to communication links with emergency care providers. In fact, the device provided a link, but not a direct link, to a 911 number; some interlink delay would occur in notifying emergency personnel. The devices, worn around the neck, were in fact a means of effecting communication when the wearer could not get to a phone. However, the device was not directly linked to a 911 number.

Officials in Arizona brought charges against the company for deceptive advertising. Standards in Arizona require proof only that someone could be misled by the commercials; actions against advertisers do not require proof that someone was actually misled. The devices have been a help to many people, bringing assistance to those who would otherwise, because of temporary or permanent mobility impairment, be unable to call for help. Officials in other states did not find the ads misleading. Does Arizona have jurisdiction?

If you were an official for the company, would you change all of your ads or modify only those in Arizona? Were the ads unethical?

ETHICS & THE LAW

The Dismissal of a Lawyer

Timothy J. Mayopoulos was the general counsel for Bank of America (B of A) until shortly before its merger/acquisition of Merrill Lynch was approved by B of A shareholders. Mr. Mayopoulos was fired from his position on the day he met with the board and the board was told that Merrill Lynch had heretofore undisclosed losses that had not been disclosed to B of A shareholders. He was escorted out of the Charlotte, North Carolina, B of A headquarters by security personnel and was not permitted to return to his office and collect his belongings. The merger was approved and the shareholders brought suit for the bank's failure to disclose the full scope of the Merrill Lynch losses.

Mr. Mayopoulos gave testimony to New York Attorney General Andrew Cuomo, the official who had been investigating whether information about the scope of the losses was withheld prior to the shareholder vote on the Merrill Lynch merger/acquisition. Mr. Mayopoulos, however, declined to disclose to Mr. Cuomo's office the content of the advice he gave to the bank, citing legal ethics rules.

Mr. Cuomo asked B of A to waive "the privilege" because its refusal was hindering his office's ability to investigate what happened in the days leading up to the merger/acquisition. B of A initially refused to waive its attorney–client privilege. However, when an SEC investigation began, the bank waived the privilege and then settled the SEC case for a $150 million fine. The shareholder litigation is ongoing.

B of A's then CEO, Kenneth D. Lewis, testified that Mr. Mayopoulos was fired because B of A had more executives than it needed following the merger.

Mr. Mayopoulos went on to become general counsel for Fannie Mae, and ultimately, its CEO, but, in an ironic note, Mr. Mayopoulos still resides in Charlotte, North Carolina on the same street as Mr. Lewis. The neighborhood block parties during the summer of 2009 must have been tense.

What is the lawyer–client privilege and when does it apply? Does it apply to general counsel as well as to outside counsel? When is the privilege waived? Why do you think Mr. Mayopoulos stood so firm on his refusal to answer questions about what happened in the days leading up to the merger and his termination? What do you think really happened in the lead-up to the merger?

For More Information

Louise Story, "Bank Firing of Counsel Is Examined," *New York Times*, September 9, 2009, p. C1.

Dan Fitzpatrick, "New York Nears Charges on Merrill Deal," *Wall Street Journal*, September 9, 2009, p. C1.

© Ron and Joe/Shutterstock.com

Note

1. The U.S. Supreme Court ruled that Mr. Newdow lacked standing to challenge the "under God" clause in the pledge of allegiance because he was not the custodial parent of his daughter. [542 U.S. 1 (2004)] The other cites for this case are 124 S.Ct. 2301(2004) and 159 L.Ed.2d 98(2004).

4 MANAGING DISPUTES:
Alternative Dispute Resolution and Litigation Strategies

The study of business regulation to this point has involved an overview of ethics, law, and the courts responsible for enforcing, interpreting, and applying the law. This chapter focuses on disputes and answers the following questions: How can businesses best resolve disputes? What strategies should a business follow if litigation is inevitable? How do courts proceed with litigation?

For up-to-date news on law, ethics, and economics, go to **mariannejennings.com**

Bo Chambers/Flickr/Getty Images

Consider...

Craig Walters slipped and fell on a piece of banana in the meat department of a Kroger store and landed on his left hip and left elbow. Initially, Walters did not experience pain or other symptoms. Peyton Kelley, the store co-manager, came to the scene, and concluded that something "mushy" and smelling like banana caused the fall. Kroger had video cameras that would have filmed both the fall as well as the regularity of clean-up in the aisles of the store. Kelley, however, did not retain the video films and allowed them to be automatically purged after the 17-day automatic preservation period. Walters filed suit and recovered over $1.6 million, partly because the jury was permitted to assume that there would have been negative evidence on the purged videos. Kroger filed an appeal objecting to that assumption about the purged videos. What happens when a business destroys evidence?

4-1 What Is Alternative Dispute Resolution?

Alternative dispute resolution (ADR) offers parties alternative means of resolving their differences outside actual courtroom litigation and the costly preparation for it. ADR ranges from informal options, such as a negotiated settlement between the CEOs of companies, to the formal, written processes of the American Arbitration Association. These processes may be used along with litigation or in lieu of litigation.

4-2 Types of Alternative Dispute Resolution

4-2a ARBITRATION

Nature of Arbitration

Arbitration is the oldest form of ADR and was once the most popular form of alternative dispute resolution, but its increasing costs and time commitment have found businesses and lawyers labeling it "no different from litigation."[1] As of 2012, arbitration cases were down and motions to set aside arbitration awards or obtain exemptions from mandatory arbitration clauses were up.[2] Mandatory arbitration clauses have even been abandoned by the American Institute of Architects, a pioneer in ADR that had the mandatory clauses in its model contract from 1888 through 2010. The AIA has moved to mandatory mediation. Bank of America has eliminated mandatory arbitration from its credit card, bank account, and auto loan contracts. Because of this shift in ADR, arbitration is no longer the preferred method for business dispute resolution.

The one remaining area of growth in arbitration is through state courts, which, in order to encourage ADR, now impose mandatory arbitration in all cases involving amounts below a certain dollar limit, generally $25,000 or $50,000. In Arizona, these mandatory arbitration proceedings are arbitrated by lawyers in the state, who are required to accept such assignments on a rotating basis either for a fee or as part of their *pro bono* activities. Such mandatory arbitration requirements have reduced the civil caseloads in many states by as much as 50 percent.

Binding vs. Nonbinding vs. Mandatory Arbitration

An agreement to submit to arbitration is an enforceable clause in consumer and commercial contracts. The parties may also agree to submit to arbitration after their dispute arises even though they do not have such a clause in their contract. Arbitration can be binding or nonbinding. **Binding arbitration** means that the decision of the arbitrators is final. Appeals of the decision are limited (see discussion that follows). **Nonbinding arbitration** is a preliminary step to litigation. If one of the parties is not satisfied with the result in the arbitration, the case may still be litigated.

A contract can also require arbitration, something known as mandatory arbitration. Under mandatory arbitration, the parties cannot choose court action first. Mandatory arbitration clauses have been a focus of court challenges. However, the Federal Arbitration Act (FAA) permits mandatory arbitration in consumer contracts and has been upheld by the U.S. Supreme Court. [*Green Tree Financial Corp. v Randolph*, 531 U.S. 79 (2000)] Arbitration clauses can be set aside if they are included in a contract due to misrepresentation or fraud. Case 4.1, *College Park Pentecostal Holiness Church v General Steel Corp.*, deals with an issue of whether an arbitration clause can be set aside.

CASE 4.1

College Park Pentecostal Holiness Church v General Steel Corp.
847 F.Supp.2d 807 (D. Md. 2012)

When a Church Gets Snookered Into a Building and Arbitration

FACTS

In December 2006, Pastor Jamil Kahn of the College Park Pentecostal Church (plaintiff) discussed by phone with Christopher Davis, an employee of General Steel Corporation (Defendants), the possible construction of a building on the Church's property in College Park, Maryland. Davis told Pastor Kahn that General Steel would provide a "turnkey" building ready for occupancy and would handle all zoning, design, site planning, and general contracting work. General Steel faxed the contract to Kahn on January 11, 2007.

The cover page of the contract, which was marked "Urgent," stated that the contract had to be signed that day and directed Kahn to initial the "CONDITIONS" page before faxing the document back to General Steel. The contract outlined the Church's "STEEL BUILDING SPECIFICATIONS," and farther down the page, in small block print, the contract stated, "… ALL DISPUTES SHALL BE ARBITRATED PURSUANT TO PARAGRAPH 6 OF THE CONDITIONS PAGE." Paragraph 6 provided:

Any controversy or claim arising out of or relating to this contract, or the breach thereof, shall be resolved by arbitration before the Judicial Arbiter Group, Inc. in Denver, Colorado. Any challenge relating to the entire agreement or any subpart thereto, arbitration of any controversy, and confirmation of any arbitration award shall be only in Denver, Colorado. Any such challenge that relates to whether claims are arbitrable shall obligate the challenging party to pay the attorney's fees and costs of defense to the non-challenging party. The party initiating arbitration shall advance all costs thereof. This agreement shall be governed by and interpreted in accordance with the laws of the State of Colorado. The Federal Arbitration Act

CONTINUED

shall govern the interpretation, enforcement, and proceedings pursuant to the arbitration clause in this agreement.

On January 12, Pastor Kahn sent General Steel a check for $45,000 as a deposit. In January 2008, Pastor Kahn signed a "Building Change Order," which added a mezzanine level to the planned building, and sent General Steel another check for $50,000. Due to the increased price of the mezzanine, however, the parties later executed a second Change Order that restored the original design of the building. General Steel never returned the $50,000.

Following payment of the deposits, General Steel informed the church that they would provide no assistance with site planning, zoning, or construction and would only supply materials for the building. The Church demanded return of the deposits, claiming it had no intention of entering into a "materials only" contract, but General Steel refused. The church filed suit for breach of contract.

General Steel filed a motion to dismiss the suit and refer the case to arbitration, but the court requested more information in order to determine the validity of the arbitration clause, given the obvious distance, cost, and inconvenience to the Church of having to arbitrate in Colorado.

JUDICIAL OPINION

MESSITTE, Judge

The U.S. Supreme Court in *Green Tree Financial Corp.-Alabama v Randolph* ruled that a party challenging an arbitration agreement on the basis of financial hardship might be able to show that the likelihood of incurring prohibitive costs effectively deprives it of its ability to seek redress. But the underlying claim in *Green Tree* was based on two federal statutes, the Truth in Lending Act, 15 U.S.C. §§ 1601–1616, and the Equal Credit Opportunity Act, 15 U.S.C. §§ 1691–1691f, not state law. At least three federal courts of appeals have held that the prohibitive cost doctrine articulated in *Green Tree* is limited to agreements where federal statutory rights are at issue.

On the other hand, notwithstanding the limited reach of *Green Tree*, the Church may still argue that the arbitration clause in this case, or some portion of it, is unenforceable because it runs afoul of generally applicable state contract law. Several state courts, for example, have considered the issue of prohibitive cost under the rubric of unconscionability in cases involving state law claims. Here, the pertinent question, then, is the enforceability of what may be unconscionable provisions of an arbitration clause under Colorado law.

Under Colorado law, an arbitration clause, as with any clause in a contract, may be invalidated if it is deemed unconscionable.

Defendants advance two arguments why the arbitration clause in this case should be enforced as written, neither of which the Court finds persuasive. They first maintain that an arbitrator, not this Court, must resolve the parties' dispute, including the viability of the venue provision, because the Church challenges the contract as a whole, not the arbitration clause specifically. In its supplemental brief, the Church specifically attacked the "enforceability of the arbitration clause" as "part of a multiple part analysis" that courts use in examining "such issues as venue under the principle of forum non-convenience [sic]." [T]he Church asserted the hardship of "litigating and/or arbitrating in Colorado." The Church's assets included a savings account totaling $32,736.00 and a checking account, after deducting outstanding liabilities, consisting of $2,319.00. The Church received an income of approximately $24,000.00 per month in donations but incurred approximately $20,000.00 per month in expenses. [T]he Judicial Arbiter Group in Denver, Colorado would charge on average $395.00 per hour for an arbitrator's services. The Church estimated that an arbitrator would spend between twenty-six to thirty-six hours resolving this case—consisting of two days of hearings and ten additional hours of work—for an arbitrator's fee of approximately $14,220.00. Additional costs of arbitration would include the cost of retaining Colorado counsel and transportation and housing expenses for a minimum of three days for at least two individuals representing the Church. To date, the Church's Maryland counsel has charged only expenses for his legal representation, and has stated that he is unable to devote the time necessary to handle arbitration in Colorado. The Church has contacted several attorneys in Denver, all of whom indicated that it would take some 50 hours to handle the arbitration and draft a post-hearing memorandum. These attorneys reported on average a fee of $325.00 per hour, which would bring their fees to a total of about $17,500.00. As for travel and accommodations expenses for two Church representatives, those may be estimated at $700.00 and $1,275.00, respectively, a total of $1,975.00. Given an approximate total cost of $33,695.00 to arbitrate in Colorado, arbitrating the dispute would effectively eliminate all of the Church's remaining assets and likely jeopardize its continued existence. The cost of arbitration that the Church would incur if Defendants' arbitration clause were fully enforceable can only be described as unconscionable.

The Court finds the Church's challenge sufficiently specific to the arbitration clause that it may be considered by the Court.

Defendants next argue that the Church's challenge to enforcement of the arbitration clause fails because the Church cannot invoke *Green Tree Financial Corp.* and its progeny, say Defendants, because those

CONTINUED

cases involved alleged violations of federal statutory rights. [However], the Church nevertheless remains able to raise the issue of prohibitive cost by challenging the provision under state law generally applicable to contracts. Determining whether an agreement is unconscionable under Colorado law requires consideration of the "terms of the contract, including substantive unfairness."

Fully cognizant that Colorado public policy "strongly favors the resolution of disputes through arbitration," the Court concludes that some terms of the clause are indeed unconscionable and therefore unenforceable.

It is readily apparent that the arbitration clause was part of a standardized agreement executed by parties of unequal bargaining strength. General Steel sent Pastor Kahn the front and back of its [purchase agreement] and pressured him to sign and return it the same day he received it. The terms and conditions of the contract, including the arbitration clause, were not subject to negotiation. According to General Steel's website, it is a "worldwide leader" in the steel building industry with "years of building design experience." See General Steel, http://www.gensteel.com. In contrast, from all appearances neither Kahn nor the Church possessed the least business sophistication, including experience with contracts or in the field of construction generally. Additionally, Khan conducted his discussions with Defendants without the benefit of counsel, and signed the Purchase Agreement as the Church's representative again without the benefit of counsel. This factor weighs heavily against enforceability of the forum selection clause.

It is also clear that the Church had little time to read and familiarize itself with the Purchase Agreement before signing it. Kahn received the contract on January 11, 2007 and was obliged to execute the contract and return it on the same day he received it. [T]he same day turn-around hardly gave the Church the opportunity to appreciate the significance of its terms, especially the potential onerousness of having to arbitrate in Colorado should it find it necessary to challenge any aspect of Defendants' performance.

The Court is hard pressed to conclude that it is commercially reasonable to require the representatives of a financially modest church to travel three-quarters of the way across the country to arbitrate its claims, pay Defendants' attorneys' fees and costs if it challenges arbitrability (whether the challenge is successful or not), and advance all costs of arbitration.

The Court [must] examine the terms of the arbitration clause and determine whether they are substantively unfair. The Court has done so and concludes that most of the provisions are clearly lopsided in favor of

Defendants. The Court finds no reason to challenge the *bona fides* of the designated arbitrator, the Judicial Arbiter Group, Inc. But the fact remains that General Steel is located in Lakewood, Colorado. The Church is located in College Park, Maryland, over 1,400 miles away. And again, if the Church merely undertakes to challenge enforcement of any aspect of the arbitration clause, it must "pay the attorney's fees and costs of defense to the non-challenging party," i.e., Defendants, whether the Church prevails on the point or not.

Perhaps more important, the Church is apparently obliged to "advance all costs thereof." In other words, even if the Church were to obtain a favorable outcome through arbitration, it would still be obligated to put forward Defendants' fees and costs and the arbitrator's fees and costs. Nothing in the contract allows for deferral of payments or shifting fees and costs to the losing party. Courts have expressed concern about fee-splitting provisions in arbitration clauses that require an aggrieved party to pay even one half of an arbitrator's fees.

Defendants' argument that hiring new counsel might not be necessary, the implication being that the Church could either appear without counsel, or that current Maryland counsel, presumably out of the goodness of his heart, could offer his services without charge, is altogether fatuous. This case is far too complex for the Church members to handle by themselves, and their counsel has already voiced his understandable unwillingness to handle the arbitration in Colorado *pro bono*. Defendants' contention that if Colorado counsel were needed, the Church has overestimated the average hourly rate and ignored the possibility of contingency fee arrangements, is also fatuous. Even $250.00 rather than $325.00 per hour would result in a significant sum over the projected 50 hours of attorney time. Moreover, it is highly unlikely that any Colorado counsel worth his or her salt would be willing to sign onto this case on a contingency basis. Finally, Defendants' suggestion that "telephonic appearances or preservation depositions" might suffice ignores the fact that they would be clearly weak substitutes for live appearances.

The Church alleges, and Defendants have yet to deny, that the latter's representative told Kahn that General Steel would provide a "turnkey" building ready for occupancy and would handle all zoning, design, site planning, and general contracting work, a representation the Church maintains was totally false when made.

Finally, it does not pass notice that Defendants' sales practices have been seriously called into question in other jurisdictions. The Church asserts that Defendants have yet again engaged in sharp dealings. Perhaps so, perhaps not. What is undisputed, however,

CONTINUED

is that as a result of signing the contract with General Steel and making the required deposits, the Church has lost $95,000, which Defendants claim is non-refundable, including—incredibly—the $50,000 deposit the Church made for a change Defendants agree was duly cancelled.

This case involves more than just a disparity of bargaining strength and a "'simple old-fashioned bad bargain.'" This is a case where "no decent, fair[-] minded person would view the ensuing result" of enforcement of the arbitration provisions "without being possessed of a profound sense of injustice …."

Accordingly, the Court will excise the unconscionable provisions of the arbitration clause. The Court will STRIKE those portions of the arbitration clause (1) designating "the Judicial Arbiter Group, Inc. in Denver, Colorado," as the sole arbitrator for any controversy or claim; (2) declaring that "Denver, Colorado" is the only place where any challenge relating to the agreement; (3) compelling the party that challenges arbitrability "to pay the attorney's fees and costs of defense to the non-challenging party;" and (4) requiring the party "initiating arbitration" to "advance all costs thereof."

The Court will direct that the arbitration go forward, but that it be held in this District, minus the described unconscionable provisions.

CASE QUESTIONS

1. What does the court find was unconscionable about the contract and negotiations?

2. What is severed from the contract and why?

3. How will the case now proceed?

4-2b ARBITRATION PROCEDURES

Once the parties agree to arbitrate, they usually notify the American Arbitration Association (AAA) (www.adr.org), which, for a fee, will handle all the steps in the arbitration. The AAA is the largest ADR provider in the country for commercial disputes, and the National Arbitration Forum is the largest for consumer contracts.

The parties submit names for arbitration and a mutually agreeable arbitrator or panel is appointed. A hearing date is set at a mutually agreeable time. Between the time the date is set and the actual hearing, the parties have the responsibility of gathering their evidence and necessary witnesses. The parties are, in effect, doing their preparation or discovery (see pp. 120–123). The parties can also request that the other party bring certain documents to the hearing. Some arbitrators are given subpoena power in certain states; that is, they have the power to require the production of documents or to have a witness testify.

The parties need not have lawyers but have the right to use one under AAA rules. AAA rules require notification to the other parties about the use and identity of counsel. Although the atmosphere is more relaxed, an arbitration hearing parallels a trial. Each of the parties has the opportunity to present evidence and witnesses. Each has the right to cross-examination and a closing statement. Some of the emotion of a trial is missing because, although emotional appeal influences juries, an expert arbitrator is not likely to be swayed by it. After the close of the hearing, the arbitrator has 30 days to make a decision.

In binding arbitration, the arbitrator's award is final. The award and decision cannot be changed, modified, or reversed. Only the parties can agree to have the case reopened; the arbitrator cannot do so. The courts are strict in their hands-off policy on private arbitration decisions that result from the parties' contractual agreement to submit to arbitration. The grounds for setting aside an arbitration finding under federal law are (1) the award resulted from corruption, fraud, or undue influence; (2) partiality or corruption occurred among the arbitrators; (3) the arbitrators were guilty of misconduct, which prejudiced the rights of one of the parties; or (4) the arbitrators exceeded their powers.

FOR THE MANAGER'S DESK

Re: Understanding the Disillusionment with ADR

The issues lawyers raise about arbitration include the following:

- Increasingly, arbitrations are as time-consuming and costly as trials.

- Too many arbitrators are allowing extensive discovery.

- Some arbitrators are requiring $40,000 retainers just for agreeing to begin hearing a case.

- The panel of arbitrators may consist of people who, while knowledgeable in their fields, are beholden to the industry, such as an engineer siding with an engineer defendant.

Some businesses are revisiting their mandatory arbitration clauses because they are looking at some of the arbitration decisions and saying, "Maybe the court system isn't so bad—at least you get due process at some point."

The concern of many lawyers and court administrators is the loss of common law and statutory interpretation when too many cases opt for the ADR route, which does not include published decisions or rationale.

What are the theoretical benefits of arbitration? What are its drawbacks?

Sources: Leigh Jones, "Gotcha Game," *National Law Journal*, February 11, 2011, p. 1; Michael Orey, "The Vanishing Trial," *BusinessWeek*, April 30, 2007, pp. 38–39.

© bloomua/Shutterstock.com

Consider...

Nicholas Sharp and Barry and Rhonda Downey own adjacent tracts of land, and for almost eight years, they have been engaged in litigation over land and easement rights. One tract of land involved in the dispute was landlocked and the other was not, with the main issue being whether there was an easement for the landlocked property and where that easement would be located. At the end of the eight years, they agreed to submit their issues for binding arbitration.

The arbitrator reached a decision that resulted in the granting of an implied easement to one owner, but not to the owner of the landlocked property. The arbitrator found that the landlocked property did not need an implied easement. Further, the arbitrator's decision on the location of the easement resulted in an easement that was not actually connected on the land. When one party moved for the court to set aside the decision of the arbitrator as an "arbitrary, irrational decision in manifest disregard of the law," the court agreed and stated that "While parties to arbitration agree to accept the arbitrator's interpretation of the law, this does not mean that they agree to permit the arbitrator to fabricate the law from whole cloth." [*Sharp v Downey*, 13 A.3d 1 (Md. App. 2010)] The case was appealed to the Maryland Supreme Court on the grounds that an arbitration award cannot be set aside when there are factual issues that could have influenced the arbitrator's decision. What should the Maryland Supreme Court do? [*Downey v Sharp*, 51 A.3d 573 (Md. 2012)]

4-2c MEDIATION

Other forms of ADR are readily available and relatively inexpensive, especially when compared to arbitration. **Mediation** is one such alternative. Mediation is a process in which both parties meet with a neutral mediator who listens to each side explain its position. The mediator is trained to get the parties to respond to each other and their concerns. The mediator helps break down impasses and works to have the parties arrive at a mutually agreeable solution. Unlike an arbitrator, the mediator does not issue a decision; the role of the mediator is to try to get the parties to agree on a solution. Mediation is completely confidential. What is said to the mediator cannot be used later by the parties or their lawyers if litigation becomes necessary. Mediation does not require that the parties be represented by lawyers. Mediation is not binding unless the parties have agreed to be bound by the decision.

4-2d MEDARB

Mediation arbitration (medarb) is a recent creation in which the arbitrator begins by attempting to negotiate between the two parties. If the arbitrator is unable to reach a settlement, the case proceeds to arbitration with the same party serving as arbitrator. One percent of the AAA's cases each year are decided by a medarb process.

4-2e THE MINITRIAL

In a **minitrial**, the parties have their lawyers present the strongest aspects of their cases to senior officials from both companies in the presence of a neutral advisor or a judge with experience in the field. At the end of the presentations by both parties, the neutral advisor can provide several forms of input, which are controlled by the parties. The advisor may be asked to provide what his or her judgment would be in the case, or the advisor may be asked to prepare a settlement proposal based on the concerns and issues presented by the parties. Minitrials are more adversarial than mediation, but they are confidential; and the input from a neutral but respected advisor may help bring the parties together. A minitrial is not binding.

4-2f RENT-A-JUDGE

Many companies and individuals are discovering that the time that elapses between the filing of a lawsuit and its resolution is too great to afford much relief. As a result, a kind of private court system, known as **rent-a-judge**, is developing in which parties may have their case heard before someone with judicial experience without waiting for the slower process of public justice. These private courts are like "Judge Judy" without the television cameras. The parties pay filing fees and pay for the judges and courtrooms. These private courts also offer less expensive settlement conferences to afford the parties a chance at mediation prior to their private hearing. This and the other methods of ADR previously discussed offer the opportunity to obtain final dispositions of cases more quickly and at less cost.

4-2g SUMMARY JURY TRIALS

Under this relatively new method of ADR, the parties are given the opportunity to present summaries of their evidence to a judge and jurors. The jurors then give an advisory verdict to start the settlement process. If the parties are unable to agree on a settlement, a formal trial proceeds. This means of resolution gives the parties an idea of a jury's perception and assists in setting guidelines for settlement. A **summary jury trial** occurs late in the litigation process, after the costs of **discovery** have been incurred. It can, however, save the expense of a trial.

4-2h EARLY NEUTRAL EVALUATION

Early neutral evaluation requires another attorney to meet with the parties, receive an assessment of the case by both sides, and then provide an evaluation of the merits of the case. The attorney, who is either a paid consultant or a volunteer through the state bar association, renders an opinion on the resolution of the case. The idea in this method of resolution is to encourage settlement. Because early neutral evaluation occurs before the discovery phase of the case, it can save time and money if the parties are able to settle.

Business Planning Tip

Mediation has been a popular form of dispute resolution among business-to-business (B2B) e-commerce companies. Amazon.com and eBay have used mediation regularly in the resolution of disputes.

© Grounder/Shutterstock.com

FOR THE MANAGER'S DESK

Re: Southwest Airlines and Creative Dispute Resolution

In 1991, Dallas-based Southwest Airlines began a marketing campaign using the slogan "Just Plane Smart." Greenville-based Stevens Aviation had been using the slogan "Plane Smart" to market its airline service business. Following posturing by lawyers, Kurt Herwald, the chairman of Stevens Aviation, called Herb Kelleher, then chairman of Southwest Airlines, and offered to arm wrestle for the rights to the slogan. Mr. Kelleher rented a wrestling auditorium, sold tickets to the event, and offered the proceeds to charity. Mr. Kelleher, then 61, lost to Mr. Herwald, then 38, who is also a weightlifter. Mr. Herwald said, "Just to show sympathy for the elderly and that there's no hard feelings, we've decided to allow Southwest Airlines to continue using our slogan." After the event, a commentator noted, "Not only did the companies save a court battle that would have taken years and cost several hundred thousand dollars, they gained loads of free publicity. They also made donations to charities."

4-2i PEER REVIEW

Peer review has become popular particularly for disputes between employers and employees and is used by Darden Industries (Red Lobster, Olive Garden), TRW Inc., Rockwell International Corp., and Marriott International, Inc. Peer review, which is generally conducted within three weeks of demand, is a review by coworkers of the action taken against an employee (demotion, termination, discipline). These panels of fellow employees (one chosen by management, one chosen by the employee, and one chosen randomly) can take testimony, review documents, and make decisions that can include an award of damages.

Employers say that sometimes their decisions are reversed in peer review, but Darden Industries indicates that peer review has reduced employee litigation and legal fees. Of the 100 disputes handled each year in peer review, only 10 proceed to litigation.

Experiments in the use of peer review for customers, contractors, and physicians are ongoing around the country. Many see the perception of fairness as an important quality that has resulted in the growth of the use of peer review.

4-3 Resolution of International Disputes

Arbitration has been used in the international business arena since 1922. The **International Chamber of Commerce** (ICC) is a private organization that handles arbitration cases from parties in 139 countries. In 2012, the Arbitration Court of the ICC handled 759 requests for arbitration and issued 491 arbitration awards. Most requests for ICC arbitration come from 139 countries, and the typical subject matters are trade transactions, contracts, intellectual property, agency, and corporate law. The following statistics were taken from the ICC's annual report for 2012, the latest data available.

- Arbitrators of 76 different nationalities were appointed or confirmed under the ICC Rules.
- Hearings were held in 59 different countries.
- The amount in dispute exceeded $1 million (U.S.) in 76.2 percent of new cases.

© bloomua/Shutterstock.com

The ICC process is similar to that discussed earlier for the American Arbitration Association. The award of the ICC is final, and payment must be made at the location of the hearing.

The ICC also provides mediation, referred to as conciliation, services. In conciliation, the court assigns an expert to work with the parties to try to achieve a settlement of the case.

In addition to the ICC, the World Bank has established the International Center for Settlement of Investment Disputes (ICSID). The ICSID is an arbitral organization created specifically to hear disputes between investors and the nations in which they have made investments. This arbitration forum was created because of investors' fears that the courts of the nation in which they have invested may favor the government of that nation.

The American Arbitration Association created the International Centre for Dispute Resolution (ICDR), with offices in New York City, Dublin, and Mexico City to provide an international AAA service for global U.S.-based companies that face contract and other types of disputes in their international operations. The ICDR has partnering agreements with ADR organizations in 92 countries, including the AAA, and uses those partnerships to manage disputes that occur primarily in other countries. The United Nations Commission on International Trade Law (UNCITRAL) adopted a Model Law for Arbitration that deals with where arbitration should be held (the parties can decide) and which country's laws should apply.

4-4 Litigation versus ADR: The Issues and Costs

4-4a SPEED AND COST

Speed and cost are two compelling reasons businesses turn to ADR to resolve disputes. Costs of ADR have increased substantially over the past five years, and the speed has slowed down considerably.

4-4b PROTECTION OF PRIVACY

Whatever matter is in dispute can be kept private if referred directly to ADR, which means that no public court documents are available for examination. Even when a suit is filed, the negotiated settlement achieved through alternative means can be kept private to protect the interests of the parties. When Dillard's, a national department store chain, and Joseph Horne Company, a department store based in Pittsburgh, were litigating over Dillard's conduct in a Horne's takeover, the parties' dispute centered on whether Dillard's was conducting due diligence in obtaining access to Horne's facilities and records, or whether Dillard's was actually running the stores in an attempt to drive down the acquisition price. The business press reported on the litigation and the underlying dispute. The information was not flattering to either party. Dillard's was portrayed as a large firm taking advantage of a small chain and engaging in unethical conduct when it was supposed to be obtaining just financial information prior to finalizing the acquisition (a process called due diligence). Horne's was portrayed as naive and inept. Dillard's and Horne's settled the dispute, and both agreed to keep the terms of the settlement confidential. As a result, the public litigation ended, and the focus on alleged misconduct changed because of the settlement and its private nature.

4-4c CREATIVE REMEDIES

Often, without the constraints of court jurisdiction and the restraints of legal boundaries, a creative remedy can be crafted that helps both sides. For example, Intel, a computer chip manufacturer, experienced ongoing disputes with employees who left the company to begin their own businesses with products and in areas that would compete with Intel. Intel's concern was whether the departing employees were taking with them technology that had been developed at and belonged to Intel. Using only the courts, Intel would have found itself in lengthy, expensive, and complex litigation over engineering and developmental issues. Such litigation is costly not only in a monetary sense but also to the morale of employees charged with product development. Constant legal battles with former employees are not healthy for a corporate image within a company or from the outside.

After filing suit against one group of employees, Intel agreed, along with the former employees, to have an expert oversee the former employees' work in their business. The expert would have knowledge of Intel's product development efforts that the employees had been involved with and would agree to notify all sides if the new company was infringing on any of Intel's patents. The expert agreed to oversee the new company's work for one year, at which point technology would make obsolete anything developed by the former employees while they were still at Intel. This creative solution permitted the former employees to operate their business, but it also provided Intel officials with the reassurance that their intellectual property was not being taken.

4-4d JUDGE AND JURY UNKNOWNS

Even though a good case and preparation are often offered as explanations for victory in a lawsuit, many good cases are lost despite excellent preparation. Various unknowns characterize all forms of litigation and ADR. The unknowns are judges, juries, and arbitrators and their perceptions and abilities. Research shows that 80 percent of all jurors make up their minds about a case after only the opening statements in a trial have been made. Further research has shown that juries use their predetermined ideas in reaching a verdict. Finally, research shows that juries employ hindsight bias in their deliberation processes; that is, juries view the outcome of a set of facts and conclude that one party should have done more. Knowing that someone was injured often clouds our ability to determine whether that person should have been able to prevent the injury.

Based on information about juries, many businesses opt for a trial in which a judge, not a jury, renders a decision. However, research with judges has demonstrated that even their case judgments are affected by predetermined ideas and hindsight bias, although to a lesser extent than those of jurors. "The Wild Card in Complex Business Litigation: The Jury" provides background information on the risks that juries pose for businesses in litigation.

4-4e ABSENCE OF TECHNICALITIES

Under ADR, the parties have the opportunity to tell their stories. The strict procedural rules and evidentiary exclusions do not apply in these forums, and many companies feel more comfortable because ADR seems to be more of a search for the truth than a battle of processes. A mediator can serve as a communication link between the parties and help them focus on issues and concerns. As one

FOR THE MANAGER'S DESK

Re: The Wild Card in Complex Business Litigation: The Jury

Most criticisms regarding the use of juries in complex suits are focused on civil cases and not on criminal prosecutions.

In the 1978 IBM antitrust case, a jury heard five months of testimony on IBM's alleged monopolization of various market segments in the computer industry. The jury was deadlocked, and an interview with one of the jurors afterward gave some indication of the level of comprehension that resulted from the trial. The concept of "interface" was critical in the trial since the ability to interface would largely control whether there was ease of market entry and product compatibility.

Stephen J. Adler documents the following exchange in the case in *The Jury*:

Judge: "What is software?"

Juror: "That's the paper software."

Asked to define "interface," the juror said: "Well, if you take a blivet, turn it off one thing and drop it down, it's an interface change, right?"

The judge asked a second juror, "What about barriers to entry?"—to which she answered, "I would have to read about it."

A mistrial was declared.

Additional difficulties arise with finding available jurors. Complex civil suits are quite lengthy, a problem that continues to grow. The question that arises about the jurors is, in cases like the five-month IBM trial, who were these people who were able to spend every day for five months sitting on a jury? Many critics noted that the result is an overabundance of retired individuals, housewives, and the unemployed, and an absence of professionals and businesspeople who might have some experience with the issues. A cultural and financial gap is created when a jury has limited cross-sectional representation. The perceptions of individuals differ according to their circumstances. For example, the American Bar Association's study of juror deliberations indicated the verdict figures in a trade secret case ranged from $1 to $1.5 million, and one juror commented as follows:

"When you start talking millions, I can't relate to that. It doesn't mean anything to me. I have trouble paying $8 for parking every day."

Source: Adapted from Marianne Jennings and Chris P. Neck, "The Wild Card in Complex Business Litigation: The Jury." Reprinted with permission from *Commercial Law Journal* 96, No. 1, p. 45. Copyright © 1991 by the Commercial Law League of America. All rights reserved.

EXHIBIT 4.1 Benefits of ADR versus Litigation

LITIGATION	ALTERNATIVE DISPUTE RESOLUTION
Technical discovery rules	Open lines of communication
Judicial constraints of precedent	Parties can agree to anything
Remedies limited (by law and precedent)	Creative remedies permitted
Backlog	Parties set timetable
Public proceeding	Privacy
Control by lawyers	Control by parties (or mediator/arbitrator)
Expensive	Expertise of arbitrator/mediator
Strict procedures/timing	More flexibility
Judge/jury unknowns	Parties select mediator/arbitrator
Those who can afford to stay in win	Positions examined for validity
Judicial enforcement tools	Enforcement by good faith

© Cengage Learning

mediator described ADR, "If you've done your job … everyone goes home with big smiles."

Exhibit 4.1 provides a list of the benefits of ADR versus litigation.

© bloomua/Shutterstock.com

FOR THE MANAGER'S DESK

Re: A Checklist for When to Litigate

Costs

Every lawsuit costs time and money. Costs of litigation include but by no means end with attorneys' fees, and other significant costs are often not considered before a business decides to become embroiled in a legal battle.

Legal Costs

The total legal fee must be considered in every case of possible litigation. A lawyer should be required to give an estimate of fees for any suit before the suit begins. The estimate should always include discovery costs… .

Time Costs (Hidden Downtime)

Litigation costs time as well as money. Indeed, in many cases, the loss of time can be more devastating to a firm than the financial loss. If a firm takes part in major litigation, chances are that its officers and possibly its directors will be involved in depositions, other forms of pretrial discovery and paperwork, and eventually in the trial itself.

Image Costs

If a lawsuit attracts the attention of the media, a firm may incur money and time costs stemming from public relations. Someone must be available to explain the firm's position to reporters and perhaps initiate an affirmative campaign to minimize negative publicity about the suit.

Capital Costs

Auditors require that pending litigation be listed in the financial reports of the company. Ongoing litigation that carries the potential for great financial loss to a business can have a negative effect on the firm's financial rating and the ability to raise capital.

Costs of Alternatives to Litigation

The costs of litigation should be compared with the costs of alternatives to litigation. (See discussion of alternatives.)

Costs of Not Litigating

There are costs for litigating, but there are also costs for not litigating. If the stakes are high enough, litigation may be worth pursuing regardless of the expense. For example, if a suit challenges the land records and thus the title to the land on which the business is located, the cost of not responding to the suit may be the loss of the property and the expense of reestablishing the business at another site. In a trademark or trade name suit, the cost may be a product or company name or label. In a patent infringement case, the failure to sue an infringer may undermine a company's sales and its exclusivity in the marketplace.

Public Relations Issues

Litigation is not a private matter. In every city, at least one reporter is assigned to the clerk's office in the state and federal courts for the purpose of checking on suits filed.

Many an electric bill goes unpaid simply because it is not good public relations for a utility company to appear in the newspapers and on television as the "bad guy" when a retired widow explains that the big power company has just filed suit because she has no money to pay her bill. …

Jury Appeal

When considering the effects of publicity on a case, a company should also consider the closely related matter of jury appeal. In some cases, it will not matter how correct a business may be, how much of a remedy the law provides, or how wrong the other side is; the jury will simply side with the "little guy," and the business will have no chance of succeeding in the courtroom. For example, the Arthur Murray Dance Studios once fully litigated a case in which a man who had been severely injured in a car accident and was unable to complete the lessons in his contract with Arthur Murray (some 2,734 lessons, for which he had paid $24,812.40) sought to recover his payments on the grounds that performance had become impossible. It is difficult to build jury appeal into such a case.

Discussion Questions

1. List the factors you should consider as you make a decision to litigate.

2. At the awards show for the Academy of Motion Picture Arts and Sciences (Academy), a character dressed as Snow White appeared in the opening musical number and sang with actor Rob Lowe. Walt Disney, Inc., had not given the Academy permission to use the Snow White likeness, a trademarked Disney character. If you were the Walt Disney Corporation, would you sue the Academy?

3. List concerns you would have as an employer litigating a sexual harassment case.

Source: Frank Shipper and Marianne Jennings. *Avoiding and Surviving Lawsuits: The Executive Guide to Strategic Legal Planning for Business,* Jossey-Bass Publishing, Inc., pp. 59–73. Copyright © 1989. Excerpted and reprinted with permission of the authors.

4-5 **When You Are in Litigation**

At times, a business must face litigation and ADR is not possible. This portion of the chapter explains the language, process, and strategies of civil litigation.

4-5a **HOW DOES A LAWSUIT START?**

Lawsuits are based on feelings. Whether rights have actually been violated and what damages were caused as a result are the questions addressed through the trial process. The only restriction on the filing of a suit is that the plaintiff's claim of right must be based on some statutory law or common law.

People begin lawsuits. The judicial system does not unilaterally undertake the enforcement of civil rights. Individuals must assume responsibility for protecting their rights. The judicial system determines what and whose rights have been violated.

Although procedures vary from state to state, the following sections offer a general discussion of the procedures involved in a civil lawsuit. Exhibit 4.2 summarizes the trial process.

4-5b **THE COMPLAINT (PETITION)**

The first step in a lawsuit is the filing of a document called a **complaint** or **petition**. The plaintiff must file the petition or complaint within certain time limits each state has for filing suit. These time limits are called **statutes of limitations**. They vary depending on the type of rights involved in a suit. The typical statute of limitations for personal injuries is two years; the typical limitation for contracts is four years.

A complaint is a general statement of the plaintiff's claim of rights. For example, if a plaintiff is suing for a breach of contract, the complaint must describe the contract, when it began, and what the defendant did that the plaintiff says is a breach. Exhibit 4.3 shows a sample complaint in a suit over a car accident.

The complaint need not have every detail described in it. The standard for a valid complaint is that it must be definite enough in its description of what happened for the defendant to understand why the suit has been brought.

EXHIBIT 4.2 The Trial Process

© Cengage Learning

EXHIBIT 4.3 Sample Complaint

Reed C. Tolman, Esq. (006502)
TOLMAN & OSBORNE, PC.
1400 E. Southern, Suite 625
Tempe, Arizona 85282
Attorneys for Plaintiffs

SUPERIOR COURT OF ARIZONA

MARICOPA COUNTY

CRAIG CONNER and KATHY CONNER,   )
husband and wife, individually   )   CV92–91319
and on behalf of their minor   )
son, CASEY CONNER,   )   COMPLAINT
)   (Tort—Motor Vehicle)
            Plaintiffs,   )
)
            v.   )
)
CARMEN A. CHENAL and THOMAS K.   )
CHENAL, wife and husband,   )
)
            Defendants.   )
_____)

For their complaint, plaintiffs allege:

1. Plaintiffs and defendants are residents of Maricopa County, Arizona.

2. This Court has jurisdiction over the subject matter under the Arizona Constitution, Art. 6, § 14.

3. Casey Conner is the minor son of Craig and Kathy Conner.

4. Carmen A. Chenal and Thomas K. Chenal are wife and husband. At all times relevant hereto, Carmen A. Chenal was acting for and on behalf of the marital community of which she is a member.

5. On or about July 20, 1990, defendant Carmen A. Chenal was driving her motor vehicle in the vicinity of Primrose Path and Cave Creek Road in Carefree, Arizona. At the time, Casey Conner was a passenger in the back seat of defendants' vehicle, a 1976 Mercedes, ID No.11603312051326.

6. At all times relevant hereto, defendant Carmen A. Chenal had a duty to care properly for the safety of Casey Conner. That duty included the responsibility to place Casey in an appropriate and functioning seat belt.

7. Prior to the accident that resulted in injuries to Casey Conner, Carmen A. Chenal knew that the right rear door of her vehicle was damaged and not functioning properly.

8. Despite the duty Carmen A. Chenal had to care properly for the safety of Casey Conner, and despite her knowledge of a malfunctioning right rear door, Carmen A. Chenal negligently failed to place Casey in an appropriate and functioning seatbelt and negligently and carelessly operated her vehicle in such a way that the right rear door opened and allowed Casey to be ejected from the vehicle while the vehicle was in operation.

9. Carmen A. Chenal's failure to exercise reasonable care for the safety of Casey and the failure to operate her vehicle in a careful and safe manner proximately caused Casey to suffer personal injuries.

10. As a result of Casey Conner's injuries, he has experienced physical and psychological suffering, and his parents have incurred medical and other expenses, as well as lost earnings.

WHEREFORE, plaintiffs request judgment against defendants for compensatory damages in an amount to be determined at trial.

DATED: this _____ day of July, 1992.
                    TOLMAN & OSBORNE
        By: _____
                    Reed C. Tolman
                    1400 E. Southern
                    Suite 625
                    Tempe, Arizona 85282

All complaints must establish the subject matter jurisdiction of the court (see Chapter 3 for a discussion of this concept). For example, for a federal district court action, the complaint would have to allege either diversity of citizenship between the parties and a damage claim of more than $75,000, or that a federal question is involved.

In some cases, the complaint is filed by a group of plaintiffs who have the same cause of action against one defendant. These types of suits, called **class action suits**, are typically filed in antitrust cases, shareholder actions against corporations, and employment discrimination cases. The class action suit enables a group of plaintiffs to share one lawyer and minimize litigation expenses while at the same time preserving their individual rights. Perhaps the most widely publicized type of class action lawsuit is the suit that results when a large jet airliner crashes and causes multiple deaths and injuries. All the plaintiffs were injured in the same event, and the defendant then litigates once with a group of plaintiffs. (See Chapter 14 for more information on product liability class action litigation.)

Another form of class action suit is the **derivative suit**, in which shareholders sue a corporation to recover damages for actions taken by the corporation. (See Chapter 18 for more information.)

The final paragraphs of a complaint list the damages or remedies the plaintiff wants. The damages may be a **legal remedy** such as money, in which case a dollar amount is specified. The plaintiff may seek an **equitable remedy**, such as specific performance in the case of an action for breach of contract. **Specific performance** is an order of the court requiring a defendant to perform on a contract. In some cases, the plaintiffs just want the defendants to stop violating their rights. In those complaints, plaintiffs ask for **injunctions**, which are court orders requiring the defendant to stop doing the act complained of. In an action for nuisance, for example, an injunction orders the defendant to stop engaging in the conduct that causes the nuisance or orders the defendant to comply with a law or a previous decision. As another example, an injunction could order a website to stop infringement of copyright music or material.

4-5c THE SUMMONS

The complaint or petition of the plaintiffs is filed with the clerk of the appropriate court—that is, the court with subject matter jurisdiction, *in personam* jurisdiction, and venue. The defendant, however, will not know of the suit just because it is filed. The second step in a lawsuit is serving the defendant with a copy of the complaint and a **summons**, which is a legal document that tells the defendant of the suit and explains the defendant's rights under the law. Those rights include the opportunity to respond and the grant of a limited amount of time for responding. Exhibit 4.4 shows a sample summons.

A summons must be delivered to the defendant. Some states require that the defendant be given the papers personally. Other states allow the papers to be given to some member of the defendant's household or, in the case of a business, to an agent of that business. (See Chapter 17 for a discussion of an agent's authority to receive the papers notifying the business of a lawsuit.)

The summons is delivered by an officer of the court (such as a sheriff or magistrate) or by private firms licensed as **process servers**. Once the defendant is served, the server must file an affidavit with the court to indicate when and where the service was made. In rare circumstances, courts allow service of process by mail or by publishing the summons and complaint. These circumstances, however, are limited and are carefully supervised by the courts.

EXHIBIT 4.4 Sample Summons

Name:
Address:
City, State, Zip:
Telephone:
State Bar Code:
Client:

ARIZONA SUPERIOR COURT, County of

ACTION NO:

SUMMONS

THE STATE OF ARIZONA TO THE DEFENDANTS:

YOU ARE HEREBY SUMMONED and required to appear and defend, within the time applicable, in this action in this court. If served within Arizona, you appear and defend within 20 days after the service of the Summons and Complaint upon you, exclusive of the day of service. If served out of the State of Arizona—whether by direct service, by registered or certified mail, or by publication you shall appear and defend within 30 days after the service of the Summons and Complaint upon you is complete, exclusive of the day of service. Where process is served upon the Arizona Director of Insurance as an insurer's attorney to receive service of legal process against it in this state, the insurer shall not be required to appear, answer or plead until expiration of 40 days after date of such service upon the Director. Service by registered or certified mail without the State of Arizona is complete 30 days after the date of receipt by the party being served. Service by publication is complete 30 days after the date of first publication. Direct service is complete when made. Service upon the Arizona Motor Vehicle Superintendent is complete 30 days after filing the Affidavit of Compliance and return receipt or Officer's Return. RCP 4; ARS §§ 20-222, 28-502, 28-503.

Copies of the pleadings filed herein may be obtained by contacting the Clerk of Superior Court, _____ County, located at _____, Arizona. RCF 4.1 (e).

SUMMONS
(Continued on Reverse Side)

1-1 ©LawForms 10-92 1-93

YOU ARE HEREBY NOTIFIED that in case of your failure to appear and defend within the time applicable, judgment by default may be rendered against you for the relief demanded in the Complaint.

YOU ARE CAUTIONED that in order to appear and defend, you must file an Answer or proper response in writing with the Clerk of this Court, accompanied by the necessary filing fee, within the time required, and you are required to serve a copy of any Answer or response upon the Plaintiffs' attorney. RCP 10(D); ARS 12-311; RCP5.

The name and address of plaintiffs' attorney is:

SIGNED AND SEALED this date:_____

....
Clerk

Method of Service:
☐ Private Process Service
☐ Sheriff or Marshall
☐ Personal Service
☐ Registered/Certified Mail (out of State)

By ....
Deputy Clerk

SUMMONS

1-1 ©LawForms 11-67, 3-84, 1-93

© Cengage Learning

4-5d THE ANSWER

The parties' positions in a case are found in the **pleadings**. The complaint or petition is a pleading. The defendant's position is found in the **answer**, another pleading in a case. The defendant must file an answer within the time limits allowed by the court or risk default. The time limits are typically 20 days for in-state defendants and 30 days for out-of-state defendants. A failure to answer, or a **default**, is like a forfeit in sports: The plaintiff wins because the defendant failed to show up. The plaintiff can then proceed to a judgment to collect damages.

The defendant's answer can do any or all of several different things. The defendant may admit certain facts in the answer. Although it is rare for a defendant to admit the wrong alleged by the plaintiff, the defendant might admit parts of the plaintiff's complaint, such as those that establish jurisdiction and venue. If the plaintiff already has correct venue, fighting that issue is costly, and admitting jurisdiction is a way to move on with the case. If, however, the court lacked *in personam* jurisdiction over the defendant, the defendant could deny the jurisdiction. (See Chapter 3 for more discussion of *in personam* jurisdiction.)

A denial is a simple statement in the answer whereby the defendant indicates that the allegation is denied. An answer might also include a statement that the defendant does not know enough to admit or deny the allegations in the complaint and might include a demand for proof of those allegations.

An answer might also include a **counterclaim**, with which the defendant, in effect, countersues the plaintiff, alleging a violation of rights and damages against the plaintiff. The plaintiff must respond to the counterclaim using the same answer process of admitting or denying the alleged wrong. Exhibit 4.5 shows a sample answer.

The answer must be filed with the clerk of the court and a copy sent to the plaintiff. With the exception of amendments to these documents, the pleadings are now complete.

4-5e SEEKING TIMELY RESOLUTION OF THE CASE

The fact that a suit has been filed does not mean that the case will go to trial. A great majority of suits are disposed of before trial because of successful motions to end them. **Motions** are requests to the court that it take certain action. Motions usually involve filed documents and include citations to precedent that support granting the motion. Often the judge will have the attorneys present oral arguments for and against the motion, after which the court then issues a ruling on the motion. For example, in 2012, a federal judge quickly dismissed Lance Arsmtrong's suit against the USADA as it prepared to take disciplinary action against Mr. Armstrong because the complaint had no legal cause of action, but was only a "a lengthy and bitter polemic against the named defendants." Following Mr. Armstrong's admissions of the use of performance-enhancing drugs, the judge's rapid dismissal proved prescient.

Motion for Judgment on the Pleadings

Either in the answer or by separate motion, a defendant can move for judgment based just on the content of the pleadings. The theory behind a **motion for judgment on the pleadings** is that the plaintiff has no cause of action even if everything the plaintiff alleges is true. For example, a plaintiff could file suit claiming the defendant is an annoying person; but unless the defendant is annoying to the extent of invading privacy or not honoring contracts, the plaintiff has no right of recovery. The

EXHIBIT 4.5 Sample Answer

Grand, Canyon & Rafts
12222 W. Camelback
Phoenix, Arizona
555-5555
Attorneys for Defendant

SUPERIOR COURT OF ARIZONA

MARICOPA COUNTY

CRAIG CONNER and KATHY CONNER,)
husband and wife, individually)
and on behalf of their minor)
son, CASEY CONNER,)
)
    Plaintiffs,)
)
    v.)
)
CARMEN A. CHENAL and THOMAS K.)
CHENAL, wife and husband,)
)
    Defendants.)
_____)
	CV92–91319
	
	ANSWER

For their answer, defendants respond to plaintiffs'
complaint as follows:
    1. Admit paragraph one.
    2. Admit paragraph two.
    3. Have no knowledge to admit or deny paragraph three.
    4. Have no knowledge to admit or deny paragraph four
    5. Admit paragraph five.
    6. As for paragraphs 6 through 10, inclusive of plaintiffs'
complaint, defendants have no knowledge of the statements alleged and
deny all statements made therein.

    Defendents deny any and all parts of plaintiffs' complaints
not specifically mentioned herein.
    DATED: this_____ day of August, 1992.
        Grand, Canyon & Raft

    By: _____
        Robert C. Canyon
        12222 W. Camelback
        Phoenix, Arizona

© Cengage Learning

defendant in this case could win a motion for judgment on the pleadings because
the law (perhaps unfortunately) does not provide a remedy for annoying people.
A denial of a motion for judgment on the pleadings does not imply victory for the
plaintiff. It simply means that the case will proceed with the next steps.

Motion to Dismiss

A **motion to dismiss** can be filed any time during the proceedings but usually is part of the defendant's answer. Such a motion can be based on the court's lack of subject matter or *in personam* jurisdiction. Again, if the case is not dismissed, it does not mean that the plaintiff wins; it just means that the case will proceed to the next steps and possibly trial.

Motion for Summary Judgment

A **motion for summary judgment** has two requirements. Summary judgment is appropriate only when (1) the moving party is entitled to a judgment under the law and (2) no issues of fact remain disputed. Actions brought on the basis of motor vehicle accidents, for example, always involve different witnesses' testimonies and variations in facts. These types of cases cannot be decided by summary

---

BUSINESS STRATEGY

The Most-Sued Companies in America

The list is surprising, but there is a top group of companies with the most suits filed in federal district court. (See Chapter 3 for a discussion of how cases enter federal district court.)

COMPANY	2010	2009	2008	2007
General Electric	9,359	12,356	20,498	3,887
Goodyear	4,989	14,393	13,330	2,661
Bank of America	3,285	2,569	1,196	775
Wells Fargo	3,092	2,428	1,413	969
Toyota Motor	1,873	154	185	158
Walmart	1,672	1,765	1,452	1,538
JPMorgan	1,150	1,149	471	275
General Motors	299	1,817	2,524	2,331
Morgan Stanley	261	405	273	236
Goldman Sachs	180	115	105	79
US Bancorp	59	74	19	25

Source: Public Access to Court Electronic Records (PACER)

The common theme in the list is consumer. Car companies, banks, a tire company, and a consumer appliance company—all of them face the highest levels of federal court litigation because of consumer rights under federal law. In addition, the banks on the list are facing all of the litigation (most settled in early 2013) related to subprime mortgages and foreclosure suits.

Interestingly, Walmart was once the number one company for suits, but it has dropped down to position 6. Walmart has employed a strategy of not settling suits filed against it and the result has been a decrease in the number of suits filed against it. These numbers do not include state court litigation, something that could alter the numbers of suits significantly. For example, Walmart slip-and-fall cases (injuries occurring in their stores) would be state court actions and, as a retailer, Walmart would face a significant number of such suits, as do all major retailers.

For More Information

http://www.foxbusiness.com/markets/2011/01/18/sued-companies-america/#ixzz2Ki6VpsDF.

http://us1.institutionalriskanalytics.com/www/index.asp.

judgment. In other cases, however, the parties do not dispute the facts but differ on the applications of law. Consider, for example, a dispute involving a contract for the repair of a computer, including service and parts. Different laws govern contractual provisions for services and provisions for goods. The parties do not dispute the facts: They agree goods and services are covered in the contract. At issue is the question about which law applies, and a summary judgment appropriately will resolve it. A suit may involve other factual disputes about contract performance, but the partial summary judgment will determine which contract law will apply.

4-5f HOW A LAWSUIT PROGRESSES: DISCOVERY

Trials in the United States are not conducted by ambush. Before the trial, the parties engage in a mandatory process of mutual disclosure of all relevant documents and other evidence. This court-supervised process of gathering evidence is called *discovery*. Under procedural rules that govern discovery, the parties must provide to each other lists of witnesses, all relevant documents, tangible evidence, and statements related to the case. Under the old discovery rules, the expense and difficulty of discovery techniques often meant the search for the truth was a cat-and-mouse game won by those with the most funds. Armed with the evidence from a full-disclosure approach, the parties to a case are more prepared, and perhaps more inclined, to negotiate a settlement. Discovery rules provide for sanctions (penalties) for not turning over relevant documents at the start of a case. Sanctions can include fines against the party who withheld the evidence, findings of contempt against the lawyers, including fines, and the exclusion of responses to the withheld evidence. The following sections cover the traditional tools of discovery.

Requests for Admissions and Interrogatories

A **request for admissions** asks the other side to admit a certain fact. **Interrogatories** ask questions about facts. The parties have some incentive to admit the facts requested if they are true because if these facts are denied and then proved at trial, the party who had to prove those true facts can recover the costs of proof. Requests for admissions request the other party to admit that a document is authentic. For example, the parties might have a dispute about the amount due under a contract but should be willing to admit that they signed the contract and that it is authentic. These requests for admission reduce the length of trials.

Depositions

Depositions are the oral testimony of parties or witnesses that are taken under oath but outside the courtroom and before the trial. They can be taken long before a trial and help preserve a witness's or party's recollection. Depositions are also helpful in determining just how strong a case is. It is far better to discover damaging information in a deposition than to have surprises at trial.

Requests for Production

A **request for production** requires the other side to produce requested documents. For example, if a business is suing to recover lost profits, the defendant will probably want to request the income statements and perhaps the income tax returns of that business in order to prepare for the presentation of damages issues at trial. A request for production can include medical records as well as tangible evidence. In *Kroger Co. v Walters* (Case 4.2), the destruction of physical evidence is an issue in a case that provides an answer to the opening "Consider..."

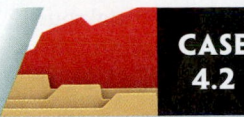

| CASE 4.2 | *Kroger Co. v Walters*
735 S.E.2d 99 (Ga. App. 2012) |

A Slip on the Banana Video

FACTS

On May 25, 2008, Craig Walters slipped and fell on a piece of banana in the meat department of a Kroger store and landed on his left hip and left elbow. Initially, Walters did not experience pain or other symptoms. Peyton Kelley, the store co-manager, came to the scene, and described the cause of the fall as something "mushy" and smelling like banana. Kelley spoke with Walters and a customer who witnessed the fall. Kelley asked Walters if he was okay, and Walters replied that he appeared to be fine. But Kelley also remembered that Walters said he was a little sore, and Kelley noticed that Walters was limping. Walters gave Kelley his name and resumed shopping. When Walters got in his car to go home, he began to experience unusual symptoms, including tingling in his toes, numbness in his legs, and, eventually, loss of balance, which grew worse over time.

In the meantime, Kelley followed Kroger's procedure to investigate every such incident. Kelley spoke to store employees, including the employee nearest to the fall. He also downloaded from a company website a six-page "Customer Incident Report & Investigation Check List," which he completed, partially that day and partially thereafter, based on his notes from the day of the incident, including a diagram of where Walters fell. That diagram is marked as having been drawn on May 25, and every page of the customer incident report, including the diagram, states that it was made "in anticipation of litigation under the direction of legal counsel."

Kelley admitted, however, that he did not follow store policy regarding his investigation. Kelley reviewed video from the security cameras located in the vicinity of the fall, including camera 17, the camera closest to that area. The cameras' hard drives retain their video for 17 days but are then erased and reused; to retain a video for a longer time, one must transfer the file to a CD or DVD. Store policy dictated that if the video covered the area of the fall, it should be retained. After viewing the video captured at the time of the fall, Kelley decided not to save any video despite the company policy. He testified that none of the cameras captured the incident. He did not know why he did not make a copy, and that he could not be sure the system was actually working at the time. Kelley admitted that, in addition to the fall itself, the videos might have shown when the store aisles were inspected, how and when banana came to be on the floor in the meat department, and whether any store

employees were in the vicinity of the fall. Kelley also testified that if he had looked at the video, he should have recorded his findings in the incident report, yet the report does not reference any video.

Walters saw Kelley from time to time thereafter when he went shopping. Walters first saw an orthopedist on July 3, 2008. On July 9, 2008, more than 17 days after the fall, Walters again spoke to Kelley and reported having problems with his back and legs beginning a month after the fall; he also stated that he needed help with his medical bills. During that conversation, Kelley obtained a telephone number and address for Walters and said he was going to submit the claim.

Walters and his wife filed suit on March 6, 2009. At his deposition, Kelley testified that camera 17 had not been moved or re-aimed since the day of the fall. Subsequently, Kroger produced exemplar video (taken from each camera on January 7, 2010), showing each camera's field of view, and camera 17 did not point directly at the place where Walters fell. On August 3, 2010, store manager Harry Turner testified that none of the indoor cameras had been re-aimed, including camera 17, since he began managing the store in 2004 and that the cameras could not be moved electronically; rather, a person would have to climb a ladder to adjust them. Following a discussion among the lawyers, the live feed was shown, and it was discovered that the camera was not pointed in the same direction as the exemplar and that, instead, the camera pointed directly at the location of Walters's fall.

Walters filed a motion for sanctions, and the court entered an order finding that Kroger had destroyed the video from the date and time of the incident by not preserving it. The case went to trial and Walters was able to show the fall caused a severe spine injury that required surgery and resulted in a lifelong disability. A jury awarded $1,689,456 in damages and $675,782.40 in attorney fees. Kroger appealed challenging the spoliation ruling.

JUDICIAL OPINION

BRANCH, Judge

A trial court's decision imposing sanctions for spoliation is reviewed for abuse of discretion. [*Wal-Mart Stores v Lee*, 290 Ga.App. 541, 546(1), 659 S.E.2d 905 (2008)] The evidence outlined above shows that the court's factual findings are supported by some evidence in the record.

CONTINUED

Kroger argues, however, that the court's order cannot be sustained because the facts fail to show it had notice at the time the video was erased that Walters was contemplating litigation, as is required in spoliation cases. But Walters deposed that he returned to the store "a week and a half, two weeks" after his fall and told Kelley about his upcoming doctor's appointment. Further, beginning on the day of the fall, Kelley began to prepare a report which states that it was made in anticipation of litigation. And some evidence supports the trial court's conclusion that during discovery Kroger submitted a false exemplar from camera 17, from which an inference could arise that Kroger knew the original video should not have been deleted.

The video might have established either actual or constructive knowledge by Kroger of a foreign substance on the floor. The exemplar video showed the general area but not the exact location of the fall, but that the subsequent deposition revealed that the camera was "centered on the exact location of Walters' fall and not the location shown in the prior images produced by Kroger and could have clearly shown the exact conditions at the time of Walters' fall and whether Kroger employees knew or should have known of the dangerous condition in that area." The court concluded that Kroger had spoliated the video evidence, which could have been maintained at minimal expense; that the spoliation prejudiced Walters; and that Kroger "acted in bad faith in failing to preserve the evidence and manipulating evidence to excuse its actions." The facts taken as a whole are sufficient to support the trial court's findings

In *Baxley*, the Supreme Court reversed the trial court and this court and found that evidence similar to that presented here was sufficient to raise an issue of spoliation. As the Supreme Court explained,

> There was proof of spoliation here, as [the defendant's] manager was aware of her customer's involvement in the accident at issue and took steps to investigate the day after it occurred, yet failed to preserve the recording of the pertinent events and allowed any potential videotaped evidence to be destroyed … the recording could have contained evidence relevant to the critical issue.

The high court concluded, "Thus, because [defendant's] manager was aware of the potential for litigation and failed to preserve whatever videotaped evidence may have been captured as to whether [the customer] would soon be driving, a rebuttable presumption arose against [the defendants]."

In sum, we find no abuse of discretion in the trial court's finding of spoliation. Reversed on other grounds.

CASE QUESTIONS

1. What does the court say the Kroger manager should have done and why?

2. What general rules would you develop for store managers based on this case?

3. What should plaintiffs who are injured learn from this case?

Consider...

The obstruction of justice trial against the accounting firm of Arthur Andersen found the prosecution using the following types of evidence:

- Testimony from partners, employees, and consultants with Andersen
- E-mails among Andersen partners, employees, and consultants; both saved and deleted e-mails were introduced into evidence
- A videotape of a partner making a presentation to employees on the pending SEC investigation in which he urged employees to get rid of excess files so that "nosy plaintiffs' lawyers" wouldn't be able to find damaging evidence
- The statistics on the e-mail deletions by Andersen employees, including the peak in e-mail deletions following the presentation that was shown on video and the instruction to get rid of unnecessary files
- The articles clipped and saved by Andersen employees relating to Enron and SEC investigations

What would the government need to show to establish that Andersen had engaged in spoliation through their e-mail deletions?

THINK: In the *Kroger* case, the court held that the video was destroyed knowing that a suit was likely.

APPLY: What is different in this Andersen situation? What is the same?

ANSWER: The evidence shows that the Andersen employees had been briefed on at least the investigations, a likely source of litigation. With the investigations pending, the destruction of e-mails and other documents at that time meets the test for spoliation.

ETHICAL ISSUES

Evaluate the ethics of the Andersen employees. Why do you think they followed orders to destroy the e-mails and other documents so willingly? Is "I was just following orders" a defense in criminal and civil cases? Is it a justification for conduct?

Limitations on Discovery

Discovery has the general limitation of relevance. Only things that are evidence or could lead to the discovery of evidence are discoverable. However, discovery also has a specific limitation. Discovery cannot require the production of **work product**, which consists of the attorney's legal research, comments or reactions to a witness, thoughts, analysis, and case or trial strategy. Discovery affords the parties the right to know all the evidence (if it asks for it), but it does not give them the right to know how that evidence will be used or what legal precedent supports a party's position.

Certain evidence in cases is not discoverable. Communications between lawyers and their clients is protected by a privilege and, except in certain limited circumstances, cannot be discovered or used by the opposition. (See Chapter 3 for a complete discussion of privilege.)

Cyber Law and Discovery

Businesses are required to preserve their business records. The so-called smartphones create problems because smartphones can be configured in different ways, sometimes with very limited archiving capability. In certain configurations, a message deleted can be lost forever. There are programs that permit hackers to download everything from a smartphone in about 30 seconds. There is a risk of everything from corporate espionage to the loss of privilege on documents that become public via hackers or theft.

CYBERLAW

Companies should develop policies on the use of smartphones by executives, policies that cover the following:

- Configuration of smartphones, access, and archiving. For example, the executive branch of the federal government has configured the smartphones of government officials so that the messages are archived (as required by law for government business) and then stored by a contractor who then manages and indexes the messages so that they are not lost.

- The requirement of a password for access to the phone

- No sharing your passwords with others

- If your smartphone is lost, notify the IT staff immediately so that they can take protective and preventive action

- Topics that should and should not be discussed on social media and smartphones

- Discussion of risks of social media and smartphone communication

- Deletion of messages on smartphones

4-5g RESOLUTION OF A LAWSUIT: THE TRIAL

If a case is not settled (and many are settled literally on the courthouse steps), the trial begins.

The Type of Trial—Jury or Nonjury

Occasionally, the parties agree not to have a jury trial and instead have a trial to the court. In these cases, the judge acts as both judge and jury—both running the trial and determining its outcome. In highly technical cases, it is sometimes better for both sides to have a knowledgeable judge involved than to try to explain the complexities of the case to a jury of laypersons.

If the parties do not agree on a nonjury trial, then certain types of cases carry a constitutional right to a trial by jury. The Seventh Amendment of the U.S. Constitution covers the jury requirement in civil trials:

In suits at common law, where the value in controversy shall exceed twenty dollars, the right of trial by jury shall be preserved, and no fact tried by a jury shall be otherwise re-examined in any court of the United States other than according to the rules of common law.

Although this right is limited to what existed at common law at the time the U.S. Constitution was adopted, many states have expanded the right under their state constitutions. The absolute right to a jury exists in criminal cases as covered in Article III and the Fifth and Sixth Amendments of the U.S. Constitution.

The size of a jury varies; some states require only six jurors. A jury may have 12 to 18 members, which include alternates, particularly in long trials, to ensure that a panel of 12 participates fully in the trial.

The Trial—Jury Selection

The pool of potential jurors and the selection of those jurors are resolved before trial. Usually, voting lists, alone or combined with other lists (e.g., rosters of licensed drivers), are used as pools for potential jurors. People on these lists are randomly notified of a period of time during which they should report for jury duty. Many states excuse from jury duty certain individuals, such as doctors and emergency workers, because of the needs they serve in society. Students are often excused if they are summoned for duty during the semester because of their peculiar obligations and time limitations on completing classes. Judges also usually have the power to excuse certain individuals who would experience hardship if they were required to serve. For example, a sole proprietor of a service business would have no income during the time of jury service and would probably be excused on a hardship basis.

Many more jurors than are actually needed are summoned to serve. These extra numbers are required because all the parties to a dispute participate in the selection of a jury. Once a pool is available, the court begins the process of *voir dire*, which determines whether a potential juror is qualified to serve. Most states have jurors complete a questionnaire on general topics so that the selection process can move quickly. The questionnaire covers personal information—age, occupation, and so on. The questionnaire might also ask whether the person has ever been a juror, a party to a lawsuit, or a witness.

A juror can be removed from a jury panel for two reasons. First, a juror can be removed for cause, which means the juror is incapable of making an impartial decision in the case. If a juror is related to one of the attorneys in the case, for example, the juror would be excused for cause. Some jurors reveal their biases or prejudices, such as racial prejudice, in the questionnaire they are required to complete. Others may express strong feelings of animosity toward the medical profession. Clearly, the removal of such jurors for cause in cases involving civil rights and malpractice suits, respectively, is an important part of trial strategy.

Sometimes a juror cannot be excused for cause but an attorney feels uncomfortable about the juror or the juror's attitudes. In these circumstances, the lawyer issues a **peremptory challenge**, which excuses the juror. The peremptory challenge is the attorney's private tool. However, the use of peremptory challenges is limited. All states have a statute or court rule limiting the number of peremptory challenges an attorney may use in a trial. The U.S. Supreme Court ruled that the use of peremptory challenges is subject to some limitations. The Court indicated that such a challenge cannot be based on either race or gender. If the trial judge suspects that either of these factors may have induced one of the lawyers to seek a peremptory challenge, the lawyer will be required to produce a plausible explanation for the use of the peremptory challenge that is unrelated to race or gender.

Consider...

Winona Ryder was arrested for shoplifting from Saks Fifth Avenue. The charges against her included theft and burglary for taking $5,600 in merchandise from Saks's Beverly Hills store.

The jury selection process in the trial uncovered the fact that Peter Guber, a Hollywood executive who was in charge of three films that starred Ms. Ryder (*Bram Stoker's Dracula, The Age of Innocence, Little Women*), was among the pool of jurors. When questioned by the judge, Mr. Guber assured him that he could be impartial in judging the evidence. Mr. Guber was allowed to remain on the jury.

What argument could the prosecution have made against keeping Mr. Guber? What argument could the defense have made against Mr. Guber? What process could each side have used to have him removed from the jury?

Source: Rick Lyman, "For the Ryder Trial, a Hollywood Script," *New York Times*, November 3, 2002, p. SL-1.

Jury selection is an art and a science. Jury consulting firms specialize in providing data to attorneys for jury selection. These firms do thorough checks of the potential jurors' backgrounds (including through their Facebook pages and even the types of bumper stickers on their cars) and offer statistics on the reactions of certain economic and social groups to trials and trial issues. Much about a case at trial is uncontrollable, but jury selection is a part of the process that, with thorough preparation, can increase the likelihood of desired results by ensuring an optimally favorable jury panel.

Jury or trial consultants perform jury profiles, find surrogate juries, and often conduct mock trials. The use of trial consultants has increased dramatically since the 1970s, and membership in the American Society of Trial Consultants has grown from 19 members in 1983 to 300 members today. Jury consultants were used to assist in defense victories in the Sean "Puffy" Combs shooting trial and the O. J. Simpson double homicide trial.[3]

The Trial Process

Opening Statements and Burden of Proof   It is often difficult to piece together all the witnesses and evidence in a trial. A lengthy trial may leave the jurors confused. The attorney for each party, therefore, is permitted to make an **opening statement** that summarizes what that party hopes to prove and how it will be proved. Most attorneys also mention the issue of **burden of proof**, which controls who has the

FOR THE MANAGER'S DESK

Re: Jury Selection in High-Profile Cases

Even though the criminal rape charges against him were eventually dismissed, NBA basketball star Kobe Bryant's trial still had progressed to the point of jury selection. As part of the *voir dire* questions for the potential Bryant jurors, the 276 jury panelists were asked the following as part of their 82-question background sheet:

- What are your feelings about the sexual assault laws in Colorado?

- Do you think that people who make a lot of money are treated better by our court system than other people?

- Have you ever been afraid of or had any negative experience with an African American individual?

- In your opinion, in general do African Americans in our society experience (check one): a great deal of racial discrimination; some amount of racial discrimination; or no racial discrimination?

- How do you feel about interracial relationships?

- Do you have particularly strong feelings about, or have you or anyone close to you ever been affected by or involved in, a situation of marital infidelity? [At the time of the alleged rape, Mr. Bryant was married and had one child.]

- Which of the following best describes your opinion of professional basketball players: very positive; positive; negative; very negative?

responsibility for proving what facts. Although the plaintiff has the burden of proving a case, the defendant has the burden of proving the existence of any valid defenses. Various standards are used for meeting the burden of proof. In criminal cases, the standard is proof beyond a reasonable doubt. In civil cases, the standard is proof by a preponderance of the evidence, or more likely than not.

Presentation of the Case and Evidence Because the plaintiff has the burden of proof, the plaintiff presents his or her case and evidence first. The attorney for the plaintiff decides the order of the witnesses; questioning of these witnesses under oath is called **direct examination**. Although the defense cannot present witnesses during this part of the trial, it can question the plaintiff's witnesses after their direct examination is completed. The defense questioning of plaintiff witnesses is called **cross-examination**, after which, the plaintiff may again pose questions to clarify under **redirect examination**.

By the end of the case, the plaintiff must show enough evidence to establish a **prima facie case**, one in which the plaintiff has offered some evidence on all the elements required to be established for recovery. Although the evidence may be subjected to credibility questions and challenged by defense evidence, some proof is required for each part of the claim. If the plaintiff does not meet this standard, the defendant can and may make a motion for a **directed verdict**. This motion for a directed verdict is made outside the jury's hearing and argued to the judge. If it is not granted, the trial proceeds with the defendant's case.

The defendant then has the same opportunity to present witnesses and evidence. Throughout the trial, the judge will apply the rules of evidence to determine what can and cannot be used as evidence. All trials have some form of witness testimony. However, tangible evidence is also often presented. In a contracts case, for example, a great deal of paper evidence—letters, memos, and cost figures—is likely.

One of the evidentiary issues that has been debated and litigated over the past few years is the use of expert testimony in cases. The issue the courts face is determining whether the expert's testimony reflects scientific knowledge or whether the testimony is contrived for the trial (often called "junk science"). In *Daubert v Merrell Dow Pharmaceuticals, Inc.*, 509 U.S. 579 (1993), the U.S. Supreme Court provided guidance for the standards judges should use in determining whether the studies and testimony of experts and their experiments and analysis should be allowed as evidence in a case. One expert, who was testifying in a suit against Merrell Dow (defendant) about birth defects allegedly caused by pregnant women's use of the anti-nausea drug Bendectin, filed an affidavit in the case stating that the use of Bendectin during the first trimester had not been shown to be a risk factor for birth defects. On the other hand, eight experts for the plaintiff parents in the case concluded, based on animal and epidemiological studies, that Bendectin can cause birth defects. The court ruled that the decision to admit the expert's evidence must be based on an examination of the study methodology as well as whether the expert's work had been subjected to peer review, the means that academics use for testing the validity of new studies and theories. The court noted that studies developed for purposes of the litigation require higher levels of scrutiny than studies that existed under the expert's work prior to the litigation. However, the expert's work does not require general acceptance and still will be subject to the scrutiny of the opposing parties' experts as well as the rigor of cross-examination.

Consider...

Karsten Manufacturing Corporation filed suit against the Professional Golf Association (PGA) because the PGA had proposed a ban of Karsten's U-groove Ping brand clubs from professional play. Karsten hired Richard Smith, then an Arizona State University finance professor, to develop an economic model to correlate professional and consumer usage. Professor Smith's model showed that if pros play with Ping clubs, a proportionate number of duffers will play with them. If the pros cannot use Ping clubs, Karsten is out of business because amateur golfers will not purchase Karsten products. Professor Smith said he conducted valid regression analysis. The attorney for the PGA, Larry Hammond, called it "junk science" that interferes with the real issues in the case. Should the Smith model be admitted? Does it make a difference that the model was developed only for the case? Does it make a difference that Professor Smith's consulting firm was paid more than $1 million for the model?

The forms and types of evidence that can be used at trial are subject to some restrictions. Most people are familiar with the hearsay rule of evidence. Hearsay is evidence offered by a witness who does not have personal knowledge of the information being given but just heard it from someone else. For example, suppose that Arkansas Sewing and Fit Fabric are involved in contract litigation. Fit Fabric says there was no contract. Arkansas Sewing has a witness who overheard the president of Fit Fabric talking to someone on a plane saying he had a contract with Arkansas Sewing but had no intention of performing on it. The witness's testimony of the airplane conversation is hearsay and cannot be used to prove the contract existed. The reason for the hearsay rule is to keep evidence as reliable as possible. The person testifying about the hearsay may not know of the circumstances or background of the conversation and is testifying only to what someone else said.

Closing Arguments and the Jury's Role. Once the evidence is presented and the parties are finished with their cases, the parties have one final "go" at the jury. The parties are permitted to make **closing arguments**, which review the presented evidence, highlight the important points for the jurors, and point out the defects in the other side's case. After the cases and closing arguments are presented, the jurors are given their **instructions**. These instructions tell the jurors what the law is and how to apply the law to the facts presented. The instructions are developed by the judge and all the attorneys in the case.

Jury deliberations are done privately; they cannot be recorded, and no one can attend the deliberations except the jurors. Jurors can, but are not required to, discuss what happened during the deliberations after they are ended and a decision is returned to the court.

The U.S. Supreme Court has ruled that jury verdicts need not be unanimous. A state can adopt a rule that requires only a simple majority or three-fourths of the jury to agree on a verdict. In those states requiring unanimous verdicts, it is not unusual for juries to be unable to agree on a verdict. The jurors have then reached a deadlock, which is called a **hung jury**. If a trial results in a hung jury, the case can be retried.

The result of jury deliberations is the **verdict**. The verdict is given to the judge and is usually read by the judge's clerk.

FOR THE MANAGER'S DESK

Re: The "Googling" Jurors

Defense lawyers are calling it the first "Google Mistrial." A federal judge in Florida had to declare a mistrial after a juror told that judge that he had been doing research on the Internet about the drug trial in which he was serving as a juror. The Internet surfing was a direct violation of the judge's instructions to the jurors to not read information about the case or discuss it with others. When the judge declared the mistrial, eight other jurors confessed that they had been doing the same thing. After the mistrial was declared, the jurors shared with the defense attorney in the case that he was on the verge of winning the case.

Google may be the least of the problems judges and lawyers are grappling with. A judge in Arkansas is reviewing a request for a $12.6 million jury verdict against a company from one of the company's lawyers based on the discovery that one of the jurors was using Twitter to send out postings on how the trial was proceeding. An excerpt from the posting appears here:

"oh, and nobody buy Stoam. Its bad mojo and they'll probably cease to Exist now that their wallet is $12m lighter.… So, Jonathan, what did you do today? Oh nothing really, I just gave away TWELVE MILLION DOLLARS of somebody else's money."[4]

Jurors are using smartphones to gather and send out information as they are serving on juries. Some jurors are using Facebook to announce when verdicts are coming.

Judges have been warning jurors for some time about not using the Internet to find additional information about a case. However, their universal access to the Internet through their phones has proved to be tempting. One juror even looked up evidence that had been excluded by the judge in the case. When asked why he violated the judge's order, the juror said simply, "Well, I was curious."

What is the problem with jurors using Google to investigate their cases?

Post-Trial Proceedings

Even after the verdict, the case is not over. The losing party can make several motions to get around the verdict. One such motion is for a new trial, wherein the attorney argues the need and reason for a new trial to the judge.

Another motion after the verdict, one that a judge is less likely to grant, is a motion for a **judgment NOV**. *NOV* stands for *non obstante veredicto*, which means "notwithstanding the verdict." In other words, the moving attorney is asking the trial judge to reverse the decision of the jury. The basis for granting a judgment NOV is that the jury's verdict is clearly against the weight of the evidence. Occasionally, juries are swayed by the emotion of a case and do not apply the law properly. It is, however, a strong show of judicial authority for a judge to issue a judgment NOV, and they are rare.

Even if no motions are granted, the case still may not be over; it can go to an appellate court for review. Such an appeal must be done within a specified time limit in each state. Here the trial has come full circle to the principle of judicial review and *stare decisis*. Exhibit 4.6 summarizes the steps in civil litigation.

4-6 Issues in International Litigation

As noted earlier, international courts have no enforcement powers. They serve as avenues for voluntary mediation. However, courts in each nation in which a firm is doing business would have jurisdiction over that firm in the nation's court system. In a recent infringement dispute over Mattel's "Barbie" and the French doll "Sindy," the parties litigated in London, where both firms were doing business and the dolls were selling well.

Among the critical questions that arise in international litigation are the following: Which set of laws applies? What court is the appropriate forum for a lawsuit that involves citizens of different countries? For example, many non–U.S. citizens who are injured in their own countries by products made by U.S. firms will generally be able to recover more under the product liability and tort laws of the United States. In *Piper Aircraft Co. v Reyno*, 454 U.S. 235 (1981), the pilot and five passengers were killed when a charter flight from Blackpool to Perth, Scotland, crashed in the Scottish highlands. The pilot and passengers were traveling in a twin-engine Piper Aztec, an aircraft manufactured in Pennsylvania by Piper Aircraft Co. The British Department of Trade conducted an investigation of the crash and determined that its cause was mechanical failure. The relatives and estates of the passengers brought suit in the United States against Piper Aircraft. Scottish law does not recognize strict tort liability (see Chapter 10), and U.S. laws on liability and damages are far more favorable than those of Scotland. The U.S. Supreme Court held that the case was properly heard in Scotland because the accident was in Scotland, and all the parties in the case were either English or Scottish.

A similar ruling was made with respect to the 2,500 victims of the Union Carbide gas leak in Bhopal, India. Some of the victims filed suit in the United States because the law and damages provisions here afforded them much greater relief. Their suit was dismissed to India, and the court added that Union Carbide would be required to submit to the jurisdiction of Indian courts and to follow discovery rules of the United States.

EXHIBIT 4.6 Steps in Civil Litigation

BIOGRAPHY The Lawyer's Lawyer Who Bribed a Judge

Class-action lawyer Dickie Scruggs played himself in the 1999 movie "The Insider," which starred Russell Crowe as Jeffrey Wigand, the tobacco industry whistle-blower who obtained a $206 billion settlement from the tobacco companies. Mr. Scruggs used Mr. Wigand as a key witness in his multistate litigation against the tobacco companies. His suits changed forever the way the tobacco companies did business and his fee for the case was $1 billion. Mr. Scruggs was the lawyer every lawyer wanted to be—one of his large verdicts served to help millions and changed the fabric of society. However, almost a decade after "The Insider" premiered, Scruggs would be the lawyer in every lawyer's nightmare. Mr. Scruggs entered a guilty plea to bribery and was sentenced to five years in prison for his role in an attempt to bribe a federal judge.

Mr. Scruggs had been representing insurance claimants against insurers for their damages from Hurricane Katrina. The judge presiding over the case contacted the FBI about a bribery attempt. One of the four lawyers working with Scruggs was approached by the FBI and agreed to wear a wire to catch Scruggs. The content of the tapes revealed the lawyers' clumsy attempts to buy a federal judge. Zachary Scruggs, Dickie's son, also entered a guilty plea. All of the remaining lawyers involved in the bribery scheme entered guilty pleas as well.

Those in the legal profession were baffled because Scruggs's extraordinary talent gave him what he needed to win any case. "He didn't need to cheat," was the comment of a representative from the American Trial Lawyers Association. Scruggs's words at his sentencing were poignant: "I could not be more ashamed to be where I am today, mixed up in a judicial bribery scheme.... I realized I was getting mixed up in it. And I will go to my grave wondering why. I have disappointed everyone in my life—my wife, my family, my son, particularly.... I deeply regret my conduct. It is a scar and a stain on my soul that will be there forever."

Source: Abha Bhattarai, "Class-Action Lawyer Given 5 Years in a Bribery Case," *New York Times,* June 28, 2008, B3.

© Fekete Tibor/Shutterstock.com

Summary

How can businesses resolve disputes?

- Alternative dispute resolution (ADR)—means of resolving disputes apart from court litigation

Types of ADR:

- Arbitration—hearing with relaxed rules of evidence
- Mediation—third party acts as go-between
- Conciliation—international term for mediation
- Medarb—combination of mediation and arbitration
- Minitrial—private judge and courtroom; shortened trial
- Rent-a-judge—disputes resolved by hired judge
- Summary jury trial—advisory verdict by jurors in a mock trial
- Early neutral evaluation—third-party evaluation before litigation proceeds
- International Chamber of Commerce (ICC)—voluntary international court that offers arbitration in international disputes

What strategies should businesses follow if litigation is inevitable?

- Evaluate cost, including the unknowns such as jury reaction
- Consider privacy and creative remedies

How do courts proceed with litigation?

- Complaint—plaintiff's statement of a case
- Summons—document to serve defendant with lawsuit
- Answers—defendant's response to complaint
- Statute of limitations—time limit for filing suit
- Discovery—advance disclosure of evidence in case
- Production—obtain and produce document
- Deposition—questioning of witnesses under oath
- Interrogatories—information questions to other party
- Admissions—acknowledgment of facts in a case

- Trial—court proceeding for hearing evidence
- *Voir dire*—jury selection method to screen for bias
- Opening statements—frame by parties' lawyers of the case
- Plaintiff's case—facts for proving complaint presented
- Defendant's case—defenses to allegations presented
- Evidence—testimony and documents presented in the case; no hearsay

Questions and Problems

1. While stocking merchandise, a Walmart employee accidentally knocked at least one and possibly more decorative reindeer from a high shelf onto Monroe Johnson's head and arm. Mr. Johnson's fiancée, now his wife, was with him and heard but did not see the accident. When she went to investigate, she found her fiancé dazed but still standing, with a cut on one arm and several reindeer lying at his feet. At the scene, Mr. Johnson told Phyllis McClane, a Walmart supervisor who had come to investigate, that he was not hurt. After a Walmart employee cleaned and bandaged his cut, Mr. Johnson and his fiancée left the store.

During her investigation, Ms. McClane took notes, photographed the reindeer, and obtained a written statement from the employee who caused the accident. She recorded the results of her investigation on a Walmart form entitled "Report of Customer Incident." She attached the photo and the employee's statement, sending copies to the district manager and claim management personnel. According to the incident report, Mr. Johnson neither threatened to sue nor indicated that Walmart should pay any medical costs or other damages. After completing the report, Ms. McClane discarded her notes.

That evening, Mr. Johnson's neck and arm began to hurt, and he could not sleep. The next day, his doctor prescribed muscle relaxers, pain killers, and physical therapy. Still in pain six months later, Mr. Johnson and his wife sued Walmart. While suit was pending, Mr. Johnson consulted three more physicians and tried additional treatments without success. About seventeen months after the accident, a surgeon performed an anterior cervical discectomy and fusion on Mr. Johnson's neck.

During discovery, the Johnsons asked whether Walmart still possessed the reindeer that fell on him. At trial, the parties offered sharply divergent evidence about the composition and weight of the reindeer in question. Mr. Johnson testified that they were made of wood, each weighing as much as ten pounds. Ron Wheeler, the store manager, countered that the reindeer were made of papier-mâché and weighed only

five to eight ounces each. Walmart argued that such flimsy reindeer could not have proximately caused Mr. Johnson's neck problems, which it claimed resulted from an automobile accident years earlier. Mr. Wheeler also testified that Walmart could not produce any of the reindeer because they had all been sold or, if broken, thrown away. Only the photograph of the reindeer was introduced in evidence, but its quality was too poor to substantiate or rebut either party's description.

Based on Walmart's failure to keep the reindeer, the judge gave the following jury instruction:

> You are instructed that, when a party has possession of a piece of evidence at a time he knows or should have known it will be evidence in a controversy, and thereafter he disposes of it, makes it unavailable, or fails to produce it, there is a presumption in law that the piece of evidence, had it been produced, would have been unfavorable to the party who did not produce it. If you find by a preponderance of the evidence that Wal-Mart had possession of the reindeer at a time it knew or should have known they would be evidence in this controversy, then there is a presumption that the reindeer, if produced, would be unfavorable to Wal-Mart.

The jury found for Mr. and Mrs. Johnson and awarded damages. Walmart appealed the jury instruction. Discuss whether the jury instruction was proper. [*Wal-Mart Stores, Inc. v Johnson*, 106 S.W.3d 718 (Tx. 2003)]

2. In the Johns-Manville asbestos litigation, Samuel Greenstone, an attorney for 11 asbestos workers, settled their claims for $30,000 and a promise that he would not "directly or indirectly participate in the bringing of new actions against the Corporation." The 1933 case settlement was documented in the minutes of Johns-Manville's board meeting. Could the information in the minutes be used in later litigation against Johns-Manville? How could a plaintiff's attorney obtain the information? Do you feel Mr. Greenstone made an ethical decision in his agreement? Wasn't his loyalty to his 11 clients and his obligation to obtain compensation for them? Would you have agreed to the no-further-participation-in-a-lawsuit clause? Would you, if you had been an executive at Johns-Manville, have supported the clause?

3. Suppose that your company had received a letter complaint about one of the prescription drugs that it sells. The customer and his physician have complained that there were cardiovascular effects from use of the drug over the past 12 months. You know about the complaint and you also have e-mails from one of your friends in the company, a research scientist who was in your fraternity in college, that indicate he sees some cardiovascular side effects from the same drug. If you deleted the e-mail, would it be spoliation?

What would be required to prove spoliation in this case?

4. After she was found guilty of obstruction of justice and conspiracy (see Chapter 8), lawyers for Martha Stewart filed a motion for a new trial on the grounds that a juror on the case had possible undisclosed bias. The defense lawyers pointed out that juror Chappel Hartridge had checked "No" on the juror questionnaire when asked whether he had been accused of, charged with, or convicted of a crime. The lawyers for Ms. Stewart filed an affidavit from a former girlfriend of Mr. Hartridge's who indicated that he had been arrested and arraigned on charges of assaulting her. Mr. Hartridge's former girlfriend ultimately dropped the charges against him. What bias do you think Ms. Stewart's lawyers alleged? Are they right? Should the juror have been eliminated for cause? [*U.S. v Stewart*, 317 F.Supp.2d 432 (S.D.N.Y.2004)]

5. A discrimination suit by a former flight attendant against Atlantic East Airlines is going to trial. Jury selection has begun. An executive from Atlantic East notices that a member of the potential juror panel was a flight attendant responsible for pregnancy leave reforms among airline flight attendants during the early 1980s. This potential juror is no longer a flight attendant and is raising two small children at home. The executive informs Atlantic East's lawyer. Can the lawyer do anything to prevent the woman from sitting on the jury?

6. Applegate is in litigation with Magnifium over a contract breach. Applegate has been approached by a former janitor for Magnifium who can testify regarding conversations about the contract between Magnifium

executives. The janitor heard them when the executives had stayed late at work and he was cleaning. Can Applegate use the statements at trial?

7. Robert Joiner began work as an electrician in the Water & Light Department of Thomasville, Georgia, in 1973. Mr. Joiner worked with and around electrical transformers that contained a fluid. In 1983, the city of Thomasville discovered that this fluid contained polychlorinated biphenyls (PCBs), a substance considered hazardous.

Mr. Joiner was diagnosed with lung cancer in 1991 and filed suit against General Electric, the manufacturer of the transformers, for negligence and product liability. Mr. Joiner had been a smoker, his parents were smokers, and his family had a history of lung cancer.

Mr. Joiner offered expert testimony on studies involving the injection of PCB into the stomachs of infant mice and resulting cancer. The experts had no epidemiological studies on PCB exposure. Should the expert testimony be admitted? [*General Electric Co. v Joiner*, 522 U.S. 136 (1997)]

8. In a case in which a widow was seeking to recover damages for the death of her husband in a train accident, the lawyer for the railroad sought to strike a juror who was a widow whose husband had died in a car accident. Discuss whether the juror could be struck from the panel for the case.

9. The SEC investigation of Tyco International for possible securities law violations produced several e-mails. The e-mails focused on two concerns about the company: accounting improprieties and the use of company funds by then-CEO Dennis Kozlowski. The e-mails were written by outside lawyers from the firm of Wilmer Cutler to former Tyco General Counsel Mark Belnick. The e-mails are as follows.

March 23, 2000: E-mail from a Wilmer Cutler Partner, Lewis Liman, to Mark Belnick

There are payments to a woman whom the folks in finance describe to be Dennis's girlfriend. I do not know Dennis's situation, but this is an embarrassing fact.

(Note: The payments were later verified as being made from the Key Employee Loan Account to Karen Mayo, who subsequently became Karen Kozlowski, who has now divorced the imprisoned Mr. Kozlowski.)

May 25, 2000: E-mail from a Wilmer Cutler Partner, William McLucas, to Mark Belnick

We have found issues that will likely interest the SEC; creativeness is employed in hitting the forecasts.

There is also a bad letter from the Sigma people just before the acquisition confirming that they were asked to hold product shipment just before closing....

(This e-mail also went on to suggest that there was, in regard to Tyco's financial reports, "something funny which is likely apparent if any decent accountant looks at this.")

Although Mr. McLucas and Mr. Liman could not comment because of attorney–client privilege, others indicate that they followed up on the e-mails and asked officials at Tyco to correct the concerns and problems raised in the e-mails.

Are the e-mails privileged? How did the SEC gain access to them? Can they be used as evidence? Are they discoverable? (Laurie P. Cohen and Mark Maremont, "E-Mails Show Tyco's Lawyers Had Concerns," *Wall Street Journal*, December 27, 2002, pp. C1, C5)

10. In October 1995, Saint Clair Adams applied for a job at Circuit City Stores, Inc., a now-defunct national retailer of consumer electronics. Mr. Adams signed an employment application that included the following provision.

I agree that I will settle any and all previously unasserted claims, disputes or controversies arising out of or relating to my application or candidacy for employment, employment and/or cessation of employment with Circuit City, exclusively by final and binding arbitration before a neutral Arbitrator. By way of example only, such claims include claims under federal, state, and local statutory or common law, such as the Age Discrimination in Employment Act, Title VII of the Civil Rights Act of 1964, as amended, including the amendments of the Civil Rights Act of 1991, the Americans with Disabilities Act, the law of contract and the law of tort.

Mr. Adams was hired as a sales counselor in Circuit City's store in Santa Rosa, California.

Two years later, Mr. Adams filed an employment discrimination lawsuit against Circuit City in state court, asserting claims under California's Fair Employment Act. Circuit City filed suit in the U.S. District Court seeking to stop the state court action and to compel arbitration under the FAA. Mr. Adams says the arbitration clause violates his statutory rights for protection against employment discrimination and that he has the right to go to court, not arbitration. Who is correct? Can Mr. Adams be required to submit to arbitration? [*Circuit City Stores, Inc. v Adams*, 532 U.S. 105 (2001)]

ECONOMICS, PUBLIC POLICY, THE LAW

Japan's Changing Legal System

Many businesspeople have argued that too many lawyers and lawsuits hurt the United States in the competitive international market. However, Japan is a country that has been moving toward the U.S. model for the role of lawyers in the judicial system even as it preserves some limitations on the standards for civil recovery and the types of recoveries available in those cases.

Lifting Limits on the Number of Lawyers

Prior to 2000, in order to become a *bengoshi* (lawyer) in Japan, an individual had to win a slot at the Legal Training and Research Institute. This government-run school accepted only 2 percent of the 35,000 annual applicants. As a result, only 400 new *bengoshi* were added each year to Japan's bar. However, in 2000, the government allowed the opening of private law schools that are operated in a manner similar to those in the United States. With more slots available for education, there are now 29,000 lawyers in Japan, a more-than-double increase from the 14,336 lawyers there in 1992. There is also increased competition among lawyers. Japan now permits lawyer advertising. Japanese law firms are also now permitted to merge with other firms to increase the services offered and compete effectively.

Limits on Recovery

Japanese courts allow recovery only for actual losses. There is no recovery for mental anguish. Class actions are rare in Japan and it is very difficult to get a court's approval to go forward with such a suit. The Toyota recall of so many cars in the sudden acceleration issues of 2010 resulted in great activity in Japanese courts for class actions and recovery.

Costs to Plaintiffs

Plaintiffs are required to pay money to their lawyers up front. The amount required is 8 percent of the recovery sought plus the nonrefundable filing fee.

Limits on Damage Awards

Judges, not juries, determine damages, and even in wrongful death cases, the damages may not include punitive damages.

Encouragement of Settlement and Cultural Disdain for Confrontation

In Japan, a cultural pride exists in being able to resolve disputes outside the courtroom; those who must litigate are looked down upon. However, the Japanese culture and judicial system are moving toward the use of litigation as a means of correcting company behaviors. One financial analyst concluded that litigation is good as he discussed the Toyota issues: "Toyota has been arrogant. It's good that lawsuits are taking place now so Toyota will go through soul-searching."

Discussion Questions

1. Should the United States move more toward some of the rules of the Japanese litigation system as Japan moves toward ours? Why or why not? Are there benefits to the openness of one and the limitedness of the other? What are they?

2. In the English court system, the loser pays court costs and the costs of the other party involved in the litigation. Should such a rule be adopted in the United States? For all cases? Would you be less willing to pursue a case for yourself or your company if you knew that you would be required to pay if you lost the case?

Sources: Michele Galen et al., "Guilty," *BusinessWeek*, April 13, 1992, pp. 60–66; *ABA Report on International Lawyers* (1990); Yuka Hayashi, "Japanese Culture Shifting on Suits," *Wall Street Journal*, February 23, 2010, p. A4.

Notes

1. Alan Dabdoub and Trey Cox, "Which Costs Less: Arbitraton or Litigation?" *Inside Counsel*, December 6, 2012, http://www.insidecounsel.com/2012/12/06/which-costs-less-arbitration-or-litigation. In fact, the study concludes arbitration is higher in costs as well as attorneys' fees.

2. Leigh Jones, "Gotcha Game," *National Law Journal*, February 4, 2011, p. A1.

3. Bob Van Voris, "Voir Dire Tip: Pick Former Juror," *National Law Journal*, November 1, 1999, pp. A1, A6.

4. John Schwartz, "As Jurors Turn to Google and Twitter, Mistrials Are Popping Up," *New York Times*, March 18, 2009, p. A1.

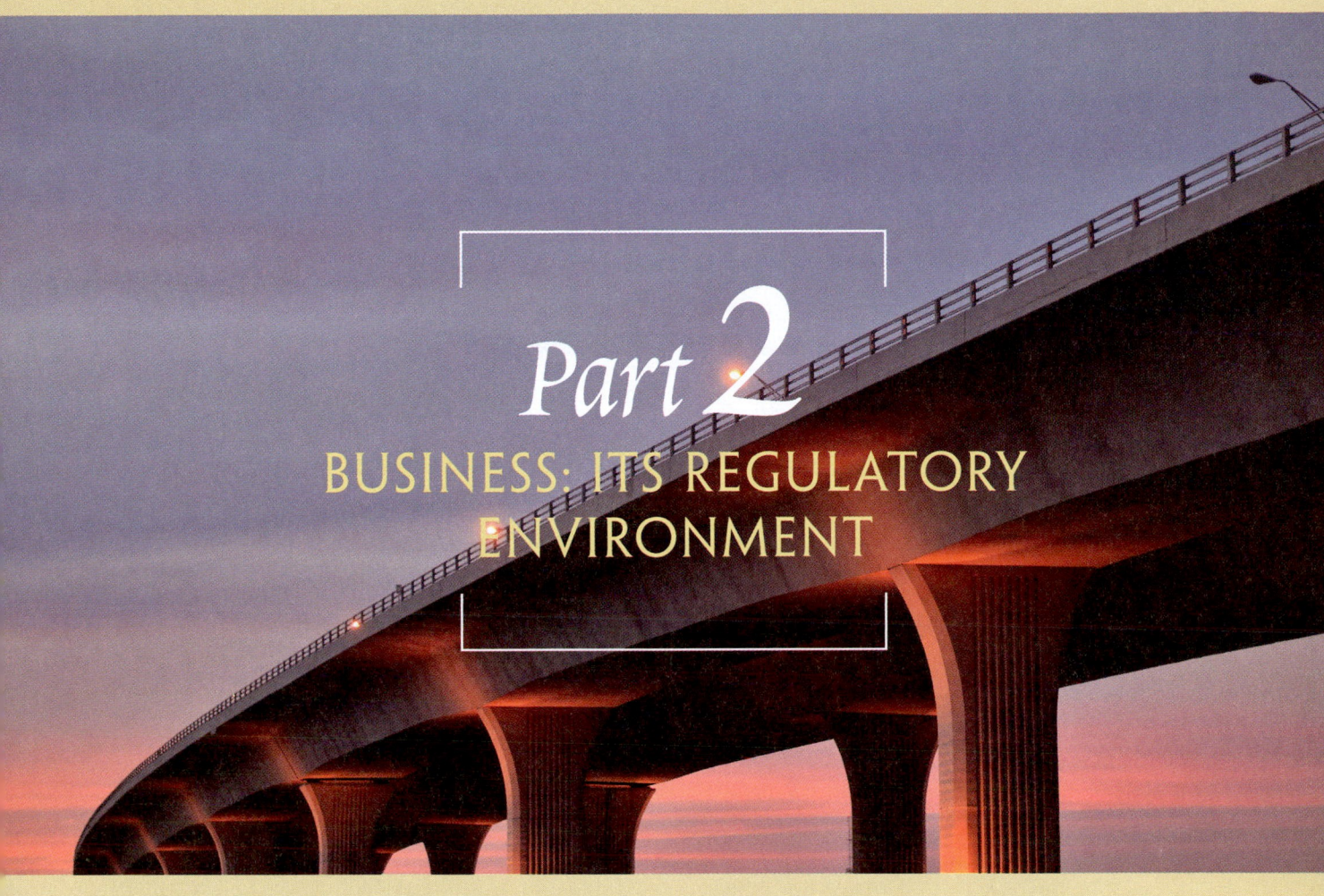

Part 2
BUSINESS: ITS REGULATORY ENVIRONMENT

A business is regulated by everything from the U.S. Constitution to the rules of the Consumer Product Safety Commission. Managers must know codified law, as well as the law that develops as cases are litigated and new issues of liability arise. The regulatory environment of business includes penalties for criminal conduct and punitive damages for knowingly causing injuries to customers. Part 2 describes the laws that regulate businesses and business operations, including cyber and environmental law, the sanctions that are imposed for violation of these laws, and the manner in which businesses can make compliance with the law a key part of their values.

Chapter 5

BUSINESS AND THE CONSTITUTION

The U.S. Constitution is a remarkable document. It was drafted by a group of independent states more than 200 years ago in an attempt to unify the states into one national government that could function smoothly and efficiently without depriving those independent states of their rights. The fact that it has survived so many years with so few changes indicates the flexibility and foresight built into the document.

This chapter covers the application of the U.S. Constitution to business and answers several questions: What are the constitutional limitations on business regulation? Who has more power to regulate business—the states or the federal government? What individual freedoms granted under the Constitution apply to businesses?

Consider...

Congress passed the Patient Protection and Affordable Care Act (also known as Obama Care) in order to increase the number of Americans covered by health insurance and decrease the cost of health care. One key provision in the law is the individual mandate, which requires most Americans to maintain "minimum essential" health insurance coverage. Attorneys general and businesses from several states challenged this requirement (and other provisions of the law) as being unconstitutional under the Commerce Clause. From a series of federal decisions from the courts below, some finding the law constitutional and others not, the affected parties appealed to the U.S. Supreme Court. What does the Commerce Clause have to do with this law? Is the law constitutional?

5-1 The U.S. Constitution

5-1a AN OVERVIEW OF THE U.S. CONSTITUTION

Although virtually all constitutional issues and all court decisions on those issues are complicated and detailed, the **U.S. Constitution** itself is a simple and short document. Contained within it is the entire structure of the federal government, its powers, the powers of the states, and the rights of all citizens. The exact language of the U.S. Constitution is presented in Appendix A.

5-1b ARTICLES I, II, AND III—THE FRAMEWORK FOR SEPARATION OF POWERS

The first three articles of the U.S. Constitution set up the three branches of the federal government. Article I establishes the **legislative branch**. The two houses of Congress—the House of Representatives and the Senate—are created, their method of electing members is specified, and their powers are listed.

Article II creates the executive branch of the federal government. The office of president, along with its qualifications, manner of election, term, and powers are specified.

Article III establishes the judicial branch of the federal government. This article creates only the U.S. Supreme Court and establishes its jurisdiction. Congress, however, is authorized to establish inferior courts, which it has done in the form of federal district courts, specialized federal courts, and U.S. courts of appeals (see Chapter 3, Exhibit 3.1).

The first three articles establish the nature of the federal government as involving the separation of powers. Each of the branches of government is given unique functions that the other branches cannot perform, but each branch also has curbing powers on the other branches through the exercise of its unique powers.

For example, the judicial branch cannot pass laws, but it can prevent a law passed by Congress from taking effect by judicially interpreting the law as unconstitutional. The executive branch does not pass legislation but has veto power over legislation passed by Congress. The executive branch has responsibility for foreign relations and treaty negotiation. However, those treaties do not take effect until the Senate ratifies them. This system of different powers that can be used to curb the other branches' exercise of power is called a system of checks and balances.

The drafters of the U.S. Constitution designed the federal government this way to avoid the accumulation of too much power in any one branch of government. In *Nixon v Administrator of General Services*, 433 U.S. 425 (1977), the Supreme Court held that former President Nixon was required to turn over to Congress any records and materials of the executive branch that were relevant to the congressional inquiry into the Watergate scandal (a break-in at the Democratic Party's national headquarters that was masterminded by members of the Nixon administration). In *Clinton v Jones*, 520 U.S. 681 (1997), the Supreme Court ruled that even the president is subject to the laws of the land and is accountable for civil wrongs alleged by private citizens. In the case, Paula Corbin Jones alleged that Mr. Clinton had sexually harassed her while he was governor of Arkansas. The Court ruled that the president cannot be above the law or judicial process when he has violated the rights of a citizen in his private conduct and wrote, "… even the sovereign is subject to God and the law."

5-1c OTHER ARTICLES

Article IV deals with states' interrelationships. Article V provides the procedures for constitutional amendments. Article VI is the **Supremacy Clause** (discussed later in this chapter), and Article VII simply provides the method for state ratification of the Constitution.

FOR THE MANAGER'S DESK

Re: The President, Justice Alito, Congress, and the Balance of Powers

During President Obama's State of the Union address on January 27, 2009, he made reference to *Citizens United v Federal Election Commission*, 558 U.S. 310 (2010) (see pp. 158–160). The decision dealt with the constitutionality of portions of the McCain–Feingold campaign and campaign contributions law. The president made the following statements about the decision:

With all due deference to separation of powers, last week the Supreme Court reversed a century of law that, I believe, will open the floodgates for special interests, including foreign corporations, to spend without limit in our elections. Well I don't think American elections should be bankrolled by America's most powerful interests, or worse, by foreign entities. They should be decided by the American people, and that's why I'm urging Democrats and Republicans to pass a bill that helps to right this wrong.

Following the statement, U.S. Supreme Court Justice Alito could be seen (as he was picked up by the cameras) shaking his head and mouthing what appears to be "not true" or "definitely not true."

What can be done with regard to the decision? Who was right on what the decision did—Mr. Obama or Justice Alito? (See p. 158.)

5-1d THE BILL OF RIGHTS

In addition to the seven articles, the U.S. Constitution has 27 amendments, the first 10 of which are the **Bill of Rights**. Although these rights originally applied only to federal procedures, the **Fourteenth Amendment** extended them to apply to the states as well. These amendments establish rights ranging from freedom of speech (First Amendment) to the right to a jury trial (Sixth Amendment) to protection of privacy from unlawful searches (Fourth Amendment) to due process before deprivation of property (Fifth Amendment). The amendments as they apply to businesses are covered later in this chapter and in Chapter 8.

5-2 The Role of Judicial Review and the Constitution

The Supreme Court and its decisions are often in the news because the cases decided by the Court are generally significant ones that provide interpretations of the U.S. Constitution and also define the extent of the rights we are afforded under it. The role of the U.S. Supreme Court is to decide what rights are provided by the general language of the U.S. Constitution. For example, the Fifth Amendment guarantees that we will not be deprived of our life, liberty, or property without "due process of law." Due process of law, interpreted by the courts many times now, includes such rights as the right to a hearing before a mortgage foreclosure, or at least the right of notice before property is sold after repossession as a result of nonpayment of the underlying debt.

The First Amendment protects the simple right to freedom of speech, but the Supreme Court has been faced with issues such as whether restrictions on membership in student clubs at state universities are an infringement of the First Amendment.[1] The Fourth Amendment, the "privacy amendment," protects us from warrantless searches. This general idea has been analyzed in the context of garbage taken from cans waiting for pickup on the street and unannounced inspections of company workplaces by OSHA regulators (see Chapter 20 for more information on OSHA—the Occupational Safety and Health Administration).

The U.S. Supreme Court has the responsibility of determining the extent and scope of the rights and protections afforded by the U.S. Constitution. In addition, the Supreme Court plays the unique role of reviewing the actions of the other branches of government. The Court is a crucial part of the checks-and-balances system set up in our Constitution. As noted in the "For the Manager's Desk" on p. 138, the court recently dealt with the issue of the constitutionality of legislation passed by Congress.

5-3 Constitutional Limitations of Economic Regulations

5-3a THE COMMERCE CLAUSE

The **Commerce Clause** is found in Article I, Section 8, Part 3 of the U.S. Constitution and provides Congress with the power "[t]o regulate Commerce with foreign Nations, and among the several States." Although the language is short and simple, the phrase "among the several states" has created much controversy. The clause limits Congress to the regulation of interstate commerce. The regulation of local and intrastate commerce is left to the states. Defining interstate commerce has been the task of the courts. The standards are defined from two perspectives: federal regulation of state and local commerce, and state and local regulation of interstate commerce.

Standards for Congressional Regulation of State and Local Business Activity

The issue, as defined by the U.S. Supreme Court, is whether the situation involves sufficient interstate contact or effects for the application of federal standards. The Constitution gives Congress authority to regulate interstate matters and vests all the remaining regulatory authority in the states.

The U.S. Supreme Court initially gave a very narrow interpretation to the scope of the Commerce Clause. In the beginning of the Court's interstate commerce jurisprudence, federal regulation applied to commercial activity if the commercial activity had a "direct and immediate effect" on interstate commerce. In 1918, the Court ruled that manufacturing was not "commerce" (because it was solely intrastate) and struck down an act of Congress that attempted to regulate goods manufactured in plants using child labor. [*Hammer v Dagenhart*, 247 U.S. 251 (1918)] During the 1930s, Congress and President Roosevelt bumped heads with the Court many times in their attempts to legislate a recovery from the Depression. The Court consistently refused to validate federal legislation dealing with manufacturing, operations, and labor. [*Schechter Poultry v United States*, 295 U.S. 495 (1935); *Carter v Carter Coal*, 298 U.S. 238 (1936)] Roosevelt refused to accept a judicial roadblock to his legislation and initiated his court-packing plan to increase the number of members of the court with Roosevelt appointees.

The Court responded in *NLRB v Laughlin Steel*, 336 U.S. 460 (1940), by ruling that intrastate activities, even though local in character, may still affect interstate commerce and thus be subject to federal regulation. The "affectation" doctrine expanded the authority of the federal government in regulating commerce. In the words of the Court, "If it is interstate commerce that feels the pinch, it does not matter how local the squeeze" (336 U.S. at 464). The Commerce Clause has had a critical role in the elimination of discrimination because the Court's liberal definition of what constitutes interstate commerce has permitted the application of federal civil rights laws to local economic activities. However, some recent refinements limit federal authority. For example, in *U.S. v Lopez*, 514 U.S. 564 (1995), the court held that the Gun-Free School Zones Act of 1990, 18 U.S.C. § 922(q)(1)(A), which made it a federal crime to knowingly possess a firearm in a school zone, exceeded Congress's authority under the Commerce Clause because Congress was not regulating any form of commerce through the law but imposing criminal sanctions on a local activity. Because there was no commerce or economic activity involved, federal authority to regulate was limited by the Commerce Clause. Congress has the authority to regulate in those areas where what they are regulating substantially affects interstate commerce. Likewise, in *U.S. v Morrison*, 529 U.S. 598 (2000), the Court struck down the federal Violence Against Women Act because the law, which provided for a federal cause of action for women who had been assaulted, did not deal with any underlying economic activity and the Court held that allowing Congress to regulate the right to file suit for criminal activity would allow Congress to use the Commerce Clause to completely obliterate the Constitution's distinction between national and local authority.

National Federation of Independent Business v Sebelius (Case 5.1) is a landmark case that also limits the scope of federal power under the Commerce Clause, but expanded other federal powers, including that of taxation (see discussion of taxation powers on p. 145).

CASE 5.1

National Federation of Independent Business v Sebelius
132 S.Ct. 2566 (2012)

Mandating Health Insurance under the Commerce Clause

FACTS

Congress passed the Patient Protection and Affordable Care Act (also known as Obama Care) in order to increase the number of Americans covered by health insurance and decrease the cost of health care. One key provision in the law is the individual mandate, which requires most Americans to maintain "minimum essential" health insurance coverage. Attorneys general from several states, along with businesses, challenged this requirement (and other provisions of the law) as being unconstitutional under the Commerce Clause. From a series of federal court decisions below, some finding the law constitutional and others not, the affected parties appealed and the Supreme Court granted *certiorari*. Their cases were consolidated for the court's review.

JUDICIAL OPINION

ROBERTS, Chief Justice

The Constitution grants Congress the power to "*regulate* Commerce." (Art. I, § 8, cl. 3.) The power to *regulate* commerce presupposes the existence of commercial activity to be regulated. If the power to "regulate" something included the power to create it, many of the provisions in the Constitution would be superfluous. For example, the Constitution gives Congress the power to "coin Money," in addition to the power to "regulate the Value thereof." And it gives Congress the power to "raise and support Armies" and to "provide and maintain a Navy," in addition to the power to "make Rules for the Government and Regulation of the land and naval Forces." If the power to regulate the armed forces or the value of money included the power to bring the subject of the regulation into existence, the specific grant of such powers would have been unnecessary. The language of the Constitution reflects the natural understanding that the power to regulate assumes there is already something to be regulated.

Our precedent also reflects this understanding. As expansive as our cases construing the scope of the commerce power have been, they all have one thing in common: They uniformly describe the power as reaching "activity." It is nearly impossible to avoid the word when quoting them.

The individual mandate, however, does not regulate existing commercial activity. It instead compels individuals to *become* active in commerce by purchasing a product, on the ground that their failure to do so affects interstate commerce. Construing the Commerce Clause to permit Congress to regulate individuals precisely *because* they are doing nothing would open a new and potentially vast domain to congressional authority. Every day individuals do not do an infinite number of things. In some cases they decide not to do something; in others they simply fail to do it. Allowing Congress to justify federal regulation by pointing to the effect of inaction on commerce would bring countless decisions an individual could *potentially* make within the scope of federal regulation, and—under the Government's theory—empower Congress to make those decisions for him.

Indeed, the Government's logic would justify a mandatory purchase to solve almost any problem. To consider a different example in the health care market, many Americans do not eat a balanced diet. That group makes up a larger percentage of the total population than those without health insurance. The failure of that group to eat a healthy diet increases health care costs more than the failure of the uninsured to purchase insurance. Those increased costs are borne in part by failure of that group to have a healthy diet increases health care costs, to a greater extent than other Americans who must pay more, just as the uninsured shift costs to the insured. Congress addressed the insurance problem by ordering everyone to buy insurance. Under the Government's theory, Congress could address the diet problem by ordering everyone to buy vegetables.

People, for reasons of their own, often fail to do things that would be good for them or good for society. Those failures—joined with the similar failures of others—can readily have a substantial effect on interstate commerce. Under the Government's logic, that authorizes Congress to use its commerce power to compel citizens to act as the Government would have them act.

That is not the country the Framers of our Constitution envisioned. James Madison explained that the Commerce Clause was "an addition which few oppose and from which no apprehensions are entertained." The Federalist No. 45, at 293. While Congress's authority under the Commerce Clause has of course expanded with the growth of the national economy, our cases have "always recognized that the power to

CONTINUED

regulate commerce, though broad indeed, has limits." The Government's theory would erode those limits, permitting Congress to reach beyond the natural extent of its authority, "everywhere extending the sphere of its activity and drawing all power into its impetuous vortex." The Federalist No. 48, at 309 (J. Madison). Congress already enjoys vast power to regulate much of what we do. Accepting the Government's theory would give Congress the same license to regulate what we do not do, fundamentally changing the relation between the citizen and the Federal Government.

[There were other issues covered in the 106-page opinion. The complicated decision resulted in the lower court decisions being both affirmed and reversed, but the individual mandate was declared unconstitutional under the Commerce Clause.]

CASE QUESTIONS

1. What was missing that the Court indicated was needed in order to find that the mandate was constitutional?

2. What was the purpose of the court's discussion of a healthy diet?

3. What sources does the court rely on for constitutional interpretation?

Consider...

Ollie's Barbecue is a family-owned restaurant in Birmingham, Alabama, specializing in barbecued meats and homemade pies, with a seating capacity of 220 customers. It is located on a state highway 11 blocks from an interstate highway and a somewhat greater distance from railroad and bus stations. The restaurant caters to a family and white-collar trade, with a takeout service for "Negroes." (*Note:* The court uses this term in the opinion on the case.)

In the 12 months preceding the passage of the Civil Rights Act, the restaurant purchased locally approximately $150,000 worth of food, $69,683 or 46 percent of which was meat that it bought from a local supplier who had procured it from outside the state.

Ollie's has refused to serve Negroes in its dining accommodations since its original opening in 1927, and since July 2, 1964, it has been operating in violation of the Civil Rights Act. A lower court concluded that if it were required to serve Negroes, it would lose a substantial amount of business.

The lower court found that the Civil Rights Act did not apply because Ollie's was not involved in "interstate commerce." Will the Commerce Clause permit application of the Civil Rights Act to Ollie's?

THINK: What did the *Morrison* case require for the Commerce Clause to allow Congressional action on intrastate activities? If Congress was to have the authority to regulate seemingly intrastate activities, there had to be some underlying economic activity and, whatever that economic activity was, it had to have some relation to or an impact on interstate activity.

APPLY: What is different about Ollie's Barbecue's activities and the activities cited in support of the federal legislation on violence against women?

Ollie's Barbecue is a commercial enterprise involved in producing and selling food. This is economic activity, and *Morrison* found that the underlying activity being regulated must be economic in nature before the findings of interstate economic activity can be made.

Ollie's has an impact on interstate commerce because it orders goods in interstate commerce, and it serves travelers who are moving from state to state. The impact may be smaller than that outlined in Congress for VAWA, but it is all pure economic activity.

ANSWER: Congress had the authority under the Commerce Clause to pass the Civil Rights Act and have it apply to intrastate businesses such as Ollie's Barbecue.

[*Katzenbach v McClung*, 379 U.S. 294 (1964)]

Standards for State Regulation of Interstate Commerce

The Commerce Clause also deals with issues beyond those of federal power. The interpretation of the clause involves how much commerce the states can regulate without interfering in the congressional domain of interstate commerce. In answering this question, the courts are concerned with two factors: (1) whether federal regulation supersedes state involvement, and (2) whether the benefits achieved by the regulation outweigh the burden on interstate commerce. These two factors are meant to prevent states from passing laws that would give local industries and businesses an unfair advantage over interstate businesses. In some circumstances, however, the states can regulate interstate commerce. Those circumstances occur when the state is properly exercising its **police power**.

What Is the Police Power? The police power is the states' power to pass laws that promote the public welfare and protect public health and safety. Regulation of these primary concerns is within each state's domain. It is, however, inevitable that some of the laws dealing with public welfare and health and safety will burden interstate commerce. Many of the statutes that have been challenged constitutionally have regulated highway use. For example, some cases have tested a state's power to regulate the length of trucks on state highways. [*Raymond Motor Transportation v Rice*, 434 U.S. 429 (1978)] In *Bibb v Navajo Freight Lines, Inc.*, 359 U.S. 520 (1959), the Supreme Court analyzed an Illinois statute requiring all trucks using Illinois roads to be equipped with contour mudguards. These mudguards were supposed to reduce the amount of mud splattering the windshields of other drivers and preventing them from seeing. Both cases revolved around the public safety purpose of the statutes.

The Balancing Test. A statute is not entitled to constitutional protection just because it deals with public health, safety, or welfare. Although the courts try to protect the police power, that protection is not automatic. The police power is upheld only so long as the benefit achieved by the statute does not outweigh the burden imposed on interstate commerce. Each case is decided on its own facts. States present evidence of the safety benefits involved, and the interstate commerce interests present evidence of the costs to and effects on interstate commerce. The question courts must answer in these constitutional cases is whether the state interest in public health, welfare, or safety outweighs the federal interest in preventing interstate commerce from being unduly burdened. In performing this balancing test, the courts of course examine the safety, welfare, and health issues. However, the courts also examine other factors, such as whether the regulation or law provides an unfair advantage to intrastate or local businesses. For example, a prohibition on importing citrus fruits into Florida would give in-state growers an undue advantage.

Courts also examine the degree of the effect on interstate commerce. State statutes limiting the length of commercial vehicles would require commercial truck lines to buy different trucks for certain routes, or in some cases to stop at a state's border to remove one of the double trailers being pulled. Such stops can have a substantial effect on interstate travel. On the other hand, a state law that requires travelers to stop at the border for a fruit and plant check is not as burdensome: Only a stop is required, and the traveler would not be required to make any further adjustments. Also, the state's health interest is great; most fruit and plant checks are done to keep harmful insects from entering the state and destroying its crops. In the *Bibb* case, the courts found that the evidence of increased safety was not persuasive enough to outweigh the burden on interstate commerce.

Another question courts answer in their analysis is whether the state could accomplish its health, welfare, or safety goal in any other way with less of a burden on interstate commerce. Suppose a state has a health concern about having milk properly processed. One way to cover the concern is to require all milk to be processed in state. Such a regulation clearly favors that state's businesses and imposes a great burden on out-of-state milk producers. The same result, however, could be produced by requiring all milk sellers to be licensed. The licensing procedure would allow the state to check the milk-processing procedures of all firms and accomplish the goal without imposing such a burden on out-of-state firms. In *Granholm v Heald* (Case 5.2), the court dealt with states' regulation of imported wines versus its differing regulation of their domestic wine producers.

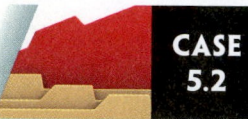

CASE 5.2   *Granholm v Heald*
544 U.S. 460 (2005)

Whining About Wine

FACTS

The regulations and statutes in both New York and Michigan prohibit out-of-state wine producers from selling their wines directly to consumers there. In-state wineries can sell directly to consumers. Out-of-state wine producers are required to pay wholesaler fees and cannot compete with in-state wine producers on direct-to-consumer sales. The direct-to-consumer sales avenue, especially through the Internet, has been a means for small wineries to compete.

Several out-of-state wine producers as well as consumers in both Michigan and New York filed suit in their federal districts challenging these laws that prohibit direct shipment. The Sixth Circuit Court of Appeals held that the out-of-state restrictions violated the Commerce Clause. The state of Michigan appealed. In the New York case, the Second Circuit Court of Appeals upheld the New York statute as constitutional. Michigan and the wine producers from the New York case appealed.

JUDICIAL OPINION

KENNEDY, Justice

Under Michigan law, wine producers, as a general matter, must distribute their wine through wholesalers. There is, however, an exception for Michigan's approximately 40 in-state wineries, which are eligible for "wine maker" licenses that allow direct shipment to in-state consumers.

New York's licensing scheme is somewhat different. As in Michigan, the result is to allow local wineries to make direct sales to consumers in New York on terms not available to out-of-state wineries. Wineries that produce wine only from New York grapes can apply for a license that allows direct shipment to in-state consumers. These licensees are authorized to deliver the wines of other wineries as well, but only if the wine is made from grapes "at least seventy-five percent the volume of which were grown in New York state." An out-of-state winery may ship directly to New York consumers only if it becomes a licensed New York winery, which requires the establishment of "a branch factory, office or storeroom within the state of New York."

We consolidated these cases and granted *certiorari* on the following question: "Does a State's regulatory scheme that permits in-state wineries directly to ship alcohol to consumers but restricts the ability of out-of-state wineries to do so violate the ... Commerce Clause ... ?"

State laws violate the Commerce Clause if they mandate "differential treatment of in-state and out-of-state economic interests that benefits the former and burdens the latter." This rule is essential to the foundations of the Union. The mere fact of nonresidence should not foreclose a producer in one State from access to markets in other States. States may not enact laws that burden out-of-state producers or shippers simply to give a competitive advantage to in-state businesses. This mandate "reflect[s] a central concern of the Framers that was an immediate reason for calling the Constitutional Convention: the conviction that in order to succeed, the new Union would have to avoid the tendencies toward economic Balkanization that had

CONTINUED

plagued relations among the Colonies and later among the States under the Articles of Confederation."

Laws of the type at issue in the instant cases contradict these principles. They deprive citizens of their right to have access to the markets of other States on equal terms. The perceived necessity for reciprocal sale privileges risks generating the trade rivalries and animosities, the alliances and exclusivity, that the Constitution and, in particular, the Commerce Clause were designed to avoid. The current patchwork of laws—with some States banning direct shipments altogether, others doing so only for out-of-state wines, and still others requiring reciprocity—is essentially the product of an ongoing, low-level trade war. Allowing States to discriminate against out-of-state wine "invite[s] a multiplication of preferential trade areas destructive of the very purpose of the Commerce Clause."

The discriminatory character of the Michigan system is obvious. The differential treatment requires all out-of-state wine, but not all in-state wine, to pass through an in-state wholesaler and retailer before reaching consumers. These two extra layers of overhead increase the cost of out-of-state wines to Michigan consumers. The cost differential, and in some cases the inability to secure a wholesaler for small shipments, can effectively bar small wineries from the Michigan market.

The New York regulatory scheme differs from Michigan's in that it does not ban direct shipments altogether. Out-of-state wineries are instead required to establish a distribution operation in New York in order to gain the privilege of direct shipment. This, though, is just an indirect way of subjecting out-of-state wineries, but not local ones, to the three-tier system.

It comes as no surprise that not a single out-of-state winery has availed itself of New York's direct-shipping privilege. We have no difficulty concluding that New York, like Michigan, discriminates against interstate commerce through its direct-shipping laws.

Affirmed as to judgment of the Sixth Circuit Court of Appeals; reversed and remanded as to judgment of the Second Circuit Court of Appeals.

Note: Strong dissent in the case indicated that because of the Twenty-First Amendment the federal government (and the court) could not be involved in state liquor regulation.

CASE QUESTIONS

1. What do the Michigan and New York statutes require?

2. Why did the U.S. Supreme Court grant *certiorari* in the cases? Why do you think the court heard and decided the two cases together?

3. What is the economic impact of the statutes on wineries, both in- and out-of-state? On wholesalers? On consumers?

Congressional Regulation of Foreign Commerce

The Commerce Clause also grants Congress the power to regulate foreign commerce. The case of *Gibbons v Ogden*, 9 Wheat. 1 (1824) defined foreign commerce as any "commercial intercourse between the United States and foreign nations." This power to regulate applies regardless of where the activity originates and where it ends. For example, many international trade transactions begin and end in the city of New York. Although the paperwork and delivery of the goods may be solely within one state (here within one city), the foreign commerce power is not restricted by intrastate standards. If the transaction involves foreign commerce, congressional regulation applies (such as customs controls and fees) regardless of the place of transaction.

5-3b CONSTITUTIONAL STANDARDS FOR TAXATION OF BUSINESS

Article I, Section 8, Paragraph 1 of the Constitution gives Congress its powers of taxation: "The Congress shall have Power To lay and collect Taxes, Duties, Imposts and Excises… ." In addition, the Sixteenth Amendment to the Constitution gives this power: "The Congress shall have power to lay and collect taxes on incomes, from whatever source derived, without apportionment among the several States, and without regard to any census or enumeration."

The U.S. Supreme Court has consistently upheld the authority of Congress, and local governments as well, to impose taxes. However, one area in taxation

Business Planning Tip

Know state taxation laws before you decide where to locate a plant, office, or warehouse. For example, Nevada does not have an inventory tax, so many manufacturers have large warehouse facilities there, including Spiegel and Levi Strauss. Other states have no sales tax but have high property tax rates. Still other states have high sales tax and low income tax rates. Structuring a nationwide business requires an understanding of intrastate as well as interstate taxes.

still results in considerable litigation. This area involves state and local taxation of interstate commerce. Interstate businesses are not generally exempt from state and local taxes just because they are interstate businesses. However, the taxes imposed on these businesses must meet certain standards.

First, the tax cannot discriminate against interstate commerce. A tax on milk could not be higher for milk that is shipped in from out of state than for milk produced within the state.

Second, the tax cannot unduly burden interstate commerce. For example, a tax on interstate transportation companies that is based on the weight of their trucks as measured upon entering and leaving the states would be a burdensome tax.

Third, some connection—"a sufficient **nexus**"—between the state and the business being taxed must be established. The business must have some activity in the state, such as offices, sales representatives, catalog purchasers, or distribution systems.

Finally, the tax must be apportioned fairly. Apportionment prevents having businesses taxed in all 50 states for their property. Apportionment also avoids the unjust result of having businesses pay state income tax on all their income in all 50 states. Their income and property taxes must be apportioned according to the amount of business revenues in each state and the amount of property located in that state. General Motors does not pay an inventory tax to all 50 states on all of its inventory, but it does pay an inventory tax on the inventory it holds in each state. Perhaps the most significant decision on state taxation is the U.S. Supreme Court case on catalog sales, *Quill Corporation v North Dakota*, summarized in Case 5.3.

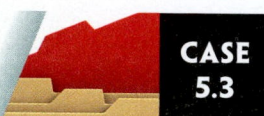

CASE 5.3   *Quill Corporation v North Dakota*
504 U.S. 298 (1992)

Is North Dakota a Taxing State?

FACTS

Quill is a Delaware corporation with offices and warehouses in Illinois, California, and Georgia. None of its employees works or lives in North Dakota, and it owns no property in North Dakota.

Quill sells office equipment and supplies; it solicits business through catalogs and flyers, advertisements in national periodicals, and telephone calls. Its annual national sales exceed $200 million, of which almost $1 million are made to about 3,000 customers in North Dakota. The sixth largest vendor of office supplies in the state, it delivers all of its merchandise to its North Dakota customers by mail or common carriers from out-of-state locations.

As a corollary to its sales tax, North Dakota imposes a use tax upon property purchased for storage, use, or consumption within the state. North Dakota requires

every "retailer maintaining a place of business in" the state to collect the tax from the consumer and remit it to the state. In 1987, North Dakota amended its statutory definition of the term "retailer" to include "every person who engages in regular or systematic solicitation of a consumer market in th[e] state." State regulations in turn define "regular or systematic solicitation" to mean three or more advertisements within a 12-month period. Thus, since 1987, mail-order companies that engage in such solicitation have been subject to the tax even if they maintain no property or personnel in North Dakota.

Quill has taken the position that North Dakota does not have the power to compel it to collect a use tax from its North Dakota customers. Consequently, the state, through its tax commissioner, filed an action to require Quill to pay taxes (as well as interest and penalties)

CONTINUED

on all such sales made after July 1, 1987. The trial court ruled in Quill's favor on a motion for summary judgment. The North Dakota Supreme Court reversed, and Quill appealed.

JUDICIAL OPINION

STEVENS, Justice

This case, like *National Bellas Hess, Inc. v Department of Revenue of Ill.*, 386 U.S. 753, 87 S.Ct. 1389, 18 L.Ed.2d 505 (1967), involves a State's attempt to require an out-of-state mail-order house that has neither outlets nor sales representatives in the State to collect and pay a use tax on goods purchased for use within the State. In *Bellas Hess* we held that a similar Illinois statute violated the Due Process Clause of the Fourteenth Amendment and created an unconstitutional burden on interstate commerce. In particular, we ruled that a "seller whose only connection with customers in the State is by common carrier or the United States mail" lacked the requisite minimum contacts with the State.

In this case the Supreme Court of North Dakota declined to follow *Bellas Hess* because "the tremendous social, economic, commercial, and legal innovations" of the past quarter-century have rendered its holding "obsole[te]."

The Due Process Clause "requires some definite link, some minimum connection, between a state and the person, property or transaction it seeks to tax," and that the "income attributed to the State for tax purposes must be rationally related to 'values connected with the taxing State.'" Prior to *Bellas Hess*, we had held that that requirement was satisfied in a variety of circumstances involving use taxes. For example, the presence of sales personnel in the State, or the maintenance of local retail stores in the State, justified the exercise of that power because the seller's local activities were "plainly accorded the protection and services of the taxing State." We expressly declined to obliterate the "sharp distinction … between mail order sellers with retail outlets, solicitors, or property within a State, and those who do no more than communicate with customers in the State by mail or common carrier as a part of a general interstate business."

Our due process jurisprudence has evolved substantially in the 25 years since *Bellas Hess*, particularly in the area of judicial jurisdiction. Building on the seminal case of *International Shoe Co. v Washington*, 326 U.S. 310, 66 S.Ct. 154, 90 L.Ed. 95 (1945), we have framed the relevant inquiry as whether a defendant had minimum contacts with the jurisdiction "such that the maintenance of the suit does not offend 'traditional notions of fair play and substantial justice.'"

Applying these principles, we have held that if a foreign corporation purposefully avails itself of the benefits of an economic market in the forum State, it may subject itself to the State's *in personam* jurisdiction even if it has no physical presence in the State.

Comparable reasoning justifies the imposition of the collection duty on a mail-order house that is engaged in continuous and widespread solicitation of business within a State. In "modern commercial life" it matters little that such solicitation is accomplished by a deluge of catalogs rather than a phalanx of drummers: the requirements of due process are met irrespective of a corporation's lack of physical presence in the taxing State. Thus, to the extent that our decisions have indicated that the Due Process Clause requires physical presence in a State for the imposition of duty to collect a use tax, we overrule those holdings as superseded by developments in the law of due process.

In this case, there is no question that Quill has purposefully directed its activities at North Dakota residents. We therefore agree with the North Dakota Supreme Court's conclusion that the Due Process Clause does not bar enforcement of that State's use tax against Quill.

Our interpretation of the "negative" or "dormant" Commerce Clause has evolved substantially over the years, particularly as that Clause concerns limitations on state taxation powers. Contrary to the suggestion of the North Dakota Supreme Court, this does not mean that *Bellas Hess* [is] "obsolete."

[w]e will sustain a tax against a Commerce Clause challenge so long as the "tax [1] is applied to an activity with a substantial nexus with the taxing State, [2] is fairly apportioned, [3] does not discriminate against interstate commerce, and [4] is fairly related to the services provided by the State." A vendor whose only contacts with the taxing State are by mail or common carrier lacks the "substantial nexus" required by the Commerce Clause.

The nexus requirements of the Due Process and Commerce Clauses are not identical. The two standards are animated by different constitutional concerns and policies.

Due process centrally concerns the fundamental fairness of governmental activity. Thus, at the most general level, the due process nexus analysis requires that we ask whether an individual's connections with a State are substantial enough to legitimate the State's exercise of power over him. We have, therefore, often identified "notice" or "fair warning" as the analytic touchstone of due process nexus analysis. In contrast, the Commerce Clause and its nexus requirement are informed not so much by concerns about fairness for the

CONTINUED

individual defendant as by structural concerns about the effects of state regulation on the national economy. That Clause prohibits discrimination against interstate commerce, and bars state regulations that unduly burden interstate.

The first and fourth prongs, which require a substantial nexus and a relationship between the tax and state-provided services, limit the reach of state taxing authority so as to ensure that state taxation does not unduly burden interstate commerce. Accordingly, contrary to the State's suggestion, a corporation may have the "minimum contacts" with a taxing State as required by the Due Process Clause, and yet lack the "substantial nexus" with that State as required by the Commerce Clause.

[a]lthough our Commerce Clause jurisprudence now favors more flexible balancing analyses, we have never intimated a desire to reject all established "bright-line" tests.

The bright-line rule of *Bellas Hess* furthers the ends of the dormant Commerce Clause. Undue burdens on interstate commerce may be avoided not only by a case-by-case evaluation of the actual burdens imposed by particular regulations or taxes, but also, in some situations, by the demarcation of a discrete realm of commercial activity that is free from interstate taxation. *Bellas Hess* followed the latter approach and created a safe harbor for vendors "whose only connection with customers in the [taxing] State is by common carrier or the United States mail." Under *Bellas Hess*, such vendors are free from state-imposed duties to collect sales and use taxes.

Like other bright-line tests, the *Bellas Hess* rule appears artificial at its edges: Whether or not a State may compel a vendor to collect a sales or use tax may turn on the presence in the taxing State of a small sales force, plant, or office. This artificiality, however, is more than offset by the benefits of a clear rule. Such a rule firmly establishes the boundaries of legitimate state authority to impose a duty to collect sales and use taxes and reduces litigation concerning those taxes.

Moreover, a bright-line rule in the area of sales and use taxes also encourages settled expectations and, in doing so, fosters investment by businesses and individuals. Indeed, it is not unlikely that the mail-order industry's dramatic growth over the last quarter century is due in part to the bright-line exemption from state taxation created in *Bellas Hess*.

Accordingly, Congress is now free to decide whether, when, and to what extent the States may burden interstate mail-order concerns with a duty to collect use taxes.

Reversed and remanded.

CASE QUESTIONS

1. Did Quill Corporation own any property in North Dakota? Were any Quill offices or personnel located in North Dakota?

2. What is the Commerce Clause issue in the case? Where does the "bright-line rule" fit into the decision?

3. What is the standard now for states collecting taxes from out-of-state companies?

4. What is the requirement for a presence in a state for collecting taxes?

Consider...

Amazon.com closed its Irvine, Texas center because of a dispute with the Texas state comptroller over $269 million that the controller says Amazon owes to the state in sales taxes for goods shipped to Texas residents. Despite state budget deficits, the revenue pot from online purchases remained largely untapped due to questions about the ability of states to tax companies based on the question of those companies' "presence" in a state. The National Conference of State Legislatures found that the amount of uncollected taxes on online and catalog sales totals $8.6 billion. Collecting those taxes by states all depends on the meaning of "physical presence" in each state. When Texas state controller Susan Combs concluded that the physical presence of a warehouse is enough of a physical presence to require Amazon.com to pay taxes on sales to Texas residents she unleashed reform in this area. (See "Business Strategy" on p. 149.)

BUSINESS STRATEGY — Amazon's Internet Sales Tax Strategy

Amazon.com has been very careful about state sales tax issues. The company has even controlled how often employees can travel to certain states so that it does not reach the level of a physical presence for purposes of being subject to sales tax in those states. However, Amazon, along with other Internet retailers, reached an agreement with the states for a type of uniform sales tax application that simplified what had become a complicated sales tax structure during the height of catalog sales. By 2013, Amazon was supporting federal legislation, known as the Marketplace Fairness Act, that would require all online retailers with over one million dollars in annual revenue to pay state and local taxes on transactions completed on the Internet by any customers located within those taxing jurisdictions. The costs of computing those taxes and handling audits by sales tax authorities would give Amazon less competition because smaller businesses could not maintain the staff or expertise to handle these complexities.

Amazon also established a division within its organization that would provide contract services to smaller businesses to help them in collecting their sales taxes on Internet sales. Amazon's approach to the confusing constitutional standards was to solve the problem with its own legislative proposals and to find a business niche to operate in helping others to solve the problems of tax collection for Internet sales. Amazon worked strategically with government and emphasized its business strengths to find a solution to a complex and uncertain legal issue.

5-4 State versus Federal Regulation of Business—Constitutional Conflicts: Preemption and the Supremacy Clause

Although the Constitution has sections that deal with the authority of the federal government and some that deal with state and local governments, some crossovers between state and federal laws still occur. For example, both state and federal governments regulate the sale of securities and both have laws on the sale of real property. Such crossovers create conflicts and a constitutional issue of who has the power to regulate. These conflicts between state and federal laws are governed by Article VI of the Constitution, sometimes called the **Supremacy Clause**, which provides: "This Constitution, and the Laws of the United States which shall be made in Pursuance thereof; and all Treaties made, or which shall be made, under the Authority of the United States, shall be the supreme Law of the Land… ."

The Supremacy Clause provides that when state and local laws conflict with federal statutes, regulations, executive orders, or treaties, the federal statute, regulation, executive order, or treaty controls the state or local law. However, in a variety of cases, a state law does not directly conflict with the federal law. Sometimes, the federal government just has extensive regulations in a particular area. In those areas of extensive federal regulation, the issue of which laws control can be resolved in Congress, which specifies its intent in an act. For example, Congress has provided that many federal workplace safety laws can be circumvented by state law as long as the state law provides as much employee protection as the federal laws. In other words, Congress allows the states to regulate the field in some instances and sets the standards for doing so. Most statutes, however, do not include the congressional intent on **preemption**. Whether a field has been preempted is a question of fact, of interpretation, and of legislative history. The question of preemption is determined on a case-by-case basis using the following questions:

1. What does the legislative history indicate? Some hearings offer clear statements of the effect and scope of a federal law.

2. How detailed is the federal regulation of the area? The more regulation there is, the more likely a court is to find preemption. Volume itself indicates congressional intent.

3. What benefits exist from having federal regulation of the area? Some matters are more easily regulated by one central government. Airlines fly across state lines, and if each state had different standards there would be no guarantee of uniform standards. The regulation of aircraft and their routes is clearly better handled by the federal government.

4. How much does a state law conflict with federal law? Is there any way that the two laws can coexist?

Mutual Pharmaceutical Co., Inc. v Bartlett (Case 5.4) deals with a preemption issue.

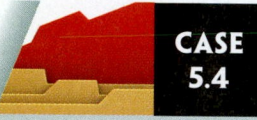

CASE 5.4   *Mutual Pharmaceutical Co., Inc. v. Bartlett*
133 S.Ct. 2466 (2013)

An Anti-Inflammatory Drug and an Inflammatory Decision

FACTS

In 1978, the FDA approved an anti-inflammatory pain reliver called "sulindac" under the brand name of "Clinoril." When the patent expired, the FDA approved several generic versions of sunlindac for sale, including one developed by Mutual Pharmaceutical (Petitioner). The warnings for Clinoril included the possibility of developing toxic epidermal necorlysis. Karen Bartlett (respondent) took a generic form of sulindac in December 2004 and developed an acute case of toxic epidermal necrolysis. Sixty to sixty-five percent of Ms. Bartlett's body deteriorated, was burned off, or turned into an open wound. She spent months in a medically induced coma, underwent 12 eye surgeries, and was tube-fed for a year. She is now severely disfigured, has a number of physical disabilities, and is nearly blind.

At the time Ms. Bartlett got her sulindac prescription, the label did not refer to toxic epidermal necrolysis, but warned that the drug could cause "severe skin reactions" and "fatalities." Toxic epidermal necrolysis was listed as a side effect in the package insert. After Ms. Bartlett was suffering from toxic epidermal necrolysis, the FDA did a comprehensive study and recommended that the product label include more explicit warnings about toxic epidermal necrolysis.

Ms. Bartlett t sued Mutual in New Hampshire state court, and Mutual removed the case to federal court. Ms. Bartlett initially asserted both failure-to-warn and design-defect claims, but the District Court dismissed her failure-to-warn claim based on her doctor's "admi[ssion] that he had not read the box label or insert." After a 2–week trial on a design-defect claim, a jury found Mutual liable and awarded Ms. Bartlett over $21 million in damages. The Court of Appeals affirmed, and Mutual appealed. The U.S. Supreme Court granted *certiorari*.

JUDICIAL OPINION

ALITO, Justice

We must decide whether federal law pre-empts the New Hampshire design-defect claim.

The Supreme Clause provides that the laws and treaties of the United States "shall be the supreme Law of the Land ... any Thing in the Constitution or Laws of any State to the Contrary notwithstanding." "[U]nder the Supremacy Clause, from which our pre-emption doctrine is derived, any state law, however clearly within a State's acknowledged power, which interferes with or is contrary to federal law, must yield."

Federal law prevents generic drug manufacturers from changing their labels. When federal law forbids an

CONTINUED

action that state law requires, the state law is "without effect." Because it is impossible for Mutual and other similarly situated manufacturers to comply with both state and federal law, New Hampshire's warning-based design-defect cause of action is pre-empted with respect to FDA-approved drugs sold in interstate commerce.

The Court of Appeals reasoned that Mutual could escape the impossibility of complying with both its federal- and state-law duties by "choos[ing] not to make [sulindac] at all." We reject this "stop-selling" rationale as incompatible with our pre-emption jurisprudence. Our pre-emption cases presume that an actor seeking to satisfy both his federal- and state-law obligations is not required to cease acting altogether in order to avoid liability. Indeed, if the option of ceasing to act defeated a claim of impossibility, impossibility pre-emption would be "all but meaningless."

The dreadful injuries from which products liabilities cases arise often engender passionate responses. But sympathy for respondent does not relieve us of the responsibility of following the law.

The dissent accuses us of incorrectly assuming "that federal law gives pharmaceutical companies a right to sell a federally approved drug free from common-law liability." But we make no such assumption. Rather, we hold that state-law design-defect claims like New Hampshire's that place a duty on manufacturers to render a drug safer by either altering its composition or altering its labeling are in conflict with federal laws that prohibit manufacturers from unilaterally altering drug composition or labeling. The dissent is quite correct that federal law establishes no safe-harbor for drug companies—but it does prevent them from taking certain remedial measures. Where state law imposes a duty to take such remedial measures, it "actual[ly] conflict[s] with federal law" by making it "'impossible for a private party to comply with both state and federal requirements.'"

Finally, the dissent laments that we have ignored "Congress' explicit efforts to preserve state common-law liability." We have not. Suffice to say, the Court would welcome Congress' "explicit" resolution of the difficult pre-emption questions that arise in the prescription drug context. That issue has repeatedly vexed the Court—and produced widely divergent views—in recent years.

As the dissent concedes, however, the [federal law's] treatment of prescription drugs includes neither an express pre-emption clause nor an express non-pre-emption clause. In the absence of that sort of "explicit" expression of congressional intent, we are left to divine Congress' will from the duties the statute imposes. That federal law forbids Mutual to take actions required of it by state tort law evinces an intent to pre-empt.

Congress [has made the] decision to regulate the manufacture and sale of generic drugs in a way that reduces their cost to patients but leaves generic drug manufacturers incapable of modifying either the drugs' compositions or their warnings. Respondent's situation is tragic and evokes deep sympathy, but a straightforward application of pre-emption law requires that the judgment below be reversed.

CASE QUESTIONS

1. Explain why the extra labeling could not be placed on the generic version of the drug that Ms. Bartlett purchased.

2. Discuss the relationship between state product liability laws and the duty of manufacturers and federal regulation of generic labels.

3. How does the court address the issue of the tragedy of the case?

Consider...

Diana Levine, a folk singer from Vermont, suffered from migraine headaches. She was being administered Wyeth Laboratory's Phenergan through an IV drip. Either because the IV needle entered Levine's artery or the drug escaped from the vein into her surrounding tissue, Ms. Levine developed gangrene. Doctors amputated her right hand and eventually her forearm. Levine could no longer work as a professional musician. Levine filed suit against both the clinic that administered the drug and Wyeth. She was awarded $7.4 million and Wyeth appealed on the grounds that the Food and Drug Administration approval of the drug preempted state tort suits by patients.

[*Wyeth v Levine*, 555 U.S. 555 (2009)]

ETHICAL ISSUES

Evaluate the ethics of a generic drug manufacturers using the same label instead of asking for updates when they are aware of risks and harms from usage of the drug.

5-5 Application of the Bill of Rights to Business

Certain of the amendments to the U.S. Constitution have particular significance for business, especially the First Amendment on freedom of speech and the Fourteenth Amendment for its issues of substantive and procedural due process and equal protection. The Fourth, Fifth, and Sixth Amendments on criminal procedures also have significance for business; those issues are covered in Chapter 8.

5-5a COMMERCIAL SPEECH AND THE FIRST AMENDMENT

The area of First Amendment rights and freedom of speech is complicated and full of significant cases. The discussion here is limited to First Amendment rights as they apply to businesses. The speech of business is referred to as **commercial speech**, which is communication used to further the economic interests of the speaker. Advertising is clearly a form of commercial speech.

5-5b FIRST AMENDMENT PROTECTION FOR ADVERTISING

Until the early 1970s, the U.S. Supreme Court held that commercial speech was different from the traditional speech afforded protection under the First Amendment. The result was that government regulation of commercial speech was virtually unlimited. The Court's position was refined in the 1970s, however, to a view that commercial speech was entitled to First Amendment protection but not on the same level as noncommercial speech. Commercial speech was not an absolute freedom; rather, the benefits of commercial speech were to be weighed against the benefits achieved by government regulation of that speech. Several factors are examined in performing this balancing test.

1. Is a substantial government interest furthered by restricting the commercial speech?
2. Does the restriction directly accomplish the government interest?
3. Is there any other way to accomplish the government interest? Can it be accomplished without regulating commercial speech? Are the restrictions no more extensive than necessary to serve that interest?

These standards clearly provide authority for regulation of fraudulent advertising and advertising that violates the law. For example, if credit terms are advertised, Regulation Z requires full disclosure of all terms (see Chapter 12 for more details). This regulation is acceptable under the standards just listed. Further, restrictions on where and when advertisements are made are permissible. For example, cigarette ads are not permitted on television, and such a restriction is valid.

Exhibit 5.1 illustrates the degrees of protection afforded business speech. The overlapping area represents those cases in which the need to disseminate information conflicts with regulations on ad content or form.

EXHIBIT 5.1 Commercial Speech: First Amendment Protections and Restrictions

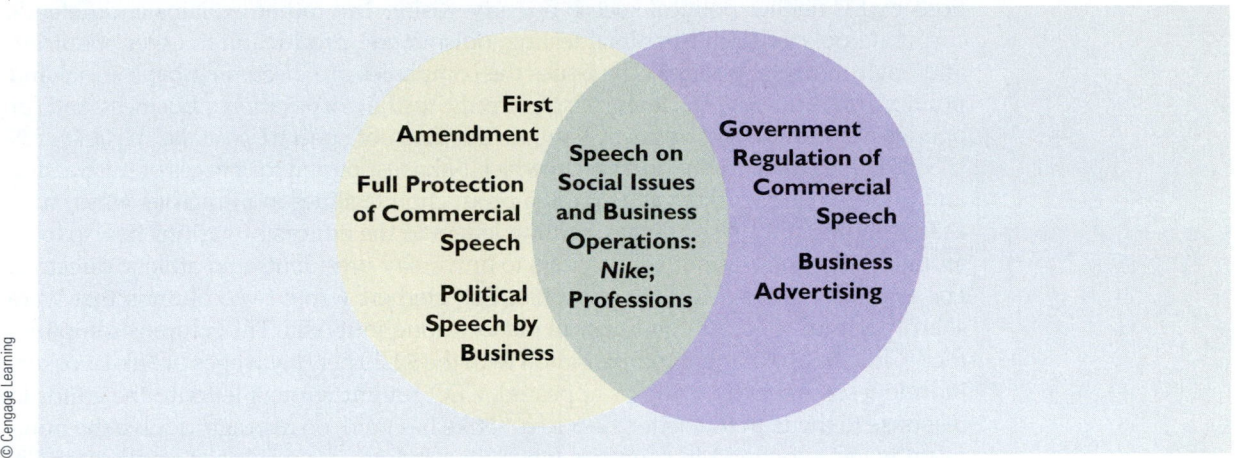

© Cengage Learning

The overlapping area of the diagram shows that during the 1970s cases were introduced that reformed the commercial speech doctrine by limiting restrictions on professional advertising. In *Virginia State Board of Pharmacy v Virginia Citizens Consumer Council, Inc.*, 425 U.S. 748 (1976), the Supreme Court dealt with the issue of the validity of a Virginia statute that made it a matter of "unprofessional conduct" for a pharmacist to advertise the price or any discount of prescription drugs. In holding the statute unconstitutional, the Court emphasized the need for the dissemination of information to the public. In a subsequent case, the Court applied the same reasoning to advertising by lawyers. [*Bates v State Bar of Arizona*, 433 U.S. 350 (1977)]

Consider...

The award-winning film *Zero Dark Thirty* came under federal investigation when then-acting director of the Central Intelligence Agency, Michael Morell, was asked by the Senate Intelligence Committee to provide the Committee with "all information and documents" that the agency had provided to filmmakers, as well as the records that reflected meetings and discussions between employees of the agency and the filmmakers. The reason for the request was the Committee's statement that it found the movie to be "grossly inaccurate." The alleged inaccuracies centered on whether information obtained through torture (waterboarding) was key in the killing of Osama bin Laden. The Senate Intelligence Committee maintains that "such information was not used in tracking down and killing bin Laden and believes that the film allows viewers to draw that conclusion from the way the story is presented."

The film's director, Kathryn Bigelow, told TV host Steven Colbert that she canceled an appearance on his show because she was "spooked" by the investigation. Christopher Dodd, a former U.S. Senator who is now the president of the Motion Picture Association of America, has objected to the investigation, saying "There could, in my view, be a chilling effect if, in the end of all this, you have a screenwriter or a director called before an investigating committee."

What type of speech is a film? Is it protected under the First Amendment? What could happen if the government were free to investigate those who express differing views and takes on issues, whether through statements or through art and films?

Sources: Alan Ziebel, "'Zero Dark Thirty' Writer Slams Probe," *Wall Street Journal*, January 28, 2013, p. B4; Michael Cieply, "Hollywood Makes Case for 'Zero Dark Thirty,'" *New York Times*, January 19, 2013.

An evolving area that is part of the overlapping portion of the two circles is that of corporate speech in defense of corporate decisions and policies—speech by corporations that is neither political speech nor advertising, but rather explains and defends corporate policies such as animal testing, outsourcing production to other countries, and environmental policies. The issues the companies are discussing have social and political implications, but they relate directly to the corporation's business and/or operations. Can the government regulate this form of speech? *Nike, Inc. v Kasky*, 539 U.S. 654 (2003) involved a situation in which Nike responded to charges of mistreating and underpaying workers at its foreign production facilities in numerous ways, such as by sending out press releases, writing letters to the editors of various newspapers around the country, and mailing letters to university presidents and athletic directors. For example, *New York Times* columnist Bob Herbert wrote two columns that were sharply critical of Nike's conditions in plants throughout Asia. The columns compared then-CEO Philip Knight's compensation with the $2.20 per day wages of Nike workers in Indonesia. After the columns appeared, CEO Knight wrote a letter to the editor in response to them. In that letter, he wrote, "Nike has paid, on average, double the minimum wage as defined in countries where its products are produced under contract. History shows that the best way out of poverty for such countries is through exports of light manufactured goods that provide the base for more skilled production."

Marc Kasky sued Nike for unfair and deceptive practices under California's Unfair Competition Law and False Advertising Law for alleged false statements in those materials and op-eds.

Nike contended that Mr. Kasky's suit was absolutely barred by the First Amendment. The trial court dismissed the case. Mr. Kasky appealed, and the California Court of Appeal affirmed, holding that Nike's statements "form[ed] part of a public dialogue on a matter of public concern within the core area of expression protected by the First Amendment."

On appeal, the California Supreme Court reversed and remanded for further proceedings. Nike appealed. The Supreme Court granted *certiorari* but later dismissed the case with a ***per curiam*** opinion (an unsigned opinion that comes from the majority of the court) that indicated only that *certiorari* was granted improvidently. The court said it would need to have the California authorities issue a decision and penalties in the case before it could be heard. Nike settled the case, so there was never a definitive decision. However, it is likely that the Court would have classified Nike's efforts as fitting into the territory between advertising and political speech, an area that would enjoy great First Amendment protection.

5-5c FIRST AMENDMENT RIGHTS AND PROFITS FROM SENSATIONALISM

In the past few years, a number of book publishers and movie producers have pursued criminal figures for the rights to tell the stories of their crimes in books, television programs, and movies. Many of the victims of the crimes and their families have opposed such moneymaking ventures as benefits that encourage the commission of crimes. The state of New York, for example, passed a statute requiring that earnings from sales of such stories be used first to compensate victims of the crimes. Statutes such as the one in New York create dilemmas between First Amendment rights and public policy issues concerning criminal activities. In *Simon & Schuster, Inc. v Members of the New York State Crime Victims Board*, 502 U.S. 105 (1991), the U.S. Supreme Court addressed the constitutionality of New York's statute. Simon & Schuster had entered into a contract in 1981 with organized crime figure Henry Hill (who was arrested in 1980) and author Nicholas Pileggi for a book about Mr. Hill's

ETHICAL ISSUES

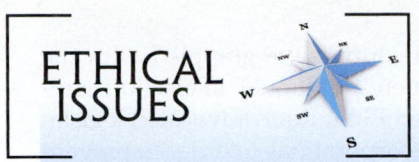

Orenthal James (O. J.) Simpson was charged with murder in June 1994 in the double homicide of his ex-wife, Nicole Brown Simpson, and her friend Ronald Goldman.

Because Mr. Simpson was charged with a capital crime, he was incarcerated upon being charged. California's version of the Son of Sam law prevents profits from crimes only after there has been a conviction. Mr. Simpson authored a book, *I Want to Tell You*, while he was incarcerated and his nine-month trial in progress. Mr. Simpson also signed autographs and sports memorabilia and sold them from the Los Angeles County jail. Mr. Simpson's cottage industry from jail netted him in excess of $3 million. Could a law that passes constitutional muster be implemented to prevent crime-related profits like those Mr. Simpson was able to obtain?

Mr. Simpson was acquitted of the murders. Following his acquittal, prosecutors in the case, Christopher Darden, Marcia Clark, and Hank Goldberg, signed multi-million-dollar book contracts to write about their experiences during the trial. Alan Dershowitz, the late Johnnie Cochran, and Robert Shapiro, members of the Simpson defense team, signed six-figure contracts to write books about the trial from the defense perspective. Daniel Petrocelli, the lawyer who represented the Goldmans in their civil suit against Mr. Simpson, also wrote a book, *Triumph of Justice: The Final Judgment on the Simpson Saga*.

In 2007, a book by Mr. Simpson, *If I Did It*, was released by the Goldman family. The Goldmans had acquired the rights to the Simpson book because of their $33 million judgment against Mr. Simpson following the civil case for wrongful death. They were assigned the rights to the book's royalties as a means of collecting the judgment. Upon its release, the book soared to number 1 on Amazon.com even as Mr. Simpson was arrested in Las Vegas for his alleged role in a robbery of sports paraphernalia.

Is it moral to profit from a crime and a trial? Are these book contracts a form of making money from the deaths of two people? Many publishers refused to publish *If I Did It*, and networks refused to air interviews with Mr. Simpson about the book. Would you have declined the book for publication? Or to air an interview that would have brought in ad revenues?

life, *Wiseguy*, a book full of colorful details and the day-to-day workings of organized crime, primarily in Mr. Hill's first-person narrative. Throughout *Wiseguy*, Mr. Hill frankly admits to having participated in an astonishing variety of crimes.

The book was also a commercial success: Within 19 months of its publication, more than 1 million copies were in print. A few years later, the book was converted into a film called *Goodfellas*, which won a host of awards as the best film of 1990.

When the Crime Victims Board requested that Simon & Schuster turn over all monies paid to Mr. Hill and that all future royalties be payable not to Mr. Hill but to the statutorily prescribed escrow account, Simon & Schuster brought suit maintaining that the so-called "Son of Sam law" violated the First Amendment. The U.S. Supreme Court agreed and held that the statute was overly broad, would have a chilling effect on authors and publications, and required a redrafting of the statute to tailor its scope more narrowly so it could still accomplish the public purpose.

5-5d FIRST AMENDMENT RIGHTS AND CORPORATE POLITICAL SPEECH

Not all commercial speech is advertising. Some businesses engage in **corporate political speech**. Corporate political speech generally takes three forms:

1. Through financial support such as from employee and political action committee (PAC) donations to political candidates
2. Through financial support such as party donations
3. Through direct communications and ads about issues, ballot propositions, and funding proposals (such as bond elections)

For more than a century, both legislators and courts have grappled with the balancing of First Amendment rights and the influence of money in election campaigns. "More than a century ago the 'sober-minded Elihu Root' advocated legislation that would prohibit political contributions by corporations in order to prevent 'the great aggregations of wealth from using their corporate funds, directly or indirectly,' to elect legislators who would 'vote for their protection and the advancement of their interests as against those of the public.'" [*United States v Automobile Workers*, 352 U.S. 567, 571 (1957)]

As a result, Congress, state legislatures, and the U.S. Supreme Court have all addressed corporate speech in all three of these categories. The first legislative prohibition came in 1907 when the Tillman Act completely banned corporate contributions of "money … in connection with" any federal election. Since that time corporations have been banned from making direct political donations to political candidates. In 1925, Congress extended the prohibition of contributions "to include 'anything of value,' and made acceptance of a corporate contribution as well as the giving of such a contribution a crime" (Federal Corrupt Practices Act, 1925, §§ 301, 313, 43 Stat. 1070, 1074). With corporate donations in tow, Congress realized through several election cycles that union contributions were equally plentiful and as powerful as corporate ones. Congress first restricted union contributions in 1940 with the passage of the Hatch Act. Congress later prohibited "union contributions in connection with federal elections … altogether" (18 U.S.C. § 610). During the passage of these limitations, PACs began. PACs are independent of corporations and labor unions, although they may be formed by those affiliated with both. For example, Coors Brewing has its corporate PAC, known as the Six Pac. Employees of companies and members of labor unions make donations to their PACs. Other PACs include trade association PACs (such as the American Medical Association and the American Association of Trial Lawyers), cooperative PACs, and PACs formed along ideological lines, such as the Right-to-Life PAC or Emily's List (Early Money Is Like Yeast, a PAC that supports pro-choice candidates beginning in the early primary stages of an election cycle).

As the Supreme Court has noted in its opinions on the topic of donations, "Money is like water and it always finds an outlet," and the donations and PAC activity became a concern. As a result, in 1972 and 1974, Congress passed and amended the Federal Election Campaign Act (FECA), which limited individual donations, required reporting and public disclosure of contributions and expenditures exceeding certain limits, and established the Federal Election Commission (FEC) to administer and enforce the legislation (2 U.S.C. § 431(8)(A)(i)).

The limitations in FECA were challenged and the U.S. Supreme Court ruled on their constitutionality in *Buckley v Valeo*, 424 U.S. 1 (1976). The court struck down the expenditure limitations of the federal law but upheld the $1,000 donation limitation as being sufficiently narrowly tailored to address the corruption concerns without infringing on the speech elements of donation. Individuals remained free to spend as much as they wanted on their own campaigns for federal office. FECA does not apply to state and local elections.

In *First National Bank of Boston v Bellotti*, 435 U.S. 765 (1978), the U.S. Supreme Court developed what has become known as the *Bellotti* doctrine, which gives corporations the same degree of First Amendment protection for their political speech that individuals enjoy in their political speech. Although commercial speech can be regulated, political speech enjoys full First Amendment rights. That is, when a corporation takes a position on a proposed ballot initiative, its right to participate in public discussion of that issue cannot be restricted.

BUSINESS STRATEGY — Where the Money Flows

A look at the following list of top corporate and trade PACs (hard dollars, not including soft dollars) indicates that those businesses whose markets or prices are controlled by the government are the most active political voices. Why do you think these particular PACs are so active?

Rank/Name (2008 Election)

Top 20 PAC Contributors to Candidates, 2011–2012

PAC NAME	TOTAL AMOUNT	DEM. PERCENT	REPUB. PERCENT
National Association of Realtors	$3,960,282	44	55
National Beer Wholesalers Association	$3,388,500	41	59
Honeywell International	$3,193,024	41	59
Operating Engineers Union	$3,182,887	84	15
International Brotherhood of Electrical Workers	$2,853,000	97	2
American Bankers Association	$2,736,150	20	80
AT&T Inc.	$2,543,000	35	65
American Association for Justice	$2,512,500	96	3
Credit Union National Association	$2,487,600	47	52
Northrup Grumman	$2,416,400	42	58
Plumbers/Pipefitters Union	$2,380,550	94	5
American Federation of State/County/Municipal Employees	$2,279,140	1	99
Lockheed Martin	$2,258,000	41	59
Blue Cross/Blue Shield	$2,177,898	33	66
Machinists/Aerospace Workers Union	$2,173,500	98	1
American Federation of Teachers	$2,171,144	99	0
Every Republican Is Crucial PAC	$2,086,000	0	100
Teamsters	$2,053,410	96	4
Boeing Co.	$2,044,000	44	56

Source: FEC, www.fec.gov.

Under FECA, contributions made with funds that are subject to the act's disclosure requirements and source and amount limitations are thus known as "federal dollars" or "hard dollars." Corporations and unions, as well as individuals who had already made the maximum permissible contributions to federal candidates, could still contribute "nonfederal money"—also known as "soft money"—to political parties for activities intended to influence state or local elections. The FEC ruled that political parties could fund mixed-purpose activities—including get-out-the-vote drives and generic party advertising—in part with soft money. In 1995, the FEC concluded that the parties could also use soft money to defray the costs of "legislative advocacy media advertisements," even if the ads mentioned the name of a federal candidate, as long as they did not expressly advocate the candidate's election or defeat.

The so-called soft money donations became extensive. As a result, Congress passed the Bipartisan Campaign Reform Act of 2002 (BCRA, 2 U.S.C.A. § 431 et seq.). Often referred to as the McCain–Feingold law, Title I of the BCRA regulates the use of soft money by political parties, officeholders, and candidates. The BCRA was immediately challenged by 11 different parties in different federal courts, and the cases were consolidated and eventually heard by the U.S. Supreme Court in *McConnell v Federal Election Comm'n*, 540 U.S. 93 (2003). The Supreme Court, in a 500-page opinion (including the dissents), upheld most of the then-new law, but the court was forced to revisit the constitutionality in *Citizens United v FEC*, the decision that the president urged Congress to reverse (see p. 138).

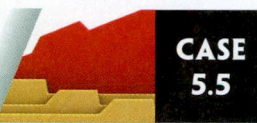

CASE 5.5	*Citizens United v Federal Election Commission* 558 U.S. 310 (2010)

Hillary: It's a Movie! It's a Campaign! It's Free Speech!

FACTS

Citizens United is a nonprofit corporation with an annual budget of about $12 million, most of which comes from donations by individuals.

In January 2008, Citizens United released a film entitled *Hillary: The Movie*. It is a 90-minute documentary about then-Senator Hillary Clinton, who was a candidate in the Democratic Party's 2008 Presidential primary elections. *Hillary* mentions Senator Clinton by name and depicts interviews with political commentators and other persons, most of them quite critical of Senator Clinton. *Hillary* was released in theaters and on DVD, but Citizens United wanted to increase distribution by making it available through video-on-demand.

In December 2007, a cable company offered, for a payment of $1.2 million, to make *Hillary* available on a video-on-demand channel called "Elections '08." Citizens United was prepared to pay for the video-on-demand; and to promote the film, it produced two 10-second ads and one 30-second ad for *Hillary*. Each ad includes a short (and, in our view, pejorative) statement about Senator Clinton, followed by the name of the movie and the movie's website address. Citizens United desired to promote the video-on-demand

offering by running advertisements on broadcast and cable television.

BCRA § 203(§441) prohibits any "electioneering communication." An electioneering communication is defined as "any broadcast, cable, or satellite communication" that "refers to a clearly identified candidate for Federal office" and is made within 30 days of a primary or 60 days of a general election. The Federal Election Commission's (FEC's) regulations further define an electioneering communication as a communication that is "publicly distributed." "In the case of a candidate for nomination for President … *publicly distributed* means" that the communication "[c]an be received by 50,000 or more persons in a State where a primary election … is being held within 30 days." Corporations and unions are barred from using their general treasury funds for express advocacy or electioneering communications. They may establish, however, a "separate segregated fund" (known as a political action committee, or PAC) for these purposes. The moneys received by the segregated fund are limited to donations from stockholders and employees of the corporation or, in the case of unions, members of the union.

Citizens United wanted to make *Hillary* available through video-on-demand within 30 days of the 2008 primary elections. It feared, however, that both the film and the ads would be covered by § 441b's ban on

CONTINUED

corporate-funded independent expenditures, thus subjecting the corporation to civil and criminal penalties. In December 2007, Citizens United sought declaratory and injunctive relief against the FEC. It argued that (1) § 441b is unconstitutional as applied to *Hillary*; and (2) BCRA's disclaimer and disclosure requirements are unconstitutional as applied to *Hillary* and to the three ads for the movie.

The District Court denied Citizens United's motion for a preliminary injunction (*per curiam*), and then granted the FEC's motion for summary judgment. The court held that § 441b was facially constitutional, and that § 441b was constitutional as applied to *Hillary* because it was "susceptible of no other interpretation than to inform the electorate that Senator Clinton is unfit for office, that the United States would be a dangerous place in a President Hillary Clinton world, and that viewers should vote against her." The court also rejected Citizens United's challenge to BCRA's disclaimer and disclosure requirements. It noted that "the Supreme Court has written approvingly of disclosure provisions triggered by political speech even though the speech itself was constitutionally protected under the First Amendment." Citizens United appealed to the U.S. Supreme Court, where the case was argued twice, once before the retirement of Justice David Souter and again following the addition of Justice Sotomayor.

JUDICIAL OPINION

KENNEDY, Justice

The narrative [of Hillary] may contain more suggestions and arguments than facts, but there is little doubt that the thesis of the film is that she is unfit for the Presidency.

Citizens United argues that Hillary is just "a documentary film that examines certain historical events." We disagree. The movie's consistent emphasis is on the relevance of these events to Senator Clinton's candidacy for President. The narrator begins by asking "could [Senator Clinton] become the first female President in the history of the United States?" And the narrator reiterates the movie's message in his closing line: "Finally, before America decides on our next president, voters should need no reminders of … what's at stake—the well-being and prosperity of our nation."

Courts, too, are bound by the First Amendment. We must decline to draw, and then redraw, constitutional lines based on the particular media or technology used to disseminate political speech from a particular speaker.

The law before us is an outright ban, backed by criminal sanctions. Section 441b makes it a felony for all corporations—including nonprofit advocacy

corporations—either to expressly advocate the election or defeat of candidates or to broadcast electioneering communications within 30 days of a primary election and 60 days of a general election. Thus, the following acts would all be felonies under § 441b: The Sierra Club runs an ad, within the crucial phase of 60 days before the general election, that exhorts the public to disapprove of a Congressman who favors logging in national forests; the National Rifle Association publishes a book urging the public to vote for the challenger because the incumbent U.S. Senator supports a handgun ban; and the American Civil Liberties Union creates a Web site telling the public to vote for a Presidential candidate in light of that candidate's defense of free speech. These prohibitions are classic examples of censorship.

Section 441b's prohibition on corporate independent expenditures is thus a ban on speech. Were the Court to uphold these restrictions, the Government could repress speech by silencing certain voices at any of the various points in the speech process. If § 441b applied to individuals, no one would believe that it is merely a time, place, or manner restriction on speech. Its purpose and effect are to silence entities whose voices the Government deems to be suspect.

Speech is an essential mechanism of democracy, for it is the means to hold officials accountable to the people.

The First Amendment protects speech and speaker, and the ideas that flow from each. The Court has recognized that First Amendment protection extends to corporations. This protection has been extended by explicit holdings to the context of political speech. Under the rationale of these precedents, political speech does not lose First Amendment protection "simply because its source is a corporation… ." Government lacks the power to ban corporations from speaking.

It is irrelevant for purposes of the First Amendment that corporate funds may "have little or no correlation to the public's support for the corporation's political ideas." All speakers, including individuals and the media, use money amassed from the economic marketplace to fund their speech. The First Amendment protects the resulting speech, even if it was enabled by economic transactions with persons or entities who disagree with the speaker's ideas.

There is simply no support for the view that the First Amendment, as originally understood, would permit the suppression of political speech by media corporations. The Framers may not have anticipated modern business and media corporations. Yet television networks and major newspapers owned by media corporations have become the most important means of mass communication in modern times. The First Amendment was certainly not understood to condone

CONTINUED

the suppression of political speech in society's most salient media. It was understood as a response to the repression of speech and the press that had existed in England and the heavy taxes on the press that were imposed in the colonies. The great debates between the Federalists and the Anti-Federalists over our founding document were published and expressed in the most important means of mass communication of that era—newspapers owned by individuals.

When Government seeks to use its full power, including the criminal law, to command where a person may get his or her information or what distrusted source he or she may not hear, it uses censorship to control thought. This is unlawful. The First Amendment confirms the freedom to think for ourselves.

When word concerning the plot of the movie *Mr. Smith Goes to Washington* reached the circles of Government, some officials sought, by persuasion, to discourage its distribution. [I]t, like *Hillary*, was speech funded by a corporation that was critical of Members of Congress. *Mr. Smith Goes to Washington* may be fiction and caricature; but fiction and caricature can be a powerful force.

Modern day movies, television comedies, or skits on Youtube.com might portray public officials or public policies in unflattering ways. Yet if a covered transmission during the blackout period creates the background for candidate endorsement or opposition, a felony occurs solely because a corporation, other than an exempt media corporation, has made the "purchase, payment, distribution, loan, advance, deposit, or gift of money or anything of value" in order to engage in political speech. Speech would be suppressed in the realm where its necessity is most evident: in the public dialogue preceding a real election. Governments are often hostile to speech, but under our law and our tradition it seems stranger than fiction for our Government to make this political speech a crime. Yet this is the statute's purpose and design.

"The First Amendment underwrites the freedom to experiment and to create in the realm of thought and speech. Citizens must be free to use new forms, and new forums, for the expression of ideas. The civic discourse belongs to the people, and the Government may not prescribe the means used to conduct it."

The judgment of the District Court is reversed with respect to the constitutionality of § 441b's restrictions on corporate independent expenditures.

CASE QUESTIONS

1. Why does the Court say it cannot be involved in ongoing monitoring of political ads, documentaries, and other forms of communication?

2. Why are independent expenditures by corporations different from corporate donations and funding of candidates?

3. Are time restrictions and unflattering portraits grounds for regulating political speech? Why or why not?

5-5e EMINENT DOMAIN: THE TAKINGS CLAUSE

The right of a governmental body to take title to property for a public use is called **eminent domain**. This right is established in the Fifth Amendment to the Constitution and may also be established in various state constitutions. Private individuals cannot require property owners to sell their property, but governmental entities can require property owners to transfer title for public projects for the public good. The Fifth Amendment provides that "property shall not be taken for a public use without just compensation." For a governmental entity to exercise properly the right of eminent domain, three factors must be present: public purpose, taking (as opposed to regulating), and just compensation.

Public Purpose

To exercise eminent domain, the governmental authority must establish that the taking is necessary for the accomplishment of a government or public purpose. When eminent domain is mentioned, we think of the use of property for highways and schools. However, the right of the government to eminent domain extends much further. For example, the following uses have been held to constitute public purposes: the condemnation of slum housing (for purposes of improving city areas), the limitation of mining and excavation within city limits, the declaration of property as a historic landmark, and the taking of property to provide a firm that is a town's economic base with a large enough tract for expansion. According to the U.S. Supreme Court, the public purpose requirement for eminent domain is to be interpreted broadly, and "the role of the judiciary in determining whether that power is being exercised for a public purpose is an extremely narrow one." [*United States ex rel. TVA v Welch*, 327 U.S. 546 (1946)] The *Kelo v City of New London* case (Case 5.6) was the U.S. Supreme Court decision that changed the eminent domain landscape, as it were.

| CASE 5.6 | *Kelo v City of New London* 545 U.S. 469 (2005) |

Yes, Actually, They Can Take That Away From You

FACTS

In 1978, the city of New London, Connecticut, undertook a redevelopment plan for purposes of creating a redeveloped area in and around the existing park at Fort Trumbull. The plan sought to develop the related ambience a state park should have, including the absence of pink cottages and other architecturally eclectic homes. Part of the redevelopment plan was the city's deal with Pfizer Corporation for the location of its research facility in the area. The preface to the city's development plan included the following statement of goals and purpose:

> To create a development that would complement the facility that Pfizer was planning to build, create jobs, increase tax and other revenues, encourage public access to and use of the city's waterfront, and eventually "build momentum" for the revitalization of the rest of the city, including its downtown area.

The affected property owners, including Susette Kelo, live in homes and cottages (15 total) located in and around other existing structures that would be permitted to stay in the area designated for the proposed new structures (under the city's economic development plan) that would be placed there primarily by private land developers and corporations. The city was assisted by a private, nonprofit corporation, the New London Development Corporation (NLDC), in the development of the economic plan and piloting it through the various governmental processes, including that of city council approval. The central focus of the plan was getting Pfizer to the Fort Trumbull area (where the homeowners and their properties were located) with the hope of a resulting economic boost that such a major corporate employer can bring to an area.

Kelo and the other landowners whose homes would be razed to make room for Pfizer and the accompanying and resulting economic development plan filed suit challenging New London's legal authority to take their homes. The trial court issued an injunction preventing New London from taking certain of the properties but allowing others to be taken. The appellate court found for New London on all the claims, and the landowners (petitioners) appealed.

JUDICIAL OPINION

STEVENS, Justice

Two polar propositions are perfectly clear. On the one hand, it has long been accepted that the sovereign may not take the property of A for the sole purpose of transferring it to another private party B, even though A is paid just compensation. On the other hand, it is equally clear that a State may transfer property from one private party to another if future "use by the public" is the purpose of the taking; the condemnation of land for a railroad with common-carrier duties is a familiar example. Neither of these propositions, however, determines the disposition of this case.

The disposition of this case therefore turns on the question whether the City's development plan serves a "public purpose." Without exception, our cases have defined that concept broadly, reflecting our longstanding policy of deference to legislative judgments in this field.

In *Berman v Parker*, 348 U.S. 26, 75 S.Ct. 98, 99 L.Ed. 27 (1954), this Court upheld a redevelopment plan targeting a blighted area of Washington, D.C., in which most of the housing for the area's 5,000 inhabitants was beyond repair. Under the plan, the area would be condemned and part of it utilized for the construction of streets, schools, and other public facilities. The remainder of the land would be leased or sold to private

CONTINUED

parties for the purpose of redevelopment, including the construction of low-cost housing.

The owner of a department store located in the area challenged the condemnation, pointing out that his store was not itself blighted and arguing that the creation of a "better balanced, more attractive community" was not a valid public use. Writing for a unanimous Court, Justice Douglas refused to evaluate this claim in isolation, deferring instead to the legislative and agency judgment that the area "must be planned as a whole" for the plan to be successful. The Court explained that "community redevelopment programs need not, by force of the Constitution, be on a piecemeal basis—lot by lot, building by building." "We do not sit to determine whether a particular housing project is or is not desirable. The concept of the public welfare is broad and inclusive…. The values it represents are spiritual as well as physical, aesthetic as well as monetary. It is within the power of the legislature to determine that the community should be beautiful as well as healthy, spacious as well as clean, well-balanced as well as carefully patrolled. In the present case, the Congress and its authorized agencies have made determinations that take into account a wide variety of values. It is not for us to reappraise them. If those who govern the District of Columbia decide that the Nation's Capital should be beautiful as well as sanitary, there is nothing in the Fifth Amendment that stands in the way."

In *Hawaii Housing Authority v Midkiff*, 467 U.S. 229, 104 S. Ct. 2321, 81 L.Ed.2d 186 (1984), the Court considered a Hawaii statute whereby fee title was taken from lessors and transferred to lessees (for just compensation) in order to reduce the concentration of land ownership. We unanimously upheld the statute and rejected the Ninth Circuit's view that it was "a naked attempt on the part of the state of Hawaii to take the property of A and transfer it to B solely for B's private use and benefit." Reaffirming *Berman*'s deferential approach to legislative judgments in this field, we concluded that the State's purpose of eliminating the "social and economic evils of a land oligopoly" qualified as a valid public use.

Those who govern the City were not confronted with the need to remove blight in the Fort Trumbull area, but their determination that the area was sufficiently distressed to justify a program of economic rejuvenation is entitled to our deference. The City has carefully formulated an economic development plan that it believes will provide appreciable benefits to the community, including—but by no means limited to—new jobs and increased tax revenue. To effectuate this plan, the City has invoked a state statute that specifically authorizes the use of eminent domain to promote economic development. Given the comprehensive character of the plan, the thorough deliberation that preceded its adoption, and the limited scope of our review, it is appropriate for us, as it was in *Berman*, to resolve the challenges of the individual owners, not on a piecemeal basis, but rather in light of the entire plan. Because that plan unquestionably serves a public purpose, the takings challenged here satisfy the public use requirement of the Fifth Amendment.

Petitioners contend that using eminent domain for economic development impermissibly blurs the boundary between public and private takings. Again, our cases foreclose this objection. We cannot say that public ownership is the sole method of promoting the public purposes of community redevelopment projects. It is further argued that without a bright-line rule nothing would stop a city from transferring citizen A's property to citizen B for the sole reason that citizen B will put the property to a more productive use and thus pay more taxes. Such a one-to-one transfer of property, executed outside the confines of an integrated development plan, is not presented in this case. While such an unusual exercise of government power would certainly raise a suspicion that a private purpose was afoot, the hypothetical cases posited by petitioners can be confronted if and when they arise. They do not warrant the crafting of an artificial restriction on the concept of public use.

Just as we decline to second-guess the City's considered judgments about the efficacy of its development plan, we also decline to second-guess the City's determinations as to what lands it needs to acquire in order to effectuate the project. "It is not for the courts to oversee the choice of the boundary line nor to sit in review on the size of a particular project area. Once the question of the public purpose has been decided, the amount and character of land to be taken for the project and the need for a particular tract to complete the integrated plan rests in the discretion of the legislative branch."

The judgment of the Supreme Court of Connecticut is affirmed.

DISSENTING OPINION

O'CONNOR, Justice, joined by Justices SCALIA, THOMAS and REHNQUIST

Under the banner of economic development, all private property is now vulnerable to being taken and transferred to another private owner, so long as it might be upgraded—i.e., given to an owner who will use it in a way that the legislature deems more beneficial to the public—in the process. To reason, as the Court does, that the incidental public benefits resulting from the subsequent ordinary use of private property render economic development takings "for public use" is to wash out any distinction between private and public use of property—and thereby effectively to delete the words "for public use" from the Takings Clause of the Fifth Amendment. Accordingly I respectfully dissent.

CONTINUED

Where is the line between "public" and "private" property use? We give considerable deference to legislatures' determinations about what governmental activities will advantage the public. But were the political branches the sole arbiters of the public-private distinction, the Public Use Clause would amount to little more than hortatory fluff. An external, judicial check on how the public use requirement is interpreted, however limited, is necessary if this constraint on government power is to retain any meaning.

Even if there were a practical way to isolate the motives behind a given taking, the gesture toward a purpose test is theoretically flawed. If it is true that incidental public benefits from new private use are enough to ensure the "public purpose" in a taking, why should it matter, as far as the Fifth Amendment is concerned, what inspired the taking in the first place? And whatever the reason for a given condemnation, the effect is the same from the constitutional perspective— private property is forcibly relinquished to new private ownership.

CASE QUESTIONS

1. What is different between this case and a case in which property is taken for constructing a freeway?

2. What is the concern of the dissent about the decision?

3. Why does the majority state that the courts should be reluctant to get involved in local government eminent domain activities?

The impact of the *Kelo* case has been substantial. Following the November 2006 general elections, nearly one-half of the states had passed ballot propositions limiting the exercise of eminent domain, adopted constitutional amendments restricting economic development eminent domain, or passed legislation with similar limitations.[2] Today, nearly all states have reformed their takings laws and the requirements for a "public purpose." The outcome of the *Kelo* case was sad. Pfizer merged with Wyeth in 2009 and closed all company operations in New London. The Fort Trumball area has no houses, no research park, no businesses, and is now undeveloped land. However, following Hurricane Irene in 2011, officials from the city of New London announced that the citizens could dump their branches and fallen trees at the site where Ms. Kelo's home once sat. In short, the Fort Trumball area is now a landfill. Justice Richard Palmer, who was the swing vote in the Connecticut Supreme decision in the case, apologized to Ms. Kelo when he encountered her at a reception for the launch of a reporter's book on her story. He said that had he known everything revealed in the book he would have voted differently.

Taking or Regulating

For a governmental entity to be required to pay a landowner compensation under the doctrine of eminent domain there must be a taking of the property. Mere regulation of the property does not constitute a taking, as determined by *Village of Euclid, Ohio v Ambler Realty Co.*, 272 U.S. 365 (1926). Rather, a taking must go so far as to deprive the landowner of any use of the property. In the landmark case of *Pennsylvania Coal v Mahon*, 260 U.S. 393 (1922), the Supreme Court established standards for determining a taking as opposed to mere regulation. At that time Pennsylvania had a statute that prohibited the mining of coal under any land surface where the result would be the subsidence of any structure used as a human habitation. The owners of the rights to mine subsurface coal brought suit challenging the regulation as a taking, and the Supreme Court ruled in their favor, holding that the statute was more than regulation and, in fact, was an actual taking of the subsurface property rights.

Because of the vast amount of technology that has developed since that case was decided, many new and subtly different issues affect what constitutes a taking. For example, in some areas, the regulation of cable television companies is an infringement on air rights. Such specialized areas of real estate rights are particularly difficult to resolve. In *Loretto v Teleprompter Manhattan CATV Corp.*, 458 U.S. 100 (1982), the U.S. Supreme Court held that the small invasion of property by the placement of cable boxes and wires did constitute a taking, albeit very small, and required compensation of the property owners for this small but permanent occupation of their land.

The issue of taking has arisen because of local zoning restrictions on development. These restrictions focus on beaches, wetlands, and other natural habitats. For example, in *Nollan v California Coastal Commission*, 483 U.S. 825 (1987), the Nollans sought permission from the California Coastal Commission to construct a home on their coastal lot where they currently had only a small bungalow. The commission refused to grant permission to the Nollans for construction of their home unless they agreed to give a public easement across their lot for beach access. The Supreme Court held that the demand by the commission for an easement was a taking without compensation and, in effect, prevented the Nollans from using their property until they surrendered their exclusive use.[3]

Yet another issue that arises in taking occurs when regulations take effect after owners have acquired land but before it is developed. In *Lucas v South Carolina Coastal Council*, 505 U.S. 1003 (1992), the U.S. Supreme Court declared that *ex post facto* legislation that prevents development of previously purchased land is a taking. In *Lucas*, David Lucas purchased for $975,000 two residential lots on the Isle of Palms in Charleston County, South Carolina. In 1988, the South Carolina legislature enacted the Beachfront Management Act, which barred any permanent habitable structures on coastal properties. The court held South Carolina was required to compensate Mr. Lucas because his land was rendered useless.

Just Compensation

The final requirement for the proper exercise by a governmental entity of the right of eminent domain is that the party from whom the property is being taken be given **just compensation**. The issue of just compensation is difficult to determine and is always a question of fact. Basic to this determination is that the owner is to be compensated for loss and that the compensation is not measured by the governmental entity's gain. In *United States v Miller*, 317 U.S. 369 (1943), the Supreme Court held that in cases where it can be determined, fair market value is the measure of compensation; and, in *United States ex rel. TVA v Powelson*, 319 U.S. 266 (1943), the Supreme Court defined fair market value to be "what a willing buyer would pay in cash to a willing seller."

Possible problems in applying these relatively simple standards include peculiar value to the owner, consequential damages, and greater value of the land because of the proposed governmental project. Basically, the issue of just compensation becomes an issue of appraisal, which is affected by all the various factors involved. In determining just compensation, the courts must consider such factors as surrounding property values and the owner's proposed use.

5-5f PROCEDURAL DUE PROCESS

Both the Fifth and the Fourteenth Amendments require state and federal governments to provide citizens (businesses included) due process under the law. **Procedural due process** is a right that requires notice and the opportunity to be heard before rights or properties are taken away from an individual or business.

Most people are familiar with due process as it exists in the criminal justice system: the right to a lawyer, a trial, and so on (discussed in Chapter 8). However, procedural due process is also an important part of civil law. Before an agency—whether state or federal—can take away a business license, suspend a license, or impose a fine for a violation, it must ensure due process.

Businesses encounter the constitutional protections of due process in their relationships with customers. For example, the eviction of a nonpaying tenant cannot be done unilaterally. The tenant has the right to be heard in the setting of a hearing. The landlord must file an action against the tenant, and the tenant will have the opportunity to present defenses for nonpayment of rent. The Due Process Clause of the U.S. Constitution provides protection for individuals before their property is taken. Property includes land (as in the case of eminent domain, discussed previously); rights of possession (tenants and leases); and even intangible property rights. For example, students cannot be expelled from schools, colleges, or universities without the right to be heard. Students must have some hearing before their property rights with respect to education are taken away.

All proceedings designed to satisfy due process requirements must provide notice and the right to be heard and present evidence (see Chapter 6 for more details). If these rights are not afforded, the constitutional right of due process has been denied and the action taken is rescinded until due process requirements are met. Suppose that OSHA charges a company with safety violations in its plants. Before a fine or order can be imposed, procedural due process requires that the company have the right to be heard and to present evidence on the violations. In court cases, a matter reduced to a judgment entitles the victorious side to collect on that judgment. However, under due process, even the proceedings for collection allow the losing party or debtor to be notified of the proceedings and to be heard.

Consider...

When the Crafts moved into their residence in October 1972, they noticed two separate gas and electric meters and only one water meter serving the premises. The residence had been used previously as a duplex. The Crafts assumed, based on information from the seller, that the second set of meters was inoperative.

In 1973, the Crafts began receiving two bills: their regular bill and another with an account number in the name of Willie C. Craft, as opposed to Willie S. Craft. In October 1973, after learning from a Memphis Light, Gas & Water (MLG&W) meter reader that both sets of meters were running in their home, the Crafts hired a private plumber and electrical contractor to combine the meters into one gas and one electric meter. Because the contractor did not combine the meters properly, they continued to receive two bills until January 1974. During this time, the Crafts' utility service was terminated five times for nonpayment.

Mrs. Craft missed work several times to go to MLG&W offices to resolve the "double billing" problem. She sought explanations on each occasion but was never given an answer.

In February 1974, the Crafts and other MLG&W customers filed suit for violation of the Due Process Clause. The district court dismissed the case. The court of appeals reversed, and MLG&W appealed.

Have the Crafts been given due process?

[*Memphis Light, Gas & Water Div. v Craft*, 436 U.S. 1 (1978)]

5-5g **SUBSTANTIVE DUE PROCESS**

Procedural rules deal with how things are done. All rules on the adjudication of agency charges are procedural rules. Similarly, all rules for the trial of a civil case—from discovery to jury instructions—are also procedural. These rules exist to make sure the substantive law is upheld. **Substantive law** consists of rights, obligations, and behavior standards. Criminal laws are substantive laws, and criminal procedure rules are procedural laws. **Substantive due process** is the right to have laws that do not deprive businesses or citizens of property or other rights without justification and reason. The issue of whether a statute was "void for vagueness" and denied due process was a central one in *F.C.C. v Fox Television Stations, Inc.*, 132 S.Ct. 2307 (2012). In the case, which appears in Chapter 6, the court held that the Federal Communications Commission (FCC) regulations did not give the television networks enough information to understand the standards for the use of expletives on television as well as the limits on momentary nudity. Justice Kennedy wrote, "A fundamental principle in our legal system is that laws which regulate persons or entities must give fair notice of conduct that is forbidden or required. This requirement of clarity in regulation is essential to the protections provided by the Due Process Clause of the Fifth Amendment.

5-5h **EQUAL PROTECTION RIGHTS FOR BUSINESS**

The Fourteenth Amendment grants citizens the right to the **equal protection** of the law. Lawmakers, however, are often required to make certain distinctions in legislating and regulating that result in classes of individuals being treated differently.

Such different or **disparate treatment** is justified only if some rational basis for it is determined. In other words, a rational connection is necessary between the classifications and the achievement of some governmental objective. Most classifications survive the rational basis test. An example of a classification that would not survive is one requiring the manufacturers of soft drinks to use only unbreakable bottles for their product but allowing juice manufacturers to use glass bottles; this classification is irrational. If a public safety concern is raised about glass bottles, it must apply equally to all beverage manufacturers.

5-6 **The Role of Constitutions in International Law**

Although the U.S. Constitution is the basis for all law in the United States, not all countries follow a similar system of governance. The incorporation of other systems (such as a constitution or code) depends on a nation's history, including its colonization by other countries and those countries' forms of law. The United States and the United Kingdom (and countries established through British colonization) tend to follow a pattern of establishing a general set of principles, as set forth in a constitution, and of reliance on custom, tradition, and precedent for the establishment of law in particular legal areas.

In countries such as France, Germany, and Spain (and nations colonized through their influences), a system of law that is dependent on code law exists. These countries have specific codes of law that attempt to be all-inclusive and cover each circumstance that could arise under a particular provision. These nations do not depend on court decisions, and often the application of the law leads to inconsistent results because of the lack of dependence on judicial precedent.

Approximately 27 countries follow Islamic law in some way. When Islamic law is the dominant force in a country, it governs all aspects of personal and business life. The constitutions in these lands are the tenets of the nation's religion.

Consider...

Following a boom in cruise ship construction, ships are now looking for ports at which they can dock in order to begin voyages, most of which start in the United States. With so many new ships, the companies are trying to establish connections with cities that are not ordinarily considered for cruise ship docks. The companies pursue these alternatives because the traditional docking cities of New York, Seattle, Miami, Los Angeles, and Houston have become crowded with cruise ship traffic. The result has been a burden on the facilities and staff at the ports.

Most cruise-ship lines are incorporated outside of the United States, do not pay federal income taxes, and are not subject to state income taxes even though the bulk of their passengers come from the United States. (See the section "5-3b Constitutional Standards for Taxation of Business" earlier in this chapter.)

Can the ships be taxed to cover the harbor expenses? Can they be required by states and cities to pay docking fees, or are they internationally exempt companies?

Source: Nicole Harris, "Big Cruise Ships Cause Traffic Jams in Ports," *Wall Street Journal*, August 20, 2003, pp. B1, B6.

BIOGRAPHY

John Glover Roberts: The Chief Justice of the U.S. Supreme Court and the Swing Vote on the Constitutionality of Obama Care

When he was sworn in on September 29, 2005, as the Chief Justice of the United States Supreme Court, John G. Roberts brought a unique perspective and depth of experience.

Justice Roberts's family moved from Buffalo, New York, where he was born in 1955, to Indiana, where he worked summers in the steel mills and graduated with honors from his high school. There, he was also the captain of his high school football team despite being, by his own account, "a slow-footed linebacker." He finished his undergraduate degree in history at Harvard, *summa cum laude*, in just three years, paying his way by working summers in the Indiana steel mills once again. His honors thesis, which was titled "Marxism and Bolshevism: Theory and Practice," won the award for best essay in 1976. He immediately went on to Harvard Law School, where he was managing editor of the *Harvard Law Review* and graduated in 1979 *magna cum laude*. Following his graduation from Harvard Law School, Mr. Roberts served as a law clerk for Judge Henry T. Friendly of the Second Circuit Federal Court of Appeals. From there he spent 1980–1981 as a clerk for U.S. Supreme Court Justice William Rehnquist. Shortly after Mr. Roberts left to go to the Justice Department, Mr. Rehnquist was named Chief Justice.

Following service in the Justice Department from 1981 to 1982, Mr. Roberts became associate general counsel to the White House during the Reagan administration. In 1986, he left the White House and went into private practice. Mr. Roberts argued his first case before the U.S. Supreme Court in 1989. After winning that case on a double-jeopardy issue as a court-appointed lawyer, Mr. Roberts was appointed as Principal Deputy Solicitor General of the United States, a position he would hold until 1992 when he was nominated by President Bush (41) to the Second Circuit Court of Appeals. With the political winds changing at that time, Mr. Roberts's nomination "languished" in the Senate and he returned to private practice. He argued 39 cases before the U.S. Supreme Court, a number that ranks him as one of the country's top five lawyers for appearances at the high court. In 2001, President Bush (43) nominated Mr. Roberts to the D.C. Circuit Court of Appeals, and his nomination was finally approved by the Senate in 2003. After Judge Roberts had served two years there, President Bush nominated him to fill the vacancy created by Sandra Day O'Connor's resignation. However, during Judge Roberts's Supreme Court confirmation process, his former boss and mentor, Chief Justice William Rehnquist, died. President Bush nominated Judge Roberts for Chief Justice rather than Associate Justice, and he was confirmed by the Senate with a 78–22 vote, a departure from previous near-unanimous confirmation of high court nominees.

Known for his clear writing style and warm personality, the Chief Justice shared, during his confirmation hearings, a story on one of his losses at the high court. He lost a case before the court on a 9–0 vote. When a client called to ask how it was possible that they could lose their case by a 9–0 vote, then-Judge Roberts said that he responded, "Because they only have nine justices on the U.S. Supreme Court!"

In 2012, Justice Roberts, in switching his vote on Obama Care, created a firestorm of controversy regarding the role of the Supreme Court, because of the controversial nature of finding the law unconstitutional under the Commerce Clause but upholding the law on other grounds. For the first time in the court's history, other justices reflected publicly on their feelings about the switch in his vote by the chief justice after their opinions were determined and the fate of the case was quite different from the original decision.

Summary

What is the Constitution?

- U.S. Constitution—document detailing authority of U.S. government and rights of its citizens

What are the constitutional limitations on business regulations?

- Commerce Clause—portion of the U.S. Constitution that controls federal regulation of business; limits Congress to regulating interstate and international commerce

  - Intrastate commerce—business within state borders

  - Interstate commerce—business across state lines

  - Foreign commerce—business outside U.S. boundaries

Who has more power to regulate business—the states or the federal government?

- Supremacy Clause—portion of the U.S. Constitution that defines relationship between state and federal laws

- Taxation—authority to tax interstate businesses

What individual freedoms granted under the Constitution apply to businesses?

- Bill of Rights—first 10 amendments to the U.S. Constitution, providing individual freedoms and protection of individual rights

- First Amendment—freedom-of-speech protection in U.S. Constitution

  - Commercial speech—ads and other speech by businesses

  - Corporate political speech—business ads or positions on candidates or referenda

- Due process—constitutional guarantee against the taking of property or other governmental exercise of authority without an opportunity for a hearing

- Equal protection—constitutional protection for U.S. citizens against disparate treatment

- Substantive due process—constitutional protection against taking of rights or property by statute

Questions and Problems

1. A group of smokers (Respondents) brought suit against tobacco producer Altria, alleging that they were misled by the Altria and other cigarette producers' (Petitioners) ads and labels on its cigarettes touting "light" and "low-tar." By covering filter ventilation holes with their lips or fingers, taking larger or more frequent puffs, and holding the smoke in their lungs for a longer period of time, smokers of "light" cigarettes unknowingly inhale as much tar and nicotine as do smokers of regular cigarettes. "Light" cigarettes are in fact more harmful because the increased ventilation that results from their unique design features produces smoke that is more mutagenic per milligram of tar than the smoke of regular cigarettes. The smokers argued that the tobacco companies violated the Maine Unfair Trade Practices Act (MUTPA) by fraudulently concealing that information and by affirmatively representing, through the use of "light" and "lowered tar and nicotine" descriptors, that their cigarettes would pose fewer health risks.

The District Court entered summary judgment in favor of the tobacco companies on the ground that the state-law claim is preempted by the Federal Cigarette Labeling and Advertising Act. The Court of Appeals reversed that judgment, and the U.S. Supreme Court granted *certiorari* to review its holding that the Labeling Act neither expressly nor impliedly preempts state law. What should the court decide and why? [*Altria Group, Inc. v Good*, 555 U.S. 70 (2008)]

2. Mrs. Florence Dolan owned a plumbing and electric supply store on Main Street in Portland, Oregon. Fanno Creek flows through the southeastern corner of Mrs. Dolan's lot, on which her store is located. She applied to the city for a permit to redevelop her lot. Her plans included the addition of a second structure.

The City Planning Commission granted Mrs. Dolan's permit but included the following requirement:

> *Where landfill and/or development is allowed within and adjacent to the 100-year floodplain, the city shall require the dedication of sufficient open land area for greenway adjoining and within the floodplain. This area shall include portions at a suitable elevation for the construction of a pedestrian/bicycle pathway within the floodplain in accordance with the adopted pedestrian/bicycle plan.*

Mrs. Dolan maintained that the requirements were a taking of her property because she would be required to reserve a portion of her property for the pedestrian/bike path, and her plans would have to be redone to accommodate the city's requirements. The city maintains that its requirements are all simply part of a redevelopment plan for the city and a means of working with the floodplain created by Fanno Creek. Mrs. Dolan says the city has imposed additional expense and forced her to dedicate a large portion of her lot to public use. Who is correct? Is Portland taking property from Mrs. Dolan? Is the city required to pay compensation to her? [*Dolan v City of Tigard*, 512 U.S. 374 (1994)]

3. The Heart of Atlanta Motel, which has 216 rooms available to transient guests, is located on Courtland Street, two blocks from downtown Peachtree Street in Atlanta, Georgia. It is readily accessible to interstate highways 75 and 85 and state highways 23 and 41. The motel does advertise outside Georgia through various national advertising media, including magazines of national circulation; it maintains more than 50 billboards and highway signs within the state, soliciting patronage for the motel; it accepts convention trade from outside Georgia; and approximately 75 percent of its registered guests are from out of state.

Prior to passage of Title II of the Civil Rights Act, the motel had followed a practice of refusing to rent rooms to Negroes, and it alleged that it intended to continue to do so. The motel filed suit, challenging Congress for passing this act in excess of its power to regulate commerce under Article I, Section 8, Part 3 of the Constitution of the United States.

Section 201 of Title II provides: "All persons shall be entitled to the full and equal enjoyment of the goods, services, facilities, privileges, advantages, and accommodations of any place of public accommodation, as defined in this section, without discrimination or segregation on the ground of race, color, religion, or national origin." Section 201(b) covers four classes of business establishments, each of which "serves the public" and "is a place of public accommodation": *any inn, hotel, motel, or other establishment which provides lodging; (2) any restaurant, cafeteria; (3) any motion picture house; and (4) any establishment which is physically located within the premises of any establishment otherwise covered by this subsection.*

Is Title II of the Civil Rights Act constitutional? Is this case different from Ollie's Barbecue? From *Morrison*? [*Heart of Atlanta Motel, Inc. v U.S.*, 379 U.S. 241 (1964)]

4. Bruce Church, Inc. is a company engaged in extensive commercial farming in Arizona and California. A provision of the Arizona Fruit and Vegetable Standardization Act requires that all cantaloupes grown in Arizona "be packed in regular compact arrangement in closed standard containers approved by the supervisor." Arizona, through its agent Pike, issued an order prohibiting Bruce Church from transporting uncrated cantaloupes from its ranch in Parker, Arizona, to nearby Blythe, California, for packing and processing.

It would take many months and $200,000 for Bruce Church to construct a processing plant in Parker. Further, Bruce Church had $700,000 worth of cantaloupes ready for transportation. Bruce Church filed suit in federal district court challenging the constitutionality of the Arizona statutory provision on shipping cantaloupes. The court issued an injunction against the enforcement of the act on the grounds that it was an undue hardship on interstate commerce. Will the regulation withstand Commerce Clause scrutiny? [*Pike v Bruce Church, Inc.*, 397 U.S. 137 (1970)]

5. Customers of AT&T brought a class action suit against the telephone company, alleging that the company's offer of a free phone to anyone who signed up for its cell phone service was fraudulent because AT&T charged the customers sales tax on the retail value of the free phone. The suit was based on California's consumer protection laws. AT&T defended on the grounds that the federal government controlled the program. What should the court decide in the case, and what are the rights of the consumers and the federal program? [*AT&T Mobility v Concepcion*, 131 S.Ct. 1740 (2011)]

6. For the past 62 years, Pacific Gas & Electric (PG&E) has distributed a newsletter in its monthly billing envelopes. The newsletter, called *Progress*, reaches more than 3 million customers and contains tips on conservation, utility billing information, public interest information, and political editorials.

A group called TURN (Toward Utility Rate Normalization) asked the Public Utility Commission

(PUC) of California to declare that the envelope space belonged to the ratepayers and that TURN was entitled to use the *Progress* space four times each year. The PUC ordered TURN's request, and PG&E appealed the order to the California Supreme Court. When the California Supreme Court denied review, PG&E appealed to the U.S. Supreme Court, alleging a violation of its First Amendment rights. Is PG&E correct? [*Pacific Gas & Electric v Public Utility Commission of California*, 475 U.S. 1 (1986)]

7.   The Minnesota legislature enacted a 1977 statute banning the retail sale of milk in plastic nonreturnable, nonrefillable containers but permitting such sale in other nonrefillable containers, such as paperboard milk cartons. Clover Leaf Creamery brought suit challenging the constitutionality of the statute under the Equal Protection Clause, alleging that there was no rational basis for the statute. The Minnesota legislature's purpose in passing the statute was to control solid waste, arguing that plastic containers take up more space in solid waste disposal dumps. The Minnesota Supreme Court found evidence to the contrary: The jugs took up less space and required less energy to produce. On appeal to the U.S. Supreme Court, can the statute survive a constitutional challenge? Is there a "rational basis" for the statute? What effect does the evidence to the contrary have on the statute's constitutionality? [*Minnesota v Clover Leaf Creamery*, 449 U.S. 456 (1981)]

8.   Iowa passed a statute restricting the length of vehicles that could use its highways. The length chosen was 55 feet. Semitrailers are generally 55 feet long; double or twin tracks (one cab pulling two trailers) are 65 feet long. Other states in the Midwest have adopted the 65-foot standard. Consolidated Freightways brought suit, challenging the Iowa statute as an unconstitutional burden on interstate commerce. The Iowa statute meant Consolidated could not use its twins in Iowa. The Iowa legislature claims the 65-foot doubles are more dangerous than the 55-foot singles. However, the statute did provide a border exception: Towns and cities along Iowa borders could make an exception to the length requirements to allow trucks to use their city and town roads. Can Iowa's statute survive a constitutional challenge? Is the statute an impermissible burden on interstate commerce? [*Kassel v Consolidated Freightways Corp.*, 450 U.S. 662 (1981)]

9.   In 1989, the city of Cincinnati authorized Discovery Network, Inc., to place on public property 62 freestanding news racks for distributing free magazines that consisted primarily of advertising for Discovery Network's service. In 1990, the city became concerned about the safety and attractive appearance of its streets and sidewalks and revoked Discovery Network's permit on the grounds that the magazines were commercial handbills whose distribution was prohibited on public property by a preexisting ordinance. Discovery Network argues that the prohibition is an excessive regulation of its commercial speech and a violation of its rights. The city maintains the elimination of the news racks decreases litter and increases safety. Is the ban on news racks constitutional? [*City of Cincinnati v Discovery Network, Inc.*, 507 U.S. 410 (1993)]

10.   Maine passed a law that prohibited anyone other than a Maine-licensed tobacco retailer from accepting an order for delivery of tobacco. The law required the retailer to arrange for delivery with a special receipt showing that someone over the age of 18 had received and signed for the tobacco products delivered. Out-of-state shippers and tobacco sellers challenged the law as one that favored Maine tobacco retailers. The state of Maine argued that its law was passed to prevent the public health hazard of minors becoming addicted to tobacco. The federal district court granted summary judgment for the shippers, and the court of appeals affirmed. The state of Maine appealed. What constitutional issues are involved? What should the U.S. Supreme Court do with the case and why? [*Rowe v New Hampshire Motor Transport Association*, 552 U.S. 364 (2008)]

ECONOMICS & THE LAW
The Perils of Eminent Domain

The bittersweet ending to the *Kelo* case presents some interesting economic issues. The city spent $87 million razing the homes to make room for the Pfizer project, which failed. Many eminent domain projects for economic developments do fail as businesses withdraw due to economic factors and other developments.

Consider whether these types of projects are good investments for local governments. Who are the stakeholders in eminent domain cases? Who is affected by the takings? What lessons do we glean about business and government partnerships?

Notes

1. *Christian Legal Society Chapter of the University of California, Hastings College of the Law v Martinez*, 130 S.Ct. 2971.

2. Florida, Georgia, Louisiana, Michigan, New Hampshire, North Dakota, and South Carolina passed constitutional amendments. Florida, Georgia, Michigan, and New Hampshire, along with Alabama, Alaska, Colorado, Illinois, Kansas, Maine, Minnesota, Missouri, Nevada, Pennsylvania, South Dakota, Utah (which had reform prior to Kelo), Vermont, West Virginia, Wisconsin, and Texas passed legislation limiting eminent domain reforms. The ballot states are Oregon, California, Idaho, Washington, Montana, and Arizona. Oregon has already codified its ballot proposition. In November 2005, the U.S. House of Representatives passed the Private Property Rights Protection Act of 2005 (also known as House Resolution 4128) by a vote of 376 to 38. The bill died in the Senate.

3. In *Koontz v St. Johns River Water Management District*, 133 S.Ct. 2586 (2013), the U.S. Supreme Court held that a landowner could not be required to fund offsite projects in order to obtain land use permits for his property.

Chapter 6 Administrative Law

The regulations of administrative agencies at the federal and state levels affect the day-to-day operations of all businesses. From permits to labor regulations, every business is affected. Agencies are the enforcement arm of governments. Created by one of the branches of government, they affect the way businesses operate. This chapter answers the following questions: What is an administrative agency? What does it do? What laws govern the operation of administrative agencies? How do agencies pass rules? How do agencies enforce the law?

Bo Chambers/Flickr/Getty Images

UPDATE
For up-to-date legal and ethical news, go to **mariannejennings.com**

Lord's Prayer	*66 words*
Gettysburg Address	*286 words*
Declaration of Independence	*1,322 words*
Federal regulations on the sale of cabbage	*26,911 words*
Internal Revenue Code and Regulation	*12,800,000 words (as of 2011)*

THIS TAG NOT TO BE REMOVED EXCEPT BY THE CONSUMER.

Modified warning tag (which previously read, "DO NOT REMOVE UNDER PENALTY OF LAW") required on mattresses
The change was made because the agency needed to reduce the number of calls from consumers who were concerned about removing their mattress tags

Consider...

The Center for Science in the Public Interest studied the calorie and fat content of movie theater popcorn and found the following information about the three largest theater chains:

Regal	60 grams of saturated fat	1,200 calories (add 260 calories for butter topping)
AMC	50 grams of saturated fat	1,030 calories
Cinemark	4 grams of saturated fat	910 calories of saturated fat (chain uses canola)

As a result, the Food and Drug Administration (FDA) proposed a rule change that would require business owners to disclose the number of calories in each standard menu item, provide information about calories to consumers on request, and notify consumers about the availability of nutrition information.

Because the regulation would apply to all businesses with 20 or more outlets that serve food, theater owners would be required to post information about their snacks, including popcorn. The theater owners are concerned that the disclosures will end sales of popcorn and maintain that the obesity of most Americans is not caused by theater popcorn. What can they do to let their concerns be heard? Can the proposed rule be challenged?

6-1 What Are Administrative Agencies?

An **administrative agency** is best defined by what it is not: It is not a legislative or judicial body. An administrative agency is a statutory creation within the executive branch with the power to make, interpret, and enforce laws. Such agencies exist at practically every level of government, and their names vary considerably. Exhibit 6.1 is a list of all the federal administrative agencies.

States also have administrative agencies that are responsible for such things as the licensing of professions and occupations. Architects, contractors, attorneys, accountants, cosmetologists, doctors, dentists, real estate agents, and nurses are all professionals whose occupations are regulated in most states by some administrative agency. Utility and worker compensation regulations are also handled by administrative agencies in each of the states.

All these agencies at every level of government derive their authority from the legislative body responsible for their creation. Congress creates federal agencies, state legislatures create state agencies, and city governments create their cities' administrative agencies.

The structures of agencies may differ significantly, but most will have an organizational chart to show how different departments operate. Exhibit 6.2 is an organizational chart for the Securities and Exchange Commission (SEC). The SEC consists of five commissioners, six divisions, and eleven regional offices.

EXHIBIT 6.1 Major Federal Administrative Agencies

EXECUTIVE OFFICE OF THE PRESIDENT

Executive Departments
Department of Agriculture
Department of Commerce
Department of Defense
Department of the Air Force
Department of the Army
Department of the Navy
Department of Education
Department of Energy
Department of Health and Human Services (HHS)
Department of Homeland Security
Department of Housing and Urban Development (HUD)
Department of the Interior
Department of Justice
Department of Labor
Department of State

Department of Transportation
Department of the Treasury

Selected Independent Agencies
Commodity Futures Trading Commission (CFTC)
Consumer Product Safety Commission (CPSC)
Environmental Protection Agency (EPA)
Equal Employment Opportunity Commission (EEOC)
Federal Aviation Administration (FAA)
Farm Credit Administration (FCA)
Federal Communications Commission (FCC)
Federal Deposit Insurance Corporation (FDIC)
Federal Election Commission (FEC)

Federal Emergency Management Agency (FEMA)
Federal Maritime Commission (FMC)
Federal Mine Safety and Health Review Commission
Federal Reserve System
Federal Trade Commission (FTC)
General Services Administration (GSA)
Interstate Commerce Commission (ICC)
National Aeronautics and Space Administration (NASA)
National Credit Union Administration (NCUA)
National Highway Traffic Safety Administration (NHTSA)
National Labor Relations Board (NLRB)

National Science Foundation (NSF)
National Transportation Safety Board (NTSB)
Nuclear Regulatory Commission (NRC)
Occupational Safety and Health Administration (OSHA)
Overseas Private Investment Corporation (OPIC)
Patent and Trademark Office
Pension Benefit Guaranty Corporation
Securities and Exchange Commission (SEC)
Selective Service System (SSS)
Small Business Administration (SBA)
Tennessee Valley Authority (TVA)
U.S. Postal Service (USPS)
Veterans Administration (VA)

Note: Some historical agencies are listed here and in CFR for topical and historical purposes. Current agency structures may include absorption of older agencies.

© Cengage Learning 2015

Legislators begin the creation of an administrative agency with the recognition of a problem and the passage of a law designed to remedy the problem. The enacted law gives the overview—what the legislature wants to accomplish and the penalties for noncompliance with the law. The law may also establish an administrative agency with the power to adopt rules to deal with the problems of enforcement of the statute. The law, referred to as an **enabling act**, gives the agency the power to deal with the issues and problems the act addresses.

6-2 Roles of Administrative Agencies

6-2a SPECIALIZATION

Administrative agencies are specialists in their particular areas of law, and this type of specialization is needed because of both the complexities of law and the areas of regulation. For example, securities regulation involves both the complexity of financial reporting and the underlying technical accounting rules. The SEC has a special division headed by its chief accountant, and that division deals with all current and evolving accounting and financial reporting issues. The people who work as staff members in these agencies are chosen for their knowledge and experience, which helps them provide protection for the public as well as an understanding of the issues members of the regulated industries face.

EXHIBIT 6.2 Securities and Exchange Commission (SEC) Organizational Chart

6-2b PROTECTION FOR SMALL BUSINESS

An individual or competitor who finds a false advertisement in a newspaper would probably not take the time or effort to bring a private suit to collect damages for the false advertisement. But an agency created to oversee truth in advertising would undertake routine enforcement against such advertisements, affording small business competitors and consumers the protection and rights they might not otherwise have.

6-2c FASTER RELIEF

If enforcement of all government regulations depended on court hearings, courts would be backlogged and the goals of swift action and enforcement defeated. Administrative agencies help expedite investigations and enforcement and penalties for violations. In addition, administrative agencies serve as review boards for granting licenses. License and permit applications can be processed far more quickly than they could be handled legislatively.

6-2d DUE PROCESS

Administrative agencies provide the opportunity to be heard, a form of due process before property, rights, or income is taken. *Goldberg v Kelly*, 397 U.S. 254 (1970), was the seminal judicial decision responsible for creating administrative agency procedures that provide timely due process. In *Goldberg*, the Supreme Court ruled that before a benefit (such as aid to dependent children) could be taken away, the agency must present its evidence and allow those who have been receiving the aid an opportunity to respond. Administrative hearings provide citizens and businesses with a process for seeing the evidence against them and presenting their side of the story (see Chapter 5 for more insight on due process).

6-2e SOCIAL GOALS

Some experts see administrative agencies as a means for accomplishing social goals that might otherwise be delayed or debated until no resolution could be reached. For example, the Environmental Protection Agency is assigned the goal of creating a cleaner environment. If Congress had to debate every permit for a factory or rule on discharges, the goal might be lost in the political arena. Further, having judicial review and determination of these issues would result in a delay that might make the goal moot. Administrative agencies can function independently of the judicial and legislative branches (however, see the *Massachusetts v EPA* case later in the chapter). Often, these agencies are created in response to a pressing social issue. For example, the Department of Homeland Security was established to combine several agencies to allow more coordinated responses to terrorism, such as the attacks on the World Trade Center and Washington, D.C., in 2001, as well as natural disasters. The goal was a more centralized means of information distribution and relief.

6-3 Laws Governing Administrative Agencies

Apart from their enabling acts, administrative agencies are also subject to some general laws on the functioning of agencies. This section covers those laws.

6-3a ADMINISTRATIVE PROCEDURES ACT

This act was the first to deal with administrative agency procedures. It was passed in 1946 after some agencies had been in existence long enough for some standard procedures to be established. The **Administrative Procedures Act (APA)** requires agencies to follow certain uniform procedures in making rules (those procedures are covered later in this chapter). The APA has been amended a number of times by the Freedom of Information Act, the Federal Privacy Act, and the Government in the Sunshine Act, among others.

6-3b FREEDOM OF INFORMATION ACT

The **Freedom of Information Act (FOIA)** allows access to certain information federal agencies possess and requires that the agencies publicly disclose their procedures and decisions. The types of procedures that must be publicly disclosed relate to agencies' structures: where the central and regional offices are located and which office or office division will respond to requests for information. Agencies must also publish their rules, regulations, procedures, policy statements, and reports.

Some agency information, not published but available to the public, can be obtained by an **FOIA request**, which must be written and must describe the documents sought. For example, you could request the results of the Federal Trade Commission's study of coaching programs for college entrance exams. The agency can charge for time and for copying costs in processing the request, although these charges must be published and applied uniformly to all requests. Agencies can waive fees for nonprofit public interest groups.

If an agency wrongfully refuses to supply the information requested, the party requesting it can bring a court action to enforce the request, with all costs paid by the agency.

Some information is exempt from FOIA requests. The nine categories of exemptions would include, for example, requests that would reveal trade secrets or private information about individuals, such as government workers' personnel records. There are ongoing legislative proposals to curb government access to certain records such as the one in New York in 2013 that now prevents government agencies from releasing the names and addresses of gun owners in the state. The effect of the release of that information was that certain police officers' home addresses became known to criminals who then threatened the officers and also caused homes that did not have firearms to become targets for robberies and burglaries. In some cases, families have an interest in protecting the privacy of loved ones. For example, when Sea World animal trainer Dawn Brancheau was killed by a killer whale during a show at the company's Florida facility, there were numerous pictures taken by OSHA as part of its investigation into the facility's compliance with federal safety standards. Ms. Brancheau's family brought suit to stop the public release of the photos because they were "death-scene

Consider...

The recordings of 9-1-1 calls have long been subject to FOIA requests by newspapers and television stations. However, the content of those calls often reveals private information or discloses health information about individuals who have not committed a criminal wrong. For example, in 2011, the release of a 9-1-1 call made by friends of actress Demi Moore from her residence as they sought help revealed the actress to be in a disoriented and under-the-influence state, in other words, an unflattering portrait of a person at an emotional and physical low in her life. However, the recording, obtained by news outlets, also revealed that agencies involved with the call were slow to respond and confused about jurisdiction in the case. Legislation was proposed to ban the public release of these types of calls when there was no criminal behavior. However, opponents of the bill pointed out that the purpose of FOIA requests is often to allow the public to hold government agencies, whether police or administrative agencies, accountable for their conduct and decisions. Discuss whether there should be an exemption or the FOIA should apply to such circumstances.

ETHICAL
ISSUES

Is the FOIA a means for legal industrial espionage? Could a competitor use an FOIA request as a means of gaining information about another firm that would not otherwise be available? For example, one firm could determine whether another is having product liability safety problems with its product and could alter its product to prevent such problems. Should any further controls be placed on FOIA requests?

materials." However, there is no such exemption under the FOIA. [*Brancheau v Secretary of Labor*, 2011 WL 4105047 (M.D.Fla.)] Courts are sensitive to the purpose of FOIA in the public oversight of government agencies and read exemptions strictly. Trade secrets are protected from FOIA disclosure, but disturbing materials are not.

Agencies can also waive exemptions. Some requests have resulted in court cases brought by the parties protected by the exemptions. For example, suppose that one company requests the government bid contract submitted by another company (its competitor for the bid) to the Department of Defense. The bidding company could bring suit to stop the disclosure. Such suits are called "reverse FOIA suits." However, the U.S. Supreme Court held in *Chrysler Corp. v Brown*, 441 U.S. 281 (1979), that the right to stop or grant disclosure rests with the agency and not with the party who supplied the information to the agency.

6-3c FEDERAL PRIVACY ACT

In 1974, Congress passed the **Federal Privacy Act (FPA)** to reduce exchanges of information between agencies about persons (individuals and businesses). The FPA prohibits federal agencies from communicating any records to another agency or person without first obtaining the consent of the person whose record is being communicated. The FPA protects all records about individuals that might be in the possession of the agency, including medical and employment histories.

Because law enforcement agencies would have a difficult time trying to conduct investigations if they had to get permission from the individuals being investigated in order to obtain information, law enforcement agencies are exempt from the FPA. Congress can also obtain information without consent. Routine agency tasks are also exempt from the prior permission requirement. For example, employees of the SEC need constant access to information about stock sales by corporate directors so that the SEC can perform its role of preventing insider trading. Because of terrorist attacks, some exchanges of information among federal agencies were broadened by the USA Patriot Act.

6-3d GOVERNMENT IN THE SUNSHINE ACT

The **Government in the Sunshine Act** is often called an **open meeting law**. Its purpose is to require prior public notice of meetings of those agencies with heads appointed by the president. All the agencies with the word *commission* in their names have agency heads appointed by the president.

This open meeting law applies only to meetings between or among agency heads. For example, when the commissioners of the FTC meet together, that meeting must be public and held only after there has been prior notice. Staff members can hold meetings in private without giving notice. Meetings on law enforcement investigations are also exempt.

ETHICAL ISSUES

In 1997, the Internal Revenue Service (IRS) disciplined employees who, out of curiosity, were looking up tax returns of famous people. The employees were not working on the taxpayers' returns; they were not obtaining information for investigations; they were simply checking to see who made how much income. The IRS fired 23 employees, disciplined 349, and provided counseling for 472. During 1996 and 1997, the IRS investigated 1,515 cases of snooping among its 102,000 employees. By 2007, the number of snooping investigations was increasing by about 400 per year, with employee disciplinary actions taken in about one-half of the cases. About 25 cases per year are referred for criminal prosecution of employees. By 2012, the IRS had implemented an audit program that tracked employee searches of records to detect access in comparison to the employees' work assignments and whether the files of individual taxpayers that employees pulled up were related to the audit or review functions that they had been assigned. The report concluded that the tracking was deficient in determining authorization for the employees to access certain files and needed to be improved.

Is this practice so bad? What is wrong with just looking at data accessible at work? The IRS employees said they did not disclose the data and therefore didn't violate federal privacy laws. Are ethics and laws the same thing?

© martan/Shutterstock.com

FOR THE MANAGER'S DESK

Re: The Size and Scope of Federal Regulation

The CFR has increased in size, from 19,335 pages in 1949 to 169,301 pages in 2011. A study by Professor John W. Dawson and John L. Seater concludes the following about the CFR:

The fastest percentage growth occurred in the early 1950s. High growth also occurred in the 1970s even though there was extensive deregulation in transportation, telecommunications, and energy. Deregulation in that period was more than offset by increased regulation in other areas, notably pertaining to the environment and occupational safety. Total pages decreased in only one year, 1985.[1]

The passage of the Dodd–Frank Wall Street Reform and Consumer Protection Act has resulted in the creation of a new federal agency, the Bureau of Consumer Financial Protection, and has increased the size of the Code of Federal Regulations (see p. 182) by 7.4 percent since its implementation beginning in 2009. There have been new federal rulemaking processes at 11 federal agencies related to the act, including rulemaking by the Federal Reserve, the FTC, the SEC, the Treasury Department, the FDIC, and the Commodities Futures Trading Commission.

For an economic analysis of the impact of regulation, go to www.cei.org. For an analysis of the new legislation, go to www.financialservices.house.gov and click on the Dodd–Frank Act link under the "Hearings/Legislation" tab.

© bloomua/Shutterstock.com

6-3e FEDERAL REGISTER ACT

Although the **Federal Register Act (FRA)** is not a part of the APA, its provisions are necessary for all the acts under the APA to work. The FRA created the **Federal Register System**, which oversees publication of federal agency information. This system provides the means for Sunshine Act notices and publication of agency rules and procedures.

Three publications make up the Federal Register System. The first is the *U.S. Government Manual*. This publication is reprinted each year and lists all federal agencies and their regional offices along with addresses. In addition, the *Manual* contains statistics about the agencies and their sizes.

The second publication of the Federal Register Act is the *Code of Federal Regulations*. (The U.S. Code is covered in Chapter 1.) The *Code of Federal Regulations* contains all the regulations of all the federal agencies. The volumes are in paperback, and the entire Code is republished each year because of tremendous changes in the regulations.

The third publication under the Federal Register System provides a daily update on changes in the regulations. This publication, called the *Federal Register*, is published every government working day and contains proposed regulations, notices of meetings (under the Government in the Sunshine Act), notices of hearings on proposed regulations, and the final versions of amended or new regulations. The *Federal Register* totals about 83,000 pages a year, or about 320 pages every working day.

6-4 The Functions of Administrative Agencies and Business Interaction

Administrative agencies have three functions: promulgating regulations, enforcing rules, and adjudicating rules. Businesses will find themselves interacting with agencies in all three areas of operation.

6-4a PROVIDING INPUT WHEN AGENCIES ARE PROMULGATING REGULATIONS

The legislative function of administrative agencies has two forms: **formal rulemaking** and **informal rulemaking**. Some agencies combine them into a type of rulemaking that is a cross between formal and informal—**hybrid rulemaking**. This section focuses on formal rulemaking.

6-4b FORMAL RULEMAKING

Exhibit 6.3 diagrams the steps involved in formal rulemaking.

Congressional Enabling Act

Congress is responsible for passing statutes designed to remedy a perceived problem that is within federal jurisdiction. As legislation progresses through Congress, constituents have an opportunity to voice their views and concerns about problem areas.

The chapter opening "Consider…" illustrates an agency carrying out a legislative mandate. The Patient Protection and Affordable Care Act ("Affordable Care Act" or "Obama Care") required the FDA to develop and enforce rules of disclosure on sales of food in restaurants. Its proposed rule on disclosure of theater popcorn was part of the agency's assignment under the enabling act legislation. Section 4205 of the Patient Protection and Affordable Care Act (PPACA) requires that companies with over 20 restaurants or vending machines must post nutrition content for standard menu items, and that vending machines must "provide a sign in close proximity to each article of food or the selection button that includes a clear and conspicuous statement disclosing the number of calories contained in the article." The law took effect immediately when it was declared constitutional (see Chapter 5 for the case decision), but restaurants and grocery stores needed more guidance in

---

EXHIBIT 6.3 Stages in Formal Rulemaking by Administrative Agencies

terms of what those labels must include. The result was the FDA's proposed regulations in 2011 regarding content and location of the labels and disclosures, as well as details on exemptions from disclosures. Those proposed rules resulted in extensive push-back from those affected and an 18-month-long rulemaking process, which involved the popcorn regulation proposals noted in the chapter opening.

Agency Research of the Problem

Any regulation passed by an administrative agency must have some purpose and evidence to show that the regulation will accomplish the purpose. Rules passed without some study and evidence supporting their need or effectiveness could be challenged as "arbitrary and capricious" (discussed later in this chapter) by the persons or industries affected by the questioned rules.

Agency staff can perform the study, or the agency can hire outside experts to conduct it. The study will examine issues such as whether the regulation will be cost effective. Some regulations may cost billions of dollars for industries to follow. The food-labeling regulations fell into that category. As the costs of disclosure were explored, the FDA granted more and more exemptions because of the impact on businesses, including the cost of lab analysis for determining label information, costs of printing labels, and the prohibitive costs of developing new products, due to new labeling certification, including the barriers to developing lower calorie or low-fat versions of food products. The agency study focuses not only on monetary costs but also on the problems the regulation is trying to correct and the cost of those problems to the individual and to society.

Proposed Regulations

Based on the needs and costs shown by the completed study, the agency will publish its proposed rules or rule changes in the *Federal Register*. To be valid, the notice in the *Federal Register* must contain certain information. If notice is not given or is given improperly, a court can set aside the action taken by the agency and require the rulemaking process to be repeated with proper notice.

EXHIBIT 6.4 Proposed FDA Rule on Food Labeling Rules

FOOD AND DRUG ADMINISTRATION

ACTION: Proposed Labeling Rules for Menus in Retail Food Establishments 7 CFR Part 1215

AGENCY: Food and Drug Administration

SUMMARY: To implement the menu labeling provisions of the Patient Protection and Affordable Care Act of 2010 (Affordable Care Act or Obama Care), the Food and Drug Administration (FDA) is proposing requirements for providing certain nutrition information for standard menu items in certain chain restaurants and similar retail food establishments. The Affordable Care Act amended the Federal Food, Drug, and Cosmetic Act to require restaurants and similar retail food establishments that are part of a chain with 20 or more locations doing business under the same name and offering for sale substantially the same menu items to provide calorie and other nutrition information for standard menu items, including food on display and self-service food. Providing calorie and other nutrition information in restaurants and similar retail food establishments would assist consumers in making healthier dietary choices.

Although not required to do so, some agencies provide background information in the notice so that some history and the function of the rules are given. In addition to publishing the notice of proposed rules in the *Federal Register*, an agency is required under the **Regulatory Flexibility Act** to publish a notice in the publications of those trades and industries that will be affected by the rule. For example, the regulation governing food labeling was published in both restaurant and grocery association magazines. Exhibit 6.4 is the original proposed FDA rule on food labeling.

The Public Comment Period

One of the purposes for publishing proposed rules is to allow the public an opportunity to review and provide input on the proposed rules. The period during which the agency accepts comments on the rule is called the **public comment period**. Under the APA, the public comment period cannot be fewer than 30 days, but most agencies make the public comment period much longer. The FDA food labeling rules were so controversial that the comment period lasted for over one year.

Private citizens, government officials, industry representatives, businesspeople, and corporations can all send in comments. With this opportunity, businesses can provide information and express concerns about proposals. A comment to an agency on a proposed rule need not use a formal format; most just appear in letter form. Exhibits 6.5, 6.6, and 6.7 illustrate the types of comments that were submitted by companies and organizations to the FDA about the proposed food labeling regulations. Comments such as these, along with comments on any other agencies' proposed regulations, are available through an FOIA request if the agencies have not already made the comments available online.

EXHIBIT 6.5 Comments in Favor of the Proposed Labeling Rules

From the Obesity Society

The Obesity Society supports this effort to empower consumers with the information they need to make food choices that will help them to manage their weight, should they wish to do so. And increasing millions of Americans are indeed attempting to manage their weight. The proposed labeling initiatives will provide them with the most important data this side of their bathroom scale: the calorie content of food items that often account for a large part of their intake. Information is power, and this initiative will give that power to the millions of Americans who wish to take more responsibility for their health.

EXHIBIT 6.6 Comments That Oppose the Proposed Labeling Rules

From the International Association of Amusement Parks and Attractions
The sale of food is not our members' primary business purpose. The amusement and attractions industry comprises very different types of entities that may sell food to a varying degree in a variety of ways. For example, mobile hand-carts sell a variety of products and do not have large surfaces on which to write the labeling and nutritional information. In the case of amusement parks and attractions, the park or attraction would have no way of knowing whether franchise restaurants [within the park] meet the requirements for compliance.

The regulation has the potential to be very far reaching and will impose a large cost on business, many of which are not primarily restaurants or food-service establishments.

EXHIBIT 6.7 Comments That the Proposed Labeling Rules Require Change and Clarification

The National Association of County and City Health Officials (NACCHO) submitted the following:
Because menu labeling has been conceptualized as a policy that was locally enforced (including those mandated by the state), many local health departments (LHDs) are skeptical about the FDA's ability to effectively enforce the new national menu labeling law. NACCHO members' experience at implementing menu labeling and other ordinances and regulations involving food establishments (e.g., tobacco smoking and trans fats bans) suggests that there is a potential for a great deal of confusion during FDA implementation of the new national menu labeling law. The confusion is likely to be compounded in municipalities where existing menu labeling regulations, statutes, and ordinances are in place or where LHDs were spearheading voluntary efforts.

To limit the potential for confusion and disrupted LHD operations, we recommend the following:

1. The FDA should hold forums for state and local health departments that spell out clearly what role state and local government would have during implementation.
2. The FDA should provide funds for a mass media campaign to educate the public about menu labeling, their rights under the law, the establishments covered under the law, and what citizens should do if the nutrition information is not available.
3. The FDA should create and maintain an accurate and up-to-date list of food establishments covered under the law.
4. The FDA should also establish a toll-free telephone number for local health inspectors or the general public to call in the event of noncompliance.

From the National Automatic Merchandising Association (NAMA), www.vending.org
NAMA offers the following comments to the FDA regarding potential rules regarding Section 4205:

1. The FDA must allow maximum flexibility in how disclosure can take place, such as allowing one menu with calorie counts for an entire bank of machines,
2. The FDA must permit options for posting calorie information that allows multiple products to be placed in the same vending coils or stacks,
3. The FDA must allow vending operators to have the same technical allowances as chain restaurants,
4. The FDA must provide legal protection for minor and inadvertent mistakes in calorie disclosure,
5. The FDA must provide sufficient time to implement any new regulations, and
6. The FDA must take into consideration and reduce the economic impact of all such rules.

We propose that the industry be allowed at least two years after rules are finalized to implement calorie disclosure. Depending on how the rules are written, for example, the industry may have to create a data bank with product calorie counts which operators could access to print menus or labels that would fit the specific vending machines. Electronic devices or digital displays would have to be designed, programmed and installed.

NAMA also argues that vending machines manufactured prior to the implementation date of the regulations should be "grandfathered" and should not be forced to disclose calories. This may help lessen the economic impact and reduce the extremely wide variety of machines on the market.

From the Beer Institute and Brewers Association
The Beer Institute and Brewers Association and their members are pleased to offer this comment to FDA Docket No. FDA-2010-N-2098. As has been the case historically, we trust that FDA has been consulting and will continue to

consult with the Tax and Trade Bureau (TTB) of the Department of Treasury to ensure that any requirements FDA adopts are consistent with TTB's rules and guidelines governing alcohol beverage labeling and advertising, such as the Statement of Average Analysis. The TTB policy is based on longstanding federal law. Formal agency guidance was first published in 1976 and has been revised periodically to inform consumers of the calories, carbohydrates, protein and fat in a consistent manner.

From Domino's

Pizza is a shared occasion. As FDA and Weight Watchers have already recognized, consumers should be provided nutrition information on a per slice basis. The average individual does not consume an entire pizza.

Pizza is unique in that consumers "build their own," and offering a standard pizza calorie count and information is most helpful to consumers. Presenting all options would not be possible.

From Starbucks

Starbucks recommends that the new regulations:

- Provide flexibility with regard to the format and location of the suggested daily caloric statement on menus and menu boards
- Provide flexibility with regard to the font size and type of calorie listings on menus, menu boards, and food tags
- Exempt custom orders from the definition of a standard menu item
- Exempt marketing materials
- Allow current establishments at least six months to comply with the new requirements before enforcement
- Establish a petition process to approve alternative methods of disclosure

Other Issues in the Comment Period.   Some agencies hold public hearings on proposed regulations. The purpose of the hearings is to take input on the proposals and consider additional evidence and factors relevant in promulgating the final version of the rule.

One of the important distinctions between the legislative process and the regulatory rulemaking process is the nature of the role of those involved. Legislators, such as representatives and senators, can accept campaign contributions and meals from lobbyists. However, those who work in administrative agencies fulfill both rulemaking and enforcement roles and cannot accept such gifts. Case 6.1 illustrates what can happen when businesses and regulators cross the fine line on influence. *U.S. v Sun-Diamond Growers of California* (Case 6.1) is a criminal prosecution for alleged bribery of officials in order to persuade them to abandon or change proposed regulations before the agency.

CASE 6.1   *U.S. v Sun-Diamond Growers of California*
526 U.S. 398 (1999)

Gratitude Can't Be in Cash or Kind or Can It?

FACTS

Sun-Diamond Growers (respondent) is a trade association that engaged in marketing and lobbying activities on behalf of its member cooperatives, which were owned by approximately 5,000 individual growers of raisins, figs, walnuts, prunes, and hazelnuts. The United States (petitioner) is represented by Independent Counsel Donald Smaltz, who, as a consequence of his investigation of former Secretary of Agriculture Michael Espy, charged Sun-Diamond with making illegal gifts to Mr. Espy in violation of

§ 201(c)(1)(A). That statute provides, in relevant part, that anyone who

otherwise than as provided by law for the proper discharge of official duty … directly or indirectly gives, offers, or promises anything of value to any public official, former public official, or person selected to be a public official, for or because of any official act performed or to be performed by such public official, former public official, or person selected to be a public official … shall be fined under this title or imprisoned for not more than two years, or both.

CONTINUED

© Harper 3D/Shutterstock.com

Count One of the indictment charged Sun-Diamond with giving Mr. Espy approximately $5,900 in illegal gratuities: tickets to the 1993 U.S. Open Tennis Tournament (worth $2,295), luggage ($2,427), meals ($665), and a framed print and crystal bowl ($524). The indictment alluded to two matters in which Sun-Diamond had an interest in favorable treatment from the Secretary at the time it bestowed the gratuities. First, Sun-Diamond's member cooperatives participated in the Market Promotion Plan (MPP), a grant program administered by the Department of Agriculture to promote the sale of U.S. farm commodities in foreign countries.

Second, Sun-Diamond had an interest in the federal government's regulation of methyl bromide, a low-cost pesticide used by many individual growers. In 1992, the Environmental Protection Agency announced plans to promulgate a rule to phase out the use of methyl bromide in the United States. The jury convicted Sun-Diamond, and the District Court sentenced the respondent on this count to pay a fine of $400,000. The Court of Appeals reversed the conviction on Count One and remanded for a new trial, stating

> Given that the "for or because of any official act" language in § 201(c)(1)(A) means what it says, the jury instructions invited the jury to convict on materially less evidence than the statute demands—evidence of gifts driven simply by Espy's official position.

The Supreme Court granted *certiorari.*

JUDICIAL OPINION

SCALIA, Justice

Talmudic sages believed that judges who accepted bribes would be punished by eventually losing all knowledge of the divine law. The Federal Government, dealing with many public officials who are not judges, and with at least some judges for whom this sanction holds no terror, has constructed a framework of human laws and regulations defining various sorts of impermissible gifts, and punishing those who give or receive them with administrative sanctions, fines, and incarceration. One element of that framework is 18 U.S.C. § 201(c)(1)(A), the "illegal gratuity statute," which prohibits giving "anything of value" to a present, past, or future public official "for or because of any official act performed or to be performed by such public official." In this case, we consider whether conviction under the illegal gratuity statute requires any showing beyond the fact that a gratuity was given because of the recipient's official position.

Bribery requires intent "to influence" an official act or "to be influenced" in an official act, while illegal gratuity requires only that the gratuity be given or accepted "for or because of" an official act. In other words, for bribery there must be a *quid pro quo*—a specific intent to give or receive something of value in exchange for an official act. An illegal gratuity, on the other hand, may constitute merely a reward for some future act that the public official will take (and may already have determined to take), or for a past act that he has already taken.

The District Court's instructions in this case, in differentiating between a bribe and an illegal gratuity, correctly noted that only a bribe requires proof of a *quid pro quo.* The point in controversy here is that the instructions went on to suggest that § 201(c)(1)(A), unlike the bribery statute, did not require any connection between respondent's intent and a specific official act.

In our view, this interpretation does not fit comfortably with the statutory text, which prohibits only gratuities given or received "for or because of any official act performed or to be performed." It seems to us that this means "for or because of some particular official act of whatever identity"—just as the question "Do you like any composer?" normally means "Do you like some particular composer?"

Why go through the trouble of requiring that the gift be made "for or because of any official act performed or to be performed by such public official," and then defining "official act" (in § 201(a)(3)) to mean "any decision or action on any question, matter, cause, suit, proceeding or controversy, which may at any time be pending, or which may by law be brought before any public official, in such official's official capacity," when, if the Government's interpretation were correct, it would have sufficed to say "for or because of such official's ability to favor the donor in executing the functions of his office"? The insistence upon an "official act," carefully defined, seems pregnant with the requirement that some particular official act be identified and proved.

Besides thinking that this is the more natural meaning of § 201(c)(1)(A), we are inclined to believe it correct because of the peculiar results that the Government's alternative reading would produce. It would criminalize, for example, token gifts to the President based on his official position and not linked to any identifiable act—such as the replica jerseys given by championship sports teams each year during ceremonial White House visits. Similarly, it would criminalize a high school principal's gift of a school baseball cap to the Secretary of Education, by reason of his office, on the occasion of the latter's visit to the school. That these examples are not fanciful is demonstrated by the fact that counsel for the United States maintained at oral argument that a group of farmers would violate § 201(c)(1)(A) by providing a complimentary lunch for the Secretary of Agriculture in conjunction with his speech to the farmers concerning various matters of USDA policy—so long as the Secretary had before him,

CONTINUED

or had in prospect, matters affecting the farmers. Of course the Secretary of Agriculture *always* has before him or in prospect matters that affect farmers, just as the President always has before him or in prospect matters that affect college and professional sports, and the Secretary of Education matters that affect high schools.

All of the regulations, and some of the statutes, contain exceptions for various kinds of gratuities given by various donors for various purposes. Many of those exceptions would be snares for the unwary, given that there are no exceptions to the broad prohibition that the Government claims is imposed by § 201(c)(1). More important for present purposes, however, this regulation, and the numerous other regulations and statutes littering this field, demonstrate that this is an area where precisely targeted prohibitions are commonplace, and where more general prohibitions have been qualified by numerous exceptions. Given that reality, a statute in this field that can linguistically be interpreted to be either a meat axe or a scalpel should

reasonably be taken to be the latter. Absent a text that clearly requires it, we ought not expand this one piece of the regulatory puzzle so dramatically as to make many other pieces misfits.

We hold that, in order to establish a violation of 18 U.S.C. § 201(c)(1)(A), the Government must prove a link between a thing of value conferred upon a public official and a specific "official act" for or because of which it was given. We affirm the judgment of the Court of Appeals, which remanded the case to the District Court for a new trial on Count One.

Reversed and remanded.

CASE QUESTIONS

1. Are administrative agency employees permitted to accept gifts from those affected by their regulations and policies?

2. What is required for proof of criminal wrongdoing in making a gift?

3. What happens with the conviction, and why?

ETHICAL ISSUES

When the Commodities Futures Trading Commission (CFTC) proposed new rules to regulate the sales of derivatives and disclosure requirements in those sales, it received hundreds of comment letters. However, an investigation revealed that many of those letters were forged comment letters that were purportedly from an H.J. Heinz Company executive; a Burger King Corporation franchise; and at least five other Arkansas-based officials, including a judge, a county sheriff, and one mental health counselor. The letters contained identical passages criticizing banks for their "cartel-like control" of the $583 trillion derivatives market. The CFTC contacted the purported authors of the letters and confirmed them as forgeries. One agency observer noted, "This is just like the fake reviews we read all the time on the Internet from product buyers and services users. Everyone expects the seller to make these up or at least ask to write letters for others." Is he right? What is the problem with the forgeries? Is this type of input different from e-Bay seller evaluations?

Deciding What to Do with the Proposed Regulation

After the comment period is over, the agency has three choices about what to do with the proposed rules. The first choice is simply to adopt the rules. The second choice is to modify the proposed rules and go through the process of public comment again. The FDA took this second option of modifying the food-labeling rules by exempting theaters and popcorn and allowing another round of public comment on the modified rules. If the modification is minor, however, the APA allows the agency to adopt a modified version of the rule without going through the public comment period again. The final choice of the proposing agency is to withdraw the rule. Some rules have so many comments pointing out their impracticability, inflexibility, or prematurity that they are withdrawn from the promulgation process. For example, when the EEOC proposed guidelines on religious harassment in the workplace, including regulations on employees wearing necklaces with crosses on them, business comments and concerns about those guidelines resulted in the U.S. Senate passing a resolution 94–0 urging the EEOC to drop the guidelines. Religious and business groups flooded the EEOC with more than 100,000 letters of protest. EEOC attorneys advised that banning such personal expression, a form of speech, would result in a flood of First Amendment suits. The EEOC withdrew the proposed rules. EEOC spokesman Mike Widomski explained that "the public outcry and the number of comments that were received" triggered the reversal. Public comments and input have an impact in the regulatory process.

Court and Legislative Challenges to Proposed Rules

Those parties who made comments on the rules during their proposal stage can challenge the validity of the rules in court. An administrative rule can be challenged on several different grounds.

The Arbitrary and Capricious Standard for Challenging an Agency Action.   The first ground on which to challenge an agency rule is that it is arbitrary, capricious, an abuse of discretion, or in violation of some other law. This standard is generally applied to informal rulemaking and simply requires the agency to show evidence to support the proposed rule. Without such evidence, the rule can be held to be **arbitrary and capricious**. *Hornbeck Offshore Services, L.L.C. et al. v Salazar* (Case 6.2) addresses the issue of whether an agency's action is arbitrary and capricious.

CASE 6.2	*Hornbeck Offshore Services, L.L.C. et al. v Salazar* 696 F. Supp. 2d 627 (E.D. La. 2010)

Drilling Down to the Facts Supporting a Rule

FACTS

Hornbeck and others (plaintiffs) provide services to support offshore oil and gas drilling, exploration, and production activities in the Gulf of Mexico. Kenneth Salazar is the Secretary of the Department of Interior (DOI), a federal agency that includes the Minerals Management.

Following the BP Deepwater Horizon drilling platform explosion on April 20, 2010, and the resulting devastation and unprecedented disaster, the President asked DOI to conduct a study to determine what steps needed to be taken to prevent another problem with oil rigs in the Gulf.

DOI did a thirty-day study, consulting respected experts from state and federal governments, academic institutions, and industry and advocacy organizations.

On May 27, 2010, DOI issued a Report that recommended a six-month moratorium on permits for new wells and an immediate halt to drilling operations on the 33 permitted wells in the Gulf of Mexico. The DOI report also stated that "the recommendations contained in this report have been peer-reviewed by seven experts identified by the National Academy of Engineering." The experts pointedly observed this statement was misleading and called it a "misrepresentation." Although the experts agreed with the safety recommendations contained in the body of the main Report, five of the National Academy experts and three of the other experts publicly stated that they "do not agree with the six month blanket moratorium" on floating drilling. They envisioned a more limited kind of moratorium, but a blanket moratorium was added after their final

CONTINUED

review and was never agreed to by them. The plaintiffs moved for a preliminary injunction against the DOI moratorium.

JUDICIAL OPINION

FELDMAN, District Judge

The Administrative Procedure Act authorizes judicial review of final agency action. The APA cautions that an agency action may only be set aside if it is "arbitrary, capricious, an abuse of discretion, or not otherwise in accordance with law." The reviewing court must decide whether the agency acted within the scope of its authority, "whether the decision was based on a consideration of the relevant factors and whether there has been a clear error of judgment."

Normally, an agency rule would be arbitrary and capricious if the agency has relied on factors which Congress has not intended it to consider, entirely failed to consider an important aspect of the problem, offered an explanation for its decision that runs counter to the evidence before the agency, or is so implausible that it could not be ascribed to a difference in view or the product of agency expertise.

After reviewing the Secretary's Report and the Moratorium Memorandum, the Court is unable to divine or fathom a relationship between the findings and the immense scope of the moratorium. The Report describes the offshore oil industry in the Gulf and offers many compelling recommendations to improve safety. But it offers no time line for implementation. The Report patently lacks any analysis of the asserted fear of threat of irreparable injury or safety hazards posed by the 33 permitted rigs also reached by the moratorium. It is incident-specific and driven: Deepwater Horizon and BP only. None others. While the Report notes the increase in deepwater drilling over the past ten years and the increased safety risk associated with deepwater drilling, the parameters of "deepwater" remain confused. And drilling elsewhere simply seems driven by political or social agendas on all sides. The Report seems to define "deepwater" as drilling beyond a depth of 1,000 feet by referencing the increased difficulty of drilling beyond this depth; similarly, the shallowest depth referenced in the maps and facts included in the Report is "less than 1,000 feet." But while there is no mention of the 500 feet depth anywhere in the Report itself, "deepwater" [is now anything] more than 500 feet.

The Court recognizes that the compliance of the 33 affected rigs with current government regulations may be irrelevant if the regulations are insufficient or if MMS, the government's own agent, itself is suspected of being corrupt or incompetent. Nonetheless, the Secretary's determination that a six-month moratorium on issuance of new permits and on drilling by the 33 rigs is necessary does not seem to be fact-specific and refuses to take into measure the safety records of those others in the Gulf. There is no evidence presented indicating that the Secretary balanced the concern for environmental safety with the policy of making leases available for development. There is no suggestion that the Secretary considered any alternatives: for example, an individualized suspension of activities on target rigs until they reached compliance with the new federal regulations said to be recommended for immediate implementation.

The Deepwater Horizon oil spill is an unprecedented, sad, ugly, and inhuman disaster. What seems clear is that the federal government has been pressed by what happened on the Deepwater Horizon into an otherwise sweeping confirmation that all Gulf deepwater drilling activities put us all in a universal threat of irreparable harm. While the implementation of regulations and a new culture of safety are supportable by the Report and the documents presented, the blanket moratorium, with no parameters, seems to assume that because one rig failed and although no one yet fully knows why, all companies and rigs drilling new wells over 500 feet also universally present an imminent danger.

[T]he Court has found the plaintiffs would likely succeed in showing that the agency's decision was arbitrary and capricious. An invalid agency decision to suspend drilling of wells in depths of over 500 feet simply cannot justify the immeasurable effect on the plaintiffs, the local economy, the Gulf region, and the critical present-day aspect of the availability of domestic energy in this country.

The plaintiffs' motion for preliminary injunction is granted.

CASE QUESTIONS

1. Why is the problem with the experts' objections important in determining whether DOI's moratorium was arbitrary and capricious?

2. What is the significance of the difference between the factual information in the report and the terms of the moratorium?

3. What does the court see as alternatives to the moratorium?

BUSINESS STRATEGY

How Companies Respond to Regulations

When companies take federal agencies to court, they do so as a last resort because the companies remain subject to the agency's regulation after the litigation ends, even when the companies win. Litigation, such as that in the *Hornbeck* case is undertaken only after careful study and some assurance that the companies can win as well as an examination of what is lost if they do not litigate. In this case, the loss of drilling rights was worth the litigation risk.

The Substantial Evidence Standard for Challenging an Agency Action. A second theory for challenging an agency's regulation is that the regulation is unsupported by substantial evidence. This **substantial evidence test** is applied in the review of formal and hybrid rulemaking. Where the arbitrary and capricious standard simply requires some proof or basis for the regulation, substantial evidence requires that more convincing evidence exist in support of the regulation than against it. A third ground on which to challenge an agency's regulation involves the rule that a regulation can be set aside if the agency did not comply with the APA requirements of notice, publication, and public comment or input. The procedures for rulemaking must be followed in order for the regulatory process and resulting rules to be valid. An agency that seeks public comment for the purposes of drafting regulations cannot then turn the proposed regulations into agency rules after the comment period. The promulgated rules must be the result of the proceedings.

The Constitutional Standard for Challenging an Agency's Action. Another basis for challenging a regulation is that the regulation is unconstitutional. Many challenges based on constitutional grounds deal with regulations that give an agency authority to search records or that impose discriminatory requirements for licensing professionals. For example, a requirement of a minimum residency period before allowing an applicant to become licensed in a particular profession has been challenged successfully. Zoning board regulations that discriminate against certain classes or races as to the use of property have also been successfully challenged as unconstitutional. Further, broadcasters often depend on freedom of speech—the First Amendment—to challenge new Federal Communication Commission (FCC) regulations. For example, in *FCC v Fox Television Stations, Inc.*, 556 U.S. 502 (2009), the court dealt with a problem on television decency standards. During the 2002 Billboard Music Awards, broadcast by Fox Television, the singer Cher exclaimed during an unscripted acceptance speech: "I've also had my critics for the last 40 years saying that I was on my way out every year. Right. So f * * * 'em." At the 2003 Billboard Music Awards, Nicole Richie made the following unscripted remark while presenting an award: "Have you ever tried to get cow s* * * out of a Prada purse? It's not so f * * * ing simple." The third incident involved an episode of NYPD Blue, a regular television show broadcast by respondent ABC Television Network in which there was brief nudity in one episode. The Federal Communications Commission (FCC) found that the networks had broadcast content that violated decency standards and fined them $1.4 million. The networks appealed and the U.S. Supreme Court held that the standards were unclear and the fines not related to warnings about issues related to decency standards. The court held that the FCC could have decency standards but that it needed to make them clear to networks before it could fine them for violations [132 S.Ct. 2307 (2012)].

Consider...

The FDA was challenged by tobacco companies for its new rules that required the tobacco companies to put one of the FDA's 12 picture labels on its packaging. The tobacco companies argued that their First Amendment rights were violated by the rules, forcing them to speak in a certain way using government-mandated materials. The new labels were promulgated by both the FDA and the Department of Health and Human Services (HHS) pursuant to authority granted by Congress in 2009 under the Family Smoking Prevention and Tobacco Control Act.

Under the law, the following nine textual statements were to be included on cigarette labels:

WARNING: Cigarettes are addictive.
WARNING: Tobacco smoke can harm your children.
WARNING: Cigarettes cause fatal lung disease.
WARNING: Cigarettes cause cancer.
WARNING: Cigarettes cause strokes and heart disease.
WARNING: Smoking during pregnancy can harm your baby.
WARNING: Smoking can kill you.
WARNING: Tobacco smoke causes fatal lung diseases in nonsmokers.
WARNING: Quitting smoking now greatly reduces serious risks to your health.

The act required that these warnings and graphic labels take up 50 percent of the cigarette package label and 20 percent of all cigarette ads.

After publishing the proposed rule and receiving more than 1,700 comments, the FDA published its final rule in June 2011. Explain how the tobacco companies could challenge the rules. Discuss whether the rules will be set aside.
[*In the case of R.J. Reynolds Tobacco Company, et al. v FDA et al.*, 696 F.3d 1205 (D.C. Cir. 2012)]

THINK: The arbitrary and capricious and substantial evidence doctrines require that any agency action, whether a promulgation of a rule or its withdrawal, be supported by evidence and APA processes. That process requires some evidence related to the action taken or rule promulgated. There must be a full public airing of the issues. Whatever labels and disclosures the agency requires must be supported by evidence.

APPLY: In this case study, the use of pictures and conclusions is a form of interpretation and not really scientifically grounded statements about the health effects of smoking.

ANSWER: The purpose of the APA requirements is to curb the emotion of the moment and ensure that agencies do not take action without having followed a process for input and before obtaining evidence that the actions taken are necessary. The court concluded that the FDA had gone too far in its zeal to warn smokers, stepping beyond the science and into emotional appeals. The court held:

> *The graphic images here were neither designed to protect the consumer from confusion or deception, nor to increase consumer awareness of smoking risks; rather, they were crafted to evoke a strong emotional response calculated to provoke the viewer to quit or never start smoking.*

The *Ultra Vires* Standard for Challenging an Agency's Action.   Another theory for challenging a regulation in court is ***ultra vires***, a Latin term meaning "beyond its powers." An *ultra vires* regulation is one that goes beyond the authority given to the agency in its enabling act. Although most agencies stay clearly within their authority, if an agency tries to change the substance and purpose of the enabling act through regulation, the regulations would be *ultra vires*. For example, the intent of the 1933 Securities Act was to provide full disclosure to investors about a securities sale. The SEC could not, on the basis of its authority, pass a rule that eliminated securities registration in favor of an unregulated securities market. In *Massachusetts v EPA* (Case 6.3), the court dealt with greenhouse gases as well as their regulation within the context of challenges to the EPA based on *ultra vires*, substantial evidence, and the administrative regulation process. (Uniquely, the agency's defense was that the actions groups were demanding were *ultra vires*.)

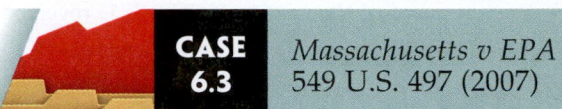

CASE 6.3	*Massachusetts v EPA* 549 U.S. 497 (2007)

Who Has Jurisdiction Over Hot Air? Congress? EPA? The Supreme Court?

FACTS

On October 20, 1999, a group of 19 private organizations (petitioners) filed a rulemaking petition asking EPA to regulate "greenhouse gas emissions from new motor vehicles under § 202 of the Clean Air Act." Petitioners maintained that greenhouse gas emissions have significantly accelerated climate change; and that "carbon dioxide remains the most important contributor to [man-made] forcing of climate change."

Fifteen months after the petition was filed, the EPA requested public comment on "all the issues raised in [the] petition," adding a "particular" request for comments on "any scientific, technical, legal, economic or other aspect of these issues that may be relevant to EPA's consideration of this petition," including whether there was global warming due to carbon emissions. The EPA received more than 50,000 comments over the next five months.

On September 8, 2003, EPA entered an order denying the rulemaking petition because (1) the Clean Air Act does not authorize EPA to issue mandatory regulations to address global climate change; and (2) even if the agency had the authority to set greenhouse gas emission standards, it would be unwise to do so at this time. Massachusetts, other states, and private organizations filed suit challenging the EPA denial as arbitrary and capricious, violative of the APA, and *ultra vires* because of statutory mandates for EPA action. The court of appeals dismissed the appeal from the agency denial and the Supreme Court granted *certiorari*.

JUDICIAL OPINION

STEVENS, Justice

In concluding that it lacked statutory authority over greenhouse gases, EPA observed that Congress "was well aware of the global climate change issue when it last comprehensively amended the [Clean Air Act] in 1990," yet it declined to adopt a proposed amendment establishing binding emissions limitations. Congress instead chose to authorize further investigation into climate change. In essence, EPA concluded that climate change was so important that unless Congress spoke with exacting specificity, it could not have meant the agency to address it.

According to the climate scientist Michael MacCracken, "qualified scientific experts involved in climate change research" have reached a "strong consensus" that global warming threatens (among other things) a precipitate rise in sea levels by the end of the century.[2]

While it may be true that regulating motor vehicle emissions will not by itself *reverse* global warming, it by no means follows that we lack jurisdiction to decide whether EPA has a duty to take steps to *slow* or *reduce* it. Because of the enormity of the potential consequences associated with man-made climate change, the fact that the effectiveness of a remedy might be delayed during the (relatively short) time it takes for a new motor-vehicle fleet to replace an older one is essentially irrelevant.

We find such action is "… arbitrary, capricious, an abuse of discretion, or otherwise not in accordance with law."

… The first question is whether § 202(a)(1) of the Clean Air Act authorizes EPA to regulate greenhouse gas emissions from new motor vehicles in the event that it forms a "judgment" that such emissions contribute to climate change.

The Clean Air Act's sweeping definition of "air pollutant" includes "*any* air pollution agent or combination of such agents, including *any* physical, chemical … substance or matter which is emitted into or otherwise enters the ambient air …" § 7602(g) (emphasis added). On its face, the definition embraces all airborne compounds of whatever stripe, and underscores

CONTINUED

that intent through the repeated use of the word "any." Carbon dioxide, methane, nitrous oxide, and hydrofluorocarbons are without a doubt "physical [and] chemical … substance[s] which [are] emitted into … the ambient air." The statute is unambiguous. If EPA makes a finding of endangerment, the Clean Air Act requires the agency to regulate emissions of the deleterious pollutant from new motor vehicles. Under the clear terms of the Clean Air Act, EPA can avoid taking further action only if it determines that greenhouse gases do not contribute to climate change or if it provides some reasonable explanation as to why it cannot or will not exercise its discretion to determine whether they do. To the extent that this constrains agency discretion to pursue other priorities of the Administrator or the President, this is the congressional design.

EPA finally argues that it cannot regulate carbon dioxide emissions from motor vehicles because doing so would require it to tighten mileage standards, a job (according to EPA) that Congress has assigned to DOT. But that DOT sets mileage standards in no way licenses EPA to shirk its environmental responsibilities. EPA has been charged with protecting the public's "health" and "welfare," a statutory obligation wholly independent of DOT's mandate to promote energy efficiency. The two obligations may overlap, but there is no reason to think the two agencies cannot both administer their obligations and yet avoid inconsistency.

Because greenhouse gases fit well within the Clean Air Act's capacious definition of "air pollutant," we hold that EPA has the statutory authority to regulate the emission of such gases from new motor vehicles.

… the use of the word "judgment" is not a roving license to ignore the statutory text. It is but a direction to exercise discretion within defined statutory limits.

Nor can EPA avoid its statutory obligation by noting the uncertainty surrounding various features of climate change and concluding that it would therefore be better not to regulate at this time. If the scientific uncertainty is so profound that it precludes EPA from making a reasoned judgment as to whether greenhouse gases contribute to global warming, EPA must say so. That EPA would prefer not to regulate greenhouse gases because of some residual uncertainty—which, contrary to Justice SCALIA's apparent belief, is in fact all that it said, is irrelevant. The statutory question is whether sufficient information exists to make an endangerment finding.

In short, EPA has offered no reasoned explanation for its refusal to decide whether greenhouse gases cause or contribute to climate change. Its action was therefore "arbitrary, capricious …, or otherwise not in accordance with law." We need not and do not reach the question whether on remand EPA must make an endangerment finding, or whether policy concerns can inform EPA's actions in the event that it makes such a finding. We hold only that EPA must ground its reasons for action or inaction in the statute.

The judgment of the Court of Appeals is reversed, and the case is remanded.

DISSENTING OPINION

Chief Justice ROBERTS, with whom Justice SCALIA, Justice THOMAS, and Justice ALITO join, dissenting
Global warming may be a "crisis," even "the most pressing environmental problem of our time." Indeed, it may ultimately affect nearly everyone on the planet in some potentially adverse way, and it may be that governments have done too little to address it. It is not a problem, however, that has escaped the attention of policymakers in the Executive and Legislative Branches of our Government, who continue to consider regulatory, legislative, and treaty-based means of addressing global climate change.

Apparently dissatisfied with the pace of progress on this issue in the elected branches, petitioners have come to the courts claiming broad-ranging injury, and attempting to tie that injury to the Government's alleged failure to comply with a rather narrow statutory provision. I would reject these challenges as nonjusticiable. Such a conclusion involves no judgment on whether global warming exists, what causes it, or the extent of the problem. Nor does it render petitioners without recourse. This Court's standing jurisprudence simply recognizes that redress of grievances of the sort at issue here "is the function of Congress and the Chief Executive," not the federal courts. I would vacate the judgment below and remand for dismissal of the petitions for review.

Justice SCALIA, with whom THE CHIEF JUSTICE, Justice THOMAS, and Justice ALITO join, dissenting
EPA's interpretation of the discretion conferred by the statutory reference to "its judgment" is not only reasonable, it is the most natural reading of the text. The Court nowhere explains why this interpretation is incorrect…. Although there have been substantial advances in climate change science, there continue to be important uncertainties in our understanding of the factors that may affect future climate change and how it should be addressed.

CONTINUED

[The] Court invents a multiple-choice question that the EPA Administrator must answer when a petition for rulemaking is filed. The Administrator must exercise his judgment in one of three ways: (a) by concluding that the pollutant *does* cause, or contribute to, air pollution that endangers public welfare (in which case EPA is required to regulate); (b) by concluding that the pollutant *does not* cause, or contribute to, air pollution that endangers public welfare (in which case EPA is *not* required to regulate); or (c) by "provid[ing] some reasonable explanation as to why it cannot or will not exercise its discretion to determine whether" greenhouse gases endanger public welfare, (in which case EPA is *not* required to regulate).

I am willing to assume, for the sake of argument, that the Administrator's discretion in this regard is not entirely unbounded-that if he has no reasonable basis for deferring judgment he must grasp the nettle at once. The Court, however, with no basis in text or precedent, rejects all of EPA's stated "policy judgments" as not "amount[ing] to a reasoned justification." Judgment can be delayed *only* if the Administrator concludes that "the scientific uncertainty is [too] profound." The Administrator is precluded from concluding *for other reasons* "that it would … be better not to regulate at this time." Such

other reasons—perfectly valid reasons—were set forth in the agency's statement.

I simply cannot conceive of what else the Court would like EPA to say.

The Court's alarm over global warming may or may not be justified, but it ought not distort the outcome of this litigation. This is a straightforward administrative-law case, in which Congress has passed a malleable statute giving broad discretion, not to us but to an executive agency. No matter how important the underlying policy issues at stake, this Court has no business substituting its own desired outcome for the reasoned judgment of the responsible agency.

CASE QUESTIONS

1. What authority is given to the EPA by statute? Why does the EPA not want to exercise authority over greenhouse gases?

2. Why does the majority conclude that greenhouse gases are included within that authority?

3. List the arguments the dissent makes against requiring the EPA to take action on greenhouse gases. What do you learn about the role of the issue of global warming in the dissent's analysis of the case versus the analysis of the majority?

6-4c PROACTIVE BUSINESS STRATEGIES IN REGULATION

Some administrative regulations can be eliminated through the use of legislation. In an enabling act called a **sunset law**, Congress creates an agency for a limited period of time during which the agency must establish its benefits and other justification for its continuation. The enabling act may provide for an audit to determine effectiveness after the agency has been in existence for two years. Without renewal by Congress, the "sun sets" on the agency and it is terminated. Some businesses lobby for the creation of sunset agencies to better control the number of agencies and their effectiveness.

Some agencies' power is controlled through congressional purse strings. With **zero-based budgeting**, the agency does not automatically receive a budget amount but rather starts with a zero budget each year and then is required to justify all its needs for funds. This type of control gives Congress some say each year in how the agency is operating. For example, the budget could be renewed only on the condition that the agency not promulgate certain regulations opposed by Congress.

6-4d INFORMAL RULEMAKING

The process for informal rulemaking is the same as that for formal rulemaking, with the exception that no public hearings are held on the rule. The only input from the public comes in the form of comments, using the same procedures discussed earlier.

Consider...

The use of snowmobiles in Yellowstone and Grand Teton National Parks was first permitted in 1963, and their use has been a topic of ongoing concern because of their impact on park resources. In 2003, the National Park Service (NPS), part of the Department of the Interior, groomed over 180 miles of park roads at least every other night. As many as 1,700 snowmobiles enter the parks on peak days.

The Fund for Animals and other environmental groups objected to the snowmobile use, and in December 2000, the NPS issued a proposed rule that capped snowmobile use in the winters of 2001–2002 and 2002–2003 and completely eliminated snowmobile use by the 2003–2004 winter season. The NPS received 5,273 comments during the 30-day public comment period; over 4,300 of these comments supported the proposed phase-out rule. On January 22, 2001, the NPS published the final rule, which allowed snowmobile use to continue but phased out all forms of mechanized snow vehicles, including snowmobiles, by the 2003–2004 winter season.

The 2001 Rule, promulgated by the Clinton administration, was published the day after President George W. Bush took office and was immediately stayed pending a review by the new administration. Meanwhile, the International Snowmobiler Manufacturers Association filed suit, challenging the 2001 Rule as an unsupported decision to ban snowmobiling. The NPS settled the litigation and agreed to consider data on new snowmobile technologies.

Pursuant to the settlement, in March 2002, the NPS issued another proposed rule. NPS received over 350,000 pieces of correspondence from the public; over 80 percent of the public comments supported the phase-out of snowmobiles. Despite this opposition, on November 18, 2002, one month before the phase-out was scheduled to go into effect, the NPS released a final rule delaying the implementation of the phase-out for an additional year. Snowmobile use was allowed to continue during the 2002–2003 winter season.

The Fund for Animals filed suit, challenging the postponement as arbitrary and capricious. In 2007, former National Park Director Fran Mainella called for using science, including studies of their impact, to make the rules on snowmobile use in national parks. Why is her recommendation relevant?

[*The Fund for Animals v Norton*, 390 F. Supp. 2d 12 (2005)]

6-5 Business Rights in Agency Enforcement Action

Administrative agencies not only make the rules; they enforce them. In so doing, the agencies are also responsible for adjudicating disputes over the scope or interpretation of the rules. Exhibit 6.8 is a chart of the steps involved in agency enforcement and adjudication.

6-5a LICENSING AND INSPECTIONS

Much of an administrative agency's role in enforcement is carried out by requiring the submission of certain types of paperwork. Many agencies issue licenses or permits as a way to enforce the law. For example, state administrative agencies may require building contractors to be licensed so that their dues can finance a recovery fund for the victims of bankrupt or negligent contractors. The idea behind the licensing and permit method of enforcement is to curtail illegal activity up front and also to have records in case problems arise.

EXHIBIT **6.8** Steps for Administrative Agency Enforcement and Adjudication

© Cengage Learning

Agencies also have the authority to conduct inspections, such as when an agency responsible for restaurant licenses inspects restaurant facilities to check for health code violations. The Occupational Safety and Health Administration (OSHA) at the federal level has the authority to inspect plants to check for violations of OSHA standards. This power of inspection at unannounced times is an enforcement tool by itself and provides strong incentive to comply with regulations. A business can refuse an inspection, but an agency can obtain a warrant and return for a mandatory inspection.

ETHICAL ISSUES

Three Chippewa Indian tribes submitted applications to the U.S. Department of the Interior seeking approval to convert a greyhound racing facility in Hudson, Wisconsin, to an off-reservation casino.

On June 8, 1995, the Indian Gaming staff in the department issued a draft report recommending approval of the Chippewa application.

While final decision on the application was pending in the agency, Harold Ickes (then White House Deputy Chief of Staff for Policy and Political Affairs) received a letter from Patrick O'Connor, a lobbyist for tribes that opposed the Chippewa application. The O'Connor letter explained the significance of the Chippewa decision, that the opposition tribes were important contributors to the Democratic Party, and that the Chippewa tribes were Republican supporters. In addition, Donald Fowler, the Democratic National Committee chairman, met with Mr. Ickes and "discussed the basis for the opposition to creating another gaming casino." Further, there were faxes regarding the application between White House staff and Department of the Interior staff.

On June 27, 1995, the Chippewa application was denied. The decision cited "community opposition" but did not incorporate or discuss the lengthy and detailed reports the staff had prepared for its June 8 recommendation of approval.

Interior Secretary Bruce Babbitt told Paul Eckstein, a lawyer for the Chippewa and a lifetime friend of Mr. Babbitt, that Mr. Ickes required him to issue the decision on June 27.

What ethical issues arise when political activities cross into administrative proceedings? How would the Chippewa perceive this series of events?

6-5b PROSECUTION OF BUSINESSES

Administrative agencies are also given the authority to prosecute violators. These agency prosecutions, however, are not traditional criminal prosecutions; the sanctions imposed for agency violations are not jail terms but rather fines, penalties, and injunctions, which are civil penalties, not criminal ones. For example, in the case of false advertising—a violation of Federal Trade Commission (FTC) rules—the agency could impose restitution as a sanction: The violator would have to reimburse all those individuals who bought the product based on false advertising. In some cases, an agency may merely want a violator to stop certain conduct and promise not to engage in that type of conduct again.

6-5c BEGINNING ENFORCEMENT STEPS

Regardless of the remedy an agency seeks, all action begins when the agency issues a **complaint** against the violating party. The complaint describes when and what the company did and why it is a violation.

Once a complaint is filed, an agency can negotiate with a party for an order or proceed to a hearing to obtain an order from an administrative law judge. The remedies in an order vary according to the type of violation and whether it is ongoing. The FTC could, and typically does, order companies running deceptive ads to stop using the ads and promise not to use them again in the future. These sanctions usually come in the form of an **injunction**, which is a court order that prohibits specifically described conduct. Many statutes are unclear about the extent of authority an agency is given in enforcement proceedings and what types of sanctions an agency can impose for violations. The authority to assess civil penalties, for example, varies from agency to agency.

6-5d CONSENT DECREES

Rather than go through a hearing and the expense of the administrative process, some companies agree to penalties proposed by an agency. They do so in a document called a **consent decree**, which is comparable to a *nolo contendere* plea in the criminal system. The party does not admit or deny a violation but simply negotiates a settlement with the administrative agency. The negotiated settlement includes the same types of sanctions the agency would have the power to impose if the case went to a hearing. The agency may be willing to give up a little in exchange for the violator's willingness to settle and save the agency the time and costs of full prosecution. The consent decree is a contract between the charged party and the regulatory agency. Exhibit 6.9 provides an example of an FTC consent decree.

6-5e HEARINGS

If the parties cannot reach an agreement through a consent decree, the question of violations and penalties will go to an administrative hearing, which is quite different from the litigation procedures described in Chapter 4. This type of hearing does not involve a jury. The plaintiff or prosecutor is the administrative agency, represented by one of its staff attorneys. The defendant is the person or company accused of violating an administrative regulation. The judge is called

---

EXHIBIT 6.9 Excerpts from an FTC Consent Decree

In the matter of the National Media Group, Inc. et al. Consent Order, etc., in regard to Alleged Violation of The Federal Trade Commission Act

This consent order, among other things, requires a King of Prussia, Pa. firm and a corporate officer engaged in the advertising and sale of "Acne-Statin," an acne "treatment," to cease disseminating or causing the dissemination of advertisements that represent that Acne-Statin cures acne, eliminates or reduces the bacteria and fatty acids responsible for acne blemishes, and is superior to all other acne preparations and soap for the antibacterial treatment of acne... . Additionally, they are required to establish an independent, irrevocable trust account containing sixty thousand dollars ($60,000) to be used to pay half of all requests for restitution by Acne-Statin purchasers; and obligated to conduct and be totally responsible for the administration of the restitution program.

(The original complaint appeared here.)

Order

It is ordered, That respondents, The National Media Group, Inc. a corporation ... and the corporate respondent's officers, agents, representatives, and employees ... do forthwith cease and desist from:

A. *Disseminating or causing the dissemination of any advertisement by means of the United States mails or by any means in or affecting commerce ... which directly or indirectly:*

1. *Represents that use of Acne-Statin will cure acne or any skin condition associated with acne.*
2. *Represents that Acne-Statin will eliminate or reduce the bacteria responsible for pimples, blackheads, whiteheads, or other acne blemishes or any skin condition associated with acne.*
3. *Represents that Acne-Statin will eliminate or reduce the fatty acids responsible for pimples, blackheads, whiteheads, other acne blemishes or any skin condition associated with acne.*
4. *Represents that Acne-Statin is superior to prescription or over-the-counter antibacterial acne preparations in the treatment of acne.*
5. *Represents that Acne-Statin is superior to soap in the antibacterial treatment of acne.*

It is further ordered, That:

A. *Within thirty (30) days of final acceptance of this consent order by the Federal Trade Commission (hereinafter the "Commission"), respondent, The National Media Group, Inc., shall establish an interest-bearing trust account containing the sum of sixty thousand dollars ($60,000), for the purpose of paying restitution to Acne-Statin purchasers....*

---

an **administrative law judge (ALJ)** at the federal level, and is called a **hearing examiner** or **hearing officer** in some state-level agencies. The defendant can be represented by an attorney.

An ALJ has all the powers of a judge. He or she conducts the hearing, rules on evidentiary and procedural questions, and administers oaths. The ALJ also has certain unique powers, such as the ability to hold settlement conferences between the parties. The ALJ also has the responsibility of making the decision in the case. That decision is cast in the form of a written opinion that consists of findings of facts, conclusions of law, and an order specifying the remedies and sanctions.

The ALJ also has the ethical responsibilities of a trial judge; that is, the judges are prohibited from having *ex parte* **contacts**, which are contacts with one side or one of the parties in the dispute without the knowledge of the others. Staff members of the agency are prohibited from supplying information to the ALJ except when they are witnesses or attorneys in the hearings.

Administrative hearings can have as participants more than just the agency and the party charged with a violation. Other parties with an interest in the case can intervene. These **intervenors** file motions to intervene and are usually permitted to do so at any time before the start of a hearing. Typical intervenors are industry organizations: Should the FCC hold hearings on charges against a television station on the content of ads on the station, the National Association of Broadcasters would probably want to intervene in the hearing.

The rules of evidence and procedure are somewhat relaxed in administrative hearings. Agencies involved in the hearings can issue subpoenas for documents, but the subpoenas can only be enforced by the courts. All of the investigation and adjudication processes of administrative agencies are subject to the constitutional standards of due process, which include the following rights: right to notification of the charges; right to notification of the hearing day; right to present evidence; right to be represented by an attorney; right to an impartial judge; right to a decision based on the law or regulation; and right to cross-examine the witnesses of the agency or intervenors.

6-5f ADMINISTRATIVE LAW OF APPEALS

Once the ALJ has issued a decision, the decision can be appealed. However, the appellate process in administrative law is slightly different. The first step in an appeal of an ALJ decision is not to a court but to the agency itself. This step gives the agency a chance to correct a bad decision before the courts become involved.

The appeal is to the next higher level in the agency. For example, in the FTC, an appeal of an ALJ's decision goes to the five commissioners of the FTC for reconsideration.

In some agencies, the structure is such that appeals may be made to more than one person in the structure. Those appealing an ALJ decision, however, must go through all the required lines of authority in the agency before they can go to court. This process is known as **exhausting administrative remedies**. An appeal made before administrative remedies are completed will be rejected for the failure to exhaust available administrative processes and remedies.

The exhaustion rule does allow some exceptions. A decision by a zoning board to allow construction of a building project could go directly to court because, if the building is started but the decision to allow construction later overruled, the builder is damaged. Alternatively, if the building is not started, other purchasers of the land and the builder are harmed. In other words, fast action is required to maintain all parties' positions.

If an agency has gone beyond its enabling act, a party can also go directly to court. This matter is more of a challenge to a regulation than it is to the agency's decision, and direct appeal is therefore permitted.

Finally, an agency decision can be appealed directly to court if exhaustion of administrative remedies would be futile, as evidenced by public statements of officials of the agency. When the FTC was trying to develop rules on children's TV advertising, for example, a group of interested parties brought a court action to have then-FTC chairman Michael Pertschuk removed from the rulemaking process because he had indicated strong feelings in the press about his position. It would

EXHIBIT **6.10** The Roles of Administrative Agencies

ACTIVITY	STEPS	PARTIES	RESULTS
Passing rules	Rule proposed	Agency	New rules
	Comments	Consumers	Modified rules
	Modification, withdrawal, or promulgation	Business Congress Agency	Withdrawn rules
Enforcement	Licensing	Agency	
		Business	
	Inspections	Agency	
		Courts (if warrant is required) Business	Search and inspection
	Complaints	Agency	Fines
			Penalties
			Injunctions
			Consent decrees
			Hearings

have been futile to try administrative remedies because the appeal would have been taken to the party they were trying to remove.

A decision of a federal administrative agency is appealed to one of the U.S. courts of appeals (as indicated in Chapter 3). An appellate court can simply affirm an agency action, find that an agency has exceeded its authority, find that an agency has violated the U.S. Constitution, or rule that an agency has acted arbitrarily or that an agency's decision or action is not supported by the evidence. The *Hornbeck* case (see Case 6.2 earlier in the chapter) is an example of a court's reversal of administrative agency action in the area of rulemaking.

Exhibit 6.10 provides a summary of the roles of administrative agencies.

6-6 The Role of Administrative Agencies in the International Market

The United States wins the award for having the most administrative agencies and regulations. Some businesses have argued that the amount of regulation hinders them in the international marketplace. For example, the readability level of regulations, as shown in Exhibit 6.11, demands much time and energy as companies attempt to interpret and comply with the laws.

Many regulators, legislators, and businesses have advocated elimination and streamlining of existing regulations, as well as careful consideration before new regulations are promulgated.

EXHIBIT 6.11 Various Reading Levels of Documents and Populations

DOCUMENTS AND POPULATIONS	GRADE LEVEL
1. *Love Story*	7.64
2. Reading level of U.S. population over age 65	9.71
3. *Playboy*	11.46
4. Reading level of general U.S. population	11.68
5. *Sports Illustrated*	12.82
6. Your Medicare Handbook	14.94
7. ERISA Summary Plan Description	15.29
8. *Wall Street Journal*	16.34
9. *Social Security Handbook*	17.51
10. Reading level of lawyers	19.00
11. *Albemarle* (U.S. Supreme Court ruling)	20.30
12. Occupational Safety and Health Act	30.79
13. Employment Retirement Income Safety Act	32.10
14. Section 18 of the Social Security Act	41.04

Sources: Warren S. Blumenfeld et al., "Readability of an ERISA Summary Plan Description vis-à-vis Intended Readership: An Empirical Test of Local Legal Compliance with a Federal Regulation." Paper presented at the Western American Institute for Decision Science Meeting, Reno, Nevada, March 1979; Warren S. Blumenfeld et al., "Readability of the Real Estate Settlement Procedures Act." Paper presented at the Southeastern Regional Business Law Association Meeting, Chapel Hill, North Carolina, October 1980.

ETHICAL ISSUES

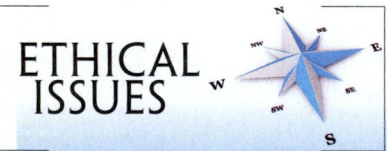

Some businesses are able to take advantage of one government's regulations. For example, the Energy Policy Act of 1992 requires that toilets installed after the act took effect (1994) use only 1.6 gallons of water rather than the nearly century-old standard of 3.5 gallons. As of 2000, about one-fourth of the nation's toilets were the 1.6-gallon types.

As homeowners have remodeled bathrooms and replaced older toilets, they have learned that the 3.5-gallon toilets are no longer sold in the United States. However, just across the U.S./Canadian border near Detroit, Canadian hardware stores are doing a land-office business selling 3.5-gallon tanks to U.S. citizens.

Those who are remodeling, and even some who are building new homes, generally install a $100 toilet from Home Depot in order to pass inspection. They then purchase a Canadian toilet, which costs in the neighborhood of $500 to $1,000 for a standard fixture because the demand is so high, and install it. Plumbing stores all over Canada report sales are brisk. In a survey conducted in May 2000, owners of Canadian plumbing stores said that they sell, on average, one toilet per day to U.S. citizens via either direct sale or shipment.

Do the citizens break any laws by what they do? Is what they do ethical?

BIOGRAPHY

Earl Devaney: An Auditor Who Kept Federal Agencies Clean

Earl Devaney served as the Inspector General (IG) for the Department of Interior (DOI) from 1999 to 2009. He later became the auditor for the funds dispersed under the Recovery Act of 2009. Mr. Devaney's reports as Inspector General were known for their forthrightness, insights, and color. When the Denver office of the Minerals Management Service of the DOI received an anonymous complaint from an employee in the Denver office that asked the IG to look into "ethical issues" there, Mr. Devaney responded. He found that agency employees were accepting lodging, gifts, alcohol, and other perks from industry executives in exchange for favorable treatment for the companies. Mr. Devaney also found that agency employees were having affairs with industry executives.[3] The agency employees defended these relationships as "arm's length." Mr. Devaney's report concluded, "Sexual relationships cannot, by definition, be arm's length."

Mr. Devaney spoke truth to power in a way that resulted in reorganization of the DOI. As a result of his investigation of lobbyist Jack Abramoff on behalf of Indian tribes, DOI secretary Gale Norton resigned. In testimony before Congress on his reports and recommendations, Devaney testified, "Short of a crime, anything goes at the highest level of the Department of Interior. Ethics failures on the part of senior department officials—taking the form of appearances of impropriety, favoritism and bias—have been routinely dismissed with a promise of not to do it again."

Mr. Devaney was appointed by President Obama to oversee the use of $787 billion in federal money under the American Reinvestment and Recovery Act. Mr. Devaney served in the role until 2013 when he retired from government service. He now serves as a consultant to Oversight Systems, an analytics systems company where he will be advising the company on audit and detection processes to detect fraud in corporate and government organizations.

Summary

What is an administrative agency?

- Administrative agency—statutory entity with the ability to make, interpret, and enforce laws

What laws govern the operation of administrative agencies?

- Administrative Procedure Act—general federal law governing agency process and operations
- Government in the Sunshine Act—federal law requiring public hearings by agencies (with limited exceptions)
- Federal Privacy Act—federal law protecting transfer of information among agencies unless done for enforcement reasons
- Freedom of Information Act—federal law providing individuals with access to information held by administrative agencies (with some exemptions such as for trade secrets)

What do administrative agencies do?

- Rulemaking—process of turning proposed regulations into actual regulations; requires public input
- *Federal Register*—daily publication that updates agency proposals, rules, hearing notices, and so forth
- *Code of Federal Regulations*—federal government publication of all agency rules
- Licensing—role in which an agency screens businesses before permitting operation
- Inspections—administrative agency role of checking businesses and business sites for compliance

How do agencies pass rules?

- Study issue, develop evidence of the need for the rule
- Public comment period—period in rulemaking process when any individual or business can provide input on proposed regulations

- Promulgation—approval of proposed rules by heads of agencies
- Rule must survive challenges based on standards of "arbitrary and capricious," "substantial evidence," "*ultra vires*," and "procedural errors."

How do agencies enforce the law?

- Consent decree—settlement (*nolo contendere* plea) of charges brought by an administrative agency
- Administrative law judge (ALJ)—overseer of hearing on charges brought by administrative agency

Questions and Problems

1. Florida State University (FSU) was under investigation by the NCAA for various types of violations. FSU created a special website where the NCAA and university officials could communicate, send documents, and post transcripts that were part of the investigation. Associated Press (AP) filed a Freedom of Information Act (FOIA) request with FSU for the release of the information on the special website. FSU refused to release the information, maintaining that because the information and documents were posted on a private website, they were not public records and, therefore, not subject to FOIA requests. Applying the principles of law from this chapter as well as what you have learned about precedent and interpretation, decide whether the court granted the FOIA request. [*Associated Press v Florida State University Board of Trustees, National Collegiate Athletic Ass'n v Associated Press*, 18 So.3d 1201 (Fla. App. 2009)]

2. The Consumer Product Safety Commission is reconsidering a rule it first proposed in 1997 that would require child-resistant caps on household products, including cosmetics. When the rule was first proposed, it was resisted by the cosmetics industry and abandoned. However, in May 2001, a 16-month-old baby died after drinking baby oil from a bottle with a pull-tab cap.

    The proposed rule would cover products such as baby oil and suntan lotion and any products containing hydrocarbons such as cleansers and spot removers. The danger, according to the commission, is simply the inhalation by children, not necessarily the actual ingestion of the products. Five children have died from inhaling such fumes since 1993, and 6,400 children under the age of five were brought into emergency rooms and/or hospitalized for treatment after breathing in hydrocarbons. There is no medical treatment for the inhalation of hydrocarbons.

    Several companies in the suntan oil/lotion industry have supported the new regulations. The head of a consumer group has said, "We know these products cause death and injury. That is all we need to know."[4]

    What process must the CPSC follow to promulgate the rules? What do you think of the consumer group

head's statement? Will that statement alone justify the rulemaking?

3. Because of overcrowded conditions at the nation's airports during the late 1960s, the Federal Aviation Administration (FAA) promulgated a regulation to reduce takeoff and landing delays at airports by limiting the number of landing and takeoff slots at five major airports to 60 slots per hour. The airports were Kennedy, LaGuardia, O'Hare, Newark, and National. At National Airport (Washington), 40 of the 60 slots were given to commercial planes, and the commercial carriers allocated the slots among themselves until October 1980. In 1980, New York Air, a new airline, requested some of the 40 slots, but the existing airlines refused to give up any. The secretary of transportation, in response and "to avoid chaos in the skies" during the upcoming holidays, proposed a rule to allocate the slots at National. The allocation rule was proposed on October 16, 1980, and appeared in the *Federal Register* on October 20, 1980. The comment period was seven days starting from the October 16, 1980, proposal date. The airlines and others submitted a total of 37 comments to the secretary. However, Northwest Airlines filed suit on grounds that the APA required a minimum of 30 days for a public comment period. The secretary argued that the 30-day rule was being suspended for good cause (the holiday season). Who is correct? Should an exception be made, or should the FAA be required to follow the 30-day rule? [*Northwest Airlines, Inc. v Goldschmidt*, 645 F.2d 1309 (8th Cir. 1981)]

4. Richardson-Vicks, Inc. is the manufacturer and seller of Vicks Pediatric Formula 44 (Pediatric 44), a cough medicine for children. In its ads for Pediatric 44, Vicks claims that the syrup contains active ingredients that enable it to begin working instantly. However, Pediatric 44 is considered to have only inactive ingredients, according to FDA regulations on "active" and "inactive" ingredients. A competitor has alleged that Vicks is "misbranding" its products. Can the FDA take any action? What steps could it take? Will the FDA be required to make an interpretation of the "active"/"inactive" regulation? [*Sandoz Pharmaceuticals v Richardson-Vicks, Inc.*, 902 F.2d 222 (3rd Cir. 1990)]

5. Rhonda Kallman founded a company that produces Moonshot 69, a caffeinated beer. Each bottle of beer contains about twice as much caffeine as a can of Pepsi. In 2011, Ms. Kallman, along with three other manufacturers, was served with a cease and desist notice from the FDA to remove the caffeine from her beer or stop selling the product. Ms. Kallman has said that what the FDA is doing is like Prohibition 2010 and that it has no authority to regulate the sale or production of alcohol. She also indicates that Moonshot 69 is not an energy drink like those that are subject to FDA regulation. She says that agencies should regulate and not ban products. What information could you share with Ms. Kallman that would help determine what the FDA is trying to accomplish?

6. San Diego Air Sports Center (SDAS) operates a sports parachuting business in Otay Mesa, California. SDAS offers training to beginning parachutists and facilitates recreational jumping for experienced parachutists. The majority of SDAS jumps occur at altitudes in excess of 5,800 feet.

The jump zone used by SDAS overlaps the San Diego Traffic Control Area (TCA). Although the aircraft carrying the parachutists normally operate outside the TCA, the parachutists themselves are dropped through it. Each jump must be approved by the air traffic controllers.

In July 1987, an air traffic controller in San Diego filed an Unsatisfactory Condition Report complaining of the strain that parachuting was putting on the controllers and raising safety concerns. The report led to a staff study of parachute jumping within the San Diego TCA. In October 1987, representatives of the San Diego Terminal Radar Approach Control (TRACON) facility met with SDAS operators. In December 1987, the San Diego TRACON sent to SDAS a draft letter of agreement outlining agreed-upon procedures and coordination requirements. Nonetheless, the San Diego TRACON conducted another study between January 14, 1988, and February 11, 1988, and about two months after the draft letter was sent, the San Diego TRACON withdrew it.

SDAS states that the air traffic manager of the San Diego TRACON assured SDAS that it would be invited to attend all meetings on parachuting in the San Diego TCA. However, SDAS was not informed of or invited to any meetings.

In March 1988, the Federal Aviation Administration (FAA) sent a letter to SDAS informing SDAS that "[e]ffective immediately parachute jumping within or into the San Diego TCA in the Otay Reservoir Jump Zone will not be authorized." The FAA stated that the letter was final and appealable.

SDAS challenged the letter in federal court on grounds that it constituted rulemaking without compliance with required APA procedures. Evaluate SDAS's challenge to the letter by applying administrative law and procedure. [*San Diego Air Sports Center, Inc. v Federal Aviation Administration*, 887 F.2d 966 (9th Cir. 1989)]

7. Hooked on Phonics is a reading program that departs from the current educational reading philosophy of "whole-language learning." The program emphasizes the more traditional reading process of having children sound out letters and combinations of letters. The Federal Trade Commission (FTC) filed a false advertising complaint against Gateway Educational Products, Inc., the owner of the Hooked on Phonics program. The FTC claimed that Gateway's television claims that those with reading disabilities would be helped "quickly and easily" and that Hooked on Phonics could "teach reading in a home setting without additional assistance" were misleading. Gateway does not feel the claims are false, but it does not want to have bad publicity. What advice can you give Gateway on handling the FTC charges?

8. In March 1992, the Federal Communications Commission (FCC) proposed rules that would increase the maximum number of radio stations a company could own from 12 AM stations and 12 FM stations to 30 of each. The FCC proposed the changes because more than half of the nation's 11,000 radio stations are unprofitable and larger ownership blocks would allow some economies of scale. Critics were vocal about domination and monopolization. As a result, the FCC changed the ownership maximums to 18 FM and 18 AM stations and issued its final rules on August 5, 1992. Describe the process the FCC employed to make these changes. Explain what public outcry accomplished.

9. The Food and Drug Administration (FDA) is concerned about laser eye surgery, noting that an industry concerned with correcting vision is spawning joint ventures, holding wine-and-cheese seminars to court potential investors, and creating databases of nearsighted consumers. The corrective laser surgery costs $2,000 per eye and is not covered by insurance. Calls to the available 800 numbers have noted some dissatisfaction among the 700 patients who've had the surgery, including complaints of farsightedness. Further, the only regulation the FDA has in the field covers granting laser manufacturers permission to sell their machines to ophthalmologists. The FDA would like to know more and perhaps control some aspects of patients' care. Describe the steps the FDA must take.

10. Countrywide, the problem mortgage company that was acquired by Bank of America, was once the largest mortgage lender in the country and the biggest supplier

NAME	TITLE	AMOUNT	RATE	TERM
Franklin Raines	Former Chair	$982,253	5.125	10 yrs.
Jamie Gorelick	Former Vice Chair	$960,149	5.000	10 yrs.
Christopher Dodd	Chair, Senate Finance Comm. (Oversight for Fannie Mae)	$506,000	4.250	5 yrs.
James Johnson	Former CEO	$971,650	3.875	5 yrs.
Franklin Raines	Former Chair	$986,340	4.125	10 yrs.
Daniel Mudd	Former CEO	$2,965,000	4.250	7 yrs.

Source of Data: Real estate records.

of mortgages to Fannie Mae's secondary market program. (Fannie Mae has since collapsed.) Countrywide released information that indicated it made additional loans to Fannie Mae officials at favorable rates. Referred to as the Friends of Angelo group, these officials received favorable rates and expedited service. The following chart shows the officials, their titles at Fannie Mae, and their loan amounts, rates, and terms.

In the last years before the Countrywide problems and Fannie's collapse, the two firms reached an agreement whereby Countrywide would funnel most of its loans to Fannie in exchange for a special rate. At the time they reached the special arrangement, the "Friends of Angelo" program was created. The FOA, as it was known, gave officials an expedited path for processing

as well as a one-point reduction in rate. Former Fannie Mae vice chair Jamie Gorelick said, "I don't believe there was any special treatment given." However, an employee at the time said, "I know 100 percent she went through the VIP department." In response, Ms. Gorelick said, "You'd think if somebody was trying to do me a favor, they would tell me they were doing me a favor, and I am unaware of any such treatment. When I did this transaction, I was decidedly a has-been. I had no favor to give."[5]

Apply what you know about conflicts of interest to Ms. Gorelick's responses to the inquiries about her loan. Did former CEO Daniel Mudd have a conflict? What is the relationship of corporate officers to customers? What is the role of regulators? Senators?

STRATEGY & THE LAW

When Your Product Is Under Regulatory Scrutiny

The Yamaha Rhino is an off-road vehicle that looks like a golf cart with four-wheel drive. Some have called it an all-terrain cycle (ATC) with a front seat and a steering wheel. With the rise in popularity over two decades ago of the ATC, increasing numbers of accidents (100 deaths and 100,000 injuries) resulted in extensive federal regulation of the design of ATCs, including the requirement of four wheels (rather than three). The Consumer Product Safety Commission (CPSC) also required extensive training, disclosures, warnings, and prohibitions on children driving ATCs. However, the Rhino is not subject to the ATC regulations because it has a steering wheel rather than handlebars. The Rhino is also not subject to federal regulations for cars because

it meets neither the size nor the structure thresholds for autos.

In this regulatory no-man's-land, the Rhino has emerged as a popular seller. The vehicle weighs 1,100 pounds, costs $11,000, and has been a popular seller since 2003. The 2008 model was the first of the Rhinos to have doors on the side. Owners say the Rhino offers the comfort of a golf cart but the ability to fit on trails as well as on the back of a pickup truck.

However, there have been 30 deaths caused by Rhino accidents and there are now 200 lawsuits around the country that seek recovery from Yamaha for injuries caused by what the suits claims is the Rhino's defective design. The Rhino is 54.4 inches long, but is narrower than any of its competitors (the design's goal is to allow the Rhino to fit on trails). The cases involve mostly rollover accidents.

Yamaha has always warned its buyers to wear seat belts and helmets when operating the Rhino. In 2006 and 2007, Yamaha sent out stickers to purchasers that read, "Abrupt maneuvers or aggressive driving have caused rollovers—even on flat, open areas." Yamaha also sent out a letter that offered to install doors on doorless Rhinos and extra handholds. The letter also added that drivers should be at least 16 years old.

The death rate for the Rhino (number of deaths in relation to number of vehicles sold per year) is 1 in 10,000.[6] However, the actual death rate for 2006, as provided by Yamaha, was 8 in 10,000. Yamaha said the death rate stat is skewed because you must include the number of hours operated to have the rate mean anything. Yamaha sold 42,000 Rhinos in 2007.

Along with other off-road vehicle manufacturers, Yamaha has formed a voluntary trade association group that has the goal of establishing voluntary safety standards. The Recreational Off-Road Vehicle Association has already proposed changing the generic name of the vehicles to Recreational Off-Highway Vehicle (ROV) from utility terrain vehicle (UTV). Yamaha and other manufacturers say that many accidents are caused by driver error and recklessness.

What are your obligations when you operate in a loophole area of the law? Is Yamaha liable if it complied with any regulations and laws that applied? What is the responsibility of a company to report accidents related to its product?

Notes

1. "Federal Regulation and Aggregate Economic Growth," *Regulation and the Macroeconomy* (2004), as updated by the authors on their websites, 2008. See also, Susan E. Dudley and Richard D. Otis, Jr., "eRulemaking: A Case Example of eGov Transformation," Mercatus Center Working Papers, #57 (2010), http://mercatus.org/sites/default/files/publication/eRulemaking-DudleyOtis.pdf.

2. Since the time of the decision reported here, the emergence of troubling e-mails on the data and the peer review process for climate scientists has raised questions about the validity of the "strong consensus." Patrick J. Michaels, "The Climategate Whitewash," *Wall Street Journal*, July 12, 2010, p. A15.

3. In 2010, the DOI found similar issues of conflicts in the Minerals Management Office, which was responsible for the Deepwater Horizon well off the coast of Louisiana. The problems emerged after the explosion at that deepwater offshore rig and the resulting oil leak that damaged the coasts of all the Gulf states.

4. Julian E. Barnes, "Safety Caps Are Considered for Cosmetics," *New York Times*, October 10, 2001, pp. C1, C8.

5. Glenn R. Simpson, "Countrywide Made Home Loans to Gorelick, Mudd," *Wall Street Journal*, September 25, 2008, p. A10.

6. Melanie Trottman and Christopher Conkey, "U.S. Probes Off-Road Vehicles After a String of Accidents," *Wall Street Journal*, November 4, 2008, pp. A1, A16.

Chapter 7 INTERNATIONAL LAW

Shakespeare was ahead of his time when he wrote that "the world is your oyster." Today's global business environment is the dream of economists, who have fostered the notion of free trade since the publication of Adam Smith's *The Wealth of Nations* 250 years ago. Trade barriers are down, resources are flowing, and even the smallest businesses are involved in international trade. Trade across borders, however, involves additional issues and laws and carries risks that do not exist in transactions within nations. Litigation across borders is expensive and complex, so businesses must understand the legal environment of international trade, including contracts, customs and duties, and antibribery provisions, in order to minimize their legal risks. This chapter helps with understanding the laws that influence international business. What and whose statutes affect businesses in international trade? What international agreements affect global businesses? How do businesses deal with the complexities of international contracts, disputes, and differing cultures and legal systems?

UPDATE
For up-to-date legal and ethical news, go to **mariannejennings.com**

Bo Chambers/Flickr/Getty Images

Consider...

James H. Giffen, owner of Mercator Corporation, a New York company, made $78 million in payments to two government officials in Kazakhstan. He was charged with violations of the Foreign Corrupt Practices Act (FCPA). Giffen moved to have the charges dismissed because he had been named a Counselor to the President of Kazakhstan and was immune from prosecution under the act of state doctrine. He also asked that the charges be dismissed because any payments he made to the officials were for facilitation and access and were not bribes for contracts with his company. Is he correct? Does the act of state doctrine apply? Did he bribe, or did he facilitate?

7-1 Sources of International Law

"When in Rome, do as the Romans do" is advice that can be modified for business: When in Rome, follow Roman law. In each country where a business has operations, it must comply with the laws of that nation. Just as each U.S. business must comply with all the tax, employment, safety, and environmental laws of each state in which it operates, each international business must comply with the laws of the countries in which it operates.

7-1a TYPES OF INTERNATIONAL LAW SYSTEMS

The various systems of laws can be quite different, and businesses are well advised to obtain local legal counsel for advice on the peculiarities of each nation's laws. Generally, a nation's laws are based on one of three types of systems. The United States, like England, has a **common law** system. Our laws are built on tradition and precedent (see Chapter 1). Not every possible situation is codified; we rely on our courts to interpret and apply our more general statutes and, in many cases, to develop principles of law as cases are presented (as with the common-law doctrine of negligence; see Chapter 9).

Other countries rely on civil law or code law. This form of law is the foundation of legal systems in France, Germany, Spain, and other European countries. Code law systems do not rely on court decisions but rely instead on statutes or codes that are intended to cover all types of circumstances and attempt to spell out the law, leaving little need for interpretation.

A final system of law is Islamic law, which is based on religious tenets and governs all aspects of life, from appropriate dress in public to remedies for contract breaches. Many of the Islamic countries have a combination of civil and Islamic systems as a result of the influences of both colonization and Islam.

Before its collapse in the former Soviet Union and Eastern Europe, communism was also classified as a legal system. Now the former communist nations struggle

ETHICAL ISSUES

PricewaterhouseCoopers is one of the United States' "Big 4" accounting firms. PwC, as it is known, has had a tax practice in Russia since the time that country changed from communist rule. One of PwC's clients in Russia was Yukos, a major Russian oil company that is now bankrupt.

Russia's Federal Tax Service, an agency similar to the IRS in the United States, has filed suit against PwC, alleging that it concealed tax evasion by Yukos for the years 2002–2004. The Tax Service also announced a criminal probe of PwC's conduct with regard to its tax services for Yukos. Twenty Tax Service agents searched PwC's offices in Moscow and questioned PwC employees about the Yukos account. Yukos lost its tax case and has paid $9.2 million in charges for the nonpayment of taxes. However, Yukos and PwC do have the case on appeal.

Many see the battle between PwC and the Tax Service as part of the Russian government's ongoing battle to sell off the assets of Yukos and avoid the surrender of the company's assets to investors and creditors who have filed claims. Those suits are pending in courts in The Hague. Some analysts believe that the Russian government is hoping to press PwC into revealing information that would help it take back the Yukos assets.

If PwC is found to have engaged in evasion, it loses its license to do business in Russia, and if it turns over information, it is likely to lose its clients in Russia.

What issues should a company consider before doing business in an economically developing country? What are the risks? Did this ethical dilemma begin long before the Russian government's demands of PwC? What international law, culture, and ethical issues should a company consider before deciding to do business in another country?

Source: Neil Buckley and Catherine Belton, "Moscow Raids PwC Ahead of Yukos Case," *Financial Times*, March 11, 2007, p. 1.

with evolving cultural, market, and governmental systems. Likewise, countries such as Iraq and Afghanistan struggle in their postwar eras to establish constitutions, free elections, and the rule of law.

7-1b NONSTATUTORY SOURCES OF INTERNATIONAL LAW

Customs and values in a culture often have a controlling effect on negotiations, contracts, and performance in international business. The American Bar Association recommends that businesspeople and their lawyers examine seven cultural factors and do background work in these cultural areas before attempting negotiations and business in a particular country. Referred to as the LESCANT factors, the following issues should be researched as if they were legal background for doing business: language, environment and technology, social organization, contexting, authority, nonverbal behavior, and time concept.

Language

Businesspeople should determine which language a particular country prefers for conducting business. Mexico and other Latin American countries are accustomed to doing business in English. In Quebec, Canadian government regulations mandate the use of French in conducting business. English has become the dominant language for contracts, even for contracts among natives of some countries that do not have English as the official language. The trend is attributed by some to the Internet. Those in non–English-speaking countries became increasingly familiar with English as they interacted on social media and the Internet. One French businessman learned the language so that he could enjoy the English jokes his son e-mailed him. His son was stunned when he visited and found his father so fluent in English following several years of joke exchanges.

Environment and Technology

Communications systems vary in quality and universality in countries around the world. Because U.S. companies are accustomed to rapid communication and verification of offers and acceptances (see Chapter 12 on contract formation), doing business in a country where technology is less developed and communication is slower and by different means requires advance knowledge and appropriate adjustments and provisions for contract negotiations.

Social Organization

Businesspeople should know a country's social order: May women negotiate deals? Is it appropriate to discuss business during a meal?

Contexting

Low-context cultures are those that rely on the written word as the controlling factor in their relationship. Little weight is given to the context in which that agreement is reached. Low-context cultures include the North American countries, Switzerland, Germany, and Scandinavian countries (although not Finland). Mid-level-context cultures are France, England, and Italy; high-context cultures are Latin American countries, Arabic nations, and Asian countries, including Japan. In high-context cultures, how and in what setting an agreement is reached are as important as the words in the document itself.

Authority

Who has negotiating authority is important in a business meeting, and who is sent to a meeting sends a signal about importance in high-context cultures. Lawyers are not considered part of the negotiating team in Japan but are considered critical in the United States. Often, in Asian cultures, the negotiators do not have the authority to commit to a deal and must take proposals back to their companies and those who do have authority.

Nonverbal Behavior

In the United States, the tendency is to interpret nonverbal behavior differently from the way it is perceived in other cultures. For example, silence during negotiations in the United States creates a compulsion for businesspeople to fill the awkward silence or interpret the silence as a rejection. In Asian cultures, such silence is simply a method of contemplating and considering and does not indicate a rejection.

Time Concept

The United States is a monochronic nation: Time is everything, and the goal of businesspeople is to get the deal done. Other monochronic nations include Great Britain, Germany, Canada, New Zealand, Australia, the Netherlands, Norway, and Sweden. Countries that operate with great flexibility regarding time and negotiate within the context of building a relationship as opposed to completing a deal are called polychronic nations. The remainder of the world operates within this flexible form of time culture.

7-1c CONTRACTS FOR THE INTERNATIONAL SALE OF GOODS (CISG)

Sometimes referred to as the Vienna Convention, the U.N. Convention on Contracts for the International Sale of Goods (CISG) began its development in 1964 as an idea that was later discussed and formulated at the 1980 Vienna Convention. The CISG first became effective in 1988 with its adoption in the United States along with a small group of other countries. Today, CISG has been adopted in 60 countries, with ratification processes under way in many other countries. However, its use is voluntary, even in adopting countries. Businesses can opt out of using the CISG to govern their contracts.

The CISG is designed to provide international contracts the convenience and uniformity that the Uniform Commercial Code provides for contracts across state lines in the United States. Although it includes some differences (see details in Chapters 12 and 13), the CISG is a reflection of the Uniform Commercial Code.

7-1d TREATIES, TRADE ORGANIZATIONS, AND CONTROLS ON INTERNATIONAL TRADE

In international trade, a number of treaties, tariffs, and organizations govern and guide international contracts. This section discusses some of the most important ones.

Whether supported or despised by economists, tariffs and restrictions on trade have existed for as long as trade itself. Duties, quotas, and tariffs have all been used to control the flow of goods over and across national boundaries. For most of history, these limits on trade have been imposed on a nation-by-nation basis. However, new forms of trade agreements are developing, and nations are organizing in larger groups in an attempt to eliminate many of the individually based barriers to trade.

The European Union

As discussed in Chapter 1, the European Union (EU) was established with the goal of removing barriers to the free movement across borders of goods, people, services, and capital. The Treaty on European Union (Maastricht Treaty) established the goals of free trade, a single currency, and uniform laws on commerce and security. Today, for example, the EU handles antitrust violations by companies in any of the EU's member nations.[1]

In addition to the European Commission, the EU created other institutions to help it carry out its goal of unified European commercial operations. The European

FOR THE MANAGER'S DESK

Re: Charting Unknown Legal Territory: Pirates

AARRGGGGGG! Shiver me timbers, and all that other Johnny Depp stuff. We have pirates, savvy? The pirates are from Somalia and they are wreaking havoc on international commerce off the coast of Africa. NATO has sent ships to patrol the African coasts and rescue ships and hostages. However, there are international law issues regarding what is to be done about—and with—the captured pirates.

In a 1718 trial of pirates, Judge Nicholas Trott ruled, "It is lawful for any one that takes them, if they cannot bring them under some government to be tried, to put them to death." More recent due process, human rights, and individual country laws require that the pirates receive a trial. However, the questions still remain: How? By whom? Where?

The conduct of pirates violates international norms of behavior, but what specific laws are broken? Who has jurisdiction when the pirates take ships in international waters? The principles of autonomy apply here: What country has the right to try a citizen of another country for crimes not committed in either country?

Trials for pirates were historically handled in military tribunals. However, the backlash today against military tribunals because of treatment of prisoners of war, as well as court rulings that have transferred the cases to civil courts, means that pirates end up being released. Released pirates are free to pirate another day and, perhaps, another sea.

Countries have come up with different solutions. The British Royal Navy has instructed its military not to detain pirates because such detention violates the pirates' human rights. Instructions for the French military are to return the pirates to Somalia. The U.S. policy is to return pirates to their home governments, but only if given assurances that the pirates will be detained and prosecuted. The civil and political unrest in Somalia often means that groups are able to secure the freedom of the pirates through the use of force against the government. In the meantime, companies doing international shipments are vulnerable. There were 300 pirate attacks of shipping vessels in 2009 and by 2012, there were 315, including 28 hijackings.

Council, which consists of the heads of state of the various members, is the policy-making body and establishes the broad directives for the operation of the EU. The next step below the council is the European Commission, the body charged with implementation of Council policies. At the third level is the European Parliament, an advisory legislative body with some veto powers. Finally, the European Court of Justice (ECJ) is the judicial body created to handle disputes and any violations of regulations and the EU treaty itself. The EU has in place nearly 300 directives that govern everything from health and safety standards in the workplace to the sale of mutual funds across national boundaries.

The WTO

In 1994, the General Agreement on Tariffs and Trade (GATT), a **multilateral treaty** (treaty among more than two nations) (see Chapter 1), was adopted and established the World Trade Organization (WTO). The WTO lists 159 countries as members, including the United States. The WTO is the body charged with the administration and achievement of the GATT objectives. GATT's primary objectives are trade without discrimination and protection through tariffs. Trade without discrimination is achieved through GATT's most-favored-nation (MFN) clause. The issue of China's membership as a most-favored nation was debated extensively, particularly in the political and social context of human rights issues in that country, prior to its admission in 2001. Russia was admitted as a member at the end of 2011 on the condition that it would take steps to ensure that its legal system will enforce contract rights.

Under MFN status, subscribing countries treat each other equally in terms of import and export duties and charges. Subscribing countries do not give more favorable treatment to one country as opposed to another. Domestic production is protected by tariffs and not through any other commercial measures.

Some exceptions under GATT for regional trading arrangements are undertaken through other treaties, such as the North American Free Trade Agreement and the European Union.

The WTO also established a Dispute Settlement Body (DSB), which is an international arbitration body created to bring countries together to resolve trade disputes rather than have those nations resort to trade sanctions. If a WTO panel finds that a country has violated the provisions of GATT, it can impose trade sanctions on that country. The sanctions imposed are generally equal to the amount of economic injury the country caused through its violation of GATT. For example, in 2012, the DSB found that the Philippines was charging differential tax rates on domestic versus imported distilled spirits and government officials there agreed to stop the practice.

The North American Free Trade Agreement (NAFTA)

The North American Free Trade Agreement (NAFTA) is a treaty among Canada, the United States, and Mexico that took effect in 1994 and eliminated all tariffs among the three countries over a 15-year period.

Products covered under NAFTA include only those that originate in these countries. All goods traded across the boundaries of these countries must carry a NAFTA certificate of origin, which verifies the original creation of the goods in the country from which they are being exported. NAFTA is unlike the EU in that NAFTA focuses only on free trade and does not create a common labor market, governing body, or currency.

Prohibitions on Trade: Individual Nation Sanctions

In some countries, international tensions have resulted in sanctions being imposed, including trade prohibitions. Countries can impose two types of trade sanctions. With primary trade sanctions, companies based in the United States are prohibited from doing business with certain countries. For example, the United States prohibited or regulated trade with Iraq since the time of the 1991 Gulf War and lifted those sanctions only over the past few years as the country's new government took hold. Currently, the United States has prohibitions on trade with Iran. Primary boycotts can be limited to certain categories of goods. Other category restrictions can include extreme limitations such as limiting trade to food and medical supplies. In some restrictions, the United States prohibits domestic companies from selling certain types of equipment to certain nations. For example, U.S. firms have severe restrictions on selling certain component parts to Iran. These parts are primarily those that could be used in the development of nuclear weapons and other military capabilities.[2]

The second form of trade prohibition is the secondary boycott, which is a step beyond the primary boycott in that companies from nations doing business with a sanctioned country will also experience sanctions for such an activity. For example, in 1996, the United States passed the Iran and Libya Sanctions Act (ILSA) as a secondary boycott against two nations on which the United States already had imposed trade restrictions. This law was passed because of active lobbying by the families of those killed when Pan Am Flight 103 exploded over Lockerbie, Scotland, as a result of bombs planted on the flight by Libyan terrorists. Under the secondary boycott trade prohibition, the United States will not grant licenses to permit its financial institutions to loan money to, award government contracts to, or allow imports from any company that finances, supplies, or constructs oil procurement in Iran or Libya. Generally, these types of secondary boycotts do not apply retroactively so that companies need not divest themselves of their holdings already invested in these countries. However, no new business is allowed once the act takes effect if the companies wish to continue trading with the United States.

The International Monetary Fund (IMF) and the World Bank

Created at Bretton Woods, New Hampshire, the International Monetary Fund (IMF) was established following World War II with the goal of expanding international trade through a bank with a lending system designed to bring stability to national currencies. The IMF created the International Bank for Reconstruction and Development (commonly called the World Bank), which allows signing nations to have Special Drawing Rights (SDR) or the ability to draw on a line of credit in order to maintain the stability of their currency.

The idea of the IMF was to enhance and encourage international trade through assurances about monetary stability in various countries. Each time a particular nation, such as Greece or Russia, experiences a difficult economic swing, significant debate occurs about the use of IMF funds to buoy that nation's currency so that international trade with that country is not destroyed.

The Hague Convention

Although largely thought of as the multilateral treaty that deals with issues of war, the Hague Convention has become increasingly important to businesses because of a 1954 addition that deals with discovery in civil cases across borders. Countries that are signatories to this 1954 treaty agree to cooperate with civil litigation discovery requests (see Chapter 4 for more information on discovery), provided that the request is made for documents that are clearly enumerated in the request and which bear a direct connection to the subject matter of the litigation. In other words, a signatory country has the right to refuse to provide the information if the request appears to be part of a fishing expedition to obtain information for reasons other than the litigation itself. As businesses deal with international copyright, patent, and trademark infringement, litigation across borders has become necessary, and cooperation under the Hague Convention Civil Procedure agreement has proven invaluable in obtaining information that can identify the perpetrators who are selling counterfeit and gray-market goods.

The Kyoto Treaty

The Kyoto Protocol, often called the Kyoto Treaty or the global warming treaty, would have required signatory countries to reduce emissions "by at least 5% below 1990 levels." The United States would have been required to reduce its emissions by at least 7 percent had it signed the treaty. China, India, and Mexico are excluded from the treaty's coverage. By the time of the Copenhagen climate summit late in 2009, the Kyoto Treaty was just a bit of history. The nations in attendance were unwilling to commit to its standards.

The Organization of Petroleum Exporting Countries (OPEC)

The Organization of Petroleum Exporting Countries (OPEC) is a cartel that works together to control oil supplies and production, prices, and taxes. The result of the OPEC cooperation has been increased royalties to participating countries.

7-2 Trust, Corruption, Trade, and Economics

Perhaps the greatest activity in multilateral agreements among countries has been in the area of curbing bribes because of their devastating impact on trust and the chilling of investment, which can stall economic development in a country. In his departure speech as Secretary of the U.S. Treasury, Robert Rubin cautioned government employees to never accept any sort of gift as part of their duties because, he noted, "Corruption and bribery benefit a few at the expense of many."

7-2a FOREIGN CORRUPT PRACTICES ACT (FCPA)

Perhaps the most widely known criminal statute affecting firms that operate internationally is the **Foreign Corrupt Practices Act** (FCPA; 15 U.S.C. §§ 78dd-1). The FCPA applies to business concerns that have their principal offices in the United States. It contains antibribery provisions as well as accounting controls for these firms and was passed to curb the use of bribery in foreign operations of these companies.

History, Purpose, and Application of the FCPA

First passed in 1977, the FCPA is the result of an investigation by the Securities and Exchange Commission (SEC) that uncovered questionable foreign payments by large stock issuers who were based in the United States. Approximately 435 U.S. corporations made improper or questionable payments totaling $300 million in Japan, the Netherlands, and Korea.

The FCPA prohibits making, authorizing, or promising payments or gifts of money or anything of value to government and NGO officials with the intent to corrupt for the purpose of *obtaining* or *retaining business* for or with or *directing business*. That one-sentence prohibition has many components. What is a payment? The decisions in cases and Justice Department guidelines have given us the following: cash, country club memberships, excessive comped travel (travel that does not include seminars or

Business Planning Tip

Many companies are unsure about the nature of certain payments and what would be considered a red flag. In 2012, the Justice Department published its *Resource Guide to the U.S. Foreign Corrupt Practices Act*. The 130-page guide, which is available online, includes the kinds of things companies can do that are not prohibited. For example, the following are not violations of FCPA according to the *Guide*:

1. Small gifts of expressions of gratitude, provided there is transparency in the giving

2. Small gifts to local charities, provided the gift is consistent with the company's general philanthropic goals and is not "large"

3. Wedding gift to a government official (if not too large)

4. Hats, t-shirts, pins, and pens that companies offer at trade show booths and that government officials take

5. Payment of the bar tab for drinks for government officials at a group meeting

6. Payment for travel to the United States for training at a company's facility; foreign dignitaries can even take in a baseball game at company expense during such training without the company risking an FCPA violation.

Companies can now provide training with these specifics to guide employees who are working in other countries.

BUSINESS STRATEGY

The Costs of Slipping on the FCPA

In companies with hundreds of thousands of employees worldwide, supervision of employees with regard to the FCPA can be difficult. Without clear signals from executive management and strong policies, even companies with the best intentions in terms of compliance with the law can fall short. For example, IBM entered into a consent decree with the SEC on charges that it engaged in bribery in violation of the FCPA. The charges filed by the SEC alleged that an IBM subsidiary, IBM Argentina S.A., was awarded a $250 million contract for modernizing the systems of Banco de la Nacion Argentina (BNA), a government-owned commercial bank in Argentina. As part of the arrangement, the IBM subsidiary entered into a $37 million contract to do business with a corporation owned by directors of BNA, with the directors receiving $4.5 million of that $37 million contract as compensation. Those directors then voted to award IBM the contract.

The consent decree requires IBM to pay a $300,000 fine. The fine is minimal because IBM did conduct its own internal investigation to uncover what had happened and fired 13 employees in its subsidiary when the preceding relationships were uncovered.

BNA revoked the contract after paying IBM $80 million, and IBM has agreed to reimburse BNA $34 million of that amount. Other Argentine agencies also revoked their contracts with IBM, and the total amount of business lost in the Argentina market is estimated to be $500 million.

IBM now has a company policy that prohibits company bids for government projects that are not done in an open bidding process with full public access to documents.

The costs to IBM in this situation, both in terms of its lost contracts and revenues and its reputation, are nearly incalculable. Many companies take the position that they will not even make facilitation payments so that their worldwide staff members understand a clear and definitive line. A Procter & Gamble executive explains that, once a government official knows that a company will pay to get things done or get them done quickly, the price keeps rising and that such payments never serve the shareholders well. Long-term growth in a country is limited when even facilitation payments become part of a company's operations there. Strategically, more than ethically and legally, these types of payments are questionable in their benefits and results.

[*In the Matter of International Business Machines Corp.,* Administrative Proceeding File No. 3–13097, Rel. No. 34–43761 (December 21, 2000)]

presentations and consists of, for example, shopping trips to Paris for government officials or their spouses), cash donations to political parties, payment of cell phone or utility bills for government officials, and giving luxury gifts such as sports cars and furs to government officials or their spouses.

The types of activities included under "obtaining, retaining, or directing business" are the following: winning contracts, influencing a procurement process, circumventing rules in order to get products imported, gaining access to non-public bid information, evading taxes or penalties, influencing the outcome of lawsuits or regulatory actions, obtaining exceptions to regulations, avoiding contract termination, asking regulators or officials to exclude your competitors from their country, evading customs duties, and extending drilling contracts.

The types of officials covered under the FCPA (to whom gifts may not be directed) include foreign officials, political parties, party officials, candidates for office, and any NGO. Using any person who will transmit the gift or money to one of the other types of people also is prohibited. Changes in 1998 added the NGO coverage so that officials such as those with the United Nations, the Olympics, or the IMF are now covered under the act. The bribery involved in awarding the 2002 Olympics held in Salt Lake City resulted in this expansion of the statute's coverage.

Use of Agents and the FCPA

When the FCPA was passed initially, many companies tried to find ways around the bribery prohibitions. Companies would hire foreign agents or consultants to help them gain business in countries and allowed these "third parties" to act independently. However, many of these consultants paid others who then paid bribes to officials. Under the FCPA, even these types of arrangements can constitute a violation if the consulting fees are high, odd payment arrangements occur, or the company has reason to know of a potential or actual violation. Companies must be able to establish that they have performed "due diligence" in investigating those hired as their agents and consultants in foreign countries. For example, if a U.S. company hired a consultant who charged the company $25,000 in fees and $250,000 in expenses, the U.S. company would be, under Justice Department guidelines, on notice for excessive expenses that could signal potential bribes being paid. These types of expenses are known as *red flags* for U.S. companies. The Justice Department uses this information as a means of establishing intent, even when the company may not know precisely what was done with the funds and what was paid to whom.

The FCPA and "Grease" or Facilitation Payments

Payments to foreign officials for "facilitation," often referred to as **grease payments**, are not prohibited under FCPA so long as these payments are made only to get the officials to do jobs that they might not do ordinarily or would do slowly without some payment. These grease payments can be made for obtaining permits, licenses, or other official documents; processing governmental papers such as visas and work orders; providing police protection and mail pickup and delivery; providing phone service, power, and water supply; loading and unloading cargo or protecting perishable products; and scheduling inspections associated with contract performance or transit of goods across the country.

Penalties for Violation of the FCPA

Penalties for individuals who have violated the FCPA can run up to $250,000 per violation and five years' imprisonment. Corporate fines can be up to $2 million per violation. Also, under the Alternative Fines Act, the Justice Department can seek to obtain two times the benefit the bribe attempted to gain, known as *disgorgement*. For example, if a company paid a bribe to obtain a $100 million contract for computer services for a foreign government, the potential fine could be $20 million and 20 years ($25 million for corporations).

The Justice Department has stepped up its enforcement of the FCPA. During 2010, FCPA charges peaked at 74. The Department says that the key to its increased enforcement is going after industry sectors. Enforcement efforts have resulted in greater compliance efforts on the part of companies

Business Planning Tip

How Companies Stay Out of FCPA Trouble

1. Know thy competition. If you are doing business in a country where corruption is known to be common, don't suspect your competitors. Look at the practices of your salespeople and agents. A good question to ask is, "How are we able to do business here so successfully if we are not doing what everyone else is doing?"

2. Focus your audits on payments in the countries that you know condone bribery. How much went to whom, why, and were there are any changes in amounts, frequency, or method of payment?

3. If someone makes an anonymous report, don't ignore it. For example, Avon's then CEO, Andrea Jung, received an anonymous tip about the company's new operations in China but did not conduct a timely or expansive enough investigation. The result was more trouble for the company, particularly because they failed to look at operations in other countries to check for similar behaviors.

4. If your investigations and audits discover misconduct on the parts of managers or employees, terminate them. The termination communicates to local employees that what is customary in their country in terms of how to do business is not consistent with company standards. For example, Alcoa terminated one of its foreign managers when an investigation revealed that the manager was demanding payments from employees who wanted their jobs back after a period of lay-offs for economic reasons ended.

5. If you find an FCPA violation, report it to the Justice Department. The Justice Department advises companies to "come knocking on our door before we come knocking on yours."[3]

Consider...

American Ri, Inc. (ARI), a Houston-based company, exports rice to foreign countries, including Haiti. Rice Corporation of Haiti, a wholly owned subsidiary of ARI, was incorporated in Haiti to represent ARI's interests and deal with third parties there. Haiti's customs officials assess duties based on the quantity and value of rice imported into the country. Haiti also requires businesses that deliver rice there to remit an advance deposit against Haitian sales taxes, based on the value of that rice. The businesses are then given a credit for the deposit when they file their Haitian sales tax returns. David Kay and Douglas Murphy, executives of ARI, were charged with violations of the Foreign Corrupt Practices Act (FCPA) for allegedly bribing Haitian officials to accept false bills of lading that reflected total rice imports to be about one-third of actual levels so that ARI would owe less in taxes. Is this type of an arrangement a bribe? Does it violate the FCPA? [*U.S. v Kay*, 359 F.3d 738 (5th Cir. 2004)]

THINK: The FCPA criminalizes payments that are intended to (1) influence a foreign official to act or make a decision in his official capacity, or (2) induce such an official to perform or refrain from performing some act in violation of his duty, or (3) secure some wrongful advantage to the payor.

APPLY: Securing reduced taxes and duties on imports through bribery enables ARI to reduce its cost of doing business, thereby giving it an "improper advantage" over actual or potential competitors, and enabling it to do more business or remain in a market it might otherwise leave.

ANSWER: Bribing foreign officials to lower taxes and customs duties certainly can provide an unfair advantage over competitors and thereby be of assistance to the payor in obtaining or retaining business. The FCPA applies broadly to payments intended to assist the payor, either directly or indirectly, in obtaining or retaining business for some person, and that bribes paid to foreign tax officials to secure illegally reduced customs and tax liability constitute a type of payment that can fall within this broad coverage.

covered under the act. In 2011, there were 48 charges, and in 2012, only 23. Currently targeted for FCPA enforcement are the medical device and pharmaceutical industries. Another target area focuses on government programs that provide government or NGO payment for supplies. The "Oil for Food" investigations have also yielded a number of corporate defendants. The "Oil for Food" program, established in 1995 by the United Nations, permitted U.S. companies to trade oil in exchange for food, medicine, and other basic supplies with Iraq. The program was terminated in 2003, but the prosecution of companies involved still continues.

The FCPA and U.S. Competitiveness

One of the long-standing concerns about the FCPA is whether it has placed U.S. businesses at a competitive disadvantage in those countries in which bribery is generally accepted as a way to win contracts and government benefits. However, a survey by the U.S. Government Accounting Office of the companies affected by the FCPA found that the ability of companies from other countries to bribe officials did not give them a competitive advantage. The survey found that U.S. trade increased in 51 of 56 foreign countries after the FCPA went into effect. The increase was attributed to the position adopted by U.S. companies with respect to their competitors—if they could not bribe government officials, they would disclose publicly information about bribes made by any of the companies from other nations.

FCPA and the Organization for Economic Cooperation and Development (OECD)

The Organization for Economic Cooperation and Development OECD is now supportive of the U.S. FCPA and its principles. Member countries have enacted legislation for compliance with its international pact against bribery. The OECD's 38 members[4] now work together to investigate companies' activities across borders.[5] However, only the United States, Germany, Norway, and Switzerland actively enforce their antibribery statutes. The British version of the FCPA took effect in July 2011 and has required significant changes in companies in terms of compliance and monitoring payments.

When Congress amended the FCPA to implement the OECD Convention on Combating Bribery of Foreign Public Officials in International Business Transactions, the amendments expanded the act's jurisdiction to cover all U.S. citizens acting outside the United States and all non-U.S. citizens acting inside the United States. The convention basically adopts the standards of the United States under the FCPA and requires nations signing the agreement to impose criminal penalties, seize profits earned through bribery, and rein in government officials who accept illicit payments by actively prosecuting them along with the companies making the payments.

7-3 Resolution of International Disputes

As discussed in Chapters 1, 3, and 4, there really is no way to enforce international laws. The International Court of Justice established by the United Nations is a court of voluntary jurisdiction for disputes between nations; it is not a court for the resolution of business disputes between nations. More and more companies and individuals favor arbitration to resolve disputes. The most popular forum chosen for such arbitrations and quasi-trials is London's Commercial Court, which was founded on March 1, 1895, when it heard its first case, a dispute over the quality of cloth a Flemish manufacturer sold to a London agent. The court was perhaps the first to recognize the role of arbitration in deciding international business disputes; such innovation restored the confidence of business in the settlement of disputes by third parties. The London Commercial Court is viewed as a neutral forum with highly experienced judges who are also experienced commercial litigators.

7-4 Principles of International Law

The sources of international law simply serve to govern businesses as they operate in a particular country, and the laws may vary from country to country. However, some principles of international law apply to all countries and people in the international marketplace. The principles of international law do affect the decisions and operations of businesses, regardless of the availability of court resolution of rights.

7-4a ACT OF STATE DOCTRINE

The act of state doctrine gives every sovereign state respect from other sovereign states for its laws, actions, decisions, and policies. The act of state doctrine confirms the independence of sovereign nations and their courts. No country will intervene in the judicial and legislative processes of another country because those actions are inconsistent with that country's standards. Courts of one country will not undertake the responsibility of providing their citizens with remedies against another country, even when that other country has violated the rights of a citizen of the first country. For example, when Union Carbide's plant in Bhopal had a high-fatality accident, Union Carbide's CEO was arrested and taken into custody when he went to Bhopal to ensure appropriate relief efforts. Although his imprisonment would have violated his rights in the United States, the U.S. courts did not intervene in India's criminal processes. Lawyers for the CEO had to work through the courts of India.

7-4b SOVEREIGN IMMUNITY

The concept of **sovereign immunity** is based on the notion that each country is a sovereign nation. This status means that each country is an equal with other countries; each country has exclusive jurisdiction over its internal operations, laws, and people; and no country is subject to the jurisdiction of another country's court system unless it so consents. Our court system cannot be used to right injustices in other countries or to subject other countries to penalties. For example, in *Schooner Exchange v McFaddon*, 7 Cr. 116 (1812), a group of American citizens attempted to seize the vessel *Exchange* when it came into port at Philadelphia because the citizens believed that the ship had been taken improperly on the high seas by the French emperor Napoleon and that the ship rightfully belonged to them. The U.S. Supreme Court held that the ship could not be seized because sovereign immunity applied, and France could not involuntarily be subjected to the jurisdiction of U.S. courts.

The Foreign Sovereign Immunities Act of 1976 clarified the U.S. government's position on sovereign immunity and incorporated the *Schooner Exchange* doctrine. Not only are countries immune but the act also adds a clarification to the concept of sovereign immunity of sovereign nations for illegal acts. For example, in *Argentine*

ETHICAL ISSUES

Transnational is an international company that arranges transportation for large cargo items and shipments of large orders. Transnational has a fleet of cargo ships. Each cargo ship has a crew of 25 employees.

Transnational's head of security, Jack Davis, is a retired U.S. Navy officer who, until January 2009, worked for the United States Department of Homeland Security. Since his hiring by Transnational, Davis has alerted senior management to the evolving issue of pirates. Despite an international incident involving a U.S. ship in the spring of 2009, the response of management to Davis's concerns has been one of postponement.

A group of pirates have boarded a Transnational ship that was, at the time of the takeover, sailing off the coast of Africa. The pirates have demanded payment of $25 million or $1,000,000 for each crew member. The pirates have imposed a deadline of five hours for Transnational's decision and promise of payment. The pirates have also indicated that they will begin killing crew members one at a time if their deadline for Transnational's agreement to the payment is not met. Davis advised Transnational to go ahead and pay the pirates because "Lives of employees are at stake and my job is protecting employees." However, a Transnational senior officer cautioned in a meeting, "That's a bribe, and Transnational has a long-standing practice of not paying bribes."

The officers, the board, and Davis seek your advice.

Republic v Amerada Hess Shipping Co., 488 U.S. 428 (1989), the Supreme Court dismissed a suit brought in a U.S. federal court by a Liberian-chartered commercial ship company against the government of Argentina for its unprovoked and illegal attack on a company ship. The ship was in neutral waters when the war between Great Britain and Argentina broke out over the Falkland Islands. The attack by the Argentine Navy was unprovoked and in clear violation of international law. However, the U.S. Supreme Court clarified that under the Sovereign Immunities Act and principles of international law, all sovereign nations are immune from suits in other countries, even for those acts—like that of Argentina—that are clear violations of international law.

There is a distinction, however, under both the Foreign Sovereign Immunities Act and the courts with respect to the commercial transactions of a sovereign nation. For example, the sale of services and goods; loan transactions; and contracts for marketing, public relations, and employment services entered into by a country are, in essence, voluntary agreements that subject that country's government to civil suits in another nation's courts according to the terms of the agreement or according to the basic tenets of judicial jurisdiction (see Chapter 3).

The *U.S. v Giffen* case (Case 7.1) deals with issues of the FCPA and the act of state doctrine as well as sovereign immunity and provides answers for the chapter opening "Consider..."

CASE 7.1	*U.S. v Giffen* 326 F. Supp. 2d 497 (S.D.N.Y. 2004)

Getting a Government Title to Avoid FCPA Issues

FACTS

Kazakhstan, formerly a republic in the Soviet Union, became a sovereign nation in 1991 and has vast oil and gas reserves, which are the property of the Kazakh government. With its independence, Kazakh officials had the opportunity to sell oil and gas rights to companies from around the world. James H. Giffen was the principal shareholder in Mercator Corporation, a New York Company.

Between 1995 and 1999, Giffen was alleged to have made $78 million in payments to Nurlan Balgimaev, the former Prime Minister and Oil Minister of the Republic of Kazakhstan, and Nursultan Nazarbaev, the President of Kazakhstan, in violation of the FCPA. Giffen moved to have the charges dismissed because he had been named, on August 1, 1995, a Counselor to the President of Kazakhstan. The Counselor position was a semiofficial title and Giffen advised the officials on oil and gas deals. Indeed, Giffen's advice tended to favor contracts with Mercator. However, Giffen argued that he was a government official in Kazakhstan and thereby immune from prosecution under the act of state doctrine and, that, as a public official of the Kazakh

government he was immune from prosecution. He also asked for dismissal on the grounds that his payments were facilitating—that he merely made the payments to gain access to the officials and that there were no direct contracts in play when he made the payments.

JUDICIAL OPINION

PAULEY III, District Judge

I. FOREIGN CORRUPT PRACTICES ACT

The FCPA makes it illegal for an individual or company in the United States to make illicit payments to a foreign official to cause that foreign official to assist in obtaining or retaining business for the payor.

Despite the FCPA's prohibition on bribery of foreign officials, an exception exists for "facilitating" payments to "expedite or to secure the performance of a routine governmental action by a foreign official, political party, or party official. The term "routine governmental action," however, does not extend to decisions by a foreign official to award new business or continue business with a particular contractor.

CONTINUED

Giffen does not dispute the FCPA's applicability to the actions charged in the indictment. Accepting those allegations as true, the illicit payments to senior Kazakh officials were for the sole purpose of obtaining and retaining business for Mercator. Giffen does not argue that the $78 million was a "facilitating" payment. Nor could the alleged payments be characterized as "facilitating" a routine governmental action because, as alleged in the indictment, they were primarily intended to influence the senior Kazakh officials to award new business to Mercator.

II. ACT OF STATE DOCTRINE

"[T]he act of state doctrine … 'precludes the courts of this country from inquiring into the validity of the Public acts a recognized foreign sovereign power committed within its own territory.'" While a United States court may question the wisdom of a foreign sovereign act, it may not rule on its legality or validity. "The major underpinning of the act of state doctrine is the policy of foreclosing court adjudications involving the legality of acts of foreign states on their own soil that might embarrass the Executive Branch of our Government in the conduct of our foreign relations."

Giffen argues that the activities charged in the indictment were all performed in his capacity as an agent of the Kazakh government. Giffen contends that because he was acting as an official of the Kazakh government, this Court must consider the "validity of the law of Kazakhstan and the official acts of its leaders."

As a preliminary matter, this Court must decide whether it will have to invalidate any official act of Kazakhstan. Giffen is charged with bribing the senior Kazakh officials. Factual findings in this case might impugn the motives of the Kazakh government in its dealings with Mercator. However, this Court will not need to rule on the legality of any public acts of the Kazakh government. In essence, Giffen's argument is that his de facto position within the Kazakh government enabled him to pay the senior Kazakh officials—not that his official duties required him to make secret payments.

The act of state doctrine also has a territorial dimension in that it is limited to "acts done within their own States, in the exercise of Governmental authority."

Here, the illicit activities occurred in the United States and Switzerland—not Kazakhstan. Moreover, Giffen allegedly transferred funds from Swiss bank accounts to non-Kazakh corporations. Because these transactions were dehors the geographic boundaries of Kazakhstan and involved transactions among foreign corporations, the act of state doctrine does not prohibit this Court from ruling on their legality. Further, some courts have determined that the act of state doctrine does not reach "acts committed by foreign sovereigns in the course of their purely commercial operations." The indictment alleges deposits of monies into foreign banks, which were then used by Giffen to fund offshore entities for the personal benefit of the senior Kazakh officials. These actions were commercial—not governmental, and are not immune under the act of state doctrine.

The FCPA countenances an affirmative defense where the payments were "lawful under the written laws and regulations of the foreign official's … country." But, Giffen does not assert that the challenged payments were lawful under Kazakh law. Rather, he argues that his actions were effected pursuant to the powers conferred by the Kazakh government. Because Giffen claims to have acted as a Kazakh government representative, he argues that his payments to senior Kazakh officials are shielded from FCPA scrutiny. The letters of appointment that Giffen offers, however, fail to show that his secret payments constituted official acts of Kazakhstan. Giffen's various official titles do not exempt his actions from prosecution by the United States.

Accordingly, this Court concludes that the act of state doctrine does not bar Giffen's prosecution.

CASE QUESTIONS

1. Why does the court conclude that Giffen was making more than facilitation payments?

2. Why is the question of whether the payments were legal under Kazakh law important in the act of state analysis?

3. What lessons should companies learn from the experiences of Giffen and Mercator?

7-4c　PROTECTIONS FOR U.S. PROPERTY AND INVESTMENT ABROAD

Expropriation

The effect of nationalization is that the private property of citizens and businesses operating in that country can be taken by the government, an act referred to as expropriation. While courts do not interfere with a sovereign's actions, the effect of

Consider...

In 2009, the top aides to Libya's then–leader, the late Col. Muammar e-Qaddafi, held a meeting with 15 executives from global energy companies that had oil operations in Libya. The United States had reopened trade with Libya in 2004 after nearly a decade-long boycott because the Libyan government played a role in the explosion of Pan Am Flight 103 at 34,000 feet over Scotland caused by a bomb onboard the plane.

At the meeting of these executives, the Qaddafi aides asked them to ante up the $1.5 billion Libya was being asked to pay for the compensation of the Pan Am 103 victims' families. The aides referred to the payments as "signing bonuses" or "consultancy fees" for their companies being permitted to continue oil operations in Libya.

A State Department 2009 cable contained the following warning for U.S. companies: "Libya is a kleptocracy in which the regime—either the al-Qadhafi [sic] family itself or its close political allies—has a direct stake in anything worth buying, selling, or owning." Some of the U.S. companies paid into the $1.5 billion fund; some did not.

Did those who paid violate the FCPA? What strategic issues do you see in the State Department's warning?

Source: Eric Lichtblau, David Rohde, and James Risen, "Business Payoffs Helped Qaddafis Solidify Control," *New York Times*, March 24, 2011, p. A1.

expropriation, combined with the act of state doctrine and sovereign immunity, has a chilling effect on U.S. investments in foreign countries. To discourage expropriation, the Foreign Assistance Act of 1962 contained what has been called the Hickenlooper Amendment, which requires the president to suspend all forms of assistance to countries that have expropriated the property of U.S. citizens or regulated the property in such a way as to effectively deprive a U.S. citizen of it (through taxation or limits on use).

Minimizing Expropriation. Many trade treaties that have been negotiated or are being negotiated with other countries contain protections against expropriation. Some treaties provide U.S. companies and investors with the same levels of protection as the citizens of those countries. For example, if a country affords its citizens due process before taking over private property, U.S. citizens and companies must be afforded those same protections prior to expropriation.

Finally, Congress has created a federal insurer for U.S. investments abroad. The Overseas Private Investment Corporation (OPIC) is an insurer for U.S. investment in those countries where the per capita annual income is $250 or less. OPIC will pay damages for expropriation, inability to convert the currency of the country, or losses from war or revolution.

Consumer protections in other countries depend on those countries' laws. For example, many U.S. citizens have constructed luxury homes along the coast near Ensenada in Baja California. They did so because the land and construction were so much cheaper than in the United States that they could afford large, luxurious homes. However, the land on which many of the homes were located was the subject of 14 years of litigation and more than 60 court decisions over disputed ownership rights. With the Mexican Supreme Court's decision on land ownership, most of the current U.S. owners have been told that they must vacate their homes and leave everything behind. Despite due process and property rights in the United States, the homeowners in Ensenada have no hope as long as the Mexican Supreme Court has declared the law for its country and land.

7-4d REPATRIATION

Repatriation is the process of bringing back to your own country profits earned on investments in another country. Some nations establish limits on repatriation; businesses can remove only a certain amount of the profits earned from the operations of a business within a country. Repatriation limits are considered acts of state and are immune from litigation in the United States.

7-4e *FORUM NON CONVENIENS*, OR "YOU HAVE THE WRONG COURT"

The doctrine of *forum non conveniens* is a principle of U.S. justice under which cases that are brought to the wrong court are dismissed. The doctrine allows judicial discretion whereby such issues as the location of the evidence, the location of the parties, and the location of the property that will be used to satisfy any judgment are examined. For example, when the Union Carbide disaster occurred at its Bhopal plant in India, victims and families brought suit against Union Carbide in New York City. A U.S. court of appeals dismissed the case and sent it back to India on the grounds of *forum non conveniens*. [*In re Union Carbide Corp. Gas Plant Disaster*, 809 F.2d 195 (2nd Cir. 1987); *cert. denied*, 484 U.S. 871 (1987)]

7-4f CONFLICTS OF LAW

No two countries match in terms of the structure of their legal system or their laws. For example, the law in the United States, codified by the widely adopted Uniform Commercial Code (UCC), is that all contracts and contract relationships are subject to a standard of good faith. In Canada, the good faith exists only if the parties place such a provision in their agreement. Under German law, protections are given not on the basis of good faith but, rather, on the basis of who is the weaker party. Just among these three major commercial powers, laws on contracts are significantly different. The rules on conflicts of law in international transactions are as follows: (1) If the parties choose which law applies, that law will apply, and (2) if no

Consider...

International Ambassador Programs, Inc. is a Washington-based nonprofit organization that arranges tours and informational visits in foreign countries, including Russia. Archpexpo, once a Soviet state enterprise and now a Russian limited partnership, facilitates and expedites tours such as those sponsored by Ambassador to Russia and the other former Soviet republics.

Archpexpo and Ambassador entered into several agreements relating to tours. An April 1989 agreement provided that "all disputes and differences without recourse to courts of law shall be referred to the arbitration tribunal with the USSR Trade and Industry Chamber for resolution, such resolution acknowledged as final by the parties."

A dispute arose between the parties when Archpexpo alleged that it had not been paid certain fees due, and Ambassador claimed it was entitled to an offset of $20,000 for refunds it had to give to travelers who were dissatisfied with Archpexpo's service.

Archpexpo filed for arbitration, and Ambassador brought suit in federal district court in the United States. Does the federal district court have jurisdiction? Must Ambassador submit to arbitration in Russia? What if Ambassador had more than one contract with Archpexpo and some of the contracts contained the arbitration clause and some did not? Would Ambassador then be required to submit to arbitration?

[*International Ambassador Programs, Inc. v Archpexpo*, 68 F.3d 337 (9th Cir. 1995)]

provision is made, the law of the country where the contract is performed will be used. Agreeing to and understanding the set of laws to be applied in a contract are critical parts of international transactions. The U.S. Supreme Court held in *Carnival Cruise Lines v Shute*, 499 U.S. 585 (1991) that, even in consumer types of contracts, the parties can agree on how and where their disputes will be resolved and which law will apply as long as the place and law selected bear some relationship to the nature of the contract and its place of performance. In that case, the court held that Carnival Cruise Lines could require its passengers to come to its place of business, Miami, to bring suit for any breaches of contract or injuries while sailing on a Carnival ship. The Miami location was not only Carnival's U.S. place of business but also a major port from which many of its cruises departed.

7-5 Protections in International Competition

Although trade barriers are coming down and a global marketplace is a reality, international competition is still subject to much regulation found in the forms of antitrust laws, protections for intellectual property, and trade treaties.

7-5a THE INTERNATIONAL MARKETPLACE AND MONETARY ISSUES: THE DISCLOSURE ROLE OF BANKS

The 2013 corporate tax rate in the United States is 35 percent, the highest rate in the world. As a result of this high rate, Apple, Google, HP, Starbucks, Amazon, and hundreds of other U.S.-based companies keep large portions of their taxable revenue in other countries: Google has $9.8 billion in Bermuda. Apple has $80 billion of its $121 billion in cash in other countries. HP keeps all of its cash in other countries. Google and Amazon were investigated by the United Kingdom tax tribunal for underpayment of taxes there. Many companies simply make a voluntary donation to these countries' treasuries when they are questioned about their cash assets and the amount of tax paid. This form of asset-parking is permitted as long as the cash assets are not concealed through complex structural webs. In fact, if the companies brought the cash back to the United States (repatriation) for distribution, both it and its shareholders would be taxed at U.S. rates on the income.

Individuals who place large amounts of cash in banks of other countries have been the subject of increasing numbers of audits because their cash assets are in other countries through tax shelters designed to help them avoid taxation on the money when it is first earned. Tax evasion is criminal, and those found to have used fraudulent shelters for their cash in foreign banks have been required to pay taxes, penalties, and interest on income placed in these shelters. In addition, the U.S. government has been indicting and imposing penalties on foreign banks that held these accounts and then refused to disclose who their customers were when tax officials conducted investigations. Getting information from banks in other countries continues to be problematic for regulatory agencies as well as for businesses that are seeking help in identifying those engaged in commercial activity that affects their products and or ability to sell those products.

U.S. courts can order foreign banks to make account disclosures as part of discovery proceedings under what is known as Hague proceedings. Named after the Hague Treaty, these proceedings are a form of international regulatory and judicial cooperation in which other nations seek to help each other in stopping criminal or infringement activities in business. Hague proceedings are a substitute for subpoenas, which are granted only if Hague proceedings would be futile because of the international respect for nation sovereignty. *Tiffany and Company v Andrew* (see Case 7.2) provides a look at this bank process and the applicable international standards that apply to bank disclosure of information for purposes of identifying those who have harmed U.S. companies through infringement or counterfeiting of goods.

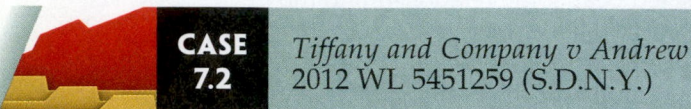

CASE 7.2   *Tiffany and Company v Andrew*
2012 WL 5451259 (S.D.N.Y.)

Looking for Counterfeiters' Bank Accounts

FACTS

Tiffany (plaintiffs) alleges that Andrew and others (defendants) sold counterfeit Tiffany products through several websites hosted in the United States. Andrew accepted payment in U.S. dollars, used PayPal, Inc. to process customers' credit card transactions, and then transferred the sales proceeds to accounts held by the Bank of China ("BOC"), Industrial and Commercial Bank of China ("ICBC"), and China Merchants Bank ("CMB") ("Banks").

Andrew defaulted on the suit, and Tiffany sought discovery from the Banks by serving subpoenas seeking the identities of the holders of the accounts into which the proceeds of the counterfeit sales were transferred and the subsequent disposition of those proceeds. The Banks involved all maintained branch offices in the Southern District of New York, and the subpoenas were served on those branch offices.

The Banks responded to the subpoenas by explaining that the information sought was all maintained in China and that the New York branches of the Banks lacked the ability to access the requested information. China's internal laws prohibited the disclosure of the information except under certain conditions. The Banks proposed that the plaintiffs pursue the requested discovery pursuant to the Hague Convention.

The court concluded that Tiffany should pursue discovery through the Hague Convention. Tiffany submitted its Hague Convention application to China's Central Authority in November 2010, and on August 7, 2011, the Ministry of Justice of the People's Republic of China ("MOJ") responded by producing some of the documents requested. For each of the Banks, the MOJ produced account opening documents (including the government identification card of the account holder), written confirmation of certain transfers into the accounts, and a list of transfers out of the accounts. With respect to CMB, the records indicate that all funds in the account were withdrawn through cash transactions at

either an ATM or through a teller. BOC and CMB each produced documents concerning a single account; ICBC produced documents for three accounts.

In its cover letter, the MOJ noted that it was not producing all documents requested. Specifically, the letter stated, "Concerning your request for taking of evidence for the Tiffany case, the Chinese competent authority holds that some evidence required lacks direct and close connections with the litigation. As the Chinese government has declared at its accession to the Hague Evidence Convention that for the request issued for the purpose of the pre-trial discovery of documents only the request for obtaining discovery of the documents clearly enumerated in the Letters of Request and of direct and close connection with the subject matter of the litigation will be executed, the Chinese competent authority has partly executed the requests which it deems conform to the provisions of the Convention."

On the grounds that the MOJ's production is deficient, Tiffany moved to enforce the subpoenas previously served on the New York branches of the Banks. The deficiencies Tiffany claims are (1) whether any of the defendants have any additional accounts at the Banks, and (2) detailed wire transfer records concerning the deposits into and withdrawals from the CMB and ICBC accounts.

JUDICIAL OPINION

PITMAN, Magistrate Judge

The principal issue to be resolved is whether the Banks' production through the MOJ has been so limited that resort to the Hague Convention process can be characterized as futile. Although the Banks' document production has been more limited than it would have been under the Federal Rules of Civil Procedure, I cannot conclude that it is so limited that the process has been futile.

The Banks, through the MOJ, have unquestionably produced relevant, responsive documents. In addition,

CONTINUED

although the MOJ took approximately nine months to respond to the Hague Convention request, this period is not inordinately long given the delays inherent in international discovery proceedings. Although I am not aware of any statistical compilations, based on my experience as a Magistrate Judge, China's nine-month response time is, at most, only slightly longer than the response time I have seen in other cases involving Hague Convention requests; it is not so long that the process can be described as futile.

Second, the scope of the Banks' production has not been so narrow that resort to the Convention can fairly be described as futile. The account holders' identities and addresses have been identified as well as transaction histories. Plaintiffs' argument that additional documents concerning transfers into and out of the accounts will lead to a fuller understanding of the trademark counterfeiting operation is extremely speculative. While I understand plaintiffs' desire to identify the source of the counterfeit merchandise, the bank transfer information they are seeking will be at, at most, a small step that may or may not lead to that goal. In an effort to frustrate detection and tracing, many domestic transactions in illegal or contraband merchandise are conducted in cash. The possibility that individuals in China who deal in counterfeit trademarked jewelry follow a similar practice is a further reason to believe that additional bank transaction documents will not provide fruitful information.

Finally, the fact that the MOJ China takes a narrower view concerning the appropriate scope of pretrial discovery does not render the Hague Convention process futile. The high cost of discovery in federal litigation is well known, and the fact that another sovereign chooses to take a more restrictive view of the appropriate scope of pretrial discovery is not unreasonable. In addition, as noted above, China is not unique in reserving its right to limit production in response to a Hague Convention request to documents that it considers to bear a direct and close connection with the litigation; many other countries have made the same reservation.

Absent extraordinary circumstances, it would not comport with considerations of "practicality and wise administration of justice" for the courts of one nation as a matter of course to sit in judgment of the adequacy of due process and the quality of justice rendered in the courts of other sovereigns. There can be no room for arrogance or presumption, or for extravagant rules or practices that may encourage insularity or chauvinism rather than respect for comity. It cannot be the proper province of any one judge in any one country, giving expression to the push of a moment or the pull of the immediate case, to promulgate judgments that impose that court's rule and will across all sovereign borders so as to reach the rest of humankind.

Concluding that the broad scope of Federal Rules discovery is the only fair manner in which to conduct discovery would be "the essence of sanctimonious chauvinism."

In summary, resort to the Hague Convention here has not proven futile. Although China, pursuant to its reservation of rights under the Convention, has not produced all the documents that would be required under the Federal Rules of Civil Procedure, its production is sufficient for plaintiffs to continue their investigation concerning the counterfeit goods at issue in their subpoenas against the Banks' New York branches is, therefore, denied.

CASE QUESTIONS

1. What information was provided by the Chinese government?
2. What did Tiffany hope for?
3. Why will the court not issue subpoenas to the Chinese government?

7-5b ANTITRUST LAWS IN THE INTERNATIONAL MARKETPLACE

All U.S. firms are subject to the antitrust laws of the United States, regardless of where their operations and anticompetitive behavior may occur. Firms from other countries operating in the United States or engaging in trade that has a substantial impact in the United States are also subject to U.S. antitrust laws. These firms are not covered under the act of state doctrine because they are not governmental entities and are engaging in commercial activity. Likewise, U.S. firms that are operating in other countries are subject to those countries' antitrust laws. For example, several major U.S. corporations have faced stiff antitrust penalties from the EU. In 2013, Microsoft was required to pay a $732 million penalty to the EU for its failure to comply with an earlier EU order on its anticompetitive behavior related to its browser. Citing a technical error, Microsoft took full responsibility for its conduct and apologized for failing to give European consumers their choice of Web browsers on about 15 million copies of the Windows 7 operating system that the company had shipped to them. Although Google was able to settle its antitrust suit with the U.S. government, it still had to work through the same allegations with the EU. Also, U.S. firms seeking to merge with competitors must obtain approval from both the U.S. Department of Justice and the EU. Microsoft and GE have been limited in their acquisitions in the EU because of EU antitrust provisions. Generally, if the EU does not approve a merger, the firms drop their plans because it is unlikely they will receive approval from the United States.

The converse is also true. Firms outside the United States may enjoy the protections and benefits of our antitrust laws and bring suit for violations if it can be established that the violations they are alleging had a substantial impact on trade in the United States.

The Export Trading Company Act of 1982 carved an exception to the antitrust laws for U.S. firms that combine to do business in international markets. Large U.S. firms that would otherwise be prohibited from merging for anticompetitive reasons are permitted to form export trading companies (ETCs) for the purpose of participating in international trade. The Justice Department approves applications for ETCs in advance, provided the applicants can demonstrate that the proposed joint venture will not reduce competition in the United States, increase U.S. prices, or cause unfair competition. ETCs such as Mobil and Exxon worked together to explore Siberian oil fields in a combination that would otherwise be prohibited both under the antitrust laws and for ongoing operations. These combinations allow effective negotiation of large foreign contracts. ExxonMobil is now one firm, a result of its joint drilling ventures.

7-5c TARIFFS

Tariffs are taxes on goods as they move in and out of countries (import and export tariffs, respectively). Import tariffs are, in effect, a tax on goods coming into a country. Tariffs increase the cost of those goods, particularly in comparison with domestic goods, and therefore limit the competitiveness of foreign goods within a country.

There are also nontariff barriers to certain goods entering the United States. For example, there are many prohibitions on businesses importing certain types of wood for use in their products. Gibson Guitars was raided by federal agents who seized guitars, pallets of wood, and electronic files. The Justice Department had obtained the warrants for purposes of seizing evidence that Gibson violated the Lacey Import Act, a federal law under which businesses can be prosecuted for the importation of "fish or wildlife taken, possessed, transported, or sold in violation of … any foreign law." [16 U.S.C. § 3372(a)(2)(A)] The Justice Department seized the guitars and wood because its theory is that Gibson's use of wood from India that is not finished by Indian workers is illegal, something that it believes to be a violation of the Lacey Act if the export of the wood to Gibson was done prior to it being finished. Gibson could not use the wood in India because of government regulations there and issues of resulting tariffs for imports from India. Gibson eventually ended up paying a penalty to Customs and switching woods

ETHICAL ISSUES

When the Taliban was in power in Afghanistan, it banned watching television. The result of the ban was the creation of a substantial market for smuggling television sets into Afghanistan. For example, a Sony TV set smuggled into Pakistan would cost about $400. The legal cost, paying tariffs, would be $440. The same set smuggled into Afghanistan could bring twice as much. Sony gets the same amount, or $220, for every set sold, regardless of where it is sold and what happens to it in terms of its final destination.

The Taliban decided to impose tariffs and taxes on TV sets even as it held to the ban because the ban resulted in the smuggling market from which they could extract substantial sums.

Do you think Sony had an ethical obligation to not sell to the Taliban? Does it have an ethical obligation to police what happens to its products? What happens when a company profits from a government making money from its own ban?

Source: Daniel Pearl and Steve Stecklow, "Taliban Banned TV but Collected Profits on Smuggled Sonys," *Wall Street Journal*, January 9, 2002, pp. A1, A8. (Note that the source for this ethical issue was an article co-authored by Daniel Pearl, the U.S. journalist who was kidnapped by terrorists who eventually killed him and shared graphic coverage of the execution.)

for its guitar production. The smallest of businesses have to be concerned with import and export regulations, even on raw materials used in their production processes.

In the United States, the U.S. Customs Service is responsible for developing the tariffs according to a tariff schedule and for enforcing the tariffs on imported goods. The tariff is based on the computed value of the goods coming into the country and is computed at the time of their entry. That computed value depends on how the goods are classified under the schedule. For example, if potato chips are classified as bread, they are tariff- or duty-free. If they are classified as snacks, they carry a tariff. [*Sabritas v U.S.*, 998 F. Supp. 1123 (Ct. Int'l Trade 1998)] The federal government has created a specialized court to handle the many disputes that arise over the application of the tariffs and the underlying classification of goods.

Competition may also be controlled by import restrictions, a resulting control on trade balance and prices. By limiting the amounts of certain products or products from certain countries, supply and demand (and, through economic principles, price) are affected. These nontariff regulations also control competition and the flow of goods across borders.

As noted earlier, some countries also limit exports, particularly of technologies to certain countries that could use them to harm others through, for example, the development of nuclear technology.

Exhibit 7.1 provides a summary of international law principles and doctrines.

7-5d　PROTECTIONS FOR INTELLECTUAL PROPERTY

Protections for intellectual property in the international marketplace are constantly undergoing refinements. Worldwide registration for patents, copyrights, and trademarks are goals that are within reach as the mechanisms for administration are being put into place. Details on international protections are found in Chapter 15.

© martan/Shutterstock.com

EXHIBIT 7.1 The Treaties, Principles, and Statutes of International Law

NAME	PURPOSE
North Atlantic Treaty North Atlantic Treaty Organization (NATO)	Treaty between U.S. and European nations that establishes a deployment of armed forces and security setup in Europe
Foreign Sovereign Immunities Act of 1976	U.S. statute that clarifies the immunity of foreign countries and officials from prosecution for crimes in the United States
Act of state doctrine (expropriation)	Recognition of a foreign government's actions as valid; U.S. courts may not be used to challenge another country's actions, even toward U.S. citizens
Foreign Assistance Act of 1962 (Hickenlooper Amendment)	Authorization given to president to cut off aid to countries where U.S. citizens' property has been taken by the government or regulated so as to deprive owner of use
Overseas Private Investment Corporation (OPIC)	Federal insurer for U.S. companies' investments in countries with low per capita income
Expropriation	Act of a sovereign state in taking property from its citizens or businesses operating there
Repatriation	Bringing back to your own country money earned on investments in other countries
Export Trading Company Act of 1982	Antitrust combination exemption for companies joining to compete in international markets
Maastricht Treaty	Agreement that created European Union
General Agreement on Tariffs and Trade (GATT)	Agreement among 150 countries to increase trade by reducing tariffs
North American Free Trade Agreement (NAFTA)	Agreement among United States, Canada, and Mexico with the goal of tariff elimination
The Iran Threat Reduction and Syria Human Rights Act of 2012	U.S. law that requires company disclosures about business by them and affiliates in Iran and Syria

© Cengage Learning 2015

7-5e CRIMINAL LAW PROTECTIONS

All persons and businesses present within a country are subject to that nation's regulatory scheme for business as well as to the constraints of the country's criminal code. Compliance with the law is a universal principle of international business operations. Expulsion, fines, penalties, and imprisonment are all remedies available to governments when foreign businesses break the law in a particular nation.

Often, the complexities of international operations produce layers of business organizations throughout the world. These layers are often necessary for individual countries and proper business structure under the law. The layers of organizations may provide opportunities for laundering of money, concealment of transactions, and other complex transactions that can escape regulatory detection for a time. However, the activities are eventually discovered, and countries are cooperating more to be certain the complexities of international business do not conceal illicit activities.

BIOGRAPHY

Siemens: The Company That Paid the Largest Fines Ever for FCPA Violations

COUNTRY	PRODUCT	BRIBES PAID	DATE
Russia	Medical devices	$55 million	2000–2007
Argentina	Identity cards project	$40 million	1998–2004
China	High-voltage transmission lines	$25 million	2002–2003
China	Metro trains	$22 million	2002–2007
Israel	Power plants	$20 million	2002–2005
Bangladesh	Mobile telephone works	$5.3 million	2004–2006
Venezuela	High-speed trains	$16.7 million	2001–2007
Russia	Traffic control systems	$0.75 million	2004–2006
Vietnam	Medical devices	$0.5 million	2005
China	Medical devices	$14.4 million	2003–2007
Nigeria	Telecommunications projects	€4.2 million	2003
Iraq	Power station	$1.7 million	2000
Italy	Power station	€6.0 million	2003
Greece	Telecommunications	€37 million	2006

© Cengage Learning

Siemens is a German conglomerate that has been in business since 1847. It has three divisions: energy, health care, and industry. Siemens has 428,200 employees and operates in 190 countries. The above chart shows the countries where Siemens paid bribes for contracts in violation of the FCPA. The multination investigation of the company's bribery activity resulted in Siemens agreeing to pay a fine that was the largest ever paid in the history of the FCPA.

Both the SEC and the U.S. Department of Justice (DOJ) were investigating Siemens. The two agencies concluded that Siemens had paid more than 4,283 bribes totaling $1.4 billion to government officials to secure contracts. The SEC concluded that the bribes resulted in the company obtaining $1.1 billion in profits.

The DOJ and Siemens AG reached an agreement to settle the company's ongoing violations. As a result of these violations, Siemens agreed to pay $800 million to the United States, a fine 20 times higher than the largest fine ever collected under the FCPA. Siemens also settled charges with 10 other countries and paid total fines of $5.8 billion. The SEC complaint

(www.sec.gov) against Siemens cited the involvement of employees at all levels of the company and a culture that had long been at odds with the FCPA.

The company's cooperation with the U.S. government since 2006, as well as its efforts to correct the violations, caused government officials to reduce the fine from $2.7 billion to $800 million. Siemens's efforts to correct its culture included cooperating with the government, turning over all documents it found, and replacing all but one officer and all board members.

Business Planning Tip

Siemens did follow what is known as "the four-eyes principle" of internal control for the FCPA, meaning all payments required two signatures. However, the company had made so many exceptions to the four-eyes principle that as a practical matter it was not in effect. Rules and processes in companies do protect the company. Exceptions should be rare, if ever.

© Fekete Tibor/Shutterstock.com

© Grounder/Shutterstock.com

Summary

What laws affect businesses in international trade?

- Foreign Sovereign Immunities Act of 1976
- Foreign Assistance Act of 1962 (Hickenlooper Amendment)
- Overseas Private Investment Corporation (OPIC)
- Export Trading Company Act of 1982
- Contracts for the International Sale of Goods (CISG)

What treaties, agreements, practices, and principles affect international business and trade?

- North Atlantic Treaty
- North Atlantic Treaty Organization (NATO)
- Maastricht Treaty
- General Agreement on Tariffs and Trade (GATT)
- North American Free Trade Agreement (NAFTA)
- International Monetary Fund (IMF)
- Duties, quotas, tariffs—controls on prices and quantities of goods by nations with the goal of balancing imports and exports
- Foreign Corrupt Practices Act (FCPA)—controls on means of accessing governments
- The Iran Threat Reduction and Syria Human Rights Act of 2012

What principles of international law affect business?

- Sovereign immunity—freedom of one country from being subject to orders from another country
- Expropriation; act of state doctrine—recognition by U.S. courts of the actions of other governments as valid despite noncompliance with traditional U.S. rights and procedures
- Repatriation—returning profits earned in other countries to one's native land
- Conflict of laws—issue as to which country's law applies in international transactions
- Antitrust issues
- *Forum non conveniens*—doctrine requiring dismissal of cases that should be heard in another country's courts

What protections exist in international competition?

- Antitrust laws
- Protections for intellectual property
- Criminal law protections

Questions and Problems

1. Tom Welch and Dave Johnson, two officials of the Salt Lake City Olympic Committee, were charged with bribery and racketeering for their alleged role in paying money to and giving rather large gifts to members of the International Olympic Committee (IOC) in order to win the bid for holding the winter Olympics in Salt Lake City in 2002. Salt Lake City did win the bid, but an anonymous letter to the IOC revealed that these types of payments and gifts had been offered. Following an investigation, nine members of the IOC were removed or resigned and others were sanctioned. The Salt Lake City Olympic Committee removed Mr. Welch and Mr. Johnson and replaced them with Mitt Romney as the head of its committee. Utah declined prosecution under state law, and a federal district court judge dismissed the charges against Mr. Welch and Mr. Johnson. The U.S. Attorney for the case filed an appeal with the tenth circuit federal court of appeals asking that the charges be reinstated. He noted that the Olympics were an "international" event and mandated federal jurisdiction. He also argued in the brief that the payments, accommodations, and gifts were more than goodwill and amounted to bribery in violation of federal law.

Applying the cases and law presented in the discussion on the FCPA, determine whether there was or was not a violation of federal law. What jurisdiction do federal courts have over criminal charges? Describe the appellate process and what an appellate court can do in an appeal such as this. [*U.S. v Welch*, 327 F.3d 1081, at 1085 (10th Cir. 2003)]

2. Suppose that the Government of Brazil took possession of the cacao farms of a chocolate factory owned by a U.S. firm. What rights would the U.S. factory have? What limits exist on those rights?

3. A Philip Morris subsidiary, C. A. Tabacalera National, and a B.A.T Industries subsidiary known as C. A. Cigarrera Bigott entered into a contract with La Fundacion del Nino (the Children's Foundation)

of Caracas, Venezuela. The agreement was signed on behalf of the foundation by the foundation's president, who also was the wife of the then–president of Venezuela. Under the terms of the agreement, these two tobacco firms were to make periodic donations to the Children's Foundation totaling $12.5 million. In exchange, the two firms would receive price controls on Venezuelan tobacco, elimination of controls on retail cigarette prices in Venezuela, tax deductions for donations, and assurances that the existing tax rates applicable to tobacco companies would not be increased.

Is the donation to the charity a violation of the FCPA? [*Lamb v Philip Morris, Inc.*, 915 F.2d 1024 (6th Cir. 1990; *cert. denied*, 498 U.S. 1086 (1995))]

4. W. Christian Riedel, a resident of Ohio, had an account with Unibanco, S.A., and asked that it transfer $100,000 to Banca Metropolitana, S.A. (Bamesa) (predecessor to Bancam) for investment in a certificate of deposit (CD). Bamesa merged with another bank to form Bancam, and Mr. Riedel's CD was renewed with the newly merged bank.

Shortly after Mr. Riedel's renewal, the Government of Mexico issued new rules governing accounts from foreigners in Mexican banks. The rules required the banks to pay the CDs in pesos at a rate that was substantially below exchange rates. A month after these rules were put into effect, Bancam was nationalized.

When Mr. Riedel's CD came due, the exchange rate was 74.34 pesos to the dollar. He was paid $53,276.23 for his $100,000 investment.

Mr. Riedel brought suit in a U.S. federal district court, alleging that Bancam had violated both federal and Ohio securities laws in selling the CDs in the United States without registration. Bancam filed a motion to dismiss the suit on the ground that the Sovereign Immunities Act of 1976 precluded U.S. courts from taking jurisdiction over the matter. Bancam also claimed protection under the act of state doctrine. Finally, Bancam claimed that the CD was not a security for purposes of U.S. securities laws.

The district court dismissed Mr. Riedel's suit on the grounds that it lacked jurisdiction over the claims under Ohio law and also on grounds of sovereign immunity and the act of state doctrine. Mr. Riedel appealed. How should the court decide the case and why? [*Riedel v Bancam*, 792 F.2d 587 (6th Cir. 1986)]

5. United Arab Shipping Company (UASC) is a corporation formed under the laws of Kuwait. Its capital stock is wholly owned by the governments of Kuwait, Saudi Arabia, the United Arab Emirates, Qatar, Iraq, and Bahrain. No single government owned more than 19.33 percent of UASC's shares, and the corporation was created by a treaty among the owner nations.

Three seamen who were injured while working for UASC brought suit against it in federal district court in the United States. UASC maintains it enjoys sovereign immunity. The seamen claim it is a commercial enterprise and not entitled to immunity. Who is correct? [*Mangattu v M/V IBN Hayyan*, 35 F.3d 205 (5th Cir. 1994)]

6. Smith & Smith, a U.S. computer firm, contracted to install a computer system for Volkswagen in the company's headquarters in Berlin, Germany. Smith's contract included the following liability limitation: "We are only liable for loss of data which is due to a deliberate action on our part. We are not responsible for lost profits in any event." The contract had no provisions on choice of law. A crash in the Smith & Smith system caused a loss of 92 days' worth of financial data. Volkswagen was required to use its auditors to restructure the database at a substantial cost. Smith & Smith says it did nothing deliberate and, therefore, is not liable. Volkswagen cites German law that mandates protection by sellers against such losses and permits recovery of lost profits. U.S. law would honor the Smith & Smith clause. Which law applies? Why?

7. The Western oil firms once were the dominant players in Kazakhstan, a Central Asian country that is rich in oil resources. However, the Justice Department indicted U.S. citizen James Giffen for allegedly making $80 million in payments to government officials in Kazakhstan on behalf of Mobil and other companies so that the companies could obtain drilling rights from the government. Giffen had the touch when it came to getting the oil companies access for drilling. Once Giffen was indicted, the Western oil firms' drilling rights diminished substantially and the presence of Chinese oil firms increased. Many have pointed to this example, with direct causal connection between the elimination of U.S. firms and the increased presence of Chinese firms, as evidence that the FCPA puts U.S. firms and the U.S. economy at a distinct disadvantage to those countries that do not take enforcement action against bribery. How would you respond to this argument? Discuss the reasons behind the bribery statutes. (Nathan Wardi, "The Bribery Law Bracket," *Forbes*, May 24, 2010, p. 70.)

8. The European Union has developed a directive on privacy and e-mail. Nations within the EU are permitted to use e-mail for commercial transactions and can exchange information via e-mail. However, businesses from countries outside the EU will not be permitted access to EU business information and EDI systems for contracting purposes unless they can guarantee adequate privacy protections are in place for the data transmitted via e-mail. Most legal experts believe the EU privacy directive applies to all forms of transmissions in business, including commercial contracts and ordering information.

What would happen if a business tapped into an EU business and began entering into transactions without an adequate privacy guarantee? Would there be criminal sanctions? Trade sanctions? How does this directive affect international trade with the EU? The EU has provided that trading privileges can be withdrawn from countries with businesses that violate the privacy standards on e-mail information and data transmission. What happens when trading privileges are withdrawn? Is the EU directive a commercial control of trade?

9. Walid Azab Al-Uneizi was an employee of the Ministry of Defense of Kuwait. Liticia Guzel was an employee of the Willard Inter-Continental Hotel in Washington, DC. One of her duties was restocking

minibars in guest rooms. Al-Uneizi approached Miss Guzel outside Rooms 610 and 612 and conferred with her about restocking Room 612. After Miss Guzel finished restocking Room 612, Al-Uneizi assaulted and raped her. After the rape, Al-Uneizi gave her a Kuwaiti flag pin. Miss Guzel has brought suit against both Al-Uneizi and the Kuwaiti government, who seek a dismissal under the act of state doctrine. Should the case be dismissed against both? [*Guzel v State of Kuwait*, 818 F. Supp. 6 (1993)]

10. When the Barings Bank bankruptcy occurred in 1995, Nick Leeson, the trader responsible for the immense losses the bank experienced after heavy derivative investments, fled to Germany. He was brought back to Hong Kong, the site of his trades, for trial. He is a British citizen who was arrested in Germany. Describe all the principles and issues of international law involved in his arrest, return to, and eventual trial in Singapore. (Note: Mr. Leeson has been released from prison and now lives in Ireland.)

STRATEGY, ETHICS, & THE LAW

Why Recovery from Bribery Charges Is So Difficult

The SEC complaint in the Siemens case (see p. 231) notes how many "red flags" the board ignored in the years during which the bribery was occurring. Since 1999, when Germany signed on to the antibribery provisions of the OECD, Siemens executives had been concerned about the company's involvement in bribery around the world. The CEO at the time of the OECD adoption voiced concern to the board about the number of executives who were under investigation by the German government for bribery activities. He asked the board to take protective measures because its members could be held responsible for inaction. Despite his plea, the bribes continued, with support from some board members.

In 2001, the general counsel for the NYSE board notified its board members that in order for the company to meet U.S. standards for its new NYSE listing, it needed to end its practice of having off-the-books accounts for the payment of the bribes. The company

took no steps to investigate or end its practices. The SEC noted there was a stunning lack of internal controls as well as a tone at the top that did not take the FCPA seriously.

What should Siemens have done? Explain the following quote from a Justice Department official: "Crimes of official corruption threaten the integrity of the global marketplace and undermine the rule of law in host countries."[6] What does the quote mean?

Siemens's new CEO has said that it will take time for the company to recover because it was so dependent on such a facile business model. He explains that the company lost the skill sets of negotiating contracts, competing for projects, and submitting effective proposals. What lessons should companies learn from this observation about reliance on bribery?

For more information, the full Siemens complaint can be found at www.sec.gov.

Notes

1. The members (in the order in which they joined) are Belgium, France, West Germany, Italy, Luxembourg, the Netherlands, Denmark, Ireland, Great Britain, Greece, Spain, Portugal, Austria, Sweden, Finland, Cyprus, the Czech Republic, Estonia, Hungary, Latvia, Lithuania, Malta, Poland, Slovakia, Slovenia, Bulgaria, and Romania. Croatia, Iceland, Montenegro, Serbia, Macedonia, and Turkey are expected to join the EU in the coming years. Potential candidates are Albania, Kosovo, Bosnia, and Herzegovina.

2. The Iran Threat Reduction and Syria Human Rights Act of 2012 (the Iran Act) imposes new disclosure requirements on public reporting companies in their SEC filings (see Chapter 19 for more information). The Iran Act requires a reporting company to disclose information about activities conducted by it or its affiliates in Iran and Syria.

3. Kevin McCoy, "Over 14,700 Take Up IRS on Leniency," *USA Today*, November 18, 2009, p. 1B.

4. The OECD member countries include Australia, Austria, Belgium, Canada, the Czech Republic, Denmark, Finland, France, Germany, Greece, Hungary, Iceland, Ireland, Italy, Japan, Korea, Luxembourg, Mexico, the Netherlands, New Zealand, Norway, Poland, Portugal, the Slovak Republic, Spain, Sweden, Switzerland, Turkey, the United Kingdom, and the United States.

5. OECD also has relationships with 70 countries and NGOs.

6. Siri Schubert and T. Christian Miller, "Where Bribery Was Just a Line Item," *New York Times*, December 21, 2008, pp. SB1, SB6–7.

Business and crime have jointly occupied the headlines of newspapers for much of the past decade. In 2011, the Corporate Fraud Task Force of the U.S. Justice Department prosecuted 726 corporate fraud cases—a jump from the 661 cases in 2010 and part of a steady increase in these types of cases since 2005. The FBI had 1,846 securities and commodities fraud cases and 2,690 health card fraud cases pending in 2011. For that same year, 93,508 mortgage fraud cases were pending, a jump from 70,533 in 2010 and less than half that amount (46,717) in 2007. White-collar crime, corporate fraud, and public corruption are three of the FBI's eight priorities on criminal investigations and prosecutions.

Every businessperson is expected to know and understand the types and nature of business crimes. This chapter offers that background by answering the following questions: Why does business crime occur? Who is liable for crimes committed by businesses? What penalties are imposed for business crimes? What are the rights of corporate and individual defendants in the criminal justice system?

UPDATE
For up-to-date legal and ethical news, go to **mariannejennings.com**

Consider...

John Park is the president of Acme Markets, a national retail food chain. Acme operated 16 warehouses that were subject to inspection by the Food and Drug Administration (FDA). During 1970 and 1971, FDA inspectors found rodents in Acme's Philadelphia and Baltimore warehouses. The FDA's chief of compliance wrote to Mr. Park and asked that he direct his attention to cleaning up the warehouses. Mr. Park told a subordinate officer to take care of the problems. When the FDA inspected the warehouses again, rodent infestation was still evident. The FDA charged Acme and Mr. Park with criminal violations of the Federal Food, Drug, and Cosmetic Act. Mr. Park says he tried to clean up the warehouses but his subordinates failed and that he should not be liable. Is Mr. Park correct?

8-1 What Is Business Crime? The Crimes within a Corporation

8-1a FINANCIAL FRAUD: EMPLOYEES MANIPULATING EARNINGS NUMBERS

Many business crimes are committed because companies apply pressure to managers and employees to produce results. Economic pressure often leads managers to cross ethical and legal lines. Managers feel compelled to meet earnings goals or to reach incentive bonus plan figures, and then they pass along the pressure they feel to employees. The drive to succeed or present a good earnings record can lead many managers and employees into committing crimes on behalf of the corporation. These crimes might not directly line employee pockets. The business benefits, and then employees benefit indirectly through profit sharing, salary increases, bonuses, or through just being able to keep their jobs.

For example, in January 2004, Andrew Fastow, the former CFO of the collapsed and bankrupt energy company Enron, entered a guilty plea to two counts of conspiracy to commit securities and wire fraud. His wife, Lea Fastow, pleaded guilty to filing a false joint tax return. Mr. Fastow was the mastermind behind the creation of off-the-books partnerships to which Enron's substantial debt was transferred. The result was that Enron's financial reports made the company seem healthy because, under accounting rules that existed at that time, the debt in the entities, which included Mr. and Mrs. Fastow as principals and officers, did not have to be reported on Enron's financial statements. The Fastows and other officers, including 26 executives who were indicted, have all explained that they were simply trying to meet projected earnings statements so that they could preserve shareholder value and share price on the market. As he testified against his former boss, former Enron CEO Jeffrey Skilling, Mr. Fastow said, "I thought I was being a hero for Enron. At the time, I thought I was helping myself and helping Enron to make its numbers."

8-1b MARKETING MISSTEPS: SALES ZEAL AND CRIMES

Since 2011, a number of pharmaceutical firms have paid billions in fines for marketing techniques that crossed legal lines. The Food and Drug Administration (FDA) does not permit pharmaceutical firms to market prescription drugs for purposes other than their federally approved use. For example, AstraZeneca paid $520 million to settle federal charges related to its marketing of its antipsychotic drug Seroquel to doctors for prescriptions for children and the elderly when the drug was not approved for use with children or the elderly. In addition, AstraZeneca internal e-mails indicated its awareness that the drug resulted in weight gains and possible development of diabetes, information that was not disclosed to those who were taking Seroquel. Eli Lilly, Bristol-Myers Squibb, Johnson & Johnson, and Pfizer together paid over $6 billion in fines for similar marketing missteps. Salespeople, particularly in the pharmaceutical industry, must be supervised carefully because criminal lines are crossed quite easily in the zeal for more sales.

8-1c FRIENDLY FIRE: EMPLOYEE THEFT

In addition to pressure to meet company goals, some individual employees feel personal financial pressure and resort to embezzlement as a means of remedying their own bleak financial positions. The Association of Certified Fraud Examiners estimates that 1 of every 28 employees is caught stealing from his or her employer each year. The FBI estimates that the amount lost in financial institution fraud is 100 times the amount taken by bank robbers. The FBI also estimates that the losses attributable to business crimes are 40 times greater than losses from crimes committed on the street. Walmart loses $3 billion each year to employee theft. In February 2013, Penny Winters, a 63-year-old maintenance worker at Walmart, was arrested for felony theft because she was caught on camera eating Oreos and other snacks as she worked her third shift at a Walmart store. She had eaten so much snack food that her charges rose to the felony level of theft. Sarbanes-Oxley imposes requirements (see Chapter 19) for additional internal control certifications so that companies have adequate systems for detecting embezzlement.

Small businesses have higher employee theft costs because they cannot afford the sophisticated monitoring measures larger corporations adopt. Most employee theft is systematic: For example, Aramark, a company that specializes in vending machine sales, reported that employees had skimmed millions in revenue by underreporting sales, ever so slightly over a period of time, in its cash/coin business. Employee theft has the hallmark of small amounts taken over a period of time with well-planned and -executed schemes. For example, employees of an aircraft plant filled their pockets with nuts and bolts each day at the end of the shift. Over time, the employees had accumulated enough hardware to fill kegs, which were then sold. Garment workers for apparel manufacturers have gone home with jeans in their purses.

Whether local misdemeanor offenses or federal felonies, employee theft and fraud are part of business. In fact, forensic accounting has been labeled "the most secure job in America" because these individuals are trained to detect fraudulent conduct within companies, whether perpetrated by a management team driven to achieve goals or by individual employees in need of extra funds. Such crimes committed for and against a business are often referred to as **white-collar crime**. Exhibit 8.1 provides a partial list of the companies and business executives that have had encounters with laws, regulators, and courts.

EXHIBIT 8.1 A Roster of Wrongdoing

COMPANY/PERSON	ISSUE	STATUS
Adelphia Communications (2002)	Company guaranteed loans to another entity controlled by the Rigas family (John Rigas and his sons held the top executive spots at Adephia); result was $2.7 billion in guarantees and $1 billion in off-the-balance-sheet debt; overstatement of number of customers and cash	Annual report delayed; shares lost 70% of value from March 2002 to April 2002; Chapter 11 bankruptcy; members of the Rigas family indicted and arrested on charges of "looting" the company of more than $1 billion in one of the largest corporate frauds ever; John Rigas and one son convicted; sentenced to 15 and 20 years
Boeing (2003)	Charges of illicit use of competitor's proprietary documents; charges of recruiting government official	Loss of 7 government contracts worth $250 million; $615 million fine; guilty plea by official who was wooed; 9-month sentence
Coca-Cola (2003)	Pending investigations over Coke's admissions that product marketing tests for frozen Coke in Burger King were rigged	Coke settled issue with Burger King, with payments rumored to be $21 million; settled suit with whistleblower
Computer Associates (2004)	Securities fraud and obstruction	Top officers indicted for securities fraud; former CEO Sanjay Kumar entered guilty plea; sentenced to 12 years
Countrywide Mortgage (2009)	Insider trading; securities fraud	Former CEO Angelo Mozilo charged with insider trading, CFO and COO charged with failure to disclose firm's relaxed lending standards; settled case for fines
Enron (2001)	Earnings overstated through mark-to-market accounting; off-the-book/share-special-purpose entities (SPEs) carried significant amounts of Enron debt not reflected in the financial statements; significant offshore SPEs	Fifth largest bankruptcy in U.S. history; shareholder litigation settled; Congressional hearings held; 20 criminal convictions or pleas
Andrew Fastow, former CFO of Enron (2004)	Multimillion-dollar earnings from serving as principal in SPEs of Enron created to keep debts off the company books	Entered guilty plea to securities and wire fraud; sentenced to 6 years; helping plaintiffs in shareholder suits
Lea Fastow (2004)	Filing false income tax return	Guilty plea; sentenced to 5 months in prison and 5 months of house arrest
Kenneth Lay, former chairman of Enron (2002)	Significant sales of shares during the time frame preceding Enron collapse	Resigned as CEO and chairman; convicted of securities and wire fraud; died of a massive coronary prior to appeal and sentence; conviction removed
Jeffrey Skilling, former CEO of Enron (2004)	Questions about his role in the Enron fraud; resigned just prior to company's collapse	Found guilty of securities fraud and sentenced to 24.4 years; U.S. Supreme Court partially reversed his conviction on honest services fraud; sentence reduced to 14 years
Galleon Group (2011)	Insider trading charges related to hedge fund's operations	Twenty-three executives, including CEO, convicted or entered guilty pleas; Galleon's $3.7 billion fund liquidated; CEO (Raj Rajaratnam) sentenced to 11 years; a Goldman Sachs director (Rajat Gupta) also convicted of insider trading and sentenced to two years in prison for feeding information to Rajaratnam

CONTINUED

COMPANY/PERSON	ISSUE	STATUS
HealthSouth (2003)	$2.7 billion accounting fraud; overstatement of revenues	16 former executives indicted; 5 guilty pleas
Richard Scrushy, CEO of HealthSouth (2003)	85 federal felony counts, including violations of Sarbanes-Oxley financial certification provisions	Acquitted of financial fraud charges; found guilty of bribery and sentenced to 7 years
ImClone (2002)	Questions surrounding the timing of disclosure of FDA action relating to the company's anticancer drug, Erbitux, and its less-than-touted effectiveness	SEC civil suit; shares dropped significantly after announcement of FDA action on December 28, 2001; shares dropped again on revelations of possible insider trading
Dr. Samuel Waksal, former CEO of ImClone (2002)	Sold $50 million in ImClone shares prior to releasing to public information that FDA had rejected marketing for Erbitux	Guilty plea to insider trading entered; sentenced to 7 years and $3 million in fines
Martha Stewart, CEO of Martha Stewart Omnimedia and close friend of Sam Waksal (2003)	Sold 5,000 shares of ImClone one day before public announcement of negative FDA action on Ebritux	Convicted of making false statements and conspiracy; served 5 months in prison, 5 months of home confinement, and two years of probation; fine of $30,000
KMPG (2006)	Tax shelter fraud	Settled with federal regulators by payment of $456 million penalty
Marsh McLennan (2005)	Price-fixing	$850 million in restitution
Sotheby's (2003)	Price-fixing	Chairman given 1 year and 1 day in prison and a $7.5 million fine; CEO placed under house arrest for 1 year
L. Dennis Kozlowski, former CEO of Tyco (2003)	Accused of improper use of company funds	Indicted in New York for failure to pay sales tax on transactions in fine art; found guilty of other charges of larceny; sentenced to 15–25 years
WorldCom (2003)	Accounting issues centered on swaps—selling to other telecommunications companies and hiding expenses, thereby overstating revenue	WorldCom emerged from bankruptcy as MCI; four officers and managers entered guilty pleas; CEO Bernard Ebbers convicted and sentenced to 25 years
Bernie Madoff (2009)	$50 billion Ponzi scheme	Entered guilty plea to all charges; sentenced to 150 years (was 71 years old at time of sentencing)
BP (2013)	Violation of Clean Air Act; willful failure to correct OSHA violations; manslaughter and obstruction	$50 million fine to EPA; $58 million fine to OSHA (largest in U.S. history) for pre-Deepwater Horizon explosion; $4 billion for crimes related to Deepwater Horizon explosion
Stanford Securities (2012)	$9 billion Ponzi scheme	CEO convicted of mail, wire, and securities fraud and sentenced to 110 years; Laura Pendergest-Holt, the former chief investment officer, entered a guilty plea and was sentenced to 3 years
Massey Coal (2012)	Mine collapse resulting in the deaths of 29 miners	Two company officials entered guilty pleas and one was convicted of charges related to tipping off employees on mine inspections and destroying records to avoid government review
Peanut Corporation of America (2013)	Indictments for producing and selling product without cleaning up salmonella issue at plant and falsifying tests that showed the salmonella was gone when it was not	Four company officers, including owner and CEO, charged with criminal fraud and conspiracy; food broker also indicted for his role in test falsification

8-1d INTERNET CRIME

CYBERLAW

© iStockPhoto.com /dra_schwartz

In 2011, various agencies in the federal government received 300,000 Internet crime complaints, resulting in losses of $485.3 million. Most of the complaints were generated by fake antivirus message warnings, the stranded traveler plea for money, the fake escrow agent, the online banking phishing scam, and, finally, the notorious Nigerian letter frauds (about 14 percent). For more information on cybercrime, see Chapter 10.

8-2 What Is Business Crime? The Crimes against a Corporation

Interbusiness crime occurs among competitors and results in one business gaining a competitive advantage over others. The list of companies and misdeeds in Exhibit 8.1 provides examples of the wide variety of business crimes committed, from kickbacks to antitrust violations to securities fraud to OSHA and EPA violations to obstruction.

Once again, competitive pressure led to these types of crimes. Employees within one company postponed necessary safety fixes so as to correct OSHA violations in order to contain costs and remain competitive. However, as the remainder of the chapter shows, any competitive advantage gained through criminal activity is only temporary.

8-3 Who Is Liable for Business Crime?

One of the major differences between nonbusiness and business crimes is that more people can be convicted of business crimes. For nonbusiness crimes, only those involved in the planning or execution of the crime or assistance after it is committed can be convicted. In other words, those who were in any way involved in the criminal act or aftermath are criminally responsible. For business crimes, on the other hand, those in management positions at firms whose employees actually commit criminal acts can be held liable if they authorized the conduct, knew about the conduct but did nothing, or failed to act reasonably in their supervisory positions. Liability for crimes also extends to employees who participate with the company and its management in illegal acts. For example, employees who help their employers establish fraudulent tax shelters for customers can be held liable along with the company and its officers. The key to establishing criminal liability is showing personal knowledge of wrongdoing.

U.S. v Park (Case 8.1), a landmark case, discusses the liability standards for those who are in charge but may not themselves commit a criminal act. It also provides an answer to the chapter's opening "Consider..."

8-4 Federal Laws Targeting Officers and Directors for Criminal Accountability

8-4a WHITE-COLLAR CRIME'S ORIGINS AND HISTORY

With each wave of accounting and fraud scandals, new legislation at the federal level has increased penalties for those who are the masterminds of white-collar crimes. In 1988, following the Michael Milken junk-bond era and the Ivan Boesky

CASE 8.1

United States v Park
421 U.S. 658 (1975)

Is Chasing Rats from the Warehouse in My Job Description?

FACTS

Acme Markets, Inc., was a national food retail chain headquartered in Philadelphia, Pennsylvania. At the time of the government action, John R. Park (respondent) was president of Acme, which employed 36,000 people and operated 16 warehouses.

In 1970, the Food and Drug Administration (FDA) forwarded a letter to Mr. Park describing, in detail, problems with rodent infestation in Acme's Philadelphia warehouse facility. In December 1971, the FDA found the same types of conditions in Acme's Baltimore warehouse facility. In January 1972, the FDA's chief of compliance for its Baltimore office wrote to Mr. Park about the inspection. The letter included the following language:

> We note with much concern that the old and new warehouse areas used for food storage were actively and extensively inhabited by live rodents. Of even more concern was the observation that such reprehensible conditions obviously existed for a prolonged period of time without any detection, or were completely ignored.
>
> We trust this letter will serve to direct your attention to the seriousness of the problem and formally advise you of the urgent need to initiate whatever measures are necessary to prevent recurrence and ensure compliance with the law.

After Mr. Park received the letter, he met with the vice president for legal affairs for Acme and was assured that he was "investigating the situation immediately and would be taking corrective action."

When the FDA inspected the Baltimore warehouse in March 1972, there was some improvement in the facility, but there was still rodent infestation. Acme and Mr. Park were both charged with violations of the Federal Food, Drug, and Cosmetic Act. Acme pleaded guilty. Mr. Park was convicted and fined $500; he appealed based on error in the judge's instruction, given as follows:

> The individual is or could be liable under the statute even if he did not consciously do wrong. However, the fact that the Defendant is president and chief executive officer of the Acme Markets does not require a finding of guilt. Though he need not have personally participated in the situation, he must have had a responsible relationship to the issue. The issue is, in this case, whether the

> Defendant, John R. Park, by virtue of his position in the company, had a position of authority and responsibility in the situation out of which these charges arose.

The court of appeals reversed Mr. Park's conviction, and the government appealed.

JUDICIAL OPINION

BURGER, Chief Justice

Central to the Court's conclusion [in *United States v Dotterweich*, 320 U.S. 277 (1943)], that individuals other than proprietors are subject to the criminal provisions of the Act was the reality that "the only way in which a corporation can act is through the individuals who act on its behalf."

At the same time, however, the Court was aware of the concern … that literal enforcement "might operate too harshly by sweeping within its condemnation any person however remotely entangled in the proscribed shipment." A limiting principle, in the form of "settled doctrines of criminal law" defining those who "are responsible for the commission of a misdemeanor," was available. In this context, the Court concluded, those doctrines dictated that the offense was committed "by all who have … a responsible share in the furtherance of the transaction which the statute outlaws."

The Act does not, as we observed in *Dotterweich*, make criminal liability turn on "awareness of some wrongdoing" or "conscious fraud." The duty imposed by Congress on responsible corporate agents is, we emphasize, one that requires the highest standard of foresight and vigilance, but the Act, in its criminal aspect, does not require that which is objectively impossible. The theory upon which responsible corporate agents are held criminally accountable for "causing" violations of the Act permits a claim that a defendant was "powerless" to prevent or correct the violation to "be raised defensively at a trial on the merits." *U.S. v Wiesenfeld Warehouse Co.*, 376 U.S. 86 (1964). If such a claim is made, the defendant has the burden of coming forward with evidence, but this does not alter the Government's ultimate burden of proving beyond a reasonable doubt the defendant's guilt, including his power, in light of the duty imposed by the Act, to prevent or correct the prohibited condition.

Turning to the jury charge in this case, it is of course arguable that isolated parts can be read as intimating that a

CONTINUED

finding of guilt could be predicated solely on respondent's corporate position.... Viewed as a whole, the charge did not permit the jury to find guilt solely on the basis of respondent's position in the corporation; rather, it fairly advised the jury that to find guilt it must find respondent "had a responsible relation to the situation," and "by virtue of his position ... had authority and responsibility" to deal with the situation. The situation referred to could only be "food ... held in unsanitary conditions in a warehouse with the result that it consisted, in part, of filth or ... may have been contaminated with filth."

Park testified in his defense that he had employed a system in which he relied upon his subordinates, and that he was ultimately responsible for this system. He testified further that he had found these subordinates to be "dependable" and had "great confidence" in them.

[The rebuttal] evidence was not offered to show that respondent had a propensity to commit criminal acts, that the crime charged had been committed; its purpose was to demonstrate that respondent was on notice that he could not rely on his system of delegation to subordinates to prevent or correct unsanitary conditions at Acme's warehouses, and that he must have been aware of the deficiencies of this system before the Baltimore violations were discovered. The evidence was therefore relevant since it served to rebut Park's defense that he had justifiably relied upon subordinates to handle sanitation matters.

Reversed.

CASE QUESTIONS

1. What problems did the FDA find in the Acme warehouses, and over what period?

2. Was Mr. Park warned about the problem? What action did he take?

3. What standard of liability did the instruction given by the judge impose?

Consider...

The Drug Enforcement Administration (DEA) issued a suspension order that revoked the controlled medication licenses of two pharmacies because the pharmacies were filling prescriptions for oxycodone (the painkiller) in excess of their monthly allowances for controlled substances. In addition, the DEA alleges that the pharmacies' corporate entities failed to conduct on-site inspections and also failed to notice that 42 to 58 percent of all the sales of the substances were cash sales, a red flag in the sale and distribution of controlled substances. In addition, the number of prescriptions filled continued to escalate—increasing ninefold in one year to more than two million dosages dispensed. When investigators were present on-site at one of the pharmacies, every third car going through the drive-thru pick-up was receiving a prescription for oxycodone. Those using the drive-thru also used "street slang" for requesting certain brands of oxycodone. Pharmacists at the drug stores, in interviews with the DEA agents, indicated that the customers paying cash for the oxycodone were "shady," and that they suspected that some of the prescriptions were not valid. The shipment of oxycodone to the pharmacies was five times the amount that would have been within normal bounds for the population in the area. Many patients living at the same address had the same prescriptions for oxycodone from the same doctor.

The two pharmacies filed suit in federal district court to have the suspension order lifted, but the appellate court upheld the actions of the DEA. [*Holiday CVS, L.L.C. v Holder*, 493 Fed. Appx. 108 (C.A.D.C. 2012)] Both companies, CVS and Cardinal Health, have indicated in court filings that they have changed their practices and provided training to pharmacy personnel so that they can spot these types of illegal prescriptions and report suspicious activity.

However, the DEA seeks to hold the corporations responsible because of the lack of on-site presence and the failure to follow the numbers for sales and distribution at the pharmacies. Can the corporation be held liable when it was not actually participating in the distribution of the oxycodone?

insider trading scandal, Congress passed additional laws against and sanctions covering insider trading in the Insider Trading and Securities Fraud Enforcement Act of 1988 (ITSFEA) (see Chapter 19 for more information). Criminal and civil penalties increased at least tenfold under the law. In 1990, Congress enacted what has been called the "white-collar kingpin" law. A response to the 1980s and 1990s savings and loan scandals and the 2000 dot-com and 2008 financial market collapses, the law imposes minimum mandatory sentences (10 years in most instances) for corporate officers who mastermind financial crimes such as bank and securities fraud.

8-4b SARBANES-OXLEY (SOX)

Following the collapses of Enron, WorldCom, Adelphia, and others in the period from 2001 to 2002, Congress passed Sarbanes-Oxley, also known as the White-Collar Criminal Penalty Enhancement Act of 2002. Under SOX, as it is known among businesspeople, penalties for mail and wire fraud, which had a former maximum of five years, have been increased to 20 years in prison. (Refer to Exhibit 8.1 to see the number of wire and fraud charges that have been brought against executives.) Penalties for violation of the trust, reporting, and fiduciary duties under pension laws increased from one year to 10 years, with fines increased from $5,000 to $100,000. SOX also provides for the specific crime of false financial statement certification, a crime directed at CEOs and CFOs, who are now required to certify the financial statements issued by their companies. Top officers who certify financial statements that they know contain false information now face being charged with a specific federal crime because of SOX reforms. Richard Scrushy, the former CEO of Health-South, became the first CEO charged with a violation of these new provisions. Mr. Scrushy was acquitted of all financial fraud charges but was later convicted of bribery in connection with payments he made to the ad campaign funds of the governor of Alabama. Mr. Scrushy is currently serving a seven-year sentence.

8-4c HONEST SERVICES FRAUD

Following the Boesky and Milken scandals, part of the 1988 federal reforms included a 28-word addition to the federal mail and wire fraud statutes that provided, "For the purposes of this chapter, the term, *scheme or artifice to defraud* includes a scheme or artifice to deprive another of the intangible right of honest services." (18 U.S.C. § 1346) The provision lay fallow for some time until the Enron era of company failures attributable to accounting fraud by officers. Prosecutors began adding so-called "honest services fraud" charges to mail and wire fraud as a way to obtain harsher sentences for the white-collar criminals. Conviction on this charge requires proof that the activities of the officers deprived the shareholders of the corporation of the honest services to which they were entitled as beneficiaries of the officers' fiduciary duties. Conrad Black, Richard Scrushy, and Jeffrey Skilling all received longer sentences because they were convicted of honest services fraud. However, the U.S. Supreme Court held in *Skilling v U.S.*, 130 S.Ct. 2896 (2010) that this portion of the mail and wire fraud statute was void for vagueness in the way prosecutors were using it for convictions and pleas (see substantive due process in Chapter 5). The court held that company officers would not know when and how they had violated the law because this portion of the statute was being applied when anything went wrong in the company. In other words, it was difficult to know what conduct deprived shareholders of officers' "honest services." The court held that the statute could be applied to the conduct of officers only in those situations in which officers accepted bribes or kickbacks so that they breached their fiduciary duties to shareholders and deprived them of the honest services officers are required to provide. There must be an underlying conflict created by a bribe or a kickback for the statute to apply. This significant decision curbed the government's flexibility in prosecuting white-collar crime and resulted in a reduction in sentences for Messrs. Black and Skilling and other white-collar criminals serving their sentences at the time of the decision.

8-4d FINANCIAL SERVICES REFORMS

Following the 2008 collapses and near-collapses of so many investment firms, banks, insurers, and mortgage lenders, Congress passed the Financial Services Reform Act, also known as the Dodd–Frank Wall Street Reform and Consumer Protection Act. The act creates a Bureau of Consumer Financial Services (CFSB) (see Chapter 12 for more information) that can impose civil penalties and also refer cases to the Department of Justice for criminal prosecution for violations of disclosure requirements or misrepresentations related to financial transactions. The act covers brokers, insurers, mortgage lenders, investment firms, banks, and any company that provides consumer financial services, including additional disclosure requirements as well as prohibitions on predatory lending.

8-5 The Penalties for Business Crime

Statutes specify penalties for crimes. Some statutes have both business and individual penalties. Exhibit 8.2 provides a summary of the penalties under the major federal statutes.

8-6 Reforming Criminal Penalties

8-6a NEW PENALTIES AND NEW PROCESSES

Some regulators and legislators argue that the difficulty with most criminal law penalties is that they were instituted with "natural" persons in mind, as opposed to "artificial" corporate persons. Fines may be significant to individuals, but a $10,000 fine to a corporation with billions in assets and millions in income is simply a cost of doing business.

A recommendation advanced for the reformation of criminal penalties is that the penalties must cost the corporation as much as a bad business decision would cost. For example, if a company develops a bad product line, net earnings could decline 10 to 20 percent. Penalties expressed in terms of net earnings, as opposed to set dollar amounts, are more likely to have a deterrent effect on business criminal behavior.

8-6b CORPORATE INTEGRITY AGREEMENTS (CIAs)

Using a corporate integrity agreement (CIA), judges are able to, in effect, place corporations on probation. Under CIAs, companies are assigned monitors who are on-site and follow up to be sure the company is not committing any further violations. Most CIAs include requirements that the company create or improve its ethics and compliance program, something that can include

---

EXHIBIT 8.2 Penalties for Business Crime under Federal Law

ACT	PENALTIES
Internal Revenue Code 26 U.S.C. § 7201	$100,000 ($500,000 for corporations) and/or 5 years For evasion (plus costs of prosecution as well as penalties and assessments: 5–50%)
Sherman Act (antitrust) 15 U.S.C. § 1	$350,000 and/or 3 years; $10,000,000 for corporations Injunctions Divestiture
Sarbanes-Oxley 15 U.S.C. § 1341 (document destruction, concealment, alteration, mutilation during pending civil or criminal investigation)	20 years plus fines (25 years for perjury)
Sarbanes-Oxley (certification of financial statements)	$1,000,000 and/or 10 years If willful: $5,000,000 and 20 years; officers who earn bonuses based on falsified financial statements must forfeit them
1933 Securities Act 15 U.S.C. § 77x (as amended by Sarbanes-Oxley)	$100,000 and/or 10 years
Securities and Exchange Act of 1934 15 U.S.C. § 78ff	$5,000,000 and/or 20 years $25,000,000 for corporations Civil penalties in addition of up to three times profit made or $1,000,000, whichever is greater
Clean Air Act 42 U.S.C. § 7413	$1,000,000 and/or 5 years
Clean Water Act 33 U.S.C. § 1319	For negligent violations: $25,000 per day and/or 1 year For knowing violations: $50,000 per day and/or 3 years For second violations: $100,000 per day and/or 6 years For false statements in reports, plans, or records: $10,000 per day and/or 2 years
Occupational Health Safety Act 29 U.S.C. § 666	Willful violation causing death: $70,000 and/or 1 year; minimum of $5,000 per willful violation Giving advance notice of inspection: $1,000 and/or 6 months False statements or representations: $10,000 and/or 6 months
Consumer Product Safety Act 15 U.S.C. § 2070	$50,000 and/or 1 year Tampering: up to $500,000 and/or 10 years

additional staffing and mandatory training for all employees. A CIA is a form of a deferred prosecution agreement. If the corporation has no further violations during the time of the CIA, which is generally three to five years, then the CIA is lifted and prosecutors do not go forward with a criminal case against the company.

Monitors

One portion of a corporate integrity agreement is generally the assignment of monitors to corporations to follow up on corporate activity. Monitors have offices within the corporation and are permitted to attend meetings, make observations, and provide feedback. The monitors are also there to report back to prosecutors any missteps. For example, ConEd was assigned a Natural Resources Defense Council lawyer as a monitor for its asbestos activity. Although their cases were not criminal in nature, both Coca-Cola and Mitsubishi agreed to a panel of monitors as part of their settlements in civil discrimination cases. America Online, Bank of New York, Blue Cross Blue Shield, Boeing, KPMG, and Monsanto are all examples of companies that have had monitors on-site as part of their criminal CIAs.

8-6c CRIMINAL INDICTMENTS OF CORPORATIONS ON COMMON LAW CRIMES

Another recommendation for reforming criminal penalties requires corporations to stand criminally responsible under traditional criminal statutes for corporate wrongs. For example, when Ford Motor Company manufactured the Pinto automobile with a design flaw involving the gas tank location, many civil suits were brought for deaths and injuries caused by the exploding gas tank. However, Ford was also indicted for a criminal charge of homicide. In 1999, the state of Florida charged ValuJet, Inc., with murder and manslaughter for carelessly handling deadly materials for shipment after an investigation showed that company procedural omissions resulted in an airplane crash and the deaths of 110 passengers and the crew. A traditional common-law crime was applied to corporations for the wrongful deaths of their customers. The owner of Imperial Foods Company in North Carolina pled guilty to workplace hazards that resulted in the burn deaths of 25 employees at his chicken-processing plant and received a 19-year prison sentence. Even though the crimes with which he was charged were violations of business laws, the sentence was traditional in the sense that an individual within a company was held personally and criminally responsible for the crimes.

8-6d SHAME PUNISHMENT

"Shame punishment" has been on the increase in corporate criminal cases. Shame punishment involves public disclosure of an offense. For example, a Delaware federal judge ordered Bachetti Brothers Market to take out an ad for three weeks confessing to its crime of violating federal law by selling meat consisting "in whole or in part of filthy, putrid and contaminated substances." Another federal judge, Ricardo Urbina, sentenced a former Bristol-Myers Squibb executive to write a book about his criminal misdeeds in reaching an agreement with a competitor to keep its generic drug off the market. The executive had to write, publish, and distribute the book to other pharmaceutical executives at his own expense. The executive was also sentenced to two years probation and a $5,000 fine. The book was completed, as required, by the end of his probation.

U.S. v Allegheny Bottling Co. (Case 8.2) involves a creative sentence imposed by a judge on a corporation.

CASE 8.2

United States v Allegheny Bottling Co.
695 F. Supp. 856 (E.D. Va. 1988); *cert. denied,* 493 U.S. 817 (1989)

Coke and Pepsi Wars Turn Criminal: Imprisonment for Price-Fixing

FACTS

Mid-Atlantic Coca-Cola Bottling Company and Allegheny Pepsi-Cola Bottling Company were charged with conspiracy to fix prices on Coke and Pepsi in order to avoid the ruinous competition that price wars were causing. Several officers pleaded guilty to the charges, and some were found guilty by a jury.

The trial evidence showed that in the Baltimore market, Coke sold from 6,200,000 to 7,000,000 cases of soft drinks a year. Prior to the price-fixing agreement, the price per case was $6.00 to $6.40. After the price-fixing agreement with Pepsi in 1982, the price was $6.80 per case, and it remained there for a full year. This additional 40 cents per case allowed the companies to earn over $1 million more. In pronouncing sentence on the corporate defendants, the judge used a creative solution (later affirmed by the appellate court).

JUDICIAL OPINION

DOUMAR, District Judge

The Lord Chancellor of England said some two hundred years ago, "Did you ever expect a corporation to have a conscience when it has no soul to be damned, and no body to be kicked?" Two hundred years have passed since the Lord Chancellor espoused this view, and the whole area of what is and is not permitted or what is or is not prohibited, has changed both in design and application. Certainly, this Court does not expect a corporation to have a conscience, but it does expect it to be ethical and abide by the law. This Court will deal with this company no less severely than it will deal with any individual who similarly disregards the law.

…Allegheny Bottling Company [parent of Allegheny Pepsi] is sentenced to three (3) years imprisonment and a fine of One Million Dollars ($1,000,000). Execution of the sentence of imprisonment is suspended and all but $950,000 of said fine is suspended, and the defendant is placed on probation for a period of three years.

As special conditions of the probation, in addition to the normal terms of probation, the defendant, Allegheny Bottling Company, shall provide:

(a) An officer or employee of Allegheny of comparable salary and stature to Jerry Polino (former vice president of sales who pled guilty to the conspiracy charges) to perform forty (40) hours of community service per week in the Baltimore, Maryland area for a two (2) year period without compensation to the defendant. [The court required 40 hours of community service from someone of equal stature for each of the four officers of Allegheny who had been convicted or pleaded guilty to the price-fixing conspiracy charges.]

Corporate imprisonment requires only that the Court restrain or immobilize the corporation. Such restraint of individuals is accomplished by, for example, placing them in the custody of the United States Marshal. The United States Marshal would restrain the corporation by seizing the corporation's physical assets or part of the assets or restricting its actions or liberties in a particular manner.

Cases in the past have *assumed* that corporations cannot be imprisoned, without any cited authority for that proposition. This Court, however, has been unable to find any case which actually held that corporate imprisonment is illegal, unconstitutional, or impossible. Considerable confusion regarding the ability of courts to order a corporation imprisoned has been caused by courts mistakenly thinking that imprisonment necessarily involves incarceration in jail. But since imprisonment of a corporation does not necessarily involve incarceration, there is no reason to continue the assumption, which has lingered in the legal system unexamined and without support, that a corporation cannot be imprisoned. Since the Marshal can restrain the corporation's liberty and has done so in bankruptcy cases, there is no reason he cannot do so in this case as he himself has so stated prior to the imposition of this sentence.

Corporate imprisonment not only promotes the purposes of the Sherman Act but also promotes the purposes of sentencing. The purposes of sentencing, according to the United States Sentencing Commission, include incapacitating the offender, deterring crime, rehabilitating the offender, and providing just punishment. The corporate imprisonment imposed today is specifically tailored to meet each of these purposes.

CASE QUESTIONS

1. Is corporate imprisonment illegal?
2. How will the corporation be imprisoned?
3. Is community service a sufficient punishment for the corporation?

ETHICAL ISSUES

In 1994, Congress passed a law that permitted nonviolent convicts to cut up to 12 months from their sentences if they complete a drug rehab/counseling program. When the program was first created, 3,755 inmates entered the program. In 2008, 18,000 federal prisoners were in the program, and there was a waiting list of 7,000 inmates.

The program has had some big names. For example, Dr. Sam Waksal, the former CEO of ImClone, served nine fewer months than his original seven-year sentence because he participated in a prison rehab program for inmates who have a problem with substance abuse. When Dr. Waksal was interviewed for the presentencing report, he told the probation officer that he was a "social drinker" and had perhaps five glasses of wine per week. One month after the interview with the probation officer, Waksal's lawyers informed a federal judge that Waksal had a "dependence on alcohol" and requested approval for Waksal's entry into a prison rehab program.

The former mayor of Atlanta, Bill Campbell, was admitted into a federal rehab program and got a

9-month reduction on his 30-month sentence for tax evasion. He was admitted to rehab despite the fact that his lawyers argued at his sentencing hearing that he had no substance abuse problem and that he hated the taste of alcohol and therefore urged the judge to conclude that Campbell's imprisonment was not necessary.

There are consulting firms that advise white-collar criminals on submitting their applications for the program. The firms also advise their clients (for a $5,000 fee) on how to maximize the sentence write-down for completing the rehab program.

The Bureau of Prisons indicates that it is cracking down on admissions to the program, looking more closely at doctors' letters and past histories of the inmates.

Evaluate the ethics of the inmates who feign addiction. Evaluate the ethics of the consulting firms that help them get into the program.

Source: Kai Falkenberg, "Time Off for Bad Behavior," *Forbes*, January 12, 2009, pp. 64–65.

8-6e OFFICER AND EXECUTIVE BANISHMENT

One of the rapidly increasing forms of business crime punishment is barring executives and officers from working in their fields if they have a criminal conviction. For example, the SEC can bar those who are convicted from the securities industry for a period of years or even for life (as in the case of Michael Milken). In the health care field, federal agencies use the "responsible corporate officer" (RCO) doctrine to hold those who head up companies criminally responsible when their hospitals submit false Medicare claims or their drug firms misbrand prescription drugs. In addition to holding these RCOs criminally responsible, the agencies prosecuting the cases often seek to have the RCOs barred from the health care industry for periods that range from one year to life, with the typical time being 12 to 20 years. In some cases, a banishment from the field for eight years or more means that their careers as health care officers are ended.

8-6f NEW AND HIGHER PENALTIES FOR CORPORATE CRIME

Criminal penalties have been increased to allow judges to fine corporations according to how much a bad decision would cost. For example, if a company develops a faulty product, net earnings could decline 10 to 20 percent. Criminal penalties can be assessed as a percentage of net income. Rather than using fixed-amount fines for corporations, statutes and courts apply percentage of revenue penalties. For example, a bad decision on a product line would cost a company 10 percent to 20 percent of its earnings. A criminal penalty could be imposed in the same percentage fashion with the idea that the company made a bad legal decision that should be reflected in reduced earnings.

8-6g CORPORATE SENTENCING GUIDELINES: AN OUNCE OF PREVENTION MEANS A REDUCED SENTENCE

The U.S. Sentencing Commission (USSC), established by Congress in 1984, has developed both federal sentencing guidelines and a carrot-and-stick approach to fighting white-collar crime. Under the commission's guidelines, companies that take substantial steps to prevent, investigate, and punish wrongdoing and cooperate with federal investigators can be treated less harshly in sentencing. The goal of the commission was to ensure that companies would establish internal crime prevention programs. The guidelines were revamped following the Boesky/Milken issues and again following the Enron era.

The sentencing guidelines permit judges to place guilty companies on probation for a period of up to five years if their offense or offenses occurred during a time when they had no crime prevention programs in place. In addition, the Justice Department has the option of agreeing to a deferred prosecution agreement (DPA) or non-prosecution agreement (NPA). The guidelines are a form of mandatory sentencing. If certain factors are present, the judge must order prison times. Corporate officers who are proven to have masterminded criminal activity must be sentenced to some prison time. However, the U.S. Supreme Court has placed some limits on the authority of judges to mete out sentences. In *U.S. v Booker*, 543 U.S. 220 (2005), the court held that when judges are determining sentences for defendants under the guidelines, any facts, other than the defendant's prior conviction, must be established by a jury beyond a reasonable doubt. In the case, Booker had been convicted of possession of 50 grams of crack cocaine. The sentencing judge considered additional evidence in the sentencing hearing that Booker had 566 additional grams of crack that was not used as evidence at the trial. The result was that Booker was not eligible under the sentencing guidelines for a lesser sentence of 21 years and 10 months, and the judge imposed a sentence of 30 years. The Supreme Court reversed the sentencing portion of the case, remanded the case for resentencing, and held that if the judge was going to consider additional facts that affected the length of sentence, such as the additional crack, those additional facts must be proved in the same way as the crime—before a jury and beyond a reasonable doubt. The impact of the *Booker* case has been widespread and many defendants are now in the process of being resentenced, including many of the business executives convicted and sentenced as a result of the Enron-era scandals.

How the Sentencing Guidelines Work and What Companies Can Do to Minimize Sentences

The federal sentencing guidelines provide for a score that determines the extent of the sentence of the company and individual officers, managers, and employees. The guidelines use a formula that takes into account the seriousness of the offense, the company's history of violations, its cooperation in the investigation, the effectiveness of its compliance program, and the role of senior management in the wrongdoing. A company's "culpability multiplier" can range from 0.05 to 4.00, which is then used to convert a business's culpability score (a number that ranges

BUSINESS STRATEGY

Much More Than Compliance

Businesses should follow these basic principles of the sentencing guidelines.

1. Have a code of ethics in place.

2. Conduct training on the code of ethics.

3. Have a company hotline and ombudsperson for employees to use anonymously to report violations. A third-party computer reporting system is also considered a "best practice" for ethics and compliance programs.

4. Protect employees who report violations.

5. Investigate all allegations regardless of their source.

6. Report all violations immediately and voluntarily.

7. Offer restitution to affected parties.

8. Cooperate and negotiate with regulators.

9. Admit your mistakes and shortcomings.

10. Be forthright and public with your code of ethics. Discuss ethics with employees via website examples or illustrations of good ethical choices in the news among companies and employees.

from 0 to 10 or above). Every company begins with a score of 5, which can be added to or subtracted from depending on various factors in the guidelines. The larger the organization, the greater the number of points added. Involvement of top officers in criminal conduct also adds to the score. Prior violations increase a company's score, as do attempts to cover up the conduct (obstruction of justice).

A company's score is decreased by the presence of effective compliance programs designed to prevent and detect violations. If a company comes forward and reports the violations voluntarily, the score is decreased. Cooperation with investigators and acceptance of responsibility also reduce the score.

These multipliers are also used in the computation of fines for a business and its employees and officers. Restitution made by a company before sentencing reduces penalties and fines. For example, a fine of $1 million to $2 million could be reduced to as low as $50,000 for a company with the following: (1) a code of conduct, (2) an ombudsperson, (3) a hotline, and (4) mandatory training for executives. The sentencing guidelines have been referred to as a "quiet revolution" in changing corporate conduct.

8-6h CORPORATE BOARD CRIMINAL RESPONSIBILITY

In *In re Caremark International, Inc.*, 698 A.2d 959 (Del. Ch. 1996), a court concluded that corporate boards could be held liable for their failure to institute and monitor adequate internal controls to prevent fraud in the company. This landmark case dealt with a company indicted for its physician referrals fees that were paid in violation of federal laws under the Medicare and Medicaid programs. The court noted that it is the responsibility of the board of directors to ensure that the company's compliance program is in place and functioning effectively. Since the time of this case, directors have been held personally liable for fraud and resulting shareholder losses committed while they were board members. For example, several board members from WorldCom, a company that had an $11 billion overstatement of revenues due to accounting fraud, were required to pay personally in order to settle civil cases brought against them by both the SEC and shareholders.

FOR THE MANAGER'S DESK

Re: Who Really Ends Up Going to Jail for Corporate Crime?

For the most part, those who were sentenced in federal court in the pre-Enron era for white-collar crimes tended to come from the middle classes rather than the upper classes. From 1988 to June 30, 1995, the federal government, through the Office of the Special Counsel of the Justice Department, was given the charge of investigating the collapse of the country's savings and loans "to find and prosecute those who looted our financial institutions." The Office of Special Counsel finished with the following results:

Number of defendants charged: 6,405

Convictions: 5,506 defendants convicted (96.5% conviction rate)

Types of persons convicted: Officers, directors, or CEOs: 29%; accountants, attorneys, and consultants: 71%

Types of persons charged: Directors and officers: 1,268 (97.5%) convicted; presidents or CEOs: 484 (95.1%) convicted

Prison time: Of the 5,506 defendants convicted: 75.5% sentenced to prison

Criminal violations committed by *Fortune* 500 corporations over a two-year period in the post-S&L scandal showed that executives were convicted in only 1.5 percent of the cases. However, managers were more likely than not to be sentenced in such cases. And employees, particularly in securities fraud cases, were more likely to be sentenced to prison than the executives for whom they worked. However, executives are far more likely than both groups to be given civil sanctions.

Since the time this data was gathered, there has been a dramatic shift in sentencing for the top executives, as the following list reflects:

Bernie Madoff (Madoff Securities)	150 years
R. Allen Stanford (Stanford Securities)	110 years
WorldCom CEO Bernie Ebbers	25 years

On the other hand, the employees who were simply following orders were given far lesser sentences:

Peter Madoff, chief operating officer	10 years
21 Madoff employees	License suspensions
Standford Chief Investment officer	3 years
Andrew Fastow (Enron CFO)	6 years
Average sentence of other Enron employees	2.75 years
WorldCom Controller David Myers	1 year and 1 day
WorldCom Accounting Director Buford Yates	1 year and 1 day
WorldCom Director of Management Reporting Betty Vinson	5 months
WorldCom Director of Legal Entity Accounting Troy Normand	3 years probation

Prosecutors now take a bottom-up approach—that is, they work their plea deals with employees in order to build their cases carefully against those at the top.

Source: Jane Sasseen, "White-Collar Crime: Who Does Time?" *BusinessWeek,* February 6, 2006, pp. 60–61.

8-7 Elements of Business Crime

The **elements**, or requirements for proof, of a business crime vary according to type. Crimes are violations of written laws, such as statutes or ordinances. But all crimes' specific elements can be classified into two general elements: *mens rea* (or *scienter*) and *actus reus*.

8-7a *MENS REA, SCIENTER,* OR CRIMINAL INTENT

A **crime** requires calculated or intentional conduct; this mental intent or knowledge of wrong (*scienter*) is the ***mens rea*** of a crime. *Mens rea* is the required state of mind for a crime—the intent to commit the act that is a crime. A criminal wrong is not based on an accident unless a person was forewarned about the accident or the accident arose from criminal conduct. Driving while intoxicated is a crime, and an accident that happens while a driver is intoxicated is also a criminal wrong. Concealing income is intentional conduct calculated to avoid paying taxes; it is willful and criminal conduct. An oversight in reporting income is not a crime. *U.S. v Ahmad* (Case 8.3) discusses the issue of intent in an environmental case.

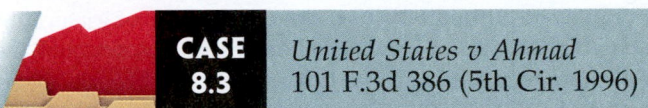

CASE 8.3

United States v Ahmad
101 F.3d 386 (5th Cir. 1996)

Gasoline, Drains, and Knowledge of the Two Together: A Crime?

FACTS

Mr. Ahmad owns a Spin-N-Market located in Conroe, Texas. Shortly after he purchased the combination gas and convenience store in 1992, he discovered a leak in one of the high-octane gasoline tanks at the location. The leak was at the top of the tank and did not present problems with gasoline seeping out. However, the leak did allow water to get into the tank and contaminate the gas. Because water is heavier than gas, the water sank to the bottom of the tank, and because the tank was pumped from the bottom, Mr. Ahmad was unable to sell gas from it.

In October 1993, Mr. Ahmad hired CTT Environmental Services, a tank-testing company, to examine the tank. CTT determined that the tank contained 800 gallons of water and the rest was mostly gasoline. Jewel McCoy, a CTT employee, told Mr. Ahmad that the leak could not be repaired until the tank was completely empty, which CTT offered to do for 65 cents per gallon plus $65 per hour of labor. After Ms. McCoy gave Mr. Ahmad this CIT estimate, he asked whether he could empty the tank himself. Ms. McCoy told him that it would be dangerous and illegal for him to do so. Mr. Ahmad then responded, "Well, if I don't get caught, what then?"

On January 25, 1994, Mr. Ahmad rented a handheld motorized water pump from a local hardware store, telling a hardware store employee that he was planning to use it to remove water from his backyard. Mr. Ahmad hooked the pump up to his tank at the Spin-N-Market and pumped 5,220 gallons of fluid into a manhole near the store and into Lewis Street alongside the store. Of the fluid pumped, 4,690 gallons were gasoline.

The gasoline from Lewis Street made its way to a storm drain and the storm sewer system and eventually into Possum Creek. When city officials discovered the gasoline in Possum Creek, several vacuum trucks were required to decontaminate it.

The gasoline from the manhole made its way to the city sewage treatment center. The gasoline was diverted into a different storage pool in order to avoid shutting down the plant altogether, but the plant had to evacuate all but essential personnel, and firefighters and hazardous materials crews from the city had to be called to restore the plant to a safe condition. While the crews worked, two area schools had to be evacuated for safety reasons.

Mr. Ahmad was indicted for three violations of the Clean Water Act (CWA), of knowingly discharging a pollutant into navigable waters without a permit, knowingly placing others in imminent danger through a pollutant, and knowingly operating a source in violation of pretreatment requirements. Mr. Ahmad did not dispute the conduct; he said he did not meet the "knowingly" requirements because he believed he was discharging water.

The jury found Mr. Ahmad guilty on two of the three charges and deadlocked on the charge of imminent danger. Mr. Ahmad appealed.

JUDICIAL OPINION

SMITH, Circuit Judge

Ahmad contends that the jury should have been instructed that the statutory *mens rea*—knowledge—was required as to each element of the offenses, rather than only with regard to discharge or the operation of a source.

The language of the CWA is less than pellucid. Title 33 U.S.C. § 1319(c)(2)(A) says that "any person who knowingly violates" any of a number of other sections of the CWA commits a felony. The principal issue is to which elements of the offense the modifier "knowingly" applies. The matter is complicated somewhat by the fact that the phrase "knowingly violates" appears in a different section of the CWA from the language

CONTINUED

defining the elements of the offenses. Ahmad argues that within this context, "knowingly violates" should be read to require him knowingly to have acted with regard to each element of the offenses. The government, in contrast, contends that "knowingly violates" requires it to prove only that Ahmad knew the nature of his acts and that he performed them intentionally. Particularly at issue is whether "knowingly" applies to the element of the discharge's being a pollutant, for Ahmad's main theory at trial was that he thought he was discharging water, not gasoline.

The Supreme Court has spoken to this issue in broad terms…. "[T]he presumption in favor of a *scienter* requirement should apply to each of the statutory elements which criminalize otherwise innocent conduct."

Indeed, we find it eminently sensible that the phrase "knowingly violates" in § 1319(c)(2)(A), when referring to other provisions that define the elements of the offenses § 1319 creates, should uniformly require knowledge as to each of those elements rather than only one or two. To hold otherwise would require an explanation as to why some elements should be treated differently from others, which neither the parties nor the case law seems able to provide.

The government also protests that CWA violations fall into the judicially created exception for "public welfare offenses," under which some regulatory crimes have been held not to require a showing of *mens rea*. On its face, the CWA certainly does appear to implicate public welfare.

The fact that violations of § 1319(c)(2)(A) are felonies punishable by years in federal prison confirms our view that they do not fall within the public welfare offense exception…. [P]ublic welfare offenses have virtually always been crimes punishable by relatively light penalties such as fines or short jail sentences, rather than substantial terms of imprisonment. Serious felonies, in contrast, should not fall within the exception "absent a clear statement from Congress that *mens rea* is not required"…. [W]e hold that the offenses charged in counts one and two are not public welfare offenses and that the usual presumption of a *mens rea* requirement

applies. With the exception of purely jurisdictional elements, the *mens rea* of knowledge applies to each element of the crimes.

At best, the jury charge made it uncertain to which elements "knowingly" applied. At worst, and considerably more likely, it indicated that only the element of discharge need be knowingly. The instructions listed each element on a separate line, with the word "knowingly" present only in the line corresponding to the element that something was discharged. That the district court included a one-sentence summary of each count in which "knowingly" was present did not cure the error.

The obvious inference for the jury was that knowledge was required only as to the fact that something was discharged, and not as to any other fact. In effect, with regard to the other elements of the crimes, the instructions implied that the requisite *mens rea* was strict liability rather than knowledge.

There was at least a reasonable likelihood that the jury applied the instructions in this way, so we conclude that the instructions misled the jury as to the elements of the offense. Because the charge effectively withdrew from the jury's consideration facts that it should have been permitted to find or not find, this error requires reversal.

Most of Ahmad's defense, after all, was built around the idea that he thought water, rather than gasoline, was being discharged. A rational jury could so have found, and at the same time could have found that he did not actually know that he was pumping gas.

Reversed and remanded.

CASE QUESTIONS

1. What does the court require for criminal intent under the Clean Water Act?

2. Of what significance is Jewel McCoy's testimony? Mr. Ahmad's testimony?

3. What is the difference between knowledge of the law and knowledge of conduct?

Consider…

Eric Ho is a naturalized citizen who emigrated to Houston from the Republic of China in the 1970s. An experienced businessperson, he owns and operates a produce supply company, Houston Fruitland, and a trucking company, Ho Ho Ho Express, Inc.

Ho purchased the abandoned Alief General Hospital and Professional Building in Houston. During negotiations for the purchase, the owner's agent told Ho that a 1994 environmental site assessment revealed extensive asbestos in the hospital's fireproofing; that asbestos abatement could cost as much as $400,000; and that the owner was selling the property "as is." The owner and Ho ultimately agreed to a price of $700,000 instead of the initial asking price of $1.1 million. The contract included a Commercial Property Condition Statement to the effect that the property contained asbestos. Ho signed the statement, thereby acknowledging the presence of asbestos.

Ho contacted a licensed asbestos abatement company to obtain a bid for asbestos removal. Ho was given bid of $325,000 to remove and dispose of all asbestos, which Ho quickly rejected as too high. The firm then offered a second bid of cost plus ten percent; Ho never responded.

Instead, Ho initiated his own hospital renovation project. He did not give advance notice to the EPA or state authorities of his intent to renovate a building with asbestos. Ho hired Manuel Escobedo, his sometimes handyman, to supervise the work, though Ho often visited the hospital site himself. Ho also hired Corson Tate to begin renovations in the professional building.

Escobedo hired 10 Mexican nationals—apparently in the United States illegally—to perform the asbestos removal work. Escobedo paid the workers by submitting their time sheets to Ho's accountant, receiving and cashing a check, and paying the workers in cash. The workers, who had no experience or training in asbestos removal, began removing the asbestos. Neither Ho nor Escobedo disclosed to the workers that asbestos is a dangerous carcinogen, nor did they provide the workers with adequate safety equipment.

Against customary asbestos abatement practices, the workers used no water as they removed the fireproofing, but only scraped off the fireproofing, which produced large amounts of asbestos-containing dust inside the hospital. The hospital remained unsealed throughout, with several open doors and windows and a large hole in the second floor exterior wall. None of these practices complied with asbestos work practice standards.

Tim Stewart, a building inspector for the City of Houston, visited the hospital to investigate a complaint of renovation work without a city permit. Stewart issued a stop-work order and placed a red tag on the main entrance to the hospital indicating that work could not proceed without a city building permit.

Ho then contacted an operations manager at Alamo Environmental, a licensed asbestos abatement company in San Antonio, for an estimate to remove the remaining asbestos-containing material. The manager gave Ho an estimate of $159,876 on February 13. Ho decided not to hire Alamo Environmental but, instead, rehired the Mexican workers and instructed them to work at night. Ho also visited the hospital frequently and on a few occasions personally supervised the workers. Ho also hired Tate to provide supplies to the workers and monitor their hours.

The workers completed the asbestos removal and Ho told Tate to wash down the inside of the hospital using a water line outside the hospital. Unfortunately, the "water line" was in fact a pressurized gas line. After Tate removed the cap on the line, he started his nearby van. The spark from the ignition and the open gas line caused an explosion. The explosion burned Tate, three workers, and the van and blew a hole in the exterior wall of the hospital.

Ho was convicted of failure to comply with asbestos work practice standards and failure to give notice of intent to remove asbestos. He appealed his conviction on the grounds that there was a lack of criminal intent on his part because he was not aware of all the federal laws that applied to his work on the hospital. Analyze whether there is sufficient evidence of criminal intent. [*U.S. v Ho*, 311 F.3d 589 (5th Cir. 2002)]

THINK: From the *Ahmad* case, you learned that for someone to be convicted of a crime, they must be aware that they are actually violating the laws on discharge. From the *Park* case, you learned that executives are liable for the conduct of others in running the company if they are aware of violations and continue to allow those violations to occur without taking action.

APPLY: Ho was aware of the presence of asbestos (from the purchase documents for the hospital). Ho twice contacted asbestos removal firms for estimates, but declined to hire them because of the costs. Ho had the work done at night after he was warned by the city inspector about the asbestos removal requirements and the need for a permit. Ho paid untrained workers in cash so as to avoid questions about the project.

ANSWER: The jury correctly concluded that there was enough evidence of intent. Although Ho might not have known all of the nuances of asbestos removal, he had sufficient warnings from the seller, the removal contractors, and the inspector about the need for certain requirements and standards for removal. He chose to ignore their advice and disclosures and, in fact, tried to conceal his work by having cash-paid workers work only at night.

8-7b *MENS REA,* CONSCIOUS AVOIDANCE, AND CORPORATE OFFICERS

Criminal intent has been a particularly significant issue in business crimes. The intent element is significant because two intents are actually involved when a corporation is prosecuted for a crime: the intent of the corporation to commit the crime and the intent of those in charge of the corporation, officers, and directors to direct the corporation to commit the wrong. Officers may have intent, but the company may not be aware of these pockets of deceit and malfeasance. However, courts have also developed the doctrine of **conscious avoidance** as a means of establishing *mens rea* for officers as well as a pattern of behavior that established an unwillingness to curb deception. Under this theory, executives cannot "consciously try to avoid knowledge" about the actions and activities of those within the company. For example, under the criminal portions of SOX that apply to CEOs and CFOs for certification of a company's financial statements, an executive cannot isolate himself from information that the financial reports were inaccurate by not attending meetings or not reading the reports that are disclosed to the public. [*U.S. v Ebbers*, 549 U.S. 1274 (2007)] The *U.S. v Park* case has modern application in that these top executives are fully accountable for the information in their companies' financial statements even when they do not actually prepare those statements. Richard Scrushy's statement, "I certainly had no knowledge of anything they were doing in terms of moving numbers around in the company," is not a defense for a CEO.[1] Bernie Ebbers, the former CEO of WorldCom, denied knowing that information in the company's financial statements was false. In fact, he indicated he did not always read the 10-Ks and 10-Qs. However, testimony of witnesses at his trial showed that he attended the "Close the Gap" meetings in which managers discussed how to have actual numbers meet projections. Mr. Ebbers could not avoid criminal culpability by avoiding the final reports when he was aware of trouble brewing.

8-7c *ACTUS REUS*

All crimes include, in addition to the mental intent, a requirement of some specific action or conduct, which is the *actus reus* of the crime. For example, in embezzlement, the *actus reus* is the taking of an employer's money. Various types of criminal conduct, or *actus reus* examples, are found in subsequent sections on specific crimes.

8-8 Examples of Business Crimes

8-8a THEFT AND EMBEZZLEMENT

The action of employees who take their employers' property is **theft** or **embezzlement**. For theft, the following elements are necessary: (1) intent to take the property, (2) actual taking of the property for permanent use, and (3) no authorization to take the property. These three elements are the *actus reus* of the crime. The *mens rea* is the taking of the property with the intent of permanently depriving the owner of use and possession.

For embezzlement, the elements are the same as for theft, with the addition of one more element: The person commits the crime while in the employ or position of trust of the property owner. In other words, embezzlement is theft from a specific type of person—an employer. Although it is usually limited to funds, embezzlement can cover such items as inventory and equipment of a business.

Consider...

Dennis Kozlowski and Mark Swartz, the former CEO and CFO, respectively, of Tyco International, initially had a hung jury in their trial for larceny.

Mr. Kozlowski and Mr. Swartz, who were eventually convicted of embezzlement, enjoyed extensive personal benefits from Tyco, an embarrassment of personal acquisition at company expense. Prosecutors must show *mens rea*, criminal intent. The defense that both men raised to counter intent, and apparently successfully enough to flummox some jurors in their first trial, was that none of what they obtained through the various company agreements and programs was done secretly. Both men produced evidence related to board knowledge of their perks and approvals through the established and proper company procedures for personal loans and the use of company funds for refurbishing and furnishing their homes. Along the lines of a "Why would I be such an idiot?" defense, the two approached their case as one in which the blatancy of their conduct would work in their favor in mitigating intent, or *mens rea*.

None of the loans was made to the men without some form of authorization, however perfunctory. Many in the executive ranks and perhaps even some board members were aware of the loans, the officer loan policy, and the processes used for booking and forgiving the loans. The issue of board approval on the loans remains a question, but compensation committee minutes from February 21, 2002, show that the committee was given a list of loans to officers and also approved all compensation packages. There was no public disclosure of these developments or the committee's review.

Do you believe these facts supported the jury's finding of *mens rea* in the retrial of the cases against Mr. Kozlowski and Mr. Swartz? Was their conduct ethical?

Sources: Adapted from Andrew Ross Sorkin, "Judge Ends Trial When Tyco Juror Reports Threat," *New York Times*, April 3, 2004, pp. A1, B4; Andrew Ross Sorkin, "After a Mistrial, Choices to Make," *New York Times*, April 5, 2004, pp. C1, C6; Jonathan D. Glater, "Prosecutors See More Time in Another Tyco Case," *New York Times*, April 8, 2004, p. C4; Mark Maremont, "Kozlowski's Defense Strategy: Big Spending Was No Secret," *Wall Street Journal*, February 9, 2004, pp. A1, A23; Andrew Ross Sorkin and Jonathan D. Glater, "Some Tyco Board Members Knew of Pay Packages, Records Show," *New York Times*, September 23, 2002, p. A1; Laurie P. Cohen, "Tyco Ex-Counsel Claims Auditors Knew of Loans," *Wall Street Journal*, October 22, 2002, p. A6.

8-8b OBSTRUCTION OF JUSTICE

Because of the cases involving the destruction of documents, SOX amended the federal law on obstruction of justice to make document destruction a specific crime and to increase its penalties. The new obstruction section makes it a felony for anyone, including company employees, auditors, attorneys, and consultants, *to alter, destroy, mutilate, conceal, cover up, falsify, or make a false entry with the "intent to impede, obstruct, or influence the investigation or proper administration of any matter within the jurisdiction of any department or agency of the United States."*[2] Obstruction can be committed by destroying or altering documents that are subject to a subpoena, or that are related to a pending investigation, and also by encouraging

Business Planning Tip

Do not ever try to withhold a violation or restructure paperwork to cover it up. The truth comes out. Concealment is an additional crime.

others to alter or destroy those types of documents. Encouraging or giving false testimony is also a form of obstruction of justice. Martha Stewart was convicted of obstruction of justice for her alteration of phone logs, backdating of an order to her broker, and encouraging a broker's assistant to lie to support her backdating story.

The SOX provisions on obstruction also cover audit records and require auditors to retain their work papers related to a client's audit for at least five years. Any destruction of these documents prior to the expiration of that period would constitute a felony and carries a penalty of up to 10 years.

ETHICAL ISSUES

As the financial performance of the infamous energy company Enron dipped, its audit firm, Arthur Andersen, worried that Enron's accounting and financial statements were doubtful. On October 16, 2001, Enron refused to change its earnings release in response to Andersen's concerns. Andersen was preparing a statement about the release. Nancy Temple, legal counsel for Arthur Andersen, e-mailed back and forth with David Duncan, the audit partner for the Enron account in Houston, about the content of the Andersen statement on Enron.

Later that same day, Temple also sent an e-mail to Andersen's internal team of accounting experts and attached a copy of the company's document policy. On October 20, the Enron crisis-response team held a conference call, during which Temple instructed everyone to "[m]ake sure to follow the [document] policy." On October 23, 2001, then–Enron CEO Kenneth Lay declined to answer questions during a call with analysts because of "potential lawsuits, as well as the SEC inquiry." After the call, Duncan met with other Andersen partners and told them that they should ensure that team members were complying with the company's document policy. Another meeting for all team members followed, during which Duncan distributed the policy and told everyone to comply. These, and other smaller meetings, were followed by considerable shredding and destruction of both paper and electronic documents.

On October 26, 2001, one of Andersen's senior partners circulated a *New York Times* article discussing the SEC's response to Enron. His e-mail commented, "the problems are just beginning and we will be in the crosshairs. The marketplace is going to keep the pressure on this and is going to force the SEC to be tough." On October 30, the SEC opened a formal investigation and sent Enron a letter that requested accounting documents. The document destruction continued despite reservations by some of Andersen's managers. On November 8, 2001, Enron announced that it would issue a comprehensive restatement of its earnings and assets. Also on November 8, the SEC served Enron and Andersen with subpoenas for records. On November 9, Duncan's secretary sent an e-mail that stated, "Per Dave—No more shredding … We have been officially served for our documents." Enron filed for bankruptcy less than a month later. Duncan was fired and later pleaded guilty to witness tampering, a plea he later withdrew.[3]

Applying the *Park* case, who is criminally liable for the document shredding? The employees who actually did it? The managers who ordered it to begin? The company itself? Were they technically not in violation of the law during the document destruction because there was no formal notice until November 8?
[*Arthur Andersen LLP v U.S.*, 544 U.S. 696 (2005)]

CYBERLAW

8-8c **COMPUTER CRIME**

What Is a Computer Crime?

The term **computer crime** is used as though it were a completely separate body of law from criminal law. Although certain crimes can only be committed using a computer, the nature of crime, with both *mens rea* and *actus reus*, does not change. Specific statutes addressing the unique means by which property is taken and covering the unique type of property found in computer software and hardware make establishing computer crimes easier than reliance on traditional crimes such as larceny and embezzlement.

Some computer crimes may involve a computer without making direct use of one. Ordinary criminal statutes can apply to these types of crimes. For example, a person who mails flyers that falsely advertise a service as computerized is guilty of committing the federal crime of using the mail to defraud.

For more serious and costly computer-related wrongs that do not fit the ordinary definitions of crime, the trend is toward adopting statutes that define specific computer crimes. Chapter 10 provides the details on computer crimes.

8-8d CRIMINAL FRAUD

Business crimes against individuals usually result from sales transactions. **Criminal fraud** is an example of this type of crime, the elements of which are the same as those the person defrauded would use to establish a contract defense: A false statement was made; the statement was material—that is, it was information that would affect the buying decision; and the person relied on the statement. The only difference between contract fraud and criminal fraud is that criminal fraud requires proof of intent that the seller intended to mislead the buyer for the purpose of effecting the transaction and making money. In the mortgage fraud cases brought against borrowers during 2008–2012, the basis for the fraud is that documents and appraisals were forged or falsified. In many cases, criminal intent was established because the loans had two sets of documents and always the same buyers.

8-8e COMMERCIAL BRIBERY

Most states have provisions that govern both the giving and receiving of gifts or funds in exchange for a contract or favor. A supplier offering a purchasing agent of a company $25,000 in cash as an incentive or reward for choosing that supplier has committed commercial bribery. The purchasing agent has betrayed his employer's interest and compromised his judgment by accepting benefits for himself. This condemnation of bribery in commercial transactions dates back to the first eras of business activity because of concerns that quality and pricing would suffer if corruption were introduced into the bargaining process.

8-8f RACKETEER INFLUENCED AND CORRUPT ORGANIZATIONS (RICO) ACT

The RICO Act (18 U.S.C. §§ 1961–1968), a complex federal statute, was passed with the intent of curbing organized crime activity. The ease of proof and severity of penalties for RICO violations have made it a popular charge in criminal cases in which organized crime may not actually be involved.

For RICO to apply, a "pattern of racketeering activity" must be established. That pattern is defined as the commission of at least two racketeering acts within a 10-year period. Racketeering acts are defined under the federal statute to include murder; kidnapping; gambling; arson; robbery; bribery; extortion; dealing in pornography or narcotics; counterfeiting; embezzlement of pension, union, or welfare funds; mail fraud; wire fraud; obstruction of justice or criminal investigation; interstate transportation of stolen goods; white slavery; fraud in the sale of securities; and other acts relating to the Currency and Foreign Transactions Reporting Act (an act passed to prevent money laundering).

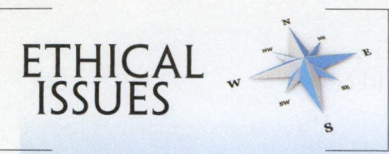

ETHICAL ISSUES

Jim G. Locklear was a purchasing agent. His spectacular career as a buyer began in 1977 with Federated Stores in Dallas, Texas. Federated officers described him as a man with an eye for fashion and a keen ability to negotiate. In 1987, Mr. Locklear was offered a position with Jordan Marsh, a retailer in the Boston area, with an annual salary of $96,000.

Citing a desire to return to Dallas, Mr. Locklear left the Jordan Marsh position after only three months. He returned to Dallas as a buyer for JCPenney at an annual salary of $56,000. Mr. Locklear did a phenomenal job as the buyer for the JCPenney Home Collection. JCPenney was the first department store to feature coordinated lines of dinnerware, flatware, and glasses. During Mr. Locklear's tenure as a purchasing agent, Penney's annual sales for his area of its tabletop line went from $25 million to $45 million.

After receiving an anonymous tip, JCPenney hired an investigator to look into Mr. Locklear's conduct. The investigator found and reported that Mr. Locklear had personal financial difficulties. He had a $500,000 mortgage on his home and child support payments of $900 a month for four children from four previous marriages. Mr. Locklear also had a country club membership, luxury vehicles, and large securities accounts, and he was known to take vacations at posh resorts. Despite the puzzling lifestyle revealed by the investigator, JCPenney took no action.

In 1992, JCPenney received an anonymous letter disclosing a kickback situation between Mr. Locklear and a manufacturer's representative. JCPenney investigated a second time, referred the case for criminal prosecution, and filed a civil suit against Mr. Locklear.

The investigation conducted by authorities found that Mr. Locklear received payments from vendors through several corporations he had established. During the five-year period from 1987 to 1992, Mr. Locklear had received $1.5 million from vendors, manufacturers' representatives, and others.

Mr. Locklear was charged with commercial bribery and entered into a plea agreement. Mr. Locklear also served as a witness for the prosecution at the trials of those who paid him the bribes. A vendor described his payment of a $25,000 fee to Mr. Locklear as follows: "It was either pay it or go out of business." Mr. Locklear was sentenced to 18 months in federal prison, less than the five-year maximum, due to his cooperation.

Should JCPenney have known of the difficulties earlier? Was Mr. Locklear's personal life responsible for his poor value choices at work? Is anyone really harmed by Mr. Locklear's activity? Wasn't he a good buyer?

RICO provides for both criminal penalties and civil remedies. In a RICO civil suit, injured parties can recover treble damages, the cost of their suit, and reasonable attorney fees. According to the *Journal of Accountancy*, 91 percent of all RICO civil actions have been based on the listed pattern crimes of mail fraud, wire fraud, or fraud in the sale of securities. The statute has been used frequently against corporations. For example, Northwestern Bell Telephone Company lobbyists, who took public utility commissioners to dinner and hired two of them as consultants after they left their commission jobs, were sued under RICO. A lawyer representing phone company customers brought a RICO civil suit based on an alleged pattern of bribing the utility regulators. [*H. J., Inc. v Northwestern Bell Telephone Co.*, 492 U.S. 229 (1989)]

Another portion of the RICO statute permits prosecutors to freeze defendants' assets to prevent further crimes. When RICO charges are brought against corporations, the seizure of corporate assets can mean the termination of the business. The Justice Department has issued guidelines requiring prosecutors to seek a forfeiture of assets in proportion to the crime rather than seize all of the business assets. A growing number of states have enacted their own versions of the RICO statute for application at the state level. Some state RICO laws are specifically directed at narcotics, but more than 20 include securities fraud as one of the covered acts.

RICO violations have become added charges in many criminal cases. For example, if someone is charged with ongoing bribery of a state or local official, RICO charges can be added because of the pattern of corruption. Only one U.S. Supreme Court case has restricted RICO's application. In *Reves v Ernst & Young*, 507 U.S. 170 (1993), the accounting firm of Arthur Young (later merged into Ernst & Young) was hired to conduct audits for the Farmer's Cooperative of Arkansas and Oklahoma. An investment by the co-op in a gasohol plant proved to be a financial disaster, and the farmers who held co-op notes that had served as the organization's means of financing over the years lost their investment when the co-op filed for bankruptcy. The investors filed suit against Arthur Young for violations of federal securities laws (see Chapter 19) and RICO. However, the Supreme Court exempted the accounting firm from RICO charges because it found that the firm did not participate in the management of the co-op. The auditor's participation was not that of directing the co-op's affairs, only that of offering its opinions on the financial statements of the firm. The case represents one of the few restrictions on RICO application.

Over the years, businesses have lobbied heavily for reforms to the broad civil and criminal liabilities created by RICO. It seems unlikely that Congress will change the rights of plaintiffs to bring treble damage suits under the act's protective and deterrent mechanisms.

8-8g BUSINESS CRIME AND THE USA PATRIOT ACT

Prior to September 11, 2001, the federal government had the Money Laundering Control Act (MLCA), 42 U.S.C. § 5301, that prohibited the knowing and willful participation in any type of financial transaction that was set up in order to conceal or disguise the source of funds. However, investigations into the backgrounds of those who had flown the planes that destroyed the World Trade Center and a portion of the Pentagon revealed intricate financial networks in which the sources of their funds were concealed through various business transactions in different types of industries. As a result, provisions of the USA Patriot Act, passed fewer than two months after the September 11 destruction, include substantial expansion of the Money Laundering Control Act as well as the Bank Secrecy Act (BSA).

Regulation of Money Laundering

Under these changes, title and escrow companies; brokerage firms; travel agents; check-cashing firms; auto, plane, and boat dealers; loan and finance companies; casinos; currency exchanges; branches of foreign banks located in the United States; and even small businesses are subject to disclosure and reporting requirements for transactions involving cash or transactions of more than $10,000. In addition, the types of accounts covered under the disclosure requirements include not just savings accounts but also money market savings and brokerage accounts. Few financial institutions are exempt from reporting and disclosure requirements for cash transactions.

Businesses affected by these amendments developed new policies and procedures for preventing and detecting money laundering. Under the Federal Sentencing Guidelines, businesses subject to these anti-money-laundering provisions must have a "Know Thy Customer" program that trains employees in how to spot money laundering and suspicious activities by customers.

Funneling Money to Terrorist Groups

Another portion of the Patriot Act makes it a crime for companies to pay monies to terrorist groups in other countries. For example, a company that pays a mercenary group for protection for its employees or facilities would violate this provision of the act. Under federal law, once an organization is designated by the U.S. government as a terrorist organization, companies cannot continue to do business with them because the purpose of the law is to curb funding to and money laundering by terrorist groups. The list of terrorist groups is available from a website the government provides to businesses via subscription.

Consider...

Between 1997 and 2004, executives in Chiquita operations in Colombia paid $1.7 million to the United Self-Defense Forces of Colombia (known as AUC, its initials in Spanish). The AUC, according to the U.S. Justice Department, "has been responsible for some of the worst massacres in Colombia's civil conflict and for a sizable percentage of the country's cocaine exports. The U.S. government designated the right-wing militia a terrorist organization in September 2001."[4] The payments were made through a Chiquita wholly owned subsidiary known as Banadex, the company's most profitable unit by 2003.

The payments began in 1997 following a meeting between the then-leader of the AUC, Carlos Castaño, and a senior executive of Banadex. No one disputes that during that meeting, Castaño implied that Chiquita's failure to make the payments could result in physical harm to Banadex employees and property. No one disputes either that the AUC was known for such violence and had been successful in obtaining payments from other companies, either following Castaño's meetings with company officials or, when the companies declined, by carrying out the threat of harm as a form of warning. By September 2000, Chiquita's senior executives were aware that the payments were being made and were also aware that the AUC was a violent paramilitary organization. Chiquita officers, directors, and employees were aware of the Banadex payments to the AUC. Chiquita recorded these payments in its financial reports and other records as "security payments" or payments for "security" or "security services."

Beginning in June 2002, Chiquita began paying the AUC in cash according to new procedures established by senior executives of Chiquita. These new procedures concealed direct cash payments to the AUC. From September 10, 2001, through February 4, 2004, Chiquita made 50 payments to the AUC totaling over $825,000, part of the $1.7 million paid from 1997 through 2004.

On February 20, 2003, a Chiquita employee, aware of the payments to the AUC, told a senior Chiquita officer that he had discovered that the AUC had been designated by the U.S. government as a foreign terrorist organization (FTO). The Justice Department discovered the following sequence of events in response to the employee having raised the issue:

> *Shortly thereafter, these Chiquita officials spoke with attorneys in the District of Columbia office of a national law firm ("outside counsel") about Chiquita's ongoing payments to the AUC. Beginning on Feb. 21, 2003, outside counsel emphatically advised Chiquita that the payments were illegal under United States law and that Chiquita should immediately stop paying the AUC directly or indirectly. Outside counsel advised Chiquita:*
> *"Must stop payments."*
> *"Bottom Line: CANNOT MAKE THE PAYMENT [.]"*
> *"Advised NOT TO MAKE ALTERNATIVE PAYMENT through CONVIVIR [.]"*
> *"General Rule: Cannot do indirectly what you cannot do directly [.]"*
> *Concluded with: "CANNOT MAKE THE PAYMENT [.]"*
> *"You voluntarily put yourself in this position. Duress defense can wear out through repetition. Buz [business] decision to stay in harm's way. Chiquita should leave Colombia."*

> *"[T]he company should not continue to make the Santa Marta payments, given the AUC's designation as a foreign terrorist organization[.]"*
>
> *"[T]he company should not make the payment."*
>
> *On April 3, 2003, a senior Chiquita officer and a member of Chiquita's Board of Directors first reported to the full Board that Chiquita was making payments to a designated FTO. A Board member objected to the payments and recommended that Chiquita consider taking immediate corrective action, including withdrawing from Colombia. The Board did not follow that recommendation, but instead agreed to disclose promptly to the Department of Justice the fact that Chiquita had been making payments to the AUC. Meanwhile, Banadex personnel were instructed to continue making the payments.[5]*

On April 24, 2003, Roderick M. Hills, a member of Chiquita's board and head of its audit committee, Chiquita general counsel Robert Olson, and, some reports indicate, the company's outside counsel met with members of the Justice Department to disclose the payments and explain that they had been made under duress. Mr. Hills, a former chairman of the Securities Exchange Commission, and the Chiquita officer were told that the payments were illegal and had to stop. The payments did not stop, and the company's outside counsel wrote to the board on September 8, 2003, advising that "[Department of Justice] officials have been unwilling to give assurances or guarantees of non-prosecution; in fact, officials have repeatedly stated that they view the circumstances presented as a technical violation and cannot endorse current or future payments."[6]

Nonetheless, the payments continued. From April 24, 2003, through February 4, 2004, Chiquita made 20 payments to the AUC totaling $300,000. On February 4, 2004, Chiquita sold the Banadex operations to a Colombian-owned company.

Chiquita then cooperated with the government by making its records available. In March 2007, Chiquita entered a guilty plea and agreed to pay a $25 million fine. Chiquita was on probation for five years and agreed to create and maintain an effective ethics program. Mr. Hills and four former Chiquita officers, including Mr. Olson, were given a no-prosecution agreement under the terms of the company's guilty plea. A Justice Department official said of the investigation, "If the only way that a company can conduct business in a particular location is to do so illegally, then the company shouldn't be doing business there."[7]

Is there an *actus reus* for violation of the Patriot Act? A *mens rea*? What lessons on ethics in international business should companies take from the Chiquita experience?

8-8h ADDITIONAL FEDERAL CRIMES

Many of the statutes on business crimes are found at the federal level. Violations of the Securities Exchange Acts (Chapter 19), the Sherman Act (Chapter 16), the Internal Revenue Act, the Pure Food and Drug Act, the environmental statutes (Chapter 11), the Occupational Safety and Health Act (Chapter 20), and Consumer Product Safety statutes (Chapter 14) carry criminal penalties.

8-8i STATE CRIMES

Similar criminal statutes at the state level cover such areas as criminal fraud and securities. In addition, states have particular regulations and laws for certain industries. The sale of liquor in most states is strictly regulated. The result is an increase in bribes and kickbacks in these highly regulated industries as businesses try to work around the regulatory restrictions. Since 2002, the state attorneys general have been especially active in white-collar financial crimes. State attorneys general have taken the lead on prosecutions related to the financial market collapses in 2007–2008.

8-9 Procedural Rights for Business Criminals

Business criminals are treated procedurally in the same manner as other criminals. They have the same rights under the criminal justice system. The U.S. Constitution guarantees protection of certain rights. The **Fourth Amendment** protects the individual's privacy and is the basis for requiring warrants for searches of private property. The **Fifth Amendment** provides the protection against self-incrimination and is also the "due process" amendment, which guarantees that an accused individual has the right to be heard. The **Sixth Amendment** is meant to ensure a speedy trial; it is the basis for the requirement that criminal proceedings and trials proceed in a timely fashion. These constitutional rights are discussed in the following sections.

8-9a FOURTH AMENDMENT RIGHTS FOR BUSINESSES

The Fourth Amendment to the U.S. Constitution provides that "the right of the people to be secure in their persons, houses, papers, and effects, against unreasonable searches and seizures, shall not be violated." This amendment protects individual privacy by preventing unreasonable searches and seizures. Before a government agency can seize the property of individuals or businesses, it must obtain a valid **search warrant**—or have an applicable exception to the warrant requirement—which must be issued by a judge or magistrate and be based on probable cause. In other words, authorities must have good reason to believe that instruments or evidence of a crime are present at the business location to be searched.

There must also be an expectation of privacy in the area being searched. In *Kyllo v United States*, 533 U.S. 27 (2001), the court dealt with a Fourth Amendment issue of agents using an Agema Thermovision 210 to scan for heat on Danny Kyllo's triplex at 3:20 A.M. to determine whether the heat emissions were unusual and therefore consistent with using heat lamps for growing marijuana. In other words, was Mr. Kyllo entitled to privacy from street scanners used on his home?

The scan showed that the roof over the garage and a side wall of Mr. Kyllo's home were relatively hot compared to the rest of the home and substantially warmer than neighboring homes in the triplex. Based on tips from informants, utility bills, and the thermal imaging, a federal magistrate judge issued a warrant authorizing a search of Mr. Kyllo's home, and the agents found an indoor growing operation involving more than 100 plants. Mr. Kyllo was indicted on one count of manufacturing marijuana.

The court held that there was a physical intrusion by the agents because they used sense-enhancing technology to obtain evidence that could not otherwise have been obtained without physical "intrusion into a constitutionally protected area"—Mr. Kyllo's home.

The Fourth Amendment applies equally to individuals and corporations. In an unauthorized search, a corporation's property is given the same protection. If an improper search is conducted (without a warrant and without meeting an exception, see p. 266), any evidence recovered is inadmissible at trial for the purposes of proving the crime. The *Dow Chemical Co. v U.S.* case (Case 8.4) deals with a Fourth Amendment issue as to whether a warrant is necessary for aerial surveillance of a company's operations. Drone activity in the United States has brought this case to the forefront once again.

CASE 8.4

Dow Chemical Co. v United States
476 U.S. 227 (1986)

Low-Flying Federal Agents: Photographic Searches

FACTS

Dow Chemical (petitioner) operates a two-thousand-acre chemical plant at Midland, Michigan. The facility, with numerous buildings, conduits, and pipes, is visible from the air. Dow has maintained ground security at the facility and has investigated flyovers by other, unauthorized aircraft. However, none of the buildings or manufacturing equipment is concealed.

In 1978, the Environmental Protection Agency (EPA) conducted an inspection of Dow. EPA requested a second inspection, but Dow denied the request. The EPA then employed a commercial aerial photographer to take photos of the plant from 12,000, 3,000, and 1,200 feet. The EPA had no warrant, but the plane was always within navigable air space when the photos were taken.

When Dow became aware of the EPA photographer, it brought suit in federal district court and challenged the action as a violation of its Fourth Amendment rights. The district court found that the EPA had violated Dow's rights and issued an injunction prohibiting the further use of the aircraft. The court of appeals reversed, and Dow appealed.

JUDICIAL OPINION

BURGER, Chief Justice

The photographs at issue in this case are essentially like those used in map-making. Any person with an airplane and an aerial camera could readily duplicate them. In common with much else, the technology of photography has changed in this century. These developments have enhanced industrial processes, and indeed all areas of life; they have also enhanced enforcement techniques. Whether they may be employed by competitors to penetrate trade secrets is not a question presented in this case. Governments do not generally seek to appropriate trade secrets of the private sector, and the right to be free of appropriation of trade secrets is protected by law.

That such photography might be barred by state law with regard to competitors, however, is irrelevant to the questions presented here. State tort law governing unfair competition does not define the limits of the Fourth Amendment. The Government is seeking these photographs in order to regulate, not compete with, Dow.

Dow claims first that the EPA has no authority to use aerial photography to implement its statutory authority of "site inspection" under the Clean Air Act.

Congress has vested in EPA certain investigatory and enforcement authority, without spelling out precisely how this authority was to be exercised in all the myriad circumstances that might arise in monitoring matters relating to clean air and water standards.

Regulatory or enforcement authority generally carries with it all the modes of inquiry and investigation traditionally employed or useful to execute the authority granted. Environmental standards cannot be enforced only in libraries and laboratories, helpful as those institutions may be.

The EPA, as a regulatory and enforcement agency, needs no explicit statutory provisions to employ methods of observation commonly available to the public at large; we hold that the use of aerial photography is within the EPA's statutory authority.

DISSENTING OPINION

Powell, Marshall, Brennan, and Blackmun, Justices

The Fourth Amendment protects private citizens from arbitrary surveillance by their Government. Today, in the context of administrative aerial photography of commercial premises, the Court retreats from that standard. It holds that the photography was not a Fourth Amendment "search" because it was not accompanied by a physical trespass and because the equipment used was not the most highly sophisticated form of technology available to the Government. Under this holding the existence of an asserted privacy interest apparently will be decided solely by reference to the manner of surveillance used to intrude on that interest. Such an inquiry will not protect Fourth Amendment rights, but rather will permit their gradual decay as technology advances.

EPA's aerial photography penetrated into a private commercial enclave, an area in which society has recognized that privacy interests may legitimately be claimed. The photographs captured highly confidential information that Dow had taken reasonable and objective steps to preserve as private.

CONTINUED

CASE QUESTIONS

1. Of what significance is the fact that Dow's plant could be seen from the air? Did Dow take any steps to protect its privacy?

2. Is the EPA specifically given aerial surveillance authority?

3. What objections do the dissenting judges raise to the decision?

Consider...

The IRS attached levies to the property and other assets of G.M. Leasing Corp. for nonpayment of taxes. To satisfy the levy, the IRS seized several automobiles from the street in front of G.M.'s offices. Also, without a warrant, the IRS entered G.M.'s offices and seized business books and records. Has the Fourth Amendment been violated with the seizure of the cars? Of the books and records?

[*G.M. Leasing Corp. v United States*, 429 U.S. 338 (1977)]

8-9b EXCEPTIONS TO THE WARRANT REQUIREMENT

Emergencies and Risk of Loss of Evidence

There are exceptions to the warrant requirements, such as when there is evidence in a burning building and evidence within the building is being destroyed. The emergency exception requires proof of risk of loss of fruits or evidence of the crime. In *Arizona v Gant*, 556 U.S. 332 (2009), the U.S. Supreme Court limited the use of evidence that is obtained from a driver's vehicle when that driver has been hand-cuffed and locked in the rear of a squad car. Most officers were in the habit of routinely searching the driver's vehicle on-site at the time of the detention/arrest. In the case of Rodney Gant, who was arrested for driving with a suspended license, the officers searched Mr. Gant's car while he was handcuffed in the backseat of the squad car and found cocaine in the pocket of a jacket lying on the backseat of Gant's vehicle. Mr. Gant was charged with possession (as well as with driving with a suspended license).

Mr. Gant's lawyer challenged the search of his client's vehicle on the grounds that there were no exigent circumstances—that is, locked in and handcuffed as he was, there was no emergency or reason to believe that Mr. Gant would spring into action and hide, destroy, or swallow the cocaine. The court held that the officers needed to impound the vehicle and obtain a warrant to search it. Without a warrant, the cocaine was not admissible for purposes of prosecuting Mr. Gant on the cocaine charges. Without the cocaine evidence, unless Mr. Gant confesses, that charge had to be dropped. Searches require warrants or a valid exception.

The Plain View Exception

Another exception to the warrant requirement is the "plain view" exception. This exception allows police officers to seize evidence that is within their view.

CYBERLAW

© iStockPhoto.com /dra_schwartz

Warrants and Technology: Texts, E-Mails, and ISPs

One of the technological areas that is still evolving deals with the rights of anonymous posters in chat rooms and the identity of those sending e-mails to others. Must the ISP turn over to law enforcement officials the identity of those who are behind their Internet activities? With a warrant, the answer is clearly yes. And warrants are relatively easy to obtain because law enforcement agencies simply need to furnish the magistrate or judge with the content the poster or e-mailer posted on the Internet. If those postings involve criminal activities or conspiracies, the court can find probable cause. Without a warrant, law enforcement officials' behavior needs to fit into an applicable exception. The details on warrants and exceptions in cyberactivities are covered in Chapter 10.

Privileged Documents and the Fourth Amendment

In many business crimes, the records used to prosecute the defendant are not in the possession of the defendant. The records are, instead, in the hands of a third party, such as an accountant or a bank. Does the Fourth Amendment afford the defendant protection in documents that discuss the defendant or reflect the defendant's finances and transactions when those documents are in the hands of another? In some cases, a privilege exists between the third party and the defendants, and certain documents are protected and need not be turned over. Notes on trial strategy, audit procedures, and other plans and thoughts are not discoverable because such communications are privileged between lawyers and clients. Some states recognize an accountant–client privilege. The priest–parishioner privilege generally exists; however, under certain exceptions, such as in cases of abuse, reporting is required.

8-9c FIFTH AMENDMENT RIGHTS FOR BUSINESSES

The Fifth Amendment provides several protections for those facing criminal charges.

Self-Incrimination

The statement "I take the Fifth" is used so often that it has made the Fifth Amendment well known for its protection against self-incrimination. For example, former MLB player Mark McGwire took the Fifth Amendment before a congressional committee investigating MLB's policies on testing players for steroids and suspensions for their use. Retired IRS administrator Lois Lerner took the Fifth Amendment

FOR THE MANAGER'S DESK

Re: Knowing When to Hold and When to Fold: What to Do When Your Company Is in Big Trouble

The *Wall Street Journal* grappled with a question that affects many business professionals in today's economy: What do you do when a scandal at your former employer has caused you to lose your job? How do you handle such a situation on your résumé?

Investment advisers from Stanford Financial Group, Madoff Securities, and a host of Wall Street firms such as Lehman Brothers and Bear Stearns find themselves looking for employment because of their defunct employers. Some executive search firms will not consider former employees from scandal-rocked companies, even if the executives worked at subsidiaries or were not involved in the fraud, even remotely. Most agree there is a long path back from such an employment history, but the following tips might help:

- Leave when the indictments and/or arrests occur—don't hang on.

- Don't lie on your résumé.

- Describe your work at the company and others without naming names and wait until the interview to disclose for whom you worked.

- Don't badmouth your former employer in your interview—this is often taken as a sign of guilt; rather, explain how difficult it is to be blindsided, something that most managers can identify with because it happens to the best.

Source: JoAnn S. Lublin, "When Scandal Rocks a Résumé," *Wall Street Journal*, August 4, 2009, p. D1.

when testifying before Congress about politically targeted activities by her agency. We cannot be compelled to be witnesses against ourselves. However, this protection applies only to natural persons; corporations are not given this privilege. A corporation cannot prevent the required disclosure of corporate books and records on grounds that they are incriminating.

Corporate officers cannot assert Fifth Amendment protection to prevent compulsory production of corporate records. Nor can corporate officers use the Fifth Amendment to prevent the production of corporate records on grounds that those records incriminate them personally. The rules applicable to corporate officers have been extended to apply to those involved in labor unions, close corporations, and even unincorporated associations. The same rule is applicable to sole shareholders of small corporations as well.

Miranda *Rights*

The famous *Miranda* doctrine resulted from an interpretation of the Fifth Amendment by the U.S. Supreme Court in *Miranda v Arizona*, 384 U.S. 436 (1966). **Miranda warnings** must be given to all people who are subjected to custodial interrogation. Custody does not necessarily mean "locked in jail," but it is generally based on an individual's perceptions of a situation. If a person feels he is without freedom to leave a place by choice, the level of custody at which *Miranda* rights must be issued has been reached. However, in *Missouri v Seibert*, 542 U.S. 600 (2004), the U.S. Supreme Court provided further clarification on when *Miranda* warnings must be given. A law enforcement official cannot coax a confession from an individual and then provide the warnings. If the individual then refuses to answer questions or offer the same information after the warnings are given, the law enforcement officials cannot use the prior confession, given before the warnings, as evidence in court. The warnings tell those in custody of their Fifth Amendment right to say nothing, as well as their right to an attorney. The failure to give *Miranda* warnings is not fatal to a case as long as the crime can be proved through evidence other than the statement of the defendant; the prosecution can still proceed based on other evidence.

Due Process Rights

The Fifth Amendment also contains due process language. The same language is found in the Fourteenth Amendment and made applicable to the states. **Due process**, as Chapters 5 and 6 discuss, means that no one can be convicted of a crime without the opportunity to be heard, to question witnesses, and to present evidence.

Due process in criminal proceedings guarantees certain procedural protections as a case is investigated, charged, and taken to trial. The Sixth Amendment complements due process rights by requiring that all these procedures be completed in a timely fashion. The following subsections discuss the basic steps in a criminal proceeding, as diagrammed in Exhibit 8.3.

Warrant and/or Arrest. A criminal proceeding can begin when a crime is witnessed, as when a police officer attempts to apprehend a person who has just robbed a convenience store. When the convenience store is robbed but the robber escapes, and if the police can establish that a certain individual was probably responsible for the robbery, a **warrant** can be issued and the individual then arrested. Whether with or without a warrant, the due process steps begin with the arrest.

Initial Appearance. Once an arrest has been made, the defendant must have an opportunity to appear before a judicial figure within a short time period (usually 24 hours) to be informed of his charges, rights, and so on. This proceeding is generally referred to as an **initial appearance**. Dates for other proceedings are

---

Exhibit 8.3 Steps in Criminal Proceedings

```
                    Warrant  ───────────  Arrest
                                 │
                             Initial
                            Appearance
                                 │
            ┌────────────────────┴────────────────────┐
      Preliminary                                   Grand
        Hearing                                      Jury
            │                                          │
       Information                                 Indictment
            └────────────────────┬────────────────────┘
                            Arraignment
                                 │
                             Discovery
                                 │
                             Pretrial
                            Conference
                                 │
                             Omnibus
                             Hearing
                                 │
                               Trial
                                 │
                              Appeal
```

© Cengage Learning

set at this time and, if the individual can be released, the terms of the release are also established. The individual may be required to post a bond to be released; others are held without release terms (release terms generally depend on the nature of the crime and the defendant). The terms *released on his own recognizance* and *released OR* mean the defendant is released without having to post a bond.

Preliminary Hearing or Grand Jury. Up to this step in the criminal proceedings, the defendant's charges are based on the word of a police officer; no proof has yet been brought forth linking the crime and the defendant. The purpose of a preliminary hearing or grand jury proceeding is to require the prosecution to establish that there is some evidence that the defendant committed the crime.

In a **preliminary hearing**, the prosecution presents evidence to a judge to indicate that the accused committed the crime. The prosecution presents witnesses, and the defendant and the defendant's attorney are present for cross-examination of those witnesses. The defense does not present its case at this time but might make an offer of proof to show that the defendant could not have committed the crime. If the judge finds sufficient proof, an **information** is issued. The information is to a criminal proceeding what a complaint is to a civil proceeding: It establishes what the defendant did and when and what crimes were committed.

In some crimes, the evidence of the crime is presented to a **grand jury**, which is a panel of citizens who serve for a designated period of time (usually six months) and act as the body responsible for the review of evidence of crimes. If the grand jury finds sufficient evidence that a crime was committed, it issues an **indictment**, which is similar to an information and serves the same function.

Grand jury proceedings are conducted secretly, whereas preliminary hearings are public. Grand juries also have the authority to conduct investigations to determine whether crimes were committed and who did so. Perhaps one of the most famous grand juries was the San Francisco grand jury investigating steroid use in baseball. The grand jury heard testimony from some of baseball's biggest stars. However, the content of their testimony remains sealed and secret unless and until it is used at a trial.

Arraignment. An **arraignment** is the proceeding at which the defendant enters a plea of guilty, not guilty, or no contest (*nolo contendere*). If a not guilty plea is entered, a date for trial is set. If the defendant enters a guilty or no contest plea, chances are the plea is the result of a **plea bargain**, which is the term used in criminal proceedings for a settlement. The defendant may plead guilty to a lesser offense in exchange for the prosecution's promise to support a lesser sentence, such as probation or minimum jail time.

Discovery. If the case is going to trial, the parties then enter a **discovery** period. Many states have mandatory criminal discovery laws that require each side to turn over certain types of information to the other side, including lists of witnesses they will call and lists of exhibits that will be used at trial. Exhibits include documents, murder weapons, and pictures.

Omnibus Hearing. In some cases, the defense attorney wishes to challenge the prosecution evidence on grounds that it was obtained in violation of any of the constitutional protections discussed earlier. Some documents, for example, may have been seized without a warrant. The **omnibus hearing** is the forum wherein all of these challenges can be presented for the judge's ruling as to the admissibility of evidence. This hearing is held before the trial so the jury is not exposed to evidence that should not have been admitted. In the O. J. Simpson double-homicide trial, an omnibus hearing was held on the admissibility of evidence gathered at Mr. Simpson's estate without a warrant.

Trial. If no plea agreement is reached before trial, the case then proceeds to **trial**.

8-10 Business Crime and International Business

As noted in Chapter 7, businesses are subject to the laws of all countries in which they do business. In many situations, authorities from several countries are working together to bring criminal charges against businesses located in different countries. There is now a cross-border system for criminal prosecutions of businesses. For example, during 2012, British and U.S. authorities uncovered a longstanding scheme at banks in the United Kingdom to fix the London Interbank Offer Rate (LIBOR). The rates were fixed so that the banks could profit from their positions in derivatives tied to that rate. Cooperation among authorities in countries around the world led to the discovery of substantial evidence as well as criminal cases around the world. The banks in Britain faced charges, but so also were the traders in Scotland, Japan, Britain, Canada, and the United States charged with conspiracy and fraud for their participation in the rate-fixing scam, which was reflected in their e-mails that authorities in their own countries discovered and then tied to the British banks.

BIOGRAPHY

Peanut Corporation of America: Knowledge Shows Intent

The Peanut Corporation of America was a supplier of processed peanuts to some of the largest food production companies in the United States. The company was founded by Hugh Parnell, Sr. when he was selling ice cream vending machines in the 1960s. When he was restocking a machine, he noticed that the peanuts on the Nutty Buddy ice cream cones came from a plant in the North. He decided to begin a company that processed peanuts in the South, where they were grown. The company grew and had plants in Virginia, Georgia, and Texas. Hugh's son Stewart Parnell entered the business in the 1970s after complaining to his father that graduates in his major, oceanography, often ended up working on oil rigs. His father offered him a job, and Stewart left college to begin work in the Virginia facilities.

Major food producers were customers of Peanut Corp. ConAgra, a major peanut butter producer, was a large customer of Peanut Corp. Peanut Corp.'s peanut product base was used in peanut butter, ice cream, cookies, and crackers. Peanut Corporation was known for its cost cutting. When a customer came back with a bid from another peanut product base supplier that was lower, Stewart Parnell, who became the CEO of Peanut Corp., would always cut the price by a few cents in order to win over the potential customer.

E-mails reflect Parnell's concerns about costs. When a salmonella test at the factory was positive, Peanut Corp. was required to hold off shipment for a retest. Parnell wrote in an e-mail, "We need to discuss this. Beside the cost, this time lapse is costing us $$$$ and causing us obviously a huge lapse from the time when we pick up the peanuts until the time we can invoice." He also wrote, about products he was informed had tested positive for salmonella, "Turn them loose." When the FDA made the connection between Peanut Corp. and salmonella poisonings that sickened 700 people in 44 states, which resulted in nine deaths, Mr. Parnell wrote to his managers, "Obviously we are not shipping any peanut butter products affected by the recall but desperately at least need to turn the raw peanuts on the floor into money."

Congress held hearings into Peanut Corp.'s operations. Stewart Parnell took the Fifth Amendment when members of the Commerce Committee in the House of Representatives asked him questions about his company.

The company declared Chapter 7 bankruptcy on February 13, 2009. However, the end of the company was not the end of the liability, civil and criminal. In early 2013, Mr. Parnell and four others were indicted: Michael Parnell, Stewart's brother who served as a food broker for the company; along with Samuel Lightsey, Mary Wilkerson, and Daniel Kilgore, all managers and supervisors at Peanut Corporation. They were charged with conspiracy, fraud, and falsification of reports. The information on Mr. Kilgore and the indictments of Mr. Parnell and the others charged the group with falsifying salmonella reports to indicate that the company's products were salmonella free when, in fact, the products contained salmonella.

Experts note that criminal charges in food-poisoning cases are rare because the proof of intent or *mens rea* is difficult or impossible when there is a one-time problem. However, as the indictment notes, Mr. Parnell was being notified by customers that his company's product was testing positive, yet he still continued production without cleaning up the plant. The indictment also alleges that the four who are charged misled FDA inspectors in January 2009, conduct that added obstruction of justice to the charges in the indictment.

Mr. Parnell's lawyer vows to fight the charges and to demonstrate that Mr. Parnell and the others never intentionally shipped tainted product. However, one portion of the indictment includes an e-mail from an employee that indicated the peanut meal containers at the plant (in 2007) were covered with dust and rat feces. Mr. Parnell responded to the employee, "Clean 'em all up and ship them." 'Tis a tall order for his lawyer to explain that one and stick with his story on lack of intent.

Sources: Adapted from "The Ethical Barometer," mariannejennings.com; Jane Zhang and Julie Jargon, "Peanut Corp. Emails Cast Harsh Light on Executive," *Wall Street Journal*, February 12, 2009, p. A3.

Summary

Who is liable for business crimes?

- Vicarious liability—holding companies accountable for criminal conduct of their officers
- Elements—requirements of proof for crimes
- *Mens rea*—requisite mental state for committing a crime
- *Actus reus*—physical act of committing a crime

What penalties exist for business crimes?

- Penalties—punishments for commission of crimes; include fines and imprisonment
- Corporate sentencing guidelines—federal rules used to determine level of penalties for companies and officers; a system that decreases penalties for effort toward prevention of wrongdoing and cooperation with investigations and increases penalties for lack of effort and other problems in company operations

What is the nature of business crime?

- Obstruction—under Sarbanes-Oxley, prohibits destruction of documents when civil or criminal investigations are pending
- Computer crime—crimes committed while using computer technology
- Criminal fraud—misrepresentation with the intent to take something from another without that person's knowledge; to mislead to obtain funds or property
- Racketeer Influenced and Corrupt Organizations (RICO) Act—federal law designed to prevent racketeering by intensifying the punishments for engaging in certain criminal activities more than once
- USA Patriot Act—federal law that deals with due process rights as well as substantive issues such as money laundering prohibitions and mandatory disclosures by those involved in financial transactions, including banks, escrow and title companies, and other financial institutions

What are the rights of corporate and individual defendants in the criminal justice system?

- Fourth Amendment—provision in U.S. Constitution that protects against invasions of privacy; the search warrant amendment
- Fifth Amendment—the self-incrimination protection of the U.S. Constitution
- Sixth Amendment—the right-to-trial protection of the U.S. Constitution
- Search warrant—judicially issued right to examine home, business, and papers in any area in which there is an expectation of privacy
- *Miranda* warnings—advice required to be given to those taken into custody; details the right to remain silent and the right to have counsel
- Due process—right to trial before conviction
- Warrant—public document authorizing detention of an individual for criminal charges; for searches, a judicial authorization
- Initial appearance—defendant's first appearance in court to have charges explained, bail set, lawyer appointed, and future dates set
- Preliminary hearing—presentation of abbreviated case by prosecution to establish sufficient basis to bind defendant over for trial
- Information—document issued after preliminary hearing requiring defendant to stand trial
- Grand jury—secret body that hears evidence to determine whether charges should be brought and whether defendant should be held for trial
- Indictment—document issued by grand jury requiring defendant to stand trial
- Arraignment—hearing at which trial date is set and plea is entered
- Plea bargain—settlement of criminal charges
- Omnibus hearing—evidentiary hearing outside the presence of the jury
- Trial—presentation of case by each side

Questions and Problems

1. Timothy Moher owns 440 acres of land on Sugar Island, Michigan. Sugar Island is located on the St. Mary's River, which marks the international border between Canada and the United States. Mohr's land is two miles from Canada. Two United States Customs and Border Protection (CBP) patrol officers entered Mr. Moher's land in order to patrol for illegal immigration activity. Mr. Moher filed suit for invasion of privacy on the grounds that the officers needed a warrant to enter his land and did not have one nor had they obtained Mr. Mohr's consent. Can you explain Mr. Mohr's rights in this situation? [*Moher v U.S.*, 875 F. Supp. 2d 739 (W.D. Mich. 2012)]

2. Rooney Enterprises, Inc., operated a cemetery in Franklin County, Virginia. A state law requires companies that receive advance payments for funeral expenses and burial plots to put those funds into a special trust account. Instead of doing so, Rooney used such funds for operating expenses. It later became insolvent, so all those customers who had prepaid their burial plots and expenses lost both their money and their plots. The Virginia Attorney General brought criminal charges against Patrick Rooney, as president, for his failure to follow the requirements for trust fund deposits. Mr. Rooney said he was unaware of the requirement, that the requirement was not in effect when his company purchased the cemetery, and that only the company could be prosecuted for the failure to follow trust-fund requirements. Decide whether Mr. Rooney should be convicted. [*Rooney v Com.*, 500 S.E.2d 830 (Va. App. 1998)]

3. Michael Friedman, Paul Goldenheim, and Howard Udell were executives at Purdue Frederick Company when it misbranded the drug OxyContin. The misbranding dealt with their company's marketing and promotion of OxyContin as "less addictive, less subject to abuse and diversion, and less likely to cause tolerance and withdrawal than other pain medications"—representations that are false.

The three were convicted of felony charges of misbranding the drug as responsible corporate officers at a company at the time the misbranding occurred. The three appealed both their convictions as responsible corporate officers as well as their 12-year suspension from participation as an executive in a health care company. Can the three be held criminally responsible for the problems with the drug labels? Explain. Also, discuss the sanction of their banishment from the health care field. [*Friedman v Sebelius*, 686 F.2d 813 (C.A.D.C. 2012)]

4. Emma Mary Ellen Holley and David Holley, an interracial couple, tried to buy a house in Twenty-Nine Palms, California. A real estate corporation, Triad, Inc., had listed the house for sale. Grove Crank, a Triad salesman, prevented the Holleys from obtaining the house for racially discriminatory reasons.

The Holleys brought a lawsuit in federal court against Mr. Crank and Triad. They claimed, among other things, that both were responsible for a fair housing law violation. The Holleys later filed a separate suit against David Meyer, the sole shareholder of Triad and its president and CEO. They claimed that Mr. Meyer was vicariously liable in one or more of these capacities for Mr. Crank's unlawful actions, which were a violation of the Fair Housing Act. Are the Holleys correct? [*Meyer v Holley*, 537 U.S. 280 (2003)]

5. The owner of a construction firm in New York City, William Lattarulo, has been charged with manslaughter in the death of one of his workers. Lauro Ortega suffocated when the foundation of a building next to where he was digging at a Lattarulo site collapsed on him. Mr. Ortega's head was all that was uncovered when the foundation collapsed, but the pressure of the dirt and debris that rendered him immobile constricted his chest and made him unable to breathe. He suffocated as his coworkers tried to dig him out from the debris.

Mr. Ortega's coworkers as well as a safety consultant had warned Mr. Lattarulo that the trench was unsafe and needed to have some supports placed in it to prevent a collapse. When he was warned a second time by his workers, Mr. Lattarulo said, "Don't worry about it."

In addition, digging operations require that a contractor hire a consultant to oversee site safety. While Mr. Lattarulo listed a company as a consultant for the site safety, he did not actually have or pay a consultant, something that saved him $90,000 on the job. On the day of the collapse, a building inspector for the city visited the site following the fatality and said there were "shoddy work conditions." She also found eight violations of city construction codes at the site.

The Lattarulo site involved digging a foundation next to another building, but the Lattarulo building required a deeper dig. The result was that the foundation of the building next to the site was weakened and required support until the Lattarulo concrete was poured to provide a substitute for the former ground support. A consultant working nearby did warn Mr. Lattarulo about the foundation's risk of collapse if the digging went deeper.

When the criminal manslaughter charges were brought, contractors had questions about their criminal liability when there are accidents on job sites. How would you advise these contractors? When is an owner criminally liable for actions and work conducted by employees? (Michael Wilson, "Manslaughter Charge for Builder in Brooklyn Collapse," *New York Times*, October 12, 2008, p. A24.)

6. Bernard Saul was a salesperson for A. P. Walter Company, a wholesale auto parts business, assigned to the D&S Auto Parts account. Mr. Saul took inventory at D&S each week and phoned in an order to Walter to cover the needed inventory replacements. Between 1976 and 1982, Mr. Saul ordered parts from Walter and invoiced D&S, but he actually kept a portion of the parts for himself, sold them to other dealers, and pocketed the money. Through an audit, D&S discovered that it had paid $155,445.20 for parts that were not received. Can Mr. Saul be charged with any crimes? Can Walter be charged with any crimes? [*D&S Auto Parts, Inc. v Schwartz*, 838 F.2d 965 (7th Cir. 1988)]

7. Odessa Mae French operated the Pines Motel as a house of prostitution for seven years. During that time, Ms. French avoided any local law enforcement action by allowing the sheriff to have free services at the Pines. Eventually, the federal government brought charges against the operation for tax evasion and RICO violations. Would the services to the sheriff constitute a form of bribe that would support a RICO charge? [*United States v Tunnell*, 667 F.2d 1182 (5th Cir. 1982)]

8. The New York City Department of Health is responsible for the inspection of Manhattan restaurants to determine whether they comply with the city's health code. Forty-six of the department's inspectors were inducing restaurateurs to pay money to them for permit approval or for a favorable inspection.

Is this activity a basis for a crime? What crime? What would a prosecutor be required to prove? Are the officers and the restaurateurs equally criminally liable? [*U.S. v Tillem*, 906 F.2d 814 (2nd Cir. 1990)]

9. Jason Jones, a 19-year-old U.S. Naval Academy midshipman, killed John and Carole Hall when he collided with the rear of their car, which was on the shoulder of the road. Mr. Jones was driving 80–105 mph and talking on a cell phone when he struck the Halls' car.

He was prosecuted for manslaughter and negligent driving. Negligent driving is a misdemeanor and carries a $500 fine. Manslaughter requires proof that the defendant knew the conduct was likely to cause death or severe bodily harm.

Testimony by experts for the prosecution indicated that cell phone use while driving is an enormous distraction. The increased accident rate during cell phone use while driving is placed at between 34 and 300 percent by various experts.

It is not illegal in Maryland to use a cell phone while driving. Can someone be convicted for crimes related to conduct that is not illegal? Was the *mens rea* present here?

10. Harlan Nolte and others invested in IFC Leasing Company, a master music recording leasing program. The company was created to acquire and lease master music recordings. Jerry Denby, the executive vice president of IFC, contacted Stephen Weiss, a partner in the law firm of Rosenbaum, Wise, Lerman, Katz & Weiss, to draft the prospectus for investors. Mr. Weiss drafted four documents used in the recruitment of investors for IFC. The complex structure of the investments, according to the documents, would have substantial tax consequences (to their benefit) for the investors.

After Mr. Nolte and others had made their investments, the IRS issued an opinion that the deductions explained in the prospectus and other documents would not be allowed. Criminal fraud actions were brought against IFC and its officers, as well as Mr. Weiss. The Justice Department also indicted both Mr. Weiss's law firm and his partners. Mr. Weiss's partners and the firm, through its management committee, maintain they cannot be held criminally liable for the actions of one partner. The Justice Department maintains that the firm and the partners were negligent in their supervision of Mr. Weiss and should, therefore, be held criminally liable. Do you agree with the Justice Department's position? Why or why not? [*Nolte v Pearson*, 994 F.2d 1311 (8th Cir. 1993)]

ETHICS, STRATEGY, & THE LAW

Particularly When a Company Faces Criminal Charges

In what was called the largest criminal tax fraud case in the history of the United States, 16 former partners and employees of the accounting firm KPMG were charged with criminal tax fraud. The case was so complex that the government alone had produced in discovery, in electronic or paper form, at least five million to six million pages of documents *plus* transcripts of 335 depositions and 195 income tax returns.

KPMG, following a dismal performance by its partners at a congressional hearing, began negotiations with the Justice Department for the settlement of the case against the firm itself. As a result of those negotiations, KPMG agreed to stop paying the legal fees for the 16 former partners and employees, to waive indictment, to be charged in a one-count information, to admit extensive wrongdoing, to pay a $456 million fine, and to accept restrictions on its practice. In turn, the Justice

Department agreed that the information against KPMG would be dismissed if KPMG met all of its obligations under the agreement. Those negotiating on behalf of KPMG had stated to the Justice Department attorneys that their goal was to avoid the fate of Arthur Andersen and save the firm. With KPMG saved, however, the 16 former partners and employees were left without means for paying what had been and would be an expensive defense to the tax shelter fraud accusations.

The 16 argued that the failure of KPMG to pay those fees, as it had done in the past, deprived them of their constitutional rights under the Fifth and Sixth Amendments on self-incrimination as well as the right to a speedy trial. They challenged the agreement in federal court.

The court found that in obtaining the agreement from KPMG, federal prosecutors, acting under Justice

Department policy established in the so-called Thompson memo, indicated to KPMG that the firm's continuing to pay the legal fees of the 16 would be considered evidence of the firm's guilt. Federal District Court Judge Lewis Kaplan found that the prosecutors had acted improperly in pressuring KPMG to throw its employees under the bus in order to preserve the firm. Judge Kaplan wrote:

> An employer often must reimburse an employee for legal expenses when the employee is sued, or even charged with a crime, as a result of doing his or her job. Indeed, the employer often must advance legal expenses to an employee up front, although the employee sometimes must pay the employer back if the employee has been guilty of wrongdoing.
>
> This principle is not the stuff of television and movie drama. It does not remotely approach Miranda warnings in popular culture. But it is very much a part of American life. Persons in jobs big and small, private and public, rely on it every day. Bus drivers sued for accidents, cops sued for allegedly wrongful arrests, nurses named in malpractice cases, news reporters sued in libel cases, and corporate chieftains embroiled in securities litigation generally have similar rights to have their employers pay their legal expenses if they are sued as a result of their doing their jobs. This right is as much a part of the bargain between employer and employee as salary or wages.

The Thompson memo, written by U.S. Deputy Attorney General Larry D. Thompson, was called *Principles of Federal Prosecution of Business Organizations* and was written to give prosecutors guidelines and policies on the decision to prosecute or not to prosecute companies. Two of the principles in the memo provided as follows:

> (1) [I]n gauging the extent of the corporation's cooperation, the prosecutor may consider the corporation's willingness to identify the culprits within the corporation, including senior executives, to make witnesses available, to disclose the complete results of its internal investigation, and to waive attorney-client and work-product

privileges. (2) *Another factor to be weighed by the prosecutor is whether the corporation appears to be protecting its culpable employees and agents. Thus, while cases will differ depending upon the circumstances, a corporation's promise of support to culpable employees and agents, either through the advancing of attorneys fees, through retaining the employees without sanction for their misconduct, or through providing information to the employees about the government's investigation pursuant to a joint defense agreement, may be considered by the prosecutor in weighing the extent and value of a corporation's cooperation.*

Mr. Thompson defended the use of pressure to have companies cut off payment of defense costs for their employees on the ground that "they [the employees] don't need fancy legal representation" if they do not believe that they acted with criminal intent. (The Thompson Memo was later replaced by the McNulty Memo, but its provisions on fee payment remained intact.)

However, Judge Kaplan ruled that the pressure the Justice Department had placed on KPMG was improper, that there were either explicit or implicit agreements to pay the attorneys' fees for the former partners and employees, and that, as a result, they had been deprived of the constitutional rights to which they were entitled in criminal proceedings. Judge Kaplan found that KPMG had a conflict of interest in representing to the government that it did not have an obligation to pay the attorneys' fees and that KPMG was so anxious to "curry favor" with the government that the government should not have relied on KPMG's representations about its obligations.

Once Judge Kaplan made the attorneys' fees ruling, the case developed other issues and problems, and the government dismissed most of the charges against the 16 former partners and employees.

Make a list of the lessons employees and companies can learn from this experience.

Source: Laurie P. Cohen, "In the Crossfire: Prosecutors' Tough New Tactics Turn Firms Against Employees," *Wall Street Journal*, June 4, 2004, p. A1.

Notes

1. Valerie Bauerlin, "Scrushy Denies Role in HealthSouth Fraud," *Wall Street Journal*, May 21, 2009, p. B4.

2. 15 U.S.C. § 1512.

3. Mr. Duncan withdrew his plea when the Andersen case was decided by the U.S. Supreme Court in Andersen's favor. The government has not pursued prosecution against him.

4. U.S. Department of Justice, press release #07-161:03, http://www.doj.gov.

5. U.S. Department of Justice, press release #07-161:03, http://www.doj.gov.

6. U.S. Department of Justice, press release #07-161:03, http://www.doj.gov.

7. Neil A. Lewis, "Inquiry Threatens Ex-Leader of Security Agency," *New York Times*, August 16, 2007, p. A18.

Chapter 9 BUSINESS TORTS

Criminal wrongs require guilty parties to pay a debt to society through a fine, imprisonment, and/or community service. However, criminal wrongs also have victims who have suffered financial losses, injuries, and, sometimes, permanent disabilities. Those who are harmed by the conduct of others are the victims of torts. Torts are civil wrongs that provide remedies. This chapter answers these questions: What are the different types of torts? What must you prove to recover for these torts? What are the business and public policy issues in torts?

Consider...

Gwyneth Williams, then 83, was housesitting for her daughter and son-in-law at The Landings, a planned residential development with a golf course located on Skidaway Island off the Georgia coast. Before The Landings was developed, the land within and surrounding its boundaries was largely marsh, where indigenous alligators lived and thrived. In order to develop the property, The Landings entities installed a lagoon system that allowed enough drainage to create an area suitable for a residential development. After the project was completed in the 1970s, the indigenous alligators began to move in and out of The Landings through its lagoon systems.

Although alligators inhabited the area, no person had ever been attacked until the night of October 5, 2007, when Mrs. Williams went for a walk near one of the lagoons close to her daughter's home some time after 6:00 P.M. The following morning, Mrs. Williams's body was found floating in the lagoon. Williams's right foot and both forearms had been bitten off. Later, an eight-foot alligator was caught in the same lagoon, and, after the alligator was killed, parts of Williams's body were found in its stomach.

Williams's family filed suit against The Landings for negligence in developing and operating the area. The Landings countered with a defense of contributory negligence— that Mrs. Williams assumed the risk of walking alone among the lagoons at night. Can her heirs recover?

9-1 What Is a Tort? Roots of Law and Commerce

Tort comes from the Latin term *tortus*, which means "crooked, dubious, twisted." A **tort** is some type of interference with someone or with someone's property that results in injury to persons or property. For example, using someone else's land without permission is interference with that person's property rights and is the tort of trespass. If you held a concert on someone else's land and the concert crowds destroyed the property's vegetation or left litter that had to be removed, then you committed the tort of trespass. Tort law provides the basis for recovering the costs of restoring the property damaged by the concertgoers.

9-1a TORT VERSUS CRIME

A tort is a private wrong. When a tort is committed, the party who was injured is entitled to collect compensation for damages from the wrongdoer for the private wrong. A crime, on the other hand, is a public wrong and requires the wrongdoer to pay a debt to society through a fine or by going to prison. For example, the crime of assault results in imprisonment, probation, and/or a fine. However, the assault victim could bring suit against the charged assailant to recover damages, such as medical bills, lost wages, and pain and suffering. The suit would be for the tort of assault.

9-1b TYPES OF TORTS

The three types of tort liability include intentional torts, negligence, and strict tort liability. **Intentional torts** are those that involve deliberate actions. For example, a battery, or hitting another person, is an intentional tort. Hitting someone in the nose deliberately is the tort of battery. Suppose that you stretch your arms in a crowd and you hit a man in the nose and hurt him. You have not committed the tort of battery, but you may have committed the tort of **negligence**. You were carelessly swinging your arms in a crowd of people. Such careless conduct, or actions done without thinking through the consequences, is the tort of negligence. You are still responsible for damages to the nose because when you fail to act cautiously and thoughtfully, you are negligent. **Strict tort liability** does not turn on state of mind or knowledge of possible harm. For example, when contractors use dynamite to raze a building, they have strict liability because the incendiary devices are so risky and consequences could be so great that we hold them responsible regardless of the precautions they take. Product liability, discussed in Chapter 14, is a form of strict liability. You will see that a company can be held liable for injuries when a customer has misused its product because even the failure to provide enough warnings results in strict liability.

9-2 The Intentional Torts

9-2a DEFAMATION

Defamation is an untrue statement made by one party to another about a third party. It consists of either slander or libel; **slander** is oral or spoken defamation, and **libel** is written (or, in some cases, broadcast) defamation. The elements of defamation are

1. A statement about a person's reputation, honesty, or integrity that is untrue
2. Publication
3. A statement that is directed at a particular person
4. Damages
5. In some cases, proof of malice

Publication

Defamation requires that whatever is said or written be communicated to a third party. A contractor who untruthfully tells developers that one of his competitors uses workers who are undocumented aliens has met the publication element. So has a supplier who notifies other suppliers that a business is insolvent when it is not. The more folks who hear the statement, the greater will be the defamation damages.

Internet messages and blog postings meet the publication requirement. They provide instantaneous and international communication, so damages can be substantial.

Statement About a Particular Person

To qualify as defamation, the statement made must be about an individual or a small enough group that all in the group are affected. For example, the general statement "All accountants are frauds" is too broad to be defamatory. But the statement "All the Andersen audit partners who worked on the Enron accounts were dishonest" is specific enough to meet this requirement.

CYBERLAW

Consider...

Lavely & Singer has become the law firm that celebrities turn to when they are concerned about a pending story in anything from the *National Enquirer* to the *Wall Street Journal*. Lavely & Singer represented Britney Spears against *US Weekly* in a libel suit for its publication of a story it ran on a sexually explicit home video that she and her ex-husband made. A California court dismissed the suit, explaining, basically, that given Ms. Spears's reputation it was difficult to defame her. The court said that because Ms. Spears has "put her modern sexuality squarely, and profitably, before the public eye," the publication of such information could not be considered harmful to her reputation, thereby meaning that one of the elements of defamation could not be established. Is the court correct on the Britney Spears decision?

Source: Peter Lattman, "When Celebrities Fear Sting of Publicity, Who Do They Call?" *Wall Street Journal,* December 9, 2006, pp. A1, A6.

Product disparagement is defamation of a product. For example, a *Consumer Reports* evaluation of a product that is not truthful about its qualities or abilities would be product disparagement. In *Bose Corporation v Consumers Union of United States, Inc.*, 466 U.S. 485 (1984), the U.S. Supreme Court dealt with whether product disparagement of the Bose speaker system actually occurred when *Consumer Reports* described individual sounds from the speakers, such as those of violins, as growing to gigantic proportions. The court held that even though Consumers Union had not given the Bose speakers a favorable review, it also did not say anything false about them in its negative review. There was, as a result, no disparagement (see Chapter 15).

Damages

The person who is defamed must be able to establish damages, such as lost business, lost profits, lost advertising, lost reputation, or some economic effect that has resulted from the defamatory statements.

Malice

Malice must be proved in defamation cases that involve public figures. Public figures are those voluntarily in the public eye, such as elected officials, recording artists, actors, sports figures, and media magnets (think Lindsay Lohan). However, someone who is injured by Justin Bieber's driving and experiences the resulting extensive media coverage is not a public figure simply because Paris-watchers brought him or her into the limelight. Such individuals would become public figures only if they used their newfound fame to launch their own careers in the spotlight. Kato Kaelin, for example, was a media hot-spot witness in the O. J. Simpson double-murder trial but not a public figure. He became a public figure when he followed up his trial testimony with voluntary and paid appearances and interviews. An example of someone who was not a voluntary public figure is the late Richard Jewell. Several

Consider...

The bases for Richard Jewell's suit against NBC were the following sentences from a broadcast by Tom Brokaw: "Look, they probably got enough to arrest him. They probably have got enough to try him." Mr. Brokaw finished his on-air commentary by adding, "Everyone, please understand absolutely he is only the focus of this investigation—he is not even a suspect yet."

Decide whether Jewell was defamed by the remarks.

Sadly, Mr. Jewell passed away in 2007 at the age of 44 from a heart attack.

news sources labeled Jewell as being a suspect or focus of the investigation into the blast that resulted in two deaths and hundreds of injuries at Olympic Park in Atlanta during the 1996 Summer Olympics. Mr. Jewell settled a defamation case with NBC without having to prove malice on its part because he was not a public figure, only a person with notoriety. As a result of the Jewell case, note that media sources and law enforcement officials no longer refer to individuals as "suspects." The term that allows them to escape defamation liability is *person of interest*. That label is used until the individual is charged or law enforcement agents clear the individual. In addition, even after charges are brought, media sources phrase their descriptions carefully by stating, for example, "He is alleged to have embezzled $5 million from his employer over three years," or "He is charged with the crime of embezzlement."

Malice provides the balance between personal rights and the protections the First Amendment provides for the media. **Malice** requires proof that the information was published or broadcast knowing that it was false or with reckless disregard for whether it was true or false.

The Defenses to Defamation

Truth.   A statement may be damaging, but, if it is the truth, it is not defamation. For example, you could publicly disclose that your boss took LSD during the late 1960s when he was in college. The remark might hurt your employer's reputation, but if it is the truth, it is not the tort of defamation despite the harm it may do to him.

Opinion and Analysis.   One of the current issues in defamation cases is whether the statements made are protected when they are a columnist's analysis of a situation. Courts are trying to determine what level of protection is given for viewpoints when someone objects to the conclusions drawn rather than the statements of fact. A fine line is often all that separates statements of fact from expressions of opinion. In business publications, those opinions can be devastating to companies and their stock performance. In *Wilkow v Forbes, Inc.*, 241 F.3d 552 (7th Cir. 2001), the court dealt with an opinion column in *Forbes* magazine. According to the article, a partnership led by Marc Wilkow "stiffed" the bank, paying only $55 million on a $93 million loan while retaining ownership of the building.

FOR THE MANAGER'S DESK

Re: Dirty Hotels and Defamation

In *Grand Resort Hotel v TripAdvisor*, 2012 WL 3637394 (E.D. Tenn. 2012), the Grand Resort filed suit against TripAdvisor for defamation. TripAdvisor is a website that provides customer feedback on hotels so that those considering booking at the hotel can obtain firsthand information about the hotel. Generally, these sites are protected against defamation suits because the information posted there is primarily opinion. However, the Grand Resort, which was included as one of TripAdvisor's "dirtiest hotels," argued that such lists were beyond protected opinion and that the comments posted in determining the list were factual, such as this one about the Grand Resort Hotel, "There was dirt at least ½-inch thick in the bathtub which was filled with lots of dark hair."

However, the court held that the statement was not defamatory because of the nature of the communication and anonymous feedback. The information on the site was protected as opinion and therefore requires business managers to understand the importance of customer service and satisfaction.

Consider...

Paul Calden, a 33-year-old, low-level manager, was fired from his job at Allstate Insurance Company in St. Petersburg, Florida, for carrying a gun to his job. His supervisors at Allstate would later describe him as a "total lunatic."

Mr. Calden applied for a job with Fireman's Fund Insurance in Tampa, Florida. Fireman's Fund contacted the Allstate offices for a reference. Allstate sent a letter signed by a vice president that was neutral in its description of Mr. Calden and did not disclose the true reasons for his termination. Mr. Calden had threatened litigation, there was some fear among the employees about him, and Allstate had agreed to a four-month severance package despite his having worked at Allstate for only nine months. Allstate also agreed to draft and send the neutral letter.

After Mr. Calden was terminated by Fireman's Fund, he shot and killed three executives of the company while they were having lunch at a café. One of the executives' wives filed suit against Fireman's Fund and Allstate. The suit against Allstate was based on its failure to disclose Mr. Calden's bizarre behavior and the risk that he was in the workplace.

Allstate defended its actions on the grounds that the average verdict in a defamation suit by a former employee against his former employer for a job reference was $57,000. In one Florida case, a former employee was awarded $25 million in damages. Allstate argued that the cost to businesses would be too high. Is Allstate liable? Be sure to discuss the privilege, defamation, and reference issues involved.

The court held that if it is plain that the columnist "is expressing a subjective view, an interpretation, a theory, conjecture, or surmise, rather than claiming to be in possession of objectively verifiable facts, the statement is not actionable." "Stiffing," as the court noted, may "drip of disapproval," but it is an interpretation of values and is not defamation.

Privileged Speech. Some speech is privileged—that is, strong public interest supports protecting the speech regardless of whether it is true. For example, members of Congress enjoy an **absolute privilege** when they are speaking on the floor of the Senate or House because of a strong public policy to encourage free debate of issues. The same is true of judicial proceedings; in order to encourage people to come forward with the truth, witnesses enjoy an absolute privilege when testifying about the matters at hand. For example, Roger Clemens sued his former trainer, Brian McNamee, for defamation after McNamee testified before a congressional committee that Clemens had used steroids during his professional baseball career. The defamation suit was dismissed because McNamee had an absolute privilege to testify. [*Clemens v McNamee*, 608 F. Supp. 2d 811 (S.D. Tex. 2009)[1]]

There are also some **qualified privileges**, or privileges that provide limited liability for defamation. In nearly all states, there is a qualified privilege for those who have a moral obligation to speak. These types of privilege statutes provide protection for whistleblowers (see Chapter 20), in that a controlled (limited) disclosure of information made in good faith will not subject a businessperson to liability for defamation. However, verification of the truth of such statements is critical.

Another qualified privilege exists for former employers when discussing former employees as the following "For the Manager's Desk" discusses.

FOR THE MANAGER'S DESK

Re: Those Glowing Letters of Recommendation vs. Truth vs. Defamation

One area of legal complexity is the intersection of letters of recommendation, the duty to disclose dangerous conduct by former employees, and defamation. Most employers follow a practice of simply disclosing for new employers whether a former employee in fact worked at their company, and for how long. In order to avoid liability for disclosing negative information in a defamation action by the former employee, employers are hesitant to offer any additional information beyond these perfunctory facts.

However, such an approach is not without risk. In *Randi W. v Muroc Joint Unified School District*, 929 P.2d 582 (Cal. 1997), a California court grappled with the problems that arose from glowing letters of recommendation from a former employer. In the case, Randi W., a 13-year-old minor who attended the Livingston Middle School, was molested and sexually touched on February 1, 1992, by Robert Gadams, who served as vice principal at the school. When her parents filed suit against the school district, they uncovered some disturbing facts.

Mr. Gadams had previously been employed at three other school districts:

- Mendota Unified School District (1985–1988). During his time of employment there, Mr. Gadams had been investigated and reprimanded for improper conduct with female junior high students, including giving them back massages, making sexual remarks to them, and being involved in "sexual situations" with them. Gilbert Rossette, an official with Mendota, provided a letter of recommendation for Mr. Gadams in May 1990. The recommendation was extensive and referred to Mr. Gadams's "genuine concern" for students, his "outstanding rapport" with everyone, and concluded, "I wouldn't hesitate to recommend Mr. Gadams for any position."

- Mr. Gadams had also previously been employed at the Tranquility High School District and Golden Plains Unified District (1987–1990). Richard Cole, an administrator at Golden Plains, also provided a letter of recommendation that listed Mr. Gadams's "favorable" qualities and concluded that he "would recommend him for almost any administrative position he wishes to pursue." At that school, Mr. Gadams had been the subject of various parents' complaints, including that he "led a panty raid, made sexual overtures to students, sexual remarks to students." Mr. Cole also knew that Mr. Gadams had resigned under pressure because of these sexual misconduct charges.

- Mr. Gadams's last place of employment (1990–1991) before Livingston was Muroc Unified School District, where disciplinary actions were taken against him for sexual harassment. When allegations of "sexual touching" of female students were made, Mr. Gadams was forced to resign from Muroc. Nonetheless, Gary Rice and David Malcolm, officials at Muroc, provided a letter of recommendation for Mr. Gadams that described him as "an upbeat, enthusiastic administrator who relates well to the students," and who was responsible "in large part," for making Boron Junior High School (located in Muroc) "a safe, orderly and clean environment for students and staff." The letter concluded that they recommended Mr. Gadams "for an assistant principalship or equivalent position without reservation."

The court held the districts liable to Randi W. and her guardians for their glowing letters, which withheld information important for the safety of children at the schools where Mr. Gadams had worked. The districts' issuance of glowing recommendations when there was troubling information resulted in liability.

Nearly all states provide a qualified privilege for letters of recommendation. A survey indicates that without such protection, disclosures about violent tendencies will not be made and the risk to employees at a new firm is high.

Under this privilege, employers are not liable for defamation if the information they disclose about a former employee is provided in "good faith" or "absence of bad faith." The statutes vary in their language from state to state but they do provide immunity for factual statements. For example, a letter on Gadams that said, "The man is a child molester," would not enjoy immunity. However, a letter from a principal that said, "Several parents complained about Mr. Gadams's inappropriate touching of their children," would enjoy the statutory protection. Also adding to the complexity of the reference issue is a U.S. Supreme Court decision in which the court held that giving a negative reference on a former employee who has sued the company for discrimination can be considered retaliatory and a violation of Title VII (see Chapter 21). [*Robinson v Shell Oil Co.*, 519 U.S. 337 (1997)]

Most employers do not rely on the immunity, and opt to disclose nothing other than the time of employment. Fifty-four percent of all employers indicate they would not disclose violent behavior when asked for a reference. However, keep the *Gadams* case in mind because there can be liability for misleading other employers into hiring those who ultimately cause harm that was predictable based on the facts the previous employer knew. In 2010, Dr. Amy Bishop, a professor at the University of Alabama, was accused of killing three of her colleagues in a dispute over her being denied tenure. As the case was investigated, law enforcement agencies discovered a history of queries about Dr. Bishop over everything from alleged threats to others at work to questions surrounding what was then called the "accidental" shooting of her brother. None of this sordid past had been disclosed when she applied for the position at the University of Alabama. The risks of nondisclosure are often life and death matters.

Another qualified privilege applies when public figures are involved in the defamation. For public figures, the media also have a qualified privilege. If the news organization prints a retraction of a published statement, it has a defense to defamation. Perhaps one of the most famous libel cases addressing the defense of the media privilege involves Donald Trump and a book that included estimates of his wealth. The case decision on this issue follows in *Trump v O'Brien* (Case 9.1).

CASE 9.1

Trump v O'Brien
29 A.3d 1090 (N.J. Super. 2011)

Truth Trumps

FACTS

Donald Trump (plaintiff) sued Timothy O'Brien, the author of *Trump Nation, the Art of Being the Donald*, and his publisher (defendants) for defamation by the book's representations about Mr. Trump's net worth. To determine Mr. Trump's net worth, Mr. O'Brien interviewed and reinterviewed three anonymous sources who eventually lowered their estimates of Trump's net worth to be, at that time, between $150 million and $250 million. Their lowered estimates resulted from the decreased value of Trump's casino holdings at the time O'Brien was writing the book. O'Brien, who also interviewed Trump, wrote:

> So I asked around for guidance. Three people with direct knowledge of Donald's finances, people who had worked closely with him for years, told me that they thought his net worth was somewhere between $150 million and $250 million. By anyone's standards this still qualified Donald as comfortably wealthy, but none of these people thought he was remotely close to being a billionaire.

That passage was followed by:

> Donald dismissed this as naysaying. "You can go ahead and speak to guys who have four-hundred-pound wives at home who are jealous of me, but the guys who really know me know I'm a great builder," he told me.

Trump alleged in his suit that these and other statements such as those that referred to Mr. Trump's "verbal billions" and "[T]rump's ability to float above the wreckage of his financial miscues and magically add zeroes to his bank account ensured that he remained an object of fascination" were false statements that harmed his reputation. The trial court granted summary judgment for Mr. O'Brien and Mr. Trump appealed.

JUDICIAL OPINION

PAYNE, Appellate Division Judge
Because there is no doubt that Trump is a public figure, the alleged defamatory statements by O'Brien must have been uttered or published with "actual malice." [*N.Y. Times Co. v Sullivan*, 376 U.S. 254 (1964)] To establish actual malice, Trump was required to demonstrate by clear and convincing evidence, that O'Brien published his statements "with knowledge that [they were] false or with reckless disregard of whether [they were] false or not."

In this context, "reckless disregard" refers to "the publishing of defamatory statements with a 'high degree of awareness of their probable falsity.'" In fact, "the recklessness in publishing material of obviously doubtful veracity must approach the level of publishing a 'knowing, calculated falsehood.' Negligent publishing does not satisfy the actual-malice test."

A determination of the existence of actual malice requires a subjective inquiry focusing on the defendant's state of mind. "To find actual malice, the factfinder must determine that the defendant in fact entertained serious doubts about the truth of the statement or that

CONTINUED

defendant had a subjective awareness of the story's probable falsity." [C]ourts have recognized that an analysis of a defendant's state of mind in a defamation action "'does not readily lend itself to summary disposition.'"

O'Brien has certified that he re-interviewed his three confidential sources prior to publishing their net worth estimates, and he has produced notes of his meetings with them both in 2004 and in 2005. The notes are significant, in that they provide remarkably similar estimates of Trump's net worth, thereby suggesting the accuracy of the information conveyed.

Further, the accounts of the sources contain significant amounts of additional information that O'Brien was able to verify independently.

In the book, O'Brien did not cite the sources' views as fact, but instead utilized their lower figures as an illustration of the spread in estimates of Trump's wealth, while suggesting that, in his own view, Trump's net worth was far less than he claimed it to be. O'Brien's opinions in this regard were not actionable, because they were absolutely privileged. O'Brien reported Trump's denial of the accuracy of the low net worth figures, although his statement, touting his abilities as a builder, can be construed as less of a denial than an avoidance of the issue presented. Even if that denial had been absolute, which it certainly was not, publication of a statement in the face of denial, however vehement, does not constitute actual malice.

Trump relied in large measure on a 2004 Statement of Financial Condition prepared by Weiser L.L.P., Certified Public Accountants, to which O'Brien was allegedly given access on three occasions including during the course of the April 21, 2005 meeting. However, a preface to that Statement demonstrates its limited value as an accurate representation of Trump's net worth. There,

the accountants cautioned that they had "not audited or reviewed the accompanying statement of financial condition and, accordingly, do not express an opinion or any other form of assurance on it." Further, the accountants noted significant departures from generally accepted accounting principles, and stated "[t]he effects of the departures from generally accepted accounting principles as described above have not been determined."

Defendants quote a September 9, 2004 article in *The Washington Post*, which stated:

> "Actually, it's hard to know exactly what percent of Trump's net worth is tied to the casino business, because most of Trump's portfolio is in privately held companies that don't report earnings. He's described himself as "a billionaire many times over," but who knows? There are skeptics out there who believe Trump has $300 million, tops. And the guy has a reputation for, let's say, shading the news in a light that reflects his enthusiasm."

[W]e find no triable issue as to the existence of actual malice in this matter, and for that reason, affirm summary judgment for O'Brien. Absent actual malice on his part, *respondeat superior* liability [for the publisher] cannot arise. Thus we find that summary judgment was also properly granted to the publishing defendants.

Affirmed.

CASE QUESTIONS

1. Explain why the court focuses on the fact-finding efforts of Mr. O'Brien.
2. What is the significance of others raising doubts about Mr. Trump's net worth?
3. What lessons should writers and reporters learn from this case? Editors? Publishers?

Consider...

The *National Enquirer* published a supposed interview with actor Clint Eastwood. The interview had never taken place, and Mr. Eastwood said the publication of such an interview in a sensationalist newspaper made it seem as if he was "washed up as a movie star." Could Mr. Eastwood recover for the publication of the fake interview? What tort has occurred, if any?

THINK: Recall the elements for defamation: a false statement that impugns the integrity of a specific person.

APPLY: We don't have the content of the interview, but it is false that the interview occurred, and Mr. Eastwood argues that just the suggestion that he would be interviewed by the *National Enquirer* harms his career.

ANSWER: Mr. Eastwood took the case to trial and won, precisely because no interview ever took place and the content and even the suggestion of him granting an interview were false.

9-2b CONTRACT INTERFERENCE

The tort of **contract interference** or **tortious interference with contracts** or tortious interference occurs when parties are not allowed the freedom to contract without interference from third parties.

A basic definition for tortious interference is that someone intentionally persuades another to break a contract already in existence. Bryan A. Garner, the author of *Tortious Interference*, offers the following examples: "Say you had a contract with Joe Blow, and I for some reason tried to get you to break that contract. Or say that Pepsi has an exclusive contract with a hotel chain to carry Pepsi products, and Coke tries to get the hotel to carry Coke despite that contract. That's tortious interference."

One of the most famous cases involving the question of tortious interference relates to interference with an inheritance. A former Playmate of the Year, the late Anna Nicole Smith (a.k.a. Vicki Lynn Marshall), married 90-year-old J. Howard Marshall II, a wealthy oil company owner. Mr. Marshall died shortly after, leaving a $1.6 billion estate. Ms. Smith was given $90 million by Mr. Marshall's son for what Ms. Smith proved was his interference with the execution of a will by the late Mr. Marshall that would have allowed her to be an heir [*In re Marshall*, 253 B.R. 550, 553 (Bankr. C.D. Cal. 2000)], and certain issues in the case made it to the U.S. Supreme Court, where Ms. Smith was in the courtroom for the oral argument of the case [*Marshall v Marshall*, 545 U.S. 1165 (2005)]. Following this decision, Ms. Smith's estate (she died before the final lower court decision following a remand from the U.S. Supreme Court) received nothing from her husband's estate.

9-2c FALSE IMPRISONMENT

False imprisonment is often referred to as "the shopkeeper's tort" because it generally occurs as a result of a shoplifting accusation in a store. **False imprisonment** is the detention of a person for any period of time (even a few minutes) against his will. No physical harm need result; the imprisoned party can collect minimal damages simply for being imprisoned without consent. Because shopkeepers need the opportunity to investigate matters when someone is suspected of shoplifting, the tort of false imprisonment does carry the defense of the **shopkeeper's privilege**. This privilege allows a shopkeeper to detain a suspected shoplifter for a reasonable period of time while the matter or incident is investigated. In most states, the shopkeeper must have a reasonable basis for keeping the person—that is, the shopkeeper must have reason to suspect the individual even if it turns out later that the individual has an explanation or did not do what the shopkeeper suspected. For example, Patricia Holguin went into a Sally's Beauty Supply store carrying her "eco-friendly canvas shopping tote," a large bag, and picked up a can of mousse that was not exactly what she wanted and started to carry it in her tote toward the front counter to ask the cashier a question about it. As she walked toward the front of the store, the assistant manager approached her and asked what was in the bag. She was detained by this manager, who told her that once she put the hair mousse in her tote bag, she was shoplifting. Holguin filed suit for false imprisonment and the court found in her favor because she did not take the mousse to the door and had no intent to conceal or take it.

Business Planning Tip

Invoking the shopkeeper's privilege involves seven key elements:

1. Stop shoppers discreetly.

2. Don't use physical force unless it is in response to the shopper's physical force.

3. Don't question shoppers publicly or make accusations within earshot of others.

4. Call the police quickly to allow them to take over.

5. If you detain shoppers, be certain the physical conditions are appropriate.

6. Don't detain shoppers except for their detention for the police and questioning that resolves the matter.

7. Be especially careful in detaining minors; allow them to call their parents or guardians.

In other words, the manager acted too quickly based on too little information. [*Holguin v Sally's Beauty Supply, Inc.*, 264 P.3d 732 (N.Mex. App. 2011)]

9-2d INTENTIONAL INFLICTION OF EMOTIONAL DISTRESS

This tort imposes liability for conduct that goes beyond all bounds of decency and results in emotional distress in the harmed individual. One of the difficulties with this tort is that the only damage the plaintiff is required to prove is that of emotional distress. Although "pain and suffering" damages have been awarded for some time in negligence actions in which the plaintiff recovers damages for physical and property injuries, the awarding of damages for mental distress alone is a relatively new phenomenon. However, the tort of **intentional infliction of emotional distress** has been used quite often by debtors who are harassed by creditors and collection agencies in their attempts to collect funds.

9-2e INVASION OF PRIVACY

The intentional tort of *invasion of privacy* is actually three different torts.

1. **Intrusion into the Plaintiff's Private Affairs.** This tort results in liability when photographers or others stalk individuals, such as in *Galella v Onassis*, 353 F. Supp. 196 (S.D.N.Y. 1972). In the case, the late Mrs. Jacqueline Kennedy Onassis brought suit against Ron Galella, a photojournalist, for invasion of her privacy. As a result of the case, Mr. Galella was ordered to remain at least 50 yards from Mrs. Onassis and 100 yards from her children.

2. **Public Disclosure of Private Facts.** This tort occurs when a company makes information about an employee public, such as disclosing the medical records that indicate that a CEO was treated for meth addiction or when a hospital employee takes a picture of a patient's tattoo and posts it on Facebook. The information disclosed is not defamation because it is true, but it may well be the tort of invasion of privacy.

   Public disclosure protections are now a statutory issue because of evolving technologies such as e-mail and Internet access. Computer-stored information also carries ease of access. But ease of access does not mean that privacy rights are lost. Statutes now control use of and rights related to computer-stored information. One such statute is the Health Insurance Portability and Accountability Act of 1996 (HIPAA) (42 U.S.C. 1320d-1320d-8). HIPAA controls how medical information is collected, used, and conveyed. For example, doctors must be careful that computer screens of their office personnel are not visible by other patients. HIPAA has resulted in the complex paperwork we sign when we receive medical care that discloses our rights to access our records. It also led to the marked lines at pharmacies behind which we must stand so that we cannot overhear the pharmacy worker's discussions with other customers.

HIPAA has made privacy front and center and introduced some new complexity. One patient services director explained HIPAA's impact as follows: "In the old days, a social worker could pick up the phone and ask Meals on Wheels to deliver lunch to Mrs. Jones five days a week. Under the federal rules, we'll now have to get a release from Mrs. Jones so we can tell Meals on Wheels that, as a diabetic with cardiac problems, she has special dietary needs."[2]

3. **Appropriation of Another's Name, Likeness, or Image for Commercial Advantage.** This final form of the privacy tort involves using someone's name, likeness, or voice for commercial advantage without his or her permission constitutes the tort of unauthorized **appropriation**. For example, if a gas station used your picture in its window to show you as a satisfied customer, you might not be harmed greatly, but your privacy is invaded because you have the right to decide when, how, and where your name, face, image, or voice will be used. *Midler v Ford Motor Co.* (Case 9.2) addresses the unauthorized appropriation of a singer's voice.

Business Planning Tip

There has been a recent string of lawsuits in which those applicants who have not been hired have sought recovery from employers who found personal information about them on Facebook, YouTube, and other social networking sites. In some cases, their friends have posted unflattering photos or information about them that resulted in the employers not offering them a job. The courts have held consistently that information posted on the web is not part of your private affairs and denied recovery. Professor Harold Abelson has explained your rights, privacy, and the Internet as follows, "In today's online world, what your mother told you is true, only more so: People can really judge you by your friends."[3] (See Chapter 10 for more information on this issue.)

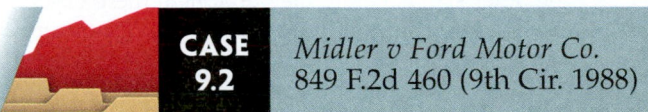

CASE 9.2

Midler v Ford Motor Co.
849 F.2d 460 (9th Cir. 1988)

Ford to Bette, "Do You Wanna Dance?" Bette to Ford, "Not Really!"

FACTS

In 1985, Ford Motor Company and its advertising agency, Young & Rubicam, Inc., advertised the Ford Lincoln Mercury with a series of nineteen 30- or 60-second television commercials in its "The Yuppie Campaign." The aim was to make an emotional connection with yuppies, bringing back memories of when they were in college. The agency tried to get the "original people"—that is, the singers who had popularized the songs—to sing them. When those efforts failed, the agency decided to go with "sound-alikes."

When Young & Rubicam was preparing the Yuppie Campaign, it presented the commercial to its client by playing an edited version of Bette Midler (plaintiff/appellant) singing "Do You Want to Dance?" taken from the 1973 Midler album, *The Divine Miss M.*

After Ford accepted the idea and the commercial, Young & Rubicam contacted Ms. Midler's manager, Jerry Edelstein. The conversation went as follows: "Hello, I am Craig Hazen from Young & Rubicam. I am calling you to find out if Bette Midler would be interested in doing…?" Mr. Edelstein: "Is it a commercial?" "Yes." "We are not interested."

Undeterred, Young & Rubicam sought out Ula Hedwig, who had been one of the "Harlettes," the backup singers for Midler for 10 years. Ms. Hedwig was told by Young & Rubicam that "they wanted someone who could sound like Bette Midler's recording of ['Do You Want to Dance?']." She was asked to make a demo tape. She made an a cappella demo and got the job. At the direction of Young & Rubicam, Ms. Hedwig made a record for the commercial. She first had to listen to

CONTINUED

Ms. Midler's recording of it and was then told to "sound as much as possible like the Bette Midler record."

After the commercial aired, Ms. Midler was told by a number of people that it sounded exactly like her. Friends told Ms. Hedwig that they thought it was Ms. Midler.

Ms. Midler, a nationally known actress and singer, won a Grammy in 1973 as Best New Artist of the Year. She has had both gold and platinum records. She was nominated in 1979 for an Academy Award for Best Female Actress in *The Rose*, in which she portrayed a pop singer. *Newsweek* described her as an "outrageously original singer/comedienne." *Time* hailed her as "a legend" and "the most dynamic and poignant singer-actress of her time."

Ms. Midler filed suit against Ford and Young & Rubicam for appropriation. Young & Rubicam had a license from the song's copyright holder to use it. Neither the name nor the picture of Ms. Midler was used in the commercial. The district court entered judgment for Ford and Young & Rubicam, and Ms. Midler appealed.

JUDICIAL OPINION

NOONAN, Circuit Judge

At issue in this case is only the protection of Midler's voice. The district court described the defendant's conduct as that "of the average thief." They decided, "If we can't buy it, we'll take it." The court nonetheless believed there was no legal principle preventing imitation of Midler's voice and so gave summary judgment for the defendants.

The First Amendment protects much of what the media do in the reproduction of likenesses or sounds. A primary value is freedom of speech and press. The purpose of the media's use of a person's identity is central. If the purpose is "informative or cultural" the use is immune; "if it serves no such function but merely exploits the individual portrayed, immunity will not be granted." It is in the context of these First Amendment and federal copyright distinctions that we address the present appeal.

Nancy Sinatra once sued Goodyear Tire and Rubber Company on the basis of an advertising campaign by Young & Rubicam featuring "These Boots Are Made for Walkin'," a song closely identified with her; the female singers of the commercial were alleged to have imitated her voice and style and to have dressed and looked like her. The basis of Nancy Sinatra's complaint was unfair competition; she claimed that the song and the arrangement had acquired "a secondary meaning" which, under California law, was protectible. This court noted that the defendants "had paid a very substantial sum to the copyright proprietor to obtain the license for the use of the song and all of its arrangements." To give Sinatra damages for their use of the song would clash with federal copyright law. Summary judgment for the defendants was affirmed. If Midler were claiming a secondary meaning to "Do You Want to Dance" or seeking to prevent the defendants from using that song, she would fail like Sinatra. But that is not this case. Midler does not seek damages for Ford's use of "Do You Want to Dance," and thus her claim is not preempted by federal copyright law. What is put forward as protectible here is more personal than any work of authorship.

Bert Lahr once sued Adell Chemical Co. for selling Lestoil by means of a commercial in which an imitation of Lahr's voice accompanied a cartoon of a duck. Lahr alleged that his style of vocal delivery was distinctive in pitch, accent, inflection, and sounds. The First Circuit held that Lahr had stated a cause of action for unfair competition, that it could be found "that defendant's conduct saturated plaintiff's audience, curtailing his market." That case is more like this one.

A voice is as distinctive and personal as a face. The human voice is one of the most palpable ways identity is manifested. We are all aware that a friend is at once known by a few words on the phone. At a philosophical level it has been observed that with the sound of a voice, "the other stands before me." *A fortiori*, these observations hold true of singing, especially singing by a singer of renown. The singer manifests herself in the song. To impersonate her voice is to pirate her identity.

We need not and do not go so far as to hold that every imitation of a voice to advertise merchandise is actionable. We hold only that when a distinctive voice of a professional singer that is widely known is deliberately imitated in order to sell a product, the sellers have appropriated what is not theirs and have committed a tort in California. Midler has made a showing, sufficient to defeat summary judgment, that the defendants here for their own profit in selling their products did appropriate part of her identity.

Outcome: Ms. Midler's case was tried, and she recovered $400,000 from the defendants in October 1989.

CASE QUESTIONS

1. In what context was Ms. Midler's voice sought?
2. Was there some confusion about who was singing in the commercial?
3. What is the difference between this case and the Nancy Sinatra case? Between this case and the Bert Lahr case?

Consider...

Catherine Balsley (known in the reporting business as "Catherine Bosley") worked as a television news reporter for WKBN, Channel 27, the CBS television affiliate in Youngstown, Ohio. She worked for WKBN as a news anchor for approximately 10 years, making her a regional celebrity.

In March 2003, while she was on vacation, Ms. Bosley and her husband went to a Florida nightclub where there was a "wet t-shirt" contest. Ms. Bosley participated with great verve in the contest and removed her clothing. Without either Ms. Bosley's notice or consent, Dream Girls Inc. videotaped Ms. Bosley's actions that night and released them on videos and DVDs. Dream Girls is a video production company to Girls Gone Wild.

Since the incident, images of Ms. Bosley have been displayed on the Internet through a series of websites, advertising pictures and videos of the "naked anchor woman." Ms. Bosely filed suit against Dream Girls for invasion of privacy. Dream Girls has responded that it filmed Ms. Bosley in a public place. What should the court do with the case?

[*Bosley v Wildwett.com*, 310 F. Supp. 2d 914 (N.D. Ohio 2004)]

BUSINESS STRATEGY: Profiting from Amateurs

The NCAA rules are quite simple: A collegiate athlete loses his or her "amateur" status if (1) the athlete "[u]ses his or her athletics skill (directly or indirectly) for pay in any form in that sport," § 12.1.2, or (2) the athlete "[a]ccepts any remuneration or permits the use of his or her name or picture to advertise, recommend or promote directly the sale or use of a commercial product or service of any kind." In fact, if the student-athlete knows that his or her name or image is being used for commercial purposes, the student athlete or the school must take steps to stop the use.

However, the NCAA's use of college athletes' likenesses is quite complex. Through its licensing arm, Collegiate Licensing Co., the NCAA licenses the use of school and team names, uniforms, and all things related to college sports. Electronic Arts Inc., with permission from and rights payment to Collegiate Licensing, created the NCAA Football videogame. In the game, the video quarterback has all the markings of being Rutgers University's famed quarterback, Ryan Hart: same color hair, shirt number, same Scarlet Knights colors, height, weight, and even the same helmet visor and wrist band on the left wrist. Players even referred to the quarterback as "Hart." However, no one had ever paid Mr. Ryan for the use of his image or likeness. In fact, no one had ever asked Mr. Ryan if his image and likeness could be used in the videogame. The NCAA simply licensed the rights away to Electronic Arts. Mr. Hart, and other former collegiate players whose likenesses had been used, filed suit for appropriation of their images. Initially, the suit was dismissed, but a federal appeal court held that it could go forward because there was appropriation.

The issue centers on the rights of these college athletes when their likenesses continue to be licensed and used *after* they are no longer student-athletes. For example, Mr. Hart's image was used in 2004–2006 versions of NCAA Football and his college football career was during 2002–2005. The licensing agreement goes on even after his collegiate career is finished and he could collect payments for use of his image.

Strategically, the NCAA will need to reexamine its licensing arrangements to limit them to the time of the student-athletes' collegiate careers or limit the use of team colors and names and prohibit individual likenesses in the videogames and depictions. The key to avoiding appropriation suits is permission, from those whose images are used, not from those authorized to license organizational names and symbols.

[*Hart v Electronic Arts, Inc.*, 717 F.3d 141 (3rd Cir. 2013)]

9-3 Negligence

The tort of **negligence** is one that applies in a variety of circumstances, but it is always used when the conduct of one party did not live up to a certain minimal standard of care we are all expected to use in driving, in our work, and in the care of our property. Negligence imposes liability on us when we are careless. The elements of and defenses to negligence are covered next.

9-3a ELEMENT ONE: THE DUTY

Each of us has the duty to act like an **ordinary and reasonably prudent person** in all circumstances. We do not always live up to the standard of the ordinary and reasonably prudent person; when we do not, we are negligent. The standard of the ordinary and reasonably prudent person is not always what everyone else does or what the law provides. For example, suppose you are driving on a curvy highway late at night and it is raining quite heavily. The posted speed limit is 45 mph. However, the ordinary and reasonably prudent person will not drive 45 mph because the road and the weather conditions dictate that slower driving is more appropriate. The level of care imposed on us by the ordinary and reasonably prudent person standard is one that requires an examination of all conditions and circumstances surrounding an event that leads to an injury. Many negligence cases struggle with the difficult task of determining whether a duty exists.

Duties, for purposes of negligence actions, can arise because of an underlying statute. Every traffic law carries a criminal penalty (fine and/or imprisonment) for violations of it. However, that law imposes a duty of obedience. A violation of that law is also a breach of duty for purposes of a civil or negligence action. When you run a red light, you have not only committed a crime; you have also breached a duty and are liable for injuries and damages resulting from that breach.

Professionals such as doctors, lawyers, and dentists have the duty of practicing their professions at the level of a reasonable professional. Failure to do so is a breach of duty and a basis for malpractice (negligence by professionals) lawsuits.

Landowners owe duties to people who enter their property. For example, the duty to trespassers, such as thieves, is not to intentionally injure them. Placing mantraps would be a breach of this duty.

There are also the duties we owe one another as fellow journeymen in society. However, those duties that are not defined by statute are becoming more difficult to define and impose. Courts deal with a difficult balance as they define duty, and what constitutes negligence is fulfilling those duties. Only a few states impose a duty to stop and help, but all states provide some form of immunity for those who stop to help but make mistakes in offering their assistance. *Van Horn v Watson* (Case 9.3) deals with these complex issues of duty.

CASE 9.3

Van Horn v Watson
197 P.3d 164 (Cal. 2008)

Tugging on the Injured While Loaded

FACTS

On October 31, 2004, Alexandra Van Horn (plaintiff), Jonelle Freed, and Lisa Torti smoked and inhaled marijuana together at Ms. Torti's home. They were joined there by Anthony Glen Watson and Dion Ofoegbu, who also joined in on the marijuana. At 10:00 P.M., they all headed to a local bar where they drank until 1:30 A.M. At 1:30 A.M., Ms. Van Horn and Ms. Freed left with Mr. Watson, leaving Ms. Torti to ride with Mr. Ofoegbu. Mr. Watson struck a curb and then a light pole whilst going 45 mph. After Mr. Watson

CONTINUED

© Harper 3D/Shutterstock.com

crashed, both Mr. Ofoegbu and Ms. Torti stopped and got out of their car to render aid. Mr. Watson got out of the car by himself, Mr. Ofoegbu helped Ms. Freed out by opening a door for her, and Ms. Torti pulled Ms. Van Horn from the car. Ms. Van Horn said Ms. Torti pulled on her arm and dragged her from the car like a "rag doll."

Ms. Torti testified that the crashed car was smoking and that she felt she should save Ms. Van Horn before flames ensued. Emergency personnel arrived moments later. Ms. Van Horn had a lacerated liver and damaged vertebrae that rendered her paraplegic. Ms. Van Horn filed suit claiming that Ms. Torti's pulling her from the wreck contributed to her paralysis. Ms. Van Horn also filed suit against all the other party animals riding in the two vehicles for their negligence. Ms. Torti claimed immunity under California's Good Samaritan statute.

Ms. Van Horn alleged that Ms. Torti was negligent in pulling her from the car and not waiting for trained personnel. There were differing accounts on whether the car was smoking and if there were flames. In other words, the danger to Van Horn was not clear. In fact, given the evening's activities, not one of them was operating in anything less than a fog at the time of the accident.

The trial court granted summary judgment for Ms. Torti on the grounds that she enjoyed immunity from suit for negligence under the California Good Samaritan law. The Court of Appeal reversed, holding that the Good Samaritan law applied only to those rendering medical care, and that Torti had not provided medical care. Ms. Torti and the others appealed.

JUDICIAL OPINION

MORENO, Justice

Section 1799.102 provides, "No person who in good faith, and not for compensation, renders emergency care at the scene of an emergency shall be liable for any civil damages resulting from any act or omission. The scene of an emergency shall not include emergency departments and other places where medical care is usually offered." The parties identify two possible constructions of this provision: Torti urges us to conclude that it broadly applies to both nonmedical and medical care rendered at the scene of any emergency; plaintiff, on the other hand, argues that section 1799.102 applies only to the rendering of emergency medical care at the scene of a medical emergency.

Although the phrase "emergency care" is not separately defined, section 1797.70's definition of "emergency" certainly supports the conclusion that the

Legislature intended for "emergency care" to be construed as meaning emergency medical care. After all, if the "scene of an emergency" (§ 1799.102) means a scene where "an individual has a need for immediate medical attention" (§ 1797.70), it logically follows that the Legislature intended for the phrase "emergency care" in section 1799.102 to refer to the medical attention given to the individual who needs it.

This construction also comports with the second sentence of section 1799.102, which reads: "The scene of an emergency shall not include emergency departments and other places where medical care is usually offered." While this sentence does not directly shed light on the intended meaning of the phrase "emergency care" in the previous sentence of section 1799.102, the fact that the Legislature excluded "emergency departments and other places where medical care is usually offered" from section 1799.102's immunity supports construing "emergency care" as meaning emergency medical care—the exclusion suggests that "emergency departments and other places where medical care is usually offered" are locations where the Legislature did not need (or want) to encourage ordinary citizens to provide emergency medical care because trained medical personnel are available to better render such care.

Torti's expansive interpretation of section 1799.102 would undermine long-standing common law principles. As we previously noted, the general rule is that "one has no duty to come to the aid of another." "The origin of the rule lay in the early common law distinction between action and inaction, or 'misfeasance' and 'non-feasance.'" (Rest.2d Torts, § 314, com. c, p. 116.) Courts were more concerned with affirmative acts of misbehavior than they were with an individual "who merely did nothing, even though another might suffer serious harm because of his omission to act."

While there is no general duty to help, a good Samaritan who nonetheless "undertakes to come to the aid of another… is under a duty to exercise due care in performance…" "'[i]t is ancient learning that one who assumes to act, even though gratuitously, may thereby become subject to a duty of acting carefully, if he acts at all.'"

The broad construction urged by Torti—that section 1799.102 immunizes any person who provides any emergency care at the scene of any emergency—would largely gut this well-established common law rule. As we recently noted, "'[w]e do not presume that the Legislature intends, when it enacts a statute, to overthrow long-established principles of law unless such intention is clearly expressed or necessarily implied.'" Torti does not identify anything that would overcome the presumption that the Legislature did not intend to work such a radical departure.

CONTINUED

As the Court of Appeal points out, Torti's sweeping construction of section 1799.102 would render other "Good Samaritan" statutes superfluous. For example, Government Code section 50086 immunizes anyone with first aid training who is asked by authorities to assist in a search and rescue operation and who renders emergency services to a victim. The statute defines "emergency services" to include "first aid and medical services, rescue procedures, and transportation or other related activities." It is difficult to see what conduct Government Code section 50086 immunizes that would not already be protected under section 1799.102 as it is interpreted by Torti.

In light of the foregoing reasons, we conclude that the Legislature intended for section 1799.102 to immunize from liability for civil damages only those persons who in good faith render emergency medical care at the scene of a medical emergency.

Affirmed.

CASE QUESTIONS

1. What is the relationship between statutory immunity and common-law duty here?

2. Would it have been better for Ms. Torti to argue that she was providing medical treatment and have the court deal with the issue of what constitutes medical care, rather than the issue of immunity?

3. What are the implications of this decision for people who are trying to offer assistance at the scene of an accident?

9-3b ELEMENT TWO: BREACH OF DUTY

Once the standard of care and the duty are established under element one, there must be a determination that the defendant fell short of that standard or breached that duty for the plaintiff to recover on the basis of negligence. For example, an accountant owes a duty to his client to perform an audit in a competent and professional manner and to conform the audit to the standards and rules established by the American Institute of Certified Public Accounts (AICPA). Failure to comply with these standards would be a breach of duty and would satisfy this second element of negligence.

In many cases, courts try to determine whether the duty was breached to determine whether the defendant's action satisfied the standard of care established in element one.

Barton v Whataburger, Inc. (Case 9.4) focuses on the issues of safety and the liability of businesses and property owners for injuries that result from the acts of third parties.

**CASE
9.4**

Barton v Whataburger, Inc
276 S.W.3d 456 (Tex. App. 2008)

What a Robbery at Whataburger: A Foreseeable Fatality?

FACTS

On a night in May 2003, Gregory Love was working as a night manager at a Whataburger restaurant in northwest Houston. Love arrived early for his shift that evening, allowing Arthur Murray, another manager, to leave. Murray and Love agreed that Love would count the cash accumulated during Murray's shift and place it in the store safe. Also on duty that night was Christopher Dean, a mentally impaired employee who had worked for Whataburger for 14 years.

Shortly after Murray left the Whataburger, Love called Murray and told him that he also needed to leave work. Love asked Murray if he could leave Dean

CONTINUED

© Harper 3D/Shutterstock.com

in charge of the restaurant. Murray responded that Dean was capable of running the restaurant, but he could not authorize Love to delegate his managerial power to Dean.

Love did not ask Murray to return, and instead disregarded Murray's warnings, left the restaurant, and put Dean in charge. Love did not count the money in the cash registers or deposit any money in the safe before he left. When Dean discovered that Love had not counted the money in the registers, he counted it and deposited the excess in the safe. Love never returned to the restaurant that night.

At around 4:00 A.M., three men, later identified as Gerald Marshall, Ronald Worthy, and Kenny Calliham, attempted to rob the Whataburger. Marshall climbed through the drive-through window and chased Dean, eventually into the back of the restaurant, where he demanded that Dean give him the key to the safe. Marshall told Dean that if Dean did not give him the key to the safe, Marshall would shoot him. When Dean, who did not have the key, failed to produce it, Marshall shot him in the face and fled the scene with Worthy and Calliham. Dean died immediately. The robbers left with nothing, but afterward robbed a Shipley Doughnut store equipped with video surveillance.

Police later connected Love to the robbery, and the State charged him with capital felony murder. A jury found Love guilty, and the trial court assessed punishment of life in prison. The court affirmed the conviction.

Rose Barton, individually and on behalf of the estate of her son, Christopher Dean, filed suit against Whataburger, Inc. The trial court granted summary judgment for Whataburger, holding that the shooting death of Dean was not a foreseeable event. Barton appealed.

JUDICIAL OPINION

BLAND, Justice
A negligence cause of action has four elements: (1) a legal duty owed by one person to another, (2) a breach of that duty, and (3) damages (4) proximately caused by the breach. In the context of the employer-employee relationship, a company has a duty (1) to provide rules for the safety of employees, and to warn them of reasonably foreseeable hazards; (2) to furnish reasonably safe machinery and equipment; (3) to furnish a reasonably safe place to work; and (4) to exercise ordinary care to select careful and competent fellow employees.

Whataburger does not dispute that it owed a duty to Dean, as its employee, but observes that its duty is to protect its employees from foreseeable harms. The issue in this case, whether analyzed as a part of the duty element of negligence or the causation element, is the foreseeability of the criminal conduct that led to Dean's murder. As the Texas cases that discuss the foreseeability of intervening criminal conduct do so, in the main, in the context of the element of duty, we do so as well.

The threshold inquiry in a negligence case is duty. As a general rule, "a person has no legal duty to protect another from the criminal acts of a third person." However, if a criminal's conduct is a foreseeable result of the prior negligence of a party, the criminal act may not excuse that party's liability. To impose liability on a defendant for negligence in failing to prevent the criminal conduct of another, the facts must show more than conduct that creates an opportunity to commit crime—they must show both that the defendant committed negligent acts and that it knew or should have known that, because of its acts, the crime (or one like it) might occur.

Thus, to impose a legal duty to prevent the criminal conduct of another, the crime must have been reasonably foreseeable at the time the defendant engaged in negligent conduct. Foreseeability exists if the actor, as a person of ordinary intelligence, should have anticipated the dangers his negligent act creates for others. Importantly, "[f]oreseeability requires more than someone, viewing the facts in retrospect, theorizing an extraordinary sequence of events whereby the defendant's conduct brings about the injury."

NEGLIGENT HIRING

Barton first contends that Whataburger's negligence in hiring Love as a restaurant manager caused the aggravated robbery that led to Dean's murder. Barton produced evidence of an investigative report that revealed Love was convicted of a felony offense of "dealing cocaine" in Indiana in September 1993, and served one year in jail. Love was convicted of felony nonpayment of child support in Texas, in November 2002, the week before he applied for a managerial position at Whataburger. Whataburger performed a background check on Love before hiring him, but only searched for criminal convictions in Harris County that occurred between November 1995 and November 2002. The search did not reveal either of the two felony convictions. Barton alleges that Whataburger's failure to conduct an adequate background check ultimately caused the aggravated robbery that led to Dean's murder.

CONTINUED

While Love's convictions, if discovered, should have raised Whataburger's suspicions about his fitness to manage a restaurant, under Texas law, they did not make his eventual participation in an aggravated robbery leading to murder reasonably foreseeable. Even assuming that information about Love's prior convictions, if known, would have torpedoed Love's employment with Whataburger, his criminal acts of selling cocaine and failing to pay child support are different from an aggravated robbery—neither crime inherently requires violence or theft, the two essential ingredients of an aggravated robbery. The record contains no evidence that the events underlying either of Love's convictions involved violence or theft, or that Love engaged in any conduct during the seven months he was employed at Whataburger that would have made his participation in an aggravated robbery foreseeable. Even viewed in hindsight, Love's convictions for selling cocaine and nonpayment of child support do not indicate a propensity for violent criminal conduct, like aggravated robbery and murder.

Barton calls our attention to criminal cases that note the connection between drugs and violence. We acknowledge that courts, including ours, have recognized a street-level connection between drugs, weapons, and violence. This connection provides police officers with the constitutionally required reasonable suspicion to conduct a *Terry* stop, or a legislature with a justification for imposing harsher sentences on drug offenders.

A stereotypical connection, however, is insufficient to raise more than a scintilla of evidence that a person convicted of selling cocaine, without any accompanying evidence of violence, will foreseeably commit aggravated robbery leading to murder in the future. While the smell of marijuana or the suspicion that a defendant possesses narcotics might provide a police officer sufficient justification to frisk a suspect for weapons under Terry, a seven-year-old conviction for "dealing" cocaine, standing alone, does not make it foreseeable that a defendant will commit a violent crime in the future.

FAILURE TO PROVIDE A SAFE WORKPLACE

Barton further contends that, even if it was not legally foreseeable that Love would engineer the crime that resulted in Dean's murder, Whataburger generally knows of an increased risk of a violent crime occurring at restaurants open late at night and should have taken reasonable security measures to prevent it.

Employees are the invitees of their employer. "[w]hen general danger to invitees is the risk of injury from criminal activity by third parties, the evidence must reveal specific previous crimes on or near the premises in order to establish foreseeability of harm."

The incidence of violent crime, the foreseeability of violent crime on Whataburger's premises, and the preventative measures that Whataburger could or did implement in view of the risk of such crime were the same for Whataburger in its capacity as employer as they were for Whataburger in its capacity as premises occupier.

Barton produced some evidence of criminal activity at the Whataburger in the years preceding Dean's murder: in July 1997, six years before the incident, a customer was shot in the parking lot, and another customer in the drive-through lane was robbed and shot in the thigh; in July 1998, a customer was robbed in the drive-through lane; in June 1999, a customer's purse was stolen; in July 2000, a customer reported an assault (without injury); in April 2001, a woman sought help in the Whataburger, reporting that she had been shot; in August 2001, a woman reported an assault (without injury); in February 2002, a woman reported that her car was stolen from her in the parking lot; in April 2002, one customer intentionally hit another customer's vehicle in the drive-through lane (with property damage but not injury); and, in February 2003, police arrested a person who refused to leave the premises.

In contrast… no crime similar to this one had ever occurred: no one had ever robbed the restaurant before, nor had it ever been the scene of any workplace violence, nor had anyone ever committed any sort of crime against a Whataburger employee, nor had anyone ever been murdered.

… the evidence does not show the rampant, violent criminal activity sufficient to raise a fact issue about the foreseeability of the aggravated robbery that resulted in Dean's murder.

… general evidence of crime rates and of robberies in other locales cannot create "an industry standard of foreseeability" sufficient to impose a duty to prevent crime.

Finally, Barton's contention that Whataburger's earlier employment of a security guard on the weekends proves the foreseeability of the robbery is unavailing. "The mere act of taking preventative measures to protect against the possibility of future crime is not the same as foreseeing that criminal activity." If we equated preventative measures to foreseeability, we would "virtually eliminate the foreseeability requirement for a negligence claim against a person who

CONTINUED

installs a security system or takes other preventative measures to guard against crime."

We hold that the trial court properly granted summary judgment because the diabolic conduct of others—men who committed aggravated robbery and murder—was a superseding cause of Dean's death that was not reasonably foreseeable to Whataburger.

Affirmed.

CASE QUESTIONS

1. After reading the court opinion, list the type of evidence that Dean's mother would have to offer to establish foreseeability.

2. What policies should employers establish based on what happened in this case?

3. What lessons do you learn about employee screening from this case?

Consider...

Dorothy McClung went shopping at the Walmart in the Delta Square Shopping Center in Memphis, Tennessee, around noon. After she completed her shopping and was returning to her car, she was abducted at gunpoint and forced into her car. She was later found dead in the trunk of her car after it was spotted by some hunters in a remote area in Arkansas. Roger McClung, her husband, filed suit against Walmart and the owner of the shopping center, Delta Square. Are these companies liable for the criminal acts of another when those acts occurred in their parking lot? [*McClung v Delta Square Limited Partnership*, 937 S.W.2d 891 (Tenn. 1996)]

9-3c ELEMENT THREE: CAUSATION

After establishing a duty and breach of duty, the plaintiff in a negligence suit must also establish that the breach of the duty was the cause of the damages. A test often used to determine **causation** is the **"but for" test**—"but for the action or lack of action of the defendant, the plaintiff would not have been injured." For example, suppose that a guest is enjoying a scenic view of the ocean from a cliff near his hotel. At the edge of the cliff, the hotel had installed a fence, but the hotel does not keep it in good repair. When the guest leans against the fence to take a picture, the fence breaks and the guest falls over the cliff. The hotel breached its duty to keep its premises in reasonably safe condition, and its failure to do so caused the guest's injury. The "but for" test is limited by the so-called zone of danger rule, which requires that the plaintiff be in the zone of danger when the injury occurs. The zone of danger includes all those people who could foreseeably be injured if a duty is breached. For example, the hotel would also be liable to those injured by the guest as he fell through the weak fence because they are in the zone of danger.

9-3d ELEMENT FOUR: PROXIMATE CAUSE

Some cutoff line must be drawn between the "but for" causation and events that contribute to the injury of the plaintiff—an element of a negligence case called **proximate cause**. Suppose that you have a tire replaced at a

Business Planning Tip

All businesses should help create a safe environment for their customers and discourage criminal acts by providing the following:

1. Good lighting
2. Access to public phones or call boxes
3. Security patrols
4. Locked gates to parking lots; gate or security access
5. Escorts for customers and employees to their vehicles after closing hours
6. Camera security
7. Assigned parking spaces for tenants and employees
8. Warning signs to use caution and be alert

Many hotels change key access codes with each guest and post security personnel near guest elevators at night in order to limit access to the elevators unless you can show your room key. Some hotels have floors for women who are traveling alone, and extra security is provided on those floors.

© Grounder/Shutterstock.com

ETHICAL ISSUE

Is there an ethical obligation on the part of bar owners to prevent intoxicated patrons from leaving their bars? Suppose, for example, that the intoxicated patron does not have a car and will not be driving home. Does the bar owner have any responsibilities regarding this type of patron? What if the bar owner entrusts the non-driving, intoxicated patron to another bar patron? Are there any legal and ethical issues with that approach?

© martan/Shutterstock.com

FOR THE MANAGER'S DESK

Re: Bars and Dram Shop Liability

David Huffman had a blood alcohol level that was three times the legal limit when he slammed the car of Meredith and Mary Eastridge at a speed over 100 mph. The Eastridges were critically wounded, and Mrs. Eastridge lost their unborn son. The two spent over one month in the hospital.

Mr. Huffman, who was killed in the accident, had been served 10 drinks over a two-hour-and ten-minute time frame at Eddie's Place, a bar and restaurant located in South Charlotte, North Carolina.

The Eastridges filed suit under North Carolina's dram shop act, a type of law that allows victims of accidents caused by drunk drivers to recover from bars and restaurants that serve alcohol to obviously intoxicated or underage people. The jury awarded the Eastridges $1.7 million.

North Carolina is one of 43 states that have a dram shop act. The laws vary by state, but North Carolina's statute imposes liability when a bar or restaurant serves someone who is obviously intoxicated when they know that the patron is driving. In this case, employees of Eddie's arranged for Huffman to get a ride home with another customer who lived in Huffman's apartment complex. However, it was after

he got home that Huffman got into his own car and drove anyway. The Eastridge case presented an interesting legal issue because the lawyers for Eddie's Place argued that the dram shop law in North Carolina does not impose liability for allowing someone who is legally intoxicated to leave the bar; liability results only when they allow someone to leave who they have reason to believe is going to drive. Given the arrangements for transportation the bar employees made, their lawyer argued that they did everything that they could. Eddie's Place has been in business for 15 years and never had a problem with any accidents or conduct by its patrons.

The dram shop acts also do not require proof of legal intoxication, the blood-alcohol content used for criminal prosecution for DWI or DUI cases. The dram shop statutes only require proof of visible intoxication.

Other states impose liability even on servers in restaurants who serve the visibly intoxicated. In other states, limits are placed on the extent of the liability of the bars and restaurants.

Source: Larry Copeland, "N.C. Crash Spotlights Dram Shop Laws," *USA Today,* November 29, 2012, p. 3A.

© bloomua/Shutterstock.com

tire store and the technician fails to tighten the wheel sufficiently. As you drive down the street, the tire comes loose, rolls off, and strikes another car. Did the tire store cause the damage to the other car? Yes. Any accidents caused by that car? Yes. Suppose the tire comes off, rolls onto the sidewalk, and strikes a pedestrian. Did the tire store cause that injury? Yes. Suppose the pedestrian sees the tire coming and jumps out of the way but, in so doing, injures another pedestrian. Did the tire store cause that injury? Yes. In all of these accidents, the following statement can be made: "But for the failure to tighten the wheel, the accident would not have occurred." Suppose that the tire injures a pedestrian, although not fatally, but a doctor treating the pedestrian, through malpractice, causes the pedestrian's death. Did the tire store cause the death? No; another's negligence intervened.

Case 9.5, *Palsgraf v Long Island Ry. Co.,* is a landmark case on the element of proximate cause.

CASE 9.5

Palsgraf v Long Island Ry. Co.
162 N.E. 99 (N.Y. 1928)

Fireworks in the Passenger's Package and Negligence in the Air

FACTS

Helen Palsgraf (plaintiff) had purchased a ticket to travel to Rockaway Beach on the Long Island Railway (defendant). While she was standing on a platform at the defendant's station waiting for the train, another train stopped at the station. Two men ran to catch the train, which began moving as they were running. One of the men made it onto the train without difficulty, but the other man, who was carrying a package, was unsteady as he tried to jump aboard. Employees of the defendant helped pull the man in and push him onto the train car, but in the process the package was dropped. The package contained fireworks, and when dropped, it exploded. The vibrations from the explosion caused some scales (located at the end of the platform on which Ms. Palsgraf was standing) to fall. As they fell, they hit and injured Ms. Palsgraf. She filed suit against the railroad for negligence.

JUDICIAL OPINION

CARDOZO, Chief Justice

Negligence is not actionable unless it involves the invasion of a legally protected interest, the violation of a right. "Proof of negligence in the air, so to speak, will not do." The plaintiff, as she stood upon the platform of the station, might claim to be protected against intentional invasion of her bodily security. Such invasion is not charged. She might claim to be protected against unintentional invasion by conduct involving in the thought of reasonable men an unreasonable hazard that such invasion would ensue. These, from the point of view of the law, were the bounds of her immunity, with perhaps some rare exceptions, survivals for the most part of ancient forms of liability, where conduct is held to be at the peril of the actor. If no hazard was apparent to the eye of ordinary vigilance, an act innocent and harmless, at least to outward seeming, with reference to her, did not take to itself the quality of a tort because it happened to be a wrong, though apparently not one involving the risk of bodily insecurity, with reference to someone else.

A different conclusion will involve us, and swiftly too, in a maze of contradictions. A guard stumbles over a package which has been left upon a platform. It seems to be a bundle of newspapers. It turns out to be a can of dynamite. To the eye of ordinary vigilance, the bundle is abandoned waste, which may be kicked or trod on with impunity. Is a passenger at the other end of the platform protected by the law against the unsuspected hazard concealed beneath the waste? If not, is the result to be any different, so far as the distant passenger is concerned, when the guard stumbles over a valise which a truckman or a porter has left upon the walk? The passenger far away, if the victim of a wrong at all, has a cause of action, not derivative, but original and primary. His claim to be protected against invasion of his bodily security is neither greater nor less because the act resulting in the invasion is a wrong to another far removed. In this case, the rights that are said to have been violated, the interests said to have been invaded, are not even of the same order. The man was not injured in his person or even put in danger. The purpose of the act, as well as its effect, was to make his person safe. If there was a wrong to him at all, which may very well be doubted, it was a wrong to a property interest only, the safety of his package. Out of this wrong to property, which threatened injury to nothing else, there has passed, we are told, to the plaintiff by derivation or succession a right of action for the invasion of an interest of another order, the right to bodily security. The diversity of interests emphasizes the futility of the effort to build the plaintiff's right upon the basis of a wrong to some one else. The gain is one of emphasis, for a like result would follow if the interests were the same. Even then, the orbit of the danger as disclosed to the eye of reasonable vigilance would be the orbit of the duty. One who jostles one's neighbor in a crowd does not invade the rights of others standing at the outer fringe when the unintended contact casts a bomb upon the ground. The wrongdoer as to them is the man who carries the bomb, not the one who explodes it without suspicion of the danger. Life will have to be made over, and human nature transformed, before prevision so extravagant can be accepted as the norm of conduct, the customary standard to which behavior must conform.

Here, by concession, there was nothing in the situation to suggest to the most cautious mind that the parcel wrapped in newspaper would spread wreckage through the station. If the guard had thrown it down knowingly and willfully, he would not have threatened the plaintiff's safety, so far as appearances could warn

CONTINUED

him. His conduct would not have involved, even then, an unreasonable probability of invasion of her bodily security. Liability can be no greater where the act is inadvertent.

DISSENTING OPINION

ANDREWS, Justice
Assisting a passenger to board a train, the defendant's servant negligently knocked a package from his arms. It fell between the platform and the cars. Of its contents the servant knew and could know nothing. A violent explosion followed. The concussion broke some scales standing a considerable distance away. In falling, they injured the plaintiff, an intending passenger.

Upon these facts, may she recover the damages she has suffered in an action brought against the master? The result we shall reach depends upon our theory as to the nature of negligence. Is it a relative concept—the breach of some duty owing to a particular person or to particular persons?

Or, where there is an act which unreasonably threatens the safety of others, is the doer liable for all its proximate consequences, even where they result in injury to one who would generally be thought to be outside the radius of danger? This is not a mere dispute as to words. We might not believe that to the average mind the dropping of the bundle would seem to involve the probability of harm to the plaintiff standing many feet away whatever might be the case as to the owner or to one so near as to be likely to be struck by its fall. If, however, we adopt the second hypothesis, we have to inquire only as to the relation between cause and effect. We deal in terms of proximate cause, not of negligence.

Negligence may be defined roughly as an act or omission which unreasonably does or may affect the rights of others, or which unreasonably fails to protect one's self from the dangers resulting from such acts.

Where there is the unreasonable act, and some right that may be affected there is negligence whether damage does or does not result. That is immaterial. Should we drive down Broadway at a reckless speed, we are negligent whether we strike an approaching car or miss it by an inch. The act itself is wrongful. It is a wrong not only to those who happen to be within the radius of danger, but to all who might have been there—a wrong to the public at large.

Negligence does involve a relationship between man and his fellows, but not merely a relationship between man and those whom he might reasonably expect his act would injure; rather, a relationship between him and those whom he does in fact injure. If his act has a tendency to harm someone, it harms him a mile away as surely as it does those on the scene.

The proposition is this: Every one owes to the world at large the duty of refraining from those acts that may unreasonably threaten the safety of others. Such an act occurs. Not only is he wronged to whom harm might reasonably be expected to result, but he also who is in fact injured, even if he be outside what would generally be thought the danger zone.

As we have said, we cannot trace the effect of an act to the end, if end there is. Again, however, we may trace it part of the way. An overturned lantern may burn all Chicago. We may follow the fire from the shed to the last building. We rightly say the fire started by the lantern caused its destruction. A cause, but not the proximate cause. What we do mean by the word "proximate" is that, because of convenience, of public policy, of a rough sense of justice, the law arbitrarily declines to trace a series of events beyond a certain point. This is not logic. It is practical politics.

This last suggestion is the factor which must determine the case before us. The act upon which defendant's liability rests is knocking an apparently harmless package onto the platform. The act was negligent. For its proximate consequences the defendant is liable. If its contents were broken, to the owner; if it fell upon and crushed a passenger's foot, then to him; if it exploded and injured one in the immediate vicinity, to him. Mrs. Palsgraf was standing some distance away. How far cannot be told from the record—apparently 25 to 30 feet, perhaps less. Except for the explosion, she would not have been injured.... The only intervening cause was that, instead of blowing her to the ground, the concussion smashed the weighing machine which in turn fell upon her. There was no remoteness in time, little in space. And surely, given such an explosion as here, it needed no great foresight to predict that the natural result would be to injure one on the platform at no greater distance from its scene than was the plaintiff. Just how no one might be able to predict. Whether by flying fragments, by broken glass, by wreckage of machines or structures no one could say. But injury in some form was most probable.

Under these circumstances I cannot say as a matter of law that the plaintiff's injuries were not the proximate result of the negligence.

CASE QUESTIONS

1. Who was carrying the package?

2. How far away from the incident was Ms. Palsgraf, and why is this significant?

3. What does Justice Cardozo find? Why does the dissent disagree?

9-3e ELEMENT FIVE: DAMAGES

The plaintiff in a negligence case must be able to establish damages that resulted from the defendant's negligence. Such damages could include medical bills, lost wages, and pain and suffering, as well as any property damages. In many of the cases in this chapter, plaintiffs have also recovered punitive damages. Often referred to as "smart money," punitive damages are similar to civil penalties that are paid to plaintiffs because of the high level of carelessness involved on the defendant's part.

9-3f DEFENSES TO NEGLIGENCE

Contributory Negligence

In some cases, an accident results from the combined negligence of two or more people. A plaintiff who is also negligent gives the defendant the opportunity to raise the defense of **contributory negligence**. Contributory negligence is simply negligence by the plaintiff that is part of the cause of an accident. For example, suppose that a boat owner is operating his boat late at night on a lake in which the water is choppy and when he is intoxicated. An intoxicated friend is sitting at the bow of the boat trying to put her feet into the water when the owner takes the boat up to high speed. She falls in and is injured. The issue of causation becomes complicated here because there were breaches of duties by both parties. Did he cause the accident by driving at high speed late at night on a choppy lake while intoxicated? Or did she cause the accident by sitting without protection or restraint on the bow of the boat when the boat was being driven like that? The effect of the defense of contributory negligence is a complete bar to both from recovery.

Comparative Negligence

Many states, in order to eliminate the harsh effect of contributory negligence, have adopted a defense of **comparative negligence**. Under this defense, the jury simply determines the level of fault for both the plaintiff and the defendant and, based on this assessment of fault, determines how much each of the parties will be awarded. Using our boat example, the jury could find that the boat owner was 75 percent at fault and the passenger was 25 percent at fault. Under comparative negligence, the passenger could recover for her injuries, but the amount recovered would be 25 percent less because of her fault in causing the accident.

The defense of comparative negligence was developed largely because of the perceived unfairness of contributory negligence, which was a complete bar to recovery. The concept of comparative negligence has resulted in more litigation and more verdicts for plaintiffs permitted to use the defense.

Assumption of Risk

The **assumption of risk** defense requires the defendant to prove that the plaintiff knew of potential risk of injury in the conduct he or she undertook but decided to go forward with it anyway. For example, some dangers are inherent in activities such as skydiving, skiing, and roller-skating. You assume the inherent risks in these activities, but you do not assume the risks caused by the owners of the premises or equipment. For example, when you ski, you assume the natural risks that exist in skiing, but you do not assume the risk of faulty equipment you rent. If the failure of that equipment causes your injuries, the rental company would be responsible for that injury. To assume the risk, you must be completely aware of the risk and you must assume the risk voluntarily. *The Landings Assoc. Inc. v Williams* (Case 9.6) deals with the issue of assumption of risk and provides the answer for the chapter's opening "Consider..."

CASE 9.6

The Landings Assoc. Inc. v Williams
728 S.E.2d 577 (Ga. 2012)

Snapping at the Homeowner's Association

FACTS

Gwyneth Williams, then 83, was housesitting for her daughter and son-in-law at The Landings, a planned residential development with a golf course located on Skidaway Island off the Georgia coast. Before The Landings was developed, the land within and surrounding its boundaries was largely marsh, where indigenous alligators lived and thrived. In order to develop the property, The Landings entities installed a lagoon system that allowed enough drainage to create an area suitable for a residential development. After the project was completed in the 1970s, the indigenous alligators began to move in and out of The Landings through its lagoon systems.

Although alligators inhabited the area, no person had ever been attacked until the night of October 5, 2007, when Mrs. Williams went for a walk near one of the lagoons close to her daughter's home some time after 6:00 P.M. The following morning, Mrs. Williams's body was found floating in the lagoon. Williams's right foot and both forearms had been bitten off. Later, an eight-foot alligator was caught in the same lagoon, and, after the alligator was killed, parts of Williams's body were found in its stomach.

Williams's family filed suit against The Landings for negligence in developing and operating the area. The Landings countered with a defense of contributory negligence—that Mrs. Williams assumed the risk of walking alone among the lagoons at night. The trial court denied a motion for summary judgment in part. The court of appeals reversed in part, and the parties appealed.

JUDICIAL OPINION

MELTON, Justice

The record shows that, prior to the attack, Williams was aware that the property was inhabited by alligators. Williams' son-in-law testified that, on at least one occasion, he was driving with Williams on property in The Landings when he stopped the car to allow Williams to look at an alligator. Williams' son-in-law also testified that Williams was, in fact, aware that there were alligators in the lagoons at The Landings and that he believed that Williams had a "normal" respect for wild animals. When asked whether he had ever discussed how to behave around wild alligators with Williams, her son-in-law responded: "No. There was never—quite frankly, there was never any reason to. I mean she was an intelligent person. She would—there was no question in my mind that—I guess I have to answer that as it's not like talking to a five year old child… stay away from alligators." In addition, Williams' son recalled a similar instance when he stopped the car to allow his mother to look at an alligator. At that time Williams mentioned that she did not like alligators and did not want to go anywhere near them.

One who is familiar with the premises cannot rely for recovery upon the negligence of the defendant in failing to correct a patent defect where such party had equal means with the defendant of discovering it or equal knowledge of its existence."

In this case, testimony shows that Williams was aware that wild alligators were present around The Landings and in the lagoons. Therefore, she had knowledge equal to The Landings entities about the presence of alligators in the community. In addition, the record shows that Williams knew that the wild alligators were dangerous, saying herself that she would not want to be anywhere near them. Nonetheless, Williams chose to go for a walk at night near a lagoon in a community in which she knew wild alligators were present. This act undisputably shows that Williams either knowingly assumed the risks of walking in areas inhabited by wild alligators or failed to exercise ordinary care by doing so. Under these circumstances, the trial court should have granted the motions for summary judgment brought by the Landings entities regarding Williams' premises liability claims.

While there is no doubt that Williams' death was a tragic event, Williams was not incompetent. A reasonable adult who is not disabled understands that small alligators have large parents and are capable of moving from one lagoon to another, and such an adult, therefore, assumes the risk of an alligator attack when, knowing that wild alligators are present in a community, walks near a lagoon in that community after dark.

The motion for summary judgment is granted.

DISSENTING OPINION

BENHAM, Justice

Notably absent from the majority's opinion are facts which, if construed in appellees' favor, require the denial of appellants' motions for summary judgment.

CONTINUED

© Harper 3D/Shutterstock.com

For example, the Landings Association had an advertised policy that it removed from the 151 lagoons in the community alligators which were seven feet long or larger and/or alligators which were aggressive toward humans or pets; the appellants did not patrol or inspect the lagoons in order to remove large or aggressive alligators according to its policy, but rather relied on residents and employees to report said animals; and appellants did not post signs near the lagoons warning guests about alligators. One expert opined that the over eight foot long, 130 pound alligator that attacked the decedent had likely been in the lagoon where the decedent's body was found for some time because such mature alligators tend to be territorial and nest. There was also evidence in the record that the decedent called for help during the attack, but that appellants' security forces, which were not trained in dealing with alligators, responded to the wrong location and then stopped investigating, assuming that the sounds in question were bird calls.

Based on the facts presented at the time of summary judgment in this case, reasonable minds could differ as to the essential elements of appellees' premises liability claim. Indeed, there are very specific questions in this case that must go to a jury: whether decedent knew that large and aggressive alligators were living on the premises and in the lagoon in which her body was discovered; and whether appellants exercised reasonable care in inspecting and keeping the premises safe from alligators—in particular, alligators that were over seven feet long and alligators that were aggressive toward humans and pets as per appellants' removal policy. Rather than allowing this evidence to be reviewed by a fact-finder, the majority opinion bars appellees' premises liability claim simply because the decedent once observed an alligator standing on the roadside.

CASE QUESTIONS

1. What fact is used to show that Ms. Williams assumed the risk on alligators?
2. Why does the dissent differ with the finding on assumption of risk?

Consider...

Lisa Winters signed up to take a Latino dance class at the Santa Monica Family YMCA, sort of a dancing-with-the-neighbors experience. However, when she arrived for class on April 17, 2002, the Latino dance instructor was ill and the jazz instructor had agreed to fill in so that the class would proceed. The jazz instructor, however, taught jazz. No one was wearing the appropriate shoes for jazz dance, the floor was made of wood, and the instructor asked the students to perform a pivoting spin maneuver. After Ms. Winters attempted the maneuver, the jazz instructor asked her to put more effort into the move. Ms. Winters first performed the maneuver with no difficulty. During her second attempt, she performed four leaps (e.g., running-type steps with both feet off the ground). As she attempted to perform the pivoting half-spin maneuver, her left foot stuck to the floor. She fell to the floor and sustained personal injuries. She filed suit against the YMCA for her injuries. The YMCA's defense is assumption of risk. Will the defense fly (as it were)? Be sure to explain why all of the facts stated are important in reaching your conclusion. [*Winter v Santa Monica Family YMCA*, 2005 WL 1713936 (Cal. App. 2 Dist)]

9-4 New Verdicts on Tort Reform

Although nearly all states have adopted some form of limitations in tort recovery, these reforms are a maze of laws differing from state to state and are in a fluid state of judicial review.

In *BMW of North America, Inc. v Gore*, 517 U.S. 559 (1996), the U.S. Supreme Court concluded that $4,000,000 in damages was excessive (reduced to $2 million by the judge on a judgment *NOV*) for the dealer's failure to disclose to a BMW buyer that his car had been refinished. The actual damages were only $4,000, and the court held, "When the ratio [of punitive damages to actual damages] is a breathtaking 500 to 1, however, the award must surely 'raise a suspicious judicial eyebrow.'" The dissent raised the question courts still labor to resolve: How much is too much?

Consider...

The Mathiases checked into a Motel 6 and were bitten extensively by bedbugs. Upon investigation, they learned that the managers and owners of the motel had been warned by guests, employees, and exterminators alike that there were bedbugs in the rooms. The exterminator offered to spray the motel each year for $600, but the motel refused. As a result, the bugs remained and propagated. The Mathiases filed suit, seeking punitive damages. The trial court awarded them $5,000 compensatory damages and $186,000 punitive damages. The motel appealed the punitive damage award as excessive. Is the award excessive? Should the punitive damages award be reversed? Why do you think the hotel wants to have a court decision on this suit?
[*Mathias v ACCR Economy Lodging, Inc.*, 347 F.3d 672 (7th Cir. 2003)]

A number of significant decisions have chipped away at answering that question. In *State Farm Mutual Auto Insurance Co. v Campbell*, 538 U.S. 408 (2003) (originally a Utah case), the U.S. Supreme Court held that a punitive damage award of $145 million in punitive damages and $1 million in compensatory damages against an insurance company for its wrongful refusal to pay a claim violated the due process clause. Because the highest criminal penalty available for fraud in Utah was $10,000, the court could not find a justification for the large punitive damage award. Neither could the court find that including out-of-state activities of a company in determining damages for conduct within the state was not proper.

In *Exxon Shipping Co. v Baker*, 554 U.S. 471 (2008), the U.S. Supreme Court found that the maximum amount for punitive damages in that case (which had peculiar maritime underpinnings) was an amount equal to the compensatory damages. These types of decisions continue to place limits on punitive damages.

9-4a   STRICT LIABILITY

Strict liability is absolute liability for conduct with few, if any, defenses available. Some activities are so dangerous that engaging in them results in liability. Use of explosives, as in building razing, is a strict liability activity.

For example, an Illinois court discussed that keeping a tiger in your backyard results in strict liability because the danger is so great.

BIOGRAPHY   The Kitty Genovese Story and Duty

Richmond, California, is a suburb of San Francisco and is an industrial area that was ranked the ninth most dangerous city in the United States in 2008. Richmond has received national attention and scorn because of the alleged gang rape of a high school student at the homecoming dance at Richmond High School, which occurred as 20 people watched the horrific conduct of the young men.

No one witnessing the brutality notified the police of the ongoing rape until a woman overheard two people discussing it and called 911.

The Richmond witnesses were overcome by what is known as the "bystander effect," the label given to the apartment dwellers who witnessed the attack and

eventual murder of Kitty Genovese in Queens, New York, in 1964. As they heard the screams of Miss Genovese while she was being beaten and stabbed, those living in the complex did nothing because of their fear of getting involved, their assumptions that someone else would take care of it, or perhaps callous disregard.

There is no statutory duty in California (yet) to report an ongoing crime and no statutory duty in most states to help another who is in danger. Indeed, many who do help have had liability imposed on them for not helping in a crackerjack fashion (see the *Van Horn v Watson* case on pp. 290–292). What are our ethical responsibilities to render aid?

Summary

What types of civil wrongs create a right of recovery for harm?

- Tort—a civil wrong; action by another that results in damages that are recoverable

- Intentional tort—civilly wrong conduct that is done deliberately

- Negligence—conduct of omission or neglect that results in damages

- Strict tort liability—imposition of liability because harm results

What are the types and elements of torts?

- Defamation—publication of untrue and damaging statements about an individual or company

- Product disparagement—the tort of defamation of products

- Malice—publication of information knowing it is false or with reckless disregard for whether it is false

- Privilege—a defense to defamation that protects certain statements because of a public interest in having information such as testimony in a trial or media coverage protected from suit

- Interference—the wrong of asking a party to breach a contract with a third party

- False imprisonment—wrongful detention of an individual; shopkeepers have a privilege to reasonably detain those they have good cause to believe have taken merchandise

- Shopkeeper's privilege—defense to torts of defamation, invasion of privacy, and false imprisonment for merchants who detain shoppers when shopkeepers have reasonable cause to believe merchandise has been taken without payment

- Intentional infliction of emotional distress—bizarre and outrageous conduct that inflicts mental and possible physical harm on another

- Invasion of privacy—disclosing private information, intruding upon another's affairs, or appropriating someone's image or likeness

- Appropriation—the use, without permission, of another's likeness, image, voice, or trademark for commercial gain

What are the elements and defenses in negligence?

- Reasonable and prudent person—the standard by which the conduct of others is measured; a hypothetical person who behaves with full knowledge and alertness

- Causation—the "but for" reason for an accident

- Proximate cause—the foreseeability requirement of causation

- Contributory negligence—negligence on the part of a plaintiff that was partially responsible for causing injuries

- Comparative negligence—newer negligence defense that assigns liability and damages in accidents on a percentage basis and thus reduces a plaintiff's recovery by the amount his negligence contributed to the cause of the accident

- Assumption of risk—plaintiff's voluntary subjection to a risk that caused injuries

What are the public policy and business issues in tort recovery?

- Tort reform—political and legislative process of limiting damages and changing methods of recovery for civil wrongs

- Amount of punitive damages

Questions and Problems

1. In the May 31, 2004, issue of *The Weekly Standard*, editor Fred Barnes wrote the following commentary:

A FEW YEARS AGO Michael Moore, who's now promoting an anti-President Bush movie entitled Fahrenheit 9/11, *announced he'd gotten the goods on me, indeed hung me out to dry on my own words. It was in his first bestselling book,* Stupid White Men. *Moore wrote he'd once been "forced" to listen to my comments on a TV chat show,* The McLaughlin Group. *I had*

whined "on and on about the sorry state of American education," Moore said, and wound up by bellowing: "These kids don't even know what The Iliad *and* The Odyssey *are!"*
Moore's interest was piqued, so the next day he said he called me. "Fred," he quoted himself as saying, "tell me what The Iliad *and* The Odyssey *are." I started "hemming and hawing," Moore wrote. And then I said, according to Moore: "Well, they're... uh... you know... uh... okay, fine, you got me—I don't know what they're*

about. Happy now?" He'd smoked me out as a fraud, or maybe worse.

The only problem is none of this is true. It never happened. Moore is a liar. He made it up. It's a fabrication on two levels. One, I've never met Moore or even talked to him on the phone. And, two, I read both The Iliad *and* The Odyssey *in my first year at the University of Virginia. Just for the record, I learned what they were about even before college. Like everyone else my age, I got my classical education from the big screen. I saw the Iliad movie called* Helen of Troy *and while I forget the name of the Odyssey film, I think it starred Kirk Douglas as Odysseus.*

So why didn't I scream bloody murder when the book came out in 2001? I didn't learn about the phony anecdote until it was brought to my attention by Alan Wolfe, who was reviewing Moore's book for the New Republic. *He asked, by email, if the story were true. I said no, not a word of it, and Wolfe quoted me as saying that. That was enough, I thought. After all, who would take a shrill, lying lefty like Moore seriously?*

Was Mr. Barnes defamed? Could he bring suit now?

2. Douglas Margreiter was severely injured in New Orleans on the night of April 6, 1976. He was the chief of the pharmacy section of the Colorado Department of Social Services and was in New Orleans to attend the annual meeting of the American Pharmaceutical Association.

On Tuesday evening, April 6, Mr. Margreiter had dinner at the Royal Sonesta Hotel with two associates from Colorado who were attending the meeting and were staying in rooms adjacent to Mr. Margreiter's in the New Hotel Monteleone. Mr. Margreiter returned to his room between 10:30 P.M. and 11:00 P.M.; one of his friends returned to his adjoining room at the same time. Another friend was to come by Mr. Margreiter's room later to discuss what sessions of the meetings each would attend the next day.

About three hours later, Mr. Margreiter was found severely beaten and unconscious in a parking lot three blocks from the Monteleone. The police who found him said they thought he was highly intoxicated, and they took him to Charity Hospital. His friends later had him moved to the Hotel Dieu.

Mr. Margreiter said two men had unlocked his hotel room door and entered his room. He was beaten about the head and shoulders and had only the recollection of being carried to a dark alley. He required a craniotomy and other medical treatment and suffered permanent effects from the incident.

Mr. Margreiter sued the hotel on grounds that the hotel was negligent in not controlling access to elevators and hence to the guests' rooms. The hotel says Mr. Margreiter was intoxicated and met his fate outside the hotel. Is the hotel liable? [*Margreiter v New Hotel Monteleone*, 640 F.2d 508 (5th Cir. 1981)]

3. The A & N Food Market in Flushing, New York, has adopted the following procedures when its security cameras observe shoppers stealing store merchandise:

- The alleged thief's identification is taken.
- The alleged thief is photographed holding the items they are alleged to have taken.
- The store security guards tell the alleged thieves that their pictures (with them holding the merchandise) will be displayed publicly in the store unless they pay for the items and pay a fine of $400.
- If they do not have $400 to pay the fine, the store holds their identification until they return with the $400.

This store, whose customers are almost all Chinese, is using the same system to curb shoplifting that is used in China. A slogan is posted at most retailers in China that warns of the store's fine policy: "Steal one, fine 10." The owners of the A & N Food Market maintain that their policies and procedures are legal because they are covered under the shopkeeper's privilege. Are they correct? Are their actions covered under the privilege? (Corey Kilgannon and Jeffrey E. Singer, "Shoplifting Suspects' Choice: Pay or Be Shamed," *New York Times*, June 22, 2010, p. A1.)

4. The CBS news show *60 Minutes* pulled from programming a scheduled airing of an interview with a Jeffrey S. Wigand, a former tobacco executive, when threats of both libel and tortious interference with contract suits arose. Brown & Williamson lawyers notified CBS News that Wigand had signed a confidentiality agreement and that the company would sue CBS News for interference with that contract if the interview were run. *60 Minutes* ran a story on tobacco companies without the interview. CBS correspondents Mike Wallace and Morley Safer protested the decision of CBS News executives. However, the *Wall Street Journal* ran a story describing CBS News's unusual arrangements with Wigand, including the payment of a consulting fee of

$12,000 and the promise of full indemnification. Did CBS commit tortious interference of contract?

5. Two disc jockeys at WPYX-FM radio in Albany, New York, were sued for intentional infliction of emotional distress by Annette Esposito-Hilder, who was identified on the air by the two disc jockeys as the "winner" of the "ugliest bride" contest. The two disc jockeys sponsored an ugliest bride contest based on wedding pictures in the daily newspaper. Viewers were invited to call in with their guesses as to which bride had been chosen. Generally, the disc jockeys did not reveal last names of the brides. However, in Ms. Esposito-Hilder's case, they broke with past practice and revealed her name.

On appeal of the case from an earlier dismissal, the court held that no defamation was involved in their statements because they were "pure, subjective opinion." The court did hold, however, that a suit for intentional infliction of emotional distress could go forward. The court held, "Comedic expression does not receive absolute First Amendment protection."

Is this defamation? Is opinion protected by the First Amendment? Does it make any difference that Ms. Esposito-Hilder was employed by a competing radio station in the area at the time she "won" the contest? [*Esposito-Hilder v SFX Broadcasting, Inc.*, 665 N.Y.S.2d 697 (1997)]

6. Ads on Times Square that feature well-known personalities clad in brand-name items are not unusual. However, the building-size photo of President Obama in a Weatherproof Garment Company jacket in an ad touting the company's apparel was out of the ordinary. The ad caught the attention of more than the millions filing through the public square. The office of White House Counsel also took note. "The White House has a long-standing policy disapproving of the use of the president's name and likeness for commercial purposes." Mr. Obama had not granted permission for use of his photo.

The photo used in the ad was one taken while the president was at the Great Wall of China in November. Freddie Stollmack, president of Weatherproof Garment Company, spotted the photo in the news and, using a magnifying glass, was able to identify the company's logo and zipper. The company did pay the licensing fees for use of the photo, one taken by the Associated Press (AP). AP, however, noted that it is the user's responsibility to obtain permission and clearances for how the photo is used. The *New York Times*, the *New York Post*, and *Women's Wear Daily* turned down the presidential ads Weatherproof had tried to place with them.

Weatherproof is known for its publicity-grabbing advertising techniques. In 2008, it issued a press release touting its unique approach of running the shortest ads on the Super Bowl—2 seconds. A later press release confirmed that no ad would be run because 2-second ads are not available during the Super Bowl. In 2006, Weatherproof photographed company representatives putting a coat on the Naked Cowboy, a well-known street performer in New York City.

The White House legal counsel had its hands full with ads because during the week prior to the jacket hoopla, People for the Ethical Treatment of Animals (PETA) ran an anti-fur ad that featured Michelle Obama on billboards in the Washington, DC, area. Mrs. Obama had also not given permission. The White House did contact PETA about the ad but did not discuss whether the parties had reached a resolution.

What are the rights of those whose images or likenesses are used for commercial purposes without their permission? Is there something different about public figures? What about First Amendment issues? Could Weatherproof argue that it was simply revealing what type of coat the president was wearing, just as newspapers reveal which designers the First Lady uses for her wardrobe? Evaluate the ethics of PETA and Weatherproof in their use of the First Family's images. (Stephanie Clifford, "A Coat Endorsed by the President? The White House Says No," *New York Times*, January 7, 2009, p. B3.)

7. On the day after Thanksgiving, November 28, 2008, Walmart held a nationwide sale of a limited number of sharply discounted televisions, computers, and video game sets. The "blitz sale" had been advertised heavily in newspapers and on television. At the Valley Stream Walmart store in Long Island, New York, 2,000 shoppers lined up hours before the scheduled 6 A.M. store opening, forming a line at a place marked by a handwritten sign: Blitz Line Starts Here. The crowd became unruly at one point and the store manager called the police. However, the police left after concluding that things were under control. Shortly afterward, at 5 A.M., the crowd broke through the glass doors of the store in a stampede. Jdimytai Damour, a Walmart maintenance worker, was trampled by the crowd and died from asphyxiation. OSHA has imposed a $7,000 fine on Walmart for its failure to take appropriate steps to control the crowd. Walmart is fighting the fine because it maintains the stampede and the trampling were not foreseeable simply because Walmart held a post–Thanksgiving day blitz sale. Walmart has argued that OSHA is asking it to predict events and that there were, at that time, no laws or rules on crowd control or so-called "blitz sales" (sales in which there are a limited number of items at a reduced price). Walmart's lawyers argued, "If this was a foreseeable event, why did the police feel comfortable in leaving the scene?"

Walmart has already entered into an agreement with the Nassau County, New York, district attorney to adopt crowd control policies at its 92 stores in New York, create a $400,000 fund to compensate trampling victims, and donate $1.5 million to various community organizations in Nassau County. Walmart also implemented crowd-control policies at its stores nationwide. Evaluate the duty, breach of duty, and foreseeability issues in the Long Island stampede. Be sure to discuss whether Walmart breached any duty to the maintenance worker and why Walmart would push back against the small fine. (Ann Zimmerman, "Walmart Fights Safety Fine, Worried About Precedent," *Wall Street Journal*, July 9, 2010, p. B3; Steven Greenhouse, "Wal-Mart Displays Its Legal Might Fighting $7,000 Fine in Trampling Case," *New York Times*, July 7, 2010, p. B1.)

8. E*Trade Financial Corporation ran a memorable ad during the 2010 NFL Super Bowl in which a baby boy and a baby girl are chatting online via the use of a web camera. The dialogue between the two babies, who have the voices of adults, is as follows:

Baby boy: "So, yea, sorry about last night."

Baby girl: "I just don't understand why you didn't call last night."

Baby boy: "I was on E*Trade, you know, diversifying my portfolio, taking control like a wolf."

Baby girl: "Right."

Baby boy: "That volatility in the market, taken care of, wolf-style… (howls)."

Baby girl: "And that milkaholic Lindsay wasn't over?"

Baby boy: "Lindsay?"

Second baby girl pops in front of the web camera: "Milkawhat?"

Lindsay Lohan, a 23-year-old actress who has been required to attend drug rehabilitation programs and has served time in jail for various drug charges, has filed a $100 million suit against E*Trade for appropriation of her likeness and image. Ms. Lohan's lawyers have statements from friends and others who indicate that Ms. Lohan was the first person who came to mind when they saw the ad. Is this appropriation?

9. KSL Recreation Corp. and Boca Partnership signed an agreement on February 23, 1994, to form a joint venture to renovate and expand the 356-acre Boca Raton Hotel & Club resort in Palm Beach County, Florida. The joint venture did not go through because KSL demanded an additional $3.5 million in expenses and fees. Boca then negotiated a loan with Olympus Real Estate Corporation. Boca was about to close on the financing of the renovation with Olympus when KSL faxed a copy of a lawsuit against Boca to Olympus. The lawsuit was not yet filed. Boca had a litigation clause in its agreement with Olympus, and it was required to pay more fees and a higher interest rate. Did KSL interfere with Boca's contract with Olympus?

10. Joseph Mosca and 23 others boarded a sportfishing boat for a day of fishing off San Clemente Island. David Lichtenwalter, one of the fishermen, was fishing off the stern near Mr. Mosca. Mr. Lichtenwalter's line became entangled in kelp and he was unable to get it released. A deckhand approached Mr. Lichtenwalter to help him. Mr. Lichtenwalter backed up and handed the pole to the deckhand just as the line "slingshotted" over the rail toward Mr. Mosca, who was struck in the eye with the sinker, which caused a partial vision loss.

Mr. Mosca filed suit against Mr. Lichtenwalter and others. The trial court, using the defense of assumption of risk, dismissed the case, and Mr. Mosca appealed. Discuss the issues and determine liability. [*Mosca v Lichtenwalter*, 68 Cal. Rptr. 2d 58 (Cal. App. 1997)]

MANAGEMENT & THE LAW

A Primer on References

If you are assigned the task of developing a new reference policy for your company, remember the following guidelines.

1. Stick with factual disclosures: Use "There was an accusation of embezzlement and he resigned," not "He is an embezzler."

2. Stick with easily defined terms: Use "Angers easily," not "He is a lunatic."

3. Report what happened, not your view: Use "Other staff members complained about her conduct and work," not "She was a constant pain in the neck."

4. Implement an exit interview policy in which you disclose the information you have on file that will be given when references are requested.

5. Verify the protections afforded under your state law, if any.

© Ron and Joe/Shutterstock.com

Notes

1. There was an interesting personal jurisdiction issue in the case—whether Brian McNamee could be required to come to Texas to defend against the defamation suit. The court upheld Texas's jurisdiction over the case. [*Clemens v McNamee*, 615 F.3d 374 (5th Cir.2010); *certiorari denied*, *Clemens v McNamee*, 131 S.Ct. 3091 (2011).] Refer to Chapters 3 and 4 for more information on jurisdiction.

2. Robert Pear, "Health System Warily Prepares for Privacy Rules," *New York Times*, April 6, 2003, pp. A1, A19.

3. "Quotation of the Week," *New York Times*, March 21, 2010, p. SB2.

As the below quotes indicate, we have a complicated and very communicative world because of the Internet and other forms of technology that permit rapid information and photo exchanges. There are tensions between and among users and providers of technology and employers and employees' cyberlaw is the field of law that deals with these issues. Cyberlaw sounds as if it is a separate body of law. However, cyberlaw is simply a collection of the other types of laws you have studied that now apply to our new technological world. We know our rights of privacy under the Constitution, tort law, and statutory protections. Where does social media fit in those protections? Do you waive certain privacy rights because of what you post online? We know the law on search and seizure and when government officials can obtain records, but how are those records obtained from a third-party server whose customers are not identified online? Contracts are formed with negotiations and paperwork, but can they be formed through electronic media?[1]

The purpose of this chapter is to take the laws you have studied or will soon study and apply them to the issues that technology brings to us. There have been and will continue to be changes in the law to accommodate new ways of doing business, but there has also been and will continue to be reliance on the fundamental principles that underlie our laws and the rights they protect. This chapter provides a framework for the challenges of legal issues in cyberspace.

The legal issues of cyberspace can be broken down into four main areas: employment issues, user issues, appropriation and competition issues, and contract issues. Within each of these four areas are several new legal issues that have arisen because of the unique nature of cyberspace and how business is conducted there. That various cyberlaw issues can be grouped into traditional areas of law demonstrates the not-so-new nature of cyberlaw.

UPDATE
For up-to-date legal news, go to **mariannejennings.com**

Consider...

Jeff Quon, a sergeant and member of the city of Ontario, California's SWAT team, sent racy text messages to several colleagues, as well as to his wife, using Arch Wireless text-messaging services that were provided for Quon through the city of Ontario's contract with Arch. Quon exceeded the maximum number of characters for texting, the department reviewed his messages through Arch, found the racy material, and disciplined Quon. Quon claimed a violation of his Fourth Amendment and privacy rights because Arch turned over his text messages to his employer. Is he correct? Can your employer get your text messages?

10-1   Employers, Employees, and Cyberlaw

The lines between our jobs and personal lives are increasingly blurred. Just three years ago, the focus in case law was on employee use of company e-mail systems to send personal messages. Today, personal blogs, social media profiles (such as Facebook), Tweets, LinkedIn, and other online activities by employees result in increasing challenges for employers as they try to protect company information and balance employee rights and privacy.[2] Blogging has often resulted in employees disclosing private and/or negative information about their companies. Tweeting is instant and ongoing communication that could reveal, prematurely, information that the company does not want public. The introductory quotes provide examples of the kinds of problems Instagram and tweeting can cause for companies. On the other hand, there are issues related to employees' rights in terms of opinion, speech, and the ability to organize for workplace benefits and terms and conditions of employment. E-mails, Internet surfing, and blogging require a delicate balancing of both employer and employee rights and interests.

10-1a   EMPLOYERS ARE ACCOUNTABLE FOR EMPLOYEE ELECTRONIC CONTENT

Employers are held responsible for the content of employee e-mails, and employers must have access and control rights over employee information that is released publicly through various electronic means. For example, e-mails that contain off-color jokes or suggestive comments create an atmosphere of harassment.[3] (See Chapter 21 for more information on sexual harassment.) Employers are also responsible when employees use e-mail or the Internet at work to violate intellectual property rights. Employers are accountable when employees use e-mails and blogs to defame fellow employees or competitors, vendors, or even customers.

Employee e-mail is spontaneous, candid, and discoverable. As a result, the content of employees' e-mail is often fertile territory for prosecutors who can find evidence of intent in employee e-mails and blogs. For example, in 2008, investigators uncovered e-mails of employees at Standard & Poor's, the investment rating agency, that indicated that while the employee/analysts were rating debt instruments as AAA, they were also having doubts about them. One employee wrote, "These deals could have been structured by cows and we would still rate them."[4] Another e-mail read, "Rating agencies continue to create [an] even bigger monster—the CDO market. Let's hope we are all wealthy and retired by the time this house of cards falters." These candid e-mails were a foundation for settlements paid by the analysts' firms and resulted in general reforms of the analyst industry.

E-mails provide a contemporaneous record of events that often defy our recollections. And e-mails on a company's computers and servers are always subject to employer review and use for purposes of disciplining employees (see the discussion in the following section). For example, in 2011, the indictment of former Penn State assistant football coach, Jerry Sandusky, for child sexual abuse resulted in questions about whether university officials had failed to report past incidents of Mr. Sandusky's inappropriate involvement with children. The late and then–head football coach, Joe Paterno, denied any knowledge of a 1998 incident in the football program showers with a young boy. However, a subsequent investigation uncovered e-mails that contradicted Coach Paterno's recollection. On May 13, 1998, Tim Curley, the university's athletic director, sent an e-mail to Gary Schultz, a university vice president of finance and operations, with the caption, "Jerry," and this message, "Anything new in this department? Coach is anxious to now where it stands."[5] Mr. Curley also requested updates on May 18 and May 30, 1998. As a result, Mr. Curley and Mr. Schultz were charged with perjury regarding their testimony of not knowing about previous incidents and Coach Paterno and Penn State were disciplined by the NCAA. The e-mail era means our own words often determine our consequences.

10-1b EMPLOYER MONITORING: WHAT IS LEGAL?

Because they are held accountable for what employees do in cyberspace, employers use various methods for monitoring employees, including random reviews of e-mails, investigations that utilize e-mail content, and even key-stroking software that allows the employer to see messages that employees typed but did not send. Employers also limit or control employee web access by using blocking software that limits sites employees can visit, monitoring blogs for content, and examining items posted on Facebook, Twitter, and YouTube.

Any existing laws related to telecommunications and privacy do not have a solid fit when it comes to tackling the privacy issues of employees when using the Internet. In the early days of cyberspace, some efforts were made to apply the **Electronic Communications Privacy Act of 1986 (ECPA)**, which prohibits the unauthorized access of "live" communications, as when someone uses a listening device to intercept a telephone conversation. However, e-mail and social media are stored information, and the question of this act's application for resolving the privacy issue is doubtful.[6] ECPA also has an exception for consensual interception, as when an employee consents to being monitored as a term and condition of employment.

The **Stored Communication Act (SCA)** prohibits the unauthorized interception of electronic communications, generally meaning stored communication, not ongoing communication such as text messaging, tweeting, and instant messaging.

However, the courts have held consistently that employees give consent to such monitoring, and there are no statutory violations when employers do live listening, interception, or recovery of sent communication that is stored and available electronically. When employers have informal policies or policies that allow employees to reimburse their employers for private use of text services, the courts have held that monitoring and disclosure of those messages is a violation of the law. The *City of Ontario v Quon* case (Case 10.1) deals with this issue between employees and employers and their text, e-mail, and privacy policies and provides the answer for the chapter's opening "Consider…"

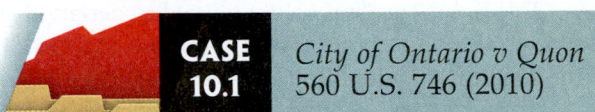

CASE 10.1 *City of Ontario v Quon*
560 U.S. 746 (2010)

Employees Exceeding their Text Characters and Employers Exceeding their Right to See the Texts

FACTS

Jeff Quon, a sergeant and member of the city of Ontario's SWAT team, sent personal and sometimes racy text messages to Sergeant Steve Trujillo, dispatcher April Florio, and his wife Jerilyn Quon (respondents) using Arch Wireless text-messaging services that were provided for Quon through the city.

Ontario Police Department (the city) (OPD) (petitioners) had no official policy directly addressing the use of text messaging. However, the city did have a general "Computer Usage, Internet, and E-mail Policy" applicable to all employees. The policy provided that all software, programs, networks, Internet, e-mail, and other systems were to be used only for city of Ontario–related business. The policy also said, "Users should have no expectation of privacy or confidentiality when using these resources," and indicated that usages were monitored and recorded. Quon attended a meeting during which SWAT team members and others were told that text messages would fall under the city's policy as public information, and be therefore eligible for auditing.

Under the city's contract with Arch Wireless, each pager was allotted 25,000 characters, after which the city was required to pay overage charges. Quon's supervisor told him that he was over by more than 15,000 characters and that he should reimburse the city for the overage charges so that he (the supervisor) would not have to audit the transmission and see how many messages were non–work related. Quon refused to pay and was told to cut down on his transmissions.

When Quon and another officer again exceeded the 25,000-character limit, his supervisor told the officers that he was "tired of being a bill collector with guys going over the allotted amount of characters on their text pagers." Ontario's chief of police, Chief Scharf, then requested an audit of the text messages.

Because city officials were not able to access the text messages themselves, they requested and obtained the messages from Arch Wireless. The audit of the messages revealed abuse of on-the-clock time through sheer numbers of personal texts and their sexually explicit content. The officers were disciplined, and they subsequently challenged the discipline by claiming violation of their Fourth Amendment rights. The trial court found that there was a Fourth Amendment violation, but granted Arch Wireless a summary judgment on Quon's claims of invasion of privacy. The Ninth Circuit held that the search was unreasonable and the city appealed.

JUDICIAL OPINION

KENNEDY, Justice

The City's Computer Policy stated that "[u]sers should have no expectation of privacy or confidentiality when using" City computers. Chief Scharf's memo and Duke's statements made clear that this official policy extended to text messaging. The disagreement, at least as respondents see the case, is over whether Duke's later statements overrode the official policy. Respondents contend that because Duke told Quon that an audit would be unnecessary if Quon paid for the overage, Quon reasonably could expect that the contents of his messages would remain private.

Cell phone and text message communications are so pervasive that some persons may consider them to be essential means or necessary instruments for self-expression, even self-identification. That might strengthen the case for an expectation of privacy. On

CONTINUED

the other hand, the ubiquity of those devices has made them generally affordable, so one could counter that employees who need cell phones or similar devices for personal matters can purchase and pay for their own.

Even if Quon had a reasonable expectation of privacy in his text messages, petitioners did not necessarily violate the Fourth Amendment by obtaining and reviewing the transcripts. Although as a general matter, warrantless searches "are *per se* unreasonable under the Fourth Amendment," there are "a few specifically established and well-delineated exceptions" to that general rule. The Court has held that the "'special needs'" of the workplace justify one such exception.

The search here was reasonable under that approach. The search was justified at its inception because there were "reasonable grounds for suspecting that the search [was] necessary for a non investigatory work-related purpose." As a jury found, Chief Scharf ordered the search in order to determine whether the character limit on the City's contract with Arch Wireless was sufficient to meet the City's needs. This was, as the Ninth Circuit noted, a "legitimate work-related rationale."

The City and OPD had a legitimate interest in ensuring that employees were not being forced to pay out of their own pockets for work-related expenses, or on the other hand that the City was not paying for extensive personal communications.

As for the scope of the search, OPD requested transcripts for only the months of August and September 2002. While it may have been reasonable as well for OPD to review transcripts of all the months in which Quon exceeded his allowance, it was certainly reasonable for OPD to review messages for just two months in order to obtain a large enough sample to decide whether the character limits were efficacious. And it is worth noting that during his internal affairs investigation, McMahon redacted all messages Quon sent while off duty, a measure which reduced the intrusiveness of any further review of the transcripts.

Even if he could assume some level of privacy would inhere in his messages, it would not have been reasonable for Quon to conclude that his messages were in all circumstances immune from scrutiny. Quon was told that his messages were subject to auditing. As a law enforcement officer, he would or should have known that his actions were likely to come under legal scrutiny, and that this might entail an analysis of his on-the-job communications. Under the circumstances, a reasonable employee would be aware that sound management principles might require the audit of messages to determine whether the pager was being appropriately used. Given that the City issued the pagers to Quon and other SWAT Team members in order to help them more quickly respond to crises—and given that Quon

had received no assurances of privacy—Quon could have anticipated that it might be necessary for the City to audit pager messages to assess the SWAT Team's performance in particular emergency situations.

OPD's audit of messages on Quon's employer-provided pager was not nearly as intrusive as a search of his personal e-mail account or pager, or a wiretap on his home phone line, would have been. That the search did reveal intimate details of Quon's life does not make it unreasonable, for under the circumstances a reasonable employer would not expect that such a review would intrude on such matters.

This Court has "repeatedly refused to declare that only the 'least intrusive' search practicable can be reasonable under the Fourth Amendment." That rationale "could raise insuperable barriers to the exercise of virtually all search-and-seizure powers," because "judges engaged in *post hoc* evaluations of government conduct can almost always imagine some alternative means by which the objectives of the government might have been accomplished." Even assuming there were ways that OPD could have performed the search that would have been less intrusive, it does not follow that the search as conducted was unreasonable.

Finally, the Court must consider whether the search violated the Fourth Amendment rights of Jerilyn Quon, Florio, and Trujillo, the respondents who sent text messages to Jeff Quon. Petitioners and respondents disagree whether a sender of a text message can have a reasonable expectation of privacy in a message he knowingly sends to someone's employer-provided pager. It is not necessary to resolve this question in order to dispose of the case, however. Respondents argue that because "the search was unreasonable as to Sergeant Quon, it was also unreasonable as to his correspondents." They make no corollary argument that the search, if reasonable as to Quon, could nonetheless be unreasonable as to Quon's correspondents. In light of this litigating position and the Court's conclusion that the search was reasonable as to Jeff Quon, it necessarily follows that these other respondents cannot prevail.

The judgment of the Court of Appeals for the Ninth Circuit is reversed.

CASE QUESTIONS

1. What general advice could you give a business about its access to employees' text messages based on the decision in this case?

2. Why are alternative methods for searching the text messages not relevant?

3. How does the court deal with the issue of expectation of privacy on the part of the officer's family and friends?

10-1c EMPLOYERS' RIGHT OF ACCESS TO EMPLOYEE E-MAILS

Because employers are accountable for the content of employee e-mail, it is not a breach of privacy for employers to monitor employee e-mail and Internet usage. Monitoring the content of employee e-mails is important for keeping companies out of legal difficulties. However, employees may believe they have an expectation of privacy in their e-mails, even when those e-mails are sent from work. That belief may spring from the tort standards that protect private lives, communications, and information. Employers cannot disclose private employee information over the Internet, but that would be different from employers monitoring employee e-mail for purposes of controlling sexual harassment, disclosure of proprietary or statutorily protected information, and employee defamation of the company and company managers.

Employers generally require employees to sign a document in which they acknowledge that by working at the company and using the company's e-mail and server that they have waived their right to privacy. Former Sun Microsoft Systems CEO Scott McNealy summed up employee rights to privacy when it comes to Internet use: "You have zero privacy. Get over it."[7] Despite this wide latitude, employers do not have the right to publish, release, or forward information in employee e-mails when that information is private.

The scope of employer monitoring of e-mails includes monitoring electronic communications from employees that are marked as private; e-mails that are sent from home and from private computers that use the company server; e-mails that do not involve company business; text messages sent using company phones (as in the *Quon* case); and Tweets sent over company iPhones, BlackBerries, and other phone communication systems.

Employees should be careful when using their work laptops for private communications. Courts have reached different conclusions, for example, on whether employees waive their attorney–client privilege when using their work computers or employer-issued cell phones to communicate with their employers. Communicating with your lawyer over the company e-mail system is risky when it comes to protecting the privilege.[8] *Holmes v Petrovich Development Company, LLC* (Case 10.2) covers some critical issues about e-mail disclosures and uses by employees and managers.

Business Planning Tip

What Employees Should Know and Remember About Internet Communication:

1. Nothing is private on the Internet. People can see everything.

2. Be careful what you blog.

3. Protect your identity when in chat rooms.

4. Assume that everything you write and post will be seen.

5. You can clean up your name on Google using several services, but having no hits at all can lead to suspicions.

6. Think before you write, blog, post, or do anything on the Internet.

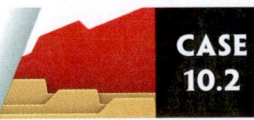

CASE 10.2   *Holmes v Petrovich Development Company, LLC*
119 Cal.Rptr.3d 878 (Cal. App. 2011)

FACTS

Gina Holmes began working for Paul Petrovich as his executive assistant in early June 2004. The employee handbook, which Ms. Holmes read and signed, contained the following warnings,

> "[e]mployees who use the Company's Technology Resources to create or maintain personal information or messages have no right of privacy with respect to that information or message," and,

> "E-mail is not private communication, because others may be able to read or access the message. Email may best be regarded as a postcard rather than as a sealed letter. . . ."

The employee handbook also states that the company may "inspect all files or messages . . . at any time for any reason at its discretion."

Ms. Holmes told Petrovich in July 2004 that she was pregnant and that her due date was December 7, 2004.

CONTINUED

During her pregnancy, Ms. Holmes was put off when coworkers asked her questions about maternity leave and made "belly-monitoring" comments. She asked "[t]hat little group of hens" to stop, and they complied. Ms. Holmes discussed her belly getting big and baby names with Mr. Petrovich and felt the discussions were inappropriate but never said anything about being offended.

On Friday morning, August 6, 2004, Mr. Petrovich and Ms. Holmes discussed her maternity leave, which he assumed would start December 7. A few hours later, Ms. Holmes e-mailed back that she estimated starting her maternity leave around November 15. Mr. Petrovich responded, "I need some honesty. How pregnant were you when you interviewed with me and what happened to six weeks? You have rights for sure and I am not going to do anything to violate any laws, but I feel taken advantage of and deceived for sure."

Ms. Holmes responded by explaining that she disclosed her pregnancy as soon as the tests from her amniocentesis came back that everything was "normal" with the baby. An amnio cannot be performed until the fourth month of pregnancy. Ms. Holmes added, "I am 39 years old, and therefore, there was a chance that there could be something 'wrong' or 'abnormal' with the baby. If there had been, I had decided not to carry the baby to term. That is a very personal choice, and not something that I wanted to have to share with people at work; so in order to avoid that, I waited until I knew that everything was o.k. before telling anyone I was pregnant. I've also had 2 miscarriages at 3 months into my pregnancy, and could not bear having to share that with coworkers again, as I have in the past. I feel that I have the right to make these decisions, and there is no deceipt[sic] or dishonesty involved with this. [t]here is no requirement in a job interview or application to divulge if you are pregnant or not; in fact, I believe it's considered unethical to even inquire as to such."

Mr. Petrovich forwarded the e-mail exchange to other employees who would need to be aware of the staffing and payroll issues.

On Monday morning, August 9, 2004, Holmes sent an e-mail to Petrovich indicating that she was very flexible and that she wanted to "work out the bumps along the way." Mr. Petrovich replied that he was pleased with her work and commitment to the job and concluded, "I want you to stay. It will work."

On August 10, 2004, Ms. Holmes used the company computer to e-mail an attorney, Joanna Mendoza. Ms. Holmes asked for a referral to an attorney specializing in labor law, specifically relating to pregnancy discrimination. Ms. Holmes forwarded a few of Mr. Petrovich's e-mails.

At 4:42 P.M. on the same day, Ms. Mendoza e-mailed Ms. Holmes that she should delete their attorney–client communications from her work computer because her employer might claim a right to access it. After a meeting with Ms. Mendoza, Ms. Holmes e-mailed Mr. Petrovich saying that she had cleared her things from her desk and would not be returning to work.

Ms. Holmes then filed a lawsuit against Mr. Petrovich and his company for sexual harassment, retaliation, wrongful termination in violation of public policy, violation of the right to privacy, and intentional infliction of emotional distress. She alleged that she was constructively terminated. The trial court granted Mr. Petrovich a motion for summary judgment. Ms. Holmes appealed.

JUDICIAL OPINION

SCOTLAND, Judge

Holmes points to the e-mails she exchanged with Petrovich on August 6 and 9, 2004, in which he implied she had deceived him about her pregnancy, stated he was offended that she had changed the period of time she would be absent for maternity leave, and asserted that her pregnancy was an extreme hardship on his business. She also complains that Petrovich unnecessarily forwarded to others her e-mail containing personal information. Holmes asserts that Petrovich did this to humiliate her. Petrovich said he sent the e-mails to in-house counsel and employees involved in human relations because he thought that Holmes was about to quit.

When viewed in context, the e-mails show nothing more than that Petrovich made some critical comments due to the stress of being a small business owner who must accommodate a pregnant woman's right to maternity leave. He recognized Holmes's legal rights, stated he would honor them, said he was not asking for her resignation, noted he had been pleased with her work, and simply expressed his feelings as a "human in a tough business where people are constantly trying to take advantage of me." He assured Holmes that "it will work." Rather than giving him a chance to honor his promise, Holmes quit.

"Constructive discharge occurs only when the employer coerces the employee's resignation, either by creating working conditions that are intolerable under an objective standard, or by failing to remedy objectively intolerable working conditions that actually are known to the employer."

Holmes argues that she was subjected to negative comments and accusations about her pregnancy, followed by Petrovich's retaliatory conduct when she told

CONTINUED

him she planned to exercise her leave rights; he retaliated by forwarding her sensitive personal information to others in the office, who had no reason to know about her prior miscarriages, amniocentesis, and potential termination of her pregnancy.

Here, Petrovich did not reduce Holmes's salary, benefits or work hours, and did not terminate her. He assured Holmes that she still had a job and that they would work things out. Holmes chose to quit because Petrovich expressed his concerns about the changes in her pregnancy leave dates and the need to replace her while she was on leave, and because he forwarded an e-mail that she wished to keep private. But she failed to demonstrate there was a triable issue of fact concerning whether he did these things to retaliate against her; she simply concluded that this was his motivation by taking out of context certain comments that he made. A reasonable person would have talked to Petrovich, expressed dismay at his actions, given him an opportunity to explain or apologize, and waited to see if conditions changed after the air had cleared. Instead, Holmes chose to quit despite Petrovich's assurances that he wanted her to stay and that things would work out.

Holmes's remaining claims of error all arise from an alleged violation of her attorney–client privilege.

[A] "confidential communication between client and lawyer" is "information transmitted between a client and his or her lawyer in the course of that relationship and in confidence by a means which, so far as the client is aware, discloses the information to no third persons other than those who are present to further the interest of the client in the consultation or those to whom disclosure is reasonably necessary for the transmission of the information or the accomplishment of the purpose for which the lawyer is consulted. . . ."

The court ruled that Holmes's e-mails using defendants' company computer were not protected by the attorney–client privilege because they were not private. When Holmes e-mailed her attorney, she did not use her home computer to which some unknown persons involved in the delivery, facilitation, or storage may have access. Had she done so, that would have been a privileged communication unless Holmes allowed others to have access to her e-mails and disclosed their content. Instead, she used defendants' computer, after being expressly advised this was a means that was not private and was accessible by Petrovich, the very person about whom Holmes contacted her lawyer and whom Holmes sued. This is akin to consulting her attorney in one of defendants' conference rooms, in a loud voice, with the door open, yet unreasonably expecting that the conversation overheard by Petrovich would be privileged.

Holmes used her employer's company e-mail account after being warned that it was to be used only for company business, that e-mails were not private, and that the company would randomly and periodically monitor its technology resources to ensure compliance with the policy.

Holmes emphasizes that she believed her personal e-mail would be private because she utilized a private password to use the company computer and she deleted the e-mails after they were sent. However, her belief was unreasonable because she was warned that the company would monitor e-mail to ensure employees were complying with office policy not to use company computers for personal matters, and she was told that she had no expectation of privacy in any messages she sent via the company computer. Likewise, simply because she "held onto a copy of the fax," she had no expectation of privacy in documents she sent to her attorney using the company's facsimile machine, a technology resource that, she was told, would be monitored for compliance with company policy not to use it for personal matters.

It is inaccurate to say only one person had the ability to monitor e-mail sent and received on company computers. The company's controller, who had an administrative password giving her access to all e-mail sent by employees with private passwords, testified that the company's "IT person" as well as company owner Cheryl Petrovich also had such access to e-mail sent and received by company computers. And at no time during her testimony did Holmes claim she knew for a fact that, contrary to its stated policy, the company never actually monitored computer e-mail. She simply said that, to her knowledge, no one did so.

The judgment is affirmed.

Note: The court did allow the case on intentional infliction of emotional distress and breach of privacy to continue with respect to the forwarded e-mail Mr. Petrovich sent to the group of employees.

CASE QUESTIONS

1. Why did the court conclude that there was not an atmosphere of harassment?

2. Why does having a password not mean that your e-mail is private?

3. What can you learn about employer policies on e-mail from this case? What are some best practices employers should follow?

BUSINESS STRATEGY

E-Mails Make Prosecutors' Cases for Them

Perhaps the most difficult to prove of any of the elements of any of the crimes, particularly white-collar crimes, is that of intent. However, e-mails have made that task much easier for prosecutors because we do put what we are doing and thinking in e-mails. For example, former Goldman Sachs' executive Fabrice Tourre tried to have his e-mails excluded as evidence in the SEC's action against him for securities fraud because those e-mails included his bragging to a girlfriend about how he had duped investors into buying debt instruments that were set up to have them lose money. The SEC's case against hedge fund billionaire Steven Cohen is tied to the timing of information received in his e-mails and the quickly following stock sales and purchases that he made based on the information. Likewise, the SEC's case against Edith O'Brien, who was the guardian of funds at now-collapsed MF Global,

is based on her statements in e-mails about her knowledge that the firm was using, illegally, client funds to cover its margins.

As a result of these cases and the strength of e-mails, many companies are providing training for employees on the use of e-mail as a means of communication. Some companies are requiring that e-mails be marked as "privileged and confidential" as a means of avoiding disclosure of e-mail information to prosecutors. E-mails directed at those other than lawyers are generally not confidential, so the best advice for potential white-collar criminals is not to limit your e-mail or guard what you say. Instead, the important strategy lesson is for employees, executives, analysts, and traders, to comply with the law. The cases show that your e-mails are a window into your mindset and a means of proving intent.

10-1d EMPLOYER SCREENING: GOOGLING APPLICANTS AND FOLLOWING EMPLOYEES

Business Planning Tip

If the employer will be doing prehiring monitoring, such as looking at Facebook—and/or Googling the applicant's name—the applicant must be told of this monitoring at the time of the application. The information that we post on publicly available sites is not considered private, so employers, as long as they are maintaining consistent standards for all applicants, can examine what you have posted on the Internet.

Beyond the initial screening process, employers are also using Google and other Internet sources to track employee work excuses. One company's human resources official was on the phone with the company employment lawyer seeking to determine what action could be taken against an employee who was absent frequently but who claimed he was absent to care for his ill grandmother. While they were talking, the lawyer Googled the employee's name and found that he was being arraigned in federal court.[9]

What Employers Should Know and Remember About Social Media Policies:

1. What your employees post on the Internet can hurt you—and it can also result in liability.

2. Let your employees know that you are watching them on the Internet. Put your policies in writing. Train employees on those policies. Explain why the policies are important.

3. Use caution on drawing from the Internet for applicant screening—develop a policy on this issue and follow it.

4. Do monitor the blogs, websites, and other social media to which the public has access in order to detect problems as they evolve.

5. Follow state laws on requesting Facebook access.

6. Enforce your policy often and consistently.

The bottom line is, as always, be careful what you post. It may be personal, but it is not private.

CYBERLAW

© iStockPhoto.com /dra_schwartz

10-1e EMPLOYER MONITORING: WHEN EMPLOYERS WANT TO BE FRIENDED INTO EMPLOYEES' ONLINE ACTIVITY

One of the significant evolving issues is whether employers can require employees to provide access to their Facebook account as part of the hiring process and then as a term and condition of employment. Currently, six states have laws prohibiting employers from requiring employees or applicants to allow access to their social media sites, and six other states have proposed legislation to do the same.[10] In those states in which there are no statutory protections, applicants and employees should know their employers' policies with regard to their personal online activity. Employers must use caution in developing and implementing any policies related to social media.

10-1f EMPLOYER CONTROL OF EMPLOYEE INTERNET ACTIVITY AND LABOR ISSUES

One additional issue in the employer/employee/Internet interaction is how control of employee posts and chats figure into their rights to organize. This labor law issue is covered in Chapter 20.

ETHICAL ISSUES

A 2012 survey revealed that 27 percent of college admissions officers Google candidates and 26 percent use Facebook to gain background information on them. Of those who use these Internet tools, 35 percent indicated that they found negative information about the applicant that resulted in them being declined.[11] In some cases, admissions officers and their staff indicated that they created a Facebook profile with a fake identity in order to be able to follow applicants on the social media site. The kinds of negative information admissions officers uncover includes incidents of bullying, use of alcohol or drugs, or inappropriate types of posting (language and content).

Because of the legal parameters and potential discrimination issues, colleges and universities are now developing policies for the use of Google and Facebook and other Internet tools in admissions processes. Currently, 15 percent of colleges and universities have a policy on admissions use of Internet tools. About 66 percent of colleges and universities indicate that they will not use the tools.

The legal issues surround the right of privacy of the applicants, and the discrimination issue is grounded in the fact that admissions officers cannot always secure online information about applicants. As a result, those who have a high-profile presence might be the victims of unintended discrimination because of a higher standard of screening being applied to them.

The policy of asking for Facebook access would eliminate some of the discrimination risks, but the privacy issue remains. In fact, California passed a law in 2012 that prohibits college admissions offices from asking for asking to applicants' Facebook pages and other social media sites. The applicants could always deny the requests, but, according to those who sponsored the legislation, they feel obligated to allow access so the law was drafted as a prohibition to prevent that obligatory feeling.

Discuss the risks and benefits of college admissions offices and officers having access to applicants' social media information.

© martan/Shutterstock.com

Business Planning Tip

Top Ten Tips for Employer Regulation of Social Media and E-Mail Content:

1. Create policies for e-mail and social media use by employees.

2. Train employees on the policies and post the policies.

3. Be sure all employees have a copy of the policies.

4. Have employees sign off on the policies every year.

5. Help employees understand what can happen as a result of misuse of e-mail and social networking outlets.

6. Enforce your policies.

7. Explain that you cooperate with law enforcement agencies on e-mail and social media content.

8. Update policies as avenues for social media change and expand.

9. Have an electronic retention policy and train employees on retention of e-mails and other postings.

10. Tell employees that you monitor all sites and uses of company computers, phones, and social media accounts.

© Grounder/Shutterstock.com

10-1h EMPLOYEE MISUSE OF COMPUTERS

There are laws at both the state and federal levels that prohibit the unauthorized access of computers and computer files. These types of statutes cover the "hacking" crimes, wherein employers tap into the websites of competitors, or tap into the Outlook calendar of one of their company executives to see what issues are percolating into meetings, discussions, and documents, or they tap into employee personnel files that are private and confidential. Unauthorized computer access is a crime in all states and at the federal level. For example, Matthew Keys was employed at a Sacramento-based television station and he is now charged with several federal crimes for giving a username and password to hackers. The hackers then used that information to gain access to online databases of the station's parent company, which owned a newspaper.

The key to prosecution is the proof that the access was not authorized. The *New Jersey v Riley* case (Case 10.3) deals with an issue of whether an employee could be prosecuted for unauthorized access.

CASE 10.3

New Jersey v Riley
988 A.2d 1252 (N.J. 2009)

Pulling Up Videos for the Goods on Your Fellow Officers

FACTS

Sergeant Kenneth Riley twice viewed digitally stored videotape from his department's computerized system. The tapes he viewed were of the traffic stops of another officer, Sergeant Robert Currier, an officer not in his unit. Sergeant Riley did not like Sergeant Currier and there was animosity between them. Sergeant Riley also permitted police personnel below sergeant's rank to view the video. His motivation for doing so was not to train officers in his own squad, but to cause injury to Sergeant Currier by subjecting him to embarrassment and discipline.

Under the user terms of the department, an administrative officer or sergeant had a password to the video database that could be used to access the whole database. However, the videos were to be used for training purposes. A grand jury returned an indictment against Sergeant Riley for use of computer data

without authorization and unlawful access and disclosure of computer data. Sergeant Riley moved to have the indictment dismissed.

JUDICIAL OPINION

OSTRER, Justice

It is uncertain what it means, first, to access computerized data, and second, what it means to do so "without authorization" or "in excess of authorization." It is also unclear whether unauthorized access may be proved solely with evidence that a defendant, who is an employee or other "insider" with current password-access, knowingly violated internal guidelines regarding *use* of computer-based information.

A hypothetical can demonstrate the uncertainty. One can posit a member of the information technology (I.T.) department of a business who possesses all the employees' passwords in order to maintain the

CONTINUED

© Harper 3D/Shutterstock.com

business's computer system, but internal policy directs him not to read employees' documents. In one sense, the I.T. professional is authorized to access every employee's files. If a worker asks the I.T. professional to help retrieve a sensitive trade-secret-related document that the worker accidentally deleted, the I.T. professional can do so, using the passwords already provided to him. In another sense, if the I.T. professional reads the worker's document, he may be acting in excess of his authorization. Reference to the plain language of the statute does not clearly indicate which reading is correct.

On one hand, the definitions of "authorization" and "access" can be read broadly to expand the statute's reach.

On the other hand, [the law may] be read more narrowly. One may construe "authorization" to refer only to a password, or other code-based restrictions to utilizing a computer. Thus, the I.T. worker posited above did not access the document without, or in excess of authorization. The worker had the password. Thus, he had the "permission, authority or consent" to enter the employee's document files.

Federal law defines the term, "exceeds authorized access," to mean "to access a computer with authorization and to use such access to obtain or alter information in the computer that the accesser is not entitled to so obtain or alter." That also is not unambiguous, as one may ponder what it means to be "not entitled to obtain or alter" data. Arguably, one is entitled if he has a password or code-based right to obtain or alter the data.

In *White v White*, 781 A.2d 85 (Ch. Div. 2001), a wife had retrieved her husband's stored e-mails to a girlfriend from the family computer. The court held that the wife's access was not unauthorized because she did not use her husband's password or code without permission. In other words, unauthorized access meant access by use of another's password or code-based right of entry.

The State's prosecution depends on reading the computer crime act to criminalize what amounts to breach of employment contracts, or even less formal employment policies, governing use of workplace computers by insiders or employees already granted some level of access to them. In effect, according to the State, the criminal law has incorporated by reference those often unclear and informal workplace policies. Actual notice to employees, let alone their explicit acceptance, is often non-existent.

In considering the potential for arbitrary enforcement of the computer crime law, this court recognizes the ubiquity of computers today in the workplace, in schools, public institutions, and in government, and the prevalence of agreements and policies governing such use. Many of these impose unrealistic rules honored in the breach. It takes no imagination to conjure up a multitude of trivial and not so trivial violations that take place every day in the workplace. Workers use workplace computers for personal use in violation of requirements that they use their computers for business only. Workers violate policies prohibiting access to social networking sites. Reportedly, fifty-four percent of companies ban workers from accessing social networking sites like Twitter, MySpace and Facebook, yet seventy-seven percent of workers with a Facebook account use it during work hours.

In sum, assuming that a broad range of the population violates internal workplace computer use policies at one point or another, then deeming such violations a crime would empower the State, unguided by firm definitional standards, to choose to prosecute whomever it wishes from that broad cross-section of the population. The vagueness doctrine is designed to prevent that. In short, the criminal law should not be some pliable material that the State may bend and mold at will to fit an unwarned defendant.

Although there is a split among other jurisdictions, there is ample precedent in federal and state courts for adopting the narrow construction of "without or in excess of authorization" found in the New Jersey law.

The indictment is dismissed.

CASE QUESTIONS

1. Explain why the purpose of Sergeant Riley's actions became an issue.

2. Discuss how the court uses the IT example to illustrate its point.

3. What are the court's fears about a broad interpretation of "unauthorized access"?

10-2 User Issues in Cyberspace

A second series of issues in cyberlaw is the use of information that websites have gleaned from their users.

10-2a USE OF USER INFORMATION

Each time you are online, it is possible that someone is gathering information about you—what you buy, what you are interested in, and even those to

ETHICAL ISSUES

When social media get back at employers:

A teacher posts negative information about her high school students on her Facebook page.

A flight attendant posts provocative pictures of herself in her airline's uniform on her Facebook page.

Medical students post information about their patients on their Facebook pages.

Domino's employees post a video on YouTube that shows them putting mucus on Domino's food as they prepare it.

Discuss the ethical obligations of employees to their employers when they are posting information on their Facebook pages.

Source: From Michelle Conlin, "You Are What You Post," *Business Week,* March 27, 2006, pp. 52–53.

whom you are linked. For example, if you use an airline's website to book your travel arrangements, that website has a profile of your travel habits. The airline knows how frequently you travel and where you travel. Other websites and retailers are willing to pay dearly for that type of targeted customer information because they know their product is being considered by those most likely to purchase it. If you use Amazon.com to buy books, that website has relevant information about the types of books you read, your interests, and even some indications about your income level based on your spending habits. Even your e-mails are scanned by certain service providers for information that can be sold for targeted marketing.

Even though this issue of privacy may seem new and peculiar to cyberspace, it is, in fact, a rather old issue. It has long been a concern of credit card companies, whose use and sale of information about their customers are restricted. Customers must be given the right to refuse such use of their names and other information for sale as part of lists for target marketing. Some state attorneys general are utilizing these credit card privacy rights to enforce privacy rights against website owners who sell information about their users. The Federal Trade Commission (FTC) has begun to take positions on all Internet issues that are identical to its stances on other types of commerce issues. For example, if catalog companies are required to provide notice to customers about delays in shipment of goods to customers, Internet companies must comply with the same notification rules.

10-2b YOUR USERNAME, YOUR IDENTITY, PRIVACY, AND FREEDOM OF SPEECH

Privacy issues arise when there is litigation related to what is posted on the Internet. For example, suppose that you or your company has been defamed by statements made on blogs, websites, or chat rooms. How do you identify who posted the false statements? In the case of law enforcement agencies, the identity of those who seem to be involved in potential criminal activity becomes critical in preventing crimes. Finally, copyright holders also have legal rights when websites infringe on music and movie rights. In these situations, plaintiffs and law enforcement agencies have been able to successfully subpoena **Internet service providers (ISPs)** to obtain the identity of individuals behind the usernames who post statements on the Internet that are defamatory, offer programs that facilitate the downloading of music and movies through their sites, and even allow the sale or sharing of term papers or **proprietary** exam information.

There are now clear standards for determining disclosure of identity that tend to favor disclosure. However, the courts have been very careful to distinguish releasing identity information when there is no illegal activity and what is posted on the Internet or through tweets is simply an expression of opinion. The key to releasing identity of posters is whether the posters were engaged in illegal or harmful activity. There is a difference between posting a nasty opinion and posting false information. Posting false information requires ISPs to disclose identity. Nasty opinions enjoy some First Amendment protection. Access to ISP identity information for illegal or actionable behavior on the Internet is now relatively routine. The *Varrenti v Gannett Co., Inc.* case (Case 10.4) deals with an issue of First Amendment expression rights, defamation, and the rights of ISP users to protection of their identities.

CYBERLAW

© iStockPhoto.com /dra_schwartz

© Harper 3D/Shutterstock.com

CASE 10.4 *Varrenti v Gannett Co., Inc.*
929 N.Y.S.2d 671 (2011)

When the Police Have a Taxcut Nemesis

FACTS

The local police chief and officers (Daniel P. Varrenti, Brian Winant, Adam Mesiti, and Stephen Mesiti) (plaintiffs) filed suit against Gannett Co. (specifically its newspaper the *Democrat & Chronicle*, a newspaper for Brockport, New York) and four John/Jane Does (defendants) who posted allegedly defamatory comments about the officers. The four posters are known online as "Taxcut," "brockportonian," "BkptStar," and "TaxpayerBWare."

The alleged defamatory statements were posted between January 17, 2011, and January 20, 2011, in response to two articles that were posted on the *Democrat & Chronicle's* website, one of which was "Brockport, Sweden and Clarkson Feud Over Fire, Ambulance Services." The following comments were posted by the four on January 17, 2011, and January 18, 2011:

Tom MudGun is Tom MudGun by any other name, and he smells as foul as the venom he dispenses. Now. According to Mr. Varrenti, we had almost 16,000 calls for service in Brockport. We have about 8,000 residents. That's 2 calls per resident. Have you made your call today? Chief V counts as a call for service every time an officer touches a doorknob, every call received for any reason, and I believe every time an officer waves at you. My! Crime has sure soared in Broke-port since Mr. V was hired. Mr. V has a 10 year, million dollar contract

with Broke-port. He has found the pot of gold at the end of the rainbow. Just call him "The Million Dollar Dan"

Regarding the competence of Broke-port's 100K a year cops, consider the following, Broke-port cops don't stop for pedestrians.

Officer Masseti broke into a home thru a basement window (without a warrant) and arrested the residents. The case was thrown out of court, and no discipline given to officer. Why?

Officers beat up a deaf kid because he could not hear their commands. Could that be a liability?

"The Million Dollar Dan" could reign in over time, but he has a sweet heart deal with the cops. They both look the other way and ignore their mutual misdeeds.

We don't need cops who harass and intimidate taxpayers who complain about the high cost, and we don't want them to manipulate elections so they can control the village board.

In response to the second article, "Municipalities Discuss Forming Fire District," "BkptStar," wrote the following comment on January 20, 2011:

Dear Loone,

If BPD is the best in the county, we are all in real trouble. They are sure not the cheapest. Why Varrenti didn't

CONTINUED

discipline the officers that beat up a deaf kid because he could not hear their commands? Why is Varrenti allowing his cops to rake in all the overtime they want?

In addition, "brockportonian" and "TaxpayerBWare," wrote the following series of comments on January 20, 2011, in response to the second article, "Municipalities Discuss Forming Fire District":

Mesiti is the least of the ones there to worry about. Someone should check into the cover ups, yes plural, of trouble the current union president got into. And, I wonder how much money was donated to the campaigns of the three blind mice by Broke-port police officers. THAT would be interesting to find out. It would definitely show allegiance.

Replying to brockportonian: Regarding cover ups and the current union president, Brian Winant, are you referring to marijuana? Evidently the investigation will turn up more than the hours that they actually work. We keep hearing about all the overtime worked. I understand that their time sheets will be available to the public soon. If there are more cover ups regarding the corruption that has been allowed by the chif, million dollar dan, laughing all the way to the bank, I can't wait.

"brockportonian":

No, I am not talking about marijuana; that would be the least of their worries. Maybe the MCSO deputies who had to deal with the problem child would cooperate if forced through an investigation. What a shame, Brockport's good cop gone bad; hiding behind the badge. I feel sorry for the reputation he is giving all the other officers. I am sure they aren't like him. He sure puts on a good show.

The court was asked to order Gannett to provide any identifying information regarding the four anonymous John/Jane Doe defendants so that the suit for defamation could proceed.

JUDICIAL OPINION

BARRY, Judge

It is well settled that the First Amendment protects anonymous speech. However, defamatory speech, whether anonymous or from identifiable sources, is not protected by the First Amendment. What this Court must decide is whether plaintiffs have stated a prima facie cause of action for defamation.

The elements of a cause of action for defamation are "a false statement, published without privilege or authorization to a third party, constituting fault as judged by, at a minimum, a negligence standard, and, it must either cause special harm or constitute defamation per se." As public officials, the plaintiffs here must also prove that the asserted defamatory statements were made "with actual malice—that is, with knowledge that it was false or with reckless disregard of whether it was false or not."

However, "[e]xpressions of opinion, as opposed to assertions of fact, are deemed privileged and, no matter how offensive, cannot be the subject of an action for defamation." Whether a particular statement constitutes an opinion or an objective fact is a question of law for the Court to decide.

"In distinguishing between actionable factual assertions and non-actionable opinions, courts must consider the content of the communication as a whole, as well as its tone and apparent purpose." Instead of "sifting through a communication for the purpose of isolating and identifying assertions of fact, the court should look to the over-all context in which the assertions were made and determine on that basis whether the reasonable reader would have believed that the challenged statements were conveying facts about the libel plaintiff. "

Here, the Court concludes that based on the overall context in which the alleged defamatory statements were made, a reasonable reader would conclude that the statements were the opinions of the anonymous John/Jane Doe defendants. The anonymous comments expressed opinions that the Village of Brockport Police Department was not properly serving the citizens of Brockport. The tone of the comments was sarcastic, hyperbolic, and based on rumors that the anonymous posters heard around the Village of Brockport and about the Department. Moreover, the apparent purpose of the comments made by the John/Jane Doe defendants was to call for an investigation into the Department's practices.

Here, the forum itself is inviting readers to comment on the articles posted on the *Democrat & Chronicle's* website, and the readers are expected to give their opinions in the comments section of the online article. As the Appellate Division observed, the culture of Internet communications, as distinct from print media such as newspapers and magazines, has been characterized as encouraging a "freewheeling, anything-goes writing style."

Given this contextual background, the Court finds that the comments posted by the four John/Jane Doe defendants on the *Democrat & Chronicle's* website constitute expressions of protected opinion, and because opinions cannot form the basis of a defamation claim, defendant Gannett is not required to unmask the

CONTINUED

identities of the four anonymous internet commentators. Therefore, plaintiffs' applications by Order to Show Cause for an order compelling defendant Gannett to provide the names, addresses, and identities and/or any relevant pedigree information for the four John/Jane Doe defendants "Taxcut," "brockportonian," "BkptStar," and "TaxpayerBWare" are hereby denied.

CASE QUESTIONS

1. Why is the context important in determining whether there is defamation?

2. Is Internet communication different from other forms of communication?

3. Why does the court not release the identity of the posters?

Consider...

John Wiley & Sons, Inc. is a publisher that discovered several ISP users (known as Does 1–30) who were sharing downloaded copies of several of Wiley's books, including *The Fat Burning Bible*, *Windows 7 Secrets*, *The Six-Figure Second Income*, *How to Build a Super Vocabulary*, *Presentation Secrets 2011*, and *101 Small Business Ideas for Under $5000*. Wiley sought to stop the users' distribution of the books' content and requested that their ISPs reveal their identity. Does 1–30 responded through their lawyers that they were simply exchanging information over the Internet, a form of free speech that is protected by the First Amendment. Determine whether the court should release the identities of Does 1–30.
[*John Wiley & Sons, Inc. v Does Nos. 1–30*, 284 F.R.D. 185 (S.D.N.Y. 2012)]

THINK: From the text discussion and the *Varrenti v Gannett* case, you learned that the courts do honor the First Amendment right to anonymous speech as long as the speech does not involve any illegal activity. Illegal activity would include planning crimes (such as terrorist attacks) or infringement.

APPLY: In this situation, the Does 1–30 are not just involved in an exchange of ideas and opinions over the Internet. They are exchanging fully downloaded copies of books, something that involves infringement of Wiley's copyrights in the books.

ANSWER: The court held that while there is a protectable interest in anonymous speech over the Internet, that speech did not include the carte blanche reproduction of the copyrighted works of others. The Does 1–30 could quote from the books, discuss the books, and recommend the books, but the First Amendment did not entitle them to the downloading of the books. The court granted the motion to have the ISP disclose the identities of Does 1–30.

10-2c THE CLOUD AND PRIVACY

Cloud computing is another technological development that has resulted in complex legal issues. With cloud computing (such as Google Docs, Carbonite, and others), the information these cloud computing companies have in their clouds from various customers, who are generally paying for cloud back-up and storage services and space, could be intermingled with other users' information. In addition, the information in the clouds is completely within the hands of a third party. Trust, service levels, and technological flaws are all issues in these relationships.

One of the benefits of cloud computing is that companies have instantaneous access to computer processing services for a fee, something that does not require substantial capital expense and allows for rapid growth. However, legal rights, in terms of ready customer access to information in the cloud, privacy rights with respect to the cloud companies' use and examination of the information, and glitches in information retrieval remain unresolved.

10-2d COOKIES AND PRIVACY

Technology has permitted companies to plant "cookies" on the computers of those who are using certain Internet sites. With those "cookies" in place, the website owner has a way to track the computer owner's activity. At least one court has held that a website operator's placing cookies on a user's computer is a violation of an unauthorized access statute that would provide the computer owner a right of action for that breach of the statute and privacy.

CYBERLAW
© iStockPhoto.com /dra_schwartz

10-2e CYBERBULLYING, CYBERSTALKING, AND PRIVACY

In 2008, a federal jury convicted Lori Drew, a 49-year-old Missouri mother of three, on misdemeanor charges of computer fraud for her actions in creating a phony MySpace account in order to trick 13-year-old Megan Meier into believing she had a secret admirer, Josh. Megan was apparently Ms. Drew's daughter's archrival and Ms. Drew plotted revenge via the MySpace medium.[12] Megan committed suicide following Josh's posting of a rejection and devastating personal comments at the site, such as "The world would be a better place without you." While the prosecutors used the Computer Fraud and Abuse Act (CFAA) (see the next section for a discussion) as the basis for the charges against Ms. Drew, there was not a good fit. As a result, many states now have anti-cyberbullying criminal statutes that define the crime in detail and provide specific penalties. The statutes are basically anti-harassment statutes that prohibit harassment involving the medium of computer communication.

Cyberbullying also raises First Amendment questions as courts balance the rights of students, for example, to public expression over the Internet, and the need for protection of the students, teachers, and administrators who are the targets of the cyberexpressions of the students. Some federal courts have ruled that schools cannot infringe on the rights of students to express themselves online during off hours when they are not using school property or servers. Other cases have held that the schools could discipline the students if the result is a "substantial disruption" of the educational environment. For example, in *Wisniewski v Bd. of Educ.*, 494 F.3d 34 (2nd Cir. 2007), the court held that administrators could expel a student who created an instant messaging icon that depicted a pistol firing, blood spatter, and the words, "Kill Mr. VanderMolen" (the student's English teacher) without creating a First Amendment problem.

One of the newer forms of statutory controls regarding some types of harassment are **anti-cyberstalking laws**. These laws impose criminal sanctions on those who send threatening e-mails to others. For example, in *People v Suic*, 928 N.E.2d 1231 (Ill. App. 2010), the court upheld the conviction of Zlatan Sucic for cyberstalking under Illinois's statute that defines the crime as follows:

(a) A person commits cyberstalking when he or she, knowingly and without lawful justification, on at least 2 separate occasions, harasses another person through the use of electronic communication and:

1. at any time transmits a threat of immediate or future bodily harm, sexual assault, confinement, or restraint and the threat is directed towards that person or a family member of that person, or

2. places that person or a family member of that person in reasonable apprehension of immediate or future bodily harm, sexual assault, confinement, or restraint

In his e-mails to Heather Stern, Mr. Sucic threatened suicide, threatened to take her life, and followed through on threats to try and enter her apartment. The court found that the statute was sufficiently specific to define the crime and that Mr. Sucic's e-mails met the standard of threats outlined in the statute.

There is also a federal anti-cyberstalking law, 18 U.S.C. §§ 2261A (1)-(2), 876(c), which parallels the Illinois law and has been upheld as constitutional. [*U.S. v Walker*, 665 F.3d 212 (1st Cir. 2011)] The distinction is that the cyberstalking must be conducted against a person in another state or territory. The federal government leaves the crime of cyberstalking within states to be handled by local authorities.

10-2f STATUTORY PROTECTIONS FOR PRIVACY IN CYBERSPACE

Several federal laws and some state laws provide privacy protections, although somewhat limited, for Internet users. The **Privacy Act of 1974** controls the use of information gathered about consumers, but it applies only to government-collected information. There have been significant questions about the information that has been gathered by the Social Security Administration, the National Security Administration (NSA), and the Internal Revenue Service, such as whether the types of information gathered were within statutory authority and whether its use by the agency, in terms of sharing or for political purposes, has been proper. For example, there was a national debate in the summer of 2013 as well as several congressional hearings on whether the NSA had exceeded its authority in tracking the phone calls of citizens. The agencies are permitted to use the information for "routine use." But the definition of routine use is a matter of interpretation as well as vigilance by the public in determining the extent of monitoring being done. It is difficult for individuals to discover when and how their information is being used, transferred, or whether they are being targeted. For example, the IRS is facing a class-action suit for its alleged release of PDF documents that contained taxpayer information about individuals who donated to political groups formed for the purpose of opposing or supporting ballot initiatives.

There are some statutory prohibitions on the use of information, but they are limited in scope. For example, some segments of the **Computer Fraud and Abuse Act (CFAA)** and the ECPA provide privacy protection for certain types of communications, such as financial information and its use and transfer. The **Children's Online Privacy Protection Act (COPPA)** targets online informational privacy but applies only to websites that collect information from children.

Numerous state laws on privacy exist; the problem comes in enforcing those laws against website sponsors who have no presence in the state. (See the discussion of long-arm jurisdiction in Chapter 4.)

CYBERLAW

10-2g WHAT IF THE INFORMATION POSTED IS TRUE BUT DANGEROUS OR ILLEGAL?

Another issue that arises frequently with information on the Internet is whether the site where the information appears is liable for injuries and damages that result from the information or connections that are made. For example, YouTube had many videos placed on its site that were subject to copyright protections. However, YouTube was not posting the videos; its users were, and those at YouTube would not be aware that there was infringement. Likewise, Craigslist might not be aware that the ads on its site are for illegal activity or placed by individuals trying to lure minors into dangerous activities. Using a standard that applied to newspaper publications in the 1980s, site owners and operators are not generally liable for infringement, injury to users, and other postings that cause damage unless and until they become or are made aware of the problem. The reasoning behind this legal standard for liability is that it would be impossible for sites to exist if every posting had to be screened by the owner/operator. However, if, for example, Universal Studios notifies YouTube that an infringing post is on its site, then YouTube must take action to remove the clip or movie that has been posted.

Craigslist, referred to as the world's largest classified advertising, came into the public spotlight after medical school student Philip H. Markoff was charged with the murder of a young woman he contacted and met through classifieds placed on Craigslist. Craigslist was not held responsible for the murder because the parties involved were connected through Craigslist personal ads. Unless Craigslist was aware of the danger of the personal ads or individuals posting them, then the company is not responsible for resulting criminal and/or harmful activity. However, in response to a series of criminal issues connected to postings on the site and the negative publicity and investigation, Craigslist removed erotic ads and shifted them to a new category called "Adult Services," where Craigslist employees do screen for suspicious posts.

Consider...

Match.com matched Nevada real estate agent Mary Kay Beckman with Wade Ridley in September 2010. After knowing him online for only eight days, she broke off their relationship. However, in January 2011, Mr. Ridley, angry that Ms. Beckman would not agree to meet in person, hid in her garage armed with a knife. When she entered the garage, he stabbed and beat her so severely that she was hospitalized and placed on a ventilator. In February 2011, Mr. Ridley was arrested in Phoenix in connection with the stabbing death of Anne Simenson, who was killed in a manner similar to the lying-in-wait attack Mr. Ridley had committed against Ms. Beckman. Mr. Ridley entered a no-contest plea to criminal charges and was sentenced to 70 years in prison. He committed suicide there in 2012. Ms. Beckman has filed a suit in federal district court seeking $10 million in damages from Match.com, a dating website owned by IAC/InterActive Corp. The suit alleges that Match.com failed to warn Ms. Beckman about the dangers of online dating. Her lawyer refers to online dating services as "absolutely not safe." The suit also alleges that the service, through its site language and advertising, leads users to believe that the service is safe. Is there liability for match.com?

10-3 Appropriation and Other Forms of Unfair Competition in Cypberspace

Competition on the Internet is intense. Competitors have many opportunities for expanding their customer bases. However, they still must expand their businesses within the legal standards that apply to competition, regardless of where that competition occurs.

10-3a APPROPRIATION ONLINE

The tort of appropriation involves taking an image, likeness, or name for purposes of commercial advantage. A business cannot use someone's name or likeness for advertising or endorsement without permission. The use of that name or image in cyberspace does not change the nature of the protection that this form of the privacy tort provides. For example, the use of Tiger Woods's name or picture on the website of a yacht company, without his permission, is appropriation, even if Mr. Woods owns one of the company's yachts. A screen saver program that uses a likeness of Richard, the million-dollar winner on the CBS television program *Survivor*, without his permission violated his privacy rights. The use of his likeness for the Conniver screen saver program with the *Survivor* logo was appropriation.

10-3b UNFAIR METHODS OF COMPETITION IN CYBERSPACE

Concealed identity bloggers can wreak havoc on competitors. For example, John Mackey, the CEO of Whole Foods, using the name Rahodeb (his wife's name, Deborah, jumbled), posted over 1,000 messages in chat rooms that were dedicated to stock trading. During the period that Mr. Mackey was posting messages, Whole Foods stock quadrupled in value. The messages were flattering to Whole Foods and negative about Wild Oats, a competitor. On February 24, 2005, Mackey posted the following comment about Wild Oats CEO Perry Odak: "Perhaps the OATS Board will wake up and dump Odak and bring in a visionary and highly competent CEO [like Mackey]." Referred to as "sock-puppeting," this common practice also raises ethical issues.

Using Computers to Commit Economic Espionage
The **Economic Espionage Act (EEA)** is a federal law [18 U.S.C. §§ 1831–1839] passed in response to several cases in which high-level executives were taking downloaded proprietary information from their computers to their new employers. In one case, an executive was accused of taking General Motors' full plan for supply chain management in Europe. The EEA makes it a felony to steal, appropriate, or take a trade secret and also makes it a felony to copy, duplicate, sketch, draw, photograph, download, upload, alter, destroy, replicate, transmit, deliver, send, mail, or communicate a trade secret. The penalties for EEA violations are up to $500,000 and 15 years in prison for individuals and $10 million for organizations. When employees take new positions with another company, their former employers are permitted to check the departing employees' computer e-mails and hard drives to determine whether the employees have engaged in computer espionage.

Using Computers to Circumvent Copyright Protection Devices
The **Digital Millennium Copyright Act (DMCA)** makes it a federal offense to circumvent or create programs to circumvent encryption devices that copyright holders place on copyrighted material to prevent unauthorized copying. For example,

CYBERLAW

© iStockPhoto.com /dra_schwartz

circumventing the encryption devices on software or CDs would be a violation of the DMCA. Dmitry Sklyarov, a Russian computer programmer, became the first person charged with a violation of DMCA. Mr. Sklyarov was arrested in early 2002 at a computer show after giving a speech on the product he developed that permits the circumvention of security devices on copyrighted materials. Specifically, his program unlocked password-protected e-books and PDF files. He gave his speech in Las Vegas at the Defcon convention, a convention billed as "the largest hacker convention on the planet." He was returned to Russia in exchange for his agreement to testify in a case that will determine the constitutionality of the DMCA. The issues tried in the case included the determination that the development and use of devices and programs to circumvent encryption devices was prohibited under DMCA and could result in criminal liability for those who develop and/or distribute the programs. [*U.S. v Elcom Ltd.*, 203 F. Supp. 2d 1111 (N.D. Cal. 2002)]

In addition, the **No Electronic Theft Act** was passed at the end of 1997, making it a federal criminal offense to willfully infringe copyrighted material worth more than $1,000 using the Internet or other electronic devices even when the infringer does not profit from the use of the material. For example, many Internet users clip articles from subscriber services on the Internet and then send them along via e-mail to nonsubscriber friends. Even though no transaction for profit occurs, the transfer of such copyrighted material still violates this federal law.

Using Computer Access for Unauthorized Advertising: Spamming

Spamming, or the practice of sending out thousands of e-mails at once to many different computer users, is an ever-increasing problem. The issues involved include First Amendment rights, privacy, and theft of property. Congress passed the **Controlling the Assault of Non-Solicited Pornography and Marketing (CAN-SPAM) Act**, which allows private companies to bring suit against spammers for their unauthorized use of ISPs. Microsoft was one of the first companies to use CAN-SPAM when it filed suit against eight spammers under CAN-SPAM in January 2004.

An industry group called the Anti-Spam Technical Alliance has been formed and has endorsed several e-mail authentication technologies. Under CAN-SPAM, the FTC is also authorized to bring suit against spammers. Some states have made it a misdemeanor to send out e-mails with a misleading title line; Virginia was the first state to make spamming a criminal act. Under the Virginia statute, spamming becomes a felony when the volume of spam e-mails sent exceeds 10,000 in 24 hours, 100,000 in 30 days, or 1 million in one year.

10-4 Contract Issues in Cyberspace

10-4a FORMATION OF CONTRACTS IN CYBERSPACE

Formation of a contract in cyberspace is simply the result of the desire for speed and better communication in business. If you wanted to form a contract with a New York seller 20 years ago and you were in Los Angeles, you drafted a proposal and mailed it to the seller. The back-and-forth negotiations took time through the mail. Then overnight delivery service arrived to speed up cross-country negotiations. Next came faxes and their instantaneous exchanges of terms and negotiations. The amount of paperwork involved in transactions was still unchanged. Paperless contracts were born with the availability of electronic digital interchange (EDI). EDI is simply the electronic exchange of business forms. Contracts are formed using purchase orders and invoices submitted via computer.

FOR THE MANAGER'S DESK

Re: SPAM and International Computing

Distributed denial of service, also known as DDoS, sends dummy traffic to certain web servers resulting in a struggle for those who are legitimately trying to access the site. Experts compare it to being stuck in a traffic jam when no one can move or the movement is very slow—one car at a time because movement is in inches, not feet.

In March 2013, security experts said we experienced what was "the biggest cyberattack in history." At the root of it was a fight over spam. Spamhaus, a Dutch company that fights spam, added Cyberbunker to its so-called blacklist. Spamhaus's blacklist consists of companies e-mail providers use as a screen to weed out spam. Cyberbunker is a web-hosting service that, by its own description, will host any site except "child porn and anything related to terrorism." As an aside, Cyberbunker got its name from its building—it occupies a former NATO bunker. Cyberbunker wants to spam and Spamhaus wants to protect e-mail servers from spam, so there is a war in cyberspace.

The DDoS began on March 19, 2013, and employed botnets that spray a site with activity. In this round, a Silicon Valley security firm has found that the data stream being used for DDoS has grown to 300 billion bits per minute. Spamhaus has experienced the brunt of the attacks and Cyberbunker explained its reasons for the online sabotage, "Nobody ever deputized Spamhaus to determine what goes and does not go on the Internet."[13]

The attacks illustrate the vulnerability of the Internet's basic structure of the Domain Name System (DNS). The domain name, such as Facebook.com, is similar to a listing in a telephone book. The Internet translates the name into numbers and then sends the traffic to the domain. However, with the release of the botnets, the Cyberbunker folks have been able to inundate the servers that direct the Internet traffic with data that overloads the system. The problem cannot be fixed by any repair to the Internet because the problem is the basic structure of the Internet. The only fix is to find who is doing the bombarding and arrest them. The difficulty is tracking down who is doing it, determining where they are, and finding a legal basis for arresting them for this international activity. Cyberbunker sources say Dutch authorities have tried to storm the bunker but have been unsuccessful.

This combination of cyberlaw with international law makes for a legal no-man's land in an area of commerce that cannot afford a slowdown. The solution may be negotiations on how to handle spam.

With the Internet, e-mail, and the ability to attach documents, cyberspace has provided business yet another method for forming contracts. While the method is different, the rules for formation have not changed. The same laws that apply when contracts are formed in a business office govern the formation of contracts in cyberspace: there must be offer and acceptance.

Some issues that arise in contract formation in the new economy are, for example, whether a contract is formed when someone downloads a program from the Internet. The person may have paid for the program by credit card and simply downloaded it on the computer. Acceptance occurs when the click occurs—a contract is formed. (See Chapters 12–13 for more information on contracts in cyberspace.) The **Electronic Signatures in Global and National Commerce Act** (called E-sign) is a federal law that recognizes digital signatures as authentic for purposes of contract formation. Even though E-sign recognizes the validity of electronic signatures, state laws regulate the authenticity and security of signatures. The **Uniform Electronic Transactions Act (UETA) and the Uniform Computer Information Transaction Act (UCITA)** are two model laws drafted to allow states to adopt a uniform position. UETA is a uniform law that 46 states plus the District of Columbia have adopted. Two states have adopted UCITA.

10-4b MISREPRESENTATION AND FRAUD IN CYBERSPACE

The types of misrepresentation and fraud on the Internet range from promises of delivery not fulfilled to promises of performance not met. The majority of the fraud complaints received by the FBI relate to Internet auctions. These issues are not new legal issues; only the form of misrepresentation or fraud has changed. For example, seven retailers signed a consent decree with the FTC, which required them to pay fines totaling $1.5 million to settle a complaint against them for late delivery of Christmas merchandise ordered over the Web. The consent decree that the retailers signed was based on the FTC mail-and-telephone rule requiring retailers to let customers know when they do not have a product or that there will be a delay in the shipment. The existing notification rule was simply applied to Internet transactions.

In marketing search engines, some companies have misrepresented the capabilities of their products or have failed to disclose the methods they use to give preference to certain links and their order of listing when the search engine is used. The remedy for such misrepresentations and fraud on the Internet is the same as the remedy in situations with paper contracts. Misrepresentation and fraud are defenses to formation and entitle the party who was misled or defrauded to rescind the agreement and/or collect money damages.

In addition to contract remedies available for misrepresenting the nature of the search engine products and capabilities, a small group of search engine companies have proposed a code of ethics for search engine firms.

10-4c CONTRACTS AND TAX ISSUES ON CONTRACTS IN CYBERSPACE

The U.S. Constitution requires that there be some "nexus" between the taxing authority and the business paying the tax (see Chapter 4 for more information on constitutional issues in taxation), and many questions arise about the constitutionality of taxing Internet sales because of the lack of "bricks and mortar" in these businesses. Some Internet retailers are located in one state and have no contact, physically, with any other states. Their only contact is through the computers of their customers, who may be located in all 50 states. Is it constitutional for Colorado to tax a New Jersey company operating out of a small office in Trenton? Courts will simply apply the standards of fairness and allocation that they have relied on in other eras as businesses grew in reach even though their physical locations did not change.

The Internet Tax Freedom Act (ITFA) has been renewed. The ITFA provides that states and local governments cannot tax Internet access. Contrary to popular belief, ITFA does not suspend sales taxes on transactions over the Internet. To tax Internet sales, the seller must have some physical presence in the state or a pattern of distribution doing business there. For example, Nordstrom might not have stores located in a particular state, but it would be required to collect sales tax from sales to residents of that state if it had warehouse facilities in that state. (Refer to Chapter 5 for a full discussion of the Internet and sales tax.) Online retailers have been negotiating tax rates and procedures with states. However, several states have passed laws that require those who purchase merchandise over the Internet to declare the amount of goods they purchased and then pay sales tax on those goods on their state income tax returns.

BIOGRAPHY

Kim Dotcom, a Man without a Country When It Comes to Criminal Charges

Kim Dotcom, aka Kim Schwarz, is the founder and owner of Megaupload, which is based in Hong Kong and is a very successful file-sharing site with millions of songs, movies, and other copyrighted materials. He has been charged by U.S. authorities with several felony violations for racketeering and money laundering related to the operation of Megaupload. However, Megaupload has no U.S. address and has a home (a compound, really) in New Zealand where he is under house arrest as New Zealand authorities work to cooperate with U.S. authorities. However, New Zealand authorities have refused to recognize the basis for U.S. search warrants and, as a result, they have been unable to gather evidence in the case. Kim's lawyers are challenging U.S. jurisdiction to prosecute because Megaupload is an Internet company with no physical presence in the United States.

Apple's Steve Wozniak believes that prosecution of Kim will have a chilling effect on the development of the Internet. The prosecutor in the case, however, notes that, "This case isn't about Internet freedom. It's about a career criminal and his associates profiting by stealing the hard work of people who make creative works that audiences love."

Source: William M. Welch, "Prosecutors: Megaupload Case Takes Bizarre Turn," *USA Today,* July 30, 2012, p. 5B.

Summary

What are the areas of focus in cyberlaw?

- Rights of employers and employees in the workplace cyberspace including information on websites, e-mails, Twitter, and Facebook.

- Rights and responsibilities of users of the Internet, such as when and if their anonymous identity online can be revealed by those who provide Internet services. The courts balance the right of free expression under the First Amendment with issues of illegal activity. The courts also balance the free and open commerce nature of the Internet with the right of users' privacy and potential invasions of that privacy through the use of data and tracking mechanisms.

- Appropriation and competition issues in cyberspace; the use of trademarks and trade names on the Internet as well as the ongoing issues related to copyright infringement of music, movies, and television shows.

- Contract issues; the issues of formation, misrepresentation, and how contracts are formed online; the responsibilities of online retailers to prevent fraud and collect sales taxes for residents of states in which they may not have any physical presence.

What should employees know about their rights in cyberspace?

- Employers have the right to monitor their e-mails, text messages, and other communications sent electronically using company equipment and servers.

- The issue of employers requiring employees and applicants to provide access to their private Facebook and other accounts is an area of change in the law, with states moving to introduce legislation to make it illegal for employers to request such access as a precondition or condition of employment.

- "You have no privacy on the Internet," especially at work.

What should employers know about monitoring employee cyberspace activity?

- Have a policy in place.

- Make full disclosures about that policy and require that employees sign off on their awareness of the policy.

- Use caution in posting or forwarding employee e-mails that have been monitored or were sent to an individual only.

What are users' rights to privacy in cyberspace?

- Your identity is protected for purposes of your First Amendment rights.

- Your ISP can be required to reveal your identity from your online username if you are engaged in illegal activity, such as in copyright infringement or terrorism threats.

- The use of the cloud for storage carries cheaper costs in terms of capital investment, but there are risks with access and third-party knowledge and use of cloud information.

- Statutes do provide protections to stop cyberbullying and cyberstalking through injunctions and also make such activities crimes so that individuals can be punished with a statute that applies directly to this form of cyberspace activity.

How are intellectual property rights and competition protected on the Internet?

- The unauthorized use of copyrighted and trademarked materials on the Internet can be stopped through injunctions and owners can collect damages for such unauthorized use. Infringement requires owners to constantly review materials on the Internet to check for infringement.

- The tort of appropriation also applies to unauthorized use on the Internet of proprietary information, symbols, and other forms of intellectual property.

- Unfair competition on the Internet would include the posting of false information about a competing business or posting fake product reviews not really written by real users of a product or service. Because identities are concealed on the Internet, it is difficult to question product and service endorsers directly. Commercial speech requires accuracy in order to increase competition.

What should businesspeople know about contract formation in cyberspace?

- Make sure there is an electronic record and preserve it so that the terms and formation are clear.

- Know your rights on misrepresentation and fraud on the Internet.

Questions and Problems

1. Discuss whether employees would have the right of privacy in the following e-mail situations:
   a. E-mail sent in a company in which there is no warning given about the lack of privacy in emails [*Smyth v Pillsbury*, 914 F. Supp. 97 (E.D. Pa. 1996)]
   b. An e-mail sent to coworkers from home using the employee's AOL account
   c. An e-mail sent from a laptop while the employee is traveling for the company
   d. An e-mail sent to a coworker over a company Internet system in a company in which the employer has promised privacy in e-mail [*Commonwealth v Proetto*, 771 A.2d 823 (Pa. Super. Ct.2001)]
   e. Employer monitoring the e-mails of any employee when those e-mails were stored in a file folder marked "Personal" [*Mclaren v Microsoft Corp.*, 1999 WL 339015 (Tex. App.)]

2. Hard Drive Productions discovered that there were 1,495 unidentified users of a peer-to-peer file-sharing protocol called BitTorrent, which was used by all of them to download and distribute Hard Drive's copyrighted motion picture, "Amateur Alleur—Maelynn," which was an infringement. Hard Drive brought suit seeking to have the ISPs for the Does disclose their identities. Through their lawyers, the Does argued that they were just sharing information and having discussions about pornography over the Internet, part of their First Amendment rights, something that entitled them to privacy. Who is correct and why? Should the ISPs disclose the identity of their users? [*Hard Drive Productions, Inc. v Does 1-1,495*, 892 F. Supp. 2d 33 (D.D.C. 2012)]

3. Colleges and universities continue to work to help students understand that what they post on the Web is not private information and can often have unintended consequences. The following examples resulted in student disciplinary proceedings:

Several students at Ohio State University boasted on Facebook (a networking/socializing site) that they had stormed the field after Ohio State beat Penn State and had taken part in what erupted into a riot. Law enforcement officials were able to trace the students through the university system, and 50 Ohio State students were referred to the office of judicial affairs.

Students at the University of Mississippi stated on an open site that they wanted to have sex with a professor. A student at Fisher College threatened to take steps to silence a campus police officer. Another problem with the open sites is that the students are posting personal information with which stalkers and others can access them. These nefarious individuals can then easily obtain students' cell phone numbers, addresses, whereabouts, and other information.

The most popular college site, Facebook, indicates that students spend an average of 17 minutes per day on the site. A great deal of information can be conveyed during that time period. Students often do so without thinking through the possibility that outsiders with bad intentions could be seeking and using information about them that is posted.

What legal and ethical issues do you see in the types of comments that students make on these sites and in the sites themselves? Why and how can the colleges and universities obtain information from these sites without a warrant?

4. Glenayre Electronics announced to its employees that it could inspect the laptops it furnished for its employees to use. An employee challenged the inspection of his laptop as a violation of his privacy. Could the company search the laptops? [*Muick v Glenayre Electronics*, 280 F.3d 741 (7th Cir. 2002)]

5. The administrators at a high school expelled a student for creating a website that requested assistance for hiring a hitman to kill a high school teacher. The student created the website on his home computer. What cyberlaw issues are involved here? Can the school legally expel the student? Does it matter that the threat was unlikely to come to pass—that is, a hitman was not likely to be hired? Be sure to refer to the chapter discussion on cyberbullying. [*J.S. ex re. H.S. v Bethlehem Area Sch. Dist*, 807 A.2d 847 (Pa. 2002)]

6. Jane Doe filed a complaint against Richard Lee Russell and America Online (AOL) to recover for alleged emotional injuries suffered by her son, John Doe. Doe claimed that in 1994, Russell lured then–11-year-old John Doe and two other minor males to engage in sexual activity with each other and with Russell. She asserted that Russell photographed and videotaped these acts and used AOL's chat rooms to market the photographs and videotapes and to sell a videotape. In her six-count complaint, Doe claimed that AOL violated criminal statutes and that AOL was negligent *per se* in distributing an advertisement offering "a visual depiction of sexual conduct involving [John Doe]" and by allowing Russell to sell or arrange to sell child pornography, thus aiding in the sale and distribution of child pornography, including obscene images of John Doe. Does Mrs. Doe have a cause of action? What laws discussed in this chapter apply? [*Doe v America Online, Inc.*, 783 So.2d 1010 (Fla. 2001)]

7. In February 2003, while serving as a civilian contractor, Michael D. King resided in a dormitory at the Prince Sultan Air Base in Saudi Arabia. During his stay in the dormitory, King kept his personal laptop computer in his room and connected it to the base network. All users of the base network signed agreements indicating that they understood their communications over and use of the base network were subject to monitoring.

An enlisted airman was searching the base network for music files when he came across King's computer on the network. The airman was able to access King's hard drive because it was a "shared" drive. The airman discovered a pornographic movie and text files "of a pornographic nature." The airman reported his discovery to a military investigator who in turn referred the matter to a computer specialist. This specialist located King's computer and hard drive on the base network and verified the presence of pornographic videos and explicit text files on the computer. She also discovered a folder on the hard drive labeled "pedophilia."

Military officials seized King's computer and also found CDs containing child pornography. Two years later, the government obtained an indictment charging King with possession of child pornography. After his arrest, the government searched his residence pursuant to a search warrant and found additional CDs and hard drives containing over 30,000 images of child pornography.

King entered a guilty plea and was sentenced to 108 months in prison. King then appealed his conviction on the grounds that there had been an illegal search and seizure of his computer and files. Explain whether there was a Fourth Amendment violation. [*U.S. v King*, 509 F.3d 1338 (11th Cir. 2007)]

8. Jessica Cutler, a staff member for Senator Mike DeWine, began a blog that detailed her sexual encounters with various government officials in Washington, DC. Ms. Cutler did not identify anyone by name in her blog, but the level of detail in her posts had most of Washington figuring out who was who in the Cutler blog. Ms. Cutler was fired for "misusing an office computer." What ethical issues exist in Ms. Cutler's public revelations? Was it legal for the senator to terminate her employment? What advice could you offer employers that is relevant to this experience? If her partners are not identified by name, can defamation still be proved? (April Witt, "Blog Interrupted," *Washington Post*, April 15, 2004, p. W12.)

9. If a coworker gave you access to her computer by giving you her password, would you be entitled to look at anything on her computer? Could you continue to log onto her computer to gather information? Discuss whether such a delegation allows the employee authorized access that would preclude prosecution for unauthorized access.

10. The late Aaron Swartz broke into a computer wiring closet at MIT and connected a computer to MIT's computer system. The result was that he was able to give free access to JSTOR, a service that provides, for a subscription price, access to millions of academic journals. The free access used by the students via the Swartz connection cost JSTOR $1,000,000. Mr. Swartz did not charge for the computer access and he did not profit from what he did. He simply believed that all knowledge should be free. He was charged with several federal crimes. Can you determine which crimes would apply to his conduct?

STRATEGY THE LAW

Not Stopping Technology; Working with It

When the first form of consumer videotaping became available (the Sony Betamax), the movie and television industries attempted to obtain injunctions, court decisions on infringement, and damages. [*Sony Corporation of America v Universal City Studios, Inc.*, 464 U.S. 417 (1984)] However, the companies were bucking a juggernaut of technology that was working to find easier ways for consumers to watch movies and television. Instead of using the legal strategies to halt the development, a better strategy would have been to embrace the technology and change marketing styles and product deliveries in order to be a first mover in what would continue to be a growing market for consumer access to films and television shows. [*Metro-Goldwyn Mayer Studios, Inc. v Grokster, Ltd.*, 545 U.S. 913 (2005)] Because the courts would not enjoin Sony's videotaping product or require that it pay royalties, the market grew from Blockbuster rentals all the way to Netflix Internet products for both movies and television.

Likewise, the music industry succeeded for a time in shutting down file-sharing sites. Napster was forced to shut down [*A & M Records, Inc. v Napster, Inc.*, 239 F.3d 1004 (9th Cir. 2001)], but the technology kept improving and the consumer demand for music, on an immediate and song-by-song basis, resulted in the Apple phenomenon of iTunes, a site that allows the downloading of music by consumer choice in exchange for royalties paid to Apple and then to the artists and record producers. While hardcopy CD sales dropped, the availability of music on the Internet increased and the royalties continued to be paid, just through a different mechanism. Record producers and artists were trying to stop technology. A strategic move was to work with the technology to provide consumers new products that met their changing demands.

The law often does take time to catch up with issues technology brings. However, relying on the law alone is a strategic risk. Law always provides remedies for legal wrongs. However, strategy requires leaders to ask a different question, "What is the consumer need that is causing the legal problem?" Understanding that need can result in a problem solved through use of technology and not through attempts to halt it permanently. Managers need to study the litigation in the context of these two product and industry changes, the end result of which was to bring more earnings to all of the companies involved.

Notes

1. A survey found that 72 percent of businesses use social media for marketing purposes. Robert Ball, "Social Media Marketing: What's the Payoff for Your Business," *Huffington Post*, February 24, 2011, http://www.huffingtonpost.com.

2. In 2009, Facebook had over one billion users and accounted for 72 percent of online social networking, including MySpace, Twitter, and LinkedIn. Nicholas Carlson, "Chart of the Day: How Many Users Does Twitter Really Have?" *Business Insider*, March 31, 2011, http://www.businessinsider.com.

3. See *Garrity v John Hancock Mut. Life Ins. Co.*, 2002 WL 974676 (D. Mass. 2002) (memorandum opinion), in which an employer's termination of an employee for sending an e-mail entitled, "The Top Ten Reasons Cookie Dough Is Better Than Men" was upheld on grounds that such content created an atmosphere of harassment. An employer was held liable for its failure to take action against an employee who used a company computer to post nude photographs of his daughter. [*Doe v XYC Corp.*, 887 A.2d 1156 (N.J. Super.Ct. 2005)]

4. Summary Report of Issues Identified in the Commission's Examination of Select Credit Rating Agencies, July 8, 2008.

5. Freeh Sporkin Sullivan, LLP, Report of the Special Investigative Counsel Regarding the Actions of the Pennsylvania State University Related to the Child Sexual Abuse Committed by Gerald A. Sandusky (2012), at p. 4.

6. "Every circuit court to have considered the matter has held that an 'intercept' under the ECPA must occur contemporaneously with transmission." [*Fraser v Nationwide Mut. Ins. Co.*, 352 F.3d 107, 113 (3rd Cir. 2003)]

7. A. Michael Froomkin, "The Death of Privacy," 52 *Stanford Law Review*, 1461, 1462 (2000). Presented at the Cyberspace and Privacy: A New Legal Paradigm? Symposium, Stanford, CA, 2000.

8. *Scott v Beth Israel Med. Ctr.*, 847 N.Y.S.2d 436 (2007).

9. For detailed information on this issue, see Patricia Sanchez Abril, Avner Levin, and Alissa Del Riego, "Blurred Boundaries: Social Media Privacy and the Twenty-First-Century Employee," 49 *American Business Law Journal* 63 (2012).

10. California, Delaware, Illinois, Maryland, Michigan, and New Jersey have laws on employer access. Massachusetts, Minnesota, Missouri, New York, Ohio, Pennsylvania, South Carolina, and Washington have legislation pending.

11. Douglas Belkin and Caroline Porter, "Web Profiles Haunt Students," *Wall Street Journal*, October 4, 2013, p. A3.

12. It is interesting that Sarah Drew, the daughter, testified against her mother in the case in exchange for immunity from prosecution. Jennifer Steinhauer, "Woman Guilty in Web Fraud Tied to Suicide," *New York Times*, November 27, 2008, pp. A1, A25.

13. John Markoff and Nicole Perlroth, "Dispute on Spam Stirs Big Assault on the Internet," *New York Times*, March 27, 2013, p. A1.

11 ENVIRONMENTAL REGULATION AND SUSTAINABILITY

Apart from the damage claims and penalties that can result from unlawful pollution of the environment, social responsibility emerges again as a business concern. Sustainability, or keeping a clean environment in all aspects of business operations, is a now a long-range goal for companies because both businesses and citizens benefit from efforts to preserve and improve the environment. As the author explained in a conference on the social responsibility of business, "It is not a matter of business profits versus preserving the environment. You can't keep the first going without taking responsibility for the second. We are all in this together and what each of us does affects the rest." This chapter answers the following questions: What are the public and private environmental laws? What are the protections and requirements in environmental laws? Who enforces environmental laws? What are the penalties for violations?

UPDATE
For up-to-date legal news, go to **mariannejennings.com**

Consider...

Shell Oil sold products to Brown & Bryant, Inc. (B & B), an agricultural chemical distribution business. B & B was what many characterized as a "sloppy" operator. Shell provided guidelines to its distributors, including B & B, for handling its products. Shell also inspected one of B & B's facilities and requested that the company make operational changes. B & B promised to make the changes but did not follow through. B & B went bankrupt, and state and federal authorities found contaminated soil on B & B's largest site. Both the EPA and state agencies sought to recover the cost of cleanup for the B & B site from Shell. Shell maintains that it did not spill the chemicals, could not control the behavior of B & B, and therefore could not be held liable. Is Shell correct?

By the shores of Gitche Gumee,
By the shining Big-Sea-Water . . .
How they built their nests in summer,
Where they hid themselves in winter,
How the beavers built their lodges,
Where the squirrels hid their acorns,
How the reindeer ran so swiftly,
Why the rabbit was so timid . . .

Henry Wadsworth Longfellow
"Hiawatha's Childhood"

11-1 Common Law Remedies and the Environment

From earliest times, landowners have enjoyed the protections of the courts and various doctrines to prevent bad smells, noises, and emissions.

11-1a NUISANCES

The common law doctrine of nuisance provides relief to adjoining landowners and communities when activities of one landowner interfere with the use and enjoyment of others' properties. Bad smells, ongoing damage to paint on buildings, excessive noise, polluted air, and the operation of facilities that present health problems can all be enjoined as **nuisances**. In many environmental problems, landowners and members of the communities who are affected do not want money for damages as much as they want the harmful activity halted. The courts have the power to issue **injunctions** against those who are causing the harm to land, individuals, communities, or the environment. Courts grant injunctions in those cases in which those who request the injunctive relief can establish ongoing harm as a result of the activities. In *Spur Industries, Inc. v Del E. Webb Dev. Co.* (Case 11.1), the Arizona Supreme Court was faced with issues of property, smells, and the issue of a developer's new project reaching a preexisting nuisance.

CASE 11.1

Spur Industries, Inc. v Del E. Webb Dev. Co.
494 P.2d 700 (Ariz. 1972)

Cattle and Flies and Retirees, Oh, My!

FACTS

Spur Industries operated a cattle feedlot near Youngtown and Sun City, Arizona (communities 14 to 15 miles west of Phoenix). Spur had been operating the feedlot since 1956, and the area had been agricultural since 1911.

In 1959, Del E. Webb began development of the Sun City area, a retirement community. Webb purchased the 20,000 acres of land for about $750 per acre.

In 1960, Spur began an expansion program in which it grew from an operation of five acres to 115 acres. At the time of the suit, Spur was feeding between 20,000 and 30,000 head of cattle, which produced 35 to 40 pounds of wet manure per head per day, or over 1 million pounds per day, and despite the admittedly good feedlot management and good housekeeping practices by Spur, the resulting odor and flies produced an annoying if not unhealthy situation as far as the senior citizens of southern Sun City were concerned. There is no doubt that some of the citizens of Sun City were unable to enjoy the outdoor living that Del Webb had advertised. Del Webb was faced with sales resistance from prospective purchasers as well as strong and persistent complaints from the people who had purchased homes in that area. Nearly 1,300 lots could not be sold. Webb then filed suit alleging Spur's operation was a nuisance because of flies and odors constantly drifting over Sun City. The trial court enjoined Spur's operations and Spur appealed.

JUDICIAL OPINION

CAMERON, Vice Chief Justice

It is clear that as to the citizens of Sun City, the operation of Spur's feedlot was both a public and a private nuisance. They could have successfully maintained an action to abate the nuisance. Del Webb, having shown a special injury in the loss of sales, had standing to bring suit to enjoin the nuisance. The judgment of the trial court permanently enjoining the operation of the feedlot is affirmed.

In addition to protecting the public interest, however, courts of equity are concerned with protecting the operator of a lawfully, albeit noxious, business from the result of a knowing and willful encroachment by others near his business.

In the so-called "coming to the nuisance" cases, the courts have held that the residential landowner may not have relief if he knowingly came into a neighborhood reserved for industrial or agricultural endeavors and has been damaged thereby:

"Plaintiffs chose to live in an area uncontrolled by zoning laws or restrictive covenants and remote from urban development. In such an area plaintiffs cannot complain that legitimate agricultural pursuits are being carried on in the vicinity, nor can plaintiffs, having chosen to build in an agricultural area, complain that the agricultural pursuits carried on in the area depreciate the value of their homes. The area being primarily agricultural, any opinion reflecting the value of such property must take this factor into account. The standards affecting the value of residence property in an urban setting, subject to zoning controls and controlled planning techniques, cannot be the standards by which agricultural properties are judged."

"People employed in a city who build their homes in suburban areas of the county beyond the limits of a city and zoning regulations do so for a reason. Some do so to avoid the high taxation rate imposed by cities, or to avoid special assessments for street, sewer and water projects. They usually build on improved or hard surface highways, which have been built either at state or county expense and thereby avoid special assessments for these improvements. It may be that they desire to get away from the congestion of traffic, smoke, noise, foul air and the many other annoyances of city life. But with all these advantages in going beyond the area which is zoned and restricted to protect them in their homes, they must be prepared to take the disadvantages."

"The case affords, perhaps, an example where a business established at a place remote from population is gradually surrounded and becomes part of a populous center, so that a business which formerly was not an interference with the rights of others has become so by the encroachment of the population...."

There was no indication in the instant case at the time Spur and its predecessors located in western Maricopa County that a new city would spring up, full-blown, alongside the feeding operation and that the developer of that city would ask the court to order Spur to move because of the new city. Spur is required to move not because of any wrongdoing on the part of Spur, but because of a proper and legitimate regard of the courts for the rights and interests of the public.

CONTINUED

Del Webb, on the other hand, is entitled to the relief prayed for (a permanent injunction), not because Webb is blameless, but because of the damage to the people who have been encouraged to purchase homes in Sun City. It does not equitable or legally follow, however, that Webb, being entitled to the injunction, is then free of any liability to Spur if Webb has in fact been the cause of the damage Spur has sustained. It does not seem harsh to require a developer, who has taken advantage of the lesser land values in a rural area as well as the availability of large tracts of land on which to build and develop a new town or city in the area, to indemnify those who are forced to leave as a result.

Having brought people to the nuisance to the foreseeable detriment of Spur, Webb must indemnify Spur for a reasonable amount of the cost of moving or shutting down. It should be noted that this relief to Spur is limited to a case wherein a developer has, with foreseeability, brought into a previously agricultural or industrial area the population which makes necessary the granting of an injunction against a lawful business and for which the business has no adequate relief.

It is therefore the decision of this court that the matter be remanded to the trial court for a hearing upon the damages sustained by the defendant Spur as a reasonable and direct result of the granting of the permanent injunction. Since the result of the appeal may appear novel and both sides have obtained a measure of relief, it is ordered that each side will bear its own costs.

Affirmed in part, reversed in part, and remanded for further proceedings consistent with this opinion.[2]

CASE QUESTIONS

1. What were the factors that made Spur's activities a nuisance?

2. Should it make any difference that Spur was there first?

3. How does the court balance retirement communities and beef production, two of Arizona's biggest industries? (Note: The case was settled when Del Webb agreed to pay Spur $11 million.)

BUSINESS STRATEGY

Data Barns and Nuisances

CYBERLAW Data barns are Internet services centers that are generally located in rural areas. They are becoming increasingly important with more and more reliance on cloud storage technology. For example, Microsoft bought 75 acres of bean fields in Grant County, Washington, to set up a digital warehouse.[1] Although county officials initially were thrilled with the presence of Microsoft, the issue of nuisance arose because Microsoft installed 40 diesel generators that operate as a backup source of power when there are transmission failures. The generators are located next to an elementary school and the smoke and noise from the generators have affected the learning environment of the school. The emissions from the generators are now classified as a toxic pollutant under Washington state law.

There were also contract disputes with the local Grant County power company. One of the provisions in service contracts for large commercial facilities is a requirement that the user estimate power use so that the utility can be certain to have an adequate supply on hand and to prevent overpurchasing of power when it is not needed.

Commercial entities are penalized under the terms of their contracts. Microsoft's contract with Grant County required the payment of a penalty for underestimating its power needs. When Microsoft was assessed a $210,000 penalty for underestimating its needs, the company began to use power excessively and the county's utility was faced with costs associated with its failure to meet other customers' demands. Facing its own penalties with customers, Grant County was forced to agree to reduce Microsoft's penalty.

As the data barn has increased in size (four buildings were added by 2012), the power demand has increased. Expansion of the Grant County utility to meet the energy demands resulted in rate increases for all consumers. Both Microsoft and county officials agree that they needed to know more about each other before welcoming the large technological facility. Indeed, Grant County and the state of Washington are rethinking the tax incentives and other programs created to encourage placement of data barns in rural areas. The costs in terms of power needs, pollution, and effects on residents are important considerations for both sides before building data barns.

ETHICAL ISSUES

Evaluate Microsoft's actions from an ethical perspective, including its response to a contract penalty as well as its use of diesel generators. When you think of companies such as Microsoft and Google, you think of them as "green" companies. What does the data barn scenario teach you about their environmental impact?

Business Planning Tip

The groups that protest locations of factories, cell phone towers, plants, and other development efforts raise political and public relations issues that require businesses to do advance planning and work with local authorities so that proposed projects are not derailed. With advance discussions, the projects can perhaps be tailored to address concerns of those activists.

11-1b NIMBYS AND NUISANCES

Environmental activists who rely on nuisance theories and local zoning laws have emerged as powerful forces in community development. Groups sometimes referred to as NIMBYs (Not In My Back Yard) challenge the placement of everything from power plants to refineries to cell phone towers to Walmarts as nuisances, backing their protests with data on traffic, crime, health and safety, and risk. Another group of activists, called the BANANAs (Build Absolutely Nothing Anywhere Near Anything), deals with the more generic issues of preventing urban sprawl and encouraging urban redevelopment. Using the legal theory of nuisance, they attempt to stop development and change, but the courts use a balancing approach in these nuisance cases.

11-2 Statutory Environmental Laws

At the federal level, most environmental laws can be placed in one of three categories: those regulating air pollution, those regulating water pollution, and those regulating solid waste disposal on land. This subsection also covers some specialized areas of regulation.

11-2a AIR POLLUTION REGULATION

Early Legislation

The first legislation dealing with the problem of air pollution, the Air Pollution Control Act, was passed in 1955, but it lacked teeth for enforcement. Federal regulation in this area continued to be ineffective in the 1960s. However, under the Air Quality Act of 1967, the federal government was given the authority to oversee the states' adoption of air quality standards and the implementation of those plans. Still, by 1970, because of little enforcement power, no state had adopted a comprehensive plan.

1970 Amendments to the Clean Air Act: New Standards

Because the states did not take action concerning air pollution, Congress passed the 1970 amendments to the original but ineffective 1963 **Clean Air Act** (42 U.S.C. § 7401); these amendments constituted the first federal legislation with any real authority for enforcement. The act created the **Environmental Protection Agency (EPA)**, a federal agency authorized to establish air quality standards. Once those standards were developed, states were required to adopt implementation plans to achieve the federally developed standards. These **state implementation plans (SIPs)** had to be approved by the EPA, and adoption and enforcement of the plans were no longer discretionary but mandatory. To obtain EPA approval, the SIPs had to meet deadlines for compliance with the EPA air quality standards, and lack of technology could no longer be used as a defense to air pollution or as a justification for state delays in meeting those standards. The 1970 amendments were the first in a series of federal laws that were known as technology forcing, or statutes that required developments of the means for achieving standards.

1977 and 1990 Amendments

The 1977 Clean Air Act amendments gave the EPA the authority to regulate business growth in order to achieve air quality standards. The EPA developed two categories for determining areas for business growth. **Nonattainment areas** included those areas with existing, significant air-quality problems, the so-called dirty areas. The second classification, called **prevention of significant deterioration (PSD) areas**, provides the EPA with a means for monitoring these areas to stop increased pollution.

New Forms of Control: EPA Expansion through Administrative Procedures

For nonattainment areas, the EPA developed its **emissions offset policy**, which requires three elements before a new facility can begin operation in an area: (1) The new plant must have the greatest possible emissions controls; (2) the proposed plant operator must have all its other operations in compliance with standards; and (3) the new plant's emissions must be offset by reductions from other facilities in the area.

In evaluating permissions for the new facility, the EPA follows the **bubble concept**, which examines all the air pollutants in the area as if they came from a single source. If a new plant will have no net effect on the air in the area (after offsets from other plants), the EPA allows the new facility to operate. This bubble concept approach also now applies in PSD areas. PSD regulations give the EPA the right to review proposed plant constructions and modifications before they can be started. Facility operators must establish that air quality will not experience any significant effects and that emissions will be controlled with appropriate devices.

In addition to the economic forces being applied to permits, the courts have upheld the authority of the EPA to increase permit requirements for plant modification. For example, in *Environmental Defense v Duke Energy*, 549 U.S. 561 (2007), the U.S. Supreme Court supported the EPA's PSD role in plant modifications, even when those modifications are not major ones. Duke Energy had begun implementing modifications to one of its coal-fired electricity plants without first seeking EPA approval. Duke was relying on past EPA procedures that had required approval for major modifications only. An environmental group brought suit against the company to require EPA approval and the agency agreed. The EPA explained to the Court that its policy shift was due to the increased need for controlling carbon emissions. The Court held, as explained in administrative law and procedure in Chapter 6, that the EPA was acting within the authority granted to it by Congress and that requiring permits for all modifications was not beyond the agency's authority under the Clean Air Act. The Court also held that the EPA could step up its standard for permit requirements to one that goes beyond best available technology (BAT) to **maximum achievable control technology (MACT)**, a standard that is not controlled by cost alone.

Since the time of the court's decision, the EPA has proposed or promulgated dozens of new standards and rules related to all forms of pollution. As a result of the extensive regulatory reforms, litigation continues, particularly challenging the new rules as *ultra vires*.

FOR THE MANAGER'S DESK

Re: Upwind and Downwind Liability and Business Relationships with the EPA

The Cross-State Air Pollution Rule (the Transport Rule), enacted by the EPA in 2011, was a rule promulgated to address downwind pollution from coal- and gas-fired power plants—that is, pollution that drifts from one state to others. These power plants generate the majority of electricity used in the United States, but they also emit pollutants that affect air quality. The authority for the rule is the Clean Air Act, which authorized the EPA to require the upwind states to reduce omissions that were causing the problems downwind. Upwind states (there are 28) must prevent sources within their borders from emitting pollution that travels across state lines and "contributes significantly" to a downwind state's "nonattainment" of federal air quality standards. This requirement on downwind responsibility is sometimes called the "good neighbor" provision. The impact of the rule has been the shutdown of many coal-fired utility plants.

Several groups and businesses filed suit against the EPA, challenging the Transport Rule, *Eme Homer City Generation, L.P. v EPA*, 696 F.3d 7 (C.A.D.C. 2012), as *ultra vires*. The court found that under the Transport Rule, upwind states may be required to reduce emissions by more than what they had contributed to a downwind state and that state's resulting nonattainment of EPA standards. The court also found that the EPA was using the good neighbor provision to impose massive emissions reduction requirements on upwind states without regard to the limits imposed by the statutory text. In addition, the Clean Air Act grants to the states the initial opportunity to implement reductions required by EPA under the good neighbor provision. However, the EPA did not allow the states to exercise this statutorily provided initial opportunity to implement the required reductions. Instead, the EPA designed Federal Implementation Plans and imposed them on the states.

The court concluded that such steps were *ultra vires* because they "transgressed statutory boundaries." The court noted that while Congress could decide to alter the statute to permit or require the EPA's approach, unless and until Congress does so, the agency must follow the statute. The court concluded, "It is not our job to set environmental policy. Our limited but important role is to independently ensure that the agency stays within the boundaries Congress has set. EPA did not do so here."

When businesses are affected by administrative rules, they can submit comments and provide testimony. However, once the rules are promulgated, their challenges lie with administrative law and the concept of *ultra vires*—that is, whether the agency exceeded its statutory authority. In this case and others like it related to other regulations, businesses rely on industry trade groups to pool their resources for litigation.

The states are Alabama, Arkansas, Florida, Georgia, Illinois, Indiana, Iowa, Kansas, Kentucky, Louisiana, Maryland, Michigan, Minnesota, Mississippi, Missouri, Nebraska, New Jersey, New York, North Carolina, Ohio, Oklahoma, Pennsylvania, South Carolina, Tennessee, Texas, Virginia, West Virginia, and Wisconsin.

New Forms of Control: EPA and Global Warming

In *Massachusetts v EPA*, 549 US 497 (2007), the Court held that the Clean Air Act mandated EPA action on greenhouse gases and global warming. With this decision and the change of administration in 2009, the EPA has been developing new expansive regulations under the Clean Air Act.

New Forms of Control: EPA and Small Businesses

The impact of the 1990 Clean Air Act amendments was more substantial on smaller businesses, such as dry cleaners, paint shops, and bakeries, because the definition of a major source of pollution was changed from those businesses emitting 100 tons or more a year to those emitting 50 tons or more per year. Many dry cleaners impose an environmental surcharge on their customers to cover the cost of emissions compliance. Emissions from dry cleaning operations have been a concern across the environmental statutes. When a dry cleaner has occupied a property, real

Consider...

Union Electric Company is an electric utility serving St. Louis, Missouri, and large portions of Illinois and Iowa. It operates three coal-fired generating plants in metropolitan St. Louis that are subject to sulfur dioxide restrictions under Missouri's SIP. Union Electric did not seek review of the implementation plan but applied for and obtained variances from the emissions limitations. When an extension for the variances was denied, Union Electric challenged the implementation plan on the grounds that it was technologically and economically infeasible and should therefore be amended. Will Union Electric succeed in having the plan amended?
[*Union Electric Co. v EPA*, 427 U.S. 246 (1976)]

estate agents recommend soil evaluation before buying that property because of the possibility that the chemicals used in processing have made their way into the soil. (See the discussion of due diligence on p. 347.)

New Forms of Control: EPA and Economic Forces

The Clean Air Act Amendments of 1990 also resulted in an exchange for the buying and selling of EPA permits for sulfur dioxide emissions. If, for example, a utility has an EPA permit to discharge one ton of sulfur dioxide per year, but its equipment permits it to run "cleaner" so that it discharges less than the one ton, the utility can sell the emissions savings portion of its permit to another utility.

11-2b WATER POLLUTION REGULATION

Early Legislation

In 1965, the first federal legislation on water quality standards was passed— the **Water Quality Act**. The act established a separate enforcement agency—the **Federal Water Pollution Control Administration (FWPCA)**—and required states to establish quality levels for the waters within their boundaries. Once again, the absence of enforcement procedures resulted in only about one-half of the states developing zones and standards by 1970. None of the states were engaged in active enforcement of those standards with their implementation plans.

The **Rivers and Harbors Act of 1899**, which prohibits the discharge into navigable rivers and harbors of refuse that causes interference with navigation, was used for a time to enforce water standards because state action was minimal. Specifically, the act prohibited the release of "any refuse matter of any kind or description" into navigable waters in the United States without a permit from the Army Corps of Engineers.

Present Legislation

Not until 1972 was meaningful and enforceable federal legislation enacted. With the passage of the **Federal Water Pollution Control Act of 1972** (33 U.S.C. § 1401), Congress set two goals: (1) swimmable and fishable waters by 1983 and (2) zero discharge of pollutants by 1985. The act was amended in 1977 to allow extensions and flexibility in meeting the goals and was renamed the **Clean Water Act**. This amendment transferred water pollution regulation from local to federal control. The EPA established federal standards for water discharges on an industry-wide basis, and all industries, regardless of state location, are required to comply.

The EPA, with the FWPCA merged into it, establishes ranges of discharge allowed for each industrial group. The ranges for pulp mills, for example, differ from those for textile manufacturers, but all plants in the same industry must comply with the same ranges.

Consider...

Inland Steel Company applied for a permit from the EPA under the Federal Water Pollution Control Act of 1972. Although Inland was granted the permit, the EPA made the permit modifiable because new standards for toxic releases and treatment were being developed. Inland filed suit, claiming the modification restriction on the permit was invalid because the EPA did not have such authority and also because Inland would be subject to every technological change or discovery made during the course of the permit. Was the restriction invalid?
[*Inland Steel Co. v EPA*, 574 F.2d 367 (7th Cir. 1978)]

The ranges of discharges permitted per industrial group are referred to as **effluent guidelines**. In addition, the EPA has established within each industrial group a specific amount of discharge for each plant, which is the effluent limitation. Generally, the standards set depend on the type of substance to be released. For setting standards, the EPA has developed three categories for pollutants: **conventional**, **nonconventional**, and **toxic pollutants**.

Finally, for a plant to be able to discharge wastes into waterways, it must obtain a National Pollution Discharge Elimination System (NPDES) permit from the EPA. This type of permit is required only for direct dischargers, or *point sources*, and is not required of plants that discharge into sewer systems (although these secondary dischargers may still be required to pretreat their discharges). Obtaining a permit is a complicated process that requires not only EPA approval but also state approval and public hearings.

The permits also impose requirements on the permit holder. If the plant is going to release a conventional pollutant, the EPA can require the plant to pretreat the substance with the **best conventional treatment (BCT)**. However, the EPA can also require the **best available treatment (BAT)** standard, which is the highest standard imposed. Until 2009, the standard for requiring BAT was solely the consideration of environmental effects and not the economic effects on the applicant. However, in *Entergy Corporation v Riverkeeper, Inc.*, 556 U.S. 208 (2009), the U.S. Supreme Court held that the EPA can use cost-benefit analysis to allow variances from those standards. In the case, Entergy's cost of bringing cooling water intake structures to the higher level the EPA requires for new structures would have been nine times the existing costs. The court held that the additional benefit achieved was too small to justify the cost of bringing the cooling water facilities up to current standards.

11-2c OTHER WATER LEGISLATION

In 1986, Congress passed the **Safe Drinking Water Act** (42 U.S.C. § 300f), which requires the EPA to establish national standards for contaminant levels in drinking water. The states are primarily responsible for enforcement and can have higher standards than the federal standards, but they must at least enforce the federal standards for their drinking water systems.

In 1990, Congress passed the **Oil Pollution Act** (OPA; 33 U.S.C. § 1251). The act was passed in response to large oil tanker spills, such as the one resulting from the grounding of the *Exxon Valdez* in Prince William Sound, Alaska, that resulted in a spill of 11 million gallons of crude oil that coated 1,000 miles of Alaskan coastline. The OPA applies to all navigable waters up to 200 miles offshore and places the federal government in charge of all oil spills. The Oil Spill Liability Trust Fund, established by a five-cent-per-barrel tax, covers cleanup costs when the party responsible is financially unable to do the cleanup. By the summer of 2010, the *Exxon Valdez* oil spill seemed to be a relatively small environmental disaster, despite its scope, in light of the April 2010 explosion and subsequent 90-day leak from BP's Deepwater Horizon rig in the Gulf Coast, which resulted in 200 million gallons of oil flowing into the Gulf before the well was capped on August 3, 2010.

11-2d SOLID WASTE DISPOSAL REGULATION

Early Regulation

During the 1970s, two major toxic waste debacles resulted in a new federal regulatory scheme of toxic waste disposal. In 1978, "Love Canal," as it came to be called, made national news as 80,000 tons of hazardous waste were found in the ground in an area that was primarily residential and included an elementary school. Epidemiological studies of cancer and illness rates in the area led to the discovery and eventual cleanup. Also, in Sheppardsville, Kentucky, an area that came to be called "Valley of the Drums," 17,000 drums of hazardous waste leaked tons of chemicals into the ground and water supply before their removal.

The emotional reaction to these two problem areas and the public outcry resulted in the passage of legislation that provided the federal government with some enforcement power for improper solid waste disposal. The **Toxic Substances Control Act** (TOSCA; 15 U.S.C. § 601), passed in 1976, authorized the EPA to control the manufacture, use, and disposal of toxic substances. Under the act, the EPA can stop the manufacture of substances that the agency concludes are dangerous.

In reaction to dangerous dumping practices, Congress passed the **Resource Conservation and Recovery Act of 1976** (RCRA; 42 U.S.C. § 6901). The two goals of the act are to control the disposal of potentially harmful substances and to encourage resource conservation and recovery. A critical part of the act is a permit system that requires manufacturers to obtain a permit for the storage or transfer of hazardous wastes so that the location of such wastes can be traced through a federal permit system.

CERCLA and the Superfund

In 1980, Congress passed the **Comprehensive Environmental Response, Compensation, and Liability Act** (CERCLA; 42 U.S.C. § 9601), which authorized the president to issue funds for the cleanup of areas that were once disposal sites for hazardous wastes. CERCLA established a **Hazardous Substance Response Trust Fund** to provide funding for cleanup. If federal funds are used for cleanup, the company responsible for the disposal of the hazardous wastes can be sued and required to repay the amounts expended from the trust fund. Often called the **Superfund**, the funds are available for governmental use but cannot be obtained through suit by private citizens affected by the hazardous disposals. Under the **Superfund Amendment and Reauthorization Act**, the EPA can recover cleanup funds from those responsible for the release of hazardous substances. Approximately 700 hazardous substances are now covered. (They are listed at 40 C.F.R. § 302.)

CERCLA Lender Liability. One of the more intriguing issues under CERCLA liability is whether a lender has the responsibility of cleanup because it took back the property and was in possession of the property as the result of a foreclosure sale or a deed in lieu of foreclosure. The **Asset Conservation, Lender Liability, and Deposit Insurance Protection Act of 1996** provides a specific exclusion for lenders. This provision has been called the "secured lender exemption" from CERCLA liability. However, these lender amendments also provide that lenders can lose their status if they "actually participate[s] in the management or operational affairs of a vessel or facility." A lender can do the following and still not be subject to environmental liability:

- Monitor or enforce terms of the security agreement.
- Monitor or inspect the premises or facility.
- Mandate that the debtor take action on hazardous materials.
- Provide financial advice or counseling.
- Restructure or renegotiate the loan terms.
- Exercise any remedies available at law.
- Foreclose on the property.
- Sell the property.
- Lease the property.

CERCLA—Four Classes of Liability Rules. Four classes of parties can be held liable under CERCLA. The present owners and operators of a contaminated piece of property comprise one group. While *owner* is self-explanatory, *operator* includes those who lease property and then contaminate it, such as those who lease factories, operate storage facilities, and so forth. The owners and operators at the time the property was contaminated form the second group. This group brings under CERCLA jurisdiction those who were responsible for the property contamination, as opposed to present owners who had the problem deeded to them. For example, many gas stations have been converted to other businesses. Suppose that one of the underground gas tanks once used by the gas station has been leaking hazardous materials into the surrounding soil. Not only would the present owners be liable; so also would be all those who owned the gasoline station previously.

The final two groups consist of those who transport hazardous materials and those who arrange for the transportation of hazardous materials. Virtually no liability exemptions are available to those who fit into these four groups. *Burlington Northern Railway/Shell Oil Co. v U.S* (Case 11.2) deals with a corporation's CERCLA liability and provides the answer to the chapter opening "Consider…"

CASE 11.2

Burlington Northern Railway/Shell Oil Co. v U.S.
556 U.S. 599 (2009)

Am I My Customer's Keeper? I'm Only the Arranger

FACTS

In 1960, Brown & Bryant, Inc. (B & B) began operating an agricultural chemical distribution business (the Arvin facility). B & B applied its products to customers' farms. B & B opened its business on a 3.8-acre parcel of former farmland and then expanded operations onto an adjacent 0.9-acre parcel of land owned jointly by the Atchison, Topeka & Santa Fe Railway Company and the Southern Pacific Transportation Company (Railroads). Wastewater and chemical runoff from the facility were allowed to seep into the groundwater below it.

B & B purchased chemicals from Shell. Shell would arrange for delivery by common carrier, f.o.b. destination. When the product arrived, it was transferred from tanker trucks to a bulk storage tank located on B & B's primary parcel. During each of these transfers, leaks and spills could—and often did—occur.

CONTINUED

In the late 1970s, Shell took several steps to encourage the safe handling of its products. Shell provided distributors with detailed safety manuals and instituted a voluntary discount program for distributors that made improvements to their bulk handling and safety facilities. Later, Shell required distributors to obtain an inspection by a qualified engineer and provide self-certification of compliance with applicable laws and regulations. B & B's Arvin facility was inspected twice, and B & B told Shell that it had made a number of recommended improvements to its facilities. Despite these improvements, B & B remained a "'[s]loppy' [o]perator."

The EPA discovered significant contamination of soil and groundwater, and in 1989, B & B's land was designated as a Superfund site. However, B & B went bankrupt that year. By 1998, the Governments had spent more than $8 million in cleanup costs.

In 1991, the EPA (referred to in the case as "Governments") ordered the Railroads to conduct certain cleanup processes. The Railroads did so, incurring expenses of more than $3 million in the process. The parties ended up in court seeking a determination of their share of cleanup liability. The U.S. District Court held that both the Railroads and Shell were potentially responsible parties (PRPs) under CERCLA: the Railroads because they were owners of a portion of the facility, and Shell because it had "arranged for" the disposal of hazardous substances through its sale and delivery of chemicals. The court did not impose joint and several liability on Shell and the Railroads for the entire response cost incurred by the Governments. The court apportioned the Railroads' liability as 9 percent of the Governments' total response cost. Based on estimations of chemicals spills of Shell products, the court held Shell liable for 6 percent of the total site response cost.

Shell and the Governments appealed. The Ninth Circuit held that Shell had arranged for the disposal of a hazardous substance and held Shell and the Railroads jointly and severally liable for the Governments' costs.

The Railroads and Shell appealed.

JUDICIAL OPINION

STEVENS, Justice

… [A]n entity could not be held liable as an arranger merely for selling a new and useful product if the purchaser of that product later, and unbeknownst to the seller, disposed of the product in a way that led to contamination. Less clear is the liability attaching to the many permutations of "arrangements" that fall between these two extremes—cases in which the seller has some knowledge of the buyers' planned disposal or whose motives for the "sale" of a hazardous substance are less than clear.

The Governments assert that by including unintentional acts such as "spilling" and "leaking" in the definition of disposal, Congress intended to impose liability on entities not only when they directly dispose of waste products but also when they engage in legitimate sales of hazardous substances knowing that some disposal may occur as a collateral consequence of the sale itself. The Governments contend that Shell arranged for the disposal by shipping to B & B under conditions it knew would result in spilling by the purchaser. Because these spills resulted in waste, a result Shell anticipated, the Governments insist that Shell was properly found to have arranged for the disposal. Shell was aware that minor, accidental spills occurred during transfer….

[t]he evidence does not support an inference that Shell intended such spills to occur. To the contrary, the evidence revealed that Shell took numerous steps to encourage its distributors to reduce the likelihood of such spills, providing them with detailed safety manuals, requiring them to maintain adequate storage facilities, and providing discounts for those that took safety precautions.

Although Shell's efforts were less than wholly successful, given these facts, Shell's mere knowledge that spills and leaks continued to occur is insufficient grounds for concluding that Shell "arranged for" the disposal. Accordingly, we conclude that Shell was not liable.

The District Court calculated the Railroads' liability based on three figures. First, the court noted that the Railroad parcel constituted only 19% of the surface area of the Arvin site. Second, the court observed that the Railroads had leased their parcel to B & B for 13 years, which was only 45% of the time B & B operated the Arvin facility. Finally, the court found that the volume of hazardous-substance-releasing activities on the B & B property was at least 10 times greater than the releases that occurred on the Railroad parcel, The District Court's detailed findings make it abundantly clear that the primary pollution at the Arvin facility was contained in an unlined sump and an unlined pond in the southeastern portion of the facility most distant from the Railroads' parcel and that the spills of hazardous chemicals that occurred on the Railroad parcel contributed to no more than 10% of the total site contamination, some of which did not require remediation. With those background facts in mind, we are persuaded that it was reasonable for the court to use the size of the leased parcel and the duration of the lease as the starting point for its analysis.

Although the Court of Appeals faulted the District Court for relying on the "simplest of considerations: percentages of land area, time of ownership, and types

CONTINUED

of hazardous products," these were the same factors the court had earlier acknowledged were relevant to the apportionment analysis.

Although the evidence adduced by the parties did not allow the court to calculate precisely the amount of hazardous chemicals contributed by the Railroad parcel to the total site contamination or the exact percentage of harm caused by each chemical, the evidence did show that fewer spills occurred on the Railroad parcel and that of those spills that occurred, not all were carried across the Railroad parcel to the B & B sump and pond from which most of the contamination originated. The fact that no spills on the Railroad parcel required remediation lends strength to the District Court's conclusion… any miscalculation on that point is harmless.

Because the District Court's ultimate allocation of liability is supported by the evidence and comports with the apportionment principles, we reverse the Court of Appeals' conclusion that the Railroads are subject to joint and several liability for all response costs arising out of the contamination of the Arvin facility.

For the foregoing reasons, we conclude that the Court of Appeals erred by holding Shell liable as an arranger under CERCLA. Furthermore, we conclude that the District Court reasonably apportioned the Railroads' share of the site remediation costs at 9%.

The judgment is reversed.

CASE QUESTIONS

1. Where do you think the term "arranger" fits in the categories of those who are responsible for cleanup costs under CERCLA?

2. What do you think the practical effect of this decision will be on companies who own Superfund sites? Does the complexity of analysis for liability help companies in cleanup cases?

3. What do you think will happen to government agencies in their efforts to seek reimbursement for their cleanup efforts?

CERCLA and Corporate Liability. CERCLA liability has also extended to corporate board members and corporate successors and officers in cases where a company is purchased by another firm. Those who merge or buy corporations also buy into CERCLA liability—liability under CERCLA continues after a transfer of ownership. The U.S. Supreme Court ruled in *United States v Bestfoods*, 528 U.S. 810 (1999), that a parent corporation is not automatically liable under CERCLA for a subsidiary corporation's conduct, but it may be responsible if the subsidiary is simply a shell. In other words, CERCLA liability of parent corporations for the actions of their subsidiaries is governed by corporate law on piercing the corporate veil. Under the *Bestfoods* case, liability of the parent corporation for actions of a subsidiary results if

a. the parent corporation operates the facility, is a joint venturer in the operation of the facility, or works side by side with the subsidiary in operations;

b. the parent and subsidiary corporations share officers and directors such that it becomes impossible to separate out the decision-making processes; or

c. an officer of the parent corporation (or other designated or authorized employee) operates the facility of the subsidiary.[3]

CERCLA and Buying Land Liability. The best safeguard against stepping into CERCLA liability is screening the property carefully before buying it or, in the case of lenders, accepting it as collateral. When lenders sell foreclosed property to a third party, the lender is in the position of trying to sell property with a CERCLA problem. The value of the collateral is reduced substantially. Lenders and any purchasers of a piece of property should conduct a *due diligence review* of the property. A due diligence review consists of three phases. Phase I consists of a search to determine whether evidence of past or current environmental problems

Consider...

For some 30 years, GE manufactured electric capacitors containing Pyranol at its plants located in New York. GE met its Pyranol needs by purchasing "virgin" PCBs that the Monsanto Company marketed. GE then refined the PCBs it purchased from Monsanto until the PCBs attained the level of purity necessary for use in electric capacitors. The end result was Pyranol.

To be of use to GE, the processed Pyranol had to meet and retain demanding purity specifications. Pyranol that fell short of these standards was deemed "scrap Pyranol" and was stored in 55-gallon drums in designated scrap areas.

Over time, GE accumulated a glut of scrap Pyranol and contacted Frederic H. "Fred" Fletcher, local manufacturer, "chemical scrapper," and businessman, and through an informal agreement Fletcher purchased scrap Pyranol from GE at bargain prices for his industrial needs.

For approximately 10 years ending in 1967, Fletcher regularly purchased 55-gallon drums of scrap Pyranol from GE, about 200,000 gallons or 3,600 55-gallon drums. By August 1967, when GE notified him by means of a collection letter, Fletcher's account was delinquent by over six thousand dollars for failure to pay for fourteen shipments of scrap Pyranol. Fletcher responded with a letter informing GE that the quality of the scrap Pyranol he received had markedly declined in recent years. Fletcher's letter marked the end of his relationship with GE.

In 1987, EPA found hundreds of drums containing scrap Pyranol and other chemicals at the Fletcher Site. The drums were unmarked and several had leaked. Subsequent testing detected hazardous substances at the site. The EPA filed suit against GE to recoup costs associated with the Fletcher site's cleanup as an arranger. Explain whether GE is an arranger and whether GE should be held liable for the cost of the Fletcher cleanup.
[*U.S. v General Elec. Co.*, 670 F.3d 377 (1st Cir. 2012)]

THINK: In the *Burlington* case, the court refused to hold Shell liable for the "sloppy" conduct of a customer in receiving goods purchased from Shell because Shell had made legitimate sales to customers and had provided information on the proper transport of its goods. Shell was not involved in the spills, and mere knowledge was not enough to result in its liability under CERCLA.

APPLY: The situation in the *GE* case is slightly different. This was a situation where GE had contaminated materials and had made arrangements with Fletcher to buy the materials from it. The goods being transferred were the contaminants and there was a need for disposal. A company cannot isolate itself from responsibility for disposal simply by hiring a contractor. There is a requirement to follow through with the reliability and responsibility of that contractor.

ANSWER: In this case, GE, in one of the longest lasting EPA cases in history, was held liable. GE had a duty to follow through on the conduct of the party with whom it had contracted for disposing of its PCB materials.

is present on the property. The EPA has established the "all appropriate inquiries" rule for Phase I, which requires the use of experts and documentation. A Phase I search must examine private and public records and include a site inspection. If Phase I reveals some concerns, the parties proceed to Phase II, which consists of chemical analysis of soil, structures, and water from the property. If Phase II finds the presence of contaminants, the report for Phase II estimates the cost of cleanup. Phase III is the actual cleanup plan.

New Developments under CERCLA

CERCLA Challenges. Courts have begun to examine the issue of causation between the contaminants present on a piece of property and its relation to any injury as a means of a cost-benefit analysis. For example, in *Licciardi v Murphy Oil U.S.A.*, Ill F.3d 396 (5th Cir. 1997), one federal circuit court held that some causation must be established between the cleanup and what the owner or operator is alleged to have dumped at the site. However, not all the federal circuit courts have followed that line of reasoning in their decisions. [*Johnson v James Langley Operation Co., Inc.*, 226 F.3d 957 (8th Cir. 2000)]

Another basis for CERCLA judicial challenges has been one grounded in the basic administrative law principle of an arbitrary and capricious challenge to an EPA demand for cleanup of a site when the demand for cleanup is not linked to any danger. For example, in *U.S. v Broderick Investment Co.*, 200 F.3d 679 (10th Cir. 1999), a company challenged the costly cleanup demands that required the cancer rate in the area to be reduced to 1 in 100,000, a rate higher than in non–Superfund sites. However, because a day care center was planned for the land, the court upheld the cleanup standards as neither arbitrary nor capricious. These types of challenges to CERCLA, including allocation issues, continue their advancement through the judicial system.

Insurers and CERCLA. Another judicial issue that continues to evolve is whether property insurance policies include coverage for CERCLA liability. Courts are left with interpretation issues on these policies. Ambiguities in the meaning of the term *pollution* in a policy are construed against the insurer in favor of coverage for the property owner. One court has held that there is no other way to interpret "pollution" other than to include CERCLA liability. [*Sulphuric Acid Trading Co., Inc. v Greenwich Ins. Co.*, 211 S.W.3d 243 (Tenn. App. 2006)] CERCLA coverage is available, but it is a policy rider, which requires additional premiums. Many insurers exclude coverage without a specific rider.

CERCLA and the Self-Audit. The EPA encourages companies to self-identify problem lands and areas in exchange for reduced fines. Companies and the EPA work together to solve the problem and be certain cleanup is done where warranted. These self-audits and disclosures also help the companies be more accurate in their disclosures to shareholders and analysts.

Under the EPA's program called Incentives for Self-Policing, Disclosure, Correction, and Prevention of Violations, those companies that come forward voluntarily, having met certain conditions, will have their penalties reduced for any violations uncovered. The conditions for reduced penalties are

1. The violations were uncovered as part of a self-audit or due diligence done on property.

2. The violations were uncovered voluntarily.

3. The violations were reported to the EPA within 10 days.

4. The violations were discovered independently and disclosed independently, not because someone else was reporting or threatening to report.

5. There is correction of the violation within 60 days.

6. There is a written agreement that the conduct will not recur.

7. There can be no repeat violations or patterns of violations.

8. There is no serious harm to anyone as a result of the violation.

9. The company cooperates completely with the EPA.

The EPA will reduce fines and penalties by 75 percent if substantially all the conditions are met. If a company falls into the 75 percent mitigation category, the EPA will not recommend criminal prosecution to the Department of Justice. The documents related to the audit can be protected by the attorney–client privilege, even those that are disclosed to the EPA. The clarification of the privilege has resulted in most companies taking advantage of the EPA's self-reporting protections.

CERCLA and Brownfields

CERCLA has been so effective that designated Superfund sites that remained undeveloped as of 2012 totaled 425,000. Called *brownfields*, these sites are defined by the EPA as "real property, the expansion, redevelopment, or reuse of which may be complicated by the presence or potential presence of a hazardous substance, pollutant, or contaminant." Brownfields often contribute to urban blight and present barriers to economic development and revitalization.[4]

The Small Business Liability Relief and Brownfields Revitalization Act was passed to allow 75 federal agencies to work together through the *Federal Partnership Action Agenda*. This agency provides funding for proposals to clean up and use these brownfields (42 U.S.C.A. § 9601). EPA rules promulgated under the act now provide a process for application to become an "innocent landowner," or someone who seeks to develop the brownfield but wants an exemption from CERCLA exposure. That designation then allows the applicant to obtain federal funding for purposes of cleaning up and developing the brownfield.

11-2e ENVIRONMENTAL QUALITY REGULATION

As part of its environmental control scheme, Congress also passed an act that regulates what governmental entities can do in the use of their properties. The **National Environmental Policy Act (NEPA)** of 1969 (42 U.S.C. § 4321) was passed to require federal agencies to take into account the environmental impact of their proposed actions and to prepare an **environmental impact statement (EIS)** before taking any proposed action.

An EIS must be prepared and filed with the EPA whenever an agency sends a proposed law to Congress and whenever an agency will take major federal action significantly affecting the quality of the environment. The information required in an EIS is as follows:

1. The proposed action's environmental impact
2. Adverse environmental effects (if any)
3. Alternative methods
4. Short-term effects versus long-term maintenance, enhancement, and productivity
5. Irreversible and irretrievable resource use

Examples of federal agency actions that have required the preparation of an EIS include the Alaskan oil pipeline, the extermination of wild horses on federal lands, the construction of government buildings such as post offices, and any highway construction paid for with federal funds. Even the North American Free Trade Agreement (NAFTA) was challenged on the basis that an EIS was required.

In 2008, the U.S. Supreme Court held there was an exigency exception to the EIS requirements in a case in which Navy training that was necessary for national defense would have been unduly delayed and the resulting harm from the Navy's use of sonar was not irreparable. [*Winter v National Resources Defense Council*, 555 U.S. 7 (2008)] The case introduces some cost-benefit analysis into the EIS process.

Sierra Club v United States Dep't of Transportation (Case 11.3) involves the question of whether an EIS was needed.

CASE 11.3

Sierra Club v United States Dep't of Transportation
753 F.2d 120 (D.C. 1985)

Skiing and Landing at Jackson Hole

FACTS

In 1983, the Federal Aviation Administration (FAA) issued two orders amending the operations specifications for Frontier Airlines, Inc., and Western Airlines, Inc. These amendments gave the airlines permanent authorizations to operate Boeing 737 jet airplanes (B-737s) out of Jackson Hole Airport, which is located within the Grand Teton National Park in Wyoming. These two airlines are the only major commercial carriers that schedule flights to and from Jackson Hole.

Private jets have flown into the airport since 1960, and Western Airlines has been flying into Jackson Hole since 1941. The airport is the only one in the country located in a national park, and Congress has continually funded expansions and improvements of the once-dirt, single-runway airport.

In 1978, Frontier applied for permission to fly B-737s into the Jackson Hole Airport. The FAA released its EIS on the application in 1980, which found that B-737s were comparable with C-580 propeller aircraft (the type then being used by Western and Frontier) for noise intrusion but were substantially quieter than the private jets using the airport. The study also showed that fewer flights would be necessary because the B-737 could carry more passengers and that different flight paths could reduce noise. Based on this EIS, Frontier was given the right to use B-737s for two years. When Frontier applied for permanent approval, the FAA used the 1980 EIS and found that with flight time restrictions, the impact would not harm the environment.

Following FAA orders allowing the runway expansion, the Sierra Club (petitioner), a national conservation organization, brought suit for the FAA's failure to file an EIS for the 1983 amendments and for the use of national park facilities for commercial air traffic without considering alternatives. (Because this is an appeal of an administrative agency's order, the case goes directly to the federal appellate level.)

JUDICIAL OPINION

BORK, Circuit Judge

We do not think the FAA violated NEPA by failing to prepare an additional EIS. Under NEPA, an EIS must be prepared before approval of any major federal action that will "significantly affect the quality of the human environment." The purpose of the Act is to require agencies to consider environmental issues before taking any major action. Under the statute, agencies have the initial and primary responsibility to determine the extent of the impact and whether it is significant enough to warrant preparation of an EIS. This is accomplished by preparing an Environmental Assessment (EA). An EA allows the agency to consider environmental concerns, while reserving agency resources to prepare full EIS's for appropriate cases. If a finding of no significant impact is made after analyzing the EA, then preparation of an EIS is unnecessary. An agency has broad discretion in making this determination, and the decision is reviewable only if it was arbitrary, capricious or an abuse of discretion.

This court has established four criteria for reviewing an agency's decision to forego preparation of an EIS. First, the agency must have accurately identified the relevant environmental concern. Second, once the agency has identified the problem, it must take a "hard look" at the problem in preparing the EA. Third, if a finding of no significant impact is made, the agency must be able to make a convincing case for its finding. Last, if the agency does find an impact of true significance, preparation of an EIS can be avoided only if the agency finds that changes or safeguards in the project sufficiently reduce the impact to a minimum.

The first test is not at issue here. Both the FAA and Sierra Club have identified the relevant environmental concern as noise by jet aircraft within Grand Teton National Park. The real issues raised by Sierra Club are whether the FAA took a "hard look" at the problem, and whether the methodology used by the agency in its alleged hard look was proper.

We find that the FAA did take a hard look at the problem. The FAA properly prepared an EA to examine the additional impact on the environment of the plan. The EA went forward from the 1980 EIS. The 1980 EIS, which was based on extensive research by Dr. Hakes of the University of Wyoming, noise testing by the FAA, and data derived from manufacturer information, showed that noise intrusions of B-737 jets over the level caused by C-580 propeller aircraft amounted to only 1 dbl near the Airport and decreased in proportion to the distance from the Airport. The agency, exercising its expertise, has found that an increase this minute is not significant for any environment. In addition, the EIS and Hakes studies were based on a worst-case scenario, and it was determined that if certain precautions were taken the actual noise levels could be diminished greatly.

CONTINUED

Petitioner argues that because Jackson Hole Airport is located within national parkland a different standard—i.e., individual event noise level analysis—is mandated. Both individual event and cumulative data were amassed in preparing the 1980 EIS on which the EAs were based. The fact that the agency in exercising its expertise relied on the cumulative impact levels as being more indicative of the actual environmental disturbance is well within the area of discretion given to the agency. We agree with petitioner that although noise is a problem in any setting, "airplane noise is fundamentally inconsistent with the type of recreational experience Park visitors are seeking" and should be minimized. Here the FAA found that a cumulative noise increase

of 1 dbl or less is not significant—even for the pristine environment in which Jackson Hole Airport is located.

Given all of these facts, we think the FAA was not required to prepare yet another EIS before granting permanent authorizations for the use of B-737s.

The orders of the FAA are hereby affirmed.

CASE QUESTIONS

1. What airport noise is at issue, and who was concerned about the issue?

2. What is the basis for the appeal?

3. What has the FAA allowed? Will the authorizations stand?

11-2f OTHER FEDERAL ENVIRONMENTAL REGULATIONS

In addition to the previously discussed major environmental laws, many other specific federal statutes protect the environment.

Surface Mining

The **Surface Mining and Reclamation Act of 1977** (42 U.S.C. § 6907) requires those mining coal to restore land surfaces to their original conditions and prohibits surface coal mining without a permit.

The Fracking Issue

Currently, several federal agencies, including the EPA, the Department of Energy (DOE), the Bureau of Land Management (BLM), the Centers for Disease Control (CDC), the Department of Agriculture (USDA), and the Securities and Exchange Commission (SEC), have adopted or are working on promulgating regulations related to hydraulic fracturing (fracking). First used in 1947, this process is now employed at 60 percent of oil and gas wells to bring those resources to the surface. This technique has become a lightning rod for opposition based on questions about its safety and impact on the environment. For example, the 2010 movie, *Gasland*, resulted in public reaction based on the film's representation of water contamination. The regulations proposed or being promulgated by federal agencies range from required disclosures in shareholder materials about a company's fracking activity to prohibitions of fracking on federal lands.

Noise Control

Under the **Noise Control Act of 1972** (42 U.S.C. § 4901), the EPA, along with the FAA, can control the amount of noise emissions from low-flying aircraft for the protection of landowners in flight paths.

Pesticide Control

Under the **Federal Environmental Pesticide Control Act**, the use of pesticides is controlled. All pesticides must be registered with the EPA before they can be sold, shipped, distributed, or received. Also under the act, the EPA administrator is given the authority to classify pesticides according to their effects and dangers.

OSHA

The **Occupational Safety and Health Administration (OSHA)** is responsible for workers' environments. OSHA controls the levels of exposure to toxic substances and requires safety precautions for exposure to such dangerous substances as asbestos, benzene, and chloride.

Asbestos

Buildings that contain asbestos materials remain a problem for buyers, sellers, and occupants. The **Asbestos Hazard Emergency Response Act (AHERA)**, passed in 1986, required all public and private schools to arrange for the inspection of their facilities to determine whether their buildings had asbestos-containing materials. Schools are required to develop plans for containment, but other buildings are not regulated. The Clean Air Act does, however, define airborne asbestos as a toxic pollutant, and liability may result from the release of fibers from this known carcinogen. Further, an amendment to the Superfund Act classified asbestos as a **community-right-to-know substance**, which means a probable duty exists to disclose the presence of asbestos to buyers, tenants, and employees. Numerous ethical questions arise about the presence of asbestos and the obligations of landowners to replace the asbestos given that the phaseout of its use did not end until 1997. Questions such as the impact of the release of asbestos from the walls when tenants, employees, and others hang photos and other objects by nailing them into the walls remain. The issues of the degree of harm and the cost of replacement continue to be debated among property owners.

Endangered Species

In 1973, Congress passed the **Endangered Species Act (ESA)**, a law that has been a powerful tool for environmentalists in protecting certain species through their advocacy of restrictions on commercial use and development when the habitats of certain species are interfered with. Under the act, the secretary of the interior is responsible for identifying endangered terrestrial species, and the secretary of commerce identifies endangered marine species. In addition, these cabinet members must designate habitats considered crucial for these species if they are to thrive. In many instances, litigation results over questions about which species should or should not be on the list. Once a species is on the list, its critical habitat cannot be disturbed by development, noise, or destruction. *Babbitt v Sweet Home Chapter of Communities for a Great Oregon* (Case 11.4) has given federal agencies broad authority in protecting endangered species.

CASE 11.4   *Babbitt v Sweet Home Chapter of Communities for a Great Oregon*
515 U.S. 687 (1995)

Jobs Versus Owls: Lumber Versus Endangered Species

FACTS

Two U.S. agencies halted logging in the Pacific Northwest because it endangered the habitat of the northern spotted owl and the red-cockaded woodpecker, both endangered species. Sweet Home Chapter (respondents) is a group of landowners, logging companies, and families dependent on the forest products industries in the Pacific Northwest. They brought suit, seeking clarification of the authority of the secretary of the interior and the director of the Fish and Wildlife Service (petitioners) to include habitation modification as a harm covered by the ESA.

The federal district court found for the secretary and director and held that they had the authority to protect the northern spotted owl through a halt to logging. The

court of appeals reversed. Bruce Babbitt, the secretary of the interior, appealed.

JUDICIAL OPINION

Stevens, Justice

Section 9(a)(1) of the Endangered Species Act provides the following protection for endangered species:

> *Except as provided in sections 1535(g)(2) and 1539 of this title, with respect to any endangered species of fish or wildlife listed pursuant to section 1533 of this title it is unlawful for any person subject to the jurisdiction of the United States to—(B) take any such species within the United States or the territorial sea of the United States. [16 U.S.C. § 1538(a)(1)]*

CONTINUED

Section 3(19) of the Act defines the statutory term "take":

The term "take" means to harass, harm, pursue, hunt, shoot, wound, kill, trap, capture, or collect, or to attempt to engage in any such conduct. [16 U.S.C. § 1532(19)]

The Act does not further define the terms it uses to define "take." The Interior Department regulations that implement the statute, however, define the statutory term "harm":

Harm in the definition of "take" in the Act means an act which actually kills or injures wildlife. Such act may include significant habitat modification or degradation where it actually kills or injures wildlife by significantly impairing essential behavioral patterns, including breeding, feeding, or sheltering. [50 CFR § 17.3 (1994)]

We assume respondents have no desire to harm either the red-cockaded woodpecker or the spotted owl; they merely wish to continue logging activities that would be entirely proper if not prohibited by the ESA. On the other hand, we must assume *arguendo* that those activities will have the effect, even though unintended, of detrimentally changing the natural habitat of both listed species and that, as a consequence, members of those species will be killed or injured. Under respondents' view of the law, the Secretary's only means of forestalling that grave result—even when the actor knows it is certain to occur—is to use his § 5 authority to purchase the lands on which the survival of the species depends. The Secretary, on the other hand, submits that the § 9 prohibition on takings, which Congress defined to include "harm," places on respondents a duty to avoid harm that habitat alteration will cause the birds unless respondents first obtain a permit pursuant to § 10.

The text of the Act provides three reasons for concluding that the Secretary's interpretation is reasonable. First, an ordinary understanding of the word "harm" supports it. The dictionary definition of the verb form of "harm" is "to cause hurt or damage to: injure." *Webster's Third New International Dictionary* 1034 (1966). In the context of the ESA, that definition naturally encompasses habitat modification that results in actual injury or death to members of an endangered or threatened species.

Respondents argue that the Secretary should have limited the purview of "harm" to direct applications of force against protected species, but the dictionary definition does not include the word "directly" or suggest in any way that only direct or willful action that leads to injury constitutes "harm." Moreover, unless the statutory term "harm" encompasses indirect as well as direct injuries, the word has no meaning that does not duplicate the meaning of other words that § 3 uses to define "take." A reluctance to treat statutory

terms as surplusage supports the reasonableness of the Secretary's interpretation.

Second, the broad purpose of the ESA supports the Secretary's decision to extend protection against activities that cause the precise harms Congress enacted the statute to avoid. As stated in § 2 of the Act, among its central purposes is "to provide a means whereby the ecosystems upon which endangered species and threatened species depend may be conserved."

Third, the fact that Congress in 1982 authorized the Secretary to issue permits for takings that § 9(a)(1)(B) would otherwise prohibit, "if such taking is incidental to, and not the purpose of, the carrying out of an otherwise lawful activity," 16 U.S.C. § 1539(a)(1)(B), strongly suggests that Congress understood § 9(a)(1)(B) to prohibit indirect as well as deliberate takings. The permit process requires the applicant to prepare a "conservation plan" that specifies how he intends to "minimize and mitigate" the "impact" of his activity on endangered and threatened species, 16 U.S.C. § 1539(a)(2)(A), making clear that Congress had in mind foreseeable rather than merely accidental effects on listed species.

The Court of Appeals made three errors in asserting that "harm" must refer to a direct application of force because the words around it do. First, the court's premise was flawed. Several of the words that accompany "harm" in the § 3 definition of "take," especially "harass," "pursue," "wound," and "kill," refer to actions or effects that do not require direct applications of force. Second, to the extent the court read a requirement of intent or purpose into the words used to define "take," it ignored § 9's express provision that a "knowing" action is enough to violate the Act. Third, the court employed *noscitur a sociis* to give "harm" essentially the same function as other words in the definition, thereby denying it independent meaning. The canon, to the contrary, counsels that a word "gathers meaning from the words around it." The statutory context of "harm" suggests that Congress meant that term to serve a particular function in the ESA, consistent with but distinct from the functions of the other verbs used to define "take." The Secretary's interpretation of "harm" to include indirectly injuring endangered animals through habitat modification permissibly interprets "harm" to have "a character of its own not to be submerged by its association."

When it enacted the ESA, Congress delegated broad administrative and interpretive power to the Secretary. See 16 U.S.C. §§ 1533, 1540(f). The task of defining and listing endangered and threatened species requires an expertise and attention to detail that exceeds the normal province of Congress. Fashioning appropriate standards for issuing permits under § 10 for takings that would otherwise violate § 9 necessarily requires

CONTINUED

the exercise of broad discretion. The proper interpretation of a term such as "harm" involves a complex policy choice. When Congress has entrusted the Secretary with broad discretion, we are especially reluctant to substitute our views of wise policy for his. In this case, that reluctance accords with our conclusion, based on the text, structure, and legislative history of the ESA, that the Secretary reasonably construed the intent of Congress when he defined "harm" to include "significant habitat modification or degradation that actually kills or injures wildlife."

In the elaboration and enforcement of the ESA, the Secretary and all persons who must comply with the law will confront difficult questions of proximity and degree; for, as all recognize, the Act encompasses a vast range of economic and social enterprises and endeavors. These questions must be addressed in the usual course of the law, through case-by-case resolution and adjudication.

The judgment of the Court of Appeals is reversed.

CASE QUESTIONS

1. Is habitat modification harming endangered species?

2. Does the Court's interpretation mean no intent is required to violate ESA?

3. Did Congress intend to give the secretary authority to shut down an industry?

Aftermath: In August 1995, Congress passed, as a rider to a budget-reduction bill, a provision that suspended environmental laws in some national forest areas in Washington and Oregon through 1996.

In *Bennett v Spear*, 520 U.S. 154 (1997), the U.S. Supreme Court held that the ESA also permits lawsuits by landowners affected by the statute's application. Landowners have equal rights along with environmental groups to challenge ESA applications and restrictions. However, in a 2009 decision, the U.S. Supreme Court limited somewhat the ability of individuals and groups to bring suit under the ESA. In *Summers v Earthland Institute*, 555 U.S. 488 (2009), the U.S. Supreme Court held that the claim that the plaintiffs would be using various national parks around the country at some point in the future was not sufficient standing to bring suit to halt the U.S. Forest Service's policies and regulation on forest clearing. The decision means that those who bring such challenges must have an "active, ongoing dispute" that is specific to the activity. In addition, the species themselves cannot bring suit. In *Cetacean Cmty. v Bush*, 386 F.3d 1169 (9th Cir. 2004), the court held that the Cetacean community, consisting of whales, dolphins, and porpoises, lacked standing to sue the federal government under the ESA in claiming that the Navy's proposed deployment of low-frequency active sonar harmed them. The court held that the ESA authorizes only persons to sue and that animals were meant to be protected rather than protectors under the statute.

BUSINESS STRATEGY

Cooperation as an Alternative Strategy to Litigation

Since the time of these head-on confrontations, the logging and paper industries have adopted a "Sustainable Forestry Initiative." The Initiative, adopted by 200 members of the American Forest and Paper Association, supports eco-friendly logging. The Nature Conservancy supports the Initiative, which has had the effect of negotiated solutions to the issue of logging versus environmental prohibitions. No further legislation has been needed at the federal level because of the cooperation between and among these groups.

ETHICAL ISSUES

Asia Pacific Resources International Holdings, Ltd. (called April) signed a landmark agreement with the World Wildlife Fund, an environmental activist group. April agreed to curb timber-cutting areas in Sumatra, Indonesia, to preserve a natural rainforest with great biodiversity. Over the past 20 years, more than half of the forest has been cut down for lumber.

April's customers, such as Procter & Gamble (makers of Charmin toilet paper and Bounty paper towels), were shunning April as a supplier because of its damage in Indonesia. While April complied with Indonesian law (leaving 20 percent of the forest untouched), it left long ribbon strips that could not support the local wildlife. Terms of the deal include the following:

- April will not allow other loggers to use its transportation system (barges and roads).
- April will verify the source of all logs it purchases.
- April will plant tree plantations and was expected to be able to sell only plantation-grown wood by 2009.

Local residents resent these agreements with environmental groups because their livelihoods have been blocked when April closes its road and prohibits use by illegal loggers. What advantages do you see in these private contract promises on environmental policy? What disadvantages do you see? What ethical issues prompted April's voluntary actions?

Source: Steve Stecklow, "Environmentalists, Loggers Near Deal on Asian Rainforest," *Wall Street Journal*, February 23, 2006, pp. A1, A14.

Consider...

Arizona Cattle Growers' Association and Jeff Menges, a rancher seeking a grazing permit on the lands at issue (together called "ACGA"), sued the Fish and Wildlife Service and the BLM to challenge Incidental Take Statements (ITSs) issued by the Fish and Wildlife Service in a biological opinion for certain grazing lands. Mr. Menges sought livestock grazing permits for land within the area supervised by the BLM's Saffold and Tucson, Arizona, field offices, and the Association represented members who claimed to be harmed by the government action. The BLM's livestock grazing program for this area affects 288 separate grazing allotments that in total comprise nearly 1.6 million acres of land. The Fish and Wildlife Service's biological opinion, issued on September 26, 1997, analyzed 20 species of plants and animals and concluded that the livestock grazing program was not likely to jeopardize the continued existence of the species affected, nor was it likely to result in destruction or adverse modification of the designated or proposed critical habitat. The Fish and Wildlife Service did, however, issue ITSs for various species of fish and wildlife listed or proposed as endangered.

ACGA's suit challenged both the ITSs and their terms and conditions. The challenge was based on the fact that the razorback sucker and the cactus ferruginous pygmy owl were in abundance and not endangered. The environmental groups challenged ACGA's right to challenge the conclusions of the agency. Who is correct?

[*Arizona Cattle Growers' Ass'n v U.S. Fish and Wildlife, Bureau of Land Management*, 273 F.3d 1229 (9th Cir. 2001)]

11-3 State Environmental Laws

In addition to federal enactments, all the states have enacted some form of environmental law and have established their own environmental policies and agencies. Some states may require new industrial businesses to obtain a state permit along with the required federal permits for the operation of their plants. Some states regulate the types of fuels that can be used in vehicles and offer incentives for carpooling.

All states have some form of regulation on hazardous waste, a sort of CERCLA statute at the state level. Some states require sellers of real estate to furnish property disclosure statements to buyers prior to the closing of a sale. All states have some system of fines for environmental violations.

11-4 Enforcement of Environmental Laws

Federal environmental laws can be enforced through criminal sanctions, penalties, injunctions, and suits by private citizens.

11-4a PARTIES RESPONSIBLE FOR ENFORCEMENT

Although many federal agencies are involved with environmental issues, the EPA is responsible for the promulgation of specific standards and the enforcement of those standards with the use of the remedies discussed in the following subsections. The federal EPA may work in conjunction with state EPAs in the development and enforcement of state programs.

The **Council on Environmental Quality (CEQ)** was established in 1966 under the National Environment Act and is part of the executive branch of government. Its role in the environment regulatory scheme is that of policymaker. The CEQ is responsible for formulating national policies on the quality of the environment and then making recommendations to lawmakers regarding its policy statements.

Other federal agencies are involved in enforcement of environmental issues, such as the Department of the Interior, the Forest Service, the BLM, and the Department of Commerce. Basically, all federal agencies that deal with the use of land, water, and air are involved in compliance with and enforcement of environmental laws.

11-4b CRIMINAL SANCTIONS AND PENALTIES FOR VIOLATIONS

Nearly all of the federal statutes previously discussed carry some form of sanctions, including criminal penalties for violations.

Penalties for Clean Air Act Violations
Exhibit 11.1 summarizes the various penalties, which include fines, criminal convictions, and civil penalties. The fines are assessed on the basis of days or per incident. In exercising its enforcement power, the EPA may require businesses to maintain records or to install equipment necessary for monitoring the amounts of pollutants being released into the air or water.

Penalties for Water Violations
The Clean Water Act carries criminal penalties of up to $25,000 per day and one year's imprisonment. For violations that are willful, the penalties increase to $50,000 and/or three years, with repeat violation carrying penalties of $100,000 and/or six years.

Those responsible for oil spills are liable for penalties of $25,000 per day or $1,000 per barrel spilled. If the spill is the result of negligence or willful misconduct, the penalties are $3,000 per barrel spilled. Failure to report a spill can bring a $250,000 fine for an individual (sole proprietor or officer, according to agency and criminal liability principles) and up to five years imprisonment or $1 million for a corporation. Civil penalties run higher and include the full cost of cleanup

EXHIBIT 11.1 Penalties for Violation of Federal Environmental Laws

ACT	PENALTIES	PRIVATE SUIT
Clean Air Act	$25,000 per day, up to one year imprisonment; 15 years for willful or repeat violations; $10,000 rewards	Citizen suits; authorized EPA suit for injunctive relief
Clean Water Act	$25,000 per day, up to one year imprisonment, or both; $50,000/three years for violations with knowledge; $100,000/six years for subsequent violations	Citizen suits; authorized EPA suit for injunctive relief
Resource Conservation and Recovery Act (Solid Waste Disposal Act)	$250,000 and/or 15 years for intentional; $1,000,000 for corporations; $50,000 and/or 5 years for others	Citizen and negligence suits after EPA refuses to handle
Oil Pollution Act	$25,000 per day, or $1,000 per barrel; $3,000 per barrel if willful or negligent; $250,000 and/or 5 years for failure to report	Hazardous Substance/Response Trust Fund for cleanup; EPA suit for injunctive relief and reimbursement of trust funds; private actions in negligence

© Cengage Learning

(up to $50 million) should those responsible not clean up the oil spill. In 2013, BP agreed to pay a $4.5 billion fine for its 2010 Deepwater Horizon Spill. In addition, two supervisors were indicted for various federal violations related to the deaths of 11 workers in the explosion and, because of BP's admissions related to the settlement, BP is banned from federal contracts for two years. The ban means that BP is not able to submit bids for drilling rights on federal lands, something estimated to result in a cost of 25 percent of the company's revenues.

U.S. v Apollo Energies, Inc. (Case 11.5) deals with the issue of criminal liability for environmental law violations.

CASE 11.5 *U.S. v Apollo Energies, Inc.*
611 F.3d 679 (10th Cir. 2010)

No Slick Way Out of Environmental Crimes

FACTS

Heater-treaters are cylindrical equipment up to 20 feet high and more than three feet wide that oil companies use to separate oil from water when the mixture is pumped from the ground. The heater-treaters can include exhaust pipes or movable louvers that can be opened to access heating equipment at the base. Birds can crawl into the exhaust pipes or through the louvers to form nests. Once inside the heater-treaters, the birds are often trapped.

Acting on an anonymous tip, an agent with the U.S. Fish and Wildlife Service inspected more than a dozen of Apollo's heater-treaters and those of other companies in December 2005. He found bird remains in about half of the heater-treaters.

Fish and Wildlife did not bring any charges based on these initial inspections, but began an education campaign to let oil companies know about the birds, sending out over 300 letters to companies to tell them to take precautions to prevent the birds from nesting in heater-treaters because they risked violation of the Migratory Bird Treaty Act (MBTA) by not fixing the problem.

After the grace period, inspections of heater-treaters at Apollo Energies and Dale Walker, dba Red Cedar Oil (defendants) revealed dead birds in their heater-treaters.

© Harper 3D/Shutterstock.com

CONTINUED

They were charged with and convicted of violations of the MBTA. They appealed on the grounds that the MBTA is unconstitutional for vagueness and lack of fair notice as applied to their conduct.

JUDICIAL OPINION

TYMKOVICH, Circuit Judge

The MBTA is not unconstitutionally vague. It criminalizes a range of conduct that will lead to the death or captivity of protected migratory birds, including to "pursue, hunt, take, capture, [and] kill…." 16 U.S.C. § 703. The actions criminalized by the MBTA may be legion, but they are not vague.

Appellants also contend the statute does not provide fair notice of prohibited conduct because of the sheer breadth of the Act. They argue the Act applies to innocuous conduct several steps removed from bird deaths or takings. No reasonable person, they contend, would be on notice that those predicate acts are potentially criminal.

Recognizing these notice and causation concerns, the district court attempted to cabin the MBTA's reach by holding the defendants must "proximately cause" the MBTA violation to be found guilty, and that they did so here. In other words, the court found the government had found "'proximate causation' or 'legal causation' beyond a reasonable doubt" by "showing that trapped birds are a reasonably anticipated or foreseeable consequence of failing to cap the exhaust stack and cover access holes to the heater/treater."

As to Apollo, the record shows it had notice of the heater-treater problem for nearly a year-and-a-half before the bird death resulting in its conviction. Indeed, Apollo admitted at trial that it failed to cover some of the heater-treaters' exhaust pipes as Fish and Wildlife had suggested after the December 2005 inspection. In effect, Apollo knew its equipment was a bird trap that could kill.

Walker was charged and convicted for dead birds found in both the April 2007 and April 2008 inspections. Walker contends the conviction arising from the April 2008 inspection should be reversed because on that occasion the bird was found in his heater-treater's louvers, not the exhaust pipe, for which he had no knowledge of a problem. Fish and Wildlife argues it warned Walker of the louver problem when, in its 2007 letter, it admonished Walker to secure all heater-treater cavities in which a protected bird might become trapped. Regardless, we find that once Walker was alerted to protected birds' proclivity to crawl into the heater-treaters' exhaust pipes, it was reasonably foreseeable protected birds could become trapped in other of the heater-treaters' cavities.

The conviction for the April 2007 bird death is a different matter. Walker's testimony—which the Fish and Wildlife agent does not dispute—is that prior to April 2007, he was not aware of problems with heater-treaters in the oil industry or in his specific operations. Fish and Wildlife did not send him a letter about the issue before the April 2007 inspection, and he was not a member of the trade association to which the Service advertised the oil field equipment problem. Nor was Walker aware of the one television report or newspaper article about heater-treaters. Given the state of this record, we agree no reasonable person would conclude that the exhaust pipes of a heater-treater would lead to the deaths of migratory birds.

Therefore, the magistrate judge's finding as to the April 2007 bird death is reversed.

We affirm in part, and reverse in part.

CASE QUESTIONS

1. Of what significance is Apollo's receipt of the letter from Fish and Wildlife?

2. Why is Walker's 2007 conviction reversed?

3. Does the breadth of the MBTA make it vague and unconstitutional?

11-4c GROUP SUITS: THE EFFECT OF ENVIRONMENTALISTS

In many circumstances, private suits have had the most effect either in terms of obtaining compliance with environmental regulations or in terms of abating existing nuisances affecting environmental quality. The reason for the success of these suits may be the ultimate outcome of the litigation—possible business shutdowns and, at the least, the payment of tremendous amounts of damages and costs.

Private suits have been brought by environmental groups that have both the organizational structure and sufficient funding to initiate and complete such suits. In some cases, environmental groups are formed to protest one specific action, as is the case of Citizens Against the Squaw Peak Parkway; other groups are national organizations that take on environmental issues and litigation in all parts of the country. Examples of these national groups include the Sierra Club, the Environmental Defense Fund, Inc., the National Resources Defense Council, and the League of Conservation Voters. Some environmental groups represent business interests in environmental issues, as does the Mountain States Legal Foundation, which becomes involved in presenting business issues when private organizations and individuals bring environmental suits.

These environmental groups have been successful not only in bringing private damage and injunctive relief suits but also in forcing agencies to promulgate regulations and to enjoin projects when EISs should have been filed but were not.

11-5 International Environmental Issues

11-5a THE EU AND ENVIRONMENTALISM

The European Union (EU) has passed more than 200 environmental directives that focus on noise restrictions; protection of endangered species; energy efficiency; recycling; and air, land, and water quality. The view of the EU is that environmental planning is to be conducted by member states as part of their economic development plans and processes. The EU's European Environment Agency serves as a clearinghouse for environmental information; eventually the agency will operate for members in a manner similar to the EPA.

Many EU directives are designed to eliminate the need for regulation by encouraging different business choices and educating consumers. One directive requires manufacturers to make 90 percent of all packaging materials recyclable. Another directive awards companies the use of an "eco-audit" sticker on their labels and stationery if they comply with an annual environmental audit of their manufacturing, waste management, materials use, and energy choices. An innovative directive of the EU created an EU-wide "eco-label" to be placed on all consumer goods to provide information about the environmental impact of a product's production, distribution, life, and disposal.

11-5b ISO 14000

The International Organization for Standardization (ISO) has developed its ISO 14000 series of international environmental standards.

Under ISO 14000, companies can become ISO certified, which will permit them to place special insignias on their materials, correspondence, and products to indicate their ISO standing. ISO standards emphasize not only compliance but also self-audits and self-correction. Genuine dedication to improvement is a key standard for this environmental certification.

11-5c LEED CERTIFICATION

LEED (Leadership in Energy and Environmental Design) is a voluntary international sustainability program that provides third-party verification of green buildings. LEED standards deal with the energy sources and uses in buildings and also require that owners think through the full lifecycle of a building in making design, energy, and materials decisions. The organization not only offers certification but also issues awards for creativity and design to architects, owners, and builders in meeting LEED standards.

BIOGRAPHY

The Story of BP's Deepwater Horizon Well and Oil Spill

Before the April 20, 2010, explosion of the BP Deepwater Horizon rig in the Gulf Coast, BP was in the midst of a culture change undertaken in response to three previous incidents that injured employees and damaged the environment. BP's Prudhoe Bay pipeline burst in March 2006 and resulted in a spill of 267,000 gallons of oil. Industry standards require smart pigging of pipelines every five years. However, BP had not done smart pigging on the Prudhoe Bay line since 1998. BP had a request from a board member to look into maintenance issues at Prudhoe Bay; he indicated that he was concerned about serious corrosion issues. A 2004 internal report written by an external consultant warned the company about accelerated corrosion on the Prudhoe pipeline, but BP did not undertake maintenance, nor did it develop a plan for testing the pipeline.

In addition, in 2005, BP had entered into an agreement with OSHA to fix the safety violations at its Texas City Refinery. OSHA had found 271 violations at the refinery. The Chemical Safety Board (CSB) report on the refinery concluded that cost cutting played a role in BP's failure to address the ongoing OSHA violations. BP had commissioned a series of audits and studies in 2002 that revealed serious safety problems at the Texas City refinery, including a lack of necessary preventive maintenance and training, and although these audits and studies were shared with BP executives in London and were provided to at least one member of the executive board, few changes were made. Instead, in 2004, BP executives challenged their refineries to cut yet another 25 percent from their budgets for the following year."[5]

Tragically, the inattention and cost cutting were a direct contributor to the explosion at BP's Texas City Refinery that resulted in a loss of 15 lives and injuries to 500 workers. The CSB investigation into the refinery tragedy was headed by James Baker, former U.S. secretary of state, who found "instances of a lack of operating discipline, toleration of serious deviations from safe operating practices and apparent complacency toward serious process safety risks at each refinery." The OSHA investigation of the refinery found a total of 439 "willful and egregious" violations, a finding that resulted in the largest fine in OSHA's history, $87 million.

The Texas City tragedy and the Prudhoe Bay spill were so public and resulted in such negative publicity that the BP board made a change in the company's leadership. CEO Lord Browne was removed and Mr. Tony Hayward, a reserved geologist, was expected to help the company turn the corner on its safety and prudence issues. However, Mr. Hayward was not able to make the cultural corrections the board hoped would happen. A 2007 internal report, issued one year into Mr. Hayward's tenure, concluded that there had been "unprecedented levels of issues and accidents at BP and that there was a culture of pervasive unwillingness to stop work when something was clearly wrong."[6]

All employees were reminded of Mr. Hayward's singular message, "Safety is our first priority."[7] But as the safety program was continued in earnest, there were increasing problems with both the decisions about, and the conduct on, BP's offshore rigs.

Almost two years after Texas City and Prudhoe Bay, and nearly two years before the Deepwater Horizon spill, was the June 5, 2008, 193-barrel oil spill at BP's Atlantis rig (also in the Gulf of Mexico). The internal report included the following information:

> "[Managers] put off repairing the pump in the context of a tight cost budget."
>
> "Leadership did not clearly question the safety impact of the delay in repair."
>
> A BP safety officer told company investigators, "You only ever got questioned on why you couldn't spend less."[8]

During this period of ongoing safety lapses and resulting casualties, BP continued its stellar financial performance. In 2007, BP's shares were at $77. Its debt/equity ratio was 0.31, its dividend rate 15 percent, and it had a 20 percent ROE, with gross margins of 27 percent and net margins of 7.47 percent. EPS growth in 2008 was at 64 percent.

The evidence that has emerged on Deepwater Horizon followed the patterns in place at the refinery and other rigs. A whistleblower allegation based on e-mails expressed concern about whether crucial engineering drawings and paperwork necessary prior to operation of offshore rigs had been completed. The e-mails also reveal that engineers who asked for an additional 10 hours in the critical path to address their concerns about the well by installing 21 centralizers instead of just 6 were dismissed by the lead engineer with "I do not like this."[9]

At hearings before the House of Representatives, other oil company CEOs testified that BP did not follow appropriate design standards in drilling the well.[10] A *Wall*

Street Journal study found that BP used a risky design that was cheaper for one out of three of its deep-water wells. The so-called "long-string" design is one that uses a single pipe for bringing the oil to the surface. Experts indicate that the result of using one long pipe is that natural gas accumulates around the pipe and can rise unchecked. Most experts recommend its use only in low-pressure wells, not wells such as Deepwater Horizon. They also note that long-string drilling would not be appropriate when a company does not know the area, something that was true about this well for BP.

The Costs

Following the spill, which is the largest in history, BP lost $30 billion, or 16 percent, of its market value.[11] Prior to the Deepwater Horizon explosion and spill, BP's share price was at $62. By July, the share price was $38, a loss of 33 percent. BP certainly has displaced Exxon and its Valdez as the bad poster child for oil companies. Retail sales at BP stations dropped 8 to 10 percent after the spill.[12]

The costs, in terms of cash outlays, continue for BP. From April through July, BP spent $7 million per day trying to contain the spill. BP was given an ultimatum by the Obama administration. Shortly after a White House meeting, BP placed $20 billion in an escrow account for the United States government to distribute to those in the Gulf-area states who have been harmed by the spill. BP sold off $7 billion in assets to cover the expenses and the $20 billion. BP took a $32 billion charge in July 2010 for the Gulf oil spill costs.

As noted earlier in the chapter, BP paid a $4.5 billion fine in 2013 for the spill and is under a two-year ban from federal contracts, or until the company is able to demonstrate that ethical standards have been restored at the company.

Summary

What are the public and private environmental laws? What protections and requirements are present in environmental laws?

- Nuisance—bad smells, noises, or dirt from one property that interferes with another's use and enjoyment of their own property
- Nonattainment areas—areas with significant air pollution problems
- Emissions offset policy—new plants not built until new emissions are offset by reductions elsewhere
- Bubble concept—EPA policy of maximum air emissions in one area
- Clean Air Act—federal law that controls air emissions
- Maximum Achievable Control Technology (MACT)—best means for controlling emissions
- Clean Water Act—federal law that regulates emissions in various water sources
- Effluent guidelines—EPA maximum allowances for discharges into water
- Safe Drinking Water Act—federal law establishing standards for contaminants
- Oil Pollution Act (OPA)—federal law imposing civil and criminal liability for oil spills
- Resource Conservation and Recovery Act (RCRA)—federal law controlling disposal of hazardous waste through a permit system
- Superfund—funds available for government to use to clean up toxic waste sites
- Comprehensive Environmental Response, Compensation, and Liability Act (CERCLA)—federal law providing funds and authority for hazardous waste site cleanups
- Endangered Species Act (ESA)—powerful federal law that can curb economic activity if it presents harm to endangered species or their habitat

Who enforces environmental laws?

- Environmental Protection Agency (EPA)—federal agency responsible for enforcement of environmental laws at the federal level
- National Environmental Policy Act (NEPA)—federal law that requires federal agencies to assess environmental issues before taking actions
- Environmental impact statement (EIS)—report by federal agency on study of proposed action's effect on the environment

What are the penalties for violations?

- Injunction—judicial order halting an activity
- Fines and criminal penalties

Questions and Problems

1. American Rivers, a national river conservation organization, the Environmental Defense Fund, and several national and local environmental organizations brought suit against the U.S. Army Corps of Engineers, the Secretary of the Army, and the Secretary of the Interior, seeking to protect the endangered least tern, the endangered pallid sturgeon, and the threatened Great Plains piping plover, all of which are protected by the ESA.

The groups allege that the manner in which the Corps has operated the extensive dam and reservoir system on the Missouri River has adversely affected the three species. Do the groups have the right to assert the claim? What response can the government agencies offer? What should the court do? [*American Rivers v U.S. Army Corps of Engineers*, 271 F. Supp. 2d 230 (D.D.C. 2003)]

2. Philip Carey Company owned a tract of land in Plymouth Township, Pennsylvania, on which it deposited a large pile of manufacturing waste containing asbestos. Carey sold the land to Celotex, and Celotex sold the land to Smith Land & Improvement Corporation. The EPA notified Smith in July 1984 that unless Smith took steps to eliminate the asbestos hazard, the EPA would do the work and pursue reimbursement. Smith proceeded with the cleanup to the EPA's satisfaction at a total cost of $218,945.44. Smith then turned to Celotex and Carey, as previous owners of the property, for reimbursement. These firms say they have no liability under CERCLA. Which firms are liable? [*Smith Land & Improvement Corp. v Celotex*, 851 F.2d 86 (3rd Cir. 1988)]

3. A group of landowners situated near the Sanders Lead Company brought suit to recover for damages to their agricultural property from accumulations of lead particulates and sulfur oxide deposits released in Sanders's production process. The landowners' property had increased in value because of its commercial potential in being close to the plant. Sanders employs most of the town's residents in its operations. What common-law and statutory rights do the landowners have, and what relief can be obtained? [*Borland v Sanders Lead Co., Inc.*, 369 So.2d 523 (Ala. 1979)]

4. In 1985, Manufacturers National Bank of Detroit issued a letter of credit for Z&Z Leasing, Inc., an industrial firm, to enable Z&Z to obtain bond financing from Canton Township, Michigan.

After six years of operation, Z&Z was not doing well and had defaulted on its bond obligations. A consultant for the bank found underground storage tanks on Z&Z's site. The tanks contained a yellowish liquid that was found to be a solvent and a hazardous substance. The bank paid off the Canton township bond obligation and foreclosed on the Z&Z property. By 1993, Z&Z had still not sold the property, and the EPA sought to hold the bank liable as an operator for the costs of cleaning up the tanks.

Can the bank be held liable? [*Z&Z Leasing, Inc. v Graying Reel, Inc.*, 873 F. Supp. 51 (E.D. Mich. 1995)]

5. Reynolds Metal has been held to the same technological standards in its pollution control for can-manufacturing plants as those applied to aluminum manufacturers. Reynolds claims the processes are different and that the technology for pollution control in can manufacturing is not yet available. Does Reynolds have a point? [*Reynolds Metals Co. v EPA*, 760 F.2d 549 (D.C. 1985)]

6. Joseph Marcantuone and Robert Gieson owned a shopping center in which one of the spaces was always leased as a dry cleaners. Eventually, the city of East Orange, New Jersey, took the property by eminent domain in order to expand the facilities for a school located next to the shopping center. In performing due diligence, the city learned that solvents from the dry cleaner operations had made their way into the soil beneath the property. The city asked that Messrs. Marcantuone and Gieson pay over $200,000 for the cleanup. Can they be held liable for what the dry cleaner tenants did? [*New Jersey Schools Development Authority v Marcantuone*, 54 A.3d 830 (N.J.Super. 2012)]

7. The Natural Resources Defense Council, Inc., the Humane Society of the United States, Cetacean Society International, League for Coastal Protection, Ocean Futures Society, and Jean-Michel Cousteau filed suit in federal district court to obtain a preliminary injunction against federal officials to prevent the U.S. Navy's peacetime use of a low-frequency sonar system for training, testing, and routine operations. This new technology, Low Frequency Active Sonar (LFA), sends out intense sonar pulses at low frequencies that travel hundreds of miles in order to timely detect increasingly quiet enemy submarines. The complaint alleges that the use of LFA is a violation of the Marine Mammal Protection Act, the ESA, the NEPA, and the Administrative Procedures Act. The complaint claims that these violations will cause irreparable injury to sea creatures, many of them rare and endangered, including whales, dolphins, seals, sea turtles, and salmon.

The Navy argues that enjoining the peacetime use of LFA sonar would harm national security, even though the Navy would still be free to use it during wartime or periods of heightened threat because training and testing are necessary for military readiness.

Do the groups and Mr. Cousteau have standing to challenge the Navy's work? Can the Navy's work be enjoined? What should the court decide and why? [*Natural Resources Defense Council, Inc. v Evans*, 232 F. Supp. 2d 1003 (N.D. Cal. 2002)]

8. The Sawtooth National Forest established its first travel plan map in 1989. The travel plan map was reprinted in 2002. The maps show visitors to the area the system of roads and trails available for their use as well as how and when they could use them. The National Forest Service decided to revise the current travel plan map to restrict motor vehicle use to designated roads and trails. The revision was initiated in response to the 2005 Travel Management Rule, which mandated certain changes to the management of motor vehicle use on National Forest System lands. Prior to the 2005 Travel Management Rule, motor vehicle use on public lands was largely unregulated, resulting in uncontrolled cross-country motor vehicle use, unplanned routes, and damage to the resources. New maps were printed with designated routes, which included some motor vehicle access but limited those routes as compared with previous route use. Any motor vehicle other than designated in the new maps is prohibited under federal law. The Wilderness Society filed suit to stop the new route use plan on the grounds that the Forest Service did not file an EIS. The Forest Service responded that its new plan restricted motor vehicle transport and did not expand it and did not require that an EIS be filed. What should the court decide about the transportation plan? [*Wilderness Society v U.S. Forest Service*, 850 F. Supp. 2d 1144 (D. Idaho 2012)]

9. CNH owns approximately 100 acres of land near Lake Michigan and operated a foundry and tractor assembly plant there. In July 2004, CNH and Champion entered into a contract that required Champion to remove dismantled equipment, property, materials, and debris from the property and dispose of it legally. Champion was also required to fill all pits, basements, utility tunnels, and other subsurface openings with crushed construction-grade fill concrete. The contract specified that Champion was to comply with all applicable laws.

In 2007, a CNH employee saw a Champion truck delivering fill material to fill a large basement area, which had been the tractor assembly portion of the plant. The CNH employee said the fill had a noticeable diesel odor. Although the parties' contract required that the material used for fill was to be obtained from the site, Champion's truck came from outside CNH's Property. Champion's then–Vice President told CNH managers that the fill material came from Racine Steel Castings and that it had delivered 20–25 truckloads to CNH property for fill.

CNH had an environmental consulting firm test the fill material, and the lab concluded that the fill material was contaminated with PCBs, gasoline range organics, and diesel range organics. CNH then notified state and federal authorities of the problem. The government agencies held CNH liable for the cost of cleanup. Discuss whether CNH has any right of recovery from Champion. What happens if Champion is insolvent? What if all of the substances found in the fill were also found on other parts of CNH's property? [*CNH America, LLC v Champion Environmental Services, Inc.*, 863 F. Supp. 2d 793 (E.D.Wis., 2012)]

10. Larry Dobbs, Frances Dobbs, Wayne Richard, and Lorena Richard live in rural Illinois next to Donald Wiggins. The Dobbses and Richards have lived on their properties for 30 years. Mr. Wiggins purchased his property in 1995 and built a home and dog kennels on that property and began raising, training, and kenneling dogs.

At first, Wiggins did not have many dogs, and the dogs did not bark much. However, the noise from barking dogs kenneled on Wiggins's property grew worse over time. Larry planted a row of cedar trees on his property to try and cut down on the barking noise.

However, the Dobbses' house was approximately 200 to 250 yards from a barn where Wiggins kenneled many of his dogs. The barking was constant, day and night. The dogs might bark for two straight hours, take a break, and start barking again, but there was never any extended period of time in which they completely quit barking. There was rarely a complete hour in which the dogs did not bark. The dogs barked more when they were being fed or when they thought they were going to be taken out of their kennels. In addition, deer and other wildlife running across the property and coyotes howling at night tended to stir up the dogs.

The Dobbses and Richards filed suit seeking an injunction against the dog kenneling operation and, at that time, there were a total of 69 dogs on Wiggins's property. Based on your study of nuisances in this chapter, explain what the court should do. [*Dobbs v Wiggins*, 929 N.E.2d 30 (Ill. App. 2010)]

SUSTAINABILITY & THE LAW

Animal Rights and Double Shower Heads

Sustainability requires us to think beyond environmental law to consequences and impact. Review the following two situations and develop an analysis that addresses consequences and impact.

People for the Ethical Treatment of Animals (PETA) has been a powerful force in demanding changes in corporate behavior. Its latest target has been Burger King for its treatment of chickens—the group wants the company to stop removing the beaks of laying hens and also to enlarge the animals' cages. Also, PETA would like Burger King to ensure that its animals are stunned before they are slaughtered. PETA has developed a new logo and name for the company, MURDER KING. Burger King is suffering from flat sales and does not welcome the negative publicity. How would you respond to PETA's concerns? Visit the websites of both PETA and Burger King for more information on these issues: www.bk.com and www.peta.org.

A federal regulation promulgated by the EPA restricts the amount of water than can flow from showerheads to a rate of 2.5 gallons per minute. When the regulation took effect, many hotel chains had complaints from their guests about the slow water flow and the difficulty they had in bathing. Westin Hotels and Resorts announced that it would install two showerheads in the baths and showers of its hotel rooms to accommodate its guests. Each showerhead will meet federal requirements, but if the two are both turned on, the guests will have water at a rate of five gallons per minute. Westin maintains that it is in compliance with the law. A federal employee responded, "But we didn't anticipate the loophole of two shower heads per shower."[13] Discuss the Westin approach to compliance with the law.

Notes

1. James Glanz, "Data Barns in a Farm Town, Gobbling Power and Flexing Muscle," *New York Times*, September 24, 2012, p. A1.

2. The decision in this case does differ from decisions in other states. For example, in *Toftoy v Rosenwinkel*, 983 N.E.2d 463 (Ill. 2012), the Illinois Supreme Court relied on that state's Farm Nuisance Act that prohibits neighbors from bringing private nuisance actions against farming operations and concluded that cattle and stable operations that result in flies and smell were not subject to injunctions. Such statutes were passed to protect farms and farming operations that predated the subdivision and development of surrounding land. In other words, some states balance nuisance cases by favoring farming.

3. The work of Professors Cindy A. Schipani and Lynda J. Oswald is an excellent resource for discussions on parent liability for CERCLA violations as well as a history of the development and scope of CERCLA. See, for example, Oswald and Schipani, "CERCLA and the 'Erosion' of Traditional Corporate Law Doctrine," 86 *Northwestern Law Review* 259 (1990). Their work was referred to in the *Bestfoods* case.

4. For more information about brownfields, go to http://www.epa.gov/brownfields.

5. Sheila McNulty, "BP Safety Culture under Attack," *Financial Times*, March 20, 2007, p. 15. The report recommended that

BP comply with 29 C.F.R. 1910.119, Process Safety Management of Highly Hazardous Chemicals and implement an effective means of process safety management.

6. Guy Chazan, Benoit Faucon, and Ben Casselman, "Safety and Cost Drives Clashed as CEO Hayward Remade BP," *Wall Street Journal*, June 30, 2010, p. A1.

7. Sarah Lyall, Clifford Kraus, and Jad Mouawad, "In BP's Record, a History of Boldness and Blunders," *New York Times*, July 13, 2010, p. A1.

8. Guy Chazan, Benoit Faucon, and Ben Casselman, "Safety and Cost Drives Clashed as CEO Hayward Remade BP," *Wall Street Journal*, June 30, 2010, p. A1.

9. Neil King Jr. and Russell Gold, "BP Crew Focused on Costs: Congress," *Wall Street Journal*, June 15, 2010, pp. A1, A5.

10. Julie Schmit, "Oil Execs: BP Didn't Meet Standards," *USA Today*, June 16, 2010, p. 1B.

11. Peter Coy and Stanley Reed, "Lessons of the Spill," *Bloomberg BusinessWeek*, May 10–May 16, 2010, p. 48.

12. Naureen S. Malik, "Protests Target BP But Hit Independents," *Wall Street Journal*, June 16, 2010, p. A4.

13. Chris Woodyard, "Dual Shower Heads Land Hotel in Hot Water," *USA Today*, May 22, 2001, p. 1B.

Part 3

BUSINESS SALES, CONTRACTS, AND COMPETITION

This section of the book covers the laws and regulations on what a business sells, how it sells its product, the condition of that product, and how the sales are financed. Do you have the right to sell a product, or have you appropriated someone else's idea? What can you say and write in your advertising? What is fair and legal in competition? When do you have a contract, and what kinds of terms do you need to have in it? In this era of electronic commerce, what exactly is a contract, and when is it formed? When has a contract been performed, and what is a breach? Can you be compensated if the other side fails to perform? How are transactions financed, and what disclosures do you need? What are a seller's rights for collecting payments due from buyers? An overarching issue in all sales is whether businesses are competing on the merits of their products or whether they are colluding on price or bids. If you build a better mousetrap, you are entitled to the customers that quality brings. But, if you refuse to deal with your bug spray customers unless they buy your inferior mousetrap, then the antitrust laws apply. The level playing field is what antitrust laws protect in competition.

This portion of the text covers the issues of contracts, production, advertising, property ownership and rights, and competition. The materials walk through the heart of business operations all the way from contract performance to receivables collection.

Chapter 12

CONTRACTS AND SALES:
Introduction and Formation

Contracts allow businesses to count on money, supplies, and services. Contracts are the private law of business; the parties develop their own private set of laws through their contracts. These private laws can be enforced by the courts in all states. This chapter covers contract basics: What is a contract? What laws govern contracts? What are the types of contracts? How are contracts formed? What statutes apply to consumer contract formation and credit extension? What contracts must be in writing?

UPDATE
For up-to-date legal and ethical news, go to **mariannejennings.com**

Bo Chambers/Flickr/Getty Images

A verbal contract isn't worth the paper it's written on.

Samuel Goldwyn

Consider...

In the summer of 1996, PepsiCo, Inc., ran a marketing campaign involving Pepsi Points. The Pepsi Points, obtained by drinking Pepsi, could be redeemed for prizes. One television ad promoting Pepsi Points shows a Harrier jet outside a schoolyard with the campaign's slogan beneath it: DRINK PEPSI GET STUFF. The jet pictured in the ad was generated by computer. The ad said the jet could be yours for 7 million Pepsi Points. PepsiCo maintains the ad was a spoof. John Leonard, then a 21-year-old business student, saw the ad and delivered to Pepsi 15 original Pepsi Points plus a check for $700,008.50—sufficient for the cost of a Harrier jet, plus shipping and handling.

Pepsi refused to deliver the jet. A Pentagon spokesman indicated that no Harrier jets were available at that time because the jets must be demilitarized before a member of the public can buy one. Pepsi also said that because the ad was a joke, it was not an offer. Mr. Leonard said that the ad induced conduct on his part, as would all Pepsi Points ads, and that Pepsi was required to deliver to him a Harrier jet.

Who was correct? Was the ad an offer?

12-1 What Is a Contract?

Businesses cannot expand and grow without being able to rely on commitments; resources are wasted if promises are not fulfilled. For example, suppose that Aunt Hattie's Bread Company constructs a new wing and buys new equipment to expand production, but when the wing is ready to operate, its wheat supplier backs out of a supply contract it has with Aunt Hattie's. Aunt Hattie's has relied on that promise, spent money counting on delivery on that promise, and now cannot expand because that promise was broken. The failure to honor a promise is more than just a breach of contract; economic ripple effects occur when businesses cannot rely on contractual promises.

"A **contract** is a promise or set of promises for breach of which the law gives a remedy, or the performance of which the law in some way recognizes as a duty." This definition comes from the *Restatement (Second) of Contracts*, a statement of contract law by the American Law Institute (ALI) and means that contract promises not kept require remedies or compensation for the private parties involved. This chapter focuses on the creation, performance, and enforcement of those promises.

12-2 **Sources of Contract Law**

The two general sources of contract law for contracts entered into the United States are common law and the Uniform Commercial Code (UCC). Some specific federal and state laws, covered later in the chapter, deal with unique issues in e-commerce contracts.

12-2a **COMMON LAW**

Common law was the first law of contracts. As discussed in Chapter 1, common law today consists of those traditional notions of law along with law developed by judicial decisions dealing with contract issues. Traditional English common law of contracts has been modified by statute in some states. Certain types of contracts have unique and specific content requirements—for example, listing agreements for real estate agents, insurance policies, and consumer credit contracts (see p. 376 for more information on the statutory requirements in consumer credit contracts). However, the statutory language and statutory requirements do not generally control the basic concepts of formation and enforcement of contracts. Common law applies to contracts that have land or services as their subject matter. Contracts for the construction of a home and employment contracts are governed by common law. A rental agreement for an apartment may be covered by specific landlord–tenant statutes in addition to common law.

A general treatment of the common law for contracts can be found in the *Restatement (Second) of Contracts*. A group of legal scholars wrote the *Restatement*, and similar groups work together to consider market changes and dynamics and modify contract law as necessary.

12-2b **THE UNIFORM COMMERCIAL CODE**

One of the problems with common law is its lack of uniformity. The states do not follow the same case decisions on contract law, and some states do not follow the *Restatement*; the result is that different rules apply to contracts in different states.

Consequently, businesses experienced great difficulty and expense when they contracted for the sale of goods across state lines because of differences in state contract common law. To address the need for uniformity, the National Conference of Commissioners on Uniform State Laws and the ALA worked to draft a set of commercial laws that would function well with business (ALI) needs. The result of the efforts of businesspeople, lawyers, and lawmakers working together was the **Uniform Commercial Code (UCC)**. The final draft of the UCC first appeared in the 1940s. With several revisions and much time and effort, the Code was adopted, at least in part, in all the states.

Article 2 of the UCC governs contracts for the sale of goods and has been adopted in all states except Louisiana. Although sections of Article 2 may have various forms throughout the states, the basic requirements for contracts remain consistent. Under Article 2, contracts can be formed more easily, the standards for performance are more readily defined, and the remedies are more easily determined. (Excerpts of Article 2 are reproduced in Appendix C.) Determining which contracts are UCC contracts and which are common law contracts is often difficult. The questions applied in the determination of UCC versus common law include the cost of the goods versus the cost of services in the contract, the parties' intent, and even some public policy issues. *Paramount Contracting Co. v DPS Industries, Inc.* (Case 12.1) addresses an interesting factual issue involving a question of goods and the application of UCC Article 2.

CASE 12.1

Paramount Contracting Co. v DPS Industries, Inc.
709 S.E.2d 288 (Ga. App. 2011)

Dirt Is Cheap, But It Is Still a Good

FACTS

Paramount, a civil engineering firm and general contractor, submitted a bid to perform the construction of runway improvements at the Atlanta Hartsfield–Jackson International Airport. Paramount included DPS's quote for supplying the fill dirt for the project in its bid. DPS's written quote described its work as "furnish[ing] and haul[ing]/deliver[ing] borrow dirt from DPS's location to the job site," and specifically excluded the provision of "traffic control, dust control, security and escort services" from the scope of work. The quote provides that the dirt would be delivered for a price of "$140/Truck Load."

After Paramount was awarded the airport project, it contacted DPS about the amount of dirt and numbers of trucks it would need for the airport project. DPS believed that the parties had a contract, and it sent a letter to Paramount confirming that it was "holding approximately 45,000 [cubic yards] of borrow dirt ready to be hauled in to your project once we receive [the] 10–day notice from you." Paramount did not respond.

Over the next two months, DPS sent other letters to Paramount about their agreement, but Paramount did not respond. After a meeting of executives from the two companies, Paramount sent the following:

> [Y]ou insisted that we give commitment to you for buying the dirt before you will give us price [for other work]. This really was a surprise to us…. Also please note that we have never committed to buy all the fill materials from you. In the last meeting you were informed that we intend to purchase some materials from you and it may be through other subcontractors. Our decisions will be conveyed to you as soon as possible.

Ultimately, Paramount bought the dirt it needed from another vendor. DPS sued Paramount for breach of contract. The jury found for DPS. Paramount appealed.

JUDICIAL OPINION

BLACKWELL, Judge

The question of formation depends on [whether the contract is] governed by Article 2 of the Commercial Code or the common law. []it is easier, generally speaking, to form a binding contract under Article 2 than under the common law. Article 2 applies only to contracts for the sale of goods, and it does not apply to contracts for the mere provision of services or labor. When a transaction involves both the sale of a good and the provision of services or labor, whether the transaction is governed by Article 2 depends upon the "predominant purpose" of the transaction. When the predominant element of a contract is the sale of goods, the contract is viewed as a sales contract and [Article 2] applies, even though a substantial amount of service is to be rendered in installing the goods.

DPS said that the parties contemplated only that DPS would sell and deliver dirt, and DPS urged that Article 2 applies because the sale of goods—the dirt that DPS offered to furnish to Paramount—was the predominant purpose of the contemplated transaction. Paramount, on the other hand, said that the parties also contemplated that DPS would perform other tasks, such as placing and compacting dirt at the construction site.

It was for the jury to weigh the conflicting evidence, resolve this disputed issue of fact, and determine exactly what the contemplated transaction involved. So long as the evidence would permit a rational jury to resolve this issue in a way that would lead to a conclusion that the sale of goods was the predominant purpose of the contemplated transaction.

The evidence is consistent with a finding that the sale of dirt was the predominant purpose of the contemplated transaction. The DPS quote contains representations and warranties about the quality of the dirt. The pricing was based on the quantity of dirt furnished, not the miles driven or time spent to deliver the dirt. DPS did not provide separate pricing for the sale of the dirt and its delivery. Paramount itself characterized the transaction repeatedly as one for the sale and furnishing of dirt, not the hauling of dirt.

Paramount relies on testimony that the costs of furnishing and hauling dirt would amount to approximately $70 or $80 per load, and that these costs would include both the expenses of operating a backhoe to load trucks and the expenses of operating the trucks. Paramount says that these cost factors all relate to hauling dirt and establish, therefore, that most of the transaction costs were related to hauling, not furnishing, the dirt.

Under Article 2, dirt is a "good" only if it is severed from the land by the seller, so the separation of dirt

CONTINUED

from the land is a necessary component of the sale of dirt, not its transportation after sale.

Finally, Paramount asks us to attribute the majority of the costs to hauling on the basis of the conventional wisdom that "dirt is cheap." We decline this invitation. Dirt might well be cheap, but we have no reason to believe that it is free and no basis for knowing just how cheap it is. We are not prepared to speculate that the commercial value of such dirt is negligible, much less to reverse a judgment entered on a jury verdict based on such speculation.

Judgment affirmed.

CASE QUESTIONS

1. Why is it important that DPS was not doing anything else at the airport site other than delivering the dirt?

2. Why is the concept of predominant importance important in determining UCC versus common law contracts?

3. Is the cost of the backhoes needed to remove the dirt considered by the court as part of the services versus goods cost component of the contract? Why or why not?

Consider...

Click2Boost, Inc. (C2B) entered into an Internet marketing agreement with the *New York Times* (NYT) (respondents) for C2B to solicit subscribers for home delivery of the *New York Times* newspaper through "pop-up ads" on websites with which C2B maintained "[m]arketing [a]lliances." The agreement required NYT to pay C2B a fee or commission for each home delivery subscription C2B submitted to NYT.

NYT paid C2B about $1.5 million in subscription submission fees from May 2002 to September 2003, but most of the subscriptions were ended, so NYT terminated the C2B agreement.

Wall Street Network (WSN) then took over C2B and filed suit for breach of contract against NYT, claiming that NYT had breached the agreement by terminating it. The contract was one for goods and C2B had furnished those goods. WSN made its claim under the UCC because the pop-up ads were sold independently as goods. NYT argued that the contract was one for services—for furnishing subscribers—something C2B did not do successfully.

WSN countered that the customers generated from the pop-up ads were what was being sold, and that this was just like selling a list of names, something that would be considered a good. The trial court granted the NYT summary judgment and WSN appealed.

[*Wall Street Network, Ltd. v New York Times Company*, 164 Cal. App. 4th 1171, 80 Cal Rptr. 3d 6, 66 UCC Rep Serv. 2d 261 (2008)]

THINK: The discussion of UCC versus common law has us examine the following:

- The essence of the parties' agreement—what was its purpose? What was to be provided under its terms?

- The general nature of the subject matter of the contract.

- The amount of service provided under the contract.

APPLY: In this case, under the agreement, C2B was obliged to place pop-up ads at the websites of its marketing partners and then relay information from customers who responded to the ads to NYT. C2B was providing a service from which it was able to obtain information.

ANSWER: C2B did not sell NYT names and addresses of persons to whom NYT intended—by its own efforts—to send solicitations for subscriptions; rather, C2B agreed to solicit subscribers for NYT by placing subscription advertisements for NYT in designated locations, and to forward responses to the advertisements. The contract is covered by the common law.

Now apply these reasoning skills to determine whether the following subject matters would be governed by the UCC or by common law:

- Electricity [*Gordonsville Energy, L.P. v Virginia Electric & Power Co.*, 29 U.C.C. Rep. Serv. 2d 849 (Va. Cir. 1996)]

- Boats [*Standing v Midgett*, 22 U.C.C. Rep. Serv. 2d 472, 850 F. Supp. 396 (E.D.N.C. 1993)]

- Software to provide voice messaging, described as a "turnkey" system—that is, it operates without additional work [*Pentagram Software Corp. v Voicetek Corp.*, 22 U.C.C. Rep. Serv. 2d 646 (Mass. Super. 1993)]

- Golf irrigation systems [*Champion Turf, Inc. v Rice, Papuchis Const. Co.*, 21 U.C.C. Rep. Serv. 2d 519, 853 S.W.2d 323 (Mo. App. 1993)]

- Wheat [*Mogan v Cargill, Inc.*, 21 U.C.C. Rep. Serv. 2d 661, 856 P.2d 973 (1993)]

- Standing timber [*Bohle v Thompson*, 8 U.C.C. Rep. Serv. 2d 897, 78 Md. App. 614, 554 A.2d 818 (1989)]

- Mobile homes [*Aslakson v Home Sav. Ass'n*, 6 U.C.C. Rep. Serv. 2d 35, 416 N.W.2d 786 (Minn. App. 1987)]

- High-frequency on-board battery chargers for electric golf carts and the installation and service of the system that charges them [*TK Power, Inc. v Textron, Inc.* 433 F. Supp. 2d 1058 (N.D. Cal. 2006)]

- Diamonds [*Wixon Jewelers, Inc. v Di-Star, Ltd.*, 218 F.3d 913, 42 U.C.C. Rep. Serv. 2d 94 (8th Cir. 2000)]

- Livestock [*Flanagan v Consolidated Nutrition, L.C.*, 627 N.W.2d 573 (Iowa Ct. App. 2001)]

- Degas painting [*Weil v Murray*, 161 F. Supp. 2d 250, 44 U.C.C. Rep. Serv. 2d 482 (S.D.N.Y. 2001)]

- Ticket to an amusement park ride [*Dantzler v S.P. Parks, Inc.*, 40 U.C.C. Rep. Serv. 2d 955, 1988 WL 131428 (E.D. Pa. 1988)]

- Concert tickets [*State v Cardwell*, 38 U.C.C. Rep. Serv. 2d 1158, 718 A.2d 954 (1998)]

Article 2A—Leases

The UCC has added a section called Article 2A Leases, which applies to leases of goods. Over the past 10 years, many new forms of goods transactions have developed, such as the long-term auto lease, which appears to be more of a sale than a lease. Because of the nature of these agreements, leases did not fit well under common law or traditional Article 2. The Leases section, drafted for these types of contracts, covers such issues as the statute of frauds (leases in which payments exceed $1,000, for example, must be in writing), contract formation, and warranties associated with a lease.

E-Commerce Contract Law: Uniform Computer Information Transactions Act

The **Uniform Computer Information Transactions Act (UCITA)** was promulgated in 1999 and has been adopted in two states (Virginia and Maryland) and proposed in others.[1] The UCITA would govern all contracts involving the sale, licensing, maintenance, and support of computer software. Those contracts not involving software that are contracts for the sale of other goods would still be governed by the UCC along with the UETA, if adopted in the state.

The UCITA allows terms that are not revealed to the buyer until after payment and delivery to become part of the contract. Typically, these terms are presented in what are often called "shrink-wrap" or "clickwrap" contracts. Once you open the shrink-wrap on the product, you have agreed to the terms, or, once you click "OK" in an electronic transaction, you have agreed to the terms. The UCITA also treats software and digital content contracts as "licenses" rather than sales of goods or sales of copies of software. This classification and treatment creates some questions about these types of contracts and whether they are governed by UCC or common law.

12-3 Types of Contracts

The following sections cover the various types of contracts and offer an introduction to contract terminology.

12-3a BILATERAL VERSUS UNILATERAL CONTRACTS

A contract can result from two parties exchanging promises to perform or from one party exchanging a promise for the other party's actions. A **bilateral contract** is one in which both parties promise to perform certain things. For example, if you sign a contract to buy a used red Mini Cooper for $2,000, you have entered into a bilateral contract with the seller. The seller has promised not to sell the car to anyone else and will give you the title to the car when you pay the $2,000. You have promised to buy that red Mini Cooper and will turn over the $2,000 to the seller in exchange for the title. The contract consists of two promises: your promise to buy and the seller's promise to sell.

FOR THE MANAGER'S DESK

Re: A Unilateral Tattoo

In a case bound to leave an imprint in the halls of justice, David Winkleman and Richard Goddard filed suit against the owner of a Davenport, Iowa, radio station (KORB-FM), Cumulus Broadcasting, because they allege that they had "93 Rock" tattooed on their foreheads in response to a disc jockey's promise. According to the permanently tattooed men, they heard disc jockey Ben Stone say on November 29, 2000, that the radio station would pay anyone who got "93 Rock" tattooed on their foreheads $30,000 per year for five years plus concert tickets, backstage passes, and a TV satellite dish.

Mr. Winkleman and Mr. Goddard say that when they called to confirm the offer, someone at the station referred them to a tattoo parlor. The station refused to pay the men, asserting that the statements by Mr. Stone were simply a joke and no one would assume otherwise.

The two men also say that they have been unable to get jobs since the tattoos and that they have been "publicly scorned and ridiculed for their greed and lack of common good sense."

The case was dismissed in 2003 because the court found no evidence that such an offer had been made. The audiotapes from the interchange indicated that the disc jockey actually said the men could go ahead and tattoo all they wanted, but that there "wasn't even a free CD in it for you." Subsequently, the two tattooed men were involved in dramatic incidents at their trailer park homes, including attempted murder of one by a neighbor wielding a ball-peen hammer. Another incident dealt with accusations of arson involving his mobile home because the fire that destroyed the home followed on the heels of his garage sale of all of his personal items that were in the mobile home.

Source: Annie Hsia, "Here's my tattoo. Where's the cash?" *National Law Journal,* June 24–July 1, 2002, p. A4.

Some contracts have one party issuing a promise and the other party simply performing. This type of contract is called a **unilateral contract**. For example, suppose that your uncle said, "I will pay you $500 if you will drive my new Mercedes to San Francisco for me within the next five days." Your uncle has promised to pay, but you have not promised to do anything. Nonetheless, you can hold your uncle to his promise if you drive his car to San Francisco. Your agreement is a promise in exchange for performance. If you drive the car to San Francisco, your uncle's promise will be enforceable as a unilateral contract.

12-3b EXPRESS VERSUS IMPLIED CONTRACTS (*QUASI* CONTRACTS)

Some contracts are written, signed (even notarized), and very formal in appearance. Others are simply verbal agreements between the parties (see p. 397 for a discussion of the types of contracts that can be oral). Still others are electronic contracts entered into via e-mail and the Internet. A contract that is written or orally agreed to is an **express contract**. In still other situations, the parties do not discuss the terms of the contract but nonetheless understand that they have some form of contractual relationship. A contract that arises from circumstances and not from the express agreement of the parties is called an **implied contract**, as when you go to a doctor for treatment of an illness. You and the doctor do not sit down and negotiate the terms of treatment, the manner in which the doctor will conduct the examination, or how much you will pay. You understand that the doctor will do whatever examinations are appropriate to determine the cause of your illness and that a fee is associated with the doctor's work. The payment and treatment terms are implied from general professional customs. You have an **implied-in-fact contract**.

A second type of implied or enforceable agreement is called an **implied-in-law contract** or a *quasi* contract. The term *quasi* means "as if" and describes the action of a court when it treats parties who do not have a contract "as if" they did. The courts enforce a *quasi* contract right if one party has conferred a benefit on another, both are aware of the benefit, and the retention of the benefit would be an enrichment of one party at the unjust expense of the other.

The theory of *quasi* contracts is not used to help "the officious meddler." The officious meddler is someone who performs unrequested work or services and then, based on a *quasi* contract theory, seeks recovery. For example, you could not be required to compensate a painting contractor who came by and painted your house without your permission because the contractor acted both without your knowledge and without your consent. However, if you are aware the painting is going on and you do nothing to stop it, you would be held liable in *quasi* contract.

12-3c VOID AND VOIDABLE CONTRACTS

A **void contract** is an agreement to do something that is illegal or against public policy, or one that lacks legal elements (see Chapter 13). For example, a contract to sell weapons to a country under a weapons ban is a void contract. Neither side can enforce the contract, even if the weapons have already been delivered, because allowing the seller to collect payment would encourage further violations of the law banning the weapons sales.

A contract may be partially void—that is, only a portion of the contract violates a statute or public policy and is therefore unenforceable. For example, in many states, it is illegal to charge excessive rates of interest (known as usury). In a usurious loan contract, the loan repayment would be enforceable, but the interest terms would not be. As another example, suppose that an owner has sold her business and in the contract has agreed never to start another similar business. Although the buyer deserves some protection for the payment of goodwill, the complete elimination of the seller's right to start a business is an excessive restraint of trade that is against public policy and would not be enforced, even though the actual sale of the business would be enforced.

A **voidable contract** is a contract that can be unenforceable at the election of one of the parties. For example, a minor who signs a contract can choose to be bound by the agreement or can choose to disaffirm the contract. Voidable contracts give one party the option of disaffirming the contract.

12-3d UNENFORCEABLE CONTRACTS

An **unenforceable contract** is a contract that cannot be honored judicially because of some procedural problem. A contract that should be in writing to comply with the statute of frauds but is not written is unenforceable. Another example of an unenforceable contract is when a party who wishes to enforce a contract does not bring suit within the time limits of the statute of limitations. Filing suit too late means the contract is unenforceable.

12-3e EXECUTED VERSUS EXECUTORY CONTRACTS

Contracts are **executed contracts** when the parties have performed according to their promises or required actions (under unilateral agreements). Contracts are **executory contracts** when the promise to perform is made but the actual performance has not been done. If you sign a contract to buy a house but have not obtained a loan or deposited monies in escrow, you have an executory contract. A contract may be wholly executed, wholly executory, or partially executed. For example, when a business files for bankruptcy, some of its contracts are executory and some are partially executed, such as those contracts in which the business has paid for goods but the goods have not been delivered. The bankruptcy trustee has the option of canceling executory contracts but will generally complete or require other parties to complete partially executed contracts. Courts often distinguish between executed and executory contracts in determining both the rights of the parties (particularly with respect to issues of public policy and capacity) and the remedies available to the parties.

12-4 Consumer Credit Contracts

12-4a DISCRIMINATION IN CREDIT CONTRACTS

Under the Equal Credit Opportunity Act (ECOA), it is unlawful to discriminate against an applicant for credit on the basis of race, color, religion, national origin, gender, marital status, or age; because all or part of the applicant's income is obtained from a public assistance program; or because the applicant has in good faith exercised any right under the Consumer Credit Protection Act (CCPA). When a credit application is refused, the lender must provide the applicant with a written explanation, such as high credit card balances or no credit history on installment loans.

Under the ECOA, debtors can recover actual damages for embarrassment and emotional distress and for punitive damages of up to $10,000. If a group of debtors brings a class action against a creditor, they can collect punitive damages of up to the lesser of $500,000 or 1 percent of the creditor's net worth. *A.B.&S. Auto Service, Inc. v South Shore Bank of Chicago* (Case 12.2) involves an ECOA issue.

CASE 12.2

A.B.&S. Auto Service, Inc. v South Shore Bank of Chicago
962 F. Supp. 1056 (N.D. Ill. 1997)

Do the Crime, Forget the Loan

FACTS

A.B.&S. Auto Service, Inc. (AB&S) is an automobile repair shop located in Chicago, Illinois. Jerry L. Bonner is AB&S's president, and he is an African-American. South Shore is a commercial bank that participates in the Small Business Administration's (SBA) loan guarantee program.

The SBA requires all applicants for the loan guarantee program to fill out an SBA Form 912 Statement of Personal History. SBA Form 912 asks applicants if they have ever been charged with or arrested or convicted for any criminal offense other than a minor motor vehicle violation and, if so, asks applicants to provide details. In February 1995, AB&S applied for a $230,000 business loan from the bank. Mr. Bonner submitted Form 912 and in his response to its question about arrests and convictions, Mr. Bonner noted the following:

1. Domestic matters between 1982 and 1984
2. Conviction for aggravated battery and assault (1983) (claims self-defense)
3. Possession of a controlled substance in 1985
4. Disorderly conduct between 1985 and 1990
5. Possession of a controlled substance in 1990
6. Possession of a stolen car in September 1994

Leslie Davis, an African-American vice president at South Shore Bank, recommended approval of Mr. Bonner's application. However, the loan committee agreed that because of Mr. Bonner's criminal record, the application should be denied. The bank then decided to deny the loan.

During the last 15 years, the South Shore Bank has made at least three business loans to applicants with criminal records. One of these three applicants was an African-American. South Shore evaluates each application on an individual basis and examines criminal record and other information for purposes of determining character.

Mr. Bonner and his company (plaintiffs) filed suit under the ECOA because the bank's practice of considering criminal record has an unlawful disparate impact on African-American men. South Shore Bank (defendants) moved for summary judgment as did Mr. Bonner.

JUDICIAL OPINION

WILLIAMS, Anne Claire, District Judge

In order to prove discrimination under the disparate impact analysis or "effects" test, an applicant must show how "a policy, procedure, or practice specifically identified by the [applicant] has a significantly greater discriminatory impact on members of a protected class."

Plaintiffs traditionally establish this prima facie case by making "a statistical comparison of the representation of the protected class in the applicant pool with representation in the group actually accepted from the pool…. If the statistical disparity is significant, then plaintiff is deemed to have made out a prima facie case."

Plaintiffs claim that South Shore Bank's practice of considering an applicant's criminal record in making commercial lending decisions has a disparate impact on African-Americans. To make the prima facie case plaintiffs offer the testimony of Dr. Jaslin U. Salmon.

Dr. Salmon testified that any decision that is based on arrest records would militate against people of color. He suggests that, based on his research, there are many cases in which the black applicant is qualified, creditworthy, but was not given the loan for other reasons and among those reasons, arrest records had been taken into consideration. However, the bank disputes this point because Dr. Salmon was unable to identify a single study showing that consideration of arrest records has a disproportionate impact on African-American applicants for any type of credit, much less any study addressing the impact on business loan applicants.

Both the statistics and Dr. Salmon's supporting testimony do not answer the following questions: (1) how many African-Americans with convictions or arrests are otherwise qualified for the loan; and (2) how many African-Americans are deterred from applying because of the bank's practice…. [t]he bank has made at least three business loans to applicants with criminal records. One of these three applicants with criminal records is African-American.

South Shore Bank's practice of inquiring into a credit applicant's criminal history is legitimately related to its extension of credit for two reasons. First, the regulations require the SBA, in evaluating a loan guarantee application, to consider "the character, reputation, and credit history of the applicant, its associates, and guarantors."

CONTINUED

Secondly, the bank's inquiry into an applicant's criminal record provides relevant information about an applicant's creditworthiness, particularly his judgment and character. Plaintiff Bonner admits that several of the incidents described in his completed SBA Form 912: possession of a controlled substance, domestic abuse, and disorderly conduct, reflected negatively on his judgment and character. Specifically, Bonner admits that these incidents involved an exercise of bad judgment.

Therefore, the court finds that the bank has successfully demonstrated that its practice of inquiring into a credit applicant's criminal record is legitimately related to the extension of credit.

For the foregoing reasons, the court grants defendant South Shore Bank's motion for summary judgment and denies plaintiff Bonner and AB&S's motion for summary judgment.

CASE QUESTIONS

1. What, according to Mr. Bonner's expert, is the impact of considering criminal records of applicants? Did the evidence support the expert's testimony?

2. Is the use of a criminal record in making a decision to extend credit a violation of the ECOA? Explain.

3. Do you think a criminal record is an indication of character? Explain.

12-4b SUBPRIME OR PREDATORY LENDING

With the economic crisis of 2008, the federal government passed significant reforms in credit contracts. Part of the reforms focused on the subprime lending market. This credit market makes loans to consumers who have bankruptcies, no credit history, low-to-moderate incomes, or a poor credit history. Because of the higher risk of these types of loans, these credit contracts involve lower loan amounts; higher origination costs, brokers' fees, credit insurance fees; higher interest rates; significant collateral pledges; large prepayment penalties (meaning that the consumer debtor is locked into the high interest rate); and faster repayment requirements. Subprime loans have had notoriously difficult-to-read contracts. Determining all of the charges and fees from the contract was a tall order. Regulations and laws at the state and federal level have changed and simplified contract disclosures for subprime loans.

Part of the subprime lending market includes lenders who take advantage of less sophisticated consumers or even consumers who are just desperate for funds. These lenders use their superior bargaining positions to obtain credit terms that go well beyond compensating them for their risk. For example, title loans (loans made in exchange for title to a car or house if the borrower defaults) have been widely used in subprime markets. These types of loans, sometimes called predatory lending, are now highly regulated by both the states and the federal government. The new wave of consumer protection on subprime loans includes limitations on interest rates, 10-day rescission periods, additional contract disclosures requirements, and the requirement of credit counseling before consumers may sign for certain types of subprime loans.

12-4c CREDIT DISCLOSURES

Federal laws require the disclosure of all interest charges, points, and fees for all types of loans and credit contracts. These laws require disclosure of an annual percentage rate (APR) so that the consumer can see just how much the transaction costs per year and can compare alternatives. The **Truth in Lending Act (TILA)** provides the requirements for disclosures in credit contracts and consumer rights when full disclosure is not made. When a consumer sale or contract provides for payment in more than four installments, it is subject to the TILA. The application of the TILA is required even when there is no service or finance charge for the installment payments. There are additional obligations of disclosure under the Fair Credit and Charge Card Disclosure Act, the Home Equity Loan Consumer

Protection Act, and the Credit Card Accountability, Responsibility and Disclosure (CARD) Act of 2009.

In 2009, the new Bureau of Consumer Financial Protection (BCFP or Bureau), created under the Dodd-Frank Wall Street Reform and Consumer Protection Act (DFCPA), also known as the Wall Street Reform and Consumer Financial Protection Act or the Consumer Financial Protection Act (CFPA), was designated to assume the enforcement role on consumer credit contracts. Housed within the Federal Reserve, the BCFP now serves the combined roles that the Federal Reserve as well as the Federal Trade Commission (FTC) and other federal agencies played in dealing with consumer credit laws, regulations, and issues.

12-4d CONTROLLING CREDIT CARD CONTRACTS

Federal regulations prohibit the unsolicited distribution of credit cards to persons who have not applied for them. The practice of simply sending credit cards through the mail to consumers is now illegal. The problems with rising identity theft have made this protection especially important to consumers because identity thieves were able to intercept the mail and seize the unsolicited credit cards.

Credit Cards for Those Under the Age of 21

The CARD Act substantially restricts the solicitation of credit card accounts from those under the age of 21. Credit card companies must have a written application in hand from those under 21 and those applications must carry the signature of a parent, guardian, or someone over the age of 21 who has the means to repay debt. The line of credit on a co-signed card for someone under the age of 21 cannot be increased without the co-signer's permission.

Colleges and universities are now restricted in their partnering with credit card companies, arrangements that allowed the colleges and universities and their alumni associations to receive funds from the credit card companies in exchange for access to their students and alumni. The CARD Act limits locations for college student credit card solicitations, requires colleges and universities to disclose their financial relationships with such credit card companies, and also requires colleges and universities to provide debt counseling for their students.

Liability Limitations

A cardholder is not liable for more than $50 for the unauthorized use of a credit card. To even recover the $50 amount, the credit card issuer must show that (1) the credit card was an accepted card, (2) the issuer gave the holder adequate notice of possible liability in such a case, (3) the issuer furnished the holder with notification means in the event of loss or theft of the credit card, (4) the issuer provided a method by which the user of the card could be identified as the person authorized to use it, and (5) unauthorized use of the card had occurred or might occur as a result of loss, theft, or some other event. The burden of proof is on the card issuer to show that the use of the card was authorized or that the holder is liable for its unauthorized use.

Transfer Terms

Transfers of consumer credit balances to new credit cards were once a lucrative area for banks and credit card companies. However, the CARD Act has changed everything from the maximum fees allowed with these transfers to how quickly credit card companies can change the advertised terms of the transfer. New disclosure requirements mandate the upfront disclosure of transfer fees as well as potential changes in the APR once the transfer has occurred. The CARD Act also places limits on how often companies can change a credit card holder's interest rate.

12-5 **Formation of Contracts**

A contract is formed when two parties with the correct mental intent, under the correct circumstances, within the boundaries of the law, and with some detriment to each of them agree to do certain acts in exchange for the other's acts. Formation elements are like ingredients in a recipe: If you leave one ingredient out of the recipe, the final result will be off in some way. So it is with the elements of a contract. You can have all the elements of formation, but if the subject matter is illegal, it will invalidate the contract. Exhibit 12.1 illustrates all elements necessary for the formation of a valid contract.

12-5a **OFFER**

The **offer** is the first part of a contract. The person who makes the offer is called the **offeror**, and the person to whom the offer is made is called the **offeree**. The following sections cover the requirements for a valid offer.

Intent to Contract versus Negotiation

The offeror must have the proper intent (mental state) to contract. Intent is gleaned from the language the offeror uses. This intent requirement distinguishes offers from negotiations. For example, a letter from a businessperson may contain the following: "I am interested in investing in a franchise. I have heard about your opportunities. Please send me all necessary information." The letter expresses an interest in possibly contracting in the future, but it does not express present intent to enter into a contract. But suppose this letter of inquiry was followed by another letter with the following language: "I have decided to invest in one of your

EXHIBIT 12.1 Overview of Contracts

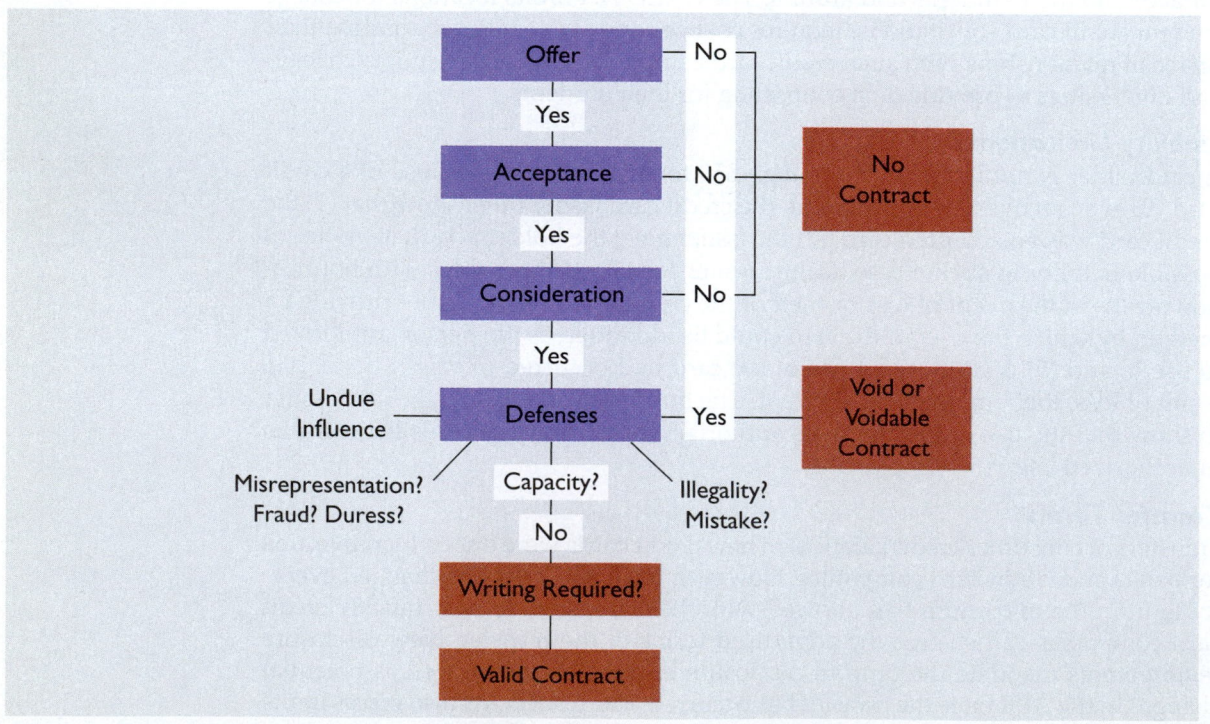

© Cengage Learning

franchises. Enclosed are the necessary documents, signatures, and a deposit check." Here the parties have passed the negotiation stage and entered into part one of the contract—an offer.

Courts use an objective standard in determining the intent of the parties, which means that courts look at how a reasonable person would perceive the language, the surrounding circumstances, and the actions of the parties in determining whether a contract was formed. For example, a businessperson who is exasperated with the poor financial performance of her firm may say jokingly to someone over lunch, "I'd sell this company to anyone willing to take it." If that statement is made in the context of a series of complaints about the firm and the workload, it would not be an offer. That same language used in a luncheon meeting with a prospective buyer would create a different result.

In many situations, one party has simply requested bids or is inviting offers. The frustrated business owner could say, "I am interested in selling my firm. If you run into anyone who is interested, have them call me." The owner has not made an offer to sell but, rather, has made an invitation for an offer.

Ads are simply invitations for offers. *Leonard v PepsiCo* (Case 12.3) provides the answer for the chapter's opening "Consider..." because it deals with an issue of the role of an ad in contract formation.

CASE 12.3

Leonard v PepsiCo
210 F.3d 88 (2d Cir. 2000)[2]

Does "Pepsi Stuff" Include a Harrier Jet?

FACTS

PepsiCo (defendant/appellee) ran a promotion titled "Pepsi Stuff," which encouraged consumers to collect Pepsi Points from specially marked packages of Pepsi or Diet Pepsi and redeem these points for merchandise featuring the Pepsi logo. John Leonard (plaintiff/appellant) saw the Pepsi Stuff commercial featuring the Harrier Jet as an example of "stuff." The ad shows a teenager in awe of the jet and the subtitles on the screen are descriptions of what the teen sees: "T-SHIRT 75 PEPSI POINTS," subtitle "LEATHER JACKET 1450 PEPSI POINTS," and "SHADES 175 PEPSI POINTS." A voiceover then intones, "Introducing the new Pepsi Stuff catalog," as the camera focuses on the cover of the catalog.

Following these lesser items, a Harrier jet swings into view and lands by the side of the teen's school building, next to a bicycle rack. The cockpit opens and the teen, inside the cockpit of the Harrier jet, holding a Pepsi exclaims, "Sure beats the bus!" A military drum-roll sounds as the following words appear: "HARRIER FIGHTER 7,000,000 PEPSI POINTS." A few seconds later, the following appears in more stylized script: "Drink Pepsi—Get Stuff."

Inspired by this commercial, Mr. Leonard set out to obtain a Harrier jet. The catalog notes that in the event that a consumer lacks enough Pepsi Points to obtain a desired item, additional Pepsi Points may be purchased for 10 cents each; however, at least 15 original Pepsi Points must accompany each order.

Mr. Leonard could not collect 7,000,000 Pepsi Points by consuming Pepsi products fast enough, so through acquaintances, Mr. Leonard raised about $700,000. On March 27, 1996, Mr. Leonard submitted an order form, 15 original Pepsi Points, and a check for $700,008.50. At the bottom of the order form, Mr. Leonard wrote in "1 Harrier Jet" in the "Item" column and "7,000,000" in the "Total Points" column. In a letter accompanying his submission, Mr. Leonard stated that the check was to purchase additional Pepsi Points "expressly for obtaining a new Harrier jet as advertised in your Pepsi Stuff commercial." On May 7, 1996, PepsiCo rejected Mr. Leonard's submission and returned the check, explaining that

> The item that you have requested is not part of the Pepsi Stuff collection. It is not included in the catalogue or on the order form, and only catalogue merchandise can be redeemed under this program.

CONTINUED

The Harrier jet in the Pepsi commercial is fanciful and is simply included to create a humorous and entertaining ad. We apologize for any misunderstanding or confusion that you may have experienced and are enclosing some free product coupons for your use.

Mr. Leonard responded via his lawyer:

Your letter of May 7, 1996 is totally unacceptable. We have reviewed the video tape of the Pepsi Stuff commercial … and it clearly offers the new Harrier jet for 7,000,000 Pepsi Points. Our client followed your rules explicitly …

This is a formal demand that you honor your commitment and make immediate arrangements to transfer the new Harrier jet to our client. If we do not receive transfer instructions within ten (10) business days of the date of this letter, you will leave us no choice but to file an appropriate action against Pepsi …

Mr. Leonard filed suit, and PepsiCo moved for summary judgment. The court granted summary judgment, and Mr. Leonard appealed.

JUDICIAL OPINION

WOOD, District Judge
PER CURIAM
We affirm for substantially the reasons stated in Judge Wood's opinion. See 88 F. Supp. 2d 116 (S.D.N.Y.1999). [To help you understand the issues in the case, portions of Judge Wood's opinion follow.]

The general rule is that an advertisement does not constitute an offer.

An advertisement is not transformed into an enforceable offer merely by a potential offeree's expression of willingness to accept the offer through, among other means, completion of an order form.

Under these principles, plaintiff's letter of March 27, 1996, with the Order Form and the appropriate number of Pepsi Points, constituted the offer. There would be no enforceable contract until defendant accepted the Order Form and cashed the check.

The exception to the rule that advertisements do not create any power of acceptance in potential offerees is where the advertisement is "clear, definite, and explicit, and leaves nothing open for negotiation," in that circumstance, "it constitutes an offer, acceptance of which will complete the contract." *Lefkowitz v Great Minneapolis Surplus Store*, 251 Minn. 188, 86 N.W.2d 689, 691 (1957). In *Lefkowitz*, defendant had published a newspaper announcement stating: "Saturday 9 AM Sharp, 3 Brand New Fur Coats, Worth to $100.00, First Come First Served $1 Each." Mr. Morris Lefkowitz arrived at the store, dollar in hand, but was informed that under defendant's "house rules," the offer was open to ladies, but not gentlemen. The court ruled that because plaintiff had fulfilled all of the terms of the advertisement and the advertisement was specific and left nothing open for negotiation, a contract had been formed.

The present case is distinguishable from *Lefkowitz*. First, the commercial cannot be regarded in itself as sufficiently definite, because it specifically reserved the details of the offer to a separate writing, the Catalog. The commercial itself made no mention of the steps a potential offeree would be required to take to accept the alleged offer of a Harrier Jet. The advertisement in *Lefkowitz*, in contrast, "identified the person who could accept." Second, even if the Catalog had included a Harrier Jet among the items that could be obtained by redemption of Pepsi Points, the advertisement of a Harrier Jet by both television commercial and catalog would still not constitute an offer.

The Court finds, in sum, that the Harrier Jet commercial was merely an advertisement.

[P]laintiff largely relies on a different species of unilateral offer, involving public offers of a reward for performance of a specified act. Because these cases generally involve public declarations regarding the efficacy or trustworthiness of specific products, one court has aptly characterized these authorities as "prove me wrong" cases. The most venerable of these precedents is the case of *Carlill v Carbolic Smoke Ball Co.*, 1 Q.B. 256 (Court of Appeal, 1892), a quote from which heads plaintiff's memorandum of law: "[I]f a person chooses to make extravagant promises . . . he probably does so because it pays him to make them, and, if he has made them, the extravagance of the promises is no reason in law why he should not be bound by them."

The case arose during the London influenza epidemic of the 1890s. Among other advertisements of the time, for Clarke's World Famous Blood Mixture, Towle's Pennyroyal and Steel Pills for Females, Sequah's Prairie Flower, and Epp's Glycerine Jube-Jubes, appeared solicitations for the Carbolic Smoke Ball. The specific advertisement that Mrs. Carlill saw, and relied upon, read as follows:

£100 reward will be paid by the Carbolic Smoke Ball Company to any person who contracts the increasing epidemic influenza, colds, or any diseases caused by taking cold, after having used the ball three times daily for two weeks according to the printed directions supplied with each ball. £1000 is deposited with the Alliance Bank, Regent Street, shewing our sincerity in the matter.

During the last epidemic of influenza many thousand carbolic smoke balls were sold as preventives against this disease, and in no ascertained case was

CONTINUED

the disease contracted by those using the carbolic smoke ball.

Mrs. Carlill purchased the smoke ball and used it as directed, but contracted influenza nevertheless. The advertisement was construed as offering a reward because it sought to induce performance, unlike an invitation to negotiate, which seeks a reciprocal promise. As Lord Justice Lindley explained, "advertisements offering rewards . . . are offers to anybody who performs the conditions named in the advertisement, and anybody who does perform the condition accepts the offer." Because Mrs. Carlill had complied with the terms of the offer, yet contracted influenza, she was entitled to £100.

In the present case, the Harrier Jet commercial did not direct that anyone who appeared at Pepsi headquarters with 7,000,000 Pepsi Points on the Fourth of July would receive a Harrier Jet. Instead, the commercial urged consumers to accumulate Pepsi Points and to refer to the Catalog to determine how they could redeem their Pepsi Points. The commercial sought a reciprocal promise, expressed through acceptance of, and compliance with, the terms of the Order Form. As noted previously, the Catalog contains no mention of the Harrier Jet. Plaintiff states that he "noted that the Harrier Jet was not among the items described in the catalog, but this did not affect [his] understanding of the offer."

In evaluating the commercial, the Court must not consider defendant's subjective intent in making the commercial, or plaintiff's subjective view of what the commercial offered, but what an objective, reasonable person would have understood the commercial to convey.

Plaintiff's insistence that the commercial appears to be a serious offer requires the Court to explain why the commercial is funny. Explaining why a joke is funny is a daunting task; as the essayist E. B. White has remarked, "Humor can be dissected, as a frog can, but the thing dies in the process . . ." The commercial is the embodiment of what defendant appropriately characterizes as "zany humor."

In light of the obvious absurdity of the commercial, the Court rejects plaintiff's argument that the commercial was not clearly in jest.

For the reasons stated above, the Court grants defendant's motion for summary judgment. Summary judgment granted and affirmed.

CASE QUESTIONS

1. When does the court think an offer was made?
2. Why is whether the ad is funny an important issue?
3. Will Mr. Leonard get his Harrier jet? Why or why not?

Consider...

Review the following language and determine whether an offer has been made.

TO: Brit Ripley

FROM: Yachts International

RE: Sailing Vessel *Infinity*

We are prepared to make an offer to purchase the U.S. Coast Guard Documented Vessel *Infinity* for the price of $600,000 on the following terms and conditions:

Price: $600,000

Terms: Cash $300,000 at close of escrow

Note: $300,000 (unsecured) due in one year

Interest: 0.5% per month on unpaid balance versus 100,000 shares of stock of a public company

Will guarantee $3.00 per share in one year. Buyer reserves the right to repurchase shares at $3.00 in one year if guarantee given.

Escrow: ASAP

Conditions:

1. All insurance to remain in effect until close.
2. Seller to deliver to Port of San Francisco in seaworthy and sailable condition.

/s./ J. P. Morgan

Yachts International

Certain and Definite Terms

One of the ways to determine whether the contract is based on intent is also the second requirement for a valid offer. The offer must contain certain and definite language and cover all the terms necessary for a valid contract, which include the following:

- Parties
- Subject matter of the contract
- Price
- Payment terms
- Delivery terms
- Performance times

Under the UCC, the requirements for an offer are not as stringent as the requirements under common law. So long as the offer identifies the parties and the subject matter, the Code sections can cover the details of price, payment, delivery, and performance (see § 2–204 in Appendix C).

Also under the UCC, courts give great weight to industry custom and the previous dealings of the parties in determining whether the terms are certain and definite enough to constitute an offer (see § 2–208 in Appendix C). For example, the parties may have done business with each other for 10 years and their agreement simply contains a quantity and a price. Whatever payment and delivery terms have been used in their relationship in the past (their *course of dealing*) will be the terms for their ongoing relationship.

Communication of the Offer

An offer must be communicated to the offeree before it is valid. A letter in which an offer is made is not an offer until the letter reaches the offeree. For example, suppose OfficeMax had prepared an offer letter to be sent to Renco Rental Equipment and other customers. The letter included an offer for a substantial price discount for computers so that Renco and its regular customers might buy computers at that discount. Before the letter is mailed to Renco, OfficeMax decides that because the computers are in such high demand it will not send the offer and will just sell them at their full retail price. The letter to Renco and other OfficeMax customers is never mailed. Renco, realizing the value of the computers and learning of the unmailed letter, cannot accept the discount computer offer because it was never communicated to them.

Termination of an Offer by Revocation

Because an offer is one-sided, it can be revoked anytime before acceptance by the offeree. **Revocation** occurs when the offeror notifies the offeree that the offer is no longer good.

Revocation is subject to some limitations. One such limitation has already been mentioned: Acceptance by the offeree cuts off the right to revoke. Also, under common law, **options** cannot be revoked. An option is a contract in which the offeree pays the offeror for the time needed to consider the offer. For example, suppose that Yolanda's Yogurt is contemplating opening a new restaurant, and Yolanda has a property location in mind but is uncertain about the market potential.

Yolanda does not want the property to be sold to someone else until she can complete a market study. Yolanda could pay the seller (offeror) a sum of money to

ETHICAL ISSUES

Anticipating Morality

When they are at the top of their games, Olympic and professional athletes are able to command multi-million–dollar endorsement contracts.

Lance Armstrong, who was recently stripped of his Tour de France wins, was once ranked as the 60th most effective product spokesperson. He was right up there with Brad Pitt. Now, he is ranked 1,410 with rapper Nicki Minaj. The companies that have not renewed Mr. Armstrong's endorsement agreements or have terminated them include Nike, Radio Shack, Trek Bicycle, Easton-Bell (the makers of the Giro helmets Mr. Armstrong wore in his races), FRS Energy Foods, Anheuser-Busch, 24 Hour Fitness, and Nissan. Mr. Armstrong earned between $15 and $17 million per year from the endorsement contracts. When the charges leveled by the U.S. Anti-Doping Agency were detailed, Nike originally stood by Mr. Armstrong. However, when the agency released its documentation, Nike called the evidence "insurmountable" that Mr. Armstrong had participated in doping for more than a decade. Nike withdrew its contract with Mr. Armstrong but agreed to continue to support his LiveStrong Foundation.

In 2013, Chef Paula Deen lost her Food Network contract as well as endorsement contracts with Smithfield Foods, Walmart, Target, and others for her admission that she had use a racial slur.

Celebrity endorsement contracts always have a form of a morals clause, a clause that allows the sponsor to terminate the contract for a variety of reasons such as an arrest. The athletes' falls from grace are for very different reasons, and those reasons are difficult to anticipate in terms of contract language. However, businesses still place morality clauses in contracts—clauses that cover moral missteps. Defining those missteps can be difficult and some contracts resort to nonspecific language such as "conduct that results in a negative response to the product or company" or "conduct that reduces the credibility of the endorser."

However, the clauses generally have additional grounds for termination such as conduct by the celebrity that brings negative publicity or boycotts to the company. The termination rights are basically a judgment call on the part of the company. There is not much wiggle room for the celebrities. In fact, there is a long history of terminations.

Olympian Michael Phelps lost his endorsement contract with Kellogg's when photos of him smoking a bong at a campus party showed up on the Internet in 2009. Model Kate Moss lost her endorsement contracts with Burberry and Chanel when, in 2005, a grainy videotape emerged that showed her using cocaine. In 2007, Verizon withdrew its sponsorship of the Gwen Stefani tour when a raunchy video of her opening act, Akon, appeared online. The video showed Akon engaged in questionable on-stage behavior with a fan under the age of 18. The video resulted in considerable coverage and outrage from parents and commentators. Uniquely, the Stefani endorsement contract was terminated for her association with another artist who had questionable behavior.

Perhaps the best example of discretion in using the morals clauses came when Tiger Woods was in a car crash near his Florida home and the extent of his marital infidelity came to light. Mr. Woods lost endorsement contracts with Accenture, AT&T, and Gatorade. Gatorade did continue its relationship with the Tiger Woods Foundation. Nike did not drop its sponsorship and Nike chairman and co-founder Phil Knight explained that these problems with athletes are just "part of the game" when you sign them. TAG Heuer did not drop Woods because, as a spokesperson explained, "He's the best in his domain. We respect his performance in the sport. Woods' personal life is not our business." TAG Heuer did, however, stop running its ads featuring Mr. Woods. Gillette also stopped running Woods ads but did not terminate the relationship until later.

Are morality clauses appropriate in these contracts? Should athletes be role models? Is termination of a contract for personal conduct ethical?

hold the offer open for 30 days. During that 30-day period, the offeror can neither revoke the offer nor sell to anyone else.

Under the UCC, one form of an option makes an offer irrevocable, even without the offeree's payment. Under a **merchant's firm offer** (see § 2–205 in Appendix C), the offer must be made by a merchant, put in some form of record,[3] and signed by the merchant. If these requirements are met, the merchant must hold the offer open for a definite time period (but no longer than three months). A merchant is someone who is in the business of selling the goods that are the subject matter of the contract or who holds particular skills or expertise in dealing with the goods. A rain check for sale merchandise from a store is an example of this type of offer. The firm offer cannot be revoked if the requirements are met, and money or consideration is not one of those requirements.

Termination of an Offer by Rejection

An offer carries no legally binding obligation for the offeree, who is free to accept or reject the offer. Once the offeree rejects the offer, the offer is ended and cannot later be accepted unless the offeror renews the offer.

Rejection by Counteroffer Under Common Law.   An offer also ends when the offeree does not fully reject the offer but rejects some portion of the offer or modifies it before acceptance. These changes and rejections are called **counteroffers**.

The effect of a counteroffer is that the original offer is no longer valid, and the offeree now becomes the offeror as the counteroffer becomes the new offer. Consider the following dialogue as an example:

Alice: I will pay you $500 to paint the trim on my house.
Brad: I will do it for $750.

Alice made the first offer. Brad's language is a counteroffer and a rejection at the same time. Alice is now free to accept or reject the $750 offer. If Alice declines the $750 counteroffer, Brad cannot then force Alice to contract for the original $500 because the offer ended. The following "Consider..." deals with an issue of offers and counteroffers.

Rejection by Counteroffer Under the UCC.   Under the UCC, modification by offerees was seen as a necessary part of doing business, and § 2–207 (see Appendix C) allows flexibility for such modifications. Under § 2–207 (not Revised UCC Article 2 because this new version has not enjoyed acceptance by the states), two separate rules apply for modifications: one governs merchants, and the other governs nonmerchant transactions. Exhibit 12.2 shows a chart of the rules.

Business Planning Tip

The docketing of deadlines is important for businesses. Also, checks that a company receives should be reconciled with the purpose of payment to be certain that accidental overpayments (or acceptances, as in the *Hancock* case discussed in the following "Consider...") do not occur through oversight.

© Grounder/Shutterstock.com

Consider...

December 30, 1977: John Hancock Insurance Company sent a commitment letter to Houston Dairy offering to loan Houston $800,000 at 9.25 percent interest; the letter provided that acceptance must be in writing within seven days and must be accompanied by a $16,000 letter of credit or cashier's check.

January 17, 1978: The president of Houston Dairy sent a letter of acceptance to Hancock along with a cashier's check.

January 23, 1978: Hancock cashed the check, which went through standard company processing.

Hancock claims there is no contract because the acceptance occurred after the offer had expired. Houston Dairy maintains that its letter of acceptance was a new offer that was accepted by Hancock with the cashing of the check.

Who is correct? Is there a contract?

[*Houston Dairy v John Hancock Mutual Life Insurance Co.*, 643 F.2d 1185 (5th Cir. 1981)]

EXHIBIT **12.2** UCC Rules for Additional Terms in Acceptance Under Article 2

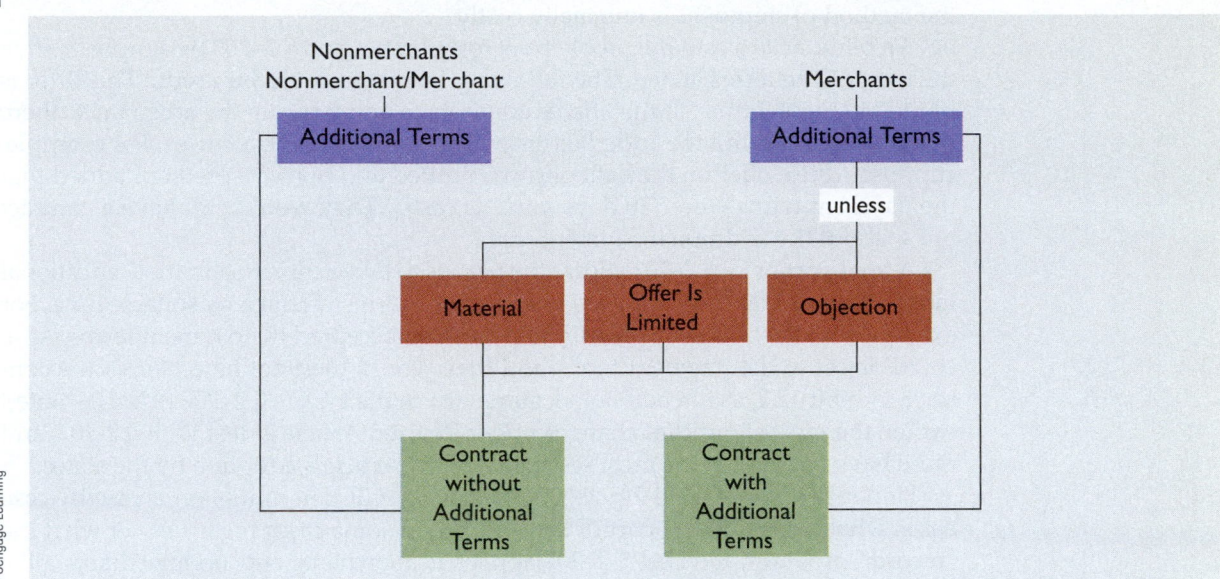

© Cengage Learning

For nonmerchants, the addition of terms in the counteroffer does not result in a rejection; there will still be a contract if there is a clear intent to contract, but the additional terms will not be a part of the contract.

For example, consider the following dialogue:

Joe: I will sell you my pinball machine for $250.
Jan: I'll take it. Include $10 in dimes.

Joe and Jan have a contract, but the $10 in dimes is not a part of the contract. If Jan wanted the dimes, she should have negotiated before formally accepting the offer.

For merchants (both parties must be merchants), § 2–207 has more complicated rules and details on additional terms in acceptance. Section 2-207 covers situations, sometimes called the battle of the forms, in which offerors and offerees send purchase orders and invoices back and forth with the understanding that they have a contract. Under § 2–207, if the parties reach a basic agreement but the offeree has added terms, there will be an enforceable contract; the added terms are not a rejection under § 2–207. Whether the added terms will become a part of the contract depends on the following questions:

1. Are the terms material?

2. Was the offer limited?

3. Does one side object?

If the terms the offeree adds to the original offer terms are *material*, they do not become a part of the contract. For example, suppose that Alfie sends a purchase order to Bob for 12 dozen, red, four-inch balloons at four cents each. Bob sends back an invoice that reflects the quantity and price, but Bob's invoice also has a section that states, "There are no warranties express or implied on these goods." Do Alfie and Bob have a contract with or without warranties? The waiver of warranties is a material change in what Alfie gets: now a contract without warranties. Because it is material, § 2–207 protects Alfie and the warranty waiver is not part of the contract.

Terms that can be added but are not considered material are such payment terms as "30 days same as cash." Shipment terms are generally immaterial unless the method of shipment is unusually costly.

An offeror can avoid the problems of form battles and § 2–207 by simply *limiting* the offer to the terms stated. The following language could be used: "This offer is limited to these terms." If the offeree attempts to add terms in the acceptance, there will be a contract, but the added terms will not be part of the contract. For example, suppose Alfie's offer on the balloons was limited and Bob accepted but added that the payment terms were "30 days same as cash." They would still have a contract but without the additional payment term.

A final portion of § 2–207 allows the parties to take action to eliminate additional terms. They can do so by *objecting* to any added terms within a reasonable time. For example, if Alfie's offer was not limited and Bob accepted the payment terms, Alfie could object to the payment terms and they would then not be a part of the contract. Exhibit 12.2, as already noted, summarizes the UCC's § 2–207 rules. As noted earlier, the most significant changes under Revised Article 2 deal with § 2-207, and these have resulted in the most resistance to the Article's adoption by the states.

Under Revised Article 2 § 2–207, the courts will determine, on a case-by-case basis, what is included as part of the contract, in some cases regardless of what the "record" provides. Revised § 2–207 applies to merchants and nonmerchants alike and regardless of whether the parties use forms. The new UCC § 2–207 is often called the "terms later" provision because it permits parties to go forward with contract performance and decide on terms later or resolve any disputes only if they arise during the course of performance. One writer has referred to "terms later" as bad economics because of the inability of parties to rely on definitive laws in making contracts and then performing under them.[4]

Consider...

Schulze and Burch Biscuit Company (Schulze) purchased low-moisture 16-mesh dehydrated apple powder from Tree Top, Inc., to use in making strawberry and blueberry "Toastettes," which it sells to Nabisco, Inc.

On April 27, 1984, E. Edward Park, Schulze's director of procurement, telephoned Rudolph Brady, a broker for Tree Top, and ordered 40,000 pounds of Tree Top's apple powder. Mr. Park told Mr. Brady that the purchase was subject to a Schulze purchase order and gave Mr. Brady the number of the purchase order, but Mr. Park did not send the purchase order or a copy of it to Mr. Brady or to Tree Top. On the front of the purchase order was the following clause:

> **Important:** *The fulfillment of this order or any part of it obligates the Seller to abide by the terms, conditions and instructions on both sides of this order. Additional or substitute terms will not become part of this contract unless expressly accepted by Buyer; Seller's acceptance is limited to the terms of this order, and no contract will be formed except on these terms.*

Shortly after the telephone conversation, Mr. Brady sent Schulze a form entitled simply "Confirmation" that listed Mr. Brady as broker, Schulze as buyer, and Tree Top as seller as well as the quantity, price, shipping arrangements, and payment terms. It also showed the purchase order number that Mr. Park had given to Mr. Brady. Several preprinted provisions, including an arbitration clause, stood on the lower portion of the form:

> *Seller guarantees goods to conform to the national pure food laws. All disputes under this transaction shall be arbitrated in the usual manner. This confirmation shall be subordinate to more formal contract, when and if such contract is executed. In the absence of such contract, this confirmation represents the contract of the parties. If incorrect, please advise immediately.*

Mr. Brady had sent a similar confirmation form to Schulze in each of at least 10 previous transactions between Tree Top and Schulze. Schulze had never objected to any of the pre-printed provisions. Schulze had sent Mr. Brady a purchase order in two of those transactions; in each of the other transactions, as in the present case, Schulze simply informed Mr. Brady of the number of the appropriate purchase order.

Subsequently, Schulze brought suit seeking damages for breach of contract, alleging that the dehydrated apple powder had been so full of apple stems and wood splinters that it clogged the machinery of Schulze's Toastette assembly line, causing the line to shut down, with various financial losses. Schulze alleged that the powder thus failed to meet Schulze's specifications, which had governed the previous sales of apple powder. Tree Top alleged that the dispute was subject to arbitration because of the arbitration clause in the confirmation sent by Mr. Brady to Schulze.

Does the arbitration clause apply? Discuss the issues under UCC § 2–207.

[*Schulze and Burch Biscuit Co. v Tree Top, Inc.*, 831 F.2d 709 (7th Cir. 1987)]

C9 Ventures v SVC-West, L.P. (Case 12.4) deals with layers of issues in contract formation, bringing together both common law and UCC principles in formation and determining terms.

CASE 12.4

C9 Ventures v SVC-West, L.P.
202 Cal. App.4th 1483, 136 Cal. Rptr.3d 550 (Cal. App. 2012)

The Helium Contract That Tanked

FACTS

SVC–West, L.P. (SVC) did time-share presentations at hotels and ordered helium tanks quite often for balloons. SVC placed a rush order with C9 Ventures (C9) for eight helium-filled tanks used to inflate festive balloons. C9 accepted the order and later that day delivered the tanks.

On the reverse of the invoice was an indemnification provision requiring SVC to indemnify C9 for any loss arising out of the use or possession of the helium-filled tanks. C9 later picked up the tanks, and, weeks later, SVC paid the invoice. SVC had obtained helium-filled tanks from C9 on prior occasions.

The invoice was on a single piece of paper, on the reverse side of which was a section entitled

"INDEMNITY/HOLD HARMLESS" (boldface omitted), which stated in part: "Customer agrees to indemnify[,] defend and hold harmless C9 … from and against any and all liability, claims, judgments, attorneys fees and cost of … every[ ] kind and nature, including, but not limited to injuries or death to persons and damage to property, arising out of the use, maintenance, instruction, operation, possession, ownership or Rental & Decor of the items rented, however cause[d], except claims or litigation arising through the solo [sic] gross negligence or willful misconduct of C9…."

The reverse side of the invoice also included a section entitled "LEGAL FEES," which provided, in essence, that in an action to enforce "this Rental & Decor Agreement," the prevailing party would be entitled to recover attorney fees.

Before then, C9 had presented the same or similar invoice to SVC 10 times, but had received the signature of an SVC employee only six times. SVC never attempted to substitute its own form agreement for C9's form.

C9 typically delivered the tanks in the morning when no SVC guests were present, but on July 3, C9's employee, Ernesto Roque, did not arrive at the SVC premises to make the delivery until about 5:00 P.M. Roque asked an SVC employee, Zayra Renteria, where to place the eight helium-filled tanks. Renteria, who was expecting the delivery during her shift, instructed Roque to bring the tanks up to the mezzanine level of the resort, at which point she would inform him where to place them. Roque wrote the following on the invoice, "[N]obody would sign all running around in lobby nobody knew who … After accident nobody got signatures."

Roque stacked five to seven tanks against the walls next to the service elevator. He was in the process of bringing up another tank when a young boy, whose parents were attending the time-share presentation, ran up to the tanks and hugged one of them, pulling it over.

CONTINUED

The tank, which was about five feet tall and weighed 130 pounds, fell on the boy's hand. He was hospitalized and underwent surgery for his injuries.

SVC and C9 each paid the boy's family to settle a lawsuit brought to recover for his injuries. C9 filed a cross-complaint against SVC to enforce the indemnification provision on the back of the unsigned invoice. The trial court found for C9 and SVC appealed.

JUDICIAL OPINION

FYBEL, Judge

This case could serve as a question on a law school final examination for a course on the Uniform Commercial Code. As in a law school examination, the facts are undisputed. The question: Is the indemnification provision on the back of the unsigned invoice enforceable against SVC?

The trial court answered the question yes, finding under California Uniform Commercial Code section 2207, the indemnification provision did not materially alter the contract and therefore became an added term.

We answer the question differently and hold the indemnification provision is not binding on SVC. SVC and C9 entered into an oral contract when C9 accepted SVC's telephone order for eight helium-filled tanks. The oral lease was sufficiently definite, although it left open various terms. Under section 2207, on which the trial court relied, additional terms proposed in an acceptance or confirmation may become terms of the contract in certain situations. Section 2207 is part of division 2 of the California Uniform Commercial Code, and division 2 governs transactions in goods. The oral contract between SVC and C9, however, was a lease of personal property (the helium-filled tanks), and personal property leases are governed by division 10, not division 2, of the California Uniform Commercial Code.

Division 10 of the California Uniform Commercial Code, which governs the oral contract between SVC and C9, does not have an analog to section 2207. The terms on the back of the unsigned invoice would have become part of the parties' oral contract only if SVC manifested assent to those terms. SVC did not manifest such assent by course of dealing or course of performance, or under basic contract law. SVC did not sign the invoice or otherwise expressly agree to its terms. An unsigned invoice itself is not a contract, and repeated delivery of a particular form does not make the form part of the parties' agreement. Payment of the invoice merely constituted SVC's performance of the obligation under the oral contract to pay for the rental of the helium-filled tanks.

To cover all bases (as one should when answering a law school examination question), we also construe the oral contract between SVC and C9 as if it were a transaction in goods governed by division 2 of the California Uniform Commercial Code and address whether the indemnification provision would have become an additional term under section 2207, as the trial court found. We conclude it would not. If SVC is not a merchant, the terms of the invoice are considered to be mere proposals for additional terms, which SVC did not accept. If SVC is a merchant, the indemnification provision would not have become part of the contract if the provision materially altered the contract. Because an indemnification provision is deemed a material alteration to an agreement as a matter of law, the indemnification provision on the back of the invoice would not, under section 2207, become part of the contract between SVC and C9.

We therefore reverse the judgment and remand with directions to enter judgment in SVC's favor. Because we reverse the judgment on which attorney fees were awarded, we also reverse the order awarding attorney fees.

CASE QUESTIONS

1. Why is it important to determine whether the contract involved a sale or lease of goods?

2. Is the indemnification clause material?

3. Would it be important to know if SVC is a merchant? Why?

Consider...

In the following three dialogues, determine whether a contract is formed under UCC § 2–207.

1. A: "I'll sell you my Peugeot bicycle for $100."
   B: "I'll take it. Include your tire pump."

2. A: "I'll sell you my white 1974 Ford Torino for $358. This offer is limited to these terms."
   B: "I'll take it. Furnish a history of repairs."

3. A: "I'll sell you my antique Coca-Cola sign."
   B: "I'll take it if you will deliver it."

Termination by Offer Expiration

An offer can end by expiring and, once expired, can no longer be accepted by the offeree. For example, if an offer states that it will remain open until November 1, it automatically terminates on November 1, and no one has the power to accept the offer after that time. The death of the offeror also ends the offer, unless the offeree holds an option. Even offers without time limits expire after a reasonable time has passed. For example, an offer to buy a home is probably only good for one or two weeks because the offeror needs to know whether to try for another house. The offeror's offer terminates naturally if the offeree fails to accept within that time frame.

FOR THE MANAGER'S DESK

Re: Checklist for Contract Preliminaries

1. Do your contract homework.

   a. Do background checks—check references, complaints at state and private agencies, court dockets.

   b. Learn the nature of the business and industry custom—learn to use the language.

2. Negotiate details.

   a. Agree on terms that help you accomplish your purpose ("apple powder for bakery equipment," not just "apple powder").

   b. Make sure your written agreement is complete.

FOR THE MANAGER'S DESK

Re: Checklist for Drafting Contracts

1. Identify both parties clearly. Be certain corporate names are correct. Make sure the parties have the proper authority to enter into the transaction. (Are copies of board resolutions approving the contract available?)

2. Define the terms used in the contract, including industry terms.

3. List all terms: price, subject matter, quantity, delivery, payment terms.

4. Answer "what-if" questions. (What if payment is not made? What if deliveries are late?)

12-5b ACCEPTANCE: THE OFFEREE'S RESPONSE

An **acceptance** is the offeree's positive response to the offeror's proposed contract, and only persons to whom the offer is made have the power of acceptance. That acceptance must be communicated to the offeror using the proper method of communication, which can be controlled by the offeror or left to the offeree. In either case, the method of communication controls the effective time of the acceptance.

EXHIBIT 12.3 Timing Rules for Acceptance

TYPE OF OFFER	METHOD OF ACCEPTANCE	ACCEPTANCE EFFECTIVE?
No means given	Same or reasonable method of communication*	When properly mailed, dispatched (mailbox rule)
No means given	Slower or unreasonable method of communication	When received, if offer still open
Means specified (specified or stipulated means)	Stipulated means used	Mailbox rule
Means stipulated (specified or stipulated means)	Stipulated means not used	Counteroffer and rejection

*Some states still follow the common low rule that requires the same method of communication in order to have the mailbox rule apply, even in UCC transactions.

© Cengage Learning

Acceptance by Stipulated Means

Some offerors give a required means of acceptance called a specified or **stipulated means**. If the offeree uses the stipulated means of acceptance, the acceptance is effective sooner than the offeror's receipt; the acceptance is effective when it is properly sent. For example, if the offeror has required the acceptance to be mailed and the offeree properly mails the letter of acceptance, the acceptance is effective when it is sent. This timing rule for acceptance is called the **mailbox rule**, and it applies in stipulated means offers so long as the offeree uses the stipulated means to communicate acceptance.

Acceptance with No Stipulated Means

If the offeror does not stipulate a means of acceptance, the offeree is free to use any method for communication of the acceptance. If the offeree uses the same method of communication or a reasonable means, the mailbox rule also applies. If the offeree uses a slower method of acceptance, the acceptance is not effective until it is received. Exhibit 12.3 summarizes the timing of acceptance rules. *Kass v Grais* (Case 12.5) deals with an issue of timing on offer and acceptance.

CASE 12.5

Kass v Grais
887 N.Y.S. 2d 578 (N.Y. Div. One 2009)

The FedEx Difference on Delivery and Acceptance

FACTS

Loryn Kass (plaintiff) made an offer to purchase land from David Grais and others (defendants). Twenty minutes after she revoked her offer, she received a FedEx package that included all the signed documents from Mr. Grais for the sale of the land to Ms. Kass.

Mr. Grais filed suit seeking to enforce their contract on the grounds that the mailbox rule applied and that his acceptance of her offer occurred when he sent the FedEx package, thus making the acceptance effective before her revocation. The trial court granted summary judgment to Ms. Kass and Mr. Grais appealed

CONTINUED

© Harper 3D/Shutterstock.com

JUDICIAL OPINION

MAZZARELLI, Presiding Judge

Although the mailbox rule has never been extended to encompass the delivery of a contract by Federal Express, defendants propose applying the rule to this purchase contract, notwithstanding the postdating of such contract to the date of delivery. Pursuant to section 25 of the purchase contract, "any notice to Escrowee shall be deemed given only upon receipt by Escrowee and each Notice delivered in person or by overnight courier shall be deemed given when delivered." It is undisputed that plaintiff withdrew her offer to purchase defendants' property before the fully executed contract was delivered. Defendant argues for excluding the executed contract from the ambit of section 25 because that provision uses the word "notice." To the extent section 25 could be considered ambiguous, which it is not, it is well settled that any ambiguity must be construed in plaintiff's favor and against defendants, who drafted it.

Affirmed.

CASE QUESTIONS

1. Is this a stipulated means offer? Explain why or why not.

2. Why does the language change the mailbox rule?

3. Does the court decide the issue of FedEx delivery and the mailbox rule?

12-5c E-COMMERCE AND CONTRACT FORMATION

The Internet has provided a means for contracting online. However, the courts have been left to deal with the issue of whether and when a contract has been formed. The new rules that have emerged regarding cyberspace contracts focus on whether the parties knew the terms and whether they voluntarily accepted those terms once aware of them. In other words, the rules on contract formation in cyberspace require that the parties prove that a click was something more than an accidental action and that the click was made after there had been full disclosure of the terms.

A new section of revised Article 2 deals with electronic communication of acceptance, including the timing issues. Section 2–213 provides that "receipt of an electronic communication has a legal effect, it has that effect even though no individual is aware of its receipt," and that acknowledgment of the receipt of an electronic communication is receipt, but, "in itself, does not establish that the content sent corresponds to the content received." So, receipt is required for electronic communication and receipt occurs when the e-mail arrives, even if the receiver does not know it has arrived. Also, the parties are left to use other means of proof to establish that all of the message made it from one party to another because acknowledging receipt does not mean that all terms arrived.

Sellers generally accomplish these two goals by establishing on their websites "clickon," "clickthrough," or "clickwrap" agreements. The company or offeror simply lists all the terms of the agreement that the visitor/offeree is about to enter into. The visitor/offeree must click on "I agree" or "I agree to these terms," or he or she cannot proceed to the completion of the contract segments of the site. The terms include cost, payment, warranties, arbitration provisions, and so on, and all applicable terms must be spelled out in advance of the "I agree" click point.

Because this type of contract formation is so new, case law is rare, but *Home Basket Co., LLC. v Pampered Chef, Ltd.* (Case 12.6) is one example of a contract-formed-on-the-Internet dispute.

CASE 12.6

Home Basket Co., LLC. v Pampered Chef, Ltd.
55 UCC Rep. Serv. 2d 792 (D. Kan 2005)

Making a Basket Case

FACTS

The Greenbrier Basket Company (GBC), a goods distributor (plaintiff) (seller) agreed in October 2003 to sell woven baskets to The Pampered Chef (TPC) (defendant) (buyer). On October 28, 2003, an executive sales agreement was drafted but never signed by the parties. GBC had, however, accepted purchase orders from TPC.

Cyndee Pollock (a manager at GBC) received offers to purchase goods via e-mail from TPC and would then tell an employee, Mark Beal, to accept these purchase orders via TPC's Internet site. GBC denies knowing that there were terms and conditions, including a forum selection clause, on TPC's Internet acceptance site. TPC sent Mark Beal an e-mail with an attachment showing him how to use TPC's purchase order management system and included instructions regarding the use of the purchase order management system, including, in section 4, three paragraphs under the title "Accepting and Rejecting Purchase Orders," the following:

> *Clicking on the Accept P.O. button will cause the terms and conditions of the purchase order to pop-up. The user should review these terms and conditions and click the Accept P.O. button at the bottom of the pop-up screen . . . . If the purchase order is not acceptable in it's [sic] current form, the user may click on the Reject and Request Changes button. This causes a pop-up window to appear where the user may enter a free-form text describing the reason for rejecting the purchase order and request changes that would make the purchase order acceptable.*

Clause 17 of the Terms and Conditions in TPC's purchase management order system states:

> *This Purchase Order shall be deemed to have been made in Addison, Illinois USA and shall be governed by and construed in accordance with the laws of State of Illinois [sic]. The sole and exclusive jurisdiction for the purpose of resolving any dispute shall be the United States District Court, Northern District of Illinois, Eastern Division.*

When disputes over orders and payments arose, GBC filed suit against TPC in Kansas for breach of contract. TPC moved to dismiss the suit for improper venue (wrong geographic court; see Chapter 3) because the terms of its purchase order called for suits in Illinois. GBC maintains it did not agree to that term because it never signed a contract and did not agree to it via their Internet contract.

JUDICIAL OPINION

BROWN, Senior J.

Plaintiff does not dispute that the forum selection clause is valid. Plaintiff instead argues that the forum selection clause was never part of the parties' contract.

TPC's e-mails containing purchase order information constituted an offer to buy baskets. The e-mails consisted of information about the quantity of baskets to be bought, price, shipment information and delivery dates. None of the e-mails had any forum selection clause; however, they did state a specific manner of acceptance:

1. *Upon receipt of order, please acknowledge via Internet at [website]. By acknowledging this P.O. [purchase order], you also acknowledge the terms and conditions of this P.O.*

2. *To accept this P.O. via Internet, visit [website].*

The evidence shows at least nine such e-mail offers. GBC consistently went to the TPC website to accept these offers.

GBC makes several arguments, without supporting case law, that the forum selection clause should not be part of the parties' contract. None of these arguments dispute when acceptance was made.

Plaintiff first argues that the e-mail offers are ambiguous because it did not alert GBC to the forum selection clause that had to be accepted on the website. The TPC e-mails state that the way to acknowledge (i.e. accept) the purchase order was to go to the website. The e-mail is not ambiguous as it also alerted GBC that there were terms and conditions associated with acknowledging the P.O. on the website.

GBC next argues that it should not be held to the terms and conditions accepted on the website because plaintiff thought that the e-mails' terms and conditions were all inclusive.

It is a well-established rule of law that contracting parties have a duty to learn the contents of a written contract before signing it, and such duty includes reading the contract and obtaining an explanation of its terms. The negligent failure of a party to read the

CONTINUED

written contract entered into will estop the contracting party from voiding the contract on the ground of ignorance of its contents. Therefore, a party who signs a written contract is bound by its provisions regardless of the failure to read or understand the terms, unless the contract was entered into through fraud, undue influence, or mutual mistake.

In determining intent to form a contract, the test is objective, rather than subjective, meaning that the relevant inquiry is the "manifestation of a party's intention, rather than the actual or real intention." Put another way, "the inquiry will focus not on the question of whether the subjective minds of the parties have met, but on whether their outward expression of assent is sufficient to form a contract."

This was a website that required action on the part of GBC. Plaintiff objectively agreed to the forum selection clause by scrolling through the terms and conditions and clicking on the "Accept P.O." button. Plaintiff's subjective beliefs that it was the e-mail and not the website terms and conditions that governed the contract are both misplaced and irrelevant. Plaintiff was under a duty to read and understand the terms and conditions prior to clicking the "Accept P.O." button as this was the formal acceptance required by TPC's offer to purchase baskets. Failure to read or understand the terms and conditions is not a valid reason to render those provisions nugatory.

Plaintiff next argues that the forum selection clause should not be read into the contract because GBC rejected an Exclusive Sales Agreement containing such a clause. Plaintiff claims that the failure to sign this agreement shows that they did not intend that a forum selection clause be part of the contract. The evidence shows that the Exclusive Sales Agreement was discussed on October 28, 2003. The date of the first e-mail inviting GBC to accept a purchase order was October 7, 2003. Plaintiff's subjective reasons for refusing to sign the Exclusive Sales Agreement are irrelevant as GBC consistently agreed, in an objective manner prior to the Exclusive Sales Agreement, to contracts with the terms and conditions on TPC's website. The Court will not alter the plain terms in the parties' contract because GBC refused to sign the Exclusive Sales Agreement.

Plaintiff also argues that there was no meeting of the minds regarding the forum selection clause on the website. A meeting of the minds requirement is proved when the evidence shows with reasonable definiteness that the minds of the parties met upon the same matter and agreed upon the terms of the contract. Part of clause 17 states "each shipment received by Buyer from Seller shall be deemed to be only upon the terms and conditions as set forth in this Purchase Order . . ." GBC agreed upon these terms and conditions published on TPC's website by clicking the "Accept P.O." button and this satisfied the meeting of the minds standard.

The Court holds that the forum selection clause in the terms and conditions on TPC's website are a part of the parties' contract. GBC must file suit in Illinois.

CASE QUESTIONS

1. Describe the ordering process between the two parties.
2. Does it matter to the court that neither side ever signed a written agreement?
3. What responsibility does the court impose on those who use websites for contracting purposes?

12-5d CONSIDERATION

Consideration is what distinguishes gifts from contracts and is what each party—offeror and offeree—gives up under the contract; it is sometimes called **bargained-for exchange**. If you sign a contract to buy a 1990 Mercedes for $17,000, your consideration is the $17,000 and is given in exchange for the car. The seller's consideration is giving up the car and is given in exchange for your $17,000. On the other hand, if your grandmother tells you that she will give you her Mercedes, the lack of consideration on your part means your grandmother's promise (unfortunately) is not a contract and is not enforceable.

The courts are not concerned with the amount or nature of consideration as long as it is actually passed from one party to the other. A contract is not unenforceable because a court feels you paid too little under the contract terms. The amount of consideration is left to the discretion of the parties, but one party cannot demand greater consideration once the contract is finalized.

Consider...

In 1977, George Lucas granted Kenner Toys the exclusive right to produce *Star Wars* toys—the action figures and other replicas from the movie—in perpetuity for $100,000 per year. At the time the contract was negotiated, no one understood how valuable the contract rights were.

In 1991, Hasbro Toys purchased Kenner. By this time, the sales of Princess Leia dolls and R2D2 replicas were nonexistent. Because there was no market for the toys, the toys were no longer produced, and an accountant with Kenner decided to save $100,000 and not send the check to Mr. Lucas.

In 1992, an employee of Mr. Lucas saw a line of Galoob toys at a trade show and asked if Galoob was interested in making the *Star Wars* toy line. Galoob jumped at the chance and did quite well marketing the toys. Some executives believe that the popularity of the toys motivated Mr. Lucas to rerelease the movies, which turned out to be a moneymaker for Mr. Lucas as well as for the Galoob toy line.

In 1996, Mr. Lucas did grant some rights to Hasbro, but it has lost market share and footing to Galoob. Was the failure to make the payment a failure of consideration? Has Hasbro lost its rights?

Unique Consideration Issues

The concept of consideration and its requirement for contract formation has presented courts with some unique problems. Often an element of fairness and reliance exists in circumstances in which an offer and acceptance are made but no consideration. For example, many nonprofit organizations raise funds through pledges. Such pledges are not supported by consideration, but the nonprofit organizations rely on those pledges. Called **charitable subscriptions**, these agreements are enforced by courts despite the lack of consideration.

Consider...

Alan Fulkins, who owns a construction company that specializes in single-family residences, is constructing a small subdivision with 23 homes. Tretorn Plumbing, owned by Jason Tretorn, was awarded the contract for the plumbing work on the homes at a price of $4,300 per home.

Plumbing contractors complete their residential projects in three phases. Phase 1 consists of digging the lines for the plumbing and installing the pipes that are placed in the foundation of the house. Phase 2 involves the placement of pipes within the walls of the home, and phase 3 handles the surface plumbing, such as sinks and tubs. However, industry practice dictates that the plumbing contractor receive one-half of the contract amount after completion of phase 1.

Mr. Tretorn completed the digs of phase 1 for Mr. Fulkins and received payment of $2,150. Mr. Tretorn then went to Mr. Fulkins and demanded an additional $600 per house for completion of the work. Mr. Fulkins said, "But you already have a contract for $4,300!" Mr. Tretorn responded, "I know, but the costs are killing me. I need the additional $600."

Mr. Fulkins explained the hardship of the demand: "Look, I've already paid you half. If I hire someone else, I'll have to pay them two-thirds for the work not done. It'll cost me $5,000 per house." Mr. Tretorn responded, "Exactly. I'm a bargain because the additional $600 I want only puts you at $4,900. If you don't pay it, I'll just lien the houses and then you'll be stuck without a way to close the sales. I've got the contract all drawn up. Just sign it and everything goes smoothly."

Should Mr. Fulkins sign the agreement? Does Mr. Tretorn have the right to the additional $600? Was it ethical for Mr. Tretorn to demand the $600? Is there any legal advice you can offer Mr. Fulkins?

The doctrine of **promissory estoppel** is also used as a substitute for consideration in those cases in which someone acts in reliance on a promise that is not supported by consideration. For example, suppose an employer said, "Move to Denver and I'll hire you." There is no detriment on your part until you begin work. The employer has no detriment either. However, if you sold your home in Phoenix and incurred the expense of moving to Denver, it would be unfair to allow the employer to claim the contract did not exist because of no consideration. You have acted in reliance on a promise, and that reliance serves as a consideration substitute.

12-5e CONTRACT FORM: WHEN A RECORD IS REQUIRED

Some contracts can exist just on the basis of an oral promise. Others, however, must be evidenced by a record to be enforceable, and these contracts are covered under each state's **statute of frauds**.

Common Law Statute of Frauds

The term *statute of frauds* originated in 1677 when England passed the first rule dealing with written contracts: the Statute for the Prevention of Frauds and Perjuries.

The purpose of the first statute and the descendant statutes today is to have records of agreements for the types of contracts that might encourage conflicting claims and possible perjury if oral agreements were allowed. The following is a partial list of the types of contracts required to be in writing under most state laws.

1. Contracts for the sale of real property. This requirement includes sales, certain leases, liens, mortgages, and easements.

2. Contracts that cannot be performed within one year. These contracts run for long periods and require the benefit of written terms.

3. Contracts to pay the debt of another. Cosigners' agreements to pay if a debtor defaults must be in writing. A corporate officer's personal guarantee of a corporate note must be in writing to be enforceable.

UCC Statute of Frauds

Under the UCC, a separate statute of frauds applies to contracts covering the sale of goods. Contracts for the sale of goods costing $500 or more must be evidenced by a record to be enforceable. As noted earlier, a record can be in the form of an electronic communication. Under Revised Article 2, the amount was increased from $500 to $5,000.

Consider...

Which of the following contracts must be in writing to be enforceable? Answer for both the old and revised UCC for those problems that involve UCC subject matter.

1. A contract for the sale of an acre of land for $400

2. A contract for management consulting for six months for $353,000

3. A contract for the sale of a car for $358

4. A contract for a loan cosigned by a corporation's vice president

5. A contract for the sale of a mobile home for $12,000

Sununu v Philippine Airlines, Inc. (Case 12.7) is a case that involves several issues related to contract formation, writing, and terms.

CASE 12.7

Sununu v Philippine Airlines, Inc.
792 F. Supp. 2d 39 (D. D.C. 2011)

A Turbulent Negotiation Contract with the Airline and a Contract That Never Took Off

FACTS

Because of financial setbacks, Philippine Airlines (PAL) wanted to renegotiate its aircraft leases, including those it had with World Airlines (WA). WA refused to negotiate with PAL. PAL retained John Sununu, the former Governor of New Hampshire and the former Chief of Staff to President George H. W. Bush, and Sununu's partner, Victor Frank, to try their hands at a renegotiation. Sununu and Frank sent a contract proposal to PAL, which included a proposed "success fee" of $600,000 if they persuaded WA to accept a modification of the lease contract. PAL gave Sununu and Frank a verbal go-ahead but did not sign the proposed contract. PAL then sent a contract with terms that were different from what Sununu and Frank had proposed. The PAL terms included a success fee of 4 percent of savings on the aircraft leases if Sununu and Frank were able to reach a settlement that met two very detailed settlement offers PAL had put into its contract proposal. Because they were so busy with contract renegotiations, Sununu and Frank did not review the PAL agreement and simply signed the contract.

Sununu and Frank were able to successfully renegotiate the lease contract with WA, saving PAL $12.8 million on the lease payments. PAL refused to pay Sununu and Frank their success fee of $520,000 because the actual settlement they had negotiated with WA did not meet the very specific contract terms that WA had put into the unsigned written agreement. Sununu and Frank filed suit against PAL in May 1998, alleging breach of contract, unjust enrichment, and fraud. The litigation went into a nine-year holding pattern while PAL endured financial reorganization proceedings in the Philippines. After reemerging from bankruptcy, PAL moved to dismiss the complaint. This Court granted PAL's motion on the breach of contract claim but allowed discovery to proceed on unjust enrichment. PAL now moves again for summary judgment.

JUDICIAL OPINION

LAMBERTH, Chief Judge

Sununu and Frank first argue that their contract with PAL was invalid because it was rescinded. They note that, under D.C. contract law, rescission can occur "when one party offers the rescission and the other party neither accepts nor rejects the offer." They claim that they rescinded the contract when they "offered a different deal, to which PAL never responded" after they learned about the severity of the lease termination dispute from WA.

There are several problems with this argument. First, Sununu and Frank present no evidence that their discussions with PAL constituted an offer to *rescind* the contract and not merely to *modify* it. ("Mr. Frank and I approached PAL about *modifying* our remuneration.") (emphasis added). Under traditional contract law principles, an unanswered proposal to modify a contract operates as unaccepted offer—leaving the underlying contract unchanged—not as a rescission of the agreement. For example, if an employee asks his boss for a raise and the boss doesn't answer, the employee continues to work at his existing wage. No one would suggest that his employment contract is terminated.

The facts alleged by the plaintiffs make rescission even less plausible here. Sununu and Frank claim they proposed amending the contract with PAL to make it more favorable to PAL by replacing the four-percent success fee with a fixed figure. To return to the example above, this is the equivalent of the employee asking his boss for a pay cut. Even if Sununu and Frank are correct that PAL did not respond to their allegedly generous offer, it makes little sense to conclude that they would opt to rescind a contract they believed disproportionately benefited them. Moreover, Sununu's deposition directly contradicts the allegation that the contract was rescinded. When asked if he had tried to rescind his contract with PAL, he answered, "No, I don't do that to clients."

Even if the Court sets aside the argument above and assumes that Sununu and Frank did intend to rescind, D.C. contract law provides that rescission must be total, not partial. Here, however, Sununu and Frank seek to have their contract and rescind it too. They invoiced and accepted payment of the $50,000 fee provided in the contract, yet they claim to have rescinded the other part of the contract and now seek unjust enrichment on that provision. The law will not allow them to have it both ways.

CONTINUED

Similarly, D.C. law provides that affirming a contract—continuing to carry it out—negates the opportunity to rescind. If a party "affirms the contract through continued performance, that party is precluded from seeking rescission." Sununu and Frank affirmed the contract by seeking to perform it, invoicing on it, and collecting on it. Finally, even if Sununu and Frank could show that the contract was rescinded and replaced by their modified proposal, they would have a claim for breach of the new contract, not unjust enrichment.

The crux of Sununu and Frank's theory is that PAL fraudulently concocted contract terms that it knew Sununu and Frank could not meet, thus sending them on the consulting equivalent of *Mission Impossible* and allowing the Manila airline "to obtain Sununu and Frank's valuable services, without having to pay [the] Success Fee."

To grant PAL's summary judgment motion is not to condone its conduct. The airline can rightly be accused of stinginess for enforcing the formalistic terms of the contract in spite of the plaintiffs' earnest efforts on its behalf. PAL's shifting explanations for why it would not pay Sununu and Frank do not reflect well on the airline's approach to business dealings. But because the airline ultimately had no obligation to pay, the facts surrounding this issue are not material to resolving the case. PAL may have violated Sununu and Frank's trust, but it did not violate the law.

For their part, Sununu and Frank seem to have done their best to serve their client, but they made a reckless bet by trusting PAL. They were accustomed to handshake deals in which personal relationships count for more than legal documents, so they made little effort to put their understandings with PAL on paper. When they ran into a client who didn't play by the same rules, they paid the price. The lesson is one that should be taught in law and business schools across America: When in doubt, write it out.

CASE QUESTIONS

1. What is the significance of the rescission argument?
2. Is there a contract? Explain why or why not.
3. Evaluate PAL's ethics in this situation.

Exceptions to the Statute of Frauds

Some exceptions to the UCC and common law statute of frauds provisions were created for situations in which the parties have partially or fully performed their unwritten contract. Under both the UCC and common law, if the parties perform the oral contract, courts will enforce the contract for what has already been done. For example, if Alan agreed to sell land to Bertha under an oral contract and Bertha has paid, has the deed, and has moved in, Alan cannot use the statute of frauds to remove Bertha and get the land back.

What Form of Writing Is Required?

The form of writing required under the statute of frauds is not formal. Evidence of a written agreement can be pieced together from memos and letters.

12-5f WRITING AND E-COMMERCE: THE UNIFORM ELECTRONIC TRANSACTIONS ACT

The **Uniform Electronic Transactions Act (UETA)**, drafted in adopted, as of mid-2013, in 47 states and the District of Colum the agenda of state legislatures in the remaining states. How the UETA are not nearly as uniform as those of the UCC, a stitutes a valid signature and the effect of electronic ve

The UETA is state recognition of the **Electro National Commerce Act of 2000 (ESIGN)**, 15 J mandates the recognition of electronic signa Although states may vary in their specifi legal effect to contracts that are entered signatures. ESIGN means that faxes "I accept" can all be used to form exempt from this equal treatment,

been adoptions of what con continue to evolve. natures in Global and 7001, the federal law that for the formation of contracts. under the UETA, they cannot deny electronically and that bear electronic online clicks on a tab that reads, valid contract. However, some documents are including wills, trusts, checks, letters of credit,

CYBERLAW

court documents, and cancellation of health and life insurance policies. States may require paper documentation for protection of legal rights in these transactions.

Rosenfeld v Basquiat (Case 12.8) deals with the issues of types of writings as well as whether a writing is sufficient to satisfy the statute of frauds requirements.

CASE 12.8

Rosenfeld v Basquiat
78 F.3d 84 (2d Cir. 1996)

The Artist, the Crayon, and the Contract

FACTS

Michelle Rosenfeld, an art dealer, alleges she contracted with artist Jean-Michel Basquiat to buy three of his paintings. The works that she claims she contracted to buy were entitled *Separation of the K, Atlas, and Untitled Head.* Ms. Rosenfeld testified that she went to Mr. Basquiat's apartment on October 25, 1982; while she was there, he agreed to sell her three paintings for $4,000 each, and she picked out three. Mr. Basquiat asked for a cash deposit of 10 percent; she left his loft and later returned with $1,000 in cash, which she paid him. When she asked for a receipt, he insisted on drawing up a contract and got down on the floor and wrote it out in crayon on a large piece of paper, remarking that some day this contract would be worth money. The handwritten document listed the three paintings, bore Ms. Rosenfeld's signature and Mr. Basquiat's signature, and stated: "$12,000— $1,000 DEPOSIT—Oct 25 82." Ms. Rosenfeld later returned to Mr. Basquiat's loft to discuss delivery, but Mr. Basquiat convinced her to wait for at least two years that he could show the paintings at exhibitions.

Before Mr. Basquiat's death, the estate argued that the contract because the statute of frauds statement unenforceable. The estate con-contract for the sale of goods must delivery. From a judgment in favor appealed.

JUDICIAL OP

CARDAMONE, J.

. . . Because this case invo the sale of three paintings, any Statute of Frauds is governed by the bility to "transactions in goods") (contr more is unenforceable "unless there is some ficient to indicate that a contract for sale has been or between the parties and signed by the party [charged]". Under the U.C.C., the only term that must appear in the writing is the quantity. See N.Y.U.C.C. § 2–201.

Beyond that, "[a]ll that is required is that the writing afford a basis for believing that the offered oral evidence rests on a real transaction." The writing supplied by the plaintiff indicated the price, the date, the specific paintings involved, and that Rosenfeld paid a deposit. It also bore the signatures of the buyer and seller. Therefore, the writing satisfied the requirements of § 2–201.

Citing *Berman Stores Co. v Hirsh*, 240 N.Y. 209 (1925), the estate claims that a specific delivery date, if agreed upon, must be in the writing. *Berman Stores* was decided before the enactment of the U.C.C. and was based on the principle that "the note or memorandum . . . should completely evidence the contract which the parties made." 240 N.Y. at 214 (quoting *Poel v Brunswick-Balke-Collender Co.*, 216 N.Y. 310, 314 [1915]). The rule that a specific delivery date is "an essential part of the contract and must be embodied in the memorandum," *Berman Stores*, 240 N.Y. at 215, was rejected by the legislature— at least for sale-of-goods cases—when it enacted the U.C.C. That rule and the statute upon which it was based were repealed to make way for the U.C.C.

. . . Because the writing, allegedly scrawled in crayon by Jean-Michel Basquiat on a large piece of paper, easily satisfied the requirements of § 2–201 of the U.C.C., the estate is not entitled to judgment as a matter of law. It is of no real significance that the jury found Rosenfeld and Basquiat settled on a particular time for delivery and did not commit it to writing . . . As a consequence . . . the alleged contract is not invalid on Statute of Frauds grounds . . .

Judgment reversed.

CASE QUESTIONS

1. Why was the contract required to be in writing?
2. Did the contract comply with the statute of frauds?
3. Does a writing that does not comply with the stat-of frauds make the alleged contract void?

EXHIBIT 12.4 Common Law versus UCC Rules on Formation

AREA	UCC	COMMON LAW
Application	Sales of goods	Services, real estate, employment contracts
Offers	Need subject matter (quantity); code gives details	Need subject matter, price, terms, full details agreed upon
Options	Merchant's firm offer; no consideration needed	Need consideration
Acceptance	Can have additional terms; mailbox rule works for reasonable means of acceptance	Mirror image rule followed; must use same method to get mailbox rule*
Consideration	Required for contracts but not for modification or firm offers	Always required
Writing requirement	Sale of goods for $500 or more	Real estate, contracts, not to be performed in one year, paying the debt of another
Defenses	Must be free of all defenses for valid contract	Must be free of all defenses for valid contract

*Some courts have adopted the UCC rule for common low contracts.

© Cengage Learning

Under the UCC, merchants can meet the statute of frauds by sending confirmation memos (see § 2–201 in Appendix C). These **merchants' confirmation memoranda** summarize the oral agreement and are signed by only one party, but they can be used to satisfy the statute of frauds so long as the memo has been sent to the nonsigning party for review and no objection is raised upon that party's receipt. The confirmation memoranda could be done via e-mail. Exhibit 12.4 provides a summary of provisions for contract formation under UCC and common law.

The Effect of the Written Contract: Parol Evidence

Once a contract is reduced to its final written form and is complete and unambiguous, the parties to the contract are not permitted to contradict the contract terms with evidence of their negotiations or verbal agreements at the time the contract was executed. This prohibition on extrinsic evidence for fully integrated contracts is called the **parol evidence** rule and is a means for stopping ongoing contradictions to contracts that have been entered into and finalized. It is a protection for the application of the document to the parties' rights as well as a reminder of the need to put the true nature of the agreement into the contract.

Some exceptions apply to the parol evidence rule. If a contract is incomplete or the terms are ambiguous, extrinsic evidence can be used to clarify or complete the contract, as in the case of UCC contracts in which price, delivery, and payment terms can be added (see § 2–202 in Appendix C). Also, if one of the parties to the contract is alleging a defense to the contract's formation, details on the circumstances creating that defense can be used as evidence. Evidence of lack of capacity or fraud does not violate the parol evidence rule.

12-6 Issues in Formation of International Contracts

International business contracts are similar to domestic contracts. However, the unique aspect of international contracts is that additional risks and questions arise over the choice of currency, the impact of culture on contract interpretation and performance, and the stability of the governments of the parties involved in the contract. In other words, international contracts carry certain risks that are not part of contracts between businesses in the same country. Over the past few years, the increased number of international transactions has resulted in recognition of the need for a more uniform law on international contract formation and performance.

12-6a CISG—UCC FOR THE WORLD

The United Nations has developed such a set of laws, called the **United Nations Convention on Contracts for the International Sale of Goods (CISG)** (see Chapter 7).

The CISG applies to those contracts in which buyer and seller have their businesses in different countries (unless the parties agree otherwise). There are similarities between the CISG and UCC, such as requirements for offers and acceptance, including a merchant's firm offer provision (without the three-month limitation from the UCC). However, under the CISG, acceptance is effective only upon receipt, and, whenever forms do not match, there is no contract unless the nonmatching terms are immaterial. The CISG also requires an agreement on price for an offer to be definite enough to be valid. Merchants' firm offers exist under the CISG, but their validity is not subject to time limitations, as with the UCC three-month limit. Parties in international trade need to be familiar with the hybrid nature of the CISG in order to protect their contract rights.

Party autonomy is a priority under the CISG. The parties can always choose the applicable law, the nation for the location of courts for resolving disputes, and remedies. Those firms and countries not relying on the CISG should be familiar with the nuances of commercial law in the countries in which they are doing business. The tendency of many U.S. businesses is to draft a form contract using the home country legal concepts and carry them over to other countries. As Exhibit 12.5 indicates, such a practice and reliance on form contracts can be dangerous.

EXHIBIT 12.5 Avoiding Legal Pitfalls in International Transactions

1. Use short, simple contracts. The tendency to place all possibilities in a contract is a U.S. tradition. In Germany, for example, the parties have a one-page agreement that references and incorporates terms and conditions of one of the parties.

2. Watch unconscionability protections. The United States focuses its unfairness protections on consumers, but other countries afford these same protections to commercial transactions.

3. Some disclaimers are void in other countries. For example, the clause, "We are only liable for loss of data which is due to a deliberate act on our part. We are not responsible for lost profits in any event," would be valid in the United States but void in Germany. In Germany, sellers of software must assume liability for at least gross negligence.

4. One party's attempt to limit liability would be void in Germany. Any liability limitation must be specifically addressed and negotiated for such a clause to be valid.

5. Unusually long periods for performance are typical in the United States but void in Germany.

6. Price increase limitations are typical in non–U.S. contracts.

7. In other countries, parties can refuse to pay on a current contract if performance on an earlier contract was less than satisfactory and damages are owed.

© Cengage Learning

12-6b **THE PAYMENT ISSUES IN INTERNATIONAL CONTRACTS**

One of the content and interpretation issues in international contracts focuses on the method of payment. Is payment to be made in pesos? Japanese yen? Euros? With significant country-by-country economic collapses, the currency to be used for contract payment has become a critical component of contract negotiations.

In addition to the risks of changing currency exchange rates and political instability, international contracts are performed through long distances in transportation and the ever-present difficulties with collection of payments. The *Sununu* case (p. 396) in an excellent illustration of the need to pin down, in writing, precise terms on international contracts. Most international contracts have built-in performance guarantees. For example, a seller ships goods with a **bill of lading** (a document of title that the carrier will have). To be able to pick up the goods from the carrier, the buyer must have a copy of the bill of lading. The seller can have a bank release the bill of lading to the buyer when the buyer has paid or when the buyer's bank issues a letter of credit (which is the bank's commitment to pay) to the seller for the amount due for the goods. The effect of these two documents is that the seller or carrier does not release the goods until the payment is made or assured. The flow of goods is controlled across borders through documents that travel with the goods and through banks that issue the payment for them. At the same time, the buyer is assured that the goods are there before payment is made or authorized.

In *Intershoe, Inc. v Bankers Trust* (Case 12.9), confusion on payment issues proved expensive for one party.

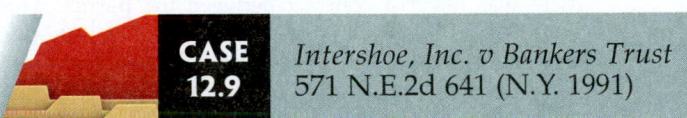

| CASE 12.9 | *Intershoe, Inc. v Bankers Trust*
571 N.E.2d 641 (N.Y. 1991) |

Lira, Shoes, and Exchange Rates

FACTS

Intershoe, Inc. (plaintiff) is a shoe importer that uses various foreign currencies, including Italian lira, in its business.

On March 3, 1985, Intershoe phoned Bankers Trust (defendant) and entered into several foreign currency transactions, one being a futures transaction involving lira. On March 13, Bankers Trust sent Intershoe a confirmation slip with the following terms: "WE [Bankers] HAVE BOUGHT FROM YOU [Intershoe] ITL 537,750,000" and "WE HAVE SOLD TO YOU USD 250,000.00."

The confirmation slip specified a rate of 2,151 lira per dollar and called for delivery of the lira approximately seven and a half months later, between October 1 and October 31, 1985. Intershoe's treasurer signed the slip and returned it to Bankers Trust on March 18, 1985.

By letter dated October 11, 1985, Bankers Trust notified Intershoe that it was awaiting instructions as to Intershoe's delivery of the lira. Intershoe responded in a letter dated October 25, 1985, that the transaction was a mistake and that it would not go through with it. To cover commitments in other currency transactions, Bankers Trust was forced to purchase lira on the open market at a higher price than that on March 13, 1985, resulting in a loss of $55,014.85. Intershoe filed suit claiming that it had purchased, not sold, lira and that it had sustained damages of $59,336.40. Bankers Trust counterclaimed for its damages.

The trial court held that there were issues of fact. Bankers Trust maintained that the case should be decided in its favor by summary judgment because of the parol evidence rule and appealed.

CONTINUED

JUDICIAL OPINION

HANCOCK, Jr., Justice

We turn to defendant's argument that UCC § 2–202 bars the parol evidence submitted in opposition to its motion.

There seems to be no question that the UCC applies to foreign currency transactions. Plaintiff does not dispute this point. Instead, plaintiff simply asserts that UCC § 2–202 has no application because defendant has not made a sufficient showing that the confirmation slip was "intended by the parties as a final expression of their agreement with respect to such terms as are included therein." Something more is required, plaintiff says, either language in the confirmation slip indicating that it was intended to be the final expression of the parties' agreement or uncontroverted evidence that the writing was so intended. Otherwise, according to plaintiff, there are factual issues as to the effect the parties intended the confirmation slip to have and summary judgment must be denied. We disagree.

Here, the essential terms of the transaction are plainly set forth in the confirmation slip: that plaintiff had sold lira to defendant, the amount of the lira it sold, the exchange rate, the amount of dollars to be paid by defendant for the lira, and the maturity date of the transaction. The signature of plaintiff's agent who signed and returned the confirmation slip five days later on March 18, 1985, signifies plaintiff's acceptance of these terms. Nothing in the confirmation slip suggests that it was to be a memorandum of some preliminary or tentative understanding with respect to these terms. On the contrary, it is difficult to imagine words which could more clearly demonstrate the final expression of the parties' agreement than "WE HAVE BOUGHT FROM YOU ITL 537,750,000" and "WE HAVE SOLD TO YOU USD 250,000.00."

The confirmation is not of some bargain to be made in the future but expresses the parties' meeting of the minds as to a completed bargain's essential terms—a sale of 537,750 lira at a rate of 2151 for 250,000 dollars—made in a telephone conversation on March 13, 1985. The only evidence plaintiff has tendered does no more than contradict the stated terms of the confirmation slip—the very evidence which UCC § 2–202 precludes. It does not address the critical question of whether the terms in the confirmation slip were intended to represent the parties' final agreement on those matters. We conclude that where, as here, the form and content of the confirmation slip suggest nothing other than that it was intended to be the final expression of the parties' agreement as to the terms set forth and where there is no evidence indicating that this was not so, UCC § 2–202 bars parol evidence of contradictory terms.

We reject plaintiff's contentions that UCC § 2–202 requires that there be some express indication in the writing itself or some other evidence that the parties intended it to be the final expression of their agreement. . . . To require that the record include specific extraneous evidence that the writing constitutes the parties' final agreement as to its stated terms would in many instances impose a virtually insurmountable obstacle for parties seeking to invoke UCC § 2–202, particularly in cases involving large commercial banks and other financial institutions, which typically close hundreds of transactions over the telephone during a business day. As a practical matter, a confirmation slip or similar writing is usually the only reliable evidence of such transactions, given the unlikely prospect that one who makes scores of similar deals each day will remember the details of any one particular agreement. Indeed, this case is illustrative inasmuch as neither of the participants had a specific recollection of the March 13, 1985, telephone conversation.

Plaintiff also argues that UCC § 2–202 does not bar the parol evidence submitted in opposition to defendant's motion because it is offered to show that there was never a contract between the parties. This argument is unavailing. Plaintiff does not dispute that it entered into a foreign currency transaction with defendant; its only contention is that the transaction called for it to purchase and not sell lira. Hence, the parol evidence is being used to contradict a term of the contract, not to show that there was no contract, and UCC § 2–202 applies.

Reversed.

CASE QUESTIONS

1. Describe the transaction, the parties, and who sold what to whom.

2. Is the memo a final writing?

3. What dangers would the court introduce if orders such as this were contradicted by oral testimony?

4. Did someone fail to read a document carefully before signing? Does the parol evidence rule allow "failure to read" as a defense?

12-6c RISK IN INTERNATIONAL CONTRACT PERFORMANCE: *FORCE MAJEURE*

International contracts carry peculiar and additional risks. One of the lessons of the wars in the Middle East, for example, is that international contracts should have provisions for war, interruption of shipping lines, and other political acts. Often referred to as *force majeure* clauses, these provisions in international contracts allow the parties to agree on what will happen in the event of sudden changes in government or in the global political climate rather than rely on a court to determine after the fact what rights, if any, the parties had. (See Chapter 13 for more details on contract issues.)

Consider...

Terrorist acts, such as the September 11, 2001 destruction of the World Trade Center towers in New York City, have become more frequent over the past few years. What happens when substantial interruption in a business's operations occurs because a bombing destroys or damages its leased facilities? Would you add provisions and protections to your lease? What terms would you want if you were the landlord?

BIOGRAPHY — Facebook Contract Formation and Internet and Litigation History

Discovery during the litigation by Cameron and Tyler Winklevoss and Divya Narendra against Facebook and Mark Zuckerberg indicates that Mr. Zuckerberg had a contract to write software for "Harvard Connection," or ConnectU, a social network site conceived by the Winklevosses. Mr. Zuckerberg did not complete the software work and instead developed his social network, Facebook, a site that has attracted 1 in every 14 people in the world. Mr. Narendra provided funding to get Facebook up and running. However, the agreements between and among the parties was oral and the terms were not clear. When Facebook started up, ConnectU, the Winklevosses, and Narenda filed suit (in 2004) against Mr. Zuckerberg and

Facebook. The result was years of litigation, a settlement by Zuckerberg and Facebook with the Winklevosses for $65 million and with Mr. Zarenda for $18.6 million. The twins' settlement consisted of $20 million in cash and $45 million in Facebook stock options.

The moral of these stories is to have something more than an oral agreement. Spell out each side's obligations and be sure to include an ani-compete clause, particularly in your agreement with the fellow who is going to develop your program and your ideas.

Sources: L. Gordon Crovitz, "The More Exciting Story of Facebook," *Wall Street Journal*, October 11, 2010, p. A17; Jon Swartz, "Facebook Lawsuit Settled For Good," *USA Today*, April 12, 2011, p. 3B.

Summary

What are contracts?

- Contract—promise or set of promises for breach of which the law gives a remedy, or the performance of which the law in some way recognizes as a duty

What laws govern contracts?

- Common law—traditional notions of law and the body of law developed in judicial decisions
- *Restatement (Second) of Contracts*—general summary of the common law of contracts
- Uniform Commercial Code (UCC)—set of uniform laws (49 states) governing commercial transactions
- Federal Consumer Contract Laws—Dodd-Frank Wall Street Reform and Consumer Protection Act (which created the Bureau of Consumer Financial Protection); Credit Card Accountability, Responsibility and Disclosure Act of 2009 (CARD), Truth in Lending Act (TILA), and Equal Credit Opportunity Act (ECOA)

What are the types of contracts?

- Bilateral contract—contract of two promises; one from each party
- Unilateral contract—contract made up of a promise for performance
- Express contract—written or verbally agreed-to contract
- Implied contract—contract that arises from parties' voluntary conduct
- *Quasi* contract—theory for enforcing a contract even though there is no formal contract because the parties behaved as if there were a contract
- Implied-in-fact contract—contract that arises from factual circumstances, professional circumstances, or custom
- Implied-in-law contract—legally implied contract to prevent unjust enrichment
- Void contract—contract with illegal subject matter or against public policy
- Voidable contract—contract that can be avoided legally by one side
- Unenforceable contract—agreement for which the law affords no remedy
- Executed contract—contract that has been performed
- Executory contract—contract not yet performed

How are contracts formed?

- Offer—preliminary to contract; first step in formation
- Offeror—person making the offer
- Offeree—recipient of offer
- Course of dealing—UCC provision that examines the way parties have behaved in the past to determine present performance standards
- Revocation—offeror canceling offer
- Options—offers with considerations; promises to keep offer open
- Merchant's firm offer—written offer signed by a merchant that states it will be kept open
- Counteroffer—counterproposal to offer
- Battle of the forms—UCC description of merchants' tendency to exchange purchase orders, invoices, confirmations, and so on; under Revised UCC, the court determines terms after the fact looking at intent, forms used, and the UCC terms
- Acceptance—offeree's positive response to offer
- Mailbox rule—timing rule for acceptance
- Consideration—something of value exchanged by the parties that distinguishes gifts from contracts
- Charitable subscriptions—enforceable promises to make gifts
- Promissory estoppel—reliance element used to enforce otherwise unenforceable contracts

When must contracts be in writing?

- Statute of frauds—state statutes governing the types of contracts that must be in writing to be enforceable
- Merchants' confirmation memorandum—UCC provision that allows one merchant to bind another based on an oral agreement with one signature
- Parol evidence—extrinsic evidence that is not admissible to dispute an integrated unambiguous contract

What issues for contracting exist in international business?

- CISG—Contracts for the International Sale of Goods; a uniform law for international commercial transactions that countries can choose to adopt and contracting parties can choose to use

Questions and Problems

1. In September of 1988, Jane Pittsley contracted with Hilton Contract Carpet Co. for the installation of carpet in her home. The total contract price was $4,402. Hilton paid the installers $700 to put the carpet in Ms. Pittsley's home. Following installation, Ms. Pittsley complained to Hilton that some seams were visible, that gaps appeared, that the carpet did not lie flat in all areas, and that it failed to reach the wall in certain locations. Although Hilton tried several times to fix the installation by stretching the carpet and other methods, Ms. Pittsley was not satisfied with the work. Eventually, Ms. Pittsley refused to allow Hilton to try to fix the carpet. Ms. Pittsley had paid Hilton $3,500, but she refused to pay the remaining balance of $902.

Ms. Pittsley filed suit, seeking rescission of the contract, return of her $3,500, and incidental damages. Hilton answered and counterclaimed for the balance remaining on the contract. Hilton also defended on the grounds that the only issue was the installation and that the damages were minimal. Ms. Pittsley argued that the contract was under the UCC and that she was entitled to remedies because the carpet was defective. Hilton disagreed on the application of the UCC. Who is correct? Does the UCC apply to the contract for the carpet sale and installation? Is Ms. Pittsley entitled to the warranty protection of the UCC? [*Pittsley v Houser*, 875 P.2d 232 (Idaho 1994)]

2. Maria Cantu had a teaching contract with the San Benito Consolidated Independent School District. She hand-delivered to her supervisor a written offer to resign. Three days later, the superintendent of schools mailed her a letter accepting the offer of resignation. Ms. Cantu then changed her mind and the next day hand-delivered a letter withdrawing her resignation. The superintendent refused to recognize the attempted rescission of the resignation. Ms. Cantu appealed to the state district court. It decided against her, and she again appealed. Is there a contract or not? Explain your answer. [*Cantu v Central Education Agency*, 884 S.W.2d 565 (Tex. App. 1994)]

3. Dr. Cook is a licensed dentist who devotes less than 50 percent of his practice to the work of fitting and making dentures. Mrs. Downing is a patient of Dr. Cook who was fitted for dentures. Mrs. Downing filed suit against Dr. Cook after she took delivery of her dentures because she said they were ill fitting and produced sore spots in her mouth. Dr. Cook's expert witness testified that Mrs. Downing's problems were probably due to candidiasis, an autoimmune reaction, or an allergy to the dental material. No expert testified that her problems were due to ill-fitting dentures.

The trial court awarded damages to Mrs. Downing on the basis of a breach of UCC Article 2, implied warranty of fitness for a particular purpose. Dr. Cook appealed, maintaining that the dentures were not a sale of goods. Explain who is correct about UCC versus common law. [*Cook v Downing*, 891 P.2d 611 (Ok. Ct. App. 1995)]

4. Consider the following sequences of offers and acceptances and determine whether in each case there would be a contract.

a. September 1, 2014: A mails an offer to B.

September 2, 2014: B receives the offer.

September 3, 2014: A mails a revocation.

September 4, 2014: B mails an acceptance.

September 5, 2014: B receives the revocation.

September 6, 2014: A receives the acceptance.

RESULT: _____

b. September 1, 2014: A mails an offer to B.

September 2, 2014: B receives the offer.

September 3, 2014: B wires an acceptance.

September 4, 2014: B wires a rejection.

September 4, 2014 (later): A receives the acceptance.

September 5, 2014: A receives the rejection.

RESULT: _____

c. September 1, 2014: A mails an offer to B.

September 2, 2014: B receives the offer.

September 3, 2014: A wires a revocation.

September 3, 2014: B wires an acceptance.

September 4, 2014: B receives the revocation.

September 5, 2014: A receives the acceptance.

RESULT: _____

Would your answers be different under the UCC from those under common law?

5. Mace Industries, Inc., sent a quotation to Paddock Pools for water treatment equipment.

Paddock responded with a purchase order that had the following written on its reverse side:

"THE SELLER AGREES TO ALL OF THE FOLLOWING TERMS AND CONDITIONS."

The clause was then followed by language stating that acceptance was expressly conditional upon Mace's acceptance of the terms.

Problems between the parties developed. Paddock says there is no contract because of its conditional acceptance. Mace maintains that § 2-207 applies and that there was a contract, with the only issues being the additional terms Paddock wrote on its purchase order and whether they are part of the contract. Who is correct? [*Mace Industries, Inc. v Paddock Pool Equipment Co., Inc.*, 339 S.E.2d 527 (S.C. 1986)]

6. On March 23, 1994, Northern Distributing Company made two offers to purchase two brands of beer carried by Keis Distributors, Inc.: 683,136 cases of Genesee beer at $1.75 per case and 95,632 cases of Labatt/Rolling Rock beer at $2 per case. The offer contained a termination date of April 11, 1994 and directed Keis to "accept this offer by signing below." Keis countersigned as requested and sent the offer back to Northern with a cover letter that stated both sides should retain counsel to work out "the wording of the final details." A proposed "closing and consulting agreement" was drafted but never signed, and Keis then withdrew from these distribution areas. Northern did purchase some of Keis's inventory after the distributorship termination, and a dispute arose as to the price due on that inventory. Northern claimed the contract price, and Keis said they had no contract, so the price was higher. Who is correct? Read the case and decide. [*Keis Distributors, Inc. v Northern Distributing Co.*, 641 N.Y.S. 2d 417 (App. Div. 1996)]

7. Lucas Rosa, a biological male, went to Park West Bank & Trust dressed in traditionally feminine attire. He requested a loan application from Norma Brunelle, a bank employee. Ms. Brunelle asked Mr. Rosa for identification. Mr. Rosa produced three forms of photo identification: (1) a Massachusetts Department of Public Welfare Card, (2) a Massachusetts Identification Card, and (3) a Money Stop Check Cashing ID Card. Ms. Brunelle looked at the identification cards and told Mr. Rosa that she would not provide him with a loan application until he "went home and changed." Mrs. Brunelle said that he had to be dressed like one of the identification cards in which he appeared in more traditional male attire before she would give him a loan application and process his loan request. Rosa sued the Bank for violations of the ECOA. The bank moved for summary judgment, and the court granted judgment

for the bank, finding that there could be no possible theory under the ECOA for discrimination. Did the bank violate ECOA? Explain your answer. [*Rosa v Park West Bank & Trust Co.*, 214 F.3d 213 (1st Cir. 2000)]

8. Procter & Gamble (P&G) began a Pampers catalog promotional offer in 1981. A statement on each box of Pampers explained that by saving the teddy bear proof-of-purchase symbols (Teddy Bears points) on packages of Pampers diapers, a customer could order various baby items from the Pampers Softouches Baby Catalog at a reduced cost. The catalog would be sent free to consumers upon request. Included in the catalog were pictures of the items for sale and the designated amount of Teddy Bears points and cash necessary for purchase. All sale terms, including the dates during which the offer was in effect, were described in each catalog. The only method for ordering merchandise was the use of the specific order form included in each catalog.

About April 1989, P&G sent out its final catalog. On the front of the catalog was a statement that it was the final catalog and that the offer would expire on February 28, 1990.

Ms. Alligood and others had cut out and saved the teddy bear symbols. The diaper purchasers claim that each package of Pampers contained an offer to enter into a unilateral contract, which they accepted by purchasing Pampers and saving the teddy bear proof-of-purchase symbols.

The precise language of the advertisement printed on packages of Pampers states:

Save these Teddy Bears points and use them to save money on toys, clothes, furniture, and lots of other baby things when you shop the Pampers Baby Catalog. For your free copy of the Catalog, send your name, complete address and youngest baby's date of birth to:

Pampers Baby Catalog
P.O. Box 8634,
Clinton, Iowa 52736.

If P&G refused to redeem the Teddy Bears points, would the purchasers have any contract rights to force P&G to deliver the catalog merchandise? [*Alligood v Procter & Gamble Co.*, 594 N.E.2d 668 (Ohio App. 1991)]

9. Aon Risk Services, Inc. (ARS Arkansas), and Combined Insurance Companies are subsidiaries of Aon Corporation. Aon issued an "Interdependency Memo" in February 2000, which was designed to motivate ARS brokerage offices to place insurance business with Aon-affiliated companies through a bonus pool for revenues generated under the plan. Under the terms of the memo, Aon agreed to pay "30% of annualized premium on all life products over 15-year term plus 15% 1st year for all other products." John Meadors saw the memo in February 2000 and believed it would entitle him to this compensation over and above his employment contract.

Meadors put Combined in touch with Dillard's Department Stores and on March 24, 2000, Dillard's and Combined executed a five-year agreement whereby Dillard's employees could purchase life, disability, and other insurance policies through workplace enrollment. When Meadors did not receive bonus-pool money generated by the transaction, he sued his employer for breach of contract. His employer's defense was that the memo was not sufficiently definite to constitute an offer. Discuss whether there was a contract formed for the bonus compensation system. Are you able to classify the type of contract? [*Aon Risk Services Inc. v Meadors*, 267 S.W.3d 603 (Ark. App. 2007)]

10. Nation Enterprises, Inc., purchased a large (36 by 3 feet) gas-fired convection oven from Enersyst, Inc., to make its pizza crusts. The oven had problems that the parties were working to resolve, but Nation needed a second oven. It was going to purchase one from someone else, but Enersyst orally promised to fix the first oven if Nation bought the second oven from it. (Oven 1 was beyond its 60-day warranty.) Nation bought the second oven, but Enersyst did not fix the first one. Nation sued, but Enersyst claims its promise on the first oven is inadmissible under the parol evidence rule. Is this correct? [*Nation Enterprises, Inc. v Enersyst, Inc.*, 749 F. Supp. 1506 (N.D. Ill. 1990)]

CONTRACTS, ETHICS, ECONOMICS, THE LAW

Lying to Each Other—An Efficient Way to Conduct Business?

Donald Trump described his contract negotiation methods and pricing as follows, "*When I build something for somebody, I always add $50 million or $60 million onto the price. My guys come in, they say it's going to cost $75 million. I say it's going to cost $125 million and I build it for $100 million. Basically, I did a lousy job. But they think I did a great job.*"

Evaluate this quote, thinking through the economic implications of this pricing. Who is affected by the Trump approach? Is he simply managing expectations? Is he misleading the other party? Is he taking unfair advantage? What happens if pricing does not reflect cost? What would happen if all contractors did this?

Notes

1. UCITA was formerly Article 2B of the Uniform Commercial Code. It was separated out because reforms for the UCC on Article 2 were pending and the controversy related to Article 2B (now UCITA) was isolated. UCITA remains controversial. See Americans for Fair Electronic Commerce Transactions at http://www.ucita.com for a summary of the concerns and issues.

2. The appellate court affirmed the federal district court opinion in a brief affirmation. The bulk of the facts and discussion presented here are taken from the lower court's decision, 88 F. Supp. 2d 116 (S.D.N.Y. 1999).

3. With the UCC modifications and ESIGN, a writing is no longer required. However, there must be some type of record, which could come in the form of an electronic submission.

4. Roger C. Bern, "'Terms Later' Contracting: Bad Economics, Bad Morals, and a Bad Idea for a Uniform Law, Judge Easterbrook Not Withstanding," 12 *Journal of Law and Policy* 641 (2004).

13 CONTRACTS AND SALES:
Performance and Remedies

Once the parties have formed a contract with an offer, acceptance, and consideration (as discussed in Chapter 12), it would seem that their troubles are over and that all they need to do is carry through with performance. However, sometimes new information arises and one party challenges the formation as invalid; or perhaps what one party believes is performance is just not enough for the other party, or is not what was contemplated when they formed the contract. This chapter focuses on contract problems and answers the following questions: What if the assumptions made in formation turn out to be untrue? Must the parties go through with the contract? If one party does not perform, is the other excused? When is performance required, and when is it sufficient? What are the credit, payment, and collection issues in performance? What remedies exist? What happens if a party to a contract declares bankruptcy? Do third parties have rights in a contract?

UPDATE
For up-to-date legal news, go to **mariannejennings.com**

Bo Chambers/Flickr/Getty Images

Consider...

Several students from a high school in Fairfax County, Virginia, and another in Tucson, Arizona, filed suit against iParadigms for copyright infringement. iParadigms is the company that owns and operates Turnitin, a software program that allows educational institutions to check student term papers against previous students' papers to detect plagiarism. The students wanted their papers removed from Turnitin because no contract was ever formed to allow their papers to be posted to Turnitin, that there was duress involved when they clicked to submit their papers because they had no choice but to post them in order to turn in their papers, and that they were minors and could not make valid contracts.

Are the students correct? Or was there a valid contract?

13-1 Defenses in Contract Formation

Even though a contract may have been formed with the three elements of offer, acceptance, and consideration, one of the elements may be flawed. The result is a contract that may be void, voidable, or unenforceable. When one of the required elements of formation is flawed, the contract is subject to a defense. A **contract defense** is a situation, term, or event that makes an otherwise valid contract invalid. These defenses ensure that the parties enter into contracts voluntarily and on the basis of accurate information. The defenses are displayed in Exhibit 13.1 and are discussed in the following sections.

EXHIBIT 13.1 Defenses in Contract Formation

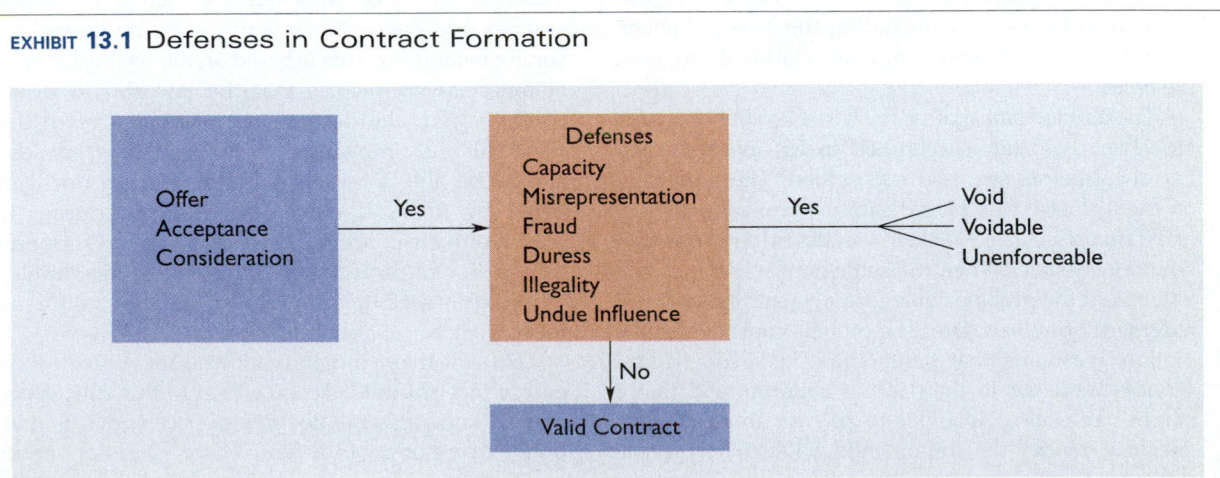

© Cengage Learning 2015

13-1a CAPACITY

Both parties to a valid contract must have **capacity**, which includes both age and mental capacity.

Age Capacity

Age capacity requires that both parties be at least the age of majority. In most states, that age is 18. Contracts entered into by **minors** (sometimes called **infants**) are voidable. A **voidable contract** of a minor allows the minor to choose not to honor the contract, in which case the other party to the contract will have no remedy. But some exceptions apply to the minors' contracts rules. Some statutes make certain contracts of minors enforceable; for example, student loan agreements are enforceable against minors, as are agreements to enter the military. Minors' contracts for such necessities as food and clothing are still voidable, but courts do hold minors liable for the reasonable value of those necessities.

Yale Diagnostic Radiology v Estate of Fountain (Case 13.1) deals with an issue of a minor's liability under a contract.

CASE 13.1	*Yale Diagnostic Radiology v Estate of Fountain* 838 A.2d 179 (Conn. 2003)

Shooting for Payment from a Minor

FACTS

In March 1996, Harun Fountain was shot in the back of the head at point-blank range by a playmate. As a result of his injuries, including the loss of his right eye, Fountain required extensive lifesaving medical services from a variety of medical services providers, including Yale Diagnostic Radiology (plaintiff). The expenses at Yale totaled $17,694. Yale billed Vernetta Turner-Tucker (Tucker), Fountain's mother, but the bill went unpaid and, in 1999, Yale obtained a judgment against her. In January 2001, all of Tucker's debts were discharged in bankruptcy, including the Yale judgment. There was no reference to Fountain's father throughout the cases.

Tucker filed suit against the boy who shot Fountain. However, Fountain succumbed to his injuries, passing away before the case was settled. The settlement on the tort case was placed into probate court as part of Fountain's estate. Tucker was the administrator of Fountain's estate. When the settlement was deposited, Yale asked the probate court for payment of its $17,694 judgment from the estate. The probate court denied the motion, reasoning that parents are liable for medical services rendered to their minor children, and that a parent's refusal or inability to pay for those services does not render the minor child liable. The probate court held that Yale could not get payment from the estate. Yale appealed to the trial court, and the trial court held for Yale. Tucker and the estate (defendants) appealed.

JUDICIAL OPINION

BORDEN, Justice

Connecticut has long recognized the common-law rule that a minor child's contracts are voidable. Under this rule, a minor may, upon reaching majority, choose either to ratify or to avoid contractual obligations entered into during his minority. The traditional reasoning behind this rule is based on the well-established common-law principles that the law should protect children from the detrimental consequences of their youthful and improvident acts, and that children should be able to emerge into adulthood unencumbered by financial obligations incurred during the course of their minority. The rule is further supported by a policy of protecting children from unscrupulous individuals seeking to profit from their youth and inexperience.

The rule that a minor's contracts are voidable, however, is not absolute. An exception to this rule, eponymously known as the doctrine of necessaries, is that a minor may not avoid a contract for goods or services

CONTINUED

© Harper 3D/Shutterstock.com

necessary for his health and sustenance. Such contracts are binding even if entered into during minority, and a minor, upon reaching majority, may not, as a matter of law, disaffirm them.

The parties do not dispute the fact that the medical services rendered to Fountain were necessaries; rather, their dispute centers on whether Connecticut recognizes the doctrine of necessaries.

…[W]e conclude that Connecticut recognizes the doctrine of necessaries. We further conclude that, pursuant to the doctrine, the defendants are liable for payment to the plaintiff for the services rendered to Fountain.

Courts in other jurisdictions that have held that minors may be liable pursuant to the doctrine of necessaries for medical services have done so by applying varying legal theories. For example, some courts have held minors liable only if the creditor can show that the minor was not living with or being supported by his or her parents at the time the contract arose or the services were rendered. Still other courts have held minors liable after determining that the goods or services rendered were necessaries, and the minor's parent or guardian was unwilling or unable to pay for them. See *Schmidt v Prince George's Hospital*, 366 Md. 535, 555, 784 A.2d 1112 (2001) (minor's father's use of insurance proceeds to buy minor car sufficient for finding that father was unwilling to pay minor's medical expenses). Still other courts have reasoned that the minor's ever present secondary liability for payment for medical services rendered to him gives rise to an implied-in-law contract.

…when a medical service provider renders necessary medical care to an injured minor, two contracts arise: the primary contract between the provider and the minor's parents; and an implied-in-law contract between the provider and the minor himself. The primary contract between the provider and the parents is based on the parents' duty to pay for their children's necessary expenses, under both common law and statute. Such contracts, where not express, may be implied in fact and generally arise both from the parties' conduct and their reasonable expectations. The primacy of this contract means that the provider of necessaries must make all reasonable efforts to collect from the parents before resorting to the secondary, implied-in-law contract with the minor.

The present case illustrates the inequity that would arise if no implied in law contract arose between Fountain and the plaintiff. Fountain was shot in the head at close range and required emergency medical care. Under such circumstances, a medical services

provider cannot stop to consider how the bills will be paid or by whom. Although the plaintiff undoubtedly presumed that Fountain's parent would pay for his care and was obligated to make reasonable efforts to collect from Tucker before seeking payment from Fountain, the direct benefit of the services, nonetheless, was conferred upon Fountain. Having received the benefit of necessary services, Fountain should be liable for payment for those necessaries in the event that his parents do not pay.

Fountain received, through a settlement with the boy who caused his injuries, funds that were calculated, at least in part, on the costs of the medical services provided to him by the plaintiff in the wake of those injuries. This fact further supports a determination of an implied-in-law contract under the circumstances of the case.

Nothing in either the language or the purpose of [Connecticut's statutes on minors] indicates an intent on the part of the legislature to absolve minors of their secondary common-law liability for necessaries.

To the contrary, the purposes behind the statutory rule that parents are primarily liable and the common-law rule, pursuant to the doctrine of necessaries, that a minor is secondarily liable, when read together, serve to encourage payment on contracts for necessaries. Those purposes are (1) to reinforce parents' obligation to support their children, and (2) to provide a mechanism for collection by creditors when, nonetheless, the parents either refuse or are unable to discharge that obligation.

The undisputed facts show that Tucker had four years to pay the plaintiff's bill for the services rendered to Fountain. She did not pay that bill even when the plaintiff pursued a collection action against her. These facts are sufficient to show that Tucker was unwilling or unable to pay for Fountain's necessary medical services.

The fact that Tucker may be supplying other necessaries, such as food and shelter, does not undermine the claim that she has not made payment for this necessary medical service, which was already provided by the plaintiff to Fountain.

The judgment is affirmed.

CASE QUESTIONS

1. Describe the series of events that led to Yale requesting that the minor pay for the medical services.

2. What public policy issues and concerns result from this decision?

3. What benefits does the decision provide?

Mental Capacity

Contracting parties must also have *mental capacity*, which is the ability to understand that contracts are enforceable, that legal documents have significance, and that contracts involve costs and obligations. Contracts of those lacking mental capacity are voidable. Moreover, if a party to a contract has been declared legally incompetent, that person's contracts are void. A **void contract** is one the courts will not honor, and neither party is obligated to perform under that agreement.

13-1b MISREPRESENTATION

When one party to a contract is not given full or accurate information by the other party about the contract subject matter, there is **misrepresentation**. In the case of misrepresentation in the formation of a contract, the law allows a **rescission** of the contract. Rescission means the contract is set aside. Misrepresentation occurs when a seller makes inaccurate statements about its product or fails to disclose pertinent information about its product that would affect someone's decision to enter into the contract. For example, failure to disclose that a deluxe model car has a standard car engine is misrepresentation. The elements required for innocent misrepresentation are as follows:

1. Misstatement of a material fact (or the failure to disclose a material fact)
2. Reliance by the buyer on that material misstatement or omission
3. Resulting damages to the buyer

To be a basis for rescission, the misrepresentation must have been one regarding a **material fact**. A material fact is the type of information that would affect someone's decision to enter into the contract. For example, if a buyer for your stock in XYZ Corporation failed to disclose that a takeover was pending, it would be considered misrepresentation of a material fact. A takeover affects the price of stock, and the price of stock in the future affects your decision to buy and sell presently.

Misrepresentation cannot be based on sales **puffing**, which is opinion about the subject matter of a contract. For example, suppose that a real estate agent told you a house you were considering buying was located in the "best area in town." Such a statement is an opinion and cannot be a basis for misrepresentation.

Consider...

Analyze the following statements. Are they opinion, or could they be the basis for a misrepresentation claim?

This lightbulb will last 200 hours.

THINK: Misrepresentation requires a statement of fact or a promise of performance that is a basis for entering into a contract.

APPLY: This statement about the lightbulb is a promise of performance. It is the type of information someone relies on when making a buying decision.

ANSWER: The statement is a basis for claiming misrepresentation if it turns out to be false.

These suits are 100 percent wool.

THINK: Misstatement of a material fact that the buyer relies on when making decisions can be the basis for a claim of misrepresentation.

APPLY: Saying that the suits are 100 percent wool is a statement of fact about the goods.

ANSWER: If the goods are not 100 percent wool, the statement is a basis for claiming misrepresentation.

Now use this approach to analyze the following statements.

This fabric is the finest money can buy.

This sweater is 50 percent cashmere.

This toothpaste reduces cavities by 20 percent.

This car gets 22 miles to the gallon.

This stock has never decreased in value.

This house has no easements running through the backyard.

This car has not been in an accident.

These bicycle locks are theft-proof.

This carpet-cleaning machine will remove every type of spot on your rugs.

ETHICAL ISSUES

Nine graduates of New York University Law School (NYLS) brought suit against their alma mater, alleging that the school misled them with the data it released about the school's graduates' employment and salaries.

The nine plaintiffs had all paid $47,800 per year in tuition and sought to recover damages of the difference between the alleged inflated tuition they paid because of the inflated data on placement and the "true value" of their education.

The nine plaintiffs had varying experiences following their graduation in terms of professional success. Plaintiff Alexandra Gomez–Jimenez attended NYLS between 2004–2007 and after graduating in 2007, Ms. Gomez–Jimenez secured full-time, permanent employment in April 2008 and now "enjoys a thriving practice as an immigration attorney" with her own office.

However, Plaintiff Chloe Giligan first worked as a saleswoman in a department store and then as a legal secretary in a small law firm, and now does not practice law. Other plaintiffs work as contract attorneys, one works as a paralegal, and some remain unemployed.

The NYLS data allegedly omitted facts which would have given a better picture on post-graduation employment prospects. For example, the data consistently reported that approximately 90 to 92 percent of NYLS graduates secured employment within nine months of graduation but did not report the percentage of graduates employed in part-time or temporary positions. A graduate could be working part-time as a barista in Starbucks and be deemed employed in business, although such employment is temporary and does not require a law degree. A contract attorney, without permanent employment, working in document review projects in a law firm would be deemed employed in private law practice under the NYLS profile.

The graduate mean salaries were computed from a selected, intensely solicited, subset of graduates. The subset consisted of only 22 to 26 percent of graduates and the mean salary information did not disclose that the salaries represented only a subset or how that subset was chosen.

What would the students need to show in order to establish fraud? Misrepresentation? Is not being transparent an ethical issue?

[*Gomez–Jimenez v New York Law School*, 943 N.Y.S.2d 834 (N.Y. Supp. 2012)]

Business Planning Tip

When employees and agents are working for commissions as well as salary (or are on commission alone), they are subject to great temptation to engage in misrepresentation. For example, in the Sears Roebuck & Company controversy over the allegations that its auto repair centers overcharged customers, Sears's then–CEO Edward Brennan issued a statement indicating that the presence of incentives for selling parts and services may have contributed to poor decisions by employees in handling customers. Incentive-based pay systems must also have ethical guidelines.

The buyer must rely on or attach some importance to the statement that was made. A buyer who is buying cars only to take them apart for their used parts does not rely on a misrepresentation that the car has not been in an accident. Whatever information is given must be part of the reason the buyer has agreed to enter into the contract.

13-1c FRAUD OR FRAUDULENT MISREPRESENTATION

Although misrepresentation can result simply because of inaccurate information, **fraud** is the knowing and intentional disclosure of false information or the knowing failure to disclose relevant information. Fraud has the same elements of proof as misrepresentation, with the added element of *scienter*, or knowledge that the information given is false. An example of the distinction is a situation in which the seller of a home obtains an exterminator's report that says the house is clear of termites and passes the report along to the buyer. If the house actually has termites, it is a case of misrepresentation but not fraud because the seller was simply passing along the information without knowledge of its accuracy. If, however, that same seller received a report from an exterminator that indicated there were termites and then found another exterminator to report there were no termites, and the seller passed only that second report along to the buyer, there would be fraud because there was knowledge of the false report and the intent to defraud the buyer. The failure to disclose material information about the subject matter of a contract can also constitute fraud. For example, a car dealership that fails to disclose to a customer that the car he is buying was in an accident is engaging in misrepresentation. If the car dealership performed the body work on the car in its own body shop, the failure to disclose the accident and repairs would be fraud.

Reed v King (Case 13.2) includes a discussion of the elements of misrepresentation and of when misrepresentation becomes fraud.

| CASE 13.2 | *Reed v King* 193 Cal. Rptr. 130 (1983) |

Buying Property from the Addams Family: How Scary Must It Be?

Dorris Reed (plaintiff) purchased a home from Robert King for $76,000. Mr. King and his real estate agents did not disclose to Mrs. Reed that 10 years earlier, the house had been the site of the murders of a mother and her four children. After Mrs. Reed moved into the home, neighbors disclosed to her the story of the murders and the fact that the house carried a stigma. Because of its history, appraisers evaluated the true worth of the house to be $65,000. Mrs. Reed filed suit on the basis of misrepresentation and sought rescission and damages. Her complaint was dismissed by the trial court, and she appealed.

JUDICIAL OPINION

BLEASE, Associate Justice

In the sale of a house, must the seller disclose it was the site of a multiple murder?

CONTINUED

Concealed within this question is the nettlesome problem of the duty of disclosure of blemishes on real property which are not physical defects or legal impairments to use.

Reed seeks to state a cause of action sounding in contract, i.e., rescission, or in tort, i.e., deceit. In either event her allegations must reveal a fraud. "The elements of actual fraud, whether as the basis of the remedy in contract or tort, may be stated as follows: There must be (1) a *false representation* or concealment of a material fact (or, in some cases, an opinion) susceptible of knowledge, (2) made with *knowledge* of its falsity or without sufficient knowledge on the subject to warrant a representation, (3) with the *intent* to induce the person to whom it is made to act upon it; and such person must (4) act in *reliance* upon the representation (5) to his *damage*."

The trial court perceived the defect in Reed's complaint to be a failure to allege concealment of a material fact. "Concealment" and "material" are legal conclusions concerning the effect of the issuable facts pled. As appears, the analytic pathways to these conclusions are intertwined.

Reed's complaint reveals only nondisclosure despite the allegation King asked a neighbor to hold his peace. There is no allegation the attempt at suppression was a cause in fact of Reed's ignorance. Accordingly, the critical question is: does the seller have duty to disclose here? Resolution of this question depends on the materiality of the fact of the murders.

In general, a seller of real property has a duty to disclose: "where the seller knows of facts *materially* affecting the value or desirability of the property which are known or accessible only to him and also knows that such facts are not known to, or within the reach of … the buyer."

Materiality "is a question of law, and is part of the concept of right to rely or justifiable reliance." Accordingly, the term is essentially a label affixed to a normative conclusion.

Numerous cases have found nondisclosure of physical defects and legal impediments to use of real property are material. However, to our knowledge, no prior real estate sale case has faced an issue of nondisclosure of the kind presented here. Should this variety of ill repute be required to be disclosed?

The paramount argument against an affirmative conclusion is it permits the camel's nose of unrestrained irrationality admission to the tent. If such an "irrational" consideration is permitted as a basis of rescission the stability of all conveyances will be seriously undermined. Any fact that might disquiet the enjoyment of some segment of the buying public may be seized upon by a disgruntled purchaser to void a bargain. In our view, keeping this genie in the bottle is not as difficult a task as these arguments assume. We do not view a decision allowing Reed to survive a demurrer in these unusual circumstances as endorsing the materiality of facts predicating peripheral, insubstantial, or fancied harms.

The murder of innocents is highly unusual in its potential for so disturbing buyers they may be unable to reside in a home where it has occurred. This fact may foreseeably deprive a buyer of the intended use of the purchase. Murder is not such a common occurrence that *buyers* should be charged with anticipating and discovering this disquieting possibility. Accordingly, the fact is not one for which a duty of inquiry and discovery can sensibly be imposed upon the buyer.

Reed alleges the fact of the murders has a quantifiable effect on the market value of the premises. Reputation and history can have a significant effect on the value of realty. "George Washington slept here" is worth something, however physically inconsequential that consideration may be. Ill-repute or "bad will" conversely may depress the value of property. Failure to disclose such a negative fact where it will have a foreseeably depressing effect on income expected to be generated by a business is tortious. Some cases have held that *unreasonable* fears of the potential buying public that a gas or oil pipeline may rupture may depress the market value of land and entitle the owner to incremental compensation in eminent domain.

Whether Reed will be able to prove her allegation, the decade-old multiple murder has a significant effect on market value we cannot determine. If she is able to do so by competent evidence she is entitled to a favorable ruling on the issues of materiality and duty to disclose. Her demonstration of objective tangible harm would still the concern that permitting her to go forward will open the floodgates to rescission on subjective and idiosyncratic grounds.

CASE QUESTIONS

1. Is the kind of information that was withheld here material? What evidence could be used to show materiality?

2. Is Mrs. Reed's case dismissed, or will she be permitted to go forward with the suit?

3. Should Mr. King and the real estate agents have disclosed the information to Mrs. Reed? Did they have an ethical obligation to do so?

Most states have passed some form of disclosure statutes for real estate transactions. In some states, the history of criminal activity on a property must be disclosed. In other states, there are prohibitions on disclosure. Some of these states prohibit disclosure of information, such as whether an occupant of the property died of AIDS. However, even in states with protections and immunity from disclosure, the buyer must be told the truth if the buyer asks specifically about the occupants and their health.

Consider...

Barry Hinesley negotiated with Oakshade Town Center during the spring of 1998 for a lease to a suite within a shopping center being developed by Oakshade in Davis, California. Hinesley said that during the negotiations, Oakshade's agent and representative, Paul Petrovich, told Hinesley the regional restaurant chain Dos Coyotes, the international coffee shop chain Starbucks, and the international ice cream and yogurt chain Baskin-Robbins would be leasing and occupying suites near the suite Hinesley was to lease. All three chains, according to Petrovich, would commence operations by the end of 1998. Hinesley leased 1,200 square feet for five years. Starbucks and Baskin-Robbins never leased space from Oakshade. However, Marble Slab Creamery (an ice cream store) and Common Grounds (a coffeehouse) did become tenants. Dos Coyotes did become a tenant of Oakshade, but its lease did not commence until December 2000.

Was there misrepresentation by Petrovich? Is tenant composition of a shopping center a material issue for tenants entering into a lease agreement for that center? Is reliance on an agent's representations a basis for an action for misrepresentation?
[*Hinesley v Oakshade Town Center*, 135 Cal. App. 4th 289 (2005)]

13-1d CONSUMER CREDIT CONTRACTS AND RESCISSION RIGHTS

There is an extensive set of federal laws that apply to credit contracts, and Exhibit 13.2 provides a summary. For example, certain types of consumer credit contracts[1] must include a **three-day cooling-off period** for the debtor, which is a buyer's protection for "cold feet," something that can happen as the full nature of the contract and credit terms become clearer. The buyer has the right to rescind certain types of credit contracts anytime during the 72 hours immediately following execution of a credit contract.

The types of credit contracts covered by the cooling-off period are those in which the creditor takes a security interest in the debtor's home. For example, if Alfie is installing a solar hot water system in his home, has purchased it on credit, and is giving the solar company a lien on his house, the three-day period applies; Alfie has three days to change his mind after he signs the contract. The three-day period also applies to **home solicitation sales**, in which sellers/creditors first approach consumers in the buyers' homes. The protection here allows buyers to recoup from any sales pressure that might have been used.

Where the three-day rescission period applies, the creditor must include both a description of the rights in the contract and a full explanation of the procedures the debtor should follow to rescind the contract during the three-day period.

Under the **Home Equity Loan Consumer Protection Act of 1988** and the **Home Ownership and Equity Protection Act of 1994 (HOEPA)**, additional disclosures are required for those transactions in which consumers use their homes as security

EXHIBIT **13.2** Consumer Protection Statutes

Summary of Federal Laws on Consumer Credit

CREDIT STATUTE (FEDERAL)	PURPOSE AND SCOPE
Dodd–Frank Wall Street Reform and Consumer Financial Protection Act [aka The Consumer Financial Protection Act of 2010 (CFPA)] (amends various sections of 12 U.S.C. and 15 U.S.C)	Creates the Bureau of Consumer Financial Protection to consolidate regulation of consumer credit; includes additional consumer credit protections
Truth in Lending Act [15 U.S.C. § 1601 (1968)]	Part of CCPA that governs disclosure of credit terms
Fair Credit Billing Act	Timing and content requirements for credit card bills
Home Equity Loan Consumer Protection Act [15 U.S.C. § 1647 (1988)]	Disclosure requirements for home equity rescission period
Home Ownership and Equity Protection Act [15 U.S.C. § 1637 (1994)]	Disclosure requirements on payment amounts for home equity loans and cancellation rights
Fair Credit Billing Act [15 U.S.C. § 1637 (1974)]	Rights of debtors on open-end credit billing disputes
Fair Credit Reporting Act [15 U.S.C. § 1681 (1970)]	Right of debtors with respect to reports of their credit histories
Fair Debt Collections Practices Act [15 U.S.C. § 1692 (1977)]	Regulation of conduct of third-party bill collectors and attorneys
Bankruptcy Abuse Prevention and Consumer Protection Act of 2005	Requires strict standards for filing for bankruptcy

© Cengage Learning 2015

for the credit. The **Consumer Financial Protection Act (CFPA)** (part of the Dodd–Frank reforms) increases the disclosure requirements and grants the **Bureau of Consumer Financial Protection (BCFP)** broad authority to promulgate regulations to prevent hidden fees, deceptive terms, and abusive practices in this area. Existing regulations on mortgage and equity loans mandate that disclosures explain that consumers who do not pay these debts could lose their dwellings, which could be sold to pay the debts. The three-day rescission period also applies to home equity credit lines. If notice of this three-day rescission right is not given to the home-owner/debtor, the right of rescission will continue for three years. Most experts agree that the types of disclosures required through CFPA will increase and that lenders will need to include sample computations for consumers so that they can evaluate the total costs, potential and otherwise, of their credit transactions. The disclosures will be personalized enough for the borrower to see how that percentage of income changes as the mortgage interest rate increases. In addition, CFPA requires the lender to establish its basis for approving the loan, making a determination that the borrower is likely and able to repay the mortgage.

The three-day rescission rights also apply to home mortgage refinancings. However, if the lender failed to make the correct disclosures on the right of rescission, the consumers then have a three-year right of rescission. [*Barrett v JP Morgan Chase Bank, N.A.*, 445 F.3d 874 (6th Cir. 2006)] There are also monetary penalties for a creditor's failure to make the required and accurate disclosures, and class-action suits are available for consumers to group together to recover the lesser of $500,000 or one percent of the creditor's net worth.

13-1e CREDIT CHANGES FOLLOWING THE SUBPRIME MORTGAGE DEFAULTS AND FORECLOSURE: SUBPRIME LENDING REPRESENTATIONS AND DISCLOSURES

Part of the CFPA reforms focused on the subprime lending market. This credit market makes loans to consumers who have bankruptcies, no credit history, low-to-moderate incomes, or a poor credit history. Because of the higher risk of these types of loans, these credit contracts involve lower loan amounts; higher origination costs, brokers' fees, credit insurance fees; higher interest rates; significant collateral pledges; large prepayment penalties (meaning that the consumer debtor is locked into the high interest rate); and faster repayment requirements.

Subprime loans have had notoriously difficult-to-read contracts. Determining all of the charges and fees from the contract was a tall order. Regulations and laws at the state and federal level have changed and simplified contract disclosures for subprime loans. Part of the subprime lending market includes lenders who take advantage of less sophisticated consumers or even consumers who are just desperate for funds. These lenders use their superior bargaining positions to obtain credit terms that go well beyond compensating them for their risk. For example, title loans (loans made in exchange for title to a car or house if the borrower defaults) have been widely used in subprime markets.

All of these types of loans, sometimes called **predatory lending**, are now highly regulated by both the states and the federal government. There are now limits on interest rates as well as expanded rescission periods (such as 10 days), and lists of additional contract disclosures. Some states require credit counseling before the contract can be validly executed. Failure to comply with the requirements allows the debtor a way out of contract performance.

13-1f DURESS

Duress occurs when a party is physically forced into a contract or deprived of a meaningful choice when deciding whether to enter into a contract. Requiring employees to sell company stock holdings in order to keep their jobs is an example of duress because of a lack of choice. If duress has occurred, the contract is voidable. The party who experienced the duress has the right to rescind the agreement, but rescission is a choice; the law does not make the contract illegal or unenforceable because duress was present. The choice of enforcement or rescission is left to the party who experienced the duress.

13-1g UNDUE INFLUENCE

Undue influence occurs when one party uses a close personal relationship with another party to gain contractual benefits. Before undue influence can be established, a **confidential relationship** of trust and reliance must exist between the parties. Attorneys and clients have a confidential relationship. Elderly parents who rely on a child or children for their care have a confidential relationship with those children. To establish undue influence, abuse of this confidential relationship must occur. For example, conditioning an elderly parent's care upon the signing over of his land to a child is an abuse of the relationship. An attorney who offers advice on property disposition to his benefit is abusing the confidential relationship. Again, contracts subject to undue influence defenses are voidable. They can be honored if the party who experienced the influence desires to honor the contract.

13-1h **ILLEGALITY AND PUBLIC POLICY**

A contract that violates a statute or the general standards of public policy is void and cannot be enforced by either party. To enforce contracts that violate statutes or public conscience would encourage the commission of these illegal acts, so contract law is controlled by the statutory prohibitions and public policy concerns of other areas of law. The *A.V. ex rel. Vanderhye v iParadigms, LLC* case (Case 13.3) deals with an issue of duress as well as several other contract defenses and provides the answer to the chapter's opening "Consider..."

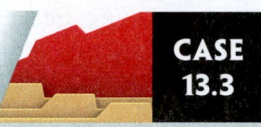

| CASE 13.3 | *A.V. ex rel. Vanderhye v iParadigms, LLC*
544 F. Supp. 2d 473, reversed on other grounds, 562 F.3d 630 (4th Cir. 2009) |

Turn It In, Then Turn It Over to the Courts

FACTS

iParadigms (defendant) owns and operates Turnitin, a proprietary technology system that evaluates the originality of written works in order to prevent plagiarism. Educational institutions contract with iParadigms and require their students to submit their written works via Turnitin. When the student work is submitted to Turnitin, the system compares the work electronically to content available on the Internet, student works previously submitted to Turnitin, and commercial databases of journal articles and periodicals. Turnitin then produces an Originality Report. The teacher evaluates the Originality Report and decides whether to address any issues with the student.

Turnitin can archive a student's work, which allows Turnitin's database to grow with each student work submitted. However, this feature must be specifically authorized by the school district.

In order to submit a paper to Turnitin, a student must click "I Agree" to the terms of the "user agreement" (also referred to as the "Clickwrap Agreement"), which is displayed directly above the "I agree" link that the student must click. The Clickwrap Agreement states: "Turnitin and its services are maintained by iParadigms, LLC ['Licensor'], and are offered to you, the user ['User'], conditioned on your acceptance without modification of the terms, conditions, and notices contained herein." The Clickwrap Agreement also contains a limitation of liability clause:

> *In no event shall iParadigms, LLC and/or its suppliers be liable for any direct, indirect, punitive, incidental, special, or consequential damages arising out of or in any way connected with the use of this web site or with the delay or inability to use this web site, or for any information, software, products, and services obtained through this web site, or otherwise arising out of the use of this web site, whether based in contract, tort, strict liability or otherwise, even if iParadigms, inc. or any of its suppliers has been advised of the possibility of damages.*

A.V., a minor, and three other students (Plaintiffs) attended high school in Virginia, in the Fairfax County Public Schools system, and in Arizona, in the Tucson Unified School District. Both school systems contracted with iParadigms to utilize iParadigms's Turnitin technology system and both authorized archiving of student-submitted work. Both school districts required their students to use Turnitin to submit their written works. If a student chose not to submit his or her work via Turnitin, that student would receive a zero on the assignment.

Each of the students read and clicked "I agree" to the terms of the Clickwrap Agreement. However, in an attempt to prevent Turnitin from archiving their written works, the students included a disclaimer on the face of their works indicating that they did not consent to the archiving of their works by Turnitin. iParadigms archived the works submitted by the four students. The students allege there was no contract entered into, that if there was a contract it was void because they were minors, and that the requirement of using Turnitin was unconscionable because it involved duress. iParadigms moved for summary judgment.

JUDICIAL OPINION

HILTON, District Judge

...iParadigms first contends that Turnitin's Clickwrap Agreement constitutes a valid contract entered into between Plaintiffs and iParadigms and that the limitation of liability clause precludes any liability in this

CONTINUED

action. In Virginia, the essential elements of a contract are offer, acceptance and consideration. As one court has stated, "[a] contract is no less a contract simply because it is entered into via a computer." In fact, many courts have found clickwrap agreements to be enforceable. Additionally, "waivers and limitation of liability clauses are enforceable."

The Court finds that the parties entered into a valid contractual agreement when Plaintiffs clicked "I Agree" to acknowledge their acceptance of the terms of the Clickwrap Agreement. The first line of the Clickwrap Agreement, which appears directly above the "I Agree" link, states: "Turnitin and its services … are offered to you, the user ['User'], conditioned on your acceptance without modification of the terms, conditions, and notices contained herein." Also, the Clickwrap Agreement provides that iParadigms will not be liable for any damages "arising out of the use of this web site." By clicking "I Agree," Plaintiffs accepted iParadigms' offer and a contract was formed based on the terms of the Clickwrap Agreement. Because a limitation of liability clause was among the terms of the Agreement, the Court finds that iParadigms cannot be held liable for any damages arising out of Plaintiffs' use of the Turnitin web site.

The existence of disclaimers on the written works indicating that Plaintiffs did not consent to the archiving of their works does not modify the Agreement or render it unenforceable. The Clickwrap Agreement itself provides that the terms of the Agreement are not modifiable. Plaintiffs had the option to "Agree" or "Disagree"; no third option was available to allow Plaintiffs to modify the Agreement. By clicking "I Agree," Plaintiffs agreed to the terms of the contract as described in the Clickwrap Agreement. Any attempted disclaimers written onto papers submitted after clicking "I Agree" did not change the terms of the Agreement.

Plaintiffs assert the defense of infancy in an attempt to void the terms of the Clickwrap Agreement. In Virginia, a contract with an infant is voidable by the infant upon attaining the age of majority. However, the infancy defense cannot function as "a sword to be used to the injury of others, although the law intends it simply as a shield to protect the infant from injustice and wrong." In other words, "[i]f an infant enters into any contract subject to conditions or stipulations, he cannot take the benefit of the contract without the burden of the conditions or stipulations."

Plaintiffs received benefits from entering into the Agreement with iParadigms. They received a grade from their teachers, allowing them the opportunity to maintain good standing in the classes in which they were enrolled. Plaintiffs cannot use the infancy defense to void their contractual obligations while retaining the benefits of the contract. Thus, Plaintiffs' infancy defense fails.

Plaintiffs also seek to invalidate the contract on the grounds of duress. In Virginia, duress is defined as the "overbearing of a person's free will by an unlawful or wrongful act or by threat such that the party's consent to a contractual agreement is involuntary."

Though Plaintiffs plead duress, there is no evidence that anyone was coerced in any fashion by Turnitin or iParadigms. Insofar as Plaintiffs' duress defense is asserted against Plaintiffs' respective schools, rather than Defendant iParadigms, there is no support for the proposition that a contract can be invalidated on the basis of third party duress. Nevertheless, even if there was evidence of coercion by iParadigms, or even if a claim of third party duress by the school systems was viable, such coercion would not rise to the level of "an unlawful or wrongful act." Schools have a right to decide how to monitor and address plagiarism in their schools and may employ companies like iParadigms to help do so. If Plaintiffs' objection is that their schools' policies requiring students to use Turnitin are wrongful, Plaintiffs' proper redress is with the school systems. Thus, Plaintiffs' duress defense fails.

CASE QUESTIONS

1. Why did the minor/infancy defense not work in this case?
2. Why did the duress defense fail?
3. Why was the students' disclaimer ineffective?

Contracts in Violation of Criminal Statutes

Contracts that are agreements to commit criminal wrongs are void. For example, the old saying that "there is a contract out on his life" may be descriptive, but it is not accurate in the legal sense. There could never be a valid contract to kill someone because the agreement is one to commit a criminal wrong and is therefore void. No one is permitted to benefit from contracts to commit illegal acts. For example, a beneficiary for a life insurance policy will not collect the proceeds from the insured's policy if the beneficiary arranged for the death of the insured (contract for murder). The following "Consider..." deals with the issue of benefits from an illegal contract.

Consider...

Janet Peterson signed a contract with Sunrider Corporation in 1976 that provided for her payment arrangements as a participant in Sunrider's sales program. Sunrider was a Utah corporation that sold herbs, dietary supplements, skin care products, and beauty aids through a multilevel marketing plan. The plan includes several "levels of achievement" through which participants may receive compensation based both on their own sales of company products and on the sales of those whom participants have "sponsored"—that is, those whom participants have brought into the company.

Peterson received commissions from Sunrider Corporation from 1976 through 1994 for sales that were made by Sunrider distributors who had been recruited by Peterson. Her payments averaged $3,500 per month. In 1994, after Sunrider had been acquired by another company, the payments ended. The new CEO stopped the payments because he claimed they were illegal. The Utah Pyramid Scheme Act (UPSA) provides that "A person may not organize, establish, promote, or administer any pyramid scheme." Part of the UPSA provides:

> receiving bonuses in a multi-level marketing business is illegal when the bonuses are based only upon sponsorship of an organization, rather than promoting a product, selling a product, or training and supervising down-line distributors.

Peterson says that her commissions from the lower levels are based on sales of products, and not just on her having recruited the people and companies to sell Sunrider. The new corporation argues that Peterson still did not make the sales herself and the payments are illegal. Peterson argues that it would be unfair not to pay the commissions.

What should the court do and why? Be sure to consider the purpose of the antipyramid statute. Think also about her reliance on the representations of the previous company's officials. Finally, think through the public policy issues in paying or not paying Peterson according to her original contract.

[*Peterson v The Sunrider Corp.*, 48 P.3d 918 (Utah 2002)]

Contracts in Violation of Licensing Statutes

In some cases, contracts are not contracts to commit illegal acts but are simply contracts for a legal act to be done by one not authorized to perform such services. Every state requires some types of professionals and technicians to be licensed before they can perform work for the public. For example, a lawyer must be admitted to the bar before representing clients. A lawyer who contracts to represent a client before having been admitted to the practice of law has entered into a void contract. Even if the lawyer successfully represents the client, no fee could be collected because the agreement violated the licensing statute, and to allow the lawyer to collect the fee, even in a *quasi* contract, would encourage others to violate the licensing requirements.

In some cases, licensing requirements are in place, not for competency reasons, but to raise revenues. For example, an architect may be required to pass a competency screening to be initially licensed in a state, and after that the license may be renewed simply by paying an annual fee. Suppose that the architect forgot to pay the annual renewal fee and, after the license had lapsed, entered into a $300,000 contract with a developer. The developer discovers the renewal problems after the work is completed and wants to get out of paying the architect. In this case, the issue is not one of competency screening but of financial oversight, and the architect would be permitted to collect the fee.

Contracts in Violation of Usury Laws

These contracts are credit or loan contracts that charge interest in excess of the state's limits for interest or finance charges. These statutes are discussed in detail in Chapter 14.

Contracts in Violation of Public Policy

Some contracts do not violate any criminal laws or statutory provisions but do violate certain standards of fairness or encourage conduct in violation of public policy. For example, many firms include **exculpatory clauses** in their contracts that purport to hold the firms completely blameless for any accidents occurring on their premises. Most courts consider a firm's trying to hold itself completely blameless for all accidents, regardless of the degree of care or level of fault, against public policy and will not, therefore, enforce such clauses.

Also grouped into the public policy prohibition are contracts that restrict trade or employment. For example, when a business is sold, part of the purchase price is paid for the business's goodwill. The benefit of that payment is lost if the seller moves down the street and starts another similar business. Hence, the courts have permitted **covenants not to compete** to be included in these contracts as long as they are reasonable in time and geographic scope. These covenants and their legality are discussed in detail in Chapter 16.

Some contracts are not actually contracts for criminal or illegal activities, but the terms of the contract are grossly unfair to one party. A contract that gives all the benefits to one side and all the burdens to the other is an **unconscionable** contract. The standards for determining whether a contract is unconscionable are the public policy standards for fairness that cover all types of contract provisions and negotiations. Many of the predatory lending contracts have been held to be unconscionable. The standards for unconscionability are set on a case-by-case basis. The courts have not given a firm definition of unconscionability. Even the UCC does not specifically define unconscionability, although one section (2–302) prohibits the enforcement of unconscionable contracts. The *Gonzalez v Wilshire Credit Corp* case (Case 13.4) deals with an issue of unconscionability in mortgage lending.

**CASE
13.4**   *Gonzalez v Wilshire Credit Corp*
25 A.3d 1103 (N.J. 2011)

Foreclosing on a Paying Borrower

FACTS

In 1994, Blanca Gonzalez (plaintiff) and Monserate Diaz purchased a home in Perth Amboy. In February 1997, Diaz borrowed $72,000 from Cityscape Mortgage Corporation and executed a Fixed Rate Balloon Note with an annual interest rate of 11.250 percent. In the note, Diaz agreed to make monthly payments of $699.31 until the loan's maturity date, March 3, 2012, when a final balloon payment of $61,384.17 would be due. Blanca did not sign the note.

As security for the loan, Blanca and Diaz pledged both of their interests in the property by executing a mortgage in favor of Cityscape. The mortgage agreement listed Blanca and Diaz as "borrower[s]." In March 1997, Cityscape assigned the note and mortgage to U.S. Bank. Wilshire Credit Corporation was U.S. Bank's servicing agent.

In 1999, Diaz died intestate. Blanca continued to live in the home and make payments on the loan. In 2001, Blanca was laid off from her factory job at Mayfair Company, where she had been employed for 17 years.

CONTINUED

After the layoff, she suffered a heart attack and other health difficulties, and in 2003 was approved for Social Security disability benefits.

Over time, Blanca fell behind on the loan payments. At some point, Wilshire refused to accept further payments. In March 2003, U.S. Bank filed a foreclosure. In September 2003, the bank notified Blanca of the foreclosure.

In April 2004, the court entered judgment in favor of U.S. Bank in the amount of $80,454.71 plus interest and costs, including $954.55 in attorneys' fees, on the defaulted loan. The court also ordered that the property be sold to satisfy the judgment. A sheriff's sale was scheduled for the next month.

Before the sheriff's sale, Blanca entered into a written agreement with Wilshire, with Wilshire agreeing to forbear pursuing the sheriff's sale contingent on Blanca paying arrears, including foreclosure fees and costs, of $17,612.84. Blanca agreed to make a lump sum payment of $11,000 and then monthly payments of $1,150 through January 20, 2006. Gail Chester, a lawyer for Central Jersey Legal Services, represented Blanca in the negotiations with Wilshire.

By the end of September 2005, Blanca had made payments totaling $24,800 under the agreement—the $11,000 lump sum payment and 12 monthly payments of $1,150. However, Blanca missed four payments during this period, leaving her $6,461.89 in arrears. A sheriff's sale was scheduled but canceled because the parties entered into a new written agreement that Blanca negotiated without Ms. Chester being present. In negotiating this second agreement, which was entirely in English, Wilshire dealt solely with Blanca, who did not speak or read English (Spanish is her native language) and who only had a sixth-grade education. Wilshire's own notes indicate that "borrower does not speak English[;] negotiating has been difficult," that Blanca was disabled and on a fixed income of $600 per month, and that Blanca did not want to sell the property because it had been in the family for many years.

In this second agreement signed by Blanca, arrearages, including foreclosure fees and costs, were fixed at $10,858.18. The arrearages in this agreement were $4,396.29 more than that calculated earlier by the trial court. Blanca agreed to make a lump sum payment of $2,200 and then monthly payments of $1,000 through October 2006. As in the first agreement, Wilshire agreed to discharge the foreclosure action when the mortgage payments became current.

In September 2006, the attorney for U.S. Bank copied Blanca on a letter stating that the previously scheduled sheriff's sale had been set for October 4, 2006. Yet Blanca had not missed a single payment required by the 2005 agreement. Indeed, Blanca had made not only all required payments through October 2006 but also additional payments. Blanca took the letter from U.S. Bank's attorney to Ms. Chester of Legal Services. Having no knowledge of the second agreement, Ms. Chester wrote to the bank's attorney that Blanca had paid $20,569.32 in excess of her regular monthly payment, $699.31, since the May 2004 agreement (the first agreement). Ms. Chester suggested that it was time to return Blanca to the monthly payment schedule of $699.31. The bank's attorney did not respond. Rather, in October 2006, Wilshire sent a letter to Blanca noting that the second agreement was about to expire and that a new agreement needed to be negotiated; otherwise, it would resume foreclosure on her property. Ms. Chester contacted the Wilshire Workout Department. Wilshire then forwarded to Ms. Chester the second agreement. Wilshire could not explain how it had come to the $10,858.18 arrears set in the October 2005 agreement, nor could it explain why Blanca was not deemed current on the loan.

In July 2007, Blanca filed suit against Wilshire and U.S. Bank (defendants) for deceptive and unconscionable practices in violation of the Consumer Fraud Act (CFA). The trial court granted summary judgment in favor of defendants. The Appellate Division reversed and reinstated.

JUDICIAL OPINION

ALBIN, Justice

We must determine whether the manner in which Wilshire secured and executed the post-foreclosure-judgment agreements, as described by plaintiff, constitutes an unconscionable practice prohibited by the CFA.

The broad language of these [CFA] provisions encompasses "the offering, sale, or provision of consumer credit." Indeed, the term "advertisement" includes within its breadth "the attempt … to induce … any person … to make any loan." Accordingly, collecting or enforcing a loan, whether by the lender or its assignee, constitutes the "subsequent performance" of a loan, an activity falling within the coverage of the CFA.

Clearly, Cityscape's loan to Diaz was contingent on plaintiff signing the mortgage papers, which listed both as borrowers. Although in any technical sense plaintiff was not a borrower, she was still in a very real sense indebted to Cityscape. The terms of the mortgage obligated plaintiff to surrender her one-half interest in her home in the event of a default and later foreclosure judgment. Plaintiff may not have been personally obligated to pay the loan, but she would not have had a roof over her head unless she did so.

Unquestionably, U.S. Bank had the right to proceed with a sheriff's sale to satisfy its judgment. Had it done

CONTINUED

so, plaintiff admittedly would have had no reason to complain. But U.S. Bank and its servicing agent, Wilshire, chose a different path. They decided to give plaintiff the opportunity to reclaim her home conditioned on her satisfying the terms of signed agreements with Wilshire.

We are in the midst of an unprecedented foreclosure crisis in which thousands of our citizens stand to lose their homes, and in desperation enter into agreements that extend credit—post-judgment—in the hope of retaining homeownership. Defendants would have us declare this seemingly unregulated area as a free-for-all zone, where predatory-lending practices are unchecked and beyond the reach of the CFA.

The victims of these unsavory practices are most often the poor and the uneducated, and in many circumstances those with little understanding of English, and therefore the "need" for the protections of the CFA is "most acute" in such cases.

Threatening a sheriff's sale of her home, Wilshire inexplicably negotiated a new agreement directly with the unrepresented plaintiff, who could neither read nor speak English, who had only a sixth-grade education, and who was disabled and on a fixed income. The chancery court had calculated plaintiff's arrearages as $6,461.89 as of October 2005, and yet defendants had plaintiff sign an agreement setting the arrearages at $10,858.18. Even though plaintiff had made every payment and was current under that second agreement, defendants nevertheless threatened another sheriff's sale in October 2006. At this time, plaintiff contacted her Legal Services attorney, Ms. Chester, who asked Wilshire to answer a few simple questions. Wilshire could not explain how it had arrived at the $10,858.18 arrearages figure in the October 2005 agreement. It also could not explain how plaintiff's loan was not current, given that plaintiff had paid $20,569.32 in excess of the regular monthly payments since May 2004.

Lending institutions and their servicing agents are not immune from the CFA; they cannot prey on the unsophisticated, those with no bargaining power, those bowed down by a foreclosure judgment and desperate to keep their homes under seemingly any circumstances. Moreover, Legal Services is only capable of representing a fraction of those low-income consumers who are similarly situated to Blanca Gonzalez, and the Attorney General has limited resources. The CFA was intended to fill that vacuum.

This case *in no way* suggests that settlement agreements in general are now subject to the CFA. Here, we are dealing with forbearance agreements. This case addresses only the narrow issue before us: the applicability of the CFA to a post-foreclosure-judgment agreement involving a stand-alone extension of credit. We hold only that, in fashioning and collecting on such a loan—as with any other loan—a lender or its servicing agent cannot use unconscionable practices in violation of the CFA.

We affirm the judgment of the Appellate Division vacating the dismissal of plaintiff's complaint. We therefore reinstate plaintiff's cause of action under the CFA.

CASE QUESTIONS

1. What should lenders and servicing agents learn from this case about settlement agreements?

2. Why is the use of Legal Aid not a defense to unconscionability in this case?

3. What does the phrase, "prey on the unsophisticated, those with no bargaining power" mean in terms of consumer protection and contracts?

13-2 Contract Performance

Once parties have contracted, they have the obligation of performance. The following subsections cover when performance is due, what constitutes performance, and when performance is excused.

13-2a WHEN PERFORMANCE IS DUE

Performance is due according to the times provided in the contract. In some contracts, however, prescribed events must occur before performance is required. These events are called **conditions**. **Conditions precedent** are events that give rise to performance. Suppose that Zelda has agreed to buy Scott's house, and their contract provides that Zelda does not have to pay until she is able to obtain a reasonable loan

BUSINESS STRATEGY

Restaurant Strategies for No-Shows

You make a reservation for dinner. The restaurant holds a place for you, and holds, and holds, but then you are a no-show. The restaurant is out the revenue it might have earned because it held, and held, and held an empty table—for you! Because costs are high, restaurants are trying new approaches to reservations, all of which involve legal issues.

The first new strategy finds restaurants tweeting the names of customers who did not show up for their reservations. One restaurant owner claims that what he does by posting their names is no worse than when customers post rants on Twitter and Facebook about his restaurant. The legal issue here is privacy. Years ago, restaurants and stores used to place bounced checks on their walls to disclose publicly those customers who had failed to pay. Such practices are considered a breach of privacy and now rarely done. However, what is posted on Twitter is not account information, just poor etiquette in failing to show and not notifying the restaurant.

A second strategy for online reservations has become popular with restaurants because many hotel concierges make reservations 30 days in advance online and just hold them for hotel guests who may want them at the last minute. However, they don't take the time to cancel if no hotel guest needs those reservations. There is no downside for the concierge because there is no name associated with the reservation. As a result, restaurants are using OpenTable.com, a generic booking site that charges $50 a head for a no-show. The use of the site is the same as the use of a hotel or airline site: The rules are clear and there are click options that indicate the customer understands the terms of the agreement and when a contract is formed.

A third strategy is one from Chicago. Diners must buy nonrefundable tickets for meals in advance. In effect, the customer pays for the meal in advance, but if they do not show up, they lose the advance payment, just as with nonrefundable airline tickets. The contract law issues here are the same as with the online booking—those who buy the meal tickets in advance must be told of the terms and conditions prior to purchase.

A final strategy is for the restaurant to take a credit card number for a deposit. Just as hotels have done for decades, restaurants are now asking diners for a credit card to secure a reservation. As they take the credit card number, they are also disclosing that unless you cancel by a certain time (some require 24 hours notice and others have a "no later than 4 P.M." stipulation on the day of the reservation), your card is still charged a deposit for the table. If you show up, the deposit goes toward paying for your meal. As part of this new contractual strategy, the restaurant also discloses that it will hold the table for a limited amount of time—15 to 30 minutes. The contract issues here are letting the customer know the terms of the reservation, including both the costs and the obligation to cancel within time limits.

to finance the purchase. This financing clause is a condition precedent to contract performance. If Zelda is denied financing, she is not required to perform under the contract. Another example of a condition precedent is in a contract for construction of jackets out of a material to be furnished by the seller. Unless the seller gives the manufacturer the fabric to work with, the manufacturer has no obligation to perform. **Conditions concurrent**, or **conditions contemporaneous**, exist in every contract; benefits are exchanged at the same time. One is willing to perform because the other side does.

13-2b STANDARDS FOR PERFORMANCE

The contract details what the parties are required to do for complete performance. In some contracts, performance is easily determined. Performance for a contract between an employment agency and a potential employee to find work for the employee is complete once the work is found.

But in some contracts, performance is complicated, and errors may occur in its execution. For example, construction contracts are long-term, complicated agreements. During the construction of a building, it is possible that some mistakes might be made. Is an owner allowed to not pay a contractor because of a mistake or two? The doctrine of **substantial performance** applies in construction contracts, and it means that the constructed building is, for practical purposes, just as good as the one contracted for. For example, a builder might have substituted a type of pipe when the brand name specified in the contract was not available. The substitution is a technical breach of contract, but it is a substitute that is just as good. The builder will be paid for the construction, but the owner will be entitled to damages.

FOR THE MANAGER'S DESK

Re: Killer Performance Requirements in Retail

It's called "the Squeeze." The Squeeze refers to the increasingly onerous logistical demands retailers place on clothing suppliers. The logistical demands add tremendous costs to suppliers, they are rigid, they are complex (some retailers' rules run 50 pages), and they carry penalties. Noncompliance with logistical requirements allows the retailer to take a "chargeback," or a deduction from its payment.

Here are some sample logistical requirements:

Shipping and Packing Guidelines from Retailers to Vendors Packing Hanging Garments
You must have written authorization from Federated to ship GOH. All ready-to-wear merchandise should be shipped in conveyable cartons in order to maximize the use of UCC-128 shipping container label....

Lazarus

Routing Instructions
Determine your RPS Zone number on the Zone Chart.... Determine your LTL [less than truckload] Zone number from the Zone Chart and follow the LTL Routing for that zone.

Kaufmann's

Paperwork Documentation
Provide a separate packing list for each store and for each purchase order, detailed as to purchase order #, department #, store # and two letter code, style #, color (when ordered by color), size (when ordered by size), number of cartons, and total units shipped.

Hecht's

Charges include $300 for incorrect labels, $500 for incorrect packing materials, and a 5 percent penalty if a shipment arrives late.

Schwab Co., the manufacturer of "Little Me" infant clothes, was charged $400 for late delivery of a $500 shipment.

A buyer for Federated Department Stores says, "... [I]t's not our responsibility to keep vendors afloat. We have a separate philanthropy program." Small vendors complain they must hire extra people to handle special boxing and that retailers' chargebacks are reversed if they offer proof of compliance.

Smaller vendors are taking their products to specialty stores and boutiques. Large retailers say, "This is all still negotiable." Some vendors say that retailers are wrong on their charges about 25–50 percent of the time, but "They throw it up to see what will stick." Vendors note that their cash flow is affected and that, until the disputes are resolved, it often takes a year for them to be paid on their invoices.

(*Lazarus, Kaufmann's, and Hecht's were regional chains that have been acquired by other national chains.*)

Is there a problem with unconscionability? Is this kind of behavior anticompetitive? Do you feel the guidelines and chargeback fees are truly negotiable? Are the chargeback levels of fees ethical?

13-2c E-COMMERCE: PAYMENT PERFORMANCE HAS CHANGED

One aspect of contract performance is payment. Internet transactions have changed dramatically how we pay for goods and services. The most common methods for electronic payment include credit cards, digital cash, and person-to-person payment, or PayPal.

13-2d WHEN PERFORMANCE IS EXCUSED

Sometimes, all conditions of a valid contract are met but performance of the contract is excused. Under common law, the parties are excused from performance if performance has become impossible. **Impossibility** means that the contract cannot be performed by the parties or anyone else. For example, performance under a contract for the purchase and sale of land that has been washed away into a lake is impossible. Completing a year of dance lessons is impossible for someone who has had a paralyzing accident.

Under the UCC (and under the *Restatement*), performance can be excused in cases of commercial impracticability. **Commercial impracticability** (see § 2–615 in Appendix C) excuses performance if the basic assumptions the parties made when they entered into the contract have changed. Although this definition makes it seem that the UCC excuses performance when wars, embargoes, and unusually high price increases occur, courts have been reluctant to apply the excuse of commercial impracticability. The standard of commercial impracticability has been interpreted to mean nothing more or less than the common law standard of impossibility.

Parties can protect themselves from unusual events by putting in their contracts *force majeure* clauses, which excuse the parties from performance in the event of such problems as wars, economic depression, or embargoes. Following the attack on the World Trade Center in New York City, performance under many contracts was excused for impossibility. For example, because air traffic was halted, all overnight shipping contract performances were excused.

Consider...

Trans World Airlines (TWA) had a sales/leaseback arrangement on 10 aircraft with Connecticut National Bank. TWA was experiencing difficulty making payments, attributing the difficulties to the Gulf War, which resulted in decreased air travel because of terrorism and decreased oil flow.

Is this situation an example of commercial impracticability?

[*Connecticut Nat'l. Bank v Trans World Airlines, Inc.*, 762 F. Supp. 76 (S.D.N.Y. 1991)]

Sons of Thunder, Inc. v Borden, Inc. (Case 13.5) deals with the issue of business needs changing and whether performance can be excused. It is a case that some experts have labeled a landmark one in terms of imposing a duty of good faith in performance. It also contains issues of performance and termination of a contract.

CASE 13.5   *Sons of Thunder, Inc. v Borden, Inc.*
690 A.2d 575 (N.J. 1997)

Ships and Liability Passing in the Night?

FACTS

Borden, Inc., owned Snow Food Products Division, a leading producer of clam products. Borden had its own four-vessel fleet as well as independent boats for obtaining clams. Boats delivered the clams to Borden's Cape May plant, where the shell stock was processed into clam meat.

In 1978, Borden hired Donald DeMusz to be the captain of the *Arlene Snow*, one of Borden's four boats. Eventually, Mr. DeMusz was hired as an independent contractor to manage Borden's boats, and Mr. DeMusz formed Sea Labor, Inc., to be the company responsible for the management of those boats. Sea Labor received five cents per bushel of clams harvested by the four boats.

At about the same time Mr. DeMusz was hired, Borden began its "Shuck-at-Sea" program, which enabled the fishermen to shuck the clams on the boat, thus allowing the boats to bring back larger amounts of clams, thereby reducing costs and eliminating the need for more plants and facilities. However, the existing boats were not large enough for the shucking equipment.

Wayne Booker, a manager for Borden, asked Mr. DeMusz to undertake the Shuck-at-Sea program. Mr. DeMusz submitted a proposal that Mr. Booker and other executives approved. Along with two partners, Mr. DeMusz formed Sea Works, Inc., and for $750,000 purchased the *Jessica Lori*, a clam-fishing boat with shucking equipment. Mr. DeMusz financed the purchase through a bank loan.

An internal company memo from Mr. Booker included the following paragraph along with a description of how Mr. DeMusz's purchase of a boat would save money:

> [W]e still have a significant mutual interest with DeMuse [sic]. His principal business will still be in chartering the Snow fleet and in captaining Arlene. He needs a dependable customer for the clams that he catches, either shell stock or meat. If we terminate our agreement with him, he would have a hard time making the payments on his boat.

Mr. DeMusz drafted a one-page contract, and Mr. Booker approved it with one small change. Mr. DeMusz then formed Sons of Thunder, Inc., with Bill Gifford and Bob Dempsey in order to purchase the second boat. The final contract was entered into on January 15, 1985, and included the following provision:

> IT IS understood and Agreed to by the parties hereto that Snow Food Products shall purchase shell stock from Sons of Thunder Corp. for a period of one (1) year, at the market rate that is standardized throughout the industry. The term of this contract shall be for a period of one (1) year, after which this contract shall automatically be renewed for a period up to five years. Either party may cancel this contract by giving prior notice of said cancellation in writing Ninety (90) days prior to the effective cancellation date.
>
> Sons of Thunder Corp. will offer for sale all shell stock that is landed to Snow Food.

In March 1985, Sons of Thunder bought a boat, the *Sons of Thunder*. The cost to rig and purchase the boat was $588,420.26. Sons of Thunder sought financing from First Jersey National Bank but was unable to obtain a loan until Mr. Booker told the bank representative that Mr. DeMusz had a solid relationship with Borden and that although the contract could be terminated within one year, Borden expected the contract to run for five years. Mr. Booker explained to the representative that the five-year term of the contract would be sufficient to pay back the loan. Ultimately, Mr. DeMusz obtained a $515,000 loan, which he, Mr. Gifford, Mr. Dempsey, and their spouses personally guaranteed. Mr. DeMusz used a personal note to cover the remaining balance.

After some preliminary testing, the *Sons of Thunder* started to operate and to fulfill its contract with Borden. For most weeks, the records show that Borden did not buy the minimum amount specified in the contract. Problems continued and the relationship between Mr. DeMusz and his companies and Borden began to deteriorate. When Borden discovered that a $500,000 accounting error had actually overstated the benefits of the Shuck-at-Sea program, Borden exercised its termination rights under the contracts and notified Mr. DeMusz of termination.

Mr. DeMusz and his companies experienced substantial losses as a result of the termination of contracts. Mr. DeMusz filed suit. Borden moved for summary judgment on the grounds that it had properly exercised its termination rights. The jury found for Mr. DeMusz, the court of appeals affirmed, and Borden appealed.

CONTINUED

JUDICIAL OPINION

GARIBALDI, Justice

The question whether Borden performed its obligations in good faith appears before the Court....

The obligation to perform in good faith exists in every contract, including those contracts that contain express and unambiguous provisions permitting either party to terminate the contract without cause. See *United Roasters, Inc. v Colgate-Palmolive Co.*, 649 F.2d 985 (4th Cir.), *cert. denied*, 454 U.S. 1054, 102 S.Ct. 599, 70 L.Ed.2d 590 (1981). In *United Roasters*, United Roasters gave Colgate the right to manufacture and distribute Bambeanos, its roasted soybean snack. The contract governing the relationship allowed Colgate to terminate its performance at any time during the test marketing period so long as it gave United Roasters thirty days' notice. After two years of testing Bambeanos, Colgate announced plans to merge with Riviana Foods, Inc., and in the next five months, it ceased producing Bambeanos, stopped advertising them, sold its entire inventory of raw soybeans and Bambeanos, and transferred its product manager to another project. Eventually, Colgate terminated the contract.

Interpreting North Carolina law in the diversity action, the Fourth Circuit concluded that North Carolina had not decided whether there was a good faith limitation on an unconditional right to terminate a contract. The Fourth Circuit did, however, evaluate United Roasters' claim that Colgate violated the covenant of good faith and fair dealing. The panel stated

> What is wrong with Colgate's conduct in this case is not its failure to communicate a decision to terminate ..., but its cessation of performance. Clearly it had an obligation of good faith performance up until its right of termination was actually effective. The contract expressly obliged it to use its best efforts in the promotion of Bambeanos. Instead of doing that, it simply ceased performance.... Quite simply, it broke its contract when it terminated its performance, which was United Roasters' contractual due.

In *Bak-A-Lum Corp.*, supra, 69 N.J. 123 (1976), this Court reached a similar conclusion even though the contract was oral and the parties had not discussed how the contract could be terminated. In that case, Bak-A-Lum and Alcoa made an oral agreement, which gave Bak-A-Lum an exclusive distributorship of aluminum siding and related products manufactured by Alcoa. Alcoa eventually terminated the exclusive part of the agreement by appointing four additional distributors. Even though Alcoa planned on terminating the distributorship, it encouraged Bak-A-Lum to expand its warehouse facilities, which substantially increased its operating costs.

Despite acknowledging Alcoa's unconditional right to terminate the contract, the Court upheld the verdict for Bak-A-Lum because it found that Alcoa had breached the implied covenant of good faith and fair dealing by withholding its plans to terminate the contract while encouraging the plaintiff to expand its facilities. As the Court explained: "While the contractual relation of manufacturer and exclusive territorial distributor continued between the parties an obligation of reciprocal good-faith dealing persisted between them." The Court found that the implied covenant of good faith and fair dealing required the defendant to give the plaintiff reasonable notice of its termination. Ultimately, the Court concluded that "a reasonable period of notice of termination of the distributorship ... would have been twenty months."

The case most heavily relied on by Borden and the majority at the Appellate Division, *Karl's Sales & Service, Inc. v Gimbel Brothers Inc.*, 249 N.J. Super. 487 (App. Div.), *cert. denied* 127 N.J. 548 (1991), is distinguishable from this matter. In that case, the Appellate Division stated that where the contractual right to terminate is express and unambiguous, the motive of the terminating party is irrelevant. As stated previously, we agree with that view of the law. However, in *Karl's Sales*, unlike this case and *Bak-A-Lum*, there were no allegations of bad faith or dishonesty on the part of the terminating party. Accordingly, *Karl's Sales* did not address the issue we are concerned with here.

Borden knew that Sons of Thunder depended on the income from its contract with Borden to pay back the loan. Yet, Borden continuously breached that contract by never buying the required amount of clams from the Sons of Thunder. Furthermore, after Gallant took Booker's place, he told DeMusz that he would not honor the contract with Sons of Thunder. Nicholson also told DeMusz that he did not plan to honor that contract. Borden's failure to honor the contract left Sons of Thunder with insufficient revenue to support its financing for the Sons of Thunder.

Borden was also aware that Sons of Thunder was guaranteeing every loan that Sea Work had taken to finance the rerigging and purchasing costs for the [boat]. Thus, Borden knew that the corporations were dependent on each other, and that if one company failed, the other would most likely fail. Borden, however, fulfilled its obligations to Sea Work only for a short time before it began to breach that agreement. Eventually, Borden terminated its contract with Sea Work even though it knew that terminating the contract would leave Sea Work with no market to fish the *Jessica Lori*.

The final issue is whether the jury's assessment of $412,000, approximately one year's worth of additional profits, for the breach of the implied covenant of good faith and fair dealing was a reasonable verdict. Specifically, can a plaintiff recover lost profits for a breach of the implied covenant of good faith and fair dealing? We agree with Judge Humphreys that

CONTINUED

the jury's award of one year's additional profits "is a reasonable and fair estimate of 'expectation damages.'" Moreover, we agree with the trial court that lost profits are an appropriate remedy when a buyer breaches the implied covenant of good faith and fair dealing.

> *In order to recover for lost profits under [Section 2-708(2)], the plaintiffs must prove the amount of damages with a reasonable degree of certainty, that the wrongful acts of the defendant caused the loss of profit, and that the profits were reasonably within the contemplation of the parties at the time the contract was entered into.*

The jury's award of $412,000, approximately one year's profit, for the breach of the implied covenant of good faith and fair dealing is reasonable and fair.

Affirmed

CASE QUESTIONS

1. Were all the DeMusz corporations completely dependent on Borden?
2. What impact does "good faith" have on termination of a contract?
3. What are the damages when there is a lack of good faith in the termination of a contract?
4. What provisions would you suggest be added to a contract such as this in which the relationship is one of contract but also one of dependence?

13-2e FINDING SOMEONE ELSE TO TAKE OVER THE CONTRACT

In some cases, the parties substitute someone else for the obligation in an agreement called a **novation**. For example, suppose that before forming a corporation, a business owner had signed a lease for store premises and then incorporates the business. The landlord agrees to substitute the new corporation as the tenant. All three parties (landlord, owner, and corporation) sign a novation. The owner is excused from individual liability and performance, and the corporation is substituted. Note that the landlord must agree; the owner cannot discharge his performance obligations by unilaterally substituting the corporation.

In other situations, the parties reach an agreement for payment in full on a contract; such an agreement is called an **accord and satisfaction**. The amount they agree to pay may be less than the original contract amount, but disputes over warranties, repairs, and other issues change the value of the contract. The accord and satisfaction serves to discharge the performance of both parties.

13-3 Nonperformance and Nonpayment— The Collection Remedies

There are times in contractual relationships where one side has clearly breached— there is no payment for goods or services delivered. How are situations involving nonpayment handled? This section covers the issues related to nonpayment.

13-3a MAKING SURE THE BILLING IS ACCURATE

In consumer credit contracts, the first step a creditor must take in enforcement is to make sure that the bills sent to the nonpaying consumer have complied with all federal laws. The **Fair Credit Billing Act** affords debtors the opportunity to challenge the figures on credit card monthly statements. Errors on credit card accounts are covered by this act and, to a lesser degree, by Regulation Z. Creditors are required to supply on the monthly statement an address or phone number to write or call in the event a debtor has questions or challenges regarding the bill. The language must read: "IN CASE OF ERRORS, CALL OR WRITE…."

Under the act, debtors can collect damages if they comply with all the act's procedural requirements. First, a debtor must notify the creditor of any errors within 60 days of the receipt of the statement. The notification must be in writing for the damage sections to apply. If a creditor supplies a phone number for inquiries, the notice must explain that oral protests do not preserve all Regulation Z rights. The written protest of the debtor must include the debtor's name, the account number, and a brief explanation of the claimed error.

The creditor has 30 days from the time of receipt of the written protest to acknowledge to the debtor receipt of the protest. The creditor has 90 days from receipt of the protest to take final action, either giving the debtor's account a credit or reaffirming that the charges are valid.

During the time the creditor is considering the debtor's protest, the debtor is not required to pay the questioned amount or any finance charges on that amount. If the charges are in fact accurate, the debtor will be charged for the finance charges during this time period. If the creditor fails to comply with any of the requirements or deadlines on bill protests, the debtor can be excused from payment even if the charges disputed were actually accurate.

13-3b COLLECTION—FAIR STANDARDS FOR OBTAINING PAYMENT

Enacted to control abuses in the collection process, the **Fair Debt Collections Practices Act (FDCPA)** controls a great deal of debt collection. Most of the states have also adopted some form of debt collection statute.

When the FDCPA Applies

The FDCPA applies to consumer debts and debt collectors. Consumer debts are defined here as they are under the TILA: debts for personal, home, or family purposes. Debt collectors are third-party collectors. The FDCPA does not apply to original creditors collecting their own debts; for example, Sears collecting Sears's debts is not governed by the FDCPA. However, if Sears referred its collection accounts to Central Credit Collection Agency, Central Credit would be under the FDCPA. If Sears created its own collection agency with a name other than Sears, the FDCPA would apply to that agency as well.

The FDCPA does not apply to the collection of commercial accounts or to banks and the Internal Revenue Service. In a rule revision, attorneys collecting debts for clients were made subject to coverage of the FDCPA.

Consider...

Telecredit Service Corporation's business is the collection of dishonored checks. Telecredit purchases these checks and then contacts the drawers to collect the funds. Stanley Holmes wrote a $315 check to Union Park Pontiac that was dishonored. Union Park sold the check to Telecredit, and Telecredit sent letters and made contacts to collect the check. Some contacts would be violations of FDCPA, but Telecredit says it is not covered by FDCPA because it is not collecting the debts of another. Is this correct?

[*Holmes v Telecredit Service Corp.*, 736 F. Supp. 1289 (D. Del. 1990)]

Collector Restrictions under the FDCPA

In addition to affirmative disclosure requirements, the FDCPA prohibits certain conduct by collectors, covered in the next sections.

Debtor Contact. One of the most frequent abuses by collectors prior to the FDCPA was constant debtor contact and harassment. The FDCPA curbs the amount of contact: Debtors cannot be contacted before 8:00 A.M. or after 9:00 P.M., and debtors who work night shifts cannot be disturbed during their sleeping hours in the daytime.

The place of contact is also controlled by the FDCPA: Collectors must avoid contact at inconvenient places. Home contact is permitted, but contact in club, church, or school meetings is prohibited. Collectors can approach debtors at their places of employment unless employers object or have a policy against such contact.

To prevent harassment, the FDCPA gives debtors a chance to "call off" a collector. If a debtor tells the collector that he wants no more contact, the collector must stop and take other steps, such as legal action, to collect the debt. If the debtor is represented by an attorney and gives the name of the attorney to the collector, the collector can contact only the attorney from that point.

Third-Party Contact. The FDCPA also prohibits notifying other parties of the debtor's debts and collection problems. However, the debtor's spouse and parents can be contacted regarding the debt. Other parties can be contacted for information, but the collector cannot disclose the reason for the contact. Further, the only information that can be obtained from these third parties is the address, phone number, and place of employment of the debtor.

These third parties cannot be told about the debt, the amount, delinquencies, or any other information about the debtor. The collector must even be careful to use appropriate stationery when writing for information so that the letterhead does not disclose the nature of the collector's business. Postcard contact with the debtor or third parties is prohibited because of the likelihood that others will see the information about the debtor.

Prohibited Acts. Collectors have certain other restrictions on their conduct under the FDCPA. The general prohibition in the FDCPA is that collectors cannot "harass, oppress, or abuse" the debtor. Continuing to make calls without identifying themselves as collectors is also a FDCPA violation. Using abusive language or physical force is prohibited. Misrepresenting the authority of a collector is also prohibited, as is posing as a law enforcement official or producing false legal documents. Debtors cannot be threatened with prison or other actions not authorized by law.

The *Gryzbowski v I.C. System, Inc.* case (Case 13.6) involves an issue of FDCPA violations.

CASE 13.6   *Gryzbowski v I.C. System, Inc.*
691 F. Supp. 2d 618 (M.D. Pa. 2010)

Cell Phones, Debts, and Anonymous Callers

FACTS

I.C. Systems, Inc. (defendant) is a debt collection company located in Minnesota that collects nationwide, particularly in Pennsylvania. Donna Gryzbowski (plaintiff) was a resident of Archibald, Pennsylvania, and was a debtor who owed money to one of I.C. Systems's clients, Washington Mutual. I.C. Systems employees called Ms. Gryzbowski's cell phone 11 times and requested that she return the call to I.C. Only one employee identified herself as a collector. On only four of the calls did the employees give their names with the request for the returned call. I.C. employees said they did not identify themselves because they thought they were calling Ms. Gryzbowski's employer. However, the greeting on the cell phone provided:

> Hi, you have reached Donna. Please leave your name, your number, and a brief message and a good time to call and I'll get back to you just as soon as I can. I appreciate your call, so I'll talk to you when I can. Thank you. Bye.

Ms. Gryzbowski filed suit alleging violations of the FDCPA for excessive contact and the failure of I.C. workers to identify themselves as debt collectors. She filed a motion for summary judgment.

CONTINUED

JUDICIAL OPINION

VANASKIE, District Judge

The FDCPA provides that a violation occurs when the debt collector fails to disclose in the initial written communication with the consumer and, in addition, if the initial communication with the consumer is oral, in the initial oral communication, that the debt collector is attempting to collect a debt and that any information obtained will be used for that purpose, and the failure to disclose in subsequent communications that the communication is from a debt collector … 15 U.S.C.A. § 1692e(11).

It is Defendant's position that based on the FDCPA's blanket prohibition regarding disclosure of debt information to third parties, Defendant does not state that it is a debt collector calling to collect a debt when it contacts a consumer at their place of employment because they want to avoid the "inadvertent or unintentional disclosure of this information" to the debtor's employer. Accordingly, the essence of Defendant's argument is that in order to guard against the potential violation of section 1692c(b), Defendant violates section 1692c(11) by failing to identify itself as a debt collector.

Just as it is not reasonable to destroy a village in order to save it, neither is it reasonable to violate an Act in order to comply with it. It was not reasonable for [the Defendant] to violate § 1692e(11) of the Fair Debt Collection Practices Act with every message it left in order to avoid the possibility that some of those messages might lead to a violation of § 1692c(b).

The defendant complained that leaving messages on answering machines would result in potential violation of § 1692c(b), therefore resulting in a rule of law forcing it not to leave any messages on answering machines. We have not decided that issue, but even if [the Defendant's] assumption is correct, the answer is that the Act does not guarantee a debt collector the right to leave answering machine messages.

[Defendant argues that] when leaving a voicemail or answering machine message, there is a concern that someone other than the consumer will hear the message. Thus, debt collectors are faced with a "Hobson's choice" of, on the one hand, leaving a "short, non-offensive message" that fails to make the necessary disclosures and thereby exposes the debt collector to claimed violations of § 1692d and § 1692e or, alternatively, leaving a message that makes the necessary disclosures but in so doing runs the risk that a third party will hear the message, thus exposing the debt collector to claimed violations of the prohibition in 15 U.S.C. § 1692c(b) on third party disclosures.

First, the calls were not placed to Plaintiff at her place of employment; they were calls to her personal cellular telephone. Although Defendant believed that the number was that of her employer, its subjective belief is irrelevant as the FDCPA is a strict liability statute. Second, Defendant has failed to cite persuasive authority that a debt collector's identification duty changes when it leaves voicemail messages on a person's cellular telephone as opposed to a home or work voicemail. As found by other courts, "leaving the recorded messages on the consumer's home telephone number [does] not cure the dilemma because the possibility still existed that a spouse, relative, or roommate would listen to the message." Accordingly, Defendant finds itself in its current "predicament" only because of the specific way that was selected to collect debts.

A message left with a co-worker, identifying the caller as a debt collector, would be a clear violation of section 1692c(b), as the co-worker is clearly a third party. A voicemail or answering machine, however, is not a third party. The potential violation of the statute does not occur when the message is left, but instead, if or when a third party overhears the debt collector's message.

As the FDCPA imposes strict liability, and Defendant admits to leaving messages on Plaintiff's voicemail without identifying itself as a debt collector, Defendant violated section 1692e(11) of the FDCPA. Defendant is not entitled to a bona fide error defense as it admits that the failure to identify itself as debt collector was intentional. Accordingly, Plaintiff's Motion for Summary Judgment based on Defendant's violation of section 1692e(11) of the FDCPA will be granted.

The statute requires that debt collectors give meaningful disclosure to the debtor, except when the communication is with a third party. Meaningful disclosure has been held to require the debt collector "to disclose the caller's name, the debt collection company's name, and the nature of the debt collector's business."

As already discussed, Defendant does not contend that it provided meaningful disclosure of its identity when it called, but instead argues that to do so would potentially violate section 1692c(d). Accordingly, Plaintiff is entitled to summary judgment as to her claim pursuant to section 1692d(6) of the FDCPA.

Plaintiff's Motion for Summary Judgment will be granted.

CASE QUESTIONS

1. What does the court mean when it uses the term "Hobson's choice"?

2. What would you advise debt collectors to do in light of this case?

3. Are the rules for cell phones the same as those for landlines under the FDCPA?

Penalties for FDCPA Violations

Under the CFPA, much of the FDCPA enforcement has been transferred to the BCFP. The BCFP will have the same enforcement authority that the FTC did, in addition to any expanded powers it promulgates under the authority it has been given under the CFPA. Those remedies include cease-and-desist orders to stop collectors from violating the FDCPA and penalties for violations. However, the greatest power of enforcement under the FDCPA lies with individual debtors. Debtors who can prove collector violations can collect for actual injuries and mental distress. Debtors can also collect up to $1,000 in addition to actual damages for actions by collectors that are extreme, outrageous, malicious, or repeated. Attorney fees incurred by debtors in bringing their suits are also recoverable.

13-3c SUITS FOR ENFORCEMENT OF DEBTS

Occasionally, collection is ineffective and there is no collateral to repossess. The creditor has few options left but to bring suit to enforce collection of the debt. In bringing a successful suit, the creditor will obtain a **judgment**, which is the court's official document stating that the debtor owes the money and the collector is entitled to that money. However, in debt cases, the judgment is only the beginning. Once the creditor has the judgment, it must be executed to obtain funds.

A judgment is executed by having it attach to various forms of the debtor's property. For example, a judgment can attach to real property. A judgment can also attach to funds by **garnishment**, which is the attachment of a judgment to an account, paycheck, or receivables. Once there is attachment, the creditor is entitled to those funds. The third party holding the funds must comply with the terms of the garnishment and release the appropriate amount of funds to the creditor.

Employees are given some protection under the Consumer Credit Protection Act with respect to garnishments. One such protection is the limitation on the employer's ability to fire employees who have their wages garnisheed by a single creditor.

Under the Consumer Credit Protection Act, the amount that consumer creditors can garnish on debtor wages is limited to 25 percent of the net wages. Garnishment for past-due child support is limited to 50 percent of net wages.

13-3d THE END OF THE LINE ON ENFORCEMENT OF DEBTS: BANKRUPTCY

Federal laws afford debtors shelter when their obligations cannot be paid. *Bankruptcy* is the legal process of having a debtor—individual, partnership, corporation, LLC (see Chapter 20)—turn over all nonexempt assets in exchange for a release from debts following the distribution of those assets to creditors. The **Bankruptcy Abuse Prevention and Consumer Protection Act of 2005 (BAPCPA)** curbed a 15-year trend of increases in the number of bankruptcies. The data indicated that bankruptcy was being used as a strategic tool by consumers and businesses alike, rather than as a relief mechanism for those who had experienced a loss of income through illness, accident, or loss of employment. Changes in the law require consumers who wish to declare bankruptcy to show through a prescribed statutory formula that they do not have the means for repaying debts.

The ability to declare bankruptcy hinges on disposable income, a figure obtained after the court allows for housing, food, and other necessary expenses. If the consumer has disposable income, then a debt adjustment plan, rather than a bankruptcy, is required.

Bankruptcy takes one of three forms. *Chapter 7* bankruptcy is the liquidation form, in which the entity is dissolved or the individual's debts are discharged. *Chapter 11* is the reorganization form, in which a business enjoys protection from collection and creditors until a new plan for satisfying the business obligations is approved. *Chapter 13* is the consumer debt adjustment plan, under which consumers can be given a new repayment plan for their debts. Before consumers can declare Chapter 7 (liquidation) bankruptcy, they must go through Chapter 13. In fact, if consumers who file directly for Chapter 7 bankruptcy do not meet the means test, the courts classify their filing as an abuse of the bankruptcy process and require Chapter 13 proceedings.

Credit repair organizations, counseling and debt service organizations that, for a fee, help consumers work through debt crises, are subject to additional disclosure requirements under the CFPA. These CROs, as they are known, must disclose fully their role, their fees, and that bankruptcy may be a result or recommendation from their efforts on behalf of the consumer debtor. CROs are regulated under the Credit Repair Organizations Act (15 U.S.C. §§ 1679–1679j) and are subject to private suit by consumer debtors for misrepresentations and failures to disclose information about fees, payments, and bankruptcy. In addition, CROs must disclose any affiliations with creditors or credit organizations. The BCFP has been given expanded authority to regulate credit counseling organizations as well.

Individuals and businesses can file a petition for bankruptcy themselves or they can be petitioned into bankruptcy through an involuntary petition. In a voluntary case, the court now must make the disposable income determination. In an involuntary case, the debtor must have a chance to present evidence against being placed into bankruptcy.

Debtors do have certain property exemptions in bankruptcy—property they do not lose to the bankruptcy estate. Those exemptions have been cut back substantially. For example, the homestead exemptions in many states protected all homes, regardless of costs. The reforms limit the amount of equity the debtor can retain following the bankruptcy and how long the protection applies.

Not all debts are discharged in bankruptcy. Alimony, child support, student loans, and taxes are examples of debts that survive bankruptcy.

13-3e IS THERE A COST TO BREACHING A CONTRACT: CREDITOR REPORTS ON NONPAYING DEBTORS

The failure to perform on a contract—that is, pay what is due—does have its reputational costs, even when the debt is discharged in bankruptcy for a very good reason such as loss of employment, health issues, or, in many cases, the economic hardships that come from the dissolution of a marriage. Creditors are able to report late payments, nonpayments, and contract defaults to credit bureaus that keep a database that future potential creditors can contact to determine the risk associated with entering into a contract with certain debtors. However, the **Fair Credit Reporting Act (FCRA)** is designed to provide debtors some rights and protections regarding the credit information held by third parties about them.

Before the passage of the FCRA, many debtors were denied the right to see their credit reports and were often victims of inaccurate reports. The FCRA brought credit reports out in the open. The enforcement of this law has been assigned to the BCFP.

When the FCRA Applies

The FCRA applies to consumer reporting agencies, which are third parties (not creditors or debtors) that compile, evaluate, and sell credit information about consumer debt and debtors. Commercial credit reporting agencies and commercial debtors are not subject to FCRA standards.

Limitations on FCRA Disclosures

Under the FCRA, consumer reporting agencies can disclose information only to the following:

1. A debtor who asks for his own report
2. A creditor who has the debtor's signed application for credit
3. A potential employer
4. A court pursuant to a subpoena

When consumers file applications for credit with lenders, they have the right to know where a credit report came from. However, the creditor cannot show the report to the debtor, who must get the report through a credit reporting agency.

Consumer agencies are limited not only as to whom disclosures can be made but also as to what can be disclosed. The following are the general limitations on debtor disclosures:

1. No disclosure of bankruptcies that occurred more than 10 years ago
2. No disclosure of lawsuits concluded more than seven years ago
3. No disclosure of criminal convictions and arrests that were disposed of more than seven years ago

When a debtor applies for a loan of more than $50,000 or a job that pays more than $20,000, these limitations on disclosures do not apply.

The Right of Debtor Correction of Information

Under the FCRA, debtors have not only the right to see reports but also the right to make corrections of inaccurate information included in those reports. A debtor simply notifies the reporting agency of the alleged error. If the agency acknowledges the error, the debtor's report must be corrected, and anyone who has received a report on that debtor during the previous two years must be notified.

If the agency still stands by the information challenged by the debtor, the debtor has the right to have included in the credit report a 100-word statement explaining his position on the matter. This statement is then included with the actual credit report in all future reports sent to third parties.

The *Morris v Trans Union LLC* case (Case 13.7) deals with a problem of an inaccurate credit report.

CASE 13.7

Morris v Trans Union LLC
987 F.2d 288 (5th Cir. 1993)

The Ex-Husband with the Wife's Target Credit Rating

FACTS

In 1997, Kenneth Morris's then–wife applied for and opened a revolving credit account at Target—the "RNB-Target" account—as a joint account. Morris did not know of the account and did not sign the application. In 2002, over a year after Morris and his wife divorced, she charged $129.91 to the account. The statement was mailed to Morris's home address, the address shown on the application. Morris forwarded the bill to his former wife, who had moved to Louisiana. Morris received a second statement showing the bill as unpaid and handled it the same way. Morris's former wife paid only $20 on the account. When Morris received another statement, he contacted RNB-Target and told them to deal with his former wife. RNB-Target nonetheless continued to send the statements to Morris, who threw them away. In May 2003, RNB-Target notified Morris that it had closed the account and charged off the unpaid amount of $253.10, including late fees and interest. RNB-Target passed the information to national credit bureaus.

In July 2003, Morris's automobile insurance quote was high because of poor credit. He downloaded a credit report that listed Morris as jointly responsible for the RNB-Target account and showed the unpaid balance charged off as a bad debt.

Morris notified Trans Union in writing that the information in the credit report about the RNB-Target account was incorrect. Morris explained that despite his request, RNB-Target had not provided any information showing that the account was in fact "ever a 'joint' account." Morris explained that the unpaid amount was charged by his former wife after their divorce. Morris asked Trans Union to correct the item and show it as disputed until then.

On July 30, 2003, Trans Union notified RNB-Target that "Consumer not liable for acct (i.e., ex-spouse, business)." Trans Union provided further explanation with the message: "ACCT NEVER JOINT." RNB-Target responded and said that the account was indeed a joint one. Morris wrote a letter of dispute, and Trans Union wrote to RNB-Target again and received the same response. Morris filed suit against Trans Union in January 2004 for violation of the Fair Credit Reporting Act. RNB-Target then instructed Trans Union to remove the account from Morris's credit report. Trans Union moved for summary judgment.

JUDICIAL OPINION

ROSENTHAL, District Judge

…Trans Union violated the FCRA only with regard to the requirement that it notify the creditor of a dispute within five days, but that the violation caused Morris no harm. Morris is correct that an inaccurate report can cause damage to a consumer in addition to the denial of credit. Each element of damage must be linked to the consumer-reporting agency's failure to comply with its FCRA obligations. With respect to Trans Union's conceded failure to comply with the five-day rule, the evidence shows no ill effects or harm to Morris as a result. Despite the initial delay, Trans Union provided Morris a timely report of its investigation. The undisputed evidence demonstrates that the information contained within Morris's credit report after his complaint was the same as it would have been had Trans Union initially given RNB-Target notice of Morris's dispute within the five-day statutory period.

On the issue of a heightened duty, this court agrees with Morris that a reporting agency may have a duty to go beyond a creditor's response. Such a heightened duty arises only when the evidence demonstrates that the agency has a basis for questioning the reliability of the creditor's information. Morris's invective-laced railing against RNB-Target is not in itself sufficient to raise a fact issue as to whether Trans Union had a basis for questioning RNB-Target's reliability. The record shows that Trans Union had worked with RNB-Target for at least eleven years and had received no report that RNB-Target had provided unreliable information. Morris simply failed to raise a fact question as to whether Trans Union's knowledge of RNB-Target's reliability required Trans Union to conduct a different kind of investigation.

Willfulness is an element of proof necessary both to show entitlement to punitive damages under the FCRA and to overcome statutory qualified immunity from state-law defamation claims. Morris asserts that Trans Union had the obligation to develop specific formal policies and procedures to measure or evaluate creditor reliability and to perform a cost-benefit analysis comparing in a given situation the cost of verifying the accuracy of

CONTINUED

the source of the credit information against the possible harm inaccurately reported information may cause the consumer. [T]he absence of formal policies and procedures to evaluate a creditor's reliability does not show that a consumer-reporting agency acted in conscious disregard for a consumer's rights in a specific case. In this case, the record contains no evidence of material misrepresentations or concealment by Trans Union.

Trans Union's motion for summary judgment is granted.

CASE QUESTIONS

1. What types of violations of the FCRA by Trans Union does Morris allege?

2. What would you recommend Trans Union and Target do as they go forward in dealing with FCRA challenges?

3. What action would you recommend to couples who obtain a divorce and still have credit accounts that were opened during the course of their marriages?

13-4 Contract Remedies for Nonperformance

If performance is not excused and there is a valid contract, the nonbreaching party can recover for damages from the nonperforming party. The purpose of such **compensatory damages** is to put the nonbreaching party in the same position he or she would have been in had no breach occurred. The law has formulas to calculate the amount of compensatory damages for breach of every type of contract. For example, if a seller has agreed to sell a buyer a car for $5,000 and the seller breaches, the buyer could collect the extra $1,000 it would cost to buy a substitute car priced at $6,000.

In addition to compensatory damages, nonbreaching parties are entitled to collect the extra damages or **incidental damages** involved because of the breach. If a seller must run an ad in a newspaper to sell a car a buyer has refused to buy, the costs of the ad are incidental damages.

Some parties agree in their contracts on the amounts they will pay in the case of nonperformance. Damages agreed upon in advance are **liquidated damages**, and the contractual clauses containing them are enforceable as long as they are not excessive and compensatory damages are not awarded in addition to the liquidated damages.

In some cases, the nonbreaching party may be able to collect **consequential damages**. Consequential damages are damages that result because of the breach and generally involve lost business, lost profit, or late penalties. For example, if a contractor must pay a penalty of $200 for each day a building is late after the completion date stipulated in the contract and the contractor is late because the steel supplier did not meet its deadline, the $200-per-day penalty would be a consequential damage that the steel supplier would be required to pay. Whether a party will

Consider...

Fingerlakes Aquaculture, LLC, an indoor fish hatchery, entered into a contract for Progas Welding Supply to build and deliver a 13,000-gallon oxygen storage tank. The contract required that the tank be delivered during the week of June 21, 1999, with a $400 per day liquidated damages provision, denoted a "fine." Throughout the year, Progas delivered smaller tanks, but was never able to deliver the 13,000-gallon tank. In June 2001, Fingerlakes Aquaculture bought a tank from another supplier and filed suit seeking the $400-per-day liquidated damages. Progas says that because of the other tanks, Fingerlakes Aquaculture had no damages and the total of $292,000 (the $400 per day for the 210 days of delay) was void as a penalty. Who is correct? Why? [*Fingerlakes Aquaculture, LLC v Progas Welding Supply, Inc.*, 825 N.Y.S.2d 559 (2006)] be able to collect consequential damages depends on whether the breaching party knew or should have known what the consequences of the breach would be.

13-5 Third-Party Rights in Contracts

Generally, a contract is a relationship between or among the contracting parties and is not enforceable by others who happen to benefit. For example, suppose a landowner and a commercial developer enter into an agreement for the construction of a shopping mall. Such a project means jobs for the area and additional business for restaurants, hotels, and transportation companies, but these businesses would not have the right to enforce the contract or collect damages for breach if the developer pulled out of the project. However, certain groups of people do have rights in contracts even though they may not have been parties to the contracts. A good example is a beneficiary of a life insurance policy. The beneficiary does not contract with the insurance company and does not pay the premiums, but the beneficiary, called a third party beneficiary, has contract rights because the purchaser of the policy directed so.

In other types of third-party contract rights, the third parties are not part of the original contract, as is the life insurance beneficiary, but are brought in after the fact. For example, suppose that a homebuilder owes a plumbing contractor $5,000 for work done on homes in the builder's subdivision. In the sales contracts for the homes, the homebuilder is the seller, and the buyer's purchase monies will go to the homebuilder. However, the homebuilder could assign payment rights to the plumber as a means of satisfying the debt. This process, called **assignment**, gives the plumber the right to collect the contract amount from the buyer. The plumber takes the place of the homebuilder in terms of contract rights.

In some cases, the duty or obligation to perform under a contract is transferred to another party. The transfer of contractual duties and obligation is called a **delegation**. Generally, a delegation of duties carries with it an assignment of benefits. For example, suppose that Neptune Fisheries, Inc., has a contract with Tom Tuna, Inc., to sell 30 fresh lobsters each day. Neptune is stopping its lobster line and delegates its duties under the Tom Tuna contract to Louie's Lobsters, Inc. Louie's takes over Neptune's obligation to furnish the 30 lobsters and is assigned the right to benefits (payment for the lobsters) under the contract. Both Louie's and Neptune are liable to Tom Tuna for performance. A delegation, unlike a novation, does not release the original contracting party.

13-6 International Issues in Contract Performance

13-6a ASSURING PAYMENT

International contract transactions for goods involve extensive shipment requirements. To control access to the goods and payment for them, many sellers use a **bill of lading** for transacting business. The bill of lading is a receipt for shipment issued by the carrier to the seller. It is also a contract for the shipment of the goods and provides evidence of who has title to the goods. If a bill of lading is used, the buyer will not gain access to the goods unless and until the seller provides the necessary documents for release of the goods. Once the seller has the bill of lading, the seller can choose to transfer title to the goods by transferring the bill of lading. The seller could also pledge the bill of lading as security for the payment of a debt. A bill of lading can be made directly to the buyer, or it can be a negotiable bill of lading that can be transferred to anyone.

The bill of lading is often used in conjunction with a line of credit in international transactions because the two together offer the seller assurance of payment and the buyer assurance of arrival of the goods. In international transactions, in which resolution of disputes over great distances can be difficult, this means of controlling access to goods and payment is helpful.

In this type of transaction, the seller delivers goods to a carrier for transportation and receives a bill of lading. The seller then sends the bill of lading through its bank to the buyer's bank to give the buyer's bank title to the goods, which will be turned over to the buyer once the funds are deducted from the line of credit established by the bank for the buyer.

The buyer may also arrange for a **letter of credit** to be used in conjunction with the bill of lading. The letter of credit is issued by the buyer's bank and is sent to a corresponding bank where the seller is located. The letter of credit lists the terms and conditions under which the seller can draw on the letter of credit or be paid. For example, turning the bill of lading over to the corresponding bank may be the condition of drawing on the letter of credit; the bill of lading is then used by the corresponding bank and the buyer's bank to allow the buyer to take possession of the goods. Because banks are involved in these transactions through credit assurances, the seller enjoys more of an assurance of payment prior to shipment because a letter of credit is actually a confirmation of payment.

13-6b ASSURING PERFORMANCE: INTERNATIONAL PECULIARITIES

International contracts have a particular need for a *force majeure* clause. Wars, revolutions, and coups are often included in international contracts as justification for noncompletion. The *force majeure* clauses are summaries of potential international events that could hamper production or trade.[2]

One other risk of international contracts is the stability of various currencies and their possible devaluation. The method and means of payment should be specified in the contract, and a clause covering devaluation may also be included so that full payment is ensured.

BIOGRAPHY Charlie Sheen: Nonperformance or Just a Lot of Trouble?

Charlie Sheen has had a history of drug and alcohol addiction and has been through several rehab programs. During a time when he admits that he was drinking, Charlie Sheen was terminated from his hit television show, *Two and a Half Men*, CBS's comedy series that was, at the time, the most successful rerun show on cable. The termination came following several public outbursts by Mr. Sheen about executives (including Chuck Lorre, the show's creator) at his network, as well as some problematic personal conduct related to his ongoing issues with drugs and alcohol.

Mr. Sheen filed suit asking to be paid for the remaining episodes. His contract does provide that, regardless of the reason for termination, he is entitled to receive full payment under his contract. Mr. Sheen's suit also

detailed that he was always at rehearsals and the show's tapings, despite his rather public escapades while under the influence of alcohol and drugs. He also noted in the suit that the network executives had not fired him during his previous absences due to rehab. In short, Mr. Sheen argued that there was no breach of contract.

The network replaced Mr. Sheen with actor Ashton Kutcher. Mr. Sheen tried to reach his fans through an Internet show, but there was little support for his offering. Mr. Sheen continued to falter, but his show was successful. The suit was settled for an undisclosed amount, but his contract called for $2,000,000 payment per episode. Mr. Sheen's career continues to wane, and *Two and a Half Men* has not done as well, critically or in the ratings, since Mr. Sheen's departure.

Summary

What if the assumptions made and the information given turn out to be untrue? Must the parties still go forward with the contract?

- Contract defense—situation, term, or event that excuses performance
- Capacity—mental and age thresholds for valid contracts
- Voidable contract—one party can choose not to honor the contract
- Puffing—statements of opinion
- Material fact—basis of the bargain
- Void contract—contract that courts will not honor
- Misrepresentation—incomplete or inaccurate information prior to contract execution
- Bureau of Consumer Financial Protection
- Consumer Financial Protection Act (Dodd–Frank)
- Three-day rescission period
- Home Equity Loan Consumer Protection Act of 1988
- Home Ownership and Equity Protection Act of 1994 (HOEPA)
- Rescission—setting aside of contract as a remedy
- Fraud—intentional misrepresentation
- *Scienter*—knowledge that information given is false
- Duress—physical or mental force that deprives party of a meaningful choice with respect to a proposed contract
- Undue influence—exerting control over another party for purposes of gain
- Confidential relationship—trust, confidence, reliance in a relationship
- Fair Credit Reporting Act
- Fair Debt Collections Practices Act
- Bankruptcy Abuse Prevention and Consumer Protection Act of 2005 (BAPCPA)
- Public policy—standards of decency
- Exculpatory clauses—attempt to hold oneself harmless for one's own conduct
- Unconscionable contract—contract that is grossly unfair

If one party does not perform, is the other side excused? When is performance required and when is it excused?

- Conditions precedent—advance events that must occur before performance is due, for example, obtaining financing
- Substantial performance—performance that, for practical purposes, is just as good as full-performance
- Commercial impracticability—defense to performance of sales contract based on objective impracticability
- Novation—agreement to change contract among all affected, for example, agreement to substitute parties
- Accord and satisfaction—agreement entered into as settlement of a disputed debt
- Obligation of good faith—must perform in a reasonable fashion; performance must meet commercial standards

What remedies exist?

- Compensatory damages—amount required to place party in as good a position as before breach
- Incidental damages—costs of collecting compensatory damages
- Liquidated damages—agreement clause in contract that preestablishes and limits damages
- Consequential damages—damages owed to third parties from a breach

What are the contract performance issues in international business?

- Bill of lading—title document used to control transfer of goods
- Letter of credit—pledge by bank of availability of funds for a transaction
- Exchange rate and risk issues in contracts

Questions and Problems

1. On December 5, 1997, Michael Dekofsky and Christopher Vrakelos sold Brea Range, Inc., an indoor shooting range, to Michael J. and Kimberly A. Hansen for $140,000. The Hansens paid $70,000 cash and assumed two promissory notes due and owing from the corporation to Mr. Dekofsky and Mr. Vrakelos. After escrow closed, the Hansens discovered that two patrons committed suicide at Brea Range, in 1995 and March 1997.

The Hansens made interest payments on the promissory notes until January 1, 1999, defaulted on the first principal payment, and ceased making payments on June 1, 1999. Mr. Dekofsky and Mr. Vrakelos sued for the balance due. The Hansens defended on the theory that the sellers had unclean hands and breached a duty to disclose material facts. In a cross-complaint, the Hansens sued for conspiracy, fraud, misrepresentation, and rescission. Do the Hansens have a valid defense to the contract's formation? Was there misrepresentation? Was there fraud? [*Dekofsky v Brea Range, Inc.*, 2001 WL 1613509 (Cal. App. 2 Dist.) (not printed in *Cal. Rptr.*—unpublished opinion)]

2. The late Tony Curtis, a respected actor, entered into a contract to write a novel for Doubleday & Company, publishers. Because of complex divorce proceedings and other personal factors, Mr. Curtis was unable to submit a satisfactory manuscript. Doubleday demanded a return of the $50,000 advance Mr. Curtis had received. Is Doubleday entitled to it? [*Doubleday & Co. v Curtis*, 763 F.2d 495 (2nd Cir. 1985)]

3. Bernina Sewing Machines imports sewing machines and parts for U.S. distribution. Its contract prices are in francs. Because of the devaluation of the U.S. dollar, Bernina wants to be excused from its contracts. Can it be excused under any contract doctrine? [*Bernina Distributors, Inc. v Bernina Sewing Machines*, 646 F.2d 434 (10th Cir. 1981)]

4. Would failure to disclose a delinquency on your mortgage on a loan application be a misrepresentation? What about not disclosing that your company was about to impose a 20 percent salary reduction on all employees? [*Barrer v Women's National Bank*, 761 F.2d 752 (D.C. 1985)]

5. Dan O'Connor paid $125 to have the University of Notre Dame's leprechaun mascot tattooed on his upper arm with the words "Fighting Irish" inscribed above the little gnome. The tattoo parlor inscribed the chosen leprechaun and "Fighing Irish."

Mr. O'Connor's girlfriend pointed out the spelling error, and Mr. O'Connor filed suit against the Tattoo Shoppe in Carlstadt, New Jersey, seeking unspecified damages.

Mr. O'Connor noted, "I was irate, and for a minute or two after I cooled down I kind of giggled. But I can't just live with this. You're not talking about a dented car where you can get another one … you're talking about flesh."

What damages should Mr. O'Connor receive? Would a refund of $125 be enough? What if the Tattoo Shoppe had a clause in its contract limiting damages to a refund? Would it be valid?

6. Jennifer Cushman has a permanent residence in Pennsylvania but attended college in Vermont. In the summer of 1993, an unknown person, possibly a member of her household in Philadelphia, applied under Ms. Cushman's name for credit cards from three credit grantors: American Express (Amex), Citibank Visa, and Chase Manhattan Bank. The person provided the credit grantors with Ms. Cushman's Social Security number,

address, and other identifying information. Credit cards were issued to that person in Ms. Cushman's name, and that person accumulated balances totaling approximately $2,400 on the cards between June 1993 and April 1994. All this occurred without Ms. Cushman's knowledge.

In August 1994, an unidentified bill collector informed Ms. Cushman that Trans Union (TUC) was publishing a consumer credit report indicating that she was delinquent on payments to these three credit grantors. Ms. Cushman notified TUC that she had not applied for or used the three credit cards in question and suggested that a third party had fraudulently applied for and obtained the cards. In response, a TUC clerk called American Express (Amex) and Chase to inquire whether the verifying information (such as Ms. Cushman's name, Social Security number, and address) in Amex's and Chase's records matched the information in the TUC report. The TUC clerk also asked if Ms. Cushman had opened a fraud investigation with the credit grantors. Because the information matched, and because Ms. Cushman had not opened a fraud investigation, the information remained in the TUC report. TUC was unable to contact Citibank, so TUC deleted the Citibank entry from the report. TUC's investigations are performed by clerks who are paid $7.50 per hour and are expected to perform 10 investigations per hour.

TUC did not obtain records to perform a handwriting comparison. Ms. Cushman was denied credit because of the report. She filed suit under the FCRA. Did TUC violate the law? [*Cushman v Trans Union Corp.*, 115 F.3d 220 (3rd Cir. 1997)]

7. Robert Hackett became a substitute fireman for the city of New Britain, Connecticut, in 1949. In 1950, he was made a full-time fireman and in 1968 became a lieutenant. After earning the highest mark on the captain's examination, he was promoted to captain in 1974. He then scored the highest score on the deputy chief exam and was promoted to that rank in 1977.

Mr. Hackett had paid an employee in the city department responsible for administering the exams to ensure that he earned the highest grades (which he did). He had, in effect, purchased his last two promotions. When these acts were discovered (after Mr. Hackett had retired), criminal charges were brought against him and the city employee. Both were convicted of felonies.

The pension board of New Britain then met and voted to reduce Mr. Hackett's pension by $5,483.97 a year because that reduction placed his pension at the level it would have been without the last two promotions. The board said the reduction was necessary because the last two promotions were obtained through illegal conduct. Mr. Hackett filed suit. Is illegality a defense to Hackett's suit for his full pension? [*Hackett v City of New Britain*, 477 A.2d 148 (Conn. 1984)]

8. Since 1978, when the first warnings emerged from medical research about using "sun tan lotion," ads for the products have created some confusion. There were "sun blocks," "sun screens," and just plain "sun tan lotion." The descriptive terms were "waterproof," "water resistant," and "sweatproof." The lotions also blocked UVB rays, but some blocked only UVA rays. The sun protection factors ranged from SPF 15 factor to SPF 60 and some consumers misunderstood what level was needed.

Consumers were experiencing sunburns despite their use of sunscreens and sun tan lotion. The Federal Trade Commission stepped in during 2012 with disclosure rules to clarify what was a material representation and what constituted puffery. Based on your knowledge of the standards for materiality in misrepresentation cases, develop a list of what the FTC rules required the manufacturers to disclose and what terms they could use.

9. Janet S. Milliken purchased a home from Kathleen and Joseph Jacono through ReMax agents Fran Day and Thomas O'Neil. Neither the sellers nor their agents disclosed to Ms. Milliken that the prior owners of the house, a husband and wife, had been involved in a murder/suicide on the property. Ms. Milliken filed suit against

the Jaconos as well as their real estate agent to have the sale set aside. Ms. Milliken said that she and her family had experienced paranormal events since moving into the home. Ms. Milliken was aware that the Jaconos had purchased their home from an estate, but did not ask any questions about why the home was held by an estate and not by individual owners. The Jacanos and their agents did contact the Pennsylvania Real Estate Commission for an opinion as to whether they had to disclose the murder/suicide. They received an opinion that it was not material and need not be disclosed. Discuss whether Ms. Milliken can set the sale aside and what legal arguments she could make. [*Milliken v Jacono*, 60 A.3d 133 (Pa. Super. 2012)]

10. Boeing Company was scheduled to deliver several of its 747-400 jumbo jetliners to Northwest Airlines by December 31, 1988. Northwest set that deadline because it needed the $16 million in investment tax credits the planes would bring. Boeing missed the December 31 deadline, and Northwest wants to recover compensation from Boeing for the lost tax credits. Could Northwest recover for these lost credits?

ORGANIZATIONAL BEHAVIOR, ECONOMICS, ETHICS, & THE LAW

Relying on Your Broker's View of the Market?

Marty Ummel, a homebuyer, brought suit against her real estate agent for his failure to disclose that homes in the area in which she bought her home had declined substantially in value. Mrs. Ummel said that she and her retired husband decided to move from the San Francisco area to the San Diego area to be near their grown children. They did market research and had already used one broker and cancelled two deals before settling on ReMax agent Mike Little, who signed the Ummels to a contract for the purchase of a home (owned by another real estate agent) for $1.2 million. Little acted as the mortgage broker for the Ummels as well.

Mrs. Ummel said that Mr. Little told them several times that the house was a good value, but Mr. Little did not disclose that there were listings down the street from her home for $105,000 less that were larger properties.

Experts say brokers aren't appraisers and can't opine on value, and that buyers should do their due diligence. However, Mrs. Ummel says that she trusted Mr. Little and that he breached that trust. Other experts note the pressure the broker feels: "Agents have a lot of fiduciary duties, but they don't make money unless they close the sale."[3] Other experts say that the Ummels just didn't do what responsible and sophisticated buyers should do in researching a property, and now seek to blame someone else for their loss.

Was there misrepresentation? Is it a defense that the agent simply cannot predict when the market has shifted? How does the real estate firm deal with the drive for commissions among their agents? What happens if you shift responsibility for market research to agents?

Notes

1. As noted in Chapter 12, consumer credit contracts are those in which the buyer is purchasing goods, services, or real property for personal and/or home use.

2. International history has played a role in the development of *force majeure* clauses because wars, trade, and international relations influence contract rights and performance.

3. David Streitfeld, "Feeling Misled on Home Prices, Buyers Are Suing Their Agent," *New York Times*, January 22, 2008, pp. A1, A14.

Chapter 14

PRODUCT ADVERTISING AND LIABILITY

The first jury verdict over $1 million in a product liability suit occurred in 1962. The top five verdicts in 2012 in the United States totaled $1.5 billion, with the largest product liability verdict being for $505.1 million.[1]

Product liability is a unique area of law. It has social roots in that it attempts to lessen the burden of losses by requiring a manufacturer or manufacturer's insurer to pay for a defective product. It also has contract roots in that if a product does not do what it is supposed to do, a breach of contract has occurred. Finally, it also has roots in tort law insofar as an injury results from someone else's carelessness. In these senses, product liability is a combination of contract law, tort law, and social responsibility.

This chapter answers the following questions: How did product liability law develop? What are the contract theories for recovery? What is required for a tort-based recovery on a defective product? How does advertising create liability for a business? What is strict tort liability for products? What reforms are proposed for cutting back liability? Are international product liability standards different?

UPDATE

For up-to-date legal and ethical news, go to **mariannejennings.com**

Bo Chambers/Flickr/Getty Images

Consider...

Ginger Smith was a passenger on Ronald Smith's boat on West Point Lake, Alabama. Ronald Smith was operating the boat, which was towing Ms. Smith's son, Shane McClellan, on an inflatable inner tube behind the boat. The inner tube was tied to the boat by a 50-foot Model 51650 polypropylene line that was manufactured by The Coleman Company and was purchased at a nearby Walmart store. While Shane McClellan was being towed on the inner tube, the line snapped, and the end connected to the boat flew back toward the boat and hit Ms. Smith in the eye, causing the loss of that eye. Ms. Smith filed suit against Coleman, Walmart, and Ronald Smith. Coleman says that its package warned against using the line for towing. Who is liable? Why or why not?

14-1 Development of Product Liability

For some time, courts followed the principle of *caveat emptor*—"Let the buyer beware." This theory meant that sellers were not liable for defects in their products and that it was the buyer's responsibility to be on the alert for defects and take the appropriate precautions.

Following a series of court decisions in which buyers were allowed recovery and courts questioned the public policy wisdom of *caveat emptor*, the *Restatement (Second) of Torts* adopted its now-famous Section 402A on strict tort liability (discussed later in this chapter). With this adoption, the area of product liability had gone full swing from no liability (*caveat emptor*) to an almost *per se* standard of liability for defective products.

14-2 Advertising as a Contract Basis for Product Liability

14-2a EXPRESS WARRANTIES

An **express warranty** as provided in the Uniform Commercial Code (UCC) is an express promise (oral or written) by the seller as to the quality, abilities, or performance of a product (UCC § 2–313). The seller need not use the words *promise* or *guarantee* to make an express warranty. A seller makes a warranty by displaying a sample or model or giving a description of the goods. Promises of how the goods will perform are also express warranties. "These goods are 100% wool," "This tire cannot be punctured," and "These jeans will not shrink" are examples of express warranties.

Ads are but one form of express warranties. The negotiation process can find the seller making express warranties to the buyer. For example, if a seller tells the buyer that a dog is a purebred, that a painting is a "painting by Francis Bacon," or that a

EXHIBIT 14.1 Statements of Fact versus Opinion

STATEMENT	FACT OR OPINION?
This car gets 20 miles per gallon.	Fact
This car gets great gas mileage.	Opinion
These goods are 100% wool.	Fact
This is the finest wool around.	Opinion
This truck has never been in an accident.	Fact
This truck is solid.	Opinion
This mace stops assailants in their tracks.	Fact (promise of performance)
This mace is very effective.	Opinion
This makeup is hypoallergenic.	Fact
This makeup is good for your skin.	Opinion
This ink will not stain clothes.	Fact
This ink is safe to use.	Opinion
This computer is IBM-compatible.	Fact
This computer is as good as any IBM.	Opinion
This watch is waterproof.	Fact
This watch is durable.	Opinion

© Cengage Learning

horse is "disease-free," the seller has made an express warranty. Statements made by the seller to the buyer before the sale that are part of the basis of the sale or bargain are express warranties. Information included on the product packaging is an express warranty if that information includes statements of fact or promises of performance.

Opinions, however, are not considered a basis for transactions and are therefore not express warranties. For example, the statement "This glassware is as good as anyone else's" is sales puffing and not an express warranty. Exhibit 14.1 gives some examples of statements of fact versus opinion.

Castro v QVC Network, Inc. (Case 14.1), deals with an issue of liability for representations via ad statements.

CASE 14.1   *Castro v QVC Network, Inc.*
139 F.3d 114 (2nd Cir. 1998)

A Turkey of a Pan: Liability on Thanksgiving Day

FACTS

In November 1993, QVC Network (appellee), an operator of a cable television home-shopping channel, advertised, as part of a one-day Thanksgiving promotion, the "T-Fal Jumbo Resistal Roaster." The roaster was manufactured by U.S.A. T-Fal Corporation. The QVC ad described the roaster as suitable for roasting a 25-pound turkey. At the time that T-Fal and QVC entered into an

agreement for the sale of the roasting pan, T-Fal did not have a pan in its line large enough to roast a 25-pound turkey. T-Fal asked its parent company in France to provide a suitable roasting pan as soon as possible. The parent company provided a larger pan to which it added two small handles.

Loyda Castro (appellant) ordered the roasting pan and used it for roasting her turkey on Thanksgiving Day, 1993. Mrs. Castro was injured when she tried

CONTINUED

© Harper 3D/Shutterstock.com

to remove the turkey from the oven. Using two large insulated oven mitts, Mrs. Castro tried to lift the pan from the oven, placing two fingers on each handle. Two fingers were the maximum grip permitted by the small handles. As the turkey tipped toward her, she lost control of the pan, spilling the hot drippings and fat that had accumulated in the pan during the cooking and basting process. Mrs. Castro suffered second- and third-degree burns to her foot and ankle, which have led to scarring, paresthesia, and swelling.

Mrs. Castro filed suit for strict liability and breach of warranty. The warranty charge was dismissed, and the jury returned a verdict for QVC and T-Fal. Mrs. Castro appealed.

JUDICIAL OPINION

CALABRESI, Circuit Judge

Products liability law has long been bedeviled by the search for an appropriate definition of "defective" product design. Over the years, both in the cases and in the literature, two approaches have come to predominate. The first is the risk/utility theory, which focuses on whether the benefits of a product outweigh the dangers of its design. The second is the consumer expectations theory, which focuses on what a buyer/user of a product would properly expect that the product would be suited for.

Not all states accept both of these approaches. Some define design defect only according to the risk/utility approach.

One of the first states to accept both approaches was California, which in *Barker v Lull Engineering Co.*, 20 Cal.3d 413, 143 Cal.Rptr. 225, 573 P.2d 443 (1978), held that "a product may be found defective in design, so as to subject a manufacturer to strict liability for resulting injuries, under either of two alternative tests"—consumer expectations and risk/utility. Several states have followed suit and have adopted both theories.

Prior to the recent case of *Denny v Ford Motor Co.*, 87 N.Y.2d 248, 639 N.Y.S.2d 250, 662 N.E.2d 730 (1995), it was not clear whether New York recognized both tests. In *Denny*, the plaintiff was injured when her Ford Bronco II sports utility vehicle rolled over when she slammed on the brakes to avoid hitting a deer in the vehicle's path. The plaintiff asserted claims for strict products liability and for breach of implied warranty, and the district judge—over the objection of defendant Ford—submitted both causes of action to the jury. The jury ruled in favor of Ford on the strict liability claim, but found for the plaintiff on the implied warranty claim. On appeal, Ford argued that the jury's verdicts on the strict products liability claim and the breach of warranty claim were inconsistent because the causes of action were identical.

This court certified the *Denny* case to the New York Court of Appeals to answer the following questions: (1) "whether, under New York law, the strict products liability and implied warranty claims are identical"; and (2) "whether, if the claims are different, the strict products liability claim is broader than the implied warranty claim and encompasses the latter."

In response to the certified questions, the Court of Appeals held that in a products liability case a cause of action for strict liability is not identical to a claim for breach of warranty.

Moreover, the court held that a strict liability claim is not per se broader than a breach of warranty claim such that the former encompasses the latter. Thus, while claims of strict products liability and breach of warranty are often used interchangeably, under New York law the two causes of action are definitively different. The imposition of strict liability for an alleged design "defect" is determined by a risk/utility standard. The notion of "defect" in a U.C.C.-based breach of warranty claim focuses, instead, on consumer expectations.

Since *Denny*, then, it has been settled that the risk/utility and consumer expectations theories of design defect can, in New York, be the bases of distinct causes of action: one for strict products liability and one for breach of warranty. This fact, however, does not settle the question of when a jury must be charged separately on each cause of action and when, instead, the two causes are, on the facts of the specific case, sufficiently similar to each other so that one charge to the jury is enough.

While eminent jurists have at times been troubled by this issue, the New York Court of Appeals in *Denny* was quite clear on when the two causes of action might meld and when, instead, they are to be treated as separate. It did this by adding its own twist to the distinction—namely, what can aptly be called the "dual purpose" requirement. Thus in *Denny*, the Court of Appeals pointed out that the fact that a product's overall benefits might outweigh its overall risks does not preclude the possibility that consumers may have been misled into using the product in a context in which it was dangerously unsafe. And this, the New York court emphasized, could be so even though the benefits in other uses might make the product sufficiently reasonable so that it passed the risk/utility test.

In *Denny*, the Ford Bronco II was not designed as a conventional passenger automobile. Instead, it was designed as an off-road, dual purpose vehicle. But in its marketing of the Bronco II, Ford stressed its suitability for commuting and for suburban and city driving. Under the circumstances, the Court of Appeals explained that a rational fact-finder could conclude that the Bronco's utility as an off-road vehicle outweighed the risk of injury resulting from roll-over accidents (thus passing the risk/utility test), but at the

CONTINUED

same time find that the vehicle was not safe for the "ordinary purpose" of daily driving for which it was also marketed and sold (thus flunking the consumer expectations test).

That is precisely the situation before us. The jury had before it evidence that the product was designed, marketed, and sold as a multiple-use product. The pan was originally manufactured and sold in France as an all-purpose cooking dish without handles. And at trial, the jury saw a videotape of a QVC representative demonstrating to the television audience that the pan, in addition to serving as a suitable roaster for a twenty-five pound turkey, could also be used to cook casseroles, cutlets, cookies, and other low-volume foods. The court charged the jury that "[a] product is defective if it is not reasonably safe[,] [t]hat is, if the product is so likely to be harmful to persons that a reasonable person who had actual knowledge of its potential for producing injury would conclude that it should not have been marketed in that condition." And, so instructed, the jury presumably found that the pan, because it had many advantages in a variety of uses, did not fail the risk/utility test.

But it was also the case that the pan was advertised as suitable for a particular use—cooking a twenty-five pound turkey. Indeed, T-Fal added handles to the pan in order to fill QVC's request for a roasting pan that it could use in its Thanksgiving promotion. The product was, therefore, sold as appropriately used for roasting a twenty-five pound turkey. And it was in that use that allegedly the product failed and injured the appellant.

In such circumstances, New York law is clear that a general charge on strict products liability based on the risk/utility approach does not suffice. The jury could have found that the roasting pan's overall utility for cooking low-volume foods outweighed the risk of injury when cooking heavier foods, but that the product was nonetheless unsafe for the purpose for which it was marketed and sold—roasting a twenty-five pound turkey—and, as such, was defective under the consumer expectations test. That being so, the appellants were entitled to a separate breach of warranty charge.

In light of the evidence presented by appellants of the multi-purpose nature of the product at issue, the district court, applying New York law, should have granted appellants' request for a separate jury charge on the breach of warranty claim in addition to the charge on the strict liability claim.

Reversed.

CASE QUESTIONS

1. Was the pan represented as suitable for roasting a turkey?

2. What is the relationship between tort liability and warranty liability?

3. What is the risk/utility test?

Consider...

John R. Klages was employed as a night auditor at Conley's Motel on Route 8 in Hampton Township. He worked from 11 P.M. until 7 A.M., five days a week. On March 30, 1968, at approximately 1:30 A.M., two individuals entered the motel and announced, "This is a stickup. Open the safe." Mr. Klages indicated that he was unable to open the safe because he did not know the combination. One of the individuals then pointed a gun at his head and pulled the trigger. Fortunately for Mr. Klages, the gun was a starter pistol, and he was not seriously injured.

The next day, Mr. Klages and a fellow employee, Bob McVay, decided that they needed something to protect themselves against the possibility of future holdups. After reading an article concerning the effects of mace, Mr. McVay suggested that they consider using mace for their protection.

After reading and discussing the literature from the Markl Supply Company with their employer, Mr. McVay purchased an MK-II mace weapon, which described the mace as follows.

Rapidly vaporizes on face of assailant effecting instantaneous incapacitation. ... *It will* instantly stop and subdue *entire groups.* ... instantly stops assailants in their tracks. ... *[A]n attacker is subdued instantly, for a period of 15 to 20 minutes.* ... Time Magazine *stated the Chemical Mace is "for police the first, if not the final, answer to a nationwide need—a weapon that* disables as effectively as a gun and yet does no permanent injury." ... *The effectiveness is the result of a unique,* incapacitating *formulation (patent pending), projected in a shotgun-like pattern of heavy liquid droplets that, upon contact with the face, cause extreme tearing, and a stunned, winded condition, often accompanied by dizziness and apathy.*

At approximately 1:40 A.M. on September 22, 1968, while Mr. Klages was on duty, two unknown individuals entered the motel office, requested a room, and announced a stickup. One of the intruders took out a gun and directed Mr. Klages to open the safe. Using the cash register as a shield, Mr. Klages squirted the mace, hitting the intruder "right beside the nose." Mr. Klages immediately ducked below the register, but the intruder followed him down and shot him in the head. The intruders immediately departed, and Mr. Klages called the police. The bullet wound caused complete loss of sight in Mr. Klages's right eye. He claims a breach of an express warranty. Is he right?

[*Klages v General Ordnance Equipment Corp.*, 19 UCC Rep. Serv. (Callaghan) 22 (Pa. 1976)]

THINK: The requirements for an express warranty are a statement of fact or a promise of performance.

APPLY: What statements of fact or promises of performance are made in the ad or on the product packaging?

"[I]nstantly stops assailants in their tracks" is a promise of performance; "subdued instantly, for a period of 15 to 20 minutes" is also a promise of performance.

ANSWER: The product failed to live up to those promises, so there was a breach of express warranty, and the company is liable for the injury Mr. Klages sustained after using the mace against his attackers.

14-2b FEDERAL REGULATION OF WARRANTIES AND ADVERTISING

Express warranties are advertisements for goods. Accurate advertising is a basis for full information, and full information is a cornerstone for competitive markets.

In 1914, Congress passed the **Federal Trade Commission Act**, which authorized the **Federal Trade Commission (FTC)** to prevent "unfair and deceptive trade practices." Congress passed the **Wheeler-Lea Act of 1938**, which clarified and expanded the FTC's power by authorizing it to regulate "unfair and deceptive acts or practices" whenever the public is being deceived, regardless of any effects on competition. The FTC has challenged unsubstantiated or ambiguous advertising claims and has reviewed and eliminated deceptive techniques in television ads.

14-2c CONTENT CONTROL AND ACCURACY

The FTC has regulated the accuracy of ads in several ways. First, the FTC challenged certain types of price claims. If an ad announces "50% off," the prices must actually be half the original prices charged for the products or services prior to the sale; that price cannot be inflated to cover the markdown. If an ad quotes a "normal" price, that price must reflect what most sellers in the area are charging.

The FTC has also challenged the accuracy of ads. Claims that goods are "100% wool" are not only the basis for express warranty recovery but also the basis for an FTC challenge. Also, the FTC challenges advertising methods. For example, using "marbles" in soup to make it look thicker as it pours is deceptive. The FTC has used its powers to ensure that ads accurately depict the product as it exists. The regulations also apply to the terms of the contract and the time for performance. For example, the FTC, through its Mail or Telephone Order Merchandise Rule, requires that catalog merchants disclose delays in delivering ordered goods to consumers and that consumers be informed up front about custom product delays, special-order delays, and direct-from-the-manufacturer delays. The ads, pamphlets, catalogs, and mailings must disclose delays known up front, and the consumer must be notified after an order is placed if the delay will exceed the maximum amount of time allowed under the rules for delivery. The FTC has enforced those disclosure requirements against Internet merchants as well. In *In the Matter of Macys.com, KBkids.com, and CDnow, Inc.*, the FTC settled charges with these three e-retailers who were alleged to have violated the Mail or Telephone Order Merchandise Rule by failing to provide buyers with adequate notice of shipping delays or had continued to promise specific delivery dates when they were aware that they were unlikely to meet those deadlines.

CYBERLAW

14-2d FTC CONTROL OF PERFORMANCE CLAIMS

Any claims of the ability or efficacy of a product must be supportable. If a sunburn-relief product claims to "anesthetize nerves," the advertiser must be able to prove that claim.

Where an advertising claim cannot be substantiated, the FTC has used **corrective advertising** as a remedy. Corrective advertising requires a seller to correct the unsubstantiated claims made in previous ads. The landmark case *Warner-Lambert Co. v FTC* (Case 14.2) involves an issue of corrective advertising.

| CASE 14.2 | *Warner-Lambert Co. v FTC*
562 F.2d 749 (D.C. Cir. 1977), *cert. den.* 435 U.S. 950 (1978) |

Does Listerine Prevent Colds?

FACTS

Listerine, a product of the Warner-Lambert Company (petitioner), has been on the market since 1879 and has been represented through advertising to be beneficial for colds, cold symptoms, and sore throats. After a 1972 complaint about Warner-Lambert advertising for Listerine, the FTC held four months of hearings on the ad issues and then ordered Warner-Lambert to do the following:

1. Cease and desist representing that Listerine will cure colds or sore throats, that it will prevent colds or sore throats, or that users of Listerine will have fewer colds than nonusers.

2. Cease and desist representing that Listerine is a treatment for, or will lessen the severity of, colds or sore throats; that it will have any significant beneficial effect on the symptoms of sore throats or any beneficial effect on symptoms of colds; or that the ability of Listerine to kill germs is of medical significance in the treatment of colds or sore throats or their symptoms.

3. Cease and desist disseminating any advertisement for Listerine unless it is clearly and conspicuously disclosed in each advertisement, in this exact language, that "Contrary to prior advertising, Listerine will not help prevent colds

CONTINUED

or sore throats or lessen their severity." This requirement extended only to the next $10 million Listerine would spend on advertising after the order.

Warner-Lambert appealed the order.

JUDICIAL OPINION

WRIGHT, Circuit Judge

The first issue on appeal is whether the Commission's conclusion that Listerine is not beneficial for colds or sore throats is supported by the evidence.

First, the Commission found that the ingredients of Listerine are not present in sufficient quantities to have any therapeutic effect.

Second, the Commission found that in the process of gargling it is impossible for Listerine to reach critical areas of the body in medically significant concentration.

Third, the Commission found that even if significant quantities of the active ingredients of Listerine were to reach critical sites where cold viruses enter and infect the body, they could not interfere with the activities of the virus because they could not penetrate the tissue cells.

… [T]he Commission found that the ability of Listerine to kill germs by millions on contact is of no medical significance in the treatment of colds or sore throats.

… [T]he Commission found that Listerine has no significant beneficial effect on the symptoms of sore throat. The Commission recognized that gargling with Listerine could provide temporary relief from a sore throat by removing accumulated debris irritating the throat. But this type of relief can also be obtained by gargling with salt water or even warm water.

Petitioner contends that even if its advertising claims in the past were false, the portion of the Commission's order requiring "corrective advertising" exceeds the Commission's statutory power. The Commission's position is that the affirmative disclosure that Listerine will not prevent colds or lessen their severity is absolutely necessary to give effect to the prospective cease and desist order; a hundred years of false cold claims have built up a large reservoir of erroneous consumer belief that would persist, unless corrected, long after petitioner ceased making the claims.

If the Commission is to attain the objectives Congress envisioned, it cannot be required to confine its road block to the narrow lane the transgressor has traveled; it must be allowed effectively to close all roads to the prohibited goal, so that its order may not be bypassed with impunity.

We turn next to the specific disclosure required: "Contrary to prior advertising, Listerine will not help prevent colds or sore throats or lessen their severity." Petitioner is ordered to include this statement in every future advertisement for Listerine for a defined period. In printed advertisements it must be displayed in type size at least as large as that in which the principal portion of the text of the advertisement appears and it must be separated from the text so that it can be readily noticed. In television commercials the disclosure must be presented simultaneously in both audio and visual portions. During the audio portion of the disclosure in television and radio advertisements, no other sounds, including music, may occur.

These specifications are well calculated to assure that the disclosure will reach the public. It will necessarily attract the notice of readers, viewers and listeners and be plainly conveyed. Given these safeguards, we believe the preamble "Contrary to prior advertising" is not necessary. It can serve only two purposes: either to attract attention that a correction follows or to humiliate the advertiser. The Commission claims only the first purpose for it, and this we think is obviated by other terms of the order. The second purpose, if it were intended, might be called for in an egregious case of deliberate deception, but this is not one. While we do not decide whether petitioner proffered its cold claims in good faith or bad, the record compiled could support a finding of good faith. On these facts, the confessional preamble to the disclosure is not warranted.

Accordingly, the order, as modified, is affirmed.

CASE QUESTIONS

1. What claims does the FTC question in the Listerine ads and why?
2. What proposals for corrective advertising are made in the order?
3. What happens to the preamble, "Contrary to prior advertising"?
4. What standard does the case establish for corrective ads once the FTC finds a company's ads have deceived the public?

Consider...

Philip Morris Inc. marketed and promoted its low-tar brands to smokers—who were concerned about the health hazards of smoking or considering quitting—as less harmful than full-flavor cigarettes. Internal industry documents revealed that by the late 1960s and early 1970s, Philip Morris and other tobacco companies were aware that lower-tar cigarettes are unlikely to provide health benefits because they do not actually deliver the low levels of tar and nicotine advertised. Smokers of low-tar cigarettes, in order to satisfy their addiction to nicotine, modify their smoking behavior to compensate for the reduced nicotine yields by "taking more frequent puffs, inhaling smoke more deeply, holding smoke in their lungs longer, covering cigarette ventilation holes with fingers or lips, and/or smoking more cigarettes." As a result of this nicotine-driven behavior, smokers of low-tar cigarettes boost their intake of tar, so that lower-tar cigarettes do not result in lower tar intake and therefore do not yield the touted health benefits or serve as a step toward quitting smoking. The FTC and other government agencies brought suit to halt the ads and require corrective advertising by the companies. Discuss whether, based on the *Listerine* case, the government would have the authority to halt the ads and require corrective advertisements.

[*U.S. v Philip Morris USA Inc.*, 566 F.3d 1095 (C.A.D.C. 2009), *cert. denied*, 130 S.Ct. 3501 (2010)]

ETHICAL ISSUES

Neiman Marcus, DrJays.com, and Eminent were accused of false marketing because they advertised shoes, coats, and other clothing items as having "faux fur." However, it turns out that the "faux fur" on the items was actually rabbit, raccoon, and, in some cases, mink. Many consumers do not want to be seen wearing real fur, and if they thought they were buying faux fur because of these three retailers' descriptions, then they were misled.

Neiman Marcus's website misrepresented the fur content and failed to disclose the animal name and fur country of origin for three products: a Burberry Outerwear Jacket, a Stuart Weitzman Ballerina Flat shoe, and an Alice + Olivia Kyah Coat. Neiman Marcus

also misrepresented the fur content of the shoe in its catalog, at bergdorfgoodman.com, and in ads mailed to consumers.

DrJays.com featured The Snorkel Jacket by Crown Holder on its website and described it as including a "faux fur-lined hood." The NY Subway Bomber jacket featured on the site included the following, "Detachable hood with faux fur lining." The Snorkel Jacket did include a label on the jacket itself that described the coat as containing "real raccoon fur." The site also included this description of a vest by Knoles: "faux fur lining."

Explain what the FTC can do with regard to these ads. Is "faux fur" an express warranty? What are the ethical issues in misrepresenting real fur as faux fur?

14-2e FTC CONTROL OF CELEBRITY ENDORSEMENTS

During the 1980s, the FTC entered a new aspect of ad content control—namely, the use of **celebrity endorsements** for products. The regulation of what celebrities say in ads and their qualifications to make the claims remains a focus for the FTC. (See the following "For the Manager's Desk.")

FOR THE MANAGER'S DESK

Re: Celebrity Tweeting

When celebrities tweet on social media site Twitter, the public responds. Advertisers know that and are willing to pay—sometimes $10,000 per tweet—when celebrities endorse a product. For example, Kim Kardashian boosted Old Navy jeans sales with her tweet that the jeans "make your butt look scary good." Lamar Odom was paid to tweet an endorsement of Jay-Z's book, "Decoded." That tweet went out to Odom's two million followers. Terrell Owens tweeted to his one million followers that Comfort Inn was offering a great deal that included free sports tickets, and the chain enjoyed a nice boost in its reservations.

There are companies, such as Izea, Ad.ly, and twtMob that pair products with celebrities in order to get those tweets out there. The success of this form of advertising and its increasing presence brought a new ruling from the FTC. The new ruling relates to a longstanding rule that resulted when former Jets quarterback, Joe Namath, endorsed pantyhose for women. The purpose of the FTC rule is very simple—to prevent consumers from being deceived about the nature of the endorsement and the product. The rule consists of four parts, as summarized by the FTC:

To thine own self be true. The bedrock principle for celebrity endorsements—and any testimonial—is that they must reflect the honest opinion or experience of the endorser. If the ad suggests that the celebrity is a satisfied customer, he or she actually must use the product.

Time will tell. You may use a celebrity's endorsement only as long as you have good reason to believe the opinions in the ad continue to be the views of the celebrity. One

way to satisfy your obligation is to check periodically that the celebrity's opinions remain the same.

Don't bury your head in the sand. A marketing campaign isn't the time for ostrich-like behavior. Even if a celebrity is given a script to read, he can't ignore signs that claims made about the product are false or misleading. For example, suppose an advertiser says its roasting bag can cook chicken in 30 minutes. During the shoot, the celebrity hired to appear in the ad watches five unsuccessful attempts to get the product to work. Each time, the chicken was raw after 30 minutes and needed a full hour to cook. However, in the commercial, the celebrity is shown placing a chicken in the bag, taking out a perfectly roasted chicken, and saying that if you want great chicken every time in only 30 minutes, this is the product you need. The celebrity could be liable for the deceptive statement about the product, and the advertiser could be liable for misrepresentations made through the endorsement.

Disclosures about connections. Financial ties between advertisers and celebrities must sometimes be disclosed. If a financial connection is obvious, disclosure is unnecessary. For example, a tennis star who appears in ads for a line of polo shirts is the type of arrangement most people expect involves payment. However, now suppose she's a guest on a morning talk show. When asked about her recent victories, she credits them to a laser vision correction procedure at a clinic she names. She doesn't disclose her contractual deal with the clinic that requires her to speak publicly about her surgery—that's a problem.

14-2f FTC CONTROL OF BAIT AND SWITCH

One of the better-known FTC ad regulations prohibits the use of **bait and switch**, a sales tactic in which a cheaper product than the one in stock is advertised to get customers into a store. The seller has no intention of selling the product and in some cases might not even have the product in stock, but the ad is used as "bait" to get the customers into the store and then present them with a "better," more expensive product. Such ad tactics are considered deceptive and subject to FTC remedy.

CYBERLAW

14-2g FTC CONTROL OF PRODUCT COMPARISONS

Another aspect of active enforcement by the FTC is in the area of product comparisons. The FTC permits and even welcomes comparisons of products, but such comparisons must be accurate. Results of surveys must be supportable, and

Business Planning Tip

Always review the language used in ads for products. Determine whether express warranties are being made. Make sure that warranties, statements of fact, and promises of performance are accurate.

© Grounder/Shutterstock.com

product preference tests must be done fairly. In the past few years, the FTC has taken a *laissez-faire* approach in ad regulation. Other agencies, such as the offices of state attorneys general, the Better Business Bureau, and private companies and individuals, have undertaken public and private enforcement of deceptive ad claims.

The bulk of litigation over comparative ads is now conducted by and against competitors. The federal trademark law permits competitors to recover from companies for ads that include misrepresentations. Litigation over comparative ads is somewhat lucrative because plaintiffs can recover treble damages, the defendant company's profits, and, in some cases, attorney fees. *McNeil-PPC, Inc. v Pfizer Inc.* (Case 14.3) involves a competitor's litigation over misrepresentation.

CASE 14.3

McNeil-PPC, Inc. v Pfizer Inc.
351 F. Supp. 2d 226 (S.D.N.Y. 2005)

© Harper 3D/Shutterstock.com

Stringing Them Along on No Floss

FACTS

In June 2004, Pfizer Inc. ("Pfizer") launched a consumer advertising campaign for its mouthwash, Listerine Antiseptic Mouthrinse. Print ads and hangtags on the bottles in the stores featured an image of a Listerine bottle balanced on a scale against a white container of dental floss.

The campaign also featured a television commercial that announced, "Listerine's as effective as floss at fighting plaque and gingivitis. Clinical studies prove it." Although the commercial cautions that "[t]here's no replacement for flossing," the commercial repeats two more times the message that Listerine is "as effective as flossing against plaque and gingivitis." The commercial also shows a narrow stream of blue liquid flowing out of a Cool Mint Listerine bottle, then tracking a piece of dental floss being pulled from a white floss container, and then swirling around and between teeth—bringing to mind an image of liquid floss.

McNeil-PPC, Inc. ("PPC") (a division of Johnson & Johnson), the market leader in sales of string dental floss and other interdental cleaning products, brought suit alleging that Pfizer engaged in false advertising and unfair competition in violation of § 43(a) of the Lanham Act, 15 U.S.C. § 1125(a). PPC contends that Pfizer's advertisements are false and misleading because the ads implicitly claim that Listerine is a replacement for floss—that all the benefits of flossing may be obtained by rinsing with Listerine.

PPC filed a motion for an injunction to stop Pfizer from running the ads.

JUDICIAL OPINION

CHIN, District Judge

Traditionally, the "most widely recommended" mechanical device for removing interproximal plaque (the deposits located in the hard-to-reach areas between the teeth) is dental floss. The ADA recommends "brushing twice a day and cleaning between the teeth with floss or interdental cleaners once each day to remove plaque from all tooth surfaces." Flossing provides a number of benefits. It removes food debris and plaque interdentally and it also removes plaque subgingivally. As part of a regular oral hygiene program, flossing helps reduce and prevent not only gingivitis but also periodontitis and caries.

Some 87% of consumers, however, floss either infrequently or not at all. Although dentists and dental hygienists regularly tell their patients to floss, many consumers do not floss or rarely floss because it is a difficult and time-consuming process.

As a consequence, a large consumer market exists to be tapped. If the 87% of consumers who never or rarely floss can be persuaded to floss more regularly, sales of floss would increase dramatically. PPC has endeavored, with products such as the RADF and the Power Flosser, to reach these consumers by trying to make flossing easier.

In the context of this case, therefore, Pfizer and PPC are competitors.

Pfizer sponsored two clinical studies involving Listerine and floss: the "Sharma Study" and the "Bauroth Study." These studies purported to compare

CONTINUED

the efficacy of Listerine against dental floss in controlling plaque and gingivitis in subjects with mild to moderate gingivitis.

The authors of the Sharma Study concluded that the study provided "additional support for the use of the essential oil mouthrinse as an adjunct to mechanical oral hygiene regimens." They cautioned that "[p]rofessional recommendations to floss daily should continue to be reinforced."

The Bauroth Study authors concluded: "[W]e do not wish to suggest that the mouthrinse should be used instead of dental floss or any other interproximal cleaning device."

The ADA reported on the Pfizer studies in its own website. The ADA wrote that "[w]hile some study results [referencing the Sharma and Bauroth Studies] indicate the use of a mouth rinse can be as effective as flossing for reducing plaque between the teeth," it continued to recommend "brushing twice a day and cleaning between the teeth with floss or interdental cleaners once each day."

A number of individual dentists and hygienists complained directly to Pfizer that consumers would get the wrong message.

From the time Pfizer launched its advertising campaign, sales of both the RADF and the Power Flosser have taken a steep decline. Consumers who use the RADF and Power Flosser … are predominantly "folks who don't like to floss," who "would love to have a replacement for flossing." These consumers "would be more susceptible to a message like the Listerine advertising campaign."

To prevail on a Lanham Act false advertising claim, a plaintiff must demonstrate the falsity of the challenged advertisement, by proving that it is either (1) literally false, as a factual matter; or (2) implicitly false, *i.e.*, although literally true, still likely to mislead or confuse consumers. The false or misleading statement must be material.

The two studies included in their samples only individuals with mild to moderate gingivitis. They excluded individuals with severe gingivitis or with any degree of periodontitis, and they did not purport to draw any conclusions with respect to these individuals. Hence, the literal claim in Pfizer's advertisements is overly broad, for the studies did not purport to prove that Listerine is as effective as floss "against plaque and gingivitis," but only against plaque and gingivitis in individuals with mild to moderate gingivitis. Consequently, consumers who suffer from severe gingivitis or periodontitis (including mild periodontitis) may be misled by the ads into believing that Listerine is just as effective as floss in helping them fight plaque and gingivitis, when the studies simply do not stand for that proposition.

Pfizer and its experts argue that the two studies are reliable, notwithstanding the indications that the participants in the flossing group did not floss properly, because these conditions reflect "real-world settings." But the ads do not say that "in the real world," where most people floss rarely or not at all, and even those who do floss have difficulty flossing properly, Listerine is "as effective as floss." Rather, the ads make the blanket assertion that Listerine works just as well as floss, an assertion the two studies simply do not prove. Although it is important to determine how a product works in the real world, it is probably more important to first determine how a product will work when it is used properly.

I find that Pfizer's false and misleading advertising also poses a public health risk, as the advertisements present a danger of undermining the efforts of dental professionals—and the ADA—to convince consumers to floss on a daily basis.

Injunction granted.

CASE QUESTIONS

1. What are the limitations of the studies on which Pfizer relied?

2. Why are mouthwash and floss competitors?

3. Evaluate Pfizer's use of the studies, the ads, and comment on the company's social responsibility posture. Comment on its competitive strategies.

14-2h FTC REMEDIES

As noted in the previous sections, the FTC has a wide range of remedies available in the event of deceptive advertising, including corrective ads, injunctions to prevent deceptive ads from being run, and reimbursement by companies and endorsers for purchasers who were misled by ads.

More often than not, these remedies come about through a consent decree. A **consent decree** is a negotiated settlement between the FTC and the advertiser.

It is the equivalent of a *nolo contendere*, or no contest plea. The FTC and the advertiser, endorser, and/or agency or website designer agree to remedies, and the case is disposed of through the decree without further action.

The FTC has focused increasingly on companies that, like Pfizer in Case 14.3, are making health claims about their products. For example, Kellogg's agreed twice in one year to change the packaging of its cereals that made health claims. It agreed to change its boxes for Frosted Mini-Wheats, which claimed to "increase your child's attentiveness by 20%," and also agreed to change its Rice Krispies packaging, which claimed, "Now helps support your child's immunity."

14-2i AD REGULATION BY THE FDA AND OTHER FEDERAL AGENCIES

Additional federal agencies have become involved in the regulation of product advertising, basing their involvement on health concerns. The Food and Drug Administration (FDA) also has authority over some forms of advertising. Several investigations are pending into energy drinks to determine whether the companies are adequately disclosing the amount of caffeine in their drinks. The investigation focuses on the fact that other ingredients in the drinks such as black tea extract and guarana are disclosed, but labels may not reflect the additional caffeine that those ingredients contain, caffeine levels that are not then disclosed in the drinks' labels.

The FDA has already issued a warning about combining these energy drinks with alcohol consumption because of several resulting deaths. In addition, the Department of Health and Human Services (HHS) has issued a report warning about the negative health effects of excessive caffeine consumption. There will be regulations on product labels, advertising, and warnings related to these products.

14-2j PROFESSIONAL ADS

Most states have limitations on the types of ads professionals (such as doctors, lawyers, dentists, and accountants) can use in reaching the public. At one time, states had complete bans on ads by professionals. However, the U.S. Supreme Court held such bans to be too restrictive and violative of First Amendment protections on commercial speech (see Chapter 5). Restrictions may include requirements on fee disclosures or caveats on distinctions in individual cases and needs. The extent and validity of the restrictions continue to be refined through judicial application of First Amendment rights.

14-3 Contract Product Liability Theories: Implied Warranties

The UCC's Article 2 governs contracts for the sale of goods and includes several provisions for implied warranties. The following sections cover the requirements for each of the implied warranties.

14-3a THE IMPLIED WARRANTY OF MERCHANTABILITY

The **implied warranty of merchantability** (UCC § 2–314) is given in every sale of goods by a merchant seller. The warranty is not given by all sellers, only by merchant sellers. Briefly defined, merchants are those sellers who are engaged in the business of selling the good(s) that are the subject of the contract. The revisions to the UCC changed the wording of this warranty slightly so that it now provides that goods sold by a merchant "(c) are fit for the ordinary purposes for which goods of that description are used." The warranty means the goods are of fair or average quality and are fit for ordinary purposes. Under this warranty, basketballs must bounce, book bindings must hold together, and food items must be free of foreign objects.

For example, in *Metty v Shurfine Central Corp.*, 736 S.W.2d 527 (Mo. 1987), the court found that a breach of the implied warranty of merchantability occurred because part of a grasshopper in a can of green beans was eaten by a pregnant woman who purchased the beans. Shurfine was liable to the woman for resulting complications in her pregnancy. But what happens if there is something naturally present, such as a cherry pit in a cherry pie, that harms someone? Is there still a breach of warranty? *Mitchell v T.G.I. Friday's* (Case 14.4) provides an answer to these questions.

CASE 14.4

Mitchell v T.G.I. Friday's
748 N.E.2d 89 (Ohio App. 2000)

Clamming Up Because of Shell Shock

FACTS

On April 11, 1996, Sandra Mitchell (appellant) was having dinner at Friday's restaurant (appellee). Ms. Mitchell was eating a fried clam strip when she bit into a hard substance that she believed to be a piece of a clamshell. She experienced immediate pain and later sought dental treatment. Some time later, the crown of a tooth came loose. The crown could not be reattached, and an oral surgeon removed the remaining root of the tooth.

Ms. Mitchell filed a product liability action against Friday's, which had served her the meal, and Pro Source Distributing (also appellee), the supplier of the fried clams. Both Friday's and Pro Source filed motions for summary judgment, which the trial court granted without explanation. Ms. Mitchell appealed.

JUDICIAL OPINION

WAITE, Judge

Appellant asserts that there is a reasonable expectation that clams are completely cleaned of their shells and free of foreign materials.

In the present case, Friday's set forth in its motion for summary judgment appellant's deposition testimony to the effect that while eating a clam strip, she bit down on "a hard, foreign substance." Appellant stated that she assumed it was a piece of a clam shell. Appellant described the size of the object as about a quarter of the size of a small fingernail or about a quarter of an inch or smaller and irregular in shape. Moreover, Friday's attached an affidavit from its manager, Eric Hicks, who

immediately responded to appellant's report of the incident. In that affidavit, Hicks confirmed that the object appellant presented to him was indeed a piece of clam shell and that it was approximately one-quarter inch in length and irregularly shaped.

Both Friday's and Pro Source presented essentially the same argument, that regardless of whether the foreign-natural test or reasonable-expectation test was applied, appellant has no claim against appellees.

The basis of appellant's argument for application of the reasonable-expectation test is found in R.C. 2307.75, which provides that a product is defective if it is more dangerous than an ordinary consumer would reasonably suspect. However, appellant has not set forth any case law or analysis that would suggest that food products fall under the purview of the statute. We can find no case that has analyzed a food item in that context. Indeed, the weight of product liability cases deal with synthetic products, for example, a cargo door hinge, a glass bottle, or a prosthetic hip joint. Thus, we see no compelling reason to abandon any established test due to the enactment of Ohio's product liability legislation.

However, it does not appear necessary to determine which test applies to the present case. Save for reference to the product liability statute, a similar argument was addressed in *Mathews v Maysville Seafoods, Inc.* (1991), 76 Ohio App.3d 624, 602 N.E.2d 764. In *Mathews*, the plaintiff suffered a bowel injury when he swallowed a fish bone while eating a fish fillet served by the defendant. The trial court granted the defendant's motion for

CONTINUED

summary judgment. On appeal, the defendant argued for the adoption of the reasonable-expectation test as opposed to the foreign-natural test.

The *Mathews* court set forth both tests. Under the foreign-natural test:

Bones which are natural to the type of meat served cannot legitimately be called a foreign substance, and a consumer who eats meat dishes ought to anticipate and be on his guard against the presence of such bones.

[Q]uoting *Mix v Ingersoll Candy Co.* (1936), 6 Cal.2d 674, 682, 59 P.2d 144, 148.

The reasonable-expectation test states:

The test should be what is "reasonably expected" by the consumer in the food as served, not what might be natural to the ingredients of that food prior to preparation.... As applied to the action for common-law negligence, the test is related to the foreseeability of harm on the part of the defendant. The defendant is not an insurer but has the duty of ordinary care to eliminate or remove in the preparation of the food he serves such harmful substances as the consumer of the food, as served, would not ordinarily anticipate and guard against.

Mathews, 602 N.E.2d at 765.

The *Mathews* court looked to *Allen v Grafton* (1960), 164 N.E.2d 167, where the plaintiff was injured after swallowing a piece of oyster shell contained in a serving of fried oysters. The Supreme Court held:

The presence in one of a serving of six fried oysters of a piece of oyster shell approximately 3 × 2 centimeters (about 11/5 inches by 4/5 of an inch) in diameter will not justify a legal conclusion either (a) that that serving of fried oysters constituted "food" that was "adulterated" within the meaning of Section 3715.59, Revised Code, or (b) that that serving constituted food not "reasonably fit for" eating.

The *Mathews* court further noted:

In the instant case, it is not necessary to hold ... that, because an oyster shell is natural to an oyster and thus not a substance "foreign" to an oyster, no liability can be predicated upon the sale of a fried oyster containing a piece of oyster shell. However, the fact, that something that is served with food and that will cause harm if eaten is natural to that food and so not a "foreign substance," will usually be an important factor in determining whether a consumer can reasonably anticipate and guard against it.

In our opinion, the possible presence of a piece of oyster shell in or attached to an oyster is so well known to anyone who eats oysters that we can say as a matter of law that one who eats oysters can reasonably anticipate and guard against eating such a piece of shell, especially where it is as big a piece as the one described in plaintiff's petition.

Despite the opposing interpretations of *Allen*, the *Mathews* court stated that "it is not necessary to decide whether the 'reasonable expectation' test or the 'foreign natural' test holds sway in Ohio." The court stated that it must be reasonably expected that even a fish fillet may contain fish bones, citing *Polite v Carey Hilliards Restaurants, Inc.* (1985). *The Mathews* court noted that in *Polite*, the court applied the foreign-natural test in affirming a summary judgment for the defendant where the plaintiff swallowed an obviously naturally occurring one-inch fish bone concealed in a fish fillet.

An occasional piece of clam shell in a bowl of clam chowder is so well known to a consumer that we can say the consumer can reasonably anticipate and guard against it.

Courts cannot and must not ignore the common experience of life and allow rules to develop that would make sellers of food or other consumer goods insurers of the products they sell.

In the present case, it cannot be disputed that the piece of clam shell that caused appellant's injury was natural to the clam strip she consumed. Turning to the question of whether appellant should have reasonably anticipated the presence of the clam shell, we are reminded of the Ohio Supreme Court's holding in *Allen, supra*, that "the possible presence of a piece of oyster shell in or attached to an oyster is so well known to anyone who eats oysters that we can say as a matter of law that one who eats oysters can reasonably anticipate and guard against eating such a piece of shell." The facts of the present case are virtually indistinguishable from *Allen* except for the type of injury and that, here, appellant was eating fried clams rather than fried oysters. We therefore hold that, as a matter of law, one who eats clams can reasonably anticipate and guard against eating a piece of shell.

As appellant's claim fails under both tests, we overrule her assignment of error and affirm the judgment of the trial court.

Judgment affirmed.

CASE QUESTIONS

1. What did the lower court do in the case that caused an admonition from the appellate court?

2. What test does Ohio follow—the foreign-natural or the reasonable-expectation test?

3. Is the reasonable-expectation test one that makes the food producer or provider an insurer?

Consider...

John Manley ate at one Wendy's restaurant during the months of February and March, 2007. He ate at no other Wendy's restaurants, but did eat at other fast-food restaurants during this period. He always had the same thing: a double-patty hamburger, garnished with cheese, tomatoes, pickles, onions, bacon, mayonnaise, and ketchup; a side of French fries or onion rings; and a soft drink. Mr. Manley always paid in cash and had no receipts from his visits to the Wendy's. When his health began to suffer with fatigue, coughing, and choking, Mr. Manley sought medical treatment and tests uncovered a piece of plastic from an eating utensil that had lodged in his lungs. The utensil fragment that was removed from his lungs was embossed with a portion of the Wendy's logo. Mr. Manley brought suit against Wendy's for breach of the implied warranty of merchantability.

Discuss the issues you see in this claim.

[*Manley v Doe*, 849 F. Supp. 2d 594 (E.D.N.C. 2012)]

14-3b THE IMPLIED WARRANTY OF FITNESS FOR A PARTICULAR PURPOSE

The **implied warranty of fitness for a particular purpose** (UCC § 2-315) arises when the seller promises a buyer that the goods will be suitable for a use the buyer has proposed. For example, the owner of a nursery makes an implied warranty for a particular purpose when telling a buyer that a weed killer will work in the buyer's rose garden without harming the roses. An exercise enthusiast is given this warranty when the seller recommends a particular shoe as appropriate for aerobics.

The requirements for this warranty are the following:

1. The seller has skill or judgment in use of the goods.
2. The buyer is relying on that skill or judgment.
3. The seller knew or had reason to know of the buyer's reliance.
4. The seller makes a recommendation for the buyer's use and purpose.

For example, if you went to a pet store and asked for two male hamsters and one cage, the salesperson who picks out the two hamsters for you is making an implied warranty of fitness for a particular purpose: that the hamsters can cohabitate without reproducing. Should your hamsters reproduce, the pet store would be responsible for whatever damage you experience, including taking the baby hamsters from the misidentified hamster couple.

Consider...

Cynthia Rubin went to Marshall Field's department store on April 5, 1986. While browsing, she got into a conversation with Julianna Reiner, a salesclerk, and told Ms. Reiner that she used Vaseline to remove her eye makeup. Ms. Reiner said Vaseline could clog her eye ducts and cause cataracts or other permanent eye damage, and she recommended Princess Marcella Borghese Instant Eye Make-Up Remover, manufactured by Princess Marcella Borghese, Inc. Ms. Rubin asked if the product was safe. Ms. Reiner showed her the box, which said, "Recommended for all skin types." Ms. Reiner said, "If it wouldn't be safe for you, it wouldn't say this on the box." Relying on Ms. Reiner's representations, Ms. Rubin purchased the product.

That night, she used the product to remove her eye makeup. Her eyelids and the skin around her eyes turned red, became taut and rough, and started to sting. She washed her skin repeatedly and kept a cold washrag on her eyes all night. Two days later, when the burning did not subside, she called an ophthalmologist and went to see him the next day. He told her that she had contact dermatitis and prescribed an ointment.

A few weeks later, because the burning and roughness of her eyelids persisted, Ms. Rubin decided to see Dr. Katherine Wier, a dermatologist. Dr. Wier prescribed a similar ointment and told Ms. Rubin that the chemical causing the burning would remain in her system for three or four months. The stinging subsided, but Ms. Rubin could not wear eye makeup again regularly until summer 1987. When she tried to wear makeup again before that, her eyelids turned bright red and began swelling upon removal of the makeup.

Ms. Rubin filed suit for breach of implied warranty of fitness for a particular purpose. Should she recover?

[*Rubin v Marshall Field & Co.*, 597 N.E.2d 688 (Ill. 1992)]

Business Planning Tip

To disclaim a warranty, follow these guidelines:

1. Use LARGE type.

2. Use a different color for the disclaimer text.

3. Place the disclaimer on the front of the contract.

4. Use proper statutory language.

5. Have buyers initial the disclaimer.

6. On electronic records, get verification of receipt of e-mail or fax with disclaimer.

14-3c ELIMINATING WARRANTY LIABILITY BY DISCLAIMERS

Warranties can be eliminated by the use of **disclaimers**. The proper method for disclaiming a warranty depends on the type of warranty. Express warranties, however, cannot be given and then taken back. Basically, an express warranty cannot be disclaimed. Exhibit 14.2 includes a summary of the means for disclaiming warranties.

The implied warranty of merchantability and the implied warranty of fitness for a particular purpose can be disclaimed by using a phrase such as "WITH ALL FAULTS," or "AS IS." Either warranty alone can be disclaimed by using the name of the warranty: "There is no warranty of merchantability given" or "There is no implied warranty of fitness for a particular purpose." For those warranty disclaimers required to be in writing, their presence in a record satisfies the writing requirements (see Chapters 12 and 13 for more information).

Even though the UCC is clear on the language to be used for warranty disclaimers and the process seems to be easy, the warranty disclaimers are still subject to the general UCC constraint of good faith. **Unconscionable** disclaimers of warranties or waiver of warranties when one party has no bargaining power may not be valid. For example, a disclaimer of liability for personal injury resulting from a breach of the warranty of merchantability for a consumer good would be unconscionable. Exhibit 14.2 summarizes the UCC warranty protections and disclaimers.

14-3d PRIVITY STANDARDS FOR UCC RECOVERY

If you have a contract to buy a car and the seller breaches the contract by refusing to deliver, you can bring suit for breach of contract based on the **privity** between you and the seller. The people in your carpool, however, could not recover from the seller for breach because you no longer have a car to use (even though they are affected). They have no privity of contract with the seller. Traditionally, a recovery for a breach of contract requires privity of contract. A breach of warranty is a breach of contract, and until the time of the UCC, privity was required to be able to recover on a breach of warranty theory.

Section 2–318 of the UCC establishes three alternatives that states can adopt, each of which provides warranty protections for *more* persons than the buyer. For example, Alternative A extends warranty protection to "any natural person who

> **EXHIBIT 14.2** UCC Warranties: Creation, Restrictions, and Disclaimers

TYPE	CREATION	RESTRICTION	DISCLAIMER
Express	Affirmation of fact or promise of performance (samples, models, descriptions)	Must be part of the basis of the bargain	Cannot make a disclaimer inconsistent with an express
Implied Warranty of Merchantability	Given in every sale of goods by a merchant ("fit for ordinary purposes")	Only given by merchants	(1) Must use disclaimer of quality or use "merchant-ability" or general disclaimer "as is" or "with all faults" (2) If written—(record) must be conspicuous
Implied Warranty of Fitness for a Particular Purpose	Seller knows of buyer's reliance for a particular use (buyer is ignorant)	Seller must have knowledge—buyer must rely	(1) Must be in writing (record) (2) Must be conspicuous (3) Must be clear there are no warranties (using specific language) or (4) Also disclaimed with "as is" or "with all faults"
Title	Given in every sale	Does not apply in circumstances where apparent warranty is not given	Must state "There is no warranty of title"

© Cengage Learning

is in the family or household … of the remote purchaser or who is a guest in the home [of the remote purchaser]." Alternative B extends coverage to "any natural person who is reasonably expected to use, consume, or be affected by the goods" or who is "injured in person" by the goods. Alternative C extends the warranty protection to "any person that may be reasonably expected to use, consume, or be affected by the goods" and is injured by them or their use. Alternative C also prohibits the disclaimer of liability for personal injury to those covered by the warranty.

14-4 Strict Tort Liability: Product Liability Under Section 402A

The discussion to this point has focused on the statutory and contract theories of product liability. Liability for making false statements about products is addressed under UCC warranty provisions or under federal and state advertising and consumer protection statutes. But these theories are grounded in contract relationships and limited statutory authority. A broader focus to product liability is grounded in tort law. Section 402A provides a remedy for those who are harmed by defective products through either a theory of strict liability or one of negligence.

The first tort theory for recovery for defective products is **strict liability** in tort. This tort was created and defined by Section 402A of the *Restatement (Second) of Torts*. Restatements of the law are developed by the American Law Institute (ALI), a group of professors and practicing attorneys. Restatements are not the law, even though they are adopted and recognized in many states as the controlling statement of law in that state. The adoption of a Restatement generally comes in the form of judicial acceptance of the doctrines provided.

> *Restatement § 402A:*
>
> *402A. Special Liability of Seller of Product for Physical Harm to User or Consumer*
>
> (1) *One who sells any product in a defective condition unreasonably dangerous to the user or consumer or to his property is subject to liability for physical harm thereby caused to the ultimate user or consumer, or to his property if*
>
> > (a) *the seller is engaged in the business of selling such a product, and*
> >
> > (b) *it is expected to and does reach the user or consumer without substantial change in the condition in which it is sold.*
>
> (2) *The rule stated in Subsection (1) applies although*
>
> > (a) *the seller has exercised all possible care in the preparation and sale of his product, and*
> >
> > (b) *the user or consumer has not bought the product from or entered into any contractual relations with the seller.*[2]

Part 2 of 402A spells out the distinction between negligence and strict tort liability. Liability results for physical harm even when sellers have exercised all possible care in developing, producing, and selling the product. The fact that the seller is in the business of making and/or selling the product and someone is injured results in the liability. No negligent error or omission is required as an element of proof for recovery. Section 402A applies to defective conditions regardless of the precautions taken by the manufacturer. Manufacturers or food processors that take great precautions in their procedures could overcome a charge of negligence; however, strict liability focuses on the fact that a defect exists, not whether the manufacturer could or could not have prevented the problem. The *Restatement (Third) of Product Liability* has been proposed and would clarify the definition of *defective* with regard to knowledge requirements and recovery.

Section 402A has no privity requirements and is not subject to the disclaimers that can eliminate warranty liability.

14-4a THE REQUIREMENT OF UNREASONABLY DANGEROUS DEFECTIVE CONDITION

The requirement of proof of an unreasonable defective condition can be produced in many different ways. Unreasonable defects can come from everything from the materials used to the manufacturing processes. Every product liability suit finds a different type of defect. A product can be unreasonably dangerous because it contains a foreign substance. Most product liability cases relating to food are based on this tenet. Rats in pop bottles, moldy bananas in cereal, parts of a snake in frozen vegetables, and stones in soup are all factual circumstances that have been recognized as Section 402A defective conditions.

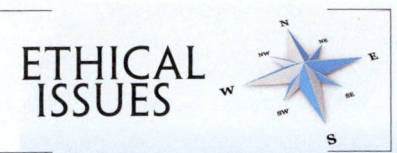

ETHICAL ISSUES

In early 2010, Toyota issued a recall for over 8,000,000 vehicles because there were increasing complaints about a sudden unintended acceleration (SUA) issue. There had been 24,000 consumer complaints about the SUA issue to dealers, to the Consumer Product Safety Commission, and via lawsuits filed against the company between 2001 through 2009. Initially, Toyota responded by claiming that the acceleration was caused by faulty floor mats and/or driver error. Causes then shifted to worn pedals, overheated pedals, condensation, and even software issues. However, the full recall was not made until January of 2010 following increasingly vocal Toyota owner complaints and a series of fatal accidents.

Discuss the possible product liability theories that would apply. If the floor mats were getting in the way of the brake pedal or pressing on the accelerator, would Toyota have liability? Evaluate the ethics of Toyota in holding off on the recalls. What if drivers made a mistake, or were just confused, and stepped on the wrong pedal? Is there product liability then?

The most common types of product liability cases are based on the following types of defects:

1. Design defects
2. Dangers of use due to lack of warnings or unclear use instructions
3. Errors in manufacturing, handling, or packaging of the product

Design Defects

A product with a faulty design exposes its users to unnecessary risks. Products must be designed with all foreseeable uses in mind. Cars must be designed in view of the probability of accidents. A design that creates an otherwise unnecessary explosion upon a rear-end collision is a faulty design. A car that suddenly accelerates because of a flaw in the auto's computer system or accelerator has a design defect.

To make the best possible case in the event of a product liability suit, it is helpful for the manufacturer to have complied with all federal and state regulations on the product. It is also helpful if the manufacturer has used the latest technology and designs available within the industry and has met industry standards in designing its product.

Improper Warnings and Instructions

Manufacturers have a duty to warn buyers of a foreseeably dangerous use of a product that the buyers are not likely to realize is dangerous. They also have a duty to supplement the warnings. For example, as defects are discovered in autos, the manufacturers send recall notices to buyers. Similarly, manufacturers of airplanes have sent warnings on problems and proper repair procedures to airlines throughout the life of a particular plane design's use.

Manufacturers must also give adequate instructions to buyers on the proper use of the product. Over-the-counter drugs carry instructions about proper dosages and the limitations on dosages. The quotes in the chapter opening give an indication of the levels of warnings required on products. The *Smith v Coleman Co.* case (Case 14.5) involves an issue of whether a warning was required, provides an answer to the chapter opening "Consider ...," and involves an integrated discussion of the various types of warranties in the sale of products.

CASE 14.5

Smith v Coleman Co.
71 UCC Rep.Serv.2d 131 (M.D. Ala. 2010)

"Towing" the Line with an Eye on Warnings

FACTS

Ginger Smith (plaintiff) was a passenger on Ronald Smith's boat on West Point Lake, Alabama. Ronald Smith (no relation to Ginger) was operating the boat, which was towing Ms. Smith's son, Shane McClellan, on an inflatable inner tube behind the boat. Shane McClellan weighed 150 pounds at the time and the tube itself weighed 5 to 10 pounds. The inner tube was tied to the boat by a 50-foot Model 51650 polypropylene line that was manufactured by Lehigh Consumer Products, LLC, but carried the label of The Coleman Company (defendants) pursuant to a licensing arrangement, and was purchased at a nearby Walmart store. While Shane McClellan was being towed on the inner tube, the line snapped, and the end connected to the boat flew back toward the boat and hit Ms. Smith in the eye, causing the loss of that eye.

The packaging of the line contained several statements. A paper insert identifies it as a "50 ft × 5/16 in UTILITY LINE." Just below that appears the phrase "Ideal for use on boat or dock." Still farther down the insert, and in an all-caps font smaller than that used in the first statement, appears, divided over two lines, "175 LBS WORKING LOAD LIMIT/STAYS AFLOAT." A longer cautionary message appears at the bottom of the insert. It states:

> *Avoid using a knot, splicing is preferable. Knots reduce the strength of the rope up to 40%. Do not use this product where personal safety could be endangered. Never stand in line with a rope under tension. Such a rope, particularly nylon rope, may recoil (snap back). Misuse can result in serious injury or death.*

There was a warning label printed on the inner tube itself, a portion of which advised boaters to "[u]se a tow rope of at least 1500 lbs average tensile strength for pulling a single person...." The overall size of this warning label is 8" × 9", and its text complies with the warning label recommended by the Water Sports Industry Association for use on inflatable tubes.

Ms. Smith filed suit against Coleman, Walmart, and Ronald Smith. (Walmart and Smith were dismissed from the case). Coleman argued that its package warned against using the line for towing and moved for summary judgment.

JUDICIAL OPINION

WATKINS, District Judge

A manufacturer has a duty "to warn users of the dangerous propensities of a product only when such products are dangerous when put to their intended use." "[A] manufacturer is under no duty to warn a user of every danger which may exist during the use of the product, especially when such danger is open and obvious." "... the warning need only be one that is reasonable under the circumstances and it need not be the best possible warning."

It is a defense to a negligent failure to warn claim that there is no evidence "that the allegedly inadequate warning would have been read and heeded and would have kept the accident from occurring." In this case, Defendants point to the deposition testimony of Ronald Smith, who purchased the line and attached it to the boat and inner tube. Mr. Smith's testimony was that he did not recall reading "any other part of the warnings on the package other than the poundage." He specifically answered a question in the negative about whether he had read the warning against tying knots in the line. According to Defendants, Mr. Smith's use of the line violated three parts of the warnings given on the package insert, which he confessed having not read: (1) the warning against tying knots in the line; (2) the warning against using the line where personal safety could be endangered; and (3) the warning against standing in line "with a rope under tension."

The court pauses to contemplate an issue not discussed by either party, but which seems so fundamental to the cause of action asserted by Ms. Smith that it is difficult to adequately address the failure-to-warn claim without touching on it. That issue is how a negligent failure-to-warn claim is affected by the plaintiff not having been the purchaser, or even the "user," of the item at issue. Both parties proceed as if the relevant inquiry is whether Mr. Smith, or perhaps either Mr. or Ms. Smith, read and followed the warnings on the package. It is undisputed that Mr. Smith purchased the rope and is the person who tied it to the boat and inner tube. Given the disposable nature of the package on which the warnings appeared, it is unclear whether Ms. Smith even had the opportunity to read the warnings—and so, in the summary judgment posture, this court must assume that she did not, if that factual question is relevant to the outcome.

CONTINUED

Conceding that Mr. Smith did not recall reading the relevant warnings, Plaintiff's argument seems to be that the phrase "warning" has a particular, technical meaning, such that the statements on the package here were not "warnings" for the purposes of the Alabama case law. The contours of this view are not very well fleshed out, but the argument is perhaps that because the statements on the packaging did not actually contain the word "WARNING," with accompanying symbols such as an exclamation mark within a triangle, they were not actually warnings at all, but merely "safety information."

The only basis for this distinction is a statement made by one of Defendants' experts that "warnings can change behavior, but it is difficult to change behavior with safety information." Perhaps there is a technical distinction, recognized by experts in product labeling or in regulations, between the two concepts, and perhaps, under that distinction, the package insert here is "safety information" rather than a "warning," although it is far from clear from the deposition excerpts before the court that this is what the expert meant. Regardless, the argument misses the point that the court must apply the word "warning" as it has been used in the Alabama case law, which governs this diversity case. The cases cited give no indication of limiting the word "warning" to a narrow, technical meaning. Certainly, the common use of the word "warning" does not limit the concept to statements appearing under the word "WARNING," accompanied by particular symbols, or colored in bright orange. The statements appearing on the utility line's package are cautionary in nature, designed to *warn*, in the ordinary sense of the term, users of the product about potential dangers of usage.

Thus, the court concludes that the statements on the package were warnings for purposes of Alabama law. As stated above, it is conceded that Mr. Smith did not read the warnings, except for the weight limitation. The only remaining question is whether failure to heed the warnings caused the accident. The court is reluctant to conclude that the warning against uses "where personal safety could be endangered" can suffice for this purpose; it is so vague as to be essentially meaningless. Any use, no matter how seemingly safe or appropriate, that actually resulted in injury could be said after the fact to have endangered personal safety. The other two warnings, however, are quite specific, and both were violated by Mr. Smith. Mr. Smith tied knots in the rope in order to attach it to the boat and the inner tube. Both Mr. Smith and Plaintiff were on board the open boat towing the inner tube behind it; in the ordinary use of language, they were both standing "in line with a rope under tension."

Indeed, it is difficult to conceive how the rope could ever be used for towing someone behind an open boat without both the person being towed and persons on board the boat violating the warning against standing in line with a rope under tension. While Plaintiff's expert prevaricates somewhat over whether Plaintiff was herself "in line" with the rope at the time it broke, heeding this warning still would have prevented the accident altogether, as there would have been no way to tow Plaintiff's son on the inner tube without putting him in line with the rope under tension.

Finally, the court does not base its ruling on Defendants' argument that towing a 150-pound child (plus a five to ten pound inner tube) would have produced a dynamic load far in excess of the 175-pound limitation on the rope, so Plaintiff's argument that there was no way for Mr. Smith or Plaintiff to be aware of the difference between static and dynamic loads is irrelevant. The court also does not base its decision on arguments concerning the warning label on the inner tube itself. Because there is no evidence that the allegedly inadequate warning was read and heeded, or that, if it had been read and heeded, the accident would have occurred anyway, the motion for summary judgment on the negligent-failure-to-warn claim is due to be granted.

With respect to the express warranty claim, Plaintiff's claim is that the statement that the line was "ideal for use on boat or dock" constitutes an express warranty. Statements "that are mere sales talk or 'puffery' do not give rise to express warranties," while "representations of fact" may give rise to such warranties. While the word "ideal" seems closer to the description of an item as "in good shape" that Alabama courts have found to constitute "puffery," *Scoggin v Listerhill Employees Credit Union*, 658 So.2d 376, 377 (Ala.1995), arguably the reference to use on a boat or dock could constitute a more specific assurance in some circumstances. Regardless, the phrase "ideal for use on boat or dock" is not the equivalent of "ideal for towing behind a boat," especially when, as explained in the previous section, the specific warnings on the package make it essentially impossible to use the utility line for towing in compliance with the packaging. There is no evidence that any express warranty was breached, and summary judgment is due to be granted on this claim.

To the extent that Plaintiff makes a claim for breach of an implied warranty of merchantability, she does not explain how that claim fits the requirements of the statute, and the claim fails for essentially the same reason as the express warranty claim. A use excluded by warning labels cannot be an "ordinary purpose [ ] for which such goods are used."

The final warranty claim is for breach of an implied warranty of fitness for a particular purpose. Plaintiff has done no more than assert that Defendants had "reason to know" that the line would be used to tow persons behind a boat; regardless, Plaintiff clearly did not "rely

CONTINUED

on the seller's skill or judgment to select or furnish suitable goods." Rather, Mr. Smith selected and purchased the utility line for himself at a Wal-Mart store. Summary judgment is due to be granted on the warranty claims.

The court need not reach Defendants' argument that Coleman is entitled to summary judgment because its only role in producing the utility line was to license its name to Lehigh.

Summary judgment for Defendants.

CASE QUESTIONS

1. What is the law with regard to product users who do not read package warnings?

2. What point does the court make about Ms. Smith not actually being the purchaser of the line?

3. What lessons should Coleman take from its experience of being a defendant along with its licensee for the line?

Errors in Manufacturing, Handling, or Packaging

This breach of duty is the most difficult form of negligence to prove. The large number of handlers in the process of manufacturing and packaging a product typically makes it difficult to prove when and how the manufacturer was negligent. One of the issues in drug manufacturing cases is whether the packaging for the materials is sufficient. Does it protect against tampering? Is it childproof? These types of dangers are foreseeable and require special duties with regard to packaging drugs.

Consider...

Classify the following as design, manufacture, or warning defects:

- Failure to disclose changes in fuel and operations for a helicopter in hot weather and higher altitudes
- A polio vaccine that produces not immunity but polio in a child
- Teflon-induced autoimmune system disease caused by Teflon used in the manufacture of an implanted TMJ jaw device
- Diamond represented as a grade VVS that is actually a lower grade
- Infant swing that causes infants to fall out backward if they fall asleep and their weight shifts
- Tobacco that causes lung cancer
- Fondue pot tipping over and burning a two-year-old child
- Bleeding of pizza-box ink onto pizza

14-4b REACHING THE BUYER IN THE SAME CONDITION

The requirement that a product reach the buyer without "substantial change" is a protection for the seller. A seller will not be liable for a product that has been modified or changed. The reason for this requirement is that once a product is modified or changed, it becomes unclear whether the original product or the modifications caused the unreasonably dangerous condition. Volkswagen would not be held liable for a dune buggy accident just because the builder and owner of the

BUSINESS STRATEGY

Nestlé and the Infant Formula and Product Marketing*

While the merits and problems of breast-feeding versus using infant formula are debated in the United States and other developed countries, the issue is not so balanced in Third World nations. Studies have demonstrated the difficulties and risks of bottle-feeding babies in such places.

First, refrigeration is not generally available, so the formula, once it is mixed or opened (in the case of premixed types), cannot be stored properly. Second, the lack of purified water for mixing with the formula powder results in diarrhea or other diseases in formula-fed infants. Third, inadequate education and income, along with cultural differences, often lead to the dilution of formula and thus greatly reduced nutrition.

Medical studies also suggest that regardless of the mother's nourishment, sanitation, and income level, an infant can be adequately nourished through breast-feeding.

In spite of medical concerns about using their products in these countries, some infant formula manufacturers heavily promoted bottle-feeding.

These promotions, which went largely unchecked through 1970, included billboards, radio jingles, and posters of healthy, happy infants, as well as baby books and formula samples distributed through the health care systems of various countries.

Also, some firms used "milk nurses" as part of their promotions. Dressed in nurse uniforms, "milk nurses" were assigned to maternity wards by their companies and paid commissions to get new mothers to feed their babies formula. Mothers who did so soon discovered that lactation could not be achieved and the commitment to bottle-feeding was irreversible.

In the early 1970s, physicians working in nations where milk nurses were used began vocalizing their concerns. For example, Dr. Derrick Jelliffe, the then–director of the Caribbean Food and Nutrition Institute, had the Protein-Calorie Advisory Group of the United Nations place infant-formula-promotion methods on its agenda for several of its meetings.

Journalist Mike Muller first brought the issue to public awareness with a series of articles in the *New Internationalist* in the 1970s. He also wrote a pamphlet on the promotion of infant formulas called *The Baby Killer*, which was published by a British charity, War on Want. The same pamphlet was published in Switzerland, the headquarters of Nestlé, a major formula maker, under

the title *Nestlé Kills Babies*. Nestlé sued in 1975, which resulted in extensive media coverage.

In response to the bad publicity, manufacturers of infant formula representing about 75 percent of the market formed the International Council of Infant Food Industries to establish standards for infant formula marketing. The new code banned the milk nurse commissions and required the milk nurses to have identification that would eliminate confusion about their "nurse" status.

The code failed to curb advertising of formulas. In fact, distribution of samples increased. By 1977, groups in the United States began a boycott against formula makers over what Jelliffe called "comerciogenic malnutrition."

One U.S. group, Infant Formula Action Coalition (INFACT), worked with the staff of Senator Edward Kennedy of Massachusetts to have hearings on the issue by the Senate Subcommittee on Health and Human Resources, which Kennedy chaired. The hearings produced evidence that 40 percent of the worldwide market for infant formula, which totaled $1.5 billion at the time, was in Third World countries. No regulations resulted, but Congress did tie certain forms of foreign aid to the development by recipient countries of programs to encourage breast-feeding.

Boycotts against Nestlé products began in Switzerland in 1975 and in the United States in 1977. The boycotts and Senator Kennedy's involvement heightened media interest in the issue and led to the World Health Organization (WHO) debating the issue of infant formula marketing in 1979 and agreeing to draft a code to govern it.

After four drafts, and two presidential administrations (Carter and Reagan), the 118 member nations of WHO finally voted on a code for infant formula marketing. The United States was the only nation to vote against it; the Reagan administration opposed the code being mandatory. In the end, WHO made the code a recommendation only, but the United States still refused to support it.

The publicity on the vote fueled the boycott of Nestlé, which continued until the formula maker announced it would meet the WHO standards for infant formula marketing. Nestlé created the Nestlé Infant Formula Audit Commission (NIFAC) to demonstrate its commitment to and ensure its implementation of the WHO code.

In 1988, Nestlé introduced a new infant formula, Good Start, through its subsidiary, Carnation. The industry leader, Abbott Laboratories, which held 54 percent of the market with its Similac brand, revealed Carnation's affiliation: "They are Nestlé," said Robert A. Schoellhorn, Abbott's chairman and CEO. Schoellhorn also disclosed that Nestlé was the owner of Beech-Nut Nutrition Corporation, officers of which had been indicted and convicted (following one reversal) for selling adulterated apple juice for babies.

Carnation advertised Good Start in magazines and on television. The American Academy of Pediatrics (AAP) objected to this direct advertising, and grocers feared boycotts.

The letters "H.A." came after the name "Good Start," indicating the formula was hypoallergenic. Touted as a medical breakthrough by Carnation, the formula was made from whey and advertised as ideal for babies who were colicky or could not tolerate milk-based formulas.

Within four months of Good Start's introduction in November 1988, the FDA was investigating the formula because of six reported cases of vomiting due to the formula. Carnation then agreed not to label the formula hypoallergenic and to include a warning that milk-allergic babies should be given Good Start only with a doctor's approval and supervision.

In 1990, with its infant formula market share at 2.8 percent, Carnation's president, Timm F. Crull, called on the AAP to "examine all marketing practices that might hinder breast-feeding." Crull specifically cited manufacturers' practices of giving hospitals education and research grants, as well as free bottles, in exchange for having exclusive rights to supply the hospital with formula and to give free samples to mothers. He also called for scrutiny of the practice of paying pediatricians' expenses to attend conferences on infant formulas.

The AAP looked into prohibiting direct marketing of formula to mothers and physicians accepting cash awards from formula manufacturers for research.

The distribution of samples in Third World countries continued during this time. Studies by the United Nations Children's Fund found that a million infants were dying every year because they were not breast-fed adequately. In many cases, the infant starved because the mother used free formula samples and could not buy more, while her own milk dried up. In 1991, the International Association of Infant Food Manufacturers agreed to stop distributing infant formula samples by the end of 1992.

In the United States in 1980, the surgeon general established a goal that the nation's breast-feeding rate be 75 percent by 1990. The rate remains below 60 percent, however, despite overwhelming evidence that breast milk reduces susceptibility to illness, especially ear infections and gastrointestinal illnesses. The AAP took a strong position that infant formula makers should not advertise to the public, but as a result, new entrants into the market (such as Nestlé with its Carnation Good Start) were disadvantaged because longtime formula makers Abbott and Mead Johnson were well established through physicians. In 1993, Nestlé filed an antitrust suit alleging a conspiracy among AAP, Abbott, and Mead Johnson.

Some 200 U.S. hospitals have voluntarily stopped distributing discharge packs from formula makers to their maternity patients because they felt it was "important not to appear to be endorsing any products or acting as commercial agents." A study at Boston City Hospital showed that mothers who receive discharge packs are less likely to continue nursing, if they nurse at all. UNICEF and WHO offer "Baby Friendly" certification to maternity wards that take steps to eliminate discharge packs and formula samples.

Discussion Questions

1. If you had been an executive with Nestlé, would you have changed your marketing approach after the boycotts began? Didn't the first mover approach make sense?

2. Did Nestlé suffer long-term damage because of its Third World marketing techniques?

3. Is the moratorium on distributing free formula samples voluntary? Would your company comply? If you were a hospital administrator, what policy would you adopt regarding discharge packs?

4. Should formula makers advertise directly to the public? What if their ads read, "Remember, breast is best"?

5. Nestlé recently turned down a merger offer from PepsiCo because it felt that PepsiCo had too many snack foods. Has Nestlé shifted its standards since the time of the infant formula crisis?

*Reprinted with permission from Marianne M. Jennings, *Case Studies in Business Ethics*, 8th ed., 2014.

Sources: "Breast Milk for the World's Babies," *New York Times*, March 12, 1992, p. A18; Thomas B. Burton, "Methods of Marketing Infant Formula Land Abbott in Hot Water," *Wall Street Journal*, May 25, 1993, pp. A1, A6; Alix M. Freedman, "Nestlé's Bid to Crash Baby-Formula Market in the U.S. Stirs a Row," *Wall Street Journal*, February 6, 1989, pp. A1, A10; Susan B. Garland, "Are Formula Makers Putting the Squeeze on the States?" *Business Week*, June 18, 1990, p. 31; Andrea Gerlin, "Hospitals Wean from Formula Makers' Freebies," *Wall Street Journal*, December 29, 1994, p. B1; Barry Meier, "Battle over the Market for Baby Formula," *New York Times*, June 15, 1993, pp. C1, C15; "Nestlé Unit Sues Baby Formula Firms, Alleging Conspiracy with Pediatricians," *Wall Street Journal*, June 1, 1993, p. B4; James E. Post, "Assessing the Nestlé Boycott: Corporate Accountability and Human Rights," *California Management Review* 27 (1985): 113–31; Marlene G. Star, "Breast Is Best," *Vegetarian Times*, June 1991, pp. 25–26.

dune buggy happened to use a Volkswagen engine in building the vehicle. Because Volkswagen's product has been taken apart and modified, its liability has ended. One issue that arises in airplane crash cases is whether the air carrier followed the manufacturer's repair procedures. The failure to follow these procedures could eliminate the manufacturer's liability because the aircraft may have been altered.

14-4c THE REQUIREMENT OF A SELLER ENGAGED IN A BUSINESS

Section 402A requires the seller to be "engaged in the business of selling the product." This requirement sounds like the merchant requirement for the UCC warranty of merchantability. However, the meaning of "selling the product" is slightly broader under Section 402A than the UCC meaning of merchant. For example, a baseball club is not a merchant of beer, but if the club sells beer at its games, it is a seller for purposes of Section 402A. Section 402A covers manufacturers, wholesalers, retailers, food sellers, and even those who sell products out of their homes.

Some courts have allowed recovery from groups of sellers. For example, in the controversy over diethylstilbestrol (DES, a drug taken by pregnant women), the plaintiffs could show that their harms resulted from DES but could not show exactly who manufactured the drug their mothers took. The courts permitted recovery against the group of manufacturers of DES during that time period. [*Sindell v Abbott Lab.*, 607 P.2d 924 (Cal. 1980)]

14-4d NEGLIGENCE: A SECOND TORT FOR PRODUCT LIABILITY

A suit for product defects can also be based in negligence. The elements for establishing a negligence case are the same as those for a Section 402A case with one addition: establishing that the product seller or manufacturer either knew of the defect before the product was sold or allowed sales to continue with the knowledge that the product had a defect. Establishing this knowledge is difficult in an evidentiary sense in court, but a plaintiff in a product liability suit who shows that the defendant-seller knew of the problem and sold or continued to sell the product can collect punitive damages in addition to damages for personal injury and property damage. Establishing knowledge in a product liability case usually produces a multimillion-dollar verdict because punitive damages are awarded in addition to compensatory ones.

Examples of cases in which establishing knowledge has been an issue include the Ford Pinto exploding gas tank cases (in which the plaintiffs used internal memos from engineers to establish the company's knowledge of defects) and the Dow Corning breast implant suits (in which an engineer, Thomas Talcott, who worked for Dow Corning in 1976, testified for the plaintiffs regarding his feelings during the product's development that leakage was possible).

14-4e PRIVITY ISSUES IN TORT THEORIES OF PRODUCT LIABILITY

Privity is not the standard for recovery in negligence actions. The standard for recovery in negligence actions is whether the injury that resulted was foreseeable and foreseeable to that particular party. For example, a manufacturer of toasters can foresee use by children and would have a duty to warn that they should not use the equipment unless supervised by adults. A manufacturer of a weed killer could foresee the presence of dogs, cats, and other pets in a yard sprayed with the killer and should either make the product not harmful to them or warn of the need to keep them away from the sprayed area for a certain period of time. Children and pets certainly have no privity with the manufacturers, but they can recover from

EXHIBIT 14.3 Comparison of Product Liability Theories

TYPE	PRIVITY REQUIRED?	KNOWLEDGE OF PROBLEM REQUIRED?	WARRANTY PROMISE REQUIRED?
Negligence	No	Yes	No
Section 402A/Strict tort liability	No	No	No
Express warranty	Yes	No	Yes
Implied warranty of merchantability	Yes	No	No
Implied warranty of fitness for a particular purpose	Yes	No	Yes

© Cengage Learning

EXHIBIT 14.4 Legal Basis for Product Liability

CONTRACT	TORT
Express warranty	402A—Strict tort liability
Implied warranty of merchantability	Elements
Implied warranty of fitness for particular purpose	(1) Defective condition unreasonably dangerous: design, manufacturing defect, or inadequate warning
	(2) Defendant in business of using, selling, or manufacturing product
	(3) Condition of product is the same Negligence elements are the same and add:
	(4) Knowledge of defect

© Cengage Learning

the manufacturer (or their parents and owners can) on the basis of the foreseeability of the children's and pets' presence and the foreseeability of the danger causing their injuries.

Likewise, parties other than the product manufacturer may be responsible for defective conditions in the products and can be held liable for their participation. For example, parts manufacturers may be held liable if it can be shown that defects in their parts resulted in a product's defect and the injury to the plaintiff. Exhibit 14.3 compares product liability theories, and Exhibit 14.4 details the basis for product liability.

14-5 Defenses to Product Liability Torts

Three defenses are available to a defendant in a product liability tort:

1. Misuse or abnormal use of a product
2. Contributory negligence
3. Assumption of risk

14-5a MISUSE OR ABNORMAL USE OF A PRODUCT

Any use of a product that the manufacturer has specifically warned against in its instructions is a **misuse**. Using a forklift to lift 25,000 pounds when the instructions limit its capacity to 15,000 pounds is a misuse of the product, and any injuries resulting from such misuse will not be the liability of the manufacturer. Product misuse also occurs when a plaintiff has used the product in a manner that the defendant could not anticipate and warn against.

14-5b CONTRIBUTORY NEGLIGENCE

Contributory negligence is traditionally a complete defense to a product liability suit in negligence. For example, although a front loader might have a design failure of no protective netting around the driver, a driver who is injured while using the front loader for recreational purposes is contributorily negligent. Contributory negligence overlaps greatly with product misuse.

Some states, as discussed in Chapter 9, have adopted a standard of **comparative negligence**, under which the plaintiff's negligence is not a complete defense: The negligence of the plaintiff merely serves to reduce the amount the plaintiff is entitled to recover. For example, a jury might find that the defendant is 60 percent at fault and the plaintiff is 40 percent at fault. The plaintiff recovers, but the amount of that recovery is reduced by 40 percent.

14-5c ASSUMPTION OF RISK

When a plaintiff is aware of a danger in the product but goes ahead and uses it anyway, **assumption of risk** occurs. If a car manufacturer recalled your car for repair and you failed to have the repair done, despite full opportunity to do so, you have assumed the risk of driving with that problem.

Patch v Hillerich & Bradsby Co. (Case 14.6) involves issues of assumption of risk and also brings together many of the issues in product liability that you have studied in this chapter.

| CASE 14.6 | *Patch v Hillerich & Bradsby Co.* 257 P.3d 383 (Mont. 2011) |

The Mighty Aluminum Bat

FACTS

While pitching in an American Legion baseball game on July 25, 2003, 18-year-old Brandon Patch was struck in the head by a batted ball that was hit using Hillerich & Bradsby's (H & B) model CB–13 aluminum bat. Tragically, Brandon died from his injuries.

The Patches brought suit against H & B for the wrongful death of their son on the grounds that the CB–13 aluminum bat was in a defective condition because of the enhanced risks associated with its use: It increased the velocity speed of a batted ball when it left

the bat, thus decreasing infielders' reaction times, and resulted in a greater number of high-energy batted balls in the infield. Some studies note that the average time needed for a pitcher to react to a batted ball is 0.4 seconds. Analysis of the sound recording from the game confirmed that the reaction time available to Brandon to turn away or defend himself was only 0.376 of a second.

Before trial, the District Court granted H & B's motion for summary judgment on Patches' manufacturing defect claim, but denied summary judgment on Patches' design defect and failure to-warn claims. The trial court excluded H & B's assumption of the

CONTINUED

risk defense. The jury concluded that the model CB–13 aluminum bat was not designed defectively, but determined that the bat was in a defective condition due to H & B's failure to warn of the enhanced risks associated with its use. The jury awarded the Patches an $850,000 verdict on their failure-to-warn claim. H & B appealed.

JUDICIAL OPINION

WHEAT, Justice

H & B asserts that only the individual batting (actual user) and the individual who purchased the bat (actual consumer) can assert a failure to warn claim in this case. H & B's narrow interpretation of the terms user and consumer is contrary to the definition of the terms as contained in the *Restatement (Second) of Torts* § 402A.

The realities of the game of baseball support the District Court's decision to submit Patches' failure to warn claim to the jury. The bat is an indispensible part of the game. The risk of harm accompanying the bat's use extends beyond the player who holds the bat in his or her hands. A warning of the bat's risks to only the batter standing at the plate inadequately communicates the potential risk of harm posed by the bat's increased exit speed. In this context, all of the players, including Brandon, were users or consumers placed at risk by the increased exit speed caused by H & B's bat. H & B is subject to liability to all players in the game, including Brandon, for the physical harm caused by its bat's increased exit speed.

In *Macrie v SDS Biotech Corp.*, 267 N.J.Super. 34, 630 A.2d 805 (N.J.Super.App.Div.1993), employees of a produce broker were seriously injured after being exposed to a toxic fungicide while they unpacked produce that had been treated with the fungicide by a farmer who had sold the produce to their employer. The employees brought a failure to warn claim against the manufacturer of the fungicide. As H & B does here, the manufacturer argued that it was not feasible, i.e., "workable," to warn the employees of the risks associated with the fungicide. The *Macrie* court rejected the manufacturer's argument and concluded that the feasibility of providing warnings is a jury question:

> [W]here a jury could find that plaintiff's foreseeable exposure [to the fungicide] would threaten them with serious physical harm, the jury could also determine that minimizing the danger warranted unusually strenuous efforts to provide them with warnings and instructions.

H & B's second argument incorrectly limits the scope of the warning by erroneously assuming that placing a warning directly on the bat is the only method

to provide a warning. While placing a warning directly on a product is one method of warning, other methods of warning exist, including, but not limited to, issuing oral warnings and placing warnings in advertisements, posters, and media releases. ("[O]ther means of communication such as advertisements, posters, releases to be read and signed … or oral warnings … could easily have been undertaken.…"). Such warnings, if issued by H & B in this case, would have communicated to all players the potential risk of harm associated with H & B's bat's increased exit speed. H & B's false assumption fails to establish the absence of genuine issues of material fact.

Because genuine issues of material fact exist regarding the scope of the warning and because the "workability" of providing a warning is a jury question, the District Court properly denied H & B summary judgment on its causation argument.

In a failure to warn case, the plaintiff has the burden of proving (1) the product was sold in a defective condition due to the lack of or an inadequate warning, (2) the defect caused the injury, and (3) the defect is traceable to the defendant. The policy underlying products liability—protecting the consuming public by requiring manufacturers to bear the burden of injuries caused by defective products—requires courts to apply a flexible standard of proof. The nature and quality of evidence used in products liability cases to demonstrate causation varies, and the death or inability of the plaintiff to testify is one of the factors influencing the requisite standard of proof.

The District Court properly allowed the jury to infer that Patches would have heeded a warning had one been given.

In certain situations … where the consequences … are severe, the lack of warning is undisputed, and the person … is dead, the jury may be permitted to infer that a warning would have been heeded and that the failure to warn was a proximate cause of the injury. Not only would it be virtually impossible to prove what the decedent would have done had he been warned, but, as a practical matter, nothing more is added in this case by having a witness merely state that, had the danger been known … he would have acted to avoid the danger. H & B argues that because Brandon had been hit by batted balls before, he knew he could be hit and, therefore, assumed the risk when he continued playing baseball. [a] manufacturer [can] assert the affirmative defense of assumption of the risk where "[t]he user or consumer of the product discovered the defect or the defect was open and obvious and the user or consumer unreasonably made use of the product and was injured by it."

Assumption of the risk was not applicable here because there is no evidence that Brandon actually

CONTINUED

knew he would be seriously injured or killed when pitching to a batter using one of H & B's model CB–13 aluminum bats. In other words, H & B failed to show that Brandon was aware of the enhanced risks associated with the model CB–13 aluminum bat, and, knowing that, he voluntarily proceeded to pitch to a batter using that bat.

The District Court properly denied H & B's motion for summary judgment on Patches' failure to warn claim because H & B is subject to liability to all players, including Brandon, for the physical harm caused by its bat's increased exit speed, and genuine issues of material fact existed regarding the causation element of Patches' claim. A new trial is not warranted.

We affirm.

CASE QUESTIONS

1. What does the court say about the argument that it was difficult to warn Brandon about the bat?

2. What does the court say about assumption of risk by Brandon in playing baseball and the fact that he had been hit by baseballs before?

3. Is Brandon a "user" or "consumer" for purposes of strict tort liability?

ETHICAL ISSUES

In 1994, a group of Chrysler engineers met to review proposals and recommendations for improving their Chrysler Caravan (a Caravan) lines in order to make them more competitive. Paul Sheridan, one of the engineers on Chrysler's Caravan Safety Team, raised the number one issue on the lists of proposals and recommendations: The latches on the Caravan rear doors appeared to be popping open, even in low-speed crashes. The Chrysler Caravan latches did not appear to have the strength of either the Ford Windstar or the Chevy van rear door latches. Mr. Sheridan proposed that Chrysler make the latches stronger and use that strength as a marketing tool.

After Mr. Sheridan made his proposal, and according to testimony in a subsequent product liability suit, a top production engineer told Mr. Sheridan, "That ship has sailed. We told you that last time. Next subject."

In *Jimenez v Chrysler Corporation*, 269 F.3d 439 (4th Cir. 2001), the jury deliberated only 2.5 hours before returning a verdict for the Jimenez family of $262.5 million, $250 million of which was punitive damages.

Chrysler replaced the latches on 4.3 million Caravans manufactured since 1984. Chrysler spent $115 million for that replacement program on everything from notification to installation and estimates that about 61 percent of the van latches have now been replaced.

The number of deaths from ejection through the rear Caravan doors is 37, which is 11 more than the fatalities from the Ford Pinto exploding gas tank defect but well short of GM's 168 fatalities in side-saddle gas tank collisions in that company's pickups.

The following evidence came out in the *Jimenez* case:

- Chrysler initially used a latch in its vans that the rest of the industry had abandoned.

- When it switched to a better latch, still not meeting federal standards for passenger vehicles, it did not notify the owners of existing vans of the change and safety issues.

- Chrysler destroyed documentation on Caravan crash tests, including films and computer records. (The company says that such destruction was part of its routine document destruction program; however, a juror noted, following the trial, that only the documentation on the collisions in which the rear door was affected was destroyed. Chrysler still had the documentation on the vans' front-end collision tests.)

- Engineers proposed adding a latch strengthener for a cost of about $0.25 per vehicle in 1990, but the plan was vetoed by Chrysler executives because it was believed such an addition would be tantamount to an admission to regulators that the latches were not safe, and Chrysler had been taking the position that the latches were indeed safe.

- Chrysler used political clout to prevent a 1994 recall by NHTSA of the vehicles for latch replacement; a letter from Chrysler Vice Chairman Tom Denomme to Chairman Robert Eaton and President Robert Lutz read, "If we want to use political pressure to try to quash a recall letter; we need to go now." Chrysler officials helped staff members for Representative John Dingell of Michigan (the ranking Democrat on the House Commerce Committee, which supervises the NHTSA) draft a letter objecting to the recall. NHTSA postponed the recall. When the recall was made in 1995, there was no acknowledgment that the latches were defective or that there was any safety issue.

Following the verdict, one juror said the evidence painted a picture of corporate indifference and added, "We want people to understand why we made the decision we did. We knew what we were doing. When you speak to a company as big as Chrysler, you've got to speak on terms they understand." Another juror noted that executives answered, "I don't know. I don't remember. I can't recall," too often to have much credibility.

Chrysler had been the first mover in the van market. Its product filled a niche in the family auto market, and it occupied a unique position in terms of federal regulation in that there were no applicable federal standards for the lifting rear door on the van. Chrysler used latch designs and parts that had been banned in passenger vehicles for years precisely because of the risk of ejection and associated high fatality rates. However, the lack of federal regulations on the vans meant that Chrysler violated no law in using the outmoded systems and parts.

When Chrysler began to receive notice of accidents and began holding design and marketing meetings in 1993, lawyers ordered that no notes be taken at meetings, and minutes of meetings were collected and destroyed.

Why were punitive damages appropriate in this case? Are they too high? What message do the punitive damages send to businesses? What should Chrysler do internally to be certain such a series of events does not happen again?

14-6 Product Liability Reform

The ALI has proposed the *Restatement (Third) of Torts,* which would change the current strict liability standard to a negligence standard for defective design and informational defect cases. In other words, plaintiffs who bring product liability cases based on defective design and instruction would have to establish negligence to recover. The strict liability standard would be eliminated under this new proposal. Strict liability would still be the standard for manufacturing defects.

14-7 Federal Standards for Product Liability

14-7a CONSUMER PRODUCT SAFETY COMMISSION

The federal level of government generally is not involved in product liability issues. However, the **Consumer Product Safety Commission (CPSC)** is a regulatory agency set up under the Consumer Product Safety Act to regulate safety standards for consumer products. The commission has several responsibilities in carrying out its purposes.

1. *To protect the public against unreasonable risks of injury from consumer products—* To perform this function, the CPSC has been given the authority to recall products and order their repair or correction. The commission also has the power to ban products completely. This ban can apply only if a product cannot be made less dangerous. In 1994, the CPSC recalled nearly all types of metal bunk beds. In 2007, the CPSC worked with Mattel on its recall of 19 million toys that had been made in China using lead-based paint, something banned in the United States. In 2008, the CPSC's authority was

expanded by the **Consumer Product Safety Improvement Act (CPSIA)** to cover secondhand sales because of the lead paint issue that affects so many used toys. Garage sales are now subject to federal product disclosure standards.

2. *To develop standards for consumer product safety*—These standards take the form of regulations and minimum requirements for certain products.

3. *To help consumers become more informed about evaluating safety*—Certain regulations require disclosure of the limits of performance and hazards associated with using a particular product.

4. To fund research in matters of product safety design and in product-caused injuries and illnesses

The act carries civil penalties of up to a maximum of $1,500,000. Knowing or willful violations carry a criminal fine of up to $100,000 and/or one year's imprisonment, and willful repeat violations carry penalties of up to $500,000 and 10 years. In addition, consumers have a right to sue in federal district court for any damages they sustain because of a violation of a regulation or law.

14-8 International Issues in Product Liability

The EU directive on product liability limits liability to "producers"; it is not as inclusive as U.S. law, which holds all sellers liable. A 10-year limit on liability and the "state-of-the-art" defense apply to most member countries: If a product upon its release was as good as any available, it is not subject to product liability.

In addition to the council's guidelines are the International Standards Organization's 9000 Guidelines for Quality Assurance and Quality Management. These directives require products to carry a stamp of compliance with standards and procedures as a means of limiting product defects.

The CISG (see Chapter 7 for more details) contains similar provisions to the UCC warranty protections for goods sold in international transactions. However, disclaimers are made more easily under the CISG and the notions of consequential damages are limited because the United States' level of damages in product liability cases far exceeds the levels for any other country in the world. Further, the notion of strict liability for products is unique to the United States, and under EU guidelines, the notion of knowledge is used as a standard for imposing liability.

Consider...

IKEA learned that one of its meat products contained horse meat. The company's Swedish meatballs were tested in the Czech Republic, and officials found traces of horse meat. IKEA withdrew its Swedish meatballs from 14 European countries. During early 2013, Nestlé and other large European food producers learned that some suppliers had been selling them meat products that were not made entirely of beef. Horse meat costs about one-fourth of the cost of beef. IKEA pulled the meatballs from its stores and in-store cafeterias. Food sales account for about 5 percent of IKEA's total store revenues.

Discuss IKEA's liability for the defective meatballs if the company did not produce them. What about the liability of the suppliers?

ETHICAL ISSUES

In some cases, products outlawed in the United States are sold outside the United States. In a practice referred to as dumping, the products are sold without mention of the U.S. recall or any litigation pending. What can be done about firms that sell defective products in third-world countries? For example, the original type of IUD and non–flame-retardant pajamas were dumped after problems developed in the United States. Discuss the ethical issues.

BIOGRAPHY

The Charming and Dangerous Toy

Buckyballs and Buckycubes were high-powered, small rare earth magnets that were imported into the United States by Maxfield and Oberton Holdings, LLC from Ningo Prosperous Imports & Exports in Ningbo City, China. The products, which consist of individual magnets packaged as aggregated masses in different size containers of 10, 125, and 216 magnets, became enormously popular with over 3,000,000 of the products sold within the United States. Initially, ads for Buckyballs compared them to the wildly successful hula hoops and Silly Putty of the 1960s. That comparison brought a new customer base for the product, and by 2009, Buckyballs were being sold as an adult executive toy and/or stress reliever. The price range for Buckyballs was $19.95 to $100.00.

Children under the age of 14 (52 of them) ingested the Buckyballs. Their powerful magnetic force caused the intestinal walls to pinch or create a trap, a condition that resulted in progressive tissue injury. Some children became septic and removal required endoscopic or surgical procedures, procedures that left children with permanent scarring. The greatest danger was that the symptoms began as simply a stomach upset and treatment was often not pursued, with the result being progressive deterioration of the intestines. Because Buckyballs were such a new and fast-moving phenomenon, many physicians were not aware of the source of the intestinal problems they were trying to diagnose, something that resulted in further delays in treatment.

The only warning that appeared on Buckyballs was, "Warning: Not intended for children. Swallowing of magnets may cause serious injury and require immediate medical care. Ages 13+." The CPSC concluded that the warning was not sufficient to reflect the real danger and consequences of ingestion. In 2010, Buckyballs had new packaging, new warnings, and new instructions, and the old products with the faulty warning were recalled. Despite these efforts, ingestion among children continued with the most severe cases causing injury to the windpipes and esophaguses of young children.

The CPSC issued a safety alert in 2011, but the ingestion continued because children thought that Buckyballs looked like candy and older children tried to mimic tongue piercing by placing them on their tongues, thereby resulting in accidental swallowing of the magnets.

At that point, the CPSC ruled that warnings could never be effective because once Buckyballs are removed from their packaging there is no longer any warning about their use. On July 25, 2012, the CPSC issued a mandatory product recall after failing to reach an agreement for a voluntary recall with the product importing company.[3]

Summary

How does advertising create liability for a business?

- Express warranty—contractual promise about nature or potential of product that gives right of recovery if product falls short of a promise that was a basis of the bargain

- Bait and switch—using cheaper, unavailable product to lure customers to store with a more expensive one, which is then substituted or offered instead

- Federal Trade Commission (FTC)—federal agency responsible for regulating deceptive ads

- Wheeler-Lea Act—federal law that allows FTC to regulate "unfair and deceptive acts or practices"

- Celebrity endorsements—FTC area of regulation wherein products are touted by easily recognized public figures

- Consent decree—voluntary settlement of FTC complaint

What are the contract theories of product liability?

- Implied warranty of merchantability— warranty of average quality, purity, and adequate packaging given in every sale by a merchant

- Implied warranty of fitness for a particular purpose—warranty given in circumstances in which the buyer relies on the seller's expertise and acts to purchase according to that advice

- Disclaimer—act of negating warranty coverage

- Privity—direct contractual relationship between parties

What is required for tort-based recovery on a defective product? What is strict tort liability for products?

- Strict liability—standard of liability that requires compensation for an injury regardless of fault or prior knowledge

- *Restatement (Second)* § 402A—American Law Institute's standards for imposing strict liability for defective products

- Negligence—standard of liability that requires compensation for an injury only if the party responsible knew or should have known of its potential to cause such injury

- Punitive damages—damages beyond compensation for knowledge that conduct was wrongful

What defenses exist in product liability?

- Misuse—product liability defense for plaintiff using a product incorrectly

- Contributory negligence—conduct by plaintiff that contributed to plaintiff's injury; serves as a bar to recovery

- Comparative negligence—negligent conduct by plaintiff serves as a partial defense by reducing liability by percentage of fault

- Assumption of risk—defense to negligence available when plaintiff is told of product risk and voluntarily uses the product

What reforms have occurred and are proposed in product liability?

- Consumer Product Safety Commission—federal agency that regulates product safety and has recall power

- Consumer Product Safety Improvement Act of 2008—expands authority to secondhand sales

Questions and Problems

1. A 30-minute infomercial for the DeLonghi America Caffe Sienna espresso/cappuccino machine included this statement from the host/announcer:

Brew cappuccino just like the pros do right at home. Up until now, the home machines, they just didn't work.

The FTC ad division approached Jim McCrusker, the president of the U.S. unit of DeLonghi, on the grounds that the ad was misleading. The ad division, reacting to complaints from competitors, wanted Mr. McCrusker to add language that indicated it wasn't that other machines didn't work. The machines worked, but their frothing processes were not good.

Mr. McCrusker brought in other machines and consumers to talk with the ad division. The presentation of competitors' machines, along with testimonials from consumers about the problems with other machines, convinced the ad council that the statement "They didn't work" was indeed accurate for more than just the frothing process.

What lessons are learned from Mr. McCrusker's experience? Is documentation for ad claims important? Is it appropriate for competitors to complain to a regulatory body about ad content? [*Sunbeam Products, Inc. v DeLonghi America, Inc.*, Not Reported in F. Supp. 2d, 2007 WL 1321134 (D.N.J.)]

2. Richard W. La Trace attended an auction at B & B Antiques, Auction & Realty, a business owned and operated by Ray Webster, Deborah Webster, Bo Webster, and Laura Webster. La Trace purchased five lamps that were identified at the auction as "Tiffany" lamps and one lampshade that was also identified at the auction as a "Tiffany" product. La Trace spent a total of $56,200 on the lamps.

La Trace contacted Fontaine's Auction Gallery to inquire about selling the lamps in an auction. Fontaine's sent Dean Lowry, an expert in Tiffany products, to examine La Trace's lamps and Lowry determined that the lamps were not authentic Tiffany products but were, in fact, reproductions.

La Trace filed suit against the Websters and B & B for fraudulent misrepresentation, breach of warranty, breach of contract, and negligence. The Websters claimed they thought the lamps were authentic and pointed out that their sales brochure and "Conditions of Auction" document contained the following disclaimer:

All property is sold AS IS WHERE IS, and we make NO guarantees, warranties or representations, expressed or implied, with respect to the property or the correctness of the catalog or other description of authenticity of authorship, physical condition, size, quality, rarity, importance, provenance, exhibitions, literature or historical relevance of the property or otherwise. No statement anywhere, whether oral or written, shall be deemed such a guarantee, warranty or representation.

The trial court granted summary judgment to the Websters, indicating that La Trace trusted blindly and should not have done so. Discuss the issues of express warranty, disclaimer, and buyer's reliance in this example and determine how the appellate court should decide the case. La Trace appealed. [*La Trace v Webster*, 17 So.3d 1210 (Ala. Civ. App. 2008)]

3. Michael Sanders was a 40-year-old man who made his living as a member of various music bands throughout Fresno. Mr. Sanders graduated from Fresno State University in May 2004 and planned to teach music. On August 20, 2004, Fresno police officers responded to a call made at the Sanders's home. When the police entered, they found Mr. Sanders, who appeared disoriented, standing unclothed behind his wife, Lavette Sanders. The officers decided to subdue Mr. Sanders by firing Tasers at his naked body, although Fresno Police Department rules and other instructions require that Tasers not come in contact with human skin. The officers fired numerous Taser darts into Mr. Sanders's body. The officers then handcuffed Sanders, placed him face down on a gurney, which suffocated him, and then placed him in an ambulance. Sanders stopped breathing. One of the officers attempted CPR, but Michael Sanders was pronounced dead at 4:30 A.M.

Mrs. Sanders filed suit against the city of Fresno as well as Taser. She based her suit against Taser on, among other things, that Taser expressly warranted that the product was "safe" and "would not cause injuries to police officers or individuals arrested by police officers." Is this the language of an express warranty? [*Sanders v City of Fresno*, 2006 WL 1883394 (E.D. Cal. 2006), 59 UCC Rep.Serv.2d 1209]

4. Wade Lederman, 31, was at a Fourth of July pool party at a relative's house in 1991. At about 10:30 P.M., Mr. Lederman, his brother, and two others decided to go swimming. They jumped from the sides of the pool into the water and also dove from the pool's diving board. At about midnight, Mr. Lederman dove into the pool from the side and struck his head on the bottom, sustaining permanent physical and neurological injuries.

The pool in which Mr. Lederman was injured is a residential swimming pool that is in-ground and oval-shaped, with a shallow end and a deep end. The pool has three steps at the shallow end by which swimmers can enter the pool. A white line one foot wide is painted on the bottom of the pool between the shallow end and the deep end. At the start of that line, the depth increases to 7 feet and then slowly descends to a depth of 10 feet at the diving-board end of the pool.

Mr. Lederman filed suit against Pacific Industries, Inc., the pool manufacturer, for its failure to display water depths in and around the pool; failure to warn as to which areas were not appropriate for diving; failure to warn that at night, with pool lights on, the depth of the pool was deceptive; and failure to warn that the white line was just the start of the deep end and not a line for diving versus nondiving areas of the pool.

Should Mr. Lederman recover from Pacific? [*Lederman v Pacific Industries Inc.*, 119 F.3d 551 (7th Cir. 1997)]

5. On August 6, 1998, Mr. Ruvolo purchased two chicken gordita sandwiches from Taco Bell. While eating the second sandwich, he felt a sharp pain in his throat and dislodged a chicken bone. The bone caused a scrape in his throat, and, as a result, he was treated at an emergency room. The following day, Mr. Ruvolo was diagnosed with acute tonsillitis, pharyngitis, sinusitis, and gastritis.

Mr. Ruvulo sued Taco Bell and its food distributors, alleging that the infections were due to the chicken bone's scratching his throat and causing an opening where germs and bacteria could enter. He further alleged that Taco Bell and its food distributors were liable because of their failure to properly inspect the chicken. Discuss the theories Mr. Ruvulo might use for recovery and who the defendants might be. [*Ruvolo v Homovich*, 778 N.E.2d 661 (Ohio App. 2002)]

6. Nintendo's Wii video game system features games with simulation of tennis and boxing. To play the game, the players use a motion-sensitive controller in their hand. When playing the game, some players, in making the motions necessary for the sport, have lost control of their controllers. The controllers have crashed into other objects, including television sets, and injured the players. Players who have been injured brought a class action suit against Nintendo for a defective wrist strap on the controllers, designed to keep the controllers from flying out of control. Could there be remedies for the design of the physical equipment used with computers? [*Elvig v Nintendo of America, Inc.*, 696 F. Supp. 2d 1207 (D. Colo. 2010)]

7. Roy E. Farrar Produce Co. ordered a shipment of boxes from International Paper Company that were to be suitable for the packing and storage of tomatoes. The dimensions of the two sizes of boxes were to be such that either 20 or 30 pounds of tomatoes could be packed without the necessity of weighing each box. Mr. Farrar requested that the boxes be the same type as those supplied to Florida packers for shipping tomatoes. Mr. Farrar told Mr. Wilson, an agent for International, to obtain the correct specifications for the Florida-type box.

International shipped Mr. Farrar 21,500 unassembled boxes at a unit price of 64 cents per box. The boxes were not tomato boxes, were not Florida boxes,

did not have adequate stacking strength, and would not hold up during shipping. Mr. Farrar had to repack 3,624 boxes (at a cost of $1.92 per box). Substitute boxes were purchased for 10 cents above the International price. The replacement boxes were Florida boxes and did not collapse. Mr. Farrar was also forced to pay growers $6 a box for tomatoes damaged during shipping. He could not use 6,100 boxes, and his sales dropped off, resulting in financial deficiencies in his operation. Can Mr. Farrar recover for his damages? Why or why not? [*International Paper Co. v Farrar*, 700 P.2d 642 (N.M. 1985)]

8. Ms. Hubbs, 80, suffered from arthritis and osteoporosis. She purchased the Clapper, a device designed to turn electrical appliances on by responding to sound, namely, the clapping of hands.

Ms. Hubbs did not follow the instructions in the product to adjust its sensitivity. As a result of continual hard clapping, Ms. Hubbs broke her wrists. Ms. Hubbs also did not follow the product instructions to use (buy) a clicker available for the product if clapping is a chore. She sued the Clapper's manufacturer for breach of the warranty of merchantability. Should she recover? [*Hubbs v Joseph Enterprises*, 604 N.Y.S.2d 292 (1993)]

9. On February 14, 1999, Garry O. Hickman opened a pack of Big Red gum, which is manufactured by Wrigley. Mr. Hickman purchased the gum at a grocery store on the evening of February 13, 1999. Mr. Hickman unwrapped the package, which was still sealed, and put two pieces of the gum into his mouth. Mr. Hickman provided the following description of the events that occurred after he began to chew the gum:

> [A]fter I started chewing the gum I bit down on it, uh, when I bit down on it the tooth exploded in my mouth. I begin to get all of this stuff out of my mouth, tooth fragments all over my mouth and everything. The screw turned up and stuck up in the top of my gum. I had to pull it out which caused me a lot of pain and all and everything and it was very uncomfortable there for a while.

Mr. Hickman sought treatment from Dr. Conly on February 18, 1999. One of Mr. Hickman's bottom teeth was fragmented. Those fragments chipped his top front teeth. Dr. Conly recommended that Mr. Hickman have surgery, which would total approximately $905, to remove the fractured tooth. However, Mr. Hickman had been unable to do so because he could not afford the surgery. His gums stayed sore for several weeks.

Mr. Hickman filed suit against Wrigley. Can he recover? What theories might he try? [*Hickman v Wm. Wrigley, Jr. Co., Inc.*, 768 So.2d 812 (La. App. 2000)]

10. New Colt Holding Corporation advertises its Model P single-action revolver as "the gun that won the west." Competitors have filed suit for false advertising because historical significance is important to gun purchasers and such false claims would draw away customers.

Also, its competitors argue that the Winchester 73 rifle is actually the gun that won the west. Is this false advertising? Analyze the statement and determine whether it is an express warranty. Also, determine if the FTC would deem the claim to be false or deceptive advertising. [*New Colt Holding Corp. v RJG Holdings of Florida, Inc.*, 312 F. Supp. 2d 195 (D. Conn. 2004)]

PUBLIC POLICY, ECONOMICS, THE LAW

What If Your Product Is Tempting, but Not Healthy?

One of the evolving product liability issues is whether sellers and manufacturers can be held liable for the dangers inherent in their products, placed there not by design but by nature. For example, eggs that contain a harmful disease or that were injected with a virus would be unreasonably dangerous and subject to product liability recovery claims. However, could there be recovery from egg producers because of the effects of eggs on body cholesterol levels? And is McDonald's liable because its high-calorie, high-fat foods have resulted in weight gains and obesity in those who frequent this restaurant chain? The courts have been fairly consistent in ruling that the use of a nondefective product with adequate warnings does not result in liability for the manufacturer because such a result would hold manufacturers liable for the criminal conduct of others.

The courts have not been willing to hold manufacturers of alcoholic beverages responsible for the deaths and injuries following accidents caused by those who have consumed their products and then driven drunk. For example, in *Greif v Anheuser-Busch Companies, Inc.*, 114 F. Supp. 2d 100 (D. Conn. 2000), a court held that beer producers could not be held liable to those killed or injured by drunk drivers because misuse of the product and its use in combination with other activities can result in dangerous conditions, but the product itself was neither defective nor inherently dangerous. In *Cook v MillerCoors, LLC*, 829 F. Supp. 2d 1208 (M.D. Fla. 2011), a motorcycle rider was injured following an accident involving a driver who had consumed "Sparks," alcoholic beverages that contain caffeine and other stimulants that are sold by MillerCoors.

The argument was that the caffeine results in more alcohol consumption because the effects of intoxication are reduced. The court held that precedent on conventional alcoholic beverage manufacturers' immunity from liability applied also in the case of alcoholic beverages mixed with stimulants. There is no duty to warn about the effects of excessive alcohol consumption, with or without caffeine. It is interesting that the court commented that there is a distinction between a "moral" duty to warn and a legal duty to do so.

Several plaintiffs attempted to bring class action suits against McDonald's as parents of obese teens who suffer from diabetes and high blood pressure that they claim resulted from their frequenting McDonald's restaurants.[4] The cases, which wound through the federal court system for over five years, sought to impose liability on McDonald's, not for defective food, but for the harms resulting from customer overindulgence in that product. The implications of a finding of liability would be tremendously costly for the restaurant industry. The courts have declined to certify class actions in these cases with the result being that the cases end.[5] There are now federal and state laws and regulations that require restaurants to make prescribed nutritional, fat, and caloric disclosures about their menu items. However, the liability of restaurants for health consequences of their food would be a destructive cost for the industry with significant economic effects. The issues of health related to "fast-food" consumption are now addressed through disclosures as well as consumer education efforts on eating a healthy diet.

Notes

1. "The Top 10 Jury Verdicts of 2012," *Lawyers USA Online*, January 21, 2013, http://lawyersusaonline.com/blog/2013/01/21/top-10-jury-verdicts-of-2012.

2. A copy of the order and complaint against the company can be found at the Consumer Product Safety Commission website, http://www.cpsc.gov//PageFiles/131696/maxfield1a.pdf.

3. The full history of the McDonald's case is summarized *Pelman v McDonald's Corp.* (*Pelman III*), 396 F.3d 508, 510 (2nd Cir. 2005), which eventually ended with four iterations and a dismissal in 2010 for the class action, but individual suits continue.

4. *Pelman v McDonald's Corp.*, 272 F.R.D. 82 (S.D.N.Y. 2010).

Chapter 15

PRODUCTS:
Business Intellectual Property

The red soles on the bottom of Louboutin designer shoes. The House of Windsor. The estates of Elvis, Princess Diana, and Albert Einstein. Louis Vuitton. NASCAR. Octomom. The common thread? They all have lucrative arrangements for their trademarks, images, and symbols. The law affords protection for these images and symbols even though the property right is a bundle of images and feelings about a person, business, or logo. This chapter covers the rights of businesses and their intellectual property. Property comes in different forms, and this chapter focuses on one form of personal property: intellectual property rights. What types of intellectual property does a business own? What are the rights and issues in this property owned by a business? What statutory protections exist for intellectual property? What issues of property protection exist in international business operations? In marketing, we learn the importance of "brand." This chapter gives the legal backdrop for ensuring a brand's exclusivity. Protecting the goodwill, symbols, names, and motifs that give a business its identity is an important part of the ongoing success of a business.[1]

UPDATE
For up-to-date legal news, go to **mariannejennings.com**

Bo Chambers/Flickr/Getty Images

Possession is nine points of the law. No, it's not. Paperwork is.

Harvard Business Review,
September/October 1995

Consider...

Joel Tenenbaum was a student at Goucher College who developed file-sharing software that permitted 30 music recordings copyrighted by Sony to be downloaded and distributed without Sony's authorization. Sony brought suit for damages and a permanent injunction. The district court entered judgment against Tenenbaum as to liability. The jury found that Tenenbaum's infringement of the copyrights at issue was willful and awarded Sony statutory damages of $22,500 for each infringed recording, for a total of $675,000. Tenenbaum was stunned and appealed because he had no intention to infringe copyrights and the damages were excessive. What should the appellate court do?

We must take care to guard against two extremes equally prejudicial: the one, that men of ability, who have employed their time for the service of the community, may not be deprived of their just merits, and the reward for their ingenuity and labour; the other, that the world may not be deprived of improvements, nor the progress of the arts retarded.

Sayre v Moore
102 Eng. Rep. 138, 140 (1785)

15-1 What Can a Business Own? Intangible Property Rights

When we see a Dreyer's or Edy's Ice Cream truck driving along beside us, we understand that Dreyer's or Edy's Ice Cream owns that truck; it is a part of the Dreyer/Edy fleet and is carried as business equipment on the books of the Dreyer/Edy corporation. If someone took that truck, it would be theft, and Dreyer's or Edy's would be entitled to compensation if the truck were damaged or destroyed by the theft. Dreyer's or Edy's would also be entitled to compensation if someone hit the truck in an accident and damaged it. Because the truck is Dreyer's or Edy's property, these companies enjoy certain rights of ownership. If someone stole or damaged the truck, the business could recover for the damages. However, the business also owns the distinctive label, colors, and stripes that are part of the Dreyer's or Edy's packaging and labels. If someone uses those symbols of their quality ice cream, the business can recover for the resulting damages.

Painted onto ice cream trucks, you see the signature brown and white stripes that are part of the ice cream's packaging. You recognize the writing, "Dreyer's (or Edy's) Grand Ice Cream." You know the truck from its distinctive paint and writing, probably before you even read the name "Dreyer's" or "Edy's." That distinctive color scheme, name, and writing are also business property. The recognition and goodwill that come from those brown stripes and the name are forms of **intangible property** that enjoy statutory protections. These protections include Dreyer's/Edy's right to prevent others from using their distinctive names and colors, which represent the goodwill and reputation of the company. The name, colors, stripes, and symbols represent a bundle of valuable rights for the business.

Forms of intangible property include patents, copyrights, trademarks, trade names, trade dress, and trade secrets. The protections for these types of property rights come from federal laws, international treaties, and common law rights of action for the damage to or taking of these forms of intangible property.

15-2 Patents

Patents are a type of legal monopoly obtained by filing certain information and forms with the U.S. Patent Office. So fundamental is the protection of new products and processes that the founding fathers placed protection for inventors in Article 1, Section 8, of the U.S. Constitution.

15-2a THE TYPES AND LENGTH OF PATENTS

There are three forms of patents. *Utility* or *function patents* cover machines, processes, and improvements to existing devices. For example, a computerized method for tracking a dry cleaner's inventory of clothing is protected by a patent. Prior to 1995, such a patent was valid for 17 years. However, in order to bring the U.S. laws into compliance with GATT provisions (see Chapter 7 for more information on this treaty), the protection was extended to 20 years. All WTO members follow the 20-year period for protection.

Design patents are those that protect the features of a product. The lace configuration on Eve of Milady bridal gowns and Procter & Gamble's method for putting elasticized legs on its disposable diapers are examples of product designs protected by patent. Design patents are granted for 14 years.

Finally, *plant patents* are obtained by those who develop new forms of plants and hybrids. Plants patents also carry a 20-year protection.

15-2b WHAT YOU CAN PATENT: PATENTABILITY

Because protection is so extensive, an idea is patentable only if it is nonobvious, novel, and useful; and the idea must be reduced to some tangible form. The categories for patent eligibility include processes and machines as well as production of new matter. Whatever the category, the invention or process must be something that is new and nonobvious. New discoveries of existing matter are not patentable, but developing a process to extract that new matter for other use would be. For example, a discovery of a reproductive hormone in the male body is not patentable but a product to stop production of that hormone for birth control purposes can be patented. A microbiologist who developed a bacterium that would break down crude oil, a valuable tool for cleaning up oil spills, was initially denied a patent because he was not manufacturing something but just using something that was living. However, the U.S. Supreme Court held that developing a method for creating something that exists in nature is protected by the patent laws. [*Diamond v Chakrabarty*, 447 U.S. 303 (1980)]

Business methods patents have been an area of judicial controversy. For example, patent number 4,022,227, called Method of Concealing Baldness, is a step-by-step process for combing hair so as to create the classic "comb-over," to attempt to conceal baldness. These types of patents, often called *junk patents*, are distinguishable from those patents that are granted for a business method tied to a machine or step-by-step process for recycling or physical production. The courts have been restricting patents on marketing methods or structuring relationships that do not involve machines and production. In *Bilski v Kappos*, 130 S.Ct. 3218 (2010), the U.S.

Supreme Court further restricted the requirements for the patent of a process. In the case, the court held that two individuals' claimed invention for helping buyers and sellers of commodities in the energy market protect, or hedge, against the risk of price changes in the form of a mathematical formula was an "abstract idea" and not a patentable "process."

15-2c THE PATENT PROCESS

The **America Invents Act (AIA)** became effective in 2011. The act is significant because it changes the effective filing date of a claimed invention as the actual filing date of the patent or application for a patent, which changes us to a "first to invent" system from a "first to file system." This timing change gives entrepreneurs and inventors greater certainty and also puts the United States on equal footing with other countries that follow this same timing system. Also, inventors can now apply for an expedited patent process, an option that allows patent application processing within 12 months, reduced from the previous average processing period of three to four years. A special speedy process is also available for inventions that reduce greenhouse emissions or provide energy conservation. Once the patent is issued it is presumed to be valid, but challenges can be made for up to nine months after the date of issue.

15-2d WHAT A PATENT DOES

During these exclusive rights periods of 14 and 20 years, the patent holder has the sole rights to profits on sales.

Anyone who sells or uses a patented product or process without the consent of the patent holder has committed patent infringement. Infringement entitles the patent holder to a statutory action for damages. The patent holder (the plaintiff) in such a case need only show patent ownership and infringement of that patent. A Patent Office registration for a product or process, however, is not a guarantee of recovery. A court must still agree with the Patent Office determination that the product or process is nonobvious, useful, and novel—that is, an issue in every infringement case is whether the patent was properly granted.

Amazon.com had a battle with Barnes & Noble over the "One-Click" shopping method. Amazon.com obtained a patent for its buyers' shopping method that permits shoppers to place items in a virtual shopping cart and then click just one button when they are ready to purchase. The buyers need not go through the process of filling in shipping, billing, and credit information for each purchase.

Barnes & Noble created a similar "One-Click" shopping experience for its online customers, and Amazon.com sued for patent infringement. On appeal, a court held that Barnes & Noble could continue to use the "One-Click" method while the parties proceeded to trial on the issue of whether the "One-Click" patent was a valid one or simply an obvious convenience for online shoppers. The parties then settled the case. [*Amazon.com, Inc. v Barnes & Noble.com*, 239 F.3d 1343 (Fed. Cir. 2001)]

On the other hand, the peculiar shading and look of Oakley sunglasses survived judicial review and the court ordered an injunction against Sunglass Hut and others from selling sunglasses that had the same green or blue lens tinting for which Oakley held a patent. [*Oakley, Inc. v Sunglass Hut Intern.*, 2001 WL 1683252, 61 U.S.P.Q.2d 1658 (C.D. Cal., Dec. 7, 2001)]

CYBERLAW

© iStockPhoto.com /dra_schwartz

Consider...

Procter & Gamble (P&G) was issued patent number 4,455,333 on June 19, 1984, for an invention entitled "Doughs and Cookies Providing Storage-Stable Texture Variety." The patent covers a method of manufacturing ready-to-serve cookies that remain crispy on the outside and chewy on the inside for an extended shelf life. P&G markets these cookies under the Duncan Hines label.

P&G brought a patent infringement action against Nabisco Brands, Inc., which markets its own lines of dual-textured cookies called "Almost Home" and "Chewy Chips Ahoy." P&G also sued Keebler Company for its dual-textured cookie called "Soft Batch" and Frito-Lay, Inc., for its "Grandma's Rich and Chewy." Each of the defendants denies infringement. They have moved for dismissal of the case on grounds that the patent is invalid because baking cookies is not patentable. Do you agree? Would you protect P&G's process?

[*Procter & Gamble Co. v Nabisco Brands, Inc.*, 604 F. Supp. 1485 (D.C. Del. 1985)]

15-2e THE REMEDIES FOR PATENT INFRINGEMENT

Two types of remedies are available for patent infringement: monetary damages and injunctions. Injunctions can be temporary, as when the court orders a halt to production or use whilst it determines whether a patent is valid. However, there is also the possibility of a permanent injunction, one that stops the other party from using the process or product for the life of the patent because the injury to the patent holder is so great that money damages are insufficient compensation. One of the patent issues that has emerged in cyberspace is the use of permanent injunctions against competitors to prevent the use of patented processes, even with compensation. In *eBay, Inc. v MercExchange* (Case 15.1), the U.S. Supreme Court dealt with this important issue.

CASE 15.1	*eBay, Inc. v MercExchange, LLC* 547 U.S. 388 (2006)

Whether "Buy It Now" Is Halted for 20 Years

FACTS

eBay and its subsidiary, half.com, operate popular websites that allow private sellers to list goods they wish to sell at either an auction or a fixed price (its "Buy it Now" feature). MercExchange, LLC, sought to license its business-method patent to eBay, but the two companies could not reach an agreement. eBay still used the "Buy It Now" process. MercExchange filed suit for patent infringement and a jury found that eBay had infringed a valid patent and awarded MercExchange $29.5 million in damages. MercExchange requested a permanent injunction against eBay for use of its process, but the trial court denied the motion. The Court of Appeals reversed and the U.S. Supreme Court granted *certiorari*.

JUDICIAL OPINION

THOMAS, Justice

According to well-established principles of equity, a plaintiff seeking a permanent injunction must satisfy a four-factor test before a court may grant such relief. A plaintiff must demonstrate: (1) that it has suffered an irreparable injury; (2) that remedies available at law, such as monetary damages, are inadequate to compensate for that injury; (3) that, considering the balance of hardships between the plaintiff and defendant, a remedy in equity is warranted; and (4) that the public interest would not be disserved by a permanent injunction…. The decision to grant or deny permanent injunctive relief is an act of equitable discretion by the district court.

CONTINUED

The Patent Act … declares that "patents shall have the attributes of personal property," including "the right to exclude others from making, using, offering for sale, or selling the invention." According to the Court of Appeals, this statutory right to exclude alone justifies its general rule in favor of permanent injunctive relief. But the creation of a right is distinct from the provision of remedies for violations of that right. Indeed, the Patent Act itself indicates that patents shall have the attributes of personal property "[s]ubject to the provisions of this title," including, presumably, the provision that injunctive relief "may" issue only "in accordance with the principles of equity," … Because we conclude that neither court below correctly applied the traditional four-factor framework that governs the award of injunctive relief, we vacate the judgment of the Court of Appeals, so that the District Court may apply that framework in the first instance. In doing so, we take no position on whether permanent injunctive relief should or should not issue in this particular case, or indeed in any number of other disputes arising under the Patent Act …

DISSENTING OPINION

Justice Kennedy, with whom Justice Stevens, Justice Souter, and Justice Breyer join, concurring …

To the extent earlier cases establish a pattern of granting an injunction against patent infringers almost as a matter of course, this pattern simply illustrates the result of the four-factor test in the contexts then prevalent. The lesson of the historical practice, therefore, is most helpful and instructive when the circumstances of a case bear substantial parallels to litigation the courts have confronted before.

In cases now arising trial courts should bear in mind that in many instances the nature of the patent being enforced and the economic function of the patent holder present considerations quite unlike earlier cases. An industry has developed in which firms use patents not as a basis for producing and selling goods but, instead, primarily for obtaining licensing fees.

For these firms, an injunction, and the potentially serious sanctions arising from its violation, can be employed as a bargaining tool to charge exorbitant fees to companies that seek to buy licenses to practice the patent.

When the patented invention is but a small component of the product the companies seek to produce and the threat of an injunction is employed simply for undue leverage in negotiations, legal damages may well be sufficient to compensate for the infringement and an injunction may not serve the public interest. In addition injunctive relief may have different consequences for the burgeoning number of patents over business methods, which were not of much economic and legal significance in earlier times. The potential vagueness and suspect validity of some of these patents may affect the calculus under the four-factor test….

Reversed and Remanded.

CASE QUESTIONS

1. Why is this type of patent different from the traditional product patents?

2. What are the risks in granting a permanent injunction in cases such as these?

3. Why are the concurring judges raising the issue of undue leverage?

15-3 Copyrights

15-3a WHAT IS A COPYRIGHT AND WHAT DOES IT PROTECT?

Patents protect inventors. **Copyrights** protect authors of books, magazine articles, plays, movies, songs, dances, recordings, architectural designs, broadcasts, photographs, computer programs, and so on. Ideas cannot be copyrighted, but the way an idea is expressed can be. Under the **Computer Software Copyright Act of 1980**, all software can be copyrighted, whether it is written in ordinary language (source code) or machine language (object code). Although software copyrights do not cover methods of operation (such as menus), they do cover the underlying programs.

A copyright gives the holder of the copyright the exclusive right to sell, control, or license the copyrighted work. A copyright exists automatically for works created after 1989. Although the placement of the traditional C or copyright symbol (©) is not required, it is recommended. Further, the existence of a copyright in the United States is recognized in all nations that have signed the Berne Convention.

For example, the transmission of NFL games by satellite to Canada is a violation of U.S. copyright laws because Canada is a signatory to the Berne Convention. Under the terms of the Berne Convention and U.S. law, copyright registration is not required, but it is recommended. Registration is a means of preventing someone violating the copyright from claiming a lack of knowledge about the work's protection. In order to register a copyright, the creator need only file two copies of the work with the Copyright Office in Washington, DC. Without copyright registration, the owner cannot bring a suit for copyright infringement.

15-3b THE RIGHTS OF COPYRIGHT HOLDERS AGAINST THIRD-PARTY INFRINGERS

Copyright holders also have the right to enforce their copyright against those who are vicariously allowing infringement. Those who develop programs or facilitate infringement can be liable for infringement vicariously, and copyright holders have the right to obtain injunctions to stop their facilitation of infringement by others. Those who distribute software that facilitates peer-to-peer file sharing can be liable for infringement by the file sharers. The *Sony BMG Music Entertainment v Tenenbaum* case (Case 15.2) deals with an issue of a student's vicarious liability for facilitating infringement and provides an answer for the opening "Consider..."

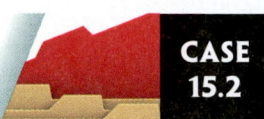

CASE 15.2   *Sony BMG Music Entertainment v Tenenbaum*
660 F.3d 487 (1st. Cir. 2011)

College Entertainment Coordinator and Infringement Facilitator

FACTS

Joel Tenenbaum was a student at Goucher College who developed file-sharing software that permitted 30 music recordings copyrighted by Sony (plaintiffs) to be downloaded and distributed without Sony's authorization. Sony brought suit for damages and a permanent injunction. The district court entered judgment against Tenenbaum as to liability. The jury found that Tenenbaum's infringement of the copyrights at issue was willful and awarded Sony statutory damages of $22,500 for each infringed recording. Tenenbaum's request for a reduction in damages (remittitur) from $675,000 was granted by the trial court and the damages were reduced by a factor of 10. Tenenbaum's request for a dismissal on the grounds that his infringement was not willful was denied. Both Sony and Tenenbaum appealed.

JUDICIAL OPINION

LYNCH, Chief Judge
Tenenbaum was an early and enthusiastic user of peer-to-peer networks to obtain and distribute copyrighted music

recordings. He began downloading and distributing copyrighted works without authorization in 1999.

Because it enabled copyright infringement, see *A & M Records, Inc. v Napster, Inc.*, 239 F.3d 1004 (9th Cir. 2001), the Napster network was shut down in 2001. This did not stop Tenenbaum from downloading and distributing copyrighted works; he instead began using other peer-to-peer networks for the same illegal purposes. These networks included AudioGalaxy, iMesh, Morpheus, Kazaa, and Limewire. Tenenbaum shifted to these other networks after Napster's termination despite his knowledge that Napster was forced to close on account of a lawsuit brought against it for copyright infringement.

Tenenbaum continued to download and distribute copyrighted materials through at least 2007. During that time span he accessed a panoply of peer-to-peer networks for these illegal purposes from several computers. From 1999 until 2002, he primarily downloaded and distributed copyrighted works to and from his desktop computer at his family's home in Providence. He left home to attend Goucher College in Baltimore, Maryland, in 2002, at which point he began using a

CONTINUED

laptop to download and distribute copyrighted works. Following his graduation from Goucher in 2006, he began using a second laptop for these purposes in tandem with his other computers. Over the duration of Tenenbaum's conduct, he intentionally downloaded thousands of songs to his own computers from other network users. He also purposefully made thousands of songs available to other network users. At one point in time in 2004 alone, Tenenbaum had 1153 songs on his "shared-directory" on the Kazaa network. Most of the networks Tenenbaum used had a "traffic tab" that informed him of the frequency with which other users were downloading his shared files. Tenenbaum regularly looked at the traffic tab, and he admitted it "definitely wasn't uncommon" for other users to be downloading materials from his computer.

While Tenenbaum was at Goucher College in 2002, his father, Dr. Arthur Tenenbaum, called him to warn him that his use of peer-to-peer networks to obtain and distribute music recordings was unlawful. Dr. Tenenbaum knew that his son was illegally downloading music because, prior to leaving for college, Tenenbaum had showed his father the array of songs that could be downloaded from the Kazaa network. After Dr. Tenenbaum became aware that lawsuits were being brought against individuals who used file-sharing programs to download and distribute music, he instructed Tenenbaum not to continue to engage in such conduct. Dr. Tenenbaum testified that, during their conversation, Tenenbaum did not appear concerned about the consequences of his actions. Despite his father's request, Tenenbaum continued his illegal activity.

Tenenbaum also received direct warnings from Goucher College. Each year Tenenbaum received a Goucher student handbook warning that using the college's network to download and distribute copyrighted materials was illegal, but he did so anyway. The handbook also warned that illegally downloading and distributing music files could subject the copyright infringer to up to $150,000 of liability per infringement, alerting Tenenbaum to his potential exposure for violating the law. Tenenbaum received handbooks containing similar language during each of his four years at Goucher, but was unfazed and continued.

Tenenbaum also knew the college took this seriously and had itself acted to stop this illegal activity. By the end of his undergraduate studies at Goucher, the school had implemented so many technological restrictions on its network—which he knew were designed to prevent illegal downloading of music files—that peer-to-peer programs "wouldn't work at all."

The Tenenbaums' Internet service provider at home in Providence, Cox Communications, also warned against using the Internet to illegally infringe copyrighted materials. In a September 2005 letter, plaintiffs

themselves informed Tenenbaum that he had been detected infringing copyrighted materials and notified him that his conduct was illegal. The letter stated: "We are writing in advance of filing suit against you in the event that you have an interest in resolving these claims." The letter urged Tenenbaum to consult with an attorney immediately, and explained that the recording companies were prepared to initiate a legal action against Tenenbaum because of the severe impact of his actions on the industry:

> Copyright theft is not a victimless crime. People spend countless hours working hard to create music—not just recording artists and songwriters, but also session players, backup singers, sound engineers and other technicians. In addition, the music industry employ thousands of other people, such as CD-plant workers, warehouse personnel, record store clerks and developers of legitimate online music services. They all depend on sale of recordings to earn a living. So do record companies, which routinely invest millions of dollars to discover and sign promising artists, and then to produce and market their recordings. In addition, piracy eats away at the investment dollars available to fund new music and, in effect, erodes the future of music.

The letter also instructed Tenenbaum to preserve any relevant evidence including "the entire library of recordings that you have made available for distribution as well as any recordings you have downloaded...."

After receiving this letter, Tenenbaum nonetheless took his laptop computer for repairs and had its operating system reinstalled and its hard drive reformatted. At trial, Tenenbaum maintained that he only had work done on the computer because "the thing wouldn't run," and that he instructed the computer repairman not to tamper with the music files stored on his computer.

Despite these warnings and his knowledge that he was and had been engaging in illegal activity which could subject him to liability of up to $150,000 per infringement, Tenenbaum continued the illegal downloading and distribution of copyrighted materials until a full two years after receiving the letter from Sony. He stopped his activity only after this lawsuit was filed against him.

Strong evidence established that Tenenbaum lied in the course of these legal proceedings in a number of ways. In his initial responses to Sony's discovery requests, Tenenbaum represented he "had no knowledge or recollection of online media distribution systems used or any dates" of such use. He also denied creating or using the "sublimeguy14@ kazaa" account name that he had used to access various peer-to-peer networks, and he denied any knowledge of whether a peer-to-peer network had been installed on his computer.

CONTINUED

At trial, however, Tenenbaum admitted that each of these statements he had made was false. He made numerous admissions in his testimony as to the scope of his conduct from 1999 until 2007.

Before the trial, Tenenbaum also attempted to shift responsibility for his conduct to other individuals by claiming they could have used his computer in order to illegally download and distribute the copyrighted works. These individuals included a foster child living in his family's home, burglars who had broken into the home, his family's house guest, and his own sisters. His sisters and others he blamed testified that they had never illegally downloaded music and had no knowledge of who installed the file sharing software on Tenenbaum's computer.

We affirm the finding of liability against Tenenbaum and in favor of plaintiffs. We affirm the injunctive relief.

We vacate the district court's due process damages ruling and reverse the reduction of the jury's statutory damages award. We reinstate the jury's award of damages and remand for consideration of defendant's motion for common law remittitur based on excessiveness.

If, on remand, the court allows any reduction through remittitur, then plaintiffs must be given the choice of a new trial or acceptance of remittitur.

CASE QUESTIONS

1. What does the court highlight as proof of his intent to infringe the copyright?

2. Explain what will be done with the damages issue.

3. What advice would you give to friends who are downloading music on peer-to-peer programs?

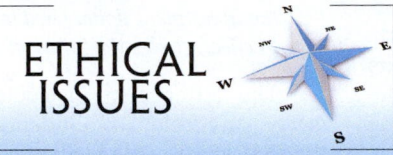

ETHICAL ISSUES

Evaluate Joel Tenenbaum's ethics in his long-standing facilitation of file-sharing copyrighted materials. Discuss his misrepresentations prior to trial.

© martan/Shutterstock.com

15-3c **HOW LONG DOES A COPYRIGHT RUN?**

Business Planning Tip

Be certain your employees understand the copyrighted nature of computer software and the protections afforded to the owners of those programs. Tell them that there are both criminal and civil penalties for infringement of software programs.

© Grounder/Shutterstock.com

Like patents, copyrights are so important that they are found in Article I, Section 8 of the U.S. Constitution, which provides that Congress can secure "for limited times to Authors and Inventors the exclusive Right to their respective Writings and Discoveries." The initial period of protection for copyrights (established in 1790), one that covered books, maps, and charts, was for 14 years with the right of renewal for another 14 years. In 1831, the protection period increased to 28 years with renewal rights for another 14. In 1909, the time expanded to 28 years with a 28-year renewal. In 1976, the time was increased to 50 years with no renewal. Under the Sonny Bono Copyright Extension Act of 1998, passed as the copyright on Mickey Mouse was about to expire, copyrights were increased to run for the life of the creator plus 70 years. If the work produced was done by an employee of a business, the business then registers the copyright. These types of business copyrights run for 120 years from the time of creation or 95 years from publication of the work, whichever is shorter. The late Representative Bono led the charge for the increased protection period concerned because copyrights he and many others held were about to expire. Even though the Constitution prohibits granting copyrights in perpetuity, a clear trend in congressional actions favors extending the protection period.

15-3d **RIGHTS OF A COPYRIGHT HOLDER**

A copyright holder has control over the use of the created work. That control includes control over reproduction, distribution, public performances, derivative works, and public displays. Some copyright holders assign or license these rights to others in exchange for royalties. For example, most songwriters assign their rights for public performances of their songs to the American Society of Composers, Authors, and Publishers (ASCAP) and Broadcast Music, Inc. (BMI), who then pay the writers each time their song is used, according to a previously determined schedule of fees. An international fee schedule for payment for tapes, CDs, and records is also in place; it could be a flat fee, a per-minute fee, a per-record fee, or a per-song fee. "Bumper" music played on talk-radio stations is always less than a minute to avoid the significant charges that would result.

Damages for copyright infringement include profits made by the infringer, actual costs, attorney fees, and any other expenses associated with the infringement action. A court can order all illegal copies destroyed and issue an injunction that halts distribution of the illegal copies. In addition to civil recovery for the damages from infringement, federal criminal penalties for copyright infringement can be imposed when the infringement is willful and for "commercial advantage or private financial gain."

Rights of Copyright Holders and the Internet

Technology has created new issues in copyright infringement, particularly in the areas of copyrighted software and music, with the availability of digital technology. For example, the *Tenenbaum* case illustrates how colleges can be used to facilitate file sharing.

CYBERLAW

© iStockPhoto.com /dra_schwartz

As a result, music producers and software developers added protection technology to their copyrighted products and lobbied for a change in copyright law, which came with the **Digital Millennium Copyright Act (DMCA)** in 1998. This act criminalizes the circumvention of protection technology in order to make copies of copyrighted materials. Assisting others, providing expertise, and manufacturing products to circumvent protection technology are also criminal activities under the DMCA. Circumvention and facilitating circumvention are now violations of copyright laws. The liability has also been extended to those who facilitate the infringement via downloading programs. Individuals who maneuver around encryption devices and those who hire them to avoid those devices, as in the case of industrial espionage, may face criminal sanctions.

However, thanks largely to the lobbying efforts of colleges and universities, the DMCA has a safe harbor provision. Internet service providers (ISPs) do not have vicarious liability for copyright infringement by their users (such as for downloading copyright music and films without payment) if the ISPs can establish that they did not know of the infringement, that they are not benefiting from the infringement, that they take action when they know of the infringement, and that they have policies and procedures in place to warn of and prevent infringement. For example, Google's YouTube has several clips from copyrighted television shows and movies. However, Google is not responsible for the posting of the clips; individuals post the clips. In *Viacom International, Inc. v YouTube, Inc.*, 676 F.3d 19 (2nd Cir. 2012) (see Case 1.2 in Chapter 1), a federal district court held that Google had not violated the DMCA by continuing to allow copyrighted clips to post on its site as long as it had the clips removed upon request by the owner. The key to infringement liability immunity is prompt removal upon request as well as advance warning. When you obtained access to the college or university's website, you agreed to abide by its

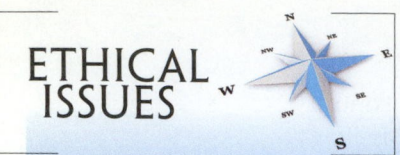

ETHICAL ISSUES

Google has been copying and posting portions of books, and, in some cases, full books, for access via the Google search system. Google refers to many of the excerpts as "snippets." However, authors have filed a class-action suit against Google for infringement. Evaluate the legal issues in the use of snippets. Evaluate the ethical issues in Google's mass reproduction of the books.

standards as well as U.S. copyright laws. In fact, you agreed that your access rights could be terminated if you violated their rules or U.S. law.

Fair Use and Copyrights

When the copyright laws were amended in 1976, one change permitted "fair use" of copyrighted materials. **Fair use** is occasional and spontaneous use of copyrighted materials for limited purposes—for example, a short quote from a copyrighted work. Fair use also allows instructors to reproduce a page or chart from a copyrighted work to use in the classroom. Copies of book pages also can be made for research purposes. The three key questions to ask on fair use are the following:

1. Is the use for commercial or nonprofit/educational use?

2. Is the work large or small, or a song, poem, or book? Using a sentence from a book is different from using a sentence from a poem.

3. What is the effect of the use on the copyrighted work? If you copy a book, the author and publisher lose sales. If you use a clip from a film, folks may rent or buy the film and you may actually increase sales.

Photocopying of articles for use in the classroom or workplace is a common practice, but it does not always comply with the protections afforded to the copyright owners of that article. For example, in *American Geophysical Union v Texaco Inc.*, 60 F.3d 913 (2nd Cir. 1995), the court held that Texaco scientists' copying of articles from journals for use by fellow scientists at the company was not fair use but infringement because it deprived the journals of subscription revenues or revenues from licenses for reproduction of the articles. Likewise, in *Princeton University Press v Michigan Document Services, Inc.*, 99 F.3d 1381 (6th Cir. 1996), the court held that the reproduction of coursepacks by the University of Michigan for sale to its students was not a fair use by a nonprofit educational institution. The failure to pay royalties to copyright holders not only deprived the holders of their rights but also placed the for-profit copy shops at a competitive disadvantage because they were required to pay such royalties. Because of that case, the reproduction of course materials is now outsourced to professional copying services that also handle the permissions rights for the materials.

One interesting question that has arisen is the relationship between the notion of fair use and the prohibitions under the Digital Millennium Copyright Act. Can a professor circumvent protection technology for fair use in the classroom? Some feel the professor can do so if he has purchased the work. In other words, the professor can use an excerpt from the Beatles' *White Album* if the professor owns that album.

Another matter in fair use involves First Amendment issues. For example, satirical works use the lyrics and speech of others as a form of social commentary such as that found in *Mad Magazine* and *Saturday Night Live*. The First Amendment protects social commentary, and the copyright laws protect original work. The *Campbell v Acuff-Rose Music, Inc.* case (Case 15.3) involves an issue of a parody of copyrighted material being used for commercial gain, dealing with the balancing of First Amendment rights and copyright protection.

CASE 15.3   *Campbell v Acuff-Rose Music, Inc.*
510 U.S. 569 (1994)

Justice Souter Does the Pretty Woman Rap

FACTS

2 Live Crew, a popular rap musical group, recorded and performed "Pretty Woman," a rap music version of Roy Orbison's famed 1964 "Oh, Pretty Woman" rock ballad. The song was written by Mr. Orbison and William Dees, and the rights to the song were assigned to Acuff-Rose Music, Inc. (respondent). 2 Live Crew's manager had written to Acuff-Rose to request permission to do the parody and offered to pay for rights to do so. Acuff-Rose's response: "I am aware of the success enjoyed by the '2 Live Crew,' but I must inform you that we cannot permit the use of a parody of 'Oh, Pretty Woman.'"

2 Live Crew recorded the parody anyway and named Mr. Orbison and Mr. Dees as the songwriters and Acuff-Rose as the publisher on the CD cover. After over 250,000 copies of the CD had been sold and over one year later, Acuff-Rose filed suit against Luther Campbell (also known as Luke Skywalker), Christopher Wongwon, Mark Ross, and David Hobbs, members of the 2 Live Crew group, for infringement. 2 Live Crew maintained that its song was a parody and fell into a fair use exception of the copyright laws. The district court granted summary judgment for 2 Live Crew. The Court of Appeals held that the commercial nature of the parody rendered it presumptively unfair. 2 Live Crew (petitioners) appealed.

JUDICIAL OPINION

SOUTER, Justice

We are called upon to decide whether 2 Live Crew's commercial parody of Roy Orbison's song, "Oh, Pretty Woman," may be a fair use within the meaning of the Copyright Act of 1976, 17 U.S.C. § 107 (1988 ed. and Supp. IV).

It is uncontested here that 2 Live Crew's song would be an infringement of Acuff-Rose's rights in "Oh, Pretty Woman," under the Copyright Act of 1976, 17 U.S.C. § 106 (1988 ed. and Supp. IV), but for a finding of fair use through parody.

The first factor in a fair use enquiry is "the purpose and character of the use, including whether such use is of a commercial nature or is for nonprofit educational purposes." The central purpose of this investigation is to see whether the new work merely "supersede[s] the objects" of the original creation, or instead adds something new, with a further purpose or different character, altering the first with new expression, meaning, or message; it asks, in other words, whether and to what extent the new work is "transformative." Although such transformative use is not absolutely necessary for a finding of fair use, *Sony Corp. of America v Universal City Studios, Inc.*, 464 U.S. 417 (1984), the goal of copyright, to promote science and the arts, is generally furthered by the creation of transformative works. Such works thus lie at the heart of the fair use doctrine's guarantee of breathing space within the confines of copyright and the more transformative the new work, the less will be the significance of other factors, like commercialism, that may weigh against a finding of fair use.

Suffice it to say now that parody has an obvious claim to transformative value, as Acuff-Rose itself does not deny. Like less ostensibly humorous forms of criticism, it can provide social benefit, by shedding light on an earlier work, and, in the process, creating a new one. We thus line up with the courts that have held that parody, like other comment or criticism, may claim fair use under § 107.

Parody needs to mimic an original to make its point, and so has some claim to use the creation of its victim's (or collective victims') imagination, whereas satire can stand on its own two feet and so requires justification for the very act of borrowing.

The fact that parody can claim legitimacy for some appropriation does not, of course, tell either parodist or judge much about where to draw the line. Like a book review quoting the copyrighted material criticized, parody may or may not be fair use, and petitioner's suggestion that any periodic use is presumptively fair has no more justification in law or fact than the equally

CONTINUED

hopeful claim that any use for news reporting should be presumed fair.

As the District Court remarked, the words of 2 Live Crew's song copy the original's first line, but then "quickly degenerate[e] into a play on words, substituting predictable lyrics with shocking ones … [that] derisively demonstrate[e] how bland and banal the Orbison song seems to them." Although the majority below had difficulty discerning any criticism of the original in 2 Live Crew's song, it assumed for purposes of its opinion that there was some.

We have less difficulty in finding that critical element in 2 Live Crew's song than the Court of Appeals did, although having found it we will not take the further step of evaluating its quality. The threshold question when fair use is raised in defense of parody is whether a periodic character may reasonably be perceived. Whether, going beyond that, parody is in good taste or bad does not and should not matter to fair use. As Justice Holmes explained, "[i]t would be a dangerous undertaking for persons trained only to the law to constitute themselves final judges of the worth of [a work]."

While we might not assign a high rank to the periodic element here, we think it fair to say that 2 Live Crew's song reasonably could be perceived as commenting on the original or criticizing it, to some degree. 2 Live Crew juxtaposes the romantic musings of a man whose fantasy comes true, with degrading taunts, a bawdy demand for sex, and a sigh of relief from paternal responsibility. The later words can be taken as a comment on the naïveté of the original of an earlier day, as a rejection of its sentiment that ignores the ugliness of street life and the debasement that it signifies. It is this joinder of reference and ridicule that marks off the author's choice of parody from the other types of comment and criticism that traditionally have had a claim to fair use protection as transformative works.

The use, for example, of a copyrighted work to advertise a product, even in a parody, will be entitled to less indulgence under the first factor of the fair use enquiry, than the sale of a parody for its own sake, let alone one performed a single time by students in school….

It is true, of course, that 2 Live Crew copied the characteristic opening bass riff (or musical phrase) of the original, and true that the words of the first line copy the Orbison lyrics. But if quotation of the opening riff and the first line may be said to go to the "heart" of the original, the heart is also what most readily conjures up the song for parody, and it is the heart at which parody takes aim. Copying does not become excessive in relation to parodic purpose merely because the portion taken was the original's heart. If 2 Live Crew had copied a significantly less memorable part of the original, it is difficult to see how its parodic character would have come through.

This is not, of course, to say that anyone who calls himself a parodist can skim the cream and get away scot-free. In parody, as in news reporting, context is everything, and the question of fairness asks what else the parodist did besides go to the heart of the original. It is significant that 2 Live Crew not only copied the first line of the original, but thereafter departed markedly from the Orbison lyrics for its own ends. 2 Live Crew not only copied the bass riff and repeated it, but also produced otherwise distinctive sounds, interposing "scraper" noise, overlaying the music with solos in different keys, and altering the drum beat. This is not a case, then, where "a substantial portion" of the parody itself is composed of a "verbatim" copying of the original. It is not, that is, a case where the parody is so insubstantial, as compared to the copying, that the third factor must be resolved as a matter of law against the parodists.

It was error for the Court of Appeals to conclude that the commercial nature of 2 Live Crew's parody of "Oh, Pretty Woman" rendered it presumptively unfair. The court also erred in holding that 2 Live Crew had necessarily copied excessively from the Orbison original, considering the parodic purpose of the use. We therefore reverse the judgment of the Court of Appeals.

The case was remanded for trial.

APPENDIX A AND B

[The U.S. Supreme Court reproduced the lyrics to the song here. However, copyright requirements prohibited this book's publisher from using those lyrics that were excerpted in the court's opinion. Placing the lyrics in a judicial opinion that resulted from litigation over those lyrics was not placing those lyrics in the public domain. It would be infringement to reproduce the lyrics here. However, the song was one of parody of the lilting lyrics of Orbison's "Oh, Pretty Woman." The 2 Live Crew version describes a woman of poor hygiene who is unfaithful and comes from a man who is grateful that the woman walking along the street is *not* his girlfriend because of her infidelity and unattractive appearance.]

CASE QUESTIONS

1. What is the significance of 2 Live Crew's commercial gain from the parody?

2. Why did 2 Live Crew's manager seek permission first?

3. Do you agree with the court's decision? Was it a fair use? Should the owner of the rights be allowed to decide how a song will be parodied for commercial gain?

Consider...

John David California has written a sequel to J.D. Salinger's *The Catcher in the Rye*. Salinger and the Salinger Literary Trust brought suit, *J.D. Salinger v John Doe*, 607 F.3d 68 (2nd Cir. 2010), seeking an injunction to halt the reproduction, publication, advertisement, distribution, or other dissemination of the book, which is entitled *60 Years Later: Coming Through the Rye*, to be published by Windupbird and Nicotext. Salinger (and subsequently his estate) alleged in the suit that the book is an unauthorized sequel of the acclaimed copyrighted novel that Salinger wrote. Salinger's estate based its suit for infringement on the use of the character Holden Caulfield of *Catcher*, who is the narrator and the very essence of the novel. At the time of the suit, the sequel was available in Britain and at Amazon.com but had not yet been distributed in bookstores.

Catcher in the Rye is one of the all-time classic American novels, named one of the 100 best novels by both *Time* magazine and The Modern Library, and is taught in schools across the country. It has been described in reviews as "a crucial American novel …," an "unusually brilliant novel," and "a cult book, a rite of passage for the brainy and disaffected" (*New York Times*).

The sequel begins, as does *Catcher*, with Holden Caulfield's departure from an institution (prep school in *Catcher*; a nursing home in the sequel) and ends with Holden and his sister Phoebe at the carousel in Central Park. In between, Holden hangs out aimlessly in New York for a few days, encountering many of the same people, visiting many of the same settings, and ruminating. The sequel is not a parody, and it does not comment upon or criticize the original.

Mr. Salinger never allowed any derivative works to be made using either *The Catcher in the Rye* or his Holden Caulfield character. Indeed, in 1980 Salinger stated to the press, "There's no more to Holden Caulfield. Read the book again. It's all there. Holden Caulfield is only a frozen moment in time."[2] Is the sequel infringement? Would the court be justified in issuing a temporary and/or permanent injunction against its publication and distribution? Why or why not?

15-4 Trademarks

15-4a WHAT ARE TRADEMARKS?

Trademarks are words, names, symbols, designs, or devices that businesses use to identify their products or services. To be protected, a trademark must have some distinctiveness. There are categories for distinctiveness including fanciful (M&Ms or Xerox), descriptive (*Sports Illustrated* or the *Wall Street Journal*), arbitrary (such as the use of the word "Apple" for computers), or acquired distinctiveness (such as the Mercedes-Benz triangle coming to represent the car and the company). Generic terms cannot be trademarks, and the failure to enforce the use of a trademark can cause it to fall into generic use. Some other examples of trademarks include Owens Corning's use of the color pink for its insulation (fanciful and distinctive). No other insulation company can have pink insulation, and the use of the Pink Panther reminds us of the company's unique product. If the symbol is one for a service, such as the symbol for "Martinizing" at the dry cleaners, it is a service mark.

15-4b WHAT ARE THE LEGAL PROTECTIONS FOR TRADEMARKS?

The **Lanham Act of 1946** is a federal law passed to afford businesses protection of their trademarks. This law is really a protection of a company's goodwill. A trademark becomes associated with that company and is used as a means of identifying that company's goods or services. The Lanham Act assures the right to retain that unique identification.

Business Planning Tip

To be certain federal protection for your intangible property rights is maximized, put either the "®" by the trade name or trademark, or place the words "Registered in U.S. Patent and Trademark Office" or "Reg. U.S. Pat. & TM. Off" on the packaging or product. Once you are registered with the U.S. Patent and Trademark Office, obtaining registrations in other countries becomes much easier. Also, a registered product means that U.S. Customs officials exclude products from entry if they infringe a registered property right.

© Grounder/Shutterstock.com

Business Planning Tip

Before you pay for a copyright or a trademark, be sure the seller owns the intellectual property and has the authority to sell it. The Lyons Group, owner and developer of Barney, the large, childlike purple dinosaur of PBS fame, purchased the rights to Barney's "I Love You" theme song from Lee Bernstein. Jean Warren, a music publisher from Everett, Washington, surfaced in 1995 and told the Lyons Group that Ms. Bernstein had sold her the rights in 1983. The result was litigation involving all the parties.

To obtain the federal protection, which lasts in perpetuity as long as the owner enforces the rights, the trademark must be registered with the Patent and Trademark Office. To be a valid trademark, the mark must serve to distinguish the company's goods or services from others. The Principal Register at the PTO is the official recording of the trademark rights. From the time of the registration, others have five years to contest the grant of a trademark. If, after five years, there has been no contest, the trademark belongs to the registered owner and is incontestable. Trademarks can also be reserved in advance of beginning a business, but the business must be started within 36 months of the time the trademark is reserved.

Trademarks are also protected internationally through the Madrid System of International Registration of Marks, known as the Madrid Protocol. The United States became a signatory to that agreement in 2003. Once a U.S. company has registered its trademark in the United States, it can then do the same in the other 60 countries that have adopted the Madrid Protocol and obtain protection in those countries as well.

15-4c ENFORCING TRADEMARKS AND THE RISK OF GOING GENERIC

Once a trademark is registered, the holder must self-enforce the unique nature of that trademark. The owner must take care so that the trademark does not fall into common use by the public as a descriptive or generic term. For example, there are "Band-Aid brand adhesive strips" instead of "Band-Aids." There is "Jell-O brand gelatin dessert" instead of "Jell-O." There are "Formica brand kitchen countertops" instead of "Formica" ones and "Rollerblade in-line skates" instead of "Rollerblades." Parker Brothers lost its "Monopoly" trademark because there is no generic term for its type of board game. Other examples of generics are "aspirin" and "cellophane."

In *Harley-Davidson, Inc. v Grottanelli*, 164 F.3d 806 (2nd Cir. 1999); *cert. denied*, 531 U.S. 1103 (2001), the court held that Harley-Davidson had lost its exclusive rights to call a Harley a "hog" because the term had become generic for describing motorcycles and not just Harley brand motorcycles.

BUSINESS STRATEGY   Infringement Suit to Protect the Brand

French footwear designer Christian Louboutin brought action against designer Yves Saint Laurent (YSL), alleging that YSL violated the Lanham Act by producing "high fashion" shoes with Louboutin's trademarked, signature-lacquered red outsoles. Louboutin claimed trademark dilution. YSL counterclaimed in the suit for cancellation of designer's trademark registration, arguing that Louboutin cannot trademark a color. Although the companies tried to settle the suit, the result was an intellectual property battle over the exclusivity of the colored sole. The federal district court denied Louboutin's 2011 motion for preliminary injunction, and Louboutin appealed.

What should the court decide? Is it possible that a color allows people to say, "That's a Louboutin shoe!" Is the colored sole a marketing strategy?
[*Christian Louboutin v Yves Saint Laurent America Holding, Inc. et al.*, 696 F.3d 206 (2nd Cir. 2012)]

Consider...

Wordspy.com is a site that specializes in noting newly coined words. The site noted that the popularity of the search engine Google has netted a verb, such as when someone says, "I went in and Googled it." A lawyer from Google has asked that the new term be deleted from Wordspy's site. Why does Google want to stop its use as a verb?

15-4d   TRADE NAMES

Not all commonly used terms, however, are generic because they may be trade names. In *San Francisco Arts & Athletics, Inc. v United States Olympic Committee*, 483 U.S. 522 (1987), the Supreme Court held that the term *Olympic* belongs to the U.S. Olympic Committee and could not be used by San Francisco Arts & Athletics, Inc. (SFAA) in promoting its "Gay Olympic Games."

The SFAA did not have permission to use the term *Olympic*. Use of a **trade name** without the registered owner's permission is infringement. The owner of the trade name can seek injunctive relief to stop the use of the trade name. The plaintiff owner can also recover all damages and attorney's fees. If the plaintiff can show a willful infringement, the Lanham Act allows the plaintiff to recover treble damages. Relief by a suit seeking an injunction is also available for using a trademark without authorization in advertising. Recent changes in the law allow a competitor to seek treble damages when its product is used deceptively in a comparative ad.

15-4e   WHAT ARE THE RIGHTS WHEN A TRADEMARK OR TRADENAME IS MISUSED?

In 1995, Congress passed the **Federal Trademark Dilution Act**, a statute that permits recovery and injunctions for "dilution" of distinctive trademarks. The purpose of the law was to prevent others from capitalizing on the recognition, familiarity, and reputation of a distinctive trademark. This statute protects the trademark owner who can establish confusion—that is, buyers assumed they were purchasing goods or services with the trademark and from the company who owns that trademark. The act covers the problem of blurring or creating confusion among consumers about the source of a product and tarnishing or portraying a product in an unsavory manner.

Moseley, dba Victor's Little Secret v V Secret Catalogue, Inc. (Case 15.4) deals with a trademark dilution issue.

CASE 15.4	*Moseley, dba Victor's Little Secret v V Secret Catalogue, Inc.* 537 U.S. 418 (2003)

The Bare Essentials on Trademark Law: Victor or Victoria's Secret?

FACTS

Victor and Cathy Moseley (petitioners) owned and operated an adult toy, gag gift, and lingerie shop that they called Victor's Little Secret near Elizabethtown, Kentucky. In the February 12, 1998, edition of a weekly publication distributed to residents of the military installation at Fort Knox, Kentucky, the Moseleys advertised the "GRAND OPENING Just in time for Valentine's Day!" of their store "VICTOR'S SECRET" in Elizabethtown. The ad featured "Intimate Lingerie for every woman," "Romantic Lighting," "Lycra Dresses," "Pagers," and "Adult Novelties/Gifts."

An army colonel, who saw the ad and was offended by what he perceived to be an attempt to use a reputable

CONTINUED

company's trademark to promote the sale of "unwholesome, tawdry merchandise," sent a copy to Victoria's Secret, Inc. (respondents).

Victoria's Secret owns 750 stores around the country and distributes 400 million catalogs each year via U.S. mail. Victoria's Secret spends $55 million annually on advertising "the VICTORIA'S SECRET brand—one of moderately priced, high quality, attractively designed lingerie sold in a store setting designed to look like a wom[a]n's bedroom." Two of Victoria's Secret's stores were located In Louisville, Kentucky, a short drive from Elizabethtown and Fort Knox.

Legal counsel for Victoria's Secret asked the Moseleys to stop using the name Victor's Secret because of possible confusion over the trademark and resulting dilution. The Moseleys changed the name of their store to Victor's Little Secret. Not satisfied, Victoria's Secret filed suit for dilution of its trademark under the Federal Trademark Dilution Act (FTDA).

The District Court granted summary judgment for Victoria's Secret under the FTDA, and the Sixth Circuit affirmed, finding that the respondents' mark was "distinctive" and that the evidence established "dilution" even though no actual harm had been proved. The Moseleys appealed.

JUDICIAL OPINION

STEVENS, Justice

Respondents described their business as follows: "Victoria's Secret stores sell a complete line of lingerie, women's undergarments and nightwear, robes, caftans and kimonos, slippers, sachets, lingerie bags, hanging bags, candles, soaps, cosmetic brushes, atomizers, bath products and fragrances." Petitioners sell a wide variety of items, including adult videos, "adult novelties," and lingerie. In answer to an interrogatory, petitioners stated that they "sell novelty action clocks, patches, temporary tattoos, stuffed animals, coffee mugs, leather biker wallets, zippo lighters, diet formula, diet supplements, jigsaw puzzles, whyss, handcufs [sic], hosiery, bubble machines, greeting cards, calendars, incense burners, car air fresheners, sunglasses, ball caps, jewelry, candles, lava lamps, blacklights, fiber optic lights, rock and roll prints, lingerie, pagers, candy, adult video tapes, adult novelties, t-shirts, etc."

Victor Moseley stated in an affidavit that women's lingerie represented only about five percent of their sales. In support of their motion for summary judgment, respondents submitted an affidavit by an expert in marketing who explained "the enormous value" of respondents' mark. Neither he, nor any other witness, expressed any opinion concerning the impact, if any, of petitioners' use of the name "Victor's Little Secret" on that value.

However, the Sixth Circuit held, "While no consumer is likely to go to the Moseleys' store expecting to find Victoria's Secret's famed Miracle Bra, consumers who hear the name 'Victor's Little Secret' are likely automatically to think of the more famous store and link it to the Moseleys' adult toy, gag gift, and lingerie shop. This, then, is a classic instance of dilution by tarnishing (associating the Victoria's Secret name with sex toys and lewd coffee mugs) and by blurring (linking the chain with a single, unauthorized establishment). Given this conclusion, it follows that Victoria's Secret would prevail in a dilution analysis."

In reaching that conclusion the Court of Appeals expressly rejected the holding of the Fourth Circuit in *Ringling Bros. Barnum & Bailey Combined Shows, Inc. v Utah Div. of Travel Development*, 170 F.3d 449 (1999). In that case, which involved a claim that Utah's use on its license plates of the phrase "greatest snow on earth" was causing dilution of the "greatest show on earth," the court had concluded "that to establish dilution of a famous mark under the federal Act requires proof that (1) a defendant has made use of a junior mark sufficiently similar to the famous mark to evoke in a relevant universe of consumers a mental association of the two that (2) has caused (3) actual economic harm to the famous mark's economic value by lessening its former selling power as an advertising agent for its goods or services." Because other Circuits have also expressed differing views about the "actual harm" issue, we granted certiorari to resolve the conflict.

Infringement law protects consumers from being misled by the use of infringing marks and also protects producers from unfair practices by an "imitating competitor."

…[w]e decide the case on the assumption that the Moseleys' use of the name "Victor's Little Secret" neither confused any consumers or potential consumers, nor was likely to do so. Neither the absence of any likelihood of confusion nor the absence of competition, however, provides a defense to the statutory dilution claim alleged….

"The term 'dilution' means the lessening of the capacity of a famous mark to identify and distinguish goods or services, regardless of the presence or absence of—

"(1) competition between the owner of the famous mark and other parties, or

"(2) likelihood of confusion, mistake, or deception."

The consequences of dilution, such as an actual loss of sales or profits, must also be proved. However, at least where the marks at issue are not identical, the mere fact that consumers mentally associate the junior user's mark with a famous mark is not sufficient to establish actionable dilution. As the facts of that case demonstrate, such mental association will not necessarily reduce the capacity of the famous mark to identify the goods of its owner, the statutory requirement for dilution under the FTDA. For even though Utah drivers may be reminded of the circus when they see a license plate referring to the "greatest snow on earth," it by no means follows that they will associate "the greatest show on earth" with skiing or snow sports, or associate it less strongly or exclusively with the circus. "Blurring" is not a necessary consequence of mental association. (Nor, for that matter, is "tarnishing.")

The record in this case establishes that an army officer who saw the advertisement of the opening of a store named "Victor's Secret" did make the mental association with "Victoria's Secret," but it also shows that he did not therefore form any different impression of the store that his wife and daughter had patronized. There is a complete absence of evidence of any lessening of the capacity of the VICTORIA'S SECRET mark to identify and distinguish goods or services sold in Victoria's Secret stores or advertised in its catalogs. The officer was offended by the ad, but it did not change his conception of Victoria's Secret. His offense was directed entirely at petitioners, not at respondents. Moreover, the expert retained by respondents had nothing to say about the impact of petitioners' name on the strength of respondents' mark.

Whatever difficulties of proof may be entailed, they are not an acceptable reason for dispensing with proof of an essential element of a statutory violation. The evidence in the present record is not sufficient to support the summary judgment on the dilution count. The judgment is therefore reversed, and the case is remanded for further proceedings consistent with this opinion.

CASE QUESTIONS

1. Describe the connection between the two companies.
2. What is Victoria's Secret concerned about?
3. What do they have to prove to get an injunction under the FTDA?
4. Why does Victoria's Secret argue against that burden of proof?

15-4f TRADE DRESS

A more recent and critical aspect of the Lanham Act is the concept of **trade dress**. Trade dress consists of the colors, designs, and shapes associated with a product. If someone copies the color schemes and shapes, they are likely to benefit from the goodwill of the owner and developer of the trade dress. The subtle copying of trade dress dilutes the value of the company's goodwill and reputation. In *Two Pesos, Inc. v Taco Cabana, Inc.*, 505 U.S. 763 (1992), the U.S. Supreme Court resolved issues related to trade dress infringement. In the case, Taco Cabana, Inc., which operated a chain of fast-food restaurants in Texas that serve Mexican food, had opened in San Antonio and had distinctive trade dress that Two Pesos used as its motif when it opened its restaurants in Houston. With expansion around Texas, the two chains ended up in head-to-head competition in Dallas, and a trade dress infringement

FOR THE MANAGER'S DESK

Re: Surveys and Trademark Confusion

Consumer surveys have become a critical part of infringement trials. Where the issue is whether the public has been misled by a trademark infringement, the responses of a representative sample are critical evidence in a case. One such case involved a survey of consumers in 24 shopping malls nationwide. The Baltimore Colts had become the Indianapolis Colts, and the Canadian Football League proposed calling one of its teams the Baltimore CFL Colts. The survey showed consumers were confused, and the data carried the case for the former Baltimore Colts' owners.

Consider...

Nautilus and ICON are direct competitors in the market for home exercise equipment. Both produce resistance-training systems that use bendable rods. In Nautilus's product, the Bowflex exerciser, the rods are arranged vertically; when a user pulls on a cable connected to the upper ends of the rods, the rods curve or "bow" outward. The rods are structured to resist this outward movement, requiring exertion by the user.

Nautilus has continuously produced the Bowflex exerciser since 1984 and holds two patents on related technology. Nautilus registered the trademark for the Bowflex brand in 1986. Since 1993, when Nautilus began to market its Bowflex exerciser directly to consumers, the company has invested in excess of $233 million in promotion efforts. Nautilus's advertising has focused on infomercials, the Internet, and print publications. As a result, over 780,000 machines have been sold, with total revenues to Nautilus of $900 million.

In 2002, ICON introduced a competing rod-based resistance training system it called Cross-Bow. In the CrossBow exerciser, the bendable rods are arranged horizontally so that they bend downward, in an inverted U-shape, rather than outward, as in Bowflex's vertical rod configuration. According to ICON, the product's resemblance to the medieval crossbow weapon inspired the brand name. In ICON's two-line logo for the machine, the "o" in "Cross" is replaced by a circular crosshairs. Beneath the mark, in smaller type, appears an additional line, "by Weider," signaling the machine's source. Since it introduced the CrossBow exerciser, ICON has spent $13 million on marketing in many of the same advertising channels as Nautilus, including infomercials and the Internet.

Nautilus commenced a suit for patent infringement against ICON. Is there infringement? What must Nautilus establish?

[*Nautilus Group, Inc. v ICON Health and Fitness, Inc.*, 372 F.3d 1330 (Fed. Cir. 2004)]

suit resulted. The U.S. Supreme Court held that a claim of trade dress infringement requires proof of the same elements as trademark infringement—that is, a company must show that its trade dress is distinctive and that consumers are likely to be confused by the similarity.

In *Wal-Mart v Samara*, 529 U.S. 205 (2000), the U.S. Supreme Court limited its ruling in *Two Pesos* to product packaging and held that no trade dress protection is available for product design absent some form of registration under federal law such as trademark or patent or the product design having achieved some level of distinctiveness. In the case, Samara designed, produced, and sold a line of seersucker children's clothes with bold appliqués and large collars. Walmart had introduced its own line of clothing that was similar. Product design trade dress enjoys no inherent protection. Product packaging, which the court noted was involved in *Two Pesos*, does enjoy protection, as in the shape of a Coca-Cola bottle. However, absent some other statutory protection, product design, with the exception of famous designers such as Tommy Hilfiger, Ralph Lauren, and Izod, requires legislative change for protection.

CYBERLAW

© iStockPhoto.com /dra_schwartz

15-4g CYBER INFRINGEMENT

What are the rights of search engines such as Google to use the symbols and trademarks of companies to direct Internet users to sites that are not affiliated with the trademark owners? Playboy Enterprises filed suit against Netscape to stop that search engine's use of the Playboy Bunny symbol in ads that directed Internet users to sites oriented toward sexual content. Netscape benefits when users click onto those sites. However, the use of the Playboy symbol allows Netscape and the sites to capitalize on Playboy's name, advertising, and goodwill. In *Playboy Enterprise, Inc. v Netscape Communications*, 354 F.3d 1020 (9th Cir. 2004), a unanimous Ninth Circuit ruled that such use was an infringement.

Companies also have the right to stop Internet sales that are not by authorized distributors. For example, in *Australian Gold, Inc. v Hatfield*, 436 F.3d 1228 (10th Cir. 2006), ETS Inc., like most beauty supply companies, sold its tanning products primarily through tanning salons. ETS, like most beauty suppliers, has distribution contracts that limit sales to beauty and tanning salons. ETS does not want its products to be available in stores because of the need for in-person consultation on their use and application. The Hatfields used a series of fictitious names to purchase ETS products through distributors and then made the products available on the Internet through seven different websites. The seven websites used the ETS trademark, product pictures, and metatags. ETS recovered $3.7 million for infringement because of the unauthorized use of the trademark and the resulting diversion of Internet traffic and sales to the Hatfields. Use of a trademark on the Internet without permission brings the resulting profits back to the owner.

Consider...

They can be spotted from a distance. The classic Ferrari design with its lined side panels and hidden headlights is unique. Although the Ferrari name is a registered trademark, the design of the Ferrari is not. Roberts Motor Company designed a car with a look similar to the Ferrari, but the Roberts car would sell for a much lower price. Ferrari brought suit against Roberts, alleging infringement. Is Ferrari correct? Can a nonpatented, noncopyrighted design belong exclusively to Ferrari?
[*Ferrari v Roberts Motor Co.*, 944 F.2d 1235 (6th Cir. 1991), *cert. denied*, 505 U.S. 1219 (1992)]

THINK: The protections for design require proof that consumers would be confused about the product, that they would likely think the Roberts car was a Ferrari. Also, where the products are the same and one company seeks to draw upon the advertising and goodwill of the other, the confusion and damages are more easily established.

APPLY: If Ferrari is able to show confusion, it can halt the design and seek damages. But proof of that confusion is necessary to seek a remedy for design infringement. Would your answer be the same if Avanti Motor Corporation designed and built a new vehicle that looks like General Motors' Hummer?

ANSWER: The court held that (1) the automobile designs had acquired secondary meaning, (2) there was likelihood of confusion between plaintiff's cars and defendant's replicas, and that (3) injunction granted by district court was proper.

15-5 **Trade Secrets**

A business often works to develop information that is not known by the public or its competitors. However, the information the business has developed may not fit into any of the federally protected categories covered earlier in the chapter. In fact, sometimes the business does not even want to make the information public in a filing for the federal protections. Therefore, the business protects its rights by keeping the information as a trade secret.

15-5a WHAT ARE TRADE SECRETS?

Trade secrets are lists of information, formulas, and even data that businesses compile for use in the marketplace, with customers, or in securing contracts. A trade secret is anything that gives the business a competitive edge and that is not known generally or by competitors. For example, products that are in development by employees cannot be taken by those employees to new employers, who might be competitors, for their competitors' use.

15-5b HOW ARE TRADE SECRETS PROTECTED?

Trade secrets are protected by the business keeping them secret. The information should have controlled access and should be available only to those within the business who have reason to know or need to use the information. Having the documents stamped to reflect their limited use, circulation, and private status is also helpful in establishing the theft or misappropriation of trade secrets because the nature of the information is clear on the face of the document.

Most companies have employees sign nondisclosure agreements so that should they leave their employment they would be subject to suit for breach of contract if they took the information with them. The biography on the nearly decade-long battle between Mattel and MGA (see p. 510), two major toy competitors, illustrates how intense the battle over trade secrets can be.

Forty-five states have adopted the Uniform Trade Secrets Act (UTSA), an act that was drafted and passed to eliminate the common-law remedies that relate to the appropriation of trade secrets by current and former employees. The law was intended to make it easier for employers to recover when employees take trade secrets and use them, either while employed or postemployment (by turning them over to another employer or using the information themselves). However, the application of UTSA has proven to be a challenge for employers because of differing interpretations and applications.

If what the employee has done fits within the definition of a trade secret under the UTSA, then all is well—that is, the employer can recover the remedies afforded under UTSA. Trade secrets have been defined to include everything from processes and procedures to customer lists and customer preferences. (The last two items are not protected under common-law theories for trade secret appropriation.) However, there are situations in which employees use something that is not considered a trade secret but by doing so they are disloyal to the employer. Some courts have held that UTSA preempts such claims and that there is no recovery unless the actions of the employee fit within the UTSA.

For example, in *Huong Que Inc. v Luu*, 58 Cal. Rptr. 3d 527 (Cal. 6th Ct. App. 2007), a California appellate court held that the customer list for a calendar company was not a trade secret and so the USTA did not apply. Mui Luu and Cu Tu Nyguyen founded a Vietnamese calendar company that was the number-one calendar company in the United States. In 2003, the husband and wife team sold their company to Huong Que, Inc., but remained as employees of the new company. Subsequently, Huong discovered an e-mail message entitled "address list" in the electronic mailbox of Mui Luu. The e-mail message was an apparent response by one Huan Nguyen to an earlier message from Luu in which she had written, "Please remember to email address list to me." His reply stated, "Attached are customers' addresses and meeting's report on 5/22/05. Please forward to other procalendar's members." Attached to the e-mail was a text file in Vietnamese, which plaintiffs later translated into English. Entitled "Minutes of meeting regard [*sic*] creation of PROCALENDAR," it called for the formation of a company using capitalization of $100,000 in five equal shares, of which two ($40,000) would be distributed to one Amy Khuu "c/o Mr. & Mrs. Nguyen Tu Cu, Mr. Phan Don." The minutes set forth, among other things, the "responsibilities of each partner...." As relevant here, they stated, "Mrs. Luu Mui will be responsible for bookkeeping, tax, contact with Taiwan for calendar/book printing for customer, and distributing calendar for customer—no direct contact with customer, and no salary. Mr. Cu will be responsible for direct sales with Mr. Xanh, no salary."

Because the list did not qualify as a trade secret, the court held the UTSA did not apply. However, the court clarified that there was a right of recovery—an independent action for breach of the duty of loyalty, which is the right of an employer to recover from an employee for what amounts to "biting the hand that feeds you." Because the two were using the information of an employer to start their own calendar company, there was a cause of action. The loyalty breach claims are based on competitive use. However, USTA does not require competitive use; rather, the employer need only prove that the information was taken by the employee.

15-5c CRIMINAL PENALTIES FOR THEFT OF TRADE SECRETS

The Industrial Espionage Act of 1996 makes it a felony to copy, download, upload, fax, or otherwise communicate trade secrets of U.S. companies to benefit anyone other than the owner of that information. Trade secrets are defined under the IEA very similarly to how they are defined under the UTSA. Again, the IEA does not apply unless the information has been treated as a trade secret.

Fines for violations by individuals are up to $500,000, and imprisonment can be for up to 15 years. For corporations that violate the IEA, the fine is the greater of up to $10,000,000 or twice the value of the secret that was communicated.

Exhibit 15.1 provides a summary of intellectual property rights and protections.

EXHIBIT 15.1 Summary of Intellectual Property Rights

TYPE OF INTELLECTUAL PROPERTY	TRADEMARKS	COPYRIGHTS	PATENTS	TRADE SECRETS
Protection	Words, names, symbols, or devices used to identify a product or service	Original creative works of authorship, such as writings, movies, records, and computer software	Utility, design, and plant patents	Advantageous formulas, devices, or compilation of information
Applicable standard	Identifies and distinguishes a product or service	Original creative works in writing or in another format	New and nonobvious advances	Not readily ascertainable, not disclosed to the public
Where to apply	Patent and Trademark Office	Register of Copyrights	Patent and Trademark Office	No public registration necessary
Duration	Indefinite so long as it continues to be used	Life of author plus 70 years; corporate, 120 years from creation or 95 years from publication of the work	Utility and plant patents, 20 years from date of application; design patents, 14 years	Indefinite so long as secret is not disclosed to public

Source: Adapted from *Anderson's Business Law,* © 2010 by David Twomey and Marianne Jennings.

15-6 International Intellectual Property Issues

15-6a PATENT PROTECTION

The period for patent protection varies from country to country. The United States does not permit patent protection for products until the patent is granted, whereas other countries afford protection from the time application is made. Procedures for obtaining patents also vary significantly from country to country. For example, many countries hold **opposition proceedings** as part of the patent process. Much like the federal regulatory promulgation steps (see Chapter 6), the process includes publishing the description of the patent and inviting the public to study the description and possibly oppose the granting of a patent.

Many countries impose working requirements on the patent holder's use of the patent, which means that the idea or product must be produced commercially within a certain period of time or the patent protection is revoked.

15-6b TRADEMARK PROTECTION

As noted earlier in the discussion of trademarks, the 1891 **Madrid Agreement** (updated in 1989) provides for the Madrid Protocol, which is central registration through the International Bureau, which is part of the World Intellectual Property Organization (WIPO) in Geneva, Switzerland. Registrations with the bureau are effective for five years in all member countries unless one of the members objects to the trademark registration, in which case the registration is not effective in that country.

In 1996, the European Union began its one-stop trademark registration, known as Community Trademark (CTM). Under the provisions of this program, U.S. companies register their trademarks once and enjoy protection in all countries that are part of the European Union. The trademark and backup materials are filed with the Office of Harmonization of the Internal Market (OHIM). The OHIM will then notify the trademark offices in each of the member states of the European Union.

Many countries have permitted the unauthorized use of trademarks in an effort to develop local economies. These countries permit the production of **knock-off goods**, which are goods that carry the trademark or trade name of a firm's product but are not actually produced by that firm. A costly problem for trademark holders

Consider...

Illia Lekach and Simon Falic are brothers-in-law who founded Perfumania, Inc. Perfumania is a chain of no-frills stores that sells 170 brands of upscale perfumes, such as Estée Lauder, Calvin Klein, and Chanel, at prices 20–70 percent below department store prices. Mr. Lekach referred to the company as the Toys "Я" Us of perfume sales.

Manufacturers of expensive perfumes like to sell only to their full-price department store customers. Perfumania must get its supplies from the gray market—unauthorized and authorized distributors in other countries where manufacturers charge less than in the United States.

Givenchy, Boucheron, and Cosmair have sued Perfumania for copyright infringement and patent violations. The manufacturers maintain that they must pay the promotion fees on the perfumes and Perfumania enjoys the benefits of the expensive promotions without paying costs. One manufacturer notes, "I don't want to sell to the gray market. It's not a strategy. You kill your name."

Evaluate the legalities and ethics of Perfumania's gray market purchases and discount sales.

is the **gray market**. Manufacturers in foreign countries are authorized to produce a certain amount of goods, but many foreign manufacturers exceed their licensed quota and dump the goods into the market at a much lower price and thereby reduce the trademark owner's market. Both knock-off and gray market goods are forms of infringement.

15-6c COPYRIGHTS IN INTERNATIONAL BUSINESS

The purpose of the Berne Convention, mentioned earlier and called the Convention for the Protection of Literary and Artistic Works, was to establish international uniformity in copyright protection. The convention was signed on September 9, 1986, and became effective in the United States on March 1, 1989. The convention is administered by WIPO and covers member countries. However, the Berne Convention gives backdoor copyright protection to works originating in non–Berne member countries if the work is simultaneously published in a Berne member country.

15-6d DIFFERING INTERNATIONAL STANDARDS

The protection of intellectual property in other countries is a difficult task, particularly when the standards of those countries do not recognize computer software as a property right.

15-7 Enforcing Business Property Rights

15-7a PRODUCT DISPARAGEMENT

When an untrue statement is made about a business product or service, the defamation is referred to as **disparagement** and is either **trade libel** (written) or **slander of title** (oral). These business torts occur when one business makes untrue statements about another business, its product, or its abilities. The elements for disparagement are as follows:

1. False statement about a business product or about its reputation, honesty, or integrity
2. Publication
3. Statement that is directed at a business (in many cases, businesses are considered public figures, and the statement must be made with malice and the intent to injure that business)
4. Damages

These elements are the same as those discussed in Chapter 9 for the personal tort of defamation. The *Bose Corporation v Consumers Union of United States, Inc.* case (Case 15.5) deals with the tort of disparagement.

15-7b PALMING OFF

Palming off, one of the oldest unfair methods of competition, occurs when one company sells its product by leading buyers to believe it is really another company's product. For example, many cases of palming off took place during the 1980s, when Cabbage Patch dolls were popular, in demand, and scarce. Many replicas were made and called "Cabbage Patch dolls" even though they were not manufactured by Coleco, the original creator.

CASE 15.5 *Bose Corporation v Consumers Union of United States, Inc.* 466 U.S. 485 (1984)

Woofers, Tweeters, and Disparagement

FACTS

Bose Corporation manufactures the Bose 901, a stereo loudspeaker. In May 1970, the Consumers Union publication *Consumer Reports* analyzed and evaluated the middle-range price group of loudspeaker systems, including the Bose 901. It was described in a two-page boxed-off section as "unique and unconventional," but the description also pointed out that a listener could "pinpoint the location of various instruments much more easily with a standard speaker than with the Bose system." The following is an excerpt from the boxed description:

> Worse, individual instruments heard through the Bose system seemed to grow to gigantic proportions and tended to wander about the room. For instance, a violin appeared to be ten feet wide and a piano stretched from wall to wall. With orchestral music, such effects seemed inconsequential. But we think they might become annoying when listening to soloists....
>
> We think the Bose system is so unusual that a prospective buyer must listen to it and judge it for himself. We would suggest delaying so big an investment until you were sure the system would please you after the novelty value had worn off.

The article was not written by the same people who made the observation of the speakers. The observers described the sound as moving around the room and the article described the sounds as wandering back and forth.

Bose Corporation took exception to many of the statements made and asked *Consumer Reports* to publish a retraction. *Consumer Reports* would not retract the statements, and Bose sued for disparagement. The district court found that Bose was a public figure and, as such, was required to prove that the statements were made with knowledge they were false (malice). However, the court did find that some of the remarks constituted disparagement and held for Bose (petitioner). The Court of Appeals reversed on the grounds that the statements were not made with malice, and that the article did not accurately reflect what evaluators heard, but was written for a mass audience and not with reckless disregard for the truth. Bose appealed.

JUDICIAL OPINION

STEVENS, Justice

...There are categories of communication and certain special utterances to which the majestic protection of the First Amendment does not extend because they "are no essential part of any exposition of ideas, and are of such slight social value as a step to truth that any benefit that may be derived from them is clearly outweighed by the social interest in order and morality." Libelous speech has been held to constitute one such category....

We agree with the Court of Appeals that the difference between hearing violin sounds move around the room and hearing them wander back and forth fits easily within the breathing space that gives life to the First Amendment. We may accept all of the purely factual findings of the District Court and nevertheless hold as a matter of law that the record does not contain clear and convincing evidence that [Consumers Union] prepared the loudspeaker article with knowledge that it contained a false statement, or with reckless disregard for the truth.

The judgment of the Court of Appeals is affirmed.

CASE QUESTIONS

1. Who prepared the *Consumer Reports* article?
2. Why is malice an important part of the case?
3. What classes of speech are exceptions to First Amendment protection?
4. Is disparagement a difficult tort to prove?

Establishing that someone is palming off requires proof that consumer confusion is likely because of the appearance or name of the competing product. For example, labeling a diamond DeBiers instead of DeBeers is likely to cause confusion. Competitors' packaging with the same colors and design as an original product creates confusion. Potential buyers are likely to be confused as to who actually made the product and who has what market and quality reputation.

15-7c MISAPPROPRIATION

The tort of **misappropriation** is a form of protection for a business whose trade secrets are taken without authorization. Misappropriation is conversion of a trade secret for self-benefit or the benefit of a new employer. For example, an employee who takes proprietary information such as a customer list from her employer and uses it to start a competing business is guilty of misappropriation. Most companies put noncompete clauses that address the issue of taking trade secrets to a new company or forming a competing company in their employment contracts. Those clauses are covered in Chapter 16.

Consider...

Ross Klein and Amar Lalvani, two former employees of Starwood Hotels & Resorts Worldwide, were hired by Hilton Hotels Corporation in the summer of 2008. A suit filed by Starwood alleged that its two former executives took with them more than 100,000 electronic documents that contained proprietary information that Hilton then used in creating its new Denizen hotel chain.

In developing a concept for a new chain (Denizen is geared at the high-end market), companies spend years and millions on studying consumer needs and preferences, social trends, lighting, costs, food choices, and even fabrics and designs. The suit alleges that all of Starwood's preliminary work on its developmental plans was taken by the executives to Hilton and that its concepts made their way into the Denizen brand. The suit maintains that the two executives sent the documents to Hilton via e-mail and through document shipments.

Starwood uncovered the alleged theft via serendipity. Starwood had begun an arbitration proceeding against Hilton for its recruitment of eight Starwood employees. While Hilton's in-house legal counsel was preparing for that arbitration, he discovered bundles of Starwood documents in the files of Mr. Klein and other Hilton employees. Hilton then sent the electronic files and documents back to Starwood. Eight boxes of materials were mailed to Starwood in February 2009. Hilton's general counsel said in a cover letter that he did not think the information was proprietary or confidential but that he was sending them back as a precaution.

However, Starwood noted that its files included its development plans for its "zen den," which it was going to put in its upscale "W" hotels. Hilton's development plans for Denizen referred to it as their "den of zen."

The Starwood complaint also alleged that the two men took along Starwood's strategic marketing plans and that Starwood has heard from existing customers that Hilton has been approaching them using the same tools and marketing techniques that Starwood has used with them.

What are the rights of companies on proprietary information? What are the rights of companies in terms of enforcing covenants not to compete against employees? Be sure to apply all the enforcement and legal tools that have been covered in this chapter. Evaluate the ethics of Hilton in hiring the two men from Starwood.

BIOGRAPHY 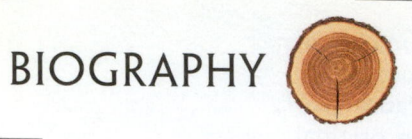   Mattel and Its Battle Over Bratz Dolls[3]

Mattel, Inc., is the world's largest manufacturer and marketer of toys, dolls, games, and stuffed toys and animals. Mattel employed Carter Bryant as a product designer from September 1995 through April 1998 and from January 1999 through October 2000. Upon starting his second term of employment in 1999, Bryant signed an Employee Confidential Information and Inventions Agreement, in which he agreed not to "engage in any employment or business other than for [Mattel], or invest or assist (in any manner) any business competitive with the business or future business plans of [Mattel]." Also, Bryant assigned to Mattel all rights, title, and interest in the "inventions" he conceived of, or reduced to practice, during his employment.

Bryant also completed Mattel's Conflict of Interest Questionnaire and certified that he had not worked for any of Mattel's competitors in the prior 12 months and had not engaged in any business dealings creating a conflict of interest. Bryant agreed to notify Mattel of any future events raising a conflict of interest.[4]

A July 18, 2003, *Wall Street Journal* article suggested Bryant had copied a scrapped Mattel project, known as "Toon Teens," in creating the Bratz line of dolls. The story reported that MGA said that the Bratz were designed by Carter Bryant, a former member of Mattel's Barbie team. Bryant didn't work on the line that Mattel scrapped in 1998. But most Barbie designers had seen the prototypes. Although the doll line that was scrapped wasn't exactly like the Bratz, they were remarkably similar with the Bratz's oversized heads, their pursed lips, cartoonish eyes, and big feet comparable to the dolls the Barbie team had created. Lily Martinez, a designer who still works at Mattel, came up with the idea for the big doll heads and posted her sketch on her cubicle where anyone could see it.[5]

By 2003, MGA's revenues were about $800 million, with 65 percent of that coming from the Bratz doll line.

After investigating the situation reported in the *Wall Street Journal*, Mattel discovered in November 2003 that Bryant had secretly entered into an agreement with MGA Entertainment, Inc., a competitor, during the time that he was employed by Mattel, to receive royalties for "works for hire." In an agreement signed September 18, 2000, Bryant agreed to provide product design services for MGA's line of "Bratz" dolls in exchange for $5,500 per month for the first six months and $5,000 per month for the next three months, as well as a 3 percent royalty on the Bratz he worked on. Mattel filed its copyright registration for the Toon Teens drawings on November 28, 2003—four years after the drawings were created.

Bryant's last day of employment at Mattel was October 20, 2000. Bryant went through the usual Mattel checkout. The checkout form used for Bryant misquoted Bryant's Inventions Agreement, which did not expressly assign to Mattel Bryant's interest in his ideas. This error may have resulted from the fact that prior versions of Mattel's Inventions Agreement expressly assigned the contracting employee's interest in his ideas. Bryant's agreement identifies "discoveries, improvements, processes, developments, designs, know-how, data computer programs and formulae, whether patentable or unpatentable"—language that was not in prior versions.

Mattel filed suit against Bryant for (1) breach of contract, (2) breach of fiduciary duty, (3) breach of duty of loyalty, (4) unjust enrichment, and (5) conversion.[6] MGA Entertainment intervened in that case. Mattel settled with Bryant but amended its complaint against MGA, alleging intentional interference with contract, aiding and abetting breach of fiduciary duty, aiding and abetting breach of duty of loyalty, conversion, unfair competition, and copyright infringement.[7] However, MGA counterclaimed against Mattel for appropriation of trade secrets. MGA's counterclaim arose out of the activities of Mattel's "Market Intelligence Group," a collection of employees dispatched to international toy fairs and directed to gather information from Mattel's competitors' private showrooms through the use of false pretenses. Allegations in the counterclaim stated that the employees had made copies of identification credentials in order to gain access to the private showrooms, showrooms that were intended for buyers to be able to see what was available for purchase from MGA in the future.

A jury found for Mattel on all counts, concluding that Bryant conceived the idea for the name Bratz and created the concept drawings and sculpt for the Bratz dolls during his second term of employment with Mattel (January 4, 1999 to October 4, 2000). The federal district court placed the Bratz trademarks in a constructive trust and enjoined MGA from continuing to sell dolls. MGA appealed, and the case was remanded for a new trial. Upon remand, both companies moved for summary judgment on various issues. The court denied summary judgment on some issues, but required a trial for others, including MGA's counterclaims on Mattel's market intelligence group.[8]

Following approximately two weeks of deliberations, the jury found that Mattel had misappropriated 26 trade secrets owned by MGA and awarded MGA $3.4 million in damages for each act of misappropriation, reaching a total award of $88.5 million. The jury also found that Mattel's misappropriation had been willful and malicious, thus entitling MGA to exemplary damages under Cal. Civ.Code § 3426.3 for a total verdict of $177.5 million, followed by an award by the court of $2.52 million in attorneys' fees and costs to MGA.[9]

However, that decision, including the determination of attorney's fees, was reversed, and is now back in federal district court.[10]

One expert commented that the litigation "killed" the Bratz line and nearly destroyed MGA as a competitor. Others have noted the lessons for all companies on preserving trade secrets, controlling access to trade secrets (such as pictures of developing products being posted in employees' carrels), and the destructive effects of litigation.

Summary

What are the types of intellectual property businesses own?

- Patents—for products, processes, discoveries
- Copyrights—for books, designs, dramatic works, photographs, films, etc.
- Trademarks—the brand protections for product symbols
- Trade names—the brand protections for product names
- Trade dress—the brand protection for those easily recognizable shapes and colors of a company and its product
- Trade secrets—the knowledge a business develops that provide its competitive edge

What are the legal protections for intellectual property?

- Patents—statutory protection of exclusivity for products and processes
- Copyrights—statutory protection of exclusivity for words, thoughts, ideas, music
- Trademarks—statutory protection of exclusivity for product symbols

- Trade names—statutory protection of exclusivity for unique product labels and names
- Trade dress—statutory protection of exclusivity for product colors and motifs
- Trade secrets—criminal sanctions for unauthorized transfer or use and violation of employer nondisclosure agreements

What issues of intellectual property protection exist in international operations?

- The Berne Convention—copyright recognition and protection across borders
- OPTH—European Community Trademark registration
- WIPO—World Intellectual Property Organization

What private remedies exist for property protections?

- Product disparagement—false and damaging statements
- Misappropriation—use of another's ideas or trade secrets
- Palming off—causing deception about the maker or source of a product

Questions and Problems

1. The San Diego Chicken, a mascot at professional baseball games, has a portion of his act in which he grabs a purple dinosaur and stomps it, stamps it, pounds it, and pummels it. Lyons Partnership, L.P., produces the *Barney the Dinosaur* television show, which features a purple dinosaur, and holds all its product

licenses. Lyons filed suit against Ted Giannoulas (the man beneath the San Diego Chicken costume) for copyright infringement.

A Texas court classified the portion of Mr. Giannoulas's act that involved a purple dinosaur as a form of parody or satire that was thereby protected by the First Amendment. Kenneth Fitzgerald, the lawyer for Mr. Giannoulas, said that Mr. Giannoulas will seek to recover his attorney's fees in the case.

Mr. Fitzgerald noted during the case that Barney has been spoofed by Jay Leno as well as on the television show "Saturday Night Live," but Lyons chose only to pursue Mr. Giannoulas.

What is wrong with selective enforcement of one's copyright protections? Is Barney the Dinosaur something that can be copyrighted? [*Lyons Partnership v Giannoulas*, 179 F.3d 384 (5th Cir. 1999)]

2. Yankee Candle Company, a leading manufacturer of scented candles, sued competitor Bridgewater Candle Company for trade name and trade dress infringement. Yankee alleged that Bridgewater's labels were the same size, had the same border, and featured similar photographs to depict the scents of the candles. For example, the Bridgewater "French Vanilla" photograph has ice cream cones filled with vanilla ice cream and the Yankee "French Vanilla" only features empty cones with no ice cream. Both the Bridgewater fragrance "Cinnamon Rolls" and the Yankee "Cinnamon" display photographs of cinnamon rolls. However, the Yankee photograph also includes cinnamon sticks, while the Bridgewater rolls highlight the sugary frosting found on a cinnamon roll. Both the Bridgewater "Apple Pie" and the Yankee "Spiced Apple" contain photographs of apple pies. However, the Yankee photograph also features a basket and several apple slices. The Bridgewater photograph contains several whole apples. In addition, in the Bridgewater photographs, the darkish filling is oozing out of the pies, while the Yankee pies are lighter in color and not leaking apple filling.

Yankee also claimed that Bridgewater had infringed its trade dress: (i) by copying Yankee's method of shelving and displaying candles in its stores, called the "Vertical Display System"; (ii) by copying the overall "look and feel" of Yankee's Housewarmer line of candles; and (iii) by copying the design of Yankee's merchandise catalog, specifically its one-fragrance-per-page layout.

Is there enough here to support any intellectual property claims by Yankee? Specify what types of and the elements required to establish any possible claims. [*Yankee Candle Co., Inc. v Bridgewater Candle Co., LLC*, 259 F.3d 25 (1st Cir. 2001)]

3. GM developed an ad for its Terrain utility vehicle that featured a tattooed, shirtless image of Albert Einstein with "his underpants on display." The body featured in the ad with Dr. Einstein's head was that of one of *People* magazine's "sexiest men alive." The ad carries the caption, "Ideas are sexy too."

The Hebrew University of Jerusalem has filed suit against GM to enforce the name and intellectual property rights that Dr. Einstein willed to the university. GM has responded that it purchased the image of Dr. Einstein for use from a licensing firm. Does the university have a basis for its claim for $75,000? Could it stop the use of Dr. Einstein's head on another body in an ad? Discuss what intellectual property rights are at issue here.

4. *The Hangover Part II* has been a hotbed of intellectual property issues. Last summer, Warner Brothers settled a lawsuit brought by the tattoo artist who did Mike Tyson's facial tattoo that was then replicated on a character in the movie. Now, Louis Vuitton has filed suit in federal court for trademark infringement of its famous bags.

The ne'er-do-well character played by Zach Galifianakis has coined a pop-culture phrase by warning his fellow imbibers when they touch his Louis Vuitton bag, "Careful, that is a Louis Vuitton." The lawsuit seeks to have the trademark bag excised from the film as well as a share of the movie's profits. The company seems most irritated because it alleges that the bag used in the movie is a knock-off. Louis Vuitton is very aggressive in enforcing its trademark rights and has brought suit against artists who have used the signature handbags and luggage in their paintings.

What is the issue in the use of trademarked products in artistic works? Why is Louis Vuitton so concerned about the use of its products in a film such as *The Hangover Part II*?

5. Rich Leivenberg and Jane Wyler, founders of the company Reuseniks, developed a new product called reusable dry-cleaning bags. Ms. Wyler met another couple in 2008 and explained to them her plan to develop the reusable dry cleaning bags. The couple was "blown away" by the idea and developed their own, "The Green Garmento." What are the rights of Reuseniks' founders? What do you need to know to be able to answer their questions about their rights?

6. LVM has registered trademarks for "LOUIS VUIT-TON" in connection with luggage and ladies' handbags (the "LOUIS VUITTON mark") and for a stylized monogram of "LV," used in connection with traveling bags and other goods (the "LV mark"). In 2005, LVM adopted other designs consisting of canvas with repetitions of the LV mark (in multiple colors of red, green, and blue) and smiling cherries on a brown background (the "Cherry design").

The Multicolor design and the Cherry design attracted immediate and extraordinary media attention and publicity in magazines such as *Vogue, W, Elle, Harper's Bazaar, Us Weekly, Life and Style, Travel & Leisure, People, In Style*, and *Jane*. The press published photographs showing celebrities carrying these handbags, including Jennifer Lopez, Madonna, Eve, Elizabeth Hurley, Carmen Electra, and Anna Kournikova, among others. *People* magazine said, "the wait list is in the thousands." The handbags retailed in the range of $995 for a medium handbag to $4,500 for a large travel bag.

Haute Diggity Dog, LLC, which is a relatively small and relatively new business located in Nevada, manufactures and sells nationally—primarily through pet stores—a line of pet chew toys and beds whose names parody elegant high-end brands of products such as perfume, cars, shoes, sparkling wine, and handbags. These include—in addition to Chewy Vuiton (LOUIS VUITTON)—Chewnel No. 5 (Chanel No. 5), Furcedes (Mercedes), Jimmy Chew (Jimmy Choo), Dog Perignonn (Dom Perignon), Sniffany & Co. (Tiffany & Co.), and Dogior (Dior). The chew toys and pet beds are plush, made of polyester, and have a shape and design that loosely imitate the signature product of the targeted brand. They are mostly distributed and sold through pet stores, although one or two Macy's stores carry Haute Diggity Dog's products. The dog toys are generally sold for less than $20, although larger versions of some of Haute Diggity Dog's plush dog beds sell for more than $100.

Haute Diggity Dog's "Chewy Vuiton" dog toys, in particular, loosely resemble miniature handbags and undisputedly evoke LVM handbags of similar shape, design, and color. In lieu of the LOUIS VUITTON mark, the dog toy uses "Chewy Vuiton"; in lieu of the LV mark, it uses "CV"; the other symbols and colors employed are imitations, but not exact ones, of those used in the LVM Multicolor and Cherry designs. LVM brought suit against Haute Diggity alleging trademark infringement, trademark dilution, copyright infringement, and common law violations. Can it recover? Why or why not? And what basis would LVM argue for its allegations? [*Louis Vuitton Malletier S.A. v Haute Diggity Dog, LLC*, 507 F.3d 252 (4th Cir. 2007)]

7. Charles Atlas has been in the business of selling bodybuilding courses for more than 70 years. Advertisements for Atlas's bodybuilding courses, which have appeared in DC Comic books, have included a one-page comic strip story titled "The Insult that Made a Man out of Mac." In the story line, (1) a bully kicks sand in Mac's face at the beach; (2) after taking the Atlas course, the skinny Mac develops a muscular physique; (3) Mac finds the bully, again on the beach, and punches him, for which he receives newfound respect, particularly from his female companion; and (4) in the final panel, the phrase "HERO OF THE BEACH" appears as a halo-like formation hovering over Mac's head. Mr. Atlas registered Mac with the Principal Register as the before and after characters of "Skinny" and "Joe." "Joe" is Mac in his muscular form with the leopard-skin trunks.

DC Comics created a character known as Flex Mentallo, who like Mac, came to be imbued with extraordinary strength. Flex Mentallo, once a scrawny weakling who has sand kicked in his face by a bully, returns to the beach with his muscular physique, and, like Mac in the Atlas comic ad, he beats up the bully and becomes "the Hero of the beach."

However, after Flex Mentallo acquires his powers the Charles Atlas tale changes a bit and Flex beats up the woman he had been with by smashing her in the face and proclaims, "I don't need a tramp like you anymore!" Mr. Atlas sued for infringement, saying that the depiction tarnished the image of Mac and, thus, the Atlas product line. DC defends its new character and story line as parody. Determine what the court should do with the Atlas infringement suit. [*Charles Atlas, Ltd. v DC Comics, Inc.*, 112 F. Supp. 2d 330 (S.D.N.Y. 2000)]

8. In 1997, Sweet Romance Jewelry Manufacturing created a piece of costume jewelry known as the "Lady Caroline Lorgnette" and began manufacturing and selling copies of the necklace in 1999 through various stores and websites. Sometime between 2005 and 2008, Home Shopping Network (HSN) began manufacturing and distributing copies of a "virtually identical" necklace.

On March 6, 2008, Sweet Romance submitted an application to the Office for Registration of its copyright in the necklace and received confirmation of receipt of the application on March 12, 2008. On March 27, 2008, Sweet Romance sued HSN for copyright infringement of the necklace. Although the Copyright Office ultimately issued a copyright registration certificate for the necklace, it did not do so before the suit was filed. HSN says that the suit must be dismissed for the failure to register the necklace as a copyrighted product. Is HSN correct?

9. Do the following slogans constitute protectable business properties?
   a. MetLife: "Get Met, It Pays"
   b. General Electric: "GE Brings Good Things to Life"
   c. Nike: "Just Do It"
   d. Toys "Я" Us: "Я Us"

10. Starbucks, Inc., the international coffeehouse, is an aggressive defender of its name as well as the names for its coffees. It has ongoing litigation for infringement:

   - A & D Café of Brooklyn, New York, uses the name "Warbucks" for its coffee, and Starbucks has filed suit against the café for dilution of its trade name.

   - Sambuck's Coffee House of Astoria, Oregon, has been sued by Starbucks for dilution. However,

the owner of the café is Samantha Buck-Lundberg, and she explains that the name of the café is a play on her name.

   - Black Bear Monster Roastery in New Hampshire uses the name "Charbucks Blend" for one of its coffees, and Starbucks has filed suit for disparagement.

   - Backwash.com had a link to Starbucks on its website. Starbucks filed suit to have the link removed, which Backwash did, citing "unappreciative" reasons.

   - Coffee Bean & Tea Leaf Co. of Los Angeles has sued Starbucks for trademark infringement for the company's use of the term "ice blended," a term that the LA company claims it coined.[11]

What protections exist for trade names? For trademarks? Do you think there is infringement in these cases?

ECONOMICS, BUSINESS STRATEGY, & THE LAW

Who Owns "A Wonderful Life"?

In 1946, director Frank Capra produced *It's a Wonderful Life*, a movie based on a short story by Philip Van Doren Stern called "The Greatest Gift." The movie, starring Jimmy Stewart, did not perform well at the box office, and, although it received five Academy Award nominations, it won no awards. The movie's copyright was allowed to lapse. Television stations showed the classic without paying fees because the copyright had lapsed.

However, the U.S. Supreme Court decision in *Stewart v Abend*, 495 U.S. 207 (1990), offering an extension of the copyright protection of the underlying story to the movie, affected Jimmy Stewart's life once again. The original story owner, Mr. Stern, held the rights to the story since the movie rights had lapsed. With

his story copyright in place, royalties for its use in the movie had to be paid once again. The owners of *It's a Wonderful Life* began charging fees to cover their fees to Mr. Stern, and the result was costly access. *It's a Wonderful Life* was seen on television day and night during the holiday season when the copyright on the movie had lapsed. Now, with the copyright clarification, the movie rights have been reprotected. The story's continuing protection and the high royalty fees make *It's a Wonderful Life* a singular holiday event.

What is the relationship between movie copyrights and the rights to the underlying story? Who owns what between story authors and movie producers? What should businesses negotiating movie rights and royalties be certain about before signing an agreement?

Notes

1. The protection of intellectual property has been important to commercial development both here and in other countries for centuries. See the *Instructor's Manual* for more information.

2. From the Salinger complaint filed with the court.

3. By way of full disclosure, the author has done ethics training work for Mattel. All information contained here is from public records.

4. *Mattel, Inc. v Bryant*, 441 F. Supp. 2d 1081 (C.D. Cal. 2005).

5. Maureen Tkacik, "Dolled Up: To Lure Older Girls, Mattel Brings in Hip-Hop Crowd; It Sees Stalwart Barbie Lose Market Share, So 'Flayas' Will Take on the 'Bratz'," *Wall Street Journal*, July 18, 2003, p. A1.

6. The case has a fascinating history of procedural questions, including an issue of diversity of jurisdiction that resulted in an appellate decision. *Mattel, Inc. v Brandt*, 446 F.3d 1011 (9th Cir. 2006).

7. *Mattel, Inc. v MGA Entertainment, Inc.*, 782 F. Supp. 2d 911 (C.D. Cal. 2011).

8. *Mattel, Inc. v MGA Entertainment, Inc.*, 2011 WL 3420571 (C.D. Cal.).

9. *Mattel, Inc. v MGA Entertainment, Inc.*, 801 F. Supp. 2d 950 (C.D. Cal. 2011).

10. *Mattel, Inc. v MGA Entertainment, Inc.*, 705 F.3d 1108 (9th Cir. 2013).

11. Emily Lambert, "The Buck Stops Here," *Forbes*, January 6, 2003, p. 52.

Chapter 16

BUSINESS COMPETITION:
Antitrust

Economic power is an inevitable result of the free enterprise system. Building a better mousetrap should result in attracting more customers and developing economic power. But gaining economic power through means other than "superior skill, foresight, and industry" destroys the free enterprise system and often means that buyers don't get a better mousetrap. They are stuck with a mediocre mousetrap built by a firm with ill-gained economic power and resulting market control.

Antitrust law exists to prevent the growth of economic or market power through means other than superior skill, foresight, and industry. Making sure that the free enterprise system has its necessary fuel of competition is the purpose of antitrust laws. This chapter answers the following questions: What interferes with competition? Or, in other words, what are restraints of trade? What forms do they take? What antitrust laws apply when concerns about competition arise? What penalties can be imposed for violations of these laws?

UPDATE
For up-to-date legal news, go to **mariannejennings.com**

Consider...

Leegin Creative Leather Products, Inc., designs, manufactures, and distributes leather goods and accessories under the brand name "Brighton." The Brighton brand, often known as the brand with the silver heart, has now expanded into a full line of women's fashion accessories and is sold across the United States in more than 5,000 retail stores. In 1997, Leegin notified its retailers that it was going to continue focusing on its strong customer service, so readily available in its smaller outlets but not in places such as Wal-Mart or Costco. To prevent the Brighton brand from being sold at warehouses and over the Internet, Leegin required its retailers to follow a minimum price policy or be terminated as a Brighton retailer. Kay's Kloset was terminated for holding sales on Brighton items in order to compete with local retailers. Kay's Kloset wants to know, "Can Leegin do that because we sold at a cheaper price? Isn't this anticompetitive?"

> *People of the same trade seldom meet together, even for merriment and diversion, but the conversation ends in some contrivance to raise prices. It is impossible indeed to prevent such meetings, by any law which would be consistent with liberty and justice. But though the law cannot hinder people of the same trade from sometimes assembling together, it ought to do nothing to facilitate such assemblies.*
>
> **Adam Smith**
> The Wealth of Nations

> *While the law of competition may be sometimes hard for the individual, it is best for the race, because it ensures the survival of the fittest in every department.*
>
> **Andrew Carnegie**

16-1 What Interferes with Competition? Covenants Not to Compete

As early as the sixteenth century, businesspeople developed agreements or covenants not to compete. The initial reaction to those agreements was not positive, with the courts issuing a resounding "No!" to those who came seeking to keep others from competing. However, by the seventeenth and eighteenth centuries, the courts began to see that some circumstances required trade restraint if competition was to flourish. As odd as it may sound, covenants not to compete can ensure competition. Through careful review of the covenants that resulted in judicial disputes, the courts began to carve out permissible types of restraints, such as protections for the buyer of a business. In these purchase agreements, the seller agreed not to open a competing business. This trade restraint, called a **covenant not to compete**, was necessary to preserve competition. A buyer purchasing a business meant someone else was entering the market. If the seller dropped down a few doors and opened the same business again, the seller would take customers and put the new buyer out of business.

So, covenants that were part of business purchase agreements are valid as long as they are reasonable in length and scope. For example, in *Mitchell v Reynolds*, 24 Eng. Rep. 347 (1711), a baker who sold his bakery agreed not to compete in the immediate area for five years, and a court held the covenant valid because it was limited in time and geographic scope.

Contracts and covenants that restrain trade are not illegal *per se*, meaning prohibited all the time no matter what. Courts continue to examine the scope of covenants and contracts that restrain trade to make sure that they are necessary for protection and not too broad in scope. For example, a covenant in a contract for the sale of a dry cleaning business that prohibits the seller from opening another dry cleaning business anywhere in the state is unreasonably broad, but a similar covenant limited to the town where the business is located is probably reasonable. The goodwill of the business must be preserved if competition is to take hold. The extent of the protection for the goodwill is determined by the economic base of the area: How many dry cleaners can the area support?

Partners' and employees' restrictions that prevent them from competing for a certain time period after they leave a partnership or corporation are also reasonable as long as they are not excessive. More details are provided in Chapter 17, but these covenants protect the investment the employers or partnerships make in recruiting and training employees or new partners.

Shopping center owners and anchor tenants may want to control the makeup of the center or even the types of merchandise sold by each retailer. In some instances, the anchor tenant stipulates that it must review and approve all potential lessees for a center. For example, in some leases, anchor tenants have clauses that disallow the leasing of space to discount merchants. This type of provision prevents the anchor tenant from being undersold on certain items.

The issue that arises from these clauses that limit the types of business operations is whether the clauses violate federal or state antitrust laws. Many such clauses have been challenged by the Federal Trade Commission and the Justice Department in an effort to eliminate them.

At this point, it is difficult to determine which clauses do or do not violate antitrust laws. Because the issues of the type of market, location, and competition vary from city to city, the validity of these clauses also varies. But, for the most part, if the clauses are reasonably necessary for shopping center survival, tenants should insist on them. In the following case, the issue of use restriction is critical. *Mark-It Place Foods, Inc. v New Plan Excel Realty Trust* (Case 16.1) deals with the issues in these shopping center restrictions.

Business Planning Tip

When negotiating valid covenants not to compete, follow these guidelines:

1. Be certain the covenant is necessary.

2. Be certain the covenant is reasonable:

   a. It covers only the geographic scope necessary. (A five-mile radius for the sale of a dry cleaning business is reasonable; a worldwide prohibition is not.)

   b. It covers only the time necessary. (Five years is reasonable; a lifetime prohibition is not.)

3. Make the covenant part of the agreement of sale, lease, or employment. Separate agreements arouse suspicions.

4. Be certain both parties initial the noncompete clause or paragraph.

5. Legal representation helps ensure validity by assumed understanding.

© Grounder/Shutterstock.com

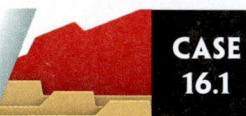

CASE 16.1 *Mark-It Place Foods, Inc. v New Plan Excel Realty Trust* 804 N.E.2d 979 (Ohio App. 2004)

FACTS

In the late 1980s, Wal-Mart Stores, Inc., retained the services of Leo Eisenberg Co., a nationwide developer and shopping center manager, to develop a shopping center in New Boston, Ohio. Eisenberg then formed the New Boston Development Company (NBDC) to build and to later own the shopping center intended to house the new Wal-Mart store. NBDC also leased 52,628 square feet in the shopping center to Scrivner, Inc., for a supermarket. That lease contained the following provision:

"Neither Lessor nor any affiliate or related party shall, … *sell or offer for sale groceries, meats, poultry, seafood, dairy products, fruits, vegetables or baked goods*, provided these restrictions shall not be deemed to prohibit a restaurant serving prepared food." (Emphasis added.)

NBDC's lease to Wal-Mart did not prohibit Wal-Mart from selling any of the items listed in the just-cited exclusive-use provision, and Wal-Mart sold foodstuffs such as "chips, nuts, beverages, cereal, cookies, canned meats, pasta, and other convenience food items."

© Harper 3D/Shutterstock.com

CONTINUED

Wal-Mart's lease provided that it could use the demised premises for "any lawful purpose."

On June 14, 1990, Scrivner assigned its leasehold interest to S.M. Flickinger Co., who sublet the premises to Festival. Fleming is the successor in interest to Flickinger.

When NBDC decided to sell the shopping center to New Plan, New Plan discovered both the exclusive-use covenant in Scrivner's lease (the property occupied by Festival Foods under the sublease) and the absence of a reciprocal restrictive-use covenant in Wal-Mart's lease. On the basis of assurances that Wal-Mart would not violate the restriction, New Plan bought the shopping center.

Fleming then sent a letter to New Plan complaining that Wal-Mart was selling foodstuffs at its store in violation of its assigned lease's exclusive-use provision. Fleming asked that New Plan promptly take action to "ensure that Wal-Mart immediately discontinue the sale of groceries, meats, poultry, seafood, dairy products, fruits, vegetables or baked goods to the public." No action was taken, and Fleming discontinued its rental payments.

Festival filed suit, alleging that New Plan and Fleming had violated the lease's terms by permitting Wal-Mart to sell foodstuffs. The trial court concluded that no breach of the lease's exclusive-use provision occurred by permitting Wal-Mart to sell particular food items. In view of the fact that Wal-Mart was not a "supermarket," and was not primarily engaged in sale of foodstuffs, the court concluded that New Plan did not violate its lease with Fleming. The court granted summary judgment in favor of New Plan.

JUDICIAL OPINION

ABELE, Judge

[T]he trial court's interpretation of the contract language is too restrictive. If the lease provision prohibited only the sale of "groceries," then we might agree that the provision could either be construed as meaning "supermarket" or that the term is sufficiently ambiguous to warrant consideration of parol evidence. We note that no case law in Ohio appears to define the term "groceries," but other jurisdictions have, at times, struggled with what is encompassed by that term. Be that as it may, the lease provision at issue here specifies more than just "groceries." It also states that the lessor shall not lease premises to any store that sells "meats, poultry, seafood, dairy products, fruits, vegetables or baked goods…." This language indicates that the parties meant to prohibit not just the sale of "groceries" by supermarkets but also the sale of other specified items by any type of store. For instance, pursuant to the lease,

"baked goods" could not be sold by any store, whether that store is a "supermarket" or is another type of store. Had the parties to the lease simply meant to exclude supermarkets, they could have used either that specific term or they could have expressly stated that no other store in the shopping center could sell "groceries." They would not have inserted a litany of other prohibited items. Moreover, by interpreting the exclusive-use provision as prohibiting other supermarkets, we would be forced to ignore the express language of the lease that prohibits any store from selling "meats, poultry, seafood, dairy products, fruits, vegetables or baked goods."

Having concluded that the exclusive-use provision of the lease has a broader meaning than was afforded to it by the trial court, we must now address whether that provision amounted to an illegal restraint of trade. New Plan argued below that if the exclusive-use provision was given its literal meaning, then it would violate state restraint-of-trade laws. The trial court essentially ruled in its March 9, 2001 judgment that the law was not violated because the lease provision prevented letting space only to "supermarkets" or to "store[s] primarily engaged in the sale of foodstuffs." Now that we have given the provision a more expansive reading, consistent with the terminology used therein, it is necessary to revisit the issue of state restraint-of-trade laws.

The gist of New Plan's argument is that by virtue of the exclusive-use provision in the lease, NBDC and Scrivner combined to form an illegal "trust" in restraint of trade. We disagree.

The Ohio Supreme Court recognized years ago that if antitrust laws were construed literally or strictly, no partnership could be formed, no corporation could be organized, no vendor could agree to a reasonable limitation upon his future business, and scores of other activities that have been permitted and approved of in this country for centuries would be banned. Thus, the court held that contracts in restraint of trade are not illegal unless they are unreasonable.

Similarly, in the instant case, the restrictive-use provision prohibits stores only from selling groceries and other specified food items in the shopping center. It did not affect the rest of the New Boston community and, thus, appears to pass muster. Moreover, we believe that the exclusive-use provision satisfies other criteria adopted by courts to determine whether such provisions are reasonable. For example, the federal District Court for the Southern District of Ohio has opined that the factors to examine when determining whether an exclusive-use provision is over-broad are (1) the relevant product and geographic markets, together with the showing of unreasonable impact upon competition in these markets due to the restrictive covenant; (2) the

CONTINUED

availability of alternate sites for the entity excluded by the operation of such covenant; (3) the significance of competition eliminated by the exclusivity clause, and whether present or future competitors were the parties excluded; (4) the scope of the restrictive covenant and whether it varies depending on the circumstances; and (5) the economic justifications for including the restrictive covenant in the lease. Weighing these factors in light of the evidentiary materials submitted below, we are not persuaded that the exclusive-use provision constitutes an unreasonable restraint of trade. As noted previously, this provision pertains only to tenants within that particular shopping center. It does not affect the rest of the community. Our review of the record has found no evidence to suggest that this provision restricted entry of, or prohibited

competition by, any grocer or seller of foodstuffs outside the shopping center and in the larger New Boston community. We emphasize that antitrust laws exist for the protection of competition, not competitors, and that the essence of competition is not within a shopping center but between shopping centers.

Therefore, New Plan has not carried its burden on summary judgment to establish that this particular provision works an illegal restraint of trade.

Affirmed on different reasoning.

CASE QUESTIONS

1. How broad does the court see the lease restriction to be?
2. Given the court's interpretation of the lease restriction, what effect is there on competition?

16-2 What Interferes with Competition? An Overview of the Federal Statutory Scheme on Restraint of Trade

During the last half of the nineteenth century, the United States experienced a tremendous change in its economy. A primarily agricultural economy changed to an industrial economy. Law on business combinations was largely undeveloped and unsuitable for the types of predatory business practices this new industrial age brought. Using the common-law standards discussed in the first section resulted in nonuniform standards for anticompetitive behavior. Congress addressed anticompetitive behavior with a series of antitrust statutes passed in the late nineteenth and early twentieth centuries. With some amendments and changes, this scheme still exists and applies today. Exhibit 16.1 summarizes the general federal statutory antitrust laws.

Federal antitrust laws apply to business conduct in interstate commerce. Even if an activity is purely intrastate, it is subject to federal laws if the activity has a substantial economic effect on interstate commerce. In only a few instances is interstate commerce not found. In *McClain v Real Estate Board of New Orleans*, 441 U.S. 942 (1980), for example, an antitrust action against real estate brokers who worked only in the New Orleans area was permitted under the Sherman Act because the U.S. Supreme Court found that the brokers facilitated the loans and insurance for the properties they sold. The loans and insurance were provided by national firms, and funding came from outside the state. This involvement of interstate commerce, even in an indirect fashion, is sufficient for **Sherman Act** jurisdiction.

The **Clayton Act** and the **Robinson–Patman Act** have more stringent requirements for federal application, such as having sales across state lines or two businesses involved in interstate commerce.

Even if the federal laws do not apply to a particular transaction, states will also have their own laws on anticompetitive behavior, with some states regulating different sorts of activities, such as price gouging, which is charging a price that produces a gross or net profit above a certain percentage determined by the statute or regulation. These statutes go into effect in situations such as post hurricane areas

EXHIBIT 16.1 Federal Antitrust Statutes

STATUTE	ORIGINAL DATE	JURISDICTION	COVERAGE	PENALTIES
Sherman Act 15 U.S.C. § 1	1890	Commerce clause	Monopolies; attempts to monopolize; boycotts; refusals to deal; price fixing; resale price maintenance; division of markets	Criminal; $100,000,000 if a corporation, or if individual, $1,000,000, or by imprisonment not exceeding 10 years, $10,000,000, for individuals if intentional; also private suits
Clayton Act 1914 15 U.S.C. § 12	1914	Persons engaged in commerce	Tying; treble damages; mergers; interlocking directorates	Private suits
Federal Trade Commission Act 15 U.S.C. § 41	1914	Commerce clause	Unfair methods of FTC competition	
Robinson–Patman Act 15 U.S.C. § 13	1936	Persons engaged in commerce and selling	Price discrimination	Private suits and criminal penalties for international acts goods across state lines
Celler–Kefauver (part of Clayton Act) 15 U.S.C. § 18	1950		Asset acquisitions	
Hart–Scott–Rodino Antitrust Improvements Act 15 U.S.C. § 1311	1976 amended 1980, 1994	Gives greater authority to Justice Department for prosecution; requires premerger notification to Justice Department		
Antitrust Modernization Commission	2002	Gave authority to study antitrust laws, and the 2007 report recommended no changes in the laws		

© Cengage Learning

when clean water is not readily available but willing sellers are offering it at prices up to five times higher than normal.

16-2a WHAT TYPES OF ACTIVITIES DO THE FEDERAL LAWS REGULATE?

The federal antitrust laws can be broken down into a chart overview that will help you understand what anticompetitive behavior is and where the federal antitrust laws apply.

Anticompetitive behavior breaks down first into two large chunks: horizontal and vertical. Horizontal behaviors are those between and among competitors, and federal law takes any activities here seriously. In these types of behaviors, the statutes and courts find *per se* **illegal** behavior, which means that courts do not analyze what the competitors did; their behavior is just plain illegal. Fixing prices and monopolizing are *per se* illegal. Vertical behaviors are those along the supply

EXHIBIT 16.2 A Look at Markets, Competition, and Antitrust Laws

HORIZONTAL MARKETS	VERTICAL MARKETS
Monopolization	Tying
(Sherman Act)	Monopsony (Sherman Act)
Price fixing	Price discrimination
(Sherman Act)	(Robinson–Patman Act)
Refusals to deal	Resale price maintenance
Group boycotts	Exclusive dealing, sole outlets, customer and territory restrictions
Mergers among competitors	Mergers along the supply chain
Interlocking directorates	Interlocking directorates
(Clayton Act)	(Clayton Act)

© Cengage Learning

chain, between manufacturer and distributor or between manufacturer and retailer. Because other manufacturers and retailers are competing with the parties in the supply chain for the same customers, arrangements that these parties make could actually help competition. Although some vertical behaviors are *per se* illegal, the courts have been chipping away to make more of the vertical activities subject to a **rule of reason** standard, which means that the courts examine whether the activities help or hinder competition. Exhibit 16.2 is a diagram of the types of activities and what laws apply.

16-3 Horizontal Restraints of Trade

Horizontal restraints of trade are designed to lessen competition among a firm's competitors. For example, the collusion on fuel surcharges discovered between Virgin and British Airways was found to be a horizontal restraint. The Sherman Act covers the horizontal restraints of **price fixing**, market division, **group boycotts** and refusals to deal, and monopolization. The Clayton Act also covers the problem of anticompetitive horizontal mergers or mergers with competitors.

16-3a MONOPOLIZATION

Section 2 of the Sherman Act prohibits the act of **monopolizing**. A Sherman Act monopolization charge requires proof of (1) market power in the relevant market and (2) some intentional or willful abuse of that power.

Market power is the power to control prices or exclude competition in a relevant market. Market power is an economic term that means the firm has a relatively inelastic demand curve. An elastic demand curve means that the firm's products have competition from other firms or from firms with substitute products. For example, cosmetic firms have an elastic demand; buyers can switch to other products when prices increase in one line, or they can even give up the use of cosmetics. On the other hand, the demand curve for gasoline is less elastic. Although substitute means of transportation are available, those who need to use their cars need gasoline.

The factors that courts examine to determine market power include the firm's market share. No set percentage figure translates into a final determination of power. However, most monopolization cases were directed at firms with market shares greater than 50 percent.

Market share is measured after determining the **relevant market**, including a look at the relevant **geographic market**. For example, a beer producer may have 50 percent of all nationwide beer sales, but in a suit involving a local competitor, the producer's share might be only 20 percent because of the local beer's popularity. This local market, or **submarket**, could be used as the relevant geographic market. A product may have an international market but may have only 10 percent market share in a particular area.

Each firm also has its own relevant **product market**, which is determined by consumers' preferences and their willingness to substitute other products for the product at issue. For example, a market could be defined as plastic wrapping materials or it could be defined as food storage materials and include wraps such as wax paper, aluminum foil, and plastic storage bags. A company may have 90 percent of the plastic wrap market, but if buyers use plastic wrap interchangeably with foil, storage bags, plastic containers, and press-and-seal wraps that share may only be 20 percent. The product market is determined by the **cross-elasticity** of demand, as explained earlier.

However, the Sherman Act does not prohibit market power or even all monopolies—certain types of monopolies are recognized as lawful exceptions. For example, a small town usually has an economic base only large enough to support one newspaper; such an operation is a lawful monopoly. Some businesses are monopolies because they make a product or provide a service that is superior or unique. When a business has obtained a large market share by **superior skill, foresight**, and **industry**, it has simply put its product in the market in a superior way and is entitled to its market share.

In order to establish a Sherman Act violation, the government agency or individual bringing suit must show that the firm acquired is maintaining monopoly power by some purposeful or deliberate act that is not "superior skill, foresight, and industry" (which, in short, is the ability to build a better mousetrap). Those who bring suit against a company alleging monopolization must have some proof of conspiratorial or nefarious activity and not just market power. In *Bell Atlantic v Twombly*, 550 U.S. 544 (2007), the U.S. Supreme Court held that companies cannot be required to figure out on their own, as defendants in an antitrust suit, what exactly they did that was monopolistic. Plaintiffs must allege enough facts to give the alleged monopolist notice of what they are defending against. In *Bell Atlantic*, the plaintiffs alleged that phone companies were engaging in parallel behaviors, or **conscious parallelism**. However, the fact that companies in the same industry might have similar practices is not enough to put the companies on notice of monopolistic behaviors. Some examples of prohibited purposeful conduct that can be used as a basis for establishing an unlawful monopoly are **predatory pricing** and **exclusionary conduct**.

Predatory pricing is pricing below actual cost for a temporary period to drive a potential competitor out of business. Exclusionary conduct is conduct that prevents a potential competitor from entering the market. For example, interfering with the purchase of a factory by a competitor would be improper exclusionary conduct. The landmark case *U.S. v Microsoft*, 253 F.3d 34 (C.A. D.C. 2001) held that Microsoft was a monopolist because of its 90 percent market share as well as its refusal to sell its products to customers who also sold Microsoft's competitors' products. The Justice Department and Microsoft settled the case. Microsoft did not have to be broken up, but it did agree to pay penalties, including donations of $180 million in software to school districts.

BUSINESS STRATEGY

The Merging Beer Market

The Justice Department filed suit to stop the proposed merger between Anheuser-Busch InBev NV, the maker of Bud Light, and Modelo, the maker of Corona. The suit alleged that combining the two companies would mean domination of the distribution chain that would result in price increases. At the time of the proposed merger, AB InBev NV held 39 percent of the beer market; Miller/Coors held 26 percent; Modelo held 7 percent; and Heineken, the last of the big four, held 6 percent. Other beer makers combined held the remaining 22 percent of the U.S. beer market.

If the Bud/Corona merger went through, the two beer producers would hold 46 percent of the country's beer market. The Justice Department suit also expressed fear about pricing, noting that when the dominant forces raise prices in the beer market the other companies follow. However, Modelo has been one of the market players that has resisted parallel price increases. The Justice Department complaint focused on the mergers resulting in the loss of one market player that has kept prices lower. The market would no longer have its low-price checks and balances.

In 2008, Crown implemented its "Momentum Plan" with Modelo's enthusiastic support. The Momentum Plan is specifically designed to grow Modelo's market share by shrinking the price gaps between brands owned by Modelo and domestic premium brands. By maintaining steady pricing while the prices of premium beer continue to rise, Modelo narrowed the price gap between its beers and ABI's premium beers, encouraging consumers to trade up to Modelo brands. These narrowed price gaps frustrated ABI and MillerCoors because they resulted in Modelo gaining market share at their expense.

The suit to stop the beer merger was based on the Sherman Act provisions on monopolization. The Justice Department has enjoyed some success in the past in stopping mergers. For example, it successfully halted the merger between AT&T and T-Mobile because of the same concerns about the combined market power. AT&T was at 32 percent market share and T-Mobile was at 11 percent, with the merger resulting in a 43 percent market share. Despite AT&T's arguments on the value to consumers of combining telecommunications hardware and software for better service, the injunction against the merger was upheld.

The Justice Department settled the case with Bud and Corona. The Justice Department allowed the merger to go through if Bud would divest itself of certain smaller breweries. Why would the sale of those breweries be a condition to the merger approval?

Consider...

Penny Stafford, the owner of Belvi Coffee and Tea Exchange, located in Bellevue, Washington, has brought an antitrust suit against Starbucks. She alleges that through its exclusive leases Starbucks bans other coffee shops from competing. Starbucks has a 73 percent market share, $8.4 billion in annual sales in the United States, and owns 7,551 of the 21,400 coffeehouses located in the United States. However, if Dunkin' Donuts, Krispy Kreme, and Tim Hortons are included in the gourmet coffee market, Starbucks holds only 43 percent of the coffee market. Starbucks purchased Seattle's Best Coffee (SBC) in 2003 and Torrefazione Italia the same year. Starbucks then closed one-half of all SBC stores and all of the Torrefazione outlets. Starbucks runs 59 stores within a two-mile radius of downtown Seattle.

Stafford said that Starbucks has exclusive leases with landlords so that the landlords cannot lease space in the same building to another coffee shop. Does such an exclusive lease violate any antitrust laws, or are such clauses permitted under the law?

FOR THE MANAGER'S DESK

Re: E-Commerce, E-Mail, and Technology

E-mail is redefining the way cases are tried. In the U.S. Justice Department's case against Microsoft, a lawyer commented, "The government does not need to put Mr. Gates on the stand because we have his e-mail and memoranda." The lawyer's comment reflects the tendency of e-mail to speak for itself. Witnesses can shrug and assert they cannot remember, but an e-mail from them is always available for recollection purposes as well as admission as evidence. At Microsoft, e-mail supplanted the telephone as the primary means of communication, and the government was able to tap into the entire e-mail system. Thirty million pages of e-mail were used as evidence in the Microsoft trial.

E-mail provides what is known as a contemporaneous record of events and has the added bonus that, for whatever psychological reason, those communicating with e-mail tend to be more frank and informal than they would be in a memo. E-mail can also contradict a witness's testimony and serve to undermine credibility. For example, when asked whether he recalled discussions with a subordinate about whether Microsoft should offer to invest in Netscape, Mr. Gates responded in his deposition, "I didn't see that as something that made sense." But Mr. Gates's e-mail included an urging to his subordinates to consider a Netscape alliance: "We could even pay them money as part of the deal, buying a piece of them or something."

E-mail is discoverable, it is admissible as evidence, and it is definitely not private. Employees should follow the admonition of one executive whose e-mail was used to fuel a million-dollar settlement by his company with a former employee: "If you wouldn't want anyone to read it, don't send it in e-mail." The impact of e-mail in the Microsoft antitrust case on companies and their e-mail policies was widespread. For example, Amazon.com launched a companywide program called "Sweep and Keep," under which employees are instructed to purge e-mail messages no longer needed for conducting business. Amazon.com is offering employees who purge immediately free lattes in the company cafeteria.

The company had a two-part program. The first portion included instructions on document retention and deletion. The second part of the program was on document creation and included the following warning for employees: "Quite simply put, there are some communications that should not be expressed in written form. Sorry, no lattes this time."

Eliot Spitzer, New York's then-attorney general, used e-mails as critical parts of his cases against analysts and investment bankers. When asked to speak at an analyst's meeting, he began by saying, "It's nice to be able to put faces with so many of your e-mails that I have read." Employees around the country report that they are now holding back on their e-mail communications and being careful about their choices of words.

Sources: Steve Lohr, "Antitrust Case Is Highlighting Role of E-Mail," *New York Times*, November 2, 1998, pp. C1, C4; John R. Wilke, "Old E-Mail Dogs Microsoft in Fighting Antitrust Suits," *Wall Street Journal*, August 27, 1998, p. B1.

ETHICAL ISSUES

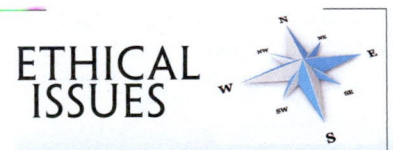

W.J. Gore & Associates, Inc., the manufacturer of Gore-Tex, a waterproof, breathable membrane that is used in everything from tents to clothing for bikers and runners, has an estimated 70 to 90 percent of the outdoor sports waterproof gear market. Examples of companies that use Gore-Tex include Adidas, Bass Pro, Ecco, LL.Bean, Nike, Patagonia, Puma, Rockport, The North Face, Timberline, New Balance, Clarks, and Mephisto. However, several of Gore's competitors have alleged that Gore refuses to sell its products to companies that carry other brands, such as the waterproof membranes offered by Columbia Sportswear Co.

Columbia alleges that its newer product (Omni-Dry) is superior to the 40-year-old Gore-Tex, but it is unable to get its foot in the door of these companies because they have agreed not to carry competitors' materials. Allegations also include information about Gore refusing to place its manufacturing with factories that do work for other manufacturers that compete with Gore. "This is the worst-kept secret in our industry…. Gore dictates what waterproof technologies they are allowed to offer consumers."[1]

There are pending antitrust investigations in the United States and Europe. Discuss what antitrust issues you see. What are the ethical issues in Gore's alleged behavior?

Business Planning Tip

The following tips can help keep trade associations free of anticompetitive behavior:

1. Do not exchange price information, including disclosures about credit terms, shipping fees, and so on.

2. Do not reveal future plans with respect to customers (e.g., "I'm not going to deal with that company anymore").

3. Do not define or reveal territories (e.g., "I'm not interested in the Yuma region anymore").

4. Do not agree to uniform pricing, commissions, or refusals to deal.

16-3b PRICE FIXING

Any agreement or collaboration among competitors "for the purpose and with the effect of raising, depressing, fixing, pegging, or stabilizing the price of a commodity" is price fixing, a *per se* violation of Section 1 of the Sherman Act.

Price fixing can take many forms, but all of them are illegal. A minimum fee or price schedule discourages competition, puts an artificial restriction on the market, and provides a shield from market forces. Even proof that the minimum price is a reasonable price is irrelevant once there is proof of an agreement. Although establishing maximum prices sounds like an excellent benefit for consumers, the effect is to stabilize prices, which translates into a restriction on free-market forces.

Some competitors have tried to use list prices as a guideline, but such lists are still a violation even though the list prices are not mandatory. Just the exchange of price information has an effect on the market and interferes with competition.

FOR THE MANAGER'S DESK

Re: Creating the Largest Airline in the World

U.S. Airways had reached an agreement to purchase American Airlines, which was then in Chapter 11 bankruptcy. The two companies announced the merger and ran extensive advertising and web campaigns about their plans for combining the two companies under the terms of their $11 billion agreement.

However, just months before the formal combination was to occur, the U.S. Justice Department filed suit to block the merger because the effect would be a lessening of competition in the airline industry. The complaint in the case noted that with the merger, four airlines would control 80 percent of the air travel market in the United States.

The important management lesson from the last-minute suit by regulators is that mergers and all proposed corporate changes and combinations of horizontal competitors require constant interaction with regulators and negotiations regarding pre-merger and post-merger requirements for approval.

Often price can be controlled through competitors' actions that affect supply. An agreement among competitors to limit production is an agreement to fix prices because the parties are controlling the supply, which in turn controls the right to demand the resulting price. Likewise, an agreement to limit or eliminate bidding, a form of a group boycott, has an effect on price because the supply is constrained. In *National Soc'y of Professional Engineers v United States*, 435 U.S. 679 (1978), a professional society agreed that there should not be bidding on engineering projects because the bidding process encouraged cost cutting and posed possible safety risks in the construction of the projects bid. Although its motives were well intentioned, it was still price fixing and a *per se* violation of the Sherman Act.

Consider...

General Electric, through its GES (General Electric Superabrasives) subsidiary, and DeBeers are both diamond processors and sellers. In 1991, both GES and DeBeers announced a price increase for their diamonds.

Edward Russell was a former GES employee who, in 1986, was promoted to the position of vice president in charge of GES. During this period, Mr. Russell exchanged notes and held meetings with the managing director of a customer who also served as a board member for DeBeers. Following the meetings, both companies announced a 1991 price increase. There was some evidence that the customer indicated to GES that DeBeers would be increasing its prices. However, the customer who offered the information about the forthcoming price increase was not authorized to negotiate contracts or agreements on behalf of DeBeers.

Mr. Russell held his position as vice president of GES until November 11, 1991, when General Electric terminated his employment. In early 1992, Mr. Russell contacted the government, alleging that General Electric employees had committed various acts of wrongdoing, including antitrust violations.

Soon after contacting the government, Mr. Russell filed a civil wrongful termination action against General Electric. He alleged that General Electric fired him because he was a whistle-blower. Mr. Russell settled his wrongful termination suit against General Electric on February 16, 1994, one day before the grand jury handed down an indictment against General Electric (GE) for price fixing in violation of the Sherman Act. Mr. Russell was a key witness for the government. His testimony was that there was advance contact between GES and DeBeers before the announcement of the price increases. GE and DeBeers do not deny the advance contact but assert that there was no agreement to increase prices.
[*U.S. v General Elec. Co.*, 869 F. Supp. 1285 (1994)]

THINK: The elements for price fixing are that competitors act together to keep prices at a certain level or agree to charge a certain price. The statute does require an agreement between the parties.

APPLY: There must be evidence of an agreement to fix prices.

ANSWER: The court held that the fact that the managing director of the customer was also the director of a company that manufactured industrial diamonds did not establish that the managing director was acting on behalf of the competitor and that the industrial diamond manufacturer knew this when the managing director and the manufacturer exchanged advance list pricing information. The court found that there was no evidence to show that the managing director's corporate links were used by the director or the competitor to form or facilitate an agreement with the manufacturer to fix prices.

ANSWER: Just because a managing director of the customer, who was also director of company that manufactured industrial diamonds under a joint venture between the customer and a competitor, supported an industrial diamond price increase did not establish that the managing director was acting on behalf of the competitor. Any exchange of information took place with both parties aware that the managing director had no authority to act on behalf of the competitor.

16-3c   DIVVYING UP THE MARKETS

Any agreement between competitors to divide up an available market is a *per se* violation under the Sherman Act. The result of such an agreement is to give the participants monopolies in their particular area. Such a market division introduces an unnatural force into the competitive market. For example, office product supply companies agreeing to operate only in certain cities throughout a state would be a division of markets and a *per se* violation.

Consider...

BRG of Georgia, Inc. (BRG), and Harcourt Brace Jovanovich Legal and Professional Publications (HBJ) are the nation's two largest providers of bar review materials and lectures. HBJ began offering a Georgia bar review course on a limited basis in 1976 and was in direct, often intense competition with BRG from 1977 to 1979. BRG and HBJ were the two main providers of bar review courses in Georgia during this period. In early 1980, they entered into an agreement that gave BRG an exclusive license to market HBJ's materials in Georgia and to use its trade name "BAR/BRI." The parties agreed that HBJ would not compete with BRG in Georgia and that BRG would not compete with HBJ outside of Georgia.

Under the agreement, HBJ received $100 per student enrolled by BRG and 40 percent of all revenues over $350. Immediately after the 1980 agreement, the price of BRG's course was increased from $150 to over $400.

Is this an illegal division of markets? Discuss any perceived economic efficiencies in the arrangement?

[*Palmer v BRG of Georgia, Inc.*, 498 U.S. 46 (1990)]

16-3d GROUP BOYCOTTS AND REFUSALS TO DEAL

A group of competitors that agrees not to deal with buyers unless those buyers agree to standard credit or arbitration clauses has committed a *per se* violation.

Some group boycotts appear to have the best intentions. Many garment manufacturers once agreed not to sell to buyers who sold discounted or pirated designer clothing. Certainly their intentions were good, but the result still has the anticompetitive effect of controlling the marketplace. Competitors cannot enforce the law through boycotts; other avenues of relief are available. The American Medical Association's rules that prohibited salaried medical practices and prepaid medical plans are illegal boycotts in spite of the protection motivations behind the restrictions. In *FTC v Superior Court Trial Lawyers Ass'n*, 493 U.S. 411 (1990), the U.S. Supreme Court held that the action of a group of well-intentioned defense lawyers who went on strike to get a higher hourly rate for public defenders was noble and perhaps in the interest of justice, but it was still an illegal boycott by horizontal market participants.

16-3e FREE SPEECH AND ANTICOMPETITIVE BEHAVIOR

Some activities by competitors are protected even though the competitors act as a group and even though the effect may be to reduce competition. One such exception is the *Noerr–Pennington* **doctrine**, under which competitors are permitted to work together for the purpose of governmental lobbying and other political action.[2] Their activity enjoys the protection of the First Amendment. For example, competitors can make appearances at new licensee hearings and oppose the granting of a license. The resulting reduction in competition enjoys First Amendment protection, which trumps the Sherman Act. In *City of Columbia v Omni Outdoor Advertising*, 499 U.S. 365 (1991), a company that was controlling the outdoor advertising market in one city attempted to use its lobbying First Amendment rights to protect its market control. An objection and suit by a competitor still resulted in the protection of *Noerr–Pennington* and First Amendment rights.

16-3f SUBTLE ANTICOMPETITIVE BEHAVIOR: INTERLOCKING DIRECTORATES

If officers of competing companies serve on each other's boards of directors, it opens the door to an exchange of information about everything from price to

Consider...

In Arizona, fees for title insurance searches and policies were established by rating bureaus established by the title companies. The bureaus recommended rates to the state, and the state adopted those rates unless some specific objection was made. The result was that title search and insurance fees were the same for all companies within the state. The FTC filed a complaint against the title companies, alleging that they were engaged in price fixing. The companies responded that government regulation of prices is not price fixing. Do you agree?
[*FTC v Ticor Title Ins. Co.*, 504 U.S. 621 (1992)]

supply chain systems to new products. Certain types of these **interlocking directorates** are prohibited under Section 8 of the Clayton Act. A director of a firm with $10 million or more in capital cannot be a director of a competing company. The risk of anticompetitive results from just the exchange of information is too great. This antitrust concern has percolated in the past several years as directors in high-tech companies have realized their overlapping business conflicts. For example, Eric Schmidt, the CEO of Google, Inc., resigned from Apple's board. Immediately following Mr. Schmidt's resignation from Apple, Arthur Levinson, the CEO of Genentech, Inc., who had served on the boards of both Google and Apple, resigned from the Google board. The two companies were increasingly competing with each other because of, among other things, Google's announcement of its own phone. The two companies were facing increased scrutiny from regulators as a result of their increasingly overlapping business areas. John Doer, a director at both Google and Amazon.com, resigned from the Amazon.com board under pressure from regulators over that interlocking directorship. Google and Amazon had become direct competitors in the electronic book markets.

ETHICAL ISSUES

The Federal Trade Commission (FTC) has charged AOL Time Warner, Inc., and its subsidiaries, Warner Music Group and Vivendi Universal SA, with price fixing in connection with the sales of the Three Tenors' audio and video CDs and tapes. (The Three Tenors are the late Luciano Pavarotti, Placido Domingo, and Jose Carreras.)

When all were alive, the Three Tenors made a recording of their live performances together—done once every four years. The first two CDs and videos in the series sold millions, with both becoming two of the highest–sales-volume opera recordings in history. However, by the third live performance and its CD and video, the public demand was not as great. The FTC charges that Warner felt the first two releases would cannibalize the sales for the third. As a result, all parties involved in the sales of these CDs and tapes had to agree not to discount the first two performance tapes so that the third would have an opportunity to sell. The FTC also alleges that there were agreements on when advertisements could run for the third series' sales and availability.

The FTC stumbled across a memo on the marketing plan and advertising constraints as it was reviewing documents in connection with the Warner/EMI Music merger proposal, a merger that fell through after European officials balked at the idea. The FTC pursued the case, and Warner settled the charges by agreeing not to restrain competition or set prices in the future.

Is it permissible for an agency investigating one issue to use evidence it comes across related to another issue? What lessons does this situation offer on the percolating nature of the truth? Is establishing a minimum price a violation of the Sherman Act? Is restricting advertising a violation of the Sherman Act?

16-3g MERGING COMPETITORS AND THE EFFECT ON COMPETITION

To determine the legality of mergers among horizontal competitors, courts have applied a test of "presumptive illegality": Any merger that produces an undue percentage share of the market or significantly increases market concentration is a violation. Courts examine market share and the relevant markets to determine whether undue concentration is a factor.

Not all horizontal mergers are prohibited. The **failing-company doctrine** allows the acquisition of a competitor that is teetering on insolvency, shut down, or bankruptcy if it is an asset or inventory acquisition. Under the **small-company doctrine**, two small companies are permitted to merge because the hope is that they will be better able to compete with the larger businesses in that market.

The trend in mergers has been to approve larger and larger combinations. In *United States v Von's Grocery Co.*, 384 U.S. 270 (1966), the Supreme Court held that a merger between Von's Grocery Company and Shopping Bag Food Stores, which would have given the two companies together a 7.5 percent share of the retail grocery market in Los Angeles, was an anticompetitive violation of the Clayton Act. However, by 1988, the Justice Department approved the merger of Von's and Safeway in southern California. The merger made the new Von's the largest competitor in terms of market percentage as well as in the number of stores. Justice Department attitudes and guidelines on mergers have changed, and geographic markets are now defined in light of international trade. As noted in the discussion of Corona and Anheuser-Busch, the standards for market share have changed, significantly since the grocery-store merger cases, with the federal government showing more leniency in approving mergers that take companies to the 50 percent or higher level of market share.

16-4 Vertical Trade Restraints

Various steps are involved in getting a product from its creation to its ultimate consumer. For example, producing packaged sandwich meats requires the manufacturer to obtain bulk-butchered meat (originally from a ranch) through a distributor and turn it into packaged sandwich meat that is sold to another distributor. This distributor sells to a grocery wholesaler, who sells to grocery stores, where consumers buy the packaged meat. This entire process has different levels of production and distribution, but it consists of one vertical chain from start to finish.

The types of vertical restraints, discussed in the following subsections, are

- Resale price maintenance
- Monopsony
- Sole outlets and exclusive distributorships
- Customer and territorial restrictions
- Tying arrangements
- Price discrimination

16-4a RESALE PRICE MAINTENANCE

Resale price maintenance is an attempt by a manufacturer to control the price that retailers charge for the manufacturer's product. Resale price maintenance is a rule-of-reason violation of Section 1 of the Sherman Act. Resale price maintenance includes either minimum or maximum prices, or both. A minimum price encourages a retailer to carry a certain product because its profit margin will be higher. One explanation offered to justify minimum prices is that without them dealers who advertise and offer service may be used by consumers for information only, after which these consumers actually buy at discount houses.

State Oil Co. v Khan (Case 16.2) deals with the issue of resale price maintenance and its change from a *per se* violation to a rule of reason standard.

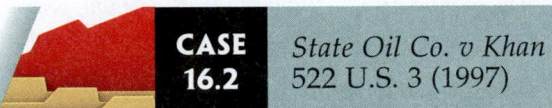

CASE 16.2 State Oil Co. v Khan
522 U.S. 3 (1997)

Fill It Up, but Only at My Price

FACTS

Barkat U. Khan and his corporation (respondents) entered into an agreement with State Oil (petitioner) to lease and operate a gas station and convenience store owned by State Oil. The agreement provided that Mr. Khan would obtain the gasoline supply for the station from State Oil at a suggested retail price set by State Oil, less a margin of 3.25 cents per gallon. Mr. Khan could charge any price he wanted, but if he charged more than State Oil's suggested retail price, the excess was rebated to State Oil. Mr. Khan could sell the gasoline for less than State Oil's suggested retail price, but the difference came out of his allowed margin.

After a year, Mr. Khan fell behind on his lease payments, and State Oil began proceedings for eviction. The court had Mr. Khan removed and appointed a receiver to operate the station. The receiver operated the gas station without the price constraints and received an overall profit margin above the 3.25 cents imposed on Mr. Khan.

Mr. Khan filed suit, alleging that the State Oil agreement was a violation of Section 1 of the Sherman Act because State Oil was controlling prices. The district court held that there was no *per se* violation and that Mr. Khan had failed to demonstrate antitrust injury. The Court of Appeals reversed, and State Oil appealed.

JUDICIAL OPINION

O'CONNOR, Justice

In *Albrecht v Herald Co.*, 390 U.S. 145, 88 S.Ct. 869, 19 L.Ed.2d 998 (1968), this Court held that vertical maximum price fixing is a per se violation of that statute. In this case, we are asked to reconsider that decision in light of subsequent decisions of this Court. We conclude that *Albrecht* should be overruled.

Although the Sherman Act, by its terms, prohibits every agreement "in restraint of trade," this Court has long recognized that Congress intended to outlaw only unreasonable restraints.

As a consequence, most antitrust claims are analyzed under a "rule of reason," according to which the finder of fact must decide whether the questioned practice imposes an unreasonable restraint on competition, taking into account a variety of factors, including specific information about the relevant business, its condition before and after the restraint was imposed, and the restraint's history, nature, and effect.

Some types of restraints, however, have such predictable and pernicious anticompetitive effect, and such limited potential for procompetitive benefit, that they are deemed unlawful per se....

In *White Motor Co. v United States*, 372 U.S. 253, 83 S.Ct. 696, 9 L.Ed.2d 738 (1963), the Court considered the validity of a manufacturer's assignment of exclusive territories to its distributors and dealers. The Court determined that too little was known about the competitive impact of such vertical limitations to warrant treating them as per se unlawful.

Four years later, in *United States v Arnold, Schwinn & Co.*, 388 U.S. 365, 87 S.Ct. 1856, 18 L.Ed.2d 1249 (1967), the Court reconsidered the status of exclusive dealer territories and held that, upon the transfer of title to goods to a distributor, a supplier's imposition of territorial restrictions on the distributor was "so obviously destructive of competition" as to constitute a per se violation of the Sherman Act. In *Schwinn*, the Court acknowledged that some vertical restrictions, such as the conferral of territorial rights or franchises, could have procompetitive benefits by allowing smaller enterprises to compete, and that such restrictions might avert vertical integration in the distribution process. The Court drew the line, however, at permitting manufacturers

CONTINUED

to control product marketing once dominion over the goods had passed to dealers.

Albrecht, decided the following Term, involved a newspaper publisher who had granted exclusive territories to independent carriers subject to their adherence to a maximum price on resale of the newspapers to the public....

Albrecht was animated in part by the fear that vertical maximum price fixing could allow suppliers to discriminate against certain dealers, restrict the services that dealers could afford to offer customers, or disguise minimum price fixing schemes. The Court rejected the notion (both on the record of that case and in the abstract) that, because the newspaper publisher "granted exclusive territories, a price ceiling was necessary to protect the public from price gouging by dealers who had monopoly power in their own territories."

Nine years later, in *Continental T.V., Inc. v GTE Sylvania, Inc.*, 433 U.S. 36, 97 S.Ct. 2549, 53 L.Ed.2d 568 (1977), the Court overruled *Schwinn*, thereby rejecting application of a per se rule in the context of vertical nonprice restrictions. The Court acknowledged the principle of *stare decisis*, but explained that the need for clarification in the law justified reconsideration of *Schwinn*:

> Since its announcement, *Schwinn has been the subject of continuing controversy and confusion, both in the scholarly journals and in the federal courts. The great weight of scholarly opinion has been critical of the decision, and a number of the federal courts confronted with analogous vertical restrictions have sought to limit its reach.*

Thus, our reconsideration of *Albrecht's* continuing validity is informed by several of our decisions, as well as a considerable body of scholarship discussing the effects of vertical restraints. Our analysis is also guided by our general view that the primary purpose of the antitrust laws is to protect interbrand competition. See, e.g., *Business Electronics Corp. v Sharp Electronics Corp.*, 485 U.S. 717, 726, 108 S.Ct. 1515, 1520–1521, 99 L.Ed.2d 808 (1988). "Low prices," we have explained, "benefit consumers regardless of how those prices are set, and so long as they are above predatory levels, they do not threaten competition." Our interpretation of the Sherman Act also incorporates the notion that condemnation of practices resulting in lower prices to consumers is "especially costly" because "cutting prices in order to increase business often is the very essence of competition." [*Matsushita Elec. Industrial Co. v Zenith Radio Corp.*, 475 U.S. 574, 594, 106 S.Ct. 1348, 1360, 89 L.Ed.2d 538 (1986)]

So informed, we find it difficult to maintain that vertically imposed maximum prices could harm consumers or competition to the extent necessary to justify their per se invalidation. As Chief Judge Posner wrote for the Court of Appeals in this case:

> As for maximum resale price fixing, unless the supplier is a monopsonist he cannot squeeze his dealers' margins below a competitive level; the attempt to do so would just drive the dealers into the arms of a competing supplier. A supplier might, however, fix a maximum resale price in order to prevent his dealers from exploiting a monopoly position.... [S]uppose that State Oil, perhaps to encourage ... dealer services ... has spaced its dealers sufficiently far apart to limit competition among them (or even given each of them an exclusive territory); and suppose further that Union 76 is a sufficiently distinctive and popular brand to give the dealers in it at least a modicum of monopoly power. Then State Oil might want to place a ceiling on the dealers' resale prices in order to prevent them from exploiting that monopoly powerfully. It would do this not out of disinterested malice, but in its commercial self-interest. The higher the price at which gasoline is resold, the smaller the volume sold, and so the lower the profit to the supplier if the higher profit per gallon at the higher price is being snared by the dealer. (93 F.3d at 1362)

Further, although vertical maximum price fixing might limit the viability of inefficient dealers, that consequence is not necessarily harmful to competition and consumers.

After reconsidering *Albrecht's* rationale and the substantial criticism the decision has received, however, we conclude that there is insufficient economic justification for per se invalidation of vertical maximum price fixing. That is so not only because it is difficult to accept the assumptions underlying *Albrecht*, but also because *Albrecht* has little or no relevance to ongoing enforcement of the Sherman Act....

We approach the reconsideration of decisions of this Court with the utmost caution. *Stare decisis* reflects "a policy judgment that 'in most matters it is more important that the applicable rule of law be settled than that it be settled right.'"

But "[s]*tare decisis* is not an inexorable command." In the area of antitrust law, there is a competing interest, well represented in this Court's decisions, in recognizing and adapting to changed circumstances and the lessons of accumulated experience. Thus, the general presumption that legislative changes should be left to Congress has less force with respect to the Sherman Act in light of the accepted view that Congress "expected the courts to give shape to the statute's broad mandate by drawing on common-law tradition."

In overruling *Albrecht*, we of course do not hold that all vertical maximum price fixing is per se lawful. Instead, vertical maximum price fixing, like the majority

CONTINUED

of commercial arrangements subject to the antitrust laws, should be evaluated under the rule of reason. In our view, rule-of-reason analysis will effectively identify those situations in which vertical maximum price fixing amounts to anticompetitive conduct....

We therefore vacate the judgment of the Court of Appeals and remand the case for further proceedings consistent with this opinion.

Remanded.

CASE QUESTIONS

1. What were the terms of Mr. Khan's lease? Include a discussion of the price terms.

2. Is vertical price fixing a *per se* violation? What does the court say about inefficient retailers and vertical price controls?

3. What does the court say about a long-standing precedent and *stare decisis*?

The "suggested retail price" has been tolerated under the rule of reason standard as long as manufacturers and distributors did not enforce that suggested price through refusals to sell. In fact, a 1975 federal law eliminated state laws that protected these enforcement arrangements, often called **fair trade contracts**. However, in 2007, the U.S. Supreme Court reversed a long-standing precedent with the *Leegin* case (Case 16.3) that has changed the nature of distribution agreements by allowing enforcement of the suggested prices. This case also provides the answer for the chapter's opening "Consider..." problem.

CASE 16.3

Leegin Creative Leather Products, Inc. v PSKS, Inc.
551 U.S. 877 (2007)

It's Not in the Bag; It's in the Service[3]

FACTS

Leegin Creative Leather Products, Inc. (Leegin) (petitioner), designs, manufactures, and distributes leather goods and accessories under the brand name "Brighton." The Brighton brand has now expanded into a full line of women's fashion accessories and is sold across the United States in over 5,000 retail stores. PSKS, Inc. (PSKS) (respondent), runs Kay's Kloset, a Brighton retailer in Lewisville, Texas, that carried about 75 different product lines but was known as the place in that area to go for Brighton. Kay's ran Brighton ads and had Brighton days in its store.

Leegin's president, Jerry Kohl, who also has an interest in about 70 stores that sell Brighton products, believes that small retailers treat customers better, provide customers more services, and make their shopping experience more satisfactory than do larger, often impersonal retailers. In 1997, Kohl released a new strategic refocus for Brighton by explaining: "[W]e want the consumers to get a different experience than they get in Sam's Club or in Wal-Mart. And you can't get that kind of experience or support or customer service from

a store like Wal-Mart." As a result, Leegin instituted the "Brighton Retail Pricing and Promotion Policy," which banished retailers that discounted Brighton goods below suggested prices. The policy had an exception for products not selling well that the retailer did not plan on reordering. The established prices gave its retailers sufficient margins to provide customers with the quality service central to Brighton's strategy.

In December 2002, Leegin discovered Kay's Kloset had been marking down Brighton's entire line by 20 percent. Kay's Kloset said it did so to compete with nearby retailers who also were undercutting Leegin's suggested prices. Leegin, nonetheless, requested that Kay's Kloset cease discounting. Its request refused, Leegin stopped selling to the store. The loss of the Brighton brand had a considerable negative impact on the store's revenue from sales (about 40–50 percent of its profits were from Brighton).

PSKS sued Leegin for violation of the antitrust laws. Leegin asked to introduce expert testimony describing the procompetitive effects of its pricing policy. The District Court excluded the testimony, relying Leegin's

CONTINUED

conduct to be a *per se* violation of federal antitrust laws. The jury awarded PSKS $1.2 million in damages and the judge trebled the damages and reimbursed PSKS for its attorney's fees and costs, for a judgment against Leegin of $3,975,000.80. The Court of Appeals affirmed. Leegin appealed. The U.S. Supreme Court granted certiorari.

JUDICIAL OPINION

KENNEDY, Justice

In *Dr. Miles Medical Co. v John D. Park & Sons Co.*, 220 U.S. 373, 31 S.Ct. 376, 55 L.Ed. 502 (1911), the Court established the rule that it is per se illegal under § 1 of the Sherman Act, 15 U.S.C. § 1, for a manufacturer to agree with its distributor to set the minimum price the distributor can charge for the manufacturer's goods. The question presented by the instant case is whether the Court should overrule the per se rule and allow resale price maintenance agreements to be judged by the rule of reason, the usual standard applied to determine if there is a violation of § 1. The Court has abandoned the rule of per se illegality for other vertical restraints a manufacturer imposes on its distributors. Respected economic analysts, furthermore, conclude that vertical price restraints can have procompetitive effects. We now hold that *Dr. Miles* should be overruled and that vertical price restraints are to be judged by the rule of reason Section 1 of the Sherman Act prohibits "[e]very contract, combination in the form of trust or otherwise, or conspiracy, in restraint of trade or commerce among the several States." The rule of reason is the accepted standard for testing whether a practice restrains trade in violation of § 1. The rule of reason does not govern all restraints. Some types "are deemed unlawful *per se*." The *per se* rule, treating categories of restraints as necessarily illegal, eliminates the need to study the reasonableness of an individual restraint in light of the real market forces at work, and, it must be acknowledged, the *per se* rule can give clear guidance for certain conduct. Restraints that are *per se* unlawful include horizontal agreements among competitors to fix prices, or to divide markets.

… [T]he *per se* rule is appropriate only after courts have had considerable experience with the type of restraint at issue, and only if courts can predict with confidence that it would be invalidated in all or almost all instances under the rule of reason.

Dr. Miles treated vertical agreements a manufacturer makes with its distributors as analogous to a horizontal combination among competing distributors…. [I]t is necessary to examine, in the first instance, the economic effects of vertical agreements to fix minimum resale prices, and to determine whether the *per se* rule is nonetheless appropriate.

Though each side of the debate can find sources to support its position, it suffices to say here that economics literature is replete with procompetitive justifications for a manufacturer's use of resale price maintenance.

The justifications for vertical price restraints are similar to those for other vertical restraints. Minimum resale price maintenance can stimulate interbrand competition—the competition among manufacturers selling different brands of the same type of product—by reducing intrabrand competition—the competition among retailers selling the same brand. The promotion of interbrand competition is important because "the primary purpose of the antitrust laws is to protect [this type of] competition." A single manufacturer's use of vertical price restraints tends to eliminate intrabrand price competition; this in turn encourages retailers to invest in tangible or intangible services or promotional efforts that aid the manufacturer's position as against rival manufacturers. Resale price maintenance also has the potential to give consumers more options so that they can choose among low-price, low-service brands; high-price, high-service brands; and brands that fall in between.

Absent vertical price restraints, the retail services that enhance interbrand competition might be underprovided. This is because discounting retailers can free ride on retailers who furnish services and then capture some of the increased demand those services generate. Consumers might learn, for example, about the benefits of a manufacturer's product from a retailer that invests in fine showrooms, offers product demonstrations, or hires and trains knowledgeable employees. Or consumers might decide to buy the product because they see it in a retail establishment that has a reputation for selling high-quality merchandise. If the consumer can then buy the product from a retailer that discounts because it has not spent capital providing services or developing a quality reputation, the high-service retailer will lose sales to the discounter, forcing it to cut back its services to a level lower than consumers would otherwise prefer. Minimum resale price maintenance alleviates the problem because it prevents the discounter from undercutting the service provider. With price competition decreased, the manufacturer's retailers compete among themselves over services.

Resale price maintenance, in addition, can increase interbrand competition by facilitating market entry for new firms and brands. "[N]ew manufacturers and manufacturers entering new markets can use the restrictions in order to induce competent and aggressive retailers to make the kind of investment of capital and labor that is often required in the distribution of products unknown to the consumer."

CONTINUED

Resale price maintenance can also increase inter-brand competition by encouraging retailer services that would not be provided even absent free riding. It may be difficult and inefficient for a manufacturer to make and enforce a contract with a retailer specifying the different services the retailer must perform. Offering the retailer a guaranteed margin and threatening termination if it does not live up to expectations may be the most efficient way to expand the manufacturer's market share by inducing the retailer's performance and allowing it to use its own initiative and experience in providing valuable services.

While vertical agreements setting minimum resale prices can have procompetitive justifications, they may have anticompetitive effects in other circumstances. Vertical price restraints also "might be used to organize cartels at the retailer level." A group of retailers might collude to fix prices to consumers and then compel a manufacturer to aid the unlawful arrangement with resale price maintenance. In that instance, the manufacturer does not establish the practice to stimulate services or to promote its brand but to give inefficient retailers higher profits. Retailers with better distribution systems and lower cost structures would be prevented from charging lower prices by the agreement.

Resale price maintenance, furthermore, can be abused by a powerful manufacturer or retailer. A dominant retailer, for example, might request resale price maintenance to forestall innovation in distribution that decreases costs. A manufacturer might consider it has little choice but to accommodate the retailer's demands for vertical price restraints if the manufacturer believes it needs access to the retailer's distribution network.

Vertical agreements establishing minimum resale prices can have either procompetitive or anticompetitive effects, depending upon the circumstances in which they are formed.

Respondent's argument, furthermore, overlooks that, in general, the interests of manufacturers and consumers are aligned with respect to retailer profit margins. The difference between the price a manufacturer charges retailers and the price retailers charge consumers represents part of the manufacturer's cost of distribution, which, like any other cost, the manufacturer usually desires to minimize. The retailers, not the manufacturer, gain from higher retail prices. The manufacturer often loses; interbrand competition reduces its competitiveness and market share because consumers will "substitute a different brand of the same product."

Resale price maintenance, it is true, does have economic dangers. If the rule of reason were to apply to vertical price restraints, courts would have to be diligent in eliminating their anticompetitive uses from the market.

Reversed.

CASE QUESTIONS

1. What reasons did Leegin give for wanting the minimum price established for its retailers?

2. What points does the court make about not having minimum prices in terms of reducing competition?

3. What risks are there in allowing minimum price requirements?

Consider...

The Federal Trade Commission is conducting an investigation into the informal agreements reached between Toys "Я" Us and toy manufacturers. Toys "Я" Us holds a 19.4 percent share of the U.S. toy market and has informal agreements with Mattel and Hasbro with respect to the sale of their toys to discount warehouse clubs such as Costco and Sam's Club. The clubs are sold toys only in more expensive packaging arrangements. For example, Hollywood Hair Barbie can be purchased at Toys "Я" Us for $10.95 but at warehouse clubs can be purchased only in a package with a dress for $15.95. Some of the most popular toy items are never sold to the warehouse clubs. For example, Hasbro has not sold its Hall of Fame GI Joe action figures to warehouse clubs, and Mattel will not sell its Fisher Price pool table to the clubs.

The FTC commissioners voted 5 to 3 to begin the investigation because toy manufacturers are put into a situation of choosing between selling to Toys "Я" Us and other retailers. Toys "R" Us maintains that the warehouse clubs do not have the overhead of advertising the toys and simply choose those items that sell the best at very low margins. The low margins can be maintained because, for example, Costco took in more in membership fees over the last 10 years than its total net profit.

Apply the *Leegin* rule of reason standard. Have the antitrust laws been violated?

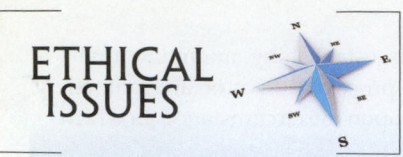

ETHICAL ISSUES

Department 56 is a company that manufactures and sells collectible Christmas village houses and other replica items to allow collectors to create the whimsical "Snow Village" town or "Dickens Christmas." Department 56 has only authorized dealers. Sam's Club, a division of Wal-Mart Stores, Inc., began selling Department 56 pieces from The Heritage Village Collection.

Susan Engel, president and CEO of Department 56, attempted to contact Wal-Mart because it is not an authorized Department 56 dealer. Wal-Mart did not respond, and Ms. Engel sent by FedEx to National Collector clubs a letter that contained the following language:

Sam's Club should not have any Department 56 merchandise. In a marketing environment where most companies are fighting to get their merchandise into the Wal-Marts of the world, we are fighting to get our merchandise out. While we recognize there is surely a place for mass market and warehouse stores, Department 56 Villages enjoy a strong heritage of dealer sales and service support. Our products simply do not fit the warehouse-style selling environment of Sam's Club.

Of strong importance to us—and we hope to you too—is the tradition of selling our villages through an exclusive dealer network made up almost entirely of independent retailers. Wal-Mart Stores, Inc., and its subsidiaries are predators on these hard-working individuals. Sales of our products mean virtually nothing to the bottom line of a company the size of Wal-Mart. But to many of our loyal dealers, healthy Department 56 product sales mean survival.

Do you really need to shop at Sam's Club or Wal-Mart? Let's refuse to purchase villages or any other products from local Wal-Mart owned stores.

The letter asked collector club members to write Wal-Mart executives and local store managers. Names, mailing addresses, and telephone and fax numbers were offered.

Has Ms. Engel violated any laws? How does this situation relate to the *Leegin* case? How do you think Sam's Club obtained the Department 56 products? Evaluate Ms. Engel's conduct in sending out the letter. Were her statements about Wal-Mart and calls to action fair? Ethical? Should Wal-Mart respond? How?

16-4b MONOPSONY

A **monopsony** exists when the buyer, rather than the seller, has the ability to control market prices. In *Weyerhaeuser v Ross-Simons*, 549 U.S. 312 (2007), the U.S. Supreme Court held that antitrust laws apply to both predatory pricing and **predatory bidding**. In the case, Ross-Simons Hardware Lumber alleged that Weyerhaeuser tried to drive it out of business by bidding up the price of sawlogs to a level that prevented Ross-Simons from being profitable. Although the lower courts found for Ross-Simons, the U.S. Supreme Court held that a plaintiff in a predatory bidding case must be able to show what a plaintiff in a predatory pricing case must show—that the bids were at such a level that below-cost pricing resulted.

In the case, Weyerhaeuser was able to show that its investment in equipment and advanced processes allowed it to process more timber and that its huge demand was driving up the price. Ross-Simons was not able to establish that the price increases were actually sought by Weyerhaeuser. The demand drove up the price, but the demand came through Weyerhaeuser's superior processing, not through nefarious means.

16-4c SOLE OUTLETS AND EXCLUSIVE DISTRIBUTORSHIPS

A **sole outlet** or **exclusive distributorship** agreement is one in which a manufacturer appoints a distributor or retailer as the sole or exclusive outlet for the manufacturer's product. This type of arrangement can be a violation of Section 1 but is subject to a rule of reason analysis. In a rule of reason analysis of sole outlets or exclusive distributorships, courts examine a manufacturer's freedom to pick and choose outlets or distributors. However, the extent of the **interbrand competition**, which is the competition available for the manufacturer's product, is critical. For example, in the case of the sandwich-meat manufacturer, as long as other manufacturers are selling their products in the area, the manufacturer could agree to sell to only one chain of grocery stores. But without interbrand competition, the antitrust laws require more **intrabrand competition**. If a manufacturer were the only one distributing sandwich meats in the area, dealing with only one grocery chain might not survive an antitrust challenge under the rule of reason.

16-4d CUSTOMER AND TERRITORIAL RESTRICTIONS

Sole outlets allow manufacturers to decide (within limitations) to whom they will sell goods. However, manufacturers are not given the right to control what the buyer does with goods and how those goods are sold. The restrictions are subject to the rule of reason because interbrand competition may be increased even though intrabrand competition is reduced. For **customer and territorial restrictions** to be valid, enough interbrand competition must balance out decreased intrabrand competition. Also, the more market power the manufacturer has, the fewer substitute goods consumers have, resulting in less interbrand competition. Vertical restrictions are likely to be reasonable when the manufacturer is new to the market or is having financial or sales difficulties. If the restrictions will help the manufacturer get started or keep going, the positive impact on interbrand competition allows the limit on intrabrand competition.

16-4e TYING ARRANGEMENTS

Tying sales require buyers to take an additional product in order to buy a needed product. For example, requiring the buyer of a copier machine to buy the seller's paper when other brands of paper are equally suitable for use in the machine is a tying arrangement. The copier machine is the tying product or the desired product, and the paper is the tied product or the required product. Tying is usually an illegal *per se* violation of Section 3 of the Clayton Act (for goods contracts) and Section 1 of the Sherman Act (for services, real property, and intangibles). The presence of market power is the key to whether tying is a violation. For example, requiring the purchase of inferior films in order to buy copyrighted quality films is an example of the presence of market power. Because the seller is the only one with the copyrighted films, market power is being used to sell another unnecessary, low-demand product. However, part of proving that there is an illegal tying arrangement is establishing market power in the product used for the tying of the low-demand product.

Two defenses have been recognized in tying cases. The first is the *new industry defense*. Under this defense, the manufacturer of the tying product is permitted to have a tied product to protect initially the quality control in the start-up of a business. For example, a cable television antenna manufacturer required purchasers to take a service contract also. The tying was upheld during the outset of the business so that the system could begin functioning properly and this new cable television industry could catch hold.

A second defense is *quality control for the protection of goodwill*. This defense is rarely supportable. This defense applies if the specifications for the tied goods were so detailed that they could not possibly be supplied by anyone other than the manufacturer of the tying product.

Illinois Tool Works Inc. v Independent Ink, Inc. (Case 16.4) involves an issue of whether a tying arrangement was valid.

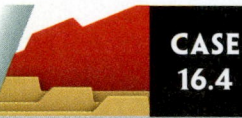

| CASE 16.4 | *Illinois Tool Works Inc. v Independent Ink, Inc.*
547 U.S. 28 (2006) |

If You Want Our Cartridges, You Have to Use Our Ink

FACTS

Trident, Inc., and its parent, Illinois Tool Works Inc. (petitioners), manufacture and market printing systems that include: (1) a patented piezoelectric impulse ink jet printhead, (2) a patented ink container, consisting of a bottle and valve cap, which attaches to the printhead, and (3) specially designed, but unpatented, ink. These products are sold to original equipment manufacturers (OEMs) who are licensed to incorporate the printheads and containers into printers that are in turn sold to companies for use in printing barcodes on cartons and packaging materials. The OEMs agree that they will purchase their ink exclusively from Illinois and that neither they nor their customers will refill the patented containers with ink of any kind.

Independent Ink, Inc. (respondent), has developed an ink with the same chemical composition as the ink sold by petitioners. Independent Ink filed suit alleging that Illinois's agreements with customers constituted an illegal tying and monopolization in violation of §§ 1 and 2 of the Sherman Act. 15 U.S.C. §§ 1, 2.

The federal district court granted summary judgment for Illinois, and Independent appealed. The appellate court reversed the decision and Illinois appealed.

JUDICIAL OPINION

STEVENS, Justice

As we explained in *Jefferson Parish*, 466 U.S., at 12, 104 S.Ct. 1551, "[o]ur cases have concluded that the essential characteristic of an invalid tying arrangement lies in the seller's exploitation of its control over the tying product to force the buyer into the purchase of a tied product that the buyer either did not want at all, or might have preferred to purchase elsewhere on different terms."

Over the years, however, this Court's strong disapproval of tying arrangements has substantially diminished. Rather than relying on assumptions, in its more recent opinions the Court has required a showing of market power in the tying product. Our early opinions consistently assumed that "[t]ying arrangements serve hardly any purpose beyond the suppression of competition."

In *Jefferson Parish*, we unanimously reversed a Court of Appeals judgment holding that an alleged tying arrangement constituted a *per se* violation of § 1 of the Sherman Act. 466 U.S., at 5, 104 S.Ct. 1551. The tying product in *Jefferson Parish*—hospital services—was unpatented, and our holding again rested on the conclusion that the plaintiff had failed to prove sufficient power in the tying product market to restrain competition in the market for the tied product—services of anesthesiologists.

In rejecting the application of a *per se* rule that all tying arrangements constitute antitrust violations, we explained:

> "[W]e have condemned tying arrangements when the seller has some special ability—usually called 'market power'—to force a purchaser to do something that he would not do in a competitive market...."

We conclude that tying arrangements involving patented products should be evaluated under the *Jefferson Parish* standards rather than under the *per se* rule. While some such arrangements are still unlawful,

CONTINUED

such as those that are the product of a true monopoly or a marketwide conspiracy, that conclusion must be supported by proof of power in the relevant market rather than by a mere presumption thereof.

Congress, the antitrust enforcement agencies, and most economists have all reached the conclusion that a patent does not necessarily confer market power upon the patentee. Today, we reach the same conclusion, and therefore hold that, in all cases involving a tying arrangement, the plaintiff must prove that the defendant has market power in the tying product.

In this case, respondent reasonably relied on our prior opinions in moving for summary judgment without offering evidence defining the relevant market or proving that petitioners possess power within it. When the case returns to the District Court, respondent should therefore be given a fair opportunity to develop and introduce evidence on that issue, as well as any other issues that are relevant to its remaining § 1 claims. The judgment of the Court of Appeals is vacated, and the case is remanded for further proceedings.

CASE QUESTIONS

1. What is the significance of the court's requirement that there must be proof of market power before tying an unpatented product to a patented product as an antitrust violation?

2. What will Independent need to establish once the case is remanded?

3. Explain when and how you could tie a product to one of your other products without running afoul of the federal antitrust laws.

Consider...

David Ungar holds a Dunkin' Donuts franchise. The terms of his franchise agreement require him to use only those ingredients furnished by Dunkin' Donuts. He is also required to buy their napkins, cups, and so on with the Dunkin' Donuts trademark on them. Is this an illegal tying arrangement? What if Dunkin' Donuts maintains that it needs these requirements to maintain its quality levels on a nationwide basis?
[*Ungar v Dunkin' Donuts of Am., Inc.*, 531 F.2d 1211 (3rd Cir. 1976)]

16-4f PRICE DISCRIMINATION

The Robinson–Patman Act prohibits **price discrimination**, which is selling goods at prices that have different ratios to the marginal cost of producing them. If two goods have the same marginal cost and are sold to different people at different prices, it is a case of price discrimination. Price discrimination is an example of the use of vertical restraints to lessen horizontal competition. Predatory pricing or pricing below cost is an example of conduct that will injure or destroy competition. Price discrimination has four elements:

1. A seller engaged in commerce
2. Discrimination in price among purchasers
3. Commodities sold that are of like grade or quality
4. A substantial lessening of competition in any line of commerce or a tendency to create a monopoly; or competition is injured, destroyed, or prevented

If all the elements are established, both the buyer and the seller have violated the Robinson–Patman Act.

Price discrimination can come in the form of the actual price charged, but can also come from indirect charges. For example, offering different credit terms to equally qualified buyers can constitute price discrimination. The products sold must be of **like grade or quality**, which means no physical differences in the product. Label differences do not make the products different. For example, the sandwich-meat manufacturer that makes a private-label meat cannot discriminate in price for the sale of that meat if the contents are the same as the manufacturer's advertised-label meat and only the label is different. However, if the private-label meat has lower-quality meat in it, a price difference can be justified because the products are not the same. In *Utah Pie Co. v Continental Baking Co.*, 386 U.S. 685, the U.S. Supreme Court held that a company that prices differently in different markets to eliminate competition, particularly when that pricing is below cost, has engaged in price discrimination. In the case, an out-of-state pie manufacturer priced its pies below cost in Utah so that it could eliminate competition from a local pie manufacturer. The mark of price discrimination is that once the competition is eliminated, prices return to a much higher level. The larger out-of-state company sustains the losses on the sales until the competitor is driven out of business. The result is less competition.

Consider...

A&P Grocery Stores decided to sell its own brand of canned milk (referred to as "private-label" milk). A&P asked its longtime supplier, Borden, to submit an offer to produce the private-label milk. Bowman Dairy also submitted a bid, which was lower than Borden's. A&P's Chicago buyer then contacted Borden and said, "I have a bid in my pocket. You people are so far out of line it is not even funny. You are not even in the ballpark." The Borden representative asked for more details but was told only that a $50,000 improvement in Borden's bid "would not be a drop in the bucket."

A&P was one of Borden's largest customers in the Chicago area. Furthermore, Borden had just invested more than $5 million in a new dairy facility in Illinois. The loss of the A&P account would result in underutilization of the plant. Borden lowered its bid by more than $400,000. The Federal Trade Commission has charged Borden with price discrimination, but Borden maintains it was simply meeting the competition. Has Borden violated the Robinson–Patman Act? Does it matter that the milk was private-label milk and not its normal trade-named Borden milk? Are the ethics of the A&P representative troublesome?
[*Great A&P Tea Co., Inc. v FTC*, 440 U.S. 69 (1979)]

Defenses to Price Discrimination

Legitimate cost differences in the manufacture or handling of a product mean price discrimination is not the issue. Additional costs of delivery or of adding specifications to a product can increase the price without violating the Robinson–Patman Act. For example, if a sandwich-meat manufacturer produces a special low-fat bologna, the price for that product can be different. If the manufacturer uses different shipping companies for its customers, a price differential may be acceptable.

Quantity discounts are permitted as long as the seller can show actual cost savings are realized in the sale of increased quantities and not just an assumption that larger sales are more economical. The law on price discrimination is based on marginal cost differences. Limiting the number of buyers who qualify for quantity discounts is some proof that the actual cost savings are not present.

Prices for products also can change according to market, inflation, material costs, and other variable factors. The seller must simply establish that a price change was initiated in response to one of these factors.

Another defense to a charge of price discrimination is **meeting the competition**. This defense must establish that a price change was made in a certain market to meet the competition there. Also, the seller must charge the same as its competitors and not a lower price. Finally, the price differences must be limited to an area or individuals. For example, a national firm may have a different price in one state because of more competition within that particular state.

16-4g VERTICAL MERGERS

Vertical mergers are between firms that have a buyer-seller relationship. For example, if a sandwich-meat manufacturer merged with its meat supplier, it would be a vertical merger. In determining whether a vertical merger violates the Clayton Act, the courts determine the relevant geographic and product markets and then determine whether the effect of the merger will be to foreclose or lessen competition.

16-5 What Are the Penalties and Remedies for Anticompetitive Behavior?

The federal antitrust laws have powerful incentives for compliance that include substantial penalties and remedies. The penalties and remedies are summarized in the following text and in Exhibit 16.3.

16-5a CRIMINAL PENALTIES

The Sherman Act carries felony criminal penalties. For individuals, the penalties are fines of up to $10 million and/or up to 10 years in prison. Corporations may be

EXHIBIT 16.3 Antitrust Remedies

	SHERMAN ACT	CLAYTON ACT	ROBINSON–PATMAN ACT	FTC ACT
Criminal	$350,000 and/or 3 years in prison for individuals; $10 million for corporations; directors and officers also liable as to intent and knowledge	None	Section 4 for intentional price discrimination	None
Civil	Treble damages plus costs and attorney fees	Same	Same	None
Equitable	Injunctions, divestitures, asset distributions, sales	Same	Same	Same
Enforcers	Justice Department; U.S. attorney; state attorneys general; private persons	Same	Same	FTC

assessed fines of up to $100 million. These criminal penalties require proof that the violator intended the anticompetitive conduct and realized the consequences of the action taken.

The FTC and Clayton Acts do not carry criminal penalties. However, Section 4 of the Robinson–Patman Act makes criminal certain forms of intentional price discrimination. Officers and directors of violating corporations can also be held criminally liable for antitrust violations, depending on their level of knowledge and involvement. For example, in the Archer Daniels Midland price-fixing case, officers were held responsible for the violations because of their direct knowledge of the price-fixing activities. The Antitrust Division of the Department of Justice or the local U.S. attorney's office is responsible for bringing criminal actions under the antitrust laws.

16-5b EQUITABLE REMEDIES

Equitable remedies consist of court orders that restrain or prevent anticompetitive conduct. Equitable remedies are available in both private and government enforcement actions. An **injunction** is a frequent form of antitrust relief; it is a court order prohibiting a violating party from engaging in anticompetitive conduct. For example, a firm can be ordered to divest itself of an acquired firm or, in an unlawful asset acquisition, a court order can require that the assets be divided with a competing firm. Contracts whose terms violate the antitrust laws can be canceled by court order. Equitable remedies give the courts discretion to fashion remedies that will eliminate the results of anticompetitive behavior.

16-5c PRIVATE ACTIONS FOR DAMAGES

Section 4 of the Clayton Act allows any person whose business or property is injured as a result of an antitrust violation to recover "threefold the damages by him sustained"—commonly referred to as **treble damages**—along with the costs of the suit and reasonable attorney fees. This section, with its substantial recovery provisions, is a strong incentive for private enforcement of antitrust laws. Consumers, businesses, and state attorneys general can all bring private damage actions under Section 4. These treble damages have found plaintiffs looking for ways to tap into the antitrust statutes, but the U.S. Supreme Court has been cautious in extending the remedies. In *Credit Suisse Securities (USA) LLC v Billing*, 551 U.S. 264 (2007), the Court held that securities investors who were bringing suit for IPO (initial primary offerings, see Chapter 21) pricing and allocation needed to turn to the securities laws for their remedies, not the antitrust laws and their treble damages. The court held that securities regulation is so extensive and investor protections so readily available that the antitrust laws did not apply to the conduct of investment bankers and brokers for purposes of investor relief.

Types of damages include lost profits, increased costs, and decreased value in property. These damage suits have a four-year statute of limitations—that is, suit must be brought within four years of the alleged violation. Those who bring private damage suits enjoy a proof benefit: If the government has brought suit and a violation is found, that judgment can be used in a private suit as *prima facie* evidence against the violating defendant. A *prima facie* case allows a plaintiff to survive a directed verdict and entitles the plaintiff to a judgment if the defendant offers no contradictory evidence (see Chapter 4 for more discussion).

16-6 What Lies Ahead in Anticompetitive Behavior: The Antitrust Modernization Commission

The Antitrust Modernization Commission (AMC), created in 2002, finished its work and completed its report in 2007. The AMC had the following general findings and recommendations:

1. Courts have been taking the correct approach in their reasoning and analyses of cases involving antitrust issues by carefully examining markets, economic systems, and individual companies and products. That approach should continue.

2. Congress does not need to change either Section 2 of the Sherman Act or Section 7 of the Clayton Act. Although some individuals and particular companies may not be happy with outcomes on monopolization and merger cases, the case law has evolved in a consistent and understandable manner.

3. The AMC also noted that change in the antitrust laws was unnecessary because, as many argued, the reality is now a "new economy" of technology-driven businesses rather than an old economy of traditional businesses. The AMC noted that the laws of economics are the same and if applied to cases with consistency, the issues of the "new economy" were resolved correctly through judicial interpretation and application.

4. The Justice Department and the FTC could help with the application of the Clayton Act if they would issue reports and findings when they make decisions with regard to mergers. These reports or findings could then serve to provide businesses with guidance for future proposed deals, mergers, and acquisitions.

5. The AMC did find some issues with regard to the interaction of patent protections with competition and that certain provisions and protections in the patent laws may actually be serving as blockades for competition. Also, the AMC noted that holding a patent does not automatically translate into monopolistic behavior. The AMC felt that Congress should address the patent law issues but not the antitrust laws.

What lies ahead is now up to Congress and its response to the findings.

16-7 Antitrust Issues in International Competition

As the level of international trade has increased, so also has the number of competitors. For example, three domestic manufacturers produce cars in the United States. However, the availability of international trade markets has resulted in the importing of cars from Japan, Great Britain, Germany, Sweden, and Yugoslavia; and international competition changes the market perspective because the relevant market is not the United States but the world. In fact, in 2007, Toyota became the number one seller of autos in the United States because of open international competition.

As a result of increased levels of international competition, more joint ventures of competitors and large companies that once would have seemed unthinkable under antitrust protections will be permitted. For example, American Telephone and Telegraph (AT&T) has entered into a joint venture agreement with the Economic

Ministry of Taiwan to improve that nation's telecommunications systems. General Mills, Inc., was permitted to acquire RJR Nabisco's cold-cereal business in both the United Kingdom and the United States so that it could compete more effectively in the large North American and European markets.

The EU has developed its own antitrust guidelines and has challenged a number of proposed U.S. firm mergers in the EU. As these large mergers are proposed, the EU and other countries are taking a closer look at their anticompetitive effects. In 2001, General Electric was handed one of the few management setbacks legendary and then-CEO Jack Welch ever experienced. The proposed acquisition of Honeywell International by General Electric was opposed by EU antitrust enforcers. The EU's Merger Task Force recommended that the $41 billion proposed merger not be permitted.

The U.S. Supreme Court has held that companies from other countries that engage in commerce in the United States will be subject to U.S. antitrust laws. Foreign corporations doing business here are subject to the same rules of competition required of U.S. corporations.

BIOGRAPHY Amazon, Apple, and E-Books: Pricing Wars

The U.S. Department of Justice (DOJ) filed an antitrust suit against Apple and five of the largest publishers in the United States (Simon & Schuster, HarperCollins, Hachette, Penguin, and Macmillan), alleging that Apple conspired with the five to battle Amazon, the market leader on e-book sales, by agreeing ahead of the release of the iPad tablet and iBook to raise their prices for e-books. The move by the publishers would thus force Amazon, if it wanted to acquire rights for the books in electronic form, to raise its prices. Amazon has traditionally charged $9.99 for its e-books, a price that other publishers could not compete with.

The government's complaint alleged that, because of the agreement, e-book prices climbed $2 to $3 per book in early 2010 when the iPad was released. The complaint also outlined the communication between and among the CEOs of Apple and the publishing houses. During December 2009 and January 2010, the publisher defendants' U.S. chief executives placed at least 56 phone calls to one another.

At the time that the CEOs were communicating (prior to Apple's iPad release), Amazon held 90 percent of the e-book market. The publishers entered into contracts with Apple that prohibited discounting of e-book pricing. And as the publishers were working with Apple as an alternative outlet, they also required Amazon, if it

wanted to purchase e-book rights from them, to agree to the same no-discounting policy.

The publishers were trying to prevent Amazon from undercutting their paper book sales with the large e-book discounts. The only way to compete with Amazon was to either lower their prices and thereby reduce sales of paper books or not compete in the electronic market. The decision to opt out of the electronic market was what Senator Charles Schumer called a Hobson's choice because it was not possible to opt out with the popularity of e-readers and customer preference. Amazon's sheer volume of e-book sales has permitted its deep discount pricing. Also, Amazon has its own publishing company that specializes in e-books.

Simon & Schuster, HarperCollins, and Hachette settled the suit with the DOJ before the suit was announced publicly. The other companies soon followed, and by February 2013, all of the publishers except Apple had settled the suit with the DOJ.

Following a long trial, a federal court found that Apple had conspired to fix prices. The penalty imposed includes several controls on Apple's contacts with the other publishers, the elimination of favorable pricing for certain retailers, and sanctions for any future retaliation. Apple is required to have an independent monitor who will work to ensure antitrust compliance at the company.

Summary

What restraints of trade are permissible?

- Covenant not to compete—clause in employment or business sale contracts that restricts competition by one of the parties; must be reasonable in scope and time

What antitrust laws exist?

- Sherman Act—first federal antitrust law; prohibits monopolization and horizontal trade restraints such as price fixing, boycotts, and refusals to deal
- Clayton Act—federal antitrust statute that prohibits tying and interlocking directorates; controls mergers
- Federal Trade Commission Act—federal law that allows the FTC to regulate unfair competition
- Robinson–Patman Act—anti–price discrimination federal statute
- Celler–Kefauver Act—regulates asset acquisitions
- Hart–Scott–Rodino Antitrust Improvements Act—antitrust law that broadened Justice Department authority and provided new merger guidelines

What penalties can be imposed for restraints of trade?

- Equitable remedies—nonmonetary remedies such as injunctions
- Treble damages—three times actual damages available in antitrust cases

What are the forms of horizontal trade restraint and defenses?

- Horizontal restraints of trade—anticompetitive behavior among a firm's competitors

- Price fixing—controlling price of goods through agreement, limiting supply, controlling credit
- Group boycotts—agreement among competitors to exclude competition
- Joint ventures—temporary combinations that may restrain trade
- *Per se* violation—violation of antitrust laws that has no defense or justification
- Monopolization—possession of monopoly power in the relevant market by willful acquisition
- Monopsony—control of a market through the control of market supply
- Market power—power to control prices or exclude competition
- Relevant market—geographic and product market used to determine market power
- Predatory pricing—pricing below actual cost to monopolize
- *Noerr–Pennington* doctrine—protection of First Amendment activities from antitrust laws

What are the forms of vertical trade restraints and defenses?

- Resale price maintenance—requiring prices be set in vertical distribution
- Exclusive distributorship—limited dealership rights; not an antitrust violation as long as horizontal competition exists
- Tying—requiring buyers to take an additional product in order to purchase the product they want
- Price discrimination—selling goods across state lines at prices that have different ratios to marginal costs

Questions and Problems

1. Harold Vogel, an experienced gem appraiser, is a member of the American Society of Appraisers. Mr. Vogel's fee for his work is based on a percentage of the value of the appraised item. The society expelled him under the authority of a bylaw that provides: "It is unprofessional and unethical for the appraiser to do work for a fixed percentage of the amount of value." Mr. Vogel brought suit under Section 1 of the Sherman Act, alleging that his expulsion was a boycott and that he no longer had referrals from the society. Mr. Vogel also claims the bylaw is a means of fixing prices. Is he right? [*Harold Vogel v American Society of Appraisers*, 744 F.2d 598 (7th Cir. 1984)]

2. Booklocker, Inc., is a print-on-demand (POD) book company that specializes in handling the printing of a run of books when there is an online order for those books. Amazon.com facilitated such orders by having customers pay up front for a print run and then placing the order with a POD company. Amazon is the dominant channel for those who wish to order books that are

not available for immediate purchase but must be done through a POD. In April 2005, Amazon acquired Book-Surge, another POD company. BookSurge's prices are generally higher than those of other POD companies. On February 10, 2008, Amazon began notifying publishers that Amazon would only continue to sell POD books through the Direct Amazon Sales Channel if the publisher agreed to print its books through BookSurge. If publishers and authors wanted to have the POD sales, they had to use Amazon's printing company. (Brick-and-mortar retailers such as Barnes & Noble do not handle PODs.) Are there any antitrust issues with this requirement? [*BookLocker.com, Inc. v Amazon.com, Inc.*, 650 F. Supp. 2d (D. Me. 2009)]

3. Amanda Reiss had completed her residency in ophthalmology in Portland, Oregon, and was moving to Phoenix, Arizona, to start her practice. She began looking for office space and met with a leasing agent who showed her several complexes of medical suites. Dr. Reiss was ready to sign for one of them when the leasing agent turned to her and said, "Oh, by the way, you're not one of those advertising doctors, are you? Because they don't want that kind in any of my complexes." Has there been a violation of the antitrust laws?

4. Budget Rent-a-Car and Aloha Airlines have developed a "fly-drive" program. Under their agreement, customers of Aloha receive a $7 first-day rental rate for car rentals (the usual rate is $14). Robert's Waikiki U-Drive has brought suit, challenging the agreement as a tying arrangement and unlawful. Is Robert's correct? [*Robert's Waikiki U-Drive v Budget Rent-a-Car*, 732 F.2d 1403 (9th Cir. 1984)]

5. In April 1965, Berkeley Heights Shopping Center leased 11,514 square feet of space to A&P Supermarkets. Under the terms of the lease, Berkeley agreed not to lease any other shopping center space to another grocery store. On April 16, 1977, A&P informed Berkeley that it was ceasing operations and subleasing the premises to Drug Fair, a modern drugstore chain that sells foodstuffs. In 1985, Berkeley sought to lease other space in the center to another grocery store, and Drug Fair objected on the grounds of the covenant not to compete. Berkeley maintains the covenant only applies when the premises Drug Fair occupies are used as a grocery store operation. Who is correct? [*Berkeley Dev. Co. v Great Atlantic & Pacific Tea Co.*, 518 A.2d 790 (N.J. 1986)]

6. Gardner-Denver, the largest manufacturer of ratchet wrenches and their replacement parts in the United States, has a dual pricing system for wrench parts and components. Its blue list had parts that, if purchased in quantities of five or more, were available for substantially less than its white list prices. Has Gardner-Denver engaged in price discrimination with its two price lists? [*D. E. Rogers Assoc., Inc. v Gardner-Denver Co.*, 718 F.2d 1431 (6th Cir. 1983)]

7. Russell Stover is a candy manufacturer that ships its products to 18,000 retailers nationwide. Stover designates resale prices for its dealers but does not request assurances from them that they are honoring the prices. It has, however, refused to sell to those retailers it believes will sell below the prices suggested. Is there an antitrust violation in this conduct? [*Russell Stover Candies, Inc. v FTC*, 718 F.2d 256 (8th Cir. 1982)]

8. William Inglis & Sons is a family-owned wholesale bakery with production facilities in Stockton, California, that manufactured and distributed bread and rolls in northern California. ITT Continental is one of the nation's largest wholesale bakeries and was a competitor of Inglis in the northern California market. Both Inglis and Continental sold their bread under a private label and an advertised label. Continental's advertised bread was "Wonder" bread, whereas Inglis's advertised bread was "Sunbeam." The private-label bread is sold at a lower price than the advertised brand, but the principal difference between the two is the profit. Inglis filed a complaint stating that Continental was selling its private-label bread at below-cost prices in a predatory price scheme designed to drive Inglis out of the market. Inglis also says the lower price on private bread earned Continental more grocery-shelf space for its "Wonder" bread. Is such conduct illegal under the Sherman Act? Is predatory pricing a *per se* violation? [*William Inglis v ITT Continental Baking Co.*, 668 F.2d 1014 (9th Cir. 1980)]

9. Christie's International and Sotheby's, international auction houses for art and estate items, are known for their handling of the estates and property of the rich and famous, such as the estate of Jacqueline Kennedy Onassis; the gowns of Diana, Princess of Wales; and the effects of Marilyn Monroe. Together, the two firms controlled 95 percent of the international auction market.

Sotheby's CEO of more than 20 years, Diana (Dede) Brooks, and Christopher M. Davidge, the CEO of Christie's, at the direction of their bosses, Sotheby's chairman, Sir A. Alfred Taubman, and Christie's chairman, Sir Anthony Tennant, met to discuss their companies' charges for commissions. Sir Alfred and Sir Anthony had met and agreed that they were "killing" each other with their competition. Both then directed Brooks and Davidge to reach agreements that ensured their firms' survivals.

Ms. Brooks and Mr. Davidge then began a series of meetings, many of which were in the backseat of

Ms. Brooks's car as she picked Mr. Davidge up from the airport, in which they discussed the following:

- Their commission rates
- An agreement to publish nonnegotiable commission rates
- An agreement as to who would publish rates first
- Exchange of customer information so that they could monitor each other's commission rates
- Eliminating interest-free loans to their seller/customers on consignment arrangements
- Eliminating charitable deductions as part of their pricing to sellers

The agreements reached in the town-car meetings worked. In March 1995, Christie's announced that it was increasing sellers' fees from a flat commission rate to a sliding scale that ranged from 2 to 20 percent. In April 1995, Sotheby's announced the same change. Their rates changed in this pattern until Mr. Davidge was fired in December 1999. Upset about a "paltry" severance package, he turned documents over to the Justice Department. When Christie's learned that the documents had been turned over, it announced that it was increasing its buyer's commission from 15.5 to 18 percent and charging its sellers less. Seller commissions would drop to between 1 and 5 percent. Sotheby's did not follow the change, the first time in the nearly five-year period that there was any difference in the two houses' commission rates.

The price-fixing charges against the two auction houses involved "conscious parallelism."

Mr. Taubman denied any involvement in the price fixing and offered a lie detector test conducted by a former FBI agent to establish that he did not know of the arrangements and communications between Ms. Brooks and Mr. Davidge. The two key questions in the polygraph exam, which Mr. Taubman passed, were the following:

Did you tell Dede Brooks to try and reach an agreement with Davidge regarding amounts to be charged to buyers or sellers?

Did Dede Brooks ever tell you that she had reached an agreement with Davidge about amounts to be charged to buyers and sellers?

Mr. Taubman's answers of "no" to each of these questions were found to be truthful by the polygraph examiner. The test was conducted without any current law enforcement agents present.

Evaluate whether the actions of "conscious parallelism" in pricing violates federal antitrust laws. Also evaluate whether the executives can be charged with criminal violations of federal antitrust laws. Which federal antitrust statute would apply?

10. Systems and Software, Inc. (SAS), located in Colchester, Vermont, designs, develops, sells, and services software that allows utility providers to organize their data, including customer information, billing, work management, asset management, and finance and accounting. In August 2002, SAS hired Randy Barnes as an at-will employee to become a regional vice president of sales. At the time he commenced work for SAS, Barnes signed a noncompetition agreement that, among other things, prohibited him—during his employment and for six months thereafter—from becoming associated with any business that competes with SAS. In April 2004, Barnes voluntarily left his position with SAS and started a partnership with his wife called Spirit Technologies Consulting Group. Spirit Technologies' only customer was Utility Solutions, Inc., which, like SAS, services municipalities and utilities nationwide with respect to customer-information-systems software. Shortly after Barnes left SAS, he represented Utility Solutions at a trade fair in a booth near SAS's booth and identified himself as Utility Solution's sales director.

SAS filed suit requesting injunctive relief and enforcement of the noncompetition agreement. Barnes says that the effect of enforcement of the clause is to prevent him from working for six months and stopping competition in Vermont. Who is correct on the noncompetition agreement? Is it valid? Why or why not? [*Systems and Software, Inc. v Barnes*, 886 A.2d 762, (Vt. 2005)]

11. British Airways and Virgin Atlantic Airlines discussed fuel surcharges at least six times during an 18-month period from 2005 through 2006. As a result, the two companies' fuel surcharges rose in tandem from 5 pounds (about $10) to 60 pounds (about $120). Would Britain's Office of Fair Trading be able to establish an antitrust violation?

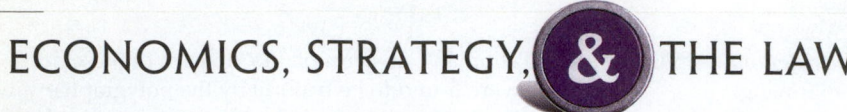

ECONOMICS, STRATEGY, & THE LAW

Reverse Payments and Competition

The Justice Department and the FTC are seeking to end "reverse-payment settlements." These are payments made by the manufacturers of brand-name drugs to generic drug manufacturers that are wrapped up in patent litigation; they are used as a way to keep generics off the market for a longer period of time.

The process works like this:

1. A generic drug manufacturer is permitted to seek FDA approval for its generic version of a branded drug based on the clinical trials of the brand manufacturer. The Hatch–Waxman Act permits this use of the brand manufacturer's clinical trials with the goal of getting generics to the market faster.

2. However, by seeking approval using the clinical trials, the generic manufacturer opens the door for patent litigation by the brand manufacturer because such a filing is an admission that the generic is the same as the branded drug.

3. The brand manufacturer then brings a patent suit against the generic manufacturer for infringement.

4. The brand manufacturer is willing to settle the case. The settlement, however, does not involve the defendant generic manufacturer paying the plaintiff brand manufacturer. Rather, the brand manufacturer pays the generic manufacturer money to agree to not market or sell its generic version. The reverse payment makes economic sense because the generic is then kept off the market for a longer period of time, and the brand manufacturer is allowed to continue its exclusive market control. For example, Bayer AG paid $398.1 million to various generic drug manufacturers for them to keep their versions of Cipro off the market.

Reverse-payment settlements have been the subject of several antitrust suits. [*In re Tamoxifen Citrate Antitrust Litigation*, 466 F.3d 187 (2nd Cir. 2006), and *In re Ciprofloxacin Hydrochloride Antitrust Litigation*, 544 F.3d 1323 (Fed. Cir. 2008)] These courts have found antitrust violations in the reverse-payment agreements. However, other courts have upheld such agreements as long as they do not cover time frames beyond the patent period.

With a split in the circuits in the law, the U.S. Supreme Court would took jurisdiction to resolve the issue of whether the agreements violate antitrust laws. In *F.T.C. v Actavis, Inc.*, 133 S.Ct. 2223 (2013), the court held that reverse-payment settlements may violate antitrust laws. The balancing the court noted that must be done comes through an examination of whether the public is benefited by the agreement or access to a needed drug is restricted. The court allowed the FTC's antitrust suit against a company that had entered into a reverse settlement agreement to proceed, with the trial court focusing on the effect of the reverse payments on availability and competition.

Explain why the payments to keep a product off the market would be an antitrust violation. What benefits are there for the companies on reverse-payment settlements? Who is harmed by these agreements? Are they anticompetitive?

[*Ark. Carpenters Health & Welfare Fund v Bayer A.G.*, 544 F.3d 1323 (Fed. Cir. 2008)]

Notes

1. Thomas Catan, "Gore-Tex Runs Into Antitrust Probes," *Wall Street Journal*, June 22, 2011, p. B1.

2. The doctrine is named after the two U.S. Supreme Court cases in which it was developed: *Eastern R.R. President's Conference v Noerr Motor Freight, Inc.*, 365 U.S. 127 (1961) and *United Mine Workers v Pennington*, 381 U.S. 657 (1965).

3. The author is grateful for the work and insights of Professor Sue Mota, Associate Dean, College of Business Administration, Bowling Green State University, Ohio. More on her work can be found at Sue Mota, "Antitrust Limited: The Supreme Court Reins in Antitrust Enforcement in 2007," 7 *Fla. St. U. Bus. Rev.* 1 (2007).

Bo Chambers/Flickr/Getty Images

Part 4
BUSINESS MANAGEMENT AND GOVERNANCE

This portion of the book covers the management of businesses, including the management of employees and the rights and duties of employers and employees as they work together to operate a business. This section of the book also covers the oversight function of boards in the operation of a business. What are the regulations and restrictions related to the hiring, retention, promotion, and firing of employees? How much authority do employees have to make decisions and take actions with respect to their work? What are the safety requirements for business operations? What responsibilities do boards have in selecting and overseeing the managers of the business? How do shareholders have input into board decisions on management and operations? What are the disclosure requirements between companies and their shareholders? How, when, and where is information disclosed to shareholders and markets? All of these questions focus on the operations of a business, making sure that there is responsibility and accountability for what businesses do and how they interact with employees, shareholders, and the capital markets.

17 MANAGEMENT OF EMPLOYEE CONDUCT:
Agency

All businesses have a common thread: employees. They need them, rely on them, pay them, and give them authority to perform certain business tasks. This chapter focuses on that delegation of authority and these questions: When does an employee act on behalf of an employer? How much authority does an employee have? What duties and obligations do employees owe employers? When is a business liable for an employee's acts?

UPDATE

For up-to-date legal news, go to **mariannejennings.com**

Consider...

Matthew Neumann and Nicholas Tides worked on Boeing's internal audit team and were working specifically on certification of Boeing's internal controls under Sarbanes–Oxley (SOX). The two men were concerned that the internal controls were not adequate and that they should not be certified as sufficient under SOX standards. The two men worked with a Seattle reporter on a story that was later published that revealed their concerns. Boeing fired Neumann and Tides for violation of Boeing's rules that prohibited public disclosure of company private or proprietary information. The two men brought suit against Boeing for retaliation, which is prohibited under SOX when employees bring concerns about financial reporting to light. Could the men be fired, or was the retaliation prohibited?

17-1 Names and Roles: Agency Terminology

A principal–agent relationship is one in which one party acts on behalf of another. A clerk who helps you to the dressing room and takes your payment in a department store is an agent. Rory McIlroy, the record-breaking PGA golfer, has an agent who negotiates his endorsement and appearance contracts for him. A **power of attorney** is a form of agency relationship that grants another authority to enter into transactions. A special power of attorney is one limited in time and/or scope, as when a landowner gives another the authority to close a particular land transaction. For example, Rory McIlroy's agent has general authority to negotiate endorsement contracts with the exception of endorsements for alcoholic beverages. Mr. McIlroy will not enter into endorsement contracts with companies whose products are alcoholic beverages and his agent has no authority to negotiate such agreements. A general power of attorney is one in which an individual gives another the rights to manage his financial affairs in everything from handling checking accounts to entering into contracts. The common thread in all of these relationships is that one party acts on behalf of another.

17-1a AGENCY

In an agency relationship, one party agrees to act on behalf of another party according to directions. The principal grants authority to an agent. Agency is a consensual relationship—both sides agree to it—and also a fiduciary relationship with duties and responsibilities on both sides. The general term *agency* can be used to refer to many different types of relationships. A real estate agent who is hired to help market your house is an agent of yours; talent agents are agents for many actors at the same time.

17-1b PRINCIPALS

In the employer–employee relationship, the employers are referred to as the **principals**. The term *principal* is used because some agents are not truly employees. A literary agent, for example, represents many authors who are the agent's principals, but the principals are not, in the usual sense, "employers" of the agent.

17-1c AGENTS

Agents are those who do a task on behalf of the principal. The agent represents the principal in such a way that if the agent negotiates a contract, the principal, but not the agent, is bound by and a party to the contract. A president of a corporation is an agent of the corporation. When the president negotiates a contract with proper authority, the corporation, not the president, is bound to perform that contract.

All employees are agents of the principal (employer), but not all agents are employees. A corporation might hire an architect to design a new office building and obtain bids for the construction of the building. The architect would be an agent for limited purposes but not an employee of the company.

17-1d EMPLOYERS AND EMPLOYEES: MASTER–SERVANT RELATIONSHIPS

A **master–servant relationship** is a relationship in which the principal (master) exercises a great deal of control over the agent (servant).[1] An employer–employee relationship for a production line worker is an example of a master–servant relationship. Among the various factors considered are whether an employee works regular hours, is paid a regular wage, and is subject to complete supervision and control by the employer during work hours. The factors used to determine whether a master–servant relationship exists are as follows:

- Level of supervision and control of the agent (most important)
- Nature of the agent's work
- Regularity of hours and pay
- Length of employment

The presence of a master–servant relationship also determines whether the principal must pay wage taxes such as FICA and FUTA and withhold income taxes. (See Chapter 18 for more details.)

17-1e INDEPENDENT CONTRACTORS

An **independent contractor** acts on behalf of another to perform a task but is not under the direct control of the other person. For example, a corporation's attorney is an agent of the corporation only for purposes of legal representation and court appearances. The attorney is not a corporate employee, and the corporation has no control over the attorney's office operations. The attorney is an independent contractor. A subcontractor hired to perform partial work on a construction site is also an example of an independent contractor.

Principals have less responsibility for independent contractors than for servants because they have little control over a contractor's conduct. The distinction between master–servant relationships and independent contractor relationships is important because a principal's liability for an agent's actions varies depending on the agent's status as servant or contractor.

17-1f AGENCY LAW

In general, agency relationships are not governed by statutory law; rather, these relationships are governed by common law. The common law of agency that the majority of states follow is found in a compilation called the *Restatement of Agency*, which is followed by many courts in deciding cases that involve agency law disputes.

Studying agency law actually involves examining three different areas. The first area deals with the creation of the agency relationship. The second area involves the relationship between principals and agents. The final area examines the relationship of the agents and principals to third parties.

17-2 Creation of the Agency Relationship

Agency relationships can be created in different ways, and the requirements vary.

17-2a EXPRESS AUTHORITY

An employee who is hired by agreement (oral or written) is an agent and has been given **express authority** to act on behalf of the business. Express authority is limited to what is spoken or written. A driver employee, for example, may only have the authority to deliver packages; a sales employee may have the authority to represent the company but may be required to obtain another employee's signature to finalize sales contracts. An **express contract** specifies the limitations of an employee/agent's authority.

17-2b THE RECORD

An agency relationship is created by agreement, which need not be evidenced by a writing or record, although it is best for both employer and employee if it is. Some form of a record, electronic or written, that specifies the agent's authority is required only if the agent will enter into contracts required to have a record or if a state statute requires an agent's authority to be in some record form. For example, most states require that real estate agents' commission contracts be evidenced by a record. That record could be a written, faxed, or PDF document that is signed by the principal.

17-2c CAPACITY

Because agents will enter into contracts for their principals, the principals must have the **capacity** to contract. *Capacity* here means capacity in the traditional contract sense: age and mental capacity (as covered in Chapter 13). In addition, the principal must be in existence for an agent to have authority. If a company has not been incorporated, those who sign for the nonexistent corporation as agents have liability.

One agency capacity issue that comes up frequently in sole proprietorships, general partnerships, and other smaller businesses that are dependent on individual personalities is the stalemate that results when mental incapacity (through accident or illness frequently) in one of these key individuals becomes a factor. For example, if one of two general partners is injured in an accident and unconscious, the remaining partner has his or her hands tied for certain types of business transactions. Under the **Uniform Durable Power of Attorney Act (UDPAA)** (a uniform law that has been adopted in most states), these key individuals can execute a type of power of attorney that comes into existence in the event of disability or incapacity of the principal. This authority then "kicks in" when needed. The UDPAA has also been helpful for children who are trying to manage their parents' financial affairs when their parents become mentally or physically disabled. The durable power of attorney allows the child or children to manage payments, accounts, and assets, depending on the scope of authority given. In many cases, the child or children need the authority just to be able to manage the medical bills and insurance claims for the parent's illness.

The contractual capacity of the agent is not an issue in the agency relationship for purposes of the agent's authority to enter into contracts. However, the capacity of the agent to drive, operate equipment, or work with the public is an issue that affects the employer's liability to third parties. Because of this liability, many employers conduct background checks, polygraph and psychological tests, and drug screening as a precondition to hiring employees. Many firms also have ongoing drug-testing programs to ensure that employees are not reporting for work—or working—under the influence of drugs or alcohol.

One of the most controversial issues in agency law concerns the **unincorporated association**, which is a group that acts as an entity but has no legal existence. Some charitable organizations—churches, for example—have an ongoing existence and have probably built buildings, had fund-raising drives, and entered into many contracts. However, because these organizations are not incorporated and do not have any legal existence, those who sign contracts for these groups are not agents. Moreover, they are liable under these contracts because the organizations are not principals with capacity. For example, suppose that a Little League coach signs a credit contract for the purchase of Little League equipment. The Little League organization is nonprofit and is not incorporated. In the event the league does not raise enough money to pay for the sporting equipment, the signing coach is liable because the league is not a principal with capacity.

The National Conference of Commissioners on Uniform State Laws proposed the Uniform Unincorporated Nonprofit Association Act (UUNAA) with revisions in 2008, and it has been adopted in 12 states. Under the UUNAA, the contract and tort liability of individual members of a nonprofit association would be eliminated if they were acting on behalf of their nonprofit unincorporated association. The UUNAA also gives unincorporated nonprofits the right to bring suits and be sued in their names and to own property in similar fashion.

17-2d IMPLIED AUTHORITY

An agent under contract not only has the authority given expressly but also has certain **implied authority**. Implied authority is the extension of express authority by custom. For example, a person who is hired as president of a corporation probably does not have his or her exact duties specified in the contract. However, corporate presidents will likely have the type of authority customarily used by presidents: to sign contracts, to authorize personnel changes, to conduct salary reviews and changes, and to institute operational changes. Customary authority is always given in the agency relationship unless the agent's contract specifies otherwise. This implied authority can be limited by agreement between the parties if they do not want custom and practice to control their relationship.

Business Planning Tip

Before you sign on behalf of an organization, be sure you understand your liability. For example, if you sign a contract with a hotel for a group's meeting, you will have personal liability if your group is not incorporated and if the hotel is not paid. If your group is incorporated, be sure to sign so that the corporation, not you, is personally liable. You can use the following format:

(Your Group Name)
By: (Your Name)
(Your Title)

Here is an example:

Weaving Through the Maze, a nonprofit corporation
By: Marianne M. Jennings
President

Together, express and implied authority are called **actual authority**. The type of authority an agent has determines the liability of the principal to third parties for contracts and torts.

17-2e APPARENT AUTHORITY

In many cases, an agency relationship arises not by express or implied contracts but because of the way a principal appears to third parties. This theory of agency law, called **apparent authority** or **agency by estoppel**, holds a principal liable if the principal makes others believe there is an agency relationship.

Apparent authority exists by appearance. A third party is led to believe that an agent, although not actually holding express and accompanying implied authority, had the proper authority to deal with the third party. The third party is led to believe that certain promises will be fulfilled. For example, a mobile home dealer who has brochures, notepads, and other materials from a mobile home manufacturer has the appearance of having the authority to sell those homes even no actual authority exists. *Cove Management v AFLAC, Inc.* (Case 17.1) deals with issues of apparent authority.

CASE 17.1	*Cove Management v AFLAC, Inc.*
	986 N.E.2d 1206 (Ill. App. 2013)

Ducking Out of a Lease

FACTS

AFLAC (defendant) is engaged in the business of underwriting and selling insurance policies in the health care field. On September 22, 2004, Darren Galgano (also a defendant) signed an "Associate's Agreement" with AFLAC, which engaged Galgano to solicit applications for insurance policies offered for sale by AFLAC. The agreement also states that Galgano is an independent contractor, without the authority to bind AFLAC for Galgano's "debts, faults, or actions." The agreement specifically states that Galgano is prohibited from entering into contracts or incurring debt on behalf of AFLAC.

On September 5, 2005, Galgano signed a "District Sales Coordinator's Agreement," which incorporated the terms of the "Associate's Agreement" and specifically withheld authority from Galgano to "rent any office space or telephone, open any bank account, or make any expenditure, obligation or commitment for any purpose in the name of AFLAC without specific written authorization from the president, a vice president, or secretary of AFLAC." On August 6, 2007, Galgano signed a "Regional Sales Coordinator's Agreement," which incorporated the "District Sales Coordinator's Agreement" and once again withheld authority from Galgano to rent office space, incur debt, or enter into a contract on AFLAC's behalf without express written authorization of the president, a vice president, or a secretary of AFLAC.

On September 4, 2009, Galgano leased retail property located in Crestwood, Illinois, from Cove Management (plaintiff). The first page of the lease listed Cove as the lessor, listed "AFLAC" as the tenant, and listed Galgano as the guarantor. The lease provided that the permitted use of the space was "insurance services." On the signature page, Joseph Bertucci, on behalf of Cove, signed under "lessor," and Galgano signed his own name under "lessee" and "guarantor." He did not indicate on the signature page that he was signing on behalf of AFLAC.

After Cove was not paid rent and the property in Crestwood was abandoned, Cove filed suit for breach of the lease agreement against both AFLAC and Galgano. The trial court granted AFLAC summary judgment on the grounds that Galgano had no authority to bind it to a lease. Cove appealed.

JUDICIAL OPINION

GORDON, Justice

AFLAC claimed that Galgano was an independent contractor who had no authority to bind AFLAC to

CONTINUED

any lease agreement. In order to determine whether Galgano was an independent contractor or an agent of AFLAC, we must first determine Galgano's authority. "An agent's authority may be either actual or apparent, and actual authority may be either express or implied." Express authority is actual authority granted explicitly by the principal to the agent, while implied authority is actual authority proven circumstantially by evidence of the agent's position. Apparent authority, by contrast, is authority imposed by equity.

Plaintiff's primary argument is that AFLAC clothed Galgano with apparent authority as its agent and thus AFLAC was liable as a lessee under the lease. Apparent authority is defined as follows:

> "Apparent authority in an agent is such authority as the principal knowingly permits the agent to assume or which he holds his agent out as possessing—it is such authority as a reasonably prudent man, exercising diligence and discretion, in view of the principal's conduct, would naturally suppose the agent to possess."

Apparent authority in an agent to do an act for his principal must be based on the words and acts of his principal and cannot be based on anything the agent himself has said or done.

The doctrine of apparent authority is rooted in the doctrine of equitable estoppel. Where a principal has created the appearance of authority in an agent, and another party has reasonably and detrimentally relied upon the agent's authority, the principal cannot deny it.

If there is no showing of reasonable and detrimental reliance upon the agent's authority, there can be no apparent authority.

The majority of evidence that plaintiff shows is evidence that came into existence after the signing of the lease, except for the statements and representations of Galgano, which cannot be considered. The business cards that Galgano gave to plaintiff showed a Chicago address with the word "AFLAC" in large letters, with phone numbers in Chicago's Loop, Chicago Ridge, and South Holland. The cards listed Galgano's email address using the domain "us.aflac.com" and "aflac.com," and designated Galgano as a "Regional Sales Coordinator" and "An Independent Associate Representing Aflac." The cards showed the name AFLAC in blue with the duck symbol on the "L" of "AFLAC." When using the Internet to look for AFLAC, plaintiff alleges that it found aflac.com listed at its Midlothian address. However, even though the sheet showing this Internet information was attached as an exhibit to plaintiff's complaint, its creation occurred after the lease was signed; thus, plaintiff could not have relied on it to its detriment. Likewise, we cannot

consider the evidence (1) that when the office was set up, the parking sign had the AFLAC symbol and duck, (2) that AFLAC's stylized blue materials were in the office, inside and out, and (3) that AFLAC was listed on the directory of the building, because they all occurred after the lease was signed and thus there was not any reliance by plaintiff on that information when entering into the lease. Without any showing of a reasonable and detrimental reliance by plaintiff, there cannot be recovery for apparent authority.

In addition, a third person dealing with a known agent may not act negligently with regard to the extent of the agent's authority or blindly trust the agent's statements in such respect. Rather, he must use reasonable diligence and prudence to ascertain whether the agent is acting and dealing with him within the scope of his powers. The mere opinion of an agent as to the extent of his powers, or his mere assumption of authority without foundation, will not bind the principal; and a third person dealing with a known agent must bear the burden of determining for himself, by the exercise of reasonable diligence and prudence, the existence or nonexistence of the agent's authority to act in the premises. The principal, on the other hand, may act on the presumption that third parties dealing with his agent will not be negligent in failing to ascertain the extent of his authority as well as the existence of his agency.

If [the third person] knows, or has good reason for believing, that the acts exceed the agent's powers or if such reasonable inquiry as he is under the duty to make, would result in discovery of the true state of the powers, and he fails to fulfill that duty, he cannot assert an apparent authority effective against the principal.

The record in the instant case does not show that plaintiff made any effort to determine whether Galgano was an independent contractor or an agent of AFLAC acting within the scope of his authority. Instead, plaintiff apparently relied exclusively on the statements and representations of Galgano that he had the authority to bind AFLAC to the lease on the premises.

The only AFLAC promotional material given to plaintiff prior to plaintiff's signing the lease was Galgano's business card and "maybe his stationary [sic]." Plaintiff's arguments that AFLAC must have known of Galgano's conduct are not the issue in this case. Since there is no showing of reasonable and detrimental reliance upon Galgano's authority, we cannot find that Galgano was acting under apparent authority. In addition, plaintiff failed to make a reasonable inquiry as they were under a duty to make.

Plaintiff next argues that the trial court improperly dismissed its count for ratification of the lease.

CONTINUED

"Ratification occurs when the principal learns of an unauthorized transaction, then retains the benefits of the transaction or takes a position inconsistent with nonaffirmation." Ratification may be inferred from surrounding circumstances, including long-term acquiescence, after notice, to the benefits of an allegedly unauthorized transaction.

Plaintiff argues that AFLAC neither objected to Galgano's actions nor made any effort to convey an objection to plaintiff. However, Lynn Fry's unchallenged affidavits explicitly state that AFLAC had no knowledge that Galgano "had signed a lease for the premises" until plaintiff filed its lawsuit. Therefore, AFLAC could not have had "full knowledge" of Galgano's actions. Although plaintiff submitted evidence that its address was listed by AFLAC on AFLAC's website, plaintiff did not attach counteraffidavits to its response to AFLAC's motions to dismiss, nor did plaintiff refute the fact asserted in Lynn Fry's affidavit. Therefore, plaintiff has admitted that AFLAC had no knowledge of the lease until plaintiff filed its lawsuit, and as a result, cannot prove that AFLAC ratified the lease.

Finally, plaintiff argues that the trial court improperly dismissed its count for unjust enrichment. Plaintiff argues that AFLAC was unjustly enriched as a result of Galgano's use of the subject premises and that plaintiff is entitled to *quantum meruit* recovery. Quantum meruit

is used as an equitable remedy to provide restitution for unjust enrichment. Plaintiffs often plead *quantum meruit* as an alternative claim in breach of contract actions so that the plaintiff may recover even if the contract is unenforceable. To recover under a *quantum meruit* theory, a plaintiff must prove that: (1) it performed a service to the benefit of the defendant; (2) it did not perform the service gratuitously; (3) defendant accepted this service; and (4) no contract existed to prescribe payment for this service.

Lynn Fry's unchallenged affidavits state that AFLAC had no knowledge of the lease until plaintiff filed its lawsuit. Without knowledge of the lease, AFLAC could not accept the services provided, and as a result, plaintiff can prove no set of facts to show that it is entitled to *quantum meruit* recovery.

The trial court properly granted defendant AFLAC's motion to dismiss.

CASE QUESTIONS

1. Why does the court find that there is no apparent authority?
2. Why does the court conclude that there was no ratification?
3. Why does the court conclude that Cove is not entitled to *quantum meruit* recovery?

Consider...

Suppose that a bar owner has employed a bouncer and the bouncer injures someone while removing him from the premises. Is the employer liable for the conduct of the bouncer? [*Byrd v Faber*, 57 Ohio St.3d 56, 565 N.E.2d 584, 587 (1991)]

THINK: The AFLAC case held that a principal is liable for the acts of an agent that a third party would perceive are within the scope of the authority of the agent.

APPLY: When an agent is hired as a bouncer, battery and assault could be within the agent's apparent scope of authority.

ANSWER: The bar owner is liable for the bouncer's conduct.

17-2f RATIFICATION

On occasion, an agent without proper authority enters into a contract that the principal later ratifies. **Ratification** occurs when the principal reviews a contract and voluntarily decides that, even though the agent did not have proper authority, the contract will be honored as if the agent had full authority. Once a contract is ratified, it is effective from the time the agent entered into it even though the agent had no authority until after the fact. Ratification is a way for a principal to give an agent authority retroactively.

Consider...

On September 20, 1973, a Beech Model 18 aircraft carrying singer Jim Croce and his entourage crashed shortly after takeoff from Natchitoches, Louisiana. All were killed.

At the time of the crash, the plane was being flown by Robert N. Elliott, an employee of Roberts Airways. Roberts had been asked by Mustang Aviation to fly the entourage according to a prepared itinerary. Mustang originally had entered into a contract with Lloyd St. Martin of Variety Artists International, a booking agent for popular singers, to fly the group itself. The agreement was entered into on September 18, 1973. Later that same day, Mustang learned that its aircraft was disabled, so Mustang's director of operations called Roberts and asked it to substitute.

Relatives of Mr. Croce and the others killed in the crash brought suit against Mustang for the crash. What, if any, agency relationships existed in this case? How did they arise? Is Mustang liable for the crash?

[*Croce v Bromley Corp.*, 623 F.2d 1084 (5th Cir. 1980)]

For example, suppose that an apartment manager does not have the authority to contract for any type of construction work except routine maintenance. Because the fence around the apartment complex is deteriorated, the manager contracts for the construction of a completely new fence at a cost that exceeds by six times any maintenance work he has had done in the past. The contractor begins work on the fence, and the apartment owner drives by, sees the work, and says nothing. By her inaction in allowing the contractor to continue building the fence, the apartment complex owner ratifies the contract.

Consider...

Benjamin Chavez served as executive director of the National Association for the Advancement of Colored People (NAACP). Mary Stansee, a former employee of the NAACP executive offices, charged Mr. Chavez with sexual harassment, and he settled the claim for $332,400. The NAACP was financially troubled at the time of the settlement, with a deficit of $2.7 million in 1993, and Mr. Chavez did not disclose the settlement to the board until after it was completed.

Did Mr. Chavez have implied authority to make the settlement? Did he have apparent authority?

17-3 The Principal–Agent Relationship

To this point, the focus of the discussion has been on the relationship between the agent and the principal on the one hand and third parties on the other. However, it is important to realize that a contractual relationship exists between the agent and the principal, so that each has certain obligations and rights. This section of the chapter covers that relationship.

17-3a THE AGENT'S RIGHTS AND RESPONSIBILITIES

Principals and agents have a fiduciary relationship, which is characterized by loyalty, trust, care, and obedience. An agent in the role of fiduciary must act in the principal's best interests.

Duty of Loyalty: General

An agent is required to act only for the benefit of the principal, and an agent cannot represent both parties in a transaction unless each knows about and consents to the agent's representation of the other. Further, an agent cannot use the information gained or the offers available to or by the principal to profit personally. For example, an agent hired to find a buyer for a new invention cannot interfere with the principal's possible sale by demonstrating his own product. Neither can an agent hired to find a piece of property buy the property and then sell it (secretly of course) to the principal. *Lucini Italia Co. v Grappolini* (Case 17.2) involves an issue of an agent's fiduciary duty in a sale transaction.

| CASE 17.2 | *Lucini Italia Co. v Grappolini*
2003 WL 1989605 (N.D. Ill. 2003)[2] |

A Slick Deal by the Olive Oil Agent

FACTS

Lucini Italia imports and sells premium extra-virgin olive oil of Italy. Lucini was formed by Arthur Frigo, a Chicago entrepreneur and adjunct professor of management and strategy at Northwestern University's Kellogg Graduate School of Management. Giuseppe Grappolini, from Loro Ciuffenna, Italy, served as a consultant to Lucini. Under the terms of his consulting contract, Mr. Grappolini was to develop Lucini Premium Select extra-virgin olive oil as well as other flavored olive oil products. Mr. Frigo had discovered a market niche in the United States for high-end olive oil ($10 to $12 per bottle).

Mr. Grappolini is also the sole owner of the Grappolini Company, an Italian limited liability company. The Grappolini Company distributes small volumes of extra-virgin olive oil in Chicago and other markets throughout the United States, but it has much larger sales volume in Europe. Between December 1997 (the date of the Grappolini consulting contract with Lucini) and June 2000, the Grappolini Company was Lucini's supplier of extra-virgin olive oil. The two companies had signed a supply agreement for this arrangement also in December 1997.

Mr. Frigo instructed Mr. Grappolini to try to negotiate an exclusive supply contract for Lucini with Vegetal, an Italian company with a unique olive oil that Mr. Frigo needed to develop another premium brand of olive oil that would have flavors such as lemon and garlic added (called the LEO project). Vegetal was the only company that could supply the type of olive oil Mr. Frigo needed for the blending process with the extra flavors. Mr. Grappolini led Mr. Frigo along with promises of a deal with the Vegetal company for nearly a year, through reports of meetings as well as with faxes and memos appearing to detail terms, conditions, and dates for delivery. At the same time, Mr. Grappolini was meeting with Mr. Frigo almost daily as they discussed the plans for the new Lucini olive oil. In the meetings, Mr. Frigo discussed the formulas, the marketing, consumer profiles, and marketing strategies for the LEO project. Apparently, Mr. Grappolini was impressed by the plans and entered into his own exclusive supply contract with Vegetal. Mr. Grappolini did not tell Mr. Frigo of the contract and continued to work as a consultant. Mr. Grappolini also assured Mr. Frigo that Lucini had a supply contract with Vegetal.

Mr. Frigo proceeded with all the contracts, ads, and plans for the LEO product launch based on assurances from Mr. Grappolini that it had the supply contract with Vegetal. However, when pressed, Mr. Grappolini could not deliver the paperwork. When Mr. Frigo requested a meeting with the CEO of Vegetal, Mr. Grappolini arranged for the meeting but cautioned Mr. Frigo not to mention the supply arrangement because such a discussion in a first-time meeting would be considered rude in the Italian culture.

With the LEO product launch approaching, and no copy of the alleged Vegetal supply contract available, Mr. Frigo had Lucini's lawyer in Italy contact Vegetal directly for a copy. The lawyer learned that Vegetal had a supply contract, but the contract was with Mr. Grappolini's company and that it was not transferable to Lucini. Mr. Frigo then confronted the officers of Vegetal and they acknowledged that they had negotiated with Mr. Grappolini for his company, not for Lucini and were not aware of Lucini's needs or Mr. Grappolini's representation of Lucini. The officers at Vegetal said that Grappolini had been a "bad boy" in negotiating the contract for himself. Vegetal agreed to supply Lucini with olive oil in the future, but could

CONTINUED

not deliver it in time for the launch of Lucini's new line. The soonest it could deliver would be after the next harvest, a time that meant the marketing and sales plans of Lucini for its new product had been wasted.

Mr. Frigo and Lucini filed suit against Mr. Grappolini and his company (defendants) for breach of fiduciary duty.

JUDICIAL OPINION

DENLOW, Magistrate

As agents, Defendants owed Lucini general duties of good faith, loyalty, and trust. In addition, Defendants owed Lucini "full disclosure of all relevant facts relating to the transaction or affecting the subject matter of the agency."

Defendants were Lucini's agents and owed Lucini a fiduciary duty to advance Lucini's interests, not their own. When Defendants obtained an exclusive supply agreement with Vegetal for the Grappolini Company instead of for Lucini, they were disloyal and breached their fiduciary duties. Lucini suffered substantial damages as a result of this breach.

Punitive damages are appropriate where the defendant has intentionally breached a fiduciary duty. Defendants' breach of their fiduciary duties was flagrant and intentional. Defendants deliberately usurped a corporate opportunity sought by Lucini, which Lucini had entrusted Defendants to secure on Lucini's behalf. Although Defendants explicitly accepted this trust and ensured Lucini that Mr. Grappolini and his company would do as Lucini requested, Defendants failed to do so and hid this fact from Lucini.

Defendants misappropriated Lucini's valuable trade secrets. Defendants acquired Lucini's trade secrets under circumstances giving rise to a duty to maintain their secrecy. Defendants' assistant Marco Milandri testified that he understood that Lucini's Premium Select and LEO product formulations were company secrets. Likewise, Grappolini testified that he understood the secrecy of trade secret information communicated to him. Indeed,

his various contracts specified that he would maintain the confidentiality of Lucini's research conclusions. After Defendants had secretly secured their own exclusive supply contract with Vegetal, they hid this fact from Lucini in order to induce Lucini to continue sharing its trade secret research, strategies, and plans with Grappolini.

Lucini's decision to focus its LEO project around essential oils from Vegetal Progress was a closely guarded trade secret. When Mr. Grappolini used this information on behalf of the Grappolini Company to allow it unfettered access to negotiate its own exclusive arrangement with Vegetal, it is necessary to conclude that the Grappolini Company "acquired" the information with full knowledge that: (i) Lucini had not consented to the use of the information by a competitor, and (ii) Mr. Grappolini had no right to transmit or use the information for his own purposes or on behalf of the Grappolini Company.

As a proximate result of Defendants' breach of their fiduciary duties, Lucini suffered lost profits damages of at least $4.17 million from selling its grocery line of LEO products from 2000 through 2003. The Court will award Lucini its lost profits of $4,170,000, together with its $800,000 of development costs for LEO project. Defendants engaged in willful and malicious misappropriation as evidenced by their use of the information for directly competitive purposes and their efforts to hide the misappropriation and, accordingly, the Court will award $1,000,000 in exemplary damages. Such an award is necessary to discourage Defendants from engaging in such conduct in the future.

CASE QUESTIONS

1. Explain how Mr. Grappolini breached his fiduciary duty.

2. What lessons can you learn about contracts, suppliers, and product launches from the case?

3. Evaluate the ethics of Mr. Grappolini's conduct. Why did Vegetal's officers refer to Mr. Grappolini as a "bad boy"?

Duty of Loyalty: Postemployment and Noncompete Agreements

Many companies have their employees sign contracts that include covenants not to compete or covenants not to disclose information about their former employers should the employees leave their jobs or be terminated from their employment.

Downsizings in the high-tech industry have brought back the issue of noncompete and confidentiality agreements. When employees were recruited by upstart firms and lured with stock options, it was difficult for them to imagine a time when the company would need to downsize or would no longer exist. As a result, most of them signed fairly restrictive covenants not to compete.

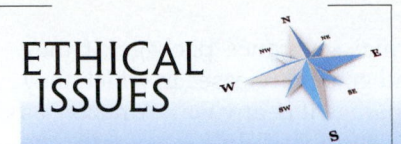

ETHICAL ISSUES

Ausaf Umar Siddiqui, a computer salesman at Fry's Electronics who worked his way up to vice president of merchandising and operations at Fry's, has been charged with receiving $65 million in kickbacks from vendors. The indictment alleges that vendors agreed to pay as much as 31 percent commission to Siddiqui in exchange for his promise to buy merchandise from them at inflated prices. The commissions he received were then paid to a company called PC International LLC. According to the IRS, the money was used to pay off gambling debts Siddiqui owed to Las Vegas casinos. Fry's has fired Siddiqui, and his coworkers at Fry's were stunned when he was arrested at work. He was released on $300,000 bond with the stipulation that he not travel to Las Vegas.

The charges came when the IRS received an anonymous tip from an upper-level manager at Fry's whose tip included copies of spreadsheets showing the payments from vendors. The anonymous tipper said that he had stumbled across the documents when he made an unannounced visit to Siddiqui's office. Vendors included U.S. Media Technology, Elitegroup Company Computer Services, Inc., Phoebe Micro, and Lead Data International, Inc. The commissions paid were 10 times the normal amounts and were sent to Siddiqui's home in Palo Alto. The IRS review of Siddiqui's bank account set up for the commissions shows that $167 million was deposited in the account during the past three years, something that leads investigators to believe that they have not uncovered all the vendors or payments.

What are the duties of an agent with respect to commissions earned? What ethical issue exists here? Is this commercial bribery? Could the vendors be charged? Why do we worry about this type of conduct by an agent?

Source: Miguel Bustillo, "Fry's Official Faces Fraud Charges," *Wall Street Journal,* December 24, 2008, p. B3.

In dealing with these covenants, courts are striking a balance between the employees' right to work and an employer's right to protect the trade secrets, training, and so forth that the former employee has and then transfers to another company or to himself or herself for purposes of starting a business.

Requirements for Noncompete Agreements.

1. The Need for Protection
The laws on noncompete agreements vary from state to state, with California and a handful of states being the most protective of employees. However, across all states, courts are clear in their positions that there must first be an underlying need or reason for the noncompete agreement—that is, the employee must have had access to trade secrets or be starting his or her own business in competition with the principal/employer.

2. Reasonableness in Scope
The covenant must also be reasonable in geographic scope and time. These factors depend on the economic base and the nature of the business. For example, a noncompete in a high-tech employee's contract could be geographically global but must be shorter in duration because technology changes so rapidly. A noncompete for a collection agency could not be global but might be longer in duration because the nature of that business is one of relationships.

3. Valid Formation
Noncompete agreements are also subject to the basics of contract law (see Chapters 12 and 13). There must be consideration and there cannot be duress. For example, one dot-com company agreed to give its employees stock options if they would sign a noncompete agreement. Amazon.com offered downsized employees an additional

10 weeks' pay plus $500, in addition to the normal severance package, if they would sign a three-page "separation agreement and general release" in which they promised not to sue Amazon over the layoff or disparage it in any way. Amazon, as a longstanding practice, has had employees sign a confidentiality agreement at the beginning of their employment that restricts their use of information and systems knowledge they gained whilst working at Amazon.

Some states provide protection for employees who refuse to sign noncompete agreements, punishing employers with punitive damages in wrongful termination cases brought by employees terminated following their refusals to sign.

4. Other Theories for Noncompete Enforcement

Some employers have begun to use the tort of tortious interference with contracts as a means of preventing former employees from working for competitors or beginning their own competing businesses. In those states in which noncompete clauses are unenforceable, the tort avenue has been used as a means of enjoining the former employee's business activities. For example, in *TruGreen Companies, LLC v Mower Brothers, Inc.*, 199 P.3d 929 (Utah 2008), the Utah Supreme Court held that a company whose former employer had gone to work for a competing company and recruited other employees to join him was liable for tortious interference and allowed recovery of lost profits.

Consider...

Eric Rush (a.k.a. Eric Romero in the dance world) was a dance instructor at a Plano, Texas, Arthur Murray dance studio. Mr. Rush says he was fired, but the attorney for the Arthur Murray studio indicates he resigned. Under the terms of his employment contract, which included a noncompete clause, Mr. Rush was prohibited from teaching dance lessons within a 25-mile radius of the Plano Arthur Murray studio. However, Mr. Rush created a Craigslist notice offering dance lessons and also contacted former students from Arthur Murray to offer dance lessons. He also taught a cha-cha lesson at Tango and Cha-Cha's Dance Studio in Dallas (to the tune of "I Left My Heart in San Francisco").

A Texas judge ordered Mr. Rush to take down the Craigslist notices and stop teaching dance through the end of 2009 within the 25-mile radius. Mr. Rush was also ordered to spend 30 days in jail for contempt of court, which consisted of his ongoing refusals to comply with the court's orders for his violations of the noncompete clause. The jail sentence represents the latest in a 10-month legal battle between Rush and his former employer. Rush's lawyer called the sentence excessive and said that the judge was "killing a fly with a bazooka."

As for Mr. Rush, he is dismayed at his clipped wings, er, silenced taps. He says that the noncompete clause "is like asking a doctor not to practice medicine."[3] He also says that if he did stop dancing "it would be, like, blasphemous."[4] Rush also adds that dancing is his calling in life and, "I just want to make a living." Mr. Rush's lawyer acknowledges that Mr. Rush could teach in cities such as Arlington and Fort Worth and not be in violation of the court order enforcing the covenant. However, Mr. Rush says that with the price of gas and the poor economy, the travel distance is prohibitive.

Mr. Rush says he is teaching dancing to his fellow inmates. From prison, Mr. Rush described dancing: "It means healing. It means grace, serenity, elegance, sex appeal. It means ambition and drive and achievement and confidence."[5]

Discuss whether the covenant is enforceable, whether it is too broad, and how a jail sentence resulted from a contract matter.

Duty of Obedience

An agent has the duty to obey reasonable instructions from the principal. The agent is not required to do anything criminally wrong or commit torts, of course; but agents are required to operate according to the principal's standards and instructions. Failure to do so could mean the agent has gone beyond the authority given and is personally liable for the conduct.

Duty of Care

Agents have a duty to use as much care and to act as prudently as they would if managing their own affairs. Agents must take the time and effort to perform their principals' assigned tasks. For example, officers of corporations must base their decisions on information, not guesses, and must ensure that their decisions are carried out by employees.

An agent who does not use reasonable care is liable to the principal for any damages resulting from a lack of care. When an agent does not make adequate travel arrangements for a speaker, the agent is liable to the speaker for damages that result from the speaker's nonappearance at an engagement.

17-3b THE PRINCIPAL'S RIGHTS AND RESPONSIBILITIES

Just like the agent on the other side of the agreement, the principal also has certain duties and obligations.

Duty of Compensation

The first obligation is that of compensation, which can take various forms that range from salary to commission to combinations of both. Some agents work for a fee on a contingency basis. A real estate agent, for example, may have an arrangement in which she receives compensation only if a buyer for the property is found. However, compensation is not required for a valid agency if the agent and principal agree that there will be no compensation.

In an agency relationship in which there will be no compensation—a **gratuitous agency**—the agent has all the same authority to act for the principal but will not be compensated. For example, some charitable organizations have agents who act in fund-raising capacities but who do not expect compensation.

Duty of Indemnification

Principals also have an obligation to indemnify agents for expenses the agents incur in carrying out the principal's orders. Corporate officers, for example, are entitled to travel compensation; sales agents are entitled to compensation for placing ads to sell goods, realty, or services.

17-4 Liability of Principals for Agents' Conduct: The Relationship with Third Parties

17-4a CONTRACT LIABILITY

Although the types of authority an agent has and the terms of the agency agreement define the authority of the agent, the contract liability of a principal is not determined by either intent or by the limitations agreed to privately by the agent and the principal. In other words, third parties have certain contract enforcement rights depending on the nature of the agent's work and the authority given by the principal.

The liability of the principal for contracts made by an agent is controlled by the perceptions created for and observed by the third party to the contract. Those perceptions vary, so the liability of the principal varies depending on the way in which the agent does business. For example, an officer of a corporation has the authority to bind the corporation, but what if the officer does not disclose that there is a principal corporation? This section deals with those issues.

The Disclosed Principal

In a situation in which a third party is aware a principal is involved and also knows who the principal is, the principal is liable to the third party but the agent is not, regardless of whether the agent has express, implied, or apparent authority. If the agent has no authority, however, then the agent, not the principal, is liable. For example, suppose that Paula Abbaduhla is the vice president of Video Television, Inc., and she signs for a line of credit for the corporation at First Bank. As long as she signed the documents "Video Television, Inc., by Paula Abbaduhla, VP," Video would be solely responsible for the line of credit. If, however, she signed that same way but had no authority, she would be liable to Video if it had to honor the agreement. As another example, most title insurers and escrow companies require corporations selling or buying real property to have board authorization in the form of a resolution. If Paula signed to buy land and did not have a resolution, she would have no express authority, and without implied or apparent authority, she would be liable for the land contract. (See Chapter 19 for a more thorough discussion of board resolutions and officers' authority.)

The Partially Disclosed Principal

In this situation, the third party knows that the agent is acting for someone else, but the identity of the principal is not disclosed. For example, an agent might be used to purchase land for development purposes when the developer does not want to be disclosed because disclosure of a major developer's involvement might drive up land prices. In this situation, the third-party seller of the land can hold either the principal or the agent liable on the contract. The agent assumes some risk of personal liability by not disclosing the identity of the principal.

The Undisclosed Principal

In this situation, an agent acts without disclosing either the existence of a principal or the principal's identity. Again, such an arrangement might be undertaken to avoid speculation, or it could be intended simply to protect someone's privacy, such as when a famous person purchases a home and does not want any advance disclosure of the purchase or its location. Here, the agent is directly liable to the third party. If the third party discovers the identity of the principal, the third party could hold either the principal or the agent liable. Exhibits 17.1 and 17.2 provide summaries of the liability of agents and principals under the three forms of disclosure of the relationship.

17-4b LIABILITY OF PRINCIPALS FOR AGENTS' TORTS

The liability of principals for torts committed by agents is controlled by the type of agency relationship—master–servant or independent contractor—and by the type of conduct.

Master–Servant Relationship

As discussed earlier in the chapter, the liability of a principal for the acts of a servant differs from that for the acts of an independent contractor. The principal is

EXHIBIT 17.1 Contract Liability of Disclosed Principal

Agent Has Actual Authority
Express Authority
Implied Authority

Principal
Agent
Third Party

Agent Has Apparent Authority but No Actual Authority

Principal
Agent
Third Party

Agent Has No Actual Authority or Apparent Authority

Principal
Agent
Third Party

EXHIBIT 17.2 Contract Liability of Undisclosed or Partially Disclosed Principal

Contract within Actual Authority
Express Authority
Implied Authority

Principal
Agent
Third Party

Contract outside Actual Authority
Express Authority
Implied Authority

Principal
Agent
Third Party

liable for the torts of the servant—an agent whose work, assignments, and time are controlled by the principal.

Scope of Employment

Employers (principals) are liable for the conduct of employees (agents/servants) while those employees are acting in the **scope of employment**. Scope of employment means that an employee is doing work for an employer at the time a tort occurs. Suppose a florist delivery driver, while delivering flowers, has an auto accident that is the delivery driver's fault. In addition to the driver's responsibility for the negligence in the accident, the florist is also liable to injured parties under the doctrine of *respondent superior*.

Scope of employment has been defined broadly by the courts. Negligent torts committed while an employee is driving to a sales call or delivery are clearly within the scope of employment.

An employee who takes the afternoon off is not within the scope of employment, and the principal is not liable if an accident occurs during that time. When an employee begins acting on personal business, the scope of employment ends. An employee who uses the lunch hour to shop is not within the scope of employment. Likewise, an employer who requires an employee to use his lunch hour to run errands for the company has changed personal time into scope-of-employment time. *Faverty v McDonald's Restaurants of Oregon, Inc.* (Case 17.3) deals with an issue of when the scope of employment ends, in a timing sense.

| CASE 17.3 | *Faverty v McDonald's Restaurants of Oregon, Inc.*
892 P.2d 703 (Ct. App. Or. 1995) |

Triple Shift Overtime: Who Is Liable for the Drive Home Afterward?

FACTS

Matt Theurer was an 18-year-old high school senior with many extracurricular activities, including being a member of the National Guard. Mr. Theurer was employed by a McDonald's restaurant (defendant) in Portland, Oregon, on a part-time basis. While his employer called Mr. Theurer an enthusiastic worker, his friends and family felt that he was doing too much and getting too little sleep.

McDonald's employed many high school students on a part-time basis, and their restaurants closed at 11:00 P.M., with cleanup and other procedures taking up another hour until midnight. McDonald's informal policy did not permit high school students to work more than one midnight shift per week or allow split shifts. Split shifts forced the students to work in the morning and then in the evening. McDonald's felt the commuting time between the shifts prevented "people from getting their rest." Despite these policies, high school employees frequently complained about being tired, and at least two of McDonald's employees had

accidents while driving home after working the closing shift until midnight.

A few times each year, McDonald's scheduled special cleanup projects at the restaurant that required employees to work after the midnight closing until 5 A.M. Student workers were to be used for cleanup shifts only on weekends or during spring break. However, for one scheduled cleanup project, there were not enough regular employees, and the manager asked for volunteers for a midnight to 5 A.M. cleanup shift. Mr. Theurer volunteered; the manager knew that Mr. Theurer had to drive about 20 minutes to and from work.

During the week of the scheduled special cleanup, Mr. Theurer had worked five nights. One night he worked until midnight, another until 11:30 P.M., two until 9 P.M., and another until 11 P.M. On Monday, April 4, 1988, Mr. Theurer worked his regular shift from 3:30 until 7:30 P.M., followed by a cleanup shift beginning at midnight until 5 A.M. on April 5, and then worked another shift from 5 A.M. until 8:21 A.M. During that shift, Mr. Theurer told his manager that he was

CONTINUED

tired and asked to be excused from his next regular shift. The manager excused him, and Mr. Theurer began his drive home.

Mr. Theurer was driving 45 miles per hour on a two-lane road when he became drowsy or fell asleep, crossed the dividing line into oncoming traffic, crashed into the van of Frederic Faverty (plaintiff), and was killed. Mr. Faverty was seriously injured. Mr. Faverty settled his claims with Mr. Theurer's estate and then filed suit against McDonald's. The jury found for Mr. Faverty, and McDonald's appealed.

JUDICIAL OPINION

LANDAU, Judge

Defendant argues that it was Theurer's employer and, because of that relationship, it was subject to a limited duty to both Theurer and plaintiff, as a matter of law.

According to defendant, there is no evidence that it knew or should have known that Theurer was so exhausted or fatigued that it should have foreseen that working him three shifts in one 24-hour period would create a foreseeable risk of harm to motorists such as plaintiff. Plaintiff argues that defendant failed to preserve that argument and that, in any event, the evidence is sufficient to support the trial court's ruling.

There is evidence that defendant controlled all work assignments. Therefore, defendant knew or had reason to know of the number of hours Theurer had been working. There also is evidence that defendant ordinarily did not use high school students to work after midnight, and when it did, it tried to limit that late shift to once a week. Defendant also had a policy of not working its employees two shifts in one day. According to at least one of the defendant's managers, those policies were adopted and enforced out of concern that employees not become overly tired on the job. In fact, defendant was aware that at least two of its employees had recently had automobile accidents as a result of falling asleep while driving home after working late shifts. There is evidence that, during and after his late-night shift, Theurer was visibly fatigued, and that defendant's managers were on site and saw Theurer throughout that shift. It is undisputed that defendant knew that Theurer was a high school student and that most of the high school students who worked there drove to work in their own cars. On the basis of that evidence, a reasonable jury could conclude that defendant knew or should have known that working Theurer so many hours would impair his ability to drive home safely.

Defendant and the dissent insist that, because Theurer "volunteered" to work so many hours, the evidence simply is insufficient to establish defendant's negligence, as a matter of law. The evidence shows that defendant—not its employees—generally controlled all work assignments and that defendant penalized its employees for not working as assigned.

Second, even indulging the assumption that Theurer volunteered for his all-night shift, the evidence still is sufficient to support the jury's verdict. Defendant's managers knew that Theurer already had been scheduled to work more than its own policies permitted. Moreover, they saw him in a visibly fatigued state and continued to work him as scheduled. In that regard, defendant was much like a bartender who served alcoholic beverages to a visibly intoxicated person who then caused an automobile accident that harmed another. No one required the intoxicated person to have the extra drink. He or she asked for the drink and "volunteered" to pay for it. Nevertheless, the courts have held that, because the bartender saw the driver in a visibly intoxicated state, and it is reasonably foreseeable that the customer will drive when he or she leaves, the bartender is liable for the consequences of the automobile accident.

Finally, defendant itself conceded at trial that, if it had allowed Theurer to "volunteer" to work around the clock three full days, the "court can almost say as a matter of law, allowing someone to work that long without any rest or sleep might very well constitute affirmative misconduct by an employer, but [it] may be a matter of degrees...."

Defendant, the dissent and the *amid curiae* the National Council of Chain Restaurants and the Defense Research Institute, Inc., implore us to reverse the trial court's judgment on the public policy ground that the result is "patently unreasonable," "shocking," "farfetched" and "goes beyond the commonsense application of tort law." However, that argument was not made to the trial court, and we will not consider it for the first time on appeal.

Affirmed.

DISSENTING OPINION

EDMUNDS, Judge

The majority need have gone no further than defendant's motion for a directed verdict in deciding this case. Defendant is entitled to a directed verdict as a matter of law because of certain uncontroverted facts. First, Theurer was not a minor, but an adult at the time of the accident. He was 18 years old and serving in the National Guard. Defendant did not owe any special responsibility to him because he also attended high school. The fact that he was a student working part time and had over-extended himself physically is of no import to defendant's liability. No rule of negligence requires an employer to inquire into the private lives of

CONTINUED

its adult employees to determine if, on a given occasion, the employee is not getting enough sleep.

Second, Theurer volunteered to work the cleanup shift. He was not sought out by defendant and "required" to work on April 5, 1988.

Third, Theurer never asked to be relieved from working the shift either before the shift started or during it; nor is there any evidence that defendant refused such a request.

Fourth, Theurer was not on defendant's business premises and was on his own time when he drove home from work that morning. Theurer was not acting on defendant's behalf, nor did defendant have actual control of or the right to control Theurer's driving conduct or where he went after he got off work. Moreover, no omission or affirmative act by defendant prevented Theurer from choosing to have someone pick him up after work, or to take a nap in his car before driving home, or some other preventive measure....

In effect, the opinion says to Oregon employers, "Do not schedule your employees in a manner that will cause fatigue, because if you do, you risk liability for negligence in the event that your employee acts in a negligent manner off-premises and after work." That is not the law of this state and it cannot be unreasonable conduct for an employer to accept an offer from an adult employee, made days in advance of the shift, to work overtime, insofar as the safety of motorists is concerned after the employee gets off work. Because the majority opinion extends the duty of care owed to the general public by employers in the scheduling of their employees' work shifts to beyond any reasonable boundary, I dissent.

CASE QUESTIONS

1. Of what significance is the fact that Mr. Theurer volunteered for the all-night shift?

2. Why would a restaurant association have an interest in the outcome of the case?

3. Did McDonald's violate any Oregon statute?

4. Was Mr. Theurer acting within the scope of employment?

5. What counterpoints does the dissenting judge make?

AFTERMATH

Some courts have declined to follow the decision in this case. In *Behrens v Harrah's Illinois Corp.*, 852 N.E.2d 553 (Ill. 2006), the court did not allow the family of an employee to recover from the employer when she experienced catastrophic injuries following a rollover accident that occurred when she was driving home from work after being required to work overtime at the casino. [See also *Barclay v Briscoe*, 47 A.3d 560 (Md. 2012).] A hospital is not liable for injuries caused by a sleep-deprived doctor working extra hours at the hospital. [*Brewster v Rush-Presbyterian-St. Luke's Medical Center*, 836 N.E.2d 635 (111. App. 2005)] However, other courts have followed the decision. In *Bussard v Minimed, Inc.*, 105 Cal.App.4th 798, 129 Cal.Rptr.2d 675 (2003), an employer was held liable to a third party under a *respondeat superior* theory where the employee became dizzy and light-headed after being exposed to pesticides at work and, while driving home, struck a car driven by the third party.

Generally, intentional acts not authorized by employers do not result in liability. However, under the theories of the **negligent failure to supervise** and **negligent hiring**, an employer may have liability for inaction when it has notice of the violent tendencies of an employee. The 1973 *Lange v National Biscuit Co.* case (Case 17.4) opened the door for recovery from employers for the intentional acts of employees in certain well-defined circumstances. This case also provides the answer for the chapter's opening "Consider..."

Negligent Hiring and Supervision

The *Lange* case provided the types of circumstances in which employers could be liable for the tort of negligent hiring and/or supervision of employees. Negligent hiring requires proof that the principal/employer hired an agent/employee whose background made her ill suited for the position. For example, a school district that does not check the background of a bus driver or teacher, particularly for past charges or history of child abuse and molestation, has committed the tort of negligent hiring. Negligent supervision liability results when an employer has been put on notice that an employee has engaged in behavior that is harmful to others but leaves the

| CASE 17.4 | *Lange v National Biscuit Co.* 211 N.W.2d 783 (Minn. 1973) |

Shelf Space Is My Life: Flipping Out over Oreos

FACTS

Jerome Lange (plaintiff) was the manager of a small grocery store in Minnesota that carried Nabisco (defendant) products. Ronnell Lynch had been hired by Nabisco as a cookie salesman–trainee in October 1968. On March 1, 1969, Mr. Lynch was assigned his own territory, which included Mr. Lange's store.

Between March 1 and May 1, 1969, Nabisco received numerous complaints from grocers about Mr. Lynch being overly aggressive and taking shelf space in the stores reserved for competing cookie companies.

On May 1, 1969, Mr. Lynch came to Mr. Lange's store to place Nabisco merchandise on the shelves. An argument developed between the two over Mr. Lynch's service to the store. Mr. Lynch became very angry and started swearing. Mr. Lange told him to either stop swearing or leave the store because children were present. Mr. Lynch then became uncontrollably angry and said, "I ought to break your neck." He then went behind the counter and dared Mr. Lange to fight. When Mr. Lange refused, Mr. Lynch viciously assaulted him, after which he threw cookies around the store and left.

Mr. Lange filed suit against Nabisco and was awarded damages based on the jury's finding that although the acts of Mr. Lynch were outside the scope of employment, Nabisco was negligent in hiring and retaining him. The judge granted Nabisco's motion for judgment notwithstanding the verdict, and Mr. Lange appealed.

JUDICIAL OPINION

TODD, Justice

There is no dispute with the general principle that in order to impose liability on the employer under the doctrine of *respondeat superior* it is necessary to show that the employee was acting within the scope of his employment. Unfortunately, there is a wide disparity in the case law in the application of the "scope of employment" test to those factual situations involving intentional torts. The majority rule as set out in Annotation, 34 A.L.R.2d 372, 402, includes a twofold test: (a) Whether the assault was motivated by business or personal considerations; or (b) whether the assault was contemplated by the employer or incident to the employment.

Under the present Minnesota rule, liability is imposed where it is shown that the employee's acts were motivated by a desire to further the employer's business. Therefore, a master could only be held liable for an employee's assault in those rare instances where the master actually requested the servant to so perform, or the servant's duties were such that that motivation was implied in law.

The fallacy of this reasoning was that it made a certain mental condition of the servant the test by which to determine whether he was acting about his master's business or not. Moreover, with respect of all intentional acts done by a servant in the supposed furtherance of his master's business, it clothed the master with immunity if the act was right, because it was right, and, if it was wrong, it clothed him with a like immunity, because it was wrong. He thus got the benefit of all his servant's acts done for him, whether right or wrong, and escaped the burden of all intentional acts done for him which were wrong. Under the operation of such a rule, it would always be more safe and profitable for a man to conduct his business vicariously than in his own person. He would escape liability for the consequences of many acts connected with his business springing from the imperfection of human nature, because done by another, for which he would be responsible if done by himself. Meanwhile, the public, obliged to deal or come in contact with his agents, for intentional injuries done by them, might be left wholly without redress…. A doctrine so fruitful of mischief could not long stand unshaken in an enlightened system of jurisprudence.

In developing a test for the application of *respondent superior* when an employee assaults a third person, we believe that the focus should be on the basis of the assault rather than the motivation of the employee. We reject as the basis for imposing liability the arbitrary determination of when, and at what point, the argument and assault leave the sphere of the employer's business and become motivated by personal animosity. Rather, we believe the better approach is to view both the argument and assault as an indistinguishable event for purposes of vicarious liability.

We hold that an employer is liable for an assault by his employee when the source of the attack is related to the duties of the employee and the assault occurs within work-related limits of time and place. The assault in this

CONTINUED

case obviously occurred within work-related limits of time and place, since it took place on authorized premises during working hours. The precipitating cause of the initial argument concerned the employee's conduct of his work. In addition, the employee originally was motivated to become argumentative in furtherance of his employer's business. Consequently, under the facts of this case we hold as a matter of law that the employee was acting within the scope of employment at the time of the aggression and that plaintiff's post-trial motion for judgment notwithstanding the verdict on that ground should have been granted under the rule we herein adopt. To the extent that our former decisions are inconsistent with the rule now adopted, they are overruled.

Plaintiff may recover damages under either the theory of *respondeat superior* or negligence. Having disposed of the matter on the former issue, we need not undertake the questions raised by defendant's asserted negligence in the hiring or retention of the employee.

Reversed and remanded.

CASE QUESTIONS

1. What previous indications did Nabisco have that Mr. Lynch might cause some problems?

2. What test does the court give for determining scope of employment?

3. What is the "motivation test," and does this court accept or reject it?

Consider...

Sean Garrick was an active-duty member of the U.S. Air Force stationed at Buckley Air Force base in Aurora, Colorado. He was given a three-day assignment in Boulder County, at which time he was to work three 12-hour shifts. During these assignments, the Air Force provided employees with hotel accommodations, a per diem allowance, and the cost of travel. During his assignment, Mr. Garrick was given a break from 1:00 to 2:30 P.M. When given breaks such as these, employees usually go back to their hotel and relax. On his way back to the hotel for a nap, Mr. Garrick struck Jason Fowler on his motorcycle and injured him.

Mr. Fowler filed suit against the United States. The United States says that Mr. Garrick was not within the scope of his employment and that it is not liable for Mr. Fowler's injuries. Is the government correct?

[*Fowler v U.S.*, 647 F.3d 1232 (10th Cir. 2011)]

employee in his position. An example is a college or university leaving a professor in the classroom after having received complaints regarding his inappropriate conduct in class and with students. If the professor then harms one of his students, the college or university would be liable to the student for the failure to make a timely termination, suspension, or other action to remove the professor from student contact or at least provide appropriate monitoring of the professor with the students.

The liability of principals for the torts of agents has become a costly part of doing business. Many firms are undertaking various forms of testing to prevent employees who could cause injuries from driving, operating machinery, or otherwise working in situations in which human safety is an issue. The courts have upheld the employer's right to test for the presence of drugs and alcohol when the firms can show a public safety need established by the employee's contact with the public during the course of employment.

Independent Contractors

Principals are not generally liable for the torts of independent contractors, but three exceptions apply to this general no-liability rule. The first exception covers **inherently dangerous activities**, which are those that cannot be made safe.

Consider. . .

Oklahoma Nursing Homes, Ltd., employed numerous health care professionals at its various nursing homes, including nurse's aides, who assisted occupants of the homes with daily activities such as eating, bathing, and dressing.

Glen Rodebush, a person with Alzheimer's disease, was a resident of one of the company's homes. His condition caused him to be combative sometimes. Mr. Rodebush's wife, Zelda, arrived one day for a visit and discovered large welts and red marks on his face. Mrs. Rodebush called her husband's doctor, who found that the marks were caused by slaps of the human hand and were 6 to 12 hours old. Earlier in the day, Mr. Rodebush had been bathed by a male nurse's aide and, during the course of the bath, Mr. Rodebush had become unruly. Following the bath, a supervisor noted that the aide smelled of liquor and saw from his time card that he had arrived 30 minutes late. The nurse's aide confessed that he had "partied all night." The aide had been hired without a background check. Following the incident and Mrs. Rodebush's complaint about the marks, the company discovered that the aide had a felony conviction for violent assault and battery with intent to kill, escape, and carrying a weapon following conviction of a felony.

The company, which had never given the aide training, had been cited by the State Department of Human Services for violations of reporting requirements as well as the failure to take proper steps against employees who report to work while intoxicated.

Mrs. Rodebush has filed suit against the nursing home on behalf of her husband. The nursing home claims it cannot be held liable for the intentional and unauthorized acts of its employees. Who is correct? Should there be recovery?
[*Rodebush v Oklahoma Nursing Homes, Ltd.*, 867 P.2d 1241 (Okl. 1993)]

For example, using dynamite to demolish old buildings is an inherently dangerous activity. Without this liability exception, a principal could hire an independent contractor to perform the task and then assume no responsibility for the damages or injuries that might result.

The second exception to the no-liability rule occurs when a principal negligently hires an independent contractor. A landlord who hires a security guard, therefore, must check that guard's background because if a tenant's property is

FOR THE MANAGER'S DESK

The National Security Agency (NSA) hired Edward Snowden to work in its Internet and phone surveillance area after it received a clear security background check from US Investigations Services LLC (USIS). This firm is the largest background check company that does background checks for the federal government.

Edward Snowden left his NSA job abruptly after releasing significant amounts of data as well as disclosures about the surveillance activities of NSA.

After Mr. Snowden leaked the highly sensitive information, he left the country and the federal government began an investigation into USIS. The information that has emerged from that investigation is that USIS was involved in "flushing," which is a process of a very fast and shallow look at an individual's background in order to get them security clearance and thereby get the money for the work paid.

What would be USIS's liability if Mr. Snowden's background check, if done thoroughly, would have revealed patterns of behavior that would not be a good fit for NSA? In order to avoid negligence hiring liability, companies need to be sure that the firms they hire to do background checks for them need to do their work thoroughly. Shortcomings in background checks translate to liability for employers.

stolen by a guard with a criminal record, the landlord is responsible. Similarly, if a principal hires independent contractors knowing of their past employment history, the principal is liable for the conduct of those independent contractors. A business that hires a collection agency to collect past-due accounts, knowing that agency's reputation for violence, is liable for the agency's torts even though they are independent contractors.

The third exception is the situation in which the principal has provided the specifications for the independent contractor's procedures or process. Because the independent contractor is required to follow the principal's directions, the principal will also have liability.

17-5 Termination of the Agency Relationship

An agency relationship can end in several different ways. First, the parties can have a definite duration for the agency relationship. A listing agreement for the sale of real property usually ends after 90 days. An agency can also end because the agent quits or the principal fires the agent. When the principal dies or is incapacitated, an agency ends automatically because the agent no longer has anyone to contract on behalf of.

Although the agency relationship ends easily when an agent is fired or quits, the authority of the agent does not end so abruptly or easily. An agent can still have **lingering apparent authority** that exists beyond the termination of the agency in relation to third parties who are unaware of the agency termination. For example, if the purchasing agent for a corporation retires after 25 years, the agency that consists of actual authority (express and implied authority) between the agent and corporation has ended. However, departure, retirement, and termination do not end apparent authority. Many customers are used to dealing with the agent and may not be aware of the end of the agency. That purchasing agent could still bind the principal corporation even though the agent's actual authority has ended.

The principal corporation can end lingering apparent authority by giving public or **constructive notice** or private or **actual notice**. Public notice is publication of the resignation. Many trade magazines and business newspapers publish announcements and personal columns about business associate changes and other personnel news. Even though not everyone dealing with the agent may see the notice, these public notices are deemed to serve as constructive notice. However, the principal must also give private notice to those firms that have dealt with the agent or have been creditors in the past. This notice is accomplished by sending a letter to each firm or individual that has dealt with the agent. Without this notice, the agent's apparent authority lingers with respect to those third parties who have not received notice.

17-6 Termination of Agents Under Employment at Will

Most employees do not have written contracts that specify the start and duration of their employment. Rather, most employees work at the discretion of their employers, which is to say that they have **employment at will**. Recent cases have placed some restrictions on this employer freedom to hire and fire at will because courts have been giving employees/agents the benefit of their reliance. Employees have based their protection rights on several theories, including implied contract and public policy. Exhibit 17.3 summarizes the "do's" and "don'ts" of disciplining employees.

EXHIBIT 17.3 The Do's and Don'ts of Working with Problem Employees

DO	DON'T
Have regular performance evaluations	Don't let annual performance reviews slip by
When disciplining employees, use a standardized procedure and have everything in writing	Don't vary from procedures
	Don't use oral communication in disciplining employees
Make sure your policies and rules are clear	Don't add to rules without notice to employees
Keep disciplinary processes private	Don't forward e-mails regarding discipline to those who have no reason to know; don't make public examples of terminated employees
Be honest in stating the reasons for termination	Don't alter the reasons for termination to make things look better
	Don't offer recommendation letters in exchange for the employee's agreement to leave

17-6a THE IMPLIED CONTRACT

Many courts have implied the existence of a contract because of the presence of promises, procedures, and policies in an employee personnel manual. Personnel manuals have been held to constitute, both expressly and impliedly, employee contracts or to become part of the employee contracts when they are given to employees at the outset. One of the factors that determines whether a personnel manual and its terms constitute a contract is the reliance of an employee on its procedures and terms.

Because the employee manual represents a potential contract for the employer, its nature and content should be considered carefully. Of the two approaches to employee manuals, one takes a detailed approach in which all rules, rights, and expectations are carefully established. Another approach is the simple one, in which overall general policies and rights are established with details to be filled in as individual issues arise. The *Dillon v Champion Jogbra, Inc.* case (Case 17.5) deals with one state's view on the issue of implied contract.

CASE 17.5 *Dillon v Champion Jogbra, Inc.*
819 A.2d 703 (Vt. 2002)

Letting a Champion Employee Go

FACTS

Linda Dillon began working for Jogbra part-time in January 1997. She was hired as a full-time employee in August 1997 in the position of charge-back analyst. In the summer of 1998, the position of sales administrator was going to become vacant. Ms. Dillon was approached by Jogbra management about applying for the position, which started on July 31. She eventually decided to apply and interviewed for the position. In the course of interviewing, Ms. Dillon recalls that she was told that she would receive "extensive training." The human resources manager told her that she would overlap with her predecessor, who would train her during those days. However, in the course of Ms. Dillon's interview with the vice president of sales, who would be her immediate supervisor, he informed her that her predecessor was actually leaving earlier and would be available for only two days of training before Ms. Dillon started the job.

CONTINUED

He reassured her, though, that the predecessor would be brought back sometime thereafter for more training. Ms. Dillon also recalls that he told her that "it will take you four to six months to feel comfortable with [the] position" and not to be concerned about it. Ms. Dillon accepted the position and spent most of her predecessor's remaining two days with her. Her predecessor then returned in early September for an additional two days of training. Ms. Dillon stated that she felt that, after the supplemental training, she had received sufficient training for the job.

On September 29, Ms. Dillon was called into her supervisor's office. The human resources manager was also present. They informed Ms. Dillon that things were not working out and that she was going to be reassigned to a temporary position, at the same pay and benefit level, which ended in December. She was told that she should apply for other jobs within the company, but if nothing suitable became available, she would be terminated at the end of December. According to Ms. Dillon, her supervisor stated that he had concluded within 10 days of her starting that "it wasn't going to work out." Prior to the meeting, Ms. Dillon was never told her job was in jeopardy, nor did Jogbra follow the procedures laid out in its employee manual when terminating her.

Ms. Dillon applied for one job that became available in the ensuing months but was not selected for it. She left Jogbra in December when her temporary position terminated. Ms. Dillon then brought suit against Jogbra for wrongful termination. She asserted claims for breach of contract and promissory estoppel. Jogbra filed a motion for summary judgment, which the trial court granted. Ms. Dillon appealed.

JUDICIAL OPINION

MORSE, Justice

We affirm with respect to Dillon's claim for promissory estoppel, but reverse and remand on her breach of contract claim.

Jogbra has an employee manual that it distributes to all employees at the time of their employment. The first page of the manual states the following in capitalized print:

> *The policies and procedures contained in this manual constitute guidelines only. They do not constitute part of an employment contract, nor are they intended to make any commitment to any employee concerning how individual employment action can, should, or will be handled.*
>
> *Champion Jogbra offers no employment contracts nor does it guarantee any minimum length of employment. Champion Jogbra reserves the right to terminate any employee at any time "at will," with or without cause.*

During the period from 1996 to 1997, however, Jogbra developed what it termed a "Corrective Action Procedure." This procedure established a progressive discipline system for employees and different categories of disciplinary infractions. It states that it applies to all employees and will be carried out in "a fair and consistent manner." Much of the language in the section is mandatory in tone.

…[A]n employer may modify an at-will employment agreement unilaterally. When determining whether an employer has done so, we look to both the employer's written policies and its practices. An employer not only may implicitly bind itself to terminating only for cause through its manual and practices, but may also be bound by a commitment to use only certain procedures in doing so.

When the terms of a manual are ambiguous, however, or send mixed messages regarding an employee's status, the question of whether the presumptive at-will status has been modified is properly left to the jury. This may be the case even if there is a disclaimer stating employment is at-will, as the presence of such a disclaimer is not dispositive in the determination. Furthermore, an employer's practices can provide context for and help inform the determination. The question of whether a written manual is ambiguous is a determination of law that we review *de novo*. In this case, we cannot agree with the trial court that the terms of Jogbra's manual are unambiguous.

Notwithstanding the disclaimer contained on the first page of the manual quoted above, the manual goes on to establish in Policy No. 720 an elaborate system governing employee discipline and discharge. It states as its purpose: "To establish Champion Jogbra policy for all employees." It states that actions will be carried out "in a fair and consistent manner." It provides that "[t]he Corrective Action Policy requires management to use training and employee counseling to achieve the desired actions of employees." It establishes three categories of violations of company policy and corresponding actions to be generally taken in each case. It delineates progressive steps to be taken for certain types of cases, including "[u]nsatisfactory quality of work," and time periods governing things such as how long a reprimand is considered "active." All of these terms are inconsistent with the disclaimer at the beginning of the manual, in effect sending mixed messages to employees. Furthermore, these terms appear to be inconsistent with an at-will employment relationship, its classic formulation being that an employer can fire an employee "for good cause or for no cause, or even for bad cause."

With respect to the record before the court on Jogbra's employment practices, Dillon herself was aware of at least one employee whose termination was carried out pursuant to the terms set forth in the manual. She also testified in her deposition to conversations with the human resources manager, with whom she was friendly, in which the manager had described certain procedures used for firing

CONTINUED

employees. She stated that the manager had told her that Jogbra could not "just get rid of" people, but instead had to follow procedures. The human resources manager herself testified that "she could only recall two instances in which the portion of the manual providing for documentation of progressive action was not followed, one of which resulted in a legal claim against the company and the other of which involved an employee stealing from the company. In fact, the manual specifically provides that stealing "will normally result in discharge on the first offense." Thus, it is not clear how that discharge deviated from the provisions of the manual.

In conclusion, the manual itself is at the very least ambiguous regarding employees' status, and Jogbra's employment practices appear from the record to be both consistent with the manual and inconsistent with an at-will employment arrangement. Therefore, summary judgment was not proper on Dillon's breach of implied contract claim....

We have held that, even if an employee otherwise enjoys only at-will employment status, that employee may still be able to establish a claim for wrongful termination under a theory of promissory estoppel if that employee can demonstrate that the termination was in breach of a specific promise made by the employer that the employer should have reasonably expected to induce detrimental reliance on the part of the employee, and that the employee did in fact detrimentally rely on the promise. We agree with the trial court in this case, however, that essential elements of promissory estoppel are absent with regard to both statements.

With respect to Jogbra's promise to Dillon that she would receive training, Dillon specifically conceded that, upon her predecessor's return in September, she had received adequate training to perform the job. In other words, Jogbra had delivered on its promise. Furthermore, even assuming that Jogbra failed to provide the full extent of promised training, Dillon has failed to explain how, as a matter of law, the promise of training modified her at-will status. In other words, it is not clear from Dillon's brief how the promise of training foreclosed Jogbra from nevertheless terminating her either on an at-will basis or for cause....

With respect to the assurance that it would take four to six months to become comfortable with the position, the statement cannot reasonably be relied upon as a promise of employment in the sales administrator position for a set period of time. Courts have generally required a promise of a specific and definite nature before holding an employer bound by it.

In sum, the trial court properly granted Jogbra summary judgment on Dillon's promissory estoppel claim. The grant of summary judgment on Linda Dillon's claim for promissory estoppel is affirmed; the grant of summary judgment on her breach of contract claim is reversed and remanded.

DISSENTING OPINION

AMESTOY, Chief Justice, dissenting

In support of employee's contention that employer's practices were at odds with an at-will policy, employee cites to her own deposition, wherein she claimed to have known of other employees who received progressive discipline prior to termination. When pressed, however, employee admitted that, of the three employees with whose discharge she was familiar, she could state with certainty that only one received progressive discipline. Moreover, employee stated that she was unfamiliar with the manner in which the other two employees' cases were handled prior to their discharge. While her own experience is relevant, it does not by itself suggest a definitive company-wide practice. Hearsay statements about what employee "had heard" is insufficient to raise a genuine issue.

Affirmed in part; reversed in part.

CASE QUESTIONS

1. What is the effect of the disclaimer in the Jogbra employment manual?

2. What changes the application of the employment-at-will doctrine to Dillon?

3. What is the dissenting justice's concern?

17-6b THE PUBLIC POLICY EXCEPTION

In a second group of employment-at-will cases, the courts have afforded protection to those employees called **whistle-blowers** who report illegal conduct and to those who refuse to participate in conduct that is illegal or that violates public policy. For example, Michael Winston won a $3.8 million verdict after being fired by Countrywide Mortgage Company (now defunct) for his refusal to write a falsified memo on succession planning at Countrywide for Moody's Investor Rating Services. John Kopchinski, a former sales rep for Pfizer who was fired for reporting to the federal

Business Planning Tip

Encourage internal whistle-blowing. Employees can benefit from following these suggestions:

1. Work within your system and through its chain of command before going public. Go through the various layers of management, even to the board of directors.

2. Voice/write your concerns; don't make accusations.

3. Maintain records of your internal contacts and their objections.

4. Find other employees who also know about this potentially volatile situation.

5. Keep a record of your information and carefully document all that you do to raise the issue.

government Pfizer's off-label marketing of Bextra for a nonapproved use, received $51.5 million of the fine collected from Pfizer.

There are significant statutory protections for whistle-blowers at the state and federal level. Two generic federal statutes afford protection for federal employees: the Civil Service Reform Act of 1978 and the Whistleblower Protection Act of 1989. The statutes protect federal employees who report wrongdoing and permit them to recover both back pay and their attorney fees in the event they litigate or protest a termination for their disclosure of possible violations of the law. The False Claims Act permits employees of government contractors whose tips and disclosures to federal investigators and agencies result in fines and penalties to collect 25 percent of those fines and penalties.

Some federal statutes also have specific provisions for certain categories of federal employees. For example, a portion of the Energy Reorganization Act provides protection for employees of nuclear facilities who report violations of federal laws and regulations at nuclear plants.

Sarbanes-Oxley (SOX) also provides antiretaliation protections for employees who raise concerns about the financial reports or internal controls of their companies. The protections apply to employees who help with an audit, employees who join in a shareholder suit against the company, employees who report financial issues to a government agency, and employees who use internal reporting systems to raise a financial concern or compliance issue. The SOX protections are unique because they are the first whistle-blower protections that go beyond those for employees who raise public safety concerns. The protections cover not only employees of companies but also analysts who raise concerns about companies they study. The research firms or investment houses the analysts work for cannot take retaliatory action against the analysts for issuing negative reports on companies that might also be clients of the analyst's employer. Companies that retaliate face criminal penalties or fines as well as imprisonment for those within the company who take action against the whistle-blower. The individual penalties for SOX retaliation are up to 10 years in prison. For the employee, damages for retaliation include back pay, actual damages, and a right to reinstatement.

Protections and rewards for whistle-blowers have been increased through statutes and regulations. Under the Dodd-Frank Wall Street Reform and Consumer Protection Act (see Chapters 12 and 19 for more information), a whistle-blower can collect between 10 and 30 percent of whatever the federal government recovers from a company for violations of the law.

In *Tides v The Boeing Company* (Case 17.6), a court deals with the issue of an employer firing an employee who has taken action by disclosing company information publicly. This case provides the answer for the chapter opening "Consider…"

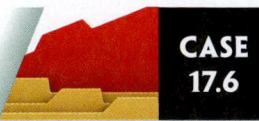

| CASE 17.6 | *Tides v The Boeing Company* 644 F.3d 809 (9th Cir. 2011) |

Going to the Newspaper to Get Results Is Not an Option

FACTS

In January 2007, Matthew Neumann and Nicholas Tides (plaintiffs) began working as auditors in Boeing's IT Sarbanes–Oxley ("SOX") Audit group. Tides worked in St. Louis, and Neumann was based in Seattle. The IT SOX Audit group was housed within Boeing's Corporate Audit organization and was responsible for helping the company comply with SOX's requirement

CONTINUED

of an annual assessment of internal controls and procedures for financial reporting. Deloitte & Touche served as Boeing's external auditor and was responsible for attesting to, and reporting on, the company's assessments of its internal controls, as required by SOX.

Tides and Neumann felt that tensions were high in the IT SOX Audit group because management feared that Deloitte & Touche might declare a "material weakness" in the company's internal controls. They alleged that managers pressured IT SOX auditors to rate Boeing's internal controls as "effective" and fostered a generally hostile work environment. Tides and Neumann began separately expressing concerns about this perceived pressure and several deficiencies in Boeing's auditing practices that they viewed as potential violations of SOX. They both believed that the system permitted unauthorized users to alter the ratings given to the company's internal controls.

In late April 2007, Andrea James, a reporter with the *Seattle Post–Intelligencer*, left messages on Tides' and Neumann's work phones asking each of them to speak with her about an article she was writing on Boeing's compliance with SOX. At the time, both were aware that Boeing had a policy that restricted the release of company information to the news media. Boeing's policy, PRO–3439, required employees to refer "[i]nquiries of any kind from the news media" to the communications department and also prohibited the release of company information without prior review by that department.

In late May 2007, James contacted Neumann again, this time showing up uninvited at his home with another *Post–Intelligencer* reporter. Neumann agreed to speak with them about Boeing's compliance with SOX. Several days after their meeting, James e-mailed Neumann an excerpt of a draft of her article. Neumann responded that the excerpt looked good and sent James the text of an e-mail that he and other IT SOX auditors recently received from a manager. The manager's e-mail reminded employees that Boeing policy prohibited the release of information to the media without prior approval from the communications department.

Tides contacted James in July 2007 after receiving what he viewed as a negative and unsubstantiated performance evaluation for the second quarter of the year. He forwarded her a series of work-related e-mails from his Boeing computer. Most of the e-mails documented the concerns he previously raised with management and human resources regarding perceived problems with the IT SOX Audit group's auditing practices. Tides also forwarded James several internal Boeing documents, including copies of the company's policies governing contract labor.

On July 17, 2007, the *Post–Intelligencer* published the article "Computer security faults put Boeing at risk," coauthored by James. The article reported that "[f]or the past three years, The Boeing Co. has failed, in both internal and external audits, to prove it can properly protect its computer systems against manipulation, theft and fraud." It detailed, among other things, a threatening company culture perceived by employees involved in SOX compliance, a record of poor internal audit results indicating that many of the company's computer system controls were failing, and an internal allegation that audit results were being manipulated.

At some point prior to the publication of the *Post–Intelligencer* article, Boeing caught on that several employees were likely releasing company information to the media. As a result, it authorized an investigation that included the monitoring of both Tides' and Neumann's work computers and e-mail accounts. The investigation revealed that the two auditors were communicating with James without permission. Two months after the publication of the *Post–Intelligencer* article, Tides and Neumann were interviewed separately by HR investigators about their communications with James. Both admitted to speaking with her about Boeing's auditing practices and to providing her with company documents. After the interviews, Boeing suspended Tides and Neumann indefinitely. Their cases were then referred to an Employee Corrective Action Review Board, a committee composed of five voting members and one nonvoting ethics advisor to evaluate charges of employee misconduct. After reviewing the applicable Boeing policies and the investigative reports detailing the two auditors' contacts with the media, the Board unanimously voted to terminate Tides and Neumann effective September 28, 2007, and October 1, 2007, respectively. Both were later informed in writing that:

> It has been determined that you created an unacceptable liability for the Company. Specifically, you violated PRO–2227, Information Protection, by disclosing Boeing information to non-Boeing persons without following appropriate procedures, obtaining necessary approvals and putting in place appropriate safeguards. In addition, you violated PRO–3439 by not referring inquiries from the news media to Communications, and by releasing information without approval in accordance with the requirements of said PRO. Your actions are aggravated by the fact that the information had an adverse effect on the Company's reputation and its relations with its employees, customers, shareholders, suppliers and other important constituents, causing significant liability. The Company deems your behavior in this incident as unacceptable and in violation of its expectations as defined in PRO–1909.

Following their terminations, Neumann and Tides filed SOX whistle-blower complaints with the Occupation Safety and Health Administration. They were given a right to sue and filed suit alleging that they were terminated in violation of 18 U.S.C. § 1514A(a)(1) for reporting violations of SOX and other securities laws. The district court granted Boeing's motion for summary judgment. Neumann and Tides appealed.

CONTINUED

JUDICIAL OPINION

SILVERMAN, Circuit Judge

SOX's whistleblower provision, 18 U.S.C. § 1514A, protects employees of publicly-traded companies from discrimination in the terms and conditions of their employment when they take certain actions to report conduct that they reasonably believe constitutes certain types of fraud or securities violations. Section 1514A claims are governed by a burden-shifting procedure under which the plaintiff is first required to establish a prima facie case of retaliatory discrimination. To make out a prima facie case, the plaintiff must show that: (1) he engaged in protected activity or conduct; (2) his employer knew or suspected, actively or constructively, that he engaged in the protected activity; (3) he suffered an unfavorable personnel action; and (4) the circumstances were sufficient to raise an inference that the protected activity was a contributing factor in the unfavorable action. If the plaintiff meets his burden of establishing a *prima facie* case, then "the employer assumes the burden of demonstrating by clear and convincing evidence that it would have taken the same adverse employment action in the absence of the plaintiff's protected activity."

The issue in this case comes down to whether the plaintiffs' disclosures to the *Post–Intelligencer* were protected under § 1514A(a)(1). To answer that question, we turn to the statute's language to determine whether it has a plain meaning.

The plaintiffs contend that their disclosures of perceived SOX violations to the *Post–Intelligencer* were protected under § 1514A(a)(1) because reports to the media may eventually "cause information to be provided" to members of Congress or federal law enforcement or regulatory agencies. We decline to adopt such a boundless interpretation of the statute. The plain language of § 1514A(a)(1) protects employees of public companies from retaliation only when they "provide information, cause information to be provided, or otherwise assist in an investigation" concerning specified types of fraud or securities violations "when the information or assistance is provided to or the investigation is conducted by" one of three individuals or entities: (1) a federal regulatory or law enforcement agency, (2) a member or committee of Congress, or (3) a supervisor or other individual who has the authority to investigate, discover or terminate such misconduct. 18 U.S.C. § 1514A(a)(1). Members of the media are not included. If Congress wanted to protect reports to the media under § 1514A(a)(1), it could have listed the media as one of the entities to which protected reports may be made. Or, it could have protected "any disclosure" of specified information, as it did with the Whistleblower Protection Act, 5 U.S.C. § 2302. But it took neither course, opting instead to limit protected activity to employees who raise certain concerns of fraud or securities violations with those authorized or required to act on the information.

When Congress wants to protect the disclosure of any information to any entity, it knows how to do so. The Whistleblower Protection Act prohibits retaliation against government employees and job applicants for "*any* disclosure of information" that the employee or applicant reasonably believes constitutes "a violation of any law, rule, or regulation, or … gross mismanagement, a gross waste of funds, an abuse of authority, or a substantial and specific danger to public health or safety" as long as "such disclosure is not specifically prohibited by law and if such information is not specifically required by Executive order to be kept secret in the interest of national defense or the conduct of foreign affairs." Relying on this language, courts and administrative bodies have interpreted the Whistleblower Protection Act to protect government employees who expose wrongdoing to members of the press. But the expansive language of that Act stands in stark contrast to the limiting text of § 1514A(a)(1). While the Whistleblower Protection Act protects "any disclosure" without limitation or qualification as to the specific types of entities to which protected whistleblower reports may be made, § 1514A(a)(1) is not so generous. This distinction lends further support to our conclusion that § 1514A(a)(1) does not protect employees of public companies who disclose information regarding fraud or certain securities violations to members of the media.

If, as the plaintiffs contend, the disclosure of information to the media is protected on the ground that it may ultimately fall into the hands of a member of Congress or a federal regulator, then virtually *any* disclosure to *any* person or entity would qualify as protected whistleblower activity, provided the information pertains to one of the statutorily-defined categories of unlawful conduct set forth in § 1514A(a)(1). We decline to afford such an expansive meaning to the statutory language.

In sum, the plain meaning of the statutory language excludes the expansive interpretation advanced by the plaintiffs. We therefore hold that § 1514A(a)(1) does not protect employees of publicly-held companies from retaliation when they disclose information regarding designated types of fraud or securities violations to members of the media.

AFFIRMED.

CASE QUESTIONS

1. What mistake did the two Boeing employees make in raising their concerns?

2. What should they have done?

3. What is the difference between the SOX whistleblower statutory protections and the protections available for federal government employees?

BUSINESS STRATEGY

The Employee Handbook as a Source of Litigation: Taking Precautionary Steps

The employee handbook continues to be a source of litigation. Every appellate court that has heard a case on the issue of employee handbooks has ruled that an implied contract results from the terms in the employee handbook.

This focus on employee handbooks has been combined with the majority of courts finding the right of an employee to recover for wrongful discharge if the employer has violated its own handbook. Here are the critical components of a good employee handbook:

1. Make sure every employee has a copy.

2. Enforce the rules. Lack of enforcement results in litigation.

3. Use clear and simple language.

4. Provide training on the handbook and the rules.

5. Give annual reminders about the rules and have employees sign off on their annual reminder.

Some companies have computer-based training that is required every year for employees to review and demonstrate understanding through questions.

6. Don't change the handbook without sufficient notice to all employees.

7. Be sure to cover the social media issues in the handbook—what employees can post on Facebook and other sites or whether managers and supervisors are permitted to ask their employees to "friend" them on Facebook.

8. Provide a contact person or department for employees who have questions about the handbook.

9. Follow the processes and rules in the handbook.

10. Refer to the handbook often when issuing reminders about policies and rules and when disciplining employees.

17-6c HANDLING EMPLOYEE TERMINATION DISPUTES

The number of suits brought by employees for improper discharge has increased tremendously. Many companies, in the interest of maintaining fairness and saving expenses, have adopted a peer review policy. **Peer review** (a process used in the *Tides v The Boeing Company* case) is a formal grievance procedure for nonunion employees. Employees who feel that they cannot get an adequate response from their supervisors or by following the lines of authority have the opportunity to present their cases to a panel of fellow employees and managers (the general configuration is three employees and two managers). Panel members listen to the presentation, can ask for more information, vote on the issue, and issue a written opinion with an explanation.

Many companies (including Coors and GTE) are avoiding lawsuits through what seems to be a mutually satisfactory resolution of wrongful termination and other grievance cases. Some employers say this process encourages both managers and employees to make better decisions. The peer review process should be in the employee handbook, should be required prior to court action, and should be widely publicized.

17-7 Agency Relationships in International Law

One of the complexities that has developed in law because of global business organizations is the liability of various subsidiaries, officers, and owners of multinational organizations when the interrelationships and operations may not be clear or even known to them. Perhaps the best example of the pitfalls of global structure is the multinational bank BCCI, a bank that proved elusive as authorities from several countries investigated it for criminal activity. BCCI was a layered, multinational organization with banks in 70 countries, including the United States (First American Bankshares, headed by the late Clark Clifford and Robert Altman). The banks and businesses in the different countries were staffed by residents of those countries, and the full global network of BCCI was not disclosed to these subsidiaries or to the individuals operating them. Regulations of operations were limited to the entities located in each of the various nations. Jurisdiction over other operations was limited. The layers of the organization made it difficult for anyone, even those in the subsidiaries, to be certain of the roles and activities of the full organization or of other subsidiaries.

BCCI collapsed and surrendered its U.S. assets to U.S. regulators in settlement of various charges. The late Clark Clifford and Robert Altman were indicted for activities involving BCCI, although they were affiliated with U.S. operations only. Mr. Altman was acquitted of the charges, and the court determined that Mr. Clifford was too ill to stand trial.

Following this complex case with its structuring of principal and agent relationships to evade the laws of any country, the United Kingdom, the United States, and other countries now work together to share information about tangled and evasive bank structures in order to prevent collapses and also detect the flow of funds by terrorist organizations. The cooperating nations now require filing and full disclosure of all principal–agent and parent–subsidiary relationships in all countries in which a bank conducts business.

Another area of agency law caution for companies in international business is the use of foreign agents in other countries for purposes of gaining access to government officials in order to win trade agreements or contracts. Companies are able to use such agents. However, they must know the agent's background and monitor carefully payments to that agent in order to avoid violations of the Foreign Corrupt Practices Act (FCPA) (see Chapter 7 for more information). Excessive payments to foreign agents is a red flag that requires the company to look into what the agent is doing and, if necessary, self-report any violations. For example, Ralph Lauren reported FCPA violations in its Argentina operations when it uncovered that excessive gifts were being transferred to government officials there in order to open up the importation process for its goods there. Ralph Lauren paid a fine and then ended its operations in Argentina.

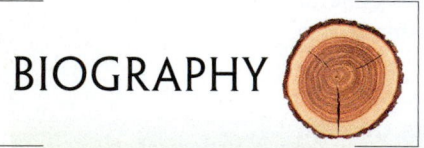

BIOGRAPHY

The Avant-Garde Ad Exec at Walmart in Arkansas: Julie Roehm

Julie Roehm was known throughout the advertising industry for her cutting-edge approach to advertising. When she worked for Chrysler, Ms. Roehm agreed to have Chrysler sponsor an alternative halftime show that would feature scantily clad models playing football, which came to be known as the Lingerie Bowl. When consumers and dealers howled, Chrysler dropped its sponsorship. She was the idea person behind the "Grab life by the horns" and "That thang got a hemi?" campaigns for Dodge Ram trucks. She also raised a few advertising eyebrows when she launched a Chrysler campaign for the Durango truck

with a television commercial that had two men at a urinal who were also having a double-entendre conversation about size. A Chrysler executive indicated Ms. Roehm was known for going over the marketing edge, but that you don't know where the edge is unless you go over it once in a while.

Walmart recruited Ms. Roehm, a fit that many of her friends felt was wrong. Ms. Roehm herself worried about moving her East Coast family to Bentonville, Arkansas. Walmart had to pull one of her first ads, one that was referred to as "sexy." The ad showed a couple having an intimate discussion about red lingerie in front of their extended family at a holiday gathering. Walmart pulled the ad after it aired on "Desperate Housewives" and Walmart received consumer complaints.

Ms. Roehm's tenure at Walmart would last only 10 months. She was hired in 2006, and by 2007, Walmart was in litigation with Ms. Roehm, who filed a wrongful termination suit against Walmart.

Walmart counterclaimed against Ms. Roehm's allegations with its allegations that Ms. Roehm had an affair with Sean Womack (both were married with children at that time), her second-in-command at the company. The filing included e-mails allegedly to Mr. Womack from Ms. Roehm that were provided by Mrs. Womack:

"I hate not being able to call you or write you. I think about us together all the time. Little moments like watching your face when you kiss me."

The filing also accuses the two of seeking employment with Draft FCB. Draft FCB was the company that was awarded the Walmart ad account by Ms. Roehm. Walmart fired Draft FCB after revelations about the conflicts and hired Interpublic Group. Walmart has since reassigned its ad contracts to three different agencies.

The Walmart counterclaim includes the following information about the perks Roehm and Womack enjoyed from Draft FCB:

- $1,100 dinner
- $700 at LuxBar in Chicago
- $440 at the bar in the Peninsula Hotel

Draft FCB cooperated with Walmart by providing copies of the e-mail communications between its employees and Roehm and Womack. However, Draft FCB also released a statement indicating that the employee communicating with Womack about employment for the two had no authority to negotiate such employment contracts or even had the authority to engage in business development.

Once Walmart counterclaimed, Ms. Roehm fired back with her own allegations, ones that basically argued, "What's sauce for the goose is sauce for the gander," a timeless legal principle in these battles of will. She alleged that Lee Scott, Walmart's then-CEO, enjoyed favorable prices from Irwin Jacobs, a Walmart supplier, on everything from jewelry to boats and that Mr. Scott's son, Eric, has worked for Mr. Jacobs for years. Her allegation was that Mr. Scott was not fired for these conflicts and, ergo, she was dismissed wrongfully. Walmart's code of ethics states that employees are not to have social relationships with suppliers if those relationships create even the appearance of impropriety.

While Walmart and Mr. Jacobs dismissed the allegations as false and outrageous, Mr. Jacobs and Mr. Scott acknowledged that their families have vacationed together and that Mr. Jacobs attended Mr. Scott's daughter's wedding. Mr. Jacobs has also stated that when the two are out together, Mr. Scott always pays and will not allow Mr. Jacobs to pay for even a lunch or other meal. Mr. Jacobs also says, 'I swear to God Lee never called me about [putting Eric to work].''

Walmart counterclaimed for its legal fees as well as for the damages (costs) it experienced when it had to re-bid the advertising agency contract Ms. Roehm had awarded. Walmart's counterclaim alleged that because Ms. Roehm had accepted expensive meals and other gifts from the agency, she violated Walmart's code of ethics, a strict one when it comes to suppliers, which prohibits employees from accepting anything from those suppliers.

The suit was dismissed and all parties agreed to walk away from the other suits that related to the situation surrounding Ms. Roehm's termination.

Sources: Louise Story and Michael Barbaro, "Wal-Mart Criticizes 2 in a Filing," *New York Times*, March 20, 2007, pp. C1, C5; Gary McWilliams and James Covert, "Roehm Claims Wal-Mart Brass Defy Ethics Rules," *Wall Street Journal*, May 27, 2007, pp. A1, A5.

Summary

When is an employee acting on behalf of an employer?

- Principal—employer; responsible party
- Agent—party hired to act on another's behalf
- *Restatement of Agency*—common-law view of agent–principal relationship
- Unincorporated association—nonlegal entity; no legal existence as natural or fictitious person

How much authority does an employee hold?

- Express authority—written or stated authority
- Implied authority—authority by custom
- Apparent authority—authority by perceptions of third parties
- Lingering apparent authority—authority left with terminated agent because others are not told of termination

- Actual notice—receipt of notice of termination
- Constructive notice—publication of notice of termination
- Ratification—after-the-fact recognition of agent's authority by principal
- Disclosed principal—existence and identity of principal are known
- Partially disclosed principal—existence but not identity of principal is known
- Undisclosed principal—neither existence nor identity of principal is known
- Gratuitous agency—agent works without compensation

When is a business liable for an employee's acts?

- Master–servant relationship—principal–agent relationship in which principal exercises great degree of control over agent
- Independent contractor—principal–agent relationship in which principal exercises little day-to-day control over agent

- Scope of employment—time when agent is doing work for the principal
- Inherently dangerous activities—activities for which, even if performed by independent contractor, principal is liable

What duties and obligations do employees owe employers?

- Fiduciary—one who has utmost duty of trust, care, loyalty, and obedience to another

How is an agency relationship terminated?

- Employment at will—right of employer to terminate noncontract employees at any time
- Protections for employees through express contract (manuals), implied contracts, and public policy
- Whistle-blowers protected by antiretaliation statutes

Questions and Problems

1. Dr. Warren Lesch had a leak in his car's gas tank that had been repaired by Malcolm Weeks, an employee of Walker's Chevron, Inc., in Bel Air, Maryland. The tank was not repaired properly, and Dr. Lesch's home and garage were destroyed when the gas tank exploded. Dr. Lesch and his wife were severely burned as a result.

Walker's Chevron is a "branded" station: It displays only Chevron signs and colors and sells only Chevron gas and oil. The Lesches have sued Mr. Weeks, Walker's Chevron, and Chevron USA. Who is liable for the explosion? [*Chevron USA, Inc. v Lesch*, 570 A.2d 840 (Md. 1990)]

2. On September 29, 1984, Wilton Whitlow was taken to Good Samaritan Hospital's emergency room in Montgomery County, Ohio, because he had suffered a seizure and a blackout. He was examined by Dr. Dennis Aumentado, who prescribed the antiepileptic medication Dilantin. Mr. Whitlow experienced no further seizures and was monitored as an outpatient at Good Samaritan over the next few weeks.

Mr. Whitlow complained to Dr. Aumentado of warm and dry eyes, and his Dilantin dose was reduced. On October 20, 1984, he was again admitted to the emergency room with symptoms that were eventually determined to be from Stevens–Johnson syndrome, a condition believed to be caused by a variety of

medications. Mr. Whitlow sued Dr. Aumentado and Good Samaritan for malpractice and Parke-Davis, the manufacturer of Dilantin, for breach of warranty.

The hospital maintains it is not liable because Dr. Aumentado was an independent contractor. Is the hospital correct? [*Whitlow v Good Samaritan Hosp.*, 536 N.E.2d 659 (Ohio 1987)]

3. On March 29, 1983, Barry Mapp was observed in the JCPenney department store in Upper Darby, Pennsylvania, by security personnel, who suspected that he might be a shoplifter. Michael DiDomenico, a security guard employed by JCPenney, followed Mr. Mapp when he left the store and proceeded to Gimbels department store. There, Mr. DiDomenico notified Rosemary Federchok, a Gimbels security guard, about his suspicions. Even though his assistance was not requested, Mr. DiDomenico decided to remain to assist in case Ms. Federchok, a short woman of slight build, required help in dealing with Mr. Mapp if he committed an offense in Gimbels.

Mr. Mapp was observed taking items from the men's department of Gimbels; when he attempted to escape, he was pursued. Although Ms. Federchok was unable to keep up, Mr. DiDomenico continued to pursue Mr. Mapp and ultimately apprehended him in the lower level of the Gimbels parking lot. When Ms. Federchok arrived with Upper Darby police, merchandise that had been taken from Gimbels was recovered. Mr. Mapp, who had been injured when he jumped from one level of the parking lot to another, was taken to the Delaware County Memorial Hospital, where he was treated for a broken ankle.

Mr. Mapp filed suit against Gimbels for injuries sustained while being chased and apprehended by Mr. DiDomenico. He alleged in his complaint that Mr. DiDomenico, while acting as an agent of Gimbels, had chased him, had struck him with a nightstick, and had beaten him with his fists. Gimbels says it is not liable because Mr. DiDomenico was not its agent. Is Gimbels correct? [*Mapp v Gimbels Dep't Store*, 540 A.2d 941 (Pa. 1988)]

4. Nineteen-year-old Lee J. Norris was employed by Burger Chef Systems as an assistant manager of one of its restaurants. On a day when he was in charge and change was needed, Mr. Norris left to get change but also decided to get Kentucky Fried Chicken at a nearby store for his lunch to take back to Burger Chef. The bank where Mr. Norris usually got change is 1.6 miles from Burger Chef, and the Kentucky Fried Chicken outlet is 2.5 miles from Burger Chef. After Mr. Norris left the bank and was on his way to the Kentucky Fried Chicken restaurant, he negligently injured Lee J. Govro in an accident. Is Burger Chef liable for the accident? [*Burger Chef Systems v Govro*, 407 F.2d 921 (8th Cir. 1969)]

5. Kevin Gardner is a driver with Loomis Armored, Inc., which is a company that supplies armored truck delivery services to banks, businesses, and others requiring secure transport of funds and other valuables. Because of the safety and liability issues surrounding armored truck deliveries, Loomis has adopted a policy for all drivers that their trucks cannot be left unattended. The policy is provided in the employee handbook and the penalty for violation of the rule is stated as follows:

Violations of this rule will be grounds for termination.

While Mr. Gardner was making a scheduled stop at a bank for a pickup of funds, he noticed a woman being threatened with a knife by an obviously agitated man. Mr. Gardner left his truck unattended as he went to the aid of the woman. The woman was saved and her assailant apprehended, and Mr. Gardner was then fired by Loomis for violating the company policy of not leaving the truck unattended. Mr. Gardner filed suit for wrongful termination in violation of public policy. [*Gardner v Loomis Armored, Inc.*, 913 P.2d 377 (Wash. 1996)]

6. Reverend John Fisher is the pastor of St. James Episcopal Church in Ohio. Catherine Davis served there as parish secretary from 1978 until six months after Reverend Fisher arrived at St. James in January 1988. Reverend Fisher fired her after she went to the bishop of the diocese to complain about sexual harassment by Reverend Fisher. The bishop promised an investigation, which was not conducted because Reverend Fisher denied the allegations. Ms. Davis then brought suit against the Episcopal Diocese. The diocese denied liability, claiming it was not in control of Reverend Fisher's actions because he was an independent contractor. Do you agree? [*Davis v Black*, 591 N.E.2d 11 (Ohio 1991)]

7. Lennen & Newell, Inc. (L&N), is an advertising agency hired by Stokely-Van Camp to do its advertising. L&N contracted for the purchase of ad time from CBS, but no Stokely representative's signature is on the contract. If L&N does not pay for the ad time, is Stokely liable? [*CBS, Inc. v Stokely-Van Camp, Inc.*, 456 F. Supp. 539 (E.D.N.Y. 1977)]

8. John Guz, 49, first hired in 1971, had worked for Bechtel Corporation for 22 years. In 1986, he was assigned to BNI, a division specializing in engineering, construction, and environmental remediation that focuses on federal government programs, principally for the Departments of Energy and Defense (BNI-MI). Mr. Guz worked his way up through Bechtel and BNI both, going from administrative assistant, beginning at a salary of $750 per month, to financial reports supervisor, earning $70,000 per year. During his time with Bechtel and BNI, Mr. Guz had been given generally favorable performance evaluations, steady pay increases, and a continuing series of promotions.

During this time, Bechtel maintained Personnel Policy 1101, dated June 1991, on the subject of termination of employment (Policy 1101). Policy 1101 stated that "Bechtel employees have no employment agreements guaranteeing continuous service and may resign at their option or be terminated at the option of Bechtel."

Between 1986 and 1991, BNI-MI's size was reduced from 13 to 6 persons, and its costs were reduced from $748,000 in 1986 to $400,000 in 1991. Bechtel eventually eliminated Mr. Guz's division. Mr. Guz was discharged, as were all the employees in the division. Mr. Guz brought suit against Bechtel alleging that he had an "implied-in-fact contract" with Bechtel that prevented the company from terminating him as long as the company was performing well financially.

The trial court granted Bechtel's motion for summary judgment and dismissed the action. In a split decision, the Court of Appeal reversed. Bechtel appealed. Who should prevail on appeal? [*Guz v Bechtel*, 8 P.3d 1089 (Cal. 2000)]

9. Bernice Bisbee is a real estate broker employed by Midkiff Realty, Inc. In September 1972, she obtained from Richard and Marian Silva an exclusive listing agreement for the sale of their property in Kaleheo,

Kauai. The land, which fronted on the Kaumualii Highway, consisted of 34,392 square feet, one two-bedroom house, and one four-bedroom house. The Silvas told Ms. Bisbee that they wanted $100,000 for the property.

Sometime later, Ms. Bisbee obtained an offer for the property from David Larsen. The down payment was set at $35,000, with payments of $2,000 a month at 8 percent a year, but Mr. Larsen backed out before closing. After that, a joint venture of six members formed the Pacific Equity Associates to buy the property. Ms. Bisbee was to manage the joint venture and would receive 10 percent of the profits for her services. One of the joint venture members, Toshio Morikawa, appeared as the buyer at the July 1973 closing of the property sale. Ms. Bisbee did not tell the Silvas of the venture nor of her pecuniary interest in it.

In August 1973, Ms. Bisbee prepared for the venture a financial statement that listed the market value of the Silva property at $149,424. Several times, the venture was late making payments, which Ms. Bisbee covered. Mr. Silva and his wife were emotionally distressed about the late payments and told Ms. Bisbee. Eventually, because of defaults on the payments, the Silvas brought suit to cancel the contract and for damages for fraud by Ms. Bisbee, naming Midkiff Realty in the suit as well.

The jury returned a verdict for $29,000 in general damages for the Silvas and $50,000 in punitive damages. Ms. Bisbee and Midkiff appealed. Was there a breach of fiduciary duty? Should the damage award stand because of Ms. Bisbee's actions? [*Silva v Bisbee*, 628 P.2d 214 (Haw. App. 1981)]

10. Recovery Express and Interstate Demolition (IDEC) are two Boston-based companies with the same business address. Albert Arillotta, who claimed to be a partner at IDEC, sent an e-mail to Leo Whitehead of CSX Transportation about purchasing rail cars for scrap purposes. The e-mail came from albert@recoveryexpress.com. The two reached an agreement, and Arillotta went to the CSX yard and disassembled rail cars and hauled them away. Mr. Whitehead sent invoices to IDEC for $115,757.36 because he believed Arillotta to be an agent for IDEC and Recovery Express. IDEC has no assets and CSX seeks to recover the amount due from Recovery Express. Recovery Express's CEO said he just allowed IDEC, a new company, to share office space and the e-mail server. Mr. Whitehead says that he assumed from the e-mail and the same address that Arillotta was an agent for Recovery as well. Who is liable? [*CSX Transportation, Inc. v Recovery Express, Inc.*, 415 F. Supp. 2d 6 (D. Mass. 2006)]

ORGANIZATIONAL BEHAVIOR THE LAW

Penn State: Oversight, Omissions, and Organizational Liability

Gerald A. Sandusky (Jerry) was a Penn State University alum who was hired in 1969 as an assistant football coach and assistant professor of physical education, a position he held until his retirement in 1999. During that time, Mr. Sandusky engaged in various acts of sexual assault with young boys who accompanied him to the campus as part of a program he had begun to help young boys who did not have father figures in their homes.

Between May 4, and May 30, 1998, there were notes and e-mails among and between Penn State University President Graham Spanier, Gary Schultz, the senior vice president for finance and business at Penn State, and Tim Curley, the Penn State athletic director regarding possible courses of action in dealing with Mr. Sandusky's actions with young boys on the campus. It is not clear how Mr. Schultz first learned of the May 4, 1998, events involving Mr. Sandusky on the campus, but his notes reflect that he knew almost

immediately and instructed the University Police Department Chief, Thomas Harmon, to let him know everything as the investigation into Mr. Sandusky's conduct proceeded. His notes concluded that Mr. Sandusky's behavior was "at best—inappropriate @ worst sexual improprieties."[6] After he received more information about a second boy's experience and the hotline report, his notes ask, "Is this opening of pandora's box? Other children?"[7]

The correspondence and notes also indicate that Mr. Curley had notified Mr. Schultz and football coach Joe Paterno, and both had asked to be kept informed about the investigation. Other documents indicate that Mr. Spanier was also notified, but he denied being aware of the issue and noted that he received many e-mails each day that keep him informed about an array of evolving concerns.

By 2011, Mr. Sandusky was indicted (and eventually convicted) for child molestation and other charges. When the charges were announced publicly, there were also charges against Mr. Curley and Mr. Schultz for perjury, conspiracy, and endangering child welfare. Mr. Spanier was later indicted for similar charges and all three entered not guilty pleas.

The trustees for Penn State fired all three men as well as Coach Paterno. There was great alumni and public backlash for the termination of the coach. The National Collegiate Athletic Association (NCAA) imposed sanctions on the university's football program—sanctions that the university accepted without protest or a hearing. The NCAA executive committee chair, Oregon State President Ed Ray, in announcing the sanctions, indicated, "I was so appalled at just the thought of those children and what was being done, and that nobody made a phone call, for God's sake."[8] When the NCAA sanctions were accepted, the University removed the statue of Coach Paterno from in front of the stadium during the wee hours of the morning.

Write a memo explaining why the trustees took the action they did. Be sure to include discussion of the principles of agency law, potential liability, and the rights of all of the terminated Penn State employees.

Notes

1. The terminology of *master* and *servant* has its roots in the historical nature of the employment relationship of indentured servants and slaves. For more information, see the course website and the *Instructor's Manual*.

2. Note: This opinion was not authorized for publication. However, the fact pattern in the case is an excellent one for analysis of fiduciary duty in agency relationships.

3. Eric Aasen, "Dancer's Misstep Lands Him in Collin County Jail," *Dallas Morning News*, October 18, 2008.

4. "Dancing Fool," *National Law Journal*, October 27, 2008, p. 16.

5. *Id.*

6. Freeh Report, at p. 47.

7. *Id.*

8. "NCAA Chair Ray: 'I was so appalled' about Penn State," *USA Today*, July 30, 2012, p. 2C.

18 GOVERNANCE AND STRUCTURE:
Forms of Doing Business

Creating a sole proprietorship is a popular way to do business, but the most popular forms of business organizations, and the ones producing the most revenues, are those formed by more than one person. Partnerships, limited partnerships, limited liability companies, and corporations are all multi-individual forms of doing business. This chapter answers the following questions: How are various business entities formed? What are the advantages and disadvantages of various entities? What are the rights, responsibilities, and liabilities of the individuals involved?

Each form of doing business is examined by reviewing its formation, sources of funding, the personal liability of owners, tax consequences, management and control, and the ease of transferring interests.

UPDATE
For up-to-date legal news, go to **mariannejennings.com**

Bo Chambers/Flickr/Getty Images

Consider...

Michael Eisner, as CEO and chairman of Disney, hired Michael Ovitz as his second-in-command at Disney. Mr. Eisner had a history of not working well with powerful seconds-in-command, and Mr. Ovitz was a powerful Hollywood talent agent and producer. In less than one year, Mr. Ovitz and Mr. Eisner were at such odds that Mr. Eisner and the board agreed to pay Mr. Ovitz more than $38 million in cash compensation and three million shares of Disney stock to leave the company. The shareholders brought suit against the Disney board alleging that the board's supervision of Eisner was lax, the hiring was a poor business decision, and the amount paid to end the arrangement constituted waste. The board says it just made a mistake. Can the shareholders recover?

18-1 Sole Proprietorships

18-1a FORMATION

A **sole proprietorship** is not a true business entity because it consists of only one individual operating a business. According to the U.S. Small Business Association, most small businesses operate as sole proprietorships, with 50 percent operating as home-based businesses. Often, a sole proprietorship is evidenced by the following language: "Homer Lane d/b/a Green Grower's Grocery"; "d/b/a" is an acronym for "doing business as." Because a sole proprietorship is not a separate organization, it has no formal requirements for formation. The individual simply begins doing business. In some states, "d/b/a" businesspeople are required to file their name(s) with a designated state agency and then publish the fictitious names under which they will be doing business.

18-1b SOURCES OF FUNDING

Most sole proprietorships have small business capital needs initially. Their financing usually comes from loans, either direct loans from banks or loans through government agencies such as the Small Business Administration.

Some sole proprietorships are started with financial backing from other people, usually in the form of personal loans. In such cases, the sole proprietor may have the skills or clients for a successful business but not the funds necessary to begin.

18-1c LIABILITY

Because financing for a sole proprietorship is based on the sole proprietor's credit rating and assets the proprietor is personally liable for the business loan, and his or her assets are subject to attachment should a default occur. To get financing, a sole proprietor takes personal financial risk.

18-1d TAX CONSEQUENCES

The positive side of a sole proprietor's unlimited personal liability is the right to claim all tax losses associated with the business. The income of the business is the income of the sole proprietor and is reported on the individual's income tax return. The IRS does not require a separate filing for the business itself; the sole proprietor files a Schedule C form with the usual 1040 form. Moreover, although sole proprietors owe all the taxes, they also get the benefit of all business deductions.

18-1e MANAGEMENT AND CONTROL

The proprietor is the manager of the business. In many businesses, the sole proprietor is both manager and employee. The proprietor makes all decisions. This form of business operation is truly centralized management.

18-1f TRANSFERABILITY OF INTEREST

Because the business is in many ways the owner, the business can be transferred only if the owner allows it. When a sole proprietor's business is transferred, the transfer consists of the property, inventory, and goodwill of the business. The sole proprietor is generally required to sign a noncompetition agreement so that the goodwill that has been paid for is preserved (see Chapters 16 and 17 for more details). In addition, upon the owner's death, the heirs or devisees of the owner inherit the property involved in the business. They may choose to operate the business, but the business usually ends upon the death of the sole proprietor.

18-2 Partnerships

Partnerships are governed by some version of the **Uniform Partnership Act (UPA)**, which has been adopted in 49 states. There is the original UPA and also the **Revised Uniform Partnership Act (RUPA)**. The states have adopted one or a combination of the UPA and RUPA. The RUPA defines a partnership as "the association of two or more persons to carry on as co-owners of a business for profit forms a partnership, whether or not the persons intend to form a partnership." "Persons" can include corporations, known as "artificial" persons, and natural persons.

18-2a FORMATION

A partnership can be formed voluntarily by direct action of the parties, such as through a partnership agreement or articles of partnership, or its formation can be implied by the ongoing conduct of the parties. (See Exhibit 18.1 for a summary of the types of business entities and Exhibit 18.2 for content of a partnership agreement.)

Conduct That Forms Partnerships by Implication

A partnership can arise even though no express agreement is made and the parties do not call themselves partners. In certain circumstances, courts infer that a partnership exists even if the persons involved say they are not partners.

Simply owning property together does not result in a **partnership by implication**. A cousin to apparent authority (see Chapter 17), a partnership by implication arises because the behaviors of the principals lead others to believe there is a partnership. Courts examine a number of factors in determining whether a partnership exists by implication. Section 7 of the RUPA provides that if two or more parties share the profits of a business, it is *prima facie* evidence that a

EXHIBIT 18.1 Comparison of Forms of Conducting Business

FORM	FORMATION	FUNDING	MANAGEMENT	TRANSFER CONTROL	TAXES	DISSOLUTION	LIABILITY
Sole proprietorship	No formal requirements	Individual provides funds	Individual	No transfer	Individual pays on individual return	Death; voluntary	Individual
Partnership	Articles of partnership	Capital contributions of partner	All partners or delegated to one	Transfer interest but not partners status	Partner takes profits and losses on individual return (flow-through)	Death; withdrawal of partner	Partners are personally liable
Limited partnership	Filing of articles of partnership	Capital contributions of general and limited partners	General partner	More easily transferred	Same as above (flow-through)	Death of general partner	General partner is personally liable; limited partners liable to extent of contribution
Corporation	Formal filing of articles of incorporation	Debt (bonds) equity (shareholders)	Board of directors, officers, or executive committee	Shares (with reasonable restrictions) are easily transferred	Corporation pays taxes; shareholders pay taxes on dividends	Dissolved only if limited in duration or shareholders vote to dissolve	No shareholder personal liability unless (1) watered or (2) corporate veil
S corporation* or Subchapter S	Same as above (special IRS filings to create special tax [flow-through] status)	Same as above	Same as above	Restrictions on transfer to comply with S corporation	Shareholders pay taxes on profits; take losses	Same as above	Same as above
C corporation†	Created as normal corporation	Same as above	Same as above	No restrictions	Corporation pays taxes; shareholders pay taxes on dividends	Same as above	Same as above
Limited liability company (LLC)	Formal filing of articles of organization	Capital contributions of members	All members or delegated to one	No admission without consent of majority	Flow-through treatment	Death; bankruptcy	Same as above (except professional negligence)
Limited liability partnership	Filing of articles of limited liability partnership	Capital contributions of partners	All partners or delegated to one	Same as above	Flow-through treatment	Death; bankruptcy	Varies by state but liability for acts of partners is limited in some way

*S corporations are formed under state incorporation laws but structured to obtain flow-through or pass-through status for income and losses under IRS regulations.

†"C corporation" is, again, a label for tax purposes.

EXHIBIT 18.2 Information Included in Articles of Partnership

MINIMUM REQUIREMENTS	SUGGESTED PROVISIONS
1. Names of the partners	1. Disability issues
2. Name of the partnership	2. Insurance coverage
3. Nature of the partnership's business	3. Sale of interest
4. The time frame of operation	4. Divorce of one of the partners
5. Amount of each partner's capital contribution	5. Indemnity agreements
6. Managerial powers of partners	6. Noncompetition agreements
7. Rights and duties of partners	7. Leaves of absence
	8. Accounting procedures for partnership books and records
	9. Methods for sharing profits and losses
	10. Salaries (if any) of the partners
	11. Causes and methods of dissolution
	12. Distribution of property if the partnership is terminated

partnership exists. (*Prima facie* evidence means the presumption that a partnership exists.) However, the presumption of partnership by profit sharing can be overcome if someone received profits for any of the following reasons:

1. Profits paid to repay debts
2. Profits paid as wages or rent
3. Profits paid to a widow or estate representative.
4. Profits paid for the sale of business goodwill

Many shopping center leases, for example, provide for the payment of both a fixed amount of rent and a percentage of net profits. The owners of the shopping center profit as the stores do, but they profit as landlords, not as partners with the shopping center businesses.

The *Byker v Mannes* case (Case 18.1) addresses the question of whether a partnership is implied by the conduct of two principals.

CASE 18.1 *Byker v Mannes*
641 N.W.2d 210 (Mich. 2002)[1]

Dumb and Dumbfounded

FACTS

In 1985, David Byker (plaintiff) was doing accounting work for Tom Mannes (defendant). The two talked about going into business together because they had complementary business skills. Mr. Mannes could locate certain properties because of his real estate

background, and Mr. Byker could raise money for their property purchases. Indeed, the parties stipulated the following as part of the litigation process in this case:

[T]he Plaintiff ... and Defendant ... agreed to engage in an ongoing business enterprise, to furnish capital, labor and/or skill to such enterprise, to raise investment

CONTINUED

funds and to share equally in the profits, losses and expenses of such enterprise.... In order to facilitate investment of limited partners, Byker and Mannes created separate entities wherein they were general partners or shareholders for the purposes of operating each separate entity.

They also stipulated that they had investment interests in five real estate limited partnerships. With regard to these partnerships in which they invested over a nine-year period, they shared equally in the commissions, financing fees, and termination costs. The two also personally guaranteed loans for these investments from several financial institutions.

The business relationship between the parties began to deteriorate after they created Pier 1000 Ltd. in order to own and manage a marina. Shortly after the creation of Pier 1000 Ltd., the marina encountered serious financial difficulties. To address these difficulties, the parties placed their profits from another partnership, the M & B Limited Partnership II, into Pier 1000 Ltd. and borrowed money from several financial institutions.

When Mr. Mannes refused to make any additional monetary contributions, Mr. Byker continued to make loan payments and incurred accounting fees on behalf of Pier 1000 Ltd. as well as on behalf of other business entities. Mr. Byker also entered into several individual loans for the benefit of Pier 1000 Ltd. These business transactions were performed without Mr. Mannes's knowledge.

The marina was returned to its previous owners in exchange for their assumption of Mr. Byker and Mr. Mannes's business obligations. At this point, the business ventures between Mr. Byker and Mr. Mannes ceased.

Mr. Byker then approached Mr. Mannes to obtain his share of the payments required as a result of the losses from the various businesses. Mr. Mannes testified that he was "absolutely dumbfounded" by the request for money.

Mr. Byker then filed suit for the payments, saying that the two had entered into a partnership. Following a bench trial, the court determined that the parties had created a general partnership that included all of the business entities. The Court of Appeals reversed that decision. Mr. Byker appealed.

JUDICIAL OPINION

MARKMAN, Justice

"[T]here is no necessity that the parties attach the label 'partnership' to their relationship as long as they in fact both mutually agree to assume a relationship that falls within the definition of a partnership."

In determining whether a partnership exists, the focus is not on whether individuals subjectively intended to form a partnership, that is, it is unimportant whether the parties would have labeled themselves "partners." Instead, the focus is on whether individuals intended to jointly carry on a business for profit regardless of whether they subjectively intended to form a partnership.

Whether Michigan partnership law, M.C.L. § 449.6(1), requires a subjective intent to form a partnership or merely an intent to carry on as co-owners a business for profit is a question of law.

...At present, partnership is defined as "an association of 2 or more persons, which may consist of husband and wife, to carry on as co-owners a business for profit ...."

In 1994, however, the UPA definition of partnership was amended by the National Conference of Commissioners. The amended definition stated that "the association of two or more persons to carry on as co-owners a business for profit forms a partnership, whether or not the persons intend to form a partnership."...

Although Michigan has not adopted the amended definition of partnership as set forth in § 202 of the Uniform Partnership Act of 1994, we believe nonetheless that M.C.L. § 449.6 is consistent with that amendment.[2]

...[I]f the parties associate themselves to "carry on" as co-owners a business for profit, they will be deemed to have formed a partnership relationship regardless of their subjective intent to form such a legal relationship. The statutory language is devoid of any requirement that the individuals have the subjective intent to create a partnership. Stated more plainly, the statute does not require partners to be aware of their status as "partners" in order to have a legal partnership.

Pursuant to this common law, individuals would be found to have formed a partnership if they acted as partners, regardless of their subjective intent to form a partnership.

If parties intend no partnership the courts should give effect to their intent, unless somebody has been deceived by their acting or assuming to act as partners; and any such case must stand upon its peculiar facts, and upon special equities.

It is nevertheless possible for parties to intend no partnership and yet to form one. If they agree upon an arrangement which is a partnership in fact, it is of no importance that they call it something else, or that they even expressly declare that they are not to be partners. The law must declare what is the legal import of their agreements, and names go for nothing when

CONTINUED

the substance of the arrangement shows them to be inapplicable.

Thus, one analyzes whether the parties acted as partners, not whether they subjectively intended to create, or not to create, a partnership....

Accordingly, we believe that our prior case law has, consistent with M.C.L. § 449.6(1), properly examined the requirements of a legal partnership by focusing on whether the parties intentionally acted as co-owners of a business for profit, and not on whether they consciously intended to create the legal relationship of "partnership."

With the language of the statute as our focal point, we conclude that the intent to create a partnership is not required if the acts and conduct of the parties otherwise evidence that the parties carried on as co-owners a business for profit. Thus, we believe that, to the extent that the Court of Appeals regarded the absence of subjective intent to create a partnership as dispositive regarding whether the parties carried on as co-owners a business for profit, it incorrectly interpreted the statutory (and the common) law of partnership in Michigan.

Accordingly, we remand this matter to the Court of Appeals for analysis under the proper test for determining the existence of a partnership under the Michigan Uniform Partnership Act.

Remanded.

CASE QUESTIONS

1. What type of relationship did Mr. Byker and Mr. Mannes have?

2. When did the relationship end? When did the parties believe it ended?

3. What does the court say about the intent of the parties?

4. Is Mr. Mannes liable to Mr. Byker for the payments Mr. Byker made with regard to their investments?

Consider...

Richard Chaiken entered into agreements with both Mr. Strazella and Mr. Spitzer to operate a barbershop. Mr. Chaiken was to provide barber chairs, supplies, and licenses. Mr. Strazella and Mr. Spitzer were to bring their tools, and the agreements included work hours and holidays for them. The Delaware Employment Security Commission determined that Mr. Strazella and Mr. Spitzer are employees, not partners, and seeks to collect unemployment compensation for the two barbers. Mr. Chaiken maintains that they are partners and not employees. Who is correct? [*Chaiken v Employment Security Comm'n*, 274 A.2d 707 (Del. 1971)]

Conduct That Forms a Partnership by Estoppel

At times, someone can be held to be a partner because he or she acted like a partner. Some court decisions have held that those who help a new business obtain a loan are holding themselves out as partners. Section 16 of the UPA provides as follows:

When a person by words spoken or written or by conduct, represents himself, or consents to another representing him to anyone as a partner in an existing partnership or with one or more persons not actual partners, he is liable to any party to whom such representation has been made.

In other words, if the conduct of two or more parties leads others to believe a partnership exists, that partnership may be found to exist legally under the notion of **partnership by estoppel**. Partnerships by estoppel arise when others are led to believe there is a partnership. Partnership by estoppel is a cousin to agency by estoppel, another ostensible relationship.

18-2b SOURCES OF FUNDING

Funding for a partnership comes from the partners who initially contribute property, cash, or services to the partnership accounts. These contributions are the capital of the partnership. Not only are these contributions put at the risk of the business, but also are each of the partners' personal assets: Partners are personally liable for the full amount of the partnership's obligations. Partners can also make loans to the partnership.

Consider...

Triangle Chemical Company supplied $671.10 worth of fertilizer and chemicals to France Mathis to produce a cabbage crop. When Mr. Mathis first asked for credit, he was denied. He then told Triangle that he had a new partner, Emory Pope. The company president called Mr. Pope, who said he was backing Mr. Mathis. Mr. Pope had loaned Mr. Mathis money to produce the crop, and Mr. Mathis said Mr. Pope would pay the bills. Mr. Pope said, "We're growing the crop together and I am more or less handling the money." When Mr. Mathis could not pay, Triangle wanted to hold Mr. Pope personally liable. Mr. Pope said his promise to pay another's debt would have to have been in writing. Triangle claimed Mr. Pope was a partner and personally liable. Is he?

[*Pope v Triangle Chemical Co.*, 277 S.E.2d 758 (Ga. 1981)]

18-2c **PARTNER LIABILITY**

Each partner is both a principal and an agent to the other partners and is liable both for the acts of others and to the others for individual acts. If one partner enters into a contract for partnership business supplies, all the partners are liable. Similarly, if partners have a motor vehicle accident while out doing partnership deliveries, the individual partners are liable for their own negligence, but because they were acting in the scope of partnership business the partnership itself is also liable. Under the RUPA, partners are jointly and severally liable for all obligations.

If partnership assets are exhausted, each partner is individually liable. Creditors can satisfy their claims by looking to the assets of the individual partners after the partnership assets are exhausted.

The *Vrabel v Acri* case (Case 18.2) deals with an issue of partnership liability.

CASE 18.2	*Vrabel v Acri*
	103 N.E.2d 564 (Ohio 1952)

Shot Down in a Ma & Pa Cafe: Is Ma Liable When Pa Goes to Jail?

FACTS

On February 17, 1947, Stephen Vrabel and a companion went into the Acri Cafe in Youngstown, Ohio, to buy alcoholic drinks. While Mr. Vrabel and his companion were sitting at the bar drinking, Michael Acri, without provocation, drew a .38-caliber gun, shot and killed Mr. Vrabel's companion, and shot and seriously injured Mr. Vrabel. Mr. Acri was convicted of murder and sentenced to a life term in the state prison.

Florence and Michael Acri, as partners, had owned and operated the Acri Cafe since 1933. From the time of his marriage to Mrs. Acri in 1931 until 1946, Mr. Acri had been in and out of hospitals, clinics, and sanitariums for the treatment of mental disorders and nervousness. Although he beat Mrs. Acri when they had marital difficulties, he had not attacked, abused, or mistreated anyone else. The Acris separated in September 1946, and Mrs. Acri sued her husband for divorce soon afterward. Before their separation, Mrs. Acri had operated

CONTINUED

© Harper 3D/Shutterstock.com

and managed the cafe primarily only when Mr. Acri was ill. Following the marital separation and until the time he shot Mr. Vrabel, Mr. Acri was in exclusive control of the management of the cafe.

Mr. Vrabel brought suit against Mrs. Acri to recover damages for his injuries on the grounds that, as Mr. Acri's partner, she was liable for his tort. The trial court ordered her to pay Mr. Vrabel damages of $7,500. Mrs. Acri appealed.

JUDICIAL OPINION

ZIMMERMAN, Judge

The authorities are in agreement that whether a tort is committed by a partner or a joint adventurer, the principles of law governing the situation are the same. So, where a partnership or a joint enterprise is shown to exist, each member of such project acts both as principal and agent of the others as to those things done within the apparent scope of the business of the project and for its benefit.

Section 13 of the Uniform Partnership Act provides: "Where, by any wrongful act or omission of any partner acting in the ordinary course of business of the partnership or with the authority of his copartners, loss or injury is caused to any person, not being a partner in the partnership, or any penalty is incurred, the partnership is liable therefore to the same extent as the partner so acting or omitting to act."

However, it is equally true that where one member of a partnership or joint enterprise commits a wrongful and malicious tort not within the actual or apparent scope of the agency, or the common business of the particular venture, to which the other members have not assented, and which has not been concurred in or ratified by them, they are not liable for the harm thereby caused.

Because at the time of Vrabel's injuries and for a long time prior thereto Florence had been excluded from the Acri Cafe and had no voice or control in its management, and because Florence did not know or have good reason to know that Michael was a dangerous individual prone to assault cafe patrons, the theory of negligence urged by Vrabel is hardly tenable.

We cannot escape the conclusion, therefore, that the above rules, relating to the nonliability of a partner or joint adventurer for wrongful and malicious torts committed by an associate outside the purposes and scope of the business, must be applied in the instant case. The willful and malicious attack by Michael Acri upon Vrabel in the Acri Cafe cannot reasonably be said to have come within the scope of the business of operating the cafe, so as to have rendered the absent Florence accountable.

Since the liability of a partner for the acts of his associates is founded upon the principles of agency, the statement is in point that an intentional and willful attack committed by an agent or employee, to vent his own spleen or malevolence against the injured person, is a clear departure from his employment and his principal or employer is not responsible therefore.

Judgment reversed.

CASE QUESTIONS

1. What was the nature of the business?
2. Why was Mr. Acri not a defendant?
3. Explain why Mrs. Acri is or is not liable for the injuries.

18-2d TAX CONSEQUENCES IN PARTNERSHIPS

A partnership does not pay taxes. It simply files an informational return. The partners, however, must report their shares of partnership income (or losses) and deductions on their individual tax returns on Schedule C, and must pay taxes on the reported share.

18-2e MANAGEMENT AND CONTROL

Partnership Authority

Unless agreed otherwise, each partner has a duty to contribute time to manage the partnership. Each partner has an equal management say, and each has a right to use partnership property for partnership purposes. No one partner controls the property, funds, or management of the firm (unless the partners so agree).

The partners may agree to delegate day-to-day management responsibilities to one or more of the partners. However, the agency rules of express, implied, and apparent authority (see Chapter 17) apply to partnerships. Each partner is an agent of the other partners, and each has express authority given by the UPA and any partnership agreement, implied authority relating to those powers, and apparent authority as is customary in their business. Some management matters are simply a matter of a vote; a majority of the partners makes the decision. The unanimous consent of the partners is required for some decisions, however, such as confessing a judgment (settling a lawsuit), transferring all the partnership's assets, or selling its goodwill. Basically, unusual transactions in which no apparent authority could be claimed require all the partners' approval.

The partners are not entitled to compensation for their management of the partnership's business, unless so specified in the partnership agreement. Under the UPA, a partner who winds up a dissolved partnership's business can be compensated.

Consider...

Silvio Giannetti, his daughter Anne Marie, and her husband Jerry Prozinsky were partners in the Giannetti Investment Company (GIC). GIC owned and operated the Brougham Manor Apartments. Mr. Prozinsky signed a contract with Omnicon to give it the right to install the equipment for and promote cable television in the apartment complex. Mr. Giannetti was most disturbed when he learned that Mr. Prozinsky had signed the agreement. He refused to allow Omnicon further access to the complex. The result was that cable service was interrupted, lines could not be repaired, and Omnicon was forced to discontinue all its cable customers in the apartment complex.

Omnicon filed suit against GIC for breach of contract. Mr. Giannetti maintains that GIC is not liable because Mr. Prozinsky did not have the authority to sign such a contract. Is Mr. Giannetti correct?

[*Omnicon v Giannetti Investment Company*, 561 N.W.2d 138 (Mich. App. 1997)]

Partner Fiduciary Duties

Because each partner is an agent for the partnership and the other partners as well, each owes the partnership and the other partners the same fiduciary duties an agent owes a principal. Partners' obligations as fiduciaries are the same as agents' duties to principals.

Partnership Property

Partnership property is defined as property contributed to the firm as a capital contribution or purchased with partnership funds. Partners are co-owners of partnership property in a form of ownership called *tenancy in partnership*. Tenants in partnership have equal rights in the use and possession of the property for partnership purposes. On the death of one of the partners, rights in the property are transferred to the surviving partner or partners. The partnership interest in the property remains, and the property or a share of the property is not transferred to the estate of the deceased partner. The estate of the deceased partner simply receives the value of the partner's interest, not the property.

Partner Interests

Partners' interests in the partnership are different from partnership property. A partner's interest is a personal property interest that belongs to the partner. It can be sold (transferred) or pledged as collateral to a creditor. Creditors (personal) can attach a partner's interests to collect a debt.

A transfer of a partner's interest affects the partnership interests in several ways. The transfer does not result in the transferee becoming a new partner because no person can become a partner without the consent of all the existing partners. Further, the transfer does not relieve the transferring partner of personal liability. A transfer of interest will not eliminate individual liability to existing creditors.

Some partnership agreements place restrictions on transfer. For example, a provision may allow the partnership the right to buy out a partner before the partner has the authority to transfer interest.

18-2f TRANSFERABILITY OF INTERESTS

A partner cannot transfer her partnership status without the unanimous consent of the other partners. However, if that transfer is approved, the departing or outgoing partner and the incoming partner should be aware of their liability. Absent an agreement from creditors, the outgoing partner remains personally liable for all partnership debts up to the time of departure. If the departing partner gives public notice of disassociation, no further personal liability results from contracts and obligations entered into after departure. The incoming partner is liable for all contracts after the date of entry into the firm. Incoming partners are liable for existing debts only to the extent of their capital contribution.

The *Byker* case also illustrates that partnership liabilities do not end when the partners no longer do business together. The debts remain and must be satisfied, even from partners no longer involved in running the business.

18-2g DISSOLUTION AND TERMINATION OF THE PARTNERSHIP

Dissolution is not necessarily termination. The UPA defines dissolution as one partner's ceasing to be associated with carrying on the business. The RUPA refers to "dissociation" of partners, which may or may not lead to dissolution. When a partner leaves, retires, or dies, the partnership is dissolved, though not terminated. Dissolution is basically a change in the structure of the partnership. Dissolution may have no effect on the business: The partnership may be reorganized and continue business without the partner who is leaving.

Dissolution *can* lead, however, to termination of the partnership. Termination means all business stops, the assets of the firm are liquidated, and the proceeds are distributed to creditors and partners to repay capital contributions and distribute profits (if any). The following events are grounds for dissolution.

Dissolution by Agreement

The partnership agreement itself may limit the partnership's time of existence. Once that time expires, the partnership is dissolved. If the agreement does not specify the time or there is no partnership agreement, the partners can (by unanimous consent) agree to dissolve the partnership.

Dissolution by Operation of Law

Another way a partnership is dissolved is by operation of law when certain events require the dissolution of the partnership. When one partner dies, the partnership is automatically dissolved. The business could go on, but the partnership as it once existed ends, and the deceased partner's estate must be paid for his or her interest. Also, if the partnership or an individual partner becomes bankrupt, the partnership is dissolved by law.

Dissolution by Court Order

The third method for dissolution of a partnership is by court order. Sometimes partners just cannot work together any longer. In such circumstances, they can petition a court for dissolution in the interest of preserving their investments.

18-3 Limited Partnerships

A **limited partnership** is a partnership with a slight variation in the liability of those involved. The types of partners in a limited partnership include at least one **general partner** and one **limited partner**. General partners have the same obligations as partners in general partnerships—full liability and full responsibility for the management of the business. Limited partners have liability limited to the amount of their contribution to the partnership, and they cannot be involved in the management of the firm. General partners run the limited partnership, and the limited partners are the investors.

The **Uniform Limited Partnership Act (ULPA)** was drafted in 1916. At that time, few limited partnerships existed and most of them were quite small. The limited partnership, however, has become a favored type of business structure, particularly for oil exploration and real estate development because of the tax advantages available through limited partnerships. The attractiveness of limited liability combined with tax advantages have resulted in an increase in the numbers and sizes of limited partnerships.

In 1976, the National Conference of Commissioners on Uniform State Laws developed the **Revised Uniform Limited Partnership Act (RULPA)**. The act was designed to update limited partnership law to address the ways limited partnerships were doing business. The RULPA was revised in 1985 and has been adopted in nearly every state.

18-3a FORMATION

A limited partnership is a statutory creature and requires compliance with certain procedures in order to exist. If these procedures are not followed, it is possible that the limited partners could lose their limited liability protection.

The RULPA requires a formal filing at the appropriate government agency in order for valid formation. That form must include certain contact information for the partnership and name a statutory agent (the individual who is authorized to receive summons for litigation against the firm and government notices). Limited partners need not be listed in the certificate, nor are they all required to sign the certificate. The size of limited partnerships makes such a listing impossible.

The formal filing is the public notice of this structure for the business, a structure that limits liability. If there are any errors in filing and formation, the limited partnership could be deemed a general partnership, and the limited partners could lose the protection of their limited liability. However, limited partners can make filings to correct any formation problems or they could withdraw from the improperly formed partnership. A limited partner would still be liable to any third parties for liabilities incurred by what was really a general partnership (because of the errors in filing).

The certificate of limited partnership is simply public disclosure of the formation and existence of the limited partnership; it does not deal with the many more rights and obligations that the partners may agree on among themselves. Those issues are generally addressed in a much longer document called a **limited partnership agreement** or the **articles of limited partnership**.

18-3b SOURCES OF FUNDING

Capital contributions supply the initial funding for a limited partnership. Both the general and limited partners make contributions upon entering the partnership. Under the RULPA, the contribution can be in the form of cash, property, services already performed, or a promissory note or other obligation to pay money or property. The RULPA requires that limited partners' promises to contribute must be in writing to be enforceable. The limited partners are always personally liable for the difference between what has actually been contributed and the amount promised to be contributed.

Some partners make **advances** or loans to the partnership. The partnership can also borrow money from third parties. However, only the general partner has any personal liability for repayment of the loan to the third party.

18-3c LIABILITY

The principal advantage of a limited partnership is the limited personal liability. To ensure personal limited liability, several requirements must be met. First, as already discussed, there must be proper formation with all required public filings. Second, at least one general partner is required. The general partner can be a corporation. Third, the limited partners cannot be involved in the management of the business because such involvement would give the appearance of general partner status. Finally, limited partners cannot use their names in the name of the partnership, which would give the wrong impression to outside parties and create an estoppel type of relationship.

Under the RULPA, a limited partner who participates in the management of the firm in the same way as does the general partner is liable only to those persons who are led to believe by the limited partner's conduct that the limited partner is a general partner. The RULPA also provides a list of activities that limited partners can engage in without losing their limited liability status, such as the following:

1. Being employed by the general partnership as an employee or a contractor
2. Consulting with or advising the general partner
3. Acting as a surety or guarantor for the limited partnership
4. Voting on amendments, dissolution, sale of property, or assumption of debt

If limited partners comply with the rules for limited liability, their liability is limited to the amount of their capital contribution. If they have pledged to pay a certain amount as capital over a period of time, they are liable for the full amount. For example, some real estate syndications that are limited partnerships allow the limited partners to make their investment in installment payments over two to four years. Limited partners in these arrangements are liable for the full amount pledged whenever an obligation to a creditor is not paid.

18-3d TAX CONSEQUENCES

Limited partnerships are taxed the same way as general partnerships. The general and limited partners report the income and losses on their individual returns and pay the appropriate taxes. A limited partnership files an information return but does not pay any taxes as an entity.

One of the benefits of limited partnership status is the combination of limited liability with direct tax benefits. In this sense, a limited partnership is the best of both worlds. Because of this ideal situation, limited partnership interests are closely scrutinized by the IRS to determine whether they are, in reality, corporations as opposed to true limited partnerships. Some of the factors examined in determining whether an organization is a corporation or a limited partnership are (1) the transferability of the interests, (2) the assets of the general partners, and (3) the net worth of the general partners. The IRS looks beyond the formal filing for creation to other factors to determine whether the organization is truly a limited partnership for tax purposes.

18-3e MANAGEMENT AND CONTROL

Profits and Distributions

The general partner in a limited partnership has absolute authority to decide not only when distributions are made but also whether they will be made; for example, the general partner might decide not to distribute funds but to put them back into the business.

Profits and losses are allocated on the basis of capital contributions. Under the RULPA, the agreement for sharing of profits and losses must be in writing.

Partner Authority

The authority of the general partner in a limited partnership is the same as the authority of the partners in a general partnership. These powers can be restricted by agreement. However, the general partner cannot perform some general activities without the consent of the limited partners, including the following:

1. Admitting a new general partner (also requires consent of other general partners)

2. Admitting a new limited partner unless the partnership agreement allows it

3. Extraordinary transactions, such as selling all the partnership assets

Limited partners can monitor the general partner's activity with the same rights provided to partners in general partnerships: the right to inspect the books and records and the right to an accounting.

18-3f TRANSFERABILITY OF INTERESTS

Although the assignment of limited partnership interests is not prohibited by the RULPA, a limited partnership agreement may provide for significant restraints on assignment. Transfer restrictions can be placed on limited partners' interests for two reasons. First, limited partnership interests may have been sold without registration as exemptions to the federal securities law (see Chapter 19 for more details on securities registrations). If those exempt interests are readily transferable, the exemption could be lost. Second, for the limited partners to enjoy the tax benefits of limited partner status, ease of transferability is a critical issue. The more easily an interest can be transferred, the more likely the limited partnership will be treated (for tax purposes) as a corporation.

The assignment of a partnership interest does not terminate a limited partnership. The assignee is entitled to receive only the distributions and profits to which the partner is entitled. The assignee does not become a partner without the consent of the other partners. Under the RULPA, a limited partnership can agree that the assigning limited partner will have the authority to make the assignee a limited partner. The effect of the RULPA provision is to simplify transfers and allow limited partners to decide whether they want to transfer their interest or their limited partner status.

18-3g DISSOLUTION AND TERMINATION OF A LIMITED PARTNERSHIP

A limited partnership can be dissolved in one of the following ways:

1. Expiration of the time period designated in the agreement or the occurrence of an event causing dissolution, as specified in the agreement
2. Unanimous written consent of all partners
3. Withdrawal of a general partner
4. Court order after application by one of the partners

Upon dissolution, a partnership can continue (assuming a general partner remains); but the partnership can also be terminated after dissolution. If termination occurs, all assets of the partnership are liquidated. The RULPA specifies that the money from the sale of the assets be used to pay partnership obligations in the following order of priority:

1. Creditors (including partners, but not with respect to distributions)
2. Partners and former partners, for distributions owed to them
3. Return of capital contributions
4. Remainder split according to distribution agreement

18-4 Corporations

Corporations have the following characteristics: unlimited duration, free transferability of interest, limited liability for shareholders/owners, continuity, and centralized management. Corporations are legal entities in and of themselves. Because they are treated as persons under the law, they can hold title to property, they can sue or be sued in the corporate name, and they are taxed separately.

18-4a TYPES OF CORPORATIONS

Each of the diverse types of corporations can be described by one or more adjectives. For example, corporations are either **profit corporations** (those seeking to earn a return for investors) or **nonprofit corporations**. In addition, they are either **domestic corporations** or **foreign corporations**. A corporation is a domestic corporation in the state in which it is incorporated and a foreign corporation in every other state. Further, corporations organized by government agencies that exist to achieve a social goal are called government corporations. **Professional corporations** are corporations organized by physicians, dentists, attorneys, and accountants; they exist by statute in most states. Professional corporation shareholders have no personal liability for any corporate debts, as in any other corporation, except for professional malpractice claims. The **corporate veil** or shield (explained later) will not give individuals personal immunity for professional negligence despite their general liability limitation through incorporation. **Close corporations** are the opposite of **publicly held corporations**—that is, the former are corporations with few shareholders. Close corporations and publicly held corporations are created in the same way, but most states then have a separate statute governing the operation of close corporations. Close corporation owners are generally given more discretion in their internal operations, and the degree of formality required for publicly held corporations is not required.

The **S corporation** (sometimes called Subchapter S or Sub S corporation) is formed no differently from any other corporation, but it must meet the IRS requirements for an S corporation and must file a special election form with the IRS indicating it wants to be treated as an S corporation. The benefit of an S corporation is that shareholders' income and losses are treated like those of partners, but the shareholders enjoy the protection of limited liability behind a corporate veil. The income earned and losses incurred by an S corporation are reported on the shareholders' individual returns, but the shareholders' personal assets are protected from creditors of the business. For tax purposes, the S corporation is like a partnership in the sense of the flow-through of profits and losses, and the shareholders avoid the double taxation of having the corporation pay tax on its earnings and the shareholders pay tax on the dividends distributed to them.

Business Planning Tip

Under the Internal Revenue Code, Subchapter corporations must meet the following requirements:

- Domestic corporations
- No more than 100 shareholders
- Limited types of shareholders
- No nonresident aliens as shareholders
- One class of stock
- Some restrictions on the types of corporations (by line of business) that qualify

© Grounder/Shutterstock.com

18-4b THE LAW OF CORPORATIONS

The **Model Business Corporation Act (MBCA)**, as drafted and revised by the Corporate, Banking, and Business Section of the American Bar Association, is the uniform law on corporations. The provisions of the MBCA are quite liberal and give management great latitude in operations. The MBCA tends to follow the principles of corporate law long established in Delaware, a state where many of the country's major companies are incorporated. Delaware boasts a rich body of case law on corporate governance that offers the stability companies want as they incorporate. Despite the ability to draw on the Delaware case law and experience, the MBCA is not adopted as widely as the UPA or the Uniform Commercial Code (UCC). Even those states that have adopted the MBCA have made significant changes in their adopted versions. As a result, each state's law on corporations is quite different. The following sections cover the revised MBCA rules, but each state may have its own variations.

18-4c FORMATION

A corporation is a statutory entity. Formal public filing is required to form a corporation. The following procedures for corporate formation are those of the MBCA. Without the filing, the corporation does not exist and liability is as if there is a general partnership. One of the complicated issues under the MBCA is what happens when there is a flaw in the corporate documents that have been filed, but the corporation operates as a corporation. In some states, the courts recognize a de facto existence and allow for a corporate existence and liability of that corporation. Other states simply conclude that either there is a valid corporation or there is not, and if there is not (because of flawed filings or paperwork), then there is liability on the part of the individuals involved.

Where to Incorporate

The following factors should be considered when determining in which state to incorporate:

1. The status of the state's corporation laws (See the preceding discussion about Delaware; also, some states' laws and judicial decisions are oriented more toward management than toward shareholders.)

2. State tax laws

3. The ability to attract employees to the state

4. The incentives that states offer to attract the business (new freeways, office space, attractive urban renewal)

The Formation Document

All states require **articles of incorporation** to be filed in order to create a corporation. These articles give the structure and basic information about the corporation. Under the MBCA, the articles of incorporation must include the following information:

1. The name of the corporation

2. The names and addresses of all incorporators (In addition, each incorporator must sign the articles of incorporation.)

3. The share structure of the corporation: (a) the common and preferred classes; (b) which shares vote; and (c) the rights of shareholders, or preemptive rights

4. The statutory agent (the party who will be served with any lawsuits against the corporation)

Who Is Incorporating

The **incorporators** (required to be listed in the articles of incorporation) are the parties forming the corporation. Under the MBCA, only one incorporator is required and that person may be a natural person, a corporation, a partnership, a limited partnership, or an association.

Incorporators are personally liable for any contracts entered into or actions taken during the pre-incorporation stage. Until the corporation exists, incorporators are acting as individuals. After incorporation, the corporation could agree to assume liability through a **novation** of the incorporators' acts.

For example, if an incorporator of a lumberyard entered into a contract for the purchase of lumber and the corporate board (after formation) agreed that the contract was a good one, the corporation could ratify it or enter into a novation to assume liability. In novation, the lumberyard agrees to substitute the corporation as the contracting party. In a **ratification**, the corporation assumes primary liability for payment, but the incorporator still remains liable. Incorporators generally are paid for their efforts in shares of the corporation's stock. They may also be the contributors of initial corporate assets and may be paid in shares for their contributions.

Postformation

After the paperwork of incorporating is complete, a corporation must begin its day-to-day operations with an **initial meeting**. At this meeting, the officers of the corporation are elected and **bylaws** are adopted to govern corporate procedures. The bylaws define the authority of each of the officers, prescribe procedures for announcing and conducting meetings (i.e., quorum numbers and voting numbers), and set the terms of officers and directors and who is eligible to serve in such offices. Articles of incorporation give an overview of a corporate entity; the bylaws constitute the operational rules.

18-4d CAPITAL AND SOURCES OF CORPORATE FUNDS

A corporation has a variety of sources of funds. It may use short-term financing, which consists of loans from banks or credit lines. The problems with short-term financing are higher interest rates and shorter payback periods. The other forms of financing used most frequently by corporations are debt and equity.

Debt Financing: The Bond Market

Long-term debt financing is available to corporations when they issue bonds. Bonds are, in effect, long-term promissory notes from a corporation to the bond buyers. The corporation pays the holders interest on the bonds until the maturity date, which is when the bonds are due or must be paid. The interest is fixed and is a fixed payment responsibility regardless of the corporation's profitability. The benefits of debt financing include the tax deductibility of interest as an expense. Further, bondholders have the benefit of first rights in corporate assets in the event of insolvency. However, a corporation cannot maintain a sound financial policy or rating with debt financing only.

Equity Financing: Shareholders

Equity financing comes through the sale of stock in a corporation. It provides a means of raising capital up front with the exchange of proportionate corporate ownership and the promise of proportionate profits. Shareholders are given shares of stock in exchange for their money. To avoid personal liability, the shareholders must pay at least par value for their shares and must honor the terms of their subscription agreement (share purchase agreement). A shareholder who has not paid at least par value is said to hold **watered shares** and is liable to creditors for the amount not paid. For example, if a shareholder paid $500 for shares with a par value of $1,000, the shareholder would be personally liable for the $500 difference. Along with those shares of stock come certain promises of future performance from the corporation. The rights of shareholders depend on the type of stock purchased. A discussion of the various types of stock follows.

Equity Financing: Common Stock

Common stock is the typical stock in a corporation and is usually the most voluminous in terms of the number of shares. Common stock generally carries voting rights so that common shareholders have a voice in the election of directors, the amendment of articles and bylaws, and other major corporate matters. Common stock generally does not have a fixed dividend rate and does not carry with it any right to have a dividend declared. Common stock dividends depend on both profitability and decisions of the board of directors. If a corporation is dissolved, the common shareholders have a right to a proportionate share of the assets (after creditors and preferred stockholders have been paid).

Equity Financing: Preferred Stock

Preferred stock is appropriately named because its owners enjoy preferred status over holders of a corporation's common stock. For example, preferred stockholders have priority in the payment of dividends. Some preferred dividends are even at a fixed rate, and **cumulative preferred stock** guarantees the payment of a dividend so that if a dividend is not paid one year, the holder's right to be paid carries over until funds are available. Preferred shareholders also have priority over common shareholders in the event the corporation is dissolved and the assets distributed.

18-4e LIABILITY ISSUES

Limited liability for shareholders is one of the advantages of corporate organization. Sometimes, however, individuals—such as shareholders, directors, and officers—can be personally liable for corporate obligations.

Shareholder Liability

Shareholders' personal liability is limited to the amount of their investment in the corporation. The personal assets of shareholders are not subject to the claims of corporate creditors. In some circumstances, however, a shareholder is liable for more than the amount of investment. For example, if a shareholder has not paid for his shares or has paid for them with overvalued property, creditors could turn to the shareholder's personal assets for satisfaction of his debt but only to the extent of the amount due on the shares.

In other more serious circumstances, shareholders can be held liable for the full amount of corporate debts. A creditor who successfully pierces the corporate veil overcomes the shield of limited liability protecting shareholders from having to accept personal liability for corporate debts. The corporate veil can be pierced for several reasons. One is inadequate capitalization. The owners of a corporation are required to place as much capital at risk in the corporation as is necessary to cover reasonably anticipated expenses of the business. The purpose of this requirement is to ensure that someone does not use the corporation to avoid liability without actually transferring to the corporation some assets for the payment of corporate liabilities.

Another theory a court can use to pierce the corporate veil is the **alter ego theory**, which means that the owners and managers of the corporation have not treated the corporation as a separate entity but have used the structure more as a personal resource. Personal and corporate assets and debts are mixed, no formality is observed with regard to operations and meetings, and transfers of property are made without explanation or authorization.

The *U.S. v Bestfoods* case (Case 18.3) deals with an issue of piercing the corporate veil in a situation involving CERCLA liability (see Chapter 11).

| CASE 18.3 | *U.S. v Bestfoods, Inc.* 524 U.S. 51 (1998) |

Lifting the Veil Is Best for Cleanup, but Not for Shareholders

FACTS

In 1957, Ott Chemical Co. manufactured chemicals at its plant near Muskegon, Michigan, and both intentionally and unintentionally dumped hazardous substances in the soil and groundwater near the plant. Ott sold the plant to CPC International, Inc.

In 1965, CPC incorporated a wholly owned subsidiary (Ott II) to buy Ott's assets. Ott II then continued both the chemical production and dumping. Ott II's officers and directors had positions and duties at both CPC and Ott.

In 1972, CPC (now Bestfoods) sold Ott II to Story Chemical, which operated the plant until its bankruptcy in 1977. Aerojet-General Corp. bought the plant from the bankruptcy trustee and manufactured chemicals there until 1986.

In 1989, the EPA filed suit to recover the costs of cleanup on the plant site and named CPC, Aerojet, and the officers of the now defunct Ott and Ott II.

The District Court held both CPC and Aerojet liable. After a divided panel of the Court of Appeals for the Sixth Circuit reversed in part, the court granted rehearing *en banc* and vacated the panel decision. This time, seven judges to six, the court again reversed the District Court in part. Bestfoods appealed (Ott settled prior to the appeal).

JUDICIAL OPINION

SOUTER, Justice

The issue before us, under the Comprehensive Environmental Response, Compensation, and Liability Act of 1980 (CERCLA), is whether a parent corporation that actively participated in, and exercised control over, the operations of a subsidiary may, without more, be held liable as an operator of a polluting facility owned or operated by the subsidiary. We answer no, unless the corporate veil may be pierced. But a corporate parent that actively participated in, and exercised control over,

CONTINUED

the operations of the facility itself may be held directly liable in its own right as an operator of the facility.

The District Court said that operator liability may attach to a parent corporation both directly, when the parent itself operates the facility, and indirectly, when the corporate veil can be pierced under state law. The court explained that, while CERCLA imposes direct liability in situations in which the corporate veil cannot be pierced under traditional concepts of corporate law, "the statute and its legislative history do not suggest that CERCLA rejects entirely the crucial limits to liability that are inherent to corporate law."

Applying that test to the facts of this case, the court found it particularly telling that CPC selected Ott II's board of directors and populated its executive ranks with CPC officials, and that a CPC official, G.R.D. Williams, played a significant role in shaping Ott II's environmental compliance policy.

> [W]here a parent corporation is sought to be held liable as an operator pursuant to 42 U.S.C. § 9607(a)(2) based upon the extent of its control of its subsidiary which owns the facility, the parent will be liable only when the requirements necessary to pierce the corporate veil [under state law] are met. In other words ... whether the parent will be liable as an operator depends upon whether the degree to which it controls its subsidiary and the extent and manner of its involvement with the facility, amount to the abuse of the corporate form that will warrant piercing the corporate veil and disregarding the separate corporate entities of the parent and subsidiary.

It is a general principle of corporate law deeply "ingrained in our economic and legal systems" that a parent corporation (so-called because of control through ownership of another corporation's stock) is not liable for the acts of its subsidiary....

But there is an equally fundamental principle of corporate law, applicable to the parent-subsidiary relationship as well as generally, that the corporate veil may be pierced and the shareholder held liable for the corporation's conduct when, inter alia, the corporate form would otherwise be misused to accomplish certain wrongful purposes, most notably fraud, on the shareholder's behalf.

Nothing in CERCLA purports to rewrite this well-settled rule, either. If a subsidiary that operates, but does not own, a facility is so pervasively controlled by its parent for a sufficiently improper purpose to warrant veil piercing, the parent may be held derivatively liable for the subsidiary's acts as an operator.

The fact that a corporate subsidiary happens to own a polluting facility operated by its parent does nothing, then, to displace the rule that the parent "corporation is [itself] responsible for the wrongs committed by its agents in the course of its business." It is this direct liability that is properly seen as being at issue here.

We are satisfied that the Court of Appeals correctly rejected the District Court's analysis of direct liability. But we also think that the appeals court erred in limiting direct liability under the statute to a parent's sole or joint venture operation, so as to eliminate any possible finding that CPC is liable as an operator on the facts of this case.

In imposing direct liability on these grounds, the District Court failed to recognize that "it is entirely appropriate for directors of a parent corporation to serve as directors of its subsidiary, and that fact alone may not serve to expose the parent corporation to liability for its subsidiary's acts."

The Government would have to show that, despite the general presumption to the contrary, the officers and directors were acting in their capacities as CPC officers and directors, and not as Ott II officers and directors, when they committed those acts. The District Court made no such enquiry here, however, disregarding entirely this time-honored common-law rule....

In sum, the District Court's focus on the relationship between parent and subsidiary (rather than parent and facility), combined with its automatic attribution of the actions of dual officers and directors to the corporate parent, erroneously, even if unintentionally, treated CERCLA as though it displaced or fundamentally altered common-law standards of limited liability....

There is, in fact, some evidence that CPC engaged in just this type and degree of activity at the Muskegon plant. The District Court's opinion speaks of an agent of CPC alone who played a conspicuous part in dealing with the toxic risks emanating from the operation of the plant. G.R.D. Williams worked only for CPC; he was not an employee, officer, or director of Ott, and thus, his actions were of necessity taken only on behalf of CPC. The District Court found that "CPC became directly involved in environmental and regulatory matters through the work of ... Williams, CPC's governmental and environmental affairs director. Williams ... became heavily involved in environmental issues at Ott II." He "actively participated in and exerted control over a variety of Ott II environmental matters," and he "issued directives regarding Ott II's responses to regulatory inquiries."

We think that these findings are enough to raise an issue of CPC's operation of the facility through Williams's actions, though we would draw no ultimate conclusion from these findings at this point. Prudence thus counsels us to remand, on the theory of direct operation set out here, for reevaluation of Williams's role, and of the role of any other CPC agent who might be said to have had a part in operating the Muskegon facility.

CONTINUED

The judgment of the Court of Appeals for the Sixth Circuit is vacated, and the case is remanded.

CASE QUESTIONS

1. Describe the corporate ownership history that surrounds the Muskegon facility.

2. What must be shown to hold a parent liable for the actions of the subsidiary? Is CERCLA liability determined under the same corporate veil standards as other issues?

3. Are joint directors of parent and corporate subsidiaries evidence of a need to pierce the corporate veil?

18-4f CORPORATE TAX CONSEQUENCES

The Double-Taxation Cost of Limited Liability

Although corporations have the benefit of limited liability, they have the detriment of double taxation. Not only does the corporation pay taxes on its earnings but shareholders must also report their dividend income on their separate returns and pay individual taxes on their dividend income. However, these shareholders pay taxes only if the dividends are paid. Unlike partnerships in which the partners pay taxes on earnings whether they are distributed or not, shareholders pay taxes on corporate earnings only when they are distributed to them.

Statutory Solutions to Double Taxation

One way to resolve the problem of the cost of double taxation is the S corporation (see p. 601).

18-4g CORPORATE MANAGEMENT AND CONTROL: DIRECTORS AND OFFICERS

Election of Directors

A corporation might be owned by a million shareholders, but its operation will be controlled by the hands of a few, the **board of directors**. The shareholders elect these directors, who serve as the corporate policy makers. The directors also have responsibility for management of the corporation. To that end, the directors usually set up an **executive committee** composed of three board members to handle the more routine matters of running the corporation so that board meetings are not required as frequently.

Role of Directors

Directors are the strategic planning and policy makers for the corporation. They are also the outside perspective for the company. They can provide insight on current management practices. They also serve a watchdog role, as with the now mandatory **audit committees** required of all stock exchange companies. Audit committees, made up of independent outside directors and at least one financial expert under Sarbanes–Oxley, none of whom have any contracts or former salary ties with the company, are responsible for assuring that the financial reports the management issues are accurate.

Institutional investors and other groups have been placing increasing pressure on boards for accountability. Some have developed standards for service on boards such as required stock ownership in the company, nominating committees to assure sufficient business background and knowledge, and term limits so that members do not become complacent. Some companies have procedures for the board to evaluate itself and its performance.

FOR THE MANAGER'S DESK

Re: CEO Compensation

The highest-paid CEOs in 2012 are summarized in the following table.

The pay levels have dropped significantly since the 2008 market crash. All of the investment banking CEOs have dropped off the top 20 list for highest-paid CEOs. For more information, go to the companies' 10-K forms at www.sec.gov/edgar.shtml.

CEO	COMPANY	COMPENSATION ($)
Lawrence J. Ellison	Oracle	96,160,696
Richard Bracken	HCA	38,600,000
Robert A. Iger	Disney	37,100,000
Mark G. Parker	Nike	35,200,000
Philippe P. Dauman	Viacom	33,400,000
John J. Donahoe	eBay	29,700,000
Howard Schultz	Starbucks	28,900,000
Stephen I. Chazen	Occidental Petroleum	28,500,000
Kenneth I. Chenault	American Express	28,000,000
Louis C. Camilleri	Philip Morris International	24,700,000
Robert J. Stevens	Lockheed Martin	23,800,000
Richard D. Fairbank	Capital One	22,600,000
Rupert Murdoch	News Corp.	22,400,000
Louis R. Chenevert	United Technologies	21,800,000
Muhtar Kent	Coca-Cola	21,600,000
James McNerney	Boeing	21,100,000
Randall L. Stephenson	AT&T	21,000,000
Alan Mulally	Ford	21,000,000
Paul E. Jacobs	Qualcomm	20,700,000
Jeff Immelt	General Electric	20,500,000

One area of director responsibility that receives ongoing attention is that of officers' compensation. Directors not only elect the officers of the corporation, they also decide the salaries for these officers and themselves. Some possible reforms are on the horizon. The issue of officer compensation has long been a contentious one for lawmakers and regulators. During the Clinton administration, Congress limited the deductibility of officer compensation to $1 million annually. Under the **Dodd–Frank Wall Street Reform and Consumer Financial Protection Act**, shareholders will have a "say on pay." At least once every three years, shareholders must have the right to cast votes (nonbinding) on executive compensation as well as golden parachutes. In addition, Dodd–Frank requires companies to have "claw-back" provisions giving them the right to take back executive compensation if it was paid as a result of inflated financial reports. The SEC will be promulgating rules on incentive compensation disclosure. In addition to the new Dodd–Frank rights, shareholders can continue to make proposals to limit executive compensation (see Chapter 19 for more information on additional regulation of pay as well as shareholder proposals) and exercise their rights of director removal if the board is not responsive to their concerns about compensation.

Director Liability

Officers and directors are **fiduciaries** of the corporation, which means they are to act in the best interests of the corporation and not profit at the corporation's expense. They are subject to the **business judgment rule**, a standard of corporate behavior under which it is understood that officers and directors can make mistakes, but they are required to show that their decisions were made after careful study and discussion. In those decisions, they may consult experts, such as attorneys, accountants, and financial analysts; but again, they need to show that these experts were well-chosen and reliable individuals.

The *Brehm v Eisner* case (Case 18.4) deals with the business judgment rule and provides the answer for the chapter's opening "Consider..."

| CASE 18.4 | *Brehm v Eisner* |
| | 746 A.2d 244 (Del. 2000) |

Kind of a Mickey-Mouse Judgment Call

FACTS

On October 1, 1995, Michael Eisner, the then CEO and chairman of Disney, hired Michael Ovitz as Disney's president. Mr. Ovitz was a long-time friend of Mr. Eisner. Mr. Ovitz was also an important talent broker in Hollywood. Although he lacked experience managing a diversified public company, other companies with entertainment operations had been interested in hiring him for high-level executive positions. Mr. Ovitz's employment agreement was unilaterally negotiated by Eisner and approved by the board. Since the hiring, there had been shareholder uprisings and director battles that resulted in a shift in the board structure. Eisner had recommended an extraordinarily lucrative contract for Ovitz, with a base salary of $1 million per year, a discretionary bonus, and two sets of stock options (the "A" options and the "B" options) that collectively would enable Ovitz to purchase five million shares of Disney common stock.

Disney needed a strong second-in-command because Mr. Eisner's health, due to major heart surgery, was in question, and there really was no succession plan. Mr. Eisner also had a rugged history when it came to working with important or well-known subordinate executives who wanted to position themselves to succeed him. Over the previous five years, Disney executives Jeffrey Katzenberg, Richard Frank, and Stephen Bollenbach had all left after short tenures under Eisner.

Following a tumultuous year that enjoyed intense media coverage about legendary battles between the two, Mr. Ovitz and Mr. Eisner negotiated Mr. Ovitz's departure on December 11, 1996. Mr. Ovitz was given a "Non-Fault Termination" that carried $38,888,230.77 as well as the option to purchase three million Disney shares under the terms of his employment agreement.

The shareholders (plaintiffs) filed suit against the directors for their failure to adequately consider the Ovitz contract initially, for not considering the issues surrounding that hiring as well as the employment package itself, and for committing waste in giving Ovitz what amounted to a $140 million severance package (when the value of the options were included). The Court of Chancery dismissed the suit and the shareholders appealed.

JUDICIAL OPINION

VEASEY, Chief Justice

This is potentially a very troubling case on the merits. On the one hand, it appears from the Complaint that: (a) the compensation and termination payout for Ovitz

CONTINUED

were exceedingly lucrative, if not luxurious, compared to Ovitz' value to the Company; and (b) the processes of the boards of directors in dealing with the approval and termination of the Ovitz Employment [this is a close case].

This is a case about whether there should be personal liability of the directors of a Delaware corporation to the corporation for lack of due care in the decision-making process and for waste of corporate assets. This case is not about the failure of the directors to establish and carry out ideal corporate governance practices. All good corporate governance practices include compliance with statutory law and case law establishing fiduciary duties. But the law of corporate fiduciary duties and remedies for violation of those duties are distinct from the aspirational goals of ideal corporate governance practices. Aspirational ideals of good corporate governance practices for boards of directors that go beyond the minimal legal requirements of the corporation law are highly desirable, often tend to benefit stockholders, sometimes reduce litigation and can usually help directors avoid liability. But they are not required by the corporation law and do not define standards of liability.

The facts in the Complaint (disregarding conclusory allegations) show that Ovitz' performance as president was disappointing at best, that Eisner admitted it had been a mistake to hire him, that Ovitz lacked commitment to the Company, that he performed services for his old company, and that he negotiated for other jobs (some very lucrative) while being required under the contract to devote his full time and energy to Disney.

All this shows is that the Board had arguable grounds to fire Ovitz for cause. But what is alleged is only an argument—perhaps a good one—that Ovitz' conduct constituted gross negligence or malfeasance.

The Complaint contends that the Board committed waste by agreeing to the very lucrative payout to Ovitz under the non-fault termination provision because it had no obligation to him, thus taking the Board's decision outside the protection of the business judgment rule. Construed most favorably to plaintiffs, the Complaint contends that, by reason of the Board's available arguments of resignation and good

cause, it had the leverage to negotiate Ovitz down to a more reasonable payout than that guaranteed by his Employment Agreement. But the Complaint fails on its face to meet the waste test because it does not allege with particularity facts tending to show that no reasonable business person would have made the decision that the Board made under these circumstances.

The Board made a business decision to grant Ovitz a Non-Fault Termination. Plaintiffs may disagree with the Board's judgment as to how this matter should have been handled. But where, as here, there is no reasonable doubt as to the disinterest of or absence of fraud by the Board, mere disagreement cannot serve as grounds for imposing liability based on alleged breaches of fiduciary duty and waste. There is no allegation that the Board did not consider the pertinent issues surrounding Ovitz's termination. Plaintiffs' sole argument appears to be that they do not agree with the course of action taken by the Board regarding Ovitz's separation from Disney. This will not suffice to create a reasonable doubt that the Board's decision to grant Ovitz a Non-Fault Termination was the product of an exercise of business judgment.

One can understand why Disney stockholders would be upset with such an extraordinarily lucrative compensation agreement and termination payout awarded a company president who served for only a little over a year and who underperformed to the extent alleged. That said, there is a very large—though not insurmountable—burden on stockholders who believe they should pursue the remedy of a derivative suit instead of selling their stock or seeking to reform or oust these directors from office.

Affirmed.

CASE QUESTIONS

1. What must the shareholders prove to recover?

2. What does the court say is the relationship between good corporate governance, liability, and business judgment?

3. What alternatives to litigation do shareholders have?

Officers and directors are also required to follow the **corporate opportunity doctrine**, under which officers and directors may not take an opportunity for themselves that the corporation might be interested in taking. For example, a director of a lumber company who discovers a deal on timberland would be required to present that opportunity to the corporation before she could take it. If the director does not first present the idea to the corporation, a constructive trust is put on the profits the director

Consider...

William Shlensky was a minority shareholder of Chicago National League Ball Club, Inc. (the Cubs). In 1966, he brought suit against the directors of the Cubs for violation of the business judgment rule because at the time of the suit the Cubs did not play night games at Wrigley Field, their home field. All of the other 19 teams in the major leagues had some night games, with substantially all of their weekday and nonholiday games scheduled under the lights. Between 1961 and 1965, the Cubs had sustained operating losses. Mr. Shlensky filed a derivative suit (a suit on behalf of shareholders) against the Cubs' directors for negligence and mismanagement.

Mr. Shlensky's suit maintained that the Cubs would continue to lose money unless night games were played. The directors' response was that baseball was a "daytime" sport and that holding night games would have a "deteriorating effect upon the surrounding neighborhood."

Why does Mr. Shlensky believe the directors did not use good judgment? Is there a difference between negligence and differing business opinions? Does the business judgment rule allow directors to make mistakes?

[*Shlensky v Wrigley*, 237 N.E. 2d 776 (Ill. 1968)]

THINK: Under the principles of liability for directors and the protection of the business judgment rule, a director and board can make mistakes. They can make decisions that ultimately prove to be big mistakes, even in judgment. However, courts do not step in and, with hindsight, second-guess the directors. So long as the directors have given their time, thought, and effort to the decision and obtained independent advice, their judgment is protected from liability to shareholders, even if they are proven completely wrong.

APPLY: While the parties disagree over whether to hold day games or night games, the Cubs organization has articulated its reasons, rightly or wrongly.

ANSWER: The reasons show that the Cubs directors have devoted the time, energy, and thought necessary to make the decision and thus enjoy protection from liability under the business judgment rule.

makes, and the corporation is the beneficiary of that trust. If, however, the director presents the opportunity and the corporation is unable or unwilling to take it, the director may go ahead with the opportunity without the problem of a constructive trust.

Officer Liability

Recent prosecutions have demonstrated an increased effort to hold corporate officers criminally responsible for the acts of the corporation. In environmental law, changes in the law and aggressive prosecutions have brought about convictions of officers, particularly concerning the disposal of hazardous waste. The issues of officer liability are covered in Chapters 8, 11, 17, and 19.

Shareholder Litigation Against Boards and Officers: Derivative Suits

Although boards and officers can be held liable to shareholders when they make missteps without following the business judgment rule, there is a preliminary step that, ironically, requires the shareholders to obtain the go-ahead for filing suit to recoup losses from the company's management. These suits by shareholders are called **derivative suits** because the shareholders have their right to sue derived from their ownership and their recovery belongs to the corporation. There are times, however, when the issue of permission to proceed becomes litigious. One of the longest-running and most contentious shareholder derivative suits is that involving AIG and Hank Greenberg. In *AIG, Inc. v Greenberg*, 965 A.2d 763 (Del. Ch. 2009), the Delaware Chancery court dealt with an issue of shareholders' rights to proceed with a derivative suit against AIG's directors and officers for its inflation of loss reserves through fictional reinsurance transactions. A special litigation committee of the board approved a shareholder suit to recover the losses from the reinsurance scam and even joined with the shareholders in their litigation. The board filed suit demanding that the shareholders obtain approval from the full board. The court held that the shareholders had followed the approval process required under AIG's bylaws and had the right to go forward with their suit and recovery.

Officers, Boards, Sarbanes–Oxley, and Dodd–Frank

Sarbanes–Oxley, the legislation passed following the collapse of companies such as Enron and WorldCom, imposed detailed requirements on boards and officers of publicly traded companies. These reforms imposed new duties beyond any statutory requirements imposed by state corporation laws such as the MBCA. In addition, the passage of the Dodd–Frank Wall Street Reform and Consumer Financial Protection Act has resulted in more regulation of board structure and directors' duties and responsibilities to shareholders.

Prohibitions on Loans to Officers. Corporations can no longer make loans to officers and directors. This provision is the result of revelations that companies such as WorldCom, Adelphia, and others had made hundreds of millions of dollars in loans to their CEOs and other executives because they had pledged their shares in the company for their personal investments. When those investments did not perform well, their shares had to be sold to satisfy the loans. A sell-off of their major holdings would have sent the company's stock into a dive. The result was a vicious circle in which more loans were made in order to prevent the sale of shares, with ever-increasing pressure to keep the share price up in order to satisfy the loans the shares secured.

Codes of Ethics for Financial Reporting. Companies must now have codes of ethics in place for the financial officers of their companies. Even though 97 percent of publicly held companies now have codes of ethics, this provision requires specific content about the standards for financial reporting and accounting in the company. These financial officers are also subject to greater federal penalties for certifying false financial statements (see Chapter 8 for more information on their criminal liability).

Role of Legal Counsel to the Company. In many of the collapsed companies, two of the questions that arose were "Where were the auditors?" and "Where were the lawyers?"[3] As Congress and the SEC grappled with these questions, they imposed extensive disclosure obligations on auditors and accountants (see Chapter 19 for those requirements), but they also imposed reporting requirements on legal counsel for corporations. Under the new requirements, lawyers have several progressive steps in their duties and disclosure requirements:[4]

- A lawyer who suspects material violations must instigate an investigation to determine whether such violations have occurred.
- The lawyer must inform the CEO of the investigation.
- The lawyer must report material violations of the law to the CEO.
- If no action is taken, the lawyer must go "up the ladder" and report the material violations to the audit committee or a group of independent board members.

- Companies must create a legal compliance committee based on the idea of strength in numbers, in that the committee will be told of investigations and findings and can take the matter "up the ladder."
- Because of concerns and objections from the American Bar Association, the SEC did not adopt the so-called noisy withdrawal rule, a process that would have required a lawyer who has found a material violation that the company will not remedy to resign from the company and report the violation to the SEC.

ETHICAL ISSUES

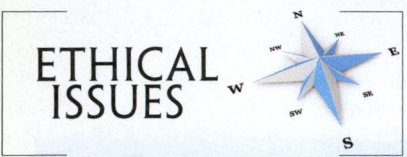

General David Petraeus, a graduate of West Point, a military scholar, and a respected general who is credited with the success of the "surge" operation in Iraq, resigned abruptly as CIA Director following an FBI investigation that uncovered an extramarital affair between the general and his biographer, Paula Broadwell. Both Ms. Broadwell and General Petraeus were married. The FBI investigation began when Jill Kelley, a social liaison at MacDill Air Force Base, began receiving threatening e-mails. When Mrs. Kelley reported the e-mails to the FBI, the agency's investigation linked them to Ms. Broadwell. Upon interviewing Ms. Broadwell and General Petraeus in late October 2012, the FBI uncovered the affair, which both admitted. General Petraeus then resigned as director of the CIA because of the fears regarding national security and, as the general explained, his "extremely poor judgment."

What has unfolded is what would be called in business "a mess." Revelations of affairs by CEOs can cause significant damage for companies, both because of market and shareholder concerns about judgment and stability (which then affects the stock price) and also because the CEOs generally must resign because their leadership ability is questioned by employees who are skeptical about leaders who do not set a good example. Companies that have suffered significant setbacks, including drops in their share prices, because of affairs or alleged harassment that involved their CEOs include Boeing, Best Buy, Stryker Corporation, and Hewlett-Packard.

Prevention is the key, and companies now follow certain best practices that might have helped General Petraeus avoid the trap of personal decadence:

- CEOs should never meet alone with outside vendors. Inappropriate advances and physical contact do not occur when a third party is present. This policy carries additional benefits in that there is always a witness to potential claims about deals and promises.

- CEOs should follow company policies on employee relationships. Most companies have policies that prohibit employees who are in a reporting-line relationship from dating. The companies offer transfers or other accommodations, but they are strict when it comes to disregarding Cupid's arrow if one employee in the relationship reports to the other employee, directly or indirectly. The potential for perceptions of favoritism or resulting harassment are too great.

- CEOs need to understand their vulnerability. An affair leaves the CEO subject to potential blackmailing because the other party has information that the CEO would not want to be disclosed. Ethical compromises or revelations of company inside information often result when a CEO tries to keep relationships and affairs secret. There is also the risk of the so-called "bunny boiler," where the person with whom the CEO has an affair begins harassing the CEO or other employees or friends and relatives.

- Companies understand that there is a fine line between wanted romance and advances and harassment and tend to be strict about policies for employees, including executives and the CEO.

- Companies audit expense reports of CEOs and executives frequently because unexplained expenses in travel and entertainment often lead to revelations about affairs that can then be investigated and ended before company information is compromised.

- Companies monitor e-mails. What you put in an e-mail is discoverable, can be reviewed, and is not private. General Petraeus would have done well to understand this principle of cyberspace.

What effect does a CEO's affair have on the company? Why does an affair leave a company vulnerable? What is the relationship between harassment and office romance?

Role of the Chairman and CEO.   Under Dodd–Frank, companies are required to inform shareholders when the offices of CEO and chairman of the board are combined or separated and provide an explanation for the decision on the role of the two offices or their combination. Some studies indicate that the separation of these two roles resulted in better governance as well as better financial performance. The 2013 shareholder meeting for JPMorgan Chase resulted in a significant battle among shareholders for separating the dual CEO/chairman role of Jamie Dimon.

Role of the Compensation Committee.   Also under Dodd–Frank, board compensation committees must be composed of independent directors, meaning directors who do not have affiliations or contractual relationships with the company. (See p. 611 for more information on the definition of "independent directors.") Board compensation committees that hire consultants (and most publicly traded companies do) must hire those consultants independently of management input, and the consultants must have a direct line of reporting to the compensation committee, not management.

Board Membership.   Under Sarbanes–Oxley, boards must consist of a majority of members who are independent. *Independent* is defined as someone who has not been an officer, employee, or manager of the company during any of the past three years; who is not related to anyone who works for the company; who is not under any type of consulting or remuneration arrangement with the company; and who is not a principal or owner of a company that does business with the board or the company. This independence requirement caused some shake-ups in boards. For example, Kenneth Chenault, the CEO of American Express, was no longer an independent member of IBM's board because IBM does business with American Express. Dodd–Frank expanded independence requirements to compensation committees. Audit committee members must all be independent directors, and at least one member of the audit committee must meet standards for certification as a financial expert.

18-4h   CORPORATE MANAGEMENT AND CONTROL: SHAREHOLDERS

Shareholder Rights: Annual Meetings

Shareholders have the opportunity to express their views at the annual meeting by electing directors who represent their interests. Annual meetings also give shareholders the opportunity to vote on critical corporate issues. Under the MBCA, the failure to hold an annual meeting does not result in dissolution or revocation of corporate status.

Shareholder Rights: Voting

At annual and special meetings, shareholders have the right to vote. Shareholders may vote their own shares or delegate their votes in a variety of ways.

The Proxy.   The most common method of delegating voting authority is the **proxy**, with which shareholders can transfer their right to vote to someone else. This type of vote assignment is temporary. Under the MBCA, a proxy is good only for 11 months, which allows a shareholder to decide to give a different proxy before the next annual meeting. Many shareholder groups solicit proxies to obtain control. Those solicitations are subject to the federal securities laws, and certain disclosures are required (see Chapter 19).

BUSINESS STRATEGY

Governing Corporate Governance

In addition to incorporating the statutory requirements under Sarbanes–Oxley, many companies are adopting new policies and procedures for corporate governance. Some of those changes, policies, and processes are mentioned here as possible strategies for effective governance.

- Some companies have created the position of a corporate ombudsperson who will monitor the audit and ethics committees in their boards and will watch for officer share trading.

- WorldCom paid Richard Breeden, a former chairman of the SEC, to prepare a 149-page report on "Restoring Trust" and will implement all of his recommended changes. The changes are part of the articles of incorporation and now cannot be changed without shareholder approval.

- Tyco is required to submit annual reports on its board and corporate governance processes.

- At some companies, an executive's salary and compensation package cannot exceed $1.5 million without shareholder approval.

- Some companies have agreed to fund university research into effective corporate governance.

Companies are also working to change their board policies and processes beyond the requirements under Sarbanes–Oxley. One company highlighted in the *Wall Street Journal* for its changes is E*TRADE, a company that got a black eye when in 2001 it revealed that its CEO had an $80 million pay package despite significant problems with the company's performance and a plunging share price. The share price had dropped from more than $60 per share to less than $5 per share when the pay package for then–CEO Christos Cotsakos was announced. (He did return $20 million of the package.)

The following changes have taken place at the E*TRADE board:

- Board meetings are now two days in length (they were four hours or fewer).

- All directors must have a three-hour orientation session before beginning their service. (Tyco also now requires this training.)

- The CFO was terminated in June when a financial restatement was necessary.

- All pay packages have been revamped, and bonuses for executives are limited to three times their annual salaries.

- The $14,000-per-month concierge service for employees has ended.

- As leases expire, the company has moved into less expensive office spaces.

- The board members who allowed the compensation package of $80 million have resigned and been replaced.

- The board has open access to all E*TRADE executives.

Ironically, Mr. Cotsakos just received his PhD from the University of London in corporate governance. E*TRADE paid for his degree.

Sources: Susanne Craig, "How One Firm Uses Strict Governance to Fix Its Troubles," *Wall Street Journal*, August 21, 2003, pp. A1, A6; Edward Iwata, "Prosecutors Slap New Rules on Companies," *USA Today*, March 22, 2004, p. 1B.

Pooling Agreements. A method of grouping shareholder votes is the **pooling agreement**, which is a contract among shareholders to vote their shares a certain way or for a certain director. One of the problems with pooling agreements is enforceability: If the agreements are breached, it is really too late to do anything about the breach because the corporation will take the action authorized by the votes or a particular director will take a seat.

Voting Trust. Another form of shareholder cooperation is the **voting trust**. In this form of group voting, shareholders actually turn their shares over to a trustee and are then issued a trust certificate. The shareholders still have the right to dividends and may sell or pledge the certificate. However, the shares remain in the hands of the trustee, and the trustee votes those shares according to the terms of

FOR THE MANAGER'S DESK

Re: The Battles for Silicon Valley Control

© bloomua/Shutterstock.com

Pooling and trust agreements are often used when shareholders are trying to work together to gain control of a company. When Silicon Valley first began, the techie entrepreneurs were willing to sign over majority interests in their companies to venture capitalists because they needed funding. Now, however, many investors are willing to simply buy an interest in the company with the founding entrepreneurs retaining majority control. For example, Mark Zuckerberg holds 57 percent of Facebook's voting shares. The remaining investors become increasingly nervous because young and untested entrepreneurs are running these companies and control the board. The arrangements have been working well because of the profitability. However, if the earnings or strategic picture changes, the investors have little recourse if they are unable to control the controlling CEO. Shareholders and board members have to work together to keep the company moving forward in a positive way so that battles for control do not hamper progress.

the trust agreement. The shareholders get their shares back only when the trust ends. Most states have specific requirements for the voting trust: A copy must be filed with the corporate offices, and some states have a maximum duration (such as 10 years) for such trusts.

Shareholder Rights in Combinations

Because shareholders' interests are involved, corporations are not free to combine at will or to merge or consolidate without shareholder input. All states have procedures for obtaining shareholder approval for business combinations.

The Procedure.   All mergers, consolidations, and sales of assets (other than in the ordinary course of business) must have shareholder approval. Further, that approval must be obtained in a manner prescribed by the MBCA.

- Board resolution. The process of obtaining shareholder approval begins with the board of directors. They must adopt and approve a resolution favoring the merger, consolidation, or asset sale.

- Notice to shareholders. Once the resolution is adopted, it must be sent to the shareholders along with a notice of a meeting for the purpose of taking action on the resolution. A notice is sent to all shareholders regardless of whether they are entitled to vote under the corporation's articles.

- Shareholder approval. The shareholders must then vote to approve the resolution at the announced meeting. In the cases of mergers and consolidations, all shareholders are entitled to vote whether they own voting or nonvoting shares because their interests are affected by the results. The number of votes needed to approve a merger under the MBCA is a majority. However, the articles of incorporation or the bylaws may require more, known as a supermajority.

Shareholder approval is not required for a short-form merger, which is one between a subsidiary and a parent that owns at least 90 percent of the stock of the subsidiary. In the absence of these narrow requirements, the long-form merger provisions of resolution and voting must be followed.

Shareholder Rights: The Dissenting Shareholder

Not all shareholders vote in favor of a merger or a consolidation. Under the MBCA and most state statutes, these **dissenting shareholders** are entitled to their appraisal rights. **Appraisal rights** allow shareholders to demand the value of their shares. Under the MBCA, a dissenting shareholder must file a written objection to the merger or consolidation before the meeting to vote on either is held.

If the merger or consolidation is approved, the corporation must notify dissenting shareholders and offer them the fair value of the shares. Fair value is determined as of the *day before* the action is taken on the merger or consolidation because the action taken will affect the value of the shares. If the dissenting shareholders do not believe the corporation's offer is fair, they can bring suit against the corporation for establishing fair value. However, if the value the corporation offered is found to be fair and the dissenting shareholders' rejection arbitrary, they will be required to pay the corporation's costs of the lawsuit.

Shareholders also enjoy some protections during merger activity that are offered under federal securities laws in terms of notice and disclosure (see Chapter 19).

Some corporations have experienced a **freeze-out**, which is a merger undertaken to get rid of the minority shareholders in a corporation. Although these minority shareholders have their dissenting rights, it is expensive to pursue a court action for a determination of fair value. The majority shareholders are able to buy out, at a low price, the minority shareholders, who are left without a remedy and usually with a loss. For this reason, many courts now impose on majority stockholders a fiduciary duty to the minority stockholders and will prevent a merger without a business purpose from freezing out minority shareholders. Courts, and some state laws (corporate constituency statutes), also require a showing that a merger or consolidation is fair to the minority shareholders. These general terms of "business purpose" and "fairness" are defined on a case-by-case basis.

Shareholder Rights: Inspection of Books and Records

The MBCA gives shareholders the absolute right to examine shareholder lists. For other records (minutes, accounting), shareholders must give notice of their request. In addition to this mechanical requirement, some courts also require a **proper purpose**, which means a shareholder has a legitimate interest in reviewing corporate progress, financial status, and fiduciary responsibilities. Improper purposes are those related to use of corporate records to advance the shareholders' moral, religious, or political ideas.

Shareholder Rights: Transfer of Shares

Stock shares can have **transfer restrictions**, which are valid as long as the following requirements are met.

1. The restrictions must be necessary. Valid circumstances include family-owned corporations, employee-owned corporations, and corporations that need restrictions to comply with SEC registration exemptions (see Chapter 19).

2. The restrictions must be reasonable. Requiring that the shares first be offered to the board before they can be sold is reasonable; requiring that the shares be offered to all the other shareholders first may be unreasonable if there are more than 5 to 10 shareholders.

3. The restrictions and/or their existence must be conspicuously noted on the stock shares.

18-4i   THE DISSOLUTION OF A CORPORATION

A corporation can continue indefinitely unless its articles of incorporation limit its duration. Long before perpetuity, however, a corporation can be dissolved voluntarily or involuntarily.

Voluntary Dissolution

Voluntary dissolution occurs when the shareholders agree to dissolve the corporation. This type of dissolution occurs in smaller corporations when the shareholders no longer get along, the business does not do well, or one of the shareholders is ill or dies.

A voluntary dissolution begins with a resolution by the board of directors, which is then put before the shareholders at a special meeting called for that purpose. Under the MBCA, all shareholders (voting and nonvoting alike) vote on the issue of dissolution because all of them will be affected by it. Once the shareholders pass the resolution (a majority or two-thirds vote in most states), the assets of the corporation are liquidated, and debts and shareholders are paid in the order of their priorities. Each state also has filing and publication requirements for dissolution.

Involuntary Dissolution

An involuntary dissolution is forced by some state agency, usually the state attorney's office. A dissolution can be forced because of fraud or failure to follow state law regarding reporting requirements for corporations.

18-5   Limited Liability Companies

The **limited liability company (LLC)**, first created in 1977, is the newest form of business structure and is now available in 48 states and the District of Columbia. The LLC has been in existence for many years in Europe (known as a GMBH) and South America (*limitada*). The LLC is more of an aggregate form of business organization than an entity such as a corporation. Owners of an LLC are called members. An LLC provides limited liability (members lose only up to their capital contributions) and flow-through tax treatment similar to a partnership in that tax liability is assessed only at the member's level of income and not at the business level. An LLC is not a corporation or a partnership. It can be taxed as a partnership, with limited liability for all its owners, unlike a limited partnership, and all personal owners can participate in management without risking liability.

It has been said that the LLC combines the best of all of the business structures: limited liability for the owners, flexibility in management in that all the owners can participate in management, and flow-through of the income directly to personal profits and losses and resulting tax liability. However, this ideal creation, in order to enjoy the flow-through characteristics necessary for the tax break, must be distinguished from a corporation. The result is that LLCs are limited in duration, with most statutes allowing them to run for periods of 30 to 40 years. The point at which LLCs dissolve by statutory limitations has not yet arrived because LLCs did not exist until 1977. However, when those dissolutions come, the restructuring and re-creation should create interesting issues among and between the owners of the LLCs.

18-5a   FORMATION

An LLC is formed through the filing of a document called the articles of organization, which is filed with a centralized state agency. The name of the business formed must contain either "limited liability company," "L.L.C.," or "LLC."

18-5b SOURCES OF FUNDING

Members of an LLC make capital contributions in much the same way as partners make capital contributions.

18-5c LIABILITY

Members of an LLC have limited liability; the most they can lose is their capital contributions. Debts belong to the LLC, and creditors' rights lie with the LLC's assets, not the personal assets of the members. However, many states require that the nature of the business organization appear on the business cards and stationery of the company so that members of the public are not misled about the nature of the business as well as the nature of the limited liability of the owners.

Consider...

Larry Clark and David Lanham formed a limited liability company in Colorado called Preferred Income Investors, LLC (PII). All of the necessary paperwork for the creation of an LLC had been filed with the secretary of state, as required by Colorado statute.

   Mr. Clark negotiated with a Westec representative about doing construction work for PII on a Taco Cabana restaurant the LLC was building. Mr. Clark gave the Westec rep his card, which had PII's name above Mr. Clark's name. Westec drew up a contract that was never signed by anyone from PII. However, Mr. Clark gave oral authorization for the work, and Westec completed it. PII did not have the assets to pay the bill for the work, and Westec sued to hold Mr. Clark liable for the contract.

   Mr. Clark said that as an owner of a limited liability company, he had no personal liability. Westec says it was never made aware that PII was an LLC and that it should have been given that information in advance. Is Mr. Clark personally liable?

[*Water, Waste, & Land, Inc., dba Westec v Lanham*, 995 P.2d 997 (Colo. 1998)]

Business Planning Tip

Getting LLC Tax Status

If an LLC is not created according to both state law and IRS guidelines, the tax benefits can be lost. The IRS has issued guidelines on the four characteristics of an LLC entitled to pass-through or flow-through status. An LLC must not have more than two of the following: limited liability for members, continuity, free transferability of interests, and no centralized management.

18-5d TAX CONSEQUENCES

The LLC enjoys the so-called flow-through treatment: The LLC does not pay taxes; income and losses are passed through to the members to be reported on their individual returns. LLC agreements must be drafted carefully to enjoy flow-through status.

18-5e MANAGEMENT AND CONTROL

Members of an LLC adopt an operating agreement that specifies the voting rights, withdrawal rights and issues, responsibilities of members, and how the LLC is to be managed. The members can agree to manage collectively, delegate authority to one member, or hire an outsider to manage the business.

18-5f TRANSFERABILITY OF INTEREST

A member's LLC interest is personal property and is transferable. However, the transferee does not become a member without approval by the majority of members. Members do not hold title to LLC property; the LLC owns the property, and each member has an interest in the LLC that reflects the property's value. Further, the owners of the LLC should structure their LLC and its operation in order to address their tax status issues.

FOR THE MANAGER'S DESK

Re: Stephen Baldwin and his LLC with Kevin Costner

Stephen Baldwin and his friend, Spyridon Contogouris, along with Kevin Costner were investors in Ocean Therapy Solutions, LLC, a company that had developed oil-separating centrifuges. These devices "eat up" the oil from spills and do so quickly enough to halt damage.

Following the April 2010 explosion at the BP Deepwater Horizon rig, BP officials met with Mr. Costner and other Ocean Therapy representatives to determine whether the centrifuges would work on the Gulf spill. As a result of the meeting, BP contracted with Ocean Therapy to spend $52 million on the devices. BP made a deposit of $18 million upon signing the contract.

At about the same time that Ocean Therapy and Mr. Costner were negotiating with BP, Mr. Baldwin and Mr. Contogouris were negotiating to sell their interests in Ocean Therapy Solutions. The two sold their interests for about $2 million ($1.4 million for Mr. Baldwin and $500,000 for Mr. Contogouris). However, they were unaware of the negotiations with BP. After they learned of the BP contract, Mr. Baldwin and Mr. Contogouris filed suit against Mr. Costner seeking an additional $21 million for the value of their interests.

The case went to trial in New Orleans and the jury deliberated for two hours before returning a verdict in favor of Mr. Costner. The jury concluded that Mr. Costner was not aware that Mr. Baldwin and Mr. Contogouris were seeking a buyout. Mr. Costner did use funds from the BP deposit to buy out the two. However, Mr. Baldwin and Mr. Contogouris had put very little cash into the company and the $2 million represented a substantial return on their investment.

Limited liability companies can place management responsibilities in the hands of one owner, as Ocean Therapy Solutions did with Mr. Costner. There is a fiduciary duty between the owners of the LLC and also between the managing owner and the "silent" owners, but daily disclosures of ongoing negotiations and contracts are not required. The jury concluded that Mr. Costner was not aware of the knowledge of Mr. Baldwin and Mr. Contogouris and could have assumed that they thought the buyout was fair, given their initial investment, even with the BP contract.

The lessons learned from the Costner experience are the importance of regular reporting of financials and transactions to owners as well as careful disclosures at the time of any buyouts of owners.

18-5g DISSOLUTION AND TERMINATION

Most LLC statutes provide that the LLC dissolves upon the withdrawal, death, or expulsion of a member. Some states permit judicial dissolution, and all states permit voluntary dissolution upon unanimous (usually written) consent of the owners.

LLC agreements can dictate terms, timing, and results of dissolution, as well as the rights of withdrawing partners.

18-6 Limited Liability Partnerships

A **limited liability partnership (LLP)** is a partnership with unique statutory protection for all its members.

18-6a FORMATION

Not all states have LLP statutes, but those with such statutes have strict formal requirements for the creation of an LLP. The failure to comply with these requirements results in a general partnership with full personal liability for all the partners. The general requirements for LLP registration are filing (1) the name of the LLP (which must include LLP or Reg LLP), (2) the name of the registered agent, (3) the address, (4) the number of partners, and (5) a description of the business.

18-6b SOURCES OF FUNDING

As in partnerships and limited partnerships, LLP partners make capital contributions.

18-6c LIABILITY

In most of the states with LLP statutes, partners are shielded from liability for the negligence, wrongful acts, or misconduct of their partners. Other states provide more extensive protection, such as limited liability even for debts entered into by other partners. In order to attain this liability limitation, some states require, upon registration, evidence of adequate liability insurance. In some states, professional negligence by partners is not covered by the shield from liability.

18-6d TAX CONSEQUENCES

All LLP income is a flow-through or pass-through to partners.

18-6e MANAGEMENT AND CONTROL

Partners can manage without risking personal liability exposure because the LLP is identified as such and registered with the state.

18-6f TRANSFERABILITY

For tax and security regulation reasons, the transferability must be restricted and is generally governed by the same principles of transfer for limited partnerships.

18-6g DISSOLUTION AND TERMINATION

Causes similar to those for the dissolution of limited partnerships and notification to the state are required.

18-7 International Issues in Business Structure

Global trade has resulted in global business structures, with many companies discovering the benefits of **joint ventures**. A joint venture is a partnership of existing businesses for a limited time or a limited purpose. The existing businesses are then partners for that limited transaction or line of business. The Justice Department has relaxed antitrust merger rules to permit joint ventures so that U.S. firms can compete more effectively internationally. For example, Mobil and Exxon formed a joint venture for oil exploration in Russia. The joint venture allows the combination of their experience and financing so that Russian negotiators can be persuaded to contract for the exploration rights.

In an attempt to break into the Japanese toy market, Toys "Я" Us, Inc., entered into a joint venture with McDonald's Co., Ltd., a Japanese toy company with 20 percent of the market. Nestlé and Coca-Cola formed a joint venture to market ready-to-drink coffees and teas; Nestlé's expertise is in dry goods (instant coffee) and Coca-Cola is a beverage company, so each plans to take advantage of the other's established reputation.

Business structures vary in other countries. In Germany, for example, a public company has both a board of directors and a shareholder advisory committee, which elects the board of directors. It is quite likely, however, that the shareholder advisory committee is composed of shareholders that are large institutional investors (such as banks) or representatives from labor unions.

BIOGRAPHY

Hank Greenberg: The Disgruntled and Former AIG CEO

Maurice R. "Hank" Greenberg was the formidable CEO of AIG, the largest insurer in the United States, for nearly four decades. Mr. Greenberg was removed from his position when the SEC raised issues regarding the company's accounting practices and the accuracy of its financial statements. Mr. Greenberg settled fraud charges with the SEC for $15 million, but he denied any wrongdoing. In addition, AIG filed suit against Mr. Greenberg for breach of his fiduciary duty as chairman for taking over $4 billion in AIG stock and placing it in another company, known as Starr International, as a means of providing under-the-SEC-radar compensation for top performers in AIG. The suit alleged that Mr. Greenberg had exceeded his authority as CEO and chairman and that the funneling off of the stock required board knowledge and approval. The jury, however, found that Mr. Greenberg had not violated his fiduciary duty and was not required to reimburse AIG for the shares that were siphoned off into the separate company. Mr. Greenberg argued that the shares were all used as a means of compensation for AIG top performers.

AIG shareholders also brought a derivative action against the board, Mr. Greenberg, and others. While Mr. Greenberg continues to maintain that he did nothing wrong, the allegations in the complaint and the opinion of the judge who heard the shareholders' case tell a different story.

According to the suit, AIG embarked on illegal activities at the direction and under the control of Mr. Greenberg. Mr. Greenberg and a core "inner circle" directly oversaw all aspects of AIG's business and kept a close watch on their subordinates. Greenberg's inner circle consisted of a small group of long-time AIG executives whom Greenberg rewarded with very lucrative compensation packages.

Most of the wrongdoing the shareholders have alleged involved action by AIG insiders to misstate AIG's financial performance in order to deceive investors into believing that AIG was more prosperous and secure than it really was. The single largest act of deception alleged involved a fraudulent $500 million reinsurance transaction in which various AIG insiders staged an elaborate artificial transaction with Gen Re Corporation. Four Gen Re executives and one AIG executive either were convicted or entered guilty pleas to criminal charges related to this transaction. Although AIG portrayed the transaction as providing Gen Re with

reinsurance, in reality the transaction had no substance and was simply staged to make AIG's balance sheet look better. In other instances, AIG insiders allegedly used secret offshore subsidiaries to mask AIG losses, blatantly misstated accounts with no basis for their adjustments, failed to correct well-documented accounting problems in an AIG subsidiary, and hid AIG's involvement in controversial insurance policies that involved betting on when elderly people would die.

Eventually, all of these schemes were uncovered. As a result, AIG was forced to restate years of financial statements, eventually reducing stockholder equity by $3.5 billion. AIG still faces litigation and regulatory proceedings on a number of fronts, an ongoing process that has already required the corporation to pay over $1.6 billion in fines and other costs necessary to resolve proceedings against it. Further, AIG became a central figure in the financial market collapses in 2008 because it was the insurer for the elaborate mortgage-backed instruments of Goldman Sachs, Bear Stearns, Lehman Brothers, Citigroup, and other investment banks that sought their payments when the real estate market collapsed and those instruments became toxic as well. One expert has concluded that AIG's legal saga will never end.

In the center of all the legal controversy and questions about AIG's business strategy and corporate governance is Mr. Greenberg. With each regulatory action and suit, Mr. Greenberg walks away with a relatively small fine and, often, vindication as regulators, prosecutors, and shareholders try to cobble together some violation of the law. A story from his youth offers some insight into his ethical philosophy. When he was stationed in London during World War II, the United States and its military command were concerned about the impression the soldiers left and their conduct. They also recognized the need for the soldiers to have some recreation. The commanding officers gave the soldiers extra leave days if they used them for cultural events. The commanding officers had the theater, the symphony, and the ballet in mind as culture, not the usual activities for leave, such as drinking and chasing women (and, all too often, catching the women). The only requirement for the extra leave day was that the soldiers had to bring back a playbill or program from whatever cultural event they had attended. Mr. Greenberg would buy a ticket to the theater, go in, collect the playbill, and then head out the side exit to spend the time on the types of activities the commanders were trying to have the soldiers avoid, to wit, carousing. Mr. Greenberg had his proof of cultural activities, but he also had his usual fun.

The litigation against Mr. Greenburg is still proceeding as of 2013, including both the shareholder action and an enduring suit brought by the state of New York.

Discussion Questions

1. Did Mr. Greenberg violate any rules as a soldier? As a board chairman and CEO? Isn't the lack of clarity on

the part of his commanding officers what caused the problem? What's wrong with using a loophole in the system?

2. The following is an excerpt from an editorial Mr. Greenberg wrote for the *Wall Street Journal*: "So, in order to stay out of the crosshairs of government regulators, companies are avoiding risks they might otherwise take to innovate or grow their businesses: 'Keep your head down.'" What does Mr. Greenberg believe is the impact of regulation? Is he correct?

Source: Maurice R. Greenberg, "Regulation, Yes. Strangulation, No," *Wall Street Journal*, August 21, 2006, p. A10.

Summary

What are the various forms of business organization?

- Sole proprietorship—individual ownership and operation of a business

- Partnership—voluntary association of two or more persons as co-owners in a business for profit

- Corporation—an entity formed by statute that has the rights of a legal person along with limited liability for its shareholder owners

- Limited liability company—newer form of business organization in which liability is limited except for conduct that is illegal

- Limited liability partnership—newest form of business organization, in which partners' liability is limited

How is a partnership formed and operated?

- Uniform Partnership Act (UPA)—law on partnerships adopted in 49 states

- Revised Uniform Partnership Act (RUPA)—update of partnership law

- Partnership by implication—creation of a partnership by parties' conduct

- Partnership by estoppel—partnership that arises by perception of third parties of its existence

- Dissolution—when partner ceases to be associated with the partnership

- Limited partnership—partnership with two types of partners: general and limited

- General partner—full and personal liability partner

- Limited partner—partner whose personal liability is limited to capital contributions

- Uniform Limited Partnership Act (ULPA)—uniform law adopted in nearly every state

- Revised Uniform Limited Partnership Act (RULPA)—update of limited partnership law

- Advances—partners' loans to partnership

How is a corporation formed and operated?

- Corporation—business organization that is a separate entity with limited liability and full transferability

- Domestic corporation—a corporation is domestic in the state in which its incorporation is filed

- Foreign corporation—category or label for corporation in all states except in state in which it is incorporated

- Professional corporation—entity with limited liability except for malpractice/negligence by its owners

- S corporation—IRS category of corporation with flow-through characteristics

- Model Business Corporation Act (MBCA)—uniform law adopted in approximately one-third of the states

- Articles of incorporation—document filed to organize a corporation

- Common stock—generally most voluminous type of corporate shares and usually allows shareholders to vote

- Preferred stock—ownership interest with priority over common stock

- Corporate veil—liability shield for corporate owners

- Watered shares—failure to pay par value for shares

- Business judgment rule—standard of liability for directors

- Corporate opportunity doctrine—fiduciary responsibility of directors with respect to investments
- Board of directors—policy-setting body of corporations
- Derivative suits—right of shareholder to recoup losses from those who made decisions not guided by proper process
- Proxy—right to vote for another
- Pooling agreement—shareholder contract to vote a certain way
- Voting trust—separation of legal and equitable title in shares to ensure voting of shares in one way
- Dissenting shareholder—shareholder who objects to merger

- Appraisal rights—value of shares immediately before merger that is paid to dissenting shareholder

How is a limited liability company formed?

- Articles of organization
- Flow-through of income

How is a limited liability partnership formed?

- Register with state
- Flow-through of income
- May need proof of liability insurance

Questions and Problems

1. Gailey, Inc., incorporated in 1980, removed asbestos and mechanical insulation on contract jobs that required union labor. Richard Gailey had been the president, controlling shareholder, and director of Gailey, Inc., from its inception.

Universal Labs, Inc., was incorporated by Mr. Gailey in March 1984 to analyze asbestos samples and air samples and to perform general laboratory work. Mr. Gailey was the sole shareholder of Universal Labs.

As president and director of Gailey, Inc., Mr. Gailey directed Gailey to pay certain debts of Universal Labs. Subsequent to that, Gailey, Inc., provided $14,500 to Universal Labs to pay for the latter's start-up expenses and costs.

Gailey, Inc., filed a voluntary petition pursuant to Chapter 11 of the Bankruptcy Code on January 28, 1985.

The case was converted to a Chapter 7 proceeding on September 30, 1985.

The trustee in bankruptcy filed suit alleging that Mr. Gailey usurped a corporate business opportunity belonging to Gailey, Inc., when he incorporated Universal Labs. Is the trustee correct? [*In re Gailey, Inc.,* 119 B.R. 504 (Bankr. W.D. Pa. 1990)]

2. Former Governor J. Fife Symington of Arizona was, during the 1980s, a director of Southwest Savings & Loan, a federal thrift headquartered in Phoenix. Mr. Symington was also a developer who constructed two major commercial projects in Phoenix, with Southwest Savings & Loan providing the loans for development. Southwest was a victim of the 1980s downturn and was taken over by the Resolution Trust Corporation (RTC). The RTC brought suit against Mr. Symington, alleging that he took advantage of his board position to obtain the loans. Mr. Symington said he was required to present the projects to the Southwest Board as part of the corporate opportunity doctrine and Southwest took the investment. Who is correct?

3. Aztec Enterprises, Inc., was incorporated in Washington with a capital contribution of $500. Aztec's incorporator and sole stockholder was H. B. Hunting. Aztec operated a gravel-hauling business and was plagued with persistent working capital problems. Carl Olson, a frequent source of loans for Aztec, eventually acquired the firm. Mr. Olson, who had no corporate minutes or tax returns, personally paid Aztec's lease fees but did not pay when he had Aztec deliver gravel to his personal construction sites. Mr. Olson never had stock certificates issued to him. Despite annual gross sales of more than $800,000, Aztec was unable to pay its debts. Truckweld Equipment Company, a creditor of Aztec, brought suit to pierce the corporate veil and recover its debt from Mr. Olson. Can it pierce the corporate veil? [*Truckweld Equipment Co. v Olson*, 618 P.2d 1017 (Wash. 1980)]

4. The Community Youth Center (CYC) corporation failed to pay its annual registration fee in 2000 and was automatically dissolved by the State Corporation Commission. CYC continued to operate as a corporation. In fact, in 2005, it obtained a loan from the First Community Bank to finance a swimming pool at its facility. The loan was signed by officers of the corporation and was secured by property owned by CYC.

CYC defaulted on the loan and First Community Bank foreclosed on the CYC property that was subject to the mortgage. First Community purchased the property at a foreclosure sale. CYC challenged the foreclosure on the grounds that the president, vice president, and treasurer of CYC had no authority to enter into the 2005 loan agreement because CYC's corporate status had been terminated and it no longer existed as a corporation. The bank responded that CYC had continued to hold itself out as a corporation and that it relied on that existence in making the loan. What should the court hold in this case and why? [*First Community Bank, N.A. v Community Youth Center*, 2010 WL 8696179 (Va. Cir. Ct. 2010)]

5. Allan Jones sold a ski shop franchise to Edward Hamilton. Although Mr. Jones did not contribute equity to the business or share in the profits, he did give Mr. Hamilton advice and share his experience to help him get started. Most of Mr. Hamilton's capital came in the form of a loan from Union Bank. When Mr. Hamilton failed to pay, Union Bank sued Mr. Jones for payment under the theory that Mr. Jones was a partner by implication or estoppel. Was he? [*Union Bank v Jones*, 411 A.2d 1338 (Vt. 1980)]

6. Heritage Hills (a land development firm) was organized on July 2, 1975, as a limited partnership, but the partnership agreement was never properly filed. Heritage Hills went bankrupt, and the bankruptcy trustee has sought to recover the debts owed by the partnership from the limited partners. Can he? [*Heritage Hills v Zion's First Nat'l Bank*, 601 F.2d 1023 (9th Cir. 1979)]

7. In June 1985, Carolyn Boose sought the dental services of Dr. George Blakeslee, who proposed to fill two cavities in her teeth. As part of the procedure, he administered nitrous oxide to Ms. Boose. She was rendered semiconscious by the drug and while she was in this state, Dr. Blakeslee lifted her shirt and fondled one of her breasts. He was subsequently charged with, and pled guilty to, the crime of indecent liberties.

Prior to the incident in question, Dr. Blakeslee had incorporated his dental practice as a professional services corporation. He was the corporation's sole shareholder, officer, and director. The corporation thereafter executed an employment agreement with Dr. Blakeslee, who signed the agreement both as an employee of the corporation and as its president.

At the time of the incident in question, Dr. Blakeslee and the corporation were covered by an insurance policy with Standard Fire Insurance Company that provided general and professional liability coverage. The general liability portion of the policy provided coverage for bodily injury or property damage caused by an "occurrence" arising out of the use of the insured premises. The insurance contract defined "occurrence" as "an accident, including continuous or repeated exposure to conditions, which results in bodily injury or property damage *neither expected nor intended by the insured*."

The professional liability portion of the policy limited coverage to damages for "injury…arising out of the rendering of or failure to render, during the policy period, professional services by the individual insured, or by any person for whom acts or omissions such insured is legally responsible… ."

In November 1985, Ms. Boose commenced an action against Dr. Blakeslee and the professional services corporation for the damages she allegedly sustained as a result of his conduct. Standard subsequently commenced a declaratory judgment action against Ms. Boose and Dr. Blakeslee in order to obtain a declaration of its rights and duties in connection with the lawsuit by Ms. Boose against Dr. Blakeslee and the corporation. All parties moved for summary judgment. The trial court granted judgment to Standard, concluding that it had no duty to defend or indemnify the insured (that is, Dr. Blakeslee and the corporation) against Ms. Boose's claim. Should the corporate veil be pierced to hold Dr. Blakeslee liable? [*Standard Fire Insurance Co. v Blakeslee*, 771 P.2d 1172 (Wash. 1989)]

8. The Orleans Parish School Board hired Johnson & Higgins (J & H) to provide consulting services. J & H provided those services over the next few years but was then acquired by Marsh & McLennan, a larger insurance firm. Marsh continued the work that J & H had been doing and submitted an invoice to the Orleans Parish School Board for reimbursement. The Board said that it had no contractual arrangement with Marsh and, as such, was not liable for the services. Is the Board correct? Describe what happened in the relationships and apply the principles of corporate law to determine whether Marsh can be paid. [*Marsh Advantage America v Orleans School Board*, 995 So. 2d (La. App. 2008)]

9. The Trapp Family Lodge, Inc. (TFL), was incorporated in 1962 as a holding company for certain assets of the Von Trapp family, including the Trapp Family Lodge, a resort hotel in Stowe, Vermont, and other assets, including certain royalty rights related to the family's story as portrayed in a Broadway musical and movie, *The Sound of Music*.

A majority of TFL shareholders approved a merger with a new corporation in 1994, and the merger took place on January 28, 1995. The dissenting shareholders, holding 75,629 of the corporation's 198,000 outstanding shares, were paid $33.84 per share as fair value by the TFL board of directors. The dissenting shareholders brought suit seeking a higher price as fair value. After the trial court set the fair value of $63.44, TFL appealed. What are the rights of dissenting shareholders who object to a merger? [*In re 75,629 Shares of Common Stock of Trapp Family Lodge*, 725 A.2d 927 (Vt. 1999)]

10. A. W. Ham Jr. served on the board of directors for Golden Nugget, Inc., a Nevada corporation. In 1969, while Mr. Ham was a director and legal counsel for Golden Nugget, he obtained a leasehold interest with an option to purchase in the California Club. The California Club is at 101 Fremont Street, Las Vegas, Nevada, and is located next to a series of properties on which Golden Nugget operates its casinos. Mr. Ham leased the property from his former wife. Golden Nugget was looking for property to expand and had, in fact, been expanding onto other lots in the area. Was there a breach of a corporate opportunity? What if Mr. Ham offers to lease the property to Golden Nugget? [*Ham v Golden Nugget, Inc.*, 589 P.2d 173 (Nev. 1979)]

HR & THE LAW

Who Says What the CEO Makes?

The so-called "say-on-pay" legislation has been kicking around Congress for a number of sessions and now, with the passage of the Dodd–Frank Wall Street Reform and Consumer Financial Protection Act, shareholders will have an advisory vote on executive compensation. Steve Hafner, the CEO of Kayak (a travel search engine), explained, "I wonder if the congressmen backing this legislation would propose similar laws governing their own compensation. I'd love to vote on congressional pay and perks."[5]

There are concerns on both sides about CEO pay. From the investors' perspective, the concerns are the following:

- Increases in pay and bonuses despite poor performance of the company and its stock

- Failure of the board to provide independent oversight on compensation

- The say-on-pay is not binding; directors can take the advice of shareholders or go against it (but they are elected by the same shareholders)

- Say-on-pay takes away shareholder frustration with the process

- In companies that are already allowing shareholders a say on pay, the shareholders appear to be fairly reasonable. For example, at Aflac, 93 percent of the shareholders voted in 2008 in favor of the multimillion-dollar pay package for CEO Dan Amos. His pay approval package rate rose to 97 percent of the shareholders in 2009 after Amos turned down the $2.8 million bonus he was entitled to under the 2008 approval.

The CEO's perspective is the following:

- There are concerns about shareholders micromanaging the company.

- There are concerns that some shareholders are fairly sophisticated and may, through the say-on-pay approval process, force CEOs into making decisions that carry a very short-term focus for the company that can prove harmful in the long run.

- This type of micro-regulation could result in a talent pool drain in what is now an international marketplace; it would allow CEOs to go to companies not subject to U.S. regulation.

- The say-on-pay rule would be another impetus for companies to go private, where there would be less transparency on true market performance.

- Say-on-pay does not promote a dialogue between management and shareholders that could bring about more meaningful self-reform on pay packages.

How will the advisory vote work? Could companies go further and ask for shareholder ratification as a required step for compensation packages? How would this work from a governance perspective? Are the roles of shareholders and managers blending together? Do you believe the advisory vote that is now law will evolve into something more?

Notes

1. This case created a bit of a tussle between the Michigan Court of Appeals and its Supreme Court. Following this decision and remand, the Court of Appeals found that there was no partnership because the parties had to be aware of it to be liable, thus defying the Michigan Supreme Court. On appeal, the Michigan Supreme Court reversed the Court of Appeals, 668 N.W.2d 909 (Mich. 2003), not offering an opinion but explaining it was reversing for the reasons stated in the dissenting opinion at the Court of Appeals on the second round.

2. Note how the court traces the history of the law of partnership. Instructors should refer to the *Instructor's Manual* for more information on the history of business organizations.

3. The questions were actually a resurrection of questions asked by Judge Stanley Sporkin when he was dealing with all of the fraud cases from the savings and loan collapses in the early 1990s. [*Lincoln Savings & Loan Ass'n v Wall*, 743 F. Supp. 901, at 920 (D.D.C. 1990)]

4. The final rules can be found at 17 C.F.R. § 205 (2013).

5. Del Jones, "CEOs Openly Pull Against Say-on-Pay," *USA Today*, July 16, 2009, p. 1B.

Chapter 19

GOVERNANCE AND REGULATION:
Securities Law

One method for raising the capital needed for a corporation or partnership is to sell interests in it. Corporations sell shares, and partnerships sell limited partnership interests. Investors provide the capital these businesses need to operate. They give the businesses their money to work with and in return are given an interest in the business. The investors' hope is that the business will give them a profit on their investment (dividends on stock and interest income on bonds and other forms of securities) and that the value of their investment will grow as the business in which they have invested increases in value (which provides them with capital gains). The investment arrangement in theory is mutually beneficial. However, because people are so eager to have their money grow and because businesses need money for growth, the interests of business and investors are often at odds. Because of this inherent conflict of interest in the investment relationship, laws regulate investments at both state and federal levels. These laws, called securities laws, govern everything from the sale of securities to soliciting proxies from owners of securities. Within these laws are mandatory governance standards. This chapter answers these questions: Why do we have securities laws, and what is their history? What requirements affect primary offerings of securities? How do securities laws regulate the secondary market? How do those laws protect shareholders in share and company acquisitions?

UPDATE
For up-to-date legal news, go to **mariannejennings.com**

Consider...

Matrixx Initiatives, Inc., the maker of Zicam Cold Remedy, began receiving questions from physicians in December 1999 about whether Zicam could cause anosmia (loss of sense of smell). Researchers at medical facilities contacted Matrixx in 2002 to offer access to studies showing that zinc sulfate (present in Zicam) was linked to anosmia. Despite these inquiries and the release of a study linking Zicam to anosmia, Matrixx executives continued to release upbeat earnings predictions through most of 2003, with no discussion about the anosmia Zicam side effects.

In November 2003, Matrixx disclosed that it was facing product liability suits from customers who experienced anosmia after using Zicam. In 2004, the Food and Drug Administration (FDA) announced its investigation into Zicam and anosmia. Matrixx's stock price fell by almost $2 per share. A group of shareholders filed suit against Matrixx and its executives for violation of Section 10(b) of the Securities Exchange Act because the company misled them about the safety of the company's product. By 2009, the FDA warned consumers about using Zicam and anosmia and ordered the product pulled from the shelves.

Can the shareholders recover for the loss in their stock value and their reliance on management's rosy picture during 2003?

19-1 History of Securities Law

Although most people think of the market crash of 1929 as the beginning of securities regulation, regulation actually began nearly 20 years earlier at the state level. In 1911, Kansas passed the first securities law, which regulated the initial sale of securities to members of the public. Some states followed the lead of Kansas, but until 1929 the field of securities was relatively free of regulation.

At that time, investors were engaging in a great deal of speculation in stocks. Investors traded "on margin," which means they borrowed money to invest in a stock and when the stock went up in value, they sold it, paid off the loan, and still made money. On a Friday in 1929, however, stock prices dropped on all the exchanges and continued to drop. Investors defaulted on the margin loans, lenders foreclosed on their properties, and the entire country was thrown into a depression.

Because of the 1929 market crash, Congress perceived a problem with the investment market. As a result, the **Securities Act of 1933** and the **Securities Exchange Act of 1934** were passed, the former to regulate initial sales of stock by businesses and the latter to regulate the secondary trading of stock on the markets. These statutes, as amended, and their accompanying regulations still govern the sale of securities today.

19-2 Primary Offering Regulation: The 1933 Securities Act

A **primary offering**—an offering by an issuer, which could be its first, known as an initial public offering (IPO)—is a sale of securities by the business itself. The 1933 act regulates these initial sales of securities.

19-2a WHAT IS A SECURITY?

The 1933 act applies only to the sale of **securities**. The language of the act itself is broad in the definition of *securities*, and approximately 20 items are considered securities, including notes; stock; bonds; debentures; warrants; subscriptions; voting trust certificates; rights to oil, gas, and minerals; and limited partnership interests. Every investment contract that gives the owner evidence of indebtedness or business participation is a security.

In interpreting the application of the 1933 act, the courts have been liberal. The landmark case on the definition of a security is *SEC v W. J. Howey Co.*, 328 U.S. 293 (1946). In holding that the sale of interests in Florida citrus groves constituted the sale of securities, the U.S. Supreme Court defined a security as "a contract, transaction, or scheme whereby a person invests his money in a common enterprise and is led to expect profits solely from the efforts of a promoter or a third party." With this even broader definition than the actual 1933 act language, known as the *Howey* **test**, courts have been reluctant to impose restrictions on the definition of a security. In recent years, the only type of arrangement the U.S. Supreme Court has excluded from this definition is an employer pension plan in which employees are not required to make contributions. The exclusion of these plans from securities laws is probably based on the fact that employees are afforded other statutory protections (see Chapter 20 and the discussion of the Employment Retirement Income Security Act and the Pension Protection Act of 2006).

Consider...

Determine whether general partnership interests would be considered securities for purposes of the 1933 Securities Act.

THINK: The *Howey* definition is that securities are investments in a common enterprise with profits to come from the efforts of others.

APPLY: Even though partnerships are investments in a common enterprise, we learned in Chapter 18 that each partner is required to contribute work and effort to the partnership. General partners, unless otherwise specified, are not paid salaries for their work and effort in making the partnership work. Because of this obligation to work and the full liability exposure, the results from investing in a partnership do not come primarily from the efforts of others but through the partnership itself.

ANSWER: A general partnership interest is not a security for purposes of the 1933 act.

Now determine whether the following are securities under the 1933 Securities Act:

- Limited partnership interests
- Limited liability company interests

- Limited liability partnership interests
- Oil and gas leases
- Limited partnership in an oil field
- An interest in a real estate investment trust
- Options to buy tickets for the World Series if your team makes it to that point

19-2b REGULATING PRIMARY OFFERINGS: REGISTRATION

The **Securities and Exchange Commission (SEC)** is the administrative agency responsible for regulating the sale of securities under both the 1933 and 1934 acts. The SEC is subject to all of the administrative rules covered in Chapter 6 because it was the administrative agency created by Congress in its enabling legislation, the 1934 Securities Exchange Act. The SEC can issue injunctions, institute criminal proceedings, bring civil suits, enter into consent decrees, handle enforcement, and promulgate rules.

The rules promulgated by the SEC provide the requirements for the registration of securities, financial reporting, and stock exchange operations. The SEC has a complete staff of lawyers, accountants, financial analysts, and other experts to assist in both the review of informational filings and the enforcement of the securities laws.

19-2c REGULATING PRIMARY OFFERINGS: EXEMPTIONS

Unless an **exemption** applies, anyone selling securities must complete certain filing requirements before the securities can be sold legally. The two types of exemptions are exempt securities and exempt transactions. These exemptions work only for the 1933 act.

Exempt Securities

Certain investments, called **exempt securities**, have been excluded specifically from coverage of the 1933 act. The following is a list of some of the exemptions:

1. Securities (bonds, etc.) issued by federal, state, county, or municipal governments for public purposes
2. Commercial paper (includes notes, checks, and drafts with a maturity date under nine months)
3. Banks, savings and loans, and religious and charitable organizations
4. Insurance policies
5. Annuities
6. Securities of common carriers (those regulated by the Interstate Commerce Commission)
7. Stock dividends and stock splits
8. Charitable bonds

Exempt Transactions

Exempt transactions are more complicated than exempt securities; more details are required to comply with the exempt transaction standards. The following subsections discuss these transaction exemptions, which are summarized in Exhibit 19.1.

EXHIBIT 19.1 1933 Securities Act Transaction Exemptions

NAME	SIZE LIMITATION	GENERAL SOLICITATION	OFFEREE/ BUYER LIMITATION	RESALE LIMITATION	DISCLOSURE	PUBLIC OFFERING	SEC FILING	TIME
Intrastate exemption, 15 U.S.C. § 77(c)(a)(11)	No	No	Buyers must be residents of state of incorporation; triple 80% requirements	Yes, stock transfer restrictions (Rule 147)–(9 months)	No	Yes, in state	No	No restriction
Small-offering exemption, 15 U.S.C. § 77D Regulation A	$5,000,000 (up to $50,000,000 if JOBS audit requirements met)	Yes	Short-form registration required (offering circular)	No	Offering circular	Yes	Short-form	12-month period
Rule 504, Regulation D	$1,000,000* or less (in 12-month period)	Yes	None, unlimited accredited and nonaccredited alike	Yes	No†	Yes	Notice of offering within 15 days of first sale	12-month period
Rule 505, Regulation D	Up to $5,000,000	No	No more than 35, excluding accredited investors (JOBS Act crowd-funding expansion)	Yes, 2 years†	Yes, to nonaccredited†	No (Yes, under JOBS)	Notice of offering (15 days)	12-month period
Rule 506, Regulation D	No	No	Unlimited accredited and 35 nonaccredited investors (nonaccredited must be sophisticated)	Yes, stock restrictions	Yes, to nonaccredited†	No (Yes, under JOBS)	Notice of offering (15 days)	12-month period
Rule 144 (Private placement)	Another name for Regulation D offerings							

*In certain circumstances. $2,000,000 if blue-sky registration (504). Up to $7,500,000 if blue-sky registration (505). Under JOBS, audits for offerings over $500,000 and financial reviews for offerings between $100,000 and $500,000.

†Must verify purchaser is buying for personal investment and shares must have restrictions on transfer.

The Intrastate Offering Exemption. This exemption exists because the Commerce Clause prohibits the federal government from regulating purely intrastate matters (see Chapter 5 for a full discussion of Commerce Clause issues). To qualify for the intrastate exemption, the investors (offerees) and issuer must all be residents of the same state. (If there is one out-of-state offeree, the exemption will not apply.) Further, the issuer must meet the following requirements:

1. Eighty percent of its assets must be located in the state.
2. Eighty percent of its income must be earned from operations within the state.

Eighty percent of the proceeds from the sale must be used on operations within the state.

Under the SEC's Rule 147, some restrictions apply to the transfer of exempt intrastate offerings, including a nine-month transfer restriction to state residents only.

Small-Offering Exemption: Regulation A. Although it is not a true exemption, **Regulation A** is a shortcut method of registration. The lengthy, complicated processes of full registration are simplified in that only a short-form registration statement is filed, a sort of fill-in-the-blanks application. Regulation A applies to issues of $5 million or less during any 12-month period. Under the Jump Start Our Business Startups Act (JOBS), which took effect in 2012, the amount can go up to $50,000,000 if the offering company has audited financial statements.

The SEC groups or "integrates" registration. Three registrations of $2 million each would not qualify for this exemption if issued within one 12-month period. They would qualify, however, if issued over three years.

Small-Offering Exemption: Regulation D. **Regulation D** is the product of the SEC's evaluation of the impact of its rules on the ability of small businesses to raise capital. It was promulgated to simplify and clarify existing exemptions, expand the availability of exemptions, and achieve uniformity between state and federal exemptions.

Regulation D creates a three-tiered exemption structure that consists of Rules 504, 505, and 506, which permit sales without registration. Sellers are, however, required to file a Form D informational statement about the sale. Rule 501 of Regulation D lists the definitions of various terms used in the three exemptions. One of the key definitions under Regulation D is that of an **accredited investor**, a term that was changed significantly by the Dodd–Frank Wall Street Reform and Consumer Financial Protection Act because so many small investors lost their investments in the 2008 subprime derivative markets.[2] Under these changes, an accredited investor is any investor who at the time of the sale falls into any of the following categories:

- Banks, insurance companies, registered investment companies, business development companies, or small business investment companies
- ERISA (see Chapter 20) employee benefit plan if the plan has a bank, insurance company, or registered investment adviser making investment decisions or if the plan has total assets greater than $5 million
- Charitable organizations, corporations, or partnerships with greater than $5 million in assets
- Directors, executive officers, or general partners of the company selling the securities

- Businesses in which all owners are accredited investors
- Individuals with net worth, or joint net worth with spouse, that exceeds $1 million at the time of the purchase, excluding the value of the primary residence of such person
- A natural person with income exceeding $200,000 in each of the two most recent years or joint income with a spouse exceeding $300,000 for those years and a reasonable expectation of the same income level in the current year
- Under JOBS, certain types of offerings under Regulation D provide accredited status for investors with net worth or income of $100,000 to invest up to 5 percent (maximum $2,000) and those worth or earning more than $100,000 to invest up to 10 percent (maximum of $100,000)
- A trust with assets in excess of $5 million, not formed to acquire the securities offered, whose purchases a sophisticated person makes

Rule 502 originally placed a number of limitations on the means an issuer could use in offering securities. JOBS allows general advertising and the use of Internet funding pools, if those pools are registered. This general access and the expansion of qualified investors has allowed what has been called "crowd funding," which is intended to allow small businesses easier and less expensive access to all types of investors. The crowd-funding portion of JOBS has been called the most dramatic change in securities laws since the 1933 original legislation was passed. The SEC has not yet promulgated its rules on this portion of JOBS. However, all of the securities sold through Regulation D exemptions are still subject to restrictions on resale in order to prevent the immediate rollover of the securities involved in these exempt transactions.

The three tiers of Regulation D exemptions are as follows.

- The **Rule 504** exemption applies to offerings of $1 million or less (within any 12-month period). Sales of stock to directors, officers, and employees are not counted in the $1 million limitation. The Rule 504 exemption applies in offerings of up to $2 million, provided the offering is registered under a state **blue-sky law**. Under JOBS, audits for offerings over $500,000 and financial reviews for offerings between $100,000 and $500,000 are required.

- The **Rule 505** exemption covers sales of up to $5 million, provided no more than 35 nonaccredited investors are involved, with JOBS expanding the definition of an accredited investor. Again, with state registration, it is possible to take a Rule 505 exemption up to $7.5 million. Also, if the issue is sold to both accredited and nonaccredited investors, the issuer must give all buyers a prospectus.

- The **Rule 506** exemption has no dollar limitation, but the number and type of investors are limited. Any number of accredited investors is allowed, but the number of nonaccredited investors is limited to 35, and these investors must meet the standards as discussed under the JOBS changes. Under a Rule 506 exemption, the resale of the shares is also subject to some restrictions.

Under Dodd–Frank, the private placement market under Regulation D was to include SEC rule changes that would prevent so-called "bad actors" from making private placement offerings. "Bad actors" are those who have a history of failed offerings and investor litigation. These types of offerors would be required to go through the supervised registration process.[3]

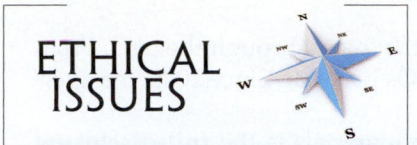

ETHICAL ISSUES

When investment banking firm Goldman Sachs's representatives appeared before Congress to testify about their failure to disclose to investors that the firm was shorting securities it was selling to its clients (betting that the securities would drop in value), members of the committee asked whether Goldman had an obligation to disclose its position to those investors. All witnesses testified with an unequivocal "No!" because of Rule 506. Rule 506 is a sale to accredited (sophisticated) investors, investors who understand how markets work, can afford to invest, and/or can afford to have advisers regarding their investments. Goldman maintains that its clients were "qualified accredited" and/or "sophisticated" investors to whom the firm was not required to provide the detailed information that is mandated for general public offerings.

Goldman's position is that the clients who purchased the instruments had enough knowledge of markets to understand and process the risk and realize that all investment bankers are positioned in the market according to their theories on risk.

Did Goldman have a fiduciary duty to its investing clients under the regulations? Evaluate Goldman's position from an ethical perspective—that is, you know Goldman met its legal requirements for disclosure—and now determine whether its conduct in nondisclosure was ethical. Discuss what role Goldman's conduct may have had in the Dodd–Frank changes to accredited investor definitions and the private placement securities market. Be sure to think back on the regulatory cycle from Chapter 2 as you provide your answer.

Under JOBS, which took effect in 2012, the SEC has proposed new rules that allow certain types of very small offerings to investors with more limited means than those eligible for Regulation D offerings.[4] These changes remain controversial because of the expansion of securities sales to those with less income and net worth without the registration disclosure requirements.

Corporate Reorganizations. If a firm is issuing new shares of stock under a Chapter 11 bankruptcy reorganization supervised by a bankruptcy court, registration is not necessary, provided court approval is obtained for the issue.

19-2d WHAT MUST BE FILED: DOCUMENTS AND INFORMATION FOR REGISTRATION

If none of the exemptions applies, the offeror of the securities must go through the registration process. In 2011, Facebook attempted to raise public offering funds without SEC involvement by issuing investment vehicles through Goldman Sachs clients. When the SEC began looking into the structure of the deals, Facebook then issued an IPO. (There is more information on the Facebook IPO under the Section 11 discussion.) The offeror (issuer) must file a **registration statement (S-1)** and sample **prospectus** with the SEC. A prospectus here means the formal document the SEC requires all shareholders to have. However, for purposes of disclosure and misrepresentation issues, a prospectus is any ad or written materials the offeror provides or places.

A filing fee is based on the aggregate offering price of the sale. The SEC has 20 days to act on the filing, after which the registration statement automatically becomes effective. The SEC takes some form of action within that time period. The SEC need not actually approve or disapprove the offering within that time limit as long as a **comment letter** or **deficiency letter** is issued. A new registration, for a first-time offeror, generally takes about six months to get through the SEC. From 1980 through 2000, there was an average of 311 IPOs per year. Since 2000, the average has dropped to 102 offerings per year.

The SEC's guide in reviewing the registration materials is the **full-disclosure standard**. The SEC does not pass on the merits of the offering or the soundness of the investment; rather, it simply requires that certain information be supplied. The SEC does not verify the accuracy of the information, only that it is on file. The following information is required in the registration statement:

1. A description of what is being offered, why it is offered, how the securities will fit into the business's existing capital structure, and how the proceeds will be used

2. An audited financial statement

3. A list of corporate assets

4. The nature of the issuer's business

5. A list of those in management and their shares of ownership in the firm

6. Other relevant and material information, such as pending lawsuits

Before and after the registration statement is filed, the issuer is very much restricted in what can be done to sell the securities. After the registration statement is filed, the issuer can run a **tombstone ad**, as shown in Exhibit 19.2, which simply announces that securities will be sold and who will have information—but clearly indicates that the ad is not an offer. Also, after filing, but before the registration statement becomes effective, the issuer can send out a **red-herring prospectus**, which has printed in red at the top that the registration is not yet effective. These red herrings are a way to get out information while waiting for SEC approval.

During this interval between filing and the effective date, no sales and no general advertising are allowed. Activity is limited until the date the registration gets SEC approval and becomes effective. Exhibit 19.3 is a diagram of federal securities registration and exemptions.

The SEC permits firms to complete *shelf registrations*. Under this process, a firm completes all the registration requirements and is then free to issue the securities any time within a two-year period, generally when market conditions are most favorable. The company's quarterly and annual filings serve to update the shelf registration. This means of filing was permitted to help corporations raise capital.

19-2e VIOLATIONS OF THE 1933 ACT

Section 11 Violations

Section 11 of the 1933 act imposes civil and criminal liability on those who do not comply with the act's requirements regarding the submission of a registration statement. Section 11 is used when full disclosure has not been made in the registration statement or if any of the information in that registration statement is false. Section 11 is a statutory fraud section that applies to security registrations. The Facebook public offering in 2012 went down in value after material information surfaced that had not been disclosed in the offering materials to all investors. For example, Facebook did not disclose that it had recently adjusted its revenue projections downward. The result was that the offering had a chilling effect on pending and future IPOs in the tech industry.

Exhibit 19.2 Sample of a Tombstone Ad

This announcement is neither an offer to sell nor a solicitation of offers to buy any of these securities. The offering is made only by the Prospectus, copies of which may be obtained in any State or jurisdiction in which this announcement is circulated only from such of the underwriters as may legally offer these securities in such State.

NEW ISSUE

January 22, 1999

$50,000,000

< a l l a i r e >

2,500,000 Shares
Common Stock

NASDAQ Symbol: "ALLR"

Price $20 Per Share

Prior to the offering there had been no public market for these securities. Allaire Corporation develops, markets and supports application development and server software for a wide range of Web development, from building static Web pages to developing high volume, interactive Web applications.

Credit Suisse First Boston

Dain Rauscher Wessels
a division of Dain Rauscher Incorporated
NationsBanc Montgomery Securities LLC

Hambrecht & Quist

Invemed Associates, Inc.

Needham & Company, Inc.

Charles Schwab & Co., Inc.

Tucker Anthony
Incorporated
C.E. Unterberg, Towbin

Wedbush Morgan Securities

CREDIT SUISSE | FIRST BOSTON

EXHIBIT **19.3** Federal Securities Registration and Exemptions

What Is Required for a Violation?

For an investor to recover civilly under Section 11, the following elements must be proved:

1. The investor purchased a security that was required to have a registration statement.

2. The registration statement contained a material misstatement or omission.

3. The investor need not show reliance unless the purchase was made over a year after the effective date.

4. The investor experienced a loss.

Who Is Liable?

Liability under Section 11 attaches to all individuals who signed the registration statement—each director and officer of the issuing corporation and every accountant, engineer, appraiser, attorney, geologist, or other expert whose input was used in the preparation of the statement. Underwriters are also included as potential defendants. Experts (such as accountants, engineers, appraisers, lawyers) are liable only for the information they provided. Directors and officers are jointly and severally liable under Section 11. Under the Dodd–Frank changes, the SEC will be studying whether to expand Section 11 liability to "aiders and abettors"—those who help offerors continue to hold out a deceptive appearance of financial solvency. (See the full discussion of this issue on p. 651.)

Defenses for Section 11 Violations

Several defenses are available to defendants. The burden of proof for these defenses rests with Section 11 defendants.

1. *Immateriality.* Because proving that a **material misstatement** or omission was made is part of the investor's case, proving that the statement or omission was immaterial is a valid defense. The standards for what is or is not material are basically the same standards used in contract misrepresentation cases.

2. *Investor knowledge.* If the investor knew of the misstatement or omission and purchased the stock anyway, there is no Section 11 liability. Section 11 defendants can offer proof of knowledge of the investor to establish a defense.

3. *Due diligence.* The **due diligence** defense is one that allows defendants (non-issuers) to show that they were acting reasonably in preparing and signing the registration statement. The experts are required to show that they acted within the standards of their profession in preparing their portions of the registration statement. Officers and directors are required to show that they had no reason to suspect or had no knowledge of an omission or misstatement.

This area of due diligence came under fire with the collapses of Enron, WorldCom, and so many dot-com IPOs. The result was an extensive network of regulation under Sarbanes–Oxley and Dodd–Frank, a network explained in the Primer on these laws found in "For the Manager's Desk" on p. 641.

Escott v BarChris Constr. Corp. (Case 19.1) is the leading case on Section 11 liability. It involves a variety of defendants, including an accounting firm and audit partners, and discusses the defense of due diligence. Ironically, although the case is from 1968, it remains the classic example of the type of financial overstatement of a company's performance that SOX was passed to address.

CASE 19.1

Escott v BarChris Constr. Corp.
283 F. Supp. 643 (S.D.N.Y. 1968)

Bowling for Fraud: Right Up Our Alley

FACTS

BarChris was a bowling alley company established in 1946. The bowling industry grew rapidly when automatic pin resetters went on the market in the mid-1950s. BarChris began a program of rapid expansion and in 1960 was responsible for the construction of over 3 percent of all bowling alleys in the United States. BarChris used two methods of financing the construction of these alleys, both of which substantially drained the company's cash flow.

CONTINUED

In 1959, BarChris sold approximately one-half million shares of common stock. By 1960, its cash flow picture was still troublesome, and it sold debentures. The debenture issue was registered with the SEC, approved, and sold. In spite of the cash boost from the sale, BarChris was still experiencing financial difficulties and declared bankruptcy in October 1962. The debenture holders were not paid their interest; BarChris defaulted.

The purchasers of the BarChris debentures brought suit under Section 11 of the 1933 act. They claimed that the registration statement filed by BarChris contained false information and failed to disclose certain material information. Their suit, which centered on the audited financial statements prepared by a CPA firm, claimed that the statements were inaccurate and full of omissions. The following chart summarizes the problems with the financial statements submitted with the registration statements.

1. *1960 Earnings*
   (a) *Sales*
Per prospectus	$9,165,320
Correct figure	8,511,420
Overstatement	$ 653,900
   (b) *Net Operating Income*
Per prospectus	$ 1,742,801
Correct figure	1,496,196
Overstatement	$ 246,605
   (c) *Earnings per Share*
Per prospectus	$ 0.75
Correct figure	0.65
Overstatement	$ 0.10

2. *1960 Balance Sheet*
   Current Assests
Per prospectus	$ 4,524,021
Correct figure	3,914,332
Overstatement	$ 609,689

3. *Contingent Liabilities as of December 31, 1960, on Alternative Method of Financing*
Per prospectus	$ 750,000
Correct figure	1,125,795
Understatement	$ 375,795
Capitol Lanes should have been shown as a direct liability	$ 325,000

4. *Contingent Liabilities as of April 30, 1961*
Per prospectus	$ 825,000
Correct figure	1,443,853
Understatement	$ 618,853
Capitol Lanes should have been shown as a direct liability	$ 314,166

5. *Earnings Figures for Quarter Ending March 31, 1961*
   (a) *Sales*
Per prospectus	$ 2,138,455
Correct figure	1,618,645
Overstatement	$ 519,810
   (b) *Gross Profit*
Per prospectus	$ 483,121
Correct figure	252,366
Overstatement	$ 230,755

6. *Backlog as of March 31, 1961*
Per prospectus	$ 6,905,000
Correct figure	2,415,000
Overstatement	$ 4,490,000

7. *Failure to Disclose Officers' Loans Outstanding and Unpaid on May 16, 1961*
	$ 386,615

8. *Failure to Disclose Use of Proceeds in Manner Not Revealed in Prospectus:*
Approx	$ 1,160,000

9. *Failure to Disclose Customers' Delinquencies in May 1961 and BarChris's Potential Liability with Respect Thereto:*
Over	$ 1,350,000

10. *Failure to Disclose the Fact that BarChris Was Already Engaged and Was About to Be More Heavily Engaged in the Operation of Bowling Alleys*

The federal district court reviewed all of the exhibits and statements included in the prospectus and dealt with each defendant individually in issuing its decisions. The defendants consisted of those officers and directors who signed the registration statement, the underwriters of the debenture offering, the auditors (Peat, Marwick, Mitchell & Co.[5]), and BarChris's attorneys and directors.

JUDICIAL OPINION

McLEAN, District Judge

Russo. Russo was, to all intents and purposes, the chief executive officer of BarChris. He was a member of the executive committee. He was familiar with all aspects of the business. He was personally in charge of dealings with the factors. He acted on BarChris's behalf in making the financing agreement with Talcott and he handled the negotiations with Talcott in the spring of 1961. He talked with customers about their delinquencies.

Russo prepared the list of jobs which went into the backlog figure. He knew the status of those jobs.

It was Russo who arranged for the temporary increase in BarChris's cash in banks on December 31, 1960,

CONTINUED

a transaction which borders on the fraudulent. He was thoroughly aware of BarChris's stringent financial condition in May 1961. He had personally advanced large sums to BarChris of which $175,000 remained unpaid as of May 16.

In short, Russo knew all the relevant facts. He could not have believed that there were no untrue statements or material omissions in the prospectus. Russo has no due diligence defenses.

Vitolo and Pugliese. They were the founders of the business who stuck with it to the end. Vitolo was president and Pugliese was vice president. Despite their titles, their field of responsibility in the administration of BarChris's affairs during the period in question seems to have been less all-embracing than Russo's. Pugliese in particular appears to have limited his activities to supervising the actual construction work. Vitolo and Pugliese are each men of limited education. It is not hard to believe that for them the prospectus was difficult reading, if indeed they read it at all.

But whether it was or not is irrelevant. The liability of a director who signs a registration statement does not depend upon whether or not he read it or, if he did, whether or not he understood what he was reading.

And in any case, Vitolo and Pugliese were not as naive as they claim to be. They were members of BarChris's executive committee. At meetings of that committee BarChris's affairs were discussed at length. They must have known what was going on. Certainly they knew of the inadequacy of cash in 1961. They knew of their own large advances to the company which remained unpaid. They knew that they had agreed not to deposit their checks until the financing proceeds were received. They knew and intended that part of the proceeds were to be used to pay their own loans.

All in all, the position of Vitolo and Pugliese is not significantly different, for present purposes, from Russo's. They could not have believed that the registration statement was wholly true and that no material facts had been omitted. And in any case, there is nothing to show that they made any investigation of anything which they may not have known about or understood. They have not proved their due diligence defenses.

Kircher. Kircher was treasurer of BarChris and its chief financial officer. He is a certified public accountant and an intelligent man. He was thoroughly familiar with BarChris's financial affairs. He knew the terms of BarChris's agreements with Talcott. He knew of the customers' delinquency problems. He participated actively with Russo in May 1961 in the successful effort to hold Talcott off until the financing proceeds came in. He knew how the financing proceeds were to be applied and he saw to it that they were so applied. He

arranged the officers' loans and he knew all the facts concerning them.

Moreover, as a member of the executive committee, Kircher was kept informed as to those branches of the business of which he did not have direct charge. He knew about the operation of alleys, present and prospective. In brief, Kircher knew all the relevant facts.

Knowing the facts, Kircher had reason to believe that the expertised portion of the prospectus, i.e., the 1960 figures, was in part incorrect. He could not shut his eyes to the facts and rely on Peat, Marwick for that portion.

As to the rest of the prospectus, knowing the facts, he did not have a reasonable ground to believe it to be true. On the contrary, he must have known that in part it was untrue. Under these circumstances, he was not entitled to sit back and place the blame on the lawyers for not advising him about it. Kircher has not proved his due diligence defenses.

Trilling. Trilling's position is somewhat different from Kircher's. He was BarChris's controller. He signed the registration statement in that capacity, although he was not a director.

Trilling entered BarChris's employ in October 1960. He was Kircher's subordinate. When Kircher asked him for information, he furnished it. On at least one occasion he got it wrong.

Trilling may well have been unaware of several of the inaccuracies in the prospectus. But he must have known of some of them. As a financial officer, he was familiar with BarChris's finances and with its books of account. He knew that part of the cash on deposit on December 31, 1960, had been procured temporarily by Russo for window dressing purposes. He should have known, although perhaps through carelessness he did not know at the time, that BarChris's contingent liability was greater than the prospectus stated. In the light of these facts, I cannot find that Trilling believed the entire prospectus to be true.

But even if he did, he still did not establish his due diligence defenses. He did not prove that as to the parts of the prospectus expertised by Peat, Marwick he had no reasonable ground to believe that it was untrue. He also failed to prove, as to the parts of the prospectus not expertised by Peat, Marwick, that he made a reasonable investigation which afforded him a reasonable ground to believe that it was true. As far as appears, he made no investigation. As a signer, he could not avoid responsibility by leaving it up to others to make it accurate. Trilling did not sustain the burden of proving his due diligence defenses.

Birnbaum. Birnbaum was a young lawyer, admitted to the bar in 1957, who, after brief periods of employment by two different law firms and an equally brief

CONTINUED

period of practicing in his own firm, was employed by BarChris as house counsel and assistant secretary in October 1960. Unfortunately for him, he became secretary and director of BarChris on April 17, 1961, after the first version of the registration statement had been filed with the Securities and Exchange Commission. He signed the later amendments, thereby becoming responsible for the accuracy of the prospectus in its final form.

It seems probable that Birnbaum did not know of many of the inaccuracies in the prospectus. He must, however, have appreciated some of them. In any case, he made no investigation and relied on the others to get it right. Unlike Trilling, he was entitled to rely upon Peat, Marwick for the 1960 figures, for as far as appears, he had no personal knowledge of the company's books of account or financial transactions. As a lawyer, he should have known his obligations under the statute. He should have known that he was required to make a reasonable investigation of the truth of all the statements in the unexpertised portion of the document which he signed. Having failed to make such an investigation, he did not have reasonable ground to believe that all these statements were true. Birnbaum has not established his due diligence defenses except as to the audited 1960 exhibits.

Auslander. Auslander was an "outside" director, i.e., one who was not an officer of BarChris. He was chairman of the board of Valley Stream National Bank in Valley Stream, Long Island. In February 1961 Vitolo asked him to become a director of BarChris. As an inducement, Vitolo said that when BarChris received the proceeds of a forthcoming issue of securities, it would deposit $1 million in Auslander's bank.

Auslander was elected a director on April 17, 1961. The registration statement in its original form had already been filed, of course without his signature. On May 10, 1961, he signed a signature page for the first amendment to the registration statement which was filed on May 11, 1961. This was a separate sheet without any document attached. Auslander did not know that it was a signature page for a registration statement. He vaguely understood that it was something "for the SEC."

Auslander attended a meeting of BarChris's directors on May 15, 1961. At that meeting he, along with the other directors, signed the signature sheet for the second amendment which constituted the registration statement in its final form. Again, this was only a separate sheet without any document attached.

Auslander never saw a copy of the registration statement in its final form. It is true that Auslander became a director on the eve of the financing. He had little opportunity to familiarize himself with the company's affairs.

Section 11 imposes liability in the first instance upon a director, no matter how new he is.

Peat, Marwick. Peat, Marwick's work was in general charge of a member of the firm, Cummings, and more immediately in charge of Peat, Marwick's manager, Logan. Most of the actual work was performed by a senior accountant, Berardi, who had junior assistants, one of whom was Kennedy.

Berardi was then about thirty years old. He was not yet a CPA. He had had no previous experience with the bowling industry. This was his first job as a senior accountant. He could hardly have been given a more difficult assignment.

After obtaining a little background information on BarChris by talking to Logan and reviewing Peat, Marwick's work papers on its 1959 audit, Berardi examined the results of test checks of BarChris's accounting procedures which one of the junior accountants had made, and he prepared an "internal control questionnaire" and an "audit program." Thereafter, for a few days subsequent to December 30, 1960, he inspected BarChris's inventories and examined certain alley construction. Finally, on January 13, 1961, he began his auditing work which he carried on substantially continuously until it was completed on February 24, 1961. Toward the close of the work, Logan reviewed it and made various comments and suggestions to Berardi.

It is unnecessary to recount everything that Berardi did in the course of the audit. We are concerned only with the evidence relating to what Berardi did or did not do with respect to those items found to have been incorrectly reported in the 1960 figures in the prospectus.

Accountants should not be held to a standard higher than that recognized in their profession. I do not do so here. Berardi's review did not come up to that standard. He did not take some of the steps which Peat, Marwick's written program prescribed. He did not spend an adequate amount of time on a task of this magnitude. Most important of all, he was too easily satisfied with glib answers to his inquiries.

This is not to say that he should have made a complete audit. But there were enough danger signals in the materials which he did examine to require some further investigation on his part. Generally accepted accounting standards required such further investigation under these circumstances. It is not always sufficient merely to ask questions.

CASE QUESTIONS

1. How much time transpired between the sale of the debentures and BarChris's bankruptcy?

2. Give a summary of the types of items that were materially misstated.

3. Who was sued under Section 11? Who was held liable?

Penalties for Violations of Section 11

Violations of Section 11 carry maximum penalties of $10,000 and/or five years' imprisonment. In addition, the SEC has the authority to bring suit seeking an injunction to stop sales based on false or omitted information in the registration statement. Purchasers harmed by the false or omitted statements have a right of civil suit in federal district court for recovery of their losses and other damages.

The Private Securities Litigation Reform Act of 1995 (PSLRA) limits attorneys' fees to a reasonable percentage of the amount recovered or the agreed-upon settlement amount. The problem of "professional plaintiffs" was also addressed through a section in the PSLRA that prevents a plaintiff from being named in more than five class action securities lawsuits in a three-year period.

One final portion of PSLRA is the so-called safe-harbor protection. With certain precautions and qualifications, companies can make forward-looking predictions for company performance in materials given to investors. The company is not held to these statements about its future as long as it makes the required SEC disclosures on forward-looking statements.

Section 12 Violations

Section 12 carries the same criminal penalties as Section 11 and covers the following offenses:

1. Selling securities without registration and without an exemption
2. Selling securities before the effective date of the registration statement
3. Selling securities using false information in the prospectus (In this case, "prospectus" includes not only the formal document but also all ads, circulars, and so on used in the sale of securities.)

The SEC also has injunctive remedies here, and buyers also have the right of civil suit. The same defenses that apply to Section 11 apply to Section 12.

FOR THE MANAGER'S DESK

Re: A Primer on Sarbanes–Oxley and Dodd–Frank

The introduction to SOX, as it has come to be known, gives the following purpose: *An Act to protect investors by improving the accuracy and reliability of corporate disclosures made pursuant to the securities laws, and for other purposes.*

The new portions of the law appear at 15 U.S.C. § 7201. However, because many of the provisions amend the Securities Exchange Act of 1934, which begins at 78 U.S.C. § 1 *et seq.,* many of the provisions can be found there.

Part I: The Creation of the Public Company Accounting Oversight Board

This section of SOX established a quasigovernmental entity called the Public Company Accounting Oversight

Board (PCAOB, but called "Peek-a-Boo") under the direction of the SEC to (1) oversee the audit of public companies covered by the federal securities laws (the 1933 and 1934 Acts), (2) establish audit report standards and rules, and (3) investigate, inspect, and enforce compliance through both the registration and regulation of public accounting firms.

Under this section of SOX, companies that conduct audits of companies covered under federal securities laws must register with PCAOB. With this registration control, PCAOB is given the power to discipline public accounting firms, including the ability to impose sanctions such as prohibitions on conducting future audits. PCAOB's powers related to intentional conduct or repeated negligent conduct by audit firms when they are doing company audits and financial certifications. PCAOB's power to regulate was upheld in *Free Enterprise Fund v Public Company Accounting Oversight Board*, 130 S.Ct. 3138 (2010). Under the Dodd–Frank changes, PCAOB will also have authority to regulate the auditors of broker/dealer firms.

The SEC is now responsible for determining what are or are not "generally accepted" accounting principles for purposes of complying with securities laws. SOX also directs the SEC to study and adopt a system of principles-based accountings.

Part II: Auditor Independence

This portion of SOX is a bit of a statutory code of ethics for public accounting firms. Accounting firms that audit publicly traded companies cannot also perform the following consulting services for the companies for which they conduct audits:

1. Bookkeeping and other services related to the accounting records or financial statements of the audit client

2. Design and implementation of financial information systems

3. Appraisal and valuation services, fairness opinions, and contribution-in-kind reports

4. Actuarial services

5. Internal audit outsourcing services

6. Management functions and human resources

7. Broker or dealer, investment adviser, and investment banking services

8. Legal services and expert services unrelated to the audit

Another conflicts prohibition is that the audit firm cannot audit, for one year, a company that has one of its former employees as a member of senior management. For example, if a partner from PwC is hired by Xena Corporation as its controller or CFO, PwC cannot be the auditor (for SEC purposes) for Xena for one year. At least one year must elapse between the hire date of the former partner and the start of the audit if PwC is to conduct the audit.

Procedural requirements in this section include rotating the audit partner for the accounting firm every five years. Also, the auditor must report directly to the audit committee of the company.

Part III: Corporate Responsibility

This section of SOX deals with the audit committees of publicly traded companies and makes these committees responsible for the hiring, compensation, and oversight of the public accounting firm responsible for conducting the company's audits and certifying its financial statements. All members of the audit committee must be members of the company's board of directors, and must be independent. *Independent* is defined by the SEC to require that the director be an outside board member (not an officer), not have been an officer for a period of time (if retired from the company), not have close relatives working in management in the company, and not have contractual or consulting ties to the company. The SEC and companies have developed complex checklists to help directors determine whether they meet the standards for independence for purposes of qualifying audit committee membership.

In addition to these structural changes in audit committees, this portion of SOX is also the officer certification section (more related to the 1934 Securities Exchange Act covered on p. 644). The company's CEO and CFO are required to certify the financial statements the company files with the SEC as being fair in their representation of the company's financial condition and accurate "in all material respects." CFOs and CEOs forfeit any bonuses and compensation that were received based on financial reports that subsequently had to be restated because they were not materially accurate or fair in their disclosures.

The SEC is given the authority to ban those who violate securities laws from serving as an officer or director of a publicly traded company if the SEC can prove that they are unfit to serve. The standard under the statute is "substantial unfitness." For example, Al Dunlap, the former CEO of Sunbeam, settled SEC charges that he oversaw an accounting fraud on its barbecue sales program by a fine and agreeing to never serve as an officer or director of a publicly traded company.

One final section in Part III was passed in response to activity at Enron in the months leading up to its collapse. At Enron, the officers were busily selling off their shares during a time when employees were prohibited from selling shares in their pension plans. Officers, such as Jeffrey Skilling and Clifford Baxter, walked away with the cash from selling at the stock's high point while employees, because of the blackout period, were left to simply watch as Enron's stock lost virtually all of its value.

During the so-called "blackout periods" on pension plans, those times when owners of the plans cannot trade in the company stock, officers of the company are also subject to the blackout periods. The penalty for violating this prohibition on stock dealing is that the officers must return any profits from blackout period trading to the company. This requirement to return the profits exists even when the trading was not intentional.

Part IV: Enhanced Financial Disclosures

This section of SOX is the accounting section. Congress directed the SEC to do something about accounting practices for off-balance sheet transactions, including special purpose entities and relationships that while immaterial in amount may have a material effect upon the financial status of the company. For example, a spin-off company that concealed $2 million in company debt is not a material amount. But if the spin-off company is involved in leveraged transactions (as was the case with Enron) and the company has agreed to serve as a guarantor to investors in the spin-off for those leveraged amounts, then the spin-off can have a material effect. The SEC changed the rules for off-balance sheet transactions quite substantially to require companies to show the economics of such off-balance sheet transactions in a transparent fashion. Lehman Brothers' bankruptcy revealed another debt spin-off strategy that company used to hide its obligations, and those types of spin-offs must also be disclosed.

A second portion of Part IV gets right to the heart of pro forma and EBITDA. Companies must use Generally Accepted Accounting Principles (GAAP) and non-GAAP, side by side.

A third segment of Part IV deals again with officers. Corporations can no longer make personal loans to corporate executives. The only exception is when the company is in the business of making loans—that is, GE executives are permitted to use GE Capital as long as they have the same types of loans that are available to the general public. Another officer requirement shortens the time for them to disclose transactions in the company's shares. Prior to SOX, executives simply had to disclose transactions within 10 days from the end of the month in which the transactions occurred. The disclosure period now is within two business days of the transaction.

As a result of the activities that led to these statutory revisions, SOX also requires companies to develop a separate code of ethics for senior financial officers, one that applies to the principal financial officer, comptroller, and/or principal accounting officer. It is interesting that Enron had just such a separate code of ethics. However, the board waived its provisions to allow former CFO Andrew Fastow to have the off-the-book transactions.

Internal Controls Certification: SOX 404

Referred to fondly now as just "404," a final portion of SOX requires companies to include an internal control report and assessment as part of the 10-K annual reports. A public accounting firm that issues the audit report must also certify and report on the state of the company's internal controls.

Although the audit committee provisions are covered in a different section, Part IV does mandate that every audit committee have at least one member who is a financial expert. The SEC has already established rules for who qualifies as a financial expert and companies' annual reports identify the financial expert and give the background.

Under JOBS, certain types of companies (often called "emerging growth companies") were given an additional three years for phasing in 404 requirements (SOX gives companies two years from their IPOS), which gives them a total of five years following their IPOs to meet SOX standards.

Title V: Analyst Conflicts of Interest

The issue of analysts and their conflicts was one that contributed to the failure of the markets to heed the warning signals at Enron and WorldCom and also contributed to the 2008 market collapse. The SEC now regulates the following:

1. Prepublication clearance or approval of research reports by investment bankers
2. Supervision, compensation, and evaluation of securities analysts by investment bankers
3. Retaliation against a securities analyst by an investment banker because of an unfavorable research report that may adversely affect an investment banker's relationship or a broker's or dealer's relationship with the company that is discussed in the report
4. Separating securities analysts from pressure or oversight by investment bankers in a way that might potentially create bias
5. Developing rules on disclosure by securities analysts and broker/dealers of specified conflicts of interest

Under Dodd–Frank, the SEC has been directed to further study analysts' relationships and roles in financial markets and is authorized to promulgate additional rules on conflicts.

Title VIII: Corporate and Criminal Fraud Accountability

This section of SOX expanded and clarified the criminal law portions of securities law by creating new crimes, increasing penalties on existing crimes, and elaborating on the elements required to prove already existing crimes. Also known as the Corporate and Criminal Fraud

Accountability Act of 2002, most of this SOX section was covered in Chapter 8.

This section amended federal bankruptcy law to make fines, profits, and penalties that result from violation of federal securities laws a nondischargeable debt in bankruptcy. Also, if common-law fraud is involved in the sale of securities, any judgment owed as a result of the fraud is also a nondischargeable bankruptcy debt.

This section also extended the time for bringing a civil law suit for securities fraud to not later than the earlier of (1) five years after the date of the alleged violation or (2) two years after its discovery.

Finally, this section prohibits retaliation against employees in publicly traded companies who assist in an investigation of possible federal violations or file or participate in a shareholder suit for fraud against the company (see Chapter 17). The protections for whistleblowers are expanded under Dodd–Frank to provide for their recovery of 10–30 percent of any fines the company must pay.

Title IX: White-Collar Criminal Penalty Enhancements

Most of this section was covered in Chapter 8, but it also contains some remarkable grants of authority to the SEC. For example, this section gives the SEC the authority to freeze bonus, incentive, and other payoffs to corporate officers during an ongoing investigation. The SEC has the authority to banish violating officers and directors from the securities markets as well as from working at a publicly traded company in the future. Auditors must keep their work papers for five years, and the penalties for destruction of documents were increased.

Source: Adapted from Marianne Jennings, Business Ethics: Case Studies and Selected Readings, 8th ed., 2014.

19-3 The Securities Exchange Act of 1934

The **Securities Exchange Act of 1934** regulates securities and their issuers once they are on the market. Securities sales, brokers, dealers, and exchanges are all regulated under the 1934 act. In addition, the act requires public disclosure of financial information for certain corporations. In effect, the 1934 act is responsible for the regulation of the securities marketplace. The SEC accomplishes its goal of regulating undesirable market practices in several ways, which are discussed in the following sections.

19-3a SECURITIES REGISTRATION

Under the 1934 act, all securities traded on a national stock exchange must be registered. Originally, any issuer with over $10 million in assets and 500 or more shareholders was required to register its equity stock (not bonds) if those shares are traded in interstate commerce. However, JOBS changed those thresholds to companies with 500 unaccredited investors or 2,000 shareholders total, including accredited and unaccredited investors. This registration is in addition to all the filing requirements for issuing securities that were discussed under the 1933 act.

19-3b PERIODIC FILING UNDER THE 1934 ACT: THOSE ALPHABET REPORTS

In addition to the one-time registration required under the 1934 act, those same companies (national stock exchange companies that meet the 500/2,000 shareholder requirements and $10 million in assets) must comply with the periodic reporting requirements imposed by the SEC. Each quarter, these firms must file a **10-Q form**, which is basically a quarterly financial report. An annual report, the **10-K form**, must be filed by the company at the end of its fiscal year. Any unusual events—bankruptcies, spin-offs, takeovers, and other changes in company control—must be reported on the **8-K form**. The 10-Qs and 10-Ks are the reports the CEO and CFO must certify under SOX. The certification means the CEO and CFO offer the following assurances:

- They have reviewed the report.
- Based on their knowledge, the report contains no untrue statements, has no omissions of fact, and includes nothing misleading.

- Based on their knowledge, the financial statements included with the periodic reports fairly present all material aspects of the company's financial performance.
- They are responsible for establishing, maintaining, and certifying internal controls for the financial operations and reporting of the company.

The increased penalties for the certifying officers run up to 20 years and $10 million.

19-3c THE 1934 ACT ANTIFRAUD PROVISION: 10(b)

In addition to regulating the reporting of information, the 1934 act regulates the propriety of sales in the marketplace. **Section 10(b)** and **Rule 10b-5** (the SEC regulation on 10(b)) are the antifraud provisions of the 1934 act. These sections are statutory versions of common law fraud. If the free market is to work, all buyers and sellers must have access to the same information. To withhold information is to commit fraud and is a violation of Section 10(b).

Application of Section 10(b)

Of all the provisions of the 1934 act, Section 10(b) has the broadest application. It applies to all sales of securities: exempt, stock-exchange-listed, over-the-counter, public, private, small, and large. The only prerequisite for 10(b) application is that interstate commerce be involved in the sales transaction. As Chapter 5 indicates, it is not difficult to find an interstate commerce connection; for example, if mail or phones were used in the transaction, 10(b) applies. The practical effect is that 10(b) applies to all sales of securities.

Proof of Section 10(b) Violation: Corporations Running Afoul

The corporate dissemination violation of 10(b) means that a corporation has not been forthcoming with material information, whether positive or negative, about the company, its performance, and its future. In 2000, the SEC promulgated the **"fair-disclosure rule" (Regulation FD)**; now, material information about the company must be made available to everyone at the same time. The Dodd–Frank legislation requires the SEC to perform several additional studies to examine the issues in disclosure, analysts' reports, and conflicts between and among underwriters and offerors.

The application and enforcement of Section 10(b) have become two of the most significant issues affecting Wall Street. Under SOX, as noted in the Primer, sales of shares by officers now require immediate reporting on 8-K forms. The previous standard of reporting by the close of the month in which the transactions occur has been changed to a two-day period.

Corporations have an obligation to disclose material information. To determine whether an item is material, the question to be answered is, "Is this the type of information that would affect the buying or selling decision?" Examples of items that have been held to be material are

1. Pending takeovers
2. Drops in quarterly earnings
3. Pending declaration of a large dividend
4. Possible lawsuit on product line

The *Siracusano v Matrixx Initiatives, Inc.* case (Case 19.2) deals with an issue of the failure of a corporation to make a material disclosure in a timely manner and provides the answer to the chapter opening "Consider…"

CASE 19.2

Siracusano v Matrixx Initiatives, Inc.
131 S.Ct. 1309 (2011)

Missing Disclosures by a Nose

FACTS

Matrixx Initiatives, Inc., is a pharmaceutical company that sells Zicam through its wholly owned subsidiary, Zicam, LLC. One of its products, responsible for 70 percent of its sales, is Zicam Cold Remedy, a homeopathic product marketed as stopping or minimizing cold symptoms.

In December 1999, Matrixx began to receive questions from physicians whose patients were developing anosmia (loss of the sense of smell). Researchers at medical facilities contacted Matrixx in 2002 to offer access to studies showing that zinc sulfate (present in Zicam) was linked to anosmia.

During this time, Matrixx's public disclosures did not discuss these inquiries and studies. In fact, on October 22, 2003, Matrixx issued an optimistic press release announcing that its net sales for the third quarter of 2003 had increased by 163 percent over the third quarter of 2002.

On an October 23, 2003, earnings conference call, executives for Matrixx expressed their "enthusiasm for the most recently completed quarter" and "optimis[m] about the future." At one point during the call, Zicam executives were asked to "make any comment on the litigation MTXX or its officers are involved in, or whether or not there is any SEC [Securities and Exchange Commission] investigation." They replied that "[t]he officers of this company are not involved in any litigation," and that they were not aware of any SEC investigation. In fact, a lawsuit alleging that Zicam caused anosmia had already been filed at this time.

By January 30, 2004, the FDA was "looking into complaints that an over-the-counter common-cold medicine manufactured by a unit of Matrixx Initiatives Inc. may be causing some users to lose their sense of smell." Matrixx's stock declined after this report, "falling from $13.55 per share on January 30, 2004, to $11.97 per share on February 2, 2004."

NECA-IBEW Pension Fund and James Siracusano (plaintiffs/appellants) brought a class action suit against Matrixx and three Matrixx executives (Appellees) alleging a violation of the Securities Exchange Act of 1934 by their failure to disclose material information regarding problems with Zicam. The district court granted

Matrixx's motion to dismiss the complaint. The court of appeals reversed. The shareholders appealed.

JUDICIAL OPINION

SOTOMAYOR, Justice

To prevail on a § 10(b) claim, a plaintiff must show that the defendant made a statement that was "misleading as to a material fact."

Matrixx urges us to adopt a bright-line rule that reports of adverse events associated with a pharmaceutical company's products cannot be material absent a sufficient number of such reports to establish a statistically significant risk that the product is in fact causing the events. Absent statistical significance, Matrixx argues, adverse event reports provide only "anecdotal" evidence that "the user of a drug experienced an adverse event at some point during or following the use of that drug." Accordingly, it contends, reasonable investors would not consider such reports relevant unless they are statistically significant because only then do they "reflect a scientifically reliable basis for inferring a potential causal link between product use and the adverse event."

A lack of statistically significant data does not mean that medical experts have no reliable basis for inferring a causal link between a drug and adverse events. As Matrixx itself concedes, medical experts rely on other evidence to establish an inference of causation.

The FDA similarly does not limit the evidence it considers for purposes of assessing causation and taking regulatory action to statistically significant data. For example, the FDA requires manufacturers of over-the-counter drugs to revise their labeling "to include a warning as soon as there is reasonable evidence of an association of a serious hazard with a drug; a causal relationship need not have been proved."

This case proves the point. In 2009, the FDA issued a warning letter to Matrixx stating that "[a] significant and growing body of evidence substantiates that the Zicam Cold Remedy intranasal products may pose a serious risk to consumers who use them." The letter cited as evidence 130 reports of anosmia the FDA had received, the fact that the FDA had received few reports of anosmia associated with other intranasal cold remedies, and "evidence in the published

CONTINUED

scientific literature that various salts of zinc can damage olfactory function in animals and humans." It did not cite statistically significant data. Given that medical professionals and regulators act on the basis of evidence of causation that is not statistically significant, it stands to reason that in certain cases reasonable investors would as well.

The information provided to Matrixx by medical experts revealed a plausible causal relationship between Zicam Cold Remedy and anosmia. Consumers likely would have viewed the risk associated with Zicam (possible loss of smell) as substantially outweighing the benefit of using the product (alleviating cold symptoms), particularly in light of the existence of many alternative products on the market. Viewing the allegations of the complaint as a whole, the complaint alleges facts suggesting a significant risk to the commercial viability of Matrixx's leading product. It is substantially likely that a reasonable investor would have viewed this information "'as having significantly altered the "total mix" of information made available.'"

Matrixx elected not to disclose the reports of adverse events not because it believed they were meaningless but because it understood their likely effect on the market. "[A] reasonable person" would deem the inference that Matrixx acted with deliberate recklessness (or even intent). We conclude, in agreement with the Court of Appeals, that respondents have adequately pleaded [materiality and] scienter.

Affirmed.

CASE QUESTIONS

1. Based on this decision, if you had been the executives at Matrixx, what would you have disclosed and when would you have disclosed it?

2. Why is it relevant that consumers would be affected by the studies, whether significant or not?

3. By 2009, the FDA required that Zicam be removed from stores and warned consumers about the risk of losing their sense of smell. What happens to the company as a result? What will be the impact on Matrixx investors? What will their damages be?

Running Afoul of 10(b): How Soon Can You Trade After Corporate Disclosures?

One of the questions asked most frequently about 10(b) cases is when trading can take place. One of the most famous corporate (and individual) 10(b) cases is *SEC v Texas Gulf Sulphur Co.*, 401 F.2d 833 (2nd Cir. 1968), a case that provides answers to that question. Texas Gulf Sulphur was involved in test-drilling operations in Canada. Early tests indicated that the company would make a substantial strike. Press releases did not indicate the richness of the strike. Corporate officers, geologists, and relatives bought stock before the richness of the find was finally disclosed, and the price of the stock soared. The court found that the overly pessimistic press release was misleading under 10(b). The company and the individual purchasers both ran afoul of 10(b).

Proof of a Violation: How Individuals Run Afoul of 10(b)

In simplest form, an individual's 10(b) violation occurs when one side to a securities transaction has information not generally available to the public and the transaction proceeds without disclosure. For example, the factual backdrop in the Galleon Hedge Fund insider trading investigation provides examples of what the SEC believes is inside information. Mr. Raj Rajaratnam, founder and CEO of Galleon, had information furnished to him by a number of individuals who were, in some way, insiders in corporations. For example, Rajat Gupta, a former McKinsey partner, served on the boards of Goldman Sachs and Procter & Gamble. Mr. Gupta had a Goldman board conference call for purposes of approving Warren Buffett's investment in the firm in exchange for Goldman stock, a move that would restore investor confidence in Goldman and increase the price of Goldman stock. That call ended at 3:55 P.M. Within seconds, Mr. Gupta's secretary connected him with Mr. Rajaratnam's direct line. The two spoke for 35 seconds, and Mr. Rajaratnam would then purchase $43 million in Goldman stock. The next day, when Goldman made the Buffett announcement, the value of Goldman shares increased 18 percent in one day. Simply put, Mr. Gupta was an insider who passed along nonpublic information to a tippee—Mr. Rajaratnam. Neither man knew that their phones had been tapped. Both were convicted of insider trading. Mr. Rajaratnam was operating a web of insider trading. As of mid-2013, he had been sentenced to 11 years, and 15 others, including his brother, are now under indictment, have been convicted, and/or sentenced on what the SEC alleges were years of insider trading in the shares of many companies.

ETHICAL ISSUES

"In my own mind, the line between permissible 'detective work' and impermissible insider trading was not always clear, especially with regard to companies broadly covered by the news media as to which there was a wealth of publicly available information, including frequent leaks, rumors and speculation about corporate transactions and other important developments."[6]

This quote was from Raja Rajaratnam when he was about to be sentenced for his convictions for insider trading. Is he correct about the use of public information? Was the information he received from Mr. Gupta public information? Is the line clear, or is Mr. Rajaratnam correct that he was confused by a gray area? Prosecutors responded to the statement by saying that the quote reflected a "serious disregard for the law." Are the prosecutors correct?

© martan/Shutterstock.com

Who Runs Afoul: The Extent of Section 10(b) Liability

Anyone who has access to information not readily available to the public is covered under 10(b). Officers, directors, and large shareholders are included in this group. However, 10(b) also applies to people who get information from these corporate **insiders**. These people are called **tippees**. For example, relatives of officers and directors would be considered tippees if they were given nonpublic information.

Who is covered under Section 10(b) has been a critical question during the past few years. The Supreme Court has made a distinction between true insiders and those who misappropriate information. *United States v O'Hagan* (Case 19.3) is a U.S. Supreme Court ruling on 10(b)'s application.

CASE 19.3 *United States v O'Hagan*
521 U.S. 657 (1997)

© Harper 3D/Shutterstock.com

Pillsbury Dough Boy: The Lawyer/Insider Who Cashed In

FACTS

James Herman O'Hagan (respondent) was a partner in the law firm of Dorsey & Whitney in Minneapolis, Minnesota. In July 1988, Grand Metropolitan PLC (Grand Met), a company based in London, retained Dorsey & Whitney as local counsel to represent it regarding a potential tender offer for common stock of Pillsbury Company (based in Minneapolis).

CONTINUED

Mr. O'Hagan did no work on the Grand Met matter, so on August 18, 1988, he began purchasing call options for Pillsbury stock. Each option gave him the right to purchase 100 shares of Pillsbury stock. By the end of September, Mr. O'Hagan owned more than 2,500 Pillsbury options. Also in September, Mr. O'Hagan purchased 5,000 shares of Pillsbury stock at $39 per share.

Grand Met announced its tender offer in October, and Pillsbury stock rose to $60 per share. Mr. O'Hagan sold his call options and made a profit of $4.3 million.

The SEC indicted Mr. O'Hagan on 57 counts of illegal trading on inside information, including mail fraud, securities fraud, fraudulent trading, and money laundering. The SEC alleged that Mr. O'Hagan used his profits from the Pillsbury options to conceal his previous embezzlement and conversion of his clients' trust funds. Mr. O'Hagan was convicted by a jury on all 57 counts and sentenced to 41 months in prison. A divided Court of Appeals reversed the conviction, and the SEC appealed.

JUDICIAL OPINION

GINSBURG, Justice
We hold, in accord with several other Courts of Appeals, that criminal liability under § 10(b) may be predicated on the misappropriation theory.

Under the "traditional" or "classical theory" of insider trading liability, § 10(b) and Rule 10b-5 are violated when a corporate insider trades in the securities of his corporation on the basis of material, nonpublic information. Trading on such information qualifies as a "deceptive device" under § 10(b), we have affirmed, because "a relationship of trust and confidence [exists] between the shareholders of a corporation and those insiders who have obtained confidential information by reason of their position with that corporation." *Chiarella v United States*, 445 U.S. 222, 228 (1980). That relationship, we recognized, "gives rise to a duty to disclose [or to abstain from trading] because of the 'necessity of preventing a corporate insider from … tak[ing] unfair advantage of … uninformed … stockholders.'" The classical theory applies not only to officers, directors, and other permanent insiders of a corporation, but also to attorneys, accountants, consultants, and others who temporarily become fiduciaries of a corporation. See *Dirks v SEC*, 463 U.S. 646, 655, n. 14 (1983).

The "misappropriation theory" holds that a person commits fraud "in connection with" a securities transaction, and thereby violates § 10(b) and Rule 10b-5, when he misappropriates confidential information for securities trading purposes, in breach of a duty owed to the source of the information. Under this theory, a fiduciary's undisclosed, self-serving use of a principal's information to purchase or sell securities, in breach

of a duty of loyalty and confidentiality, defrauds the principal of the exclusive use of that information. In lieu of premising liability on a fiduciary relationship between company insider and purchaser or seller of the company's stock, the misappropriation theory premises liability on a fiduciary-turned-trader's deception of those who entrusted him with access to confidential information.

The two theories are complementary, each addressing efforts to capitalize on nonpublic information through the purchase or sale of securities. The classical theory targets a corporate insider's breach of duty to shareholders with whom the insider transacts; the misappropriation theory outlaws trading on the basis of nonpublic information by a corporate "outsider" in breach of a duty owed not to a trading party, but to the source of the information. The misappropriation theory is thus designed to "protec[t] the integrity of the securities markets against abuses by 'outsiders' to a corporation who have access to confidential information that will affect th[e] corporation's security price when revealed, but who owe no fiduciary or other duty to that corporation's shareholders."

We agree with the Government that misappropriation, as just defined, satisfies § 10(b)'s requirement that chargeable conduct involve a "deceptive device or contrivance" used "in connection with" the purchase or sale of securities. We observe, first, that misappropriators, as the Government describes them, deal in deception. A fiduciary who "[pretends] loyalty to the principal while secretly converting the principal's information for personal gain" "dupes" or defrauds the principal.

Deception through nondisclosure is central to the theory of liability for which the Government seeks recognition.

The misappropriation theory comports with § 10(b)'s language. The theory is also well tuned to an animating purpose of the Exchange Act: to insure honest securities markets and thereby promote investor confidence. Although informational disparity is inevitable in the securities markets, investors likely would hesitate to venture their capital in a market where trading based on misappropriated nonpublic information is unchecked by law. An investor's informational disadvantage vis-à-vis a misappropriator with material, nonpublic information stems from contrivance, not luck; it is a disadvantage that cannot be overcome with research or skill.

In sum, considering the inhibiting impact on market participation of trading on misappropriated information, and the congressional purposes underlying § 10(b), it makes scant sense to hold a lawyer like O'Hagan a § 10(b) violator if he works for a law firm representing the target of a tender offer, but not if he works for a law firm representing the bidder.

CONTINUED

In sum, the misappropriation theory, as we have examined and explained it in this opinion, is both consistent with the statute and with our precedent. Vital to our decision that criminal liability may be sustained under the misappropriation theory, we emphasize, are two sturdy safeguards Congress has provided regarding scienter. To establish a criminal violation of Rule 10b-5, the Government must prove that a person "willfully" violated the provision. In addition, the statute's "requirement of the presence of culpable intent as a necessary element of the offense does much to destroy any force in the argument that application of the [statute]" in circumstances such as O'Hagan's is unjust.

The Eighth Circuit erred in holding that the misappropriation theory is inconsistent with § 10(b). The

Court of Appeals may address on remand O'Hagan's other challenges to his convictions under § 10(b) and Rule 10b-5.

Reversed.

CASE QUESTIONS

1. What does the court say the misappropriation theory is?

2. Could others have done research and obtained the same information?

3. What advice would you give to those who are employed in law and equity firms that are working on pending deals?

Running Afoul of 10(b) with Timing: When Disclosure Must Be Made

Once information becomes public knowledge, insiders and tippees are free to buy and sell the shares affected. However, the time of "public knowledge" is not always easy to determine. In *SEC v Texas Gulf Sulphur*, 401 F.2d 833 (2nd Cir. 1968), some of the insiders and tippees waited to buy Texas Gulf Sulphur stock until after a press conference announcement had been made regarding a major mineral find. However, the information released at the press conference had not yet made its way out of the press conference room; not enough dissemination had yet occurred for it to be public knowledge. Those who bought by phone immediately following the announcement were found to be in violation of 10(b).

BUSINESS STRATEGY

Huddles with Analysts or Strategists: Does It Matter?

The SEC prohibits an analyst from issuing reports on securities that run contra to the analyst's personal beliefs about the securities. The SEC also requires an investment firm to engage in "fair dealing with its customers."[7] Whether those two requirements were met at the investment firms continues to be the subject of debate. For example, Goldman Sachs held what were known as "trading huddles." The huddle found analysts and traders meeting to determine short and long investments on particular shares. The conclusions of the huddle were then shared with Goldman's traders and a selected few of Goldman's thousands of clients; those conclusions were often different from the Goldman analysts' reports and recommendations that were

issued publicly. Other firms such as Morgan Stanley also have huddles in addition to their published research recommendations, but their conclusions from the weekly meetings are then sent out in an e-mail blast to all clients.

One distinction between Goldman's huddles and those of other investment firms was that Goldman's huddles did not involve equity research analysts, the analysts who are subject to the SEC rules. Rather, those who participated in the huddle were from Goldman's "Fundamental Strategies Group," a group that would be exempt from the SEC rules.[8]

Was this change of name a good business strategy? Are there risks in this strategy?

Running Afoul Using the Net: E-Commerce and Insider Trading

One trend that has emerged in stock trading is the practice of "pump and dump." This practice uses the rapid communication of the Internet to disperse information about a company so that the market price is affected. Those who have pumped the stock then sell, or dump, their shares when their efforts on the Internet have caused a sufficient jump in the price.

For example, Mark S. Jakob was dealing in call options in Emulex stock. His prediction that Emulex stock would take a dive was wrong, and the stock in fact increased in value. He had a loss of $100,000. In order to cover his losses, the 23-year-old sent an e-mail press release to an Internet wire service. The fake press release indicated that the CEO of Emulex would resign due to the fact that earnings had been overstated. The news release was then distributed to various websites. The overall loss to shareholders in reaction to the negative news was $2.5 billion as the share price plummeted. However, Mr. Jakob made $240,000 on his trades in the stock.

Mr. Jakob was arrested for securities fraud and wire fraud.[9] However, his use of the Internet resulted in significant damage to the company's stock value. The rapid dissemination of information via the Internet and the resulting damage has resulted in significant enforcement efforts against fraud committed online.

Running Afoul of 10(b): Aiders and Abettors

One area of 10(b) liability that remained unclear for almost two decades was whether those who participated with a company in disseminating false information—that is, those who aided and abetted—could be held liable under 10(b). The U.S. Supreme Court's decision in *Stonebridge Investment Partners, LLC v Scientific-American, Inc.*, 552 U.S.148 (2008) limited the civil liability of third-party aiders and abettors to accounting manipulation and fraud. However, Dodd–Frank will expand the liability of those who participate in helping a company to overstate or understate items in financial reports that result in a rosier picture such as inflating inventory levels and valuations of accounts receivable.

In the *Stonebridge* case, the conduct of third parties helped a company appear to be in better financial condition than it really was. Scientific-Atlanta and Motorola supplied Charter Communications with the digital cable converter boxes that Charter furnished to its customers. Charter arranged to overpay these two suppliers $20 for each set top box it purchased until the end of the year, with the understanding that Scientific-Atlanta and Motorola would return the overpayment by purchasing advertising from Charter. The transactions had no economic substance; but, because Charter would then record the advertising purchases as revenue and capitalize its purchase of the boxes, in violation of generally accepted accounting principles, the transactions would enable Charter to fool its auditor into approving a financial statement that showed Charter had met projected revenue and operating cash flow numbers. So that Arthur Andersen would continue auditing in the dark and not discover or understand the link between Charter's increased payments for the boxes and the advertising purchases by Motorola and Scientific-Atlanta, the companies drafted documents to make it appear the transactions were unrelated and were just business as usual between and among friends, suppliers, and customers (although it was not entirely clear to an outsider that the two roles were being played with the same cash). Charter asked Scientific-Atlanta to send documents to Charter stating that it had increased production costs. It raised the price for boxes for the rest of 2000 by $20 per box. Charter, under a written agreement, would then purchase from Motorola a specific number of boxes and pay liquidated damages of $20 for each unit it did not take. The whole idea of the contract was to set up Charter's failure to purchase all the units and then have Charter ship the cash back by paying Motorola the liquidated damages.

To cloud the transactions for the auditor further, the new box agreements were backdated to have a different start date from the advertising agreements. The back-dating was important to convey the impression that the negotiations were unconnected; this is a point auditors get testy about.

The case resulted in outrage from the investors who lost their investments because two companies participated in obfuscation that duped the auditor and resulted in a clean audit opinion that offered investors ongoing reassurance of an investment that was actually going south very quickly. The court held, correctly as the law existed at that time, that the two companies could not be held liable because they did not assist in preparing Charter's financial statements. Aiders and abettors who help create the atmosphere for deceptive financial statements but do not prepare them can now be held liable under the changes Dodd–Frank provides for that expanded liability.

FOR THE MANAGER'S DESK

Re: What's Ethical in Insider Trading?

Insider trading is a tough area. Consider a few examples to test how well you understand the law:

1. You are employed by Marsh, a large insurance underwriter. Marsh has been charged with antitrust violations, and the price of the company's shares has taken a beating. As you and your coworkers worry about your future, you decide to have a happy hour session at a local bar. During the discussion, a coworker says, "The stock is down now, but there's still value in the company. I am buying a bunch of shares now, while the market is down on us. I can make a killing when it all comes back, and it will." You take his words to heart and on Monday buy a large block of your company's shares. Did you violate 10b?

   __Yes __No __Maybe __Ethical __Unethical

2. On March 6, 1973, Dirks, an investment analyst, received information from Secrist, a former officer of Equity Funding of America, that the assets of Equity Funding were vastly overstated, and that fraud was afoot at the company. After he did some checking, and employees confirmed to Dirks what he had heard, he told a number of clients and investors what he had discovered and they sold their shares. Neither Dirks nor his company had any shares in Equity Funding. Did Dirks and his clients violate 10b?

   __Yes __No __Maybe __Ethical __Unethical

3. Mark Cuban, the wealthy Internet entrepreneur and owner of the Dallas Mavericks, purchased a 6.3 percent interest in Mamma.com, Inc., a Canadian-based company. In June 2004, Mamma.com, Inc., executives invited Cuban to participate in a private equity placement (private investment in public equity [PIPE]) for Mamma.com. Cuban was told that the offering would be made at a discount and that it would result in dilution for existing shareholders. At the end of the call, Cuban told the CEO, "Well, now I'm screwed. I can't sell."

   The CEO called Cuban again and offered to let him speak with the investment adviser (Merriman) handling the private equity placement. Cuban did so and the investment adviser has described Cuban as angry. Within one minute of this conversation and within hours of his conversation with Mamma.com's CEO, Cuban called his broker and instructed him to sell Cuban's entire position in the company. Cuban instructed his broker, "Sell what you can tonight and just get me out the next day." On June 29, 2004, Cuban sold his remaining 590,000 Mamma.com shares during regular trading at an average cost per share of $13.2937. The SEC charged Cuban with insider trading. When the offering was publicly announced, Mamma.com's stock price opened at $11.89, down $1.215 or 9.3 percent from the prior day's closing price of $13.105. According to the complaint, Cuban avoided losses in excess of $750,000 by selling his stock prior to the public announcement of the offering. Was this insider trading?

   __Yes __No __Maybe __Ethical __Unethical

Standing to Sue Under Section 10(b)

To be able to recover under Section 10(b), a party suing must have standing. **Standing** in these cases has been defined by the U.S. Supreme Court as the actual sale or purchase of stock in reliance on the information or lack of information given. For example, persons who would have purchased stock had they known the truth could not recover for damages under 10(b). Likewise, they cannot recover damages because they would have sold their stock had they known the truth. An actual sale or purchase must have occurred for a plaintiff to satisfy the standing requirements of 10(b). In *Blue Chip Stamp v Manor Drug Store*, 421 U.S. 723 (1975), the U.S. Supreme Court held that a pessimistic statement of income and potential was not a 10(b) violation because a potentially interested buyer who did not buy because of the pessimism did not have actual damages and, hence, no standing.

The Requirement of Scienter Under Section 10(b)

A conviction under 10(b) cannot be based on negligence—that is, the failure to discover financial information. Because 10(b) is a criminal statute, violators must have some intent to defraud or knowledge of wrongdoing, or *scienter*. Convictions are only for knowing the financial information but failing to disclose it.

In *Ernst & Ernst v Hochfelder*, 425 U.S. 185 (1978), the Supreme Court held that an accounting firm that had negligently performed an audit of a business based on a fraud could not be held liable under 10(b) because, although the accounting firm made a mistake, it had no intent to defraud.

Penalties for Running Afoul of Section 10(b)

Each time a major scandal breaks, the penalties for insider trading increase. Following Boesky's insider schemes on Wall Street, the **Insider Trading and Securities Fraud Enforcement Act of 1988**, an amendment to the 1934 act, increased substantially the penalties for violations of Section 10(b). SOX changes have more than doubled the penalties of those earlier reforms. Violations of 10(b) carry prison terms of up to 25 years plus penalties. Corporate financial officers also face the increased penalties and the claw-back of bonuses and other compensation earned through false financial statements. In addition to these criminal penalties, the SEC is authorized to bring civil actions against the companies and its officers and collect civil penalties for financial reporting violations, insider trading, and other activities related to 10(b) violations.

To increase the likelihood of corporate employees coming forward with information on fraudulent financial reporting, the SEC can pay bounties in the form of a percentage of the amount recovered to informants who report violations. Sarbanes–Oxley includes protections for company whistle-blowers who report violations to the SEC. These protections are similar to many antiretaliation statutes at the federal and state levels and provide the employees with a shield against termination for reporting violations. Dodd–Frank allows the SEC to increase the bounties paid to whistle-blowers to up to 30 percent and also provides employees who are retaliated against for reporting information to the SEC a right of private action against their employers. Officers and legal counsel are also protected under this provision. The American Bar Association (ABA) amended its Model Code of Ethics to allow lawyers, without being considered in violation of their duty of client confidentiality, to report the conduct of clients who are using the lawyer's advice to commit a fraud. As noted in Chapter 18, lawyers are also required to report conduct of company officers "up the ladder" in the corporation to the board and audit committee, and the ABA changed its Model Code of Ethics to allow such reporting.

Consider...

Scott London was a senior partner at KPMG for 29 years. What began as a friendship and a case of braggadocio ended with over $100,000 in cash and gifts exchanged and criminal charges for both Mr. London and Bryan Shaw, Mr. London's golfing friend. The two met at a Los Angeles golf course and in their initial contacts made conversation about business. Mr. London let slip the names of companies KPMG was auditing and some information about those companies. Mr. Shaw used the information to position himself to profit from the advance tips on the companies' fates. For example, if the information was negative, Mr. Shaw positioned himself short. If the information was positive, Mr. Shaw simply purchased the stock ahead of the release of the positive news.

There were phone calls between the two men, some during which Mr. London read the company press releases prior to their public disclosure. Mr. Shaw was able to net $1.2 million from the stock trades based on the London tips. And after each profitable sale of stock, Mr. Shaw would meet Mr. London in a parking lot and pay him $10,000 in cash. For example, KPMG was doing the audits on Skechers and Herbalife, and Mr. Shaw, possessing negative information on those companies, was able to position himself short and profit once the questions about earnings were publicly disclosed (in the case of Herbalife, its accounting methods for pyramid sales were revealed). The FBI and the SEC have photos of those exchanges and records of those telephone calls because Mr. Shaw began cooperating with federal authorities on February 8, 2013. He wore a wire, tipped the FBI on the cash pay-off sites, and allowed his phone to be tapped.

Mr. London was charged with securities fraud—Section 10(b) of the 1934 Securities Exchange Act. Did he violate 10(b) if he did not work for the companies directly? Even if he did not work on the course directly?

19-3d INSIDER TRADING AND SHORT-SWING PROFITS

In addition to the application of Section 10(b) and Rule 10b-5 to trading on inside information, the 1934 act also has a form of a strict liability statute for insider trading. Officers, directors, and 10 percent or more shareholders have greater access to inside information. They are involved in setting a corporation's policy and directions in dividend decisions, in product decisions, and in expansion decisions. They will always have access to information that is not yet available to the public. **Section 16** of the 1934 act is a *per se* liability section designed to deal with stock trading by corporate insiders, who are defined as officers, directors, and 10 percent shareholders of those companies and are required to be registered under the 1934 act.

Under 16(a), officers, directors, and 10 percent shareholders (10 percent of any class of stock) are required to file reports declaring their holdings. In addition, they must file updated reports after any change in ownership (purchase, sale, or transfer). Any changes in ownership must be reported within two days.

Under 16(b), officers, directors, and 10 percent shareholders are required to give to the corporation any **short-swing profits**—that is, profits earned on the sale and purchase or purchase and sale of stock during any six-month period. For example, suppose Director Cadigan of a listed New York Stock Exchange company engaged in the following transactions:

April 11, 2014—Ms. Cadigan bought 200 shares of her corporation's stock at $50 each.
April 30, 2014—Ms. Cadigan sold 200 shares at $30 each.
May 15, 2014—Ms. Cadigan bought 200 shares at $20 each.

The SEC will match the highest sale with the lowest purchase. Ms. Cadigan has a profit of $10 per share even though she has a net loss. This profit must be returned to the corporation. It is irrelevant whether the officer, director, or 10 percent shareholder actually used inside information: The presumption under 16(b) for short-swing trades is that the officer, director, or 10 percent shareholder had access to inside information.

These rules also apply to stock options. However, the issue of stock options and compensation has become a sensitive one following their role in the collapse of so many companies. To minimize or eliminate the incentives for making the financial picture brighter for purposes of increasing the value of stock options, some companies, such as GE and Coca-Cola, have changed their compensation plans to eliminate options and offer employees special classes of stock that have predetermined values or that are awarded only after a period of years following the release of earnings.

19-3e REGULATING VOTING INFORMATION

At one time, shareholders could give their proxies to the company just by endorsing the backs of their dividend checks; proxies then were obtained easily and without much disclosure. The 1934 act changed the way proxies were solicited. With the same philosophy used for registration, the SEC required full disclosure to be the goal of all **proxy solicitations**. To achieve that goal, the SEC now requires prior filing and adequate representation of shareholder interests.

The Proxy Statement

Under Section 14 of the 1934 act, all companies required to register under the act must file their proxy materials with the SEC at least 10 days before those materials are to be sent. Proxy materials include the proxy statement and all other solicitation materials that will be sent to shareholders. The proxy statement required by the SEC must contain the following details:

1. Who is soliciting the proxy
2. How the materials will be sent
3. Who is paying for the costs of soliciting
4. How much has been spent to date on the solicitation
5. How much is expected to be spent on the solicitation
6. Why the proxy is being solicited—annual meeting elections, special meeting on a merger, and so on

Shareholder Proposals

Because the purpose of Section 14 is full disclosure, the representation of views other than those of corporate management is important in proxy solicitations. Shareholders can submit proposals to be included in proxy solicitation materials. If the company does not oppose what is being proposed, the proposition is included as part of the proxy materials. If management is opposed, the proposing shareholder has the right to include a 200-word statement on the proposal in the materials. These proposals are not permitted along with their 200-word statements unless they propose conduct that is legal and related to business operations, as opposed to social, moral, religious, and political views. During the Vietnam era, many shareholders wanted to include proposals in proxy materials for companies that were war suppliers. Their proposals centered on the political opposition to the war and not the business practices of the company. Through 2003, shareholders focused on social issues such as human rights initiatives for companies' international operations. However, as shown in Exhibit 19.4, attention has shifted back to corporate governance proposals.

EXHIBIT 19.4 The Top Topic Areas for Shareholder Proposals

THE TOP SHAREHOLDER PROPOSALS DURING THE 2012–2013 ANNUAL MEETING SEASON:

Approval vote on compensation	Require a majority to elect directors
Right to call a special meeting	Take action on climate change
Repeal classification of directors	End supermajority vote requirement
Review of report on company political spending	Retention period for stock awards
Independent board chairman	Report on sustainability
Disclosure of indirect lobbying activities by the corporation	Report on diversity
	Adopt sexual orientation antibias policy

Under Dodd–Frank, the SEC must issue rules permitting shareholders to use proxy solicitation materials supplied by the company in order to distribute their proposals, something that eliminates a barrier shareholders faced in getting proposals to go forward. With this access, shareholders will be able to nominate individuals for board membership.

The say-on-pay provision that was part of the Dodd–Frank revisions requires shareholders to vote on executive compensation every two years. While the vote is advisory only, this statutory requirement has emboldened shareholders and some companies now are required, through shareholder votes, to obtain their consent for compensation packages.

The focus of shareholder proposals shows a distinct shift from social and environmental issues to straight procedural and governance issues. Directors and management have also changed their approaches with shareholders, often meeting with the activists and agreeing to make changes without the need for a vote. With almost half of shareholder proposals approaching 50 percent approval, this new strategy seems to be an inevitable one.

Remedies for Violations of Section 14

If proxies are solicited without following the Section 14 guidelines, the proxies are invalid. They must then be resolicited, and if the meeting has been held in which the invalid proxies were used, the action taken at the meeting can be set aside.

ETHICAL ISSUES

Iroquois Brands, Ltd., is a food company that imports French *foie gras*, a pâté made from the enlarged livers of force-fed geese. The French method for raising the geese is to funnel corn down the geese's throats and gag them with rubber bands to keep them from regurgitating. A shareholder wishes to include in the proxy materials a proposal that the company study this method of force-feeding as an unethical business practice (cruelty to animals).

Should the proposal be included? Does Section 14 require that it be included?

[*Lovenheim v Iroquois Brands, Ltd.,* 618 F. Supp. 554 (D.C. 1985)]

19-3f SHAREHOLDER RIGHTS IN TAKEOVERS, MERGERS, AND CONSOLIDATIONS

Definitions

Mergers. A **merger** is a combination of two or more corporations, after which only one corporation continues to exist. For example, when America West Airlines merged with US Airways, the newly merged company became US Airways. US Airways owned all of America West's assets and assumed all of America West's liabilities. The three types of mergers are horizontal, vertical, and conglomerate.

Consolidations. In a **consolidation**, two or more companies combine into one new company and none of the old companies continues to exist. For example, if US Airways and America West had become America First Airlines, then both corporations give all of their rights and liabilities to the new company, which holds all assets of the consolidating companies and assumes all their liabilities.

Tender Offers. A **tender offer** is not a business combination; it is a method for achieving a business combination. An offer that is publicly advertised to shareholders for the purchase of their stock is a tender offer. The offering price for the stock is usually higher than the market price of the shares, which makes the tender offer attractive to the shareholders.

Originally, the tender offer was used as a means for a corporation to reacquire its shares. However, it has become a tool of business combinations of every sort, sometimes friendly and sometimes hostile.

Takeovers. Takeovers are accomplished through the use of tender offers and can be either friendly or hostile. A **friendly takeover** is one the management of a firm favors, whereas a **hostile takeover** is one the management of a firm opposes. Restrictions on the use of tender offers and procedures for accomplishing a takeover are discussed later in the chapter.

Acquisitions. The acquisition of another firm's assets is either a means of expanding or a way to eliminate a creditor; **asset acquisition**, however, is different from the other business combinations. Because the corporate structure does not change, shareholder approval is not required for an asset acquisition. However, asset acquisitions are subject to the constraints of the Clayton Act.

1934 Act Regulation of Takeovers

In all of these business combinations (except asset acquisitions), someone is buying enough stock to own a company. That much buying and selling has long had the attention of the SEC. The **Williams Act** amendment to the Securities Exchange Act of 1934 regulates these offers to buy stock or tender offers. The Williams Act was passed in 1968 to apply to all offers to buy more than 5 percent of a corporation's securities.

Filing Requirements Under the Williams Act. Any offeror subject to the Williams Act is required to file a tender offer statement with both the SEC and the target company. The offeror must also send or publish for shareholders of the target company all the information and details about the offer. If the target company is opposing the takeover (that is, if it is hostile), the target must also file its materials with the SEC.

A registration statement for a tender offer must include the name of the offeror, its source of funding for the offer, its plans for the company if its attempted takeover is successful, and the number of shares now owned.

Shareholders have seven days after a tender offer to withdraw their shares. This seven-day period is to prevent shareholders from being forced into a "now-or-never" transaction. The actual purchase of the shares cannot take place until at least 15 days after the tender offer began. If the offeror changes the tender offer terms, shareholders must be notified; and if a better price is offered, all shareholders must be given 10 days to tender their shares at that price (even those who have already tendered their shares at the lower price).

Williams Act Penalties for Violations. The Williams amendments provide for both civil and criminal penalties for violations of the act's procedures. The penalties are based on the same type of language used for 10(b) violations. Criminal and civil penalties are imposed for "fraudulent, deceptive or manipulative" practices used in making a tender offer. Penalties may also be assessed for omissions or misstatements of material facts in the tender offer materials.

Special Protections for the Hostile Takeover. In a noncontested takeover, the target company must declare to its shareholders one of the following within 10 days after the date the tender offer commenced:

1. That it recommends acceptance or rejection of the offer
2. That it has no opinion and remains neutral
3. That it is unable to take a position

The target company must also justify its position.

In those cases in which the target company does not want to be taken over, both the target company and the offeror develop strategies for stopping the other. Some of the tactics used by a target company to fight takeovers are the following:

1. Persuading shareholders that the tender offer is not in their best interests
2. Filing legal suits or complaints on the grounds that the takeover violates provisions of the antitrust laws
3. Matching the buyout with a target company offer
4. Soliciting a "white knight" merger or a merger from a friendly party

State Laws Affecting Tender Offers
The U.S. Supreme Court has held that state statutes that change the regulatory process for takeovers are violations of the Supremacy Clause (see Chapter 5). Congress has preempted the field by establishing a full regulatory scheme for takeovers under the Williams Act. [*Edgar v MITE Corp.*, 457 U.S. 624 (1982)] However, following the *MITE* case, the states passed a new type of antitakeover statute that permits shareholders to have some say in whether a corporation should be taken over.

Current shareholder proposal activity focuses on having their companies opt out of these state takeover requirements as a matter of governance so that managers can deal with takeover offers more efficiently.

Proxy Regulations and Tender Offers
Once some shares are acquired, a firm poised for a takeover wages a proxy battle, which means it solicits proxies in order to be able to command the number of votes needed to gain control of the board. Even though these proxy solicitations originate outside the company, the proxy statement and solicitation materials must be filed with the SEC.

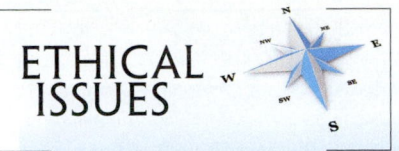

ETHICAL ISSUES

Joseph Horne Company, a department store in Pennsylvania, entered into an agreement to have Dillard's (a national retail chain) take it over. Dillard's performed its due diligence—the process of getting internal access to computers and records to verify financial statements. During due diligence, Dillard's assumed responsibility for ordering and shipping merchandise. Employees in Horne's management were told that they would no longer have jobs, and nearly 500 employees left Horne. Horne's Christmas merchandise was delayed and was often wrong, and the merger fell through. Horne says that Dillard's went too far. Dillard's says that due diligence is part of a takeover, that Horne's financial statements were inaccurate, and that Horne could have stopped the ordering and shipping at any time. One of the officers at Horne's bank says a Dillard's official told him that Dillard's would just wait until the company was in Chapter 11 bankruptcy and pick it up cheaply. Evaluate the ethics of both parties.

Failure to file these materials makes the proxies invalid, and any action taken at a meeting using the proxies can be set aside. Mergers voted on with invalid proxies can be "unwound." The SEC or the shareholders can bring an action to prevent the use or undo the use of invalid proxies. If a shareholder successfully brings an action seeking a remedy for a violation of the SEC proxy solicitation rules outlined in Section 14, the offeror must fully reimburse the shareholder for all costs of the court action.

Proxies obtained by using misleading information or by not disclosing material information are also invalid. Again, either the SEC or individual shareholders can bring suit to stop the use of these proxies or to set aside action taken with them.

Proxy contests are expensive. Who pays for their costs? If management wins, they can be reimbursed for reasonable costs. However, some courts limit this reimbursement right to battles waged over corporate policy and not over personality conflicts. If the new group wins, they can vote to reimburse for reasonable expenses, but many states require shareholders to ratify such reimbursement.

19-4 State Securities Laws

Today all states have their own securities laws. In addition to federal laws, all issuers are required to follow state blue-sky laws in all states in which their securities are sold. Two types of state securities laws govern registration: those that follow the SEC standards for full disclosure and those that follow a merit review standard. Under SEC standards, a filing is required, and as long as all the required information is there, the offering will be approved for public sale. Under a **merit review** standard, the regulatory agency responsible for securities enforcement can actually examine a filed offering for its merits as to adequate capitalization, excessive stock ownership by the promoters, and penny-stock problems. These agencies apply a general standard that the offering must be "fair, just, and equitable." This general standard gives them great latitude in deciding which issues will be approved.

Many companies do not register their offerings in states that conduct merit review. They sell in the other states to avoid the problems of being denied registration.

As on the federal level, all states have their own exemptions from registration. Most SEC exemptions also work at the state level, the only requirement being that the issuer file a notice of sale with the state agency.

EXHIBIT 19.5 State and Federal Securities Law

1933 ACT	1934 ACT	BLUE SKY
S1—Registration statement	*Application*	State securities registration
Financial information	500 or more unaccredited	Merit versus disclosure standards
Officers/directors	shareholders (or more than 2,000	Federally exempt securities may still
Prospectus 20-day effective date,	total shareholders) with $10 million	need to register at state level
deficiency letter	or more in assets or listed on national	
	exchange	
Section 11—Filing false registration	Sec. 10b—insider trading/fraud	
statement	*10K*	
Liability: anyone named in	Annual reports	
prospectus or offering expert	*10Q*	
materials for it	Quarterly report	
Material: false statement; privity	*Foreign Corrupt Practices Act*	
not required unless longer than	Financial reports	
one year	Internal controls	
Defenses: due diligence; buyer's	Applies to 1933 and 1934 act	
knowledge	registrants	
Section 12—Failure to file; selling	*Section 14*	
before effective date; false	Proxy registration	
prospectus	Compensation disclosure	
Material: false statement; privity	*Section 16A*	
required	Officers, directors, 10% shareholders	
Defenses: due diligence; buyer's	Sales registration	
knowledge	*Section 16B—short-swing profits*	
Penalties	Tender offer regulations (Williams Act)	
$100,000 and/or five years	Penalties—up to 25 years	
(criminal/civil suit)	Separate financial certification	
	penalties under Sarbanes–Oxley	

In addition to regulating securities offerings, these state agencies also control the licensing of brokers and agents of securities within the state. The licensing process consists of an application and a background check conducted by the agency to identify possible criminal problems.

Exhibit 19.5 provides a summary of securities regulation under state and federal law.

19-5 International Issues in Securities Laws

The following policy statement from the State Department summarizes the nature of international capital markets today: "The United States Government is committed to an international system which provides for a high degree of freedom in the movement of trade and investment flows."

The United States has ten stock exchanges; Germany, eight; France, seven; and Switzerland, seven. The United Kingdom, Japan, Canada, the Netherlands, Belgium, Luxembourg, Norway, Kuwait, Australia, and many other countries have at least one stock exchange each.

A directive from the European Union has developed uniform requirements for disclosure in primary offering. Often called a "listing of particulars" instead of a "prospectus," uniform information is given to shareholders prior to their purchases. One difficulty that must be resolved is that accounting practices outside the United States are not uniform. Insider trading has been prosecuted vigorously in the United States for the past 30 years. European enforcement has been limited. In addition to the lack of enforcement, little regulatory structure for investigation and prosecution is in place.

BIOGRAPHY

Bernie Madoff: The Largest and Longest Ponzi Scheme in History ($50 Billion and 18 Years)

It is a remarkable story, that of Madoff (pronounced MADE-off) Securities. An entrepreneur from his early years, Bernie Madoff, the founder of Madoff Investments, Inc., worked his way through college as a part-time lifeguard who also ran his own lawn sprinkler system company. He installed and repaired lawn sprinkler systems in the mornings and went to class in the afternoons. He graduated from Hofstra University and then went on to Brooklyn Law School, again running his business in the morning and going to classes in the afternoon. Because he was not really interested in practicing law, he left law school after the first year and, using $5,000 he had saved from his business, bought a trader position on Wall Street. He had grown up familiar with stocks, bonds, and trading because his mother had operated a small securities trading firm when Bernie was younger. She had even been investigated by the SEC, but when she withdrew her registration as a trader, the SEC withdrew its investigation.

From the time he began his Wall Street career until his arrest, Bernie was on an upward swing. Over decades, he delivered 12–18 percent returns to his investors. He was the investment firm for the rich and famous. Kevin Bacon, Kyra Sedgwick, Steven Spielberg, and others from the wealthiest sets in New York City and Palm Beach were clients of Madoff Securities. He was one of the founders of NASDAQ and served as chairman of its board in its early years. He spent a great deal of time in Washington, DC, testifying at Congressional hearings and meeting with regulators on markets, regulations, and trading issues.

Madoff and his wife were kind to employees, generous to charities, and active with colleges and universities, donating money to Hofstra, Brooklyn University, and Yeshiva University. They were also known for their wealth and spending.

Some have said the scheme began in the 1980s, but Madoff said in court that he believes it began in the 1990s. Mr. Madoff put clients' money in a Chase Manhattan bank account and then used the money to pay individual investors, trust funds, charitable organizations and others as they requested withdrawals from their accounts. He said he did not promise a specific rate of return, but his clients expected that he would outperform the market, so he concocted a bogus investment strategy that he then used to recruit new clients. Mr. Madoff was adamant in insisting that his other businesses, including a stock trading company with offices in New York and London, which were run by his sons and his brother, were not connected to his Ponzi scheme, "The other businesses my firm engaged in, proprietary trading and market-making, were legitimate, profitable, and successful in all respects. Those businesses were managed by my brother and two sons."[10]

In order to keep the funds flowing, he was dependent upon the classic Ponzi scheme model: getting more investors in with additional money, which is critical to keeping the earlier investors satisfied. However, there comes a point when there are not enough new recruits to satisfy the existing participants and the fund collapses under even just the daily demands for payouts, let alone the draw-downs that can come from fears in a bull market.

The scheme was uncovered by federal investigators in December 2008, and Mr. Madoff entered a guilty plea to criminal charges of securities fraud, wire fraud, conspiracy, and other crimes and was sentenced to 150 years in prison. When he entered his guilty plea, Mr. Madoff told the packed courtroom,

"I am actually grateful for this opportunity to publicly speak about my crimes, for which I am so deeply sorry and ashamed. I knew what I was doing was wrong, indeed, criminal. When I began the Ponzi scheme, I believed it would end shortly and I would be able to extricate myself and my clients. [Finding an exit] proved difficult and ultimately impossible. As the years went by I realized this day, and my arrest, would inevitably come.

I am painfully aware that I have deeply hurt many, many people, including members of my family, my closest friends, business associates and the thousands of clients who gave me their money. I cannot adequately express how sorry I am for what I have done."[11]

The psychology of Madoff, like that of all diabolical Ponzi schemers, is fascinating. One of his best friends, for whom Mr. Madoff served as best man, was asked to explain why Bernie would engage in such behavior and not understand the consequences of the huge fraud, "There is no way to. I can't make it add up. It doesn't make sense. I cannot take the Bernie I knew and turn him into the Bernie we're hearing about 24/7. It doesn't compute."[12]

Summary

What requirements affect primary offerings?

- Primary offering—sale of securities by the business in which interests are offered
- Security—investment in a common enterprise with profits to come from efforts of others

Why do we have securities laws, and what is their history?

- Securities Act of 1933—federal law regulating initial sales of securities
- Securities Act of 1934—federal law regulating securities and companies in the secondary market
- Amendments include SOX, PSLRA, and JOBS

How do securities laws regulate the primary market?

- Blue-sky laws—state securities registration regulations
- Merit review—regulation of merits of an offering as opposed to disclosure
- *Howey* test—Supreme Court definition of security
- SEC—federal agency responsible for enforcing federal securities laws
- Exemption—security not required to be registered
- Exempt transaction—offering not required to be registered
- Regulation D—small offering exemption rules
- Accredited investor—investor who meets threshold standards for assets and income
- Rules 504, 505, 506—portion of Regulation D affording exemptions for variously structured offerings

- Registration statement—disclosure statement filed by the offeror with the SEC
- Prospectus—formal document explaining offering or any ad or written materials describing offering
- Comment letter—request by SEC for more information
- Deficiency letter—request by SEC for more information
- Full-disclosure standard—review for information, not a review on the merits
- Tombstone ad—ad announcing offering that can be run prior to effective date of registration statement
- Red herring prospectus—redlined prospectus that can be given to potential purchasers prior to effective date of registration statement
- Shelf registrations—SEC approval process that allows approval and then waiting period for market conditions
- Material misstatement—false information that would affect the decision to buy or sell
- Section 11—portion of 1933 act that provides for liability for false statements or omissions in registration statements
- Due diligence—defense of good faith and full effort to Section 11 charges
- Section 12—portion of 1933 act that provides for liability for selling without registration or exemption before effective date or with a false prospectus
- SOX numerous protections on certifications and disclosures

How do securities laws regulate the secondary market?

- 10-Q—periodic reporting forms required of 1934 act companies

- SOX and certification of financial reports by CEO and CFO

- 10-K—periodic reporting forms required of 1934 act companies

- 8-K—periodic reporting forms required of 1934 act companies

- Section 10(b)—antifraud provision of Securities Exchange Act

- Rule 10b-5—SEC regulation on antifraud provision of Securities Exchange Act

- Insider—person with access to nonpublic information about a company

- Tippee—person who gains nonpublic information from an insider

- Fair Disclosure Rule—SEC regulation on disclosure to analysts

- Insider Trading and Securities Fraud Enforcement Act of 1988—federal law increasing penalties for insider trading violations

- Section 16—portion of 1934 act regulating short-swing profits by officers, directors, or 10 percent shareholders

- Short-swing profits—gain on sale and purchase or purchase and sale of securities within a six-month period

- Proxy solicitations—formal paperwork requesting authority to vote on behalf of another

How do securities laws protect shareholders in share and company acquisitions?

- Mergers, consolidations, tender offers, and asset acquisitions are regulated

- Williams Act regulates tender offers

- States have antitakeover statutes

Questions and Problems

1. The Farmer's Cooperative of Arkansas (Co-Op) was an agricultural cooperative that had approximately 23,000 members. In order to raise money to support its general business operations, the Co-Op sold promissory notes payable on demand by the holder. The notes were uncollateralized and uninsured and paid a variable rate of interest that was adjusted to make it higher than the rate paid by local financial institutions. The notes were offered to members and nonmembers and were marketed as an "investment program." Advertisements for the notes, which appeared in the Co-Op newsletter, read in part: "YOUR CO-OP has more than $11,000,000 in assets to stand behind your investments. The Investment is not Federal [sic] insured but it is … Safe."

Despite the assurance, the Co-Op filed for bankruptcy in 1984. At the time of the bankruptcy filing, over 1,600 people held notes worth a total of $10 million.

After the bankruptcy filing, a class of note holders filed suit against Arthur Young & Co., alleging that Young had failed to follow generally accepted accounting principles in its audit, specifically with respect to the valuation of the Co-Op's major asset, a gasohol plant. The note holders claimed that if Young had properly treated the plant in its audited financials, they would not have purchased the notes. The petitioners were awarded $6.1 million in damages by the federal district court. Are the notes securities? [*Reves v Ernst & Young*, 494 U.S. 56 (1990)]

2. In August 1994, Mervyn Cooper, a psychotherapist, was providing marriage counseling to a Lockheed executive. The executive had been assigned to conduct the due diligence (review of the accuracy of the books and records) of Martin Marietta, a company with which Lockheed was going to merge.

At his August 22, 1994, session with Mr. Cooper, the executive revealed to him the pending, but nonpublic, merger. Following his session with the executive, Mr. Cooper contacted a friend, Kenneth Rottenberg, and told him about the pending merger. They agreed that Mr. Rottenberg would open a brokerage account so they could buy Lockheed call options and common stocks and then share in the profits.

When Mr. Rottenberg went to some brokerage offices to set up an account, he was warned by a broker about the risks of call options. Mr. Rottenberg told the broker that Lockheed would announce a major business combination shortly and that he would not lose his money.

Did Mr. Rottenberg and Mr. Cooper violate Section 10(b)? What about the broker? [*SEC v Mervyn Cooper and Kenneth E. Rottenberg*, No. 95-8535 (C.D. Cal. 1995)]

3. Rollo Norton II, a.k.a. Rick, a financial planner, worked diligently for a number of years to try to keep a San Diego condo project afloat during a real estate downturn. He has confessed to forging signatures, faking loan applications, kiting checks intended for deposit in escrow accounts, and using credit of buyers to borrow money to keep his project going. He and two associates entered guilty pleas and are cooperating with federal authorities in their ongoing investigation of the project.

Fidelity National Financial, which is the largest title insurance company in the United States, was the title insurer for most of the buyers in the project. The project began to unwind in 2006 when several buyer victims filed suit and the architect for the project entered a guilty plea to fraud. However, Fidelity did not disclose the suits, suits that increased from 2006 until October 2009 when the fraud issues emerged. There is no mention in any of the company's 8-K, 10-Q, or 10-K filings about the developments in the project, the litigation, or the guilty pleas.

When Fidelity shareholders filed suit against the company for violations of 10b, company expert witnesses maintained that disclosure when there is uncertainty can harm the company's share price and result in unnecessary losses.

Should there have been disclosure? Of what, how much, and when?

4. Steve Hindi is an animal rights activist who owns $5,000 in Pepsi stock. He discovered that Pepsi advertises in bullrings in Spain and Mexico, and he has attended annual shareholder meetings and put forward shareholder proposals to have the company halt the practice. His proposal did not pass, but he did not give up easily and started a website to increase pressure on the company. (See www.sharkonline.org for an article containing more details regarding this issue.)

Pepsi has withdrawn bullfighting ads in Mexico but continues with them in Spain. Mr. Hindi continues his quest. Should the proposal have been approved? Does Mr. Hindi run any risk with his website activism?

5. Beginning in March 1981, R. Foster Winans was a *Wall Street Journal* reporter and one of the writers of the "Heard on the Street" column (the "Heard" column), a widely read and influential column in the *WSJ*. David Carpenter worked as a news clerk at the *WSJ* from December 1981 through May 1983. Kenneth Felis, who was a stockbroker at the brokerage house of Kidder Peabody, had been brought to that firm by another Kidder Peabody stockbroker, Peter Brant, Mr. Felis's longtime friend, who later became the government's key witness in this case.

Since February 2, 1981, it had been the practice of Dow Jones, the parent company of the *Wall Street Journal*, to distribute to all new employees "The Insider Story," a 40-page manual with seven pages devoted to the company's conflicts-of-interest policy. Mr. Winans and Mr. Carpenter knew that company policy deemed all news material gleaned by an employee during the course of employment to be company property and that

company policy required employees to treat nonpublic information learned on the job as confidential.

Notwithstanding company policy, Mr. Winans participated in a scheme with Mr. Brant, and later Mr. Felis and Mr. Carpenter, in which he agreed to provide the two stockbrokers (Mr. Brant and Mr. Felis) with securities-related information that was scheduled to appear in "Heard" columns; based on this advance information, the two brokers would buy or sell the subject securities. Mr. Carpenter, who was involved in a private, personal, nonbusiness relationship with Mr. Winans, served primarily as a messenger for the conspirators. Trading accounts were established in the names of Kenneth Felis, David Carpenter, R. Foster Winans, Peter Brant, David Clark, Western Hemisphere, and Stephen Spratt. During 1983 and early 1984, these defendants made prepublication trades on the basis of their advance knowledge of approximately 27 *Wall Street Journal* "Heard" columns, although not all of those columns were written by Mr. Winans. Generally, he would inform Mr. Brant of an article's subject the day before its scheduled publication, usually by calls from a pay phone and often using a fictitious name. The net profits from the scheme approached $690,000. Was this scheme a 10(b) violation? [*United States v Carpenter*, 791 F.2d 1024 (2nd Cir. 1986); *affirmed, Carpenter v United States*, 484 U.S. 19 (1987)]

6. Following the collapse of the World Trade Center (WTC) in New York City on September 11, 2001, the stock markets were closed for several days. When the stock markets reopened on Monday, September 17, 2001, there was unusual activity in stocks that were hit the hardest by the attacks and subsequent shut-down of the United States' airline industry: airlines and insurance. Investors based in Europe had purchased puts in airline and insurance companies with the expectation of earning returns based on the fall in these companies' share prices.

Puts work as follows: A company sells 1,000,000 put options on its stock (trading at $100 per share) exercisable at $100 within a month or two months or one year. Investors buy the puts at $10 a share. The company pockets $10,000,000 in cash.

When the put date arrives: If the stock price is $100 or more, the puts expire worthless. Company A has made $10,000,000. If the stock price drops to $50, the investor can buy shares at $50 and exercise the puts. Company A must buy back the shares at $100. The company loses $50 million less its $10 million for a net loss of $40 million.

In the case of the WTC disaster, someone with advance knowledge of the attacks, by buying puts, bet that the stocks of these companies would go down. They were correct, and the SEC placed a hold on the payments to the put holders as investigators looked into trading on inside information and tracing the links of those who bought the puts. Would advance knowledge of the attacks be a form of inside information? Would buying with that advance knowledge be a violation of 10(b)? What about the fact that they were foreign investors?

7. Vincent Chiarella was employed as a printer in a financial printing firm that handled the printing for takeover bids. Although the firm names were left out of the financial materials and inserted at the last moment, Mr. Chiarella was able to deduce who was being taken over and by whom from other information in the reports being printed. Using this information, Mr. Chiarella was able to dabble in the stock market over a 14-month period for a net gain of $30,000. After an SEC investigation, he signed a consent decree that required him to return all of his profits to the sellers from which he purchased during that 14-month period. He was then indicted for violation of 10(b) of the 1934 act and the SEC's Rule 10b-5. Did Mr. Chiarella violate 10b-5? [*Chiarella v United States*, 445 U.S. 222 (1980)]

8. Jeff Charleston is a retired executive of Clarkson, Inc. He retired in 2013. He has been asked to join the board and serve on the audit committee. Clarkson is a publicly traded 1934 Act reporting company. Can he serve on the board? On the audit committee?

9. William H. Sullivan, Jr., gained control of the New England Patriots Football Club (Patriots) by forming a separate corporation (New Patriots) and merging it with the old one. Plaintiffs are a class of stockholders who voted to accept New Patriots' offer of $15 a share for their common stock in the Patriots' corporation. They now claim that they were induced to accept this offer by a misleading proxy statement drafted under the direction of Mr. Sullivan, who owned a controlling share in the voting stock of the Patriots at the time of the merger. The proxy statement, plaintiffs claim, contained various misrepresentations designed to paint a gloomy picture of the financial position and prospects of the Patriots, so that the shareholders undervalued their stock. They seek to rescind the merger or to receive a higher price per share for the stock they sold. Does the court have the authority to rescind under Section 14? [*Pavlidis v New England Patriots Football Club*, 737 F.2d 1227 (1st Cir. 1984)]

10. Charles Edwards was the chairman, chief executive officer, and sole shareholder of ETS Payphones, Inc. ETS sold payphones packaged with a site lease, a five-year leaseback and management agreement, and a buyback agreement. The purchase price for the payphone packages was approximately $7,000. Under the leaseback and management agreement, purchasers received $82 per month, a 14 percent annual return. Purchasers were not involved in the day-to-day operation of the payphones they owned. ETS selected the site for the phones, installed the equipment, arranged for connection and long-distance service, collected coin revenues, and maintained and repaired the phones. The payphones did not generate enough revenue for ETS to make the payments required by the leaseback agreements, so the company depended on funds from new investors to meet its obligations.

In September 2000, ETS filed for bankruptcy. The SEC brought suit against Edwards and ETS for failure to register securities prior to sale. The district court concluded the arrangement was an "investment contract" subject to the securities laws. The Court of Appeals reversed the lower court. Which court is correct? Did the sale of securities take place? [*SEC v Edwards*, 540 U.S. 389 (2004)]

ETHICS, PUBLIC POLICY, THE LAW

Goldman Sachs: The Gold (?) Standard of Wall Street

Goldman Sachs was founded in 1869 as an originator and a clearinghouse for commercial paper. Marcus Goldman, a German immigrant, founded the company along with his son-in-law, Samuel Sachs. But the stodgy negotiable instruments market proved insufficient as the firm drifted from its founders' influence and its basic roots in tangible one-on-one business loans to more complex and sophisticated financial instruments.

In 1999, the same year Goldman itself went public, Goldman underwrote 47 companies. The 1990s investors did not know that the standard underwriting practice of requiring that a company show three years of profitability before being taken public was no longer enforced. That profitability standard had been slowly eased back to one year and then to one quarter. In fact, some Internet IPOs that Goldman underwrote had not yet seen any profits and their business plans indicated that profits were not on the immediate horizon.

In addition, Goldman engaged in laddering in the 1990s. Goldman and its best clients arranged for the allocation of a certain portion of an IPO at a pre-established price. However, those clients also had to agree to purchase a certain number of shares later during the IPO rollout at $10–$15 higher. Laddering is a trick, a sort of insider scam by the underwriter and its favored clients. The underwriter locks precommitted buyers into a price above the initial price and the shares of the IPO are guaranteed to rise. Goldman knows the fixed hand, but those in the market who are evaluating the IPO do not know that the increase in price is not due to legitimate demand for the company's shares.

For example, in 2000, Goldman was the underwriter for eToys, whose stock was priced for the IPO at $20. Goldman had laddered the shares and the price climbed to $75 per share by the end of the first day. By March 2001, eToys was in bankruptcy. Then–Goldman Chairman Hank Paulson condemned the practice when the firm received its SEC Wells notice for laddering, but denied any charges of securities fraud. Goldman settled the SEC charges of laddering by agreeing to pay a $40 million fine.[13]

In the 2000s, Goldman was a big player in mortgage-backed securities such as collateralized debt obligations (CDOs). Goldman made recommendations to clients to purchase CDOs as it was pushing to have the instruments rated high even as it was positioning itself short on the instruments. Positioning short means that Goldman stood to make money when the value of the CDOs declined. Internal e-mails at Goldman found the investment banker referring to CDO securities as "junk," "s___," or "crappy."[14] When Goldman executives were asked at a congressional hearing about their internal negative characterizations of securities the firm was touting and selling to its clients, Goldman executive David Viniar responded, "I think that's very unfortunate to have on e-mail." When his response elicited laughter in the hearing room, Mr. Viniar changed his answer to, "It's very unfortunate to have said that in any form."[15]

When the real estate market declined rapidly, the value of the CDOs plummeted to junk levels. Goldman received $10 billion from the U.S. government as a bailout. In addition, the government had to bail out AIG, the insurer Goldman had used for its hedges against the CDO market.

Goldman's 2009 annual revenues topped $13 billion, with first-quarter earnings for 2010 of $3.2 billion showing it on track for a repeat. The company has 32,000 employees worldwide and takes no new clients unless they have a minimum of $10 million to invest. The company has several management mantras. One is "long-term greedy," which Goldman executives translate to mean "don't kill the marketplace,"[16] and the other is "filthy rich by 40," a motivator for young people.

The SEC filed a civil action against Goldman for its conduct in ABACUS, a CDO deal. According to the complaint, 31-year-old Goldman employee Fabrice Tourre put together a deal of CDOs with the mortgage pool handpicked by John Paulson, a financial wizard who planned to position himself short on the securities Goldman would sell to its clients. The SEC complaint shows that Paulson chose mortgage pools that were dogs—that is, "crappy." Those mortgages were chosen because these securities "tanking" was important to Goldman and Paulson due to their positions on the mortgage instrument markets.

Goldman's position is that the clients who purchased the instruments were "qualified" or "sophisticated" investors and had a sufficient level of knowledge of markets to understand and process the risk and realize that all investment bankers are positioned in the market according to their theories on risk.

Goldman's activities have been described as "Heads Goldman wins, tails you lose."[17] And "Every game has a sucker, and in this case, the sucker was not so much AIG as it was the U.S. government and the taxpayer."[18] Goldman CEO Lloyd Blankfein defended his firm's conduct in November 2009 in an interview with the *London Times* by stating that he was just a banker "doing God's work."[19]

Discussion Questions

1. What are the results when companies create a business model based on loopholes and interpretations of the law?

2. Evaluate Goldman's ethics on the role it believed it played with its clients. Mr. Tourre was charged and found guilty of civil fraud. Goldman paid a fine. What lessons should employees learn from this result?

Notes

1. John Arlidge, "I'm Doing 'God's Work.' Meet Mr. Goldman Sachs," *London Times* interview, *The Sunday Times*, November 8, 2009, p. 1.

2. Dodd–Frank requires the SEC to review the definition of an "accredited investor" at least once every four years to be certain that the exemption is not including those who need further disclosures and protections from securities sales not subject to full registration. The Government Accounting Office (GAO) must conduct a study every three years to determine whether the private investment thresholds are appropriate for necessary protections.

3. The SEC proposed a bad-actor rule one year after Dodd–Frank was passed. However, the proposed rule has been a proposed rule for two years. The SEC has not finalized nor promulgated the proposed rule.

4. There has been significant push-back to the JOBS Act revisions to small offering exemptions. While there are proposed SEC rules, there have also been congressional hearings in support of amending the changes for small offerings in the act itself.

5. Peat, Marwick, Mitchell was one of the Big 8 accounting firms that existed during the 1960s and 1970s. These firms did all the audits on publicly traded companies. During the 1990s, the firms merged down to the Big 5. With the demise of Andersen following Enron, the Big 4 accounting firms remain.

6. David Glovin, "Galleon's Rajaratnam May Face Stiffer Jail Sentence After Questioning Law," *Bloomberg News*, September 12, 2011.

7. Susanne Craig, "Goldman's Trading Trips Reward Its Biggest Clients," *Wall Street Journal*, August 24, 2009, p. A1.

8. Andrew Ross Sorkin, "At Goldman, E-Mail Message Lays Bare Conflicts in Trading," *New York Times*, January 13, 2010, p. B1.

9. Alex Berenson, "Man Charged in Stock Fraud Based on Fake News," *New York Times*, September 1, 2000, pp. C1, C2.

10. Joanna Chung and Brooke Masters, "Madoff Says He Acted Alone," *Financial Times*, March 13, 2009, pp. 1, 7.

11. http://www.justice.gov/usao/nys/madoff/madoffhearing031209.pdf.

12. Julie Creswell and Landon Thomas, Sr., "The Talented Mr. Madoff," *New York Times*, January 25, 2009, p. SB1.

13. *SEC v Goldman Sachs*, January 25, 2005, http://www.sec.gov/litigation/complaints/comp19051.pdf. Settlement at http://www.sec.gov/litigation/litreleases/lr19051.htm.

14. Michael M. Phillips, "Senators Seek, Fail to Get an 'I'm Sorry,'" *Wall Street Journal*, April 28, 2010, pp. A3, A5.

15. Michael M. Phillips, "Senators Seek, Fail to Get an 'I'm Sorry,'" *Wall Street Journal*, April 28, 2010, p. A5.

16. Michael M. Phillips, "Senators Seek, Fail to Get an 'I'm Sorry,'" *Wall Street Journal*, April 28, 2010, p. A6.

17. Robert Farzad and Paula Dwyer, "Not Guilty, Not One Little Bit," *BusinessWeek*, April 12, 2010, p. 31.

18. Robert Farzad and Paula Dwyer, "Not Guilty, Not One Little Bit," *BusinessWeek*, April 12, 2010, p. 32.

19. John Arlidge, "I'm Doing 'God's Work.' Meet Mr. Goldman Sachs," *London Times* interview, *The Sunday Times*, November 8, 2009, p. 1.

20 MANAGEMENT OF EMPLOYEE WELFARE

The employer–employee relationship has evolved from one of a paternal nature in the 1600s and 1700s to one of a contractual nature.[1] In those earlier periods, employers often assumed responsibility for the well-being of their employees through personal relationships that were possible because of the less-complex nature of business at the time. With the Industrial Revolution, however, more employees were needed, and personal relationships were no longer possible. The employer–employee relationship became thoroughly contractual.

One effect of the change in the relationship to one of contract was that both parties behaved as parties in contracts and negotiation do: They wanted to maximize their own economic benefits. Employers wanted the most work for the least amount of money. Employees wanted maximum pay, safe working conditions, and some type of insurance for retirement, unemployment, and disability. Because employers had the upper hand—they controlled the jobs—their bargaining positions were stronger than those of employees. To balance the scales of power a bit, workers organized to give themselves more bargaining power through unionization, and the federal government enacted worker protection legislation to provide workers with some of their needs.

This chapter discusses the work and safety standards covered in federal legislation and answers the following questions: What wage and work hour protections exist for employees? Are there restrictions on children's work? What protections exist for safety in the workplace? What happens when an employee is injured in the workplace? Are workers entitled to pensions, and are they regulated? What is the Social Security system, and what benefits does it provide? What rights do unemployed workers have? How are labor unions formed, and what is their relationship with employees?

UPDATE
For up-to-date legal news, go to **mariannejennings.com**

Consider...

Boeing Company has long built many of its planes in the Puget Sound region in Washington, using a unionized workforce. In October 2009, Boeing CEO Jim McNerney announced that Boeing would be diversifying its labor force by moving production for its new 787 Dreamliner Jumbo Jet to a new plant in South Carolina due to "strikes happening every three to four years in Puget Sound." South Carolina is a right-to-work state. Mr. McNerney added that Boeing needed stability in production for its new jet in order to meet order demands, and the move to South Carolina would reduce Boeing's "vulnerability to delivery disruptions caused by work stoppages."

In April 2011, just two months prior to the ribbon-cutting ceremony for the South Carolina facility, the National Labor Relations Board (NLRB) issued a complaint against Boeing. The complaint charged Boeing with unfair labor practices because its decision to build the plant and move the 787 Dreamliner work to South Carolina interfered with the rights of employees guaranteed under the National Labor Relations Act (NLRA). The complaint also requested a remedy of transferring the 787 Dreamliner production work back to Washington.

Is the transfer of work from a unionized plant because of strikes an unfair labor practice? May an employer consider costs in making its decision to transfer work from a unionized plant? Would the transfer of work from a plant have a chilling effect on employee rights to unionize? To strike? What would happen if employers could not transfer work from plants for cost reasons?

20-1 Wage and Hours Protection

Exhibit 20.1 summarizes the series of laws affecting employee rights over the past 50 years, which are discussed in this chapter.

20-1a THE FAIR LABOR STANDARDS ACT

The **Fair Labor Standards Act (FLSA)** is commonly called by workers the "minimum wage law" or the wage and hour law. This act does establish a minimum wage, but it also includes provisions regulating child labor, overtime pay requirements, and equal pay provisions. The FLSA was originally introduced in the Senate by Hugo L. Black when he was a senator from Alabama. His 1937 appointment to the U.S. Supreme Court may have helped it pass the high court's scrutiny. Amended several times, the FLSA is an enabling statute that sets up various administrative agencies to handle the regulations and necessary enforcement.

Fatal Occupational Injuries in 2012: 4,383

Causes

Transportation: 41%

Equipment: 15%

Assaults and violence: 17%

Falls: 14%

Environmental: 9%

Fire and explosions: 3%

Data on Injuries

Highest fatality rates:

Construction: 16%

Second-highest fatality rates:

Transportation and warehousing: 16%

Third-highest fatality rate:

Mining: 15%

Accident rate in the workplace in 1995:

8.1 per 100

Accident rate in the workplace in 2011:

3.5 per 100

U.S. Department of Labor Statistics, October 2012

OSHA Violations Found in 2012 in the Workplace: 92,294

Total OSHA federal inspections 2012: 40,648

Total OSHA fines 2012: $583,386,000

Top five violations

1. *Fall protection*

2. *Inadequate training on safety procedures and hazards*

3. *Scaffolding protection*

4. *Respiratory protection*

5. *Ladders*

Occupational Safety and Health Administration
www.osha.gov

EXHIBIT 20.1 Statutory Scheme for Employee Welfare

STATUTE	DATE	PROVISIONS
Worker's Compensation (state laws)	1900	Absolute liability of employers for employee injury; no common-law tort suits by employees against employers
Social Security Act 42 U.S.C. § 301	1935	FICA contributions; unemployment compensation; retirement benefits
Fair Labor Standards Act 29 U.S.C. § 201	1938	Minimum wages; child labor restrictions; overtime pay
Equal Pay Act 29 U.S.C. § 206	1963	Amendment to FLSA; equal pay for equal work
Occupational Safety and Health Act 29 U.S.C. § 651	1970	Safety in the workplace; employee rights; employer reporting; inspections
Employment Retirement Income Security Act 29 U.S.C. § 441	1974	Disclosure of contributions, investments, loans; employee vesting; employee statements
Family and Medical Leave Act 29 U.S.C. § 2601	1993	Protection of job after family leave (for pregnancy, child care, adult illness, elderly care)
Pension Protection Act 29 U.S.C. §§ 302 et. seq.	2006	Amends ERISA to require higher funding levels as well as limits on officer stock sales during blackout periods
Patient Protection & Affordable Care Act 42 U.S.C. §§ 18001 et seq.	2010	Imposes responsibility on employers for health care coverage for employees

© Cengage Learning

Coverage of FLSA

The FLSA applies to all businesses that affect interstate commerce. As discussed in Chapter 5, "affecting" interstate commerce is a broad standard.

FLSA Minimum Wage and Overtime Regulations

Under FLSA, all covered employees must be paid a **minimum wage**. The minimum wage is established by Congress and is increased through legislation, with the latest increase taking effect in 2012. Domestic service workers, including full-time babysitters, cooks, and housekeepers must be paid a minimum wage. The minimum wage is determined after the employer deducts any expenses for housing and food.

The FLSA also includes an hours protection for covered employees in the form of time-and-one-half pay for hours worked above 40 hours per week. Regardless of the pay period for covered employees (monthly, weekly, or biweekly), overtime is computed on the basis of 40 hours per week. For example, if a covered employee worked 38, 42, 35, and 47 hours in four consecutive weeks and is paid on a monthly basis, that employee is entitled to 9 hours of **overtime pay**.

The definition of covered employees is provided in the FLSA. Some categories of employees are covered for purposes of minimum wage protections but not for overtime pay. For example, professionals, executives, and others who exercise discretion and judgment in their positions may be covered for purposes of minimum wage protections but not for purposes of overtime protections. The reason for this exemption is that these employees, often referred to as "white-collar" workers, possess sufficient training, knowledge, and experience to counter employer unfairness. The FLSA, under rules promulgated by the Department of Labor, has specific salary and job requirements for employees to be covered under the overtime exemption. The trend has been one of expanding the list of employees who are protected by overtime pay requirements. One issue that has resulted from the impact of downsizing is whether employees can be required to work overtime hours. The FLSA simply provides the right to time-and-one-half pay for overtime worked; it does not include limitations on hours (except in child labor regulations for children under the age of 18), nor does it provide a statutory right to refuse to work overtime. Union collective bargaining agreements can impose restraints, and many employers seek volunteers for overtime. However, employers should exercise caution with overly tired employees because, as *Faverty v McDonald's Restaurants of Oregon, Inc.* (Chapter 17, Case 17.3) held, employers may be liable for accidents of such employees even when employees are on their way home.

FLSA and Child Labor Provisions

The child labor provisions of the FLSA keep children in school for at least a minimum number of years. The provisions of the act govern particular ages and restrict the types of jobs those age groups can hold. For example, those over the age of 18 can work in any type of job. Those who are ages fourteen and fifteen can work only in nonhazardous, nonmanufacturing, and nonmining jobs, and only during nonschool hours.

Among the exemptions to the laws are those for young actors and actresses, for example. However, Screen Actors Guild rules place stringent limits on "set time" for children. But in the film industry, states may require approval of minors' contracts and also require that some of the earnings be put in trust for use by the child actor when he or she becomes an adult. Other exemptions apply to work-study programs and farmwork. (For information on child labor in international business, see p. 696.)

Enforcement of FLSA

Enforcement of the FLSA requirements comes about in different ways. Employees can initiate the process by filing a complaint with the U.S. Department of Labor. In some cases, employers make the laws self-enforcing by requesting interpretations from the Labor Department that are then published in the *Code of Federal Regulations*.

In a final type of case, the Labor Department initiates its own investigation of a firm for possible violations. For example, after the Labor Department reviewed car dealership programs that had high-school-age vocational students working in service departments, it halted several common practices in that industry. Although teens could train by doing mechanical work, using under-18 students as car jockeys to bring the customers' cars around to them following service work was a violation of the age restrictions on types of work under FLSA.

Penalties for FLSA Violation

The FLSA carries both civil and criminal penalties for violations. Employees have the right to sue civilly to recover from an employer any wages that were not paid or any overtime compensation that was denied, plus reasonable attorney fees required to bring the action to recover. In addition to the employees' rights, the U.S. Department of Labor's Wage and Hour Division has enforcement power for violations. A willful violation of FLSA carries a maximum $10,000 fine and possible imprisonment of up to six months.

To help employees pursue their rights, the FLSA makes it a violation for any employer to fire an employee for filing an FLSA complaint or for participating in any FLSA proceeding.

Liability for FLSA Violation

Officers of a corporation can be held individually liable for the corporation's violations. The FLSA imposes fines on both corporations and officers involved in managing employees. These personal penalties are particularly likely in cases in which the company has not kept accurate records of the wages and hours worked of its employees, a requirement of the FLSA. Case 20.1, *Chao v Hotel Oasis, Inc.*, reflects the new enforcement standards and policies of the Department of Labor.

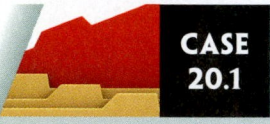

| CASE 20.1 | *Chao v Hotel Oasis, Inc.*
493 F.3d 26 (1st Cir. 2007) |

Two Sets of Books, One Big Penalty

FACTS

Hotel Oasis, Inc., operates a hotel and restaurant in southwestern Puerto Rico. Dr. Lionel Lugo-Rodríguez (defendant-appellant) (Lugo) is the president of the corporation, runs the hotel, and manages its employees. Oasis's records show that between October 3, 1990, and June 30, 1993, employees were paid less than minimum wage, were not paid for training time or meetings held during nonworking hours, were paid in cash "off the books," and were not paid correctly for overtime. Oasis also maintained two sets of payroll records for the same employees, covering the same time periods, one showing fewer hours at a higher rate, and the other showing more hours at a subminimum wage rate. Lugo maintains that the two sets of books were necessary, one for temporary employees and one for permanent employees.

On April 5, 1994, the Secretary of Labor (the "Secretary") filed a complaint in the United States District Court for the District of Puerto Rico against Oasis and Lugo ("Defendants"), alleging violations of the minimum wage, overtime, and recordkeeping provisions of the Fair Labor Standards Act ("FLSA"). The Secretary also sought liquidated damages.

After years of litigation, the district court ordered Oasis to pay $141,270.64 in back wages and an equal amount in liquidated damages to 282 current and former employees. The court also found Lugo personally liable for the back wages and penalties. Lugo and Oasis appealed.

JUDICIAL OPINION

TORRUELLA, Circuit Judge

"[T]he overwhelming weight of authority is that a corporate officer with operational control of a corporation's covered enterprise is an employer along with the corporation, jointly and severally liable under the FLSA for unpaid wages." Although we found it "difficult to accept...that Congress intended that *any* corporate officer or other employee with ultimate operational control over payroll matters be personally liable," we narrowly determined that the FLSA did not preclude personal liability for "corporate officers with a significant ownership interest who had operational

CONTINUED

control of significant aspects of the corporation's day to day functions, including compensation of employees, and who personally made decisions to continue operations despite financial adversity during the period of nonpayment."…

…[Because] not every corporate employee who exercised supervisory control should be held personally liable, we identified several factors that were important to the personal liability analysis, including the individual's ownership interest, degree of control over the corporation's financial affairs and compensation practices, and role in "caus[ing] the corporation to compensate (or not to compensate) employees in accordance with the FLSA."

Based on the above considerations, we affirm the district court's judgment holding Lugo personally liable for Oasis's compensation decisions. Lugo was not just any employee with some supervisory control over other employees. He was the president of the corporation, and he had ultimate control over the business's day-to-day operations. In particular, it is undisputed that Lugo was the corporate officer principally in charge of directing employment practices, such as hiring and firing employees, requiring employees to attend meetings unpaid, and setting employees' wages and schedules. He was thus instrumental in "causing" the corporation to violate the FLSA. The FLSA contemplates, at least in certain circumstances, holding officers with such personal responsibility for statutory compliance jointly and severally liable along with the corporation.

Finally, Defendants argue that the district court erred in awarding liquidated damages based on a finding of willfulness. The FLSA authorizes the Secretary of Labor to recover on behalf of employees unpaid wages and overtime compensation plus an equal amount in liquidated damages. The only way an employer can escape liquidated damages is to "show[] to the satisfaction of the court" that it acted in good faith and had reasonable grounds for believing that its acts did not violate the FLSA.

Here, the district court found that Defendants failed to show good faith or objective reasonableness, referring back to its findings on willfulness with respect to the applicable statute of limitations. Defendants

"intentionally and consistently failed to keep accurate records of the time worked by its employees[,]… disguised minimum wage, as well as overtime pay violations,… did not record the amounts of cash tips… [and] most salient…[to] a finding of willfulness…[paid] employees 'off the books.'"

Oasis's failure to keep adequate payroll records and its intentional manipulation of the records it did keep are sufficient grounds for concluding that Oasis did not act in good faith or with a reasonable belief that it was in compliance with the FLSA. "[T]he fact that an employer knowingly under-reported its employee's work hours could suggest to a [fact finder] that the employer was attempting to conceal its failure to pay overtime from regulators, or was acting to eliminate evidence that might later be used against it in a suit by one of its employees."

Defendants' primary argument on appeal is that the court had indicated at trial that the willfulness issue was "close" and that the Secretary had offered no evidence that Oasis acted in reckless disregard of its statutory obligations. These arguments are unpersuasive. First, the district court noted its "initial inclination against a determination of willfulness," but explained that it ultimately relied on the employees' testimony and Defendants' own documentary evidence to reach its conclusion regarding willfulness. We have already determined that the willfulness finding is not clearly erroneous. Furthermore, it is the *employer's* burden to show good faith and objective reasonableness, and therefore the Secretary's alleged failure to offer evidence of willfulness is not an impediment to the court's decision to refrain from awarding liquidated damages.

Affirmed.

CASE QUESTIONS

1. What shows willfulness of a violation?

2. What are the standards for holding an officer liable for FLSA violations?

3. Explain what liquidated damages are and when they are available for recovery.

20-1b THE EQUAL PAY ACT OF 1963

The **Equal Pay Act of 1963** is an amendment to the FLSA that makes it illegal to pay different wages based on gender to men and women who are doing substantially the same work. If the jobs involve equal responsibility, training, or skill, men and women must have equal pay. Merit systems and seniority systems instituted in good faith do not violate the Equal Pay Act even though they may result in different pay rates for the same jobs. As long as the disparate pay is based on length of employment or a merit-raise system, the disparity is within the act.

The Equal Pay Act is not an act that requires the application of comparable worth. Comparable worth requires that men and women be paid on the same scale, not just for the same jobs but when they are doing different jobs that require equal skill, effort, and responsibility. This issue came to light in 1983 when Louise Peterson, a licensed practical nurse at Western State Hospital in Tacoma, Washington, brought suit when she discovered that her salary of $1,462 per month for her supervision of the daily care of 60 men convicted of sex crimes was $192 less per month than that of the hospital groundskeeper and $700 less per month than men doing similar jobs at Washington's state prisons. A federal court found no violation of the Equal Pay Act.

20-2 Workplace Safety

20-2a THE OCCUPATIONAL SAFETY AND HEALTH ACT

One of the worker welfare concerns of Congress has been safety in the workplace. In the past, the economic concerns of employers often overshadowed their concern for proper safety precautions. To ensure worker safety, Congress passed the **Occupational Safety and Health Act of 1970**. Its application was broad, protecting virtually every employee in the country. It was an enabling statute that created three agencies responsible for worker safety standards: the **Occupational Safety and Health Administration (OSHA)**, the Occupational Safety and Health Review Commission (OSHRC), and the National Institute for Occupational Safety and Health (NIOSH). OSHA is the agency responsible for the promulgation and enforcement of workplace safety standards. OSHA's enforcement powers include investigations, record-keeping requirements, and research. The stated purpose of the act is to "assure so far as possible every working man and woman in the nation safe and healthful working conditions and to preserve our human resources."

OSHA Coverage and Duties

OSHA coverage is broad: Every employer that is in a business affecting commerce and has at least one employee is covered by OSHA. Several other federal acts regulate safety for particular industries, including the Coal Mine and Safety Act and the Railway Safety Act.

20-2b OSHA RESPONSIBILITIES

Promulgating Rules and Safety Standards

OSHA is responsible for promulgating rules and regulations for safety standards and procedures. The rules are adopted by the standard administrative process of notice in the *Federal Register*, public input, and final decision (see Chapter 6).

Inspections

OSHA inspections are an enforcement tool. Inspectors can enter the workplace "without delay and at a reasonable time" to inspect. They can check the workplace and the records and can question employees. OSHA's inspection power is limited by numbers, however. Because of OSHA's limited staff, the regulations provide for an order of priority on inspections. For example, OSHA places priorities on investigations of fatal accident sites as well as employee complaints.

OSHA must follow certain inspection procedures. An OSHA inspector who appears at a workplace must show identification and ask the employer's permission to conduct an inspection. If the employer allows the inspection, the employer or an agent of the employer can accompany the OSHA inspector. After the inspection, the inspector and employer meet to discuss violations, and the problems are often worked out on the spot and the violations remedied immediately.

Employee Rights, Inspections, and OSHA. If an inspection is the result of an employee complaint, the employer cannot take any retaliatory action against that employee. Because of OSHA's limited staff, the agency relies on those in the workplace to bring violations to its attention. If workers fear retaliation, the violations will remain unreported. An employee who is fired, demoted, or discriminated against for registering an OSHA complaint can file a complaint, and the Department of Labor can pursue the employee's rights in federal district court. In *Whirlpool Corporation v Marshall*, 445 U.S. 1 (1980), the U.S. Supreme Court held that employees could not be sent home from work or docked on their pay if they refused to work because of an unsafe condition or employer practice.

OSHA Search Warrant Requirements

Although most businesses voluntarily permit OSHA inspections, employers do have the right to refuse access. In *Marshall v Barlows, Inc.*, 436 U.S. 307 (1978), the U.S. Supreme Court ruled that OSHA inspectors must obtain warrants if employers refuse access.

OSHA Penalties

There are five types of OSHA violations, and each carries a different range of penalties. Exhibit 20.2 is a summary of OSHA penalties.

State OSHA Programs

Most federal regulatory laws preempt state laws, but state laws addressing occupational safety are not generally preempted, and the states share responsibility

EXHIBIT 20.2 OSHA Penalties

TYPE OF OFFENSE	DESCRIPTION	PENALTY
Willful	Employer aware of danger or a repeat violator	Up to $70,000 (not less than $5,000) and/or six months' imprisonment
Serious	Violation is a threat to life or could cause serious injury	$7,000
Nonserious	No threat of serious injury	Up to $7,000
De minimis	Failure to post rights	Up to $7,000 per violation
Failure to correct	Citation not followed	$7,000 per day

for workplace safety with the federal government. Some states do go beyond the federal standards. For example, some states have "right to know" laws for employees—laws that require employers to post the presence of hazardous substances at the office, plant, and so forth. Also, state criminal laws may be used to prosecute officers and companies already sanctioned by OSHA.

For a state to assume responsibility for an OSHA program, the agency must be assured that the state plan will be as effective as federal OSHA would be. Also, OSHA is in charge of the Complaints against State Program Administration, which permits those affected and interested in safety to file complaints with OSHA regarding state performance. OSHA can then investigate and, if necessary, eliminate state approval.

20-2c EMPLOYEE IMPAIRMENT AND TESTING ISSUES

One safety problem in the workplace is the presence of impaired coworkers. An employee operating equipment, whether a drill press or a delivery van, while under the influence of drugs or alcohol presents a substantial safety concern for any business. Current estimates are that between 14 and 20 percent of the U.S. workforce is impaired on the job. Employees who use drugs are almost four times more likely to be involved in workplace accidents. Further, the annual cost in reduced productivity attributable to impaired workers is $100 billion. As a result, drug-testing of employees by their employers is not only permitted but also essential for workplace safety.

FOR THE MANAGER'S DESK

Re: BP and OSHA

BP has experienced some of the largest fines imposed in the history of OSHA. For example, OSHA levied what was then the largest fine in its history against BP for its failure to correct safety violations at its Texas City, Texas, refinery, a violation that resulted in a 2005 explosion that killed 15 workers and injured 170 others. The fine was $87 million, one that is four times larger than any fine OSHA has ever issued against a company.

At the time of the explosion, BP was under an agreement with OSHA to fix the safety violations that OSHA had discovered at the plant. Not only had BP failed to fix the 271 violations that were in the agreement, OSHA's investigation and report on the explosion also found a total of 439 "willful and egregious" violations, including the unfixed 271 violations.

The fine at the refinery was so high because of the willful neglect of known violations and the fact that many of the violations resulted from overzealous cost-cutting on maintenance and safety, undue production pressures, antiquated equipment, and fatigued employees.

In 2010, BP experienced an explosion at its Deepwater Horizon rig and, following an OSHA and EPA investigation of that accident (that resulted in 13 deaths), BP agreed to settle criminal charges related to its design, construction, operation, and maintenance of the rig. There were similar findings of cost-cutting that affected safety there. The terms of the consent decree were that BP had to pay a fine of $4.5 billion and also agree to have safety monitors present on its rigs. In addition, BP was banned from having any federal contracts until it was able to demonstrate that it had an effective compliance program.

BP's operations, accidents, and resulting fines illustrate how critical OSHA compliance and safety standards are for companies. The fines as well as the costs of monitoring and loss of revenues from federal contracts cut deep into revenues and profits for years following the settlement of charges.

20-3 Employee Pensions, Retirement, and Social Security

One of the concerns of workers is what happens to them when they retire: Will they have an income? Other concerns are whether they will have a source of income in the event of disability, or whether their survivors will have income in the event of their death. Finally, what if no work is available? What income will they have until they find another job? These issues are the social issues of employment law—providing for those who, because of age, disability, or unemployment, are unable to provide for themselves.

20-3a SOCIAL SECURITY

The **Social Security Act of 1935** was a key component of the massive reforms in federal government during Franklin Roosevelt's presidency.

The idea of the Social Security system was to have those who could work shoulder the social burden of providing for those who could not. Every employer and employee is required to contribute to the Social Security programs under the **Federal Insurance Contributions Act (FICA)**. The amount employees contribute is based on their annual wage. Changes under the Patient Protection and Affordable Care Act (Obama Care) now make FICA contributions applicable to interest and dividend income as well as capital gains at a rate of nearly 4 percent. FICA contributions are paid one-half by employers and one-half by employees. Independent contractors pay their own FICA contributions. Social Security includes provision of death benefits for spouses and children as well as disability and retirement benefits.

FOR THE MANAGER'S DESK

Re: Who Is an Employee and Who Is an Independent Contractor?

For purposes of Social Security taxes, unemployment compensation, workers' compensation, and, of course, principal liability, the definition of an employee versus that of independent contractor is critical. Many businesses apply a label of "independent contractor" to agents doing work for them, but the activities of those independent contractors may, in fact, make them employees. Employers should check the status of those who are doing work so that they are paying wage taxes properly and have adequate coverage for liability.

In a 1987 revenue ruling, the Internal Revenue Service (IRS) listed the following 20 factors for determining whether an employer has sufficient control to label an agent an employee (servant) as opposed to an independent contractor, including how much the worker was controlled by the employer, in terms of instructions, schedule, and method of payment (hourly wages pointing to an employee and commissions pointing to independent contractor).

These 20 complex and burdensome factors were eventually consolidated by the courts [*Donovan v Sureway Cleaners*, 656 F.2d 1368 (9th Cir. 1981)] into six factors:

1. Degree of control over workers
2. Whether the worker has the risk of profit or loss
3. Whether the worker makes an investment
4. Level of skills and training for the work
5. Permanency of worker
6. Integration into economics of the business

One consistent factor not present in any of the evaluation lists is what the employer labels the worker—the label is irrelevant, and courts are consistent in their unwillingness to accept employers' labels of workers.

Since 2010, the IRS has been reexamining who is and who is not a federal contractor, with the scales tipping to more determinations that workers are employees and not independent contractors.

The benefits paid to retired and disabled people are based on formulas. The amount depends on how long an individual worked and within what salary range. Surviving spouse and children's benefits are likewise tied to the employee's work and salary history.

20-3b PRIVATE RETIREMENT PLANS

For many, Social Security retirement benefits do not provide enough security, and at present there is no assurance that those employed today will be able to collect their Social Security benefits upon retirement. For these reasons, many employees have invested in their own private retirement plans.

Many retirement and pension plans are set up by employers, who enjoy tax benefits from some plans. However, when evidence revealed that employees' funds in plans were being misused, not invested wisely, and in some cases embezzled, Congress enacted the **Employee Retirement Income Security Act of 1974 (ERISA)**, which was amended in 2006 by the **Pension Protection Act of 2006**.

Coverage of ERISA

ERISA applies to any employer engaged in or affecting interstate commerce and to any organization (such as a union) representing employees in interstate commerce. ERISA covers any medical, retirement, or deferral-of-income plan.

Requirements of ERISA Plans

ERISA does not require employers to have pension plans, but if an employer chooses to have a pension plan, the employer is subject to funding, accounting, and disclosure requirements imposed by federal law, including changes under the Pension Protection Act, enacted because of company and pension funding failures. As part of its 2006 Chapter 11 bankruptcy, United Airlines was relieved of its pension liabilities. However, in the GM and Chrysler bankruptcies, the pension plans were preserved. Because many former Enron employees lost their pensions when Enron declared bankruptcy because it was funded with Enron stock, there are now new regulations on disclosures to employees about stock investments in their companies for their private retirement funds as well as additional restrictions on management stock trades.

The wide disparity in the security of pension plans continues to attract Congressional attention. One discovery following the United bankruptcy was that loopholes in the accounting processes for pension fund reporting had permitted United, and many others, to report pension numbers that made the health of the fund look better than it actually was. The loopholes were Enronesque in nature, allowing obligations to be spun off the books so that the existing levels of obligations of the plan looked small and the assets rich.

Under the Pension Protection Act of 2006, Congress closed these financial reporting accounting loopholes. Companies must now fund their pension plans according to the numbers reported to the SEC in their financials. Companies reported their pension obligations and funding accurately to the SEC, but for ERISA purposes, those numbers were inflated. For example, if United had funded its plans when its SEC numbers indicated it needed to (i.e., 1998), United would have had a sufficiently funded plan at the time of its bankruptcy. However, under ERISA guidelines, United was not required to kick in funds until 2002, by which time the fund was so grossly underfunded that the company was unable to salvage the fund or provide the cash for increased levels of funding.

By 2012, another type of pension plan resulted in more bankruptcies. States, cities, counties, and towns were underfunded in pensions for government workers. The result was bankruptcies (as with Detroit, and Stockton and San Bernadino, California) as well as significant pension and contract reforms, as done in Wisconsin through a bitter political battle.

ERISA Employee Rights

Under ERISA, employees are entitled to receive an annual statement showing both their total benefits in any of the covered plans and the amount that is vested or that is nonforfeitable should they leave their jobs. In addition, ERISA sets minimum vesting requirements for employees before they will have rights in their retirement, pension, or annuity plans. To avoid the Enron problem of management sell-offs pending bad news announcements, the Pension Protection Act of 2006 added another protection for employees that prohibits officers of the company from selling their shares when employees are subject to blackout periods on their pension funds. That is, when employees cannot make changes in their pension fund allocations or deposits, officers likewise cannot trade in the company's stock. This provision was passed to prevent what happened at Enron. Enron officers sold off large blocks of stock even as the employees' pension plan was frozen by a blackout period. All the employees could do was sit and watch the values of their plans decline. They were unable to allocate pension funds to other sources.

One final protection for employees resulted from a 2008 U.S. Supreme Court decision. Employees may now bring suit against their employers for failure to honor their fiduciary duties in managing employee pension accounts. [*LaRue v DeWolff, Boberg & Associates, Inc.*, 552 U.S. 248 (2008)]

20-3c UNEMPLOYMENT COMPENSATION

Benefits Provided

Unemployment compensation programs were created under the Federal Unemployment Tax Act (FUTA). The federal government collects the FUTA tax and established the minimum standards for such programs, such as the period of time that unemployment coverage lasts. The amount is tied to the average amount earned by an individual during the months preceding employment termination. The benefits are usually paid on a weekly or biweekly basis. The federal government has increased the maximum time period for unemployment benefits to nearly two years.

Qualifying for Benefits

Each state has its own standards for payment of benefits. Generally, eligibility requirements demand that an individual be (1) involuntarily terminated from a job, (2) able and available for work, and (3) involved in seeking employment. Termination cannot be the result of voluntary action by an employee, such as quitting, or such as engaging in behavior that the employee has been warned about in the past. Willful disregard of employer rules is voluntary termination.

The payment of unemployment benefits raises many social issues regarding its effects. Many opponents of such benefits maintain that awarding them, particularly for the nearly two years now available, encourages unemployment. In addition, unemployment compensation has created some conflicts in federal labor legislation. In *Wimberly v Labor and Industrial Relations Comm'n of Missouri*, 479 U.S. 511 (1987), the U.S. Supreme Court held that leaving the workforce voluntarily because of pregnancy is still a voluntary departure from a job and does not entitle the mother to collect unemployment benefits.

Consider...

Ashok K. Gupta, a native of India, was employed at Lightbridge, Inc. as a credit analyst from November 10, 1999, until his discharge on August 20, 2001. Lightbridge operates a telephone call center where sellers of cellular telephones obtain credit checks on prospective customers. Gupta's responsibilities included answering calls and running credit checks. Lightbridge's customer service procedures explicitly state that "[a]ny incidences, i.e. disconnecting calls, not answering calls, unprofessional conduct while on the phone…or anything that causes an adverse business impact on Lightbridge, Inc. (complaint from client or agent, financial loss or client loss, etc.) may result in corrective action."

Gupta had been the subject of two complaints from callers. The first incident occurred after a dealer asked Gupta to repeat himself. Gupta replied, "[w]hat do you mean I'm speaking to you in English," and disconnected the call, after ignoring the dealer's request to speak with a supervisor. Gupta received a verbal warning and an "Employee Corrective Action Form" admonishing that he would be subject to disciplinary action for "[a]ny further infractions of this or any other company policy."

The second warning came after a different dealer called Lightbridge crying and reporting that Gupta had been rude and uncooperative. Gupta was again spoken to and received another corrective action form, which noted that "[a]ny further violations of this company policy or any other company policies will result in additional disciplinary action up to and including termination." Gupta had signed both disciplinary forms.

On August 17, 2001, a caller referred to Gupta as "[y]ou stupid Indian." Gupta replied, "Hold on you idiot." He then placed the caller on hold and attempted to locate a supervisor. Unable to find a supervisor, he returned to the call, but it had been disconnected. A short time later, the same dealer called again, but upon hearing Gupta's voice the dealer said, "Jesus," and hung up. Lightbridge lost a customer as a result. Gupta was terminated, and he applied for unemployment. The state denied his benefits because he had willfully disobeyed workplace rules.

Gupta filed suit to collect his unemployment benefits. Is he entitled to them? Explain why the state decided as it did and what the appeals court should do.

[*Gupta v Deputy Director of Div. of Employment & Training*, 818 N.E.2d 217 (Mass. App. Ct. 2004)]

Who Pays for Unemployment Benefits?

Although the idea and mandate for unemployment compensation came from the federal government, the states actually administer their own programs. Employers in each state are taxed based on the number of workers they employ and their wages. Those taxes are collected by the states on a quarterly basis. These funds are deposited with the federal government, which maintains an unemployment insurance program with the funds. Each state has an account in the federal fund on which it can draw. Employers effectively pay the costs of the unemployment compensation system.

20-4 Workers' Compensation Laws

The purpose of **workers' compensation** laws is to provide wage benefits and medical care to victims of work-related injuries. Although each state has its own system of workers' compensation, several general principles remain consistent throughout the states:

1. An employee who is injured in the scope of employment is automatically entitled to certain benefits (a discussion of work-related injuries and the scope of employment follows).

2. Fault is immaterial. Employees' contributory negligence does not lessen their right to compensation. Employers' care and precaution do not lessen their responsibility.

3. Coverage is limited to employees and does not extend to independent contractors.

4. Benefits include partial wages, hospital and medical expenses, and death benefits.

5. In exchange for these benefits, employees, their families, and dependents give up their common-law right to sue an employer for damages.

6. If third parties (e.g., equipment manufacturers) are responsible for an accident, recovery from the third party goes first to the employer for reimbursement.

7. Each state has some administrative agency responsible for administration of workers' compensation.

8. Every employer who is subject to workers' compensation regulation is required to provide some security for liability (such as insurance).

20-4a EMPLOYEE INJURIES

As they originated, workers' compensation systems were created to provide benefits for accidental workplace injuries. Over the years, however, the term *accident* has been interpreted broadly. Most injuries are those that result suddenly, such as broken arms, injured backs caused by falls, burns, and lacerations. But workers' compensation has been extended to cover injuries that develop over time. For example, workers involved in lifting heavy objects might eventually develop back problems. Even such medical problems as high blood pressure, heart attacks, and nervous breakdowns have in some cases been classified as work related and compensable.

The standard for recovery under the workers' compensation system is that the injury must originate in the workplace, be caused by the workplace, or develop over time in the workplace. Issues that arise include whether the injury occurred during work hours, whether the employee caused the injury, and scope of employment.

20-4b CAUSATION AND WORKER'S COMPENSATION

One of the most litigated areas in worker's comp involves issues about injuries that may not be exclusive to work. For example, stress can have personal and work-related causation, but when it is shown to be caused or originated by employment, is a compensable injury. The employee must tie the onset or increase in stress to job functions. Workers' compensation issues have become more complex, and many of the hearings involve the issue of determining whether a disability originated on the job or would have existed independently of the job. For example, the family of an employee of an oilfield storage facility who contracted psittacosis after he was exposed to pigeons roosting in the facility and died was not entitled to death benefits under worker's compensation. There was no evidence that pigeons or psittacosis were incidental to the character of the oilfield supply business, or that the nature of his work there was the proximate cause of his disease. However, blood pressure and alcoholism, if tied to the nature of the employee's work, are compensable under worker's compensation systems if there is a tie between these diseases and workplace stress. [*Castillo v Caprock Pipe & Supply, Inc.*, 285 P.3d 1072 (N.M. App. 2012)]

20-4c FAULT IS IMMATERIAL

The fact that an injury occurs in the workplace is enough for recovery. Employee negligence, employer precautions, contributory negligence, and assumption of risk are generally not issues in workers' compensation cases.

20-4d EMPLOYEES VERSUS INDEPENDENT CONTRACTORS

Workers' compensation applies to employees but not to independent contractors. Employees are those who are present at the workplace on a regular basis, paid a wage, and supervised. **Independent contractors** are those who work on a job basis, work irregular hours, and are not supervised by the employer. A backhoe operator working daily from 5 A.M. to 1 P.M. for a plumbing company and paid a weekly wage is an employee. A backhoe operator hired and paid on a per-job basis is an independent contractor. A more complete discussion of employee status can be found in Chapter 17.

20-4e BENEFITS

Workers' benefits can be grouped into three different categories: medical, disability, and death. Medical benefits include typical insurance-covered costs such as hospital costs, physician and nursing fees, therapy fees, and rental costs for equipment needed for recovery.

Disability benefits are payments made to compensate employees for wages lost because of a disability injury. The amount of benefits is based on state statutory figures. Most states base disability benefits on an employee's average monthly wage, and they also specify a maximum amount. State statutes also generally have a list of **scheduled injuries**, which will carry a percentage disability figure. For example, loss of a body part is a typical injury. In Arizona, the disability amount for a lost thumb is 55 percent of the average monthly wage for 15 months (Ariz. Rev. Stat. § 23–1044). For a lost foot, the amount is 55 percent of the average monthly wage for 50 months. Total disability is also defined by statute. Workers who have total disability are generally entitled to two-thirds of their average monthly salary for the period of the disability. Total disability usually includes the loss of both eyes or both hands, or complete paralysis.

Some injuries suffered by workers are not listed in statutes. Those not specifically described in statutes are called **unscheduled injuries**. The amount allowed for unscheduled injuries is discretionary and an area of frequent litigation.

Death benefits are paid to the family of a deceased employee and generally include burial expenses. In addition, survivors who were economically dependent on an employee are also paid benefits. The amount of death benefits is generally some percentage of the average monthly salary; for example, a surviving spouse might be entitled to a 35 percent benefit.

20-4f FORFEITURE OF THE RIGHT OF SUIT

The majority of states require employees to forfeit all other lawsuit rights in exchange for workers' compensation benefits. Employees receive automatic benefits but lose the right to sue their employers for covered incidents. Some states even prohibit employees from suing their coworkers under most conditions. In addition, some states allow family members to sue employers for direct injury to themselves. In those states, a spouse could bring a lawsuit against an employer for loss of consortium (marital companionship).

20-4g THIRD-PARTY SUITS

If an employee is injured by a machine malfunction while on the job, the employee is covered by workers' compensation. However, product liability may also be at issue in the accident. If suit is brought against the machine's manufacturer for product liability, any recovery goes first to the employer to compensate for the cost of the employee's benefits. In other words, third-party recovery is first used to reimburse the employer.

20-4h ADMINISTRATIVE AGENCY

Every state has some administrative agency responsible for the administration of claims, hearings, and benefits. In most states, this agency holds hearings for claims, and its decision is appealable in the same manner as any other agency decision.

The procedure for compensation requires employees to file claims with the agency along with medical documentation for the claim. Most claims are paid without contest; but if a challenge is made to a decision, a hearing with evidence and testimony is held.

20-4i INSURANCE

All states with workers' compensation systems require employers to be financially responsible for benefits under their systems. Employers can show financial responsibility by (1) maintaining an insurance policy, (2) obtaining a policy through the state agency, or (3) offering evidence of sufficient assets and resources to cover potential claims and benefits.

The *Hopkins v Uninsured Employers' Fund* case (Case 20.2) deals with various issues in a worker's compensation claim.

| CASE 20.2 | *Hopkins v Uninsured Employers' Fund*
251 P.3d 118 (Mont. 2011) |

A Bear of a Worker's Compensation Case

FACTS

Great Bear Adventures (the Park) is located near West Glacier, Montana. Visitors to the Park enjoy a drive-through experience of bears in their natural habitat. Russell Kilpatrick owns the Park and lives on adjacent property. Brock Hopkins began working there in 2002, doing various tasks, including maintenance and feeding the bears. In the past, some workers have been known to smoke marijuana on the premises. Although Kilpatrick professed to not condone marijuana use by workers, testimony established that he had smoked marijuana at the Park in the past, and on occasion had done so with Hopkins.

On November 2, 2007, Hopkins smoked marijuana on his way into work. When he arrived, Kilpatrick told Hopkins to raise the boards on the Park's front gates so they would not freeze to the ground. Hopkins asked Kilpatrick if he should feed the bears as well. Testimony regarding Kilpatrick's answer conflicted.

However, the Workers' Compensation Commission (WCC) ultimately found that Kilpatrick never told Hopkins not to feed the bears.

After completing work on the gates, Hopkins returned to Kilpatrick's house. Kilpatrick was asleep inside. Hopkins mixed food for the bears and used Kilpatrick's truck to drive into the Park. He entered the bears' pen and began to place food out. At some point while Hopkins was working, the largest bear, Red, attacked him. The bear knocked Hopkins to the ground, sat on him, and bit his leg, knee, and rear-end. While this was occurring, another bear, Brodie, came up from behind, and bit Red. In response, Red moved off Hopkins momentarily, and Hopkins escaped by crawling under one of the electrified wires surrounding the pen. Kilpatrick eventually found Hopkins, and he was transported to the hospital by helicopter. He suffered severe injuries.

Kilpatrick did not carry workers' compensation insurance. Hopkins petitioned the WCC for workers'

CONTINUED

compensation benefits from the Uninsured Employers' Fund. Both the Uninsured Employers' Fund and Kilpatrick opposed Hopkins' petition. The WCC found for Hopkins, concluding that (1) Hopkins was employed by Kilpatrick at the time of Hopkins' injuries, (2) Hopkins was in the course and scope of his employment at the time of his injuries, (3) marijuana use was not the major contributing cause of Hopkins' injuries, and (4) Hopkins was not performing services in return for aid or sustenance only. Kilpatrick appealed.

JUDICIAL OPINION

MCGRATH, Chief Justice

The WCC correctly concluded that Kilpatrick, "unquestionably controlled the details of Hopkins' work at the bear park." Hopkins had worked at the Park since 2002, received regular payments from Kilpatrick, and engaged in tasks at Kilpatrick's command. Furthermore, Kilpatrick's assertion that Hopkins was a volunteer is without support. As the WCC succinctly stated, "[t]here is a term of art used to describe the regular exchange of money for favors—it is called 'employment.'"

Factors considered in a "course and scope" analysis include (1) whether the activity was undertaken at the employer's request, (2) whether the employer, directly or indirectly, compelled the employee's attendance at the activity, (3) whether the employer controlled or participated in the activity, and (4) whether the employer and the employee mutually benefited from the activity. The presence or absence of any given factor is not dispositive, as the determination is dependent on a totality of the circumstances.

On November 2, 2007, Kilpatrick compelled Hopkins to work at the Park. Even though there was conflicting testimony as to whether Kilpatrick agreed that Hopkins should feed the bears on that day, an employee's injuries are compensable unless the employee is not "attending to employment-related matters" and has abandoned the course and scope of his employment. Feeding the bears was one of Hopkins' regular employment duties. Hopkins testified he was engaged in the "same routine" he had done for two or three years and would not have fed the bears had Kilpatrick expressly so instructed him. Feeding the bears was not a personal activity "severed"

from the continuity of Hopkins' employment-related duties at the Park. Additionally, the WCC found that "Kilpatrick benefitted from the care and feeding of the bears that Hopkins provided since presumably customers are unwilling to pay cash to see dead and emaciated bears." The WCC did not err when it concluded that Hopkins was acting in the course and scope of his employment at the time of his injuries.

Non-prescription drug consumption will preclude an injured employee's benefits if consumption was the leading cause contributing to the result, when compared to all others. No evidence was presented regarding Hopkins' level of impairment. The WCC aptly noted, "Hopkins' use of marijuana to kick off a day of working around grizzly bears was ill-advised to say the least and mind-bogglingly stupid to say the most." However, the WCC further noted that grizzlies are "equal opportunity maulers," without regard to marijuana consumption. Without evidence of Hopkins' level of impairment, the WCC correctly concluded that marijuana was not the major contributing cause of Hopkins' injuries.

Subject to exceptions that are inapplicable here, employment of a person performing services in exchange for aid or sustenance only is not covered by the Workers' Compensation Act. The Workers' Compensation Act defines aid or sustenance as a "subsidy made to provide a means of support, maintenance, or subsistence for the recipient." Kilpatrick testified that he gave money to Hopkins, not as wages, but rather "out of his heart." The WCC found this testimony to be without credibility, and the trier of fact is in the best position to weigh the respective credibility of witnesses. The WCC did not err when it concluded that Hopkins' services were not in exchange for aid or sustenance only.

Affirmed.

CASE QUESTIONS

1. Why was the question of actual employment an issue?

2. What does the court mean when it says that "bears are equal opportunity maulers"?

3. Of what significance is the confusion about the duty to feed the bears?

20-4j PROBLEMS IN WORKERS' COMPENSATION SYSTEMS

Increasingly, states and employers are experimenting with reforms to workers' compensation systems. Concerns focus on fraud that stems from incentives in the system. For example, medical benefits in workers' compensation are better than most medical plans. Because nearly all disability payments are tax-free, employees may be living on close to 90 percent of what they lived on (after taxes) before their disability.

Some doubts exist about the legitimacy of many complaints. For example, in one state, a janitor moonlighting for HGO, Inc., hurt his little finger while on the job. He collected $16,800 in disability payments over the next three years, even though he was able to continue his regular day job as a police officer.

Suggested reforms have included imposing a maximum number of years for disability payouts. Other states have hired more investigators to detect fraud. Companies are also attempting to cut costs by using staff doctors or by returning employees to other jobs that can be done despite an injury.

Workers' compensation systems were established during the Industrial Revolution, when the injuries sustained were primarily the types of factory and machinery accidents we traditionally associate with workers' compensation claims. However, the majority of jobs in the United States are now in service industries, and the nature of work-related injuries has changed from sudden-accident types to ongoing, progressive problems that are more expensive to treat and correct. For example, the repetitive hand-and-arm motions of computer keyboard operators can injure word processors, journalists, reservationists, and cashiers. This injury, often called carpal tunnel syndrome, can require expensive surgery and results in many lost workdays, if not new job assignments. Such repetitive stress injuries (RSIs) are the basis of many worker injuries.

The office environment itself is presenting new and difficult-to-control health-related problems for workers. Ergonomics is a rapidly growing field that examines the design of work areas and office equipment to minimize such worker injuries as repetitive motion syndromes and back problems. Architects and engineers are working together to design buildings that eliminate the so-called sick-building syndrome, in which poor air quality or the lack of fresh air circulation increases the incidence of illness and causes other symptoms in office workers.

A final issue in workers' compensation is the relationship between the state systems and the Americans with Disabilities Act (see Chapter 21), which prohibits discrimination against employees with disabilities and requires accommodation of employer facilities to permit disabled persons to work. Traditionally, when an accident caused disability, an employee collected payment in lieu of being rehired. An issue that arises as the systems of laws interact is whether an employer is required to rehire a disabled employee.

20-5 Statutory Protections of Employees Through Labor Unions

20-5a THE NORRIS–LAGUARDIA ACT OF 1932

The **Norris–LaGuardia Act** prohibits the use of injunctions as a remedy in labor disputes. Violent strikes can still be enjoined, provided evidence shows that violence did or would have occurred and that public officers could not control the violence and any resulting damage. Injunctions cannot be issued without first holding a hearing.

20-5b THE WAGNER ACT

The **Wagner Act**, also known as the **National Labor Relations Act of 1935 (NLRA)**, gave employees the right to organize and choose representatives to bargain collectively with their employers. Further, it established the **National Labor Relations Board (NLRB)**, which had two functions: to conduct union elections and to investigate and remedy unfair labor practices.

20-5c THE TAFT–HARTLEY ACT: THE LABOR-MANAGEMENT RELATIONS ACT OF 1947

Over President Truman's veto, Congress passed the **Taft–Hartley Act**, which was a response to the public's concern about too many strikes, secondary boycotts, and the unrestrained power of union officials. Strikes to force employers to discharge nonunion employees, secondary boycotts, and strikes over work assignments are prohibited as unfair labor practices. Employees were also given the right to remove a union they no longer wanted as their representative. The act also contains provisions that allow the president to invoke a **cooling-off period** of bargaining before a strike that threatens to imperil the public health and safety can begin. This power has been used by presidents in transportation and coal strikes.

20-5d THE LANDRUM–GRIFFIN ACT: THE LABOR-MANAGEMENT REPORTING AND DISCLOSURE ACT OF 1959

The **Landrum–Griffin Act** provides employee protection within union organizations. The act gave union members a bill of rights, required certain procedures for election of officers, prescribed financial reporting requirements for union funds, and established criminal and civil penalties for union misconduct.

In the 1950s, about one-third of U.S. workers were unionized. By the 1980s, about one-fifth of U.S. workers were unionized. As of April 2013, slightly more than one-tenth of U.S. workers are represented by unions, with membership being strongest in government unions.

CYBERLAW

20-5e UNION ORGANIZING EFFORTS AND SOCIAL MEDIA

Employees have the right to communication to organize themselves. Today, that organization effort may depend on the use of social media. That form of communication is often controlled by employer policies (see Chapter 10 for discussion of these policies) and that control has raised some interesting NLRA issues. The NLRB released a memo explaining when employees are protected in their use of social media.[2] For example, Lydia Cruz, who was a domestic violence advocate working for Hispanics United of Buffalo (HUB), frequently communicated with her coworker, Mariana Cole-Rivera. Their communications were often very critical of the job performance of other employees in HUB's housing department. For roughly six months, Cruz complained to multiple employees and management that the employees in the housing department were not doing enough for clients. Cole-Rivera, upset with Cruz's constant criticism of coworkers, planned to meet with the executive director to discuss Cruz's criticism. In preparation for the meeting, Cole-Rivera posted this public message on her Facebook page from home during off-work hours:

> [Cole-Rivera:] Lydia Cruz, a coworker feels that we don't help our clients enough at HUB I about had it! My fellow coworkers how do u [sic] feel?[3]

Four employees of HUB responded to Cole-Rivera's posting on Facebook, and the next workday, HUB's executive director fired Cole-Rivera and the other four employees who responded to Cole-Rivera's initial solicitation on Facebook. The NLRB held that the employee communication from home was protected and the ALJ affirmed that decision, so that the employer's actions constituted an unfair labor practice under the NLRA.[4] The key to their protection is that they were expressly communicating about organization—"What do you think?"

© iStockPhoto.com /dra_schwartz

BUSINESS STRATEGY

Employer Strategies for Social Media and Union Organization

CYBERLAW

1. Have a clear social media policy and educate employees about the policy.

2. Encourage open discussion with employees so that they do not resort to online postings. For example, Wells Fargo employees posted information about Wells Fargo's "unethical" policies on collecting overdraft fees, something that would cost the bank millions

in a class-action suit. Encouraging employees to raise issues prevents the social media postings.

3. Create a forum that is intra-company only for employees to post questions and encourage discussion. The more public workplace communication you have, the less likely you are to have social media negative postings.

20-5f THE UNIONIZATION PROCESS

Employees have the right to make the decision as to whether a union will represent them and, if so, which will serve as their representative. This process is called selecting a bargaining representative, and the NLRB has strict procedures for such selection. The NLRB carefully chooses how employees will be grouped together so that they share common interests.

The Collective Bargaining Unit

The first step in union organization is the establishment of a collective bargaining unit. The **collective bargaining unit** is a group of employees recognized by the NLRB as appropriate for exclusive representation of all employees in that group. Collective bargaining units are determined by the NLRB.

Some bargaining units consist of entire plants of workers, whereas others are specialized units within a plant, such as the maintenance staff or the line workers in an assembly plant. For some national companies, the bargaining unit is all employees, whereas for other national firms the bargaining unit is one particular plant or store.

The Petition, Cards, and Vote

Once the collective bargaining unit is set, the union, employees, or employers can file a petition for exclusive representation of employees within a unit. An employer can voluntarily recognize the union. However, if a majority of employees in the bargaining unit do not support the union, the employer can insist on a formal election.

The NLRB monitors closely the conduct of both employer and union as the election approaches. Employers can prohibit oral campaigning during work hours and can restrict literature distribution both during and, to a degree, before and after work hours. Employers cannot make threats about relocation or make speeches to captive audiences (employees on their shifts) in the 24 hours before an election. The *United Food v NLRB* case (Case 20.3) deals with the issue of appropriate conduct by employers and provides some insights for solving the chapter opening "Consider…"

Certification

If a majority of employees vote for the union in a secret ballot process administered by the NLRB, the union has completed its **certification**. An employer who refuses to deal with the certified union can be forced to by an injunction obtained by the NLRB.

CASE 20.3

United Food and Commercial Workers Union Local 24 v NLRB
506 F.3d 1078 (D.C. Cir. 2007)

Veiled Threat or Economic Prediction?

FACTS

In March 1999, United Food and Commercial Workers' Union (UFCW) attempted to organize a Smithfield Foods meatpacking plant in Wilson, North Carolina. After a three-month campaign, the union lost the election. The union filed a series of unfair labor practice charges against Smithfield, alleging that the company's antiunion campaign had tainted the election. An administrative law judge (ALJ) found that Smithfield executives violated NLRA section 8(a)(1) by threatening to close the company's Wilson plant if workers unionized.

On review, the NLRB found for Smithfield on the issues of threatened plant closure. The union appealed the NLRB's dismissal of the unfair labor practice charges.

JUDICIAL OPINION

TATEL, Circuit Judge

NLRA guarantees employees "the right to selforganization, to form, join, or assist labor organizations,…for the purpose of collective bargaining or other mutual aid or protection." Section 8(c), however, protects employers' First Amendment rights to convey their views on unionization to employees so long as such expression "contains no threat of reprisal or force or promise of benefit."

In a case like this, which deals only with predictions of adverse economic consequences, a two-part inquiry [is required] to distinguish "permissible predictions" from "forbidden threats." First, did the employer predict "adverse economic consequences" as a result of unionization? If not, the inquiry ends. But if the employer made such predictions, then we proceed to the second question: did those predictions rest on objective facts outside the employer's control?

Guided by these questions, we turn to the union's claim that communications by high-level Smithfield managers during the unionization campaign constituted unlawful threats of plant closure. In a series of speeches and letters designed to combat the UFCW's unionization campaign, Plant Manager Phil Price and Smithfield President and Chief Operating Officer Lewis Little repeatedly told employees that three other companies had previously operated the Wilson plant, that the UFCW had unionized the plant under each of those

companies, and that each company ultimately shut down the plant. Both managers, however, carefully avoided linking the previous closures directly to the union. For example, in one speech Price mentioned the three previous plant closures but made clear he had no idea whether the UFCW had caused them:

> In none of these three cases did a union contract provide long-term job security for employees. Maybe it was just the opposite. Maybe the union forced inflexible rules on these companies so that they could not compete in today's environment. Maybe this union made it so these companies couldn't satisfy their customers' demands. It really doesn't matter. Whether this union caused these other three plants to close is not for me to say. I don't know what happened. I do know that Smithfield wants this plant to be a success… .

Later in the unionization campaign, Price sent a letter to all Smithfield employees that again emphasized the Wilson plant's repeated failures under previous management. Offering no prediction about the company's intentions, he stated, "I can't predict the future, especially if the union were to get in," and he again disclaimed any direct link between the union and the previous plant closures. Price said:

> Did the UFCW cause these three companies to close the plant here on Wilco Boulevard? I don't know the answer to that. Maybe they did, maybe not. But I can spot a bad trend… . The UFCW is obviously a jinx for this plant. They have struck out for Wilson employees three times. It's time for another approach.

Finally, in an election-eve speech to employees, Smithfield President Lewis Little explained that he was "committed to the success of this plant." Echoing Price, however, Little made no predictions: "I cannot stand here and tell you what will happen." He concluded by urging employees not to "hang the UFCW around this plant's neck for a fourth time."

Based on full circumstances, the ALJ ruled that Price and Little unlawfully threatened employees by repeatedly mentioning the three previous plant closures without providing a sufficient objective explanation for the closures.

The Board disagreed. Reviewing all the evidence "in context," the Board, over one member's dissent, found

CONTINUED

no threat or coercion in Price's and Little's statements and concluded that they merely contained "relevant, factual information about the union's history at the facility." The Board emphasized that the two managers "never mentioned closure" and "expressly disclaimed any certainty about the connection between the previous closures at the Wilson facility and the union."

The union argues that an employer can violate the Act by merely suggesting that it may close a plant as a result of unionization; it need not definitively assert that it will do so. Placing the statements recounted above in the context of the company's overall antiunion campaign, the union contends that the unmistakable effect of Price's and Little's remarks was to threaten workers with the specter of a plant shutdown.

The Board reads the record differently. It argues that neither Price nor Little ever raised the possibility that Smithfield might shut the plant. As the Board sees it, Price and Little simply related indisputable historical facts without ever explicitly linking previous plant closures to the UFCW. Under this interpretation of the record, case law requiring an employer to provide objective justification for a predicted plant closure—the second of the two questions established in our case law—has no applicability to this appeal because here the managers never made such a prediction.

[W]e conclude that substantial evidence supports the Board's finding that neither Price nor Little threatened to close the Wilson plant in the event of unionization. As the Board found, neither executive predicted that the company would take any particular course of action, nor did either ever suggest closing the plant.

The record also reveals that when asked whether Price ever said that "the plant would close if the union got in," one employee responded, "No, he just asked what would—what do we think would happen." Finally, in a pre-election speech to employees, Little mentioned that Smithfield had dealt with the UFCW at other plants, and told employees that in the event of a strike Smithfield would "operate the plant without" the striking workers.

In upholding the Board's decision, we acknowledge that the record could be read differently. Perhaps the Board could have interpreted the managers' statements as the union does, namely as "thinly veiled prediction[s] that electing the union a fourth time would result in closure." Nevertheless, as the union acknowledges, it is the Board's duty, not ours, to "focus on the question: 'What did the speaker intend and the listener understand?'" Here, the Board determined that threats were neither intended nor understood. Had the Board reached the opposite conclusion, we likely would have deferred to that determination as well. For, as we have previously noted, "the very existence of competing views reinforces the need for reliance on the Board's experience."

The union argues that the Board departed from its own precedent, specifically *Eldorado Tool, Division of Quamco, Inc.*, 325 N.L.R.B. 222 (1997). There, the employer had displayed a poster depicting a row of tombstones bearing names of plants that had previously closed after unionization. The last tombstone bore the employing plant's own name with a question mark beneath it. Although the Board concluded that the employer's actions violated the Act, the case is both distinguishable and irrelevant. It's distinguishable because there the Board found that "no member of the [employer's] management ever sought to clarify the message, or to assure employees that it was not predicting that the same fate awaited [them] as had befallen other plants," while here the Board found exactly the opposite. [This is] nothing more than an example of the Board properly exercising its judgment to interpret arguably ambiguous statements made in the employment context.

For the reasons given above, we deny the union's petition for review.

CASE QUESTIONS

1. What does the court find is critical in the statements by the managers about the future of the plant in the event of unionization?

2. Why was the *Eldorado Tool* decision a different outcome from this case?

3. What advice would you give plant managers when faced with a unionization effort?

Consider...

Based on this case, determine the answer to the chapter opening "Consider..." on Boeing.

After a union has been certified, an election for a new union cannot be held for twelve months from the time of certification. If the union signs a collective bargaining agreement, no union certification election can be held until the collective bargaining agreement expires. These limitations on elections and certifications prevent chaos in the workplace that would result from constant changeovers in union representation.

Nonunion Members in the Certified Workplace

Although the NLRA gave unions the right to exist, it also gave workers the right to a choice. Workers are not required to join unions and cannot be coerced into supporting union action. Attempts by a union to force its members to participate in strikes and other union activities are considered unfair labor practices. In *Pattern Makers' League of North America, AFL-CIO v NLRB*, 473 U.S. 95 (1985), the U.S. Supreme Court held that a union member could not be fined for his failure to participate in a strike.

20-5g UNION CONTRACT NEGOTIATIONS

Once a union is certified as the employees' representative, one of its major roles is to obtain a contract or **collective bargaining agreement** between employer and employees. Both sides must engage in **good-faith bargaining**, which the NLRB defines as a mutual obligation of employer and union to meet at reasonable times, confer in good faith on employment issues, and execute a written agreement reflecting their oral agreement. Both parties must bargain with an open mind and the sincere intent of reaching an agreement.

Two types of subject matters can be discussed during bargaining: (1) mandatory or compulsory subject matter and (2) permissive subject matter. As to the former, the NLRA describes **mandatory bargaining terms** as those dealing with "wages, hours, and other terms and conditions of employment." Obviously, the amount to be paid as wages is included but so also are related issues, such as merit pay, vacations, overtime, work hours, leaves, and paydays. Exhibit 20.3 lists the usual topics covered in a collective bargaining agreement.

Permissive subject matters, in contrast to compulsory subject matters, would be those the parties are required to negotiate but on which they need not reach an agreement. A strike vote of employees before a strike starts is an example of a permissive subject. Any topic that does not directly concern employer–employee relations is a permissive subject. A refusal to bargain on a permissive subject is not, however, an unfair labor practice; a refusal to bargain on mandatory subject matter *is* an unfair labor practice.

EXHIBIT 20.3 Usual Topics for a Collective Bargaining Agreement

Union recognition	Insurance	Union announcements (bulletin board rights)
Wages	Pension/retirement plans	
Work hours	Employee grievances	Definition of terms
Vacations	Length of agreement/ expiration date	Leaves of absence
Sick leave		Drug testing
Seniority	Incentive plans	

© Cengage Learning

Some subjects are "unbargainable." Employers and employees cannot bargain to give away statutory rights—for example, the procedures for certifying a union. Nor can they bargain about having a **closed shop**, which requires employees to be union members before they can be hired. Such shops are illegal under the Taft–Hartley Act.

Failure to bargain on mandatory subject matter is an **unfair labor practice**, which is conduct prohibited by statute or NLRB decision. When an employer or union fails to bargain on a mandatory topic, a charge can be brought and the NLRB can proceed with a complaint.

Consider...

Are insurance plans a mandatory, permissive, or nonbargainable topic?

THINK: The law says that the terms and conditions of employment are mandatory collective bargaining topics.

APPLY: Insurance is a term and condition of employment—it determines the level of employee benefits.

ANSWER: Insurance plans are a mandatory topic.

Now determine whether the following subjects are mandatory, permissive, or nonbargainable:

- Maternity leaves
- Plant rules
- Subcontracting procedures
- Strikes
- Layoffs
- Union bookkeeping procedures
- Meal periods

20-5h PROTECTED CONCERTED ACTIVITIES

Some union activities are protected under the NLRA. Ads and handbills that explain the union's issues and position are permitted and can be an effective tool for obtaining boycotts. Employees' handbills and ads can encourage customers not to deal with their employer until the strike is settled. A union currently recognized as a certified collective bargaining agent can engage in **picketing** an employer, but picketing for recognition of a union is not permitted. The **strike** is the best-known and most widely used economic weapon of unions. A strike is a work stoppage because employees no longer report to work.

In recent years, unions have developed a new economic tool—contacting institutional shareholders and board members to put public pressure on corporate officers to work with unions. These public-attention tactics have been effective.

20-5i UNFAIR EMPLOYEE PRACTICES

Employees are also prohibited from engaging in some activities that are classified as unfair labor practices. A **slowdown** is an economic tool that interrupts the employer's business but falls short of a stoppage or strike. Slowdowns usually occur when employees refuse to perform work or use certain equipment that is in violation of their collective bargaining agreement with the employer. For example, in early 1999, American Airlines pilots staged a slowdown by calling in sick, known as a sickout. After more than 1,000 flights per day were canceled, a federal court ordered the pilots to halt their slowdown.

Featherbedding is payment for work not actually performed. It is an unfair labor practice for a union to negotiate an agreement that requires an employer to pay for work that was not actually performed. For example, some bricklayers' unions at one time required payment for a minimum number of bricks even though the work might not have actually involved that many bricks.

20-5j EMPLOYER RIGHTS

Employers have the right to give information to employees about unions and the results of union organization. The speech of employers cannot be controlled by the NLRB unless the speech is accompanied by some unlawful conduct, such as a threat of physical force or a promise of benefit. For example, an employer who threatens the loss of jobs if employees join the union is not protected by the free speech rule. An employer who tells employees that it will not negotiate with a union is also not protected by the free speech rule.

Exhibit 20.4 is a summary of management do's and don'ts when faced with an upcoming union election.

20-5k RIGHT-TO-WORK LAWS

Section 14(b) of the Taft–Hartley Act is in some ways a protection for employers as well as for employees. This section outlaws the closed shop, which, as discussed earlier, is a business that requires union membership before an employee can be hired. Based on this section of Taft–Hartley, states can pass **right-to-work laws** that give people the right to work without having to join a union. About half the states have right-to-work statutes.

EXHIBIT 20.4 Management Do's and Don'ts in the Unionization Process

DO	DON'T
Tell employees about current wages and benefits and how they compare to other firms.	Promise employees pay increases or promotions if they vote against the union.
Tell employees you will use all legal means to oppose unionization.	Threaten employees with termination or discriminate when disciplining employees.
Tell employees the disadvantages of having a union (especially cost of dues, assessments, and requirements of membership).	Threaten to close down or move the company if a union is voted in.
Show employees articles about unions and negative experiences others have had elsewhere.	Spy or have someone spy on union meetings.
Explain the unionization process to your employees accurately.	Make a speech to employees or groups at work within 24 hours of the election (before that, it is allowed).
Forbid distribution of union literature during work hours in work areas.	Ask employees how they plan to vote or if they have signed authorization cards.
Enforce in a consistent and fair manner disciplinary policies and rules.	Urge local employees to persuade others to vote against the union (such a vote must be initiated solely by the employee).

Source: R. L. Mathis and J. H. Jackson, *Human Resource Management*, 8th ed., p. 533. © 1997. Reprinted with permission of South-Western, a part of Cengage Learning.

© Cengage Learning

ETHICAL ISSUES

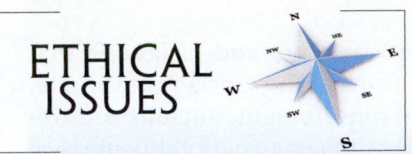

Many employers are ranking employees, or "placing them in buckets" as it is commonly called, as part of their annual performance evaluations. For example, Ford Motor Company, when it used this system, had 18,000 managers who were grouped into sets of 30 to 50. Of each group, 10 percent must be assigned an "A" grade, 80 percent must be assigned a "B" grade, and 10 percent must be given a "C" grade. Those with the bottom grades are then eased out of the company. Those with a "C" grade cannot be given a pay raise, and those with a "C" grade for two years in a row are demoted or terminated. No exceptions are made for any of the groups, but Ford did cut back on the "C" requirement to 5 percent in 2001 and changed the system in 2003.

Other companies with grading systems include Intel and Sun Microsystems.

Cisco Systems has established a goal of getting rid of 1 of every 20 employees, with the purpose of terminating employees who are given substandard performance evaluations.

GE has a 20–70–10 plan for ranking employees. GE follows a carrot approach in that it rewards the top 20 percent so well that few ever leave the company. GE uses the 10 percent group to terminate employees, and it terminates about 8,000 management and professional employees each year. Former GE CEO Jack Welch noted that employees in the 10 percent bottom group would end up leaving the company anyway because they are unhappy in not performing, and GE just makes the inevitable decision for them early.

Workers' rights groups call the systems inhumane. Some say that instead of motivating employees to do better, the result is that they are demoralized and do worse or leave the company.

Do these systems violate any laws? Are they a mandatory collective bargaining issue? Are you comfortable with them from the perspective of business ethics?

Source: Del Jones, "More Firms Cut Workers Ranked at the Bottom to Make Way for Talent," *USA Today,* May 30, 2001, pp. 1B, 2B.

20-5I ECONOMIC WEAPONS OF EMPLOYERS

Employers have economic weapons that can be used in response to employee economic weapons. In response to union certifications and strikes, some employers have opted to close the affected plants. In some cases, employers have abandoned the business altogether. It is clear that these shutdowns and closures are strong economic weapons, and their legality under the federal labor law scheme has some restrictions. In *Textile Workers Union v Darlington Manufacturing Co.*, 380 U.S. 263 (1965), the Supreme Court ruled that employers have the right to terminate their entire business for any reason. Even if the reason for the closing is vindictiveness toward the union, neither the NLRB nor the courts can require an employer to stay in business.

Employers cannot use a temporary closing with a promise of reopening after a union is defeated in an election. Further, employers cannot stage a **runaway shop**, which is when work is transferred to another plant or a new plant is opened to carry the workload of the old plant.

The concern of the NLRB in the closing of one plant is that employees in other plants, fearful that their plants will be closed, will fail to exercise their rights to unionize. For a plant closure to be an unfair labor practice, the evidence must show that the closure was done with the intent of curbing unionization in that and other plants owned by the employer.

Federal plant-closing legislation is called the **Worker Adjustment and Retraining Notification Act of 1988 (WARN)**. Under this act, employers with 100 or more workers are required to give workers 60 days' advance notice of plant shutdowns that would affect at least 50 workers and of layoffs that would last more than six months and affect one-third of the workers at the site. There are some exceptions to the 60-day notice requirement, such as unforeseeable circumstances and seasonal, agricultural, and construction businesses. Penalties for violations include back pay and benefits for employees for each day of violation and up to $500 per day for each day notice was not given. The closing of Arthur Andersen following Enron resulted in WARN litigation, but the court held the closing was not foreseeable. [*Roquet v Arthur Andersen LLP*, 398 F.3d 585 (7th Cir. 2005)]

One result of the increased globalization of business is the availability of lower-cost labor pools outside the United States. When union demands increase business costs beyond what managers feel will allow a firm to remain competitive, plants are closed and work is transferred to plants outside the United States. The global marketplace provides management with a bargaining tool that becomes difficult for unions to address. Demands for wage increases, more benefits, and better working conditions are often met with a plant closing in the United States and a plant opening in another country where the labor pool is large and the wages low.

A **lockout** is an employer's economic weapon in which the employer refuses to allow employees to work. Lockouts have been recognized by the U.S. Supreme Court as a legitimate measure to help an employer avoid a strike at an economically damaging time. The reason for an employer's lockout must be economic. A lockout to discourage union membership, therefore, is an unfair labor practice.

Employers can use benefits as economic weapons; the only restriction is the timing of those benefits. Offering them too close to an election can be an unfair labor practice. Conferring benefits on a temporary basis to gain an advantage (precluding the union) is also an unfair labor practice.

Bankruptcy has become a solution for many business problems, labor problems among them. When strikes extend for long periods of time, the financial well-being of the firms affected can deteriorate, often to the degree that some firms declare bankruptcy. The type of bankruptcy proceedings initiated will determine the fate of labor contracts. In a reorganization, the contracts remain in force. In a straight bankruptcy, the workers stand in line (although with some priority) to collect any wages due and any contributions made to the firm's retirement plan. Bankruptcy can be an escape for a firm, but the bankruptcy laws themselves limit the availability of this economic weapon. The firm must still meet the tests for declaring bankruptcy, so the weapon is not entirely optional.

Exhibit 20.5 provides a summary of labor weapons, rights, and unfair practices.

20-6 International Issues in Labor

Today's labor market is considerably different from the market that existed at the time of the enactment of federal labor legislation. Both operations within the United States and operations in other countries are affected by a new international labor force. Domestic operations must be certain that all employees from other

---

EXHIBIT 20.5 Union Disputes: Economic Weapons and Rights of Employers and Employees

Economic Weapons	Rights	Unfair Labor Practices
Employer		
Business closing	Freedom of speech	Refusal to bargain in good faith
Plant closings	Demand election	Refusal to bargain on a mandatory issue
Lockouts	Freedom of speech	Violation of collective bargaining agreement
Right to confer benefits (timing)	Right to union representation upon investigation	Interference with joining union
Employee	Right to join union	Timing of benefits
Strike	Right of members to adequate representation	Observation of union activities
Ads		Domination of labor union
Picketing	Right to union office	Discrimination in promotion of union members
Boycotts		Blacklisting
Shareholders		Violation of collective bargaining agreement
		Secondary boycotts
		Payment for union cards
		Coercion or discrimination in union membership
		Causing an employer to pay excessive amounts or for work not done

© Cengage Learning

countries are documented workers. International operations present numerous ethical and public policy issues in the conditions and operations of plants in other countries with different labor standards.

20-6a IMMIGRATION LAWS

The fluidity of commerce across borders has found companies in the United States with employees from around the world. Employers are responsible for ensuring that their employees are properly in the United States. This section deals with immigration laws, documentation for alien employees, and the penalties for employer violations of the compliance requirements.

The **Immigration and Naturalization Act (INA)**, the **Immigration Reform and Control Act of 1986 (IRCA)**, and the **Immigration Act of 1990** (8 U.S.C. § 11101 *et seq.*) are the federal laws that apply to immigrants in the United States and impose requirements on employers in the United States that employ immigrants. The Immigration Act of 1990, or IMMACT 90, increased legal immigration by 35 percent, enabled more family-sponsored immigration, and increased employment-based immigration, while providing a "diversity" program to increase the number of immigrants from countries traditionally underrepresented in the U.S. immigrant mix (e.g., Ireland and some African countries). This program is also known as the "green card visa lottery."

Two federal statutes cover the issues of immigration, deportation, and penalties for hiring illegal immigrants: the **Illegal Immigration Reform and Immigrant Responsibility Act of 1996** and the **Antiterrorism and Effective Death Penalty Act** (18 U.S.C. § 1). The statutes served to increase the types and numbers of crimes that rendered illegal immigrants deportable from the United States and denied them entry from other countries. The statutes also decreased the defenses to deportation as well as the procedural protections for opposing deportation. The enforcement of the immigration laws is now under a cabinet-level agency known as the **U.S. Department of Homeland Security (DHS)**. DHS has Immigration and Customs Enforcement (ICE) as one of its reporting agencies. The Immigration and Naturalization Service (INS), originally housed within the U.S. Department of Justice, was abolished and INS's responsibilities have been divided among separate bureaus within DHS. This reorganization and the creation and elevation of DHS to a cabinet-level position was the result of the **Uniting and Strengthening America by Providing Appropriate Tools Required to Intercept and Obstruct Terrorism Act** (**USA Patriot Act**; 18 U.S.C. § 1).

With the passage of Homeland Security Act of 2002, the nature of immigration enforcement issues changed. The USA Patriot Act toughened security clearances and background checks for nonimmigrant and immigrant admittance into the United States, tightened coordination between immigration-related government agencies, and increased the U.S. government's ability to track foreign nationals in the United States.

Before hiring a new employee, employers must verify that the employee is either a U.S. citizen or is permitted to work in the United States. All non–U.S. citizens must have an I-9 form on file with the employer. Form I-9 provides complete information about noncitizens and requires the employer to verify the information provided through an Alien Registration Card, commonly called a "green card." Verification of U.S. citizenship can be provided by a driver's license from a state in the United States, a Social Security card, or a U.S. passport. If someone with a foreign accent can provide evidence of U.S. citizenship, the employer is not permitted to question further or require additional documentation, for such questioning on the basis of the accent would be an act of discrimination under the immigration laws.

Because of lobbying from the high-tech industries, Congress has passed a series of laws that address immigration exemptions, the latest of which is the **American Competitiveness in the Twenty-First Century Act** of 2000. Under this statute, employers cannot lay off American employees within the 90 days following their submission of an application for entrance and employment of one of these highly skilled workers. Referred to as *H-1B professionals*, their pay scale is also controlled by the act so that their pay is equivalent to what an equally skilled U.S. worker would earn in the same position. This constraint on wages eliminates the incentive for companies to hire all foreign H-1B professionals at much lower salaries. Workers who have H-1 visa classification have "distinguished merit and ability" and are permitted to work in the United States on a temporary basis. These types of aliens include architects, engineers, lawyers, physicians, and teachers. H-1B visas are limited to 65,000 per annum. L-1 visas allow companies to make intracompany transfers of employees who work in other countries on temporary assignment and seek permission from the government through their visas.

20-6b WORKING CONDITIONS AND INTERNATIONAL LABOR LAW

Many countries do not have comparable Department of Labor or OSHA organizations or the experience and regulatory structures to enforce any existing laws. As a result, production is often done quite cheaply in other countries because of reduced wages and the lower costs that come from sub-par construction, ventilation, and hygiene. The result is that companies can only be urged to meet certain standards because, legally, they are not violating the law when these low-cost production facilities continue to produce cheaper goods.

FOR THE MANAGER'S DESK

Re: The High Cost of the Failure to Comply with U.S. Immigration Laws

The tale of Agriprocessors, Inc., has nearly come to an end. However, the story of the company's demise is a lesson in the importance of following labor and employment laws. The company had received more than 12 letters in 2005 and 2006 that indicated the Social Security numbers that the company was using for its workers did not match the information that the federal agency had in its files. The 3,000 discrepancies the agency found affected 78 percent of the plant's workers. The company did not respond and the Social Security Administration stopped sending letters after 2007. The following chart shows the discrepancies the SSA found:

DATE	SS# DISCREPANCIES	TAX YEAR
May 9, 2002	22	2001
May 19, 2005	500	2004
May 19, 2005	500	2003
May 19, 2005	500	2002
May 19, 2005	500	2001
May 19, 2005	461	2000
March 24, 2006	52	2004
March 24, 2006	42	2003
March 24, 2006	37	2002
March 24, 2006	24	2000
April 21, 2006	68	2005
May 5, 2006	500	2005

Elizabeth Billmeyer was the director of HR at the Agriprocessors, Inc., plant in Postville, Iowa, a company that has been called the largest kosher slaughterhouse in the country. Federal authorities conducted a raid at the plant in April 2008 and arrested 900 undocumented workers there.

Ms. Billmeyer was charged with conspiracy to harbor undocumented aliens for profit and knowingly accepting false resident alien cards. Ms. Billmeyer entered two guilty pleas to two counts, one on each charge.

In September 2008, the Iowa attorney general charged the food processor with over 9,000 violations of child labor laws. The charges focused on 32 minors who were working at the company and had been assigned work tasks or worked in areas not permitted for minors under Iowa law. The charges alleged that children under the age of 18 were exposed to poisonous chemicals and that children under 16 were employed in the operation or tending of power-driven machinery, including but not limited to conveyor belts, meat grinders, circular saws, power washers, and power shears.

Sholom Mordechai Rubashkin was the CEO of the plant that was owned by his father, Aaron. The Rubashkins were also charged with fraud and money laundering schemes, and Sholom was convicted of 86 of the 91 charges. The media coverage of the company and the raid and arrests was so extensive that the trial had to be moved to South Dakota. Following his conviction on the fraud charges, a federal judge dismissed the immigration charges against Sholom. He was sentenced to 27 years in prison.

The charges against Aaron Rubashkin were eventually dismissed. Five supervisors and managers entered guilty pleas to various federal charges.

Agriprocessors filed for bankruptcy in 2008, was purchased by a Canadian company, and is now known as AgriStar.

Using your textbook, go through this summary of events and list how many chapter topics you can find that are covered in this scenario. When you are finished, reach some conclusions about what the executives and managers could have done to avoid the company's demise and their criminal prosecution.

Sources: "H.R. Chief Pleads Guilty After Immigration Raid," *National Law Journal,* April 20, 2009, p. B5; Lynda Waddington, "Agriprocessors Ignored Government Warnings For Years," *The Iowa Independent,* May 24, 2008, www.iowaindependent.com; *U.S. v Agriprocessors,* 2009 WL 2255729 (N.D. Iowa).

20-6c SAMPLE INTERNATIONAL STANDARDS

The United Nations Commission on Human Rights has developed the International Covenant on Economic, Social, and Cultural Rights. This covenant includes the right to work; join trade unions; enjoy leisure; earn a decent living; and receive education, medical care, and Social Security. Although this international covenant would carry with it the protections outlined in this chapter for U.S. workers, enforcement of the covenant is difficult. Its real strength comes through documentation and disclosure of its violation.

One of the most successful organs of the United Nations is the International Labour Organization (ILO). This commission, founded in 1920, continues to work to develop such principles as the right to work, to join trade unions, and to have a safe work environment. Member nations submit reports on their nation's status and compliance with the standards of the ILO agreement.

The National Labor Committee (NLC), an activist group, periodically releases information on conditions in foreign factories and the companies utilizing those factories.

20-6d THE RISKS OF INTERNATIONAL SUPPLIERS

U.S. companies' investments in foreign manufacturing in major developing nations such as China, Indonesia, and Mexico have tripled in the past 15 years. However, new issues about the use of foreign labor and factories are emerging.

Quality of Goods Produced

Mattel, a company that has the majority of its inventory produced by factories in China, had to recall 70 percent of its inventory in 2007 because Chinese contractors had used paint on the toys that contained lead at levels prohibited in the United States. The recall of pet food because of another toxic material used in production in Chinese factories has required U.S. companies to rethink the foreign outsourcing process because of the damage to their brands when these massive recalls are forced on them through substandard conditions and lesser standards in other countries.

Safety Issues in Production Plants

In a practice that is widely accepted in other countries, children ages 10 to 14 labor in factories for 50 or more hours per week. Their wages enable their families to survive. School is a luxury, and children attend only until they are able to work in a factory. For example, Foxconn, a supplier for Apple and other U.S. technology firms, made international news for its use of child labor, suicides at its plants, and the long working hours demanded of employees.

Plant safety issues in production outsourced to other countries have become a subject of intense media coverage and a focus of protests in the United States. The April 2013 collapse of a clothing factory in Bangladesh resulted in 617 deaths. The tragedy was close on the heels of a November 2012 Bangladesh factory collapse that resulted in the loss of 117 lives of workers there. The site of the 2013 collapse was a building that was approved for five floors of construction, but eight floors were built. The building had never been approved for industrial use, but five different factories were operating in the building. Numerous inspections by government authorities found fire safety and ventilation issues, but no action was taken by either the factory owners or the government to address the industrial safety issues. On the day of the collapse, cracks in the building indicated unsafe stress and the police ordered the building closed. The banks and other offices located on the first floor of the building shut down their operations, but the factory workers were ordered to report for work. The result was a collapse that killed hundreds and found hundreds more trapped—some for up to 11 days.

These factories were the production locations for Walmart, Benetton, and NTD Apparel (a Canadian company). Inspections by monitors who provide information about production facilities to U.S. companies in May 2011 warned that the conditions in the Bangladesh factory required attention. After the fire in 2012, there was significant pressure from international rights groups for the companies to examine standards at their factories in Bangladesh. Benetton, despite stiff competition from Zara and other retailers on cost, has decided to pull out of Bangladesh because the country's officials cannot seem to get their arms around conditions at the factories and the enforcement of standards.

Wage Issues in Production Plants

Nike is perhaps the poster child company for wage issues at factories in countries outside the United States. The effective campaign that placed its $150 shoes next to the pennies-per-hour wages of its foreign production workers resulted in boycotts of its goods as well as cancellation of its contracts with colleges and universities because of the protests of students. The reports on Nike's factories issued by Vietnam Labor Watch included the following: women required to run laps around the factory for wearing nonregulation shoes to work; payment of subminimum wages; physical beatings, including with shoes, by factory supervisors; and employment mostly of women between the ages of 15 and 28.

20-6e NEW TRENDS IN MANAGING INTERNATIONAL WAGE AND SAFETY STANDARDS

The backlash against Nike as well as companies such as Apple resulted in the formation and activism of the American Apparel Manufacturers Association (AAMA), which counts 70 percent of all U.S. garment makers in its membership. AAMA maintains a database for its members to check labor compliance by contractors. In addition, the National Retail Federation has established the following statement of Principles on Supplier Legal Compliance (now signed by 250 retailers).

1. We are committed to legal compliance and ethical business practices in all of our operations.

2. We choose suppliers that we believe share that commitment.

3. In our purchase contracts, we require our suppliers to comply with all applicable laws and regulations.

4. If it is found that a factory used by a supplier for the production of our merchandise has committed legal violations, we will take appropriate action, which may include canceling the affected purchase contracts, terminating our relationship with the supplier, commencing legal actions against the supplier, or other actions as warranted.

5. We support law enforcement and cooperate with law enforcement authorities in the proper execution of their responsibilities.

6. We support educational efforts designed to enhance legal compliance on the part of the U.S. apparel manufacturing industry.

Some companies, including Walmart, have decided to depart from reliance on group data and have undertaken a new independent approach to confirming that their suppliers meet certain safety and wage standards. The U.S. Department of Labor has recommended that U.S. apparel importers should do more to monitor subcontractors and homeworkers (the areas where child labor violations occur) and take a more active and direct role in the monitoring and implementation of codes of conduct that the production factories sign.

BIOGRAPHY

Aaron Feuerstein: An Odd CEO

Aaron Feuerstein is the chief executive officer and chairman of the board of Malden Mills, a 93-year-old privately held company that manufactures Polartec and is located in Methuen, Massachusetts. Polartec is a fabric made from recycled plastic that stays dry and provides warmth. It is used in everything from ski parkas to blankets by companies such as L.L.Bean, Patagonia, Lands' End, and Eddie Bauer. Malden employs 2,400 locals, and Mr. Feuerstein and his family have steadfastly refused to move production overseas. Their labor costs are the highest in the industry—an average of $12.50 per hour. Malden Mills is the largest employer in one of the poorest towns in Massachusetts.

On December 11, 1995, a boiler explosion at Malden Mills resulted in a fire that injured 27 people and destroyed three of the buildings at Malden Mills' factory site. With only one building left in functioning order, many employees assumed they would be laid off temporarily. Other employees worried that Mr. Feuerstein, then 70 years old, would simply take the insurance money and retire. Mr. Feuerstein could have retired with about $300 million in insurance proceeds from the fire.

Instead, Mr. Feuerstein announced on December 14, 1995, that he would pay the employees their salaries for at least 30 days. He continued that promise for six months, when 90 percent of the employees were back to work. The cost of covering the wages was approximately $25 million to the company. During that time, Malden ran its Polartec through its one working facility as it began and completed the reconstruction of the plant, at a cost of $430 million. Only $300 million of that amount was covered by the insurance on the plant; the remainder was borrowed so that Malden Mills would be a state-of-the-art environmentally friendly plant. It is interesting to note that production output during this time was nine times what it had been before the fire. One worker noted, "I owe him everything. I'm paying him back." After the fire and Feuerstein's announcement, customers pledged their support, with one customer, Dakotah, sending in $30,000 to help. Within the first month following the fire, $1 million in donations was received.

Malden Mills was rededicated in September 1997 with new buildings and technology. About 10 percent of the 2,400 employees were displaced by the upgraded facilities and equipment, but Feuerstein created a job training and placement center on site in order to ease these employees' transition.

By the end of 2001, six years after the fire, Malden Mills had debts of $140 million and was teetering near bankruptcy. However, Malden Mills had been through bankruptcy before, in the 1980s, and emerged very strongly with its then-new product, Polartec, developed through the company's R&D program.

Some have suggested that Mr. Feuerstein's generosity during that time is responsible for the present financial crisis. However, the fire destroyed the company's furniture upholstery division and customers were impatient at that time. They were not inclined to wait for production to ramp up, and Malden Mills lost most of those customers. It closed the upholstery division in 1996.

Also, there was the threat of inexpensive fleece from the Asian markets that was ignored largely because of the plant rebuilding and the efforts focused there. Finally, in 2000, the company had a shakeup in its marketing team just as it was launching its electric fabrics—fabrics with heatable wires that are powered by batteries embedded in the fleece.

Once again, however, the goodwill from 1995 remained. Residents of the town have been sending in checks to help the company, some as small as $10. An Internet campaign was begun by town residents to "Buy Fleece." The campaign is enjoying some success as Patagonia, Lands' End, and L.L.Bean report increased demand. In addition, the U.S. military placed large orders for fleece jackets for soldiers fighting in Operation Enduring Freedom in Afghanistan.

Then–Senators Ted Kennedy and John Kerry lobbied GE not to involuntarily petition Malden Mills into bankruptcy. GE Capital held one-fourth of Malden Mills' debts. Its other creditors included Finova Capital, SAI Investment, Pilgrim Investment, LaSalle Bank, and PNC Bank. The lobbying was to no avail. By 2002, Malden Mills was in bankruptcy. Feuerstein labored to raise the money to pay off creditors and buy his company back, but he was unable to meet the bankruptcy deadline. Malden Mills emerged from bankruptcy on September 30, 2003, but under management other than Mr. Feuerstein. He still hopes to buy the company back, but the price, originally $93 million, has increased to $120 million. Feuerstein is the president of Malden Mills, serves on its board, and earns a salary of $425,000 per year, but he is no longer in charge and cannot be until the creditors are repaid.

In January 2004, members of the U.S. House and Senate lobbied to convince the Export-Import Bank to loan Mr. Feuerstein the money he needed to buy back his company. The Ex-Im Bank, swayed by Mr. Feuerstein's commitment to keep Malden's production in the United States, increased the loan amount from the $20 million it had originally pledged, to the $35 million Mr. Feuerstein needed.

By the end of January 2004, Malden Mills had three new strategies: Mr. Feuerstein was selling Polarfleece blankets on QVC, the company would be in partnership in China with Shanghai Mills, and the company announced it would expand its military contracts. Mr. Feuerstein remains as president and chairman of the board.

The company's patient union had its patience wearing thin. During the 2002–2003 time frame of the bankruptcy, the union leader said, "We're ready to make sacrifices for a little while. Whatever he asks us to do to keep the place going." However, a threatened strike in December 2004 resulted in negotiations and a new union three-year contract, a more expensive one for the company.

Mr. Feuerstein said at the time, "There are times in business when you don't think of the financial consequences, but of the human consequences. There is no doubt this company will survive."

In 2006, Malden Mills landed a multimillion-dollar contract with the U.S. Department of Defense to be a supplier of the lightweight Polartec blankets for the U.S. military branches. However, by 2007, Malden Mills filed for bankruptcy again. The Pension Benefit Guarantee Corporation took over its assets in order to satisfy the pension obligations the company could not pay. The pensions were underfunded by 49 percent. The last shipment of Polartec from the factory was in July 2007.

Evaluate Mr. Feuerstein's business strategies, his ethics, his views on social responsibility, and the company's fate. Mr. Feuerstein is a Talmudic scholar who often quotes the following proverbs:

"In a situation where there is no righteous person, try to be a righteous person."

"Not all who increase their wealth are wise."

Sources: From Marianne M. Jennings, *Business Ethics: Selected Cases and Readings*, 8th Ed. (2014); Steve Wulf, "The Glow from a Fire," *Time*, January 8, 1996, p. 49. © 1996 Time, Inc. Reprinted with permission; Rabbi Avi Shafran, "Bankrupt and Wealthy," *Society Today*, July 29, 2007 (as originally accessed for research).

Summary

What wage and hour protections exist for employees?

- Fair Labor Standards Act (FSLA)—federal law that regulates minimum wage and overtime pay
- Minimum wage—federal hourly rate of pay
- Overtime pay—rate of 1½ times the hourly rate for hours over 40 per week worked
- Equal Pay Act—equal wages for equal work regardless of gender
- Child labor standards—restrictions on hours and types of work for children under the age of 18

What protections exist for safety in the workplace?

- Occupational Safety and Health Act—federal law setting and enforcing workplace safety standards
- Occupational Safety and Health Administration (OSHA)—federal agency responsible for safety in the workplace
- Drug testing—screening of employees for impairment

What happens when a worker is injured in the workplace?

- Workers' compensation—state-by-state system of employer strict liability for injuries of workers on the job; the few exceptions to recovery include self-inflicted injuries

What is the Social Security system, and what benefits does it provide?

- Social Security Act—federal law establishing disability, beneficiary, and retirement benefits
- Federal Insurance Contributions Act (FICA)—statute establishing system for withholding contributions for Social Security benefits

Are workers entitled to pensions, and are they regulated?

- Employment Retirement Income Security Act (ERISA)—federal law regulating employer-sponsored pension plans
- Pension Protection Plan of 2006

What rights do unemployed workers have?

- Unemployment compensation—federal program handled by states to provide temporary support for displaced workers
- Workers' compensation—system of no-fault liability for employees injured on the job

How are labor unions formed, and what is their relationship with employees?

- Norris-LaGuardia Act—federal law prohibiting injunctions to halt strikes
- National Labor Relations Act (Wagner Act)—federal law authorizing employee unionization
- Labor Management Relations Act (Taft–Hartley Act)—federal law limiting union economic-weapons
- Labor–Management Reporting and Disclosure Act (Landrum–Griffin Act)—federal law regulating union membership and organizations
- National Labor Relations Board (NLRB)—federal agency responsible for enforcing labor laws
- Collective bargaining unit—group of employees recognized as exclusive bargaining agent
- Certification—recognition of union as exclusive bargaining agent
- Collective bargaining agreement—exclusive rights agreement between employer and employee
- Good-faith bargaining—requirement that parties negotiate terms in earnest
- Unfair labor practice—conduct by labor or management prohibited by statute

- Concerted activities—union-sponsored activities
- Picketing—public appearance of striking union members
- Boycotts—refusal to work for or to buy from or handle products of an employer
- Slowdown—workers report to job but do not operate at full speed
- Right-to-work laws—right to work at a company without being required to join a union
- Worker Adjustment and Retraining Notification Act (WARN)—federal law requiring employers to give 60 days' notice of plant shutdowns
- Lockout—employer closure of plant or business so workers cannot work

What are the laws and procedures related to immigrants and employment?

- Immigration and Naturalization Act (INA)
- Immigration Reform and Control Act of 1986 (IRCA)
- Immigration Act of 1990
- Illegal Immigration Reform and Immigrant Responsibility Act of 1996
- Antiterrorism and Effective Death Penalty Act
- Uniting and Strengthening America by Proving Appropriate Tools Required to Intercept and Obstruct Terrorism Act (USA Patriot Act)
- The Homeland Security Act
- American Competitiveness in the Twenty-First Century Act of 2000

Questions and Problems

1. Whirlpool, a manufacturer of household appliances, uses a system of overhead conveyor belts to send a constant stream of parts to employees on the line throughout the plant. Beneath the conveyor belt is a netting or mesh screen to catch any parts or other objects that might fall from the conveyor belt.

Some items did fall to the mesh screen, located some 20 feet above the plant floor. Maintenance employees had the responsibility for removing the parts and other debris from the screen. They usually stood on the iron frames of the mesh screen, but occasionally they found it necessary to go onto the screen itself. While one maintenance employee was standing on the mesh, it broke, and he fell the 20 feet to his death on the floor below. After this fatal accident, maintenance employees were prohibited from standing on the mesh screen or the iron

frames. A mobile platform and long hooks were used to remove objects.

Two maintenance employees, Virgil Deemer and Thomas Cornwell, complained about the screen and its safety problems. When the plant foreman refused to make corrections, Mr. Deemer and Mr. Cornwell asked for the name of an OSHA inspector, and Mr. Deemer contacted an OSHA official on July 7, 1974.

On July 8, 1974, Mr. Deemer and Mr. Cornwell reported for work and were told to do their maintenance work on the screen in the usual manner. Both refused on safety grounds, so the plant foreman sent them to the personnel office. They were then forced to punch out and were not paid for the six hours left on their shift.

Explain Mr. Deemer and Mr. Cornwall's rights under OSHA. [*Whirlpool Corporation v Marshall*, 445 U.S. 1 (1980)]

2.   Supervisors at Walmart asked employees to work off the clock, erase hours from their time cards, and not take lunch and other breaks. Determine whether there would be any FLSA violations if the employees voluntarily agreed to do what the supervisors requested.

3.   Joe Ortiz was discharged from Magma Copper Co. for absenteeism. He missed the last shift of work before he was fired because he was temporarily in custody following an arrest for a criminal offense. He filed for unemployment but was denied. Mr. Ortiz said he notified Magma that he was missing because of being detained in jail. The unemployment compensation agency says Mr. Ortiz is disqualified for benefits because he was fired for misconduct. Who is right? [*Magma Copper v Department of Employment Security*, 625 P.2d 935 (Ariz. 1981)]

4.   Casimer Gacioch began working for Stroh Brewery on February 24, 1947. When he began his work for Stroh, he was predisposed to alcoholism, but he had not yet become an uncontrolled alcoholic.

Beer was provided free at the brewery and was available to all employees on the job. This availability had been negotiated through a collective bargaining agreement. Employees could drink beer during their breaks and at lunch with no limit on the amount.

Mr. Gacioch did not drink at home during the week but drank three or four bottles of beer on the weekend. At work, he drank 12 bottles a day. He was not a test taster; he ran a machine that fed cases of beer to a soaker.

He became an alcoholic, was intoxicated on the job, and could not perform his work. He was fired on August 30, 1974.

Mr. Gacioch pursued a workers' compensation claim against Stroh because the free-beer policy accelerated his problem. Explain whether he is entitled to worker's compensation. [*Gacioch v Stroh Brewery Co.*, 396 N.W.2d 1 (Mich. 1990)]

5.   Janice W. Craig was employed by Drenberg and Associates, an insurance agency. About the time she started to work, Drenberg began a year of explosive growth. Under normal conditions, an agency with 400,000 accounts could expect to acquire approximately 40,000 new accounts in the period of a year. Drenberg grew from 400,000 to 1,200,000 in just over one year. Craig and the agency's employees worked many overtime hours.

Mrs. Craig was a conscientious perfectionist. She also took over a part of the commercial desk, handling correspondence, renewals, and changes. She was under constant pressure.

In April 1975, Drenberg purchased another agency, thereby acquiring 500 new accounts and an additional employee. Mrs. Craig was given responsibility for supervising the new employee and merging the books of the two agencies. The additional responsibility and mounting pressure began to affect her. She began to feel frustrated and ineffective. She experienced difficulty relating to her coworkers and on occasions had heated exchanges with customers. On September 25, 1975, she engaged in a particularly emotional telephone conversation with one of the agency's customers, after which she eventually left the office in tears.

In addition to Mrs. Craig's difficulties at the office, she was experiencing domestic disharmony. She and her husband argued frequently concerning his drinking habits. She encountered difficulties in relating to her daughters, and her mother's death caused additional internal pressures. On the evening of September 25, 1975, the Craigs again argued, following which she took an overdose of medication.

The following day she sought help at the Tri-City Mental Hospital and was subsequently admitted to Camelback Hospital, where her condition was diagnosed as neurotic depression, or a mental breakdown.

Mrs. Craig filed a claim for worker's compensation. Explain whether Mrs. Craig should receive workers' compensation. [*Fireman's Fund Ins. Co. v Industrial Comm'n*, 579 P.2d 555 (Ariz. 1979)]

6.   Felix Santos, Carlos Garcia, and Jose A. Valdes Prieto were stock persons for Cuba Tropical, Inc., a supermarket supplier. They regularly worked over 40 hours per week, but they were not paid overtime. They brought suit to recover their overtime pay against Cuba Tropical as well as Jose L. Rodriguez, a co-owner of Cuba Tropical. Mr. Rodriguez has no control over the hiring and firing of employers, does not establish their working hours, and did not visit the warehouse where the three employees worked. He hired managers for the business and had them handle the day-to-day operations. He was required to sign certain documents for the corporation, but he did not sign any checks personally. Can Mr. Rodriguez be held personally liable for the overtime wages that are due to the three men? [*Santos v Cuba Tropical, Inc.*, 829 F. Supp. 2d 1304 (S.D. Fla., 2011)]

7.   An employee of Walmart worked at the store on the night restocking crew. For security reasons, the manager of the store implemented a policy of locking all doors leading into and out of the store at the close of the business day. Only management personnel had keys to the store and no one in management worked on the night crew. Consequently, employees on the night crew were locked in the store without a key to exit the building until it opened the following day. While working one night, the employee suffered a stroke and collapsed, unconscious. When the emergency medical personnel arrived, approximately six minutes later, they were unable to enter the store because no one on the night crew had a key to the door. By the time the emergency crew was able to assist the employee, they were unable to revive her. The deceased employee was taken to the hospital where she was declared brain dead, and after 15 hours, the life support systems to which she was connected were discontinued. Subsequently, the executor of her estate and guardian for her child filed suit against Walmart for unlawful false imprisonment. The trial court granted Walmart's motion for summary judgment, and the executor/guardian appealed. How should the appellate court decide the case and why? [*Bryant v Wal-Mart Stores, Inc.*, 417 S.E.2d 688 (Ga. App. 1992)]

8. Michael Kittell was an employee at Vermont Weatherboard. While he was operating a saw at work, a splinter flew into his eye and went into his cranium. Kittell filed suit against his employer because he was an inexperienced employee who was put to work straightaway on the saw, without any training. He also said that his employer had removed all the safety devices from the saw thereby causing the injury to his eye and brain. Can Kittell recover from his employer? What about the manufacturer of the saw? [*Kittell v Vermont Weatherboard, Inc.*, 417 A.2d 926 (Vt. 1980)]

9. A group of exotic dancers at several clubs in the San Fernando Valley of California brought a class action suit against their employers, the club owners, for the following violations of labor law:

- Failure to provide meal breaks
- Failure to provide rest breaks
- Club managers taking 50 percent of the dancers' tips, which resulted in some dancers earning less than the minimum wage for hours worked
- Failure to reimburse dancers for the costs of their uniforms

The club owners acknowledge that the dancers worked over 40 hours each week but that they were professionals and not subject to the provisions of the FLSA. The club owners also claim that the dancers work on a type of commission basis and so are not covered by the minimum wage law. Are labor law violations going on at the clubs? Are you able to respond to the defenses that the club owners raised?

10. Alfred Smith and Galen Black were fired by a private drug rehabilitation center because they ingested peyote for sacramental purposes at a ceremony of the Native American Church, of which both are members. When Mr. Smith and Mr. Black applied for unemployment compensation from the state of Oregon, their requests were denied because they were fired for "misconduct." They challenged the decision as a violation of their religious freedom. Are Mr. Smith and Mr. Black correct? Note: You may have to think about constitutional rights in order to answer this question (refer to Chapter 5). [*Employment Div., Dep't of Human Resources of Oregon v Smith*, 496 U.S. 913 (1990)]

ECONOMICS THE LAW

The Cost of the Cheap Shirt

Economists warn about quick fixes for wages and the imposition of U.S. safety standards on foreign factories. They offer the following figures to illustrate that the issue of labor conditions in other countries is complex.

In Bangladesh, clothing factories get about $6.75 per shirt. These are the factory costs:[5]

$4.75 for the fabric and thread
$1.00 for the shirt's labels
$0.38 wage costs for each shirt (workers earn $70 to $80 a month)
$0.15 per shirt for laundering

That leaves $0.47 per shirt for facilities, shipment, marketing, and perhaps the interest on loans.

The cost of living in Bangladesh is $40 per month for rent, and food per adult is $13 per month. Milk for a child is $5 per month. Those who work in the factories are generally the main wage earners in their families because no other jobs pay as well.

Given this analysis, where do you see some fixes for the safety and wage issues? What needs to be done besides instituting codes of ethics and factory and labor standards?

Notes

1. For more information on the history of employment law see the *Instructor's Manual*.

2. NLRB, Office of Gen. Counsel, Div. of Operations-Mgmt., OM 11-74, Report of the Acting Gen. Counsel Concerning Social Media Cases (Aug. 18, 2011).

3. Hispanics United, 2011 WL 3894520, slip op. at 6.

4. Hispanics United of Buffalo, Inc., No. 3-CA-27872, 2011 WL 3894520 (N.L.R.B. Div. of Judges Sept. 2, 2011).

5. Thanks to Rubana Huk, "The Economics of a $6.75 Shirt," *Wall Street Journal*, May 17, 2013, p. A15, for his cost figures.

Employment discrimination has been one of the fastest-growing legal issues of the past decade. Few employers have remained unaffected by the impact of antidiscrimination laws and cases.

This chapter answers the following questions: What laws governing employment discrimination exist? What types of discrimination exist? Are there any defenses to discrimination? What penalties or damages can be imposed for violations?

UPDATE
For up-to-date legal news, go to **mariannejennings.com**

Consider...

Lydia Gonzalez, 58, worked as a reporter at *El Nuevo Dia*, a Puerto Rico newspaper. Her supervisor, Maria Luisa Ferre, often said that Ms. Gonzalez's demeanor and couture were "[o]ut of style" and "colorless," and her coiffure was "like Phyllis Diller." Ms. Ferre also said that Ms. Gonzalez was old-fashioned (viz., "manias de vieja," or "old person's ways") and that she should have retired and gone to live with her grandchildren in Florida long ago.

Ms. Gonzalez asked to cover fashion shows, and when Ms. Ferre balked at the idea, Ms. Gonzalez responded, "You want me to look like a *Vogue* model?" Ms. Ferre simply stared and assigned younger reporters to cover the fashion shows.

Ms. Gonzalez was terminated shortly after. Following her termination, Ms. Gonzalez filed suit for age discrimination. Can she recover?

I have a dream that one day this nation will rise up and live out the true meaning of its creed: "We hold these truths to be self-evident; that all men are created equal." I have a dream . . . I have a dream that my four little children will one day live in a nation where they will not be judged by the color of their skin but by the content of their character. I have a dream . . . .

Dr. Martin Luther King, Jr.

21-1 History of Employment Discrimination Law

Protections against employment discrimination are strictly statutory. Common law afforded employees no protection against discrimination. Indeed, common law viewed the entire employment relationship as a private contractual matter that should be free from judicial interference.[1]

Notwithstanding the **Civil Rights Acts of 1866 and 1870**, the first effective antidiscrimination employment statute was a long time in coming. The first federal legislation to deal directly with the issue of discrimination was the **Equal Pay Act of 1963** (see Chapter 20 for more details). The statutory right to equality was expanded beyond the issue of pay less than a year later by **Title VII** of the **Civil Rights Act of 1964**. Title VII is the basis for discrimination law and judicial decisions in such matters. Although it has been amended many times, its basic purpose is to prohibit discrimination in employment on the basis of race, color, religion, sex, or national origin.

Title VII was first amended by the **Equal Employment Opportunity Act of 1972**. This amendment gave the act's enforcer, the **Equal Employment Opportunity Commission (EEOC)**, greater powers—for example, the right to file suits in federal district court. In 1975, Title VII was again amended, with the **Pregnancy Discrimination Act**, which defined "sex" discrimination to include discrimination on the basis of pregnancy and childbirth.

Laws have also been enacted to protect against discrimination because of age or handicap. Discrimination on the basis of age was prohibited by the **Age Discrimination in Employment Act of 1967** (discussed later in this chapter). Under the **Rehabilitation Act of 1973**, federal contractors are prohibited from discriminating against certain employees in performing their contracts. With the **Americans with Disabilities Act (ADA)**, passed in 1990, employers of 15 or more employees are prohibited from discriminating against employees with disabilities and are required to make reasonable accommodations for qualified employees with disabilities. Although the substance of the existing antidiscrimination laws

Nature of Complaint	Number of Complaints
Total	99,412
Race	33,512
Sex	30,356
Disabilities	22,857
Age	22,857
National origin	10,883
Religion	3,811
Equal pay	1,082

EEOC 2012 Data on Employment Discrimination Cases

remains, the **Civil Rights Act of 1991** made significant changes in procedural aspects of Title VII litigation. Exhibit 21.1 provides a summary of federal antidiscrimination legislation to date.

EXHIBIT **21.1** Employment Discrimination Statutory Scheme

STATUTE	DATE	PROVISIONS
Civil Rights Acts of 1866 and 1870 42 U.S.C. § 1981	1866 1870	Prohibited intentional discrimination based on race, color, national origin, or ethnicity; permit lawsuits
Equal Pay Act 29 U.S.C. § 206	1963	Prohibits paying workers of one sex different wages from the other when the jobs involve substantially similar skill, effort, and responsibility; Wage and Hour Division of Department of Labor enforces; private lawsuits permitted; double damage recovery for up to three years' wages plus attorney fees
Civil Rights Act of 1964 42 U.S.C. § 1981	1964	Outlaws all employment discrimination on the basis of race, color, religion, sex, or national origin; applies to hiring, pay, work conditions, promotions, discipline, and discharge; EEOC enforces; private lawsuits permitted; costs and attorney fees recoverable
Age Discrimination in Employment Act 42 U.S.C. § 6101	1967	Prohibits employment discrimination because of age against employees over 40 and mandatory retirement restrictions; EEOC enforces; private lawsuits permitted; attorney fees and costs recoverable
Equal Employment Opportunity Act 42 U.S.C. § 2000	1972	Expanded enforcement power of EEOC
Rehabilitation Act 29 U.S.C. § 701	1973	Prohibits employment discrimination on the basis of handicaps
Pregnancy Discrimination Act 42 U.S.C. § 2000e	1975	Prohibits discrimination on the basis of pregnancy and childbirth
Americans with Disabilities Act 42 U.S.C. § 12101	1990	Prohibits discrimination against those with covered disabilities (plus 2008 amendments)
Civil Rights Act of 1991 42 U.S.C. § 1981	1991	Clarifies disparate impact suit requirements; clarifies the meaning of "business necessity" and "job related"; changes some Supreme Court decisions (*Wards Cove*); punitive damage recovery
Glass Ceiling Act 42 U.S.C. § 2000e	1991	Creates commission to study barriers to women entering management and decision-making positions
Family and Medical Leave Act 29 U.S.C. § 26	1993	Establishes 12 weeks of unpaid leave for medical or family reasons
Title II of the Genetic Information Nondiscrimination Act of 2008 42 U.S.C. § 2000ff	2008	Prohibits employment discrimination based on genetic information about an applicant, employee, or former employee
Lilly Ledbetter Fair Pay Act (2009) 42 USC § 2000a	2009	Changes the recovery period for back wages to the EEOC standard that existed prior to the decision in *Ledbetter v Goodyear Tire & Rubber Co., Inc.*, 550 U.S. 618 (2007); each paycheck triggers a new 180-day filing period regardless of when the discrimination began

In addition to this legislation, several executive orders that apply to administrative agencies (see Chapter 6) have been issued. These orders require federal government contractors to institute, among other things, affirmative action programs in their labor forces.

21-2 Employment Discrimination: Title VII of the Civil Rights Act

Title VII of the Civil Rights Act of 1964—also known as the **Fair Employment Practices Act**—as amended in 1991, prohibits discrimination in all areas of employment on the basis of race, color, religion, national origin, and sex (including pregnancy, childbirth, or abortion). Other acts prohibit discrimination based on physical disability or age.

21-2a APPLICATION OF TITLE VII

Groups Covered

Title VII does not apply to all employers but is limited to the following groups:

1. Employers with at least 15 workers during each working day in each of 20 or more calendar weeks in the current or preceding year (state antidiscrimination statutes may apply to employers with fewer than 15 employees)

2. Labor unions that have 15 members or more or operate a hiring hall that refers workers to covered employers

3. Employment agencies that procure workers for an employer who is covered by the law

4. Any labor union or employment agency, provided it has 15 or more employees. Companies should note, however, that even if they do not meet the minimum size requirements for federal laws, state antidiscrimination laws most likely do apply to their operations and employment practices.

21-2b EMPLOYMENT PROCEDURES COVERED

Every step in the employment process is covered by Title VII. Hiring, compensation, training programs, promotion, demotion, transfer, fringe benefits, employer rules, working conditions, and dismissals are all covered. In the case of an employment agency, the system for the agency's job referrals is also covered.

21-3 Theories of Discrimination Under Title VII

Three basic but not mutually exclusive theories of discrimination under Title VII include **disparate treatment**, **disparate impact**, and **pattern or practice of discrimination**.

21-3a DISPARATE TREATMENT

The most common form of discrimination at the time Title VII was passed was treating employees of one race or sex differently from employees of another race or sex. This different, or disparate, treatment results in unlawful discrimination when an individual is treated less favorably than other employees because of race, color, religion, national origin, or sex. The U.S. Supreme Court established the elements required to be shown to establish disparate treatment under Title VII in

McDonnell Douglas Corp. v Green, 411 U.S. 792 (1973). The case involved the rights of a black mechanic who had been laid off during a general workforce reduction and then not rehired. McDonnell claimed Mr. Green was not rehired because of his participation in a lock-in at the plant to protest racial inequality. Mr. Green brought suit for a Title VII violation, and the Supreme Court established the following elements as a *prima facie* case for discrimination.

1. The plaintiff belongs to a racial minority.
2. The plaintiff applied for and was qualified for a job with the employee.
3. The plaintiff, despite job qualifications, was rejected.
4. After the plaintiff's rejection, the job remained open and the employer continued to seek applicants.

These same elements can be applied to other forms of discrimination by just substituting, for example, "The plaintiff belongs to a protected age group," or "The plaintiff has a disability." The employer has the burden of proof to show that the employment decision was made for a nondiscriminatory reason. That burden arises when the employee-plaintiff establishes the four elements set out in *Green*. For example, a company may have retained a male supervisor when it terminated a female supervisor, but if the company can show that, because of reductions in force, it needed managers with broader experience and the male supervisor had that experience, the decision is not discriminatory. *Chescheir v Liberty Mutual Ins. Co.* (Case 21.1) deals with an issue of disparate treatment and proof of discrimination in an employment decision.

CASE 21.1

Chescheir v Liberty Mutual Ins. Co.
713 F.2d 1142 (5th Cir. 1983)

Why Can He Go to Law School But I Can't? The Case of the Law Student Claims Adjuster

FACTS

Liberty Mutual Insurance Company has a rule prohibiting its adjusters and first-year supervisors from attending law school. This "law school rule" was proposed and implemented on a national basis by Edmund Carr, a vice president and general claims manager, in November 1972.

Joan Chescheir (plaintiff) was hired by Liberty Mutual's Dallas office in March 1973 as a claims adjuster. In January 1975, she voluntarily resigned but in June of that year was hired in Liberty's Houston office as a claims adjuster.

In August 1976, Wyatt Trainer, the claims manager at the Houston office, received an anonymous letter informing him that Ms. Chescheir was attending law school. After consulting with his assistants and superior, Mr. Trainer fired her after she admitted she was attending law school.

Charity O'Connell also worked in the Houston office as a claims adjuster during the same period Ms. Chescheir did. During a coffee break with a new employee, Timothy Schwirtz (also an adjuster), Ms. O'Connell relayed the story of Ms. Chescheir's firing. Mr. Schwirtz then said, "Oh, that's strange, because when I was hired, when Wells [Southwest Division claims manager] interviewed me, he told me that I could go to law school and in fact if I came down to the Houston office, there were law schools in Houston." Ms. O'Connell then went to her supervisor and told him she also was attending law school. She refused to quit law school and was fired.

William McCarthy, Liberty's house counsel in its Houston office, attended law school while working as an adjuster and was retained as house counsel upon his graduation. The trial court found that Mr. McCarthy's supervisors were aware of his contemporaneous law school career. Alvin Dwayne White was employed as an adjuster in Liberty's Fort Worth office and asked for a transfer to Houston so he could attend law school. He was given the transfer and attended law school in Houston. James Ballard worked as an adjuster in Houston, attended law school, and was promoted

CONTINUED

to supervisor while in law school. Supervisors and employees were aware of his law school attendance, but the law school rule was not enforced against him. In short, none of the male employees known to have been attending law school was fired.

Ms. Chescheir and Ms. O'Connell both filed complaints with the EEOC, were given right of suit letters, and filed suit in federal district court. After a lengthy trial, the court found that Liberty Mutual had violated Title VII. Both women were given back pay. Liberty Mutual appealed.

JUDICIAL OPINION

GOLDBERG, Circuit Judge

Title VII applies … not only to the more blatant forms of discrimination, but also to subtler forms, such as discriminatory enforcement of work rules.

The four-part test for demonstrating a *prima facie* case for discriminatory discharge due to unequal imposition of discipline [is]:

1. That plaintiff was a member of a protected group;

2. That there was a company policy or practice concerning the activity for which he or she was discharged;

3. That nonminority employees either were given the benefit of a lenient company practice or were not held to compliance with a strict company policy; and

4. That the minority employee was disciplined either without the application of a lenient policy, or in conformity with the strict one.

Of course, if an employer is unaware that a nonminority employee is in violation of company policy, the absence of discipline does not demonstrate a more lenient policy. It follows from this that if an employer applies a rule differently to people it believes are differently situated, no discriminatory intent has been shown.

It is clear that the plaintiffs are members of a protected group and that there was a company policy or practice concerning the activity for which the plaintiffs were discharged; thus the first two elements of the test are met. It is also clear that minority employees were disciplined without the application of a lenient policy, and in conformity with a strict policy. All women known to violate the law school rule were immediately discharged. Furthermore, even potential violations of the rule by women were investigated promptly. An anonymous letter was sufficient to trigger an investigation of Chescheir, and the fact that Chescheir was attending law school moved the company to interrogate another woman.

The only remaining element of the *prima facie* case is a finding that male employees either were given the

benefit of a lenient company practice or were not held to compliance with a strict company policy. This is the element upon which Liberty Mutual focuses its attack. Recasting Liberty Mutual's argument slightly, it claims that other males were strictly disciplined in accord with the law school rule, and that Liberty Mutual never knew that McCarthy, White, and Ballard were attending law school. Thus, claims Liberty Mutual, the third element was not met.

We are not persuaded. First, our review of the record does not disclose any males in the Southwest Division who were discharged because of the law school rule. Second, even were we to accept Liberty Mutual's contention that it did not actually know McCarthy, White, and Ballard were attending law school, we would still affirm the judgment. The operative question is merely whether Liberty Mutual applied a more liberal standard to male employees. The district court found that there were widespread rumors that McCarthy and Ballard were attending law school. Also, the EEOC notified Liberty Mutual that a male adjuster was attending law school (Ballard) and requested an explanation. Key managerial employees, at a minimum, suspected McCarthy was attending law school but preferred not to ask and confirm their suspicions. One male adjuster was told when he was hired that he could attend law school. In contrast to Liberty Mutual's energetic investigation of women it believed might be attending law school, Liberty Mutual never investigated any of these allegations, suspicions, or rumors about male adjusters. The case of Mr. White is even more dramatic. After he expressed a desire to transfer to Houston in order to attend law school, that transfer was granted and he was never told he could not attend law school.

The preceding facts are more than enough to support the third leg [of the test]. Males at Liberty Mutual were subject to lenient enforcement of the law school rule. The district court's ultimate finding of fact that Liberty Mutual applied its law school rule discriminatorily finds firm support in the record; all four elements of the *prima facie* case are present.

Once Chescheir and O'Connell established a *prima facie* case of discrimination, the burden shifted to Liberty Mutual to present a justification. The district court found that Liberty Mutual offered no justification. Accordingly, the judgment of the district court is affirmed.

CASE QUESTIONS

1. Had any male employees ever been fired under the rule?

2. Were there examples of disparate use of the rule?

3. Give an example of some facts that would have supported a defense theory that there were nondiscriminatory reasons for the terminations.

Consider...

In November, 1980, Kathryn Davis Matthews was hired by A-1, Inc., a mobile home sales company, as a sales associate. She was the only female sales associate in the Lubbock, Texas, office. She was fired on July 11, 1981, for (1) violating company policy prohibiting "moonlighting" and (2) tardiness and absenteeism. Her "moonlighting" activity was selling Mary Kay cosmetics. A-1's manager, Wayne Swinney, listed three examples of Ms. Matthew's absenteeism: (1) when her mother was ill, (2) when she went to the hairdresser, and (3) when she had car trouble.

Male associates in the office with tardiness and absenteeism problems were counseled and, in some instances, had documentation placed in their files. Male associates were permitted to leave on personal errands and to go to the barbershop. Two of the office's male associates engaged in some "moonlighting" activity, even on company time. They were both given an exemption from the company rule. No male employees were terminated for tardiness and absenteeism unless there also was a problem with their productivity. Ms. Matthews had no problems with productivity given in her discharge notice. Ms. Matthews filed suit for discrimination. Does she have the elements of a sex discrimination case?

[*Matthews v A-1, Inc.*, 748 F.2d 975 (5th Cir. 1984)]

THINK: The rulings in *Green* and *Chescheir* are that employers cannot treat those who are members of different groups or protected classes (race, gender, religion) using different standards or rules, with the result being that the members of the nonprotected group are hired or retained, while those in the protected class are not.

APPLY: A-1 did not apply the same standard to all employees. Male employees were given more latitude on absences and A-1 was inconsistent in the application of its moonlighting policy.

ANSWER: The treatment was disparate and constituted discrimination.

21-3b DISPARATE IMPACT

Many employment hiring, promoting, and firing practices are not intentionally discriminatory. In fact, the basis for such decisions may be quite rational. Even so, the effect or impact of many employment standards is to discriminate against particular races or on the basis of sex.

In one case, the Alabama prison system had a minimum height requirement of 5'2" and a minimum weight requirement of 120 pounds for all of its "correctional counselors" (prison guards). The impact of the rule was to exclude many females and very few males. [*Dothard v Rawlinson*, 433 U.S. 321 (1977)] Although the rule had a purpose other than one of discrimination, namely, making sure guards were large enough to perform their jobs, the effect of the rule was to exclude women from the job position.

Disparate impact cases do not require the four steps of proof outlined in the *Green* case. Rather, the proof required in disparate impact cases is a statistical showing of the impact of an employment practice.

The 1991 amendments to the Civil Rights Act require a plaintiff to establish that a practice or practices have a disparate impact on a protected class. The burden then shifts to the employer to show "business necessity" for the practice. The employer must show that the practice is "job related for the position in question and consistent with business necessity." However, disparate impact cases cannot be based on an analysis of only the demographics of the labor market; the proper comparison is between the skilled labor force (as defined by the position in question) and those actually holding the position.

The *Ricci v DeStefano* case (Case 21.2) is a landmark U.S. Supreme Court decision on the issue of testing and disparate impact. The case focuses on an area of active litigation in employment discrimination—the validity of employer skill and knowledge tests for hiring and promoting.

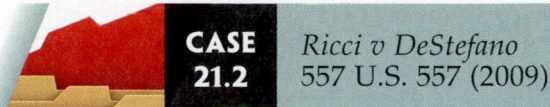

CASE 21.2   *Ricci v DeStefano*
557 U.S. 557 (2009)

Fighting Fire with Stats

FACTS

In 2003, 118 firefighters in the city of New Haven, Connecticut, took examinations to qualify for promotion to the rank of lieutenant or captain. Promotion examinations in New Haven (City) were infrequent, so the stakes were high. Exam results determined which firefighters would be considered for promotions during the next two years, and their order for consideration. Many firefighters, including Frank Ricci, studied for months, at considerable personal and financial cost.

The examination results showed that white candidates had outperformed minority candidates. Seventy-seven candidates completed the lieutenant examination—43 whites, 19 blacks, and 15 Hispanics. Of those, 34 candidates passed—25 whites, 6 blacks, and 3 Hispanics. Eight lieutenant positions were vacant at the time of the examination, which meant that the top 10 candidates were eligible for an immediate promotion to lieutenant. All 10 were white. Subsequent vacancies would have allowed at least three black candidates to be considered for promotion to lieutenant.

Forty-one candidates completed the captain examination—25 whites, 8 blacks, and 8 Hispanics. Of those, 22 candidates passed—16 whites, 3 blacks, and 3 Hispanics. Seven captain positions were vacant at the time of the examination. Nine candidates were eligible for an immediate promotion to captain—seven whites and two Hispanics.

Following a briefing on the exam results, the mayor and other local politicians opened a public debate on the results that turned rancorous. The firefighters argued that the test results should be discarded because the results were discriminatory. Some firefighters threatened a discrimination lawsuit if the city made the promotions on the basis of the tests. Other firefighters said the exams were neutral and fair, and they, in turn, threatened a discrimination lawsuit if the city, relying on the statistical racial disparity, ignored the test results and denied promotions to the candidates who had performed well. In the end, the city took the side of those who protested the test results. It threw out the examination results. Mr. Ricci and others filed suit.

The federal district court found that there was discrimination against the white and Hispanic firefighters, and the city (respondents) appealed. The appellate court reversed the district court's decision.[2] The firefighters (petitioners) appealed to the U.S. Supreme Court.

JUDICIAL OPINION

KENNEDY, Justice

The City's actions would violate the disparate-treatment prohibition of Title VII absent some valid defense. All the evidence demonstrates that the City chose not to certify the examination results because of the statistical disparity based on race—i.e., how minority candidates had performed when compared to white candidates. As the District Court put it, the City rejected the test results because "too many whites and not enough minorities would be promoted were the lists to be certified." Without some other justification, this express, race-based decision making violates Title VII's command that employers cannot take adverse employment actions because of an individual's race.

Whatever the City's ultimate aim—however well intentioned or benevolent it might have seemed—the City made its employment decision because of race. The City rejected the test results solely because the higher scoring candidates were white. The question is not whether that conduct was discriminatory but whether the City had a lawful justification for its race-based action.

Allowing employers to violate the disparate-treatment prohibition based on a mere good-faith fear of disparate-impact liability would encourage race-based action at the slightest hint of disparate impact. A minimal standard could cause employers to discard the results of lawful and beneficial promotional examinations even where there is little if any evidence of disparate-impact discrimination. That would amount to a de facto quota system, in which a "focus on statistics … could put undue pressure on employers to adopt inappropriate prophylactic measures."

Congress has imposed liability on employers for unintentional discrimination in order to rid the workplace of "practices that are fair in form, but discriminatory in operation." But it has also prohibited employers from taking adverse employment actions "because of" race. Applying the strong-basis-in-evidence standard to Title VII gives effect to both the disparate-treatment and disparate-impact provisions, allowing violations of one in the name of compliance with the other only in certain, narrow circumstances. The standard leaves ample room for employers' voluntary compliance efforts, which are essential to the statutory scheme and to Congress's efforts to eradicate workplace discrimination. And the standard appropriately constrains employers' discretion

CONTINUED

in making race-based decisions: It limits that discretion to cases in which there is a strong basis in evidence of disparate-impact liability, but it is not so restrictive that it allows employers to act only when there is a provable, actual violation.

Examinations like those administered by the City create legitimate expectations on the part of those who took the tests. As is the case with any promotion exam, some of the firefighters here invested substantial time, money, and personal commitment in preparing for the tests. Employment tests can be an important part of a neutral selection system that safeguards against the very racial animosities Title VII was intended to prevent. Here, however, the firefighters saw their efforts invalidated by the City in sole reliance upon race-based statistics.

If an employer cannot rescore a test based on the candidates' race, then it follows *a fortiori* that it may not take the greater step of discarding the test altogether to achieve a more desirable racial distribution of promotion-eligible candidates—absent a strong basis in evidence that the test was deficient and that discarding the results is necessary to avoid violating the disparate-impact provision. Restricting an employer's ability to discard test results (and thereby discriminate against qualified candidates on the basis of their race) also is in keeping with Title VII's express protection of bona fide promotional examinations.

For the foregoing reasons, we adopt the strong-basis-in-evidence standard as a matter of statutory construction to resolve any conflict between the disparate-treatment and disparate-impact provisions of Title VII.

The City argues that, even under the strong-basis-in-evidence standard, its decision to discard the examination results was permissible under Title VII. That is incorrect. Even if respondents were motivated as

a subjective matter by a desire to avoid committing disparate-impact discrimination, the record makes clear there is no support for the conclusion that respondents had an objective, strong basis in evidence to find the tests inadequate, with some consequent disparate-impact liability in violation of Title VII.

On the record before us, there is no genuine dispute that the City lacked a strong basis in evidence to believe it would face disparate-impact liability if it certified the examination results. In other words, there is no evidence—let alone the required strong basis in evidence—that the tests were flawed because they were not job-related or because other, equally valid and less discriminatory tests were available to the City. Fear of litigation alone cannot justify an employer's reliance on race to the detriment of individuals who passed the examinations and qualified for promotions. The City's discarding the test results was impermissible under Title VII, and summary judgment is appropriate for petitioners on their disparate-treatment claim.

Our statutory holding does not address the constitutionality of the measures taken here in purported compliance with Title VII. We also do not hold that meeting the strong-basis-in-evidence standard would satisfy the Equal Protection Clause in a future case.

Reversed.

CASE QUESTIONS

1. Explain what happened on the exam and why the city decided to toss the exam results.
2. What does the court establish as the law applicable to "tossing" exam results?
3. What is the court trying to balance in interpreting the law?

Business Planning Tip

Tests have become tricky for employers. Those who allege discrimination do not need to prove that there is anything discriminatory about the test. They need only allege that the employer did not choose a test with the least impact on protected classes. Employers that use testing will need to review the results of the tests and use caution in their use of those results as well as in the continuing use of the test for screening.

21-3c PATTERN OR PRACTICE OF DISCRIMINATION

The "pattern or practice" theory involves discrimination not against one person but, rather, against a group or class of persons (e.g., women or African Americans).

The standards for establishing a pattern or practice of discrimination are affected by the 1991 amendments to the Civil Rights Act; the burdens of proof are those discussed under disparate impact, with a "reasonable justification" defense for employers. The plaintiff must show causation between the practice of the employer and the disparate impact. In pattern or practice cases, the initial burden of proof of discrimination is on the plaintiff or the EEOC. For example, in one case that immediately preceded the 1991 amendments, the Seventh Circuit found that a company's low percentage of

African Americans in its workforce was due to its location in a Hispanic neighborhood and not because of its practice of hiring by word of mouth. [*EEOC v Chicago Miniature Lamp Works*, 947 F.2d 292 (7th Cir. 1991)]

Consider...

In *Dukes v Wal-Mart Stores*, 603 F.3d 571 (9th Cir. 2010), the female employees of Walmart filed suit under Title VII of the 1964 Civil Rights Act, 42 U.S.C. § 2000e *et seq.*, alleging that women employed in Walmart stores (1) are paid less than men in comparable positions, despite having higher performance ratings and greater seniority; and (2) receive fewer promotions to in-store management positions than do men, and those who are promoted must wait longer than their male counterparts to advance.

The court allowed the women to use statistical evidence as a basis for certification as a class. The statistical evidence cited was the approximate percentages of women in specific hourly and salaried management positions as follows:

Salaried Positions

- Store manager—14 percent
- Co-manager (only in larger stores)—23 percent
- Assistant manager—36 percent

Hourly Positions

- Management trainee—42 percent
- Support manager—50 percent
- Department manager—78 percent
- Customer service manager—85–90 percent
- Other hourly positions—70 percent

Walmart challenged the case (brought on behalf of 1.5 million women employed at Walmart; the largest employment class-action suit ever filed) on the grounds that mere statistics do not establish a Title VII violation. What do the women have to prove to establish discrimination? Are the statistics enough? What explanation could Walmart offer for the numbers that would evidence no discrimination on its part?
[*Wal-Mart Stores, Inc. v Dukes*, 131 S.Ct. 2541 (2011)]

21-4 Specific Applications of Title VII

The various theories of Title VII discrimination apply to specific types of discrimination. The following sections cover these types of discrimination and Title VII's application to them.

21-4a SEX DISCRIMINATION

Although Title VII included sex discrimination in its prohibitions, its presence and effects were not as obviously in existence as the more blatant racial discrimination. Many of the initial discrimination suits were brought in response to "protective legislation," which consisted of state statutes that prohibited women from working in certain fields and occupations for safety reasons. The reasons for such prohibitions were that the jobs were too strenuous, too dangerous, or too stressful. Because the effect of the statutes was to keep women from certain higher-paying occupations and men from certain female-dominated jobs, the EEOC issued guidelines providing that employers guilty of discrimination could not use these statutory cloaks. The *Dothard v Rawlinson* case [433 U.S. 321 (1977)] discussed earlier is an example of a sex discrimination case.

A *prima facie* case of sex discrimination by an employer requires proof of the same elements established in the *Green* case. The only difference is that the issue of rejection, firing, or demotion is based on sex rather than race.

Other more subtle hints of discrimination have slowly been eliminated from every area of employment. Even job listings in classified ads cannot carry any sexual preference. For example, an employer cannot advertise for just a "waitress"; the ad must be for a "waiter/waitress." Further, state laws and company policies that prohibit women from working during certain hours if they have school-age children are violations of Title VII.

Sexual Harassment

Sexual harassment is a violation of Title VII of the Civil Rights Act. Company policies on this issue should attempt to make it clear that an environment of harassment is not appropriate for any employee. Companies should also enforce policies uniformly.

Sexual harassment cases take two forms. In *quid pro quo* cases, an employee is required to submit to sexual advances in order to remain employed, secure a promotion, or obtain a raise. In the other—*atmosphere of harassment* cases—the invitations, language, pictures, or suggestions become so pervasive as to create a hostile work environment.

***Quid Pro Quo* Harassment.** This form of harassment occurs when someone in a position of authority in the workplace has made sexual advances to an employee that carry the threat of employer sanctions if the employee does not accept the advances. While a supervisor may be the individual who initiates the *quid pro quo* advance, the company or employer of the supervisor may also be liable for the supervisor's conduct in certain circumstances. *Burlington Industries, Inc. v Ellerth* (Case 21.3) deals with the issue of when an employer is vicariously liable for the sexual harassment of one of its employees by another employee.

| CASE 21.3 | *Burlington Industries, Inc. v Ellerth*
 524 U.S. 742 (1998) |

The Boorish Supervisor Meets Vicarious Liability

FACTS

Kimberly Ellerth (respondent) worked as a salesperson in one of Burlington's divisions from March 1993 to May 1994. During her employment, she reported to a midlevel manager, Ted Slowik. Ms. Ellerth worked in a two-person office in Chicago and was one of Burlington's 22,000 employees. Mr. Slowik was based in New York but was responsible for Ms. Ellerth's office. The following incidents of boorish and offensive behavior occurred during Ms. Ellerth's employment.

| Summer 1993 | While on a business trip, Ms. Ellerth accepted Mr. Slowik's invitation to the hotel lounge. Mr. Slowik made remarks about Ms. Ellerth's breasts, told her to "loosen up," and said, "You know, Kim, I could make your life very hard or very easy at Burlington." |
| March 1994 | Ms. Ellerth was being considered for a promotion, and Mr. Slowik expressed concern during the interview that she was not "loose enough." Mr. Slowik then reached out and rubbed her knee. |

CONTINUED

March 1994	Mr. Slowik called Ms. Ellerth to give her the promotion and said, "You're gonna be out there with men who work in factories, and they certainly like women with pretty butts/legs."
May 1994	Ms. Ellerth called Mr. Slowik for permission to insert a logo into a fabric sample. Mr. Slowik said, "I don't have time for you right now, Kim—unless you want to tell me what you're wearing." Ms. Ellerth ended the call.
May 1994	Ms. Ellerth called again for permission, and Mr. Slowik said, "Are you wearing shorter skirts yet, Kim, because it would make your job a whole heck of a lot easier."

In May 1994, the supervisor in the Chicago office cautioned Ms. Ellerth about returning phone calls. Ms. Ellerth quit and faxed a letter giving reasons for her decision unrelated to the alleged sexual harassment. Three weeks later, however, she sent another letter complaining of Mr. Slowik's behavior.

During her employment at Burlington, Ms. Ellerth did not tell anyone about Mr. Slowik's behavior. She chose not to tell her supervisor in the Chicago office because, "It would be his duty as my supervisor to report any incidents of sexual harassment."

Ms. Ellerth filed suit against Burlington for violation of Title VII in that the sexual harassment forced her constructive discharge.

The District Court found Mr. Slowik's behavior created a hostile work environment but found that Burlington neither knew nor should have known about the conduct. The Court of Appeals reversed, with eight separate opinions imposing vicarious liability on Burlington. Burlington appealed.

JUDICIAL OPINION

KENNEDY, Justice

The terms *quid pro quo* and hostile work environment are helpful, perhaps, in making a rough demarcation between cases in which threats are carried out and those where they are not or are absent altogether, but beyond this are of limited utility.

"*Quid pro quo*" and "hostile work environment" do not appear in the statutory text. The terms appeared first in the academic literature, see C. MacKinnon, *Sexual Harassment of Working Women* (1979); found their way into decisions of the Courts of Appeals, see, e.g., *Henson v Dundee*, 682 F.2d 897, 909 (CA11 1982); and were mentioned in this Court's

decision in *Meritor Savings Bank, FSB v Vinson*, 477 U.S. 57 (1986)….

We do not suggest the terms *quid pro quo* and hostile work environment are irrelevant to Title VII litigation. When a plaintiff proves that a tangible employment action resulted from a refusal to submit to a supervisor's sexual demands, he or she establishes that the employment decision itself constitutes a change in the terms and conditions of employment that is actionable under Title VII. Because Ellerth's claim involves only unfulfilled threats, it should be categorized as a hostile work environment claim which requires a showing of severe or pervasive conduct.

We must decide, then, whether an employer has vicarious liability when a supervisor creates a hostile work environment by making explicit threats to alter a subordinate's terms or conditions of employment, based on sex, but does not fulfill the threat. We turn to principles of agency law, for the term "employer" is defined under Title VII to include "agents." We rely "on the general common law of agency, rather than on the law of any particular State, to give meaning to these terms."…

The general rule is that sexual harassment by a supervisor is not conduct within the scope of employment.

Scope of employment does not define the only basis for employer liability under agency principles. In limited circumstances, agency principles impose liability on employers even where employees commit torts outside the scope of employment.

In a sense, most workplace tortfeasors are aided in accomplishing their tortious objective by the existence of the agency relation: Proximity and regular contact may afford a captive pool of potential victims.

Tangible employment actions are the means by which the supervisor brings the official power of the enterprise to bear on subordinates.

For these reasons, a tangible employment action taken by the supervisor becomes for Title VII purposes the act of the employer. An employer is subject to vicarious liability to a victimized employee for an actionable hostile environment created by a supervisor with immediate (or successively higher) authority over the employee. When no tangible employment action is taken, a defending employer may raise an affirmative defense to liability or damages, subject to proof by a preponderance of the evidence. The defense comprises two necessary elements: (a) that the employer exercised reasonable care to prevent and correct promptly any sexually harassing behavior, and (b) that the plaintiff employee unreasonably failed to take advantage of any preventive or corrective opportunities provided by the employer or to avoid harm otherwise. While proof that an employer had promulgated an anti-harassment

CONTINUED

policy with complaint procedure is not necessary in every instance as a matter of law, the need for a stated policy suitable to the employment circumstances may appropriately be addressed in any case when litigating the first element of the defense. And while proof that an employee failed to fulfill the corresponding obligation of reasonable care to avoid harm is not limited to showing any unreasonable failure to use any complaint procedure provided by the employer, a demonstration of such failure will normally suffice to satisfy the employer's burden under the second element of the defense. No affirmative defense is available, however, when the supervisor's harassment culminates in a tangible employment action, such as discharge, demotion, or undesirable reassignment.

Affirmed.

DISSENTING OPINION

Justice THOMAS, with whom Justice SCALIA joins, dissenting

The Court today manufactures a rule that employers are vicariously liable if supervisors create a sexually hostile work environment, subject to an affirmative defense that the Court barely attempts to define....

Sexual harassment is simply not something that employers can wholly prevent without taking extraordinary measures—constant video and audio surveillance, for example—that would revolutionize the workplace in a manner incompatible with a free society.

Indeed, such measures could not even detect incidents of harassment such as the comments Slowik allegedly made to respondent in a hotel bar. The most that employers can be charged with, therefore, is a duty to act reasonably under the circumstances.

The Court's holding does guarantee one result: There will be more and more litigation to clarify applicable legal rules in an area in which both practitioners and the courts have long been begging for guidance....

Popular misconceptions notwithstanding, sexual harassment is not a freestanding federal tort, but a form of employment discrimination. As such, it should be treated no differently (and certainly no better) than the other forms of harassment that are illegal under Title VII. I would restore parallel treatment of employer liability for racial and sexual harassment and hold an employer liable for a hostile work environment only if the employer is truly at fault. I therefore respectfully dissent.

CASE QUESTIONS

1. When will an employer be held liable (i.e., vicariously liable) for sexual harassment despite a lack of actual knowledge?

2. What is the liability of a company for harassment of an employee by an immediate supervisor?

3. What major issues does the dissenting opinion raise?

CYBERLAW

Atmosphere of Harassment. Unwanted advances are one type of sexual harassment. However, sexual harassment can also exist when the atmosphere of the workplace becomes one of sexual tone or suggestion. Derogatory, suggestive, and offensive e-mails and electronic bulletin boards on servers sponsored by an employer can be the basis for a hostile environment sexual harassment suit. Employers not only have the responsibility to prohibit employees from posting such materials; they also have a responsibility to supervise such bulletin boards and e-mails to be certain that no atmosphere of harassment results from the contents.

Further, in litigation over such materials, plaintiffs may rely on printed copies of the materials and messages to use in establishing their cases even though the materials may have already been deleted from the company system.

Consider...

Determine whether the following would constitute sexual harassment (either *quid pro quo* or atmosphere of harassment) under Title VII.

1. A manager who referred to female customers as "bitchy" or "dumb," flirted with an employee's female relatives, and told of spending a weekend at a nudist camp [*Gleason v Mesirow Financial, Inc.*, 118 R.3d 1134 (7th Cir. 1997)]

2. A manager who told a single, pregnant female employee that he disapproved of premarital sex [*Brill v Lante*, 119 R.3d 1266 (7th Cir. 1997)]

3. Calendar photographs of women in swimwear posted in a co-employee's work-station [*Guidry v Zale Corp.*, 969 F. Supp. 988 (M.D. La. 1997)]

4. A supervisor who called his wife "ignorant" and women in his department "dumb" and used the term "gals" for all his female employees [*Penry v Federal Home Loan Bank of Topeka*, 970 F. Supp. 833 (D. Kan. 1997)]

5. A supervisor who referred to the architecture of a shopping mall as looking like "two hooters" and a "bra bazaar," while having dinner with an employee on a business trip [*Penry v Federal Home Loan Bank of Topeka*, 970 R. Supp. 833 (D. Kan. 1997)]

FOR THE MANAGER'S DESK

Re: Romance at Work

A great many married couples met at work. From Barack and Michele Obama to Bill and Melinda Gates to Brad Pitt and Angelina Jolie, romance befalls many at work, whether they are working at a software company, a law firm, or making a movie together. Romance is even more prevalent among the less famous. The data indicate that 39 percent of us have dated a coworker. There is one question to ask as a follow-up: "Were your employers aware of the dating?"

Employers cannot control when and where Cupid's arrow may strike, but they do need to have rules and policies in place to deal with the potential issues that can arise from workplace romances.

Some rules can help both employers and their employees. The goal for employers is to prevent issues of favoritism and sexual harassment. Along the way, the employers' rules may save an employee from a broken heart. A few sample rules that companies use for purposes of avoiding the pitfalls of office romance follow:

1. Some companies simply prohibit employees who work together from having a relationship. Such a rule can be problematic because employees have the relationship anyway and simply hide it from the employer as other employees gossip. Often, companies accompany this policy with a policy on finding one member of the couple a different position outside the division or office where both met and are currently working.

2. Some companies prohibit relationships between employees when one reports to the other. For example, when Barack worked as a summer intern at the same law firm as Michele, she was his supervisor. Many companies would require a transfer or that one leave the firm.

3. Some companies follow this rule: Disclose to your supervisor that you are having a romantic relationship with a coworker. The purpose of such disclosure is for the supervisor to determine whether there are any issues with conflicts or if an adjustment needs to be made because of reporting lines—that is, two employees who are dating should not be in a direct report relationship. Some companies do not permit even indirect reportees to date supervisors. These companies work to find one of the employees a different position in the company outside the direct or indirect reporting lines.

4. Most companies remind employees that a consensual relationship that goes south can very often turn into allegations of sexual harassment. Employees are cautioned to proceed within company rules for their own protection. Some companies have what is called a "love contract" that the two employees sign upon disclosure of their relationship so that there is a written record that there is a consensual relationship—a protection for both the employer and the employees against sexual harassment charges.

5. Although most companies do not address the issue directly, an adulterous relationship between two employees is generally a career killer, at least within the company. During the past year, two CEOs of major firms have had to depart following disclosures of their affairs with employees.

Sex Discrimination and Pensions

Another area of sex discrimination in employment involves the statistical fact that women live longer than men. It costs more for a female employee to have a pension than a male employee because she will likely live longer after retirement. In *City of Los Angeles Department of Water v Manhart*, 435 U.S. 702 (1978), the Supreme Court held that employers could not require female employees to contribute more to their pension plans than males. The additional contributions for the female employees were required by the employer because the pension planner had statistical evidence that longevity of female employees exceeded that of male employees. If the Supreme Court had sanctioned the disparity in pension plan payments, the higher cost of having female employees could have been cited by employers as the reason for their hiring practices.

The Pregnancy Discrimination Act

This act, which revolutionized maternity issues in the employment world, prohibits an employer from forcing someone to resign because of a pregnancy, refusing to allow a mother to return to work after her pregnancy is completed, providing different benefits for sick leaves than for pregnancy, and refusing to hire or promote someone because of pregnancy or family plans.

The landmark case *International Union v Johnson Controls, Inc.* (Case 21.4) focuses on some nuances in sex discrimination issues.

CASE 21.4	*International Union v Johnson Controls, Inc.*
	499 U.S. 187 (1991)

The Acid Test for Women: The Right to Choose High-Risk Jobs

FACTS

Johnson Controls, Inc. (respondent) manufactures batteries. In the manufacturing process, the element lead is a primary ingredient. Occupational exposure to lead entails health risks, including the risk of harm to any fetus carried by a female employee.

Before the Civil Rights Act of 1964 became law, Johnson Controls did not employ any woman in a battery-manufacturing job. In June 1977, however, it announced its first official policy concerning its employment of women in jobs with lead exposure risk:

[P]rotection of the health of the unborn child is the immediate and direct responsibility of the prospective parents. While the medical profession and the company can support them in the exercise of this responsibility, it cannot assume it for them without simultaneously infringing their rights as persons....

Since not all women who can become mothers wish to become mothers (or will become mothers), it would appear

to be illegal discrimination to treat all who are capable of pregnancy as though they will become pregnant.

Consistent with that view, Johnson Controls "stopped short of excluding women capable of bearing children from lead exposure" but emphasized that a woman who expected to have a child should not choose a job in which she would have such exposure. The company also required a woman who wished to be considered for employment to sign a statement indicating that she had been advised of the risk of having a child while she was exposed to lead. The statement informed the woman that although there was evidence "that women exposed to lead have a higher rate of abortion," this evidence was "not as clear ... as the relationship between cigarette smoking and cancer," but that it was, "medically speaking, just good sense not to run that risk if you want children and do not want to expose the unborn child to risk, however small...."

In 1982, Johnson Controls shifted from a policy of warning to a policy of exclusion. Between 1979 and 1983, eight employees became pregnant while maintaining

CONTINUED

lead levels in excess of 30 micrograms per decaliter of blood. The company responded by announcing a broad exclusion of women from jobs that exposed them to lead:

> [I]t is [Johnson Controls'] policy that women who are pregnant or who are capable of bearing children will not be placed into jobs involving lead exposure or which could expose them to lead through the exercise of job bidding, bumping, transfer or promotion rights.

The policy defined "women … capable of bearing children" as "[a]ll women except those whose inability to bear children is medically documented."

Several employees (petitioners) and their unions filed suit alleging that Johnson Controls' fetal protection policy violated Title VII of the Civil Rights Act. Included in the group were

- Mary Craig—sterilized to avoid losing her job
- Elsie Nason—50-year-old divorcee who lost compensation when transferred out of lead exposure job
- Donald Penney—denied request for leave of absence to lower his lead level before becoming a father

The district court entered summary judgment for Johnson Controls. The court of appeals affirmed, and the employees appealed.

JUDICIAL OPINION

BLACKMUN, Justice

The bias in Johnson Controls' policy is obvious. Fertile men, but not fertile women, are given a choice as to whether they wish to risk their reproductive health for a particular job. Section 703(a) of the Civil Rights Act of 1964, 78 Stat. 255, as amended, 42 U.S.C. § 2000e-2(a), prohibits sex-based classifications in terms and conditions of employment, in hiring and discharging decisions, and in other employment decisions that adversely affect an employee's status. Respondent's fetal-protection policy explicitly discriminates against women on the basis of their sex. The policy excludes women with childbearing capacity from lead-exposed jobs and so creates a facial classification based on gender. Respondent assumes as much in its brief before this Court.

Nevertheless, the Court of Appeals assumed, as did the two appellate courts who already had confronted this issue, that sex specific fetal-protection policies do not involve facial discrimination. These courts analyzed the policies as though they were facially neutral, and had only a discriminatory effect upon the employment opportunities of women. Consequently, the courts looked to see if each employer in question had established that its policy was justified as a business necessity. The business necessity standard is more lenient for the employer than the statutory BFOQ [bona fide occupational qualification] defense. The court assumed that

because the asserted reason for the sex-based exclusion (protecting women's unconceived offspring) was ostensibly benign, the policy was not sex-based discrimination. That assumption, however, was incorrect.

First, Johnson Controls' policy classifies on the basis of gender and childbearing capacity, rather than fertility alone. Respondent does not seek to protect the unconceived children of all its employees. Despite evidence in the record about the debilitating effect of lead exposure on the male reproductive system, Johnson Controls is concerned only with the harms that may befall the unborn offspring of its female employees….

The Pregnancy Discrimination Act has now made clear that, for all Title VII purposes, discrimination based on a woman's pregnancy is, on its face, discrimination because of her sex. In its use of the words "capable of bearing children" in the 1982 policy statement as the criterion for exclusion, Johnson Controls explicitly classifies on the basis of potential for pregnancy. Under the PDA, such a classification must be regarded, for Title VII purposes, in the same light as explicit sex discrimination. Respondent has chosen to treat all its female employees as potentially pregnant; that choice evinces discrimination on the basis of sex.

We concluded above that Johnson Controls' policy is not neutral because it does not apply to the reproductive capacity of the company's male employees in the same way as it applies to that of the females. Moreover, the absence of a malevolent motive does not convert a facially discriminatory policy into a neutral policy with a discriminatory effect. Whether an employment practice involves disparate treatment through explicit facial discrimination does not depend on why the employer discriminates but rather on the explicit terms of the discrimination.

In sum, Johnson Controls' policy "does not pass the simple test of whether the evidence shows 'treatment of a person in a manner which but for that person's sex would be different.'"

We therefore turn to the question whether Johnson Controls' fetal-protection policy is one of those "certain instances" that come within the BFOQ exception.

Johnson Controls argues that its fetal-protection policy falls within the so-called safety exception to the BFOQ. Our cases have stressed that discrimination on the basis of sex because of safety concerns is allowed only in narrow circumstances. In *Dothard v Rawlinson*, 433 U.S. 321 (1977), this Court indicated that the danger to a woman herself does not justify discrimination. We there allowed the employer to hire only male guards in contact areas of maximum-security male penitentiaries only because more was at stake than the "individual woman's decision to weigh and accept the risks of employment." We found sex to be a BFOQ inasmuch as the employment of a female guard would create real risks of safety to others if violence broke out because the guard was a woman.

CONTINUED

Sex discrimination was tolerated because sex was related to the guard's ability to do the job—maintaining prison security. We also required in *Dothard* a high correlation between sex and ability to perform job functions and refused to allow employers to use sex as a proxy for strength although it might be a fairly accurate one.

Similarly, some courts have approved airlines' lay-offs of pregnant flight attendants at different points during the first five months of pregnancy on the ground that the employer's policy was necessary to ensure the safety of passengers.

The unconceived fetuses of Johnson Controls' female employees, however, are neither customers nor third parties whose safety is essential to the business of battery manufacturing. No one can disregard the possibility of injury to future children; the BFOQ, however, is not so broad that it transforms this deep social concern into an essential aspect of battery making....

A word about tort liability and the increased cost of fertile women in the workplace is perhaps necessary. It is correct to say that Title VII does not prevent the employer from having a conscience. The statute, however, does prevent sex-specific fetal-protection policies. These two aspects of Title VII do not conflict.

More than 40 states currently recognize a right to recover for a prenatal injury based either on negligence or on wrongful death. According to Johnson Controls, however, the company complies with the lead standard developed by OSHA and warns its female employees about the damaging effects of lead. It is worth noting that OSHA gave the problem of lead lengthy consideration and concluded that "there is no basis whatsoever for the claim that women of childbearing age should be excluded from the workplace in order to protect the fetus or the course of pregnancy." Instead, OSHA

established a series of mandatory protections which, taken together, "should effectively minimize any risk to the fetus and newborn child." Without negligence, it would be difficult for a court to find liability on the part of the employer. If, under general tort principles, Title VII bans sex-specific fetal-protection policies, the employer fully informs the woman of the risk, and the employer has not acted negligently, the basis for holding an employer liable seems remote at best.

Although the issue is not before us, the concurrence observes that "it is far from clear that compliance with Title VII will preempt state tort liability."

Our holding today that Title VII, as so amended, forbids sex-specific fetal-protection policies is neither remarkable nor unprecedented. Concern for a woman's existing or potential offspring historically has been the excuse for denying women equal employment opportunities.

It is no more appropriate for the courts than it is for individual employers to decide whether a woman's reproductive role is more important to herself and her family than her economic role. Congress has left this choice to the woman as hers to make.

The judgment of the Court of Appeals is reversed and the case is remanded for further proceedings consistent with this opinion.

CASE QUESTIONS

1. Describe Johnson Controls' evolving policy on lead exposure.
2. Are there circumstances when sex is a BFOQ?
3. What problem is presented by the exclusion of men from the policy?
4. What is the court's position on tort liability of the company with respect to the fetus?

BUSINESS STRATEGY   Dangerous Exposure

The *Johnson Controls* decision has allowed many women to work in jobs that expose them to toxins. The U.S. Supreme Court did acknowledge in its holding that tort liability might result from its decision but that such liability was often used as a guise or cover for gender discrimination. However, nearly 20 years after the decision, women who were protected by Title VII in their right to high-risk jobs are now suing their employers for the birth defects in their children. For example, IBM has several suits from employees and their children against it for

defects allegedly tied to production-line toxins. The position of many of the employers is that even if there were evidence linking the toxins to birth defects, the women took the jobs with knowledge about the risk and agreed to that risk. How can employers, legislators, and public policy specialists reconcile antidiscrimination laws and these risks of exposure?

Source: Stephanie Armour, "Workers Take Employers to Court over Birth Defects," *USA Today*, February 26, 2002, pp. 1A, 2A. For more information, visit http://www.cdc.gov/niosh.

21-4b RELIGIOUS DISCRIMINATION

Employers are required to make reasonable efforts to accommodate an employee's religious practices, holidays, and observances. Not all religious or church activities, however, are protected; for example, the observance of a religion's Sabbath is a protected activity, but taking time to prepare for a church bake sale or pageant is an unprotected activity. The 1972 amendments to Title VII defined religion to include "all aspects of religious observance and practice, as well as belief." The accommodation of religion thus defined is required unless an employer is able to establish that allowing the employee such an accommodation would result in "undue hardship on the conduct of the employer's business."

In *Trans World Airlines, Inc. v Hardison*, 432 U.S. 63 (1977), the Supreme Court confirmed the clear language of the 1972 act that requires an employer to demonstrate an ability to accommodate an employee's religious needs. As a member of a church that worshiped on Saturdays, Larry G. Hardison expressed a desire not to work that day. TWA worked through several alternatives to afford Mr. Hardison the opportunity for Saturdays off, including asking the union to waive a seniority rule that limited substitutes for him and looking for an alternative job that would not require Saturday work. The union would not waive its rule, and no managers were available to take the shift. When Mr. Hardison refused to work on Saturdays, he was dismissed and filed suit, but the Court found for TWA because of its extensive efforts and the constraints that prevented shifting of workers without substantial interference in TWA's operations.

Title VII requires only reasonable accommodation. Employees are not necessarily entitled to the accommodation they desire. For example, in *American Postal Workers Union v Postmaster General*, 781 F.2d 772 (9th Cir. 1986), several postal employees refused to work at a window in the post office where draft registration forms were handled. They asked to be able to direct draft registrants to the windows of employees who did not have religious objections to the draft. The Postal Service transferred the employees to nonwindow jobs, which was supported by the court as a reasonable accommodation.

In *TWA v Hardison*, the Court noted, "The statute is not to be construed to require an employer to discriminate against some employees in order for others to observe their Sabbath." The *Cloutier v Costco* case (Case 21.5) deals with the issues of what is protected as a religious tenet and the extent of employer accommodation required.

CASE 21.5

Cloutier v Costco
390 F.3d 126 (1st Cir. 2004)

The Costco Employee Who Worshipped at the Church of Body Modification

FACTS

Kimberly Cloutier was a member of the Church of Body Modification. In 1997, during her job interview for a position at Costco, Ms. Cloutier sported four tattoos and multiple earrings, but she had no facial piercings. She was hired and given a copy of the Costco dress code, which was modified several times between 1997 and 2001. One of the modifications prohibited employees from having facial piercings. As the policy was modified, Ms. Cloutier increased the number of body piercings she had, including an eyebrow ring. Ms. Cloutier maintained that they were part of her adherence to

CONTINUED

her faith, the Church of Body Modification (CBM), but she did not join the CBM until 2001. The CBM, which anyone can join via electronic application, had approximately 1,000 members at that time. The members participate in piercing, tattooing, branding, cutting, and body manipulation. Among the goals espoused in the CBM's mission statement are for its members to "grow as individuals through body modification and its teachings," to "promote growth in mind, body and spirit," and to be "confident role models in learning, teaching, and displaying body modification." However, the tenets of the faith do not require that body modifications be on display at all times.

Ms. Cloutier did not object to the dress code or any of the modifications on religious grounds until, in 2001, her supervisors asked her to either remove the eyebrow ring whilst she was working or cover it with some form of Band-Aid adhesive bandage. Costco also proposed having her wear a clear plastic ring in the eyebrow piercing whilst she was working so that her body modification could still be seen but would not be conspicuous. Ms. Cloutier refused the proposed accommodations and filed a complaint with the EEOC. The EEOC concluded that Costco had discriminated on the basis of Ms. Cloutier's religion and she then filed suit against Costco for religious discrimination in violation of Title VII. The district court granted summary judgment for Costco and Cloutier appealed.

JUDICIAL OPINION

LIPEZ, Circuit Judge

Cloutier asserts that the CBM mandate to be a confident role model requires her to display all of her facial piercings at all times. In her view, the only reasonable accommodation would be exemption from the no-facial-jewelry policy. Costco maintains that such an exemption would cause it to suffer an undue hardship, and that as a result it had no obligation to accommodate.

An accommodation constitutes an "undue hardship" if it would impose more than a *de minimis* cost on the employer. *TransWorldAirlines, Inc. v Hardison*, 432 U.S. 63, 84, 97 S.Ct. 2264, 53 L.Ed.2d 113 (1977). This calculus applies both to economic costs, such as lost business or having to hire additional employees to accommodate a Sabbath observer, and to non-economic costs, such as compromising the integrity of a seniority system.

Cloutier argues that Costco has not met its burden of demonstrating that her requested accommodation would impose an undue hardship. She asserts that she did not receive complaints about her facial piercings and that the piercings did not affect her job performance. Hence, she contends that any hardship Costco

posits is merely hypothetical and therefore not sufficient to excuse it from accommodating her religious practice under Title VII.

Courts are "somewhat skeptical of hypothetical hardships that an employer thinks might be caused by an accommodation that never has been put into practice." "Nevertheless, it is possible for an employer to prove undue hardship without actually having undertaken any of the possible accommodations …"

The district court acknowledged that "Costco has a legitimate interest in presenting a workforce to its customers that is, at least in Costco's eyes, reasonably professional in appearance." Costco's dress code, included in the handbook distributed to all employees, furthers this interest. The preface to the code explains that, "Appearance and perception play a key role in member service. Our goal is to be dressed in professional attire that is appropriate to our business at all times…. All Costco employees must practice good grooming and personal hygiene to convey a neat, clean and professional image."

It is axiomatic that, for better or for worse, employees reflect on their employers. This is particularly true of employees who regularly interact with customers, as Cloutier did in her cashier position. Even if Cloutier did not personally receive any complaints about her appearance, her facial jewelry influenced Costco's public image and, in Costco's calculation, detracted from its professionalism.

Costco is far from unique in adopting personal appearance standards to promote and protect its image. As the D.C. Circuit noted, "Perhaps no facet of business life is more important than a company's place in public estimation…. Good grooming regulations reflect a company's policy in our highly competitive business environment. Reasonable requirements in furtherance of that policy are an aspect of managerial responsibility." Courts have long recognized the importance of personal appearance regulations, even in the face of Title VII challenges. Such regulations are often justified with regard to safety concerns. *E.g., Bhatia v Chevron U.S.A., Inc.,* 734 F.2d 1382 (9th Cir. 1984) (affirming summary judgment for employer who refused to exempt a Sikh employee from the requirement that all machinists be clean-shaven, where the policy was based on the necessity of being able to wear a respirator with a gas-tight face seal because of potential exposure to toxic gases).

Courts considering Title VII religious discrimination claims have also upheld dress code policies that, like Costco's, are designed to appeal to customer preference or to promote a professional public image.

Costco has made a determination that facial piercings, aside from earrings, detract from the

CONTINUED

"neat, clean and professional image" that it aims to cultivate. Such a business determination is within its discretion.

Cloutier argues that regardless of the reasons for the dress code, permitting her to display her facial jewelry would not be an undue hardship because Costco already overlooks other violations of its policy. In support of her position, she cites affidavits from two Costco employees identifying co-workers who "were allowed to wear facial piercing[s] … and were not disciplined." Costco responds that any employees who displayed facial jewelry did so without its permission or knowledge, noting that constant monitoring is impossible in a facility with several hundred employees.

We find Cloutier's contention, and the affidavits underlying it, unpersuasive. To the extent that the ambiguous term "allowed" implies that Costco was aware of the piercings, the affidavits are marred by an evidentiary flaw: the affiants do not appear to have personal knowledge of Costco's awareness.

Costco's offer of accommodation was manifestly reasonable as a matter of law.

The temporary covering of plaintiff's facial piercings during working hours impinges on plaintiff's religious scruples no more than the wearing of a blouse, which covers plaintiff's tattoos. The alternative of a clear plastic retainer does not even require plaintiff to cover her piercings. Neither of these alternative accommodations will compel plaintiff to violate any of the established tenets of the CBM.

Affirmed.

CASE QUESTIONS

1. Why was it important for the court to know the tenets of Ms. Cloutier's faith?

2. What happens if an employer does not enforce the dress code standards?

3. How does this type of reasonable accommodation case differ from those of employees who object to working on certain days?

21-4c RACIAL DISCRIMINATION

When Title VII was first enacted, its clear intent was to prevent discrimination against the minority workforce. After Title VII had been in effect for several years, an unanticipated problem arose: Does Title VII's protection extend to all races? Are white employees entitled to the same protection Title VII affords other races?

In 1976, the Supreme Court provided the answer in *McDonald v Santa Fe Trail Transportation Co.*, 427 U.S. 273 (1976). Here, some black employees had been reinstated after committing the same offense as a group of white employees who were not reinstated. The Court held that Title VII prohibited such racial discrimination.

21-5 Antidiscrimination Laws and Affirmative Action

Some employers, either voluntarily or through the EEOC, have instituted affirmative action programs. Nothing prohibits such programs under Title VII, and the Supreme Court has sanctioned them as methods for remedying all the past years of discrimination. Although Title VII does not mandate such programs, employers may legally institute them.

21-5a WHAT IS AFFIRMATIVE ACTION?

Affirmative action is a remedial step taken to ensure that those who have been victims of discrimination in the past are given the opportunity to work in positions they would have attained had there not been discrimination.

Affirmative action programs are used to improve job opportunities for those in the so-called protected classes, including African Americans, Hispanics, Native Americans, Asians, women, persons with disabilities, and Vietnam veterans.

21-5b WHO IS REQUIRED TO HAVE AFFIRMATIVE ACTION PROGRAMS?

Some federal funding laws, such as those for education and state and local governments, mandate affirmative action programs.

Some employers have an obligation to take steps to equalize the representation of minorities and women in their labor forces. This equalization of representation in the labor force is the process of affirmative action. The following types of employers are obligated to undertake affirmative action programs:

1. Employers who, pursuant to consent decree or court order, must implement plans to compensate for past wrongs

2. State and local agencies, colleges, and universities that receive federal funds

3. Government contractors

4. Businesses that work on federal projects (10 percent of their subcontract work must employ minority businesses)

Affirmative action plans cannot simply be **quotas**. (A quota program is an unlawful infringement of the rights of a majority group of employees.) Rather, affirmative action programs set goals—for example, a certain number of minorities employed by a certain date. If the goal is not met, a business has not violated the law so long as it has made a good-faith effort to recruit and hire minorities. That good-faith effort can be established by a showing of internal and external advertising, monitoring of the program's progress, and changes and improvements in the program's development.

21-5c AFFIRMATIVE ACTION BACKLASH: THE THEORY OF REVERSE DISCRIMINATION

Currently, some legislative movements and grassroots referenda mandate the elimination of affirmative action programs. The University of California system eliminated affirmative action programs in 1995, but the programs were reinstated by a court after the elimination was challenged. A state referendum then passed, eliminating racial preferences by any state agency, including its colleges and universities.

In *Adarand Constructors, Inc. v Vena*, 515 U.S. 200 (1995), the U.S. Supreme Court was faced with the issue of affirmative action programs in a case brought by a contractor that challenged the federal government's program granting socially and economically disadvantaged contractors and subcontractors preferences in the awarding of government contracts. The case was remanded for trial after a ruling by the Court that such programs were subject to a standard of review known as strict scrutiny. The Court held that the government's set-aside program offering preferences to minority-owned businesses was a racial classification. To survive the strict scrutiny test, which is derived from the Equal Protection Clause of the U.S. Constitution (see Chapter 5), the federal government must be able to show, when a case goes to trial, that the contractor preferences serve a compelling government interest. *Adarand II*, heard by the U.S. Supreme Court in 2001, was upheld without opinion.[3]

In *Taxman v Board of Education of Piscataway* [91 F.3d 1547 (3rd Cir. 1996); *cert.* granted, 521 U.S. 1117 (1997); *cert.* dismissed, 522 U.S. 1010 (1997)], a school district, when facing the need to reduce the size of its teaching staff, decided to retain an African-American schoolteacher, Debra Williams. Sharon Taxman, a white schoolteacher, challenged the decision as discriminatory, and the school board defended on the grounds of its affirmative action program. On appeal, the circuit court held that the decision was unconstitutional because the school board's program was adopted to promote diversity and not to remedy any past wrongs the school district had committed. The U.S. Supreme Court granted *certiorari* to review the case, but the school board agreed to a settlement, paying Ms. Taxman $433,500, of which $308,500 was paid by national civil rights organizations. The civil rights organizations indicated that they agreed to pay the bulk of the settlement because they were fearful that the court might outlaw affirmative action programs. A few years later, and on the same day, the U.S. Supreme Court issued two landmark decisions on affirmative action in admissions programs: *Gratz v Bollinger*, 539 U.S. 244 (2003) and *Grutter v Bollinger*, 539 U.S. 306 (2003). In one case, the law school two-track admissions system was upheld, but the undergraduate two-track admission system was held to be unconstitutional. In another case, involving the admissions program at the University of Texas, the U.S. Supreme Court reexamined the issue of preferred admissions programs. [*Fisher v University of Texas at Austin*, 133 S.Ct. 2411 (2013)] The U.S. Supreme Court sent the case back for retrial because the court had not applied the strict scrutiny test that the U.S. Constitution demands when race is used as a basis for making determinations in, as in this case, admission to a public university. The summary judgment that the court granted was not appropriate when evidence related to the admissions process and whether the racial criteria were necessary to achieve a compelling state interest in diversity. There must be no workable, racially neutral standards that could be applied in order to allow the application of race-based standards in admissions.

21-6 The Defenses to a Title VII Charge

Title VII is not a strict liability statute. The act provides some defenses that employers can use to defend against a charge of discrimination.

21-6a BONA FIDE OCCUPATIONAL QUALIFICATION

A **bona fide occupational qualification (BFOQ)** is a job qualification based on sex, religion, or national origin that is necessary for the operation of business. A particular religious belief is a BFOQ for a pastor of a church. Similarly, an actor, to qualify for a role, may need to be a certain sex for purposes of realism and thus sex is a BFOQ for such employment.

The BFOQ exception has been applied narrowly, however. For a discriminatory qualification for employment to fall within the BFOQ exception, the employer must be able to establish that the job qualification is carefully formulated to respond to public safety, privacy, or other public needs; and the formulation of the policy must not be broader than is reasonably necessary to preserve the safety or privacy of individuals involved. For example, a restriction on hiring male employees for work in a nursing home occupied by women is excessive if male employees can work in jobs not involved with the personal care of the residents. Nor is personal preference a justification for a BFOQ; for example, many airlines have argued that there is a customer preference for female as opposed to male flight attendants. But customer preference is not a basis for a BFOQ; it is not a business necessity.

21-6b SENIORITY OR MERIT SYSTEMS

The goals and objectives of Title VII are often inconsistent with labor union rules of operation. Although matters of discrimination and union supervision are both covered by federal law, the two statutory schemes conflict on some points. Which controls the other: the remedial effect of Title VII or the longstanding history of seniority and other union rules?

The following criteria are used to determine whether a seniority or merit system is valid:

1. The system must apply to all employees.
2. Whatever divisions or units used for the system must follow the industry custom or pattern—that is, the divisions cannot be set up so as to discriminate against particular races or groups.
3. The origins of the system cannot lie in racial discrimination.
4. The system must be maintained for seniority and merit purposes and not to perpetuate racial discrimination.

21-6c **APTITUDE AND OTHER TESTS**

Any employer charged with Title VII discrimination because of employee aptitude testing must be able to show that the tests used are valid. Validity means that the tests are related to successful job performance and that a test does not have the effect of eliminating certain races from the employment market.

An employer can validate a test in any of several different ways. Test scores of applicants can later be compared with the applicants' eventual job performance to validate the test. An employer can also give the test to current employees and use the correlation between their scores and job performance as a means for validating the test. Some tests can be validated by their content. For example, requiring potential police officers to complete a driving course, a physical fitness test, and a marksmanship test is valid because the tests are based on the things police officers actually do. (Refer to p. 712 and the discussion of disparate impact for more information on validation of tests.)

21-6d **MISCONDUCT**

For many years, an absolute defense to discrimination was employee misconduct. If an employee violated company rules, the case did not involve discrimination. The defense was so broad that even evidence the employer acquired *after* the termination and charge of discrimination could be used as a defense. In *McKennon v Nashville Banner Publishing Co.* (Case 21.6), the Supreme Court limited this defense.

CASE 21.6	*McKennon v Nashville Banner Publishing Co.* 524 U.S. 742 (1995)

Lying Is Not a Defense for Discrimination

FACTS

For 30 years, Christine McKennon (petitioner) worked for Nashville Banner Publishing Company (respondent) (Banner), but she was terminated as part of a work reduction plan. She was 62 years old at the time of her termination. Ms. McKennon filed suit, alleging her termination was a violation of the Age Discrimination in Employment Act (ADEA).

During Ms. McKennon's deposition, she testified that during her final year of employment, she had copied several confidential documents bearing upon the company's financial condition. She had access to these records as secretary to Banner's comptroller. Ms. McKennon took the copies home and showed them to her husband. Her motivation, she averred, was apprehension that she was about to be fired because

CONTINUED

of her age. When she became concerned about her job, she removed and copied the documents for "insurance" and "protection." A few days after these deposition disclosures, Banner sent Ms. McKennon a letter declaring that removal and copying of the records was in violation of her job responsibilities and advised her (again) that she was terminated. Banner's letter also recited that had it known of Ms. McKennon's misconduct, it would have discharged her at once for that reason.

Banner conceded its discrimination in district court, which granted summary judgment for Banner on grounds that Ms. McKennon's misconduct was a defense. The court of appeals affirmed, and Ms. McKennon appealed.

JUDICIAL OPINION

KENNEDY, Justice

We shall assume that the sole reason for McKennon's initial discharge was her age, a discharge violative of the ADEA. Our further premise is that the misconduct revealed by the deposition was so grave that McKennon's immediate discharge would have followed its disclosure in any event. We do question the legal conclusion reached by those courts that after-acquired evidence of wrongdoing which would have resulted in discharge bars employees from any relief under the ADEA. That ruling is incorrect.

The ADEA and Title VII share common substantive features and also a common purpose: "the elimination of discrimination in the workplace." Congress designed the remedial measures in these statutes to serve as a "spur or catalyst" to cause employers "to self-examine and to self-evaluate their employment practices and to endeavor to eliminate, so far as possible, the last vestiges" of discrimination. The ADEA, in keeping with these purposes, contains a vital element found in both Title VII and the Fair Labor Standards Act: it grants an injured employee a right of action to obtain the authorized relief.

The objectives of the ADEA are furthered when even a single employee establishes that an employer has discriminated against him or her. The disclosure through litigation of incidents or practices which violate national policies respecting nondiscrimination in the work force is itself important, for the occurrence of violations may disclose patterns of noncompliance resulting from a misappreciation of the Act's operation or entrenched resistance to its commands, either of which can be of industry-wide significance. The

efficacy of its enforcement mechanisms becomes one measure of the success of the Act.

As we have said, the case comes to us on the express assumption that an unlawful motive was the sole basis for the firing. McKennon's misconduct was not discovered until after she had been fired. The employer could not have been motivated by knowledge it did not have and it cannot now claim that the employee was fired for the nondiscriminatory reason. Mixed motive cases are inapposite here, except to the important extent they underscore the necessity of determining the employer's motives in ordering the discharge, an essential element in determining whether the employer violated the federal antidiscrimination law. As we have observed, "proving that the same decision would have been justified … is not the same as proving that the same decision would have been made."

The ADEA, like Title VII, is not a general regulation of the workplace but a law which prohibits discrimination. The statute does not constrain employers from exercising significant other prerogatives and discretions in the course of the hiring, promoting, and discharging of their employees. In determining appropriate remedial action, the employee's wrongdoing becomes relevant not to punish the employee, or out of concern "for the relative moral worth of the parties," but to take due account of the lawful prerogatives of the employer in the usual course of its business and the corresponding equities that it has arising from the employee's wrongdoing.

The proper boundaries of remedial relief in the general class of cases where, after termination, it is discovered that the employee has engaged in wrongdoing must be addressed by the judicial system in the ordinary course of further decisions, for the factual permutations and the equitable considerations they raise will vary from case to case. We do conclude that here, and as a general rule in cases of this type, neither reinstatement nor front pay is an appropriate remedy. It would be both inequitable and pointless to order the reinstatement of someone the employer would have terminated, and will terminate, in any event and upon lawful grounds.

Where an employer seeks to rely upon after-acquired evidence of wrongdoing, it must first establish that the wrongdoing was of such severity that the employee in fact would have been terminated on those grounds alone if the employer had known of it at the time of the discharge. The concern that employers might as a routine matter undertake extensive discovery into an employee's background or performance on the job to resist claims under the Act is not

CONTINUED

an insubstantial one, but we think the authority of the courts to award attorney's fees, mandated under the statute, 29 U.S.C. §§ 216(b), 626(b), and in appropriate cases to invoke the provisions of Rule 11 of the Federal Rules of Civil Procedure will deter most abuses.

The judgment is reversed.

CASE QUESTIONS

1. Why is the timing of the misconduct disclosure important?
2. Does Banner deny discriminatory intent?
3. Why are "mixed motive" cases not relevant in this analysis?

ETHICAL ISSUES

Consider the following circumstances and decide whether there has been a violation of Title VII. Consider the ethical implications of the conduct along with the legal ones.

1. An employee must be dismissed. Two women, one white and the other black, have been with the company for the same amount of time and have the same rate of absenteeism. Their performance evaluations are about the same. Can the black employee be dismissed without violating Title VII?

2. Company B has had a significant problem with absenteeism, tardiness, and failure to follow through

on job assignments among the employees who are of a certain race. The personnel director is concerned about company productivity, the costs of training, and the costs of constant turnover. The personnel director is also aware of the constraints of Title VII. The director instructs those staffing the front office to tell members of that particular race who apply for a job that the company is not accepting applications. The director's theory is that his applicant pool will be prescreened and he will not have to make discriminatory hiring decisions. Is the director correct?

© martan/Shutterstock.com

21-7 Enforcement of Title VII

Title VII is an enabling act that created the Equal Employment Opportunity Commission for the purpose of administration and enforcement. The EEOC is a five-member commission whose members are appointed by the president with the approval of the Senate. As with all other federal commissions, no more than three members can belong to the same political party.

The EEOC was given broad powers under Title VII. In addition to its rulemaking and charging powers, the EEOC has broad investigatory authority, including the authority to subpoena documents and testimony.

21-7a   STEPS IN AN EEOC CASE

The Complaint

An EEOC complaint can be filed by an employee or by the EEOC. An employee has 180 days (in some cases, up to 300 days) from the time of the alleged violation to file a complaint. In *Ledbetter v Goodyear*, 550 U.S. 618 (2007), the U.S. Supreme Court clarified the 180-day rule for individual suits. Lilly Ledbetter filed suit against Goodyear after her retirement in 1999, following 19 years of employment at the company's plant in Gadsden, Alabama. While she filed suit within 180 days after receiving her last paycheck, the court held that she must have brought her pay discrimination suit within 180 days from when the alleged discrimination in pay occurred. The suit was dismissed, with the high court noting that employers must have current enough allegations so that they can defend the suit with their records, which may not be available after 19 years. The decision required employees to bring suit within 180 days from the time of the discriminatory conduct. In 2009, Congress passed the **Lilly Ledbetter Fair Pay Act**, which provides that each paycheck triggers a new 180-day filing period regardless of when the discriminatory practices that led to pay disparity began.

The complaint may be filed with either the EEOC or the state administrative agency set up for employment discrimination issues. For the state agency to continue handling the complaint, it must be an EEOC-approved program. If it is not, the EEOC handles the complaint. The EEOC has special forms that can be filled out by any employee wishing to file such a complaint.

Notification of the Employer

Once a complaint has been filed, the EEOC has 10 days to notify the employer of the charges. Employers are prohibited from the time of notification from taking any retaliatory action against the charging employee.

EEOC Action

After the complaint is filed, the EEOC has 180 days from that time to take action in the case before the complaining party can file suit on the matter. During this time, the EEOC can use its investigatory powers to explore the merits of the charges. In the case of *University of Pennsylvania v EEOC*, 493 U.S. 182 (1990), the Supreme Court ruled that the EEOC could have access to all information in an employee's file—even evaluation letters in which evaluators were promised confidentiality. During this conciliation period, the EEOC may also try to work out a settlement between the employer and the employee.

The Right-to-Sue Letter

If the EEOC has not settled its complaint within 180 days from the time of its filing, the employee has the right to demand a **right-to-sue letter** from the EEOC, which is a certification that the employee has exhausted available administrative remedies. If a state agency is involved, the time for its settlement of the matter must also expire before the employee can take the matter to court.

The employee has the right to this letter regardless of the EEOC's findings. Even if the EEOC has investigated and determined the charges have no merit, the employee can still pursue the case in court. Under *EEOC v Waffle House*, 534 U.S. 279 (2002), the U.S. Supreme Court held that the EEOC, as an agency, has the right to proceed with its remedies even if the private remedies are dismissed or not available to the affected employee.

21-7b REMEDIES AVAILABLE UNDER TITLE VII

Remedies available under Title VII include injunctions, back pay, punitive damages, and attorneys' fees. If a court finds a violation, it may order that corrective or affirmative action be taken to compensate for past wrongs. An injunction usually requires the employer to stop the illegal discrimination and then institute a plan to hire or promote minorities. Back-pay awards are limited to two years under Title VII. Section 706(b) of the act permits successful parties to recover "reasonable attorneys' fees."

An employer cannot take retaliatory action against employees who file charges or who are successful in a suit; Title VII makes such action unlawful.

Title VII originally allowed damages for back pay for all forms of discrimination. Punitive and compensatory damages are now permitted in racial and ethnic discrimination cases. The 1991 amendments extend the recovery of punitive and compensatory damages to cases involving sex, religion, or disability.

21-8 Other Antidiscrimination Laws

21-8a AGE DISCRIMINATION IN EMPLOYMENT ACT OF 1967

Title VII does not cover the real problem of age discrimination, which generally involves companies' hiring preference for younger people. To correct this loophole, the Age Discrimination in Employment Act (ADEA) was passed in 1967, and the EEOC was given responsibility for its enforcement. The act covers all employers with 20 or more employees and prohibits age discrimination in the hiring, firing, and compensation of employees. All employment agencies are covered. The act protects workforce members above age 40.

The elements in an age discrimination case are similar to those in other discrimination cases—simply substitute that the terminated employee was replaced with a younger employee. The replacement need not be below the age of 40. [*O'Connor v Consolidated Coin Caterers Corp.*, 517 U.S. 308 (1996)] The *Gonzalez v El Dia, Inc.* case (Case 21.7) deals with an issue of age discrimination and provides the answer for the chapter opening "Consider..."

CASE 21.7

Gonzalez v El Dia, Inc.
304 F.3d 63 (1st Cir. 2002)

¿La Empleada con Manias de Vieja y El Empresario con Responsabilidad?

FACTS

Lydia Gonzalez, 58 (plaintiff), worked as a reporter at *El Nuevo Dia*, a Puerto Rico newspaper. Her supervisor, Maria Luisa Ferre, often said that Ms. Gonzalez's demeanor and couture were "[o]ut of style" and "colorless," and her coiffure was "like Phyllis Diller." Ms. Ferre also said that Ms. Gonzalez was old-fashioned (viz., "manias de vieja," or "old person's ways") and that she should have retired and gone to live with her grandchildren in Florida long ago. Ms. Ferre also taunted Ms. Gonzalez by saying that she would not live long enough to see her grandson play major league baseball.

Ms. Gonzalez asked Ms. Ferre if she could be assigned to cover fashion shows, but Ms. Ferre balked at the idea. Ms. Gonzalez then asked, "You want me to look like a *Vogue* model?" Ms. Ferre simply stared at her and then assigned younger reporters to the fashion

shows, telling Ms. Gonzalez, "Dona Lydia, I don't know what I'm going to do with you."

Jorge Mercado, the director of the human resources department at the newspaper, frequently stated that Ms. Gonzalez had "manias de vieja." Mr. Mercado would often accost Ms. Gonzalez when he visited the department in which Gonzalez worked by calling her "Mom," and making comments such as, "Are you still here?" or "I thought you had been discharged or terminated a long time ago."

Following a serious work-related injury in April 1997, Ms. Gonzalez took medical leave while receiving treatment and rehabilitative therapy. During Ms. Gonzalez's medical leave, Ms. Ferre contacted the *El Dia* human resources department regarding retirement packages that might be offered to Gonzalez.

During one discussion during her leave, Ms. Ferre asked Ms. Gonzalez whether she would like to retire,

CONTINUED

adding, "Look, you are already 63 years old and your health is not good." Ms. Gonzaleaz offered to return to work immediately, but Ms. Ferre rejected her offer and advised Gonzalez to take a vacation and return to work on July 1. Ms. Gonzalez had no remaining paid vacation time, and was in difficult financial straits. Ms. Ferre arranged for a $6,000 advance on salary for Ms. Gonzalez, what Ms. Ferre believed was part of a voluntary retirement package the two had agreed to.

Four days later, Ms. Gonzalez was presented with a resignation, release, and compensation agreement. Ms. Gonzalez refused to retire and returned to work three days later, when she signed a note agreeing to repay the $6,000. Ms. Gonzalez then took work from a competing newspaper in order to meet her repayment obligations on the note. Working for a competing newspaper was a violation of the conflict-of-interest clause in her contract.

She was then terminated and filed suit for violations of the ADEA. The district court granted summary judgment to *El Dia*.

JUDICAL OPINION

CYR, Senior Circuit Judge

Under the ADEA, an employer may not "discharge … or otherwise discriminate against any individual with respect to [her] compensation, terms, conditions, or privileges of employment, because of [her] age." El Dia acknowledges that Gonzalez established a prima facie case under the ADEA.

[T]he burden of proof [then] shifts to the defendant employer to articulate a legitimate, nondiscriminatory basis for its adverse employment action. The plaintiff employee may meet her burden of proof by showing that the employer's proffered reason for the challenged employment action was pretextual.

El Dia met its burden by identifying a nondiscriminatory basis for the Gonzalez discharge: i.e., her acceptance of employment as a reporter for a competing newspaper, in direct violation of the conflict-of-interest provision in the employee collective bargaining agreement (CBA).… the burden then shifted back to Gonzalez to prove that the nondiscriminatory basis assertedly relied upon by El Dia was merely a pretext, and that age animus was the real reason for her termination. "[Federal courts] do 'not sit as a super-personnel department that reexamines an entity's business decisions.' 'No matter how medieval a firm's practices, no matter how high-handed its decisional process, no matter how mistaken the firm's managers, [the ADEA does] not interfere.'" Accordingly, in order to establish that an age-based animus nonetheless

constituted a motivating factor in the decision to terminate her employment, Gonzalez relies upon varieties of evidence.

THE AGEIST REMARKS

"[S]tray workplace remarks," as well as statements made either by nondecision makers or by decision makers not involved in the decisional process, normally are insufficient, standing alone, to establish either pretext or the requisite discriminatory animus.

Secondly, it is far from clear that the alleged remarks bespeak any age-based animus at all. Some statements, such as those made by Mr. Mercado, merely displayed a measure of surprise that Gonzalez was still employed at El Dia, without either asserting or implying that she was too old to be working. Moreover, Mr. Mercado's alleged use of the salutation "Mom"—though no doubt insensitive, perhaps even rude—hardly constituted a self-sufficient foundation for an ADEA claim, especially since these particular attributions—motherhood and advanced age—plainly are not synonymous.

[T]he Spanish phrase "manias de vieja" ("old ways") did not unambiguously connote that Gonzalez was old, let alone too old, but rather that she acted in ways which did not appear in keeping with a person her age. [S]uch terms "apply more to a person's state of mind than to a person's age."

THE FASHION SHOW COVERAGE

Given her acknowledged penchant for old-fashioned clothing and hairstyles, it seems much more plausible to attribute El Dia's decision to the fact that Gonzalez was insufficiently attuned to current fashions; and, therefore, that her representation of El Dia at fashion shows could very well reflect adversely upon its business image in such circles.

THE REMARKS MADE BY MS. FERRE [IN THE LEAVE DISCUSSION]

On June 12, Ms. Ferre adverted to Gonzalez' age while the two were discussing Gonzalez' vacation plans and the retirement offer which had been made to her. Of course the mere tender of a retirement proposal does not evince the requisite discriminatory animus.

Moreover, even viewed in the light most favorable to Gonzalez, Ms. Ferre's statement plainly conveyed the rational concern that retirement might prove the more prudent course, especially since Gonzalez had

CONTINUED

been experiencing serious health problems, as well as financial difficulties.

Gonzalez ignores the fact that, arguably at least, she engaged in a series of infractions. She defaulted on a promissory note which she had insisted that Mr. Mercado draw up, and thereafter deliberately went to work for a competing newspaper in direct contravention of the CBA. Thus, no rational jury reasonably could conclude that El Dia lacked "just cause" to terminate Gonzalez.

Affirmed.

CASE QUESTIONS

1. Describe how the burden of proof works in discrimination suits.
2. What workplace rules would you put in place to avoid these types of lawsuits?
3. Explain how the human resources manager and the supervisor could have handled the issues with Ms. Gonzalez in a way that would have avoided the litigation.

21-8b EQUAL PAY ACT OF 1963

The Equal Pay Act of 1963 is an amendment to the Fair Labor Standards Act. (The details of its coverage are outlined in Chapter 20.)

21-8c COMMUNICABLE DISEASES IN THE WORKPLACE

Whether employees can be fired because they may carry a communicable disease has recently become a crucial issue. Court decisions on the treatment of infected employees have varied, but the Supreme Court decision *School Board of Nassau County v Arline*, 480 U.S. 273 (1987), has been touted as a protectionist measure as a result of its finding that a school board could not discriminate against a teacher because she had tuberculosis (a contagious disease). The Americans with Disabilities Act will provide new issues and remedies with regard to communicable diseases (see the following discussion).

21-8d REHABILITATION ACT OF 1973

Congress enacted the Rehabilitation Act to prohibit discrimination in employment against handicapped persons by persons and organizations that receive federal contracts or assistance. The Labor Department is responsible for enforcing the act.

The Rehabilitation Act laid the groundwork for the Americans with Disabilities Act, but is limited in application to employers who have federal contracts and requires the same reasonable accommodation standards now required under ADA.

21-8e AMERICANS WITH DISABILITIES ACT

The intent of the Americans with Disabilities Act (ADA) was to eliminate discrimination against individuals with disabilities. The ADA has been called the "Emancipation Proclamation" for disabled U.S. citizens.

Portions of the ADA apply to employment discrimination issues, while other sections ensure that those with disabilities have access to public streets, walkways, buildings, and transportation.

Under the ADA, employers of 15 or more employees cannot discriminate in hiring, promotion, and selection criteria against a "qualified individual with a disability." A disability is defined by the ADA and its 2008 amendments as a physical or mental impairment that substantially limits one or more major life activities such as seeing, hearing, speaking, walking, breathing, learning, or self-care. Pursuant to a U.S. Supreme Court case [*Bragdon v Abbott*, 524 U.S. 624 (1998)], human immunodeficiency virus (HIV) is considered a physical impairment for purposes of the ADA. In that case, a dentist's refusal to treat an HIV-positive patient who needed a cavity filled violated the ADA public accommodation provisions.

Employers must make "reasonable accommodations" for disabled individuals to enable them to perform essential functions. Included in reasonable accommodations are providing employee facilities that are readily accessible to and usable by disabled individuals, job restructuring, allowing part-time or modified work schedules, reassigning disabled individuals to vacant positions, acquiring or modifying equipment, and providing qualified readers or interpreters. Perhaps the accommodation best known to the public is the right golfer Casey Martin won in *PGA Tour, Inc. v Martin*, 531 U.S. 1049 (2001). Martin wanted to use a cart in PGA tournaments because of his circulatory ailment. Martin has been afflicted since birth with Klippel-Trenaunay-Weber syndrome, a degenerative circulatory disorder. Walking aggravates the condition, but the PGA refused to allow him to use a cart. He filed suit for violation of the ADA, and the U.S. Supreme Court agreed.

Preemployment medical examinations are prohibited under the ADA, as are specific questions about a protected individual's disabilities. However, an employer may inquire about the ability of the applicant to perform job-related functions. "Can you carry 50 pounds of mail?" is an appropriate question; "Do you have the use of both arms?" is not.

Employers can refuse employment if an ADA-protected individual cannot perform necessary job functions. Also, employers can refuse to hire individuals who pose a direct threat to the health and safety of others in the workplace (assuming the risk cannot be minimized through accommodation).

The ADA is enforced through the EEOC and carries the same rights and remedies provided under Title VII. Exhibit 21.2 provides a list of items to help employers comply with ADA. Exhibit 21.3 examines proper and improper questions for job interviews under ADA.

EXHIBIT 21.2 Compliance Tips for ADA

MINIMIZING AN EMPLOYER'S ADA RISKS

1. Post notices describing the provisions of the ADA in your workplace.

2. Review job requirements to ensure that they bear a direct relationship to the ability to perform the essential functions of the job in question.

3. Identify, in writing, the "essential functions" of a job before advertising for or interviewing potential candidates.

4. Before rejecting an otherwise qualified applicant or terminating an employee on the basis of a disability, first determine that (a) the individual cannot perform the essential duties of the position, or (b) the individual cannot perform the essential duties of the position without imminent and substantial risk of injury to self or others, and (c) the employer cannot reasonably accommodate the disability.

5. Articulate factors, other than an individual's disability, that are the basis of an adverse employment decision. Document your findings and the tangible evidence on which a decision to reject or terminate was based; make notes of accommodations considered.

6. Ask the disabled individual for advice on accommodations. This shows the employer's good faith and a willingness to consider such proposals.

7. Institute programs of benefits and consultation to assist disabled employees in effectively managing health, leave, and other benefits.

8. Check with your insurance carrier regarding coverage of disabled employees and attempt (within economic reason) to maintain provided coverage or arrange for separate coverage.

9. Keep disabled individuals in mind when making structural alterations or purchasing office furniture and equipment.

10. Document all adverse employment actions, including reasons for the employment action with respect to disabled employees; focus on the employee's inability to do the job effectively rather than any relation to the employee's disability.

Source: EEOC Enforcement Guidance, http://www.eeoc.gov.

> **EXHIBIT 21.3** Legal and Illegal Versions of Similar Job Interview Questions
>
> | LEGAL | ILLEGAL |
> | --- | --- |
> | 1. Do you have 20/20 corrected vision? | What is your corrected vision? |
> | 2. How well can you handle stress? | Does stress ever affect your ability to be productive? |
> | 3. Can you perform this function with or without reasonable accommodation? | Would you need reasonable accommodation in this job? |
> | 4. How many days were you absent from work last year? | How many days were you sick last year? |
> | 5. Are you currently illegally using drugs? | What medications are you currently taking? |
> | 6. Do you regularly eat three meals per day? | Do you need to eat a number of small snacks at regular intervals throughout the day in order to maintain your energy level? |
> | 7. Do you drink alcohol? | How much alcohol do you drink per week? |
>
> *Source:* EEOC's "Enforcement Guidance on Pre-Employment Disability-Related Inquiries," May 12, 1994.

21-8f THE FAMILY AND MEDICAL LEAVE ACT

Passed in 1993, the **Family and Medical Leave Act (FMLA)** requires companies with 50 or more employees to provide 12 weeks' leave each year for medical or family reasons, including the birth or adoption of a child or the serious health condition or illness of a spouse, parent, or child. Although pay is not required during the leave, medical benefits of the employee must continue, and the same or an equivalent job must be available for the employee upon return.

21-9 The Global Workforce

Currently 2,000 U.S. companies have 21,000 subsidiary operations in 21 countries throughout the world. With the free trade agreements (see Chapter 7), those numbers will increase, as will the sizes of global operations.

One of the many employment issues that arises with respect to employees in subsidiary operations is whether the protections of Title VII apply to workers in these foreign operations. In *EEOC v Arabian American Oil Co.*, 499 U.S. 244 (1991), the U.S. Supreme Court was faced with the issue of whether U.S. companies could engage in employment discrimination against U.S. citizens when they are working in countries outside the United States. The Court held that the companies are governed by the employment laws of the country of operations and not the provisions of U.S. legislation.

Congress responded to the Supreme Court's ruling in *Arabian American Oil* by adding a section to the Civil Rights Act of 1991 addressing the issue of foreign operations. The statutory provision on foreign operations and civil rights protections is neither universal nor automatic. The amendment provides basically that in a case of conflict between U.S. employment discrimination laws and those of a host country, a company should follow the laws of the host country. An example is a law in the host country that prohibits the employment of women in management. The company would be required to follow that prohibition for operations located in the host country. If the host country has no laws on employment discrimination, the company is then required to follow all U.S. antidiscrimination laws.

Several multilateral treaties govern the rights of workers. In 1948, the United Nations adopted its Universal Declaration of Human Rights. The declaration supports, among other things, equality of pay and nondiscriminatory employment policies. Also, the Helsinki Final Act of 1973 supports nondiscriminatory employment policies. In 1977, the International Labor Office issued its Tripartite Declaration of Principles Concerning Multinational Enterprises, which supports equal pay and nondiscriminatory payment policies. The EU has adopted all of these treaties and policies for their implementation.

BIOGRAPHY Ann Hopkins, a Shunned Partner

Ann Hopkins was a senior manager in the Management Advisory Services division of the Price Waterhouse Office of Government Services (OGS) in Washington, DC. After earning undergraduate and graduate degrees in mathematics, she taught mathematics at her alma mater, Hollins College, and worked for IBM, NASA, Touche Ross, and American Management Systems before beginning her career with Price Waterhouse in 1977. She became the firm's specialist in large-scale computer system design and operations for the federal government. While salaries in the accounting profession are not published, estimates put her salary as a senior manager at about $65,000. Estimates of the increase in salary were that she would earn almost double that, or $125,000 annually, on average (1980 figures).

At that time, Price Waterhouse was known as one of the "Big 8," or one of the top public accounting firms in the United States. A senior manager became a candidate for partnership when the partners in her office submitted her name for partnership status. In August 1982, the partners in Hopkins's office proposed her as a candidate for the partner for the 1983 class of partners. Of the 88 candidates who were submitted for consideration, Hopkins was the only woman. Hopkins was responsible for bringing to Price Waterhouse a two-year, $25 million contract with the Department of State, the largest contract ever obtained by the firm. At that time, Price Waterhouse had 662 partners, 7 of whom were women. All of the firm's partners were invited to submit written comments regarding each candidate, but not every partner did so. Of the 32 partners who submitted comments on Hopkins, one stated that "none of the other partnership candidates at Price Waterhouse that year [has] a comparable record

in terms of successfully procuring major contracts for the partnership."

Her billable hours were 2,442 in 1982 and 2,507 in 1981, amounts that none of the other partnership candidates' billable hours even approached.

There were no limits on the number of persons to whom partnership could be awarded and no guidelines for evaluating comments about candidates. Price Waterhouse offered 47 partnerships to the 88 candidates in the 1983 round; another 27 were denied partnerships, and 20, including Ms. Hopkins, were put on hold. Ms. Hopkins had received more "no" votes than any other candidate for partnership, with most of those votes coming from members of the partnership committee outside the firm's government services unit.

Thirteen of the 32 partners who submitted comments on Hopkins supported her; three recommended putting her on hold; eight said they did not have enough information; and eight recommended denial.

The partners in Hopkins's office praised her character as well as her accomplishments, describing her in their joint statement as "an outstanding professional" who had a "deft touch," a "strong character, independence, and integrity." Clients appear to have agreed with these assessments. One official from the State Department described her as "extremely competent, intelligent," "strong and forthright, very productive, energetic, and creative." She "was generally viewed as a highly competent project leader who worked long hours, pushed vigorously to meet deadlines, and demanded much from the multidisciplinary staffs with which she worked."

On too many occasions, however, Hopkins's aggressiveness apparently spilled over into abrasiveness. Staff members seem to have borne the brunt of Hopkins's brusqueness. Long before her bid for partnership, partners evaluating her work had counseled her to improve her relations with staff members. Although later evaluations indicate an improvement, Hopkins's perceived shortcomings in this important area eventually doomed her bid for partnership. Virtually all of the partners' negative remarks about Hopkins—even those of partners who supported her—concerned her "interpersonal skills." Both "[s]upporters and opponents of her candidacy indicated that she was sometimes overly aggressive, unduly harsh, difficult to work with, and impatient with staff."

Another partner testified at trial that he had questioned her billing records and was left with concerns because he found her answers unsatisfying.

One partner's evaluation described her as "macho," while another suggested that she "overcompensated for being a woman"; a third advised her to take "a course at charm school." One partner wrote that Hopkins was "universally disliked." Several partners criticized her use of profanity. In response, one partner suggested that those partners objected to her swearing only "because it[']s a lady using foul language." Another supporter explained that Hopkins "ha[d] matured from a tough-talking, somewhat masculine, hardnosed manager to an authoritative, formidable, but much more appealing lady partner candidate." In order for Hopkins to improve her chances for partnership, Thomas Beyer, a partner who supervised Hopkins at OGS, suggested that she "walk more femininely, talk more femininely, dress more femininely, wear make-up, have her hair styled, and wear jewelry." Ms. Hopkins said she could not apply makeup because that would require removing her trifocals and she would not be able to see. Also, her allergy to cosmetics made it difficult for her to find appropriate makeup. Mr. Beyer also suggested that she should not carry a briefcase, should stop smoking, and should not drink beer at luncheon meetings.

Dr. Susan Fiske, a social psychologist and associate professor of psychology at Carnegie-Mellon University who would testify for Hopkins in her suit against Price Waterhouse, reviewed the Price Waterhouse selection process and concluded that it was likely influenced by sex stereotyping. Dr. Fiske indicated that some of the partners' comments were gender-biased, while others that were gender-neutral were intensely critical and made by partners who barely knew Hopkins. Dr. Fiske concluded that the subjectivity of the evaluations and their sharply critical nature were probably the result of sex stereotyping.

Although Hopkins and 19 others were put on hold for the following year, her future looked dim. Later, two partners withdrew their support for Hopkins, and she was informed that she would not be reconsidered the following year. Hopkins, who maintains that she was told after the second nomination cycle that she would never be a partner, then resigned and filed a discrimination complaint with the EEOC.

At that time, the law was not clear and the assumption was that Title VII did not apply to partnership decisions in companies. With the EEOC refusing to take action, Hopkins filed suit against Price Waterhouse. She has stated she filed the suit to find out why Price Waterhouse made "such a bad business decision." The U.S. Supreme Court found that Ms. Hopkins did indeed have a cause of action for discrimination in the partnership decision. The *Hopkins* case was an important employment discrimination case because the Supreme Court recognized stereotyping as a way of establishing discrimination. However, the case is also known for its clarification of the law on situations in which employers take action against employees for both lawful and unlawful reasons. Known as "mixed-motive" cases, this form of discrimination case shifts the burden of proof to the employer to establish that it would have made the same decision if using only the lawful considerations and in spite of unlawful considerations that entered into the process. The "same-decision" defense requires employers to establish sufficient grounds for termination or other actions taken against employees that are independent of the unlawful considerations.

In 1990, on remand, Ms. Hopkins was awarded her partnership and damages. She was awarded back pay plus interest, and while the exact amount of the award is unclear, Hopkins later verified that she paid $300,000 in taxes on her award that year and also paid her attorneys the $500,000 due and owing them. Ms. Hopkins rejoined Price Waterhouse as a partner in 1991.

Ms. Hopkins retired from Pricewaterhouse-Coopers in 2002, and she has written a book about her experience as a litigant. She also gardens, does carpentry work, and enjoys spending time with her grandchildren. She is still in litigation over the death of her youngest son, who was struck by a drunk driver.

Sources: Adapted from Marianne M. Jennings, *Business Ethics: Cases and Selected Readings*, 7th ed., 2011; Ann Hopkins, "Price Waterhouse v Hopkins: A Personal Account of a Sexual Discrimination Plaintiff," 22 *Hofstra Lab. & Emp. LJ.* 357 (2005).

Summary

What laws govern employment discrimination?

- Civil Rights Acts of 1866, 1964, 1991—federal statutes prohibiting discrimination in various aspects of life (employment, voting)

- Equal Pay Act—equal pay for the same work regardless of gender

- Equal Employment Opportunity Act—antidiscrimination employment amendment to Civil Rights Act

- Pregnancy Discrimination Act—prohibits refusing to hire, refusing to promote, or firing because of pregnancy

- Age Discrimination in Employment Act (ADEA)—prohibits hiring, firing, promotion, benefits, raises based on age

- Rehabilitation Act of 1973—federal statute prohibiting discrimination on basis of disability by federal agencies and contractors

- Americans with Disabilities Act (ADA)—federal law prohibiting discrimination on basis of disability by certain employees

- Family and Medical Leave Act (FMLA)—federal law providing for 12 weeks of leave for childbirth, adoption, or family illness

- Lilly Ledbetter Fair Pay Act—federal law that expands the time for filing claims for violations of Title VII for compensation

What types of discrimination exist?

- Disparate treatment—form of discrimination in which members of different races/sexes are treated differently

- Disparate impact—test or screening device that affects one group more than another

- Pattern or practice of discrimination—theory for establishing discrimination that compares population percentages with workplace percentages

- Sexual harassment—form of discrimination that involves a *quid pro quo* related to sexual favors or an atmosphere of harassment

What are the defenses to discrimination?

- Bona fide occupational qualification (BFOQ)—job qualification of sex, religion, or national origin that is necessary for the operation of a business, such as religious affiliation for the pastor of a church

- Affirmative action—programs created to remedy past wrongs that permit choices on the basis of race, sex, or national origin

Questions and Problems

1. Patrick Brady, 19, who has cerebral palsy, had worked for two years as a pharmacy assistant at a local pharmacy. He had no incidents at work there and was given a good recommendation from his employer. He then applied at Wal-Mart for a pharmacy aide position and went right to work in the Wal-Mart pharmacy. After a few days as a pharmacy aide, he was transferred to the job of collecting shopping carts and garbage in the parking lot. His supervisor, Ms. Yem Hung Chin, said Brady was "absolutely awful," and she "wanted [him] away from [her] prescriptions." Although Wal–Mart had an institutional "coaching policy," she never approached Brady about participating in it, because "I really didn't think it kind of applied. I didn't know how to teach him to find names better... ." Brady testified that he never handed out the wrong prescription, was never unable to find a prescription in the bin, and never required assistance from Ms. Chin or any other coworker to perform his job.

Brady was never given the 90-day probationary period given to other employees, nor was he given any training. When he met with the store manager about his parking lot job, he was transferred to the bakery with no training and no uniform. When he asked to return to the pharmacy, he was given a work schedule that conflicted with his community college class schedule, something he had noted on his application for employment in describing his availability. Frustrated, Brady quit and filed suit. Explain his rights under the Americans with Disabilities Act. Discuss Ms. Chin's statements and anything else Wal-Mart did that might be used as proof of discrimination. [*Brady v Wal–Mart Stores, Inc.*, 531 F.3d 127 (2nd Cir. 2008)]

2. Calvin Rhodes began as a salesman with Dresser Industries in 1955. In 1986, the oil industry experienced a severe economic downturn, and Mr. Rhodes was laid off. His severance report said he was discharged as part of a reduction in force. Within two months, Dresser had hired a 42-year-old replacement. Mr. Rhodes sued for violation of ADEA. Will he win? [*Rhodes v Guiberson Oil Tools* (subsidiary of Dresser), 75 F.3d 989 (5th Cir. 1996)]

3. Vivian Martyszenko was working as a cashier at a Safeway grocery store in Ogallala, Nebraska, when she received a call from the police informing her that her two children might have been molested. Ms. Martyszenko's supervisor gave her two weeks' vacation leave to care for her children.

The psychiatrist's exam of the children was inconclusive, and Ms. Martyszenko was told it would take time for their recovery. She asked for leave under the FMLA, which Safeway denied. She then filed suit, alleging Safeway had violated FMLA. Was the boys' condition a serious health condition covered under FMLA? [*Martyszenko v Safeway, Inc.*, 120 F.3d 120 (8th Cir. 1997)]

4. On August 11, 1980, Shelby Memorial Hospital hired Sylvia Hayes, a certified X-ray technician, to work the 3–11 P.M. shift in the hospital's radiology department. Two months later, she was fired after she informed her supervisor that she was pregnant. The supervisor fired Ms. Hayes because Dr. Cecil Eiland, the hospital's radiology director and director of radiation safety, recommended that Ms. Hayes be removed from all areas using ionizing radiation, and the hospital could not find alternative work for her. After her dismissal, Ms. Hayes filed suit for violation of the Pregnancy Discrimination Act and Title VII. Should she recover? [*Hayes v Shelby Memorial Hosp.*, 726 F.2d 1543 (11th Cir. 1984)]

5. The Masonic nursing home has mostly female occupants and hires fewer male attendants than female ones. Home administrators maintain that the female occupants (for privacy reasons) would not consent to intimate personal care by males and would, in fact, leave the home. A substantial portion of the women at the home are "total care" patients who require assistance in performing virtually all activities, including bathing, dressing, and using toilets, catheters, and bedpans. In a suit brought by a male nurse's aide who was denied employment, who would win? [*Fessel v Masonic Home*, 17 FEP Cases 330 (Del. 1978)]

6. Between 1985 and 1990, while attending college, Beth Ann Faragher worked part-time and during the summers as an ocean lifeguard for the Parks and Recreation Department of the City of Boca Raton. Ms. Faragher worked for three immediate supervisors during this period: Bill Terry, David Silverman, and Robert Gordon. Ms. Faragher resigned in June 1990 and brought a Title VII sexual harassment suit against the

City in 1992. She alleged a sexually hostile atmosphere because of "uninvited and offensive touching," lewd remarks, and Mr. Silverman's comment, "Date me or clean the toilets for a year."

Ms. Faragher had not complained to higher management, and the lifeguards had no significant contact with higher city officials. Two months before Ms. Faragher's resignation, a former lifeguard, Nancy E. Wanchew, wrote to the City's personnel director complaining about Mr. Terry and Mr. Silverman's harassment of female lifeguards. Should the City be held liable? Does it matter that Ms. Faragher asked only for nominal damages, attorney's fees, and costs? [*Faragher v City of Boca Raton*, 524 U.S. 775 (1998)]

7. After working for Ace Drill Bits for nearly 10 years as a production supervisor, Constance Price learns that she is being paid less than the other four production supervisors in her department, who are all men. Immediately after learning about the pay discrepancy, Constance files an EEOC charge alleging sex-based wage discrimination in violation of Title VII. The investigation shows that Constance generally received lower pay raises than her male counterparts as the result of lower performance ratings. These performance ratings and related pay raises all occurred more than 300 days before Constance filed her charge. Discuss whether there has been a Title VII violation. Also discuss whether Constance has filed within the time limits for an EEOC claim.

8. Would the following actions constitute sexual harassment?
  a. Making sexual comments or innuendoes; telling sexual jokes or stories
  b. Asking questions about social or sexual life
  c. Telling lies or spreading rumors about a person's personal sex life
  d. Making sexual comments about a person's body
  e. Turning work discussions to sexual topics
  f. Looking a person up and down
  g. Staring repeatedly at someone
  h. Blocking a person's path or hindering them
  i. Giving unwanted gifts of a sexual nature
  j. Invading a person's body space
  k. Making sexual gestures or kissing sounds or offering massages
  l. Displaying sexual posters, cartoons, or handouts

9. American Airlines passed a grooming rule that prohibited "cornrow" hairstyles on all employees. Renee Rogers, a black woman, brought a Title VII suit alleging that the denial of her right to wear the hairstyle intruded upon her rights and discriminated against her. What will be the result? [*Rogers v American Airlines, Inc.*, 527 F. Supp. 229 (S.D.N.Y. 1981)]

10. American Airlines has a policy of not hiring flight officers over the age of 40. The reason for their policy is that it takes 10–15 years for a flight officer to become a copilot and then another 10–15 years for a copilot to become a captain. Because the FAA requires retirement at age 60, service would be limited. Edward L. Murnane, age 43, was denied employment on the basis of age and filed an age discrimination suit. Is age a BFOQ for the job? [*Murnane v American Airlines, Inc.*, 667 F.2d 98 (D.C. 1981)]

ETHICS, ORGANIZATIONAL BEHAVIOR, THE LAW

English Only in Emergencies?

English-only policies in the workplace have become the fastest-growing area of EEOC challenges as well as litigation under Title VII. In 1996, the EEOC had 30 discrimination complaints related to English-only policies of employers. Since 1996, the EEOC has had a 500 percent increase in those complaints.[4] Employers that have implemented English-only policies include the Salvation Army, All-Island Transportation (a Long Island taxi company), a geriatric center in New York, and Oglethorpe University in Atlanta.

One lawyer noted that employers seem more willing to make the policies and risk the legal battles because they think such policies are appropriate and necessary in order to provide adequate customer service, or in the case of health operations such as the geriatric center, correct medical care. Employers are, however, warned by their lawyers that they will have "a target on their backs" if they implement the policies.

A case that an employer lost was *Maldonado v City of Altus*, 433 F.3d 1294 (10th Cir. 2006). In that case, the city of Altus promulgated an English-only policy that affected 29 of the city's employees, who are Hispanic. All 29 of the employees are fluently bilingual. In the spring of 2002, the city's street commissioner issued a rule that employees in his division could speak only English while on the job. The city's HR director told the commissioner that the policy would be upheld only if limited to when the employees were using the radio to communicate for purposes of city business. However, the rule was enforced throughout the workday, even during lunch and breaks. The employees filed suit alleging that the rule created a hostile environment for them. The 10th Circuit agreed with the employees and reversed the summary judgment for the city.

Lawyers offer the following guidelines for enforceable English-only policies:

1. Such policies are permitted if they are needed to promote safe or efficient operations.

2. Such policies are permitted where communication with customers, coworkers, or supervisors who speak only English is also important.

3. Such policies are permitted where there are frequent emergency encounters in which speaking a common language is necessary for purposes of managing such situations.

4. Such policies are necessary in situations in which cooperation and close working relationships demand a common language and some workers speak only English.

Discussion Questions

1. Is there a common thread among the companies mentioned that have English-only policies?

2. Do these language policies create a hostile environment?

3. Give a list of the types of employers you believe could qualify for an English-only policy under the EEOC guidelines.

Notes

1. See the website and the *Instructor's Manual* for additional background on the history of employment discrimination law.

2. Justice Sonia Sotomayor's confirmation to the high court was pending at the time of this decision. She was one of the appellate judges who reversed the lower court decision.

3. For updates on affirmative action and other issues in employment discrimination law, be sure to visit the course website.

4. U.S. Equal Employment Opportunity Commission (EEOC), "Litigation Statistics," http://www.eeoc.gov. At the EEOC homepage, search "Litigation Statistics." Or, click on "About the EEOC," go to "Statistics," and then click on "EEOC Enforcement and Litigation Statistics," or go to http://www.eeoc.gov /eeoc/statistics/enforcement/litigation.cfm.

The United States Constitution

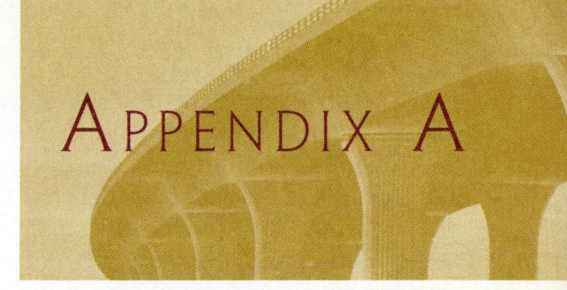

We the People of the United States, in Order to form a more perfect Union, establish Justice, insure domestic Tranquility, provide for the common defence, promote the general Welfare, and secure the Blessings of Liberty to ourselves and our Posterity, do ordain and establish this Constitution for the United States of America.

ARTICLE I

Section 1

All legislative Powers herein granted shall be vested in a Congress of the United States, which shall consist of a Senate and House of Representatives.

Section 2

The House of Representatives shall be composed of Members chosen every second Year by the People of the several States, and the Electors in each State shall have the Qualifications requisite for Electors of the most numerous Branch of the State Legislature.

No Person shall be a Representative who shall not have attained to the Age of twenty five Years, and been seven Years a Citizen of the United States, and who shall not, when elected, be an Inhabitant of that State in which he shall be chosen.

Representatives and direct Taxes shall be apportioned among the several States which may be included within this Union, according to their respective Numbers, which shall be determined by adding to the whole Number of free Persons, including those bound to Service for a Term of Years, and excluding Indians not taxed, three fifths of all other Persons. The actual Enumeration shall be made within three Years after the first Meeting of the Congress of the United States, and within every subsequent Term of ten Years, in which Manner as they shall by Law direct. The Number of Representatives shall not exceed one for every thirty Thousand, but each State shall have at Least one Representative; and until such enumeration shall be made, the State of New Hampshire shall be entitled to choose three,

Massachusetts eight, Rhode Island and Providence Plantations one, Connecticut five, New York six, New Jersey four, Pennsylvania eight, Delaware one, Maryland six, Virginia ten, North Carolina five, South Carolina five, and Georgia three.

When vacancies happen in the Representation from any State, the Executive Authority thereof shall issue Writs of Election to fill such Vacancies.

The House of Representatives shall chuse their Speaker and other Officers; and shall have the sole Power of Impeachment.

Section 3

The Senate of the United States shall be composed of two Senators from each State, chosen by the Legislature thereof, for six Years; and each Senator shall have one Vote.

Immediately after they shall be assembled in Consequence of the first Election, they shall be divided as equally as may be into three Classes. The Seats of the Senators of the first Class shall be vacated at the Expiration of the second Year, of the second Class at the Expiration of the fourth Year, and of the third Class at the Expiration of the sixth Year, so that one third may be chosen every second Year; and if Vacancies happen by Resignation, or otherwise, during the Recess of the Legislature of any State, the Executive thereof may make temporary Appointments until the next Meeting of the Legislature, which shall then fill such Vacancies.

No Person shall be a Senator who shall not have attained to the Age of thirty Years, and been nine Years a Citizen of the United States, and who shall not, when elected, be an Inhabitant of that State for which he shall be chosen.

The Vice President of the United States shall be President of the Senate, but shall have no Vote, unless they be equally divided.

The Senate shall chuse their other Officers, and also a President pro tempore, in the Absence of the Vice President, or when he shall exercise the Office of President of the United States.

The Senate shall have the sole Power to try all Impeachments. When sitting for that Purpose, they shall be on Oath or Affirmation. When the President of the United States is tried the Chief Justice shall preside: And no Person shall be convicted without the Concurrence of two thirds of the Members present.

Judgment in Cases of Impeachment shall not extend further than to removal from Office, and disqualification to hold and enjoy any Office of honor, Trust or Profit under the United States: but the Party convicted shall nevertheless be liable and subject to Indictment, Trial, Judgment and Punishment, according to Law.

Section 4

The Times, Places and Manner of holding Elections for Senators and Representatives, shall be prescribed in each State by the Legislature thereof; but the Congress may at any time by Law make or alter such Regulations, except as to the Places of chusing Senators.

The Congress shall assemble at Least once in every Year, and such Meeting shall be on the first Monday in December, unless they shall by Law appoint a different Day.

Section 5

Each House shall be the Judge of the Elections, Returns and Qualifications of its own Members, and a Majority of each shall constitute a Quorum to do Business; but a smaller Number may adjourn from day to day, and may be authorized to compel the Attendance of absent Members, in such Manner, and under such Penalties as each House may provide.

Each House may determine the Rules in its Proceedings, punish its Members for disorderly Behaviour, and, with the Concurrence of two thirds, expel a Member.

Each House shall keep a Journal of its Proceedings, and from time to time publish the same, excepting such Parts as may in their Judgment require Secrecy; and the Yeas and Nays of the Members of either House on any question shall, at the Desire of one fifth of those Present, be entered on the Journal.

Neither House, during the Session of Congress, shall, without the Consent of the other, adjourn for more than three days, nor to any other Place than that in which the two Houses shall be sitting.

Section 6

The Senators and Representatives shall receive a Compensation for their Services, to be ascertained by Law, and paid out of the Treasury of the United States. They shall in all Cases, except Treason, Felony and Breach of the Peace, be privileged from Arrest during their Attendance at the Session of their respective Houses, and in going to and returning from the same; and for any Speech or Debate in either House, they shall not be questioned in any other Place.

No Senator or Representative shall, during the Time for which he was elected, be appointed to any civil Office under the Authority of the United States, which shall have been created, or the Emoluments whereof shall have been encreased during such time; and no Person holding any Office under the United States, shall be a Member of either House during his Continuance in Office.

Section 7

All Bills for raising Revenue shall originate in the House of Representatives; but the Senate may propose or concur with amendments as on other Bills.

Every Bill which shall have passed the House of Representatives and the Senate, shall, before it become a Law, be presented to the President of the United States; If he approve he shall sign it, but if not he shall return it, with his Objections to that House in which it shall have originated, who shall enter the Objections at large on their Journal, and proceed to reconsider it. If after such Reconsideration two thirds of that House shall agree to pass the Bill, it shall be sent, together with the Objections, to the other House, by which it shall like wise be reconsidered, and if approved by two thirds of that House, it shall become a Law. But in all such Cases the Votes of both Houses shall be determined by Yeas and Nays, and the names of the Persons voting for and against the Bill shall be entered on the Journal of each House respectively. If any Bill shall not be returned by the President within ten Days (Sundays excepted) after it shall have been presented to him, the Same shall be a Law, in like Manner as if he had signed it, unless the Congress by their Adjournment prevent its Return, in which Case it shall not be a Law.

Every Order, Resolution, or Vote to which the Concurrence of the Senate and House of Representatives may be necessary (except on a question of Adjournment) shall be presented to the President of the United States; and before the Same shall take

Effect, shall be approved by him, or being disapproved by him, shall be repassed by two thirds of the Senate and House of Representatives, according to the Rules and Limitations prescribed in the Case of a Bill.

Section 8

The Congress shall have Power To lay and collect Taxes, Duties, Imposts and Excises, to pay the Debts and provide for the common Defense and general Welfare of the United States; but all Duties, Imposts and Excises shall be uniform throughout the United States;

To borrow Money on the credit of the United States;

To regulate Commerce with foreign Nations, and among the several States, and with the Indian Tribes;

To establish an uniform Rule of Naturalization, and uniform Laws on the subject of Bankruptcies throughout the United States;

To coin Money, regulate the Value thereof, and of foreign Coin, and fix the Standard of Weights and Measures;

To provide for the Punishment of counterfeiting the Securities and current Coin of the United States;

To establish Post Offices and post Roads;

To promote the Progress of Science and useful Arts, by securing for limited Times to Authors and Inventors the exclusive Right to their respective Writings and Discoveries;

To constitute Tribunals inferior to the supreme Court;

To define and punish Piracies and Felonies committed on the high Seas, and Offenses against the Law of Nations;

To declare War, grant Letters of Marque and Reprisal, and make Rules concerning Captures on Land and Water;

To raise and support Armies, but no Appropriation of Money to that Use shall be for a longer Term than two Years;

To provide and maintain a Navy;

To make Rules for the Government and Regulation of the land and naval Forces;

To provide for calling forth the Militia to execute the Laws of the Union, suppress Insurrections and repel Invasions;

To provide for organizing, arming, and disciplining, the Militia, and for governing such Part of them as may be employed in the Service of the United States, reserving to the States respectively, the Appointment of the Officers, and the Authority of training the Militia according to the discipline prescribed by Congress;

To exercise exclusive Legislation in all Cases whatsoever, over such District (not exceeding ten Miles square) as may, by Cession of particular States, and the Acceptance of Congress, become the Seat of the Government of the United States, and to exercise like Authority over all Places purchased by the Consent of the Legislature of the State in which the Same shall be, for the Erection of Forts, Magazines, Arsenals, dock-Yards, and other needful Buildings;—And

To make all Laws which shall be necessary and proper for carrying into Execution the foregoing Powers, and all other Powers vested by this Constitution in the Government of the United States, or in any Department or Officer thereof.

Section 9

The Migration or Importation of such Persons as any of the States now existing shall think proper to admit, shall not be prohibited by the Congress prior to the Year one thousand eight hundred and eight, but a Tax or duty may be imposed on such Importation, not exceeding ten dollars for each Person.

The Privilege of the Writ of Habeas Corpus shall not be suspended, unless when in Cases of Rebellion or Invasion the public Safety may require it.

No Bill of Attainder or ex post facto Law shall be passed.

No Capitation, or other direct, Tax shall be laid, unless in Proportion to the Census or Enumeration herein before directed to be taken.

No Tax or Duty shall be laid on Articles exported from any State.

No Preference shall be given to any Regulation of Commerce or Revenue to the Ports of one State over those of another; nor shall Vessels bound to, or from, one State, be obliged to enter, clear or pay Duties in another.

No Money shall be drawn from the Treasury, but in Consequence of Appropriations made by Law; and a regular Statement and Account of the Receipts and Expenditures of all public Money shall be published from time to time.

No Title of Nobility shall be granted by the United States: And no Person holding any Office of Profit or Trust under them, shall, without the

Consent of the Congress, accept of any present, Emolument, Office, or Title, of any kind whatever, from any King, Prince or foreign State.

Section 10

No State shall enter into any Treaty, Alliance, or Confederation; grant Letters of Marque and Reprisal; coin Money; emit Bills of Credit; make any Thing but gold and silver Coin a Tender in Payment of Debts; pass any Bill of Attainder, ex post facto Law or law impairing the Obligation of Contracts, or grant any Title of Nobility.

No State shall, without the Consent of the Congress, lay any Imposts or Duties on Imports or Exports, except what may be absolutely necessary for executing its inspection Laws: and the net Produce of all Duties and Imposts, laid by any State on Imports or Exports, shall be for the Use of the Treasury of the United States; and all such Laws shall be subject to the Revision and Control of the Congress.

No State shall, without the Consent of Congress, lay any Duty on Tonnage, keep Troops, or Ships of War in time of Peace, enter into any Agreement or Compact with another State, or with a foreign Power, or engage in War, unless actually invaded, or in such imminent Danger as will not admit of delay.

ARTICLE II

Section 1

The executive Power shall be vested in a President of the United States of America. He shall hold his Office during the Term of four Years, and, together with the Vice President, chosen for the same Term, be elected, as follows:

Each State shall appoint, in such Manner as the Legislature thereof may direct, a Number of Electors, equal to the whole Number of Senators and Representatives to which the State may be entitled in the Congress: but no Senator or Representative, or Person holding an Office of Trust or Profit under the United States, shall be appointed an Elector.

The Electors shall meet in their respective States, and vote by Ballot for two Persons, of whom one at least shall not be an Inhabitant of the same State with themselves. And they shall make a List of all the Persons voted for, and of the Number of Votes for each; which List they shall sign and certify, and transmit sealed to the Seat of the Government of the United States, directed to the President of the Senate. The President of the Senate shall, in the Presence of the Senate and House of Representatives, open all the Certificates, and the Votes shall then be counted. The Person having the greatest Number of Votes shall be the President, if such Number be a Majority of the whole Number of Electors appointed; and if there be more than one who have such Majority, and have an equal Number of Votes, then the House of Representatives shall immediately chuse by Ballot one of them for President; and if no Person have a Majority, then from the five highest on the List the said House shall in like Manner chuse the President. But in chusing the President, the Votes shall be taken by States, the Representation from each State having one Vote; a quorum for this Purpose shall consist of a Member or Members from two thirds of the States, and a Majority of all the States shall be necessary to a Choice. In every Case, after the Choice of the President, the Person having the greatest Number of Votes of the Electors shall be the Vice President. But if there should remain two or more who have equal Votes, the Senate shall chuse from them by Ballot the Vice President.

The Congress may determine the Time of chusing the Electors, and the Day on which they shall give their Votes; which Day shall be the same throughout the United States.

No Person except a natural born Citizen, or a Citizen of the United States, at the time of the Adoption of this Constitution, shall be eligible to the Office of President; neither shall any Person be eligible to that Office who shall not have attained to the Age of thirty-five Years, and been fourteen years a Resident within the United States.

In Case of the Removal of the President from Office, or of his Death, Resignation, or Inability to discharge the Powers and Duties of the said Office, the Same shall devolve on the Vice President, and the Congress may by Law provide for the Case of Removal, Death, Resignation, or Inability, both of the President and Vice President, declaring what Officer shall then act as President, and such Officer shall act accordingly, until the Disability be removed, or a President shall be elected.

The President shall, at stated Times, receive for his Services, a Compensation, which shall neither be increased nor diminished during the Period for which he shall have been elected, and he shall not receive within that Period any other Emolument from the United States, or any of them.

Before he enter on the Execution of his Office, he shall take the following Oath or Affirmation:— "I do solemnly swear (or affirm) that I will faithfully execute the Office of President of the United States, and will to the best of my Ability, preserve, protect, and defend the Constitution of the United States."

Section 2

The President shall be Commander in Chief of the Army and Navy of the United States, and of the Militia of the several States, when called into the actual Service of the United States; he may require the Opinion, in writing, of the principal Officer in each of the executive Departments, upon any Subject relating to the Duties of their respective Offices, and he shall have Power to grant Reprieves and Pardons for Offenses against the United States, except in Cases of Impeachment.

He shall have Power, by and with the Advice and Consent of the Senate, to make Treaties, provided two thirds of the Senators present concur; and he shall nominate, and by and with the Advice and Consent of the Senate, shall appoint Ambassadors, other public Ministers and Consuls, Judges of the supreme Court, and all other Officers of the United States, whose Appointments are not herein otherwise provided for, and which shall be established by Law: but the Congress may by Law vest the Appointment of such inferior Officers, as they think proper, in the President alone, in the Courts of Law, or in the Heads of Departments.

The President shall have Power to fill up all Vacancies that may happen during the Recess of the Senate, by granting Commissions which shall expire at the End of their next Session.

Section 3

He shall from time to time give to the Congress Information of the State of the Union, and recommend to their Consideration such Measures as he shall judge necessary and expedient; he may, on extraordinary Occasions, convene both Houses, or either of them, and in Case of Disagreement between them, with Respect to the Time of Adjournment, he may adjourn them to such Time as he shall think proper; he shall receive Ambassadors and other public Ministers; he shall take Care that the Laws be faithfully executed, and shall Commission all the Officers of the United States.

Section 4

The President, Vice President and all Civil Officers of the United States, shall be removed from Office on Impeachment for, and Conviction of, Treason, Bribery, or other high Crimes and Misdemeanors.

ARTICLE III

Section 1

The judicial Power of the United States, shall be vested in one supreme Court, and in such inferior Courts as the Congress may from time to time ordain and establish. The Judges, both of the supreme and inferior Courts, shall hold their Offices during good Behaviour, and shall, at stated Times, receive for their Services, a Compensation, which shall not be diminished during their Continuance in Office.

Section 2

The judicial Power shall extend to all Cases, in Law and Equity, arising under this Constitution, the Laws of the United States, and Treaties made, or which shall be made, under their Authority;—to all Cases affecting Ambassadors, other public Ministers and Consuls;—to all Cases of admiralty and maritime Jurisdiction;—to Controversies to which the United States shall be a Party;—to Controversies between two or more States;—between a State and Citizens of another State;—between Citizens of different States,—between Citizens of the same State claiming Lands under Grants of different States, and between a State, or the Citizens thereof, and foreign States, Citizens or Subjects.

In all Cases affecting Ambassadors, other public Ministers and Consuls, and those in which a State shall be Party, the Supreme Court shall have original Jurisdiction. In all the other Cases before mentioned, the supreme Court shall have appellate Jurisdiction, both as to Law and Fact, with such Exceptions, and under such Regulations as the Congress shall make.

The Trial of all Crimes, except in Cases of Impeachment, shall be by Jury; and such Trial shall be held in the State where the said Crimes shall have been committed; but when not committed within any State, the Trial shall be at such Place or Places as the Congress may by Law have directed.

Section 3

Treason against the United States, shall consist only in levying War against them, or in adhering to their Enemies, giving them Aid and Comfort. No Person shall be convicted of Treason unless on the Testimony of two Witnesses to the same overt Act, or on Confession in open Court.

The Congress shall have Power to declare the Punishment of Treason, but no Attainder of Treason shall work Corruption of Blood, or Forfeiture except during the Life of the Person attainted.

ARTICLE IV

Section 1
Full Faith and Credit shall be given in each State to the public Arts, Records, and judicial Proceedings of every other State. And the Congress may by general Laws prescribe the Manner in which such Acts, Records and Proceedings shall be proved, and the Effect thereof.

Section 2
The Citizens of each State shall be entitled to all Privileges and Immunities of Citizens in the several States.

A Person charged in any State with Treason, Felony, or other Crime, who shall flee from Justice, and be found in another State, shall on Demand of the executive Authority of the State from which he fled, be delivered up, to be removed to the State having Jurisdiction of the Crime.

No Person held to Service or Labour in one State, under the Laws thereof, escaping into another, shall, in Consequence of any Law or Regulation therein, be discharged from such Service or Labour, but shall be delivered up on Claim of the Party to whom such Service or Labour may be due.

Section 3
New States may be admitted by the Congress into this Union; but no new State shall be formed or erected within the Jurisdiction of any other State; nor any State be formed by the Junction of two or more States, or Parts of States, without the Consent of the Legislatures of the States concerned as well as of the Congress.

The Congress shall have Power to dispose of and make all needful Rules and Regulations respecting the Territory or other Property belonging to the United States; and nothing in this Constitution shall be so construed as to Prejudice any Claims of the United States, or of any particular State.

Section 4
The United States shall guarantee to every State in this Union a Republican Form of Government, and shall protect each of them against Invasion; and on Application of the Legislature, or of the Executive (when the Legislature cannot be convened) against domestic Violence.

ARTICLE V

The Congress, whenever two thirds of both Houses shall deem it necessary, shall propose Amendments to this Constitution, or, on the Application of the Legislatures of two thirds of the several States, shall call a Convention for proposing Amendments, which, in either Case, shall be valid to all Intents and Purposes, as Part of this Constitution, when ratified by the Legislatures of three fourths of the several States, or by Conventions in three fourths thereof, as the one or the other Mode of Ratification may be proposed by the Congress; Provided that no Amendment which may be made prior to the Year One thousand eight hundred and eight shall in any Manner affect the first and fourth Clauses in the Ninth Section of the first Article; and that no State, without its Consent, shall be deprived of its equal Suffrage in the Senate.

ARTICLE VI

All Debts contracted and Engagements entered into, before the Adoption of this Constitution, shall be as valid against the United States under this Constitution, as under the Confederation.

This Constitution, and the Laws of the United States which shall be made in Pursuance thereof; and all Treaties made, or which shall be made, under the Authority of the United States, shall be the supreme Law of the Land; and the judges in every State shall be bound thereby, any Thing in the Constitution or Laws of any State to the Contrary notwithstanding.

The Senators and Representatives before mentioned, and the Members of the several State Legislatures, and all executive and judicial Officers, both of the United States and of the several States, shall be bound by Oath or Affirmation, to support this Constitution; but no religious Test shall ever be required as a Qualification to any Office or public Trust under the United States.

ARTICLE VII

The Ratification of the Conventions of nine States, shall be sufficient for the Establishment of this Constitution between the States so ratifying the Same.

AMENDMENT I (1791)

Congress shall make no law respecting an establishment of religion, or prohibiting the free exercise thereof; or abridging the freedom of speech, or of the press; or the right of the people peaceably to assemble, and to petition the Government for a redress of grievances.

AMENDMENT II (1791)

A well regulated Militia, being necessary to the security of a free State, the right of the people to keep and bear Arms, shall not be infringed.

AMENDMENT III (1791)

No Soldier shall, in time of peace be quartered in any house, without the consent of the Owner, nor in time of war, but in a manner to be prescribed by law.

AMENDMENT IV (1791)

The right of the people to be secure in their persons, houses, papers, and effects, against unreasonable searches and seizures, shall not be violated, and no Warrants shall issue, but upon probable cause, supported by Oath or affirmation, and particularly describing the place to be searched, and the persons or things to be seized.

AMENDMENT V (1791)

No person shall be held to answer for a capital or otherwise infamous crime, unless on a presentment or indictment of a Grand Jury, except in cases arising in the land or naval forces, or in the Militia, when in actual service in time of War or public danger; nor shall any person be subject for the same offense to be twice put in jeopardy of life or limb; nor shall be compelled in any criminal case to be a witness against himself, nor be deprived of life, liberty, or property, without due process of law; nor shall private property be taken for public use, without just compensation.

AMENDMENT VI (1791)

In all criminal prosecutions, the accused shall enjoy the right to a speedy and public trial, by an impartial jury of the State and district wherein the crime shall have been committed, which district shall have been previously ascertained by law, and to be informed of the nature and cause of the accusation; to be confronted with the witnesses against him; to have compulsory process for obtaining Witnesses in his favor, and to have the Assistance of Counsel for his defense.

AMENDMENT VII (1791)

In Suits at common law, where the value in controversy shall exceed twenty dollars, the right of trial by jury shall be preserved, and no fact tried by a jury, shall be otherwise reexamined in any Court of the United States, than according to the rules of the common law.

AMENDMENT VIII (1791)

Excessive bail shall not be required nor excessive fines imposed, nor cruel and unusual punishments inflicted.

AMENDMENT IX (1791)

The enumeration in the Constitution, of certain rights, shall not be construed to deny or disparage others retained by the people.

AMENDMENT X (1791)

The powers not delegated to the United States by the Constitution, nor prohibited by it to the States, are reserved to the States respectively, or to the people.

AMENDMENT XI (1798)

The Judicial power of the United States shall not be construed to extend to any suit in law or equity, commenced or prosecuted against one of the United States by Citizens of another State, or by Citizens or Subjects of any Foreign State.

AMENDMENT XII (1804)

The Electors shall meet in their respective states and vote by ballot for President and Vice President, one of whom, at least, shall not be an inhabitant of the same state with themselves; they shall name in their ballots the person voted for as President, and in distinct ballots the person voted for as Vice-President, and they shall make distinct lists of all persons voted for as President, and of all persons voted for as Vice-President, and of the number of votes for each, which lists they shall sign and certify, and transmit sealed to the seat of the government of the United States, directed to the President of the Senate;—The President of the Senate shall, in the presence of the Senate and House of Representatives, open all the certificates and the votes shall then be counted;—The person having the greatest number of votes for President, shall be the President, if such number be a majority of the whole number of Electors appointed; and if no person have such majority, then from the persons having the highest numbers not exceeding three on the list of those voted for as President, the House of Representatives shall choose immediately, by ballot, the President. But in choosing the President, the votes shall be taken by states, the representation from each state having one vote; a quorum for this purpose shall consist of a member or members from two-thirds of the states, and a majority of all the states shall be necessary to a choice. And if the House of Representatives shall not choose a President whenever the right of choice shall devolve upon them, before the fourth day of March next following, then the Vice-President shall act as President, as in the case of the death or other constitutional disability of the President— The person having the greatest number of votes as Vice-President, shall be the Vice-President, if such number be a majority of the whole number of Electors appointed, and if no person have a majority, then from the two highest numbers on the list, the Senate shall choose the Vice-President; a quorum for the purpose shall consist of two-thirds of the whole numbers of Senators, and a majority of the whole number shall be necessary to a choice. But no person constitutionally ineligible to the office of President shall be eligible to that of Vice President of the United States.

AMENDMENT XIII (1865)

Section 1
Neither slavery nor involuntary servitude, except as a punishment for crime whereof the party shall have been duly convicted, shall exist within the United States, or any place subject to their jurisdiction.

Section 2
Congress shall have power to enforce this article by appropriate legislation.

AMENDMENT XIV (1868)

Section 1
All persons born or naturalized in the United States and subject to the jurisdiction thereof, are citizens of the United States and of the State wherein they reside. No State shall make or enforce any law which shall abridge the privileges or immunities of citizens of the United States; nor shall any State deprive any person of life, liberty, or property, without due process of law; nor deny to any person within its jurisdiction the equal protection of the laws.

Section 2
Representatives shall be apportioned among the several States according to their respective numbers, counting the whole number of persons in each State, excluding Indians not taxed. But when the right to vote at any election for the choice of electors for President and Vice President of the United States, Representatives in Congress, the Executive and Judicial officers of a State, or the members of the Legislature thereof, is denied to any of the male inhabitants of such State, being twenty-one years of age, and citizens of the United States, or in any way abridged, except for participation in rebellion, or other crime, the basis of representation therein shall be reduced in the proportion which the number of such male citizens shall bear to the whole number of male citizens twenty-one years of age in such State.

Section 3
No person shall be a Senator or Representative in Congress, or elector of President and Vice President, or hold any office, civil or military, under the United States, or under any State, who, having previously taken an oath, as a member of Congress, or as an officer of the United States, or as a member of any State legislature, or as an executive or judicial officer of any State, to support the Constitution of the United States, shall have engaged in insurrection or rebellion against the same, or given aid or comfort to the enemies thereof. But Congress may by a vote of two-thirds of each House, remove such disability.

Section 4

The validity of the public debt of the United States, authorized by law, including debts incurred for payment of pensions and bounties for services in suppressing insurrection or rebellion, shall not be questioned. But neither the United States nor any State shall assume or pay any debt or obligation incurred in aid of insurrection or rebellion against the United States, or any claim for the loss or emancipation of any slave; but all such debts, obligations and claims shall be held illegal and void.

Section 5

The Congress shall have power to enforce, by appropriate legislation, the provisions of this article.

AMENDMENT XV (1870)

Section 1

The right of citizens of the United States to vote shall not be denied or abridged by the United States or by any State on account of race, color, or previous condition of servitude.

Section 2

The Congress shall have power to enforce this article by appropriate legislation.

AMENDMENT XVI (1913)

The Congress shall have power to lay and collect taxes on incomes, from whatever source derived, without apportionment among the several States, and without regard to any census or enumeration.

AMENDMENT XVII (1913)

The Senate of the United States shall be composed of two Senators from each State, elected by the people thereof, for six years; and each Senator shall have one vote. The electors in each State shall have the qualifications requisite for electors of the most numerous branch of the State legislatures.

When vacancies happen in the representation of any State in the Senate, the executive authority of such State shall issue writs of election to fill such vacancies: *Provided*, That the legislature of any State may empower the executive thereof to make temporary appointments until the people fill the vacancies by election as the legislature may direct.

This amendment shall not be so construed as to affect the election or term of any Senator chosen before it becomes valid as part of the Constitution.

AMENDMENT XVIII (1919)

Section 1

After one year from the ratification of this article the manufacture, sale, or transportation of intoxicating liquors within, the importation thereof into, or the exportation thereof from the United States and all territory subject to the jurisdiction thereof for beverage purposes is hereby prohibited.

Section 2

The Congress and the several States shall have concurrent power to enforce this article by appropriate legislation.

Section 3

This article shall be inoperative unless it shall have been ratified as an amendment to the Constitution by the legislatures of the several States, as provided in the Constitution, within seven years from the date of the submission hereof to the States by the Congress.

AMENDMENT XIX (1920)

The right of citizens of the United States to vote shall not be denied or abridged by the United States or by any State on account of sex.

Congress shall have power to enforce this article by appropriate legislation.

AMENDMENT XX (1933)

Section 1

The terms of the President and Vice President shall end at noon on the 20th day of January, and the terms of Senators and Representatives at noon on the 3d day of January, of the years in which such terms would have ended if this article had not been ratified; and the terms of their successors shall then begin.

Section 2

The Congress shall assemble at least once in every year, and such meeting shall begin at noon on the 3d day of January, unless they shall by law appoint a different day.

Section 3

If, at the time fixed for the beginning of the term of the President, the President elect shall have died, the Vice President elect shall become President. If a President shall not have been chosen before the time fixed for the beginning of his term, or if the President elect shall have failed to qualify, then the Vice President elect shall act as President until a President shall have qualified; and the Congress may by law provide for the case wherein neither a President elect nor a Vice President elect shall have qualified, declaring who shall then act as President, or the manner in which one who is to act shall be selected, and such person shall act accordingly until a President or Vice President shall have qualified.

Section 4

The Congress may by law provide for the case of the death of any of the persons from whom the House of Representatives may choose a President whenever the right of choice shall have devolved upon them, and for the case of the death of any of the persons from whom the Senate may choose a Vice President whenever the right of choice shall have devolved upon them.

Section 5

Sections 1 and 2 shall take effect on the 15th day of October following the ratification of this article.

Section 6

This article shall be inoperative unless it shall have been ratified as an amendment to the Constitution by the legislatures of three fourths of the several States within seven years from the date of its submission.

AMENDMENT XXI (1933)

Section 1

The eighteenth article of amendment to the Constitution of the United States is hereby repealed.

Section 2

The transportation or importation into any State, Territory, or possession of the United States for delivery or use therein of intoxicating liquors, in violation of the laws thereof, is hereby prohibited.

Section 3

This article shall be inoperative unless it shall have been ratified as an amendment to the Constitution by conventions in the several States, as provided in the Constitution, within seven years from the date of the submission hereof to the States by the Congress.

AMENDMENT XXII (1951)

Section 1

No person shall be elected to the office of the President more than twice, and no person, who has held the office of President, or acted as President, for more than two years of a term to which some other person was elected President shall be elected to the Office of the President more than once. But this Article shall not apply to any person holding the office of President when this Article was proposed by the Congress, and shall not prevent any person who may be holding the office of President, or acting as President, during the term within which this Article becomes operative from holding the Office of President or acting as President during the remainder of such term.

Section 2

This article shall be inoperative unless it shall have been ratified as an amendment to the Constitution by the legislatures of three fourths of the several States within seven years from the date of its submission to the States by the Congress.

AMENDMENT XXIII (1961)

Section 1

The District constituting the seat of Government of the United States shall appoint in such manner as the Congress may direct:

A number of electors of President and Vice President equal to the whole number of Senators and Representatives in Congress to which the District would be entitled if it were a State, but in no event more than the least populous State; they shall be in addition to those appointed by the States, but they shall be considered, for the purposes of the election of President and Vice President, to be electors appointed by a State; and they shall meet in the District and perform such duties as provided by the twelfth article of amendment.

Section 2

The Congress shall have power to enforce this article by appropriate legislation.

AMENDMENT XXIV (1964)

Section 1
The right of citizens of the United States to vote in any primary or other election for President or Vice President, for electors for President or Vice President, or for Senator or Representative in Congress, shall not be denied or abridged by the United States or any State by reason of failure to pay any poll tax or other tax.

Section 2
The Congress shall have power to enforce this article by appropriate legislation.

AMENDMENT XXV (1967)

Section 1
In case of the removal of the President from office or of his death or resignation, the Vice President shall become President.

Section 2
Whenever there is a vacancy in the office of the Vice President, the President shall nominate a Vice President who shall take office upon confirmation by a majority vote of both Houses of Congress.

Section 3
Whenever the President transmits to the President pro tempore of the Senate and the Speaker of the House of Representatives his written declaration that he is unable to discharge the powers and duties of his office, and until he transmits to them a written declaration to the contrary, such powers and duties shall be discharged by the Vice President as Acting President.

Section 4
Whenever the Vice President and a majority of either the principal officers of the executive departments or of such other body as Congress may by law provide, transmit to the President pro tempore of the Senate and the Speaker of the House of Representatives their written declaration that the President is unable to discharge the powers and duties of his office, the Vice President shall immediately assume the powers and duties of the office as Acting President.

Thereafter, when the President transmits to the President pro tempore of the Senate and the Speaker of the House of Representatives his written declaration that no inability exists, he shall resume the powers and duties of his Office unless the Vice President and a majority of either the principal officers of the executive department or of such other body as Congress may by law provide, transmit within four days to the President pro tempore of the Senate and the Speaker of the House of Representatives their written declaration that the President is unable to discharge the powers and duties of his office. Thereupon Congress shall decide the issue, assembling within forty-eight hours for that purpose if not in session. If the Congress, within twenty-one days after receipt of the latter written declaration, or, if Congress is not in session, within twenty-one days after Congress is required to assemble, determines by two-thirds vote of both Houses that the President is unable to discharge the powers and duties of his office, the Vice President shall continue to discharge the same as Acting President; otherwise, the President shall resume the powers and duties of his office.

AMENDMENT XXVI (1971)

Section 1
The right of citizens of the United States, who are eighteen years of age or older, to vote shall not be denied or abridged by the United States or by any State on account of age.

Section 2
The Congress shall have power to enforce this article by appropriate legislation.

AMENDMENT XXVII (1992)

No law varying the compensation for services of the Senators and Representatives shall take effect until an election of representatives shall have intervened.

APPENDIX B

The Foreign Corrupt Practices Act (Excerpts)

15 U.S.C. § 78dd-1

§ 78dd-1. Prohibited foreign trade practices by issuers (15 U.S.C. § 78dd-2)

(a) Prohibition

It shall be unlawful for any issuer which has a class of securities registered pursuant to section 78l of this title or which is required to file reports under section 78o(d) of this title, or for any officer, director, employee, or agent of such issuer or any stockholder thereof acting on behalf of such issuer, to make use of the mails or any means or instrumentality of interstate commerce corruptly in furtherance of an offer, payment, promise to pay, or authorization of the payment of any money, or offer, gift, promise to give, or authorization of the giving of anything of value to—

(1) any foreign official for purposes of—

(A)(i) influencing any act or decision of such foreign official in his official capacity, (ii) inducing such foreign official to do or omit to do any act in violation of the lawful duty of such official, or (iii) securing any improper advantage; or

(B) inducing such foreign official to use his influence with a foreign government or instrumentality thereof to affect or influence any act or decision of such government or instrumentality, in order to assist such issuer in obtaining or retaining business for or with, or directing business to, any person;

(2) any foreign political party or official thereof or any candidate for foreign political office for purposes of—

(A)(i) influencing any act or decision of such party, official, or candidate in its or his official capacity, (ii) inducing such party, official, or candidate to do or omit to do an act in violation of the lawful duty of such party, official, or candidate, or (iii) securing any improper advantage; or

(B) inducing such party, official, or candidate to use its or his influence with a foreign government

or instrumentality thereof to affect or influence any act or decision of such government or instrumentality, in order to assist such issuer in obtaining or retaining business for or with, or directing business to, any person; or

(3) any person, while knowing that all or a portion of such money or thing of value will be offered, given, or promised, directly or indirectly, to any foreign official, to any foreign political party or official thereof, or to any candidate for foreign political office, for purposes of—

(A)(i) influencing any act or decision of such foreign official, political party, party official, or candidate in his or its official capacity, (ii) inducing such foreign official, political party, party official, or candidate to do or omit to do any act in violation of the lawful duty of such foreign official, political party, party official, or candidate, or (iii) securing any improper advantage; or

(B) inducing such foreign official, political party, party official, or candidate to use his or its influence with a foreign government or instrumentality thereof to affect or influence any act or decision of such government or instrumentality, in order to assist such issuer in obtaining or retaining business for or with, or directing business to, any person.

(b) Exception for routine governmental action

Subsections (a) and (g) of this section shall not apply to any facilitating or expediting payment to a foreign official, political party, or party official the purpose of which is to expedite or to secure the performance of a routine governmental action by a foreign official, political party, or party official.

(c) Affirmative defenses

It shall be an affirmative defense to actions under subsection (a) or (g) of this section that—

(1) the payment, gift, offer, or promise of anything of value that was made, was lawful under the written laws and regulations of the foreign official's, political party's, party official's, or candidate's country; or

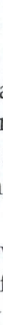

(2) the payment, gift, offer, or promise of anything of value that was made, was a reasonable and bona fide expenditure, such as travel and lodging expenses, incurred by or on behalf of a foreign official, party, party official, or candidate and was directly related to—

(A) the promotion, demonstration, or explanation of products or services; or

(B) the execution or performance of a contract with a foreign government or agency thereof.

15 U.S.C. § 78dd-2

(g) Penalties

(1)(A) Any domestic concern that is not a natural person and that violates subsection (a) or (i) of this section shall be fined not more than $2,000,000.

(B) Any domestic concern that is not a natural person and that violates subsection (a) or (i) of this section shall be subject to a civil penalty of not more than $10,000 imposed in an action brought by the Attorney General.

(2)(A) Any natural person that is an officer, director, employee, or agent of a domestic concern, or stockholder acting on behalf of such domestic concern, who willfully violates subsection (a) or (i) of this section shall be fined not more than $100,000 or imprisoned not more than 5 years, or both.

(B) Any natural person that is an officer, director, employee, or agent of a domestic concern, or stockholder acting on behalf of such domestic concern, who violates subsection (a) or (i) of this section shall be subject to a civil penalty of not more than $10,000 imposed in an action brought by the Attorney General.

(3) Whenever a fine is imposed under paragraph (2) upon any officer, director, employee, agent, or stockholder of a domestic concern, such fine may not be paid, directly or indirectly, by such domestic concern.

(h) Definitions

For purposes of this section:

(1) The term "domestic concern" means—

(A) any individual who is a citizen, national, or resident of the United States; and

(B) any corporation, partnership, association, joint-stock company, business trust, unincorporated organization, or sole proprietorship which

has its principal place of business in the United States, or which is organized under the laws of a State of the United States or a territory, possession, or commonwealth of the United States.

(2)(A) The term "foreign official" means any officer or employee of a foreign government or any department, agency, or instrumentality thereof, or of a public international organization, or any person acting in an official capacity for or on behalf of any such government or department, agency, or instrumentality, or for or on behalf of any such public international organization.

(B) For purposes of subparagraph (A), the term "public international organization" means—

(i) an organization that is designated by Executive order pursuant to section 1 of the International Organizations Immunities Act (22 U.S.C. 288); or

(ii) any other international organization that is designated by the President by Executive order for the purposes of this section, effective as of the date of publication of such order in the Federal Register.

(3)(A) A person's state of mind is "knowing" with respect to conduct, a circumstance, or a result if—

(i) such person is aware that such person is engaging in such conduct, that such circumstance exists, or that such result is substantially certain to occur; or

(ii) such person has a firm belief that such circumstance exists or that such result is substantially certain to occur.

(B) When knowledge of the existence of a particular circumstance is required for an offense, such knowledge is established if a person is aware of a high probability of the existence of such circumstance, unless the person actually believes that such circumstance does not exist.

(4)(A) The term "routine governmental action" means only an action which is ordinarily and commonly performed by a foreign official in—

(i) obtaining permits, licenses, or other official documents to qualify a person to do business in a foreign country;

(ii) processing governmental papers, such as visas and work orders;

(iii) providing police protection, mail pick-up and delivery, or scheduling inspections associated with contract performance or inspections related to transit of goods across country;

(iv) providing phone service, power and water supply, loading and unloading cargo, or protecting perishable products or commodities from deterioration; or

(v) actions of a similar nature.

(B) The term "routine governmental action" does not include any decision by a foreign official whether, or on what terms, to award new business to or to continue business with a particular party, or any action taken by a foreign official involved in the decision-making process to encourage a decision to award new business to or continue business with a particular party.

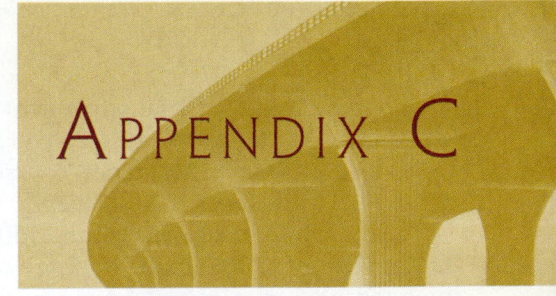

APPENDIX C

The Uniform Commercial Code (Excerpts)*

PART 1. SHORT TITLE, GENERAL CONSTRUCTION AND SUBJECT MATTER

§ 2–106. Definitions: "Contract"; "Agreement"; "Contract for Sale"; "Sale"; "Present Sale"

(1) In this Article unless the context otherwise requires "contract" and "agreement" are limited to those relating to the present or future sale of goods. "Contract for sale" includes both a present sale of goods and a contract to sell goods at a future time. A "sale" consists in the passing of title from the seller to the buyer for a price (Section 2-401). A "present sale" means a sale which is accomplished by the making of the contract.
[Note: Some notations appear regarding the Revised UCC Article 2. Because Revised UCC Article 2 has enjoyed limited adoption, it is not included here.]

PART 2. FORM, FORMATION AND READJUSTMENT OF CONTRACT

§ 2–201. Formal Requirements; Statute of Frauds

(1) Except as otherwise provided in this section a contract for the sale of goods for the price of $500 or more is not enforceable by way of action or defense unless there is some writing sufficient to indicate that a contract for sale has been made between the parties and signed by the party against whom enforcement is sought or by his authorized agent or broker. A writing is not insufficient because it omits or incorrectly states a term agreed upon but the contract is not enforceable under this paragraph beyond the quantity of goods shown in such writing.

(2) Between merchants if within a reasonable time a writing in confirmation of the contract and sufficient against the sender is received and the party receiving it has reason to know its contents, it satisfies the requirements of subsection (1) against such party unless written notice of objection to its contents is given within 10 days after it is received.

(3) A contract which does not satisfy the requirements of subsection (1) but which is valid in other respects is enforceable

(a) if the goods are to be specially manufactured for the buyer and are not suitable for sale to others in the ordinary course of the seller's business and the seller, before notice of repudiation is received and under circumstances which reasonably indicate that the goods are for the buyer, has made either a substantial beginning of their manufacture or commitments for their procurement; or

(b) if the party against whom enforcement is sought admits in his pleading, testimony or otherwise in court that a contract for sale was made, but the contract is not enforceable under this provision beyond the quantity of goods admitted; or

(c) with respect to goods for which payment has been made and accepted or which have been received and accepted (Sec. 2-606).

§ 2–202. Final Written Expression: Parol or Extrinsic Evidence

Terms with respect to which the confirmatory memoranda of the parties agree or which are otherwise set forth in a writing intended by the parties as a final expression of their agreement with respect to such terms as are included therein may not be contradicted by evidence of any prior agreement or of a contemporaneous oral agreement but may be explained or supplemented

(a) by course of performance, course of dealing, or usage of trade (Section 1-303); and

(b) by evidence of consistent additional terms unless the court finds the writing to have been intended also as a complete and exclusive statement of the terms of the agreement.

§ 2–204. Formation in General

(1) A contract for sale of goods may be made in any manner sufficient to show agreement, including conduct by both parties which recognizes the existence of such a contract.

(2) An agreement sufficient to constitute a contract for sale may be found even though the moment of its making is undetermined.

(3) Even though one or more terms are left open a contract for sale does not fail for indefiniteness if the parties have intended to make a contract and there is a reasonably certain basis for giving an appropriate remedy.

§ 2–205. Firm Offers

An offer by a merchant to buy or sell goods in a signed writing which by its terms gives assurance that it will be held open is not revocable, for lack of consideration, during the time stated or if no time is stated for a reasonable time, but in no event may such period of irrevocability exceed three months; but any such term of assurance on a form supplied by the offeree must be separately signed by the offeror.

§ 2–207. Additional Terms in Acceptance or Confirmation

(1) A definite and seasonable expression of acceptance or a written confirmation which is sent within a reasonable time operates as an acceptance even though it states terms additional to or different from those offered or agreed upon, unless acceptance is expressly made conditional on assent to the additional or different terms.

(2) The additional terms are to be construed as proposals for addition to the contract. Between merchants such terms become part of the contract unless:

(a) the offer expressly limits acceptance to the terms of the offer;

(b) they materially alter it; or

(c) notification of objection to them has already been given or is given within a reasonable time after notice of them is received.

(3) Conduct by both parties which recognizes the existence of a contract is sufficient to establish a contract for sale although the writings of the parties do not otherwise establish a contract. In such case the terms of the particular contract consist of those terms on which the writings of the parties agree, together with any supplementary terms incorporated under any other provisions of this Act.

§ 2–209. Modification, Rescission and Waiver

(1) An agreement modifying a contract within this Article needs no consideration to be binding.

(2) A signed agreement which excludes modification or rescission except by a signed writing cannot be otherwise modified or rescinded, but except as between merchants such a requirement on a form supplied by the merchant must be separately signed by the other party.

(3) The requirements of the statute of frauds section of this Article (Section 2-201) must be satisfied if the contract as modified is within its provisions.

§ 2–211. Legal Recognition of Electronic Contracts, Records and Signatures (Revised UCC) (Completely new section) (Some states have adopted some version of this electronic signature section)

(1) A record or signature may not be denied legal effect or enforceability solely because it is in electronic form.

(2) A contract may not be denied legal effect or enforceability solely because an electronic record was used in its formation.

(3) This article does not require a record or signature to be created, generated, sent, communicated, received, stored, or otherwise processed by electronic means or in electronic form.

(4) A contract formed by the interaction of an individual and an electronic agent under Section 2–204(4)(b) does not include terms provided by the individual if the individual had reason to know that the agent could not react to the terms as provided.

§ 2–213. Electronic Communication (Revised UCC) (Completely new section)

(1) If the receipt of an electronic communication has a legal effect, it has that effect even though no individual is aware of its receipt.

(2) Receipt of an electronic acknowledgment of an electronic communication establishes that the

communication was received but, in itself, does not establish that the content sent corresponds to the content received.

PART 3 GENERAL OBLIGATION AND CONSTRUCTION OF CONTRACT

§ 2–302. Unconscionable Contract or Term

(1) If the court as a matter of law finds the contract or any clause of the contract to have been unconscionable at the time it was made the court may refuse to enforce the contract, or it may enforce the remainder of the contract without the unconscionable clause, or it may so limit the application of any unconscionable clause as to avoid any unconscionable result.

(2) When it is claimed or appears to the court that the contract or any clause thereof may be unconscionable the parties shall be afforded a reasonable opportunity to present evidence as to its commercial setting, purpose and effect to aid the court in making the determination.

§ 2–312. Warranty of Title and Against Infringement; Buyer's Obligation Against Infringement

(1) Subject to subsection (2) there is in a contract for sale a warranty by the seller that

　　(a) the title conveyed shall be good, and its transfer rightful; and

　　(b) the goods shall be delivered free from any security interest or other lien or encumbrance of which the buyer at the time of contracting has no knowledge.

(2) A warranty under subsection (1) will be excluded or modified only by specific language or by circumstances which give the buyer reason to know that the person selling does not claim title in himself or that he is purporting to sell only such right or title as he or a third person may have.

(3) Unless otherwise agreed a seller who is a merchant regularly dealing in goods of the kind warrants that the goods shall be delivered free of the rightful claim of any third person by way of infringement or the like but a buyer who furnishes specifications to the seller must hold the seller harmless against any such claim which arises out of compliance with the specifications.

§ 2–313. Express Warranties by Affirmation, Promise, Description

(1) Express warranties by the seller are created as follows:

　　(a) Any affirmation of fact or promise made by the seller to the buyer which relates to the goods and becomes part of the basis of the bargain creates an express warranty that the goods shall conform to the affirmation or promise.

　　(b) Any description of the goods which is made part of the basis of the bargain creates an express warranty that the goods shall conform to the description.

　　(c) Any sample or model which is made part of the basis of the bargain creates an express warranty that the whole of the goods shall conform to the sample or model.

(2) It is not necessary to the creation of an express warranty that the seller use formal words such as "warrant" or "guarantee" or that he have a specific intention to make a warranty, but an affirmation merely of the value of the goods or a statement purporting to be merely the seller's opinion or commendation of the goods does not create a warranty.

§ 2–314. Implied Warranty: Merchantability; Usage of Trade

(1) Unless excluded or modified (Section 2-316), a warranty that the goods shall be merchantable is implied in a contract for their sale if the seller is a merchant with respect to goods of that kind. Under this section the serving for value of food or drink to be consumed either on the premises or elsewhere is a sale.

(2) Goods to be merchantable must be at least such as

　　(a) pass without objection in the trade under the contract description; and

　　(b) in the case of fungible goods, are of fair average quality within the description; and

　　(c) are fit for the ordinary purposes for which such goods are used; and

　　(d) run, within the variations permitted by the agreement, of even kind, quality and quantity within each unit and among all units involved; and

　　(e) are adequately contained, packaged, and labeled as the agreement may require; and

　　(f) conform to the promise or affirmations of fact made on the container or label if any.

(3) Unless excluded or modified (Section 2-316) other implied warranties may arise from course of dealing or usage of trade.

§ 2–315. Implied Warranty: Fitness for Particular Purpose

Where the seller at the time of contracting has reason to know any particular purpose for which the goods are required and that the buyer is relying on the seller's skill or judgment to select or furnish suitable goods, there is unless excluded or modified under the next section an implied warranty that the goods shall be fit for such purpose.

§ 2–316. Exclusion or Modification of Warranties

(1) Words or conduct relevant to the creation of an express warranty and words or conduct tending to negate or limit warranty shall be construed wherever reasonable as consistent with each other; but subject to the provisions of this Article on parol or extrinsic evidence (Section 2-202) negation or limitation is inoperative to the extent that such construction is unreasonable.

(2) Subject to subsection (3), to exclude or modify the implied warranty of merchantability or any part of it the language must mention merchantability and in case of a writing must be conspicuous, and to exclude or modify any implied warranty of fitness the exclusion must be by a writing and conspicuous. Language to exclude all implied warranties of fitness is sufficient if it states, for example, that "There are no warranties which extend beyond the description on the face hereof."

(3) Notwithstanding subsection (2)

(a) unless the circumstances indicate otherwise, all implied warranties are excluded by expressions like "as is", "with all faults" or other language which in common understanding calls the buyer's attention to the exclusion of warranties and makes plain that there is no implied warranty; and

(b) when the buyer before entering into the contract has examined the goods or the sample or model as fully as he desired or has refused to examine the goods there is no implied warranty with regard to defects which an examination ought in the circumstances to have revealed to him; and

(c) an implied warranty can also be excluded or modified by course of dealing or course of performance or usage of trade.

(4) Remedies for breach of warranty can be limited in accordance with the provisions of this Article on liquidation or limitation of damages and on contractual modification of remedy (Sections 2-718 and 2-719).

§ 2–318. Third Party Beneficiaries of Warranties Express or Implied

Alternative A

A seller's warranty whether express or implied extends to any natural person who is in the family or household of his buyer or who is a guest in his home if it is reasonable to expect that such person may use, consume or be affected by the goods and who is injured in person by breach of the warranty. A seller may not exclude or limit the operation of this section.

Alternative B

A seller's warranty whether express or implied extends to any natural person who may reasonably be expected to use, consume or be affected by the goods and who is injured in person by breach of the warranty. A seller may not exclude or limit the operation of this section.

Alternative C

A seller's warranty whether express or implied extends to any person who may reasonably be expected to use, consume or be affected by the goods and who is injured by breach of the warranty. A seller may not exclude or limit the operation of this section with respect to injury to the person of an individual to whom the warranty extends.

§ 2–615. Excuse By Failure of Presupposed Conditions

Except so far as a seller may have assumed a greater obligation and subject to the preceding section on substituted performance:

(a) Delay in delivery or non-delivery in whole or in part by a seller who complies with paragraphs (b) and (c) is not a breach of his duty under a contract for sale if performance as agreed has been made impracticable by the occurrence of a contingency the non-occurrence of which was a basic assumption on which the contract was made or by compliance in good faith with any applicable foreign or domestic governmental regulation or order whether or not it later proves to be invalid.

(b) Where the causes mentioned in paragraph (a) affect only a part of the seller's capacity to perform, he must allocate production and deliveries among his customers but may at his option include regular customers not then under contract as well as his own requirements for further manufacture.

He may so allocate in any manner which is fair and reasonable.

(c) The seller must notify the buyer seasonably that there will be delay or non-delivery and, when allocation is required under paragraph (b), of the estimated quota thus made available for the buyer.

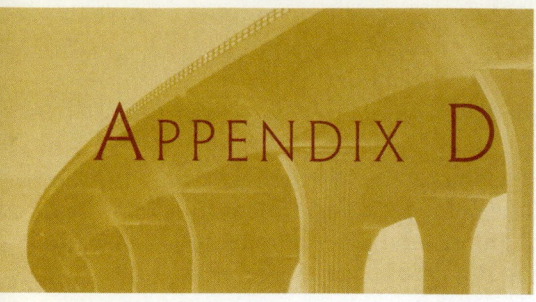

APPENDIX D

Dodd-Frank (Wall Street Reform and Consumer Financial Protection Act) Key Provisions

CORPORATE GOVERNANCE (15 U.S.C. § 78n-2)

Not later than 180 days after July 21, 2010, the Commission shall issue rules that require an issuer to disclose in the annual proxy sent to investors the reasons why the issuer has chosen—

(1) the same person to serve as chairman of the board of directors and chief executive officer (or in equivalent positions); or

(2) different individuals to serve as chairman of the board of directors and chief executive officer (or in equivalent positions of the issuer).

WHISTLEBLOWER PROTECTION (15 U.S.C. § 78u-7)

§ 78u-7. Implementation and transition provisions for whistleblower protection

(a) Implementing rules

The Commission shall issue final regulations implementing the provisions of section 78u-6 of this title, not later than 270 days after July 21, 2010. (Note: As of September 2013, the Commission (SEC) had implemented only 47 percent of the rules required for Dodd-Frank.)

(b) Original information

Information provided to the Commission in writing by a whistleblower shall not lose the status of original information (as defined in section 78u-6(a)(3) of this title) solely because the whistleblower provided the information prior to the effective date of the regulations, if the information is provided by the whistleblower after July 21, 2010.

(c) Awards

A whistleblower may receive an award pursuant to section 78u-6 of this title, regardless of whether any violation of a provision of the securities laws, or a rule or regulation thereunder, underlying the judicial or administrative action upon which the award is based, occurred prior to July 21, 2010.

SECURITIES WHISTLEBLOWER INCENTIVES AND PROTECTION (15 U.S.C § 78u-6)

In any covered judicial or administrative action, or related action, the Commission, under regulations prescribed by the Commission and subject to subsection (c), shall pay an award or awards to 1 or more whistleblowers who voluntarily provided original information to the Commission that led to the successful enforcement of the covered judicial or administrative action, or related action, in an aggregate amount equal to—

(A) not less than 10 percent, in total, of what has been collected of the monetary sanctions imposed in the action or related actions; and

(B) not more than 30 percent, in total, of what has been collected of the monetary sanctions imposed in the action or related actions.

RECOVERY OF ERRONEOUSLY AWARDED COMPENSATION POLICY (15 U.S.C. § 78j-4)

The Commission shall, by rule, direct the national securities exchanges and national securities associations to prohibit the listing of any security of an issuer that does not comply with the requirements of this section.

(b) Recovery of funds

The rules of the Commission under subsection (a) shall require each issuer to develop and implement a policy providing—

(1) for disclosure of the policy of the issuer on incentive-based compensation that is based on financial information required to be reported under the securities laws; and

(2) that, in the event that the issuer is required to prepare an accounting restatement due to the material noncompliance of the issuer with any financial reporting requirement under the securities

laws, the issuer will recover from any current or former executive officer of the issuer who received incentive-based compensation (including stock options awarded as compensation) during the 3-year period preceding the date on which the issuer is required to prepare an accounting restatement, based on the erroneous data, in excess of what would have been paid to the executive officer under the accounting restatement.

SEC. 917. STUDY REGARDING FINANCIAL LITERACY AMONG INVESTORS

(a) IN GENERAL.—The Commission shall conduct a study to identify—

(1) the existing level of financial literacy among retail investors, including subgroups of investors identified by the Commission;

(2) methods to improve the timing, content, and format of disclosures to investors with respect to financial intermediaries, investment products, and investment services;

(3) the most useful and understandable relevant information that retail investors need to make informed financial decisions before engaging a financial intermediary or purchasing an investment product or service that is typically sold to retail investors, including shares of open-end companies, as that term is defined in section 5 of the Investment Company Act of 1940 (15 U.S.C. 80a–5) that are registered under section 8 of that Act;

(4) methods to increase the transparency of expenses and conflicts of interests in transactions involving investment services and products, including shares of open-end companies described in paragraph (3);

(5) the most effective existing private and public efforts to educate investors; and

(6) in consultation with the Financial Literacy and Education Commission, a strategy (including, to the extent practicable, measurable goals and objectives) to increase the financial literacy of investors in order to bring about a positive change in investor behavior.

SECTION 929X. SHORT SALE REFORMS (15 U.S.C. § 78m(f))

(d) TRANSACTIONS RELATING TO SHORT SALES OF SECURITIES.—

It shall be unlawful for any person, directly or indirectly, by the use of the mails or any means or instrumentality of interstate commerce, or of any facility of any national securities exchange, or for any member of a national securities exchange to effect, alone or with one or more other persons, a manipulative short sale of any security. The Commission shall issue such other rules as are necessary or appropriate to ensure that the appropriate enforcement options and remedies are available for violations of this subsection in the public interest or for the protection of investors.

SEC. 1403. PROHIBITION ON STEERING INCENTIVES

Section 129B of the Truth in Lending Act (as added by section 1402(a)) is amended by inserting after subsection (b) the following new subsection:

(c) PROHIBITION ON STEERING INCENTIVES.—

(1) IN GENERAL.—For any residential mortgage loan, no mortgage originator shall receive from any person and no person shall pay to a mortgage originator, directly or indirectly, compensation that varies based on the terms of the loan (other than the amount of the principal).

(2) RESTRUCTURING OF FINANCING ORIGINATION FEE.—

(A) IN GENERAL.—For any mortgage loan, a mortgage originator may not receive from any person other than the consumer and no person, other than the consumer, who knows or has reason to know that a consumer has directly compensated or will directly compensate a mortgage originator may pay a mortgage originator any origination fee or charge except bona fide third party charges not retained by the creditor, mortgage originator, or an affiliate of the creditor or mortgage originator.

SUBTITLE B—MINIMUM STANDARDS FOR MORTGAGES

SEC. 1411. ABILITY TO REPAY

(a) IN GENERAL.—

(1) RULE OF CONSTRUCTION.—No regulation, order, or guidance issued by the Bureau under this title shall be construed as requiring a depository institution to apply mortgage underwriting standards that do not meet the minimum underwriting standards required by the appropriate prudential regulator of the depository institution.

(2) AMENDMENT TO TRUTH IN LENDING ACT.—Chapter 2 of the Truth in Lending Act (15 U.S.C. 1631 et seq.) is amended by inserting after section 129B (as added by section 1402(a)) the following new section:

§ 129C. Minimum standards for residential mortgage loans

(a) ABILITY TO REPAY.—

(1) IN GENERAL.—In accordance with regulations prescribed by the Board, no creditor may make a residential mortgage loan unless the creditor makes a reasonable and good faith determination based on verified and documented information that, at the time the loan is consummated, the consumer has a reasonable ability to repay the loan, according to its terms, and all applicable taxes, insurance (including mortgage guarantee insurance), and assessments.

(2) MULTIPLE LOANS.—If the creditor knows, or has reason to know, that 1 or more residential mortgage loans secured H. R. 4173—768 by the same dwelling will be made to the same consumer, the creditor shall make a reasonable and good faith determination, based on verified and documented information, that the consumer has a reasonable ability to repay the combined payments of all loans on the same dwelling according to the terms of those loans and all applicable taxes, insurance (including mortgage guarantee insurance), and assessments.

(3) BASIS FOR DETERMINATION.—A determination under this subsection of a consumer's ability to repay a residential mortgage loan shall include consideration of the consumer's credit history, current income, expected income the consumer is reasonably assured of receiving, current obligations, debt to-income ratio or the residual income the consumer will have after paying non-mortgage debt and mortgage-related obligations, employment status, and other financial resources other than the consumer's equity in the dwelling or real property that secures repayment of the loan. A creditor shall determine the ability of the consumer to repay using a payment schedule that fully amortizes the loan over the term of the loan.

(4) INCOME VERIFICATION.—A creditor making a residential mortgage loan shall verify amounts of income or assets that such creditor relies on to determine repayment ability, including expected income or assets, by reviewing the consumer's Internal Revenue Service Form W–2, tax returns, payroll receipts, financial institution records, or other third-party documents that provide reasonably reliable evidence of the consumer's income or assets. In order to safeguard against fraudulent reporting, any consideration of a consumer's income history in making a determination under this subsection shall include the verification of such income by the use of—

(A) Internal Revenue Service transcripts of tax returns; or

(B) a method that quickly and effectively verifies income documentation by a third party subject to rules prescribed by the Board.

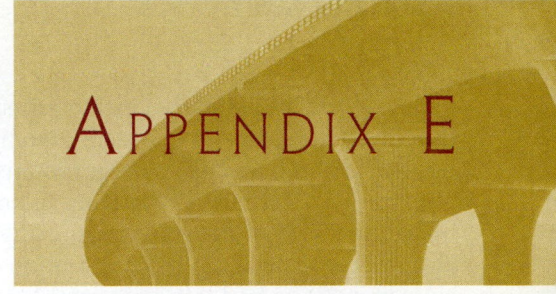

The Securities Act of 1933 and the Securities Exchange Act of 1934 (Excerpts)

SECURITIES ACT OF 1933

Civil Liabilities on Account of False Registration Statement (15 U.S.C. § 77k)
SECTION 11.

(a) In case any part of the registration statement, when such part became effective, contained an untrue statement of a material fact or omitted to state a material fact required to be stated therein or necessary to make the statements therein not misleading, any person acquiring such security (unless it is proved that at the time of such acquisition he knew of such untruth or omission) may, either at law or in equity, in any court of competent jurisdiction, sue—

(1) every person who signed the registration statement;

(2) every person who was a director of (or person performing similar functions) or partner in, the issuer at the time of the filing of the part of the registration statement with respect to which his liability is asserted;

(3) every person who, with his consent, is named in the registration statement as being or about to become a director, person performing similar functions, or partner;

(4) every accountant, engineer, or appraiser, or any person whose profession gives authority to a statement made by him, who has with his consent been named as having prepared or certified any part of the registration statement, or as having prepared or certified any report or valuation which is used in connection with the registration statement, with respect to the statement in such registration statement, report, or valuation, which purports to have been prepared or certified by him;

(5) every underwriter with respect to such security.

If such person acquired the security after the issuer has made generally available to its security holders an earning statement covering a period of at least twelve months beginning after the effective date of the registration statement, then the right of recovery under this subsection shall be conditioned on proof that such person acquired the security relying upon such untrue statement in the registration statement or relying upon the registration statement and not knowing of such omission, but such reliance may be established without proof of the reading of the registration statement by such person.

(b) Persons exempt from liability upon proof of issues

Notwithstanding the provisions of subsection (a) no person, other than the issuer, shall be liable as provided therein who shall sustain the burden of proof—

(1) that before the effective date of the part of the registration statement with respect to which his liability is asserted (A) he had resigned from or had taken such steps as are permitted by law to resign from, or ceased or refused to act in, every office, capacity, or relationship in which he was described in the registration statement as acting or agreeing to act, and (B) he had advised the Commission and the issuer in writing that he had taken such action and that he would not be responsible for such part of the registration statement; or

(2) that if such part of the registration statement became effective without his knowledge, upon becoming aware of such fact he forthwith acted and advised the Commission, in accordance with paragraph (1), and, in addition, gave reasonable public notice that such part of the registration statement had become effective without his knowledge; or

(3) that (A) as regards any part of the registration statement not purporting to be made on the authority of an expert, and not purporting to be a copy of or extract from a report or valuation of an expert, and not purporting to be made on the authority of a public or official document or statement, he had, after reasonable investigation, reasonable ground to believe and did believe, at the time such part of the registration statement became effective, that the statements therein were true and that there was no

omission to state a material fact required to be stated therein or necessary to make the statements therein not misleading; and (B) as regards any part of the registration statement purporting to be made upon his authority as an expert or purporting to be a copy of or extract from a report or valuation of himself as an expert, (i) he had, after reasonable investigation, reasonable ground to believe and did believe, at the time such part of the registration statement became effective, that the statements therein were true and that there was no omission to state a material fact required to be stated therein or necessary to make the statements therein not misleading, or (ii) such part of the registration statement did not fairly represent his statement as an expert or was not a fair copy of or extract from his report or valuation as an expert; and (C) as regards any part of the registration statement purporting to be made on the authority of an expert (other than himself) or purporting to be a copy of or extract from a report or valuation of an expert (other than himself), he had no reasonable ground to believe and did not believe, at the time such part of the registration statement became effective, that the statements therein were untrue or that there was an omission to state a material fact required to be stated therein or necessary to make the statements therein not misleading, or that such part of the registration statement did not fairly represent the statement of the expert or was not a fair copy of or extract from the report or valuation of the expert; and (D) as regards any part of the registration statement purporting to be a statement made by an official person or purporting to be a copy of or extract from a public official document, he had no reasonable ground to believe and did not believe, at the time such part of the registration statement became effective, that the statements therein were untrue, or that there was an omission to state a material fact required to be stated therein or necessary to make the statements therein not misleading, or that such part of the registration statement did not fairly represent the statement made by the official person or was not a fair copy of or extract from the public official document.

(c) Standard of reasonableness

In determining, for the purpose of paragraph (3) of subsection (b) of this section, what constitutes reasonable investigation and reasonable ground for belief, the standard of reasonableness shall be that required of a prudent man in the management of his own property.

Civil Liabilities Arising in Connection with Prospectuses and Communications (15 U.S.C. § 77l)

SECTION 12.

(a) In general

Any person who—(1) offers or sells a security in violation of section 77e or

(2) offers or sells a security (whether or not exempted by the provisions of section 77c other than paragraph (2) of subsection (a) of said section), by the use of any means or instruments of transportation or communication in interstate commerce or of the mails, by means of a prospectus or oral communication, which includes an untrue statement of a material fact or omits to state a material fact necessary in order to make the statements, in the light of the circumstances under which they were made, not misleading (the purchaser not knowing of such untruth or omission), and who shall not sustain the burden of proof that he did not know, and in the exercise of reasonable care could not have known, of such untruth or omission, shall be liable to the person purchasing such security from him, who may sue either at law or in equity in any court of competent jurisdiction, to recover the consideration paid for such security with interest thereon, less the amount of any income received thereon, upon the tender of such security, or for damages if he no longer owns the security.

Penalties (15 U.S.C. § 77x)

SECTION 24. Any person who willfully violates any of the provisions of this subchapter, or the rules and regulations promulgated by the Commission under authority thereof, or any person who willfully, in a registration statement filed under this subchapter, makes any untrue statement of a material fact or omits to state any material fact required to be stated therein or necessary to make the statements therein not misleading, shall upon conviction be fined not more than $10,000 or imprisoned not more than five years, or both.

SECURITIES EXCHANGE ACT OF 1934

Manipulative and Deceptive Devices (15 U.S.C. § 78j)

SECTION 10. It shall be unlawful for any person, directly or indirectly, by the use of any means or instrumentality of interstate commerce or of the mails, or of any facility of any national securities exchange—

(a) (1) To effect a short sale, or to use or employ any stop-loss order in connection with the purchase or sale, of any security registered on a national securities exchange, in contravention of such rules and regulations as the Commission may prescribe as necessary or appropriate in the public interest or for the protection of investors.

* * * * *

(b) To use or employ, in connection with the purchase or sale of any security registered on a national securities exchange or any security not so registered, any manipulative or deceptive device or contrivance in contravention of such rules and regulations as the Commission may prescribe as necessary or appropriate in the public interest or for the protection of investors.

Audit requirements (15 U.S.C. § 78j-1)

(a) In general

Each audit required pursuant to this chapter of the financial statements of an issuer by a registered public accounting firm shall include, in accordance with generally accepted auditing standards, as may be modified or supplemented from time to time by the Commission—

(1) procedures designed to provide reasonable assurance of detecting illegal acts that would have a direct and material effect on the determination of financial statement amounts;

(2) procedures designed to identify related party transactions that are material to the financial statements or otherwise require disclosure therein; and

(3) an evaluation of whether there is substantial doubt about the ability of the issuer to continue as a going concern during the ensuing fiscal year.

(b) Required response to audit discoveries

(1) Investigation and report to management

If, in the course of conducting an audit pursuant to this chapter to which subsection (a) of this section applies, the registered public accounting firm detects or otherwise becomes aware of information indicating that an illegal act (whether or not perceived to have a material effect on the financial statements of the issuer) has or may have occurred, the firm shall, in accordance with generally accepted auditing standards, as may be modified or supplemented from time to time by the Commission—

(A) (i) determine whether it is likely that an illegal act has occurred; and

(ii) if so, determine and consider the possible effect of the illegal act on the financial statements of the issuer, including any contingent monetary effects, such as fines, penalties, and damages; and

(B) as soon as practicable, inform the appropriate level of the management of the issuer and assure that the audit committee of the issuer, or the board of directors of the issuer in the absence of such a committee, is adequately informed with respect to illegal acts that have been detected or have otherwise come to the attention of such firm in the course of the audit, unless the illegal act is clearly inconsequential.

(2) Response to failure to take remedial action

If, after determining that the audit committee of the board of directors of the issuer, or the board of directors of the issuer in the absence of an audit committee, is adequately informed with respect to illegal acts that have been detected or have otherwise come to the attention of the firm in the course of the audit of such firm, the registered public accounting firm concludes that—

(A) the illegal act has a material effect on the financial statements of the issuer;

(B) the senior management has not taken, and the board of directors has not caused senior management to take, timely and appropriate remedial actions with respect to the illegal act; and

(C) the failure to take remedial action is reasonably expected to warrant departure from a standard report of the auditor, when made, or warrant resignation from the audit engagement; the registered public accounting firm shall, as soon as practicable, directly report its conclusions to the board of directors.

(3) Notice to Commission; response to failure to notify

An issuer whose board of directors receives a report under paragraph (2) shall inform the Commission by notice not later than 1 business day after the receipt of such report and shall furnish the registered public accounting firm making such report with a copy of the notice furnished to the Commission. If the registered public accounting firm fails to receive a copy of the notice before the expiration of the required 1-business-day period, the registered public accounting firm shall—

(A) resign from the engagement; or

(B) furnish to the Commission a copy of its report (or the documentation of any oral report given) not later than 1 business day following such failure to receive notice.

(4) Report after resignation

If a registered public accounting firm resigns from an engagement under paragraph (3)(A), the firm shall, not later than 1 business day following the failure by the issuer to notify the Commission under paragraph (3), furnish to the Commission a copy of the report of the firm (or the documentation of any oral report given).

(c) Auditor liability limitation

No registered public accounting firm shall be liable in a private action for any finding, conclusion, or statement expressed in a report made pursuant to paragraph (3) or (4) of subsection (b) of this section, including any rule promulgated pursuant thereto.

(d) Civil penalties in cease-and-desist proceedings

If the Commission finds, after notice and opportunity for hearing in a proceeding instituted pursuant to section 78u-3 of this title, that a registered public accounting firm has willfully violated paragraph (3) or (4) of subsection (b) of this section, the Commission may, in addition to entering an order under section 78u-3 of this title, impose a civil penalty against the registered public accounting firm and any other person that the Commission finds was a cause of such violation.

Proxies (15 U.S.C. § 78n)

SECTION 14.

(a) It shall be unlawful for any person, by the use of the mails or by any means or instrumentality of interstate commerce or of any facility of a national securities exchange or otherwise, in contravention of such rules and regulations as the Commission may prescribe as necessary or appropriate in the public interest or for the protection of investors, to solicit or to permit the use of his name to solicit any proxy or consent or authorization in respect of any security (other than an exempted security) registered pursuant to section 78(*l*) this title.

Directors, Officers, and Principal Stockholders (15 U.S.C. § 78p)

SEC. 16. DIRECTORS, OFFICERS, AND PRINCIPAL STOCKHOLDERS

(a) DISCLOSURES REQUIRED.—

(1) DIRECTORS, OFFICERS, AND PRINCIPAL STOCKHOLDERS REQUIRED TO FILE.—Every person who is directly or indirectly the beneficial owner of more than 10% of any class of any equity security (other than an exempted security) which is registered pursuant to section 78, or who is a director or an officer of the issuer of such security, shall file the statements required by this subsection with the Commission.

(2) TIME OF FILING.—The statements required by this subsection shall be filed—

(a) at the time of the registration of such security on a national securities exchange or by the effective date of a registration statement filed pursuant to section 78(g) of this title;

(b) within 10 days after he or she becomes such beneficial owner, director, or officer or within such shorter time as the Commission may establish by rule;

(b) Profits from purchase and sale of security within six months

For the purpose of preventing the unfair use of information which may have been obtained by such beneficial owner, director, or officer by reason of his relationship to the issuer, any profit realized by him from any purchase and sale, or any sale and purchase, of any equity security of such issuer (other than an exempted security) within any period of less than six months, unless such security was acquired in good faith in connection with a debt previously contracted, shall inure to and be recoverable by the issuer, irrespective of any intention on the part of such beneficial owner, director, or officer in entering into such transaction of holding the security purchased or of not repurchasing the security sold for a period exceeding six months. Suit to recover such profit may be instituted at law or in equity in any court of competent jurisdiction by the issuer, or by the owner of any security of the issuer in the name and in behalf of the issuer if the issuer …

Liability for Misleading Statements (15 U.S.C. § 78r)

SECTION 18.

(a) Any person who shall make or cause to be made any statement in any application, report, or document filed pursuant to this title or any rule or regulation thereunder or any undertaking contained in a registration statement as provided in subsection (d) of section 78o of this title, which statement was at the time and in the light of the circumstances under which it was made false or misleading with respect to any material fact, shall be liable to any person (not knowing that such statement was false or misleading) who, in reliance upon such statement, shall have purchased or sold a security at a price which was affected by such statement, for damages caused by such reliance, unless the person sued shall prove that he acted in good faith and had no knowledge that such statement was false or misleading. A person seeking to enforce such liability may sue at law or in equity in any court of competent jurisdiction. In any such suit the court may, in its discretion, require an undertaking for the payment of the costs of such suit, and assess reasonable costs, including reasonable attorneys' fees, against either party litigant.

(b) Every person who becomes liable to make payment under this section may recover contribution as in cases of contract from any person who, if joined in the original suit, would have been liable to make the same payment.

(c) No action shall be maintained to enforce any liability created under this section unless brought within one year after the discovery of the facts constituting the cause of action and within three years after such cause of action accrued.

§ 78n-1. Shareholder approval of executive compensation

(a) Separate resolution required

(1) In general

Not less frequently than once every 3 years, a proxy or consent or authorization for an annual or other meeting of the shareholders for which the proxy solicitation rules of the Commission require compensation disclosure shall include a separate resolution subject to shareholder vote to approve the compensation of executives, as disclosed pursuant to section 229.402 of title 17, Code of Federal Regulations, or any successor thereto.

§ 78n-2. Corporate governance

Not later than 180 days after July 21, 2010, the Commission shall issue rules that require an issuer to disclose in the annual proxy sent to investors the reasons why the issuer has chosen—

(1) the same person to serve as chairman of the board of directors and chief executive officer (or in equivalent positions); or

(2) different individuals to serve as chairman of the board of directors and chief executive officer (or in equivalent positions of the issuer).

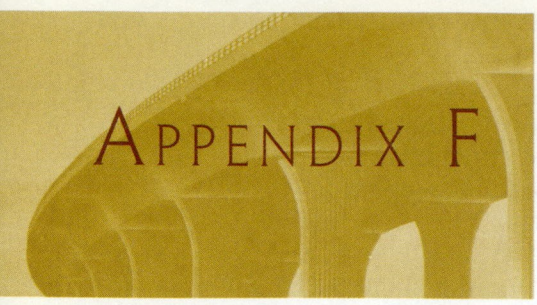

APPENDIX F

Sarbanes-Oxley Key Provisions (Excerpts)

SEE 15 § U.S.C. 78j-1 (B) IN APPENDIX E FOR DETAILS ON AUDIT REQUIREMENTS

SEC. 201. SERVICES OUTSIDE THE SCOPE OF PRACTICE OF AUDITORS

(g) Prohibited activities 15 § U.S.C. 78j-1

Except as provided in subsection (h), it shall be unlawful for a registered public accounting firm (and any associated person of that firm, to the extent determined appropriate by the Commission) that performs for any issuer any audit required by this title or the rules of the Commission under this title or, beginning 180 days after the date of commencement of the operations of the Public Company Accounting Oversight Board established under section 101 of the Sarbanes-Oxley Act of 2002 (in this section referred to as the "Board"), the rules of the Board, to provide to that issuer, contemporaneously with the audit, any non-audit service, including—

(1) bookkeeping or other services related to the accounting records or financial statements of the audit client;

(2) financial information systems design and implementation;

(3) appraisal or valuation services, fairness opinions, or contribution-in-kind reports;

(4) actuarial services;

(5) internal audit outsourcing services;

(6) management functions or human resources;

(7) broker or dealer, investment adviser, or investment banking services;

(8) legal services and expert services unrelated to the audit; and

(9) any other service that the Board determines, by regulation, is impermissible.

(h) Preapproval required for non-audit services

A registered public accounting firm may engage in any non-audit service, including tax services, that is not described in any of paragraphs (1) through (9) of subsection (g) for an audit client, only if the activity is approved in advance by the audit committee of the issuer, in accordance with subsection (i) of this section.

SEC. 203. AUDIT PARTNER ROTATION (15 U.S.C. § 78j-1(j))

(j) Audit partner rotation

It shall be unlawful for a registered public accounting firm to provide audit services to an issuer if the lead (or coordinating) audit partner (having primary responsibility for the audit), or the audit partner responsible for reviewing the audit, has performed audit services for that issuer in each of the 5 previous fiscal years of that issuer.

AUDIT COMMITTEE INDEPENDENCE (15 U.S.C. § 78j-1(m)(3))

(3) Independence

(A) In general

Each member of the audit committee of the issuer shall be a member of the board of directors of the issuer, and shall otherwise be independent.

(B) Criteria

In order to be considered to be independent for purposes of this paragraph, a member of an audit committee of an issuer may not, other than in his or her capacity as a member of the audit committee, the board of directors, or any other board committee—

(i) accept any consulting, advisory, or other compensatory fee from the issuer; or

(ii) be an affiliated person of the issuer or any subsidiary thereof.

SEC. 302. CORPORATE RESPONSIBILITY FOR FINANCIAL REPORTS

Failure of Corporate Officers to Certify Financial Reports 18 U.S.C. § 1350

§ 1350. FAILURE OF CORPORATE OFFICERS TO CERTIFY FINANCIAL REPORTS

(a) Certification of periodic financial reports

Each periodic report containing financial statements filed by an issuer with the Securities Exchange Commission pursuant to section 13(a) or 15(d) of the Securities Exchange Act of 1934 (15 U.S.C. 78m(a) or 78o(d)) shall be accompanied by a written statement by the chief executive officer and chief financial officer (or equivalent thereof) of the issuer

(b) Content

The statement required under subsection (a) shall certify that the periodic report containing the financial statements fully complies with the requirements of section 13(a) or 15(d) of the Securities Exchange Act of 1934 (15 U.S.C. 78m or 78o(d)) and that information contained in the periodic report fairly presents, in all material respects, the financial condition and results of operations of the issuer.

(c) Criminal penalties

Whoever—

(1) certifies any statement as set forth in subsections (a) and (b) of this section knowing that the periodic report accompanying the statement does not comport with all the requirements set forth in this section shall be fined not more than $1,000,000 or imprisoned not more than 10 years, or both; or

(2) willfully certifies any statement as set forth in subsections (a) and (b) of this section knowing that the periodic report accompanying the statement does not comport with all the requirements set forth in this section shall be fined not more than $5,000,000, or imprisoned not more than 20 years, or both.

SEC. 404. MANAGEMENT ASSESSMENT OF INTERNAL CONTROLS (15 U.S.C. § 78m (2))

(2) Every issuer which has a class of securities registered pursuant to section 78l of this title and every issuer which is required to file reports pursuant to section 78o(d) of this title shall—

(A) make and keep books, records, and accounts, which, in reasonable detail, accurately and fairly reflect the transactions and dispositions of the assets of the issuer;

(B) devise and maintain a system of internal accounting controls sufficient to provide reasonable assurances that—

(i) transactions are executed in accordance with management's general or specific authorization;

(ii) transactions are recorded as necessary (I) to permit preparation of financial statements in conformity with generally accepted accounting principles or any other criteria applicable to such statements, and (II) to maintain accountability for assets;

(iii) access to assets is permitted only in accordance with management's general or specific authorization; and

(iv) the recorded accountability for assets is compared with the existing assets at reasonable intervals and appropriate action is taken with respect to any differences; and

(C) notwithstanding any other provision of law, pay the allocable share of such issuer of a reasonable annual accounting support fee or fees, determined in accordance with section 7219 of this title.

SEC. 406. CODE OF ETHICS FOR SENIOR FINANCIAL OFFICERS

(a) Code of ethics disclosure

The Commission shall issue rules to require each issuer, together with periodic reports required pursuant to section 13(a) or 15(d) of the Securities Exchange Act of 1934, to disclose whether or not, and if not, the reason therefor, such issuer has adopted a code of ethics for senior financial officers, applicable to its principal financial officer and comptroller or principal accounting officer, or persons performing similar functions.

SEC. 802. CRIMINAL PENALTIES FOR ALTERING DOCUMENTS (18 U.S.C. § 1519)

§ 1519. Destruction, alteration, or falsification of records in Federal investigations and bankruptcy

Whoever knowingly alters, destroys, mutilates, conceals, covers up, falsifies, or makes a false entry in any record, document, or tangible object with the intent to impede, obstruct, or influence the investigation or proper administration of any matter within the jurisdiction of any department or agency of the United States or any case filed under title 11, or in relation to or contemplation of any such matter or case, shall be fined under this title, imprisoned not more than 20 years, or both.

§ 1520. Destruction of corporate audit records

(a)(1) Any accountant who conducts an audit of an issuer of securities to which section 10A(a) of the Securities Exchange Act of 1934 (15 U.S.C. 78j-1(a)) applies, shall maintain all audit or review workpapers for a period of 5 years from the end of the fiscal period in which the audit or review was concluded.

(2) The Securities and Exchange Commission shall promulgate, within 180 days, after adequate notice and an opportunity for comment, such rules and regulations, as are reasonably necessary, relating to the retention of relevant records such as workpapers, documents that form the basis of an audit or review, memoranda, correspondence, communications, other documents, and records (including electronic records) which are created, sent, or received in connection with an audit or review and contain conclusions, opinions, analyses, or financial data relating to such an audit or review, which is conducted by any accountant who conducts an audit of an issuer of securities to which section 10A(a) of the Securities Exchange Act of 1934 (15 U.S.C. 78j-1(a)) applies. The Commission may, from time to time, amend or supplement the rules and regulations that it is required to promulgate under this section, after adequate notice and an opportunity for comment, in order to ensure that such rules and regulations adequately comport with the purposes of this section.

(b) Whoever knowingly and willfully violates subsection (a)(1), or any rule or regulation promulgated by the Securities and Exchange Commission under subsection (a)(2), shall be fined under this title, imprisoned not more than 10 years, or both.

SEC. 1102. TAMPERING WITH A RECORD OR OTHERWISE IMPEDING AN OFFICIAL PROCEEDING (18 U.S.C. § 1512)

(c) Whoever corruptly—

(1) alters, destroys, mutilates, or conceals a record, document, or other object, or attempts to do so, with the intent to impair the object's integrity or availability for use in an official proceeding; or

(2) otherwise obstructs, influences, or impedes any official proceeding, or attempts to do so, shall be fined under this title or imprisoned not more than 20 years, or both.

The Copyright Act (as Amended) (Excerpts)

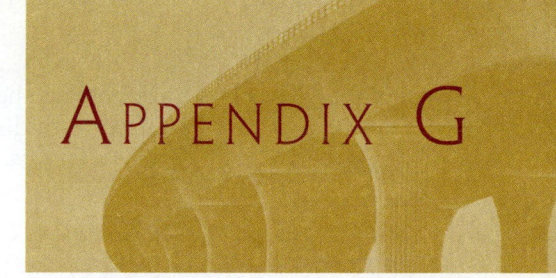

SECTION 102. SUBJECT MATTER OF COPYRIGHT: IN GENERAL (15 U.S.C. § 102)

(a) Copyright protection subsists, in accordance with this title, in original works of authorship fixed in any tangible medium of expression, now known or later developed, from which they can be perceived, reproduced, or otherwise communicated, either directly or with the aid of a machine or device. Works of authorship include the following categories:

    (1) literary works;

    (2) musical works, including any accompanying words;

    (3) dramatic works, including any accompanying music;

    (4) pantomimes and choreographic works;

    (5) pictorial, graphic, and sculptural works;

    (6) motion pictures and other audiovisual works;

    (7) sound recordings; and

    (8) architectural works.

(b) In no case does copyright protection for an original work of authorship extend to any idea, procedure, process, system, method of operation, concept, principle, or discovery, regardless of the form in which it is described, explained, illustrated, or embodied in such work.

SECTION 106. EXCLUSIVE RIGHTS IN COPYRIGHTED WORKS (15 U.S.C. § 106)

Subject to sections 107 through 120, the owner of copyright under this title has the exclusive rights to do and to authorize any of the following:

    (1) to reproduce the copyrighted work in copies or phonorecords;

    (2) to prepare derivative works based upon the copyrighted work;

    (3) to distribute copies or phonorecords of the copyrighted work to the public by sale or other transfer of ownership, or by rental, lease, or lending;

    (4) in the case of literary, musical, dramatic, and choreographic works, pantomimes, and motion pictures and other audiovisual works, to perform the copyrighted work publicly; and

    (5) in the case of literary, musical, dramatic, and choreographic works, pantomimes, and pictorial, graphic, or sculptural works, including the individual images of a motion picture or other audiovisual work, to display the copyrighted work publicly; and

    (6) in the case of sound recordings, to perform the copyrighted work publicly by means of a digital audio transmission.

SECTION 107. LIMITATIONS ON EXCLUSIVE RIGHTS: FAIR USE (17 U.S.C. § 107)

Notwithstanding the provisions of sections 106 and 106A, the fair use of a copyrighted work, including such use by reproduction in copies or phonorecords or by any other means specified by that section, for purposes such as criticism, comment, news reporting, teaching (including multiple copies for classroom use), scholarship, or research, is not an infringement of copyright. In determining whether the use made of a work in any particular case is a fair use the factors to be considered shall include—

    (1) the purpose and character of the use, including whether such use is of a commercial nature or is for nonprofit educational purposes;

    (2) the nature of the copyrighted work;

    (3) the amount and substantiality of the portion used in relation to the copyrighted work as a whole; and

    (4) the effect of the use upon the potential market for or value of the copyrighted work.

The fact that a work is unpublished shall not itself bar a finding of fair use if such finding is made upon consideration of all above factors.

SECTION 408. COPYRIGHT REGISTRATION IN GENERAL (17 U.S.C. § 408)

(a) Registration permissive

At any time during the subsistence of copyright in any published or unpublished work in which the copyright was secured before January 1, 1978, and during the subsistence of any copyright secured on or after that date, the owner of copyright or of any exclusive right in the work may obtain registration of the copyright claim by delivering to the Copyright Office the deposit specified by this section, together with the application and fee specified by sections 409 and 708. Such registration is not a condition of copyright protection.

SECTION 591. INFRINGEMENT OF COPYRIGHT (17 U.S.C. § 501)

(a) Anyone who violates any of the exclusive rights of the copyright owner as provided by sections 106 through 118 or of the author as provided in section 106A(a), or who imports copies or phonorecords into the United States in violation of section 602, is an infringer of the copyright or right of the author, as the case may be. For purposes of this chapter (other than section 506), any reference to copyright shall be deemed to include the rights conferred by section 106 (a). As used in this subsection the term "anyone" includes any State, any instrumentality of a State, and any officer or employee of a State or instrumentality of a State acting in his or her official capacity. Any State, and any such instrumentality, officer, or employee, shall be subject to the provisions of this title in the same manner and to the same extent as any nongovernmental entity.

(b) The legal or beneficial owner of an exclusive right under a copyright is entitled, subject to the requirements of section 411, to institute an action for any infringement of that particular right committed while he or she is the owner of it. The court may require such owner to serve written notice of the action with a copy of the complaint upon any person shown, by the records of the Copyright

Office or otherwise, to have or claim an interest in the copyright, and shall require that such notice be served upon any person whose interest is likely to be affected by a decision in the case. The court may require the joinder, and shall permit the intervention, of any person having or claiming an interest in the copyright.

REMEDIES FOR INFRINGEMENT: DAMAGES AND PROFITS (17 U.S.C. § 504)

Section 504.

(a) In general. Except as otherwise provided by this title, an infringer of copyright is liable for either—

1. the copyright owner's actual damages and any additional profits of the infringer, as provided by subsection (b); or

2. statutory damages, as provided by subsection (c).

(b) Actual damages and profits

The copyright owner is entitled to recover the actual damages suffered by him or her as a result of the infringement, and any profits of the infringer that are attributable to the infringement and are not taken into account in computing the actual damages. In establishing the infringer's profits, the copyright owner is required to present proof only of the infringer's gross revenue, and the infringer is required to prove his or her deductible expenses and the elements of profit attributable to factors other than the copyrighted work.

(c) Statutory damages

(1) Except as provided by clause (2) of this subsection, the copyright owner may elect, at any time before final judgment is rendered, to recover, instead of actual damages and profits, an award of statutory damages for all infringements involved in the action, with respect to any one work, for which any one infringer is liable individually, or for which any two or more infringers are liable jointly and severally, in a sum of not less than $750 or more than $30,000 as the court considers just. For the purposes of this subsection, all the parts of a compilation or derivative work constitute one work.

(2) In a case where the copyright owner sustains the burden of proving, and the court finds, that infringement was committed willfully, the court in its discretion may increase the award of statutory damages to a sum of not more than $150,000. In a case where the infringer sustains the burden

of proving, and the court finds, that such infringer was not aware and had no reason to believe that his or her acts constituted an infringement of copyright, the court in its discretion may reduce the award of statutory damages to a sum of not less than $200. The court shall remit statutory damages in any case where an infringer believed and had reasonable grounds for believing that his or her use of the copyrighted work was a fair use under section 107, if the infringer was: (i) an employee or agent of a nonprofit educational institution, library, or archives acting within the scope of his or her employment who, or such institution, library, or archives itself, which infringed by reproducing the work in copies or phonorecords; or (ii) a public broadcasting entity which or a person who, as a regular part of the nonprofit activities of a public broadcasting entity (as defined in subsection (g) of section 118) infringed by performing a published nondramatic literary work or by reproducing a transmission program embodying a performance of such a work.

SECTION 506. CRIMINAL OFFENSES (15 U.S.C. § 506)

(a) Criminal infringement

(1) In general—Any person who infringes a copyright willfully and for purposes of commercial advantage or private financial gain shall be punished as provided in section 2319 of title 18, if the infringement was committed—

(A) for purposes of commercial advantage or private financial gain;

(B) by the reproduction or distribution, including by electronic means, during any 180-day period, of 1 or more copies or phonorecords of 1 or more copyrighted works, which have a total retail value of more than $1,000; or

(C) by the distribution of a work being prepared for commercial distribution, by making it available on a computer network accessible to members of the public, if such person knew or should have known that the work was intended for commercial distribution.

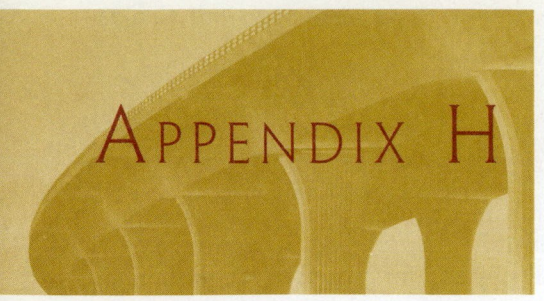

APPENDIX H

Title VII and the Civil Rights Act (Employment Provisions) (Excerpts)

§ 1981. EQUAL RIGHTS UNDER THE LAW

(a) All persons within the jurisdiction of the United States shall have the same right in every State and Territory to make and enforce contracts, to sue, be parties, give evidence, and to the full and equal benefit of all laws and proceedings for the security of persons and property as is enjoyed by white citizens, and shall be subject to like punishment, pains, penalties, taxes, licenses, and exactions of every kind, and to no other.

(b) For purposes of this section, the term "make and enforce contracts" includes the making, performance, modification, and termination of contracts, and the enjoyment of all benefits, privileges, terms, and conditions of the contractual relationship.

(c) The rights protected by this section are protected against impairment by nongovernmental discrimination and impairment under color of State law.

§ 1981A. DAMAGES IN CASES OF INTENTIONAL DISCRIMINATION IN EMPLOYMENT

(a) Right of recovery

(1) Civil rights. In an action brought by a complaining party under section 706 or 717 of the Civil Rights Act of 1964 (42 U.S.C. § 2000e-5 [or 2000e-16]) against a respondent who engaged in unlawful intentional discrimination (not an employment practice that is unlawful because of its disparate impact) prohibited under section 703, 704, or 717 of the Act (42 U.S.C. § 2000e-2 or 2000e-3 [or 2000e-16]), and provided that the complaining party cannot recover under section 1977 of the Revised Statutes (42 U.S.C. § 1981), the complaining party may recover compensatory and punitive damages

as allowed in subsection (b), in addition to any relief authorized by section 706(g) of the Civil Rights Act of 1964 [42 USCS § 2000e-5(g)], from the respondent.

SECTION 703. UNLAWFUL EMPLOYMENT PRACTICES

Employer Practices

(a) It shall be an unlawful employment practice for an employer—

(1) to fail or refuse to hire or to discharge any individual, or otherwise to discriminate against any individual with respect to his compensation, terms, conditions, or privileges of employment, because of such individual's race, color, religion, sex, or national origin; or

(2) to limit, segregate, or classify his employees or applicants for employment in any way which would deprive or tend to deprive any individual of employment opportunities or otherwise adversely affect his status as an employee, because of such individual's race, color, religion, sex, or national origin.

Employment Agency Practices

(b) It shall be an unlawful employment practice for an employment agency to fail or refuse to refer for employment, or otherwise to discriminate against, any individual because of his race, color, religion, sex, or national origin, or to classify or refer for employment any individual on the basis of his race, color, religion, sex, or national origin.

Labor Organization Practices

(c) It shall be an unlawful employment practice for a labor organization—

(1) to exclude or to expel from its membership, or otherwise to discriminate against, any individual because of his race, color, religion, sex, or national origin;

(2) to limit, segregate, or classify its membership or applicants for membership, or to classify or fail or refuse to refer to employment any individual, in any way which would deprive or tend to deprive any individual of employment opportunities, or would limit such employment opportunities or otherwise adversely affect his status as an employee or as an applicant for employment, because of such individual's race, color, religion, sex, or national origin; or

(3) to cause or attempt to cause an employer to discriminate against an individual in violation of this section.

Training Programs

(d) It shall be an unlawful employment practice for any employer, labor organization, or joint labor-management committee, controlling apprenticeship or other training or retraining, including on-the-job training programs to discriminate against any individual because of his race, color, religion, sex, or national origin in admission to, or employment in, any program established to provide apprenticeship or other training.

Businesses or Enterprises with Personnel Qualified on Basis of Religion, Sex, or National Origin; Educational Institutions with Personnel of Particular Religion

(e) Notwithstanding any other provision of this subchapter, (1) it shall not be an unlawful employment practice for an employer to hire and employ employees, for an employment agency to classify or refer for employment any individual, for a labor organization to classify its membership or to classify or refer for employment any individual, or for an employer, labor organization, or joint labor-management committee controlling apprenticeship or other training or retraining programs to admit or employ any individual in any such program, on the basis of his religion, sex, or national origin in those certain instances where religion, sex, or national origin is a bona fide occupational qualification reasonably necessary to the normal operation of that particular business or enterprise, and (2) it shall not be an unlawful employment practice for a school, college, university, or other educational institution or institution of learning to hire and employ employees of a particular religion if such school, college, university, or other educational institution

or institution of learning is, in whole or in substantial part, owned, supported, controlled, or managed by a particular religion or by a particular religious corporation, association, or society, or if the curriculum of such school, college, university, or other educational institution or institution of learning is directed toward the propagation of a particular religion.

Seniority or Merit System; Quantity or Quality of Production, Ability Tests; Compensation Based on Sex and Authorized by Minimum Wage Provisions

(h) Notwithstanding any other provisions of this subchapter, it shall not be an unlawful employment practice for an employer to apply different standards of compensation, or different terms, conditions, or privileges of employment pursuant to a bona fide seniority or merit system, or a system which measures earnings by quantity or quality of production or to employees who work in different locations, provided that such differences are not the result of an intention to discriminate because of race, color, religion, sex, or national origin, nor shall it be an unlawful employment practice for an employer to give and to act upon the results of any professionally developed ability test provided that such test, its administration or action upon the results is not designed, intended or used to discriminate because of race, color, religion, sex, or national origin. It shall not be an unlawful employment practice under this subchapter for any employer to differentiate upon the basis of sex in determining the amount of the wages or compensation paid or to be paid to employees of such employer if such differentiation is authorized by the provisions of section 206(d) of Title 29.

SECTION 704. OTHER UNLAWFUL EMPLOYMENT PRACTICES

Discrimination for Making Charges, Testifying, Assisting, or Participating in Enforcement Proceedings

(a) It shall be an unlawful employment practice for an employer to discriminate against any of his employees or applicants for employment, for an employment agency, or joint labor-management committee controlling apprenticeship or other training or retraining, including on-the-job training programs to discriminate against any individual, or for a labor organization to discriminate against any member thereof or applicant for membership, because he has opposed any practice, made an unlawful employment practice by this subchapter, or because he has made a charge, testified, assisted, or participated in any manner in an investigation, proceeding, or hearing under this subchapter.

Printing or Publication of Notices or Advertisements Indicating Prohibited Preference, Limitation, Specification, or Discrimination; Occupational Qualification Exception

(b) It shall be an unlawful employment practice for an employer, labor organization, employment agency, or joint labor-management committee controlling apprenticeship or other training or retraining, including on-the-job training programs, to print or publish or cause to be printed or published any notice or advertisement relating to employment by such an employer or membership in or any classification or referral for employment by such a labor organization, or relating to any classification or referral for employment by such an employment agency, or relating to admission to, or employment in, any program established to provide apprenticeship or other training by such a joint labor-management committee, indicating any preference, limitation, specification, or discrimination, based on race, color, religion, sex, or national origin, except that such a notice or advertisement may indicate a preference, limitation, specification, or discrimination based on religion, sex, or national origin when religion, sex, or national origin is a bona fide occupational qualification for employment.

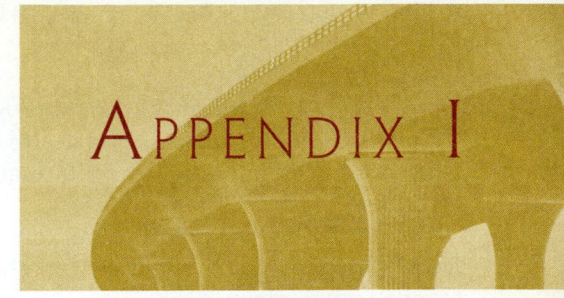

APPENDIX I

The Americans with Disabilities Act (Excerpts)

TITLE I—EMPLOYMENT (42 U.S.C. § 12102)

Sec. 101. Definitions.

As used in this chapter:

(1) Disability

The term "disability" means, with respect to an individual—

(A) a physical or mental impairment that substantially limits one or more major life activities of such individual;

(B) a record of such an impairment; or

(C) being regarded as having such an impairment (as described in paragraph (3)).

(2) Major life activities

(A) In general

For purposes of paragraph (1), major life activities include, but are not limited to, caring for oneself, performing manual tasks, seeing, hearing, eating, sleeping, walking, standing, lifting, bending, speaking, breathing, learning, reading, concentrating, thinking, communicating, and working.

(B) Major bodily functions

For purposes of paragraph (1), a major life activity also includes the operation of a major bodily function, including but not limited to, functions of the immune system, normal cell growth, digestive, bowel, bladder, neurological, brain, respiratory, circulatory, endocrine, and reproductive functions.

(3) Regarded as having such an impairment

For purposes of paragraph (1)(C):

(A) An individual meets the requirement of "being regarded as having such an impairment" if the individual establishes that he or she has been subjected to an action prohibited under this chapter because of an actual or perceived physical or mental impairment whether or not the impairment limits or is perceived to limit a major life activity.

(B) Paragraph (1)(C) shall not apply to impairments that are transitory and minor. A transitory impairment is an impairment with an actual or expected duration of 6 months or less.

(4) Rules of construction regarding the definition of disability

The definition of "disability" in paragraph (1) shall be construed in accordance with the following:

(A) The definition of disability in this chapter shall be construed in favor of broad coverage of individuals under this chapter, to the maximum extent permitted by the terms of this chapter.

(B) The term "substantially limits" shall be interpreted consistently with the findings and purposes of the ADA Amendments Act of 2008.

(C) An impairment that substantially limits one major life activity need not limit other major life activities in order to be considered a disability.

(D) An impairment that is episodic or in remission is a disability if it would substantially limit a major life activity when active.

(E) (i) The determination of whether an impairment substantially limits a major life activity shall be made without regard to the ameliorative effects of mitigating measures such as—

(I) medication, medical supplies, equipment, or appliances, low-vision devices (which do not include ordinary eyeglasses or contact lenses), prosthetics including limbs and devices, hearing aids and cochlear implants or other implantable hearing devices, mobility devices, or oxygen therapy equipment and supplies;

(II) use of assistive technology;

(III) reasonable accommodations or auxiliary aids or services; or

(IV) learned behavioral or adaptive neurological modifications.

(ii) The ameliorative effects of the mitigating measures of ordinary eyeglasses or contact lenses shall be considered in determining whether an impairment substantially limits a major life activity.

(iii) As used in this subparagraph—

Bo Chambers/Flickr/Getty Images

(I) the term "ordinary eyeglasses or contact lenses" means lenses that are intended to fully correct visual acuity or eliminate refractive error; and

(II) the term "low-vision devices" means devices that magnify, enhance, or otherwise augment a visual image.

Definitions. 42 U.S.C. § 12111

(9) Reasonable accommodation

The term "reasonable accommodation" may include—

(A) making existing facilities used by employees readily accessible to and usable by individuals with disabilities; and

(B) job restructuring, part-time or modified work schedules, reassignment to a vacant position, acquisition or modification of equipment or devices, appropriate adjustment or modifications of examinations, training materials or policies, the provision of qualified readers or interpreters, and other similar accommodations for individuals with disabilities.

(10) Undue hardship

(A) In general

The term "undue hardship" means an action requiring significant difficulty or expense, when considered in light of the factors set forth in subparagraph (B).

(B) Factors to be considered

In determining whether an accommodation would impose an undue hardship on a covered entity, factors to be considered include—

(i) the nature and cost of accommodation needed under this chapter;

(ii) the overall financial resources of the facility or facilities involved in the provision of the reasonable accommodation; the number of persons employed at such facility; the effect on expenses and resources, or the impact otherwise of such accommodation upon the operation of the facility;

(iii) the overall financial resources of the covered entity; the overall size of the business of a covered entity with respect to the number of its employees; the number, type, and location of its facilities; and

(iv) the type of operation or operations of the covered entity, including the composition, structure, and functions of the workforce of such entity; the geographic separateness, administrative, or fiscal relationship of the facility or facilities in question to the covered entity.

Sec. 102. Discrimination. 42 U.S.C. § 12112

(a) General rule

No covered entity shall discriminate against a qualified individual with a disability because of the disability of such individual in regard to job application procedures, the hiring, advancement, or discharge of employees, employee compensation, job training, and other terms, conditions, and privileges of employment.

(b) Construction

As used in subsection (a), the term "discriminate" includes—

(1) limiting, segregating, or classifying a job applicant or employee in a way that adversely affects the opportunities or status of such applicant or employee because of the disability of such applicant or employee;

(2) participating in a contractual or other arrangement or relationship that has the effect of subjecting a covered entity's qualified applicant or employee with a disability to the discrimination prohibited by this title (such relationship includes a relationship with an employment or referral agency, labor union, an organization providing fringe benefits to an employee of the covered entity, or an organization providing training and apprenticeship programs);

(3) utilizing standards, criteria, or methods of administration—

(A) that have the effect of discrimination on the basis of disability; or

(B) that perpetuate the discrimination of others who are subject to common administrative control;

(4) excluding or otherwise denying equal jobs or benefits to a qualified individual because of the known disability of an individual with whom the qualified individual is known to have a relationship or association;

(5) (A) not making reasonable accommodations to the known physical or mental limitations of an otherwise qualified individual with a disability who is an applicant or employee, unless such covered entity can demonstrate that the accommodation would impose an undue hardship on the operation of the business of such covered entity; or

(B) denying employment opportunities to a job applicant or employee who is an otherwise qualified individual with a disability, if such denial is based on the need of such covered entity to make reasonable accommodation to the physical or mental impairments of the employee or applicant;

(6) using qualification standards, employment tests or other selection criteria that screen out or tend to screen out an individual with a disability or a class of individuals with disabilities unless the standard, test or other selection criteria, as used by the covered entity, is shown to be job-related for the position in question and is consistent with business necessity; and

(7) failing to select and administer tests concerning employment in the most effective manner to ensure that, when such test is administered to a job applicant or employee who has a disability that impairs sensory, manual, or speaking skills, such test results accurately reflect the skills, aptitude, or whatever other factor of such applicant or employee that such test purports to measure, rather than reflecting the impaired sensory, manual, or speaking skills of such employee or applicant (except where such skills are the factors that the test purports to measure)....

Sec. 104. Illegal Use of Drugs and Alcohol.... 42 U.S.C. § 12114

(a) Qualified individual with a disability

For purposes of this subchapter, "a qualified individual with a disability shall" shall not include any employee or applicant who is currently engaging in the illegal use of drugs, when the covered entity acts on the basis of such use.

(b) Rules of construction

Nothing in subsection (a) shall be construed to exclude as a qualified individual with a disability an individual who—

(1) has successfully completed a supervised drug rehabilitation program and is no longer engaging in the illegal use of drugs, or has otherwise been rehabilitated successfully and is no longer engaging in such use;

(2) is participating in a supervised rehabilitation program and is no longer engaging in such use; or

(3) is erroneously regarded as engaging in such use, but is not engaging in such use; except that it shall not be a violation of this Act for a covered entity to adopt or administer reasonable policies or procedures, including but not limited to drug testing, designed to ensure that an individual described in paragraph (1) or (2) is no longer engaging in the illegal use of drugs. ...

(c) Authority of covered entity

A covered entity—

(1) may prohibit the illegal use of drugs and the use of alcohol at the workplace by all employees;

(2) may require that employees shall not be under the influence of alcohol or be engaging in the illegal use of drugs at the workplace;

(3) may require that employees behave in conformance with the requirements established under the chapter 81 of Title 41;

(4) may hold an employee who engages in the illegal use of drugs or who is an alcoholic to the same qualification standards for employment or job performance and behavior that such entity holds other employees, even if any unsatisfactory performance or behavior is related to the drug use or alcoholism of such employee; and

(5) may, with respect to Federal regulations regarding alcohol and the illegal use of drugs, require that—

(A) employees comply with the standards established in such regulations of the Department of Defense, if the employees of the covered entity are employed in an industry subject to such regulations, including complying with regulations (if any) that apply to employment in sensitive positions in such an industry, in the case of employees of the covered entity who are employed in such positions (as defined in the regulations of the Department of Defense);

(B) employees comply with the standards established in such regulations of the Nuclear Regulatory Commission, if the employees of the covered entity are employed in an industry subject to such regulations, including complying with regulations (if any) that apply to employment in sensitive positions in such an industry, in the case of employees of the covered entity who are employed in such positions (as defined in the regulations of the Nuclear Regulatory Commission); and

(C) employees comply with the standards established in such regulations of the Department of Transportation, if the employees of the covered entity are employed in a transportation industry subject to such regulations, including complying with such regulations (if any) that apply to employment in sensitive positions in such an industry, in the case of employees of the covered entity who are employed in such positions (as defined in the regulations of the Department of Transportation).

(d) Drug testing

(1) In general

For purposes of this subchapter, a test to determine the illegal use of drugs shall not be considered a medical examination.

(2) Construction

Nothing in this subchapter shall be construed to encourage, prohibit, or authorize the conducting of drug testing for the illegal use of drugs by job applicants or employees or making employment decisions based on such test results.

(e) Transportation employees

Nothing in this subchapter shall be construed to encourage, prohibit, restrict, or authorize the otherwise lawful exercise by entities subject to the jurisdiction of the Department of Transportation of authority to—

(1) test employees of such entities in, and applicants for, positions involving safety-sensitive duties for the illegal use of drugs and for on-duty impairment by alcohol; and

(2) remove such persons who test positive for illegal use of drugs and on-duty impairment by alcohol pursuant to paragraph (1) from safety-sensitive duties in implementing subsection (c) of this section.

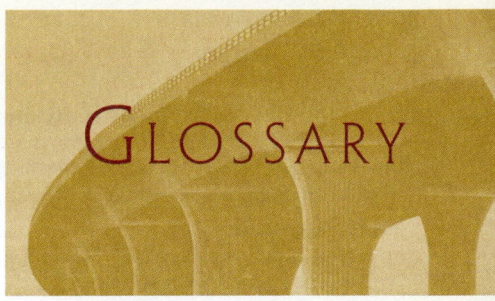

GLOSSARY

10-K form Periodic reporting forms required of 1934 act companies.

10-Q form Periodic reporting forms required of 1934 act companies.

8-K form Periodic reporting forms required of 1934 act companies.

A

absolute privilege A defense to defamation; a protection given to legislators and courtroom participants for statements made relating to the proceedings; encourages people to come forward and speak without fear of liability.

acceptance Offeree's positive response to offer.

accord and satisfaction Agreement entered into as settlement of a disputed debt.

accredited investor Investor who meets threshold standards for assets and income.

act of state doctrine In international law, a theory that each country's governmental actions are autonomous and not subject to judicial review by the courts in other countries.

actual authority Express and implied authority.

actual notice Receipt of notice of termination.

actus reus A requirement of that crimes that they include some specific action or conduct.

administrative agency Governmental unit created by a legislative body for the purposes of administering and enforcing the laws.

administrative law judge (ALJ) Special category of judicial official who presides over agency enforcement hearings.

Administrative Procedures Act (APA) Basic federal law governing the creation, operation, and reporting of federal administrative agencies.

advance Partners' loan to partnership.

affirmative action Programs created to remedy past wrongs that permit choices on the basis of race, sex, or national origin.

affirms Action taken by an appellate court on an appealed case; the effect is that the court upholds the lower court's decision.

Age Discrimination in Employment Act of 1967 Prohibits hiring, firing, promotion, benefits, raises based on age.

agent Party hired to act on another's behalf.

alter ego theory When owners and managers of the corporation have not treated the corporation as a separate entity but have used the structure more as a personal resource.

alternative dispute resolution (ADR) Means other than litigation used to resolve disputes and claims; includes arbitration, mediation, and negotiated settlements.

America Invents Act (AIA) Changes the effective filing date of a claimed invention as the actual filing date of the patent or application for a patent.

American Competitiveness in the Twenty-First Century Act A law that addresses immigration exemptions.

Americans with Disabilities Act Federal law prohibiting discrimination on basis of disability by certain employees.

answer Pleading filed by the defendant in a lawsuit; contains the defendant's version of the basis of the suit, counterclaims, and denials.

anti-cyberstalking laws Statutes that criminalize harassment via electronic communication.

Antiterrorism and Effective Death Penalty Act Federal statute that covers the issues of immigration, deportation, and penalties for hiring illegal immigrants.

apparent authority; also called **agency by estoppel** Authority by perceptions of third parties.

appellant The name on appeal for the party who appeals a lower court's decision.

appellate brief Lawyer's summation of issues of law and/or error for appellate court to consider.

appellate court A court of appeals or a court of review; a court whose function is to review the decision and actions of a trial court; does not hear witnesses; only reviews the transcript and studies the arguments and briefs of the parties.

appellee The name on appeal for the party who won a lower court's decision—that is, the party who does not appeal the lower court decision.

appraisal rights Value of shares immediately before merger that is paid to dissenting shareholder.

appropriation The use, without permission, of another's likeness, image, voice, or trademark for commercial gain.

arbitrary and capricious Standard for challenging administrative agency rules; used to show decisions or rules were not based on sufficient facts.

arraignment Hearing at which trial date is set and plea is entered.

article of incorporation Document filed to organize a corporation.

Bo Chambers/Flickr/Getty Images

Asbestos Hazard Emergency Response Act (AHERA) Act that requires all public and private schools to arrange for the inspection of their facilities to determine whether their buildings had asbestos-containing materials.

asset acquisition Acquisition for which shareholder approval is not required, but which is subject to the constraints of the Clayton Act.

Asset Conservation, Lender Liability, and Deposit Insurance Protection Act of 1996 Act that provides secured lender exemption from CERCLA liability.

assignment Process of assigning payment rights to satisfy a debt.

assumption of risk Plaintiff's voluntary subjection to a risk that caused injuries.

attorney–client privilege Protection of client's disclosures to her attorney; attorney cannot disclose information client offers (with some exceptions, such as the client telling the attorney of an ongoing or planned crime); the confession of a crime already committed cannot be disclosed by the lawyer.

audit committee Committee responsible for assuring that financial reports management issues are accurate.

B

bait and switch Using cheaper, unavailable product to lure customers to store with a more expensive one then substituted or offered instead.

Bankruptcy Abuse Prevention and Consumer Protection Act of 2005 (BAPCPA) Curbed a 15-year trend of increases in the number of bankruptcies.

battle of the forms UCC description of merchants' tendency to exchange purchase orders, invoices, confirmations, and so on; under Revised UCC, the court determines terms after the fact looking at intent, forms used, and the UCC terms.

best available treatment (BAT) Highest standard EPA imposes for treating pollutants.

best conventional treatment (BCT) If the plant is going to release a conventional pollutant, the EPA requirement to pretreat the substance.

bilateral contract Contract of two promises; one from each party.

bilateral treaty In international law, a treaty between two nations.

bill of lading Title document used to control transfer of goods.

Bill of Rights Portion of the U.S. Constitution that consists of the first ten amendments and includes such rights as freedom of speech, right to privacy, the protections afforded in criminal procedures under the Fourth Amendment search and seizure, and the Fifth Amendment protections against self-incrimination.

binding arbitration Arbitration from which there is no judicial appeal.

bluesky laws State securities registration regulations.

board of directors Policy-setting body of corporations.

bona fide occupational qualification (BFOQ) Job qualification of sex, religion, or national origin that is necessary for the operation of a business, such as religious affiliation for the pastor of a church.

brief Document prepared by lawyers on the appeal of a case to provide the appellate court with a summary of the case and the issues involved.

bubble concept EPA policy of maximum air emissions in one area.

burden of proof The responsibility of the party for proving the facts needed to recover in a lawsuit.

Bureau of Consumer Financial Protection (BCFP) Federal agency created in the Dodd-Frank Act that combines all consumer credit federal law enforcement, promulgation, and interpretation in an agency housed within the Federal Reserve.

business judgment rule Standard of liability for directors.

"but for" test But for the action or lack of action of the defendant, the plaintiff would not have been injured.

bylaws Define the authority of officers, prescribe procedures for announcing and conducting meetings, and set terms of officers and directors and who is eligible to serve.

C

capacity Capacity in the traditional contract sense: age and mental capacity.

causation The "but for" reason for an accident.

caveat emptor Let the buyer beware.

celebrity endorsement FTC area of regulation wherein products are touted by easily recognized public figures.

certification Recognition of union as exclusive bargaining agent.

charitable subscription Enforceable promise to make gifts.

Children's Online Privacy Protection Act (COPPA) Targets online informational privacy but applies only to websites that collect information from children.

citation Name given to abbreviated description of a court case or statute; for example, 355 F. Supp. 291.

cite *See* citation.

civil law Laws affecting the private rights of individuals.

Civil Rights Act of 1964 Cornerstone of the antidiscrimination statutes; the original statute passed to prevent discrimination in housing, education, and employment.

Civil Rights Act of 1991 Federal statute prohibiting discrimination in various aspects of life (employment, voting).

Civil Rights Acts of 1866 and 1870 Federal statutes prohibiting discrimination in various aspects of life (employment, voting).

class action suit In civil law, a suit by a group of plaintiffs with the same claims; generally used in antitrust and securities lawsuits.

Clayton Act Federal antitrust statute that prohibits tying and interlocking directorates; controls mergers.

Clean Air Act Federal law that controls air emissions.

Clean Water Act Federal law that regulates emissions in various water sources.

close corporation Corporation with few shareholders.

closed shop Business that requires union membership before an employee can be hired.

closing argument The summary attorneys give to the jury before it deliberates and after all the evidence has been presented.

Code of Federal Regulations (C.F.R.) Series of volumes carrying the enactments of all federal agencies.

collective bargaining agreement Exclusive rights agreement between employer and employee.

collective bargaining unit Group of employees recognized as exclusive bargaining agent.

comment letter Request by SEC for more information.

Commerce Clause Provision in the U.S. Constitution controlling the regulation of intrastate, interstate, and foreign commerce and delineating authority for such regulation.

commercial impracticability Defense to performance of sales contract based on objective impracticability.

commercial speech The speech of business in the form of advertising, political endorsements, or comments on social issues.

common law Originally, the law of England made uniform after William the Conqueror; today, the nonstatutory law and the law found in judicial precedent.

common stock Generally most voluminous type of corporate shares and usually allows shareholders to vote.

community-right-to-know substance When substance is present, there is a probable duty to disclose that presence to buyers, tenants, and employees.

comparative negligence Newer negligence defense that assigns liability and damages in accidents on a percentage basis and thus reduces a plaintiff's recovery by the amount his negligence contributed to the cause of the accident.

compensatory damages Amount required to place party in as good a position as before breach.

complaint The first pleading in a lawsuit; the document that outlines the plaintiff's allegations against the defendant and specifies the remedies sought; with respect to federal agencies, can also be a formal change of rules or statutory violations by a company or individual.

Comprehensive Environmental Response, Compensation, and Liability Act (CERCLA) Federal law providing funds and authority for hazardous waste site cleanups.

computer crime Crimes committed while using computer technology.

Computer Fraud and Abuse Act (CFAA) Federal law that makes it a crime to use computers without authorization or to harm computers and systems through actions on the Internet.

Computer Software Copyright Act of 1980 Act under which all software can be copyrighted, whether it is written in ordinary language (source code) or machine language (object code).

concurrent jurisdiction Authority of more than one court to hear a case.

conditions Events that must occur before contract performance is due.

conditions precedent Advance events that must occur before performance is due, for example, obtaining financing.

conditions concurrent (or) conditions contemporaneous In contracts, the conditions that must occur simultaneously for contract performance to be required; for example, in an escrow closing in real property, an agent collects title, insurance, funds, and other documents and sees that all the exchanges under the contract occur at the same time.

confidential relationship Trust, confidence, reliance in a relationship.

conflict of laws Issue as to which country's law applies in international transactions.

conscious avoidance Theory under which executives cannot "consciously try to avoid knowledge" about the actions and activities of those within the company.

conscious parallelism Pricing patterns when one competitor follows the lead of another.

consent decree For administrative agencies, a type of plea bargain; a settlement document for an administrative agency's charges.

consequential damages Damages owed to third parties from a breach.

consideration Something of value exchanged by the parties that distinguishes gifts from contracts; sometimes called bargained-for exchange.

consolidation When two or more companies combine into one new company and none of the old companies continues to exist.

constitution Document that contains the basic rights in a society and the structure of its government; cannot be changed without the approval of the society's members.

constructive notice Publication of notice of termination.

Consumer Financial Protection Act (CFPA) Federal law passed after the mortgage crisis that provides additional protections in mortgage loan disclosures and in foreclosures.

Consumer Product Safety Commission (CPSC) Federal agency that regulates product safety and has recall power.

Consumer Product Safety Improvement Act (CPSIA) Expands authority to secondhand sales.

contentious jurisdiction Consensual jurisdiction of a court that is consented to when the parties have a dispute; for example, UN courts.

contract Promise or set of promises for breach of which the law gives a remedy, or the performance of which the law in some way recognizes as a duty.

contract defense Situation, term, or event that excuses performance.

contract interference Tort that occurs when parties are not allowed the freedom to contract without interference from third parties.

contributory negligence Conduct by plaintiff that contributed to plaintiff's injury; serves as a bar to recovery.

Controlling the Assault of Non-Solicited Pornography and Marketing (CAN-SPAM) Act Allows private companies to bring suit against spammers for their unauthorized use of ISPs.

conventional, nonconventional, and toxic pollutants Three categories the EPA developed for pollutants.

cooling-off period Bargaining that takes place before a strike can begin that threatens to imperil the public health and safety.

copyright Protection for the creative intellectual property of its creators, such as for songs, books, plays, art, etc.

corporate opportunity doctrine Fiduciary responsibility of directors with respect to investments.

corporate political speech *See* political speech.

corporate sentencing guidelines Federal rules used to determine level of penalties for companies and officers; a system that decreases penalties for effort toward prevention of wrongdoing and cooperation with investigations and increases penalties for lack of effort and other problems in company operations.

corporate veil Liability shield for corporate owners.

corporation Business organization that is a separate entity with limited liability and full transferability; also an entity formed by statute that has the rights of a legal person along with limited liability for its shareholder owners.

corrective advertising Requires a seller to correct the unsubstantiated claims made in previous ads.

Council on Environmental Quality (CEQ) Part of the executive branch of government; responsible for formulating national policies on quality of the environment and then making recommendations to lawmakers regarding its policy statements.

counterclaim Pleading in a lawsuit in which the defendant makes allegations against the plaintiff in response to the plaintiff's complaint.

counteroffer Counterproposal to offer.

county court Lesser trial court that hears smaller disputes and misdemeanor cases; like justice of the peace courts in many states.

course of dealing UCC provision that examines the way parties have behaved in the past to determine present performance standards.

Court of Justice of European Communities The court of dispute settlement for the nations of the European Community.

courts of chancery Courts that were once separate and administered equitable remedies; now chancery courts are not separate; most courts have the authority to order legal or equitable remedies.

covenant not to compete Promise to protect employers and buyers from loss of goodwill through employee or seller competition.

Credit Card Accountability, Responsibility and Disclosure Act of 2009 (CARD) Federal law that expanded consumer credit disclosures and rights.

crime Requires calculated or intentional conduct.

criminal fraud Misrepresentation with the intent to take something from another without that person's knowledge; to mislead to obtain funds or property.

criminal law As opposed to civil law, the law on wrongs against society.

cross-elasticity Ability to substitute one good for another.

cross-examination Questioning by opposing parties of a witness in court; that is, defendant cross-examines plaintiff's witnesses and plaintiff cross-examines defendant's witnesses.

cumulative preferred stock Guarantees the payment of a dividend so that if a dividend is not paid one year, the holder's right to be paid carries over until funds are available.

customer and territorial restrictions Restrictions on geographic sales territory or customer contacts.

cyberbullying Intimidating or threatening electronic communications.

cyberstalking The crime of following, harassment, and other acts of intimidation using the Internet or other forms of electronic communication.

D

defamation Publication of untrue and damaging statements about an individual or company.

default Judgment entered when the defendant fails to file an answer in a lawsuit.

defendant The party who is alleged to have committed a wrong in a civil lawsuit; the charged party in a criminal prosecution.

deficiency letter Request by SEC for more information.

delegation Transfer of contractual duties and obligation.

deposition Form of discovery in which witnesses or parties can be questioned under oath in recorded testimony outside the courtroom.

derivative suit Lawsuit brought on behalf of another through the other's rights; for example, a shareholder suing to enforce corporation's rights.

Digital Millennium Copyright Act (DMCA) Criminalizes the circumvention of protection technology in order to make copies of copyrighted materials.

direct examination Term that describes a party's questioning of her own witness.

directed verdict Verdict entered by judge upon motion of a party after the presentation of either side's case; can be entered if the plaintiff has not met his burden of proof or if the defendant fails to rebut the plaintiff's case.

disclaimer Act of negating warranty coverage.

disclosed principal Existence and identity of principal are known.

discovery Process before trial for investigation of the case; includes collection of evidence, deposing witnesses, posing and answering interrogatories and admissions, and production of documents.

disparagement False and damaging statements.

disparate impact Test or screening device that affects one group more than another.

disparate treatment Form of discrimination in which members of different races/sexes are treated differently.

dissenting opinion In an appellate court's review of a case, an opinion written by a judge who disagrees with the decision of the majority of the court.

dissenting shareholder Shareholder who objects to merger.

dissolution When partner ceases to be associated with the partnership.

diversity of citizenship A term referring to a requirement for federal court jurisdiction that plaintiff and defendant must be citizens of different states.

Dodd–Frank Wall Street Reform and Consumer Financial Protection Act Federal law that imposed new reporting requirements on publicly traded companies and added additional disclosure requirements in consumer credit contracts.

Dodd–Frank Wall Street Reform and Consumer Protection Act Created the Bureau of Consumer Financial Protection.

domestic corporation A corporation is domestic in the state in which its incorporation is filed.

due diligence Defense of good faith and full effort to Section 11 charges.

due process Right to trial before conviction.

duress Physical or mental force that deprives party of a meaningful choice with respect to a proposed contract.

duties, quotas, tariffs Controls on prices and quantities of goods by nations with the goal of balancing imports and exports.

E

Economic Espionage Act (EEA) Federal law passed in response to several cases in which high-level executives were taking downloaded proprietary information from their computers to their new employers.

effluent guidelines EPA maximum allowances for discharges into water.

Electronic Communications Privacy Act of 1986 (ECPA) Act that prohibits the unauthorized access of "live" communications, as when someone uses a listening device to intercept a telephone conversation.

Electronic Signatures in Global and National Commerce Act (ESIGN) A federal law that recognizes digital signatures as authentic for purposes of contract formation.

elements Requirements for proof of a business crime.

eminent domain In constitutional law, the taking of private property by a government entity for a public purpose, with compensation paid to the owner.

emissions offset policy New plants cannot be built until new emissions are offset by reductions elsewhere.

Employee Retirement Income Security Act of 1974 (ERISA) Federal law regulating employer-sponsored pension plans.

employment at will Right of employer to terminate noncontract employees at any time.

enabling act Act of a legislative body establishing an administrative agency and providing it with guidelines and authority for the enforcement of the law.

Endangered Species Act (ESA) Powerful federal law that can curb economic activity if it presents harm to endangered species or their habitat.

environmental impact statement (EIS) Report by federal agency on study of proposed action's effect on the environment.

Environmental Protection Agency (EPA) Federal agency responsible for enforcement of environmental laws at the federal level.

Equal Credit Opportunity Act (ECOA) Federal law that prohibits discrimination in granting or denying credit.

Equal Employment Opportunity Act of 1972 Anti-discrimination employment amendment to Civil Rights Act.

Equal Employment Opportunity Commission Enforcer of the Equal Employment Opportunity Act of 1972.

Equal Pay Act of 1963 Equal wages for equal work regardless of gender.

equal protection Constitutional right of all citizens to be treated in the same manner and afforded the same rights under law regardless of sex, race, color, or national origin.

equitable remedy A court order remedy other than money damages, such as specific performance, injunction, and so on, that restrains or prevents anticompetitive conduct.

equity The portion of the law that originated to afford remedies when money damages were not appropriate; currently, remedies of law and equity have merged and courts can award either or both.

ethical standards Standards of conduct based on ethical principles such as honesty and fairness.

European Court of Human Rights A noncommercial court dealing with disputes over the treatment of a country's citizens.

exclusionary conduct Conduct that prohibits market entry on a basis other than competition.

exclusive jurisdiction Authority granted to only one court for particular types of cases.

exculpatory clause Attempt to hold oneself harmless for one's own conduct.

executed contract Contract that has been performed.

executive committee Committee composed of three board members to handle the more routine matters of running a corporation.

executive order Law of the executive branch; sets policies for administrative workers and contracts.

executory contract Contract not yet performed.

exempt securities Type of security that can be sold without registration.

exempt transaction Offering not required to be registered.

exemption Security not required to be registered.

exhausting administrative remedy Requirement that all procedures internal to an administrative body be exhausted before an individual pursues a remedy in court.

ex parte **contact** Latin term for a contact with a judicial figure or hearing officer outside the presence of the opposing side.

express authority Written or stated authority.

express contract Written or verbally agreed-to contract. Also, it specifies the limitations of an employee/agent's authority.

express warranty Contractual promise about nature or potential of product that gives right of recovery if product falls short of a promise that was a basis of the bargain.

expropriation Act of state doctrine; recognition by U.S. courts of the actions of other governments as valid despite noncompliance with traditional U.S. rights and procedures.

F

failing-company doctrine Allows the acquisition of a competitor that is teetering on insolvency, shut down, or bankruptcy if it is an asset or inventory acquisition.

Fair Credit Billing Act Affords debtors the opportunity to challenge the figures on credit card monthly statements.

Fair Credit Reporting Act (FCRA) Designed to provide debtors some rights and protections regarding the credit information held by third parties about them.

Fair Debt Collections Practices Act (FDCPA) Enacted to control abuses in the collection process.

"fair-disclosure rule" (Regulation FD) SEC regulation on disclosure to analysts.

Fair Employment Practices Act Prohibits discrimination in all areas of employment on the basis of race, color, religion, national origin, and sex (including pregnancy, childbirth, or abortion).

Fair Labor Standards Act (FLSA) Federal law that regulates minimum wage and overtime pay.

fair trade contract Arrangement that enforces a suggested retail price.

fair use Occasional and spontaneous use of copyrighted materials for limited purposes.

false imprisonment Wrongful detention of an individual; shopkeepers have a privilege to reasonably detain those they have good cause to believe have taken merchandise.

Family and Medical Leave Act (FMLA) Federal law that permits unpaid leave up to twelve weeks with a job guarantee upon return; allowed for birth or adoption of child or illness of parent, spouse, or child.

featherbedding Payment for work not actually performed.

federal circuits Geographic groupings of the federal district courts for purposes of appellate jurisdiction.

federal district court The trial court of the federal system.

Federal Environmental Pesticide Control Act Act controlling the use of pesticides.

Federal Insurance Contributions Act (FICA) Statute establishing system for withholding contributions for Social Security benefits.

Federal Privacy Act (FPA) Federal law that prohibits exchange of information about individuals among agencies without request and notification, unless for law enforcement purposes.

Federal Register A daily federal publication that reports the day-to-day actions of administrative agencies.

Federal Register Act (FRA) Federal law that establishes all the publications and reporting mechanisms for federal administrative law, such as the *Federal Register* and the *Code of Federal Regulations*.

Federal Register System Part of the federal government responsible for the publication of government notices and rules.

Federal Trade Commission (FTC) Federal agency responsible for regulating deceptive ads.

Federal Trade Commission Act Authorized the Federal Trade Commission (FTC) to prevent unfair and deceptive trade practices.

Federal Trademark Dilution Act Statute that permits recovery and injunctions for "dilution" of distinctive trademarks.

Federal Water Pollution Control Act of 1972 Act by which Congress set two goals: (1) swimmable and fishable waters by 1983 and (2) zero discharge of pollutants by 1985.

Federal Water Pollution Control Administration (FWPCA) Agency established to enforce the Water Quality Act.

fiduciaries Officers and directors of a corporation who are to act in the best interests of the corporation and not profit at the corporation's expense. Also, one who has utmost duty of trust, care, loyalty, and obedience to another.

Fifth Amendment The self-incrimination protection of the U.S. Constitution.

FOIA request Request to a government agency for information retained in that agency's files.

force majeure Provisions in international contracts allow the parties to agree what will happen in the event of sudden changes in government or in the global political climate.

foreign corporation Category or label for corporation in all states except in state in which it is incorporated.

Foreign Corrupt Practices Act Federal law that prohibits the payments of bribes by U.S. companies doing business in other countries.

formal rulemaking Process for developing rules in an administrative agency; involves hearings and public comment period.

forum non conveniens Doctrine requiring dismissal of cases that should be heard in another country's courts.

Fourteenth Amendment Provision of the U.S. Constitution that provides for equal protection and due process.

Fourth Amendment Provision in U.S. Constitution that protects against invasions of privacy; the search warrant amendment.

fraud Intentional misrepresentation.

Freedom of Information Act (FOIA) Federal law that permits access to information held by federal administrative agencies.

freeze-out A merger undertaken to get rid of the minority shareholders in a corporation.

friendly takeover One the management of a firm favors.

full-disclosure standard Review for information, not a review on the merits.

G

garnishment Attachment of a judgment to an account, paycheck, or receivables.

general partner Full and personal liability partner.

geographic market Relevant geographic location for a firm's market; used as a basis for determining monopoly power and market share.

good-faith bargaining Requirement that parties negotiate terms in earnest.

Government in the Sunshine Act Federal law that requires advance notice and open meetings of agency heads.

grand jury Secret body that hears evidence to determine whether charges should be brought and whether defendant should be held for trial.

gratuitous agency Agent works without compensation.

gray market When foreign manufacturers exceed their licensed quota and dump the goods into the market at a much lower price and thereby reduce the trademark owner's market; unauthorized and authorized distributors in other countries where manufacturers charge less than in the United States.

grease payment Payment to foreign officials for facilitation. Facilitation payments are those made to speed up processes, obtain licenses or approvals, but not to win business.

group boycotts Agreement among competitors to exclude competition.

H

Hazardous Substance Response Trust Fund; also called the Superfund Provides funds for cleanup of hazardous waste disposal sites.

hearing examiner or hearing officer Quasi-judicial figure for agency hearings.

Home Equity Loan Consumer Protection Act of 1988 States that additional disclosures are required for those transactions in which consumers use their homes as security for the credit.

Home Ownership and Equity Protection Act of 1994 (HOEPA) States that additional disclosures are required for those transactions in which consumers use their homes as security for the credit.

home solicitation sale Sales in which sellers/creditors first approach consumers in the buyers' homes.

horizontal restraints of trade Anticompetitive behavior among a firm's competitors.

hostile takeover A takeover the management of a firm opposes.

Howey **test** Supreme Court definition of security.

hung jury A jury unable to come to a verdict.

hybrid rulemaking Process by which agency promulgates rules with some hearings but relies mostly on public comments.

I

Illegal Immigration Reform and Immigrant Responsibility Act of 1996 Federal statute that covers the issues of immigration, deportation, and penalties for hiring illegal immigrants.

Immigration Act of 1990 Federal law that applies to immigrants in the United States and imposes requirements on employers in the United States that employ immigrants.

Immigration and Naturalization Act (INA) Federal law that applies to immigrants in the United States and imposes requirements on employers in the United States that employ immigrants.

Immigration Reform and Control Act of 1986 (IRCA) Federal law that applies to immigrants in the United States and imposes requirements on employers in the United States that employ immigrants.

implied authority Authority by custom.

implied contract Contract that arises from parties' voluntary conduct.

implied warranty of fitness for a particular purpose Warranty given in circumstances in which the buyer relies on the seller's expertise and acts to purchase according to that advice.

implied warranty of merchantability Warranty of average quality, purity, and adequate packaging given in every sale by a merchant.

implied-in-fact contract Contract that arises from factual circumstances, professional circumstances, or custom.

implied-in-law contract Legally implied contract to prevent unjust enrichment.

impossibility When a contract cannot be performed by the parties or anyone else.

***in rem* jurisdiction** Jurisdiction over the thing; a method whereby a court obtains jurisdiction by having property or money located within its geographic jurisdiction.

***in personam* jurisdiction** Jurisdiction over the person; type of jurisdiction court must have to require a party to appear before it.

incidental damages Costs of collecting compensatory damages.

incorporators Parties forming the corporation.

independent contractor Principal–agent relationship in which principal exercises little day-to-day control over agent. Also, those who work on a job basis, work irregular hours, and are not supervised by the employer.

indictment Document issued by grand jury requiring defendant to stand trial.

informal rulemaking Process by which an agency promulgates rules without formal public hearings.

information Document issued after preliminary hearing requiring defendant to stand trial. If the judge finds sufficient proof at a preliminary hearing, an information is issued.

inherently dangerous activities Activities for which, even if performed by independent contractor, principal is liable.

initial appearance Defendant's first appearance in court to have charges explained, bail set, lawyer appointed, and future dates set.

initial meeting When a corporation first begins its daily operations.

injunction Equitable remedy in which courts order or enjoin a particular activity.

insider Person with access to nonpublic information about a company.

Insider Trading and Securities Fraud Enforcement Act of 1988 Federal law increasing penalties for insider trading violations.

instructions Explanation of the law applicable in a case given to the jury at the end of the evidence and arguments.

intangible property Forms include patents, copyrights, trademarks, trade names, trade dress, and trade secrets.

intentional infliction of emotional distress Bizarre and outrageous conduct that inflicts mental and possible physical harm on another.

intentional tort Civilly wrong conduct that is done deliberately.

Inter-American Court of Human Rights In international law, the court for resolution of noncommercial issues or the violation of human rights by a particular nation in North or South America.

interbrand competition Competition available for a manufacturer's product.

interference The wrong of asking a party to breach a contract with a third party.

interlocking directorate When officers of competing companies serve on each other's boards of directors.

International Chamber of Commerce (ICC) Voluntary body with uniform rules on commerce and contracts.

International Court of Justice (ICJ) Voluntary court in the international system of law; nonbinding decisions.

Internet service provider (ISP) electronic carrier of Internet traffic such as Yahoo, AOL, and Cox.

interrogatories Method of discovery in which parties send written questions to each other, with responses required to be given under oath.

intervenors Interested parties who are permitted to participate in agency hearings even though they are not parties to the case.

intrabrand competition Competition among one producer's products; e.g., Diet Coke versus Coke Zero.

invasion of privacy Disclosing private information, intruding upon another's affairs, or appropriating someone's image or likeness.

J

JOBS Act Federal law (Jump Start Our Businesses) that made significant changes to small securities offerings exemptions.

joint venture A partnership of existing businesses for a limited time or a limited purpose. Also, a temporary combination that may restrain trade.

judge Elected or appointed government official responsible for supervising trials, hearing appeals, and ruling on motions.

judgment The court's official document stating that the debtor owes the money and the collector is entitled to that money.

judgment NOV Judgment *non obstante veredicto*; a judgment notwithstanding the verdict; a judgment issued by the judge after the jury has rendered a verdict; a trial court's reversal of a jury's decision on the grounds that the verdict was against the weight of the evidence.

judicial review Review by appellate court of decisions and actions of a lower court to determine whether reversible errors in procedure or law were made.

jurisdiction The concept of authority of a court to settle disputes.

jurisprudence The philosophy of law.

just compensation Principle in eminent domain that requires the government entity taking private property to pay the owner a fair amount.

justice of the peace court Lower court generally handling traffic citations and other lesser civil matters.

K

knock-off goods Goods that carry the trademark or trade name of a firm's product but are not actually produced by that firm.

L

Labor Management Relations Act (Taft–Hartley Act) Federal law limiting union economic weapons.

Labor–Management Reporting and Disclosure Act (Landrum–Griffin Act) Federal law regulating union membership and organizations.

Lanham Act of 1946 Federal law passed to afford businesses protection of their trademarks.

lawyer Licensed professional who serves as a representative for another in private negotiations and in judicial and other types of legal proceedings.

legal remedy In common law, a legal remedy consisted of money damages versus equitable remedies of injunctions and specific performance; different courts afforded different remedies in common law England, but the distinction has disappeared today, and all courts have authority to award legal and equitable remedies.

legislative branch One of the three branches of government; at the federal level, consists of the Congress (the Senate and the House of Representatives) and is the branch responsible for making laws.

letter of credit Pledge by bank of availability of funds for a transaction.

libel Written (or, in some cases, broadcast) defamation.

like grade or quality No physical differences in a product.

Lilly Ledbetter Fair Pay Act Federal law that expands the time for filing claims for violations of Title VII for compensation.

limited jurisdiction Specialty courts that have only limited authority over certain types of cases with distinct subject matter; probate courts have limited jurisdiction over probate matters only.

limited liability company (LLC) Newer form of business organization in which liability is limited except for conduct that is illegal.

limited liability partnership (LLP) Newest form of business organization, in which partners' liability is limited.

limited partner Partner whose personal liability is limited to capital contributions.

limited partnership Partnership with two types of partners: general and limited.

limited partnership agreement, or articles of limited partnership Document for creation of a limited partnership.

lingering apparent authority Authority left with terminated agent because others are not told of termination.

liquidated damages Agreement clause in contract that preestablishes and limits damages.

lockout Employer closure of plant or business so workers cannot work.

long-arm statutes Statutes in each state that allow the state courts to bring in defendants from outside the state so long as they have some "minimum contact" with the state.

M

Madrid Agreement Provides for the Madrid Protocol, which is central registration through the International Bureau.

mailbox rule Timing rule for acceptance.

malice Publication of information knowing it is false or with reckless disregard for whether it is false.

mandatory bargaining terms Terms dealing with wages, hours, and other terms and conditions of employment.

market power Power to control prices or exclude competition.

master–servant relationship Principal–agent relationship in which principal exercises great degree of control over agent.

material fact Basis of the bargain.

material misstatement False information that would affect the decision to buy or sell.

maximum achievable control technology (MACT) Best means for controlling emissions.

mediation Alternative dispute resolution mechanism in which a third party is brought in to find a common ground between two disputing parties.

meeting the competition A price change made in a certain market to meet the competition there.

mens rea Mental intent or knowledge of wrong (*scienter*); the required state of mind for a crime—the intent to commit the act that is a crime.

merchant's firm offer Written offer signed by a merchant that states it will be kept open.

merchants' confirmation memoranda UCC provision that allows one merchant to bind another based on an oral agreement with one signature.

merger Combination of two or more corporations, after which only one corporation continues to exist.

merit review Regulation of merits of an offering as opposed to disclosure.

minimum contacts Standard used for determining *in personam* jurisdiction over residents outside the state of the court of litigation; nonresident defendants must have some contact with the state to justify a court taking jurisdiction.

minimum wage Federal hourly rate of pay.

minitrial Alternative dispute resolution method in which the officers of two firms in a dispute listen to the key evidence in a case to see if a settlement can be determined.

minors (sometimes called **infants**) Someone who has not reached the age of majority; in most states, that age is 18.

Miranda warning Advice required to be given to those taken into custody; details the right to remain silent and the right to have counsel.

misappropriation Use of another's ideas or trade secrets.

misrepresentation Incomplete or inaccurate information prior to contract execution.

misuse Product liability defense for plaintiff using a product incorrectly.

Model Business Corporation Act (MBCA) Uniform law adopted in approximately one-third of the states.

modify An option for an appellate court in its review of a lower court case; an action that is something less than reversing a decision but something more than simply affirming it; for example, an appellate court could agree with the verdict but modify the judgment amount or the remedy.

monopolization Possession of monopoly power in the relevant market by willful acquisition.

monopsony Control of a market through the control of market supply.

moral relativism Ethical theory holding that there is no absolute right and wrong and that right and wrong vary according to circumstances, often referred to as "situational ethics."

motion for judgment on the pleadings A motion made to dismiss a suit for failure by the plaintiff to establish a cause of action in the pleadings.

motion for summary judgment A motion made for final disposition of a case in which there is no dispute of facts and only a dispute of law and its application.

motion to dismiss A motion made after the presentation of the plaintiff's case or the defendant's case for failure to establish a *prima facie* case (in the case of the plaintiff) or failure to rebut the presumption (in the case of the defendant).

motions A party's request to the court for action.

multilateral treaty Treaty among more than two nations.

N

National Environmental Policy Act (NEPA) Federal law that requires federal agencies to assess environmental issues before taking actions.

National Labor Relations Act (Wagner Act) of 1935 (NLRA) Federal law that established the right to unionize as well as fair labor practices.

National Labor Relations Board (NLRB) Federal agency responsible for enforcing labor laws.

natural law Law or principles of behavior that exist without being written; supreme laws that cannot be circumvented.

negligence Standard of liability that requires compensation for an injury only if the party responsible knew or should have known of its potential to cause such injury.

negligent failure to supervise Tort that imposes liability on a principal/employer for the failure to take steps to curb employee behavior that has resulted in or could result in injury to third parties.

negligent hiring Tort that imposes liability on principals/employers for injuries to third parties that result from their failure to perform adequate screening and background check on employees prior to hiring.

nexus Connection; a term used in constitutional analysis of the authority to tax; there must be a sufficient connection between the business and the taxing state.

No Electronic Theft Act Makes it a federal criminal offense to willfully infringe copyrighted material worth more than $1,000 using the Internet or other electronic devices even when the infringer does not profit from the use of the material.

Noerr–Pennington doctrine Protection of First Amendment activities from antitrust laws.

Noise Control Act of 1972 Act authorizing the EPA, along with the FAA, to control the amount of noise emissions from low-flying aircraft for the protection of landowners in flight paths.

nolo contendere A plea of no contest.

nonattainment areas Areas with significant air pollution problems.

nonbinding arbitration Arbitration in which the decision is not final, that is, the parties can still take the matter to court.

nonprofit corporation Those not seeking to earn a return.

Norris–LaGuardia Act Federal law prohibiting injunctions to halt strikes.

novation New contract that removes liability from original party and substitutes another party.

nuisance Bad smells, noises, or dirt from one property that interferes with another's use and enjoyment of their own property.

O

obstruction Under Sarbanes-Oxley, prohibits destruction of documents when civil or criminal investigations are pending.

Occupational Safety and Health Act of 1970 Federal law setting and enforcing workplace safety standards.

Occupational Safety and Health Administration (OSHA) Federal agency responsible for safety in the workplace.

offer Preliminary to contract; first step in formation.

offeree Recipient of offer.

offeror Person making the offer.

Oil Pollution Act (OPA) Federal law imposing civil and criminal liability for oil spills.

omnibus hearing Evidentiary hearing outside the presence of the jury.

open meeting law Law (at either state or federal level) requiring that notice be given of meetings of agency heads and that they be open to the public.

opening statement In a trial, each side's overview of the case and the evidence that will be presented.

opposition proceedings Process that includes publishing the description of the patent, and inviting the public to study the description and possibly oppose the granting of a patent.

options Offers with considerations; promises to keep offer open.

oral argument Upon appeal of a case, the attorneys' presentation of their points on appeal to the panel of appellate judges.

ordinances Laws at the city, town, or country level.

ordinary and reasonably prudent person In negligence, standard used for determining the level of care required in any given situation.

original jurisdiction Jurisdiction of trial courts; jurisdiction of courts where a case begins.

overtime pay Rate of 1½ times the hourly rate for hours over 40 per week worked.

P

palming off Causing deception about the maker or source of a product.

parol evidence Extrinsic evidence that is not admissible to dispute an integrated unambiguous contract.

partially disclosed principal Existence but not identity of principal is known.

partnership Voluntary association of two or more persons as co-owners in a business for profit.

partnership by estoppel Partnership that arises by perception of third parties of its existence.

partnership by implication Creation of a partnership by parties' conduct.

party autonomy The right of parties to determine privately their choice of law.

patent Utility or function patents cover machines, processes, and improvements to existing devices; design patents protect the features of a product; plant patents are obtained by those who develop new forms of plants and hybrids; statutory protection of exclusivity for products and processes.

pattern or practice of discrimination Theory for establishing discrimination that compares population percentages with workplace percentages.

peer review Formal grievance procedure for nonunion employees.

penalties Punishments for commission of crimes; include fines and imprisonment.

Pension Protection Act of 2006 Pension reform act that addressed financial insolvency concerns in pension plans.

per curiam A judicial opinion of the full court with no judge or justice claiming authorship.

per se "On its face"; "without further proof."

per se **illegal** Behavior that courts do not analyze regarding what the competitors did; the behavior is just plain illegal.

per se **violation** Violation of antitrust laws that has no defense or justification.

peremptory challenge Right to strike jurors with or without cause; lawyer's discretionary tool in selecting a jury; number of peremptory challenges is usually limited.

petition Often the first document in a case.

petitioner Party filing a petition; or in the case of an appeal, the party filing the appeal of a lower court decision.

picketing Public appearance of striking union members.

plaintiff Party filing suit, who is alleging a wrong committed by the defendant.

plea bargain Settlement of criminal charges.

pleadings The complaint, answer, and counterclaim filed in a lawsuit.

police power Constitutional term describing the authority given to the states to regulate the health, safety, and welfare of their citizens.

pooling agreement Shareholder contract to vote a certain way.

positive law Codified law; law created and enforced by governmental entities.

power of attorney A form of agency relationship that grants another authority to enter into transactions.

precedent Prior judicial decisions; the law as it exists; *see also stare decisis.*

predatory bidding Company with market power using high-bid pricing to drive its competitors from the market place by inflating the cost of supplies.

predatory lending Type of lending that involves high interest or forfeiture and is generally targeted to low knowledge consumers with poor credit ratings.

predatory pricing Pricing below actual cost to monopolize.

preemption Constitutional term from the Supremacy Clause, which provides that the federal government preempts state law where such preemption was intended or where the federal regulation is so pervasive that it prevents state regulation.

preferred stock Ownership interest with priority over common stock.

Pregnancy Discrimination Act Prohibits refusing to hire, refusing to promote, or firing because of pregnancy.

preliminary hearing Presentation of abbreviated case by prosecution to establish sufficient basis to bind defendant over for trial.

prevention of significant deterioration (PSD) areas Classification that provides the EPA with a means to monitor nonattainment areas to stop increased pollution.

price discrimination Selling goods across state lines at prices that have different ratios to marginal costs.

price fixing Controlling price of goods through agreement, limiting supply, controlling credit.

prima facie **case** A case establishing all the necessary elements; without rebuttal evidence from the defendant, entitles the plaintiff to a verdict.

primary offering Sale of securities by the business in which interests are offered.

principal Employer; responsible party.

Privacy Act of 1974 Controls the use of information the government gathers about consumers.

private law The law of contracts and the intrabusiness laws such as personnel rules.

privilege A defense to defamation that protects certain statements because of a public interest in having information such as testimony in a trial or media coverage protected from suit.

privity Direct contractual relationship between parties.

procedural due process Constitutional protection that gives litigants in civil cases and defendants in criminal cases the right to notice in all steps in the process and the right of participation.

procedural law Law that provides the means for enforcing rights.

process servers Individuals licensed by a state to deliver summonses and subpoenas to individuals.

product disparagement The tort of defamation of products.

product market Market determined by consumers' preferences and their willingness to substitute other products for the product at issue.

professional corporation Entity with limited liability except for malpractice/negligence by its owners.

profit corporation Those seeking to earn a return for investors.

promissory estoppel Reliance element used to enforce otherwise unenforceable contracts.

proper purpose When a shareholder has a legitimate interest in reviewing corporate progress, financial status, and fiduciary responsibilities.

Proprietary Information or content that is the property of individuals or companies and is not for sale or transfer without consent.

prospectus Formal document explaining offering or any ad or written materials describing offering.

proximate cause The foreseeability requirement of causation.

proxy Right to vote for another.

proxy solicitation Formal paperwork requesting authority to vote on behalf of another.

public comment period In administrative rulemaking, the period during which any member of the public can comment on the rule, its content, and potential efficacy.

public law Law passed by some governmental agency.

publicly held corporation Corporation with many shareholders.

puffing Statements of opinion.

punitive damages Damages beyond compensation for knowledge that conduct was wrongful.

Q

qualified privileges Privileges that provide limited liability for defamation.

quasi **contract** Theory for enforcing a contract even though there is no formal contract because the parties behaved as if there were a contract.

quota Program that is an unlawful infringement of the rights of a majority group of employees.

R

Racketeer Influenced and Corrupt Organizations (RICO) Act Federal law designed to prevent racketeering by intensifying the punishments for engaging in certain criminal activities more than once.

ratification After-the-fact recognition of agent's authority by principal. Also, when a corporation assumes primary liability for payment, but the incorporator still remains liable.

reasonable and prudent person The standard by which the conduct of others is measured; a hypothetical person who behaves with full knowledge and alertness.

red-herring prospectus Redlined prospectus that can be given to potential purchasers prior to effective date of registration statement.

redirect examination Plaintiff's questioning of his own witness after defendant's cross-examination is complete; or vice versa when defendant's witness is involved.

regional reporter Series of volumes reporting the appeals and supreme court decisions of state courts; grouped by geographic region; for example, *Pacific Reporter* for the western states.

registration statement (S-1) Disclosure statement filed by the offeror with the SEC.

Regulation A Small offering exemption that shortens registration process.

Regulation D Small offering exemption rules.

Regulatory Flexibility Act Reform act for federal agency rules promulgation; requires publication of proposed rules in trade magazines so that industries and individuals affected can properly respond during the public comment period.

Rehabilitation Act of 1973 Federal statute prohibiting discrimination on basis of disability by federal agencies and contractors.

relevant market Geographic and product market used to determine market power.

remand The action an appellate court takes when a case is sent down to a lower court for a retrial or other proceeding on the basis of the appellate court decision.

rent-a-judge Means of alternative dispute resolution in which the parties hire a former judge and a private hearing room and have the judge determine liability.

repatriation Process of bringing back to your own country profits earned on investments in another country.

request for admissions Discovery tool in which one side asks the other to admit certain facts as proven in a case.

request for production Discovery tool in which one side asks the other side to produce documents relevant to the case.

resale price maintenance Requiring prices be set in vertical distribution.

rescission Setting aside of contract as a remedy.

Resource Conservation and Recovery Act (RCRA) Federal law controlling disposal of hazardous waste through a permit system.

respondent On appeal of a case, the party who is not appealing; in a petition for a divorce, the party against whom the petition is filed.

respondent superior Let the master answer; employer is responsible for certain torts committed by employees in the scope of employment.

Restatement (Second) of Contracts General summary of the common law of contracts.

Restatement of Agency Common law view of agent–principal relationship.

reverses Action of an appellate court in changing the decision of a lower court because a reversible error has been made.

reversible error Mistake made in lower court proceedings that is ruled as improper by an appellate court and that requires a reversal of the case and possible retrial.

Revised Uniform Limited Partnership Act (RULPA) Update of limited partnership law.

Revised Uniform Partnership Act (RUPA) Update of partnership law.

revocation Offeror canceling offer.

right-to-sue letter Certification that the employee has exhausted available administrative remedies.

right-to-work laws Right to work at a company without being required to join a union.

Rivers and Harbors Act of 1899 Prohibited the release of "any refuse matter of any kind or description" into navigable waters in the United States without a permit from the Army Corps of Engineers.

Robinson–Patman Act Anti-price discrimination federal statute.

Rule 10b-5 SEC regulation on antifraud provision of Securities Exchange Act.

rule of reason A standard that the courts use to examine whether activities help or hinder competition.

Rules 504, 505, 506 Portion of Regulation D affording exemptions for variously structured offerings.

runaway shop When work is transferred to another plant or a new plant is opened to carry the workload of the old plant.

S

S corporation IRS category of corporation with flow-through characteristics.

Safe Drinking Water Act Federal law establishing standards for contaminants.

scheduled injuries Injuries that are listed by statute, along with compensation figures.

scienter Knowledge that information given is false.

scope of employment Time when agent is doing work for the principal.

search warrant Judicially issued right to examine home, business, and papers in any area in which there is an expectation of privacy.

SEC Federal agency responsible for enforcing federal securities laws.

Section 10(b) Antifraud provision of Securities Exchange Act.

Section 11 Portion of 1933 act that provides for liability for false statements or omissions in registration statements.

Section 12 Portion of 1933 act that provides for liability for selling without registration or exemption before effective date or with a false prospectus.

Section 16 Portion of 1934 act regulating short-swing profits by officers, directors, or 10 percent shareholders.

Securities Act of 1933 Federal law regulating initial sales of securities.

Securities and Exchange Commission (SEC) Administrative agency responsible for regulating the sale of securities under both the 1933 and 1934 acts.

Securities Exchange Act of 1934 Federal law regulating securities and companies in the secondary market.

security Investment in a common enterprise with profits to come from efforts of others.

sexual harassment Form of discrimination that involves a quid pro quo related to sexual favors or an atmosphere of harassment.

shelf registrations SEC approval process that allows approval and then waiting period for market conditions.

Sherman Act First federal antitrust law; prohibits monopolization and horizontal trade restraints such as price fixing, boycotts, and refusals to deal.

shopkeeper's privilege Defense to torts of defamation, invasion of privacy, and false imprisonment for merchants who detain shoppers when shopkeepers have reasonable cause to believe merchandise has been taken without payment.

short-swing profits Gain on sale and purchase or purchase and sale of securities within a six-month period.

Sixth Amendment The right-to-trial protection of the U.S. Constitution.

slander Oral or spoken defamation.

slander of title Oral disparaging statements.

slowdown Workers report to job but do not operate at full speed.

small claims court Specialized court designed to allow the hearing of claims of limited monetary amounts without the complexities of litigation and without attorneys.

small-company doctrine Two small companies are permitted to merge because the hope is that they will be better able to compete with the larger businesses in that market.

Social Security Act of 1935 Federal law establishing disability, beneficiary, and retirement benefits.

sole outlet or **exclusive distributorship** Limited dealership rights; not an antitrust violation as long as horizontal competition exists; one in which a manufacturer appoints a distributor or retailer as the sole or exclusive outlet for the manufacturer's product.

sole proprietorship Individual ownership and operation of a business.

sovereign immunity Concept that protects a country's actions based on the notion that each country is entitled to respect for its laws and system of governance.

specific performance Equitable remedy in which party asks for performance of the contract as damages.

standing Defined by the U.S. Supreme Court as the actual sale or purchase of stock in reliance on the information or lack of information given.

stare decisis Latin term for "Let the decision stand"; the doctrine of following or distinguishing case precedent.

state codes State laws passed by legislatures.

state implementation plans (SIPs) Plans states were required to adopt to achieve the federally developed EPA air quality standards.

statute of frauds State statutes governing the types of contracts that must be in writing to be enforceable.

statute of limitations Generic term referring to various state statutes controlling the time periods in which suits must be brought by plaintiffs; time varies according to the nature of the suit; for example, contract statutes of limitations are generally four years.

statutory law Law codified and written; passed by some governmental entity.

stipulated means Required means of acceptance.

Stored Communication Act (SCA) Act that prohibits the unauthorized interception of electronic communications, generally meaning stored communication, not ongoing communication such as text messaging, tweeting, and instant messaging.

strict liability Absolute liability for conduct with few, if any, defenses available.

strict tort liability Imposition of liability because harm results.

strike A work stoppage because employees no longer report to work.

submarket Local market.

substantial evidence test Basis for challenging the actions of an administrative agency on the grounds that the rule promulgated was not based on enough evidence.

substantial performance Performance that, for practical purposes, is just as good as full-performance.

substantive due process Constitutional protection that requires laws to apply equally to all and not to deny property or rights without prior notice.

substantive laws Laws that give rights and responsibilities to individuals.

summary jury trial A private method of alternative dispute resolution in which the parties present a summary of their evidence to a private jury and then agree to abide by their decision or settle, depending on what the jury concludes; held privately and can often save the cost of going to court for a real trial.

summons Court document issued to the defendant in a lawsuit that explains the requirement of filing an answer and the time period in which it must be done.

sunset law Law that places an ending date on an administrative agency; if not renewed, an agency terminates at sunset on a particular date; the sun sets on the agency.

Superfund Funds available for government to use to clean up toxic waste sites.

Superfund Amendment and Reauthorization Act Act that authorizes the EPA to recover cleanup funds from those responsible for the release of hazardous substances.

superior skill, foresight, and industry In short, the ability to build a better mousetrap.

Supremacy Clause Constitutional provision allowing federal laws to preempt state laws where Congress intended or where the regulation is pervasive.

Surface Mining and Reclamation Act of 1977 Requires those mining coal to restore land surfaces to their original conditions and prohibits surface coal mining without a permit.

T

takeover Accomplished through the use of tender offers and can be either friendly or hostile.

tender offer Method for achieving a business combination.

theft or **embezzlement** For theft, the following elements are necessary: (1) intent to take the property, (2) actual taking of the property for permanent use, and (3) no authorization to take the property. For embezzlement, the elements are the same as for theft, with the addition of one more element: The person commits the crime while in the employ or position of trust of the property owner.

three-day cooling-off period Period in which the buyer has the right to rescind certain types of credit contracts.

tippee Person who gains nonpublic information from an insider.

Title VII Prohibits discrimination in employment on the basis of race, color, religion, sex, or national origin.

tombstone ad Ad announcing offering that can be run prior to effective date of registration statement.

tort A civil wrong; action by another that results in damages that are recoverable.

tortious interference with contracts Tort that occurs when parties are not allowed the freedom to contract without interference from third parties.

Toxic Substances Control Act Authorized the EPA to control the manufacture, use, and disposal of toxic substances. Under the act, the EPA can stop the manufacture of dangerous substances that the agency concludes are dangerous.

trade dress Statutory protection of exclusivity for product colors and motifs; brand protection for those easily recognizable shapes and colors of a company and its product.

trade libel Written disparaging statements.

trade name Statutory protection of exclusivity for unique product labels and names; brand protections for product names.

trade secret Anything that gives the business a competitive edge and that is not known generally or by competitors; knowledge a business develops that provide its competitive edge.

trademark Brand protection for product symbols; statutory protection of exclusivity for product symbols.

traffic court Lesser trial court, in which traffic cases and violations of other city ordinances are tried.

transfer restriction Prohibition on transfers of shares by shareholders.

treaty In international law, an agreement between two or more nations.

treble damages Three times actual damages available in antitrust cases.

trial Presentation of case by each side.

trial court First stop in the judicial system when a suit is filed; the court where the case is presented and witnesses testify.

trial *de novo* Latin for "trial again" or "trial anew."

Truth in Lending Act (TILA) Federal law that mandates disclosures in consumer credit contract.

Tying Requiring buyers to take an additional product in order to purchase the product they want.

U

U.S. Constitution The cornerstone of the federal government's structure and the basis of private citizens' rights and protections.

U.S. Department of Homeland Security (DHS) Cabinet-level agency responsible for enforcement of the immigration laws.

U.S. Government Manual Book published by the U.S. government that includes descriptions and organizational charts for all federal agencies.

U.S. Supreme Court The highest appellate court in the federal system and also the highest appellate court for state appeals.

unconscionable Contract that gives all the benefits to one side and all the burdens to the other. Also, a contract term that is unfair, one-sided, or oppressive in requirement or cost.

undisclosed principal Neither existence nor identity of principal is known.

undue influence Exerting control over another party for purposes of gain.

unemployment compensation Federal program handled by states to provide temporary support for displaced workers.

unenforceable contract Agreement for which the law affords no remedy.

unfair labor practice Conduct by labor or management prohibited by statute.

Uniform Commercial Code (UCC) Uniform law adopted in 49 states governing sales contracts for goods, commercial paper, security interests, documents of title, and securities transfers.

Uniform Computer Information Transactions Act (UCITA) Act that governs all contracts involving the sale, licensing, maintenance, and support of computer software.

Uniform Durable Power of Attorney Act (UDPAA) When key individuals in a business can execute a type of power of attorney that comes into existence in the event of disability or incapacity of the principal.

Uniform Electronic Transactions Act (UETA) State recognition of Electronic Signatures in Global and National Commerce Act of 2000 (ESIGN).

Uniform Electronic Transactions Act (UETA) and the Uniform Computer Information Transaction Act (UCITA) Model laws drafted to allow states to adopt a uniform position on the authenticity and security of signatures.

uniform laws Series of laws drafted by groups of business people, law professors, and lawyers; adopted and codified by states to help attain a more uniform commercial environment for transactions.

Uniform Limited Partnership Act (ULPA) Uniform law adopted in nearly every state.

Uniform Partnership Act (UPA) Law on partnerships adopted in 49 states.

unilateral contract Contract made up of a promise for performance.

unincorporated association Nonlegal entity; no legal existence as natural or fictitious person.

United Nations Convention on Contracts for the International Sale of Goods (CISG) Contracts for the International Sale of Goods; a uniform law for international commercial transactions that countries can choose to adopt and contracting parties can choose to use.

United States Code (U.S.C.) Statutory volumes of congressional enactments.

Uniting and Strengthening America by Providing Appropriate Tools Required to Intercept and Obstruct Terrorism Act (USA Patriot Act) Federal law that tightened employer requirements for aliens, imposed new financial disclosures of transactions, and allowed additional federal surveillance.

universal treaty A treaty accepted and recognized by all countries; for example, the Warsaw Convention on air travel.

unscheduled injuries On-the-job injuries not specifically described in statutes.

V

venue Geographic location of a trial.

verdict The outcome or decision in a trial.

vertical merger A merger between firms that has a buyer–seller relationship.

vicarious liability Holding companies accountable for criminal conduct of their officers.

void contract Contract with illegal subject matter or against public policy.

voidable contract Contract that can be avoided legally by one side.

voting trust Separation of legal and equitable title in shares to ensure voting of shares in one way.

W

warrant Public document authorizing detention of an individual for criminal charges; for searches, a judicial authorization.

Water Quality Act The first federal legislation on water quality standards, which was passed in 1965.

watered shares Failure to pay par value for shares.

Wheeler-Lea Act of 1938 Federal law that allows FTC to regulate "unfair and deceptive acts or practices."

whistle-blower Employee who reports illegal conduct and who refuses to participate in conduct that is illegal or that violates public policy.

white-collar crime Crimes committed for and against a business.

Williams Act Regulates tender offers.

work product An attorney's thoughts, research, and strategy in a case; nondiscoverable.

Worker Adjustment and Retraining Notification Act of 1988 (WARN) Federal law requiring employers to give 60 days' notice of plant shutdowns.

workers' compensation System of no-fault liability for employees injured on the job: laws that provide wage benefits and medical care to victims of work-related injuries.

Z

zero-based budgeting Process of agency budgeting in which the budget starts with a figure of zero rather than at the level of the previous year's budget; effect is to require an agency to justify its functions and expenditures for each budget period.

TABLE OF CASES

T

U

V

W

Y

Z

TABLE OF PRODUCTS, PEOPLE, AND COMPANIES